JIM MURRAY'S
WHISKY
BIBLE
2014

This edition first published 2013 by Dram Good Books Ltd

10 9 8 7 6 5 4 3 2 1

The "Jim Murray's" logo and the "Whisky Bible" logo are trade marks of Jim Murray.

Text, tasting notes & rankings, artwork, Jim Murray's logo and the Whisky Bible logo copyright
© Jim Murray 2013

Design copyright © Dram Good Books Ltd 2013

For information regarding using tasting notes from Jim Murray's Whisky Bible contact:
Dram Good Books Ltd, 9 Edison Close, Wellingborough, Northamptonshire, UK, NN8 6AH
Tel: 44 (0)117 317 9777. Or contact us via www.whiskybible.com

ISBN: 978-0-9554729-8-5

Printed in England by Stanley L Hunt (Printers) Ltd. Rushden, Northamptonshire
www.stanleylhunt.co.uk

Written by: Jim Murray
Edited by: David Rankin
Design: James Murray, Dean Ayotte, Jim Murray
Maps and Cover Design: James Murray
Production: Dean Ayotte, James Murray, Billy Jeffrey
Sample Research: Ally Telfer, Julia Nourney, Mick Secor
Other Research: Emma Thomson
Cover Photograph: Clive Wagner

Author's Note
I have used the spelling "whiskey" or "whisky" depending on how the individual distillers
prefer. All Scotch is "whisky". So is Canadian. All Irish, these days, is "whiskey", though
that was not always the case. In Kentucky, bourbon and rye are spelt "whiskey", with the
exception of the produce of the early Times/Old Forester Distillery and Maker's Mark which
they bottle as "whisky". In Tennessee, it is a 50-50 split: Dickel is "whisky", while Daniel's is
"whiskey".

JIM MURRAY'S
WHISKY
BIBLE
2014

DRAM GOOD BOOKS

Contents

Introduction

Exactly 54 weeks ago today I sat in the same seat of the same plane looking down at the same evening sun-bathed, snow-capped, misty valleyed mountains as I headed to the same destination, London.

Just like last year I still have the taste of America's multi-dimensional whiskeys fresh on my palate and mind – and a few Scotches exclusively destined for the US market, as well. And just like that mirror trip of August last year, my laptop is doing what it says on the tin as I type the introduction of a book which has consumed four solid months of my life in order to write with maximum accuracy. You would think that this sameness suggests that everything about this job is crushed in a bore-constricting oneness. Especially when you realise that this is the tenth year of writing Jim Murray's Whisky Bible. The first was written during the Spring and Summer of 2003, a summer which brought record temperatures to England, a heat-wave which I spent sitting in a cool tasting room that saw little of the sun until after 7pm. And exactly ten years on, temperatures in the UK again rose to record-breaking levels...an uncanny reminder of and parallel to the genesis of the world's biggest selling whisky guide.

So a year...no, ten years...of same old, same old, right? Wrong. Very wrong.

Even a significant number of whiskies from a year ago have moved on, let alone from a decade ago. Especially in the world of the micro distilleries which is now reaching into mainstream availability. This was the first year that I felt that that ever-swelling and diversifying army of small independent distillers in both Europe and North America have, overall, taken their whiskies to the next level. When tasting these guys in the past, you knew that the numbers you would be able to taste in one day would be limited by the build up of feints – the mainly unwelcome oils included in the final selection of spirit destined to become whisky – which earmark a small distiller's need to produce as much whisky as possible from his distillation to be financially viable.

This year my time lost to feint overload was negligible. Ten years ago, mind you, it was virtually nil. And that was because the micro distilling boom had yet to begin. There was the odd whisky to be found in Germany and Austria. And that was about your lot. America was not even on the map: Kentucky and Tennessee was where you went to find the country's grain spirit – and invariably it was from all the large, established historic distiller.

Likewise, this year no time was lost at all to having to allow the caramel from colouring to filter out of my system. Not so in 2003, when my taste buds became clogged up every other day. That doesn't mean to say that artificial colouring has been banished, alas, from the face of whisky. But the vast majority of the 1,127 new whiskies I have tasted for this landmark edition, which very neatly, incidentally, has taken me passed the 12,500 mark for all different whiskies tasted by me especially for the Bible, have been produced for the more discerning drinker in mind. Sadly, there are still many brands which falsely colour and because the distillers are not transparent about this, so to speak, again I have repeated, purposely, my crusade from a decade ago in Bible Thumping. And on the subject of Bible Thumping I'd like to thank all those in the industry as well as consumers who took the trouble to thank me for the stance the Whisky Bible took last year against the continued use of sulphur-treated casks in whisky maturation. It was a article which hit the headlines worldwide and, hopefully, helped people understand that not all whiskies are as bad as they had begun to think.

There are so many truly astonishing, tinglingly gorgeous whiskies out there I can only reiterate what I said last year: the gap between the best whiskies and the worst is widening. This year that rate of rift had clearly gathered momentum. Back in 2003 many whiskies scored in the low-to-mid-80s because they were so dull thanks to over-zealous caramel usage. Now it is obvious that distillers are working much harder to not only cherry pick their finest whiskies warehoused, but create a style which suits the malts in question. This is a long way from dumping what was available some years back. So you will see many whiskies have scored in the 90s. Not because I am getting softer. But because, despite the wide problems still obvious with sulphur-dulled or even spoiled brands, this is a golden era of great whisky. Try the whiskies I have awarded 90 points and over and see if you can possibly disagree.

Same old, same old? Well, the sun has set over the Rockies, as they are doing now, since before mankind. And that gold and crimson glow is as beautiful now as it was 54 weeks ago today....and back in 2003. Because natural beauty is timeless. Even in a changing world...

Jim Murray
Seat 63A Flight BA48
Somewhere between Seattle and London, August 2013

How to Read The Bible

The whole point of this book is for the whisky lover – be he or she an experienced connoisseur or, better fun still, simply starting out on the long and joyous path of discovery – to have ready access to easy-to-understand information about as many whiskies as possible. And I mean a lot. Thousands.

This book does not quite include every whisky on the market... just by far and away the vast majority. And those that have been missed this time round – either through accident, logistics or design – will appear in later editions once we can source a sample.

Whisky Scoring

The marking for this book is tailored to the consumer and scores run out just a little higher than I use for my own personal references. But such is the way it has been devised that it has not affected my order of preference.

Each whisky is given a rating out of 100. Twenty-five marks are given to each of four factors: nose (n), taste (t), finish (f), balance and overall complexity (b). That means that 50% of the marks are given for flavour alone and 25% for the nose, often an overlooked part of the whisky equation. The area of balance and complexity covers all three previous factors and a usually hidden one besides:

Nose: this is simply the aroma. Often requires more than one inspection as hidden aromas can sometimes reveal themselves after time in the glass, increased contact with air and changes in temperature. The nose very often tells much about a whisky, but – as we shall see – equally can be quite misleading.

Taste: this is the immediate arrival on the palate and involves the flavour profile up to, and including, the time it reaches maximum intensity and complexity.

Finish: often the least understood part of a tasting. This is the tail and flourish of the whisky's signature, often revealing the effects of ageing. The better whiskies tend to finish well and longer without too much oak excess. It is on the finish, also, that certain notes which are detrimental to the whisky may be observed. For instance, a sulphur-tarnished cask may be fully revealed for what it is by a dry, bitter residue on the palate which is hard to shake off. It is often worth waiting a few minutes to get the full picture of the finish before having a second taste of a whisky.

Balance: This is the part it takes a little experience to appreciate but it can be mastered by anyone. For a whisky to work well on the nose and palate, it should not be too one-sided in its character. If you are looking for an older whisky, it should have evidence of oak, but not so much that all other flavours and aromas are drowned out. Likewise, a whisky matured or finished in a sherry butt must offer a lot more than just wine alone and the greatest Islay malts, for instance, revel in depth and complexity beyond the smoky effects of peat.

Each whisky has been analysed by me without adding water or ice. I have taken each whisky as it was poured from the bottle and used no more than warming in an identical glass to extract and discover the character of the whisky. To have added water would have been pointless: it would have been an inconsistent factor as people, when pouring water, add different amounts at varying temperatures. The only constant with the whisky you and I taste will be when it has been poured directly from the bottle.

Even if you and I taste the same whiskies at the same temperature and from identical glasses – and even share the same values in whisky – our scores may still be different. Because a factor that is built into my evaluation is drawn from expectation and experience. When I sample a whisky from a certain distillery at such-and-such an age or from this type of barrel or that, I would expect it to offer me certain qualities. It has taken me 30 years to acquire this knowledge (which I try to add to day by day!) and an enthusiast cannot be expected to learn it overnight. But, hopefully, Jim Murray's Whisky Bible will help...!

Score chart

Within the parentheses () is the overall score out of 100.

0–50.5 Nothing short of absolutely diabolical.
51–64.5 Nasty and well worth avoiding.
65–69.5 Very unimpressive indeed.
70–74.5 Usually drinkable but don't expect the earth to move.
75–79.5 Average and usually pleasant though sometimes flawed.
80–84.5 Good whisky worth trying.
85–89.5 Very good to excellent whiskies definitely worth buying.
90–93.5 Brilliant.
94–97.5 Superstar whiskies that give us all a reason to live.
98–100 Better than anything I've ever tasted!

Key to Abbreviations & Symbols

% Percentage strength of whisky measured as alcohol by volume. **b** Overall balance and complexity. **bott** Date of bottling. **db** Distillery bottling. In other words, an expression brought out by the owners of the distillery. **dist** Date of distillation or spirit first put into cask. **f** Finish. **n** Nose. **nc** Non-coloured. **ncf** Non-chill-filtered. **sc** Single cask. **t** Taste. ☼ New entry for 2014. ☉ Retasted – no change. ☉☉ Retasted and re-evaluated. **v** Variant

Finding Your Whisky

Worldwide Malts: Whiskies are listed alphabetically throughout the book. In the case of single malts, the distilleries run A–Z style with distillery bottlings appearing at the top of the list in order of age, starting with youngest first. After age comes vintage. After all the "official" distillery bottlings are listed, next come other bottlings, again in alphabetical order. Single malts without a distillery named (or perhaps named after a dead one) are given their own section, as are vatted malts.

Worldwide Blends: These are simply listed alphabetically, irrespective of which company produce them. So "Black Bottle" appears ahead of "White Horse" and Japanese blends begin with "Ajiwai Kakubin" and end with "Za". In the case of brands being named after companies or individuals the first letter of the brand will dictate where it is listed. So William Grant, for instance, will be found under "W" for William rather "G" for Grant.

Bourbon/Rye: One of the most confusing types of whiskey to list because often the name of the brand bears no relation to the name of the distillery that made it. Also, brands may be sold from one company to another, or shortfalls in stock may see companies buying bourbons from another. For that reason all the brands have been listed alphabetically with the name of the bottling distiller being added at the end.

Irish Whiskey: There are four types of Irish whiskey: (i) pure pot still; (ii) single malt, (iii) single grain and (iv) blended. Some whiskies may have "pure pot still" on the label, but are actually single malts. So check both sections.

Bottle Information

As no labels are included in this book I have tried to include all the relevant information you will find on the label to make identification of the brand straightforward. Where known I have included date of distillation and bottling. Also the cask number for further recognition. At the end of the tasting notes I have included the strength and, if known, number of bottles (sometimes abbreviated to btls) released and in which markets.

Price of Whisky

You will notice that Jim Murray's Whisky Bible very rarely refers to the cost of a whisky. This is because the book is a guide to quality and character rather than the price tag attached. Also, the same whiskies are sold in different countries at varying prices due to market forces and variations of tax, so there is a relevance factor to be considered. Equally, much depends on the size of an individual's pocket. What may appear a cheap whisky to one could be an expensive outlay to another. With this in mind prices are rarely given in the Whisky Bible.

How to Taste Whisky

It is of little use buying a great whisky, spending a comparative fortune in doing so, if you don't get the most out of it.

So when giving whisky tastings, no matter how knowledgable the audience may be I take them through a brief training schedule in how to nose and taste as I do for each sample included in the Whisky Bible.

I am aware that many aspects are contrary to what is being taught by distilleries' whisky ambassadors. And for that we should be truly thankful. However, at the end of the day we all find our own way of doing things. If your old tried and trusted technique suits you best, that's fine by me. But I do ask you try out the instructions below at least once to see if you find your whisky is talking to you with a far broader vocabulary and clearer voice than it once did. I strongly suspect you will be pleasantly surprised — amazed, even - by the results.

Amusingly, someone tried to teach me my own tasting technique some years back in an hotel bar. He was not aware who I was and I didn't let on. It transpired that a friend of his had been to one of my tastings a few years earlier and had passed on my words of "wisdom." I'd be lying if I said I didn't smile when he informed me it was called "The Murray Method." It was the first time I had heard the phrase... though certainly not the last!

"The Murray Method"

1. Drink a black, unsweetened, coffee or chew on 90% minimum cocoa chocolate to cleanse the palate, especially of sugars.

2. Find a room free from distracting noises as well as the aromas of cooking, polish, flowers and other things which will affect your understanding and appreciation of the whisky.

3. Make sure you have not recently washed your hands using heavily scented soap or are wearing a strong aftershave or perfume.

4. Use a tulip shaped glass with a stem. This helps contain the alcohols at the bottom yet allows the more delicate whisky aromas you are searching for to escape.

5. Never add ice. This tightens the molecules and prevents flavours and aromas from being released. It also makes your whisky taste bitter. There is no better way to get the least from your whisky than by freezing it.

6. Likewise, ignore any advice given to put the bottle in the fridge before drinking.

7. Don't add water! Whatever anyone tells you. It releases aromas but can mean the whisky falls below 40%...so it is no longer whisky. Also, its ability to release flavours and aromas diminish quite quickly. Never add ridiculous "whisky rocks" or other supposed tasting aids.

8. Warm the undiluted whisky in the glass to body temperature before nosing or tasting. Hence the stem, so you can cradle in your hand and curve the curve of the thin base. This excites the molecules and unravels the whisky in your glass, maximising its sweetness and complexity.

9. Keep an un-perfumed hand over the glass to keep the aromas in while you warm. Only a minute or two after condensation appears at the top of your glass should you extend your arms, lift your covering hand and slowly bring the glass to your nose, so the alcoholic vapours have been released before the glass reaches your face.

10. Never stick your nose in the glass. Or breathe in deeply. Allow glass to gently touch your top lip, leaving a small space below the nose. Move from nostril to nostril, breathing normally. This allows the aromas to break up in the air, helping you find the more complex notes.

11. Take no notice of your first mouthful. This is a marker for your palate.

12. On second, bigger mouthful, close your eyes to concentrate on the flavour and chew the whisky - moving it continuously around the palate. Keep your mouth slightly open to let air in and alcohol out. It helps if your head is tilted back very slightly.

13. Occasionally spit — if you have the willpower! This helps your senses to remain sharp for the longest period of time.

14. Look for the balance of the whisky. That is, which flavours counter others so none is too dominant. Also, watch carefully how the flavours and aromas change in the glass over time.

15. Assess the "shape" and mouth feel of the whisky, its weight and how long its finish. And don't forget to concentrate on the first flavours as intensely as you do the last. Look out for the way the sugars, spices and other characteristics form.

16. Never make your final assessment until you have tasted it a third or fourth time.

17. Be honest with your assessment: don't like a whisky because someone (yes, even me!), or the label, has tried to convince you how good it is.

18. When you cannot discriminate between one whisky and another, stop immediately.

10th Anniversary
Renewing Vows

It must be 15 years since I sat in the office of one of the world's biggest publishing companies and was told that the Whisky Bible would be a flop.

So I vowed on the central London street their door emptied out onto that I would go home, form my own publishers and launch a book which I knew would change the whisky appreciating landscape. It was a bright spring morning, the kind of day where green shoots form and buds begin to bloom: where nature cannot be thwarted. The perfect moment, in fact, for the blossoming of a dream.

In fact, it took until 2003 to at last get Jim Murray's Whisky Bible onto the bookshelf. But, since then we are now rapidly heading towards half a million copies sold, an extraordinary number for a book which has only ever appeared in English language. And one now having enough international influence for its World Whisky of the Year to sell more bottles in the 24 hours after the announcement of the award than it had in the entire previous year....

The reason for the delay of the initial launch was because, as it was to be funded by myself, I had to wait until exactly the right time to strike. When I knew that there were a sufficient number of independent bottlers to ensure that each new annual edition would have enough fresh contents to make it a new book in itself, then I made my move. The first year should have been 2002 for a 2003 edition, but it took too long to get the samples assembled and the marketing curtains were drawn closed on that tiny window of opportunity. Instead, I began again in the spring of 2003, this time with an impressive armada of whiskies already gathered and, after spending the hottest-ever summer in Britain indoors tasting, by the autumn of that year the Whisky Bible, comprising of 2,100 whiskies and 256 pages was being read the world over.

Now Jim Murray's Whisky Bible carries 4,500 whiskies over 384 pages. In total, over 12,500 different whiskies have now been tasted and rated by me especially for the Whisky Bible. On average, around 1,200 new whiskies are nosed and tasted by me each year. It is a punishing schedule, one my friends have tried to curtail by suggesting I publish once every two years. But that would lose the rhythm, impact and importance of the Whisky Bible: one of its beauties is that it contains all the newest whiskies from around the world that I and my team of researchers can find. Publish every two years and it would be instantly out of date.

From the very first moment, my concept of the Whisky Bible was for it to serve the general public and support the then small number of shops which were at the vanguard of the whisky movement. And the distillers, too, by rewarding those companies in the business of whisky excellence. The only way it could serve the public was by being fearlessly honest and entirely trustworthy: if a whisky was not of the highest quality, then the Bible would say so. It also had to campaign if need be: to be an independent voice.

It has meant that some distillers and bottlers have not been quite as forthcoming with samples as they might. One of the latter even told me quite recently (in front of witnesses, amazingly!) that he would not send me samples as I might give a low score. "Why don't you do what some other writers do," he suggested. "If you don't like it, don't include it."

Such a concept is such anathema to me I refuse to believe anyone could do that. Even so, I can assure you that will never be the way I work. I will, as all my professional and personal instincts and beliefs demand, write as I find...whichever the whisky. And to underscore our independence, we have never and will never carry advertising. The marking of the whiskies will be carried without fear or favour. Not as much as a single half point will be given or subtracted depending on brand or bottler: you don't punish the children because of their parents. And, contrary to what I have read on website forums, we don't take money for awards. Indeed, we don't even charge for whiskies to be included in the Bible. If a whisky gets a high score or an award it is because I, rightly or wrongly, believe it to be of that standard.

And we shall continue to campaign. The first edition carried a withering Bible Thumping on the use of caramel. It was a hard-hitting article which we know led to some independent bottlers discarding colouring altogether and a complete reassessment by many distillers. Ten years on I make no apology for repeating the dose; last year's stance on sulphur received international attention and brought about the bigest-ever debate on the subject, long overdue.

We're proud the way Jim Murray's Whisky Bible has served both the consumer and industry for ten years. Let's hope my nose and tastebuds can withstand the onslaught of ten more...

Bible Thumping
Genesis: Let There Be Lightness

Just what Charles Darwin would make of the recent evolution of the whisky industry we will never know. But I can guess.

Let's just say that had he spent the last ten years studying life in the marketing departments of certain distillers, rather than only half that time on-board The Beagle, his On the Origin of Species wouldn't quite have had the same impact on mankind's understanding of the natural world. Or, most likely, the wellbeing of his own sanity.

Where Darwin's seminal work, that bedrock upon which non-fundamentalists pitch their sturdy tent, is based upon observation and logic, much of what happens within the whisky world defies it. To understand this, you have only to find a copy of the first edition of Jim Murray's Whisky Bible, written exactly ten years ago. And turn, of course, to Bible Thumping.

It was, I am moderately proud to say, an essay which did have quite a profound effect on many corners of the whisky globe. In it I argued, forcibly but not without reason, against the use of caramel in whisky. Forever, it had seemed, the industry had claimed that the use of caramel as a colouring agent had no effect whatsoever on either the nose or taste of whisky. I rejected that claim entirely, adding that it also changed the body and feel of the whisky, too.

When I tasted the 2,100 whiskies which made up that first-ever Jim Murray's Whisky Bible 2004, I had to often stop work because my taste buds had been clogged up by the caramel which, then, was ubiquitous. And scores were lower then than now. Because a decade ago so many whiskies tasted alike, their higher notes, the personality which would differentiate them so subtly, blunted by the toffee effect dulling both the spirit and senses.

Yet a decade ago the industry was not in denial. So usual and common was the use of it, except in the US where bourbon, rye and Tennessee is banned from the inclusion of additives, that there was no reason to get twitchy about it. It is what everyone did. There had been very little writing or debate about it over the last century, so why give it a second thought?

But then, about 20 years ago, people began to take an interest in whisky. Not just how it tasted. But why it tasted. What it was that gave a certain this aroma, that flavour. What was different between the distilleries. What happened at different ages. And, of course, the industry bought into this god-sent interest and did all they could to nurture it. Advertising budgets grew and the message went out about the purity of whisky. Its natural ingredients of barley. And water. Maybe peat. The oak. The changing seasons as it matured, untouched by hand. All natural things. I cannot once, though, remember any advert mentioning the adding of caramel – burned sugar – and, contrary to popular belief, a bitter substance. That was something that for some reason was ignored by the copy writer.

So much so, I remember continually querying a particular brand about the use of caramel. Their marketing guy told me, categorically, there was none. Still I asked: why the flat finish? And why did the nose have that cardboard dusty feel peculiar to falsely-coloured whiskies? Then, one day I was in Germany and found a bottle of his whisky. I rang him and said what was written on the label. "Mit Farbstoff". With colouring. The silence at the other end of the phone could not have been more eloquent.

On another occasion, I was giving a whisky tasting in South Africa. Among the audience was the former distiller of a Scottish malt distillery, a truly talented individual, a seriously good production pro, who I must say has been responsible for the making of some of the finest whisky currently maturing in Scotland today. I argued in the tasting that if I used colouring as an aroma, flavour and texture altering device when I blended pot still rums – which I did as it, like rum, comes from sugar – what the hell was it doing to much lighter bodied whiskies? Here the ex-manager intervened with indignation: "James, you are being very naughty. You know full well that the caramel used for whisky is different to the caramel used for rum." But then I pointed out that perhaps he was the one who was mistaken: the rum I blended was vatted in a bottling hall which bottled both well-known rums and whiskies. And the caramel available for me to use was the same for all.

So you would think with the evolution of whisky, with the extraordinary interest in it on the internet, podcasts, magazines and books – none of which were available when I became the world's first full time whisky writer 21 years ago, and much still in its infancy when the Bible was launched in 2003 - distillers would go out of their way to get the true message across. Surely, there could be no hiding place for the flat earthers who subscribed to a way of thinking that was learned by rote rather than understanding.

But, no. Apparently not.

There I was at a whisky festival in northern Europe a few months back and, just before the doors were flung open to the public, I joked with heavy sarcasm to a friend about a tique-coloured blend - standing out like a blood-gorged sore thumb in a room full of light gold independent bottlings - obviously having no colouring added. A young lady standing behind the table corrected me. She was, it transpired, the Brand Ambassador. "That whisky doesn't have any colouring added." there was silence as I looked at her with amusement waiting for the punch-line. When it didn't come, I realised she was being serious.

"Excuse me?"

"I said the whisky doesn't have any colouring added. All the colour comes from the wood, especially from the sherry."

Again, I waited for a punch-line. This was too hilarious to be true. Instead, she stared at me with humourless defiance. She then pointed to a display sample of cask strength whisky, dark and mysterious, which had been taken directly from a butt.

"All the colour comes from that," she said

My god! She was being serious. Someone had been teaching her to talk complete bollocks.

"Err, I think you are pretty much mistaken," said I, trying to get my head around the fact that such garbage was still officially being spouted after all this time.

My eyes narrowed and fixed on hers and I invited her to compare the two whiskies. "Which of the two whiskies is the darker? They are about the same, right? Yet the bottled whisky is 40% abv, while the cask strength sample there is 50% stronger. So that would have to be watered down considerably – and therefore lightened in colour – to get it to the required bottling strength. Now this brand is a blend. So the vast majority of this very common product is grain whisky. Are you telling me you fill all your grain whisky into brand new, juicy, hugely expensive, first fill oloroso butts? As I've been through your warehouses a few times over the years, I can tell you they don't. I have also seen this product bottled. I have seen the spirit pre and post bottling. And I can tell you colouring is added."

She looked at me unmoved and in full patronising mode. "Then we shall just have to agree to disagree."

This is where I admit, gentle reader, I lost it a bit and my temper moved that notch up from resigned disbelief to unambiguous anger. Not least after ten years of banging the gong.... and then....this!

"I'm afraid I agree with you on nothing. You are wrong and have no idea what you are talking about. If you are telling this to the public, then shame on you. If they are talking to the brand ambassador, then they should be getting the truth: that is what they expect. And, I'm afraid, either because you know absolutely nothing about whisky or you are simply trying to hoodwink them, they are not getting the truth from you."

I can't say that, in the heat of the moment, the words came out exactly in that order, but I think that is a pretty fair facsimile.

What was interesting was that this was a new slant. This was denial of the existence of caramel in the whisky. In the past it had been admittance, but that the caramel was neutral and had no effect. In Canada once, I was giving a training session to the buyers and whisky specialists of a Province's Liquor Board. A brand ambassador was passing through and they asked if they minded me allowing her to do her piece on her product, a blended Scotch, as part of the training. Now I have always regarded "training" by distiller's reps as often as not being brainwashing. But I was happy to let it go, to see how she presented the product, but with the proviso I would step in if I felt what she was saying was incorrect. And, in fairness, the first part of her presentation was excellent: she had really understood her stuff and was doing a superb job. Until she got to the caramel bit and started telling all assembled that it had no effect on the whisky. Then I had to stop the show and give a rather more independent and informed view on things.

Likewise, an old friend of mine gave up writing on whisky as it just wasn't covering the mortgage and putting enough food on his kids' plates. He got a job as a brand ambassador for another well known blend. I asked him what he said about caramel. "I have to tell them it has no effect on the whisky."

"But that's not true and you know it."

"I know, Jim. But what can I do?"

A few months later he quit and found another job: he could simply not continue telling the public something he knew to be false.

And this is where Mr Darwin would find the evolution of whisky so puzzling. Ten years ago

I campaigned against the use of caramel in whisky. And since then distillers from Scotland to India and from Wales to Canada have bought into that philosophy...usually with stunning, award-winning success. And more than one Independent bottler has told me that that campaigning article in that first-ever Bible had a profound and policy-altering effect on the way they presented their whiskies to the public. None have yet to tell me it was for the worse.

Surely then, the evolution of whisky has to be that you give the public what they want. And expect. And what they appear to want is what is advertised. Purity. Natural ingredients. Something made from grain, water and yeast. Tradition. Of course, it can be argued that colouring with caramel is a tradition. But it can also be argued it was a tradition begun when companies wanted to make their whiskies look older than they actually were. So why when there is so much knowledge around does the industry allow false information to be fed to the public? This cannot be home something as magnificent as whisky should evolve.

And if you think I am letting the Americans get away with this scot free, then you are wrong. Recent developments in Kentucky have also left me wondering just what on earth is going on. At the moment, the bourbon and rye producers of Kentucky are having the best time of it in living memory. Demand for both styles, rye in particular, is rising faster than a banker's bonus. And yet, one of the reasons bourbon is doing so well is because it is proving a far more consistent product than Scotch, due to the cask (mis)management programme in Scotland. Bourbon and Rye, having to use virgin oak casks, is staying out of that mess. The last thing they want to do is get involved with fortified and unfortified wine casks.

Yet, so often, instead of distillers and bottlers having confidence in what they are doing, and just making sure they do it a little better if they can, panic buttons are pushed if someone tries something new. So out come copycat bottlings. The cask finishing craze in malt whisky — and not just in Scotland — is a case in point. Some were good. Many were not. Bigger distillers in the old days used to just dump the experimental whisky into a blend somewhere if it didn't turn out how they wished. Now, with the time and expense involved, finished are often bottled whether they work or not. Especially for the smaller guys. So often balance takes a fatal bullet to the head when the wine and grain styles simply fail to sync. But marketeers love the look of some exotic wine on their label...and out it comes at a premium price, good bad or ugly.

Now, in America, bourbon should be safe. But it isn't. Up to a couple of years back Darwin would have been absolutely spot on to show how bourbon has evolved by keeping to its strengths, and as the public learned more about the world's whiskies, the more likely they were to try — and appreciate — the most pure and honest of them all. But what is happening now? Cask finishes. With the word "bourbon" somewhere being used in the label. "Straight bourbon finished in..." and then fill the gap. That, of course, leads to confusion at a time when the world is just beginning to understand. I meet many people at my tastings who think that bourbon finished in Cognac or wine is still bourbon. It isn't.

As I write this, there is a website belonging to an independent bottler claiming that "our masterpiece is unlike any other bourbon." Well maybe that's because you are not any other bourbon. You have finished it in used casks. Which automatically means it just ain't bourbon at all. The law states:

"Whisky distilled from bourbon (rye, wheat, malt, or rye malt) mash" is whisky produced in the United States at not exceeding 160° proof from a fermented mash of not less than 51 percent corn, rye, wheat, malted barley, or malted rye grain, respectively, and stored in used oak containers; and also includes mixtures of such whiskies of the same type.

So the moment the spirit is transferred from virgin oak, which makes it bourbon, into used casks it has clearly crossed the border. So why doesn't the Kentucky Distillers Association crack down on both the big boys and the little ones who are claiming or even inferring their whiskey may be something it isn't? Keep things simple. In this case, the word bourbon should be nowhere on the front label, unless clearly titled: "whisky distilled from bourbon mash."

Above all, they would be protecting the hallowed names and reputations of bourbon and rye; whiskeys which have evolved over a couple of centuries and, being among the fittest, now appreciated by an entirely new whisky-savvy world. It is something causing so much concern in Kentucky right now, there is at least one senior distiller ready to resign if his bosses take the path that further leads to the obscurification in the meaning, definition and understanding of the purest of all the world's whiskeys.

Last year Kentucky's tartan counterparts, the Scotch Whisky Association, had the chance to say something meaningful to the public following the furore created by my stinging criticism of the use of sulphur-treated casks in whisky in the 2013 Bible, a story which made headlines across the world. Their insipid response, nutshelled, that these casks just added variety to whisky flavours would be funny if it were not so tragic. Evolution by the propagation and promotion of a faulty gene.

I would love to see even the great mind of Charles Darwin come up with an explanation for that one...

Jim Murray's Whisky Bible Award Winners 2014

So, Whisky of the Year again goes to a bourbon. Well, not quite....

Scotland has clinched this year's top spot. But with a very different kind of malt whisky, one that will hopefully make the industry sit up and ponder awhile. For it is one matured in the manner of straight bourbon or rye. Glenmorangie brought out this stunner of a dram doubtless helped to its complex best by being matured in virgin oak casks. In other words, the kind of barrels that legally makes bourbon bourbon and rye rye.

It beat off for top spot two whiskies which have dominated these awards in recent years: one a bourbon, the other a rye and both from Buffalo Trace. And when it comes to sheer enormity of flavour, these runners-up lead by a distance.

But the Glenmorangie Ealanta pipped them at the post because it went out and did something very different: not only did it blow me away with its deftness, beauty and elegance, but it gave an aroma and taste profile completely new to me in over 30 years of tasting whisky. Oddly enough, I actually saw these barrels sitting in the Glenmorangie warehouse about two weeks after they were first filled back in 1993. The then distillery manager Bill Lumsden showed them to me proudly. They were an experiment, he told me. As fate would decree, Bill is no longer manager of Glenmorangie. He is now the blender. So he had been keeping a special eye on them from day one to bottle when ripe. I, on the other hand, had just about forgotten about them...until I sniffed the glass....

This is by no means the first scotch I have tasted from white oak. But I cannot remember one that has been matured longer. Which was a brave thing to do. The most remarkable thing about this whisky is its hybrid nature. Even after all this time the barley is still not only recognisable but, almost miraculously, actually juicy and fresh. While the heavier oak-stained bourbon-style notes balance out beautifully. The closest I have come to it before was some of the earlier bottlings of Colorado malt whisky matured in virgin oak in the US. But this, understandably, is better quality spirit taking the style to its zenith: the longer time in a milder climate appears to have allowed the flavours to spread into uncharted territory.

So Buffalo Trace, last year's winner and runner-up, had to settle for second and third. No bad testimony to their consistency. Ditto Ballantine's 17, which held on to blend of the year and was outflanked as top Scotch only by the Glenmorangie's masterful and unique signature.

Perhaps the unluckiest distillery not to win a major award was St. George's in England. Their output was of staggeringly high quality for a distillery so young. But the Mackmyra of Sweden and Santis of Switzerland, no strangers to top class whisky, thwarted them for the top prizes.

2014 World Whisky of the Year
Glenmorangie Ealanta 1993

Second Finest Whisky in the World
William Larue Weller (123.4 proof)

Third Finest World Whisky in the World
Thomas Handy Sazerac Rye (132.4 proof)

SCOTCH

Scotch Whisky of the Year
Glenmorangie Ealanta 1993
Single Malt of the Year (Multiple Casks)
Glenmorangie Ealanta 1993
Single Malt of the Year (Single Cask)
SMWS 33.120 Ardbeg 8 Years Old
Scotch Blend of the Year
Ballantine's 17 Years Old
Scotch Grain of the Year
Clan Deny Dumbarton 48 Years Old
Scotch Vatted Malt of the Year
Six Isles St Etienne Rum Cask Finish

Single Malt Scotch

No Age Statement (Multiple Casks)
Ardbeg Corryvreckan
No Age Statement (Runner Up)
Aberfeldy Unravel
10 Years & Under (Multiple Casks)
Glen Grant Aged 10 Years Old
10 Years & Under (Single Cask)
SMWS 33.120 Ardbeg 8 Years Old
11-15 Years (Multiple Casks)
Highland Park Loki Aged 15 Years
11-15 Years (Single Cask)
The Warehouse Collection Clynelish Aged 15 Years
16-21 Years (Multiple Casks)
Glenmorangie Ealanta 1993
16-21 Years (Single Cask)
Aberfeldy Single Cask Aged 21 Years
22-27 Years (Multiple Casks)
Highland Park Aged 25 Years
22-27 Years (Single Cask)
SMWS 77.28 Glen Ord 25 Years Old
28-34 Years (Multiple Casks)
Maxwell 33 Year Old Highland Single Malt
28-34 Years (Single Cask)
Chieftain's Port Ellen Aged 30 Years
35-40 Years (Multiple Casks)
Old Pulteney Aged 40 Years
35-40 Years (Single Cask)
Glenglassaugh Massandra Collection Aleatico Aged 39 Years
41 Years & Over (Multiple Casks)
Gordon and MacPhail Glen Grant 1960
41 Years & Over (Single Cask)
Glendronach Recherche 1968

Blended Scotch

No Age Statement (Standard)
Ballantine's Finest
No Age Statement (Premium)
Johnnie Walker Blue Label Casks Edition
5-12 Years
Johnnie Walker Black Label 12 Years Old
13-18 Years
Ballantine's 17 Years Old
19 - 25 Years
Hankey Bannister 21 Years Old
26 - 50 Years
The Last Drop 50 Years Old

IRISH WHISKEY

Irish Whiskey of the Year
Redbreast Aged 12 Years Cask Strength Ed
Irish Pot Still Whiskey of the Year
Redbreast Aged 12 Years Cask Strength Ed
Irish Single Malt of the Year
Bushmills Aged 21 Years
Irish Blend of the Year
Jameson

AMERICAN WHISKEY

Bourbon of the Year
William Larue Weller 123.4
Rye of the Year
Thomas Handy Sazerac Rye. 132.4
US Micro Whisky of the Year
Cowboy Bourbon Texas Straight Bourbon Whiskey Aged Three Years
US Micro Whisky of the Year (Runner Up)
Balcones Brimstone Texas Scrub

Bourbon

No Age Statement (Multiple Barrels)
William Larue Weller 123.4
No Age Statement (Single Barrel)
Buffalo Trace Single Oak Project Barrel 101
9 Years & Under
Ridgemont Reserve 1792 Aged 8 Years
10-17 Years (Multiple Barrels)
Parker's Heritage Collection Sixth Edition Master Distillery's Blend Of Mashbills 2001
10-17 Years (Singlee Barrel)
Four Roses Single Barrel 12 Yrs 5 months
18 Years & Over (Multiple Barrels)
Evan Williams 23 Years Old

Rye

No Age Statement
Thomas Handy Sazerac Rye. 132.4
11 Years & Over
Sazerac Kentucky Straight Rye 18 YO

CANADIAN WHISKY

Canadian Whisky of the Year
Masterson's 10-year-old Straight Rye

JAPANESE WHISKY

Japanese Whisky of the Year
SMWS Cask 116.17 Aged 25 Years (Yoichi)

EUROPEAN WHISKY

European Whisky of the Year (Multiple)
Mackmyra Moment "Glod" (Glow)
European Whisky of the Year (Single)
Säntis Malt Swiss Highlander

WORLD WHISKIES

Asian Whisky of the Year
Kavalan Podium Single Malt
Southern Hemisphere Whisky of the Year
Timboon Single Malt Whisky
*Overall age category winners are presented in **bold**.*

The Whisky Bible Liquid Gold Awards (97.5-94)

Jim Murray's Whisky Bible is delighted to again make a point of celebrating the very finest whiskies you can find in the world. So we salute the distillers who have maintained or even furthered the finest traditions of whisky making and taken their craft to the very highest levels. And the bottlers who have brought some of them to us.

After all, there are over 4,500 different brands and expressions listed in this guide and from every corner of the planet. Those which score 94 and upwards represents only a very small fraction of them. These whiskies are, in my view, the elite: the finest you can currently find on the whisky shelves of the world. Rare and precious, they are Liquid Gold.

So it is our pleasure to announce that all those scoring 94 and upwards automatically qualify for the Jim Murray's Whisky Bible Liquid Gold Award. Congratulations!

97.5

Scottish Single Malt
Ardbeg Uigeadail
Scotch Malt Whisky Society Cask 33.120 Aged 8 Years (Ardbeg)
Glenmorangie Ealanta 1993 Vintage
Old Pulteney Aged 21 Years

Scottish Blends
Ballantine's 17 Years Old

Bourbon
George T Stagg
William Larue Weller
William Larue Weller bott Fall 2011

American Straight Rye
Thomas H Handy Sazerac Straight Rye
Thomas H. Handy Sazerac Straight Rye

97

Scottish Single Malt
Aberfeldy Single Cask Aged 21 Years
Ardbeg 10 Years Old
Ardbeg Day Bottling
Ardbeg Supernova
Master of Malt Ardbeg Aged 18 Years
Brora 30 Years Old
The GlenDronach Recherché 1968
Glenfiddich 50 Years Old
Master of Malt Glen Grant 31YO Lost Bott
Scotch Malt Whisky Society Cask 77.28 Aged 25 Years (Glen Ord)

Scottish Grain
Clan Denny Cambus 47 Years Old

Scottish Blends
Johnnie Walker Blue The Casks Edition
Old Parr Superior 18 Years Old

Irish Pure Pot Still
Redbreast Aged 12 Years Cask Strength

Bourbon
Parker's Wheated Mashbill Aged 10 Years
William Larue Weller

American Straight Rye
Thomas H. Handy Sazerac Straight Rye
Colonel E.H. Taylor Straight Rye

Japanese Single Malt
Nikka Whisky Single Coffey Malt 12 Years

Indian Single Malt
Amrut Fusion

Taiwanese Single Malt
Kavalan Solist Fino Sherry Cask

96.5

Scottish Single Malt
Ardbeg Corryvreckan
Balblair 1965
Provenance Benrinnes Over 18 Years
Bruichladdich 1991 Valinch Anaerobic Digestion 19 Years Old
Octomore Orpheus 5 Yrs Ed 02.2 PPM 140
Port Charlotte PC6
The Whisky Agency Caol Ila 33 Years Old
The GlenDronach 18 Years Old
Glengoyne Single Cask 24 Years Old
Glenglassaugh Massandra Collection Aleatico Aged 39 Years
Gordon and MacPhail Distillery Label Glentauchers 1994
Berry's Own Selection Glen Grant 1974
Glenmorangie Sonnalta PX
Highland Park 50 Years Old
Gordon and MacPhail Cask Strength Highland Park 2003
The Glenlivet Single Cask Inveravon 21 Yrs
Lagavulin 12 Years Old Special Release
Laphroaig Aged 25 Years Cask Strength 2011
The Macallan Masters Of Photography Annie Leibovitz 1989 "The Gallery"
Old Malt Cask Speyside's Finest Agd 43 Yrs
Old Masters Strathmill 21 Years Old
Chieftain's Port Ellen Aged 30 Years
Master Of Malt Speyside 50 Yrs 3rd Edition
Riegger's Selection Eagle of Spey Glenfarclas 1993

Scottish Grain
Clan Denny Cambus Vintage Aged 25 Years
Clan Denny Dumbarton Aged 48 Years

Scottish Vatted Malt
The Last Vatted Malt
The Six Isles St Etienne Rum Cask Finish

Scottish Blends
The Last Drop
The Last Drop 50 Years Old
Teacher's Aged 25 Years

Irish Pure Pot Still
Midleton Single Pot Still Single Cask 1991
Powers John's Lane Release Aged 12 Years
Redbreast Aged 12 Years Cask Strength

Bourbon
Blanton's Gold Original Single Barrel
Blanton's Uncut/Unfiltered

Four Roses Single Barrel
Four Roses Single Barrel 12 Years 5 Months
Four Roses 16 Years Old Single Barrel 78-3B
George T Stagg
George T. Stagg Limited Edition
Virgin Bourbon 7 Years Old

American Straight Rye
Sazerac Kentucky Straight Rye 18 Years Old

Canadian Blended
Masterson's 10 Year Old Straight Rye

Swedish Single Malt
Mackmyra Moment "Glöd" (Glow)

Swiss Single Malt
Säntis Swiss Highlander Dreifaltigkeit
Säntis Malt Swiss Highlander

Welsh Single Malt
Penderyn Cask Strength Rich Madeira
Penderyn Portwood Swansea City Special

Australian Single Malt
Sullivans Cove Rare Tasmanian Single Cask
Timboon Single Malt Whisky

Indian Single Malt
Amrut Intermediate
Paul John Edited

Taiwanese Single Malt
Kavalan Podium Single Malt

96

Scottish Single Malt
Aberfeldy Single Cask Unravel
Aberlour a'Bunadh Batch No. 33
Mo Òr Collection Aberlour 1990 20 Year Old
Ardbeg 1977
Ardbeg Kildalton 1980
Ardbeg Provenance 1974
Scotch Malt Whisky Society Cask 33.116 Aged 8 Years (Ardbeg)
Auchentoshan 1978 Bourbon Cask Ltd Ed.
Scotch Malt Whisky Society Cask 73.44 Aged 29 Years (Aultmore)
Master of Malt Balblair 35 Year Old Lost Bottling Series
Cadenhead Banff 34 Years Old
The BenRiach Single Cask 1983 Aged 30 Yrs
The BenRiach Single Cask 1996 Aged 17 Yrs
Port Charlotte PC10
Brora 25 Year Old 7th Release
Chieftain's Brora Aged 30 Years
Octomore 5 Years Old
Director's Cut Bruichladdich Aged 21 Years
Scotch Malt Whisky Society Cask 23.70 Aged 9 Years (Bruichladdich)
Duncan Taylor Octave Caperdonich 20 YO
Duncan Taylor Cardhu 26 Years Old
Duncan Taylor Cragganmore 25 Years Old
The Dalmore Candela Aged 50 Years
Gordon & MacPhail Glen Albyn 1976
Glencadam 30 Years Old Single Cask 1982
Scotch Malt Whisky Society Cask 104.13 Aged 36 Years (Glencraig)
The GlenDronach Single Cask 1992 21 Years
The GlenDronach Single Cask 1994 19 Years
The GlenDronach Single Cask 1994
Glenfarclas 1967 Family Casks Release V

Glenfarclas 1981 Family Casks Release VII
Glenfarclas 1989 Family Casks Release IX
Glenfarclas 1993 Family Casks Release IX
Glenfiddich 40 Years Old
Glenglassaugh 40 Year Old
Gordon & MacPhail Distillery Label Glen Grant 1960
Malts Of Scotland Glen Grant 1972
Gordon & MacPhail Glenlivet 1954
Rarest of the Rare Glenlochy 1980
Glenmorangie Truffle Oak
The Whisky Agency Glen Moray 35 YO
Highland Park Aged 25 Years
Highland Park 1973
Highland Park Loki Aged 15 Years
The Arran Malt 1996 'The Peacock'
Malts Of Scotland Isle of Arran 1996
Lagavulin 21 Years Old
Laphroaig PX Cask
Laphroaig Quarter Cask
Malts Of Scotland Lochside 1967
Duncan Taylor Octave Longmorn 15 Years
The Whisky Agency Longmorn 1965
Berry's Own Selection Macduff 2000
Scotch Malt Whisky Society Cask 64.34 Aged 21 Years (Mannochmore)
Scotch Malt Whisky Society Cask 64.42 Aged 22 Years (Mannochmore)
Cadenhead Miltonduff 22 years Old
Dun Bheagan Miltonduff 24 Years Old
Gordon and MacPhail Port Ellen 1979
Malts Of Scotland Port Ellen 1982
Rosebank 25 Years Old
Master of Malt Springbank Aged 19 Years

Scottish Vatted Malt
Big Peat
Big Peat Batch 20 Xmas 2011

Scottish Grain
Clan Denny Caledonian 45 Years Old

Scottish Blends
Ballantine's Finest
Dewar House Experimental Aged 17 Years

Irish Pure Pot Still
Redbreast 12 Years Old
Redbreast Aged 12 Years Cask Strength
Redbreast Aged 15 Years bott 12 Nov 12

Irish Blends
Jameson Rarest 2007 Vintage Reserve

Bourbon
Ancient Ancient Age 10 Years Old
Buffalo Trace Master Distiller Emeritus Elmer T Lee Collector's Edition
Buffalo Trace Single Oak Project Barrel #101
Four Roses Limited Edition 2012 Small Batch Barrel Strength
Old Weller Antique 107
Pappy Van Winkle's Family Reserve 15 YO
Willett Family Estate Bottled 14 Years Old

American Straight Rye
Bulleit 95 Rye
Rittenhouse Very Rare 21 YO Barrel 28
Rittenhouse Rye Aged 25 Years Barrel 19

American Small Batch
Cowboy Bourbon Texas Straight Bourbon

Whiskey Aged Three Years
Stranahan's Colorado Whiskey Batch #67
Stranahan's Colorado Whiskey Batch #90

Canadian Blended
Alberta Premium bott lott L1317
Crown Royal Special Reserve

Japanese Single Malt
Karuizawa 1967 Vintage
Scotch Malt Whisky Society Cask 116.17 Aged 25 Years (Yoichi)

Japanese Blended
Hibiki Aged 21 Years

English Single Malt
Hicks & Healey Cornish Whiskey 2004
The English Whisky Co. Chapter 6 English Single Malt Not Peated

Finnish Single Malt
Old Buck Second Release

German Single Malt
Derrina Einkorn Schwarzwälder Single Grain

Swedish Single Malt
Mackmyra Privus 03 Rökning Tillåten

Swiss Single Malt
Langatun Old Bear Châteauneuf-du-Pape

Welsh Single Malt
Penderyn Bourbon Matured Single Cask
Penderyn Portwood bott 1 Nov 12
Scotch Malt Whisky Society Cask 128.3 Aged 5 Years (Penderyn)

Australian Single Malt
Bakery Hill Classic Malt Cask Strength
Southern Coast Single Malt Batch 002

Indian Single Malt
Amrut Double Cask
Amrut Greedy Angels
Select Cask Peated
Paul John Single Malt Single Cask No 164

95.5

Scottish Single Malt
Wemyss Ardmore 1992 Single Speyside "Mellow Mariner"
The Whisky Agency Balmenach 1979
The BenRiach Aged 12 Years Sherry Wood
The BenRiach Single Cask 1988 24 Years
The BenRiach Single Cask 1990
Benromach 30 Years Old
The Whisky Broker Bowmore 14 Years Old
Bruichladdich Redder Still 1984
Scotch Malt Whisky Society Cask 127.20 Aged 8 Years (Bruichladdich)
Caol Ila 14 Years Old Unpeated Style
Caol Ila 'Distillery Only'
Caol Ila Special Release 2010 12 Years Old
The Warehouse Collection Clynelish 15 Yrs
Duncan Taylor Caol Ila 30 Years Old
Liquid Sun Caol Ila 1981
Old Malt Cask Clynelish Aged 28 Years
Cragganmore Special Release 2010 21 YO
The Dalmore Visitor Centre Exclusive
Elements of Islay Pe1
Berry's Own Selection Glencadam 1991
Cadenhead GlenDronach 21 Years Old
The Whisky Cask Glen Elgin Aged 25 Years

Glenfarclas 105
Glenfarclas 1961 Family Casks Release IX
Glen Grant Distillery Edition Cask 20 Years
The Glenlivet Founder's Reserve 21 Yrs Old
Gordon & MacPhail Glenlivet 1974
Scotch Malt Whisky Society Cask 2.80 Aged 15 Years (Glenlivet)
Glenmorangie 25 Years Old
Glen Moray 1995 Port Wood Finish
The Whisky Castle Glenrothes 21 Years Old
Single Cask Collection Glentauchers 17 Years Old
Highland Park Aged 18 Years
Highland Park Vintage 1978
Old Malt Cask Arran Aged 15 Years
Archives Laphroaig 1998 13 YO 2nd Release
Old Malt Cask Laphroaig Aged 15 Years
Scotch Malt Whisky Society Cask 29.106 Aged 13 Years (Laphroaig)
Scotch Malt Whisky Society Cask 7.75 Aged 27 Years (Longmorn)
The Macallan Fine Oak 12 Years Old
The Macallan Oscuro
Gordon & MacPhail Mortlach 1971
Longrow C.V
Chieftain's Mortlach Aged 22 Years
Gordon & MacPhail Strathisla 1969
Mo Òr Collection Tomatin 1976 34 Years Old
Mo Òr Collection Tullibardine 1965 44 YO
Glenbridge 40 Years Old
Wemyss 30 Years Islay "Heathery Smoke"

Scottish Grain
The Coopers Choice Lochside 1964 47 YO
Malts Of Scotland North British 1962

Scottish Vatted Malt
Compass Box Flaming Hart
Compass Box The Spice Tree

Scottish Grain
Clan Denny Invergordon 44 Years Old
Scotch Malt Whisky Society Cask G5.3 Aged 18 Years (Invergordon)

Scottish Blends
Johnnie Walker Black Label 12 Years Old
Royal Salute "62 Gun Salute"
William Grant's 25 Years Old

Irish Single Malt
The Tyrconnell Single Cask 11 Year Old
Bushmills Aged 21 Years
Sainsbury's Dún Léire Aged 8 Years

Bourbon
Booker's 7 Years 4 Months
Buffalo Trace Single Oak Project Barrel #27
Buffalo Trace Single Oak Project Barrel #30
Buffalo Trace Single Oak Project Barrel 63
Buffalo Trace Experiment Hot Box
Charter 101
Elijah Craig Barrel Proof Bourbon 12 Years
European Bourbon Rye Association Kentucky Straight Bourbon Whiskey 16 Years
Four Roses Limited Edition Small Batch 2011 Barrel Strength
Willett Pot Still Reserve

American Straight Rye
Sazerac Kentucky Straight Rye 18 Years Old

American Small Batch
Bad Guy Bourbon
Balcones Brimstone
Balcones Brimstone Texas Scrub Oak Smoked Corn Whisky
Balcones True Blue Cask Strength
Stranahan's Snowflake Cab Franc
The Notch Aged 8 Years
Canadian Blended
Alberta Premium
Forty Creek Port Wood Reserve
Gibson's Finest Rare Aged 18 Years
Japanese Single Malt
Golden Horse Chichibu Aged 12 Years
Hakushu Single Malt Whisky Agd 12 Yrs
Ichiro's Card "King of Hearts"
Ichiro's Malt Aged 20 Years
Japanese Single Grain
Kawasaki Single Grain
Austrian Single Malt
Pure Rye Malt J.H. bott code LPR 07
English Single Malt
Stephen Notman Whisky Live Taipei 2013
The English Whisky Co
German Single Malt
Austrasier Single Cask Grain
Swiss Single Malt
The Swiss Malt
Swedish Single Malt
Mackmyra Brukswhisky
Mackmyra Moment "Rimfrost"
Australian Single Malt
The Nant 3 Years Old Cask Strength
Release The Beast
Indian Blends
Rendezvous
Japanese Single Malt
Karuizawa 1964

95

Scottish Single Malt
Ardbeg 10
Ardbeg Mor
Auld Reekie Islay Malt
Master Of Malt Aultmore 15 Years Old
McDonald's Celebrated Ben Nevis
Bruichladdich 16 Years Old
Bruichladdich 1989 Black Art 2nd Edition
Octomore 10
Old Malt Cask Bruichladdich Aged 20 Years
Octomore 3rd Edition Aged 5 Years
Bunnahabhain Darach Ur Batch no. 4
The Warehouse Collection Bunnahabhain Aged 21 Years
Malts Of Scotland Bunnahabhain 1966
Duncan Taylor Caol Ila 28 Years Old
Old Malt Cask Caol Ila Aged 15 Years
Old Malt Cask Caol Ila Aged 16 Years
Wemyss 1996 Single Islay Caol Ila "Lemon Smoke"
Gordon and MacPhail Connoisseurs Choice Clynelish 1996
Celtique Connexion Saussignac Double Matured 1997

The Dalmore Eos Aged 59 Years
The Dalmore 62 Years Old
Dalwhinnie 15 Years Old
Glencadam Aged 10 Years
Glencadam Agd 14 Years Oloroso Finish
The GlenDronach Aged 33 Years
The GlenDronach 1991 Aged 20 Years
The GlenDronach 1993 Aged 19 Years
Glenfarclas 1962 Family Casks Release VI
Glenfarclas 1972 Family Casks Release VIII
Glenfiddich 18 Years Old
Glenfiddich Snow Phoenix
Glenglassaugh 1973 Family Silver
Glenglassaugh The Chosen Few 1st Edition "Ronnie Routledge" 35 Years Old
Glen Grant Aged 10 Years
The Glenlivet French Oak Reserve 15 YO
The Glenlivet Nadurra Aged 16 Years
Cadenhead Glenlivet 21 Years Old
Gordon & MacPhail Glenlivet 1966
Gordon & MacPhail Rare Old Glenlochy 79
Berry's Own Selection Glen Moray 1991
Glen Ord 25 Years Old
Chieftain's Glentaughers Aged 20 Years
A.D. Rattray Highland Park 1984
Old Malt Cask Inchgower Aged 16 Years
That Boutique-y Whisky Company Arran
Lagavulin Aged 16 Years
Lagavulin 12 Years Special Release 2012
Malts of Scotland Laphroaig 1996
The Warehouse Collection Linkwood 28 YO
Riegger's Selection Littlemill 1990
Gordon & MacPhail Longmorn 1973
Malts Of Scotland Longmorn 1992
The Macallan Lalique III 57 Years Old
Malts Of Scotland Macallan 1990
Mo Ôr Collection Macallan 1991 19 YO
Single Cask Collection Littlemill 21 YO
Mo Ôr Collection Miltonduff 1980 30 YO
Old & Rare Port Ellen Aged 30 Years
Old Malt Cask Tamdhu Aged 21 Years
Rosebank Aged 12 Years
Talisker Aged 20 Years
Talisker 57 Degrees North
The Perfect Dram Tomatin 34 Years Old
Tomintoul Aged 14 Years
Mo Ôr Collection Tomintoul 1967 43 YO
The Whisky Agency Tomintoul 1972
Master Of Malt Springbank 30 Year Old Lost Bottling Series
Maxwell 33 Year Old Highland Single Malt Mystery Lochside
Master Of Malt Speyside 40 YO 2nd Edition
Wemyss 1990 Highland "Tropical Spice"
Celtique Connexion Sauternes 16 Years Old
Scottish Vatted Malt
Compass Box Flaming Heart 4th Edition
Douglas Laing's Double Barrel Highland Park & Bowmore
Johnnie Walker Green Label 15 Years Old
Norse Cask Selection Vatted Islay 1992
Wild Scotsman Aged 15 Years Vatted Malt
Scottish Grain
Clan Denny Carsebridge Aged 45 Years

Jim Murray's Whisky Bible Award Winners 2014

Scottish Blends
The Bailie Nicol Jarvie (B.N.J)
Chivas Regal 25 Years Old
Clan Gold 3 Year Old
Glen Orin 30 Years old Blend
The Tweeddale Blend Aged 12 Years

Irish Pure Pot Still
Midleton 1973 Pure Pot Still

Irish Single Malt
Tyrconnell Aged 11 Years
Bushmills Select Casks Aged 12 Years
Bushmills Rare Aged 21 Years

Irish Blends
Jameson
Midleton Very Rare 2009

Bourbon
Big Bottom Straight Bourbon 91
Buffalo Trace Single Oak Project Barrel 14
Buffalo Trace Single Oak Project Barrel 132
Cougar Bourbon Aged 5 Years
Four Roses Single Barrel barrel 4-1F
Maker's 46
Woodford Reserve Master's Four Grain

American Corn Whiskey
Dixie Dew

American Straight Rye
Cougar Rye
High West Rocky Mountain 21 Year Old Rye
Rittenhouse Very Rare 21 YO Barrel 8
Sazerac Kentucky Straight Rye 18 Years Old

American Small Batch
McCarthy's Oregon Single Malt
McCarthy's Aged 3 Years batch W10-01
McCarthy's Aged 3 Years batch W12-01
Stranahan's Colorado Whiskey Batch #83
Woodstone Microspirit 5 Grain Straight
Bourbon Single Barrel No. 3

Other American Whiskey
High West Son of Bourye

Canadian Blended
Alberta Premium 25 Years Old
Danfield's Limited Edition Aged 21 Years
Wiser's Legacy
Wiser's Red Letter

Japanese Single Malt
The Hakushu Aged 15 Years Cask Strength
Hakushu 1984
Ichiro's Card "Four of Spades"
Yoichi Key Malt Agd 12 Yrs "Peaty & Salty"
Yoichi 20 Years Old
Pure Malt Black

Japanese Blended
Royal Aged 15 Years

English Single Malt
The English Whisky Co. Chapter 6 English
Single Malt Not Peated bott Jan 13
The English Whisky Co. Chapter 6 English
Single Malt Not Peated bott Apr 13
The English Whisky Co. Chapter 9 Peated/
Smokey bott 2012
The English Whisky Co. Chapter 14 English
Single Malt (unpeated)

Finnish Single Malt
Old Buck

French Single Malt
Kornog Single Malt Tourbé (Peated) Whisky
Breton Taourc'h Trived 12BC
P&M Corsican Single Malt Aged 7 Years

German Single Malt
The Alrik Smoked Hercynian 4 Years Old
Derrina Triticale Schwarzwälder Single Grain
Spinnaker 20 Years Old

Swedish Single Malt
Mackmyra Moment "Urberg"
Mackmyra Moment "Skog"
Mackmyra Moment "Mareld" (Sea Fire)

Swiss Single Malt
Interlaken Swiss Highland "Classic"

Welsh Single Malt
Penderyn Madeira bott Jun 11
Penderyn Peated bott 2 Nov 12
Penderyn Madeira bott 4 Feb 13
Penderyn Sherrywood Limited Edition

Australian Single Malt
Overeem Port Cask Matured Cask Strength
Overeem Sherry Cask Matured Cask
Southern Coast Single Malt Batch 006
Velvet Hammer 13 Years Old

Indian Single Malt
Amrut Two Continents Limited Edition
Amrut Two Continents 2nd Edition
Paul John Single Malt-Classic (Un Peated)

New Zealand Single Malt
The New Zealand Whisky Collection South
Island Single Malt Aged 21 Years

Taiwanese Single Malt
Kavalan Solist Fino Sherry Cask
Kavalan Single Malt Whisky Sherry Oak

94.5 (New Entries Only)

Scottish Single Malt
Aberfeldy Bits of Strange 16 Year Old
Scotch Malt Whisky Society Cask 33.121
Aged 8 Years (Ardbeg)
Auchentoshan Silveroak 1990 Ltd Release
That Boutique-y Whisky Aultmore
The BenRiach Single Cask 2005 8 Years
Scotch Malt Whisky Society Cask 3.192
Aged 24 Years (Bowmore)
Port Charlotte Heavily Peated
Scotch Malt Whisky Society Cask 127.28
Aged 9 Years (Bruichladdich)
Old Malt Cask Bunnahabhain 10 Years
Master of Malt Clynelish Aged 15 Years
Master of Malt Dailuaine 15 Years Old
That Boutique-y Whisky Dailuine 15 YO
The GlenDronach Single Cask 2002 10 Years
Cadenhead Glenlivet 24 Years Old
Scotch Malt Whisky Society Cask 2.83 Aged
19 Years (Glenlivet)
Scotch Malt Whisky Society Cask 35.68
Aged 25 Years (Glen Moray)
Scotch Malt Whisky Society Cask 4.173
Aged 23 Years (Highland Park)
Riegger's Selection Arran 1997
Isle of Jura 1977
Riegger's Selection Littlemill 1992
Berry's Own Selection Longmorn 1992

The Macallan Sienna

Gordon and MacPhail Distillery Label Scapa 2001

Gordon & MacPhail Distillery Label Strathisla 1965

Tomatin Legacy

Scottish Vatted Malt

Douglas Laing's Double Barrel Talisker & Craigellachie 2nd Release

Scottish Grain

Scotch Malt Whisky Society Cask G8.2 Aged 23 Years (Cambus)

The Coopers Choice Golden Grains Garnheath 1967 45 Years Old

Clan Denny North Of Scotland Vint. 38 Yrs

Clan Denny Port Dundas Vintage 24 Years

Bourbon

Buffalo Trace Single Oak Project Barrel #28

Buffalo Trace Single Oak Project Barrel #69

Buffalo Trace Single Oak Project Barrel #192

Colonel E.H. Taylor Small Batch

Parker's Heritage Collection Sixth Edition Master Distillery's Blend Of Mashbills 2001

American Small Batch

Dry Fly Cask Strength Straight Wheat

Palm Ridge Reserve Handmade Micro Batch Florida Whiskey

Wasmund's Single Malt Whisky 13 Months

Danish Single Malt

Stauning 2nd Edition Peated

Stauning Young Rye bott Aug 12

English Single Malt

The English Whisky Co. Chapter 7 Cask Strength

The English Whisky Co. Chapter 15 English Single Malt (peated) cask no. 615-618

Founders Private Cellar

French Single Malt

Kornog Single Malt Breton Sant Ivy 2013

German Single Malt

Derrina Grünkern Schwarzwälder Single Grain bott code. L11009

Spinnaker 25 Years Old

Welsh Single Malt

Penderyn Madeira bott 3 July 12

Australian Single Malt

Bakery Hill Double Wood cask no. 9078

Bakery Hill Peated Malt cask no. 6512

Indian Single Malt

Amrut Single Malt batch 41

Paul John Brilliance

Paul John Single Malt Cask No 163

94 (New Entries Only)

Scottish Single Malt

Wemyss 1998 Single Lowland Auchentoshan "Candied Fruit"

Balblair 1997 2nd Release

The Whisky Cask Ben Nevis Aged 16 Years

The BenRiach Single Cask 1984 28 Years

That Boutique-y Whisky BenRiach

Old Master Bowmore 16 Years Old

Master of Malt Braes O'Glenlivet 21 Years

Berry's Own Selection Bruichladdich 1991

Old Malt Cask Bruichladdich Aged 25 Years

Gordon and MacPhail Private Collection Caol Ila Madeira 1995

Wemyss 1980 Single Islay Caol Ila "The Smokery"

That Boutique-y Whisky Caperdonich

Master Of Malt Clynelish 16 Years Old

Provenance Clynelish Over 15 Years

That Boutique-y Whisky Deanston

The GlenDronach Cask Strength batch 2

Glenglassaugh The Chosen Few 1978

Glenglassaugh Muscat Finish

Provenance Glenlivet Over 11 Years

Gordon and MacPhail Connoisseurs Choice Glenlossie 1993

Gordon and MacPhail Distillery Label Imperial 1994

Scotch Malt Whisky Society Cask 72.25 Aged 29 Years

A.D. Rattray Ledaig 2004

Caermory Aged 20 Years

The Warehouse Collection Tomatin 19 Years

Finlaggan Old Reserve Cask Strength

Port Askaig Harbour Aged 19 Years

Scottish Vatted Malt

Compass Box The Peat Monster

Scottish Grain

Clan Denny Cameronbridge Aged 38 Years

Scotch Malt Whisky Society Cask G10.1 Aged 23 Years

Scottish Blends

Hanky Bannister 40 Year Old

Johnnie Walker X.R Aged 21 Years

The Lost Distilleries Batch 2

Bourbon

Buffalo Trace Single Oak Project Barrel #57

Buffalo Trace Single Oak Project Barrel #90

Buffalo Trace Single Oak Project Barrel #153

Buffalo Trace Single Oak Project Barrel #169

Buffalo Trace Single Oak Project Barrel #190

Buffalo Trace Experimental Wheat 125

Four Roses Single Barrel 9 Years 4 Months

Russell's Reserve Single Barrel

American Small Batch

Willett Family Estate Bottled Single Barrel Rye 4 Years Old Barrel no 45

American Small Batch

Stranahan's Colorado Whiskey Batch #94

Austrian Single Malt

Single Malt Selection J.H. bott code L7/02

Belgian Single Malt

The Belgian Owl Single Malt 60 Months

German Single Malt

The Glen Els The Journey

Blaue Maus 25 Years Old

Welsh Single Malt

Penderyn Icon of Wales Red Flag

Australian Single Malt

Bakery Hill Classic Malt cask no. 8212

The Nant Distillery 5 Year Old Cask Strength

Indian Single Malt

Amrut Bourbon

Bold (Amrut)

Paul John Single Malt

Scottish Malts

For those of you deciding to take the plunge and head off into the labyrinthine world of Scotch malt whisky, a piece of advice. And that is, be careful who you take your advice from. Because, too often, I hear that you should leave the Islays until you have tackled the featherlight Speysiders and the bolder, weightier Highlanders. This is just complete, patronising nonsense. The only time that rings true is if you are tasting a number of whiskies in one day. Then leave the smoky ones to last, so the lighter chaps get a fair hearing.

I know many people who didn't like whisky until they got a Talisker from Skye inside them, or a Lagavulin to swamp their tastebuds with oily iodine. The fact is, you can take your map of malt whisky, start at any point and head in whichever direction you feel. There are no hard and fast rules. Certainly with nearly 3,000 tasting notes for Scottish malts here you should have some help in picking where this journey of a lifetime begins.

It is also worth remembering not always to be seduced by age. It is true that many of the highest scores are given to big-aged whiskies. The truth is that the majority of malts, once they have lived beyond 25 years or so, suffer from oak influence rather than benefit. Part of the fun of discovering whiskies is to see how malts from different distilleries perform to age and type of cask. Happy discovering.

22

ORKNEY ISLANDS
Highland Park
Scapa

Wolfburn

Pultney

Clynelish
Brora

Balblair
Glenmorangie
Dalmore
Invergordon
Teaninich
Speyside see page 24
Banff ✝
Macduff
Glenglassaugh
Glen Ord
Royal Brackla
Knockdhu
Glendronach
Glenugie
Inverness ●
Glen Albyn ✝
Tomatin
Glendronach
Ardmore
Glen Mhor ✝
Glen Garioch
Millburn ✝
The Speyside Distillery
Royal Lochnagar
Aberdeen ●

Dalwhinnie
✝ Glenury Royal
Fettercairn
Glencadam
Fort William
Blair Athol
North Port
Glenesk ✝
Ben Nevis
✝ Lochside
Glenlochy ✝
Edradour
Aberfeldy
● **Dundee**

Glenturret
● **Perth**
Daftmill
Tullibardine
Deanston
Cameronbridge

Glengoyne
Rosebank
St. Magdelene
Glenkinchie
Loch Lomond
● **Edinburgh**
✝ Dumbarton
North British
✝ Interleven
✝ Littlemill
Glasgow ●
Auchentoshan
Strathclyde
Port Dundas
Kinclaith ✝

Girvan
Ailsa Bay
Ladyburn ✝

Bladnoch

Key
● **Major Town or City**
▲ Single Malt Distillery
▲ (*Italics*) Grain Distillery
✝ Dead Distillery

Speyside

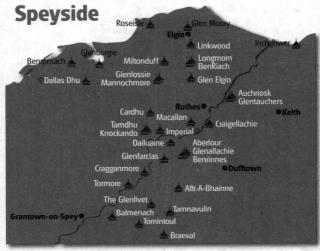

Distilleries by Town

Single Malts
ABERFELDY
Highlands (Perthshire), 1898. John Dewar & Sons. Working.

Aberfeldy Aged 12 Years db (83) n22 t21 f19 b21. The nose is superbly enriched by its usual and uniquely nutty depth. The bitter nougat delivery and finish fails to match the expectation. 40%

⋅⋅⋅ **Aberfeldy Bits of Strange 16 Year Old** db (94.5) n24 that just about unique aroma of a freshly-breeched cask: all dank oak, fruit and barley. Timeless and flawless...; t23.5 magnificent delivery with the sherry ringing loud and clear...and I mean clear...!!! Fabulous spices pepper the palate with oaky splinters; f23 long, forever drying with the oak, but enough voluptuous esters to make a big difference and balance out the finale; b24 one of those lovely casks which combines oaky and sugary bits in just the right proportions. A cracker of a cask – and sublime by present day sherry standards. The perfect way to start or end a day... 55.1%. sc. John Dewar & Sons. Matured in oak for 16 years. 318 bottles.

⋅⋅⋅ **Aberfeldy 16 Year Old Ramble** db (93.5) n23.5 even nuttier than usual, the spices positively pulse. Loads of sharp marmalade and walnut oil combine with stand-your-spoon-in oloroso; t24 heavy molasses notes arrive early and keep their foot in the door. Elsewhere the juiciest of Demerara sugars melt on the palate and begin to form a fabulous Melton Mowbray Hunt Cake richness. Again, walnuts are present and mix perfectly with the syrupy dates; f22 a slight buzz at the death tells its own tale, but before then enjoy the fade to the richest of all fruits cakes with the raisins now at their toastiest; b24 an almost flawless cask good enough for a big, robust, grape-exploding treat. 56%. 643 bottles. Whisky Shop Exclusive.

Aberfeldy Aged 18 Years "Chris Anderson's Cask" db (90) n24 plays the range from bourbon-rich red liquorice right down to diced kumquat; sharp, angular, bold, salty and very enticing; not a single blemish in distillate or wood; t23.5 sharp delivery with a mouth watering malty juiciness, but also weighty, too, with heavy oaks immediately apparent. Any threatening bitterness is seen off by a light dusting of muscovado and dried dates; f21.5 bites deep and caramels out; b22 had the natural caramels just not ticked over a little too exuberantly, this would have headed for a very high score. Aberfeldy in a very unusual light... 54.9%. 248 bottles.

Aberfeldy Aged 21 Years db (92) n24 have I just bitten into a high cocoa Lubec marzipan? The one which has an orange jam topping the almond paste? I must have. Some sublime bourbon hickory and Demerara on show, too. Superb! t23 uniquely nutty delivery screams "Aberfeldy!"; creamy texture without losing complexity. Out of the oils vanilla rises cleanly; f22 reverts to a fruitiness, including, alas, a slightly furry bitter marmalade drawl from, most probably, just one butt...; b23 a distillery I have long held in very high esteem here gives a pretty clear view as to why... 40%

Aberfeldy Aged 25 Years db (85) n24 t21 f19 b21. Just doesn't live up to the nose. When Tommy Dewar wrote, "We have a great regard for old age when it is bottled," as quoted on the label, I'm not sure he had as many as 25 years in mind. 40%. 150 bottles to mark opening of Dewar's World of Whisky.

⋰ **Aberfeldy Single Cask Aged 21 Years** bott 10 Oct 12 db (97) n24 what can you say: the colour of clear honey and with a nose to match...except the salty oakiness adds intriguing depth of fine whisky proportions; t24.5 near enough perfect mouth feel with the kind of punchy bite that every cask strength whisky should have. Actually, make that EVERY whisky. The oak skips around offering a chewy custard tart richness. But that clear honey (perfectly depicted by the bees on the label) is always there or thereabouts; f24 fantastic butterscotch layering, though with delicate marzipan and honey sub layers. The oak is profound but of the highest possible quality, injecting a fabulous drier balance, bordering on cocoa dusting; b24.5 if I find a better single cask this year, it might well be World Whisky of the Year. Just buzzes with magnificence... I have long regarded this not just one of the great distilleries of Scotland, but, even from its Diageo days, one of the true underachievers of world whisky. Not anymore. Someone who knows exactly what they are doing has invaded the Aberfeldy warehouses and made a beeline for the honey casks. This is exactly how malt whisky should bee.... 55.3%. sc. John Dewar & Sons Ltd. 172 bottles.

⋰ **Aberfeldy Single Cask Unravel** db (96) n24 a beautiful amalgam of dank oak casks (even from the outside) and freshly grated, juicy ginger. The soft distant oak-induced creamed rice and honey, topped with light molasses is superb; some major bourbon traits suggest a pretty virgin type of cask in play here; t24 intense oak but with all the bourbony sugars forming an unforgettable alliance with the black peppers which scorch into the roof of the mouth; like the other two Aberfeldys, the mouth feel is just about perfect...; f24 long, with that formidable coppery flourish sitting happily with the brown sugar and spices; so many layers, you almost give up counting... b24 this completes the best set of single cask malts I have tasted from any Scottish distillery for the last four or five years. Restores one's faith, it does... Oh, and this is supposed to be savoured while listening to some music. Don't bother; it conjures a major symphony of its own...56.5%. sc. John Dewar & Sons.

Berry's Own Selection Aberfeldy 1999 cask no. 27, bott 2012 (86) n21.5 t22 f21 b21.5. A very steady ship is kept as juicy barley struts its stuff on a quite oily base. 46%. nc ncf sc.

Gordon & MacPhail Connoisseurs Choice Aberfeldy 1991 (82) n20 t23 f19 b20. Once you'd expect nuts and raisins from this distillery in these kinds of casks, which I strongly suspect includes sherry. Not quite that now, as the finish does little for your next mouthful. But the original delivery shows just how majestic the spirit originally was. 43%

⋰ **Gordon & MacPhail Connoisseurs Choice Aberfeldy 1991** (78) n18 t22 f18 b20. Some sensational toffee and raisin moments here, while the sugar-spice combo is in perfect unison. However, also shows what a game of Russian roulette it is now using sherry butts. 46%. ncf.

James MacArthur Old Masters Aberfeldy 11 Years Old cask no. 83, dist 2000, bott Oct 11 (78.5) n18 t22.5 f19 b19. Delighted to report that the overall tasting experience is very much better than the nose, which is a fabulous example of when cask and spirit are barely on speaking terms. An old cask offering little positive life to the malt is the root cause, as the nose starkly reveals. The mouth-watering freshness of the totally immature malt on delivery is a fillip, though the finish expectedly follows the nose's lead. 55.8%. nc ncf sc.

Mo Òr Collection Aberfeldy 1994 16 Years Old first fill bourbon hogshead, cask no. 4016, dist 7 Jun 94, bott 24 Jan 11 (92) n23 recognised this as Aberfeldy even before I checked the label. Just the right degree of marzipan paste, going easy on the sugars. Also, the vaguest hint of smoke; t23.5 A fabulous layering of yet more marzipan with acacia honey and diced hazelnut; the malt is firm and even glistens with a degree of flintiness; f22.5 butterscotch and thickening strands of vanilla; b23 a typically nutty affair with perhaps an extra dollop of honey: the distillery nutshelled, in fact. When in this natural form, the distillery has the opportunity to reveal itself as a little-known gem of Scotland. 46%. nc ncf sc. Release No. 32. 460 bottles.

⋰ **Old Malt Cask Aberfeldy Aged 18 Years** refill hogshead, cask no. 8264, dist Jun 94, bott Jun 12 (92) n23 gorgeous beeswax and vanilla mix; t23.5 not sure if the humming I hear is from the bees or my own happiness: the orange blossom honey and butterscotch is pepped up with just-so black peppers; f22.5 much simpler with more butterscotch and light vanilla; b23 such a charming malt! One for the ladies, too... 50%. nc ncf sc. 306 bottles.

⊙ **That Boutique-y Whisky Company Aberfeldy** batch 1 (83) n21 t22 f19 b21. Didn't know Aberfeldy was in East Anglia. Only explanation for a malt this flat. 47%. 155 bottles.

⊙ **Wemyss Malts Aberfeldy 1994 Single Highland "Melon Cocktail"** hogshead, dist 94, bott 13 (88) n21 disappointing and enclosed. A little fruit shows promise against the so-so oak; t23 didn't quite see that coming: juicy, delicious, salivating barley of stunning intensity and empowered by a gorgeous mix of maple syrup (not always a good sign this early) and kiwi fruit; f21.5 the bittering oak confirm the nose and earlier maple syrup; b22.5 a long way from a perfect dram, but one to seek if character counts for something. 46%. sc. 311 bottles.

ABERLOUR
Speyside, 1826. Chivas Brothers. Working.

Aberlour 10 Years Old db (87.5) n22.5 t22 f21 b22. Remains a lusty fellow though here nothing like as sherry-cask faultless as before, nor displaying its usual honeyed twinkle. 43%

Aberlour 10 Years Old Sherry Cask Finish db (85) n21 t21 f21 b22. Bipolar and bittersweet with the firmness of the grain in vivid contrast to the gentle grape. 43%

Aberlour 12 Years Old Double Cask Matured db (88.5) n22 t22.5 f22 b22. Voluptuous and mouth-watering in some areas, firmer and less expansive in others. Pretty tasty in all of them. 43%

Aberlour 12 Years Old Non Chill-Filtered db (87) n22.5 impressive blood orange but a little untidy...and worrying; t22 superb weight with a surprising degree of barley coming through early on despite the close attention of the fruit; f21 the fuzzy finish confirms the fears raised on the nose...; b21.5 there are many excellent facets to this malt, not least the balance between barley and grape and the politeness of the gristy sugars. But a sulphured butt has crept into this one, taking the edge off the excellence and bringing down the score like a cold front drags down the thermometer. 48%. ncf.

Aberlour 12 Years Old Sherry Cask Matured db (88) n23 t22 f21 b22. Could do with some delicate extra sweetness to take it to the next level. Sophisticated nonetheless. 40%

Aberlour 13 Years Old sherry cask, hand fill db (84) n21 t22 f20 b21. Skimps on the complexity. 58.8%

Aberlour 14 Year Old Double Cask Matured db (84) n23 t22 f19 b20. Brilliant nose full of vibrant apples and spiced sultana, but then, after a complex, chewy, malt-enriched kick-off, falls surprisingly flat on its face. 40%

Aberlour 15 Years Cuvee Marie d'Ecosse db (91) n22 t24 f22 b23. This always was a deceptive lightweight, and it's got lighter still. It is sold primarily in France, and one can assume only that this is God's way of making amends for that pretentious, over-rated, caramel-ridden rubbish called Cognac they've had to endure. 43%

Aberlour 15 Year Old Sherry Finish db (91) n24 exceptionally clever use of oak to add a drier element to the sharper boiled cooking apple. And a whiff of the fermenting vessel, too; t22 the sharp fruit of the nose is magnified here ten times; f23 wave upon wave of malt concentrate; b22 quite unique: freaky, even. Really a whisky to be discovered and ridden. Once you acclimatize, you'll love it. 43%

Aberlour Aged 16 Years Double Cask Matured bott 23 Feb 10 db (94.5) n24 a magnificent marriage between sweet, juicy fruit and lively spice; sturdy-framed but giving grape, too; t24 the softest delivery of lightly sugared grape, salivating and sensuous; light spices struggle to free themselves from the gentle oils; f23 pithy with the vanilla determined to ensure a drier finale; b23.5 a joyous malt reminding us of just what clean, fresh sherry butts are capable of. A malt of unbridled magnificence. 43%

Aberlour 18 Years Old db (91) n22 thick milkshake with various fruits and vanilla; t22 immediate fresh juice which curdles beautifully as the vanilla is added; f24 wonderful fruit-chocolate fudge development: long, and guided by a gentle oiliness; b23 another high performance distillery age-stated bottling. 43%

Aberlour 100 Proof db (91) n23 t23 f22 b23. Stunning, sensational whisky, the most extraordinary Speysider of them all ...which it was when I wrote those official notes for the bottling back in '97, I think. Other malts have superseded it now, but on re-tasting I stand by those original notes, though I disassociate myself entirely with the rubbish: "In order to savour Aberlour 100 at its best add 1/3 to 1/2 pure water. 57.1%

Aberlour a'Bunadh Batch No. 31 db (93.5) n24 a resounding Jaffa Cake nose, except someone has extracted much of the sugar from the jam. Some big vanillas amid the cocoa, too; t23.5 a dry delivery with the spices punching hard as the grape unravels; a few maple syrup notes begin to creep in; f23 long, remains dry as the cocoa levels rise enormously; b23 chocolate, anyone...? 60.5%. nc ncf.

Aberlour a'Bunadh Batch No. 32 db (81.5) n20.5 t21 f20 b20. Decidedly acerbic, and this has nothing to do with the strength. Dries far too violently for any balance to be held. 60.4%. nc ncf.

Aberlour a'Bunadh Batch No. 33 db **(96)** n24 now there's an aroma! A good 20 minute nose, this one, as you try to follow the contours of the Demerara sugar and old sherry Dundee cake on one hand and the far drier, dustier vanillas on the other. The peppers are almost akin to those of a wheated bourbon; **t24.5** I think it's the mouth feel that grips the attention first, especially the sheer lusciousness of it. Just as you try to size that up, in pops all kinds of fruit and spice notes, framed by the almost inevitable dark chocolate; those bourbon notes on the nose are backed up by a superb honey-liquorice middle ground; **f23.5** much drier now but the vanillas and other oaky notes show not a degree of bitterness or misalignment; **b24** a masterful dram bubbling over with intense grape....and a whole lot more. Simply gorgeous: the oak involved in this is about as good as it gets. 61.1%. nc ncf.

Aberlour a'Bunadh Batch No. 34 db **(87.5)** n21 thick, fruit toffee: rather one dimensional; **t23.5** juicy and warming on delivery and then thickens and sweetens very fast. Again the toffee arrives in thick and chewy fashion, though the peppers offer welcome respite; **f21.5** spiced vanilla toffee; **b21.5** overall, impossible not to enjoy. But a bit of a roly-poly kind of malt in which you feel a little short-changed on the complexity front. 59.6%. nc ncf.

Aberlour a'Bunadh Batch No. 35 db **(90)** n22 well spiced and heading into red liquorice bourbon territory; **t22.5** silky and toffee-rich delivery. The sugars build cleverly, with the weight firmly on muscovado before the toffee fudge arrives. A light fruitiness mingles with the growing cocoa; **f23** quite complex with the vanillas and cocoa sure footed and well balanced; **b22.5** from the same school as Batch 34, but avoids being bogged down in sticky toffee; 60.4%. nc ncf.

Aberlour a'Bunadh Batch No. 36 db **(94)** n22.5 another Kentucky style nose: the liquorice and spiced vanilla take a vice-like grip and refuse to let go; **t24** big and beefy, the sugars arrive with a near treacle thickness, though it is the enormity of the spice which leaves you gasping; **f23.5** calms down but the oils ensure a more gentle version is played out to maximum complexity; the finish displays some flinty fruitiness, not unlike the crisper rye notes in a very good bourbon; **b24** can you find this year another Speyside whisky come with as much muscle as this...? I doubt it. A malt whisky that appears to have spent as much time in the gym as it did the warehouse... 60.3%. nc ncf.

Aberlour a'Bunadh Batch No. 37 db **(94.5)** n23 back to a more conventional sherry style here, or seemingly so at first, with what appears to be spiced grape turned up to full volume. However, some powerful bourbon notes are on the prowl and take over proceedings and the fruit effect crumbles...; **t24** spice, as ever, on delivery and as the juiciness grows in intensity, the peppers click up a notch or two; the sugars also arrive early, this time in much lighter mode. Possibly one of the most satisfying deliveries from this brand for some while...which is saying something; **f23.5** vanilla and late molasses interplay superbly; **b24** spice is playing a more central role in a'Bunadh these days and here it is used to excellent effect, putting quite an edge to the fruit. Really beautiful whisky. 59.6%. nc ncf.

Aberlour a'Bunadh Batch No. 38 db **(88.5)** n22 fruit toffee; **t22** kerpow...!!! the spice thumps you from every direction...hard. Lots more fruit toffee; **f22.5** fruit toffee vindaloo... with a few extra chilli peppers thrown in..; **b22** a heavyweight which maybe overdoes it on the spice. 60.5%. nc ncf.

Aberlour a'Bunadh Batch No. 39 db **(94)** n22 wonderful fruit ranging from over-ripe apple to succulent date. The spice is straining at the leash; the grape is encrusted in chocolate; **t24** a graceful dance is being choreographed on my tongue. The spices are at the centre, but swirling around them is a dizzying array of juicy grape and salivating barley. The usual big liquorice sub plot is there and the bourbon theme is underlined with honeycomb. Curiously, there is a small still coppery element to this as well. It does no harm at all; **f23.5** a fabulous denouement of Crunchy honeycomb candy and Cadbury's Fruit and Nut...though that is hardly doing justice to the quality of the cocoa...; **b24.5** when they ask for seasoned oak, I am sure the coopers must use pepper. Here, though, as spicy as it may be, everything is under control and weighted superbly. One of the great whiskies of 2012. And confirmation that the best sherry butts on the single malt scene are currently deployed in the a'Bunadh range. 59.8%. nc ncf.

Aberlour a'Bunadh Batch No. 40 db **(93.5)** n24 one of the freshest fruit noses you could hope for, with a barrow-full of greengages so ripe they are fit to explode...; **t23.5** silky and succulent, the barley and spice make a big impact after the grape skin introduction; inevitable spices lead to a drier butterscotch tart middle; **f22.5** relatively lightweight for an a'Bunadh with the accent firmly on the barley; **b23.5** a shapely malt with no little barley. 61%. nc ncf.

Aberlour a'Bunadh Batch No. 41 db **(83)** n21 t22 f20 b20. By normal standards, not too bad a malt, and another with the emphasis on the barley. But as an a'Bunadh, rather lacking... with one or two unattractive tangs too many. 59.7%. nc ncf.

Duncan Taylor Dimensions Aberlour 18 Years Old cask no. 7371, dist 1993 **(86)** n21 t22 **f21.5 b21.5.** A real steady Eddie cask which efficiently completes its task of dishing out the barley with minimum frills or fuss. 54.3%. nc ncf sc. Duncan Taylor & Co.

⸬ **Malts of Scotland Aberlour Christmas 2012** sherry hogshead, cask no. MoS 12053, dist Jun 00, bott Nov 12 (80) n19 t24 f18 b19. Classic sulphur stain on the nose and finish in particular, though this could be a lot worse. Elsewhere, there's stunning Dundee cake, groaning under the weight of burnt raisins and voluptuous spiced sultana. All the makings of a true superstar dram. What a shame. For the record, the Christmas of 2012 was my worst ever. This didn't improve it. 57.1%. ncf nc sc. 96 bottles.

Mo Ór Collection Aberlour 1990 20 Years Old first fill bourbon hogshead, cask no. 102107, dist 13 Nov 90, bott 9 Mar 11 (96) n24.5 as near as damn it perfect: the barley is not only clean and juicy, but tinged with over-ripe pear and sharpened by pear drop. Beyond fantastic! t24.5 wow! More of the same on the palate. The barley is proud and three dimensional with the spices not even thinking of hanging around and joining the fray from the third or fourth flavour wave. The sugars are crisp and diverse in style, the barley juice flows like a winter stream; f23 dries out as the first fill cask begins to exert some muscle and the sugars die quite quickly; b24 a dream cask which celebrates and perhaps even magnifies the magnificence of the classic Speyside style. Not a single note of weakness: extraordinary. Distilled on my 33rd birthday, I might well be putting this to one side to savour on my 55th! 46%. nc ncf sc. Release No. 31. The Whisky Talker. 300 bottles.

⸬ **Old Malt Cask Aberlour Aged 12 Years** refill hogshead, cask no. 9340, dist Jan 00, bott Jan 13 (82) n19 t21 f21 b21. Escapes from the tightened nose of the indifferent cask, displaying a surprising degree of malty versatility, helped by some excellent barley sugar. 50%. sc. Douglas Laing & Co. 312 bottles.

Old Malt Cask Aberlour Aged 21 Years refill sherry butt, cask no. 8230, dist Nov 90, bott Mar 12 (92) n22.5 lively and loud, the salt bites deep into the candy fruit; t23 podgy, sweet and chewy there is a fair degree of toffee raisin about this; f23 love the finale: we are now into Toffo cream toffee style candy with some muscovado sugars softening the finish further; b23.5 what a fabulous piece of oak the spirit was poured into! Brimming with character: superb! 50%. nc ncf sc. Douglas Laing & Co. 271 bottles.

⸬ **Provenance Aberlour Over 12 Years** refill hogshead, cask no. 9074, dist Summer 00, bott Autumn 12 (88) n22 suet pudding with molten iced sugar; t22 those sugars arrive early but it's the barley which stars in typical Speyside, grassy fashion; f22 soft oils lengthen the juicy finale; b22 well behaved whisky taking a singular malty path. 46%. nc ncf sc.

Riegger's Selection Aberlour 1990 bourbon cask, cask no.16915, dist 30 Oct 90, bott 25 Jan 11 (87.5) n21.5 walnut and cream cake; t22 brittle barley with a juicy, crisp sugary coating; f22 same again, except more accent on the vanilla rather than barley; b22 shows the firmer side of Aberlour, which was common in the 1980s, rarely seen today. 52.9%. nc ncf sc. 184 bottles.

Scott's Selection Aberlour 1987 bott 2012 (86.5) n22.5 t22 f21 b21. Ouch! So oaky it hurts! With some early thick honey to carry out damage limitation it starts off well enough. But then becomes just a little OTT. 54.9%. Speyside Distillers.

Single Cask Collection Aberlour 17 Years Old refill sherry hogshead, dist 1996 (87.5) n22 banana and putty; t22.5 briefly sharp and barley infested with a massive explosion of spice. But then quietens...and quietens...; f21.5 whispering vanilla; b21.5 considering that five of the six Scotch single malts I had tasted today had been tainted by sulphur, this came as something of a relief! Still not the brightest dram you'll ever find, though. 55.9%. sc.

⸬ **That Boutique-y Whisky Company Aberlour** batch 1 (92) n22 thick with grape, only the spices find a way through; t23.5 a punchy, blistering delivery with mildly burned sultanas offering a fruitcakey edge to this early on; the mid-ground goes all chocolatey on you...; sugars abound, but are kept honest by the drier, toastier oak notes; f23 long with those spices continuing their busyness. A silkier element allows the oak to enjoy centre stage late on; b23.5 the nose warns of a soupy dram. The reality is quite different, with a pleasing complexity unravelling. 53.4%. Master of Malt. 175 Bottles.

⸬ **That Boutique-y Whisky Company Aberlour** batch 2 (87.5) n22 just a soupcon of spice lifts the wallowing fruit; t23 juicy and spicy delivery excels. The caramels move in a little too quickly; f21 some spice buzz but the toffee and light molasses coats a little too well; b21.5 one of those toffee apple fruity guys. With emphasis on the toffee. 52.1%. 298 bottles.

ABHAINN DEARG

Highlands (Outer Hebrides), 2008. Marko Tayburn. Working.

Abhainn Dearg db (91) n22 the odd feint when pouring, but let the glass warm for a few minutes and the stronger elements soon burn off. What is left is a soft, pulpy gooseberry note as well as barley sugar and vague spice; t22.5 intense and chewy, the delivery confirms the wide cut and for a while the flavours are in suspension. Slowly, a meaningful dialogue with the palate begins and it's those gorgeous barley notes which are first to speak up, soon joined by maple syrup and butterscotch tart; the tongue nearly wipes a hole in the roof of your mouth as it tackles the flavour orgy; f23.5 a wonderful finish, not least because the malt appears to have relaxed into a sugary barleyfest with only a light coppery tang reminding us this is all from a brand new distillery forging its place in island folk lore; **b23** so here we go: the 1,000th new whisky of the 2013 Jim Murray Whisky Bible. And this year I give the honour of that landmark to Abhainn Dearg: the first bottling of a brand new Scotch single malt distillery is that very rarest of species. The fact it comes from Lewis really puts the icing on the cake. Some may remember that a couple of years back I made their new make the 1,001st new whisky for the 2011 edition: I have been keeping a close eye on this, now the most western scotch distillery. And it is strange to think that this is the first malt whisky to come from the Outer Hebrides with a licence attached.... My word, it was worth the wait. For after an unsteady start the quality becomes so clearly touched by angels. I can see everyone on the island having no qualms in tucking into this, even on the Sabbath. Well, maybe not... 46%. nc ncf sc.

Abhainn Dearg New Make db (92.5) n23 t23 f23.5 b23. Exceptionally well made with no feints and no waste, either. Oddly salty – possibly the saltiest new make I have encountered, and can think of no reason why it should be – with excellent weight as some extra copper from the new still takes hold. Given a good cask, no reason this impressive new born son of the Outer Hebrides won't go on to become something significant. 67%

Abhainn Dearg New Make db (88) n21.5 t23 f21.5 b22. OK. I admit that the 1,001st new whisky for the 2011 Bible wasn't whisky at all, but new make. But, as the Isle of Lewis has made it impossible for me not to visit there by now being an official whisky-making island, I thought it was worth celebrating. The new make in this form is rich, clean and malty but with a much heightened metallic feel to it, both on nose and taste, by comparison to other recently-opened distilleries. This is likely to change markedly over time as the stills settle in. So I had better start looking at the Cal-Mac Ferry timetables to go and find out for myself if it does... *Sample from cask at Whiskyfair Limburg 2010*

ALLT-Á-BHAINNE
Speyside, 1975. Chivas Brothers. Working.

Berry's Own Selection Allt-á-Bhainne 1995 cask no. 125284, bott 2011 (90.5) n22.5 just so great to find a malt so clean on the nose and allowing the complex barley almost free reign; t23 a touch oilier and more intense than the nose makes you expect; these waves thump down forcefully on the taste buds offering variation of sweetness and spice only; f22.5 just a little on the bitter side, though a touch of mocha is welcome; b22.5 if it's malt you want, it's malt you get...!! Of its type, absolutely wonderful. 53.4%. nc ncf sc. Berry Bros & Rudd.

Connoisseurs Choice Allt-á-Bhainne 1995 dist 1995 (88) n21.5 t22 f22.5 b22. Almost beautiful in its stark simplicity. 43%. Gordon & MacPhail.

James MacArthur Old Masters Allt-á-Bhainne 16 Years Old (89) n22 attractive interplay between newly cut hay and a squeeze or two of lime; t24 one of those satisfying deliveries where the malt, as this distillery has a tendency to do, appears to multiply in intensity not long after first delivery. The spices in the mid-ground are sublime; f21 lightens with almost indecent haste, leaving the vanillas to fight on alone; b22 one of those drams where the delivery is truly irresistible. 54.7%. James MacArthur & Co.

Mo Òr Collection Allt-á-Bhainne 1992 18 Years Old first fill bourbon hogshead, cask no. 12, dist 20 May 92, bott 6 Jan 11 (88) n22 a tangy, zesty maltfest which goes easy on the sugars; t23.5 clean with an exceptional emboldening of intense, sturdy malt that shows a just-so degree of give; f20.5 thins, and lightens with an accent on vanilla; b22 the nose and delivery is all you could want or ask of this distillery – and perhaps a little more besides. 46%. nc ncf sc. Release No. 33. The Whisky Talker. 460 bottles.

❖ **Old Malt Cask Allt-à-Bhainne Aged 15 Years** sherry butt, cask no. 8216, dist Dec 96, bott Mar 12 (89) n22.5 a few grapey notes rise above the intense barley; t22 clean arrival, succulent with a delicate spiced oak catch. The grape meanders gently throughout; f22.5 complex with the simple elements of fruit, barley and oak taking polite turns of dominance; b22 not just is there sherry influence, there isn't the slightest hint of an off note. Delicate and playful. 50%. nc ncf sc. Douglas Laing & Co. 273 bottles.

Old Malt Cask Allt-á-Bhainne Aged 18 Years refill hogshead, cask no. 7610, dist Feb 93, bott Aug 11 (87) n22 clean malt lightly sweetened with a touch of butterscotch; t23 soft with the light sugars seeping through ahead of the usual intense malt; f20 the malt loses ground to the thin vanillas; b22 easy going with the accent on the Speyside style. 50%. nc ncf sc. Douglas Laing & Co. 290 bottles.

❖ **Old Malt Cask Allt-à-Bhainne Aged 21 Years** sherry butt, cask no. 8820, dist May 91, bott Jul 12 (71.5) n17 t20 f16.5 b18. The thick, almost concentrated grape does its best to see off the worst excesses of the treated butt. 50%. nc ncf sc. Douglas Laing & Co. 323 bottles.

Provenance Allt-á-Bhainne Over 11 Years sherry butt, cask no. 7652, dist Summer 2000, bott Summer 2011 (82) n19 t21 f21 b21. The nose may inspire little confidence but the shape on the palate offers a never less than intriguing mix of the rich and the Spartan. 46%. nc ncf sc.

⟐ **Provenance Allt-A-Bhainne Over 12 Years** sherry butt, cask no. 9219, dist Summer 00, bott Autumn 12 (83) n21 t21.5 f20 b20.5. This may be from a sherry butt, but it has been a long time since a grape has had any kind of influence on this oak. Nothing wrong with the juicy maltiness, however. 46%. nc ncf sc. Douglas Laing & Co.

⟐ **Provenance Allt A Bhaine Over 12 Years** sherry butt, cask no. 9513, dist Summer 00, bott Winter 13 (91.5) n22.5 gooseberry tart with a porridge and molten sugar side dish; t23.5 big delivery of barley sweetened, stunningly, with coconut shards in maple syrup; the mid ground offers limited spice, more gooseberry tart; f22 the butterscotch finale is inevitable; keeps its weight and texture to near perfection to the very death; b23.5 from the boiled gooseberry school of deliciousness. And about as clean a Speysider as you'll find this year. 46%. nc ncf sc.

ARDBEG
Islay, 1815. Glenmorangie Plc. Working.

Ardbeg 10 Years Old db (97) n24 more complex, citrus-led and sophisticated than recent bottlings, though the peat is no less but now simply displayed in an even greater elegance; a beautiful sea salt strain to this; t24 gentle oils carry on them a lemon-lime edge, sweetened by barley and a weak solution of golden syrup; the peat is omnipotent, turning up in every crevice and wave, yet never one once overstepping its boundary; f24 stunningly clean, the oak offers not a bitter trace but rather a vanilla and butterscotch edge to the barley. Again the smoke wafts around in a manner unique in the world of whisky when it comes to sheer élan and adroitness; b25 like when you usually come across something that goes down so beautifully and with such a nimble touch and disarming allure, just close your eyes and enjoy... 46%

Ardbeg 10 bottling mark L10 152 db (95) n24.5 mesmerising: bigger oak kick than normal suggesting some extra age somewhere. But fits comfortably with the undulating peat and dusting of salt; captivating complexity: hard to find a ten year old offering more than this...; t23.5 a shade oilier than the norm with orange and honey mingling effortlessly with the smoke: more than a hint of icing sugar; melts in the mouth like a prawn cracker...but without the prawns...; f23.5 drying oak with cocoa powder. The oils help the sugars linger; b23.5 a bigger than normal version, but still wonderfully delicate. Fabulous and faultless. 46%. Canadian market bottling in English and French dual language label.

Ardbeg 17 Years Old earlier bottlings db (92) n23 t22 f23 b24. OK, I admit I had a big hand in this, creating it with the help of Glenmorangie Plc's John Smith. It was designed to take the weight off the better vintages of Ardbeg whilst ensuring a constant supply around the world. Certainly one of the more subtle expressions you are likely to find, though criticised by some for not being peaty enough. As the whisky's creator, all I can say is they are missing the point. 40%

Ardbeg 17 Years Old later bottlings db (90) n22 t23 f22 b23. The peat has all but vanished and cannot really be compared to the original 17-year-old: it's a bit like tasting a Macallan without the sherry: fascinating to see the naked body underneath, and certainly more of a turn on. Peat or no peat, great whisky by any standards. 40%

Ardbeg Guaranteed 30 Years Old db (91) n24 t23 f21 b23. An unsual beast, one of the last ever bottled by Allied. The charm and complexity early on is enormous, but the fade rate is surprising. That said, still a dram of considerable magnificence. 40%

Ardbeg 1977 db (96) n25 t24 f23 b24. When working through the Ardbeg stocks, I earmarked '77 a special vintage, the sweetest of them all. So it has proved. Only the '74 absorbed that extra oak that gave greater all-round complexity. Either way, the quality of the distillate is beyond measure: simply one of the greatest experiences – whisky or otherwise – of your life. 46%

Ardbeg 1978 db (91) n23 t24 f22 b22. An Ardbeg on the edge of losing it because of encroaching oak, hence the decision made by John Smith and I to bottle this vintage early alongside the 17-year-old. Nearly ten years on, still looks a pretty decent bottling, though slightly under strength! 43%

Ardbeg Alligator 1st Release db (94) n24 delicate: like a bomb aimer...steady, steady, steady...there she goes...and suddenly spices light up the nose; some coriander and cocoa, too; t22.5 surprisingly silky, soft and light; milky chocolate hides some lurking clove in the soothing smoke; f24 hits its stride for a magnificent finale: as long as you could possibly hope for and an-ever gathering intensity of busy, prickly spice. Mocha and a dab of praline see off any potential bitterness to the oaky fight back; b23.5 an alligator happy to play with you for a bit before sinking its teeth in. The spices, though big, are of the usual Ardbegian understatement. 51.2%. ncf. Exclusive for Ardbeg Committee members.

Ardbeg Alligator 2nd Release db (93) n24 clove and black pepper; a degree of bourbony polished leather and liquorice, too; t23 early Demerara sugars and smoke make way for that slow build up of spices again; though perhaps missing the subtlety of the first edition's quietness, it more than has its macho compensations; **f23** curiously, a short finale, as though more energy was expended in the delivery. Much drier with the oak having a good deal to say, though the spices nip satisfyingly; **b23** something of a different species to the Committee bottling having been matured a little longer, apparently. Well long enough for this to evolve into something just a little less subtle. The nose, though, remains something of striking beauty — even if barely recognisable from the first bottling. *51.2%. ncf.*

Ardbeg Almost There 3rd release dist 1998, bott 2007 db **(93)** n23 t24 f23 b23. Further proof that a whisky doesn't have to reach double figures in age to enter the realms of brilliance... *54.1%*

Ardbeg Blasda db **(90.5)** n23.5 distant kumquat and lime intertwine with gentle butterscotch tart; it's all about the multi-layered barley and the most vague smokiness imaginable which adds a kind of almost invisible weight; the overall clarity is like that found swimming off a Pacific atoll; **t22.5** sharp barley hits home to almost mouth-watering effect; again there is the most pathetic hint of something smoky (like the SMWS cask, perhaps from the local water and warehouse air), but it does the trick and adds just the right ballast; **f22** soft spices arrive apologetically, but here it could do with being at 46% just to give it some late lift; **b22.5** a beautiful, if slightly underpowered malt, which shows Ardbeg's naked self to glowing effect. Overshadowed by some degree in its class by the SMWS bottling, but still something to genuinely make the heart flutter. *40%*

Ardbeg Corryvreckan db **(96.5)** n23 excellent, thick, not entirely un-penetrable — but close — nascent smoke and a vignette of salty, coastal references save the day; **t24.5** amazing: here we have Ardbeg nutshelled. Just so many layers of almost uncountable personalities with perhaps the citrus leading the way in both tart and sweet form and then meaningful speeches from those saline-based, malty sea-spray refreshed barley notes with the oak, in vanilla form, in close proximity. The peat, almost too dense to be seen on the nose, opens out with a fanfare of phenols. It is slumping-in-the-chair stuff, the enormity of the peat taking on the majesty of Cathedral-esque proportions, the notes reverberating around the hollows and recesses and reaching dizzying heights; such is its confidence, this is a malt which says: "I know where I'm going...!"; **f24** long, outwardly laconic but on further investigation just brimming with complexity. Some brown sugary notes help the barley to come up trumps late on but it's the uniquely salty shield to the mocha which sets this apart. Simply brilliant and unique in its effortless enormity...even by Ardbeg standards; **b25** as famous writers — including the occasional genius film director (stand up wherever you are my heroes Powell and Pressburger) — appear to be attracted to Corryvreckan, the third most violent whirlpool found in the world and just off Islay, to boot, - I selected this as my 1,500th whisky tasted for the historic Jim Murray Whisky Bible 2009. I'm so glad I did because many have told me they thought Blasda ahead of this. To me, it's not even a contest. Currently I have only a sample. Soon I shall have a bottle. I doubt if even the feared whirlpool is this deep and perplexing. *57.1%. 5000 bottles.* ⊙

Ardbeg Day Bottling db **(97)** n24.5 a dry lead....seemingly. But it's the busy stuff behind the scenes which intrigues. In typical Ardbegian fashion it's what you have to take a little extra time to find which is the real turn on...apart from the rock pool salt, apart from the squeeze of slightly sugared lime, apart from the thinnest layer of honey, apart from the fracturing hickory, apart from the kelp;...; **t24.5** and while the nose at times seems hard and brittle, the delivery moulds itself into the shape of your palate. Soft oils fill the contours; dissolving sugars counter the well-mannered but advancing oak; the phenols take on an earthy form, languid spices and omnipresent smoke; **f23.5** dries again in a vanilla direction with the oak determined to have its say. But it is a gentle speech and one inclusive of the delicate phenols encouraging the growing citrus. The oils remain just higher than the norm and thicken the muscovado-sweetened mocha. The finish, one of the longest you will find this year, carries on beyond what you would normally expect of an Ardbeg. And that is saying something; **b24.5** I left this to be one of the last whiskies I tasted this year. I had an inkling that they might come up with something a little special, especially with the comparative disappointment of the fundamentally flawed Galileo. On first sweep I thought it was pretty ordinary. but I know this distillery a little too well. So I left the glass for some 20 minutes to breathe and compose itself and returned. To find a potential world whisky of the year... *56.8%. Available at distillery and Ardbeg embassies.*

Ardbeg Feis Ile 2011 db **(67)** n16 t19 f15 b17. If anyone asked me what not to do with an Ardbeg, my answer would be: don't put it into a PX cask. And if asked if anything could be worse, I'd day: yeah, a PX Cask reeking of sulphur. To be honest, I am only assuming this is PX, as there is no mention on my sample bottle and I have spoken to them about it. But for something to fail as completely as this my money is on PX. And sulphur. *55.4%*

Ardbeg Galileo 1999 db **(87.5)** n23 the nose is busy, with a constant criss-crossing of smoke and fruity notes...but takes all the nuances in its stride. Slightly more oak than you might expect of an Ardbeg this age, which seems to give a helping hand to the peat. Thick peaches and apricots absorb the impact of the more weighty bodies; **t23.5** the nose had already told you this was going to be a pretty thick delivery, and so it proves. Anyone old enough to remember original Old Jamaica chocolate from the 1970s (not the nonsense being sold today) will appreciate this as the cocoa and raisins are big with a kumquat sub-layer; the peat is omnipresent yet never overpowering; **f19** crashes back to earth with a fuzzy finish; **b22** today, as I taste this, I am celebrating the first birthday of my grand-daughter Islay-Mae, named after the greatest whisky island in the world. And this was one of half a dozen special whiskies I set aside to mark the event. For it is not often you get the chance to celebrate the first birthday of your first grand-daughter. Nor to taste a malt specially bottled to celebrate some of its fellow Ardbeg whisky that was sent into orbit for experimentation in the Space Station....At least I know a day like this will never be repeated. *49%*

Ardbeg Kildalton 1980 bott 2004 db (**96**) **n23 t24 f24 b25**. Proof positive that Ardbeg doesn't need peat to bring complexity, balance and Scotch whisky to their highest peaks... *57.6%*

Ardbeg Lord of the Isles bott Autumn 2006 db (**85**) **n20 t22 f22 b21**. A version of Ardbeg I have never really come to terms with. This bottling is of very low peating levels and shows a degree of Kildalton-style fruitiness. No probs there. But some of the casks are leaching a soft soapy character noticeable on the nose. Enjoyable enough, but a bit frustrating. *46%*

Ardbeg Mor db (**95**) **n24** coastal to the point of sea spray showering you, with the smell of salt all the way home until you reach the peat fire. Evocative, sharp with elements of vinegar to the iodine; **t24** one of the biggest deliveries from Ardbeg for yonks; the peat appears way above the normal 50%, thickest and gloriously bitter-sweet, the steadying vanillas carried on the soft oils; **f23** mocha enters the fray with a raspberry jam fruitiness trying to dampen the continuing smoke onslaught; **b24** quite simply Mor the merrier... *57.5%*

Ardbeg Provenance 1974 bott 1999 db (**96**) **n24 t25 f23 b24**. This is an exercise in subtlety and charisma, the beauty and the beast drawn into one. Until I came across the 25-year-old OMC verson during a thunderstorm in Denmark, this was arguably the finest whisky I had ever tasted: I opened this and drank from it to see in the year 2000. When I went through the Ardbeg warehouse stocks in 1997 I earmarked the '74 and '77 vintages as something special. This bottling has done me proud. *55.6%*

Ardbeg Renaissance db (**92**) **n22.5 t22.5 f23.5 b23.5**. How fitting that the 1,200th (and almost last) new-to-market whisky I had tasted for the 2009 Bible was Renaissance... because that's what I need after tasting that lot...!! This is an Ardbeg that comes on strong, is not afraid to wield a few hefty blows and yet, paradoxically, the heavier it gets the more delicate, sophisticated and better-balanced it becomes. Enigmatically Ardbegian. *55.9%*

Ardbeg Rollercoaster db (**90.5**) **n23** youthful malts dominate; a patchwork of smoke on many different levels from ashy to ethereal: almost dizzying; **t23** again, it's the young Ardbeg which dominates; the delivery is almost painful as you shake your head at the shock of the spices and unfettered peat. A genuine greenness to the malts though some natural caramels do make a smoky surge; **f23** long, buttery in part, limited sweetness; almost a touch of smoked bacon about it; **b21.5** to be honest, it was the end of another long day – and book – when I tasted this and I momentarily forgot the story behind the malt. My reaction to one of my researchers who happened to be in the tasting room was: "Bloody hell! They are sending me kids. If this was any younger I'd just be getting a bag of grist!" This malt may be a fabulous concept. And Rollercoaster is a pretty apt description, as this a dram which appears to have the whisky equivalent of Asperger's. So don't expect the kind of balance that sweeps you into a world that only Ardbeg knows. This, frankly, is not for the Ardbeg purist or snob. But for those determined to bisect the malt in all its forms and guises, it is the stuff of the most rampant hard-ons. *57.3%*

Ardbeg Still Young 2nd release dist 1998, bott 2006 db (**93**) **n24 t24 f22 b23**. A couple of generations back – maybe even less – this would not have been so much "Still Young" as "Getting on a Bit." This is a very good natural age for an Ardbeg as the oak is making a speech, but refuses to let it go on too long. Stylish – as one might expect. And, in my books, should be a regular feature. Go on. Be bold. Be proud say it: Ardbeg Aged 8 Years. Get away from the marketing straightjacket of old age... *56.2%. ncf.*

Ardbeg Supernova db (**97**) **n24.5** moody, atmospheric; hints and threats; Lynchian in its stark black and white forms, its meandering plot, its dark and at times indecipherable message and meaning...; **t24** at first a wall of friendly phenols but only when you stand back and see the overall picture you can get an idea just how mammoth that wall is; there are intense sugary gristy notes, then this cuts away slightly towards something more mouth-fillingly smoky but now with a hickory sweetness; a light oil captures the long, rhythmic waves, a pulse almost; **f24** gentle, sweetening cocoa notes evolve while the peat pulses... again...and again... **b24.5** apparently this was called "Supernova" in tribute of how I once described a very highly peated Ardbeg. This major beast, carrying a phenol level in excess of 100ppm, isn't quite a Supernova...much more of a Black Hole. Because once you get dragged into this one, there really is no escaping... *58.9%*

Ardbeg Supernova SN2010 db **(93.5) n24** youthful, punchy and spicy; vanillas and bananas add a sweetness to the molten peat; **t23.5** an explosion of sharp citrus and grassy malt. Not quite what was expected but the smoke and spices cause mayhem as they crash around the palate: eye-watering, safety harness-wearing stuff; **f23** the oak has a bitter-ish surprise but soft sugars compensate. Elsewhere the smoke and spice continues its rampage; **b23** there are Supernovas and there are Supernovas. Some have been going on a bit and have formed a shape and indescribable beauty with the aid of time; others are just starting off and though full of unquantifiable energy and wonder have a distance to travel. By comparison to last year's blockbusting Whisky Bible award winner, this is very much in the latter category. *60.1%*

⁙ **Ardbeg The Ultimate** ex-Manzanilla sherry cask **(78.5) n20 t22 f17.5 b19**. The best advice one can be given about bogs is to avoid them. *52.1%. Glenmorangie PLC.*

Ardbeg Uigeadail db **(97.5) n25 t24.5 f23.5 b24.5**. Massive yet tiny. Loud yet whispering. Seemingly ordinary from the bottle, yet unforgettable. It is snowing outside my hotel room in Calgary, yet the sun, in my soul at least, is shining. I came across this bottling while lecturing the Liquor Board of British Columbia in Vancouver on May 6th 2008, so one assumes it is a Canadian market bottling. It was one of those great moments in my whisky life on a par with tasting for the first time the Old Malt Cask 1975 at a tasting in Denmark. There is no masking genius.The only Scotch to come close to this one is another from Ardbeg, Corryvreckan. That has more oomph and lays the beauty and complexity on thick...it could easily have been top dog. But this particular Uigeadail (for I have tasted another bottling this year, without pen or computer to hand and therefore unofficially, which was a couple of points down) offers something far more restrained and cerebral. Believe me: this bottling will be going for thousands at auction in the very near future, I wager. *54.2%*

Ardbeg Uigeadail db **(89) n25 t22 f20 b22.** A curious Ardbeg with a nose to die for. Some tinkering - please guys, as the re-taste is not better - regarding the finish may lift this to being a true classic *54.1%*

⁙ **Ardbog The Ultimate** ex-Manzanilla sherry cask **(78.5) n20 t22 f17.5 b19**. The best advice one can given about bogs is to avoid them. *52.1%. Glenmorangie PLC*

Chieftain's Ardbeg Aged 13 Years barrel, cask no. 1779, dist Jun 98 **(87.5) n22** the most half-hearted phenols you are likely to find after the takeover from Allied; **t22** a gentle stampede of sweet, coffee enriched barley, the smoke takes time to form and intensify...but its getting there; **f21.5** thins out rather too dramatically; **b22** this bottling has gone to America. Get hold of the NYPD – now! Someone has half-inched the peat....!!! In evidence, I'd say the culprit was a certain Ed Dodson, who hadn't yet completely sorted out the non-removal of shell of the barley from the grist... No, honestly, officer, it wasn't me..!! And yes, now you come to mention it, I am a wise guy... *46%. nc ncf sc. Ian Macleod Distillers.*

Malts Of Scotland Ardbeg 1991 sherry hogshead, cask no. MoS11003, dist Feb 91, bott Oct 11 **(89) n22.5** I think there is more than the standard 50ppm at play here. A lot more. The phenols are enormous...and have to be to keep the crystalline, untainted sherry at bay... **t22** ...though on delivery guess which comes through first loud and clear: almost pure grape juice. This lessens the body and it takes a while for the peat to regroup and build up a significant body of intensity; **f22** so far this has been a battle between peat and pure sherry....and there is no clear winner on the finish, though at last some delicate though molasses-based sugars make a desired and required appearance; **b22.5** bugger me! A sherry butt Ardbeg not fatally torpedoed by sulphur...I don't believe it! *48.4%. nc ncf sc. Malts Of Scotland.*

⁙ **Master of Malt Ardbeg Aged 18 Years** refill sherry hogshead, dist 28 Oct 93, bott 29 Aug 12 **(97) n24** lack of space prevents me from giving this the full treatment. Probably lack of time, too: it would take a good two hours to get to the bottom of this. The peat is diffused evenly with primroses, nutmeg and walnut oil all playing leading roles. It is the salt which seems to lift everything above a secretive whisper and the citrus which creates the third dimension; **t23.5** the nose in fluid form and minus the primroses...; **f24.5** so, so long. The sugars are now flanked by some serious spices, but in keeping with the genteel nature of this malt, they somehow refuse to upset the balance. A sub layer of ulmo honey also keeps tabs on the neo bourbon characteristics of liquorice, hickory and toasted honeycomb; **b25** a thing of outstanding natural beauty...and probably one of the finest single casks ever commercially bottled. *56.3%. ncf sc. 252 bottles.*

Scotch Malt Whisky Society Cask 33.112 Aged 5 Years second fill sherry butt, cask no. 3965, dist 2005 **(87) n22 t23 f20 b22.** Was going along beautifully until a little historic sulphur managed to work its way into the equation. *60.8%. sc.*

Scotch Malt Whisky Society Cask 33.113 Aged 8 Years cask no. 1418, **(93.5) n23** dry, ashy, layered smoke...; **t23** dry, ashy, layered delivery...mainly of smoke. But sweetens as red liquorice and Demerara squeeze into the act; a few spicy moments; **f23** long, still retaining the oils and sugars but now extra vanillas and a hint of mocha; **b23.5** seems to go through quite a transformation of styles in a short time. As fascinating as it is delicious..! *60.4%. sc.*

Scotch Malt Whisky Society Cask 33.114 Aged 11 Years refill butt, cask no. 1553, dist 1999 **(79)** n20 t21 f19 f19. Irrespective as to whether a sherry butt is sound or sulphur-contaminated, the success of a whisky depends on whether a malt achieves an enjoyable degree of balance. This, alas, does not. And further, it also suffers from a slight sulphur taint. This is Ardbeg It should not be so. 56.3%. sc.

Scotch Malt Whisky Society Cask 33.115 Aged 11 Years refill sherry butt, cask no. 1606, dist 1999 **(73.5)** n19.5 t20 f16 b18. Syrupy. Stodgy. Bitter. Tight. Imbalanced. Sulphured. Following after 33.114, I don't know which I am most: shocked, appalled or angry. Well done, whoever is responsible. You get the world's best distillery. If not, then second only to Buffalo Trace. You have access to its stocks. And then you select, by Ardbegian standards, a complete dud. That, believe me, is some achievement! 55.4%. sc.

Scotch Malt Whisky Society Cask 33.116 Aged 8 Years first fill barrel, cask no. 1422, dist 2003 **(96)** n24 the line-up of the sweeter elements hurts the brain: from heather honey to Demerara, they run the gamut. Lavender works in tandem with the heather. And what's the peat doing all this time? Prowling like a proud lion: relaxed but ready for any trouble which might come its way...; **t23.5** hardly surprising the sugars form the vanguard of the delivery, or that soft oils usher in a smoky base. Nor is the degree of complexity, or the way the citrus cuts through the oil like some kind of smoky detergent through grease....; **f24** a succession of bourbon tannins now add a weight that is not peat-related. That said, never for a moment becomes heavy going and delicate notes, even now, abound; **b24.5** Ardbeg at its most amorous. Worth getting 33.113 as a comparison: the difference, though presumably from the same batch, makes the hair stand on end. this is what happens when all the sugars make a countering contribution, rather than being passive a la 113... 60.4%. sc.

⁙ **Scotch Malt Whisky Society Cask 33.120 Aged 8 Years** 1st fill barrel, ex bourbon dist 16 Sept 03 **(97.5)** n24.5 because it is still young enough, the gristiness hangs around the glass limp and glowing like someone prostrate having just experienced the greatest sex of their life; and because the cask is top quality there is also a maturity and depth which offers a counter to the sweet malt and slightly rancid smoke, which is a cross between a beach bonfire and an old crofter's hearth; **t24.5** if you didn't think it possible for a nose to completely come alive and be translated in the glass, then try this. Except there is unquestionably more. The relative youth offers a salivating juiciness after which appears the drier embers and charred malt husk; the mid ground really emphasises the youngest aspect, but by underlining the purity and trueness of the malt, which leaks out independently of the smoke; above all though, the sugars: layer upon layer of toasty Demerara and muscovado **f24** long, at last tapering in sweetness, with a little liquorice and mocha to add to the sugars and, finally, tip-of-the-tongue spices; **b24.5** a very simple question begs to be asked: why isn't something this quintessentially Ardbeg, a single cask which points a bright beam on the distillery's greatness, not bottled under the distillery's own label? This is about as complex as any single cask is able to be. Confirmation that the argument for an 8-year-old Ardbeg at100 per cent ex-bourbon is not as much compelling as unanswerable. For it is time to stop mucking around with the low quality wine cask nonsense and get back to the magnificent and truly unique basics. 58.5%

⁙ **Scotch Malt Whisky Society Cask 33.121 Aged 8 Years** 1st fill barrel, dist 1 Jul 04 **(94.5)** n24 adorable gristy smoke. Hard to better the balance between salt, malt, smoke and sugar. The phenols are probably lower than the norm, but the complexity is right up there...; **t23.5** as expected, it is sweet, juicy, gristy barley first to cross the threshold; the spices appear to radiate from the centre outwards, the sugars solidifying in their wake; the mid-ground has some fascinating coppery moments lubricated by the softest of oils; **f23** the copper theme continues, with the spices pinging off the metallic firmness; **b24** very unusual Ardbeg which appears to be showing some recent work to a still. The smoke, though constantly heard, is merely a spectator. 59%. nc ncf sc. 243 bottles.

⁙ **Scotch Malt Whisky Society Cask 33.123 Aged 7 Years** 2nd fill barrel, dist 1 Apr 05 **(84.5)** n21 t22 f20.5 b21. Unhelpful wood interferes on the nose and the finish hits the buffers with an unwelcome late tang, too. The peat is shunted off into an unusual cough sweet siding. 59%. nc ncf sc. 234 bottles.

⁙ **Scotch Malt Whisky Society Cask 33.128 Aged 7 Years** 1st fill barrel, dist 9 May 05 **(89)** n22.5 gruff phenols this time don't appear to be hunting for the normal complex route. A kind of Fisherman's Friend- Parma Violet sweetshop duet, though with some salt added to the mix; **t22.5** eye-watering delivery: the Demerara and phenols are scrunched up tight for maximum impact; **f22.5** liquorice and hickory form a rock-hard gate at the finish while the spices go ballistic; **b21.5** one of the most unsubtle Ardbegs I've seen in a while. But you have to admire the effect. 64.6%. nc ncf sc. 242 bottles.

⁙ **That Boutique-y Whisky Company Ardbeg** batch 4 **(86)** n21.5 t22 f21 b21.5. Surprisingly oily, overly sweet and the smoke appears to be infused with some strange and surprising botanicals. 52.4%. Master Of Malt. 427 bottles.

ARDMORE
Speyside, 1899. Beam Inc. Working.

Ardmore 100th Anniversary 12 Years Old dist 1986, bott 1999 db **(94)** n24 t23.5 f22.5 b24. Brilliant. Absolutely stunning, with the peat almost playing games on the palate. Had they not put caramel in this bottling, it most likely would have been an award winner. So, by this time next year, I fully expect to see every last bottle accounted for... 40%

Ardmore 25 Years Old db **(89.5)** n21 t23.5 f22.5 b22.5 a 25-y-o box of chocolates: coffee creams, fudge, orange cream...they are all in there. The nose maybe ordinary: what follows is anything but. 51.4%. ncf.

Ardmore 30 Years Old Cask Strength db **(94)** n23.5 the first time I have encountered a cough-sweetish aroma on an Ardmore but, like every aspect, it is played down and delicate. Melting sugar on porridge. Citrus notes of varying intensity. Fascinating for its apparent metal hand in velvet glove approach; t23.5 sweet, gristy delivery even after all these years. And a squeeze of sharp lime, too, and no shortage of spices. Does all in its power to appear half its age. This includes blocking the oaks from over development and satisfying itself with a smoky, mocha middle; the muscovado sugars are, with the smoke, spread evenly; f23 busy spices and a lazy build up of vanillas; b24 I remember when the present owners of Ardmore launched their first ever distillery bottling. Over a lunch with the hierarchy there I told them, with a passion, to ease off with the caramel so the world can see just how complex this whisky can be. This brilliant, technically faultless, bottling is far more eloquent and persuasive than I was that or any other day... 53.7%. nc ncf. 1428 bottles.

Ardmore Fully Peated Quarter Casks db **(89)** n21 t23 f23 b22. This is an astonishingly brave attempt by the new owners of Ardmore who, joy of all joys, are committed to putting this distillery in the public domain. Anyone with a 2004 copy of the Whisky Bible will see that my prayers have at last been answered. However, this bottling is for Duty Free and, due to the enormous learning curve associated with this technique, a work in progress. They have used the Quarter Cask process which has been such a spectacular success at its sister distillery Laphroaig. Here I think they have had the odd slight teething problem. Firstly, Ardmore has rarely been filled in ex-bourbon and that oak type is having an effect on the balance and smoke weight; also they have unwisely added caramel, which has flattened things further. I don't expect the caramel to be in later bottlings and, likewise, I think the bourbon edge might be purposely blunted a little. But for a first attempt this is seriously big whisky that shows enormous promise. When they get this right, it could – and should – be a superstar. Now I await the more traditional vintage bottlings... 46%. ncf.

Ardmore Traditional Cask db **(88.5)** n21.5 t22 f23 b22. Not quite what I expected. "Jim. Any ideas on improving the flavour profile?" asked the nice man from Ardmore distillery when they were originally launching the thing. "Yes. Cut out the caramel." "Ah, right..." So what do I find when the next bottling comes along? More caramel. It's good to have influence... Actually, I can't quite tell if this is a result of natural caramelization from the quarter casking or just an extra dollop of the stuff in the bottling hall. The result is pretty similar: some of the finer complexity is lost. My guess, due to an extra fraction of sweetness and spice, is that it is the former. All that said, the overall experience remains quite beautiful. And this remains one of my top ten distilleries in the world. 46%. ncf.

Teacher's Highland Single Malt quarter cask finish db **(89)** n22.5 a uniquely floral twist to the un-Ardmorish peat. Of course, there is always peat on Ardmore...but this displays an unusual salty coarseness above the usual 9ppm phenols which suits; lots of toffee-vanilla notes, but patted down by elegant kumquat; t23 they like silk in India, so this should be appreciated. Cream toffee with a two-pronged peat attack – both smoky and spicy; an interesting coppery tang in the mid-ground, as if a still had recently undergone remedial work; f21.5 just a little too heavy on the buttery toffee fudge; b22 This is Ardmore at its very peatiest. And had not the colouring levels been heavily tweaked to meet the flawed perceptions of what some markets believe makes a good whisky, this malt would have been better still. As it is: superb. With the potential of achieving greatness if only they have the confidence and courage... 40%. India/Far East Travel Retail exclusive.

⠿ **Cadenhead Ardmore 15 Years Old** **(88.5)** n22 a little mint mixed in with delicate, sweetened smoke; t22 salivating barley and tingling spices outweigh the phenols; f22.5 a touch bitter from the oak, but a good balancing of icing sugar and kumquat; b22 a malt which whispers its way through life. 46%. sc. WM Cadenhead Ltd. 366 bottles.

Dun Bheagan Ardmore 12 Years Old St Etienne rum finish, dist Jun 99 **(87)** n22.5 astonishingly complex aroma – all shadows and whispers. Perhaps a little smoke here, maybe a touch of lime peel there; t22 the barley heads the parade of delicate soft, almost guarded notes; the fruit is inconsistent though fine; f20.5 warm and a little bitter; b22 must admit: I hadn't read the label and was scratching my head wondering when I'd encountered an Ardmore like this before. Believe me: I hadn't. 46%. nc ncf sc. Ian Macleod Distillers.

Liquid Sun Ardmore 19 Years Old bourbon cask, dist 1992, bott 2011 **(91.5) n22.5** as though a kipper has been smoked after being marinated in orange juice...; **t23.5** beautiful in both texture and weight, it is not long before it becomes evident this is a more heavily peated Ardmore than the norm; the layering of phenols and liquorice is glorious; **f22.5** long with a slow melting of molassed sugars and more liquorice; the smoke bounds along beautifully; **b23** someone upped the peat smoke big time. This bottling effortlessly accentuates the greatness of this distillery. *49.9%. sc. The Whisky Agency.*

⁓ **Malts of Scotland Ardmore 1991** Rum barrel **(87) n21** stiff smoke, though hides behind the crystalline, nippy oak; **t23** salivating, juicy delivery at first offering big barley; sweetens and sharpens simultaneously; the middle heads towards a coffee theme, then abruptly closes down; **f21** thin, sugar encased, in the manner of toffee apple toffee...; **b22** an occasional problem with rum casks is that the sugary element they offer can sometimes enclose the malt it is supposedly helping to enrich. Here is a good example, though the delivery is far from lacking. *53.8%*

Mo Òr Collection Ardmore 1992 18 Years Old first fill bourbon barrel, cask no. 5013, dist 24 Jun 92, bott 21 Jan 11 **(85.5) n21 t23 f20 b21.5**. Behaves absolutely nothing like a first-fill bourbon barrel. The oak interface is barely discernible, other than a slight soapiness much more associated with a clapped out third fill. Still a malt with some outstanding moments, especially as the sugars and smoke merge into a glorious spiciness. *46%. nc ncf sc. Release No. 34. The Whisky Talker. 286 bottles.*

⁓ **Old Malt Cask Ardmore Aged 16 Years** refill hogshead, cask no. 8020, dist Feb 96, bott Feb 12 **(84.5) n21 t21.5 f21 b21**. Mild brown sugar stirred into a spiced, cocoa-rich smoky oily dram. Perhaps a little too warming. *50%. nc ncf sc. Douglas Laing & Co. 315 bottles.*

Provenance Ardmore Over 7 Years refill hogshead, cask no. 6959, dist 2003, bott 2011 **(86) n22 t22.5 f20.5 b21**. Here's a little known fact: when I am working on a blend, it is not unknown for me to take home some Ardmore aged between three and seven to drink while relaxing, so entertaining can it be. This, though, comes from a cask which is pretty well used, so that the interplay between spirit and oak doesn't trouble you too much. *46%. nc ncf sc.*

Provenance Ardmore Over 8 Years barrel, cask no. 7928, dist Autumn 2003, bott Winter 2011 **(89.5) n24** one of the most delightful experiences in Scotland is being in the mash room at Ardmore when the boiling water strikes the grist. Here you get a semblance of the aroma; a little background noise states for certain a slightly bitter finish...; **t22.5** just enough oil to stretch every last barley-peat sinew the maximum distance; **f20.5** butterscotch and citrus, then...errr...bitterish; **b22** go on, I dare you to grab a bottle of this and NOT fall in love with the aroma... *46%. nc ncf sc. Douglas Laing & Co.*

⁓ **Provenance Ardmore Over 9 Years** refill barrel, cask no. 9341, dist Autumn 2003, bott Winter 13 **(88.5) n21.5** delicate, smoky grist; **t22.5** refreshing, salivating with a busy burst of phenols; excellent spice development; **f22** long, with vanilla dissolving into soft oils; **b22.5** even when in a lazy, sleepy old cask like this, a high quality malt which refuses to let you down. *46%. nc ncf sc. Douglas Laing & Co.*

Scotch Malt Whisky Society Cask 66.35 Age 9 Years refill butt, cask no. 1064, dist 2002 **(88.5) n22** grape with all the give of a coat of armour...; the smoke rattles around somewhere inside; **t23** even the smoke feels it might splinter into a million pieces at any moment; the grape is crunchy and burnt; **f21.5** the small degree of bitterness doesn't come softly; **b22** have not been supplied with details of cask type yet, but probably refill sherry. Whichever, it certainly puts the 'ard into Ardmore.... *58.2%. sc.*

⁓ **Scotch Malt Whisky Society Cask 66.36 Aged 9 Years** refill butt, dist 17 Jul 02 **(83.5) n22.5 t21 f19 b21**. Smoke and sherry rarely works. Here, there is a poor (lightly sulphured) cask at work but the hickory and ersatz coffee combine with thick molasses to make for an interesting few moments. *58.2%. nc ncf sc. 702 bottles.*

⁓ **Scotch Malt Whisky Society Cask 66.40 Aged 10 Years** refill barrel, dist 9 Oct 02 **(87.5) n21.5** a slight bitter bite from the oak; peat and coal dust; **t22.5** busy spice, but barley dominates; **f21** the oak again seems unsettled, but is patched up by the oils; **b22.5** a bit lumpy and, for all its attractiveness, fails to find the usual distillery rhythm. *58.9%. nc ncf sc.*

⁓ **Scotch Malt Whisky Society Cask 66.41 Aged 9 Years** refill barrel, dist 17 Nov 03 **(91.5) n23** oak doesn't turn up: citrus and almost pathetic smoke all the way: delicious, though...; **t23** mouth-watering with gristy sugars zipping around the palate; a slow but telling build up of spice; **f23** at last some oak with a delicate minty cocoa finale; **b22.5** unbelievably light: molten grist. An essay on understatement. *60.2%. nc ncf sc. 130 bottles.*

Single Malts Of Scotland Ardmore 1992 (90.5) n23 remember those guns which used to fire caps...? **t23.5** soft grapefruit, a sprinkle of salt and growing acacia honey; the barley is clean and confident throughout; the smoke hovers rather than dives in; **f21.5** vanilla, cocoa and spice; **b22.5** a very lightly peated version it may be. But it certainly doesn't stint on complexity. A delight. *49.3%. ncf sc. Speciality Drinks. 207 bottles.*

Wemyss Ardmore 1992 Single Speyside "Mellow Mariner" barrel (95.5) n24 I think if I was asked to show exactly how an Ardmore should "sniff", then this would be just about it. Slightly above the usual peating level to start with, the smoke has reduced just enough over time to form the perfect frame for the charming butterscotch tart and chocolate caramel mix. Gorgeous weight, profound barley and not a single flaw; t24 off we go again: the nose but in liquid form. The delicate peat entirely envelopes the palate but it is the differing sugary tones, varying in intensity, style and weight which really press the buttons, especially as they are so in tune with the busy spices. Muscovado and liquorice are the front runners but some toasted caramel also has a telling input; f23 all the slightly drier, toastier notes converge with the sugars now more of a drier New Zealand style and the phenols now take on a more weighty smokiness; b24.5 as I write this, Grimsby Town have just been knocked out of the play offs for a place in the Football league – so this will be the only Mellow Mariner in the UK right now. Mind you, after a couple of glasses of this even the most ardent Grimsby supporter - Mariner – will have a smile on his face, and the loss to Newport will seem little more than one of life's oft dwelt deuces. Easily one of the finest whiskies unveiled by Wemyss. 46%. sc. 213 bottles.

AUCHENTOSHAN

Lowlands, 1800. Morrison Bowmore. Working.

Auchentoshan 10 Years Old db (81) n22 t21 f19 b19. Much better, maltier, cleaner nose than before. But after the initial barley surge on the palate it shows a much thinner character. 40%

Auchentoshan 12 Years Old db (91.5) n22.5 sexy fruit element – citrus and apples in particular – perfectly lightens the rich, oily barley; t23.5 oily and buttery; intense barley carrying delicate marzipan and vanilla; f22.5 simplistic, but the oils keep matters lush and the delicate sugars do the rest; b23 a delicious malt very much happier with itself than it has been for a while. 40%

Auchentoshan 14 Years Old Cooper's Reserve db (83.5) n20 t21.5 f21 b21. Malty, a little nutty and juicy in part. 46%. ncf.

Auchentoshan 21 Years Old db (93) n23.5 a sprig of mint buried in barely warmed peat, all with an undercoat of the most delicate honeys; t23 velvety and waif-like, the barley-honey theme is played out is hushed tones and unspoiled elegance; f23 the smoke deftly returns as the vanillas and citrus slowly rise but the gentle honey-barley plays to the end, despite the shy introduction of cocoa; b23.5 one of the finest Lowland distillery bottlings of our time. A near faultless masterpiece of astonishing complexity to be cherished and discussed with deserved reverence. So delicate, you fear that sniffing too hard will break the poor thing...! 43%.

Auchentoshan 1975 db (88) n22.5 a soft, pliable nose: no bites or nibbles. Just orange and caramel...; only as the glass dries does the enormity of the oak begin to reveal itself; t22.5 takes time before the age begins to tell: after a silky, if slightly untaxing, start the tannins and spices begin to roll over the palate; sharp sugars spike here and there; f21 back to sleep with the caramel, though a little spice does pulse; b22 goes heavy on the natural caramels. Does not even remotely show its enormous age for this distillery. I detest the word "smooth". But for those who prefer that kind of malt...well, your dreams have come true...; 45.6%

Auchentoshan 1977 Sherry Cask Matured oloroso sherry cask db (89) n23 t22 f22 b22. Rich, creamy and spicy. Almost a digestive biscuit mealiness with a sharp marmalade spread. 49%. sc. Morrison Bowmore. 240 bottles.

Auchentoshan 1978 Bourbon Cask Matured Limited Edition db (96) n24.5 a nose which stops you in your tracks: Taiwanese green tea sweetened with a brave and enthralling mix of muscovado sugar and manuka honey. There is essence of Kentucky, too, with a bourbony-liquorice trait while the vanillas head at you with two or three different degrees of intensity. How subtle. How complex. So beguiling, you almost forget to drink the stuff... t24 wonderful strands of sweetness of varying types and levels, from the lighter, fragile citrus notes to something sturdier and more honeyed; the middle ground has a few oily moments which allow all the elements to mix without bias or domination: a near perfectly balanced harmony; f23.5 long, lush with the barley now having the confidence to reveal itself while the toasted fudge makes an attractive and fitting bitter-sweet finale; b24 if there was a Lowlander of the Year, this'd probably wipe the floor with the rest. It's as though someone was in a warehouse, stumbled across this gem and protected it with his life to ensure it was not lost in some blend or other. Whoever is responsible should be given a gold medal, or a Dumbarton season ticket. Ensure you taste this one at body temperature for full blow-away results. 53.4%. 480 bottles.

Auchentoshan 1979 db (94) n23.5 very well aged Christmas fruit cake. With an extra thick layer of top quality marzipan; t24 sumptuous delivery with the burnt raisin biting deep; bursting with juicy barley; f23 long with the emphasis on the dryness of the sherry; b23.5 it's amazing what a near faultless sherry butt can do. 50.1%

Auchentoshan 1998 Sherry Cask Matured fino sherry cask db **(81.5)** n21 t22 f18.5 b20. A genuine shame. Before these casks were treated in Jerez, I imagine they were spectacular. Even with the obvious faults apparent, the nuttiness is profound and milks every last atom of the oils at work to maximum effect. The sugars, also, are delicate and gorgeously weighted. There is still much which is excellent to concentrate on here. *54.6%. ncf. 6000 bottles.*

⁝⁝⁝ **Auchentoshan American Oak** db **(85.5)** n21.5 t22 f20.5 b21.5. Very curious: reminds me very much of Penderyn Welsh whisky before it hits the Madeira casks. Quite creamy with some toasted honeycomb making a brief cameo appearance. *40%*

Auchentoshan Classic db **(80)** n19 t20 f21 b20. Classic what exactly...? Some really decent barley, but goes little further. *40%*

Auchentoshan Select db **(85)** n20 t21.5 f22 b21.5. Has changed shape of late, if not quality. Much more emphasis on the enjoyable juicy barley sharpness these days. *40%*

⁝⁝⁝ **Auchentoshan Silveroak 1990 Limited Release** db **(94.5)** n23.5 the softest fruit: dates and greengages suggest oloroso at its finest. Not a single off note: these are pristine butts enlivened by some of the most butterfly-minded spices you'll find this year. Love the milky-chocolate sub-plot; t23 a whispering delivery: pithy fruit here, a light burst of intense, salivating barley there, a crisp and crunchy muscovado/Demerara mix of sugars pottering about...; f24 enters into complexity overdrive as the few oils there are gather and up the varying flavours and textures, allowing them to cling...how satisfying! b24 okay...tasting pretty blind on this: have only the sample bottle, showing the name of the brand and the strength, but no accompanying production notes. Appears to have good age, probably above 17, and the sherry butts used here (and I don't think it is exclusively wine oak at work) are of rare high quality for these days. Appears to have the imprint of outstanding blender Rachael Barry. *50.9%. Exclusive for Global Travel Retail.*

Auchentoshan Solera db **(88)** n23 a tidal wave of highly attractive, lightly spiced medium sweet sherry; t22 again it is all grape though there is the faintest echo of barley; f22 late spices and drier vanilla; now in cream sherry land; b21 enormous grape input and enjoyable for all its single mindedness. Will benefit when a better balance with the malt is struck. *48%. ncf.*

Auchentoshan Three Wood db **(76)** n20 t18 f20 b18. Takes you directly into the rough. Refuses to harmonise, except maybe for some late molassed sugar. *43%*

⁝⁝⁝ **Auchentoshan Virgin Oak** db **(92)** n23.5 like a busy bourbon with the accent on the buzzing small grains: all the regulation manuka honey and liquorice there in respectful amounts; t23 big, sugary delivery, but a cushion of hickory and vanilla keeps the sweetness under control; a little molasses adds extra weight to the middle; f22.5 pretty dry, with a bit of a coppery sheen, as though some murk had recently been done to a still; b23 not quite how I've seen 'Toshan perform before: but would love to see it again! *46%*

Duncan Taylor Dimensions Auchentoshan 13 Years Old dist Dec 98, bott Jan 12 **(82)** n21 t21 f19.5 b20.5. Good sugars. but the distillate is sloppy and the cask is a little tired. *46%. nc ncf sc. Duncan Taylor & Co.*

⁝⁝⁝ **Malts of Scotland Auchentoshan 1991** bourbon barrel, cask no. MoS 13016, dist May 91, bott Mar 13 **(91.5)** n22 floral and scented: distinctly late warm summer evening, if anyone in the UK can remember what one of those is like... t23.5 absolutely textbook – for a Speyside style, that is. Well weighted barley but the honey and fudge combo is irrepressible: there is even a wonderful pollen-like breakdown to the flavours, as you sometimes get from old honey; the spices are pure entertainment; f22.5 more fudge and late mocha; b23.5 another malt distilled by bees. And much sturdier than you normally find from this distillery. A classic of its kind. *52.3%. nc ncf sc. 96 bottles.*

Malts Of Scotland Auchentoshan 1999 sherry hogshead, cask no. 155, bott 2011 **(85.5)** n22.5 t22.5 f21.5 b20. The good news: not a single atom of sulphur to be had. The bad news; an outrageously OTT barrel which so drowns the whisky in sherry that there are no malty survivors. That said, the spices do delight. *57.9%. nc ncf sc. Malts Of Scotland.*

⁝⁝⁝ **Master of Malt Auchentoshan Aged 27 Years** bourbon barrel, dist 11 Dec 84, bott 20 Nov 12 **(89)** n23 the grassy notes sway in an oaky wind; t22 salivating and simple, the barley trots off any number of sugary tones; f22 light oils soften the oaky impact; b22 warming to the point of running slightly hot, the juicy, malty blast is a treat. *58%. sc. 209 bottles.*

Old Malt Cask Auchentoshan Aged 13 Years refill hogshead, cask no. 6865, dist Dec 97, bott Jan 11 **(83.5)** n19 t22 f21 b21.5. Get past the indifferent nose and some malty little treasures are there to be had. *50%. nc ncf sc. Douglas Laing & Co. 308 bottles.*

Old Malt Cask Auchentoshan Aged 14 Years refill hogshead, cask no. 8257, dist Dec 97, bott Mar 12 **(88.5)** n22 lemon and lime cordial; t23.5 superbly intense malt-citrus melody; f21 dries a little, as it must. But decent late cocoa; b22 possibly the ultimate morning dram: few come more refreshing! *50%. nc ncf sc. Douglas Laing & Co. 303 bottles.*

⁝⁝⁝ **Old Malt Cask Auchentoshan Aged 15 Years** refill hogshead, cask no. 9807, dist Dec 97, bott May 13 **(89)** n22 sultana loaf with a squeeze of lemon; t22.5 juicy grist which revs the salivation-o-meter into the red zone...; **f22** light vanilla with a dusting of inevitable grist and castor sugar; the late spices delight and balance; **b22.5** simple, on the sweet side but rather adorable. *50%. nc ncf sc. 211 bottles.*

Premier Barrel Auchentoshan Aged 11 Years (85.5) **n20.5 t22.5 f21 b21.5**. Light, sugary and mouth-watering with the barley flickering in intensity. Some attractive spices ramp up the interest. *46%. nc ncf sc. Douglas Laing & Co. 182 bottles.*

⁖ **Provenance Auchentoshan Over 11 Years** refill hogshead, cask no. 8690, dist Autumn 00, bott Summer 12 (72) **n18 t19 f17 b18**. Fair distillate in a less than fair cask. *46% nc ncf sc. Douglas Laing & Co.*

⁖ **Provenance Auchentoshan Over 12 Years** refill hogshead, cask no. 9311, dist Autumn 00, bott Winter 12 (85.5) **n20.5 t22 f21.5 b21.5**. The kind of whisky every Chancellor hates: untaxing. Clean, grassy, mouth-watering. *46%. nc ncf sc. Douglas Laing & Co.*

⁖ **Provenance Auchentoshan Over 12 Years** hoghshead, cask no. 9755, dist Autumn 00, bott Spring 13 (87.5) **n21.5** light, though the barley sparkles; **t23** spot on: there is a real 3D clarity to this, allowing the barley to offer a gristy juiciness and deeper muscovado notes: excellent balance; **f21** bitters out a bit; **b22** clearly from the same stable as cask 9311. Except this has a little more oomph and much better use of sugars. *46%. nc ncf sc.*

⁖ **That Boutique-y Whisky Company Auchentoshan** batch 2 (86.5) **n20 t22.5 f22 b22**. Big perfumed guy giving it large with orange blossom honey. For all the dry, sherry character evident, a hint of hickory-style bourbon slips in, too. *46.6%. Master Of Malt. 295 bottles.*

⁖ **Wemyss 1998 Single Lowland Auchentoshan "Candied Fruit"** bott 13 (94) **n23** impressively sweetened, high intensity tannin; **t23.5** a stick of rock solid muscovado melts slowly to leave rock solid barley sugar; the spices make an early entry and stay; **f24** inevitable butterscotch, but works well with the toasted fudge and continuing spice; **b23.5** 'Toshan at its most spiced and most barley intense. A bit of a coup for this distillery as this is a genuinely classy piece. *46%. sc. Wemyss Malts. 294 bottles.*

Wemyss 1998 Single Lowland Auchentoshan "Lemon Sorbet" bott 2012 (87.5) **n22** busy with a twist of citrus, lime especially; **t22** big malty surge in this distillery's own inimitable juicy style: a real barley fest; **f21.5** back to the lime marmalade, but just a little heavy on the bittering; **b22** could this really be anything other than a 'Toshan? *46%. sc. 314 bottles.*

AUCHROISK

Speyside, 1974. Diageo. Working.

Auchroisk Aged 10 Years db (84) **n20 t22 f21 b21**. Tangy orange on the nose, the malt amplified by a curious saltiness on the palate. *43%. Flora and Fauna.*

⁖ **Auchroisk 30 Years Old Special Release 2012** American and European Oak refill casks, dist 1982, bott 2012 db (91.5) **n22** borderline bourbon with a wonderful hickory and liquorice edge to the duller fruit; **t23** outstanding delivery with a mouth feel to die for; the spices buzz busily and with intent, but can never get the better of the soft oils, layered hickory and dried molasses; **f23** the oils intensify, even with a degree of rum-like esters allowing the oak to surge without causing damage; **b23.5** a hugely – and surprisingly - impressive singleton of tannins. *54.7%. nc ncf. Diageo.*

Auchroisk Special Release 2010 20 Years Old American and European oak db (89) **n22.5 t22 f22.5 b22**. Can't say I have ever seen Auchroisk quite in this mood before. Some excellent cask selection here. *58.1%. nc ncf. Diageo. Fewer than 6000 bottles.*

Boisdale Auchroisk 1998 cask no. 13423, bott 2012 (84.5) **n21.5 t22 f21 b21**. A pleasant, barley-accented malt which looks pretty but has little to say. *46%. nc ncf sc.*

⁖ **Gordon & MacPhail Connoisseurs Choice Auckroisk 1996** db (84.5) **n21 t21 f21.5 b21** At its most ethereal, naturally toffeed and blendiest. *46%.*

⁖ **Kingsbury Auchroisk Aged 21 Years** sherry cask, cask no. 2554, dist 91 (91.5) **n22.5** dry grape is comfortable in its light vanilla skin; **t23.5** bigger weight and mouth feel than you'd expect, even from a sherry butt, with this cask; some serious fruit candy notes sprinkled with spice; **f22.5** returns back to its dry and moody lair; **b23** the man who would have ordered this into sherry butt, J&B blender Jim Milne, would have been as surprised as he would delighted with this. He found the spirit just too thin in its standard bourbon cask incarnation and looked for excellent sherry butts to give extra lift....he didn't see it surviving to 21 otherwise. A cracker of a cask. *46%. nc ncf. Japan Import System. 212 bottles.*

⁖ **Master Of Malt Auchroisk 23 Years Old** sherry cask, cask no. 3669, dist 1990, bott 2013 (90) **n22** crème brûlée and fudge; **t23** excellent delivery with juicy barley, spiked by crisp muscovado, rampant; the spices have just enough devil; **f22.5** the spices continue the good cause as the butterscotch sets; **b22.5** silky, but just enough spice to shake up the taste buds. *44%. sc. 99 bottles.*

Mo Ôr Collection Auchroisk 1991 19 Years Old first fill bourbon hogshead, cask no. 2560, dist 14 Feb 91, bott 28 Jan 11 (86) **n22.5 t21.5 f20.5 b21.5**. Solid if simplistic stuff. Even so, the malt holds firm and allows the better-than-average oak to stir up some spices. The gooseberry on the nose is a little treat. *46%. nc ncf sc. Release No. 36. 329 bottles.*

Old Malt Cask Auchroisk Aged 21 Years refill hogshead, cask no. 7045, dist Feb 90, bott Mar 11 **(85.5) n21 t21 f22 b21.5.** For such a light distillate the malt is stretched to impressive lengths. Surprisingly fresh and juicy. *50%. nc ncf sc. Douglas Laing & Co. 244 bottles.*

Old Malt Cask Auchroisk Aged 35 Years refill bourbon barrel, cask no. 6703, dist Apr 1975, bott Oct 2010 **(88) n21.5 t21.5 f23 b22.** I remember receiving from a wine store in Manchester the first ever bottling of this, a 12-year-old in the mid 80s. God, I'm getting old! *47.2%. nc ncf sc. Douglas Laing & Co.*

Provenance Auchroisk Over 10 Years refill hogshead, cask no. 8198, dist Spring 2002, bott Spring 2012 **(82.5) n21 t21.5 f20 b20.** Hard to imagine a whisky to be more malt-simplistic. *46%. nc ncf sc. Douglas Laing & Co.*

⁖ **That Boutique-y Whisky Company Auchroisk** batch 1 **(84) n21 t22 f20.5 b20.5.** Soft, run of the still stuff. Pretty taken aback by the nose, though, which threw me back to the Stockholm restaurants of the early '90s, when each one would offer their own aquavit. This nose is not entirely dissimilar to something found there. *44.7%. Master Of Malt. 127 bottles.*

AULTMORE
Speyside, 1896. John Dewar & Sons. Working.

Aultmore 12 Years Old db **(86) n22 t22 f20 b22.** Do any of you remember the old DCL distillery bottling of this from, what, 25 years ago? Well, this is nothing like it. *40%*

A.D. Rattray Aultmore 1982 cask no. 2215, dist 25 May 82, bott Jun 12 **(94) n22.5** quite a heavyweight with hints of cucumber lightening the honey-vanilla theme; some spiced chocolate lurks...; **t23.5** sweet and spicy kick off with a mix of molasses and fudge thickening the barley; the build up of chocolate turns into mocha with a complex liquorice/hickory backbone and dryness; **f24.5** the liquorice and mocha thread thickens and binds tightly. Even so, the chocolate reinvents itself and to delicious effect; **b24** a malt of exceptionally high quality. *53.8%. sc. A.D. Rattray Ltd.*

James MacArthur Old Masters Aultmore 15 Years Old cask no. 3592, dist 1997, bott Feb 12 **(85.5) n22.5 t22 f20 b21.** The busy, juicy delivery sees the barley dominating early on. But very little weight with the delicate smoke just apparent on the nose absent on the palate. The finish is thin and short. *54.8%. nc ncf sc. James MacArthur & Co.*

⁖ **Master Of Malt Aultmore Aged 5 Years** first fill sherry puncheon, dist 12 May 07, bott May 12 **(88) n22** far more strands of toasty bourbon than malt; **t22.5** a dry, intense delivery with the oak ganging up with intent; the barley offers a meek sugary counter; the spices are pepped up further by the strength; **f22** long, again with the oak in complete control insuring a dry mildly cocoa-dusted fade; **b21.5** exceptionally well hung and ballsy. The oak has an enormous amount to say and the sherry virtually nothing. Solid stuff with not a hint of an off note. *66.8%. ncf sc. 628 bottles.*

⁖ **Master Of Malt Aultmore 15 Years Old** hogshead, cask no. 3560, dist 15 May 97, bott 1 Apr 13 **(95) n24** adorable. Like the girl next door: pretty and seemingly unremarkable. But look closer and you will see how the mood shifts and brightens, throwing up irresistible traits, especially the spiced chocolate orange; **t24** just so much orange blossom honey, sharpened by apple and pear juice and some gorgeous spiced red liquorice as the oak gets to serious work; **f23** molasses and beech honey still show glimpses of citrus here and there while the spices are like a Rottweiler with a ragdoll; **b24** an amazing degree of apple and orange to this. Really one turn-on of a dram. *55.8%. sc.*

Mo Òr Collection Aultmore 1974 36 Years Old first fill bourbon hogshead, cask no. 3740, dist 29 Apr 74, bott 2 Dec 10 **(94) n22** aged, exotic fruit, but a slightly salty version. A few signs of wear...; **t24.5** gorgeously complex delivery: salivating with fabulous texture to the malt, which displays a pitch-perfect harmony between sugars and spices; **f23.5** some late toffee caramel; the spices linger; **b24** a few frayed edges on the nose are repaired by the colourful tapestry on the palate. *46%. nc ncf sc. Release No. 23. The Whisky Talker. 264 bottles.*

Mo Òr Collection Aultmore 1982 28 Years Old first fill bourbon hogshead, cask no. 2219, dist 25 May 82, bott 14 Mar 11 **(89.5) n22.5** spotted dog pudding; a real suet and raisin mix with an extra spoonful of spices; **t24** complex delivery, not just in flavours but texture. Malt but with a background of soft fruit and harder liquorice and mocha; **f21** bitters out slightly and becomes just too much the tough guy; **b22** you don't need a TV when you have a malt like this to get into. A psychological thriller all the way. *46%. nc ncf sc. Release No. 30. 300 bottles.*

Old Malt Cask Aultmore Aged 30 Years refill hogshead, cask no. 8533, dist May 82, bott May 12 **(88.5) n22.5** busy, a little nippy but excellent fruit custard sweetness; **t22** fresh, sweet and a little bite to the barley juice early on. But soon settles into a comfortable vanilla elegance befitting its vintage; **f22** Horlicks, with a healthy dollop of vanilla; **b22** spot on for distillery and age. *50%. nc ncf sc. Douglas Laing & Co. 238 bottles.*

Provenance Aultmore Over 11 Years refill butt, cask no. 7772, dist Autumn 2000, bott Autumn 2011 (83.5) n21 t22 f19 b21.5. A pleasant, well-weighted if plodding malt offering a big buzz to liven things up. 46%. nc ncf sc. Douglas Laing & Co.

⠿ **Provenance Aultmore Over 11 Years** sherry butt, cask no. 8188, dist Autumn 00, bott Winter 12 (89) n22.5 newly mown grass; t22.5 as clean and salivating as the nose promises; f22 delicate oak and a modicum of fruit enters the delicate fray; b22 a beautifully clean malt fest. Don't expect complexity: just enjoy the delicious simplicity. 46% nc ncf sc.

Scotch Malt Whisky Society Cask 73.44 Aged 29 Years refill sherry butt, cask no. 1672, dist 1982 (96) n23 highly evocative mix of powering tannins and rich fruit, though this is more bourbony-oak enriched than previous bottlings I can remember from the same period; the kumquat-sharp vanillas constantly pound; t24 an immediate avalanche of plain chocolate mousse with diced black cherry and Demerara sugar; f25 I doubt if I have ever tasted a richer chocolate finale in any whisky: the oils are thick and irresistible and the weight is perfect.; b24 THE single malt for hard-line chocoholics. A malt you will remember for a lifetime, this is close to being a chocolate liqueur but without all the sickly sweet stuff. Simply, and quite literally, fantastic. 53.7%. sc.

Scotch Malt Whisky Society Cask 73.45 Aged 19 Years cask no. 1391 (91.5) n22.5 laden with natural caramels and bulky tannins, this is no lightweight; t23 big mix of fat, oily barley and crisp sugars, the vanilla is a good focal point to chew on; f23 the enormous oils lengthen the experience while the sugars maintain balance as the drier, spicier notes begin to make a stand; b23 the SMWS appear to have hit a rich seam of magnificent Aultmores... 56.1%. sc.

Scotch Malt Whisky Society Cask 73.46 Aged 12 Years refill barrel, cask no. 304291, dist 1999 (89) n21.5 a touch of lime punctuates the barley oak dominance; t23 the sugars are wonderfully weighted; f22 long with the accent still on barley and vanilla. Not a hint of bitterness or unease. Impressive...; b22.5 simplistic, but forgivably so seeing the powering intensity. 576%. sc.

Scotch Malt Whisky Society Cask 73.48 Aged 9 Years refill hogshead, cask no. 305712, dist 2002 (90) n23 no half measures with the oak, though the barley clings to the citrus for grim death; t23 big, chewy vanilla-malt delivery. Excellent sharpness to the barley with the crisper sugars keeping a respectable distance; f21.5 the odd more bitter element of the oak bares its teeth; b22.5 peddles hard to keep up its early promise. 60.2%. sc.

⠿ **That Boutique-y Whisky Company Aultmore** batch 1 (94.5) n23 intense, heavy duty fruit, dates especially. Spices threaten but are kept under control by the thick, almost impenetrable dollops of mixed fruit...; t23.5 massive delivery – as expected. Again syrupy dates control the early moments, though now with those busy spices which try to be heard on the nose; f24 softens now for a more red-liquorice, bourbon-style fade, though the oak plays a big part offering both custard and spice in equal measures. The muscovado sugars melt slowly; b24 one of those rare malts which so often appears to be heading way over the top...but then throttles back so the balance is maintained. A real treat...probably at its best last thing before heading for bed, as the finish is truly fabulous. 53.4%. Master of Malt. 422 Bottles.

⠿ **That Boutique-y Whisky Company Aultmore** batch 2 (85) n21 t22 f21 b21. Big, thumping almost barley wine intensity to the malt. But not the first Boutique-y whisky to have a strange juniper-gin trace element to it. A coincidence? 56%. Master Of Malt. 226 bottles.

⠿ **The Warehouse Collection Aultmore Aged 16 Years** bourbon barrel, cask no. 3565, dist 15 May 97, bott 17 May 13 db (88.5) n21.5 sawdusty dry and of pensionable gait; t23 recovers, after the initial dry, oaky onslaught, with some amazing ulmo honey and barley speeches; after a thin start, thickens on the palate by the second; f22 dries again, but love the rhubarb tart finale; b22 just enough honey to see off the energetic oak. 56.4%. nc ncf sc. Whisky Warehouse No. 8. 186 bottles.

⠿ **Wemyss 1982 Single Speyside Aultmore "Sugared Almonds"** hogshead, bott 2012 (87.5) n23 how attractive is that?! Not sure about the sugared almonds (I had a couple for breakfast), but love the unusual and very delicate mix of freshly sliced aubergine and orange pith; excellent weight and an elegant degree of roasted yam; t22 it's the mouth feel which stars, the early oiliness allowing the barley to get off to a clean, juicy start. The middle thins quickly as the standard vanilla dominates; f21 clean, but a little too thin and bland after such a promising start; b21.5 starts outstandingly on both nose and palate but fades very quickly 46%. sc. 272 bottles.

BALBLAIR
Highlands (Northern), 1872. Inver House Distillers. Working.

Balblair 10 Years Old db (86) n21 t22 f22 b21. Such an improved dram away from the clutches of caramel. 40%

Balblair Aged 16 Years db (84) n22 t22 f20 b20. Definitely gone up a notch in the last year. The lime on the nose has been replaced by dim Seville oranges; the once boring finish reveals elements of fruit and spice. It's the barley- rich middle that shines, though, and some more work will belt this up into the high 90s where this great distillery belongs. *40%*

Balblair 1965 db **(96.5) n23** any more Kentuckian and I do declare that I'd swear this'd been matured in a log cabin with racoons for guards...; a lovely procession of manicured bourbon notes, with semi-peeled kumquats at the van; **t24.5** you will not find a more superbly complex delivery, with this seemingly possessing two bodies in one: the first is a little oily and soft but carrying the darker oaky notes, while simultaneously the mouth fills with juices from both barley and fruit; **f24.5** a mix of peach and melon yogurt mixed in with chocolate mousse, a rare but delightful concoction; light liquorice and hickory dusted with muscovado sugars reminds one of Kentucky again; **b24.5** many malts of this age have the spirit hanging on in there for grim life. This is an exception: the malt is in joint control and never for a moment allows the oak to dominate. It is almost too beautiful for words. *52.3%*

Balblair 1969 db **(94.5) n22.5** marmalade and pencil shavings; **t23.5** just so salivating as sugared orange juice intermingles with a glorious array of delicate caramel and vanilla tones, rounding off with honey; **f24** honey still, now stirred into a bowl of rice pudding; **b24.5** a charmer. Don't even think about touching this until it has stood in the glass for ten minutes. And if you are not prepared to give each glass a minimum half hour of your time (and absolutely no water), then don't bother getting it for, to be honest, you don't deserve it... *41.4%*

Balblair 1975 db **(94.5) n24.5** one of the most complex noses in the Highlands with just about everything you can think of making a starring, or at least guest, appearance at some time. That's not a taster's get-out. Nose it and then defy me...For starters, watch the clever bourbon edge alongside the crème brulee and ground cherry topping...hunt the smoke down, also... **t23.5** the barley descends in the most gentle manner possible but this does not detract from the intensity: wave upon wave of barley melts upon the tastebuds, varying only in their degree of sweetness; **f23** a few more bitter oak noises, but it remains barley all the way, even at this age. Amazing...; **b23.5** essential Balblair. *46%*

Balblair 1978 db **(94) n24** evidence of great antiquity hangs all over this nose, not least in the exotic fruit so typical of such vast aging; there is smoke, too: a delicate peat more common at the distillery in those days is evident and most welcome; **t24** the lush delivery offers up an improbably malty juiciness. But this is almost immediately countered by a spicy oakiness which offsets with great charm the salivating barley chorus and layers of delicate fruit and almost nutty vanilla: not for a second is elegance compromised; **f23** those of you with a passion for older Ballantine's will not be much surprised that this was, in its Allied days, once a vital ingredient: such is the clarity of the vanilla-led silkiness. Again, great age is never in doubt. Towards the very death the wisps of smoke found on the nose make a lingering reappearance; **b23** just one of those drams that exudes greatness and charm in equal measures. Some malts fall apart when hitting thirty: this one is totally intact and in command. A glorious malt underlining the greatness of this mostly under-appreciated distillery. *46%*

Balblair 1989 db **(91) n23 t23 f22.5 b22.5**. Don't expect gymnastics on the palate or the pyrotechnics of the Cadenhead 18: in many ways a simple malt, but one beautifully told. Almost Cardhu-esque in the barley department. *43%*

Balblair 1989 db **(88) n21.5** sharp barley untroubled by too much else; **t22** crisp sugars in tandem with no less crunchy barley; **f22.5** moves, at last, away from barley and offers a degree of vanilla-caramel complexity; **b22** a clean, pleasing malt, though hardly one that will induce anyone to plan a night raid on any shop stocking it... *46%*

Balblair 1990 db **(92.5) n24 t23.5 f22 b23.** Tangy in the great Balblair tradition. Except here this is warts and all with the complexity and greatness of the distillery left in no doubt. *46%*

⠶ **Balblair 1997 2nd Release** dist 97, bott 13 db **(94) n23.5** gooseberry tart with a curious salt and sugar seasoning; a shaving of ginger and a little physalis adds no end of complexity; **t23.5** sharp, tangy, pulsing barley both salivating and showing verve and a complex drier side: quintessential Balblair...; **f23** the vanillas walk hand-in-hand with the barley towards a cocoa-rich, late-spiced finale; **b24** a very relaxed well-made and matured malt, comfortable in its own skin, bursting with complexity and showing an exemplary barley-oak ratio. A minor classic. *46%. nc ncf.*

Balblair 2000 db **(87.5) n21.5 t22.5 f21.5 b22**. No toffee yet still a clever degree of chewy weight for all the apparent lightness. *43%*

Balblair 2001 db **(90.5) n23.5** gooseberries at varying stages of ripeness; barley so clean it must be freshly scrubbed; the kind of delicate spice prickle that is a must; **t23.5** majestic delivery: hard to imagine barley making a more clean, intense and profound entrance than that. The malt forms many layers, each one sugar accompanied but taking on a little more oak; **f21.5** dries, spices up but bitters a little; **b22.5** a typically high quality whisky from this outrageously underestimated distillery. *46%*

⠶ **Balblair 2002 1st release** bott 2012 db **(90.5) n22** lively barley dominates, though some first fill bourbons are evident, also; **t23** absolutely brilliant delivery showing the distillery in a playful mood, yet with a deeper, earthier strata. Natural caramels abound in fudgy form, with those creamy sugars thickening the feel of the barley; **f22.5** light banana and custard notes, plus barley sugar, vanilla and yet more fudge; **b23** a malt which reminds you how cold it is during Scottish winters...there is a lot of fresh-faced youth to this. But just so beautiful thanks to its understated complexity and honesty. 46%. nc ncf.

Cadenhead Balblair 20 Years Old bott 2009 **(88) n21.5** salty malt. Just a few tight wrinkles; **t23** originally sharp, it slowly evolves into a majestic malt fest; **f21.5** slightly tart, as is often the house style. But the malt is unmoved and the sugars are pretty sexy...; **b22** massively malty with the sugars almost grist concentrate. 53%. sc. WM Cadenhead Ltd.

Gordon & MacPhail Private Collection Balblair 1991 (79.5) **n20 t21.5 f20 b18.** An interesting experiment. But, as so many have been through the ages, a failure. Love the juicy delivery. But, overall, way too fussy and tart for its own good. 45%

⋯ **Master of Malt Balblair 35 Years Old Lost Bottlings Series** dist 1964, bott Aug 99 **(96) n24** so rare to find a nose so polished. The seasoning of the American oak hits the high spots with the spices just strong enough without prodding at the nose. The bitter-sweet balance, sharpened by a vague citrus and plum note, could not be better; **t24** silk, as to be expected on delivery. A procession of melt-in-the mouth sugars, with molassed at the vanguard, counter those inevitable spices; a hint of Parkin cake and walnut oil; **f24** I'm sure the toasty raisin is from char, not sherry. But sits so well with that consistently rumbling spice; a touch of late hickory; **b24** despite an outwardly fruity character, I'm pretty sure this is from a supremely high quality bourbon cask which received absolutely Rolls Royce seasoning. No idea what they are charging. Whatever it is, it's not enough...!! 43.1%

BALMENACH
Speyside, 1824. Inver House Distillers. Working.

Balmenach Aged 25 Years Golden Jubilee db **(89) n21 t23 f22 b23.** What a glorious old charmer this is! An essay in balance despite the bludgeoning nature of the beast early on. Takes a little time to get to know and appreciate: persevere with this belter because it is classic stuff for its age. 58%. Around 800 decanters.

⋯ **Gordon and MacPhail Connoisseurs Choice Balmenach 2004** **(78) n20.5 t21 f17.5 b19.** Attractive mix of cereal and sultana notes on nose and delivery. But falls to the near inevitable consequence of the modern sherry butt at the very last. 46%. ncf.

Mo Òr Collection Balmenach 1988 23 Years Old first fill bourbon hogshead, cask no. 1150, dist 4 Apr 88, bott 25 May 11 **(89) n23.5** subtlety and elegance take all the leading places here. Palma violets dovetail with delicate vanillas and a fleck here and there of kiwifruit; **t22** soft barley sugar heralds in the far brisker peppered oaky notes; lightly oiled, allowing the sugars and spices to mix with waves of barley calming matters; **f21** bitters out slightly at the death; **b22.5** a gorgeously busy dram. 46%. nc ncf sc. Release No. 51. The Whisky Talker. 440 bottles.

Provenance Balmenach Over 9 Years refill hogshead, cask no. 8496, dist 2002, bott 2012 **(79) n19 t21 f19 b20.** A seriously malty cove. But the cask injects a tang. 46%. nc ncf sc.

Provenance Balmenach Over 11 Years refill hogshead, cask no. 7827, dist Autumn 2000, bott Autumn 2011 **(71.5) n17.5 t19 f16.5 b17.5.** Juicy delivery but over influenced by wood which may have seen better days. 46%. nc ncf sc. Douglas Laing & Co.

Scotch Malt Whisky Society Cask 48.26 Aged 23 Years refill butt, cask no. 1124, dist 1988 **(91) n23** like when you open up a tin and you find an old dried up fruit cake where the nuts and molasses dominate on the nose and there is a toasty dryness from the shrivelled raisins; **t23** silky barley with a labyrinthine complexity to the suety sugars; **f22** that distant fruit on the nose now begins to show; the sugars remain consistent; **b23** far from a usual bottling, there is much here to surprise and delight. 50.5%. sc.

Scotch Malt Whisky Society Cask 48.29 Aged 12 Years first fill barrel, cask no. 800531, dist 1999 **(89) n21.5** straight as a die vanilla and malt; **t23.5** wow! Where did that salty, tangy, explosive malt come from? Fabulous malt middle and seasoned with effective salt and pepper; fudge and raisin fills the middle; **f22** comparatively bland caramel; **b22** the brightness on the palate makes a mockery of the relatively dull nose and finish. 61%. sc.

Scotch Malt Whisky Society Cask 48.30 Aged 12 Years first fill barrel, cask no. 800533, dist 1999 **(93) n23.5** I defy you not to be turned on by this most delicate and clean of citrus and barley noses; sponge cake with an orange jam filling; physalis about to burst; **t23.5** stunning delivery: almost perfect weight and the interplay between those delicate citrus notes and that barley is priceless. Retains that lovely light sponge cake feel; **f23** the oaks finally come into action, but merely add light liquorice gravitas. Oddly tangy at the death; **b23** an essay in poise...and what happens when you have a near faultless cask. 56.9%. sc.

The Whisky Agency Balmenach 33 Years Old dist 1979 **(89) n23** superb oak presence, conjuring up spiced cocoa and walnuts; **t22** teasing salts tickle the taste buds before a wave of oily sugars move us into vanilla-rich grounds; **f22** long, sweet and as oily as a second-hand car salesman...; **b22** a typically fat lad from this distillery. *52.8%. sc.*

⠿ **The Whisky Agency Balmenach 1979** ex-bourbon hogshead, dist 79, bott 12 **(95.5)** **n23.5** for all the upfront oak, the equalising sugars and barley defy the years; smoke...at first shy...more confident as the temperature raises; **t23.5** sumptuous delivery: the barley is ridiculously fresh for the age. The mid-ground moves into a gorgeous heather-honey mode, aided by a languid smokiness; **f24** fabulous finale with such charm to the peek-a-boo peat muscling in, pathetically, to the manuka honey and overdone toast; **b24.5** a must-get malt. Stunning. One of the most delicate and complex this year. *52.8%*

THE BALVENIE
Speyside, 1892. William Grant & Sons. Working.

The Balvenie Aged 10 Years Founders Reserve db **(90) n23** astonishing complexity: the fruit is relaxed, crushed sultanas and malty suet. A sliver of smoke and no more: everything is hinted and nudged at rather than stated. Superb; **t24** here we go again: threads of malt binding together barely detectable nuances. Thin liquorice here, grape there, smoke and vanilla somewhere else; **f20** Light muscovado-toffee flattens out the earlier complexity. The bitter-sweet balance remains brilliant to the end; **b23** just one of those all-time-great standard 10-year-olds from a great distillery – pity they've decided to kill it off. *40%*

The Balvenie Double Wood Aged 12 Years db **(80.5) n22 t20.5 f19 b19**. OK. So here's the score: Balvenie is one of my favourite distilleries in the world, I confess. I admit it. The original Balvenie 10 is a whisky I would go to war for. It is what Scotch malt whisky is all about. It invented complexity; or at least properly introduced me to it. But I knew that it was going to die, sacrificed on the altar of ageism. So I have tried to get to love Double Wood. And I have tasted and/or drunk it every month for the last couple of years to get to know it and, hopefully fall in love. But still I find it rather boring company. We may have kissed and canoodled. But still there is no spark. No romance whatsoever. *40%*

The Balvenie 14 Years Old Cuban Selection db **(86) n20 t22 f22.5 b21.5**. Unusual malt. No great fan of the nose but the roughness of the delivery grows on you; there is a jarring, tongue-drying quality which actually works quite well and the development of the inherent sweetness is almost in slow motion. Some sophistication here, but also the odd note which, on the nose especially, is a little out of tune. *43%*

The Balvenie 14 Years Old Golden Cask db **(91) n23.5** mildly tart: rhubarb and custard, with a vague sprinkling of brown sugar; bourbon notes, too; **t23** mouth-watering and zingy spice offer up a big delivery, but settles towards the middle towards a more metallic barley-rich sharpness; **f22** soft spices peddle towards the finish and a wave or three of gathering oak links well with the sweetened barley strands; **b22.5** a confident, elegant malt which doesn't stint one iota on complexity. Worth raiding the Duty Free shops for this little gem alone. *47.5%*

⠿ **The Balvenie Double Wood Aged 17 Years** db **(84) n22 t21 f20 b21**. Balvenie does like 17 years as an age to show off its malt at its most complex, and understandably so as it is an important stage in its development before its usual premature over maturity: the last years or two when it remains full of zest and vigour. Here, though, the oak from the bourbon cask has offered a little too much of its milkier, older side while the sherry is a fraction overzealous and a shade too tangy. Enjoyable, but like a top of the range Mercedes engine which refuses to run evenly. *43%. William Grant & Sons.*

⠿ **The Balvenie Double Wood Aged 17 Years** bott 2012 db **(91) n22.5** the sherry does a good job injecting a controlled softness to the experience, perhaps at the expense of some of the higher bourbon cask notes; **t23.5** the softness on the nose is transformed into silkiness on delivery, followed by a really outstanding layering of spice; a few apple notes thins the grape and bourbon style liquorice which piles in with early gusto; **f22** a more restrained and relaxed fade with the higher oak notes playing us out, helped by delicate muscovado sugars; **b23** a far friskier date than the 12-year-old. Here, maturity equals a degree of sophistication. Still not as outrageously sexy as a straightforward high grade bourbon cask offering from the distillery. But easily enough to get you hot under the collar. Lip smacking, high quality entertainment. *43%*

The Balvenie Roasted Malt Aged 14 Years db **(90) n21 t23 f22 b24**. Balvenie very much as you've never seen it before. An absolute, mouth-filling cracker! *47.1%*

The Balvenie Rum Wood Aged 14 Years db **(88) n22 t23 f21 b22**. Tasted blind I would never have recognized the distillery: I'm not sure if that's a good thing. *47.1%*

Balvenie 17 Years Old Rum Cask db **(88.5) n22 t22.5 f22 b22**. For all the best attentions of the rum cask at times this feels all its 17 years, and perhaps a few Summers more. Impossible not to love, however. *43%*

Balvenie New Wood Aged 17 Years db **(85) n23 t22 f19 b21**. A naturally good age for Balvenie; the nose is lucid and exciting, the early delivery is thick with rich malt. This, though, has sucked out lots of caramel from the wood to leave an annoyingly flat finish. *40%*

The Balvenie Aged 17 Years Old Madeira Cask Madeira finish, bott 2009 db **(93.5) n24** classically two-toned, with a pair of contrasting tales being told simultaneously yet in complete harmony. One is fruity (especially apple) and ripe and blended with the weighty oak; the other is barley-sweet and refreshing; **t23.5** the juicy grape takes the higher ground, joining forces with the juicier barley; some distance below the oak throbs contentedly; **f23** an oak prickle and a hint of sweet mocha on the vanilla; **b23** an essay in deportment. Every aspect appears to have been measured and weighed. Hurry this imperious whisky at your peril. *43%*

The Balvenie 17 Year Old Sherry Oak db **(88) n23 t22.5 f21 b21.5.** Clean as a nut. High-class sherry it may be but the price to pay is a flattening out of the astonishing complexity one normally finds from this distillery. Bitter-sweet in every respect. *43%*

The Balvenie Aged 21 Years Port Wood db **(94.5) n24** chocolate marzipan with a soft sugar-plum centre; deft, clean and delicate; **t24** hard to imagine a delivery more perfectly weighted: a rich tapestry of fruit and nut plus malt melts on the palate with a welter of drier, pithy, grape skin balancing the vanillas and barley oils; **f23** delicately dry with the vanilla and buttered fruitcake ensuring balance; **b23.5** what a magnificently improved malt. Last time out I struggled to detect the fruit. Here, there's no escaping. *40%*

The Balvenie Thirty Aged 30 Years db **(92) n24** has kept its character wonderfully, with a real mixture of varied fruits. Again the smoke is apparent, as is the panting oak. Astonishing thet the style should have been kept so similar to previous bottlings; **t23** big, full delivery first of enigmatic, thick barley, then a gentle eruption of controlled, warming spices; **f22** much more oaky involvement but such is the steadiness of the barley, its extraordinary confidence, no damage is done and the harmony remains; **b23** rarely have I come across a bottling of a whisky of these advanced years which is so true to previous ones. Amazing. *473%*

The Balvenie 1993 Port Wood db **(89) n21 t23 f22 b23.** Oozes class without getting too flash about it: the secret is in the balance. *40%*

The Balvenie TUN 1401 batch 1 db **(91) n22.5** one of the crispier Balvenie aromas from over the years: as though the barley has a new sugary husk; **t23** indeed, it is those sugars which arrive first on delivery, and they don't even try to be cute about it. The barley trails in behind almost as an afterthought; **f22.5** now a more composed and relaxed period, though there is a weak residual (presumably butt) buzz; **b23** I have experienced Balvenie a lot more complex than this. But there is no faulting the feel good factor... *48.3%. nc ncf.*

The Balvenie TUN 1401 batch 2 db **(89.5) n23** single plantation Santo Domingo cocoa, draped by Demerara sugar, wafts around the barley and juicy dates with ease and elegance; **t23** a more overt sherry character by comparison to batch 1 on arrival and even forms the framework for the juicy mouth feel; those Demerara sugars intercede as promised; **f21.5** the finish doesn't work along the same creaseless lines and a degree of bitterness points accusingly at a sherry butt; **b22** the odd moment here hits high notes from this distillery I only ever before experienced with the old 10-years-old some quarter of a century ago. *50.6%. nc ncf.*

The Balvenie TUN 1401 batch 3 db **(91) n22** perhaps a little tight on the nose in part, but there is also a big Kentucky feel to this, too: some of the casks have bitten deep into the American oak and extracted a chunk of toasted honeycomb and Demerara; lots of creamy toffee and raisin; **t23.5** stunning delivery: unlikely you will encounter many better mouth feels for a Speysider this year. Again, that big bourbon oak resonance makes no attempt to hide its macho character. A procession of liquorice and ulmo/manuka honey blend; **f22** some bitter marmalade takes a vaguely furry turn; **b23.5** one of those bottlings which again hits some magnificent heights; it is as though David Stewart is taking his beloved distillery through its repertoire. Still much prefer if he'd keep sherry off the programme, though. *50.3%. nc ncf.*

The Balvenie TUN 1401 batch 4 db **(80.5) n21.5 t23 f17 b19.** The finish has all the quality of an Andy Murray line call challenge. In this case it is unacceptably bitter, nowhere near matching up with the utter brilliance of the delivery. *50.4%. nc ncf.*

The Balvenie TUN 1401 batch 5 db **(87.5) n22** the most honey-rich of the five batches so far, absolutely dripping with acacia and heather honey; no shortage of cream toffee, either; **t22** a thick stream of natural caramels put a gooey lid on some other notes which think about making a challenge; prickly spices do make it through, though, and even a few citrus notes make a brave stand. Plenty of Toffee to chew on; **f21.5** a little dull and that well known buzz...; **b22** about as heavy duty a Balvenie as I can remember. Hardly surprising as the bourbon barrels appear to have had all their natural caramels dredged from them and this makes it a double whammy with the sherry. *50.1%. nc ncf.*

-:÷:- **The Balvenie TUN 1401** batch 6 db **(90) n22.5** about as thick as grapes growing in an oak forest; **t23** huge. Massive. Absolutely fills the mouth. The oak is definitely OTT, but there is something entertaining and intriguing in the way the sugars try to blast a way through with almost laser beam intensity; **f22** still too much oak, but the excesses are deflected into a disarming chocolate mousse finale; **b22.5** I'm amazed my stemmed nosing glass hasn't cracked under the weight of this Speyside monster of a dram. With the mix of fruit and big oak, probably distilled in lead stills... 49.8%. nc ncf.

⠿ **The Balvenie TUN 1401** batch 7 db **(87) n22.5** jam doughnut but a massive oak spice buzz, too; **t23** sugars arrive early with a lovely ulmo honey sub current; good juice until the raisin becomes increasingly burnt; **f20** slightly bitter, fuzzy finish; **b21.5** more juiciness to the fruit and sugar allows more clarity than the previous batch. 49.2%. William Grant & Sons.

BANFF
Speyside, 1863–1983. Diageo. Demolished.

⠿ **Cadenhead Banff 34 Years Old** bourbon cask, dist 76, bott 10 **(96) n23.5** some serious breakfast cereal notes here (especially those which have honey involved), mixing comfortably with salt and creamy, orangey tannin; **t24.5** the delivery borders perfection: all kinds of tangerine notes here, mixing easily with fresh barley, for all its years, which meld with lime and watered-down orange blossom honey; **f23.5** even the arrival of tannin and leather-style oak seems only to hit the right chord with the sugars and honey notes which linger to the end; **b24.5** I wrote long ago that it is likely that during the mid '70s Banff was making some of the best malt in the world. Don't believe me? Taste this... 53.8%. sc. 232 bottles.

Malts Of Scotland Banff 1975 bourbon barrel, cask no. MoS12015, dist Nov 75, bott Apr 12 **(87.5) n21.5** standard vanilla and malt fare; **t22** soft body; profound growth in maltiness; **f22** some late nougat and praline; **b22** very pleasant and malt mad, but absolutely refuses to do anything which celebrates its longevity. 43.8%. nc ncf sc. Malts Of Scotland.

BEN NEVIS
Highlands (Western), 1825. Nikka. Working.
Ben Nevis 10 Years Old db **(88) n21 t22 f23 b22.** A massive malt that has steadied itself in recent bottlings, but keep those knives and forks to hand! 46%

⠿ **Ben Nevis 15 Years Old 1996** sherry cask, cask no. 1654, dist Oct 96, bott Sept 12 db **(91) n23** clean as a whistle, ultra juicy grape sitting prettily with greengage and vanilla; a lot younger than its age; **t23** crisp and crunchy delivery with the barley at first forming a brittle guard of honour for the developing fruit. Then spices run amok.... **f22** the lightness of age on the nose is underlined as the oak does little more than offer a continued frame for the grape and grain; **b23** doesn't the heart sing when you find a good whisky matured in an unsullied sherry butt...? 51.7%. nc ncf sc. 523 bottles.

⠿ **Ben Nevis Synergy 13 Years Old** db **(88) n22** firm, crisp brown sugars; **t22** intense: all the emphasis on broad muscavado sugars with a degree of a taste of marmalade; **f21.5** long, dries, just a little fuzzy; **b22.5** one of the sweetest Ben Nevis's for a long time, but as chewy as ever! A bit of a lady's dram to be honest. 46%

Cadenhead Ben Nevis 20 Years Old bott Apr 12 **(82) n19 t20.5 f22 b20.5.** A brooding, bustling malt which overcomes its untidy start with impressive late panache. 56.2%. sc.

⠿ **Chieftain's Ben Nevis Aged 13 Years** hogshead, cask no. 240, dist May 99, bott Aug 12 **(93) n23** occasionally Ben Nevis takes off its heavy duffle coat and dons something of an altogether sleeker cut: here the barley, figs and blackberries are of the lightest hue imaginable; **t23.5** dulcet barley get the juices flowing; the vanilla sub plot is ridiculously polite; initially younger than its years, but revealing a depth beyond; **f23** superbly trimmed with an attractive chalky dryness to the oak, but seasoned with tingling spices; **b23.5** Ben Nevis in its Sunday finest. Immaculate. 46%. nc ncf sc. Ian Macleod Distillers. 354 bottles.

The Clan Denny Ben Nevis 42 Years Old dist 1969 **(89.5) n22** thick and heavy with some hefty barley and oak, yet citrus bursts forth like a ray of sunlight; plenty of mint too; **t23** compact and intense barley with impressive muscovado sugars; **f22** some clunking unimpressive oak at the death, but the path leading to it was strewn with delicious fudge: it carries its age well; **b22.5** a malt which needs a little time to compose itself. 47.8%. sc.

Companions of the Quaich Ben Nevis 1996 (88) n23.5 the kind of aroma which makes my nose twitch and my toes curl: the weight between the ultra clean, fizzy barley and the oak is near perfection; the faintest touch of something phenolic; **t23** superb adaptation from nose the delivery, with those barleys really belting out their fullest intensity and the spices and sugars ganging together with magnificent depth; **f20** unravels somewhat as the soft oils cannot quite overcome a late biting austerity; **b21.5** the delivery is unforgettable, displaying a very rare and compelling juiciness. 55.4%

⠿ **The Coopers Choice Ben Nevis 1996 15 Years Old** sherry cask, cask no. 1478, dist 96, bott 12 **(90.5) n22** muted honey with vanilla holding sway; a few random fruit notes buzz around; **t22** firm, semi-viperish delivery but settles down in midstream as the honey reforms and intensifies; **f23.5** a superb finale with a few tannins giving the honey a bourbon edge but now with spices and burnt raisin adding to the mix; **b23** complex and deeply satisfying malt. 56%. The Vintage Malt Whisky Co Ltd. 300 bottles.

✥ **McDonald's Celebrated Ben Nevis (95)** n23.5 a smoky broil drifts and teases. Young yet ever so light honey in every sniff; t24 superb, youthful body which holds both the malt and smoke so satisfyingly; just enough oil to spread the message far and wide; f23.5 smoked chocolate ensures a rich finale. b24 Admirable young whisky with surprising panache and not carrying the usual Ben Nevis weight. Very different - and absolutely top class. There is, indeed, much to celebrate. Wish I saw more whiskies on the market today where the young malt was given free reign - reminds me of the old five year old Bowmores bottled by Oddbins back in the very early 1990s. 46%

The Maltman Ben Nevis Aged 45 Years sherry cask, cask no. 1801, dist Mar 66 **(89)** n22 a surprising amount of butterscotch for ex-sherry; t22 chocolate Munchies plus some big time vanilla pods; the bourbon trail is an easy one to follow; f23 remains soft with a quite charming alloy of vanilla and barley; b22 though ex-sherry, the fruit influence is close to nil. Delicious, untaxing malt. 40.6%. nc ncf sc. Meadowside Blending Co.

✥ **Malts Of Scotland Ben Nevis 1996** sherry hogshead, cask no. MoS 12054, dist Jun 96, bott Nov 12 **(78.5)** n18 t21.5 f19 b19. Some decent sherry trifle moments, but never seems to find its balance – pretty dodgy when on Ben Nevis. 53.1%. nc ncf sc. 96 bottles.

✥ **Old Malt Cask Ben Nevis Aged 16 Years** sherry butt, cask no. 8228, dist Oct 96, bott Oct 12 **(86)** n20 t22 f22 b22. Pleasingly bright and sharp. The intensity of the malt impresses. 50%. sc. Douglas Laing & Co. 512 bottles.

✥ **Old Malt Cask Ben Nevis Aged 46 Years** refill hogshead, cask no. 9511, dist Jun 66, bott Feb 13 **(91)** n23 I'm in a warehouse in Guyana, surely! Big, bold sweeping muscovado notes, laced with manuka honey and milky coffee; t23 hardly silk, even after all these years: a real creaky, crankiness to this, blowing hot and cold on the sugar front but with the toasty oak merely having pot shots at the sweeter tones, rather than trying to dominate; f22.5 tangy, almost as if there has been a shortage of copper in the system – which (thinking about it) being a Long John distillery at the time, there probably was; b22.5 about as close to a pot still rum you'll ever find a whisky. Though this is bottled as a single malt, this appears to have much more of the character of the Coffey still grain distillery which was around at the time. 43.1%. sc. Douglas Laing & Co. 184 bottles.

✥ **Old Masters Ben Nevis 14 Years Old** cask no. 1499, dist 98, bott Nov 12 **(84.5)** n20 t22.5 f21 b21. A malt which appears to take delight in rolling up its sleeves and giving the taste buds a bit of a biff. A rough-house dram at its best early on when the barley is in full sparkle. 54.7%. sc. James MacArthur & Co Ltd.

Provenance Ben Nevis Over 12 Years refill hogshead, cask no. 7432, dist 1998, bott 2011 **(87)** n20.5 floral and gristy. Delicate, with just enough in reserve to see off some of the more unfriendly oak notes; t22 has that familiar Ben Nevis weighty rumble of thick, almost gelled barley. But the unfriendly fire from the cask fails to materialise, leaving the sugars to happily placate the palate; f22.5 attractively sweet with some real malty chewability; b22 the nose suggests a potential problem but on the palate it just gets better and better. 46%. nc ncf sc. Douglas Laing & Co.

Provenance Ben Nevis Over 14 Years refill hogshead, cask no. 8008, dist Autumn 1997, bott Winter 2012 **(86.5)** n20 t22.5 f22 b21 A thick, lumbering malt with the sugars, plummy fruit and opaque barley laid on with a trowel. Have to say I find it great fun. 46%. nc ncf sc.

✥ **The Warehouse Collection Ben Nevis Aged 16 Years** bourbon hogshead, cask no. 1739, dist 1 Jan 96, bott 29 Apr 13 **(86.5)** n21 t23 f21 b21.5. No shortage of delicious, clear honey on this. But for a 16-year-old, has more in common with a malt half that age; the cask must have been third fill sitting at the very bottom of a very cold warehouse. 53.6%. nc ncf sc. Whisky Warehouse No. 8. 321 bottles.

✥ **The Whisky Cask Ben Nevis Aged 16 Years** hogshead, dist 96, bott 12 **(94)** n23 the usual chunky barley. But cleaner than the norm with crispier sugars; t24 excellent dual-toned weight balance. On one hand, big, bustling, thick-cut barley, brimming with oils; the secondary plot is a much juicier barley-sugar little theme; the spices are deft; f23 chocolate with barley sugar filling; b24 another quite stunning Ben Nevis to hit the market in the last year – an absolute must find for those looking for the best from each distillery. 53%. nc ncf sc.

BENRIACH
Speyside, 1898. The BenRiach Distillery Co. Working.

The BenRiach db **(86)** n21 t22 f21.5 b21.5. The kind of soft malt you could wean nippers on, as opposed to Curiositas, which would be kippers. Unusually for a BenRiach there is a distinct toffee-fudge air to this one late on, but not enough to spoil that butterscotch-malt charm. No colouring added, so a case of the oak being a bit naughty. 40%

The BenRiach Curiositas Aged 10 Years Single Peated Malt db **(90.5)** n23 the thin smoke is losing out to the honey-fudge; t23 the peat takes a little time to gather its speech, but when it comes it is fine and softly delivered. In the meantime soft barley and that delicious but curiously dampening sweet fudge struts its stuff; f22 chalky vanillas and a squirt of chocolate like that found on ice cream cones; b22.5 "Hmmmm. Why have my research team marked this down as a 'new' whisky" I wondered to myself. Then immediately on nosing and tasting I discovered the reason without having to ask: the pulse was weaker, the smoke more apologetic...it had been watered down from the original 46% to 40%. This is excellent malt. But can we have our truly great whisky back, please? As lovely as it is, this is a bit of an imposter. As Emperor Hadrian might once have said: "ifus itus aintus brokus..." 40%

The BenRiach Aged 12 Years db (82.5) n21 t20 f21 b20.5. More enjoyable than the 43% I last tasted. But still an entirely inoffensive malt determined to offer minimal complexity. 40%

The BenRiach Aged 12 Years db (78.5) n21.5 t20 f18 b19. White peppers on the nose, then goes uncharacteristically quiet and shapeless. 43%

The BenRiach Aged 12 Years Dark Rum Finish db (85.5) n21 t22 f21 b21.5. More than a decade ago, long before it ever became fashionable, I carried out an extensive programme of whisky maturation in old dark rum casks. So, if someone asked me now what would happen if you rounded off a decently peated whisky in a rum cask, I'd say – depending on time given for the finish and type of rum – the smoke would be contained and there would be a ramrod straight, steel-hard sweetness ensuring the most clipped whisky you can possibly imagine. And this here is exactly what we have... 46%

The BenRiach Aged 12 Years Matured In Sherry Wood db (95.5) n23.5 big, juicy, compelling grape. Absolutely clean and stupendous in its multi-layering; t24 quite magnificent! How I pray whiskies to be on delivery, but find they so rarely are. Some caramels are caught up in the genteel squabble between the grape juice and the rich barley; f24 long, faultless and ushering in a chocolate raisin depth; late vanilla and any amount of spice; b24 since I last tasted this the number of instances of sampling a sherry wood whisky and not finding my taste buds caked in sulphur has nosedived dramatically. Therefore, to start my tasting day at 7am with something as honest as this propels me with myriad reasons to continue the day. A celebration of a malt whisky in more ways than you could believe. 46%. nc ncf.

The BenRiach Aged Over 12 Years "Arumaticus Fumosus" richly peated style, ex-dark rum barrels db (91) n23 t23 f22 b23. Very often finishing in rum can sharpen the mouthfeel yet at the same time add a sugary sheen. This little gem is no exception. 46%

The BenRiach Aged Over 12 Years "Heredotus Fumosus" peated PX finish db (92.5) n23 the peat is so thick you could grow a grape vine in it; t23 the sweetness of the grape arrives in spicy waves, comfortably supported by the thick, oily peat; f23 long, more sugared smoke and cocoa; b23.5 at last a PX-peat marriage not on the rocks. What an improvement from the last bottling. Smokograpus Miracalus. 46%. nc ncf.

The BenRiach Aged Over 12 Years "Importanticus Fumosus" richly peated style, ex-port hogshead db (87) n22 t22 f21 b22. Hardicus asius Nailsus. 46%

The BenRiach Aged 12 Years "Importanticus Fumosus" Tawny port wood finish db (91.5) n23 no matter here had it been finished in Short-eared, Long-eared, Little, Barn or Tawny Port, the peat would have come out tops. The smoke is enormous: owl do they do it...? t22.5 a peaty custard pie in the mush: enormous impact with more early vanilla than fruit; f23.5 now the grape begins to get its head above the smoky parapet: a beautiful balance with the smoke, vanilla and minor spices; b22.5 you'd be a twit not to buy two of 'em. 46%

The BenRiach Aged 13 Years "Maderensis Fumosus" peated madeira finish db (85.5) n20 t23.5 f21 b21. Never a shrinking violet, this still enjoys some pretty off the wall moments. But for a brief success on delivery where the richness of the sugars and smoke work in astonishing harmony, the remainder of the journey is one of vivid disagreement. 46%. nc ncf.

The BenRiach Aged 15 Years Dark Rum Finish db (86) n20 t22 f22 b22. Drier, spicier than before. Old Jamaica chocolate candy. 46%. nc ncf.

The BenRiach Aged 15 Years Madeira Wood Finish db (89.5) n22.5 t21.5 f23 b22.5. Very much drier than most Madeira finishes you will find around. Once the scramble on delivery is over, this bottling simply exudes excellence. A collector's must have. 46%

The BenRiach Aged 15 Years Pedro Ximénez Sherry Wood Finish db (94.5) n25 astonishing layering, each one delicate and fragile: vanilla and lime; gooseberry; barley; grape...a buzz of spice. Not a single bitter or off note. This is one of the world whisky noses of the year: absolute perfection; t23.5 mouth-filling barley then a spreading of a sugary but fruity theme, especially to the roof of the mouth where it sticks on a light oil; in the meantime there is a slow burn of increasing spice; f22.5 long, absolutely thick with butterscotch barley, framed by a constant drone of spicy, sugared grape; b23.5 some of the strangest Scotch malts I have tasted in the last decade have been fashioned in PX casks. And few have been particularly enjoyable creations. This one, though, bucks the trend thanks principally to the most subtle of spice imprints. All the hallmarks of some kind of award-winner. 46%

The BenRiach Aged 15 Years Tawny Port Wood Finish db (89.5) n21.5 t23 f22.5 b22.5. Now that really is the perfect late night dram. 46%

The BenRiach Aged 16 Years db (83.5) n21.5 t21 f20 b21. Although maltily enjoyable, if over dependent on caramel flavours, you get the feeling that a full works 46% version would offer something more gripping and true to this great distillery. 40%

The BenRiach Aged 16 Years db (83.5) n21.5 t21 f20 b21. Pleasant malt but now without the dab of peat which gave it weight; also a marked reduction of the complexity that once gave this such a commanding presence. 43%. nc ncf.

The BenRiach Aged 16 Years Sauternes Wood Finish db (85) n19.5 t23 f21.5 b21. One of the problems with cask finishing is that there is nothing like an exact science of knowing when the matured whisky and introduced wood gel to their fullest potential. BenRiach enjoy a reputation of getting it right more often than most other distillers and bottlers. But here it hasn't come off to quite the same effect as previous, quite sensational, versions I have tasted of the 16-y-o Sauternes finish. No denying the sheer joy of the carpet bombing of the taste buds on delivery, though, so rich is the combination of fresh grape and delicate smoke. 46%

The BenRiach Aged 17 Years "Septendecim" Peated Malt db (93.5) n24 easily one of the most complex of all the new peaty noses of the year. Both sweet and dry, with an ashy feel to the peat fire mingling with dangerous complexity. Almost perfectly weighted and balanced; t24.5 the delivery reveals a light oiliness which is entirely absent from the nose. This in turn maximises the intensity of both the sugars and smoke. When the spices arrive, the harmony is just about complete; f23 just a dash of oaky bitterness reveals a degree of discord. But the Demerara sugars are so crisp and painstaking in their efforts to ensure balance that all can be forgiven....; b24 proof, not that it is now needed, that Islay is not alone in producing phenomenal phenols... 46%. nc ncf.

The BenRiach "Solstice" 17 Years Old 2nd Edition port finish, heavily peated db (94) n23.5 a touch of the Bowmores with this: definitely a hint of Fisherman's Friend, but also creamy celery soup; t23 big and thick, coating the palate superbly, first with peat and then with a rich molassed fruitiness, especially with juicy dates to the fore; f23.5 reverts back to a Fisherman's Friend stance with the fruit now vanished and some half-hearted spices enlivening the delicate late sugars; b24 well, it's the 21st June 2012, the summer solstice. And, naturally, pouring down with rain outside. So what better time to taste this whisky? With all that heart-warming, comforting peat as thick as a woolly jumper, this is the perfect dram for a bitterly cold winter's day the world over. Or midsummer's day in England... 50%. nc ncf.

⁙ **The BenRiach 1995 Aged 17 Years** virgin American oak finish, dist 4 May 95 db (88) n23 not joking, folks: acorns!! Don't know if you've ever roasted them...but it's a bit like this! t22 a soft shuffling of power between the maple syrup and vanilla concentrate; f21 ye gods... the tannins!!! b22 from little acorns and all that.... 53.1%. Whisky Shop Exclusive.

The BenRiach Aged 18 Years Gaja Barolo Wood Finish db (89) n22 t23 f21.5 b22.5. The delivery gives one of the most salivating experiences of the year. 46%

The BenRiach Aged 18 Years Moscatel Wood Finish db (92.5) n23.5 one of those sublime noses where everything is understated: the fresh apples and grape, the most delicate of smoke, the jam on toast, the vanilla...; t23.5 textbook delivery: every note clean and clear, especially the juicy fruits melting into the lush barley. A buzz of distant background smoke all helped along by the most subtle of oils; f22 leans towards the vanilla; b23.5 one of those rare whiskies which renews and upholds any belief I have for cask finishing. Superb. 46%

The BenRiach Aged 20 Years db (85.5) n21.5 t23 f19 b22. A much more attractive version than the American Release 46%. The barley offers a disarming intensity and sweetness which makes the most of the light oils. Only a bittering finish shuts the gate on excellence. 43%. nc ncf.

The BenRiach Aged 20 Years db (78) n19 t20 f19 b20. This is big, but not necessarily for the right reasons or in the right places. A big cut of oiliness combines with some surging sugars for a most un-BenRiachy ride. 46%. US Market.

The BenRiach Aged 21 Years "Authenticus" Peated Malt db (85.5) n22 t21.5 f21 b21. A heavy malt, though the smoke only adds a small degree to its weight. The barley is thick and chewy but the oak has a very big say. 46%

The BenRiach 25 Years Old db (87.5) n21.5 t23 f21 b22. The tranquillity and excellent balance of the middle is the highlight by far. 50%

The BenRiach 30 Years Old db (94.5) n24 the fruit, though very ripe and rich, remains uncluttered and clean and is helped along the way by a superb injection of sweetened cloves and Parma Violets; the oak is present and correct offering an egg custard sub-plot; t24 how ridiculously deft is that? There is total equilibrium in the barley and fruit as it massages the palate in one of the softest deliveries of a 30-y-o around; the middle ground is creamy and leans towards the vanilla; so there are some amazingly juicy moments to savour; f23 very lightly oiled and mixing light grist and rich vanilla; b23.5 it's spent 30 years in the cask: give one glass of this at least half an hour of your time: seal the room, no sounds, no distractions. It's worth it...for as hard as I try, I can barely find a single fault with this. 50%

The BenRiach Single Cask 1976 Aged 35 Years batch 9, cask no. 6967, dist 14 Oct 76, bott 2012 db (**94.5**) **n23** creaky old leather and dusty libraries...I feel quite at home; some spiced up juicy dates, too; **t24** an engrossing experience: the grape is almost as fresh as it must have been way back in the days when Abba were topping the charts. The inevitable spices hold firm, setting into a rich fudge and mocha middle; **f23.5** some vanillas and tannins peel off from the grape and it is the popping vanilla pods which have the very last say; **b24** it is impossible to ask any more of an old sherry cask from Benriach than this: quite magnificent. 59%. nc ncf sc.

The BenRiach Single Cask 1976 Aged 35 Years batch 9, Pedro Ximenez sherry finish, cask no. 5317, dist 11 Oct 76, bott 2012 db (**86.5**) **n21.5 t20.5 f23 b21.5**. An exceptionally sticky beast on the palate and the grape works wonders to overcome some obviously exhausted oak. The mint is a bit of a give-away so far as the state of the cask is concerned. But the injection of the treacle and spice makes for an, ultimately, lovely experience. 54.1%. nc ncf sc.

The BenRiach Single Cask 1976 Aged 35 Years batch 9, peated, cask no. 8804, dist 6 Dec 76, bott 2012 db (**91.5**) **n22** the peat is shadowy and the oak just a little too laid back. Dry with some polished wooden floorboard; **t23.5** mouth-watering and what was a dormant whisky has suddenly erupted. The barley is intense and crisp sugar cranks up the salivation levels; the spices arrive pretty early and refuse to err; **f23** long, with a strange garibaldi biscuit sweetness; the spices and sugars are now in perfect rhythm; **b23** yet another cask which makes the BenRiach tasting days one of the highlights of my Whisky Bible writing year. This one shrugs aside the no-show nose and emerges as a Superwhisky, in much the same way Clark Kent finds new life each time he enters a phone box...; 54.9%. nc ncf sc.

⁙ **The BenRiach Single Cask 1976 Aged 37 Years** batch 10, hogshead, cask no. 2013, dist 19 Mar 76, bott Jun 13db (**82**) **n20 t24 f18 b20**. What can you say? The delivery, absolutely brimming with maple syrup and the lime filling which dissects the better chocolate cakes, is just so exotically right. The nose and the finish in particular are just so wrong. 49.6%. nc ncf sc.

The BenRiach Single Cask 1977 Aged 34 Years batch 9, Sauternes finish, cask no. 2598, dist 18 Aug 77, bott 2012 db (**77**) **n20 t19 f19 b19**. A real shame, as the usual rich, complex physalis and honey thread is there for all to see. Those who can't pick up sulphur will adore this one, especially as the staining is only light. 44.2%. nc ncf sc.

The BenRiach Single Cask 1977 Aged 34 Years batch 9, Rioja finish, cask no. 2588, dist 18 Aug 77, bott 2012 db (**90**) **n23** an intriguing head-on meeting of fruit salad and barley sugar...with some spiced vanilla thrown in to remind you of the age; **t22** silky yet strangely well mannered for a malt which has plenty of spices just bursting to escape; **f22.5** creamy textured, long and deliciously chewable. Some of those spices finally make it into general play; **b22.5** clean, sweet and quietly understated. 44.1%. nc ncf sc.

⁙ **The BenRiach Single Cask 1977 Aged 36 Years** batch 10, muscatel hogshead, cask no. 1031, dist 15 Apr 77, bott Jun 13 db (**87**) **n21** heavily perfumed with herb-laden grape; **t24** not just juicy, but multi-juiced. Ranging from sultana, through prunes and pear, the toasted raisin is given a helping hand with beech honey; **f20** bitters out; **b22** when the grape kicks in all its glory, it really does hit the heights. 54.9%. nc ncf sc.

The BenRiach Single Cask 1983 Aged 29 Years batch 9, cask no. 291, dist 6 May 83, bott 2012 db (**93**) **n24** a supremely stylish mix of sugars used in the '50s and '60s for candy cigarettes and playful lime...all topped with custard; **t23** firm barley captures all the early ground on delivery, slowly allowing the tannins to gather and form a dry, spicy camp; **f22.5** surprisingly oily, allowing the barley back into circulation; **b23.5** a really complex malt showing not a single degree of tiredness. Can't make up its mind to be a hard nut or a softie. 43.1%. nc ncf sc.

⁙ **The BenRiach Single Cask 1983 Aged 30 Years** batch 10, hogshead, cask no. 296, dist 20 Apr 83, bott Jun 13 db (**96**) **n24** not sure you can ask more of a cask than this: there is no telling which wins, the oak or barley. Neither, really, as the interplay glazed ginger and ulmo and manuka honey, all carried out in whispers, almost makes the mind explode. There is the faintest sliver of smoke which seems to introduce the spices. Some thin cucumber tops it off; **t24** soft, caressing...like a siren calling in the distance, the delivery is barley sugar enlivened with sterner oak which is overtaken by lilting spice and honey in the middle; **f24** long, back on to ulmo honey and still with a spicy tail; **b24** that, to me, is how a great Speyside malt of three decades maturation should taste. Classic doesn't do it justice. 43.9%. nc ncf sc.

The BenRiach Single Cask 1984 Aged 27 Years batch 9, Pedro Ximenez sherry finish, cask no. 1052, dist 19 Sep 84, bott 2012 db (**71**) **n19 t19 f15 b18**. Ungainly and falls flat on its face. 50.7%. nc ncf sc.

The BenRiach Single Cask 1984 Aged 27 Years batch 9, peated, Tawny port finish, cask no. 4050, dist 10 Oct 84, bott 2012 db (**94**) **n23** a briny, as well as smoky, aspect to the big fruit; thick and heady; hard to believe this is not from a Hebridean island... **t23.5** we can be grateful to the spice-assisted sugary grape for coming alive first, as this means a lovely juiciness thins the rampant smoke; **f24** tangy, spicy...and smoky, of course...; some excellent mocha towards the end; **b23.5** a quite beautiful whisky with much to admire and adore. Yet for all its greatness and undeniable charm you cannot help thinking that certain aspects of the two styles may have cancelled each other out. But that's me just being greedy... *52.5%. nc ncf sc.*

⁘ **The BenRiach Single Cask 1984 Aged 28 Years** batch 10, peated/PX sherry finish, cask no. 1051, dist 19 Sep 84, bott Jun 13 db **(94)** **n23** raisins pitched onto a peat-rich bonfire; **t23.5** massive delivery: a surprising amount of dried molasses and treacle at work; the peat appears to be trying to fight the fruit rather than talking to the palate; a real bite to this, part spice, part sheer violence from the warring factions; **f24** at last settles into something we can make sense of: a few buttery vanilla notes pop their head timidly above the smoky firing line; a little mocha and hickory is soothed by Demerara sugar; **b23.5** my palate just raised a white flag. My jaw literally ached from chewing this, my brain hurt trying to work out the shake and direction. Still, the cask is unusually clean for sherry, faultless in fact, and the entertainment offered cannot be matched elsewhere. One of the best peat/PX combos I've seen worldwide so far. Amazing what a difference a non-spoiled cask can make. *49.9%. nc ncf sc.*

The BenRiach Single Cask 1985 Aged 26 Years batch 9, Pedro Ximenez sherry finish, cask no. 7190, dist 13 Nov 85, bott 2012 db **(85)** **n21 t22 f21 b21.** A clean cask with no off notes. But, as is so often the case when this ultra sweet grape and big smoke get together, the picture on the palate is pretty but there is very little to look at. *48.7%. nc ncf sc.*

⁘ **The BenRiach Single Cask 1985 Aged 27 Years** batch 10, peated/virgin American oak finish, cask no. 7188, dist 13 Nov 85, bott Jun 13 db **(85)** **n22 t22 f20 b21.** Even the more sugary elements has a battle to cope with the late bitterness. At times on nose and delivery it is less of a malt than a battle plan – none of the participants too happy with the other. Nothing, if not intriguing. Save the overly bitter finale. *48.9%. nc ncf sc.*

⁘ **The BenRiach Single Cask 1988 Aged 24 Years** batch 10, tawny port hogshead, cask no. 4000, dist 12 Oct 88, bott Jun 13 db **(95.5)** **n23.5** thicker than a1970 Vintage; oakier and spicier than even a '35 Cockburn. Pulsing with orange peel; **t24.5** no let up on the delivery. Zesty with sublime spiced Dominican cocoa while the sugars never veer very far away from light molasses; **f23.5** dries but towards dates and fudge; **b24** why can't all wine cask matured whisky be like this? Hardly a single telling off note. Sublime. *52.6%. nc ncf sc.*

The BenRiach Single Cask 1990 Aged 22 Years batch 9, Tawny port finish, cask no. 2596, dist 24 Jan 90, bott 2012 db **(95.5)** **n25** there is such aplomb to the almost wafer-brittle thinness of the strand of grape which defines the nose of this whisky, one is almost tempted to put down the glass and applaud. The barley and vanilla attaches itself to the grape with a deftness which defies belief; elsewhere no less delicate stratum of aged dates, faint smoke and manuka honey add to the perfection; **t23.5** stunningly salivating and fresh on delivery, there is a busy jauntiness to this which offers great contrast to the nose. The barley really shines and it takes a little while for the grape to finally emerge. When it does, we are back to a slower, more thoughtful building and dispersal of flavours; **f23.5** all vibrancy now spent, you need about ten minutes to pick your way through the fruity finish. The peat, which you could swear was on the nose, makes a very late reprise...and stays when it gets there; **b23.5** as it happens, just a couple of days back I found a stunning 43-year-old Tawny Port being served onboard a Qatar Airlines flight. How an Arab airline got hold of something so magnificent I'd like to know. But I doubted if I would find any Tawny-related drink which would better it on the nose for the remainder of the year at least. How wrong I was... *53.4%. nc ncf sc.*

⁘ **The BenRiach Single Cask 1992 Aged 21 Years** batch 10, Pedro Ximenez sherry finish, cask no. 986, dist 19 Feb 92, bott Jun 13 db **(91.5)** **n24** any sign of malt has vanished under the incoming tide of sweet, spiced grape juice; **t24** and there goes that grape again off on full juice and treacle alert; **f21** bitters out as it becomes pithy; **b22.5** a top rate PX butt displays its sugary charms without being shrouded in a peaty smog. Even so, the malt is nowhere to be seen... *53.3%. nc ncf sc.*

⁘ **The BenRiach Single Cask 1994 Aged 18 Years** batch 10, virgin American oak hogshead, cask no. 4385, dist 27 Jul 94, bott Jun 13 db **(93)** **n23** distinctly Kentuckian in feel, especially with the ping-ponging of manuka honeys and hickory all over the show; **t24** oh, what a to-die-for delivery. The complexity levels have rattled the roof in the sugar types alone, though the pre-dominant ones are crisp and toasty. There is a buttery sub-plot, though the big spice tries to cover this; **f22** some of the older oak dives in to add a bit of a tang, but only after the last of the sugars have done their duty with something akin to a meringue and custard sign off; **b24** the weight of the malt means that this distillery is absolutely ideal to take on virgin oak. Quite lovely. *55.5%. nc ncf sc.*

⁘ **The BenRiach Single Cask 1996 Aged 17 Years** batch 10, Marsala hogshead, cask no. 10306, dist 2 Apr 96, bott Jun 13 db **(96)** **n23.5** dried dates, juicier figs and Maryland cookie mix bigging it up on the spices; **t24.5** that spice on the nose turns up on delivery en masse from the first second, as does countering acacia honey; despite the delicious grape and kumquat intervention malt comes through loud and clear; astoundingly beautiful...; **f23.5** enters complexity overdrive. The muscovado sugar and manuka honey mix is matched by deep liquorice and pulsing spice. The fruit here is restrained but still manages to hint of old fruit cake, sans nuts; **b24.5** a very high quality cask, entirely free of faults, ensures an exceptionally spicy and endearingly complex Benriach. A distillery landmark malt. *56%. nc cnf sc.*

⠴⠂ **The BenRiach Single Cask 1998 Aged 15 Years** batch 10, Pedro Ximenez sherry puncheon, cask no. 7633, dist 27 May 98, bott Jun 13 db **(71) n17 t18 f18 b18.** I have to admit, despite the low score, I love the sugars involved here. But overall... it just doesn't do it for me. *56.1%. nc ncf sc.*

⠴⠂ **The BenRiach Single Cask 2005 Aged 8 Years** batch 10, peated virgin American oak hogshead, cask no. 3782, dist 23 Feb 05, bott Jun 13 db **(94.5) n22.5** shovels full of peat here: outmuscling the thudding oak; **t24.5** absolutely typical sugars as leeched from bourbon ensuring an almost eye-watering delivery; if that isn't enough, massive phenols attack from every direction. This bizarre Kentucky meets Islay format continues with the intense muscovado sugars and hickory pitching tent for the long haul; **f23.5** sizzling smoky spice with a crisp sugary accompaniment; **b24** this is hairy, bare-chested macho, peck-thumping stuff.... the ladies will love it! *58.1%. nc ncf sc.*

⠴⠂ **The BenRiach Vestige 1966** hogshead, cask no. 2381, bott Nov 12 db **(89.5) n23** as though the tide has gone out, leaving concentrated oloroso...and oak; **t22** massive tannin intro then, thankfully, those grape notes re-form with treacle and a sliver of manuka honey to sweeten and balance; **f22** vivid vanilla, bountiful butterscotch....and oceans of oak; **b22.5** you should be able to find this in the Last Legs saloon. But enough fruit and sugar hang around to see us through this dark forest of a dram. *44.1%. 62 bottles.*

The BenRiach "Heart of Speyside" db **(85.5) n21.5 t22 f21 b21.** A decent, non-fussy malt where the emphasis is on biscuity barley. At times juicy and sharp. Just a tease of very distant smoke here and there adds weight. *40%*

The BenRiach "Horizons" db **(87) n22 t22.5 f21 b21.5.** Few mountains or even hills on this horizon. But the view is still an agreeable one. *50%. nc ncf.*

The BenRiach "Solstice" db **(94) n23.5** gorgeous non-coastal peat. By which I mean, intense smoke, but none of the brine and rock pools which sometimes accompanies it. This is simply clean, lumbering phenols, thickened still further by a good dollop of lascivious fruit...; **t24** a barrage of firm brown sugars are first to show, followed soon after by a cream sundae fruitiness. The smoke is all pervasive and intensifies as the flavours play out; there is also a decent showing of peppery spice pulsing in its intensity; **f23** an enormously long fade, a bit like a midsummer sunset. No surprises, bitterness or off notes whatsoever. Just a slow dimming of all that has gone on before; **b23.5** on midsummer's day 2011, the summer solstice, I took a rare day off from writing this book. With the maximum light available in my part of the world for the day I set off at daybreak to see how many miles I could walk along remote country paths stopping, naturally, only at a few remote pubs on the way. It was a fraction under 28 miles. Had this spellbinding whisky been waiting for me just a little further down the road, I am sure, despite my troubled left knee and blistered right foot, I would have made it 30... *50%. nc ncf.*

Birnie Moss Intensely Peated db **(90) n22** youthful, full of fresh barley and lively, clean smoke; **t23.5** juicy, fabulously smoked, wet-behind the ears gristy sugars; **f22** some vanillas try to enter a degree of complexity; **b22.5** before Birnie Moss started shaving... or even possibly toddling. Young and stunning. *48%. nc ncf.*

⠴⠂ **Gordon and MacPhail Connoisseurs Choice BenRiach 1997 (88.5) n22** molten Mars bar; **t23** big eye-watering barley moving towards a hazelnut middle; **f21.5** late spices and caramel; **b22** a toffee-nut straight down the line Speysider designed for blending, but polishing up very pleasantly, indeed. *46%. ncf.*

Liquid Sun BenRiach 15 Years Old bourbon cask, dist 1996, bott 2011 **(82.5) n20 t22 f20 b20.5.** Perhaps one more for the whisky pathologists than lovers as the lack of meaningful oak means you can work out something about what made this malt tick before it met its demise from vanilla starvation. On the subject of pathologists, I raise this dram as a toast to Jack Klugman, Quincy, who proved that being ugly and 54, like me, was no bar to pulling some highly intelligent and stunningly beautiful women. And any man who sues a big company over contractual rights is a hero in my book. To you, sir! *46%. The Whisky Agency.*

⠴⠂ **Liquid Library BenRiach 1996** ex-bourbon hogshead, dist 96, bott 12 **(90) n21.5** the tannins are little overcooked; barley a decent back up; **t22.5** punchy, concentrated barley gets chewier and chewier; **f23** goes into complexity overdrive as the spices pile in. The butterscotch is tinged with heather honey and a chalky vanilla; **b23** though patently made for blending, this bottling shows just how effortlessly good the distillery can be. *51.1%.*

Malts Of Scotland BenRiach 1991 bourbon barrel, cask no. 32283, dist 1991, bott 2011 **(94) n23** thumping malt matched by a lively liquorice and coconut oakiness; **t23.5** exemplary delivery with just the right degree of oil to maximise the limited sugars; **f23.5** the oils stretch and the waves continue to lap. A pretty sophisticated phase of dryness follows. A little cocoa and red liquorice endorse the quality of the oak; **b24** a classy, complex cask. *51.6%. nc ncf sc.*

Mo Òr Collection BenRiach 1991 19 Years Old first fill bourbon hogshead, cask no. 110681, dist 24 Sep 91, bott 9 Mar 11 **(81) n21 t21 f19 b20.** Bold barley. But the bitterness from the oak is a little severe. *46%. nc ncf sc. Release No. 37. The Whisky Talker. 300 bottles.*

Single Cask Collection BenRiach 15 Years Old bourbon hogshead, dist 1996 **(74) n17 t18 f19 b18.** Malty but thin, hot and aggressively vapourish. *54.3%. sc. Single Cask Collection.*

⁙ **That Boutique-y Whisky Company BenRiach** batch 1 **(90.5) n23** so much toasted honey comb...on even toastier toast...; **t23** again, a mega intense mix of burnt sugars and grain. Uncompromising; **f22** a serious natural dark fudge finish to the honey sweetness of the barley; inevitable butterscotch and spice...and then dries; **b22.5** as though some acacia honey has been burnt with the toast. So much sugar, yet so much balancing bitters: a fascinating, delicious whisky of extremes. *48.2%. Master of Malt. 140 Bottles.*

⁙ **That Boutique-y Whisky Company BenRiach** batch 2 **(94) n23.5** impressive light peat, slightly unusual for not dragging any gristy sugars with it; **t23.5** here we go: determined to whisper its way around the palate. Listen hard and you can just hear the smoke cloaking the tannin-rich honey; **f23** smoke signals pass the silent message that the butterscotch is clean and offering a graceful sweetness; **b24** elegant, graceful and understated from first to last. A little gem that's easy to overlook. *48.1%. Master Of Malt. 58 bottles.*

BENRINNES

Speyside, 1826. Diageo. Working.

Benrinnes Aged 15 Years db **(70) n16 t19 f17 b18.** What a shame that in the year the independent bottlers at last get it right for Benrinnes, the actual owners of the distillery make such a pig's ear of it. Sulphured and sicklysweet, this bottling has little to do with the very good whisky made there day in day out by its talented team. Depressing. *43%. Flora and Fauna.*

A.D. Rattray Benrinnes 1998 butt, cask no. 6850, dist 2 Sep 98, bott Feb 12 **(85) n21 t23 f20 b21.** A Spanish sherry butt which isn't quite as pure as the football of the country's national side. But shows some outstanding touches without doubt. *53.5%. sc. A.D. Rattray Ltd.*

⁙ **Gordon and MacPhail Connoisseurs Choice Benrinnes 1997** **(85) n20.5 t23 f20 b21.5.** Attractive, entertaining whisky in its own sweet and unencumbered way. A busy small grains feel and plentiful sugars. The quality of the oak contributes positives and negatives. But the caramel and pinging spices star. *46%. ncf.*

Hart Brothers Benrinnes Aged 14 Years cask no. 82, dist 25 Nov 97, bott 15 Apr 12 **(86) n22 t22 f21 b21.** Always fascinated by this distillery: you never know quite what awaits in the glass. This is a thoroughly enjoyable version. Distinctly single minded and complexity free. But a really enjoyable exhibition of barley at its most impervious. *46%. sc.*

⁙ **Liquid Library Benrinnes 1984** refill sherry hogshead, dist 84, bott 12 **(91.5) n22.5** a touch of green grape to the super-light barley; **t23.5** super-salivating, there is an almost unbelievable gentleness to all aspects of the recipe: even the oak offers the most graceful of banana sweetness to compliment the fruit-gristy sugars in residence; some sultana flits around the middle ground; **f22.5** long, with a lovely crème brûlée and sherry trifle flourish but some nagging, tired oak, too; good late spice; **b23** even in a softer, lightly graped, incarnation than normal there is something about the way the malts jar into the taste buds which makes the style recognisable. But being so clean and with no off notes, this is way above the distillery's norm. *46.9%. The Whisky Agency.*

⁙ **Master of Malt Benrinnes 14 Years Old (82.5) n20 t20.5 f21 b21.** Uncompromisingly Raw and ready. Expect your taste buds to be napalmed. If you like a bit of rough on the side, this is the stuff for you. Some redeeming barley juice, though. *578%*

⁙ **Master Of Malt Benrinnes 14 Years Old** sherry butt, cask no. 6841, dist 2 Sep 98, bott 1 Apr 13 **(90) n22** biting spice nibbles at the nose: a little pear and apple adds layering; **t22.5** nutty, toffee apple; juicy malt middle; **f22.5** chewy, fruit cake, going heavy on the raisin. Some attractive late spice; **b23** a high quality sherry butt which allows the barley to play. But enough spice to guarantee complexity. *55%. sc. 570 bottles.*

⁙ **Old Malt Cask Benrinnes Aged 14 Years** sherry butt, cask no. 9631, dist Dec 98, bott Mar 13 **(89) n21** suet pudding but dull, except for a strange hint of smoke; **t22.5** lively big malt arrival, some of it smoky; **f23** it's light barley throughout; **b22** curiously, a cleaner cask than its Provenance twin, 9632, technically better by far but fewer twists and turns. *50%. sc. Hunter Laing & Co. 302 bottle.*

⁙ **Old Malt Cask Benrinnes Aged 17 Years** sherry butt, cask no. 7437, dist May 94, bott Jul 11 **(87) n22** sweet chestnut stuffing embedded with raisins in nougat and toffee; **t23** a big, profound, spice- and sugar-exploding delivery. At first it skirts around the fruit like a city bypass, concentrating on the juicy barley. Finally it confronts it headlong and we are tossed into something thick, encased in demerara sugar and burnt almost to a crisp; **f20** a touch bitterish, off key for the usual sherry-related reasons but enough trusty vanilla to see it home...just; **b22** flawed genius: the delivery is worth the investment alone. *55.1%. Douglas Laing and Co. nc ncf sc. 300 bottles. The Whisky Shop Dufftown.*

⟡ **Provenance Benrinnes Over 12 Years** sherry butt, cask no. 8571, dist Summer 99, bott Summer 12 **(86) n20 t22.5 f21.5 b22.** Rattles the teeth and taste buds with a bludgeoning maltiness which displays impressive sugars. Even a surprising and beguiling hint of smoke. *46%. nc ncf sc. Douglas Laing & Co.*

⟡ **Provenance Benrinnes Over 14 Years** sherry butt, cask no. 9632, dist Winter 98, bott Spring 13 **(90) n22** not as thin as normal for this distillery with a gorgeous sweet dough theme, the odd raisin tossed into the mix; **t23.5** wow! I didn't expect that: beautifully controlled malt, crunchy – as are the generous sugars; a thread of mocha adds weight and depth; the spices represent the fruit gloriously; **f21** milky chocolate with two lumps of Demerara; a little furry at the finale; **b23.5** rare to find a crisp sherry, but this is one. And fabulously backed by a shell of sugar. *46%. nc ncf. Douglas Laing & Co.*

⟡ **Provenance Benrinnes Over 18 Years** sherry butt, cask no. 9765, dist Winter 95, bott Spring 13 **(96.5) n23.5** the grape is so thick, the spice hanging from it so deft, the sharper greengage notes so clean, you almost forget to drink the stuff...; **t24.5** luscious delivery: the grape appears to have had its sugars rationed early on leaving a concentrated mass. A light molassed note begins to filter through, though not before the spices get to work; **f24** reverts to a quiet sweetness with a spicy buzz working pleasantly on the chocolate raisin finale; **b24.5** this uncommonly good year for Benrinnes bottlings also includes an absolutely spotless sherry edition. A masterpiece from the leftfield. Superb! *46%. nc ncf sc.*

Riegger's Selection Benrinnes 1998 first fill sherry butt, cask no. 6844, dist 2 Sep 98, bott 7 Feb 12 **(77) n19 t20 f19 b19.** Forceful and unsubtle. The barley and sugars work hard to overcome some major shortcoming. *55.3%. nc ncf sc. Viktor-Riegger GmbH. 420 bottles.*

Scotch Malt Whisky Society Cask 36.56 Aged 22 Years refill hogshead, cask no. 801, dist 1989 **(91.5) n23** delicate with excellent vanilla-barley balance; a welcome touch of salt; **t23** the nose suggests a big, salivating barley fanfare...and it is deafening...; **f22.5** the barley continues its slightly salty course while the spices make a late noise; **b23** when you find a good Benrinnes, it can charm the barley from its husk... *53.6%. sc. Scotch Malt Whisky Society.*

⟡ **Stronachie Aged 12 Years Small Batch 2012 (83.5) n21 t21 f21.5 b20.** A warming – actually, slightly hot – malt which relies on the intensity of the youthful barley to fill in the gaps left by the fragility of the spirit. Decent barley sugar residue. *43%.*

⟡ **That Boutique-y Whisky Company Benrinnes** batch 1 **(93) n23** something of the sherry trifles about this...; **t23.5** ....and even more about a limited single malt thriving in a beautifully rich grape and Demerara environment: just so thick yet juicy! **f22.5** dries with an agreeable degree of spice for company; the sweet sultanas work long hours...; **b23.5** the near (though not quite) faultless sherry has polished this malt up rather impressively. *48.9%. Master of Malt. 202 Bottles.*

⟡ **That Boutique-y Whisky Company Benrinnes** batch 2 **(85) n21 t22 f21 b21.** Heavy caramel and a little sulphur dulls an otherwise pleasant bottling. *49.5%. 420 bottles.*

BENROMACH
Speyside, 1898. Gordon & MacPhail. Working.

Benromach 10 Years Old matured in hand selected oak casks db **(87.5) n22 t22 f21.5 b22.** For a relatively small still using peat, the experience is an unexpected and delicately light one. *43%*

Benromach 21 Years Old db **(91.5) n22** some exotic fruit and green banana is topped off with a splodge of maple syrup; **t23.5** excellent interplay between the sweeter, barley-rich components and the elegant, spiced oaky backbone; virtually no bite and softened further by an unfurling of vanilla on the middle; **f23** long, oak-edged with a slow, tapering dryness which does nothing to confront the sugared backnotes or even the suggesting of the most delicate smoke; **b23** an entirely different, indeed lost, style of malt from the old, now gone, big stills. The result is an airier whisky which has embraced such good age with a touch of panache and grace. *43%*

Benromach 22 Years Old Finished in Port Pipes db **(86) n22 t23 f20 b21.** Slightly Jekyll and Hyde. *45%. 3500 bottles.*

Benromach 25 Years Old db **(92) n24** seriously sexy with spices interplaying with tactile malt: the bitter-sweet balance is just so. There is even the faintest flicker of peat-smoke to underscore the pedigree; **t22** an early, surprising, delivery of caramel amongst the juicy barley; **f23** lots of gentle spices warm the enriched barley and ice-creamy vanilla; **b23** a classic old-age Speysider, showing all the quality you'd hope for. *43%*

Benromach 30 Years Old db (95.5) n23.5 spiced sultana, walnuts and polished bookcases; t24 no malt has the right to be anything near so silky. The sugars are a cunning mix of molasses and muscovado; the honey is thinned manuka. Still the barley gets through, though the vanilla is right behind; f24 drier, but never fully dries and has enough spotted dog in reserve to make for a moist, lightly spiced finish. And finally a thin strata of sweet, Venezualan cocoa; b24 you will struggle to find a 30-year-old with less wrinkles than this.. Magnificent: one of the outstanding malts of the year. 43%

Benromach Cask Strength 1981 db (91) n21.5 t23 f23.5 b23. Really unusual with that seaweedy aroma awash with salt: stunningly delicious stuff. 54.2%

Benromach Cask Strength 2001 db (89) n21.5 t23 f22 b22.5. Just fun whisky which has been very well made and matured with total sympathy to the style. Go get. 59.9%

Benromach 2002 Cask Strength db (88.5) n22 clean, sweet, gristy smoke; t22.5 big and intense peat on delivery. Soon begins soothing and stroking the taste buds with the softest barley sugar imaginable; f22 clean and simple with the vanillas showing no more inclination to aggression than the smoke; b22 most peaty malts frighten those who aren't turned on by smoky whisky. This might be an exception: they just don't come any friendlier. 60.3%

Benromach 2002 Sassicaia Wood Finish db (86) n21 t22 f21 b22. Again this entirely idiosyncratic wood-type comes crashing head to head with the smoke to form a whisky style like nothing else. Dense, breathless and crushed, there is little room for much else to get a word in, other than some oak-extracted sugars. A must experience dram. 45%

Benromach 2005 Sassicaia Finish db (92.5) n22.5 lightly smoked, well weighted and boasting a delicate degree of Turkish Delight; t24 the delivery is just a little special with a silky texture to die for and phenols and fruit that dissolve like candy; f23 an injection of vanillas stiffen things up. But the weight remains impressive; b23 a sassy dram in every way... 45%

Benromach Madeira Wood db (92) n22 some rolling smoke and chunky dried fruits almost cancel each other out; t24 voluptuous body displaying soft oils which coat the mouth with a spot on peat which is at once full and chewy yet light enough to allow the layered fruits full reign; the bitter-sweet balance just couldn't be better; f23 some touches of almost Jack Daniel hickory amid the circling smoke and juiced up fruit; mind-boggling complexity to this for so long; b23 if you want a boring, safe, timid malt, stay well away from this one. Fabulous: you are getting the feeling that the real Benromach is now beginning to stand up. 45%

Benromach Marsala Wood db (86.5) n21.5 t22 f22 b21. Solid, well made, enjoyable malt, which in some ways is too solid: the imperviousness of both the peat and grape appears not to allow much else get through. Not a dram to say no to, however, and the spices in particular are a delight. 45%

Benromach Organic db (91) n23 massive oak input and the freshest oak imaginable. But sits comfortably with the young pulsing malts. Wow!!; t23 oak arrives first again, but has enough deftness of touch to allow the rich, mouthwatering malts to prosper; f22 plenty of vanillins and natural, sweet toffee; b23 young and matured in possibly first fill bourbon or, more likely, European (even Scottish) oak; you cannot do other than sit up and take notice of this guns-blazing big 'un. An absolute treat! 43%. nc ncf.

Benromach Organic Special Edition db (85.5) n22 t21 f21.5 b21. The smoky bacon crisp aroma underscores the obvious youth. Also, one of the driest malts of the year. Overall, pretty. But pretty pre-pubescent, too... 43%

Benromach Origins db (84.5) n20 t22 f21 b21.5. You'd think after tasting over 1,250 whiskies in the space of a few months you'd have nosed and tasted it all. But no: here is something very different. Discordant noises from nose to finish, it is saved by the extraordinary richness of the coppery input and a vague smoky richness finishing with cold latte. 50%

Benromach Origins Batch 1 "Golden Promise" dist 1999 db (69.5) n17 t17.5 f17.5 b17.5. The nose is less than promising. And with good reason. 50%

Benromach Origins Batch 2 "Port Pipe" dist 1999 db (86) n22 t20.5 f23 b20.5. Dense whisky with huge spice. But it is as if in concentrate form with little room for complexity to develop into its full potential. Some charming chocolate and toffee on the finish. 50%

Benromach Origins Batch 3 "Optic" dist 2000 db (83.5) n21 t20 f21.5 b21. Another chunky, tight malt from the new Benromach. Some serious chewing, but a few feints on which to chew... 50%

Benromach Peat Smoke Batch 3 db (90.5) n22 excellent nose: pretty decent levels of peak reek evident but dried, rather than cured...; t23 the dry peat builds in intensity, though not after the clean and powering barley makes the first speech; f22.5 dry, chalky and compact; damn it – this is very good, indeed! b23 an excellent malt that has been beautifully made. Had it been bottled at 46 we would have seen it offer an extra degree of richness. 40%

Benromach Traditional db (86) n22 t21 f21.5 b21.5. Deliciously clean and smoky. But very raw and simplistic, too. 40%

Benromach Wood Finish Hermitage dist 2001 db (84) n19 t23 f21 b21. A sweet, tight dram with all the shape crushed out of it. It does have its moment of greatness, though: about three or four seconds after arrival when it zooms into the stratosphere on a massively fruity, sensuously spiced rocket. Then it just fades away... 45%

Benromach Wood Finish Pedro Ximénez dist 2002 db (85.5) n21 t22.5 f21 b21. Combining PX with peated whisky is still probably the hardest ask in the maturation lexicon. Lagavulin are still to get it right. And they have not quite managed it here, either. It's a bumpy old ride, though some of the early chewing moments are fun. Not a bad attempt, at all. Just the learning curve is still on the rise... 45%

Benromach Vintage 1968 db (94.5) n23 theoretically way over the top oak. But the sherry acts as a sponge...or, to be more precise, a very well aged fruit cake; some mega juicy plums and figs; t23 can't fault the marbelling with the fruit running thickly into the spicier, almost bourbony meat. Again the oak is over the top, yet, thanks to the depth of the cocoa and juicy grape, somehow gets away with some outrageous splinters; f24.5 now completely dazzles as all the more militant elements of the oak have been pacified and we are left with not only a sherry trifle/fruitcake mix, but chocolate cream/raspberry roll for good measure... b24 a 40 year plus whisky of astonishing quality...? A piece of cake... 45.4%

Benromach Vintage 1969 db (92) n22 a slightly tired, sappy aroma; honeycomb offers the perfect antidote; t24 the sugars are queuing to deliver and do so with a barley-rich gentleness. Some milk chocolate arrives, and then a succession of much drier, more assertive oak; f23 hangs on well and the seasoning is at times both complex and challenging; finishes with coconut shreds dunked in Golden Syrup; b23 the odd branch of the old oak too many. But still has many magical mahogany moments. 42.6%

⁖ **Gordon & MacPhail Benromach Vintage 1976** db (89) n22.5 the structure of the nose is pure oak; the cement which holds it together, honey; t22 a silky delivery which needs every last ounce of sweetness to fight off the oaky attack; fortunately the intense ulmo honey and roasty fudge make for a superb and telling combination; f22 the honey and fudge battle gamely to the last! b22.5 for all the massive oak which shapes every inch of this dram, the degree of ulmo honey at work is extraordinary. 46%. ncf.

⁖ **Gordon & MacPhail Benromach Port Wood finish 2000** db (86.5) n22 t21 f22 b21.5. A pleasant experience with a distinctive chocolate liqueur feel to it. Just a little too heavily laden with grape (though thankfully clean and entirely sulphur-free) for greatness as the malt is all but obliterated, though the spices rack up the complexity levels. 45%. ncf.

BLADNOCH

Lowlands, 1817. Armstrong Brothers. Working.

Bladnoch Aged 6 Years Bourbon Matured db (91) n21.5 young, yes. But the soft feints have nothing to do with that; t22.5 a youthful, oily delivery, not exactly a picture of harmony, gives way to a brutal coup d'etat of ultra intense prisoner-slaughtering barley; f24 intense barley-concentrate oils offer a perplexing array of sweet, grassy tones; you simply chew and chew until the jaw aches. Cocoa at last arrives, all with a spiced buzz and a smearing of vanillas. Meanwhile your tongue explores the mouth, wondering what the hell is going on; b23 the fun starts with the late middle, where those extra oils congregate and the taste buds are sent rocking. Great to see a Lowlander bottled at an age nearer its natural best and even the smaller cut, in a roundabout way, ensures a mind-blowing dram. 57.3%

Bladnoch Aged 6 Years Lightly Peated db (93) n23 a peat fire just bursting into life; t23 firm, bitter-sweet; the layering of the peat is awesome, with the youth of the malt adding an extra dimension; some citrus notes help lighten the load; f23.5 smoky hickory; the vanillas make a feeble entry, a gentle oiliness persists; b23.5 the peat has nothing to do with the overall score here: this is a much better-made whisky with not a single off-note and the cut is spot on. And although it claims to be lightly peated, that is not exactly true: such is the gentle nature of the distillate, the smoke comes through imperiously and on several levels. "Spirit of the Lowlands" drones the label. Since when has outstanding peated malt been associated with that part of the whisky world...?? 58.5%

Bladnoch Aged 6 Years Sherry Matured db (73.5) n18 t19 f18.5 b18. A sticky, lop-sided malt where something, or a group of somethings, conjures up a very unattractive overture. Feints on the palate but no excellent bourbon cask to the rescue here. 56.9%

Bladnoch Aged 10 Years db (94) n23 lemon and lime, marmalade on fresh-sliced flour-topped crusty bread; t24 immensely fruity and chewy, lush and mouthwatering and then the most beguiling build-up of spices: the mouthfeel is full and faultless; f23 long, remains mildly peppery and then a dryer advance of oak. The line between bitter and sweet is not once crossed; b24 this is probably the ultimate Bladnoch, certainly the best I have tasted in over 25 years. This Flora and Fauna bottling by then owners United Distillers should be regarded as the must-get-at-all-costs Bladnoch. If the new owner can create something even to hang on to this one's coat-tails then he has excelled himself. For those few of us lucky enough to experience this, this dram is nothing short of a piece of Lowland legend and folklore. *43%*.

Bladnoch Aged 15 Years db **(91)** n22.5 remnants of zest and barley sit comfortably with the gentle oaks; **t22.5** excellent delivery and soon gets into classic Bladnoch citric stride; **f23** wonderfully clean barley belies the age and lowers the curtain so delicately you hardly notice; **b23** quite outstanding Lowland whisky which, I must admit, is far better than I would have thought possible at this age. *55%*

Bladnoch Aged 16 Years "Spirit of the Lowlands" db **(88)** n22 t22 f22 b22. Really lovely whisky and unusual to see a Lowlander quite this comfortable at such advanced age. *46%. ncf.*

Bladnoch 18 Years Old db **(88.5)** n21 t23.5 f22 b22. The juiciness and clarity to the barley, and especially the big gooseberry kick, early on makes this a dram well worth finding. *55%*

Berry's Own Selection Bladnoch 1992 cask no. 2159, bott 2011 **(91.5)** n23 a Lowlander with a thin strata of smoke...intriguing! The barley, though, is as clean and intense as you are likely to find this year; **t23.5** just a splendid exhibition of barley: the type that blenders purr about as the clean, uncluttered intensity travels a long, long way; **f22** ...errr....barley... **b23** almost too simplistic and one dimensional, except for that most tantalizing hint of smoke. Except it is not too simplistic as the barley is so sexily shaped and nubile that you are not sure whether to drink it or sing soppy love songs to it... *46%. nc ncf sc. Berry Bros & Rudd.*

Chieftain's Bladnoch Aged 18 Years hogshead, cask no. 4195, dist Nov 92 **(82.5)** n21 t22.5 f19 b20. Made during an interesting, and uncertain, part of the distillery's history, this malt is slightly out of kilter with the standard style though the barley at full pelt is very attractive. *55.3%. nc ncf sc. Ian Macleod Distillers. USA exclusive.*

⁘ **Gordon and MacPhail Connoisseurs Choice Bladnoch 1993** **(84.5)** n21 t21 f22 b20.5. We have reached a point here where the oak and barley are not on speaking terms. Perhaps not the greatest spirit to start off with, as the nose testifies, it certainly lacks sufficient muscle to see off the more vivid embraces of the oak. Some attractive muscovado-topped butterscotch from time to time, but all too much of a mishmash. *46%. ncf.*

Malts Of Scotland Bladnoch 1990 bourbon barrel, cask no. MoS12019, dist Jul 90, bott Apr 12 **(90.5)** n22 big citrus; polished school floors; **t23** just as well I can type: I am salivating too much to speak...; **f22.5** the juicy barley withdraws slightly to allow a liquorice-chocolate fudge finale; **b23** when this was distilled I never expected to see this distillery bottled at this kind of age. Or looking quite as shapely as this... *54.4%. nc ncf sc. Malts Of Scotland.*

Old Malt Cask Bladnoch Aged 18 Years sherry finished butt, cask no. 7162, dist. Nov 92, bott Jun 11 **(76.5)** n18.5 t21 f18 b19. Probably a malt which would have done better without the sherry interference. *50%. nc ncf sc. 389 bottles.*

⁘ **Old Malt Cask Bladnoch Aged 20 Years** refill hogshead, cask no. 9431, dist Nov 92, bott Feb 13 **(71)** n18 t18 f17 b18. A malt some Germans will adore while those of us not immune to the dreaded "s" word can only weep. Some decent chocolate notes, though. *50%. sc. Hunter Laing & Co. 199 bottles.*

Scotch Malt Whisky Society Cask 50.49 Aged 21 Years refill barrel, cask no. 303511, dist 1990 **(83.5)** n20 t21.5 f21 b21. Hangs on grimly for life, literally. The oak is too aggressive and only some stunning chocolate-orange notes save the day. *55.8%. sc.*

Sestante Collection Bladnoch 21 Years Old dist 1990, bott 2011 **(82)** n21 t21 f20 b20 barley aplenty. But all a little hot and harsh. *58.7%. sc. Silver Seal Whisky Company.*

BLAIR ATHOL
Highlands (Perthshire), 1798. Diageo. Working.

Blair Athol Aged 12 Years db **(77)** n18 t19 f21 b19. Thick, fruity, syrupy and a little sulphury and heavy. The finish has some attractive complexity among the chunkyness. *43%. Flora and Fauna.*

A Fine Cigar's Pleasure Blair Athol Aged 12 Years sherry butt **(63)** n16 t18 f13 b16. If chewing on a fat cigar is a way of not tasting sulphur-wrecked whisky, I might just think about taking up smoking for the first time in my life..... *50%. Douglas Laing & Co. 443 bottles.*

Duthies Blair Athol 13 Years Old bott 2012 **(86)** n21.5 t23 f20.5 b21. An absolutely typical new style Blair Athol big juicy barley affair - a couple of decades back this was a much dirtier kind of malt unrecognisable from this. Here everything is clean and very sweet. And rather well oiled, too. *46%. nc ncf sc. WM Cadenhead Ltd.*

John Milroy Selection Blair Athol 1998 cask no. 2753, bott 2012 **(84.5)** n21 t21.5 f21 b21. A grassy, malty thirst-slaker. *46%. nc ncf sc. Berry Bros & Rudd.*

⁘ **Old Malt Cask Blair Athol Aged 15 Years** sherry butt, cask no. 9759, dist Aug 97, May 13 **(92)** n23.5 the sprinkle of cinnamon and kiwi fruit makes all the difference to an already faultless butt; **t23** the sugars arrive first, second and fourth, with a few mixed barley ale and spice notes intervening; **f22.5** the toasted raisins make their mark, settling neatly into the spotted dog finale; **b23** don't see many Blair Athols in this kind of nick. Especially from sherry. *50%. nc ncf sc. Hunter Laing & Co Ltd. 271 bottles.*

Old Malt Cask Blair Athol Aged 21 Years refill hogshead, cask no. 7561, dist Aug 90, bott Aug 11 **(88) n21** outwardly pleasant enough. But a bit of a failure on the soapy barrel front...; **t23.5** what the f...? This is whisky? Reminds me, vividly, of a strange concoction many years back I did regarding rum, cognac, vanilla and saffron; **f21.5** after that initial explosion of delicious weirdness we return to earth...and mostly a pretty boring part of it; **b22** there was I shaking my head at the nose, thinking how 21 years ago the malt made at Blair Athol was not quite of the same standard as that made a dozen years back. Then I tasted and was blasted back into my seat. This is the whisky equivalent of a slap around the chops. The finish confirms the faults. But...oh, my word....! *50%. nc ncf sc. Douglas Laing & Co. 268 bottles.*

Premier Barrel Blair Athol Aged 12 Years (90.5) n23 love the unsullied fruit and malt mix; just a hint of spice amid the diced apple; **t23.5** sublime delivery: a teasing, chewable, mouth-watering hurrah is extended about the palate by the deftest of oils; **f21.5** thins just a little too enthusiastically but the vanillas are a treat; **b22.5** Blair Athol at its most seductive. *46%. nc ncf sc. Douglas Laing & Co. 302 bottles.*

Provenance Blair Athol Over 11 Years sherry butt, cask no. 7695, dist 1999, bott 2011 **(90) n23.5** clean, subtle and with the faintest echo of grape; an equally distant sound of smoke makes for a perfect accompaniment; **t23** salivating, gentle malt is rounded off in the middle ground by buttered sultana; **f21.5** thins and warms somewhat; **b22** a steady ship which plots a course for calmer waters yet still heads into unfamiliar seas for this distillery. *46%. nc ncf sc.*

Provenance Blair Athol Over 12 Years sherry butt, cask no. 6000, dist Winter 1999, bott Winter 2011 **(84.5) n21 t21.5 f21 b21.** A bottling by no means short on charm. But the butt has done little to enhance either the malt or complexity. *46%. nc ncf sc. Douglas Laing & Co.*

⋰⋱ **Provenance Blair Athol Over 12 Years** sherry butt, cask no. 8767, dist Winter 99, bott Summer 12 **(86.5) n21 t22 f21.5 b22.** Malty, juicy, spicy though it is the lightest hint of smoke which throws up the biggest surprise. *46%. nc ncf sc. Douglas Laing & Co.*

⋰⋱ **Provenance Blair Athol Over 15 Years** sherry butt, cask no. 9757, dist summer 97, bott spring 13 **(93) n22** pear drops and hot cross buns; **t23.5** deft delivery with the spices up early. The malt has almost as big a say as the fruit; a surprising juicy volley hits the mid ground; **f24** mocha rules supreme, though the vanilla surges late and strong; **b23.5** clearly a twin butt to the OMC 15, it is seemingly flatter in most areas, but pulls together with more complexity from the mid ground onwards. *46%. nc ncf sc. Douglas Laing & Co.*

⋰⋱ **Wemyss 1986 Single Highland Blair Athol "Autumn Berries"** hogshead, bott 2012 **(86.5) n22 t22 f21 b21.5.** A light malt always going out of its way to tip-toe over the taste buds. The delivery is adorable, though, with more than a nod, on the nose too, to the venerable sweetshop, with all kinds of boiled candy of varying fruits. The finish, though clean and vanilla vibrant, is a little austere by comparison. *46%. sc. 268 bottles.*

BOWMORE
Islay, 1779. Morrison Bowmore. Working.

Bowmore Aged 12 Years db **(91) n22.5** light peats, the air of a room with a man sucking cough sweets; sweet pipe smoke; **t23.5** soft, beautiful delivery of multi-layered peats; lots of effervescent spices and molassed sugars; spices abound; **f22.5** much drier with sharper berries and barley; the peat still rumbles onwards, but has no problems with the light, sawdusty oaks; **b23.5** this new bottling still proudly carries the Fisherman's Friend cough sweet character, but the coastal, saline properties here are a notch or three up: far more representative of Islay and the old distillery style. Easily by far the truest Bowmore I have tasted in a long while with myriad complexity. Even going back more than a quarter of a century, the malt at this age rarely showed such relaxed elegance. Most enjoyable. *40% ⊙*

Bowmore "Enigma" Aged 12 Years db **(82) n19 t22 f20 b21.** Sweet, molassed and with that tell-tale Fisherman's Friend tang representing the light smoke. This Enigma hasn't quite cracked it, though. *40%. Duty Free.*

Bowmore "Darkest" Aged 15 Years db **(83) n20 t23 f19 b21.** In recent years a dram you tasted with glass in one hand and a revolver in the other. No more. But for the sulphur present, this would have been a much higher score. *43%*

Bowmore "Mariner" Aged 15 Years db **(79) n19 t21 f19 b20.** There are two ways of looking at this. As a Bowmore. Which is how I have marked it. Or a something to throw down your neck for pure fun. Which is probably worth another seven or eight points. Either way, there is something not entirely right here. *43%. Duty Free.*

Bowmore Aged 17 Years db **(77) n18 t22 f18 b19.** For all the attractiveness of the sweet fruit on delivery, the combination of butt and cough sweet makes for pretty hard going. *43%*

Bowmore Aged 18 Years db **(79) n20 t21 f19 b19.** Pleasant, drinkable Fisherman's Friend style – like every Bowmore it appears around this age. But why so toffee-dull? *43%*

⬩ **Bowmore Aged 23 Years Port Matured** db (86) n22 t22 f21 b21. Have you ever sucked Fisherman's Friends and fruit pastels at the same time, and thrown in the odd Palma Violet for good measure...? 50.8%

Bowmore Aged 25 Years db (86) n21 t22 f21 b22. Not the big, chunky guy of yore: the age would surprise you if tasted blind. 43%

Bowmore Aged 30 Years db (94) n23 intense burnt raisin amid the intense burnt peat; a deft rummy sweetness strikes an improbable chord with the sweetened lime; the oak is backward coming forward but binds beautifully with both peat and fruit; t24 near flawless delivery showing a glimpse of Bowmore in a form similar to how I remember it some 25 years ago. The peat, though intense does have a hint of the Fisherman's Friend about it, but not so upfront as today. For all the peat, this is clean whisky, moulded by a craftsman into how a truly great Islay should be; f23 dries sublimely as the oak contains the peat and adds a touch of coffee to it in unsugared form. Gentle oils cling tightly to the roof of the mouth; b24 a Bowmore that no Islay scholar should be without. Shows the distillery at its most intense yet delicate; an essay in balance and how great oak, peat and fruit can combine for those special moments in life. Unquestionably one of the best Bowmores bottled this century. 43%

Bowmore 1985 db (89) n21.5 Fisherman's Friend with a mix of muscovado and lightly molassed sugars as ballast; t24 still not technically right. But you have to be a miserable sod not to enjoy the counter-balance between the sugars and the outrageous, weirdly off key peat; f22 stays the course as a bit of a punch-drunk liquorice-sodden Fisherman's Friend addict but its sheer individuality has you in a trance of enjoyment; b21.5 I may have tasted a sweeter Islay. Just not sure when. This whisky is so wrong..it's fantastically right...! 52.6%

Bowmore 100 Degrees Proof db (90.5) n22 low key smoke. Anyone who has been to Arbroath looking for where the Smokies are cured and homed in on the spot by nose alone will recognise this aroma...; t23 delicate in all departments, including the peat. The barley is sweet but it is the tenderness of the oils which stars; f22.5 long with a tapering muscovado finale; b23 proof positive! A real charmer. 57.1%. ncf.

⬩ **Bowmore Devil's Cask** db (87.5) n22 a p-souper of a nose...peaty, that is. Just so dense, it is really a little too much; t23 there's no smoke without fire and the flames lick around a fruity Hades; f21 hints of brimstone; b21.5 not really my style of whisky, for all its obvious fun...and this little devil doesn't really even to try and balance itself out. 56.9%

Bowmore Laimrig III db (92) n23.5 so delicate is the ultra clean grape, I am assuming this is a sherry cask finish. Not usually a fan of smoke and grape, but when it is this delicate, what isn't there to like?; t23.5 the softness found on the nose is continued on the palate. The sweetness is cleverly controlled and when the Fisherman's Friend personality arrives, it is quietly muffled, if not smothered to death, by a combination of silky grape, teasing spice and melting muscovado sugars; f22.5 the oak now raises its profile, the deep vanillas and hint of honeycomb underlining a reasonable age; b23 I must ask my research team: where the hell are Laimrigs I and II....? 53.7%

Bowmore Legend db (88) n22 t22.5 f22 b22.5. Not sure what has happened here, but it has gone through the gears dramatically to offer a substantial dram with both big peat and excellent balancing molasses. Major stuff. 40%

Bowmore Small Batch Reserve db (80.5) n20 t21 f19 b20.5. With a name like "Small Batch Reserve" I was expecting a marriage between intense Kentucky and Islay. Alas, this falls well short of the mark. 40%

Bowmore Tempest Aged 10 Years Small Batch Release No.1 db first fill bourbon, bott 2009 (87) n22.5 t22 f21 b21.5. Perhaps too dependent on the fudgy character. When given a chance, its coastal attributes are set off to excellent effect. 55.3%

Bowmore Tempest Aged 10 Years Small Batch Release No.2 1st fill bourbon, bott 2010 db (93) n23.5 a rousing and strangely subtle mixture of dusty, bone-dry phenols not uncommon to non-island peated malts and a sweeter, tangier smoke, much more reminiscent of lums reeking their winter warmth; all this charged and emboldened by sly degrees of golden syrup and juicy figs; t23.5 sturdy delivery. Just a light introduction of oils help the easy passage of a more fulsome earthiness, like the nose assisted by sugars, much more gristy this time. There is also a youthful citrus tone to this, though the dissolving vanilla and icing sugars do much good work; f23 a hint of bitterness from the oak, but the smoke and spices bombard the taste buds. Some muscovado sugars and even the most playful hint of molasses ensures the salty, coastal notes don't take too great a hold...; b23.5 just turned the bottle round to find some tasting notes banging on about "lemon pepper" here there and everywhere. That is only part of the tale: this is one of the better distillery bottlings to be found at Bowmore in recent years and does much to restore a slightly jaded reputation. Less a tempest than a glide across the Sound of Islay on a sunny day, cheese and tomato sandwich in hand.. But a massive statement by Bowmore, nonetheless. 56%. ncf.

Bowmore Tempest Aged 10 Years Small Batch Release No. 4 db (**89**) **n22** even by Bowmore standards the peat is light with barely a breeze to alter the course of the smoke. A few renegade spices ping around the citrus vanilla; **t23** if my taste buds were massaged any more softly by the light smoke and spices they might doze off; **f22** lightly smoked vanilla all the way; **b22** a much tamer version than the last Tempest I tasted. Then, there was a crescendo. This one sweeps gently across the palate without kicking up anything like a storm. 55.1%. ncf.

A.D. Rattray Bowmore 1998 cask no. 800005, dist 9 Mar 98, bott Jun 12 (**89**) **n22** smoked Digestive biscuit...with a fair bit of salt, too; **t23** excellent oils and top rate molasses give the smoke some substance; even the spices fit in seamlessly; **f22** dries, but elegantly; remains smoky and sweet to the very end; **b22** an understated little island treasure. 46%. sc.

⋰ **A.D. Rattray Bowmore 1999** butt, cask no. 2262, dist 16 Sep 99, bott Nov 12 (**87**) **n22** Fisherman's Friend meets Harvey's Bristol Cream; somewhere in the background a match is struck; **t22.5** pounding peat forced into the taste buds by a combination of the weight of the sherry and the big vanilla kick; **f21** molasses and...that struck match again...; **b21.5** not quite a flawless butt, but the outstanding points outweigh the blemishes. 59%. sc. A.D. Rattray. DRCC Japan and Holland markets.

Berry's Own Selection Bowmore 1994 cask no. 1714, bott 2011 (**83.5**) **n21 t22 f20 b20.5**. Puts most of its emphasis on the muscular spice kick. Pleasant, but doesn't hang together with too much charm or style. 54.2%. nc ncf sc. Berry Bros & Rudd.

Berry's Own Selection Bowmore 1996 cask no. 1378, bott 2011 (**93.5**) **n23** two-toned peat offering soft and spiky varieties; salty, too; **t23** juicy and clean: the sugars are muscovado style and are crystal clear; **f23.5** some oily Venezuelan chocolate joins the medium roast Mysore coffee...with brown sugar, of course; **b24** doesn't try to be overtly spectacular: just does what it's meant to very well indeed. 55.9%. 55.9%. nc ncf sc. Berry Bros & Rudd.

Berry's Own Selection Bowmore 2003 cask no. 20059, bott 2012 (**91.5**) **n21.5** the smoke plays little more than peek-a-boo; **t23.5** some light orange notes drift into the peat and vanilla chorus; the sugars leave a malty residue; **f23** the complexity continues, though the phenols rarely raise their voice above a hoarse whisper; **b23.5** its understated and delicate qualities certainly do grow on you. A little gem. 57.9%. nc ncf sc. Berry Bros & Rudd.

Boisdale Bowmore 2000 cask no. 800113, bott 2012 (**83.5**) **n21.5 t21 f20 b21**. A lazy, frankly boring, beggar that really does deserve a kick up the arse. 46%. nc ncf sc.

⋰ **The Coopers Choice Bowmore 2001 10 Years Old** refill butt, cask no. 9074, dist 01, bott 11 (**91**) **n22.5** something between the Bowmore norm and Caol Ila in smokiness, with attractive light oak edges; more like a Caol Ila in its oiliness, though; **t22.5** a bigger puff of smoke than you'd normally expect, the impact broadened by the intact oils and generous sugars; **f23** long, with those muscovado sugars really determined to go all the way; **b23** Bowmore at its most relaxed and effortlessly enjoyable. Without question above the normal peating levels. 46%. The Vintage Malt Whisky Co Ltd. 360 bottles.

Duncan Taylor NC² Bowmore 1998 (**85.5**) **n22 t21 f21.5 b21**. Lightly smoked, softly oiled, delicately oaked and as though any excess sweetness has been extracted from it. 46%. nc ncf. Duncan Taylor & Co.

Duncan Taylor Rare Auld Bowmore 28 Years Old cask no. 85161, bott 1982 (**86**) **n20 t22.5 f21.5 b22**. Can't help thinking that this spirit was pumped through the stills at a rare old rate of knots. At times, thin and fiery but at others, the vanilla and smoke offers enough sweetness to genuinely charm. 51.6%. sc. Duncan Taylor & Co.

Duncan Taylor Rare Auld Bowmore 29 Years Old cask no. 85212, bott 1982 (**89.5**) **n22.5** a unique signature: Fisherman's Friend wrapped in bourbon and topped with strawberry... not something you experience every day...; **t21.5** a misfit of a delivery with the varied and contrasting flavours and weights finding difficulty in hitting a groove; **f23** a majestic finale: more bourbon and smoke but now some gorgeous vanilla and late exotic fruit; **b22.5** a malt which handsomely pays back on your invested patience. 50.1%. sc.

⋰ **Fine Malt Selection Bowmore 12 Years Old** cask no. 800252, dist 00, bott Apr 13 (**85.5**) **n21.5 t22 f20.5 b21.5**. A beauty of Bowmore is that the peating level can vary by intriguing degrees. Chewy and malty and less encumbered with salt than usual. But even the higher than normal phenols fails to fully overcome the late oak bitterness. 46%. sc.

Kingsbury Single Cask Series Bowmore Aged 14 Years Trois Riviers rum finish (**85.5**) **n21.5 t22 f21 b21**. You have to be very careful with rum casks: few ever make perfect finishes for a whisky as the sugars have a tendency to constrict the complexity. As pleasant as this virtually smokeless malt is, it is no exception. 46%. sc. Japan Import Systems.

⋰ **Kingsbury Bowmore Aged 14 Years** barrel, cask no. 800194, dist 98 (**86.5**) **n22 t22 f21 b21.5**. A delicate Bowmore which never quite hits the heights, but the gristy sweetness is soothing and pleasant. 46%. nc ncf. Japan Import System. 273 bottles.

⋰ **Kingsbury Bowmore Aged 17 Years** butt, cask no. 14, dist 95 (**88.5**) **n21.5** a pyrotechnic display of grape and earth unique to Bowmore; **t23** more of the same, but with some pretty full on molasses tipped into the mix; f22.5 sweetens and at last becomes a little more genteel; b21.5 typically disjointed yet enormous and somehow works. 53.6%. nc ncf. Japan Import System. 545 bottles.

Liquid Sun Bowmore 11 Years Old bourbon cask, dist 2000, bott 2011 (88.5) n22 a hint of mocha to the powdery peat; t22 a short sweet blast of brown sugars quickly followed by a much drier dose of vanilla; f22.5 an untaxing but entertaining intertwining of those sweet and dry notes; b22 straight as a die. 46%. sc. The Whisky Agency.

Liquid Sun Bowmore 22 Years Old bourbon cask, dist 1989, bott 2011 (84) n20 t22 f20.5 b21.5. Pleasant and attractively sweet for the first four or five big flavour waves directly after delivery. Thins dramatically on the finish. 50.7%. sc. The Whisky Agency.

Liquid Sun Bowmore 1998 bott 2011 (84.5) n21 t21.5 f21 b21. From the Fisherman's Friend school of Bowmore bottlings. Perhaps a little extra sugar than the norm, though this dissolves by the very dry finish. 53.6%. nc ncf sc. The Whisky Agency.

Malts Of Scotland Bowmore 1989 bourbon hogshead, cask no. MoS11004, dist Oct 89, bott Oct 11 (86.5) n21 t22 f21.5 b22 Very sweet and quietly smoky. The oils are pleasant but the spices do bite a little. 51.2%. nc ncf sc. Malts Of Scotland.

Malts Of Scotland Bowmore 1995 sherry hogshead, cask no. 111, bott 2011 (85) n21 t22 f20.5 b21.5. Perhaps just too much of a soup with grape thrown into the smoky mix, rather than carefully measured first. 56.5%. nc ncf sc. Malts Of Scotland.

Malts Of Scotland Bowmore 1995 sherry hogshead, cask no. MoS12018, dist May 95, bott Apr 12 (85) n21 t22 f20 b21.5. Thought I'd tasted a whisky like this some weeks back. Then spotted my notes for MOS 1985 cask 11. Peas in a pod, save the lesser finish on this one. 56.8%. nc ncf sc. Malts Of Scotland.

Malts Of Scotland Bowmore 1999 bourbon hogshead, cask no. MoS110014, dist 22 Sep 99, bott Oct 11 (88) n22.5 teasing floral notes interact beautifully with the delicate smoke; t21 perhaps a little thin on delivery but fattens out as light oils seep in with peaty vanilla; f22.5 almost cocoa oil dryness to this. The chewability climbs dramatically; b22 for all the alcoholic strength, Bowmore's lightness of touch with its peat is in full evidence. 61.2%. nc ncf sc.

⁝⁝ Malts of Scotland Bowmore 2001 bourbon hogshead, cask no. MoS 12060, dist Oct 01, bott Nov 12 (87.5) n21.5 the refreshing lemon zest and angular smoke points to something younger than it is; a little lemon curd tart nods at the oak; t22 busy, gristy sugars again bounding with sharp sugars and a rattling spiciness; f22 at last soothes slightly as hickory and liquorice melt with the smoke; b22 never low key and makes the most of its youthful anarchy. 58.2%. nc ncf sc. 96 bottles.

Mo Òr Collection Bowmore 1968 42 Years Old first fill bourbon hogshead, cask no. 3825, dist 8 Oct 68, bott 3 Nov 10 (82) n21.5 t21.5 f19 b20. Without doubt, the Mo Or collection has been one of the highlights of the whisky year. So there is no little irony that their collector's edition pales in quality to what was to follow. This guy is too old and over oaked. Still has its moments, especially when the sugars get a brief foothold and is allowed to lift the peat and above the oaky swamp. 42.4%. nc ncf sc. Release No. 1. 184 bottles.

Mo Òr Collection Bowmore 1996 13 Years Old, cask no. DL6464, dist 1996, bott 2010 (90.5) n21.5 pleasant, lightly smoked but don't hunt too hard for complexity; t24 a hugely satisfying delivery with a Jammy Dodger gloss to the delivery and a few layers of honey man-marking the phenols; f22 smoky vanilla; soft with delicate oils; b23 worth experiencing for the sublime delivery alone. A much better experience than the nose heralds. 46%. nc ncf sc. 360 bottles.

Old Malt Cask Bowmore Aged 11 Years sherry butt, cask no. 7791, dist Sep 00, bott Nov 11 (88.5) n23 the peat remains attractively defined. Something akin to a rum and raisin sweetness; t23.5 the thickness on the nose is recreated on the lightly oiled palate; some liquorice blends in beautifully with the smoked grape; f20 just a little too dry; b22 at times an exceptional sherry butt which, early on, took me back some 30-odd years when casks like this were not uncommon at Bowmore. A soupy treat. 50%. nc ncf sc. 451 bottles.

⁝⁝ Old Master Bowmore 16 Years Old cask no. 800203, dist 97, bott 13 (94) n23 pungent from so many angles: a massive saline kick to this, which fully accentuates not just the otherwise lazy phenols but the citrus curve to the vanilla; t23.5 outrageously salivating for its age: now the lemon is in free flow, ensuring the taste buds see the barley before the smoke begins to make a noise, though not a very loud one; f24 the sherbet lemon fizz continues, the delicate smoke and light cocoa coating in its wake: the best part of the experience! b23.5 love it! 57%. sc. James MacArthur & Co Ltd.

⁝⁝ Old & Rare Bowmore Aged 25 Years refill butt, dist Feb 87, bott Apr 12 (91.5) n23 a bizarre but quite delightful combination of Love Heart candy, Fisherman's Friend and stewed apple; t23 at once lush yet licentious with the puckering spices making lurid advances on the palate which prove irresistible; f22.5 seemingly simplifies out into a much more straightforward vanilla-themed dram with the smoke bubbling away in the background. But look deeper and there is a vivid complexity one normally associates with the "small grains" found in better bourbons; **b23** shows some imperfections and eccentricities reminiscent of a certain colourful period in the distillery's history. But this has moved on from the simple Fisherman's Friend of old to something altogether more complex and almost erotically enjoyable. 56.1%. *nc ncf sc. Douglas Laing & Co. 124 bottles.*

Provenance Bowmore Over 10 Years refill hogshead, cask no. 7594, dist Autumn 2000, bott Summer 2011 **(86.5) n22 t21 f22 b21.5**. An enjoyable malt, though it appears lacking in the usual coastal qualities. 46%. *nc ncf sc. Douglas Laing & Co.*

⁖ **Provenance Bowmore Over 10 Years** refill hogshead, cask no. 9325, dist Autumn 02, bott winter 12 **(84.5) n20 t22 f21 b21.5**. A sweet, warming dram perfect for a cold day. Shows impressive malt-peat complexity despite the dull oak. 46%. *nc, ncf, sc. Douglas Laing & Co.*

⁖ **Provenance Bowmore Over 10 Years** refill hogshead, cask no. 9574, dist winter 02, bott spring 13 **(89.5) n22** violets on a warm summer evening; peat reek in a florist's; **t23** texture and malt weight absolutely spot on, allowing the maple syrup and delicate smoke free reign; **f22** minimum oils allow the vanilla to grow during the elegantly slow fade; **b22.5** simplistic, yet the most complete Bowmore of this age I've seen bottled for a while. Evidence the quality is on the way back. Beautiful. 46%. *nc ncf sc.*

Riegger's Selection Bowmore 1996 bourbon cask, cask no. 1334, dist 7 May 96, bott 2 Mar 12 **(91.5) n22** tight in part, but enough movement to allow the saltiness of the sweet smoke a free hand; **t23** soft and very sweet. The delivery is less about the smoke than the intensity of the bourbon-style sugars; **f23** long, with something of the Maryland cookie about it; **b23.5** sheer entertainment. 55.7%. *nc ncf sc. Viktor-Riegger GmbH. 340 bottles.*

Robert Graham's Dancing Stag Bowmore 1990 cask no. 17520, bott Jan 12 **(73.5) n18.5 t19 f17 b18**. Entirely off key, this one gets into a rut. 46%. *nc ncf sc. 257 bottles.*

Scotch Malt Whisky Society Cask 3.179 Aged 21 Years refill hogshead, cask no. 2808, dist 1990 **(88) n21.5** untidy, higgledy-piggledy nose which refuses to find a rhythm; **t22.5** a bigger delivery than expected and wonderfully juicy, too; the mid ground goes mocha while the smoke begins upping the ante; **f22** now pure cocoa...with very indulgent smoke for a Bowmore; **b22** you just can't beat a glass of smoked chocolate! 50.3%. *sc.*

Scotch Malt Whisky Society Cask 3.181 Aged 15 Years refill hogshead, cask no. 2773, dist 1996 **(86) n22 t22 f20 b22**. Well made, but for all the rich sugars embedded in the smoke, it is let down by a less than wonderful piece of oak. 60.5%. *sc.*

Scotch Malt Whisky Society Cask 3.185 Aged 16 Years refill hogshead, cask no. 803, dist 1995 **(92) n23** much friskier smoke than the norm from Bowmore: a charming crispness is laced with gooseberry jam and orange segment; **t24** mmmm! No less sexy on delivery and is aided with a perfect degree of oil; the smoke is now less up front but delicate spices and those sweet gooseberry and sharper citrus notes cover the mid ground well; **f22** loses momentum as the oak digs deep; **b23** now that is rather good.... 573%. *sc.*

Scotch Malt Whisky Society Cask 3.189 Aged 14 Years refill butt, cask no. 2407, dist 1997 **(63) n15 t17 f14 b15**. How such a fatally sulphured malt got anywhere near bottling is beyond me. 58.4%. *sc.*

⁖ **Scotch Malt Whisky Society Cask 3.192 Aged 24 Years** 2nd fill sherry butt, dist 8 Dec 87 **(94.5) n23** the peat and fruit are good mates: this is one very clean sherry butt and delicate smoke takes full advantage to blossom; **t24** about as good a sherry delivery as you are likely to find with this distillery. The submissive nature of the peat allows the rich fruitcake to thrive and even show a nutty nature; **f23.5** must be oloroso at work as there is a rich sheen to the grape which carries the light (and spice-free) smoke effortlessly; **b24** unusually creamy and just sweet enough. Absolutely exceptional and quite fruitless sherry butt at work. Sublime. 51.8%. *nc ncf sc. 145 bottles.*

⁖ **Scotch Malt Whisky Society Cask 3.195 Aged 14 Years** 2nd fill sherry butt, dist 25 Sep 97 **(76.5) n18 t20 f18.5 b19**. Sweet, but cuts up rough. About as unbalanced as 3.192 is textbook. 58.5%. *nc ncf sc. 609 bottles.*

Scott's Selection Bowmore 1991 bott 2012 **(89.5) n22** no Bowmore from this period is complete without at least a hint of Fisherman's Friend and here it can be detected alongside the crisp sugars; **t23** lovely delivery with a texture to die for. The mid ground offers a charming nuttiness which adds to the sweet barley and drier phenol complexity; **f22** a surprising degree of standard vanilla, though some smoke lasts the course alongside the spice; **b22.5** a lovely bottling very true and sympathetic to the distillery style. 54.6%

Silver Seal Bowmore Over 16 Years Old dist 1995 **(88.5) n22** a few primroses and bluebells in the earthy lead; **t23** early sugars, some of them distinctly molassed and toasty; **f21.5** attractive vanillas come out to play; some late salt; **b22** never an easy distillery to get the measure of, this is a pretty steady ship. 54%. *sc. Silver Seal Whisky Company.*

⁖ **That Boutique-y Whisky Company Bowmore** batch 1 **(84.5) n20 t21 t22.5 b21**. Pleasant. Sweet. Very lightly smoked. Even more lightly fruited. Yet seems to struggle for a pulse. The delicate spices are the star turn. 48.7%. *Master of Malt. 263 bottles.*

⬧ **That Boutique-y Whisky Company Bowmore** batch 2 **(91)** n21.5 grapes, citrus and seaweed...; t23.5 profound sugars, some a little along the lines of gooseberry and apricot jam. The smoke builds slowly until the middle is a spicy, muscovado sugar addled hallelujah! f23 retains its now slightly more gristy sweetness to the death; b23 Bowmore in a very good form, indeed, with the smokiness decidedly enigmatic. *49%. Master of Malt. 292 bottles.*

The Whisky Broker Bowmore 14 Years Old refill bourbon barrel, cask no. 800229, dist 1997, bott 2011 **(95.5)** n23.5 if it wasn't for a dash of chocolate, the delicate smoke and honey would point me to another island; t24 the delivery offers sublime balance: all kinds of acacia and clear honey tones brought down to earth by a light rumble of smoke. Do we have the right distillery here? f24 remains lush and the citrus notes move from an original lemony deftness to a heavier kumquat. This is all encased in gorgeous Venezuelan chocolate to turn the finale into a high quality, lightly spiced candy bar; b24 what it misses in smoke it makes up for in honey! Almost an HP in disguise. *55%. nc ncf sc. 183 bottles.*

BRAEVAL
Speyside, 1974. Chivas Brothers. Working.

⬧ **Dun Bheagan Braeval Aged 16 Years** hogshead, cask no. 85163, 85165, 85166, dist May 96, bott 13 **(89)** n21.5 not dissimilar to a very malty breakfast cereal; t23 the sugars which are hidden on the nose pop up here in all their lightly molassed glory; the sweetness wears away as the more determined vanillas take hold; f22 the big malt theme persists, protected by a silky shield; b22.5 a cheery, high quality dram full of happy, uncomplicated malty notes. *43%. nc ncf. Ian Macleod Distillers. 1050 bottles.*

Duncan Taylor Dimensions Braes Of Glenlivet 22 Years Old cask no. 979, dist May 89, bott Dec 11 **(90.5)** n22 Speyside in a sniff...; t23.5 ...and on the palate, too, so clean and vivid is the grassy barley; plenty of light chewing thanks to the sugared vanilla; f22 a continuation of the same mega clean notes...; b23 the kind of just-right dram which brings tears of joy to the eye. *55.4%. nc ncf sc. Duncan Taylor & Co.*

⬧ **Master of Malt Braes O'Glenlivet Aged 21 Years** ex-bourbon cask, dist 23 Aug 92, bott 28 Nov 12 **(94)** n23.5 much more Buffalo Trace than Braeval: the tannins leap from the glass like Nureyev from the stage floor with a wonderful accompaniment of muscavado sugars and liquorice; sharp rhubarb and gooseberry preserve on mildly burned toast; t24 malts of this age rarely arrive on the palate so saturated in barley juice...it just drips with the stuff. With it comes a supreme sweet-sharp barley balance, then a slow introduction of vanilla and butterscotch.; f23 the finish reverts back to the bourbon style with toasted honeycomb walnuts in abundance; b23.5 when Braes is good it can be, like this, bloody marvellous...!! *474%. sc. 251 bottles.*

Mo Ór Collection Braeval 1995 15 Years Old first fill bourbon hogshead, cask no. 186019, dist 12 Dec 95, bott 5 Apr 11 **(84.5)** n20.5 t22 f20.5 b21.5. Surprisingly "milky" in style which belies its first fill pedigree. Huge barley statement on both nose and especially on delivery. But that oak... *46%. nc ncf sc. Release No. 39. The Whisky Talker. 480 bottles.*

Provenance Braeval Over 11 Years refill butt, cask no. 7596, dist Autumn 1999, bott Summer 2011 **(85)** n21.5 t21 f21.5 b21. Pleasant and biscuity. A kind of 52 proof Ovaltine. *46%. nc ncf sc. Douglas Laing & Co.*

Provenance Braeval Over 12 Years sherry butt, cask no. 8011, dist Autumn 1999, bott Winter 2012 **(84.5)** n21.5 t22 f20 b21. One of the weightiest Braevals ever bottled. Thick, malty and with plenty of chewy fudge. *46%. nc ncf sc. Douglas Laing & Co.*

⬧ **That Boutique-y Whisky Company Braes O'Glenlivet** batch 1 **(78)** n21 t20 f18 b19. Flat, toffeed, bitter and very disappointing for this distillery. *47.2%. 210 bottles.*

BRORA
Highlands (Northern), 1819–1983. Diageo. Closed.

Brora 25 Year Old 7th Release bott 2008 db **(96)** n24 even with the lowest peating levels you ever have nosed from this distillery, the aura of beauty is unmistakable: the soft phenol molecules appears to be perfectly matched with the oak ones. Meanwhile fragile citrus ensures a youthful charm; somewhere there is a hint of bourbon; t24.5 superb barley kick off, absolute waves of juices running about the palate, and still the smoke holds back, no more than a background murmur; as the middle fills, that bourbon on the nose become more pronounced with shades of honeyed liquorice; f23.5 long, with the sugars hanging in there allowing the vanillas to form very slowly; b24 as the distillery closed in March 1983, if memory serves me correctly, this must be coming to the end of the road for the true 25-year-old. Those looking for the usual big peat show might be disappointed. Others, in search of majesty, sophistication and timeless grace, will be blown away. *56.3%*

Brora 30 Years Old db **(97)** n24 t25 f24 b24. Here we go again! Just like last year's bottling, we have something of near unbelievable beauty with the weight perfectly pitched and the barley-oak interaction the stuff of dreams. And as for the peat: an entirely unique species, a giant that is so gentle. Last year's bottling was one of the whiskies of the year. This even better version is the perfect follow-up. 56.4%

Brora 30 Years Old Special Release refill American and European oak db **(89) n22 t23.5 f21.5 b22.** Seeing as I was the guy who proudly discovered this whisky over 20 years ago, I take more than a keen interest. But like a loved and cherished old relative, you can still adore its personality and unique independence but be aware that it is slowly fading away... 54.3%. nc ncf. Diageo. 2958 bottles.

Brora 32 Years Old Special Release 2011 db **(89) n22** toffee and orange peel; **t23** a delicate smoke creeps in through the back door of the delivery, which concentrates mainly on the same caramels which dominate the nose; the sawdusty vanilla leaves little doubt to the oak's powers; **f22** strained ulmo honey; **b22** a strange bottling containing more natural caramels from a Brora than I have ever before seen. Obviously a dumbing down effect is inevitable but enough of the original beauty remains to enthral. 54.7%. nc ncf.

⋰ **Brora 35 Years Old Special Release 2012** Refill American Oak, dist 1976 &1977, bott 2012 db **(90.5) n24.5** got a spare day or two...? This is Brora in transformation: the peat levels have dropped now to a whisper while the exotic fruit delegation, often present in very old whisky, though more normally found in Speyside, have turned up in full force. The oak notes dominate over the peat at a rate of about three to one. But, some of those vanilla and guava notes in particular are exceptionally complex; **t22.5** eye-watering oak on delivery. The oils prevent too much damage and the kumquats retain a degree of juiciness; predictable cocoa in mid-ground; the smoke has thinned like the hair on an old man's pate; **f21** there is a buzz, less of spice and more of exhausted oak. But, again, those cocoa oils fill and sooth; just enough sugars around to guarantee balance; **b22.5** perhaps 90% of other Scottish malts would have failed under such an oaky onslaught. However, the pedigree of this distillery sees it through against the odd and the nose rewards a good hour's study. Not sure how much longer this guy can hold out for, though. 48.1%. nc ncf. Diageo.

Chieftain's Brora Aged 30 Years sherry butt, cask no. 1523, dist Dec 81 **(88.5) n22** relaxed smoke lets in the fruit cocktail; **t23** the delivery surprises: far more caramel than the nose suggests, though this soon melts and helps along the golden syrup and over-ripe greengage for the softest of experiences; **f21.5** just becomes a tad bland as the caramels take too great a stranglehold; **b22** when the oak decides to go on the attack, even the world's greatest spirits can offer so much resistance. But as one of the world's great spirits you can be assured of some masterful complexity along the way, if only fleetingly. 54.6%. nc ncf sc. Ian Macleod Distillers. USA exclusive.

Chieftain's Brora Aged 30 Years sherry butt, dist Dec 81, bott 2012 **(96) n24** when you find a near perfect sherry butt these days it is a moment for almost lump in the throat joy. The way the apricot and unripe peach and juicy mango intermingles with the spicy yet earthy peat: we are talking faultless weight and major complexity here; **t24.5** no letting up of complexity here either. There is a blend of honeys – orange blossom and thyme – which link fingers and dance around the phenols which slowly transform into praline and walnut...wow! **f23.5** long, with those walnut oils lingering and softening the late phenolic glow; **b24** a malt of a lifetime which barely puts a foot wrong. Magnificent. 50%. nc ncf sc. Ian Macleod Distillers.

BRUICHLADDICH
Islay, 1881. Rémy Cointreau. Working.

Bruichladdich 10 Years Old db **(90) n22** beautifully clean and zesty, the malt is almost juvenile; **t23** sweet, fruity then malty charge along the tastebuds that geets the mouth salivating; **f23** the usual soft vanilla and custard but a bigger barley kick in the latter stages; **b22** more oomph than previous bottlings, yet still retaining its fragile personality. Truly great stuff for a standard bottling. 46%

Bruichladdich 12 Years Old 2nd Edition db **(88) n23 t22 f22 b21.** A similar type of wine involvement to "Waves", but this is oilier in the old-fashioned 'Laddie style and lacks a little of the sparkle. The fruit on the finish is outstanding, though, and I don't think you or I would turn down a third glass... 46%

Bruichladdich 15 Years Old 2nd Edition db **(86) n22 t23 f20 b21.** Delicious, as usual, but something, possibly fruity, appears to be holding back the show. 46%

Bruichladdich 16 Years Old bourbon cask db **(89) n22.5 t22.5 f22 b22.** Plucked from the cask in the nick of time. In this state rather charming, but another Summer or two might have seen the oak take a more sinister turn. 46%

Bruichladdich 16 Years Old bourbon/Chateau d'Yquem cask db **(95) n24** if you've got a good half an hour to spend, try using it intelligently by sticking your nose in this for a while: the grape is sweet and sultana juicy; the understated spices somehow hit just the right point to satisfy grape, oak and barley in one hit: some achievement... **t23.5** sweet, as the nose suggests, but the arrival is not all about grape. That sweetness also contains pristine barley... **f23.5** just so soft and subtle with the vanillas offering a discreet escort to the barley-grape marriage; **b24** possibly the most delicate and understated of all the truly great whiskies of the year. Not one for the ice and water brigade. *46%*

Bruichladdich 16 Years Old bourbon/Chateau Haut Brion cask db **(81.5)** n21 t21.5 f19 **b20.** fruity and busy for sure. But just not the kind of wine barrel effect that does much for me, I'm afraid, not least because of the background buzz on the palate. *46%*

Bruichladdich 16 Years Old bourbon/Chateau Lafite cask db **(89)** n24 t22.5 f21.5 b21.5. Ridiculously soft. Could just do with an injection of something to propel it into greatness. *46%*

Bruichladdich 16 Years Old bourbon/Chateau Lafleur cask db **(92.5)** n23 t23.5 f23 b23. So luminous on the palate, it's positively Lafleurescent... *46%*

Bruichladdich 16 Years Old bourbon/Chateau Latour cask db **(84.5)** n21 t21.5 f21 b21. Enjoyable. But there is a strange aggression to the spice which doesn't altogether sit as comfortably as it might. The fruit heads off into not just grapey but citrus territory, but there is a always a but about the direction it takes... *46%*

Bruichladdich 16 Years Old bourbon/Chateau Margaux cask db **(78.5)** n20.5 t20 f19 b19. Not 1st Cru Bruichladdich, I'm afraid. *46%*

Bruichladdich XVII Aged 17 Years bourbon/renegade rum db **(92)** n23 typical rum "clipped" nose; this one with just a shade of soft, dry rubber typical of certain Guyana (especially Enmore) or Barbados marks; a rather lovely lemon tint to the vanilla works a treat; **t23.5** super dry delivery, too, with the sugars taking time to arrive. When they do, they weld with the barley attractively; formidable balance between the barley and spices while a light sprinkling of salt seems to up the spicy oak input to counter the sugars; **f22** mainly dry and attractively layered with short, sweet bands; **b23.** always good to see the casks of drier, more complexly structured rums being put to such intelligent use. My sample doesn't tell me which rum casks were used, but I was getting vivid flashbacks here of Ruby-Topaz Hummingbirds flitting from flower to flower in the gardens of the now closed Eigflucht distillery in Guyana in the long gone days when I used to scramble around the warehouses there. That distinctive dryness though is pure Enmore, though some Barbadian rum can offer a similar effect. Something very different and a top quality experience. *46%. nc ncf.*

Bruichladdich 18 Years Old bourbon/cognac cask db **(84.5)** n23.5 t21 f20 b20. Big oak-spice buzz but thin. Sublime grapey nose, for sure, but pays a certain price, ultimately, for associating with such an inferior spirit... *46%*

Bruichladdich 18 Years Old bourbon/opitz cask db **(80.5)** n19 t22 f19.5 b20. Dry, complex; at times oak-stretched. *46%*

Bruichladdich 18 Years Old 2nd Edition bourbon/jurancon db **(86)** n22 t21.5 f21 b21.5. Plenty of fruit, including medium ripe greengages and slightly under-ripe grape. Juicy and sweet in the right places. *46%*

Bruichladdich Flirtation Aged 20 Years 2nd Edition db **(86)** n21 t22 f22 b21. Hi sugar! A Laddie for those with a sweet tooth. *46%*

Bruichladdich 21 Years Old oloroso cask db **(76.5)** n18.5 t21 f18 b19. Oops! *46%*

Bruichladdich Black Art 3rd Edition Aged 22 Years db **(83)** n22 t21.5 f20 b20.5. Where last year' Black Art II managed to get away with the odd slight off note due to its brain-exploding enormity, this year it just hasn't got what it takes to get over the hurdles. Some sumptuous fruit through the middle, but it just ain't enough... *48.7%. nc ncf.*

Bruichladdich 32 Years Old DNA 1977 bourbon cask db **(94.5)** n23 there are so many bourbon tags on this, especially the waxiness to the honey, that just for a fleeting, off-guard moment I thought I was back nosing Kentucky whisky again. Then a giveaway salty tang coupled with a delicate hint of barley reminded me that I was in the land where the bagpipe abounds...; **t24** ridiculous! I mean, bloody outrageous! No whisky has the right to a delivery that perfect with the lightly oiled texture seemingly holding both oak and grain in equal measures. Buttery and rich, it then pans out back towards Kentucky with some liquorice and threads of honey. Then propels back to Scotland with a uniquely salty toffee middle; **f23.5** relatively easy going and simplistic. But the cream toffee hangs in there and then a late breakdown of almost clichéd bourbon notes from honey to hickory...; **b24** absolutely top of the range, profound and virtually faultless whisky which makes you remember the reason why you fell so deeply in love with this stuff all those many years ago. How fitting that when this was made Laddie was the Scotch distillery closest to America. For this is as much a bourbon in style as Scotch. But who cares? It doesn't matter: great whisky is great whisky. Full stop. *474%*

Bruichladdich 37 Years Old DNA 80% bourbon/20% sherry cask, aged in Le Pin wine casks db **(87)** n23.5 t22 f20.5 b21. Balance..? What balance...? Actually, somehow, this crazy thing does find some kind of equilibrium... *41%*

Bruichladdich 1984 Golder Still bourbon cask, db **(88.5)** n22 t23 f22 b21.5. A huge amount of natural caramels leached from the oak does the joint job of ensuring extraordinary softness and eroding the higher notes. Still, there is enough eye-rolling honey and spice to keep anyone happy and the rich bourbony character on delivery really is dreamy stuff. 51%

Bruichladdich 1984 Redder Still db (95.5) n23.5 t24 f23.5 b24.5. Now it's finding whiskies like this that I became the world's first-full time whisky for. I dreamed of discovering drams which stretched my tastebuds and spoke to me with eloquence, charisma and unmistakable class. This is one such whisky: the style is highly unusual; the cleverness of the layering almost unique. This is the kind of near flawless whisky for which we were given tastebuds. Oh, and a nose... 50.4%

Bruichladdich 1989 db (75.5) n20 t19 f17.5 b19. Ouch! 52.9%. Special bottling for Alberta.

Bruichladdich 1989 Black Art 2nd Edition bourbon cask db (95) n24 a thick fruit composite of probably the juiciest dates you'll find south of the Sahara and a dense hickory and honey strain of bourbon... Not just compelling. But absolutely magnificent...and just so right!!! Sulphur? Can it be? Yes, no...? Can't quite make it out...; t24 how many deliveries allow the spice ahead of the main thrust? Perhaps more accurately, alongside. Still pretty rare and the way in which the chocolate fruit and nut melts in with the honey and liquorice bourbon notes, you feel anything can happen; f23 some wonderful oils helping those dates and now walnuts, too, all embedded in light cocoa, to their final spicy farewell; b24 Bourbon cask, it says. Right. But how did those lush dates get in there? Also, there even appears to be the very faintest (and I mean the odd molecule) of sulphur. But so miniscule it does no damage whatsoever. This is a whisky that asks ten times more questions than it answers. Time, though, not to wonder why, but just bloody well enjoy, for this is one of the great whiskies of the year. 49.7%

⁘ **Bruichladdich Black Art 1990 Aged 23 Years 4th Edition** cask no. 13/161 db (79) n20 t21 f18 b20. The same wobbly weaknesses found in the 3rd edition are back here in force once again. Big, juicy fruit notes will form a degree of compensation for some. 49.2%. nc ncf sc.

Bruichladdich 1990 Aged 18 Years db (85.5) n22.5 t21 f21 b21. Enlivened by citrus and emboldened by soft salt. 46%

Bruichladdich 1990 Aged 18 Years cognac cask db (81.5) n20.5 t21 f20 b20. Wouldn't be a far greater benefit to the spirit world if Cognac was matured in a Bruichladdich cask...? 46%

Bruichladdich 1991 Aged 16 Years Chat Margaux finish db (94) n23 t25 f22.5 b23.5. A true Premier Cru malt...I have been almost certainly the most outspoken critic of whisky finishes: trust me, if they were all like this, you would never hear the merest clack of a dissenting typing key from me again... 46%

Bruichladdich 1991 Valinch Anaerobic Digestion 19 Years Old bourbon & madeira casks db (96.5) n24.5 huge, yet cleverly weighted fruit with spiced boiled greengages oozing from the glass but very happy to allow golden syrup to share some of its limelight; t24 if the nose was excellent, the delivery is of no less quality. A light, oily bed allows the grape and sugars to land gently, then a light spicy layer forms another level entirely. All the hallmarks of a juicy first fill Madeira cask at work here...and working well; f24 perhaps drier than all else before it with the spices chipping away and a burnt raisin sharpness mingling with the latent honey; virtually a never ending tale...; b24 about 20 minutes ago I could name you 250 excellent reasons to go and visit this distillery. I can now name you 251...A potential world whisky of the year that manages to do just about everything right...!!! 52.5% ncf sc. Only available at distillery.

Bruichladdich 1992 Sherry Edition "Fino" Aged 17 Years bourbon/fino sherry db (94) n23.5 dry, suety, spotted dick; in the background, dried dates lurk deliciously; wonderful balance; t24 fabulously subtle malt-generated sweetness sits comfortably with a much drier, juicier sub-plot; the mouthfeel hovers around perfection with just enough light oil to grease the roof of the mouth and keep the barley in the ascendancy; f23 lots to chew here as the vanillas offer a custardy edge, though sugars – whilst present - are at a premium. Again we are back to the dregs of dried dates; b23.5 exceptionally good: a rare showing of Fino at its most sophisticated and unblemished. 46%. nc ncf.

Bruichladdich 1992 Sherry Edition Pedro Ximénez Aged 17 Years bourbon/PX db (83) n22 t22 f18.5 b20.5. My word, that grape really does fly relentlessly at the taste buds. Probably the hardest sherry type to get right and here it works pretty well for the most part. 46%. nc ncf.

Bruichladdich 1993 14 Years Old Bolgheri French oak db (85.5) n23 t21 f21.5 b20. The fabulous nose doesn't quite translate once on the palate. The natural caramels and barley combo never quite gets it together with the grape. Now the nose: that's a different matter! 46%

Bruichladdich 1993 14 Years Old Sassicaia French oak db (83) n20 t21 f20.5 b21. From a too tight nose to a too limp body. Just not my sac... 46%

Bruichladdich 1994 Valinch Blandola bourbon/Chateau d'Yquem casks, dist Sep 94 db (87) n21.5 t22.5 f21 b22. A bit muddled here and there but, like the distillery and staff, no shortage of personality. 55.3%. Available only from Bruichladdich's distillery shop.

Bruichladdich 1994 "Kosher" Aged 12 Years db (85.5) n22 t21 f21 b21.5. Clean. What else, my dear? 46%

Bruichladdich 1998 db **(89)** n22 t22.5 f22.5 b22. A truly unique signature to this but absolute class in a glass. *46%*

Bruichladdich 1998 bourbon/oloroso cask, dist 1998 db **(87.5)** n22.5 t22.5 f21 b21.5. Surprisingly conservative. But, joy of joys, not an atom of sulphur to be found...!! *46%*

Bruichladdich 1998 bourbon/Manzanilla cask, dist 1998 db **(82.5)** n21 t21 f20 b20.5. Fruity. But bitter where it should be sweet. *46%*

Bruichladdich 1998 Ancien Regime db **(84.5)** n22 t21.5 f20 b21 An easy, slightly plodding celebration of all things malty, caramelly, oily and vanillay... *46%*

Bruichladdich 2001 Renaissance db **(91)** n23 lively with the smoke and oak in particular going hammer and tongs; t23 brilliant delivery! Varying fruit tones hit the palate running but there is a bit of barley reinforcement flexing some considerable muscle. But the star is the ubiquitous smoke which shows a gentle iron fist; f22.5 a big surge of natural caramels but the spices make a scene; b22.5 a Big Laddie. *46%*

Bruichladdich 2001 The Resurrection Dram 23.10.01 bourbon cask, dist 2001, bott 2009 db **(90.5)** n23 so subtle! Spiced sultana on malt, laced with golden syrup; t23 grist dissolves in the mouth: molten (fruitless) barley again with a sugary sheen. Simplistic, but beautifully effective; f21.5 long, vanilla-led, spiced and a little bitter; b23 now, be honest. How can you not have a first class Resurrection in the Bible...? *46%. 24,000 bottles.*

Bruichladdich 2004 Islay Barley Valinch fresh sherry butt db **(89.5)** n22.5 t24 f21 b22. Yet another quite fabulous bottling form Bruichladdich, this one really cranking up the flavours to maximum effect. Having said all that, call me mad if you will...but seeing as this is Islay barley, would it not have been a good idea to shove it into a bourbon barrel, so we could see exactly what it tastes like? Hopefully that is on its way... *575%*

Bruichladdich Infinity Second Edition bourbon/rioja db **(94)** n24 t24 f23 b23. Wasn't it Daffy Duck who used to put on his cape and shout: "Infinity and Beyond" ? Oh, no... it was Buzz Lightyear. Anyways, he must have been thinking of this. And there's certainly nothing dethspicable about this one... *52.5%*

Bruichladdich Infinity Third Edition refill sherry tempranillo db **(94.5)** n24 the smokiness appears to have a life of its own: still cured bacon, as in previous Infinities (actually can there be such a thing...?) but perhaps a touch of Bavarian smoked cheese, perhaps, as a side dish, next to a freshly diced apple? I adore the lack of oils on the nose; the teasing dryness compensated by a distant fruit freshness; t24 and its more of the same: just so dry, the palate is parched in seconds. The smoke is ashy, the vanilla is powdery, the malt gristy...just flakes of flavour wafting into every crevice like snow falling on a silent day; f23 long, with the inevitable build up of dry, powdery spices which match the vanilla for weight and impact; b23.5 I dare anybody who says they don't like smoky whisky not to be blown away by this. Go on...I dare you... *50%*

Bruichladdich Islay Barley Aged 5 Years db **(86)** n21 t22.5 f21.5 b21. The nose suggests a trainee has been let loose at the stills. But it makes amends with an almost debauched degree of barley on delivery which lasts the entirety of the experience. Heavens! This is different. But I have to say: it's bloody fun, too! *50%. nc ncf.*

⠿ **Bruichladdich Islay Barley Rockside Farm 2007** bourbon, cask no. 13/159 db **(88)** n22 so, so young! Maybe Islay barley, but it is still pretty green; very odd molecule of smoke here and there; t22 juicy youthful barley; the final echoes of new make but otherwise absolutely pure, uncomplicated malt. Spices litter the palate, as do some hardening sugars and softer caramel; f22 a few cocoa, mildly minty notes, though this seems more like the remnants of new make than cask; b22 clean and chirpy. Great fun. *50%. nc ncf.*

Bruichladdich Laddie Classic Edition 1 db **(89.5)** n23 t23 f21 b22.5. You probably have to be a certain vintage yourself to fully appreciate this one. Hard to believe, but I can remember the days when the most popular malt among those actually living on Islay was the Laddie 10. That was a staunchly unpeated dram offering a breezy complexity. Not sure of the age on this Retroladdich, but the similarities almost bring a lump to the throat... *46%*

Bruichladdich Legacy Series 3 Aged 35 Years db **(91)** n22 t22.5 f23.5 b23. So they managed to find a whisky exactly the same age as Ladie distiller Jim. *40.7%*

Bruichladdich Links "Carnoustie" 14 Years Old db **(78)** n19 t20 f19 b20. Hits some unexpected rough. *46%*

Bruichladdich Links K Club Ireland "16th Hole" 14 Years Old bourbon/syrah, dist 1992, bott 2007 db **(93)** n23 t23 f23 b24. I quite like this, though as hard as I try I can't quite love it. The spices offer great entertainment value and the juiciness on delivery is astonishing, but... My tongue is investigating every crevice in my mouth with some urgency, so I know it's complex – and very unusual, but... It's gossamer light. It kind of teases you. It's playful. But it's not beautiful. Is it...? Third mouthful in and I'm getting hooked. Oh, sod it! I've just upped it from a 86 to 93. What can I do? I'm in love... *46%. nc ncf. 12,000 bottles.*

Bruichladdich Links "Torrey Pines" 15 Years Old db **(89.5)** n23 t22.5 f22 b22. As clean as the perfect tee shot from the 15th... *46%*

Bruichladdich Organic 2003 Anns An T-Seann Doigh bourbon db **(84.5)** n22 t22 f20 b20.5. Thick barley carrying a soft smoke. A slight bitterness threads in and out of the proceedings. *46%. nc ncf. 100% Scottish barley.*

Bruichladdich Organic Multi Vintage bourbon db **(87.5)** n22 t22 f20.5 b22. Genteel. *46%*

Bruichladdich Peat db **(89.5)** n23 peat; t22.5 peat; f22 peat; b22 peaty. *46%*

Bruichladdich Rocks db **(82)** n19 t22 f20 b21. Perhaps softer than you'd imagine something called "rocks"! Beautiful little malty charge on entry. *46%*

⋅⋅⋅ **Bruichladdich Scottish Barley The Classic Laddie** db **(78.5)** n20 t21.5 f18 b19. Not often a Laddie fluffs its lines. But despite some obviously complex and promising moves, the unusual infiltration of some sub-standard casks has undone the good of the local barley. If you manage to tune out of the off-notes, some sublime moments can still be had. *50%. nc ncf sc.*

Bruichladdich Sherry Classic Fusion: Fernando de Castilla bourbon/Jerez de la Frontera db **(91)** n23 t23 f22 b23. What a fantastically stylish piece of work! I had an overwhelming urge to sing Noel Coward songs while tasting this: for the Dry Martini drinkers out there who have never thought of moving on to Scotch... *46%*

Bruichladdich Waves db **(81.5)** n20.5 t21.5 f19.5 b20. Not sure if the tide is coming in or out on this one. Got various sugar and spice aspects which appeals, but there is something lurking in the depth that makes me a little uneasy... *46%*

Bruichladdich WMD II - The Yellow Submarine 1991 db **(75)** n20 t19 f18 b18. This one just doesn't have the balance and sinks. *46%*

Bruichladdich X4 db **(82)** n18 t22 f21 b21. Frankly, like no new make I have ever come across in Scotland before. Thankfully, the taste is sweet, malty and compact: far, far better than the grim, cabbage water nose. Doesn't really have the X-Factor too, though. *50%*

Bruichladdich X4 +3 Quadruple Distilled 3 Aged Years bourbon db **(86)** n21.5 t22 f21 b21.5. It is as if the sugars in the barley have been reduced to their most intense form: this is all about huge barley of eye-watering intensity. A novel and not unattractive experience. *63.5%. nc ncf. 15,000 bottles.*

The Laddie Ten American oak db **(94.5)** n24 a stunning balance between sea spray, the most delicate liquorice and hickory imaginable and blemish-free barley; t23.5 no let down on delivery with the barley and delicate sugars hand in hand for the first three or four very big flavour waves; the middle an oaky richness but not a single hint of weary dryness: gorgeously weighted and rich without over sweetening; f23 at last the salts form, as do the vanillins and slightly coarser oaky notes. Retains that distinctly coastal feel; b24 this, I assume, is the 2012 full strength version of an Islay classic which was the preferred choice of the people of Islay throughout the 70s, 80s and early 90s. And I have to say that this is already a classic in its own right.... *46%. nc ncf.*

Octomore 5 Years Old db **(96)** n23.5 seeing how Octomore is actually a farm on Islay, it is rather fitting that the massive peat here yields a distinctly farm-yardy aroma. Yet this is curiously low on peat reek for a dram boasting phenomenal phenols at 131 parts per million – Ardbeg is about 50; the much smokier PC7 is just 40. That said, obviously peaty, yet an age-related lemon lightness, too...and a herd of cattle...; t24.5 the oils are absolutely perfect, as is the slow unfurling of the myriad strata of peat; those youthful, zesty, citrus notes have been enriched with a perfect degree of golden syrup; a near-perfect sprinkling of spice enriches further...; f24 a wonderful array of vanillas lighten not just the peat but the sweetened mocha which is now making its mark. Long, relaxed and very assured for a malt so young... b24 forget about the age. Don't be frightened by the phenol levels. Great whisky is not about numbers. It is about excellent distillation and careful maturation. And here you have a memorable combination of both... *63.5%*

Octomore Edition 2.1 Aged 5 Years (140 ppm) bourbon cask, bott Jun 09 db **(94)** n23 a snug nose of tight, thick peat: needs a chainsaw to cut through it; t24 surprisingly sweet delivery with more than a hint of citrus: a massive gristy surge which is about as mouth-watering as heavily peated malt ever gets; the smoke is all enveloping; f23 long with some vanilla at last getting into the act; some excellent late mocha and marzipan thins the smoke; b23 talk about a gentle giant: as though your taste buds are being clubbed to death by a ton of smoky feathers. *62.5%. nc ncf. 15,000 bottles.*

Octomore Edition 2.2 "Orpheus" Aged 5 Years (140 ppm) bourbon/chateau Petrus, bott 2009 db **(96.5)** n24 when you clean out the ashes of fire that had been fed 100% by peat, that morning after the night before task, this is what you get. Well, partially. You will have to have one hand in the grate, the other around a glass of Petrus...; t24.5 let's get this right: 140ppm phenols? Check. 61% abv? Check. How then, can the landing on the palate be like jumping onto a bed of feathers? The Demerara-gristy sweetness helps. So does the smoke, which envelopes the mouth. But the peat is also dry and that means a magnificent balance with those gristy sugars, so all seems to be in harmony. Brilliant! f23.5 long, and just a gentle wind down of all before. Maybe a bit of extra fruit visible later on, as well as some Liquorice

Allsorts; **b24.5** a standing ovation for this massive performance...the quite perfect way to bring up my 900th new whisky for the 2011 Bible. Everything works; the age and freshness of the barley, the controlled enormity of the smoke...even the entirely sulphur-free wine barrel. For those with a lot of hair on their chest...and want even more. *61%. 15,000 bottles.*

⁖ **Octomore Edition 5.1** db **(91.5) n23** sooty peat with a sprig of mint; **t22.5** the youth is immediately apparent – more than usual – with the fresh gristy malt soon being lost under the sugars; **f23** after last year I was waiting for the cocoa...for a long time. A vague mocha note does appear, sweetened by several spoonfuls of smoky Demerara; **b23** a slightly less complex version, probably because of the obvious lack of years. Great fun, though. *59.9%*

⁖ **Octomore Edition 6.1 Aged 5 Years** bourbon cask db **(91.5) n24** acrid smoke. Bonfires at my Dad's old allotment back in Surrey, it's leafy sweetness mixing with the chunkier peak reek; beyond that is a mix of Fisherman's Friend and cherry cough sweet. Also detectable, if you can spot it, is very young grist...the aroma of grist mashing...; **t23** a brief new make opening amid the big sugary delivery: concentrated Demerara concentrated again. The smoke is both chewy and also acts as a counter for the staggering grist sweetness; **f22** some late coconut cake carries the smoke and mocha; **b22.5** a slightly different Octomore, a little more tart than usual and wears its youth with pride. *57%*

⁖ **Octomore Edition 6.2 Aged 5 Years** Cognac cask db **(90) n22.5** the peat is already crushed, the fruit strangles any possible movement; **t23.5** hard to imagine the smoke playing second fiddle, but it does: the sugars are so intense and the barley so salivating, for a few moments you even forget it is there; **f22** even tighter oak and crisp enough to break all your teeth; **b22** one of the sweetest bottlings from this distillery of all time. Some warming late spice, too; *58.2%. Travel Retail Exclusive Limited Edition Release. 18,000 bottles.*

Octomore 3rd Edition Aged 5 Years bourbon cask db **(95) n24.5** as someone who grew up in the countryside and, to this day, spends as much of what little spare time I get traipsing around fields and farmsteads, this is an aroma I know too well... cowsheds! Except here there is that extra element of peat, but that intense sweetness is unmistakable: It may only be a young 'un, and the youth is noticeable, but it remains one of the most distinguished and most flawless of all Scotland's whisky aromas...; **t24** as soft to the palate as a view of the sea from Port Charlotte is to the eye... The peat does not compromise, yet nor does it bully, allowing any amount of Demerara sugars to form and intensify with the vanilla and natural caramels from, I suspect, from first fill oak; **f23** much quieter than you might expect from the nose, but there is a touch of the Horlicks about the finale; **b23.5** I usually taste this late on in the Bible writing cycle: it is so important to be rewarded at the end of a long journey. This hasn't let me down and here's the rub: how something which looms so large be made from so many traits so small...? *59%*

Octomore 4th Edition Aged 5 Years (167 ppm) db **(92) n21.5** hardly believable as an Octomore: the smoke appears locked in a caramel bubble...; **t23.5** sheer power seems to allow the smoke to burst away from its shackles, but it has to work hard. But there is none of the normal peaty dryness. Instead we are directed towards a delicious praline thread with the nut oils building and a non-specific fruitiness offering little more than a hint; **f23.5** 80% cocoa smoked chocolate...outrageous! **b23.5** Choctomore, surely? *62.5%*

Octomore 10 db **(95) n24** have I ever mentioned cowsheds? This is David and Ruth Archer's threatened milking parlour...but without the milk...awww nawooo..! **t24** as ever, smoke...like someone's set fire to the barn...awww nawooo!; **f23** the most intense of all finishes, as though the excess of the cowshed has been drained by marauding badgers... awww nawoooo! **b24** when I am tasting an Octomore, it means I am in the home straight inside the stadium after running (or should I say nosing and tasting) a marathon. After this, there is barely another 20 more Scotch malts to go and I am closing in on completing my 1,200 new whiskies for the year. So how does this fair? It is Octomore. It is what I expect and demand. It gives me the sustenance and willpower to get to that crossing line. For to tell you guys about a whisky like this is always worth it...whatever the pain and price. Because honesty and doing the right thing is beyond value. Just ask David Archer... *50%. nc ncf.*

Port Charlotte An Turas Mor Multi Vintage bourbon cask db **(85.5) n23 t22 f20 b20.5** Does much right, especially the intriguing bullying of the colossal peat over what probably passes for grape. But bitters out and struggles to find a balance or plot line to keep you wanting to discover more. *46%*

⁖ **Port Charlotte Heavily Peated** db **(94.5) n23** smoke comes scudding into the nose, vigorously, giving the joint effect of death by peat and acrid burnt toast; **t24** a youthful livewire delivery with a pretty surprising degree of maple syrup and treacle latching onto the phenols: the effect and balance is wonderful; pay attention and you'll spot some juicy fruit notes popping up here and there, too; **f23.5** the lack of major oak means the finish is fractionally lighter than it might be, but the smoke is now even and pretty soft despite the late spice; **b24** rearrange the following two words: "giant" and "gentle" *50%*

Port Charlotte PC6 db **(96.5) n24.5** ohhhhhh... arrrrrrrhh... mmmmmmmmmm... oh, the peat, the peat... yesssssss... oh my god... mmmmmmm... ohhhhhhh... **t24** first you get the smoky... ooooohhhhhhh... arrrrrrrr... then the sweeter... mmmmmmmm... arrrooooohhhh... **f24** it finishes with a more gentle arghoooo... mmmmmmm... ooooophhhhhh... arrrrrrrr... **24** not many whiskies have a truly unmistakable nose... and... but this is, this... is... this... mmmmmmm..., arrrrhh. Ohhhhhhh... 61.6%

Port Charlotte PC7 dist 2001 db **(93.5) n24** dry. The most profound peat fire ashes: not for peaty amateurs... **t24** a few drops of sweetness added; a liquorice/molassed melt to the massive smoke: the phenols seems a lot higher than the 40ppm they talk about; **f22** drops down a gear or two as some bitterness creeps in, as does a secondary fizz to the spice; **b22.5** not quite as orgasmic as last year, sadly. But should still be pretty stimulating... 60.5%

Port Charlotte PC8 bourbon, dist 2001, bott 2009 db **(88) n22 t23 f21 b22.** Enjoyable, but muted by PC standards... 60.5%. 30,000 bottles.

⚜ **Port Charlotte PC10** db **(96) n24** promises to be the best PC for a few years! There is a vague kumquat undercoat that does well having itself heard amid the formidable phenols. But the weight is just so enormous, yet somehow crushes nothing; **t24.5** stunning! You know the peat is omnipotent yet, miraculously, it is the sugar-honey mix which dictates play, especially the pace of flavour development. Some oils and caramels ensure excellent shape and body; **f23.5** the smoke works hard to re-establish itself but the oak still has much to say; **b24** just so right....!!! 59.8%

⚜ **Port Charlotte The Peat Project** db **(93.5) n23.5** rhubarb and custard with an outrageous dollop of manuka honey. And a lot of soft, sweet smoke...so sweet it could be from a tobacconists; **t24** so intriguingly sweet I tried to re-create it: the closest I got was orange-blossom honey, muscovado sugar, treacle and maple syrup. Pretty close. What I couldn't copy was the enigmatic peat: one moment seeming massive, another barely noticeable; **f22.5** surprisingly low key; all kinds of butterscotch and lemon curd tart but, like the peat, only hinted at; **b23.5** a very curious, odd even, PC when much is said in the nose and glass, but few speeches are made. 46%

⚜ **The Laddie Sixteen** American oak db **(88) n22** huge natural caramels dipped in brine; **t22.5** very even and gentle with a degree of citrus perking it up; **f21.5** reverts to caramels before the tannins strike hard; **b22** oak 'n' salt all the way... 46%

⚜ **The Laddie Twenty Two** db **(90.5) n24** a breakfast plate of three pieces of toast: one with salted butter, another with ulmo honey and the last one with marmalade; light spices, too. Busy yet understated; **t23** silky salted butters again on delivery immediately backed by intense barley sugar; **f21.5** the oak cranks up significantly; **b22** fabulous coastal malt, though the oak is a presence always felt. 46%

⚜ **Berry's Own Selection Bruichladdich 1991** cask no. 2998, bott 2013 **(94) n23** a field of grass freshly mown; gooseberry tart with limited sugars; **t23.5** you expect salivating, you get salivating. In fact you get advanced salivating, for as well as the pure juiciness of it all, you also get a degree of salt and spice to zap up the sharpness; **f24.5** amid the zipping, seriously warming spice, we somehow return to those gooseberries; naturally, a little custard arrives at the end, as well as some chocolate mousse; **b24** classic Bruichladdich for those of us of a certain vintage...! Few malts over 20 are this alive. Spectacular. 51.6%. nc ncf sc.

Cadenhead Bruichladdich 20 Years Old bott Mar 12 **(91) n23** light and lithesome. Unbelievably grassy barley, seasoned with gorgeous sea salt; **t23.5** much oilier than can be detected on the nose. But that barley stays sharp and fresh and brimming with salty vanilla; **f22** does little to shift shape or tack. Just a thin layer of cocoa acknowledges the age; **b22.5** hard to imagine a whisky that outwardly does so little, yet says so much. Beautiful! 52.2%. sc.

Chieftain's Bruichladdich Aged 22 Years hogshead, dist Apr 89 **(83) n21 t22 f20 b20.** Anyone who remembers the original old Bruichladdich 10-year-old will recognise the contours here. Except this has taken on far too much oak, especially towards the austere finale. 46%. nc ncf sc. Ian Macleod Distillers.

⚜ **Director's Cut Bruichladdich Aged 21 Years** refill sherry butt, cask no. 8937, dist Oct 90, bott Sep 12 **(96) n24** it doesn't happen often these days, but a 20-y-o malt sitting in a 100% untarnished, truly perfect, sherry butt. The meeting between the prickly spiced grape and malt is something to savour for as long as you possible can...; **t24.5** absolute silk on delivery, and then all kinds of rampant spices biting and exploding, yet such is the almost barley wine thickness to the malt the impact is contained with ease; a distinctive chocolate fruit and nut bar forms in the middle ground; **f23.5** more scope for the oak as the vanillas seize control from the fruit; **b24** a couple of years ago a whisky "expert" (he has/had a web page or something in Canada, so he must be one) took me to task for saying that Bruichladdich made outstandingly good unpeated whisky during the days when they had no smoked output at all. Apparently I was wrong on both counts. They always made peated, I was lectured, and, secondly, when they made unpeated it was due to running out of peated malt and was of inferior quality. Don't remember the name of the fool, but if he is reading this...just get your kisser around this and learn....For not only is this unpeated, but it comes from a perfect sherry butt. Sensational! *57.1%. sc. Douglas Laing & Co. 255 bottles.*

⫶⫶ **Gordon and MacPhail Connoisseurs Choice Bruichladdich 1991** (92) n23.5 the oaks are mildly over enthusiastic but vanilla ice cream with a generous dollop of lime sauce bumps up the sweetness; t23 superb delivery - spices abound; the tannins boast bourbon-style liquorice and hickory but enough juicy barley to balance matters out; f22.5 consistent vanilla and spice; b23 old school Laddie which has passed its Highers. *46%.*

John Milroy Selection Bruichladdich 1992 cask no. 3791, bott 2012 (88.5) n22 a seaside freshness to the clean barley; t23 not just vivid barley but you can almost hear the gulls mewing: salty, tangy and as refreshing as a face-full of sea spray; f21.5 calms down as natural caramels and fudge smother the natural fire; b22 'Laddie, old-fashioned style! *54.6%. nc ncf sc. Berry Bros & Rudd.*

Liquid Sun Port Charlotte 2002 bott 2011 (93) n23 beautifully distilled, the peat appears happy to take a back seat to the resplendent citrus notes; t23.5 as though someone has distilled this from pure lemon juice and maple syrup, with a big chunk of peat tossed into the spirit still...; f23 some residual spices add topsoil to the smoke and extraordinary citrus; b23.5 I have never come across any whisky so bursting forth with such sexy citrus. Oh, the zest.... the zest...yes...yesssss...oh, my God...!!! *53.5%. nc ncf sc. The Whisky Agency.*

⫶⫶ **Malts of Scotland Bruichladdich 1988** sherry hogshead, cask no. MoS 12040, dist Apr 88, bott Sep 12 (80) n21.5 t21 f18 b19. Sharp on delivery with a good spice blast. But bitters out at finish. *54.3%. nc ncf sc. 96 bottles. Bottled exclusively for Islay Whisky Dinner 2012.*

⫶⫶ **Malts of Scotland Bruichladdich 2002** bourbon barrel, cask no. MoS 13026, dist May 02, bott Apr 13 (88.5) n22 smoked cream soda; t22 smoked Blackpool rock; f22.5 smoked butterscotch tart; b22 creamy, sugary, buttery....and smoky! *55.2%. nc ncf sc. 96 bottles.*

Malts Of Scotland Port Charlotte 2001 white Rioja hogshead, cask no. MoS11017, dist Dec 01, bott Oct 11 (88) n24 don't bother to look for harmony. The grape does its thing while the peat does its own merry way...; t23 now the two clash head on: at times it is spectacular! The sugars pulse, the smoke explodes, the grape whines...; f21 not a great finale with the more volatile oily elements having the biggest say; b22 It so doesn't work in so many ways...yet just so does in others...typical PC!! *66.3%. nc ncf sc.*

⫶⫶ **Malts of Scotland Port Charlotte 2001** sherry hogshead, cask no. MoS 12039, dist Nov 12, bott Sep 12 (83.5) n20.5 t22 f20 b21. Smoked raisin soup. The sherry furriness at the finish confirms suspicions on the nose... *63.3%. nc ncf sc. 96 bottles. Bottled exclusively for Islay Whisky Dinner 2012.*

⫶⫶ **Malts of Scotland Port Charlotte 2001** sherry hogshead, cask no. MoS 13013, dist 01, bott 13 (87.5) n21.5 someone's packed some knives in the smoky fruitcake: sharp and pungent; t22 though peat and sherry often get on like cats and dogs, this fights but in a more playful manner; f22 thick smoky fudge and raisin; b22 I know there are those out there who will sell their children into slavery for this, despite the modest flaw. *62.4%. nc ncf sc. 48 bottles.*

⫶⫶ **Old Malt Cask Bruichladdich Aged 20 Years** refilled sherry butt, cask no. 9037, dist Feb 92, bott Nov 12 (95) n23.5 do you remember that luscious moment when you get to the bottom of the sherry trifle...? t23.5 mouth-filling, fruity beyond measure...a Richter Scale for fruitiness would probably explode at this point. Some barley makes the odd noise, as does the oak but that grape is all consuming; f24 complexity begins to really kick in now as some cocoa filters through, then mocha. But someone is stirring some sherry into it, too; b24 restores one's faith in whisky kind when sherry butts like this turn up. Flawless and a fabulous exhibition of how a great sherry cask can do enough to influence, but leave room for the other elements to play. *50%. nc ncf sc. Douglas Laing & Co. 363 bottles.*

⫶⫶ **Old Malt Cask Bruichladdich Aged 25 Years** refill hogshead, cask no. 9810, dist Feb 88, May 13 (94) n22.5 marzipan with raspberry jam; t24 the distillery's old fashioned silk delivery brimming with concentrated barley soon loses out to a much more aggressive oakiness, though the ulmo honey soothes the spat; the balance between sugar and tannin is something to be experienced; f23.5 loads more ulmo honey and now the oak has been tamed and only purrs a butterscotch and crème brûlée finale; b24 just starting to vanish under the oak. All that is left is pure magnificence...1 *48.3%. nc ncf sc. Hunter Laing & Co Ltd. 328 bottles.*

Scotch Malt Whisky Society Cask 23.70 Aged 9 Years refill barrel, cask no. 755, dist 2001 (96) n24 classically complex in the distillery's style with a bevy of varied salty notes adding a rich hue to the already beautifully structured liquorice and hickory tones. Somehow the barley manages to make a statement amid all this with commanding eloquence; t24.5 the mouth doesn't so much water as flood: the barley is pristine and multi-dimensional while the oak makes impressive shapes of varying weight and intensity; f23.5 long, and with the noticeable lack of oils. Both the barley and oak are given the most free reign possible to continue their complex and delightfully entertaining discussion...; **b24** stunning. Simply stunning...! And proof, not that it was ever needed, that you don't need peat to make an Islay whisky of truly world class stature. *66%. sc.*

Scotch Malt Whisky Society Cask 127.15 Aged 9 Years refill barrel, cask no. 388, dist 2002 **(94.5) n23** floral as well as peaty with evening primroses having an unusually telling say. Delicate, for all its obvious oily enormity; **t24** Those oils really do make an early impact. But when that dies down, an explosion of spiced sugars makes one almost groan in delight; **f23.5** long, almost ridiculously so, with the emphasis now on molten Mars bars, with the nougat and natural caramels blending in with the cocoa; **b24** there are a few seconds right in the middle of this which are as close to perfection as I have tasted this year... *65.9%. sc.*

Scotch Malt Whisky Society Cask 127.18 Aged 9 Years refill barrel, cask no. 374, dist 2002 **(89.5) n23** weighty, with a succession of bigger dark sugar notes, especially Demerara, having a major input; really excellent spice, too...; **t22.5** dry, bordering on the austere as the oils so prevalent in 127.15 surprisingly go AWOL. The sugars are crisper, the spices a little more blatant and warming; **f22** now generally spice dependent; **b22** a most curious bottling which concentrates on solo performances rather than the entire work. *66.1%. sc.*

Scotch Malt Whisky Society Cask 127.19 Aged 9 Years refill barrel, cask no. 384, dist 2002 **(89) n22.5** natural caramels have caught up with this and have made surprising inroads into the apparently shocked phenols; **t23** even on delivery, the tannins race ahead. The mid ground makes amends with a burst of frightening complexity as the sugars, phenols and tannins each claim higher ground; **f21.5** dulls with a smoked fudgy finale; **b22** a malt which peaks and troughs but always has something to keep the taste buds on full alert. *66%. sc.*

Scotch Malt Whisky Society Cask 127.20 Aged 8 Years refill barrel, cask no. 848, dist 2003 **(95.5) n23.5** coal dust mixes in readily with the peaty phenols; far more spices than is the norm ensure a degree of major complexity; **t24.5** the enormity of the nose prepares you for what is next. The delivery is something akin to an explosion in a munitions factory: the pyrotechnics leave you gasping as the spices dazzle to an almost blinding degree. As for the amalgam between the vanillas and sugars...well, if you wondered why we were ever given taste buds, now you know... **f24** the spices never less than pulse; the vanillas are always adding a custardy or butterscotch note here and there; the barley even at the death injects a juicy, gristy quality; **b23.5** back in the 1930s, the distillers at Ardbeg always claimed their malt was at peak perfection when it reached eight years of age. There is evidence here that the new regime at Bruichladdich can reasonably make the very same claim... *64.2%. sc.*

⁙ **Scotch Malt Whisky Society Cask 127.28 Aged 9 Years** refill butt, dist 21 Jun 02 **(94.5) n23.5** thick and heady: you could stand a spoon in the aroma alone...; **t24.5** it is not the delivery, it is not the moment after the delivery: it is from about the sixth flavour pulse...then, even after the smoggy beauty of before, it becomes a work of compelling, eye-rolling beauty with the fruity sugars meeting the phenols on even ground and at equal weight; **f23** long, with soft oils helping lift the mocha; brown sugars abound; a little off key and tangy at the very death; **b24** engrossing and unmissable. *65.1%. nc ncf sc. 217 bottles.*

⁙ **Scotch Malt Whisky Society Cask 127.29 Aged 10 Years** refill butt, dist 14 Dec 01 **(73.5) n19 t19.5 f17 b18.** Ever wondered what a fumarole in the middle of an Islay peat bog might nose and taste like....? *63.8%. nc ncf sc. 73 bottles.*

⁙ **Scotch Malt Whisky Society Cask 127.30 Aged 10 Years** refill barrel, dist 21 Jun 02 **(91) n22.5** like sticking your nose inside a bag of peat soot..; **t23.5** now like swallowing that peat soot...initially so dry! As it juices out the mid-ground becomes a brown sugared bonanza; **f22** back to peat soot again as it dries until your entire mouth seems bereft of water; **b23** should be the preferred dram of the Scottish Union of Chimney Sweeps... *66.8%. nc ncf sc. 252 bottles.*

BUNNAHABHAIN
Islay, 1881. Burn Stewart Distillers. Working.

Bunnahabhain 12 Years Old (Older Bottling) db **(80) n19 t21 f20 b20.** Pleasant in its own clumsily sweet, smoky way. But unrecognisable to the masterful, salty Bunna 12 of old. *43.3%. nc ncf.*

Bunnahabhain Aged 12 Years db **(85.5) n20 t23 f21 b21.5.** Lovers of Cadbury's Fruit and Nut will adore this. There is, incongruously, a big bourbony kick alongside some smoke, too. A lusty fellow who is perhaps a bit too much of a bruiser for his own good. Some outstanding moments, though. But, as before, still a long way removed from the magnificent Bunna 12 of old... *46.3%. nc ncf.*

Bunnahabhain Aged 16 Years Manzanilla Sherry Wood Finish db **(87) n20.5 t23 f21.5 b22.** The kind of undisciplined but fun malt which just makes it up as it goes along... *53.2%*

Bunnahabhain Aged 18 Years (Older Bottling) db **(94) n24.5** chestnut colour and, fittingly, roast chestnut on the fruitcake nose: the health-conscious might say there is too much salt in the mix, but it works perfectly here...; **t24** outstanding oloroso with the clean, faultless grape dripping of the salty barley; the oak again offers a nutty background, while Demerara sugars form a crisp counter to the invading salt; burnt raisin underscores the fruitcake character; **f22.5** light mocha, as a very slight bitterness steels its way in; **b23** a triumph for the sherry cask and a reminder of just how good this distillery can be. It's been a long time since I've enjoyed a distillery bottling to this extent. *43%*

Bunnahabhain Aged 18 Years db **(93.5) n24** a sumptuous amalgam of lightly salted roasted hazelnut shimmering within its own oil. Oloroso bulging with toasted, slightly singed currants, a sliver of kumquat and topped by thick vanilla. Irresistible... **t24.5** almost impossible to fault: the oloroso grandly, almost pompously, leads the way exuding thick, Christmas pudding depth; a light muscovado sugar top dressing counters the deeper, lightly salted vanillas which begin to emerge; **f22** a very slight sulphury note sullies the tone somewhat, but there is still enough rich vanilla and spotted dick for some enjoyable afters; **b23** only an odd cask has dropped this from being a potential award winner to something that is merely magnificent... *46.3%. nc ncf.*

Bunnahabhain XXV Aged 25 Years (Older Bottling) db **(91.5) n23** hard to imagine a more coastal aroma than this: the grape tries to get a word in edgeways but the salt has formed a crusty doorway; what fruit does get through is top quality; **t23** excellent arrival, the grape forcing the pace but with a tell-tale tang of saltiness; busy with a sneaky arrival of malt through the middle; **f22.5** chocolate fruit and nut... and salt; **b23** an intense and fun-packed malt for those who like a fine sherry and a sea breeze. *43%*

Bunnahabhain XXV Aged 25 Years db **(94) n23** you almost need a blow torch to cut through the oloroso, so thick is it. A little tight thanks to a minor distortion to a butt, but I am being picky. Salty and seaweedy, the ocean hangs in the air...; **t24** glorious weight and sheen to the delivery. The early balance is nearly perfect as the thick fruit is thinned by the proud barley. The early, contemplative sweetness, buttressed by a wonderful mixture of sultana and Demerara, gives way to the drier oaks and the tingly, chalky signs of a mildly treated butt; **f23** despite the winding down of the sugars the residual fruit manages to overcome the small obstacles placed before it; **b24** no major blemishes here at all. Carefully selected sherry butts of the highest quality (well, except maybe one) and a malt with enough personality to still gets its character across after 25 years. Who could ask for more...? *46.3%. nc ncf.*

Bunnahabhain Cruach-Mhòna batch no.1 db **(83) n17.5 t24.5 f21 b20.** It appears that there is a new house style of being strangely off balance and less than brilliantly made, but making amends by offering a blistering maltiness which leaves one almost speechless. The delivery alone, with its light smokiness mixing in with the Demerara sugars and Grenadine spices, is the stuff of Islay legend. All else is skewed and out of sync. Unique, for sure. *50% nc ncf.*

Bunnahabhain Darach Ùr Batch no. 1 db **(87) n21.5 t22.5 f21 b22.** Almost milkshake thick. Not exactly a technical triumph but high marks for entertainment value! *46.3%*

Bunnahabhain Darach Ùr Batch no. 4 db **(95) n24** good grief; as though matured in a barrel full of plump sultanas... but from the depth of sweetness, rather than the fruit...if you get my drift. Just a hint of spice as well as coconut and honey. Fabulous in a bourbon kind of salty, Hebridean way...; **t24.5** as thick and richly-textured as any malt you'll find this year. Intense, lightly salted barley is a match for the brimming, fruit-like sweetness; with a salivation factor which disappears through the roof, wonderful bourbon over- and under-tones link wonderfully to the mega sugars attached to the vanilla; **f23** much drier with a tangy, kumquat fade but plenty of vigorous spice; **b23.5** because of my deep love for this distillery, with my association with it spanning some 30 years, I have been its harshest critic in recent times. This, though, is a stunner. *46.3%. nc ncf.*

Bunnahabhain Toiteach db **(78) n19 t21 f19 b19.** Cloying, sweet, oily, disjointedly smoky. Had you put me in a time capsule at the distillery 30 years ago, whizzed me forward to the present day and given me this, it would have needed some serious convincing for me to believe this to be a Bunna. *46%*

Bunnahabhain Toiteach Un-Chillfiltered db **(75.5) n18 t21 f17.5 b19.** A big gristy, peaty confrontation on the palate doesn't hide the technical fault lines of the actual whisky. *46%. ncf.*

⁙ **Abbey Whisky Bunnahabhain Aged 23 Years** The Rare Casks refill bourbon cask, dist 89, bott 13 **(86) n21.5 t23 f20 b21.5.** Any amount of complex honey and sea-salt makes for some riveting early dramming. But the eye-watering oak takes few prisoners. *44%. nc ncf sc. 96 bottles.*

⁙ **Berry's Own Selection Bunnahabhain 1989** cask no. 5756, bott 2013 **(89) n22.5** for those cake lovers: Lubeck marzipan and an under-layer of raspberry jam; **t23** soft, caressing, buttery barley lands almost without notice, a slight pinch of salt raises the profile of the tannin by a tiny amount; **f21.5** a tad lazy, allowing the natural caramels to do all the work; **b22** from a distillery which rarely ages too happily an oldie which creaks a bit but can still put on a show. *44%. nc ncf sc.*

Berry's Own Selection Bunnahabhain 1990 cask no. 20, dist 2011 **(67) n17 t18 f16 b16.** Some of the sherry butts taken in at Bunna during these Highland Distillers days of the late 80s and early 90s were among some the most heavily sulphured in Scotland. You will find worse, but this is a fair example... 54.1%. nc ncf sc. Berry Bros & Rudd.

⁘ **Chieftain's Bunnahabhain Aged 10 Years** sherry butt, cask no. 466, dist Sep 01, bott Aug 12 **(71) n16 t19 f18 b18.** Another example of what might have been. If you don't pick up sulphur on the palate, the richness of the fruit will blow you away. 46%. nc ncf sc. 778 bottles.

⁘ **The Coopers Choice Bunnahabhain 2001 9 Years Old** sherry cask, cask no. 1269, dist 01, bott 11 **(90) n23.5** a really glorious union of dry, peppery sherry, lightly salted celery and orange blossom honey and all suitably understated; **t23** textbook weight on the palate with the oils forming an attractive guard of honour for the grape which begins to take an ever-increasingly juicy form; the barley is still alive thanks to the relative youthfulness of the malt; **f21.5** the slight flaw in the cask eventually reveals itself. But before it does, the dry vanillas are very attractive; **b22** always great to see a sherry butt in near unsullied condition. And a malt reminding everyone that complexity abounds in many malts before the 10th birthday is reached. 46%. nc ncf sc. The Vintage Malt Whisky Co Ltd. 720 bottles.

Director's Cut Bunnahabhain Aged 20 Years refill hogshead, cask no. 7957, dist Dec 91, bott Dec 11 **(94) n22.5** clean but very still for a Bunna. Very light salt and citrus, but otherwise all is quiet on the Sound of Islay... **t24** as though some honey from its then sister distillery of Highland Park has crept into the barrel. No smoke but plenty of heather; big, big barley...; **f23.5** beautifully textured with a wonderful fade of lightly salted honeyed butterscotch; that huge barley hangs on to the very death; **b24** an almost emotional reminder as to exactly why this was once one of my favourite distilleries in the world... 49.6%. Douglas Laing & Co.

Duncan Taylor Rare Auld Bunnahabhain 24 Years Old cask no. 1598, dist 1987 **(90) n22** some semblance of bourbon at work: a touch of red liquorice amid the florid oak; **t24** at first the oak is a little too aggressive. Then the malt fights back with as much bloody mindedness as aplomb; spiced, busy and, frankly, delicious; there is even a banana and custard moment to savour; **f21.5** dries every bit as expected; **b22.5** holds on grimly for life as the oak does all it can to prise any grip the malt may have on proceedings. A fascinating battle to the death in the glass and on your palate.. 55.7%. nc ncf sc. Duncan Taylor & Co.

Duncan Taylor Rare Auld Bunnahabhain 32 Years Old cask no. 38408, dist 1979 **(86.5) n22 t23.5 f20 b21.** Bunna rarely sees out the years comfortably. This, though, has done better than I expected and though the finish shows the ravages of time clearly enough, the heady mix of oaky spices and intense, salty malt and exotic fruit on delivery is a treat worth discovering. The early body ain't too bad, either. 47.1%. nc ncf sc. Duncan Taylor & Co.

⁘ **Duncan Taylor Octave Bunnahabhain 33 Years Old** oak cask, cask no. 383401, dist 1979, bott 2012 **(91) n24** you know that when it comes to taste the oak is likely to be overbearing. Yet here it seems to work beautifully well with the salty citrus, boot polish and watered down manuka honey; **t21** just as well the sugars are first on the scene, backed by lemon curd tart, otherwise the oak which forms, almost to the point of saturation, would simply be too much to handle. But the intensity of the barley stretches out far enough...just! **f23.5** the oak settles for a more cocoa-dusted evenness, and the egg custard tart on the finish is thoroughly delicious; **b22.5** even an injection of massive oak which might have killed off lesser malts cannot entirely dent the enormity of this ancient beauty which finishes with surprising aplomb and dexterity. That said, a malt taken as far as it can go. 52.4%. sc. 66 bottles.

⁘ **Gordon & MacPhail MacPhail's Collection Bunnahabhain Peated 8 Years Old (88) n22** pretty basic rock pool, salty iodine; **t22.5** gristy phenols ensure plenty of juicy sugar and zest; **f21.5** the very lightest smoky oils mix attractively with the custardy vanilla; **b22** no pages on complexity could ever be written about a bottling like this. But no faulting its overall enjoyment. 43%

⁘ **Gordon and MacPhail Collection Bunnahabhain 2004 (87) n22** lemon Fairy Liquid (from a glass only ever washed in pure water) **t22** the barley is ethereal and strangely free of saltiness for a Bunna; lovely manuka honey but the oak is pure greybeard stuff and a real shock to the system; **f21.5** more rabid oak amid the barley; **b21.5** the oak is an unreconstructed fogey: an 8-y-o going on 80...!! 43%

Kingsbury "The Selection" Bunnahabhain 9 Years Old puncheons, 1266 & 3694, dist Oct & Dec 11, bott Apr 11 **(89) n22** lack of salt for a Bunna but the barley makes amends; **t23** the malt hits the taste buds like rain crashes against the Paps; **f22** a tad bitter but the rich malt shake compensates; **b22** one of the better young Bunnas for a while even though few of the usual distillery characteristics are present. 43%. nc ncf. Japan Import Systems. 1,611 bottles.

⁘ **Kingsbury Bunnahabhain Aged 14 Years** hogshead, cask no. 5384, dist 97 **(86) n21 t22 f21.5 b21.5.** Smoky and surprisingly oily – almost with a Caol Ila style weight. Light sugars make for an easy and enjoyable journey, but don't look for any complex views. 46%. nc ncf. Japan Import System. 321 bottles.

The MacPhail's Collection Bunnahabhain 2001 (78) n19 t22 f18 b19. Technically less than impressive. But the barley shines early on. 43%. Gordon & MacPhail.

Malts Of Scotland Bunnahabhain 1966 bourbon hogshead, cask no. MoS11020, bott Nov 11 (95) n23.5 bares quite a few oaky scars. But there are little tell-tale signs of green shoots...; salt and then the big physalis-led exotic fruit as it opens in the glass; t24 silky and mesmeric on delivery, the oak tries to lay down a few basic laws, only to be usurped by the gathering fruit which not only softens and sweetens the experience, but creates a path for the mocha and praline; the body, though, is the equal of any lithe being half this whisky's age...; f23.5 Mars Bars; certainly not fried as only the Scots know how, though there are oils which intensify the experience; b24 I feared the worst when I nosed this. But about 20 minutes of oxidisation in the glass brought forth the desired fruit elements, and we were away... 41.4%. nc ncf sc.

Malts Of Scotland Bunnahabhain 1973 sherry butt, cask no. 3463, dist 26 Mar 73, bott May 11 (79) n19 t21 f19 b20. Just a little furry and bitter at the wrong times. 50.2%. nc ncf sc.

Malts Of Scotland Angel's Choice Bunnahabhain 1976 sherry hogshead, cask no. MoS12005, bott Jan 12 (87.5) n22 one assumes it fino cask as the dryness of the grape almost demands an olive; t22 ramps itself up for maximum fruity richness but the bite of the vanilla ensures the barley juiciness also has a say; f21.5 a bit of a scratchy finale with the spirit having a surprising amount to say so late on; b22 you know when you are in a classic vintage car and the ancient engine is misfiring a bit...? 56.3%. nc ncf sc. Malts Of Scotland.

⋇ **Malts of Scotland Bunnahabhain 1980** bourbon hogshead, cask no. MoS 12038, dist Apr 80, bott Jun 12 (88.5) n23 not for the first time, guava on an old Bunna nose, working really well with the semi-bourbon motif and banana; t23 sensational delivery, but grab it while you can before the oak kicks in. Soft oils help allow the honey on butter sweetness max effect; some coffee notes begin to percolate; f21 the oak kicks in with a drying vengeance but enough ulmo honey to deflect damage; b21.5 just about stands the test of time and where it is good, it is magnificent. 46.8%. nc ncf sc. 96 bottles.

Malts Of Scotland Bunnahabhain 1997 sherry hogshead, cask no. 3258, bott 2011 (77) n18.5 t20 f19 b19.5. Now here's a Pavlovian thing: I set this up as my last tasting of the day without thinking, so traumatised over recent years have I become by sherry butts from Bunna. Not very much sulphur here (though some), I'm relatively delighted to report. But, nonetheless, there is a nihilistic element to this with the spirit not being exactly of the highest quality, the grape being as subtle as an egg custard pie in the mush and the peat fired at you, seemingly, from a paintball gun. 52.9%. nc ncf sc. Malts Of Scotland.

⋇ **Master of Malt Bunnahabhain Aged 23 Years** refill hogshead, dist 20 Oct 89, bott 28 Nov 12 (93) n23 tangy malt, helped along by red liquorice and lightly salted cold vegetable stew...busy stuff! t23 the barley pitches up in a surprisingly juicy uniform for its age. It takes time for the oak to filter through, but does so alongside lazy, warming spices and even a touch of coriander. The sweet-dry ratio is exemplary; f23.5 long, and the continuing, controlled, dryness – despite the obvious barley – lends towards a degree of sophistication. But even at the end, it is a sugar-light Malteser sign off which accentuates the vitality of the barley; b23.5 old style Bunna up to its full malty max. 46%. sc. 253 bottles.

⋇ **Master Of Malt Bunnahabhain 23 Years Old Lost Bottlings Series** dist 1979, bott 2002 (71.5) n16.5 t20 f17 b18. Bit of a shame this cask was ever found again. 49.7%

Mo Òr Collection Bunnahabhain 1968 42 Years Old first fill sherry butt, dist 11109, dist 2 Dec 68, bott 14 Jan 11 (94.5) n24 double-checked the label: the grapes are far too clean and crystalline to be over 30 years, surely. A refined noble rot sweetness, beautifully interlaced with a brief shake of salt, adds to the unexpected lustre and controlled depth; t23.5 ridiculous! No less than 42-years-old and it makes you salivate. What a magnificent combination of crisp, clean barley and juicy grape. And then the vanillas and spices begin to roll in like a sea mist...; f23 long, playing happily off the spices as the oak begins to build a head of steam. But never does it cross that fine line between adding and overwhelming....; b24 a surprise package: knowing Bunna as I do, and having tasted many of their sherry butts from this era over the years, I was expecting a dose of splinters. Instead, I was treated to a malt very comfortable with its old age: fit, healthy and exercising fully yet strictly within its limitations. What a treat! 46%. nc ncf sc. Release No. 13. The Whisky Talker. 254 bottles.

Old Malt Cask Bunnahabhain Aged 10 Years sherry butt, cask no. 7861, dist Dec 01, bott Dec 11 (86) n20 t22.5 f21.5 b22. Takes a little time to hit its rhythm. Certainly the nose waves the white flag with the oak offering a touch too much astringency. After the indifferent delivery, an explosion of spices shocks the malt to its senses and the juicy story is a pleasant malty and fruity one from onwards. 50%. nc ncf sc. Douglas Laing & Co. 280 bottles.

⋇ **Old Malt Cask Bunnahabhain Aged 10 Years** sherry butt, cask no. 8215, dist Dec 01, bott Mar 12 (94.5) n23.5 wonderfully clean aroma with the grape taking varying forms between lightly burnt raisins and under-ripe ones from the vine. The lightness of touch from the spice makes one purr...; t24 a fantastic delivery of very rare quality these days. The sherry influence is absolutely clean cut and embraces not just (very!) juicy grape but almost a chocolate sherry truffle of limited sweetness; the sugars are decidedly of the Demerara style; **f23.5** beautiful mocha and a mix of pith and barley; **b23.5** a phenomenal sherry butt for its era. Always heart-warming to see this one truly great distillery being shown in its brighter colours. *50%. nc ncf sc. Douglas Laing & Co. 342 bottles.*

‑❊‑ **Old Malt Cask Bunnahabhain Aged 11 Years** sherry butt, cask no. 9428, dist Dec 01, bott Jan 13 **(88) n21.5** busy: playfully spiced and diced fresh fruit aplenty; **t23** superbly juicy on delivery with the barley coming out on top. The fruit arrives by the back door with the vanilla really having a surprisingly large input; **f21.5** long, remaining dry with stewed apples offering a fruity presence; **b22** can hardly have been presented with a better weight. *50%. sc. Douglas Laing & Co. 282 bottles.*

Old Malt Cask Bunnahabhain Aged 14 Years refill hogshead, cask no. 7233, dist Aug 97, bott Aug 11 **(94.5) n22.5** a coal, anthracite and peat-mix smokiness is generously smeared with salted butter; **t24.5** there is a dreamy beauty to this one; the malt dissolves on delivery leaving myriad smoky layers; **f23.5** the complexity continues, though now the drying vanillas dig deep into the sugars. The diaphanous smoke continues to tease; **b24** a classy act entirely worthy of Bunnahabhain's great name. *50%. nc ncf sc. Douglas Laing & Co. 333 bottles.*

Old Malt Cask Bunnahabhain Aged 14 Years refill hogshead, cask no. 8616, dist Dec 97, bott Feb 12 **(90) n22** very light smoke drifts across the simplistic barley-oak mix; **t22** early emphasis on the girsty, salivating barley. The smoke arrives later, becoming surprisingly weighty; **f23** a wonderful finish thanks to a decent oak input. Love the almost Indian style spiced nuts as well as the Horlicks which help play down the smoky intensity; **b23** so delicate, you are almost frightened to chew it too hard...a charming and, actually, quite cracking whisky. *50%. nc ncf sc. Douglas Laing & Co. 335 bottles.*

Old Malt Cask Bunnahabhain Aged 21 Years refill hogshead, cask no. 7597, dist Feb 90, bott Aug 11 **(92.5) n22** some celery chopped into the nut and raisin toffee; **t24** gorgeously soft delivery with just enough spice prickle to prevent you from becoming too comfortable. An impressive array of dark sugars amid the bourbony liquorice; **f23** those spices prove persistent blighters, as do the sugars, thus guaranteeing little or no age wear; **b23.5** a compelling malt beautifully made and matured. *50%. nc ncf sc. Douglas Laing & Co. 218 bottles.*

‑❊‑ **Old Malt Cask Bunnahabhain Aged 21 Years** refill hogshead, cask no. 9819, dist Nov 91, bott May 13 **(77) n19 t21 f18 b19.** The predictable tang arrives in all the predictable places. *48.3%. nc ncf sc. Hunter Laing & Co Ltd. 256 bottles.*

‑❊‑ **Old Malt Cask Bunnahabhain Aged 25 Years** refill hogshead, cask no. 9516, dist Nov 87, bott Feb 13 **(67) n17 t17 f16 b17.** Time for some cheese and tomato...my poor ol' taste buds! *50%. sc. Douglas Laing & Co. 271 bottles.*

The Perfect Dram Bunnahabhain 35 Years Old dist 1976 **(89.5) n23.5** probes elegantly at the exotic fruit stall...so charmingly well behaved and delicate! **t22.5** soft and lacking the usual Bunna salty explosion for a malt of this age; concentrates nimbly on the barley; **f21.5** runs out of puff on the complexity front and is content with overly simplistic vanilla; **b22** a perfectly charming malt which disguises its coastal roots. One for a very late evening when the brain needs little to tax it. *48.8%. sc. The Whisky Agency.*

Provenance Bunnahabhain Over 9 Years sherry butt, cask no. 7599, dist Autumn 2001, bott Summer 2011 **(84) n21 t22 f20 b21.** Something of jammy Swiss role to this one. The copiously oily delivery is a contrast to the grindingly dry finale. The very vaguest puff of smoke disappears after a brief appearance on the nose. *46%. nc ncf sc. Douglas Laing & Co.*

Provenance Bunnahabhain Over 9 Years sherry butt, cask no. 7860, dist Winter 2001, bott Autumn 2011 **(85) n21 t21.5 f21 b21.5.** Another curiously oiled Bunna. But it is the smoke evident here (hardly at all in its sister sherry cask 7599) which is most baffling. *46%. nc ncf sc. Douglas Laing & Co.*

‑❊‑ **Provenance Bunnahabhain Young & Feisty** two refill hogsheads, cask nos. 8672 & 8673, bott Summer 12 **(85.5) n20 t22 f22 b21.5.** Young and Peaty, more like. Not sure of the age, but has the feel of a five year old in very average wood: Bambi-like in its ability to steer an even course. Juicy, too, early on, as you might expect. *46%. nc ncf. Douglas Laing & Co.*

Riegger's Selection Bunnahabhain 1977 bourbon cask, cask no. 7865 **(87.5) n23** a 35-year-old malt going on 65. Some major age issues here but the honeycomb and hickory keep this on an attractive course; **t22** beautifully sexy delivery with the barley enjoying a near silk quality. Again, the oak is on the attack and doesn't hold back. But the honeycomb on the nose does the business yet again, though now with far more salt at play; **f21** the oak finally wins through for a very toasty finale; **b21.5** just hangs on to enough honey to see off the encroaching age. *49.7%. nc ncf sc. Viktor-Riegger GmbH.*

Scotch Malt Whisky Society Cask 10.74 Aged 13 Years refill hogshead, cask no. 5408, dist 1997 **(74) n17 t21 f18 b18.** Sweet and lightly smoked. But the cuts on the stills are all wrong and the oils unacceptable for a distillery so great. *54.8%. sc. Scotch Malt Whisky Society.*

Scotch Single Malt Circle Bunnahabhain 1991 cask no. 5447, dist 2 Dec 91, bott 22 Oct 10 **(81)** n20 t22 f19 b20. A jumbled message on both nose and palate as this malt struggles to find either a coherent style or rhythm. Some attractive coppery notes, but all else is a bit of a mess. 54%. sc.

Sestante Collection Bunnahabhain 38 Years Old dist 1972, bott 2011 **(88.5)** n23 how salty can a whisky get? Lightly sugared grape preserved in a saline solution; t22.5 again, early sugars reinforced by fruit and then an almost frightening tidal wave of salt; f21.5 lovely oils develop, but so too does the oak which has been battering the proceedings throughout; b21.5 what might have been had only this cask been plucked from the warehouse a decade earlier. This is a malt haunted by the ghost of greatness past. There is the most delicate of fruit notes which shows an unforced class; the type of oak intrusion underlines that the quality of the barrel was exceptional. In fact, it was too good and someone in the company owning this should have spotted its majesty long before it was allowed to lose its defining shape and composure. 46%. sc. Silver Seal Whisky Company.

⁙ **Single Cask Collection Bunnahabhain Aged 21 Years** bourbon hogshead, cask no. 5468, dist 2 Dec 91, bott 22 Aug 12 **(92.5)** n22.5 the oak has no hesitation in taking the lead but there is a playful sweetness, too...those of us old enough to remember packs of candy cigarettes will be taken back to another world...; t23.5 a fabulously sophisticated landing: can barley be so gorgeously juicy and sweet yet held in check by firm, unblemished tannin...? f23 a slight hint of salt brings out the oakiness to a greater degree but liquorice and manuka honey thinned by barley water allows the finale to show excellent poise; b23.5 when Bunna shines, it really does sparkle. 49.1%. nc ncf sc. 290 bottles.

The Warehouse Collection Bunnahabhain Aged 14 Years bourbon hogshead, cask no. 5426, dist 8 Dec 97, bott 13 Apr 12 **(87.5)** n22 the resounding sea-breezy peat is not entirely put off course by the wide, oily cut; t23.5 the oils need a tanker to carry them. The smoke seems to be intensified while the muscovado sugars lighten the molasses. This is big, big whisky...; f20 long, with that wide cut buzzing at the back of the throat; b22 technically imperfect. But when the smoke signals are this friendly, who cares...? 58.5%. sc. 279 bottles.

⁙ **The Warehouse Collection Bunnahabhain Aged 21 Years** bourbon hogshead, cask no. 5477, dist 2 dec 91, bott 6 Feb 13 **(95)** n23 beech and ulmo honey beautifully mixed and salt-seasoned; a little dank pine forest floor; earthy, at times vaguely peaty; t24 quite superb delivery: the oak, as with most Bunnas over 12, has a big, sharp impact, but the countering weaving of the honey into the broad barley theme is stunning; a light saltiness enriches; f24 long with the oak just staying honest, though it is the red liquorice, maple syrup, molten salted butters and fabulous late introduction of black pepper to the butterscotch that keeps the pot bubbling; b24 not a distillery naturally given to good age, this is about as you'll find for the age. You'd find me Westering Home for this any day.... 49.6%. nc ncf sc. 261 bottles.

The Whisky Agency Bunnahabhain 43 Years Old bourbon cask, dist 1968, bott 2011 **(85.5)** n21 t21 f22 b21.5. I have tasted a few 40+ Bunnas over the years, some actually in their warehouse. Most were fit for blending only. This has escaped that fate and deserves to. The nose is tired though boosted by orange blossom and the delivery is shudderingly course with oak. But as the oils gel, the malt settles into a more comfortable stance so the interplay between the vanillas and molassed sugars intrigue. 45.7%. sc. The Whisky Agency for 3 Rivers.

⁙ **The Whisky Agency Bunnahabhain 'Seal Life' 1968** refill sherry butt, dist 68, bott 12 **(87)** n21.5 huge oak. A malt in decline as the tannins take a limpet-like grip; so deliciously salty, though...; t22.5 early barley sparkle gives way to a massive onslaught of OTT oak; a little salt and mocha go a long way and muscovado sugars help out more; f21.5 the pulsing oak refuses to budge, but the mocha and late praline sideshow save the day; b21.5 Bunna is not a distillery that clings to great age without casualties. Plenty of salt and honey delights but the oak gouges just a little deep for its own good. Ten years ago this would have been truly Premiership stuff. 47%

The Whisky Broker Bunnahabhain 20 Years Old hogshead, cask no. 5469, dist 2 Dec 91, bott 10 Jan 12 **(89)** n22.5 almost like a malty breakfast cereal, only with some polished oak floor for extras; t22.5 and again! Barley all the way in the most pristine salivating form; f22 a few spices buzz past, the late fudge-like sugars salute; b22 a curious Bunna. In many ways of the old school, yet sans the usual coastal qualities. I assume it has spent 20 years maturing inland. 49.7%. nc ncf sc. 286 bottles.

⁙ **Wemyss 1989 Single Islay "Maritime Embrace"** hogshead, dist 89, bott 13 **(93)** n22 the oak comes out as if wishing to brain you. The big saline counter, softened by Dundee cake, rescues a tricky situation; t24 no surprises when the oak is first over the hurdles. But the way the light molasses cushion the blow, then Sao Tome cocoa and hickory fill the middle ground; f23 bitter marmalade...with a shake of salt, of course! b24 an oaky embrace for sure. The tannins squeeze a little too tight at times, though the salt and chocolate-orange combination ensures a memorable, multi-complex performance. 46%. sc. 265 bottles.

Wemyss 1991 Single Islay "Honey Spice" butt, dist 1991, bott 2011 **(86.5) n22 t23.5 f19 b21.5.** A pretty big whisky, one which at times appears to belie its strength. The finale, alas, has a degree of furriness amid the cocoa. But this is all about the delivery and aftermath: honey spice hardly does this justice. Almost a dessert of a malt... delicious! *46%. 743 bottles.*

⁖ **Wemyss Bunnhabhain 1997 Single Islay "Billowing Embers"** hogshead **(76) n18 t19 f20 b19.** Awkward, ill-balanced and, at times, overly sweet, this is not one for the Bunna Hall of Fame. *46%. 331 bottles.*

Wemyss 1997 Single Islay "Driftwood" hogshead, bott 2012 **(78) n21.5 t21 f17 b18.5.** To quote from the label: "This Hogshead has a peaty nose, reminiscent of a walk in the bracing sea air." What? I have walked beside many oceanic masses, this year alone involving the Arabian Sea, The Dead Sea, the Red Sea, The Pacific, the Mediterranean, the North Sea, the Irish Sea, the Baltic and probably one or two others besides. And I have to admit the one thing they had in common was a general lack of a peat in the air. Come on guys, please!!! Drop the amateurish, nonsensical and pretentious prose and concentrate instead on getting good whisky bottled, as I know you can, away from the poor cask which offers up an unpleasantly lingering, biting bitterness like this! *46%. sc. 374 bottles.*

Wemyss 1997 Single Islay "The Malt Barn" hogshead, bott 2011 **(86) n22 t22 f20.5 b21.5.** A very acceptable example of the new style Bunna showing a charming smokiness to the gristy barley. Thins out just a little too energetically but the early delivery enjoys some excellent moments. *46%. sc. Wemyss Malts. 343 bottles.*

⁖ **Wemyss 2001 Single Islay Bunnahabhain "Chocolate Honeycomb"** puncheon, bott 13 **(86) n21 t22.5 f21 b21.5.** Tasted many a Bunna over the last three decades...and I mean many! But never before found one with these kinds of fingerprints. Thick to the point of being glutinous spices intervene late on to give some roughage to the otherwise ultra-silky experience. Don't get the chocolate, do get a little toasted honeycomb, but the spirit does not seem overly comfortable to begin with. Enjoyable...but a head scratcher. *46%. sc. 812 bottles.*

Whisky Antique Bunnahabhain 42 Years Old Special Bottling dist 1968, bott 2011 **(92.5) n23** the earliest Bunna in which I have ever picked up trace elements of smoke (though this did happen from time to time when they had to buy malt in from Port Ellen during storm-induced stock shortages); but there is also a touch of citrus, ultra-ripe banana and barley by the bushel; **t23.5** soft bodied yet deliciously intense and yielding barley massaged by luxurious cream toffee; **f23** some light embers of peat find their way to the finale, though now the caramels are pretty rampant; **b23** possibly not matured at the distillery, as there is far less brine apparent than would normally be the case. But a fabulous malt absolutely teeming with life even after all these years. *45.2%. sc. Silver Seal Whisky Company.*

CAOL ILA
Islay, 1846. Diageo. Working.

Caol Ila Aged 8 Years Unpeated Style dist 1999, bott 2007 db **(93.5) n23 t24 f23 b23.5.** Oh well, here goes my reputation...honest opinion: on this evidence (backed by other samples over the years) Caol Ila makes better straight malt than it does the peated stuff. Sorry, peat lovers. This should be a, if not the, mainstay of the official Caol Ila portfolio. *64.9%*

Caol Ila Aged 8 Years Unpeated Style 1st fill bourbon, dist 2000, bott 2008 db **(91.5) n23** a touch maltier than the previous bottling; salty digestive biscuit; **t23** beautifully refreshing with a real puckering, salty tartness to the barley; I seem to remember citrus here last year. But this time we have butterscotch and toffee; **f22.5** long, very delicately oiled with the vanillas and toffee in decent harmony; **b23** a bit more of a pudding than last year's offering, but delicious dramming all the way. *64.2%*

Caol Ila Aged 10 Years "Unpeated Style" bott Aug 09 db **(93.5) n24** a beautiful medley of pear and lime with a thin spread of peanut butter for good measure...not exactly what one might expect...!!! **t23.5** the barley is just so juicy from the kickoff: the citrus on the nose reappears, though any hopes of pear vanishes; the barley, so rarely heard in a Caol-Ila grows in confidence and intensity as the delivery develops; **f23** not as oily as you might expect, allowing extra oak to emerge; **b23** always fascinating to see a traditional peaty Islay stripped bare and in full naked form. Shapely and very high class indeed. *65.4%. Only available at the Distillery.*

Caol Ila Aged 12 Years db **(89) n23 t23 f21 b22.** A telling improvement on the old 12-y-o with much greater expression and width. *43%*

Caol Ila 12 Years Old Special Release 2010 1st fill bourbon oak cask, dist 1997 db **(95.5) n23** the smoke is almost an afterthought to the red liquorice lead. Bracing, tangy, full of energy...; **t24** to die for. The trademark oils arrive only as an apologetic afterthought to the delivery which takes at least six mouthfuls to get the measure of. Uniquely, the lead characteristic is sweetened cocoa, something of a bourbon front which is further backed by toasted honeycomb. The smoke offers no more than ballast and refuses to assert any authority on the salivating malt; **f24** now the limited oils have arrived they are put to excellent use by lengthening the finale. The vanillas are sweetened; the barley is galvanised by a curiously fruity earthiness and the most delicate spices imaginable tiptoe across the taste buds...; finally, a discreet muscavado sugar fanfare pipes the experience to its majestic close... **b24.5** the peat more or less takes a back seat in what is a masterful display of force and diplomacy on the palate. Most probably the best Caol Ila I have tasted in recent years. And this in a year of magnificent Caol Ilas. *57.6%. nc ncf. Diageo. Unpeated, fewer than 6000 bottles.*

Caol Ila 12 Years Old Special Release 2011 db **(89) n21.5** stretched and surprisingly thin, the bourbony vanillas are just a little too cocky; **t23.5** more at home on the palate where the vanillas continue to screech but now harmonise with the crisp sugars and peek-a-boo peat; **f22** long with some lengthy tannin-enriched speeches. The oak holds sway even as the smoke tries to muscle back into the frame late on; **b22** a sideways look at a big distillery allowing the casks to have the loudest say over the malt: not at all common with this Islay. *64%. nc ncf.*

⁙ **Caol Ila 14 Years Old Unpeated Style** First fill ex-bodega European Oak Casks, dist 1997, bott 2012 db **(95.5) n22.5** unusual for it to happen, but the tannins from the oak outgun the fruit! The vaguest hint of something smoky – perhaps from the air breathed in by the cask. But salty in a bacon sandwich kind of way...and as though it is slightly smoky bacon... and bacon that has been smeared with sugar, too...; **t24** at first the tannins explode and advance with an intensity which doesn't bode too well. Then, half way in, the malt relaxes to allow those sugars caught on the nose a freer hand while the tannins re-emerge but now with delicate spices...and that vaguest hint of smoke, though there is nothing so subtle about the hickory; **f23** dries like oak in the Spanish sun. Big burned fudge, embittered slightly by the crumbs of lightly burnt toast; the barley now rises but that too is pretty singed; **b24** what a night's entertainment to battle your way through this. In normal circumstances the astonishing machinations of this malt would be lost under a sea of peat. But the malt here – 14 going on 40 – never ceases to amaze. A whisky grey and hunched way beyond its years...but what a story it tells...! A malt that lives long on the palate...and in the memory... *59.3%. nc ncf.*

Caol Ila Aged 18 Years db **(80) n21 t20 f19 b20.** Another improvement on the last bottling, especially with the comfortable integration of citrus. But still too much oil spoils the dram, particularly at the death. *43%*

Caol Ila 1979 db **(74) n20 t19 f17 b18.** Disappointing. I could go on about tropical fruit yada, yada, yada. Truth is, it just conks out under the weight of the oak. Too old. Simple as that. *58.6%*

Caol Ila 1997 The Manager's Choice db **(93.5) n24** dry, ashy peat sweetened less by grist but mango chutney; **t23.5** the grist arrives and sharpens up quickly: a barley juiciness sets in as Lincoln biscuit/garibaldi dunked in peat hogs the middle ground; hickory and liquorice begin to form; **f23** dusty, but the liquorice and smoke hold sway; **b23** when this malt is not enveloped in taste bud-clogging oil, it really can be a little special. Here's further proof. *58%*

Caol Ila 'Distillery Only' bott 2007 db **(95.5) n24 t24 f23.5 b24.** Caol Ila is the third hardest distillery to get to in Scotland: however should you do so some time soon you can reward yourself by picking up a bottle of this. I can say honestly that the journey will be very much worthwhile... *58.4%. 5,000 bottles. Available only from the Caol Ila Distillery shop.*

Caol Ila Moch db **(87) n22 t22 f21 b22.** Easy drinking Islay. Though I think they mean "Mocha"... *43%*

Archives Caol Ila 2000 10 Years Old Inaugural Release barrel, cask no. 3309899, dist Nov 00, bott Aug 11 **(86.5) n22 t22 f21 b21.5.** Dry nose and delivery, then sweetens with a sugary injection and heads into the realms of pleasant nuttiness. *59.1%. nc ncf sc. Whiskybase B.V. 220 bottles.*

Berry's Own Selection Caol Ila 1982 cask no. 6514, bott 2011 **(77) n19 t19 f20 b19.** An uncouth dram. First it shows rather too much of the seedier side of the cask on the nose. Then the puckering spice leaves little to the imagination. *56.4%. nc ncf sc. Berry Bros & Rudd.*

Berry's Own Selection Caol Ila 1983 cask no. 4825, bott 2011 **(91) n22.5** like a middle-aged sailor: salty with the peat showing distinct signs of thinning; **t22** oily and spicy with the malt punching through rather impressively; **f23** barely any peat makes it through to the end. But the mocha finale is rather charming; the sugars are a delight: a wonderful mix of acacia honey, burned fudge and maple syrup; **b23.5** this is a malt which has battled against all the odds to present to you absolutely top class fayre from this distillery, stretching itself as far as it can go without the unwelcome interruption of tired oak to do so. *54.9%. nc ncf sc.*

Cadenhead Caol Ila 21 Years Old Apr 12 **(88) n22** age has shorn the malt of some of its smoke intensity, allowing the barley much greater say than normal; **t22** big, big barley on delivery with some pretty major oak nearby. The sugars and smoke arrive almost as an afterthought... **f22** some salt and spice intensify what had been a low key affair... **b22** I doubt if an old Islay comes more steady or sober than this... *51.9%. sc. WM Cadenhead Ltd.*

⁙ **The Coopers Choice Caol Ila 1992 18 Years Old** hogshead, cask no. 4511, dist 92, bott 10. **(78.5) n19 t21 f19 b19.5.** Tangy and off key. Not the greatest help from the oak. *46%. nc ncf sc. The Vintage Malt Whisky Co Ltd. 330 bottles.*

❧ **The Coopers Choice Cao I lla 1990 21 Years Old** hogshead, cask no. 4171, dist 90, bott 12 **(89)** n22 the oak is staking a big claim here; enough lightly smoked butterscotch sees off the drier excesses; t23 gorgeous delivery with a mocha edge to the beautifully opening smoke. This soon develops into a more toasted honeycomb and maple syrupy sweetness; the oil is sublimely weighted and holds back enough for full malt development; f22 some esters appear to cling to the smoky oils; late spices nibble; b23 wonderfully elegant and almost glassy in its mouth feel. *53%. nc ncf sc. The Vintage Malt Whisky Co Ltd. 250 bottles.*

Duncan Taylor Dimensions Caol lla 28 Years Old cask no. 3625, dist 1983, bott Jan 12 **(95)** n24.5 just about the perfect nose for such an oldie: salt leads the way, closely followed by an outwardly thick yet uber-complex interplay of fat raisin and marmalade. The smoke is deft, cleverly thickening here to fill in gaps, thinning there to allow the vanillas and molassed sugars ample scope to play. There appears to be almost a rum element to this, so happily in tandem are the spices and sugars; t24.5 absolutely dissolves on the palate with a perfect combination of spiced smoke and juicy yet oak-tinged sugars. Very little oil beyond that needed for essential maintenance work and spreading the sweet, smoky word; the spices tease and tingle, the vanillas trumpet their quality; f22.5 despite the lack of usual oils from this distillery, the length doesn't appear compromised. A light treacle touch to the growing liquorice but the subtly spiced smoke keeps all in order; b23.5 it is well known that Caol Ila doesn't rate as my favourite Islay. But Duncan Taylor have unearthed a stunner here. Seemingly from a sherry butt, there are so many sugar and spice elements at work it now gives the impression of having spent a life in a Demerara cask. Unique and truly unforgettable. *54.3%. sc.*

Duncan Taylor Dimensions Caol lla 30 Years Old cask no. 2929, dist 1981, bott 2012 **(88)** n22 expecting something along the lines of cask 2928, but this heads much more into Bowmore-ish territory with a light Fisherman's Friend character tagging onto the molasses; t22 sharp, though buttery delivery with a delicious smoked sugar edge; the barley unifies with the citrus vanilla; f22 a delicate spice buzz sees this unusual Caol lla to a close; b22 it may be next in line to the magnificent cask 2928, but they are very different animals. *54.4%. nc ncf sc.*

Duncan Taylor Rare Auld Caol lla 30 Years Old cask no. 2928, dist 1981 **(95.5)** n24 complex with an astonishing array of attractive vegetable and earthy notes entirely in kilter with subtle spiced honey and a dab of maple syrup. The peat appears to be mixed with a degree of gun smoke; t24.5 deliveries rarely come better than this either in terms of weight and mouth feel. The smoke has riches and depth but is both supported by the oak and particularly hushed by it. The sugars are diverse and no less rich and the maple syrup suspected on the nose is now proved; f23 long thanks to oils which assist rather than overkill as this distillery has the propensity of doing. Back to an attractive vegetable element to the earthiness and the oils are happy to play themselves out; b24 what can you say? The bourbon casks were better in those days, of course, and here is a rare chance to see the oak stand up to some near bullying tactics with aplomb. Huge, absolutely top class, whisky with the cask giving as good as it gets and an object lesson for the new generation of blenders and "experts" in the field to learn.... and weep. *54.8%. sc. Duncan Taylor & Co.*

❧ **Fine Old Islay Single Malt Aged 19 Years** ex-bourbon cask **(90)** n22 attractively spiky with a touch of vague citrus and even apple to balance matters; t23.5 every bit as juicy as the delicate fruit nose promises, with a stunning grassy sub strata. The smoke is delivered with an oily sheen; f22 long for a malt but medium length for a Caol lla, with a drying, dusty tail; b22.5 a pleasing complexity and a fruitiness which sits comfortably with the smoke 55.9%. *The Whisky Exchange. Caol lla.*

❧ **Gordon and MacPhail Private Collection Caol lla Sassicaia 1994 (83)** n21 t21.5 f20 b20.5. A thin warble of a dram in which the fruit tries to sing but never raises enough puff to get past the smoke or make even a balancing contribution. Pleasant, but neither fish nor fowl. *45%. ncf.*

❧ **Gordon and MacPhail Private Collection Caol lla Madeira 1995 (94)** n22.5 so heavy with grape and smoke (most of it anthracite), little else gets through; t24 Lordy, me! Just how many fronts does this work on? First, the texture on delivery is nigh perfect: the usual Caol lla oils have been tamed by the richness of the grape, the sweetness of the fruit matching the gristy contours of the smoke perfectly; elsewhere the spices sting with just the right degree of venom; f23.5 long, with a gorgeous spiced chocolate fruit and nut theme; b24 well, you know by now my feelings about grape and peat...so welcome to rare exception. This is a stunner, in anyone's money...! *45%. ncf.*

Gordon & MacPhail Cask Strength Caol lla 1999 (94) n22.5 rugged stuff: some rough and tumble to the peat with the oak no less inclined to stick the boot in; t24.5 superb delivery! Like the nose, it is a bruiser, only here we have the extra dimension of chocolate Swiss Roll and molassed fruitcake combined. Don't look for soothing silkiness: this is about controlled aggression and power; f23 that chocolate spins itself out to the very end; the fruit and cream accompaniment is superb; b24 a warlord of the isles... *61.6%. Gordon & MacPhail.*

⁘ **Gordon and MacPhail Connoisseurs Choice Caol Ila 1999** (88) n22 soft oils lighten the peaty load. A little suet pudding and maple syrup at work, too...; as gentle as a big Islay gets; t22.5 myriad sugars, of the gristy variety, shepherd the smoke to somewhere safe and compromising; lemon butter middle f21.5 the odd tired cask adds a degree of bitterness to the lightly spiced, delicately smoked fade; b22 cannot be mistaken for any other distiller: Caol Ila nutshelled. 46%. ncf.

⁘ **Kingsbury Caol Ila Aged 16 Years** hogshead, cask no. 793, dist 96 (88) n22 a light mint and lemon touch to the lively phenols; t22 regulation gristy sweetness, perhaps with the odd extra spoonful of castor sugar towards the middle; the smoke is surprisingly subdued; f22 the smoke is a lazy bleat of a thing, with the sweet vanilla persisting; chocolate mint on the death; b22 well rounded and quicksand soft. 46%. nc ncf. 359 bottles.

Liquid Library Caol Ila 11 Years Old bourbon cask, dist 2000, bott 2011 (87) n22 somewhere under all that oil you know there is some major peat smoke lurking....; t22.5 clean, malty, oily and very smoky though the peat reveals itself by degree; f21 a tiring cask bitters matters out slightly; b21.5 a Caol Ila in its oiliest livery. Delicious but don't go in search of complexity. 46%. sc. The Whisky Agency.

⁘ **Liquid Sun Caol Ila 1979** ex-bourbon hogshead, dist 79, bott 12 (86) n22 t22 f20.5 b21.5. The buttery smokiness does its best to fill some of the oaky, slightly off beam cracks. Pretty rigorous stuff – a surprise package and impressively virile for its age. 52.9%.

Liquid Sun Caol Ila 1981 bott 2011 (95.5) n24 a wonderful and quite charming compilation of delicate peaty and sooty notes: a blending of old steam trains and distant peat fires on the salty wind; t24 like the nose, this is all about hint and delicacy. There is no doubting the salt. Nor the gooseberry jam. Nor the thin spreading of honey on golden toast. What is remarkable is the deftness of touch of the smoke...; f23 remains long by virtue of the light oils which leads a train of varying sugar and honey notes. All understated, of course...; b24.5 has withstood the inquisition of time with an exhibition of great elegance. A must experience whisky. 52.9%. nc ncf sc. The Whisky Agency.

Malts Of Scotland Caol Ila 1979 bourbon hogshead, cask no. MoS12022, dist Mar 79, bott Apr 12 (84.5) n21.5 t22 f20 b21.0. You know when a malt is getting just a little ripe when the oak actually outperforms the peaty input of a Caol Ila... 52.3%. nc ncf sc.

Malts Of Scotland Caol Ila 1981 bourbon hogshead, cask no. MoS11009, dist May 81, bott Aug 11 (83) n20 t22.5 f20 b20.5. For a few brief moments this malt positively beams and glistens on the palate, its enormity writ large in spice. But the overall effect leaves you with the feeling that this would have done a better job in a 30-year-old blend, rather than standing alone with its oaky exhaustion fully exposed. 59.2%. nc ncf sc. Malts Of Scotland.

⁘ **Malts of Scotland Caol Ila 1990** bourbon hogshead, cask no. MoS 12042, dist Apr 90, bott Sep 12 (91) n22 bright and sea breezy with some lovely mix of fresh grist and peat reek on the wind; t23.5 rich in barley and mid-range in oils, the sugars are crisp and the peat crunchy, a little spicy and offering a tangy citrus edge; f22.5 cocoa oils, Demerara sugar and smoke; b23.5 always great to see Caol Ila in this kind of complex yet relaxed form. 55.6%. nc ncf sc. 96 bottles.

Malts Of Scotland Caol Ila 1995 bourbon hogshead, cask no. 9805, dist Aug 95, bott May 11 (88.5) n21 the oak almost outweighs the smoke; t23 a gorgeous liquorice injection on the delivery mingles almost perfectly with the expanding peat; f22 a much drier send off, but the vanillas play their part well; b22.5 an impressive exhibition of controlled, cleverly smoked aggression. 54.1%. nc ncf sc. Malts Of Scotland.

Malts Of Scotland Caol Ila 2000 bourbon hogshead, cask no. 309876, dist Nov 00, bott May 11 (86) n22 t22 f21 b21. Absolutely classic blending fodder, except perhaps missing the usual degree of oiliness. Juicy, lightly sugared, smoky and makes no unreasonable demands on either nose or palate. 54.6%. nc ncf sc. Malts Of Scotland.

Mo Òr Collection Caol Ila 1980 30 Years Old first fill bourbon hogshead, cask no. 2570, dist 19 Mar 80, bott 4 Feb 11 (81.5) n20.5 t22 f19 b20. An over-aged cask with the oak dominating intrusively. 46%. nc ncf sc. Release No. 15. The Whisky Talker. 300 bottles.

Mo Òr Collection Caol Ila 1983 27 Years Old first fill bourbon hogshead, cask no. 4824, dist 12 Oct 82, bott 11 Mar 11 (89.5) n22 butterscotch tart and mixed fruit; a few honeyed notes hover. The smoke is conspicuous by its absence; t23.5 the lack of peat allows the oils to reveal their intensity to the fullest. Salty barley to the fore...; f22 dries as the salt bites a little deeper; b22 if you are looking for a smoky Islay, give this a swerve. But if you want to inspect the skeleton of the malt... 46%. nc ncf sc. Release No. 48. The Whisky Talker. 400 bottles.

⁘ **Old Masters Caol Ila 12 Years Old** cask no. 3309908, dist 00, bott Nov 12 (91) n22.5 soft, playful smoke with a zesty corner; t23 brilliant brevity with just the right amount of aggression to the peat and backed and balanced by a rich wave of juicy barley; f22.5 silky and soft to the end with the sugars multiplying; b23 anyone with a sweet tooth and a penchant for smoky whisky will be in their element. 56.8%. sc. James MacArthur & Co Ltd.

Old Malt Cask Caol Ila Aged 14 Years refill hogshead, cask no. 6898, dist 1996, bott 2011 (89.5) n2.52 dry, ashy top layer, the gristy sugars lurk no great distance below; t23.5 sensual delicacy: soft and delicately oiled and brimming full of light barley and oaky-induced sugars; the peat knows exactly where not to go to allow maximum complexity; f21.5 a little on the bitter side; b22 soothingly sweet; carries its considerable smoky weight lightly. 50%. nc ncf sc.

Old Malt Cask Caol Ila Aged 15 Years refill hogshead, cask no. 8003, dist Sep 96, bott Jan 12 (95) n23 crisp barley for a Caol Ila with the smoke offering a specific, toasty shape rather than its usual oily generalisation; t24 the weight and texture are quite sublime and here we have the smoke playing a dual role: both as a lightly oiled purveyor of sweetness and as a sterner, slightly spicy lead. A gristy barley sweetness adorns the lighter vanillas; f24 long, thanks to that most subtle oil, with a light cocoa depth; b24 an unforgettable cask: this distillery rarely displays so well. 50%. nc ncf sc. Douglas Laing & Co. 299 bottles.

Old Malt Cask Caol Ila Aged 16 Years refill hogshead, cask no. 7931, dist May 95, bott Dec 11 (94) n24 smoked Swiss cheese on a plate of salted celery and spiced liquorice. As intriguing as it is sublimely aromatic and balanced; t23.5 unusual for a Caol Ila but the lively sugars surge ahead of the oils; the lightly smoked barley still retains a gristy quality; f23 an excellent sweet-dry finale which gathers the cocoa and spices and play them out to full effect. The smoke now offers its full worth; b24 a Caol Ila showing a style rarely seen since the 1980s. Of its type, a classic. 50%. nc ncf sc. Douglas Laing & Co. 189 bottles.

⁘ **Old Malt Cask Caol Ila Aged 16 Years** refill hogshead, cask no. 9512, dist Sep 96, bott Feb 13 (95) n23.5 dry: the hearth being cleaned of the previous night's burnt peats; t24 outstanding citrus attack on delivery — fresh and salivating. The peat arrives by the squadron load but the light oils carry some serious barley sugar; t23.5 more like the drier nose now as diced coconut and fudge make for a chewy finish; the confident peat makes all the right noise; b24 never one of Caol Ila's greatest fans (well, since it was rebuilt), I have to say this is a dram I could drink all day any day, simply because it is so subtle and understated....and without a single distilling or maturation blemish. Truly sublime. 50%. sc. 156 bottles.

⁘ **Old Malt Cask Caol Ila Aged 16 Years** refill hogshead, cask no. 9823, dist 1996, bott 2013 (92) n22.5 slightly estery, though the peat shines; t23.5 juicy, citrus and grist in a lovely oily base; smoked chocolate in muscovado sugars through the middle; f23 long, with a gorgeous smoked custard fade; b23.5 excellent distillate in good oak which both supports and allows the malt, and complex sugars in particular, a full view. Superb. 50%. nc ncf sc. 145 bottles.

⁘ **Old Malt Cask Caol Ila Aged 16 Years** refill hogshead, cask no. 9057, dist Sep 96, bott Sep 12 (86) n21 t22.5 f21 b21.5. Competent, gristy malt with the smoke subdued but eventually makes its mark. The delivery enjoys a juicy peak. 50%. sc. 213 bottles.

⁘ **Port Sgioba Private Cask Caol Ila Aged 12 Years** bourbon barrel, dist 3 Nov 12, bott 5 Nov 12 (89.5) n22 of the dry style with coal dust mingling with the peat; t23 the smoke makes all the early running and quickly builds in intensity, the sweetness of the barley hanging on to its coat tails... f22 probably a second fill barrel which could impart a little more tannin for complexity. As it is, the smoke dominates and the spices crank up the amps; b22.5 a spot on barrel, above average in complexity thanks probably to the lighter than the norm oils. 55.5%. nc ncf sc. Friends Over a Hogshead Syndicate. 205 bottles.

⁘ **Provenance Caol Ila Young and Feisty** two refill hogshead, cask no. 9278 & 9279, bott Winter 12 (85.5) n21 t22 f21 b21.5. Uncomplicated blending malt where the peat and early sugars would have done the job intended. The finish is a little undercooked. 46%. nc ncf sc.

Provenance Caol Ila Young & Feisty Small Batch Bottling cask no. 7767 & 7768, bott Autumn 2011 (84) n21 t22.5 f19.5 b21. Not so much young and feisty as infantile and spoilt. A fun whisky full of smoky rhetoric. But the bitter finish deserves a smacked bum. 46%. nc ncf.

Provenance Caol Ila Young & Feisty Small Batch Bottling refill hogshead, bott Spring 2012 (91) n23 sound, clean peat enjoying excellent sweet and dry undertones; t23.5 fine delivery: the smoke is to the fore, but the delicate sugars soon guide the overall shape: hugely satisfying; f22 a little disapproval from the oak but those lightly smoked sugars handle the situation well; b22.5 does most of what you hope from a Caol Ila. 46%. nc ncf sc.

Provenance Caol Ila Young & Feisty Small Batch Bottling refill hogshead, cask no. 8010 & 8124, bott Winter 2012 (82) n19 t22 f20 b21. The limitations of the cask put a muzzle on what must have been some very decent spirit. 46%. nc ncf. Douglas Laing & Co.

Scotch Single Malt Circle Caol Ila 1999 cask no. 310808, dist 23 Sep 99, bott 5 Oct 11 (89.5) n23 the peat is spray-painted on: thick, dry and salty; t22.5 beautifully clean barley makes a pleasant start, then it's peat, muscovado sugars and oaky spices all the way; f22 simplifies down to the very basics. Not a trace of bitterness or an off note, though; b22 about as subtle as a one tonne bomb. But what good clean fun! Love it!! 61.4%. sc.

Scotch Malt Whisky Society Cask 53.154 Aged 17 Years refill hogshead, cask no. 10905, dist 1993 (77) n20 19 f19 b19. How ordinary can a Caol Ila be? Surely there were better casks than this to choose from? Very poor oak. 59.8%. sc. Scotch Malt Whisky Society.

Scotch Malt Whisky Society Cask 53.156 Aged 10 Years refill hogshead, cask no. 312007, dist 2000 **(89.5) n21.5** this kipper can still bite; **t22.5** a dry nip to the smoke; mildly ashy and devoid of the usual oily coating; **f23** now really goes into complexity overdrive as the warming spices hit a perfect crescendo with the gathering muscovado sugars; **b22.5** a lovely little essay in complexity. 57.6%. sc. Scotch Malt Whisky Society.

Scotch Malt Whisky Society Cask 53.157 Aged 10 Years refill hogshead, cask no. 312008, dist 2000 **(91.5) n22.5** clean, gristy and mildly simplistic, the peat is much starker than usual for a Caol Ila; **t22.5** the delivery concentrates on the smoke ahead of the oil...hang on...what oil? Unusually crisp and almost gristy; light spices bob and weave; **f23.5** a few vanilla notes confirm some oak is involved and now the delicate sugars enter the fray and continue the salivating theme; **b23** lacking the usual oils, this is almost like seeing all the distillery's charms for a change instead of with three layers of clothing... 58%. sc.

Scotch Malt Whisky Society Cask 53.158 Aged 15 Years refill hogshead, cask no. 14551, dist 1996 **(84.5) n21 t21.5 f21 b21.** Dry yet firmly sugared. Just annoyingly underdeveloped for its age. 58.6%. sc. Scotch Malt Whisky Society.

Scotch Malt Whisky Society Cask 53.166 Aged 15 Years refill ex-bourbon hogshead, cask no. 12557, dist 1996 **(90) n22** anyone who has ever crushed a parched, fried grain of peated malt in their fingers will recognise the aroma immediately; **t24** superb delivery tasting tall to show every single one of its 35ppm phenol; some Demerara sugars rumble elsewhere while the lack of usual oils help elevate the honeycomb middle; **f21.5** falls away as the oak fails to live up to the quality of the spirit; **b22.5** a slightly better cask would have rendered this a mini classic. A real experience, though. 58.1%. sc.

⠿ **Scotch Malt Whisky Society Cask 53.170 Aged 22 Years** refill hogshead, dist 19 dec 89 **(86.5) n21 t22.5 f21 b22.** A chewy, toasty dram which doesn't over beef up on the smoke. This allows in a period of outstanding cocoa and Demerara sugar, but ultimately just a little too frenzied oak for its own good. 55.1%. nc ncf sc. 183 bottles.

⠿ **Scotch Malt Whisky Society Cask 53.174 Aged 12 Years** refill hogshead, dist 18 Nov 99 **(81.5) n22 t21 f19 b19.5.** Ye gods! Celtic must have been playing Rangers live on TV when this was made. This has been fair ripped through the stills as this is as thin and hot a Caol Ila as you'll ever encounter. 64.2%. nc ncf sc. 297 bottles.

⠿ **That Boutique-y Whisky Company Caol Ila** batch 1 **(84.5) n20.5 t22 f21 b21.** Excellent use of a salt and sugar combination. Not so sure about the juniper, though, as this has a distinct gin-like quality... 45.8%. Master Of Malt. 732 bottles.

⠿ **Wemyss 1980 Single Islay Caol Ila "The Smokery"** hogshead, dist 80, bott 13 **(94) n23.5** more lime than lemon in the citrus; the smoke has been weathered by time and clings to the vanilla for dear life; **t23.5** silky delivery with a slow but ever-growing punctuation of oaky spice; lovely hickory middle with smoky ulmo honey glaze; **f23** slightly more lightly oiled than an average Caol Ila, just enough hangs around to ensure the drier smoke elements balance against the late maple syrup and butterscotch; **b24** fabulous, understated elegance. 46%. sc. 322 bottles.

⠿ **Wemyss 1987 Single Speyside Tamdhu "The Hay Bale"** hogshead, dist 87, bott 13 **(88) n22** anyone who has dipped their face into a pile of freshly harvested, slightly dank barley will recognise this...; **t23** simplistic yet stunningly effective barley concentrate – almost from the Tomatin school of advanced malt; **f21** irritating interference from slightly sub-standard oak, but the juicy, gristy maltiness still powers through; **b22** a solid malt making few apologies for its one-dimensional maltiness. Not the greatest oak input, but the original richness of the spirit makes for an enjoyable digestive biscuit style dram. 46%. sc. 330 bottles.

⠿ **Wemyss 1996 Single Islay Caol Ila "Lemon Smoke"** hogshead, bott 2012 **(95) n23.5** astonishingly dry and oil-less for a Caol Ila with the accent on a salty, sea-breezy smokiness and crammed with rock pools and other coastline clichés; **t24.5** absolutely top-notch. Again the lack of oil is evident, allowing both the peat and impressively deft oak full reign. The sugars are pure grist, though after the smoke drifts in and out it is backed by a heavier muscovado style; the growing oak again displays a light salty seasoning; **f23** dries to allow the vanilla a much bigger (though still dry) say, almost like a smoky ice cream cone; late spices tingle and mingle with the little sugars which thrive; a light cocoa coating forms at the finish; **b24** Caol Ila at by far its most delicate and in single malt rather than blending mode. Another breath-taking connoisseur's must have from a distillery which doesn't always hit the heights, but when it does.... 46%. sc. 380 bottles.

Wemyss 1996 Single Islay "Smokehouse" hogshead, bott 2011 **(88.5) n21.5** a squeeze of grapefruit on an Arbroath Smokie; **t23** satisfying amalgam of fruit and smoke but with the grist still standing tallest; **f21.5** a tad bitter as the oak cuts in but still a good smoky send off; **b22.5** plays its drier and juicier personalities against each other with aplomb. 46%. sc. 363 bottles.

⠿ **Wemyss 1996 Single Islay Caol Ila "The Tobacconist"** hogshead, dist 96, bott 13 **(81.5) n20.5 t22 f19 b20.** Never having as much as put an unlit cigarette to my lips, let alone smoked (a reason some specialist doctors in the field have told me as to why my palate is so sensitive), I know little of what goes on in tobacconists, other than that their hovercrafts are full of eels. Bouncy, bouncy! I assume whoever picked this cask goes quite often, otherwise he or she might have spotted the bitter oak flaw. 46%. sc. Wemyss Malts. 381 bottles. Exclusive for France.

The Whisky Agency Caol Ila 33 Years Old dist 1979 **(96.5)** n24.5 for the age, pretty close to perfect. You fear that time will have thinned the peat to a mere shell. Not a bit: delicately powered, ashy and very much alive...; t24 so beautiful with its molten sugars dragging along a multitude of peaty notes. The sugars head towards more molassed pastures as the experience unfolds; f24 very late in the day, citrus pops up from somewhere. The lightly oiled phenols now carry mocha. This is dreamy stuff; b24 when you open a bottle of 33-year-old Islay, you are looking for one of the times of your life. This happily obliges. 53.7%. sc.

⁙ **The Whisky Agency Caol Ila 1982** bott 12 **(91.5)** n23.5 as soft and smoky as a loving kiss from a '40s sweetheart...; t23 doesn't take long for the spices to come crashing through the windows, though not before the silky barley pitches camp; f22 slightly aggressive now as the oak bites hard; b23 a delightfully full of character; a high quality dram which makes no secret of its age and home turf; 51.2%

⁙ **The Whisky Agency Caol Ila 'Sea Life' 1984** ex-bourbon hogshead, dist 1984, bott 2012 **(89.5)** n22 diced, dried lemon peel thins the smoke attractively; lovely salty sub-strata; t23 wonderful delivery of salivating barley and citrus with the peat wandering around the palate soothing here and there; f22 a ridiculously clean finish, much younger than its years with the toffee-butterscotch and lemon drizzle cake swamped in phenols; b22.5 the distillery at its grooviest, as opposed to grooviest as the citrus plays a massive role. 53.5%

The Whisky Agency Caol Ila 1992 bott 2011 **(87.5)** n22.5 a nose that makes you sit up and take notice: a smattering of white pepper causes chaos in the smoky lines; the citrus is a delightful distraction; t22.5 soft and melt-in-the mouth delivery with the malt cranking up the sugars and smoke in equal degrees; the spices begin their bombardment; f20.5 annoyingly bitter as the oak takes a wrong turn; b22 puckering and busy, this is less about the smoke and more about how the spices assert themselves. 50.5%. nc ncf sc. The Whisky Agency.

The Whisky Agency Caol Ila 1993 bott 2012 **(85.5)** n22 t21.5 f21 b21. A pleasant, good looking but, ultimately, lazy dram which you feel deserves a good whipping for its indolence. 56.1%. nc ncf sc. The Whisky Agency.

Whisky Antique Caol Ila 28 Years Old Special Bottling dist 1983, bott 2011 **(84.5)** n21 t22 f20.5 b21. A curious Caol ila with plenty of pepper, minimal smoke and no shortage of toffee, especially on the finale. 46%. sc. Silver Seal Whisky Company.

CAPERDONICH

Speyside, 1898. Chivas Brothers. Closed.

⁙ **Abbey Whisky Caperdonich Aged 17 Years The Rare Casks** refill bourbon barrel, dist 95, bott 12 **(86.5)** n21.5 t22.5 f21 b21.5. The ulmo honey and spices work overtime to see off the over-enthusiasm of the oak. Never less than entertaining, but the tannins win the day a little too convincingly. 578%. nc ncf. 96 bottles.

⁙ **Duncan Taylor Octave Caperdonich 20 Years Old** cask no. 413904, dist 92 **(96)** n23.5 the oak makes for a overtly dry experience, but it doesn't take too much work to locate the delicate ulmo honey and spiced peach melba; t22.5 dry delivery but enough sugars from the barley to soften things beautifully; f25 heads into overdrive as we come up with one of the most complex and beautifully weighted finishes of the year. The barley has now absorbed enough tannin to pulse a sweet sharpness and the weight and feel has altered from bone dry and heavy to semi ethereal and dusted with gentle sugars including, astonishingly, grist. Playful lemon drop notes also hint of a bygone youth: a bit like an old man still with the profile of the child he once was...; b24 just about the complete Speyside for its type and age. A finish to be revered. Superb. 54.6%. sc. Duncan Taylor & Co.

Gordon & MacPhail Connoisseurs Choice Caperdonich 1998 (82) n19 t22 f20.5 b20.5. A thin, pleasant though entirely underwhelming malt which, for all its barley theme, gives another clue as to why it was decided the distillery wasn't worth saving. 46%.

⁙ **Gordon & MacPhail Connoisseurs Choice Caperdonich 1999 (91.5)** n22.5 sandalwood and moist sawdust amongst the heather honey; t23.5 juicy barley on delivery; toastier malt on the third and fourth waves; light liquorice and hickory in the mid-ground; f22.5 the delicate spices persists amid the vanilla ice cream; b23 irresistible! 46%. ncf.

⁙ **Liquid Sun Caperdonich 1992** bott 12 **(92.5)** n22 freshly diced Granny Smith freshens up the oak; t24 exceptional texture: just enough oils brought home by the big malt to ensure serious weight; eye-watering pears instead of apples and so much spice...; f23 long and, though thinning out to a gruel at the finish, the deft maple syrup ensures balance is maintained; b23.5 the distillery may now be dead, but this is so alive on the palate...51.9%.

Malts Of Scotland Caperdonich 1994 bourbon hogshead, cask no. 625, dist Mar 94, bott May 11 **(79)** n21 t20 f19 b19. A good example of why the distillery was closed down and dismantled, though some attractive cocoa and barley sugar manage to dodge the ruthlessly searing heat of the spirit. 53.3%. nc ncf sc. Malts Of Scotland.

Mo Òr Collection Caperdonich 1972 38 Years Old first fill bourbon hogshead, cask no. 7437, dist 7 Nov 72, bott 25 Jan 11 **(87.5)** 22 huge oak impact, but the fruit is more kumquat rather than the desired mixed exotic; t22 soft delivery with the barley building a platform on the oily ground. Again the oak has a big say, but levels off with a cocoa dryness; f21.5 chocolate sponge, though with little sugar; b22 makes a bold attempt to recreate the great old Capers of six or seven years ago. But this has absorbed too much oak for any form of greatness, though it is always enjoyable. 46%. nc ncf sc. Release No. 9. The Whisky Talker. 162 bottles.

⠐⠐ **Old Malt Cask Caperdonich Aged 18 Years** refill hogshead, cask no. 8475, dist Jun 94, bott Jun 12 **(89)** n23 not the usual exotic fruit expected from a Caper: the oak here is more heavy duty and bludgeoning with an eye towards the sappy, but enough citrus to ward that off; t22 the oak again pours through early on, but the barley is rich, rounded and sweet enough. Spices abound; f23.5 settles down impressively for an outstanding fade, with the early broad strokes now more detained and busy. The oak still makes its mark but here, it is of a more chocolaty hue; b22.5 oscillates between excellence and very good. 50%. nc ncf sc. Douglas Laing & Co. 297 bottles.

⠐⠐ **Old Malt Cask Caperdonich Aged 20 Years** refill hogshead, cask no. 9321, dist Oct 92, bott Jan 13 **(92.5)** n24 almost perfumed in its fruitiness: wine gums melting in the sun. A hint of hot cross bun does for the spice and sherbet for tartness; t23 with the sherbet on the nose, the fizzing delivery seems a natural way for the barley to hit home on the palate; delicate spices pop around, as does a light creamed mocha-butterscotch middle; f22.5 much drier now and something for vanilla fans to enjoy; b23 never seen a Caperdonich perform like this before: come to think of it, its style is a first in a couple of decades of tastings. Inventive and pure fun. 50%. sc. Douglas Laing & Co. 322 bottles.

⠐⠐ **That Boutique-y Whisky Company Caperdonich** batch 3 **(94)** n24 wild mint dissolves into a subtle honey and herbal mix; t23 steady oak from delivery offers maple syrup alongside the zingy, citrusy edge; f23.5 egg custard tart with spice; very late ulmo honey; b23.5 a quality malt which is not only complex but displays a near perfect weight. 45.7%. Master of Malt. 120 bottles.

⠐⠐ **The Warehouse Collection Caperdonich Aged 18 Years** bourbon hogshead, cask no. 88853, dist 23 Jun 94, bott 28 Oct 12 **(82)** n20 t20 f21.5 b20.5. A seriously weird one. In over three decades, I have tasted Caper in all shapes, forms, ages and sizes. This is the first, though, that smells more like cider brandy and tastes something akin to slivovitz. Impossible not to enjoy in its own right, though. 62.8%. nc ncf sc. Whisky Warehouse No. 8. 278 bottles.

The Whisky Agency Caperdonich 18 Years Old dist 1994 **(81)** n22 t19 f20 b20. Sweet. But ouch!! It's hotter than the sun...! (That's for you, Armando) 52.2%. sc.

CARDHU

Speyside, 1824. Diageo. Working.

Cardhu 12 Years Old db **(83)** n22 t22 f18 b21. What appears to be a small change in the wood profile has resulted in a big shift in personality. What was once a guaranteed malt love-in is now a drier, oakier, fruitier affair. Sadly, though, with more than a touch of something furry. 40%

Duncan Taylor Rare Auld Cardhu 26 Years Old cask no. 2873, dist 1984 **(96)** n25 I'm in love: if I didn't have a deadline, this is a nose I could wallow in all day. What's ringing my bells? Well the absolutely perfect - and I mean faultless - weight balance between an allspice (almost bread pudding) richness mixing in with the diced kumquat zest. The sugars are subtle and varied but edge towards muscovado depth; this is as long, labyrinthine and mysterious as a Brazilian rain forest...; t24.5 fabulous delivery with the silky oils attached to the body grabbing the attention at first. Then a confident, striding display of bourbon oak, liquorice and tannins. But the sugars keep pace effortlessly; f23.5 at last the malt thins and the oaks encroach a little too keenly. Busy and a little biting around the tongue; the malt offers a last, sugary hurrah...; b24 a real rarity. And one worth waiting for: an essay of weighty Speyside complexity. But, please. Spend at least half an hour on the nose before you taste: no water, just body temperature. You will thank me — and Cardhu - forever. Notably, I tasted this on February 29th. I expect it'll be another four years before I find such a cask from Cardhu again... 54.4%. nc ncf sc. Duncan Taylor & Co.

⠐⠐ **Duncan Taylor Octave Cardhu 27 Years Old** cask no. 863289, dist 84 **(93.5)** n24 while virtually every aroma somehow stems from the oak, it is achieved with such effortless sophistication that there is not a hint of tired or laboured tannin; perhaps there is a hint of malt on the ulmo honey, while the spice carries the fruitiness found in rye or pure pot Irish.

Really complex stuff; **t23** translates onto the palate perfectly; the sugars lead the way, all of a silky disposition, before a few tannins hit home, as do the spices. But there is a slightly overcooked jam tart darkness to this, too: quite lovely; **f23** the spices keep up the pace and intensity while the custard pie hits the intended target; **b23.5** uber-high quality and shows its grey hairs in only a distinguished manner. Cardhu is one of the few delicate Speysiders which can translate to older ages with such grace. 51.1%. sc. Duncan Taylor & Co.

Scotch Malt Whisky Society Cask 106.18 Aged 27 Years refill hogshead, cask no. 2882, dist 1984 (91) **n23** a busy entanglement between soft oak and delicate orange blossom honey; **t23** for all the background oak, the delivery is surprisingly light with almost a whipped cream consistency; the Jamaican Blue Mountain coffee ensures a subtle middle ground; the sugars are little more than bystanders but, as ever, it is the barley which quietly steels the show; **f22** a thin spreading of marmalade on granary toast; **b23** beautiful complexity throughout from this under-rated distillery. 52.6%. sc.

The Whisky Agency Cardhu 1984 bott 2011 **(92) n22.5** as SMWS 106.18 above but with a little extra oak, or is that manuka in with the orange blossom? **t23** very similar to above but more oil to the whipped cream and the orange blossom honey produces the goods a fraction earlier than before; **f23** extra oak weight on the finish, balanced by a slightly sweeter mocha and praline finale; **b23.5** this one has had me scratching my head. Two whiskies side by side, poured from different bottles. Yet like two peas in a pod, the second showing only a marginal degree of extra oak encroachment and fractionally better balance. On checking, I spotted they were the same age and the same strength. Take your eye off the ball and you'd easily think it was the same cask. 52.6%. nc ncf sc. The Whisky Agency.

CLYNELISH
Highlands (Northern), 1968. Diageo. Working.

Clynelish Aged 15 Years "The Distillers Edition" double matured in oloroso-seco casks Cl-Br: 169-1f, bott code L6264CM000 03847665, dist 1991, bott 2006 db **(79) n20 t20 f19 b20.** Big in places, distinctly oily in others but the overall feel is of a potentially brilliant whisky matured in unsympathetic barrels. 46%

Archives Clynelish 1997 14 Years Old Inaugural Release bourbon hogshead, cask no. 4634, dist Jul 97, bott Jul 11 **(89.5) n22.5** the oak takes a back seat and allows the malt to dazzle...; incredible young and lemon drop-like; **t22.5** mouth-watering barley pulses out more and more beautifully sweetened citrus; **f22** the barley is left to itself; **b22.5** it is a rare event when a bourbon cask on perhaps its third time round does not interfere with a minor degree of negativity. Of its type, quite gorgeous. 53.9%. nc ncf sc. Whiskybase B.V. 160 bottles.

Berry's Own Selection Clynelish 1997 cask no. 6864, bott 2012 **(92.5) n22** an enticing melody of light citrus, heavier toasty oak and the very vaguest puff of smoke; **t23.5** delicate delivery with a lighter body than normal. The barley is juicy but the spices are quite astonishing, yet next out of context with the mashed banana and light honey; **f23** long with a light oil forming and lengthening the egg custard tart...with no little sugar and cocoa sprinkled on top; **b24** like so often from this great distillery, an absolute treat for the taste buds. 46%. nc ncf sc.

Boisdale Clynelish 1997 cask no. 6467, bott 2012 **(93.5) n23** artful barley at work: delicate, fragile yet bold enough to inject a degree of fruit; there is something in the wind to watch carefully late on; **t24.5** you are probably wondering where I have docked the half mark. "I mean", you will say, "where the hell can you find fault with that?" For the weight, somewhere between bantam and fly, is perfect. So too is the slow motion development of the barley. The introduction of the gristy sugars is faultless and the intertwining with some duskier oak notes is beyond reproach. The answer is just a frisson of bitterness, noticeable only because the malt is just so delicate; **f22.5** the mildly sub-standard bitter oak makes only limited impact as the sugars, picking up a fruity theme, do an excellent damage limitation job; **b23.5** Clynelish, in all its finery, makes one of the best deliveries on the palate this year... 46%. nc ncf sc.

Chieftain's Clynelish Aged 14 Years hogshead, cask no. 4717, dist Apr 97 **(91) n22.5** fascinating nose which never seems to settle: each sniff offers a slightly different view of the lightly smoked bananas and custard; **t24** one of those divine deliveries where delicate oils thrust the multi-layered lightly sugared barley directly at the more deadpan oak; mocha and caramel fills the middle; **f22** thins out somewhat as the vanilla gets a little chalkier; **b23** slightly more oaky vanilla than usual. But doesn't impact too badly on the usual high complexity. 46%. nc ncf sc. Ian Macleod Distillers. USA exclusive.

⁘ **The Coopers Choice Clynelish 1998 13 Years Old** hogshead, cask no. 7733, dist 98, bott 11 **(80) n19 t22.5 f18 b20.5.** Moist ginger cake, anyone? Proof, though, that a sub-standard cask will do damage to, or at best restrict, even arguably Scotland's finest mainland spirit. 46%. nc ncf sc. The Vintage Malt Whisky Co Ltd. 350 bottles.

Duncan Taylor Dimensions Clynelish 21 Years Old cask no. 3229, dist 1990, bott 2012 **(89.5) n22** wow! is this 21 years old only? Has the heavy fruit and tannins of a malt almost twice that age; **t23** rich delivery: profound oak is kept in check by some fabulous fudge and liquorice notes; the body is always thick, the mid-ground creaks with oak; **f22** still no need to put the Zimmer frame away; **b22.5** fruity enough, and pretty sexy in part. But prematurely aged. Discover what many top 35-40-year-old malts taste like for only half the price! *51.4%. nc ncf sc.*

Duthies Clynelish 16 Years Old sherrywood, bott 2012 **(90) n22** fruitcake with plenty of warmed nuts...; **t23.5** salivating delivery despite the burnt raisins and a buoyant follow through full of dark cherries and muscovado sugar; **f22.5** late spices jazz up the butterscotch; **b23** get spirit from one of Scotland's finest distilleries, put it into a decent, untainted sherry cask...and you are unlikely to go too far wrong. *46%. sc. WM Cadenhead Ltd.*

⸭ **Dun Bheagan Clynelish Aged 22 Years Port Hogshead Finish**, cask no. 93781, 93783, dist Dec 90, bott 13 **(87.5) n21.5** the peppery port influence is sharp, fresh and unmistakable; a very vague hint of something smoky; **t22** juicy, moderately rich with sprightly redcurrant fruitiness; **f22** chocolate liqueur with a cherry filling; **b22** a surprising lack of oak; the port pipes have taken years off this malt, though the balance has suffered a little. *46%*

⸭ **Fine Malt Selection Clynelish 15 Years Old** cask no. 4711, dist 97, bott Apr 13 **(92) n22.5** no getting away from a coastal saltiness...like Tyrrell crisps on a seaside picnic where Tunnock's caramel wafers are the main course; **t23** a sharp, juicy barley and salt bite at first, then a surprise custardy back up...with the vaguest hint of smoke; **f23** the saline sharpness lasts the entire tale and even merges with the Toffo finish; just a little glassy at the death, suggesting even greater age; **b23.5** more natural caramels and vanillas than normal for this distillery. But a stunner is a stunner... *46%. sc. James MacArthur & Co Ltd.*

⸭ **Gordon and MacPhail Connoisseurs Choice Clynelish 1996 (95) n24.5** you never need to buy a ticket to travel with a Clynelish of this era in the glass: one is transported, Business Class at least, to a world where ulmo honey drips from greengage trees and orange blossom honey fills any gaps. Something so Mediterranean about this: time after time this distillery comes up with soft, pliable aromas which near perfection; **t24** slightly more oak adorns the delivery than is noticeable on the nose. A wave of toffee fudge is interspersed by raisin and kumquats; the spices are teasing and ticklish, the balance always in tune; **f22.5** buttery barley and butterscotch fence off the advancing oak; **b24** in recent years I have been coming to the conclusion that Clynelish is probably the greatest of all the mainland Scotch distilleries. This bottling does little to dissuade me. *46%. ncf.*

Hart Brothers Clynelish Aged 14 Years cask no. 5743, dist 21 May 97, bott 30 Apr 12 **(92) n23.5** quite brilliant: some candy shop fruitiness mixed in the most delicate stem ginger imaginable plus golden syrup. Some peaches and mangoes up the fruity sweetness further; **t23** soft and silky, the malt displays a degree of gristy sweetness which appears to ramp up the juice levels without the fruit on the nose being present; **f22.5** now some spices offer late extra complexity and depth; a wave of natural caramels make for a slightly subdued finale; **b23.5** a hugely complex Clynelish, as they so very often are.... *46%. sc.*

Malts Of Scotland Clynelish 1982 bourbon hogshead, cask no. MoS11015, dist 15 Dec 82, bott Oct 11 **(93) n23** a wonderful mix of herbs and freshly diced celery; the sweetness is supplied by telling vanillins – complete with spice – and coconut. **t23.5** the big oaky thrust is softened by a further build up of mega juicy barley sugar notes; complex and wonderfully structured, as usual; **f23** a saline drip is fed into the lightly spiced finale. The continuing sugars enrich the texture; **b23.5** such a dependable distillery! *53.7%. nc ncf sc. Malts Of Scotland.*

Malts Of Scotland Clynelish 1989 bourbon hogshead, cask no. MoS12012, dist 29 Sep 89, bott Jan 12 **(90.5) n22.5** anyone who has tasted spirits in Eastern Europe will recognise this distinctive slivovitz, crushed pip style: astonishing! **t23** more of the same with the barley swamped by the juiciest light fruitiness imaginable. The sugars, distinctly of the white, icing sugar variety, are sublime; **f22.5** long with sweetened vanilla and still a fruity twist to the barley; **b22.5** quite bizarre, considering this is from a bourbon cask: has all the attributes of one that has spent some time alongside a dry grape... *53.2%. nc ncf sc. Malts Of Scotland.*

Malts Of Scotland Clynelish 1998 bourbon hogshead, cask no. MoS12025, bott 2012 **(85) n21 t22 f21 b21.** A thick, sweetened malt milkshake of a dram though undermined by a cask which ensures a degree of tartness. *50.7%. nc ncf sc. Malts Of Scotland.*

⸭ **Master of Malt Clynelish Aged 15 Years** refill hogshead, dist 3 Apr 97, bott 28 Nov 12 **(94.5) n23.5** swoon time! Massive oak, more than a usual 15-y-o Clynelish, but the tannins are so beautifully buttressed by the buttery, gently honeyed malt you could almost shed a tear of delight; **t23.5** the little honey on the nose now unleashes unexpected intensity and depth; the malt gains in juiciness; **f23.5** now the drier flip side. But true to the distillery's magnificent character, where the delicate sugars cannot be denied, wins through; **b24** hard to go wrong with Clynelish. And here you won't...at all. Another malt of thundering, yet somehow coy beauty. *56.1%. sc. 255 bottles.*

⸭ **Master Of Malt Clynelish 16 Years Old** sherry, cask no. 4033, dist 3 Apr 97, bott 1 Apr 13 **(94) n22.5** powerful cinnamon-specked grape, kumquat and greengage; **t24** for all the fruit influence, it is the concentrated honey notes which dominate and to a satisfaction which makes one purr...; the early spice makes you grip your seat with pleasure; **f23.5** surprising degree of vanilla; tangy; **b24** at times the grape looks as though it might strange the malt, but so virile are the sugars, there is just no holding this malt down. Just another astonishing whisky from what is probably Scotland's finest mainland malt. *56.7%. sc.*

Old Malt Cask Clynelish Aged 16 Years refill hogshead, cask no. 7920, dist Jun 95, bott Nov 11 **(91.5) n22.5** a thin, if unique, blend of gooseberry and kiwifruit; **t23.5** the usual Clynelish elegance fuses the malt and spices together with aplomb; elsewhere light fruit and spice dally with intent; the intensity of the juices defies belief; **f22.5** still juicy and intensely malty but now more of a cocoa theme; **b23** effortlessly superb. *50%. nc ncf sc. 287 bottles.*

⫶⫶⫸ **Old Malt Cask Clynelish Aged 16 Years** refill hogshead, cask no. 8253, dist Jun 95, bott Mar 12 **(92) n23** from the banana and custard side of the Clynelish family; **t23** tangy malt coated in lightly oiled maple syrup; a grassier side is revealed at midpoint before the oak gathers; **f23** much drier oaks now. Toasty with vanilla and just a late hint of hazel nut; **b23** unerringly gorgeous. *50%. sc. Douglas Laing & Co. 319 bottles.*

Old Malt Cask Clynelish Aged 28 Years refill hogshead, cask no. 7553, dist Dec 82, bott Aug 11 **(95.5) n24** the odd puff of peat is met with equal pathetic force by juicy pear and clinker-rich coal dust; no shortage of sweet barley; **t24.5** a near perfect delivery. The barley is intense and juicy. This comes and goes in five or six waves which get steadily more oily; arriving at the same time is an ever-enlivening spiciness; black peppers squabbling and fighting or space against the ever encroaching, thickening malt; **f23** much thinner now with perhaps an odd hint of smoke here and there; the occasional bite of pepper but a constant of delicate malt. It is the vanilla which has the big final say; **b24** it is bottlings like this which help confirm my suspicion that this is the fairest of all the Diageo distilleries... *50%. nc ncf sc.*

The Perfect Dram Clynelish 23 Years Old dist 1989 **(87) n22** lightly smoked; broad honey-spice waves; **t22.5** typical Clynelish delivery, busting with a honeyed complexity; **f20.5** a slightly unyielding cask injects a little bitterness; **b22** frustrating! *49.7%. sc.*

⫶⫶⫸ **Provenance Clynelish Over 15 Years** refill hogshead, cask no. 9660, dist Summer 97, bott Spring 13 **(94) n23.5** buttery vanilla, with a clear and ulmo honey blend; **t24** deliveries on the palate rarely come softer or more beautiful: the malt is in silky, concentrate form, while light liquorice and even lighter clove are coated with a thin layer of molasses; somehow enough barley escapes to guarantee a juicy mouthful; **f23** liquorice and butterscotch, though the oak gathers peacefully; **b23.5** this really has to be the most consistent malt distillery in Scotland. Another angle-kissed dram. *46%. nc ncf. Douglas Laing & Co.*

Robert Graham's Dancing Stag Clynelish 1995 hogshead, cask no. 8658, dist 22 Sep 95, bott Sep 11 **(81) n19 t22 f19 b21.** A far better experience than the nose will lead you to believe. The moist ginger bread on delivery is a lovely touch. But the limitations of the oak take this malt only so far. *46%. nc ncf sc. Robert Graham. 461 bottles.*

Scotch Malt Whisky Society Cask 26.82 Aged 15 Years refill sherry butt, cask no. 6119, dist 1995 **(68) n17 t18 f16 b17.** A sulphur-riddled offering. *57.9%. sc.*

Scotch Malt Whisky Society Cask 26.86 Aged 21 Years refill barrel, cask no. 7923, dist 1990 **(89.5) n23.5** the distillery's standard – and highly desirable – honeyed signature; **t23.5** busy delivery with minimal viscosity but maximum honeyed lubrication; a few butterscotch and Lubec marzipan notes massage the taste buds further; **f20** sinks a little as the oak catches up to offer a countering bitterness; **b21.5** shame about the late failure of the oak: until then things had motored along beautifully. *50.5%. sc.*

⫶⫶⫸ **Scotch Malt Whisky Society Cask 26.92 Aged 28 Years** refill butt, dist 13 dec 84 **(88) n23** soft smoke drifts around with citrus; **t22** puckering salt makes way for the juicier barley; melted sugar on porridge; **f21** the oak offers up chalky vanilla; **b22** just a little too old to ensure the usual Clynelish genius. *58.2%. nc ncf sc. 491 bottles. nc ncf. Ian Macleod Distillers. 798 bottles.*

Scotch Single Malt Circle Clynelish 1989 cask no. 3843, dist 7 Jun 89, bott 12 Feb 12 **(88.5) n22.5** a dab of something superficially fruity lightens the malty load; a real toasty, bourbon liquorice base note; **t22** superb weight and surprise package of early vanillins cranking up the early intensity; the usual honeyed suspects begin to appear as matters calm; **f22** a light finish, not entirely unlike porridge with a dollop of molten honey; **b22** the first whisky of yet another long tasting day. And it is important to start it with one which is a safe bet to get your taste buds off to a flying start. Not quite as flowing and complex as one might hope due to the big oak, but no disappointments either. *51.8%. sc. Scotch Single Malt Circle.*

Single Cask Collection Clynelish 14 Years Old refill sherry hogshead, dist 1997 **(76) n18 t22 f17 b19.** Stunning delivery...which is saying something under the circumstances. Of the ten Scotch whiskies I have tasted today, this is the fifth tainted by sulphur. *56.8%. sc.*

⫶⫶⫸ **That Boutique-y Whisky Company Clynelish** batch 2 **(85) n21.5 t22 f20.5 b21.** May be wrong, but this has all the hallmarks of a sherry-treated barrel from the distillery's United

Distillers days. The soft sulphur mixing with the trademark honey really is a very unusual combination. 56.6%. Master of Malt. 319 bottles.

⁙ **The Warehouse Collection Clynelish Aged 15 Years** bourbon barrel, cask no. 5740, dist 21 May 97, bott 5 May 13 **(95.5) n23.5** salty bite to the spiced honey; **t24.5** immediate complexity: varying honey style from beech to ulmo; the salt really does up the sharpness and intensity as hickory and liquorice finds a place; some juicy barley pulses in and out; **f23** much drier with creamy fudge and cocoa layered with molassed sugar; **b24.5** effortless brilliance from Clynelish: this is how malt whisky should be..! 55.5%. nc ncf sc. 157 bottles.

Wemyss 1997 Single Highland Clynelish "Fresh Fruit Sorbet" hogshead, bott 2012 **(92) n23.5** not so sure about the fresh fruitsorbet. Unless barley is now a fruit. From this distillery you'd expect a salad bowl on the nose. Instead we are treated to wonderful multi-directional grassy notes augmented with thin maple syrup; **t23** it's all about the barley – again. And this gives it to you in a Speyside Tomatin kind of way with the malt just getting thicker by the second; **f22.5** dries as the vanillas assemble; **b23** this distillery is just fearsomely good. How simultaneously bold yet subtle can a whisky get? 46%. sc. 331 bottles.

⁙ **Wemyss Clynelish 1997 Single Highland "Spiced Chocolate Cup"** hogshead, dist 97, bott 13 **(91.5) n23** an intriguing parade of rich oak notes: from yam to hickory via red liquorice; **t23** silky barley with spiced undertones; loses identity as the ulmo honey takes command; **f22.5** cocoa notes...? Nope! (I just don't know where these titles are coming from!!!). Quite the opposite as the barley reignites late on and it is the sugars which bathe the palate on fade; **b23** hard to go wrong with this distillery. And this doesn't... 46%. sc. 302 bottles.

The Whisky Broker Clynelish 14 Years Old refill sherry hogshead, cask no. 6884, dist 14 Jul 97, bott 28 Sep 11 **(89.5) n22.5** classic fruit cake, though this one tends to have more moist high quality marzipan than most; **t24** this distillery can't help making you swoon on delivery whichever type of sound cask it has been matured in: a magnificent almost Christmas pudding richness to this...just lacking the silver thruppencies; **f21** the big burnt raisins fight on valiantly and make light of the few late sulphur notes; **b22** my usual twitch which appeared when I read this was from refill sherry disappeared once it hit my glass. Not perfect, but some cracking moments along the way. 53.7%. nc ncf sc. 285 bottles.

⁙ **The Whisky Cask Clynelish Aged 15 Years** (see Warehouse Collection Clynelish)

COLEBURN

Speyside, 1897–1985. Diageo. Closed.

The Whisky Agency Coleburn 26 Year Old dist 1983, bott 2009 **(88.5) n22 t23 f21.5 b22.** Coleburn is a rare whisky. A thoroughly enjoyable Coleburn is rarer still. So here's one you've just got to go and track down... 49.5%. The Whisky Agency, Germany.

CONVALMORE

Speyside, 1894–1985. William Grant & Sons. Closed.

Convalmore 1977 bott 2005 db **(91) n23 t23 f22 b23**. Must be blended with Botox, as there is no detrimental ageing to either nose or delivery. A quite lovely and charming whisky to remember this lost – and extremely rare - distillery by. 57.9%. 3900 bottles.

CRAGGANMORE

Speyside, 1870. Diageo. Working.

Cragganmore Aged 12 Years db **(81.5) n20 t21 f20 b20.5.** I have a dozen bottles of Cragganmore in my personal cellar dating from the early 90s when the distillery was first bottled as a Classic Malt. Their astonishing dexterity and charm, their naked celebration of all things Speyside, casts a sad shadow over this drinkable but drab and instantly forgettable expression. 40%

Cragganmore Aged 14 Years The Distillers Edition finished in port casks, dist 1993, bott 2007 db **(85) n22 t21 f21 b21.** The tightly closed fruit on the palate doesn't quite match the more expansive and complex nose. 40%

Cragganmore Special Release 2010 21 Years Old refill American oak, dist 1989 db **(95.5) n23.5** huge age, but the close knitted nature of the clean barley ensures all the strength required to keep the oak in check; the odd pine-laden tannin and even a touch of pineapple and honeydew melon gives the nod towards something a little exotic; **t24** you can ask little more from a Speyside-style delivery at this age and from bourbon. The barley is so wholesome and well integrated that the palate goes into immediate barley-juice overdrive; the oaks offer up some half-hearted cocoa but some full blown molasses. The result is a single malt of unstinting enormity, yet unambiguous magnificence; **f23.5** some light liquorice joins forces with the cocoa and molasses to underline the bourbon credentials. Massive age, the odd creak here and there. But never for a second is the quality breeched; **b24.5** what a fascinating, awe-inspiring dram. More or less at the very time this malt was being made, I remember talking to the manager at the then barely known Speyside distillery. He told me that the new Classic Malt 12-year-old was selected at that age because it was felt that, as a singleton (though not for blending), Cragganmore did not give its best over that age. I still tend to agree, in general. But here is a bottling which is making me look at this distillery is a new light...and that light is a beacon. I think the manager and I would have stood in amazement if we knew just how fine that young spirit would be when entering its 21st year. 112 per cent proof that you should never say never... *56%. nc ncf. Diageo. Fewer than 6000 bottles.*

A.D. Rattray Cragganmore 1997 cask no. 1494, dist 28 Mar 97, bott Jun 12 **(84.5)** n21 t22 f20.5 b21. Concentrated barley, but the oak offers an unwelcome tang. *46%. sc.*

Berry's Own Selection Cragganmore 2000 cask no. 3673, bott 2011 **(86.5)** n21 t22 f22 b21.5. Craggymalt, more like...! Technically less than perfect from a distillation perspective, as the nose and finish testifies. But my word! It is hard not to be impressed by the almost Glen Grant-esque, granite-faced barley which assails the taste buds! Hard and juicy. *56.8%. nc ncf sc.*

Duncan Taylor Dimensions Cragganmore 25 Years Old dist 1986 **(96)** n24.5 earthy without being smoky; sweet yet no trace of sugars; bourbony yet with no overpowering liquorice; fruity but with little sign of grape; spicy yet without aggression: enigmatic, ultra complex and magnificent; t24.5 rarely does a single mouthful last so long or take you on a journey seemingly without end: the spices hanging around the nose here gather in nibbling, tantalising squadrons; the sugars form and reform at regular intervals, each time moving towards a honeycomb weightiness; throughout the barley perches juicily on the taste buds and the dates move from old and dry to ripe and lush; f23 the spices hint at something of the vaguest smokiness; the oak takes on new cask form; b24 just track down a bottle and be prepared to give up two or three days of your life for a journey you'll never forget. Wondrously beautiful: the very reason why I can never fall out of love with whisky. *54.6%. sc.*

Duncan Taylor Rare Auld Cragganmore 18 Years Old cask no. 1385, dist 1993 **(83)** n20 t21 f22 b20. Not a spoiled sherry butt by any means. In fact, astonishingly clean. But one which swamps all else with mushy grape and allows little else to survive. Fantastically spiced, juicy but heavier than a sumo wrestler drowned in a vat of oloroso: OTT. *55.3%. sc.*

Duncan Taylor Rare Auld Cragganmore 23 Years Old cask no. 1964, dist 1987 **(86.5)** n22 t22 f21 b21.5. An exceptionally warming malt with a tendency to overplay its floral hand, which includes no shrinking violets. Spicy and dries with intent. *55.3%. sc.*

Duthies Cragganmore 18 Years Old bott Mar 12 **(88.5)** n22 if the barley was any sharper it'd cut your nose off; t23 gorgeously mouth-watering barley where age has been eschewed for almost three-dimensional malt: intense yet with the weight of the average soufflé...; f21 thin vanilla; b22.5 a flighty little hussey. *46%. sc. WM Cadenhead Ltd.*

Malts Of Scotland Cragganmore 1999 bourbon hogshead, cask no. MoS110012, dist 11 Dec 99, bott Oct 11 **(92)** n23 some neo Kentuckian notes with a serious bourbon edge to every aspect of the sweetness. There are peppery spices, but far out-battled by a stupendous orangey-liquorice note more usually associated with Wild Turkey...; t23.5 magnificent weight from the off...or should that be oof!! Because this fair takes the breath away, the shards of manuka honey in perfect sync with the thick vanilla and persistent liquorice; f22.5 long, with the oaks still having a major say, though the sugars last the pace longest; b23 a relentless tide of vanilla and barley. For the bourbon lovers among the malt connoisseurs. *55.1%. nc ncf sc.*

Master Of Malt Cragganmore 20 Year Old cask no. 1146, dist 1991 **(87)** n22 an attractive, slightly unusual nuttiness as found in a west coast salad; lively liquorice; t22 a thick bourbon richness to the intense barely; f21.5 big, a little unwieldy and some bittering oak; b21.5 no shortage of character and class, but perhaps on the wane. *53.5%. sc. Master Of Malt.*

Mo Òr Collection Cragganmore 1989 21 Years Old first fill bourbon hogshead, cask no. 2840, dist 14 Nov 89, bott 14 Mar 11 **(87.5)** n21.5 Almost like salt and lime on a tequila. Only without the tequila; t22.5 big, big age though the barley is trimming off the grey hairs. A salty tightness to the butterscotch and vanilla cream biscuit; somewhere some juicy barley is found to breathe the required life into the malt; f21.5 dry, tired but pleasantly spiced; b22 It is unlikely you will ever come across a saltier Cragganmore. Perhaps just a shade too much age for its own good, there is easily enough sugar to make a telling contribution and ramp up the complexity. *46%. nc ncf sc. Release No. 27. The Whisky Talker. 395 bottles.*

Scotch Malt Whisky Society Cask 37.49 Aged 12 Years refill hogshead, cask no. 840, dist 1999 **(89.5)** n22.5 exemplary Speyside: big barley with a slight grassy edge but enough oak from the cask to ensure a balancing dryness and weight; t23 just love that delivery: absolutely maxes out on the barley and clean enough to make your teeth sparkle; f22 long and malty but dispenses with complexity; b22 yummy! *54.2%. sc. Scotch Malt Whisky Society.*

Scotch Malt Whisky Society Cask 37.51 Aged 18 Years first fill sherry butt, cask no. 1379, dist 1993 **(92)** n23 faultless sherry butt: clean grape with no off notes and generous enough to allow a barley-bourbon thread for added complexity; t23 dry delivery with the oloroso showing its colours – literally! But soon the oak injects a spicy edge and the barley adds a fabulous salivating quality; **f23** long with chocolate fruit and nut. Yet still the barley keeps coming...; **b23** always great to find a malt which can stand up to a massive, clean sherry butt and offer a devastating return volley. *60%. sc. Scotch Malt Whisky Society.*

⫶⫶⫶ **Scotch Malt Whisky Society Cask 37.52 Aged 9 Years** refill hogshead, dist 11 Jun 02 **(87.5) n21** the malt never seems to quite gets to grips with the stark, yet thin oak; **t22.5** an unhappy delivery at first, showing the same imbalance as the nose. But, though showing youth, recovers beautifully as the barley intensifies as the oils kick in. The mid-ground becomes a wonderful battle between juicy young barley and the first signs of more mature cocoa-induced oak; **f22** soft oils help balance the buzz from the growing oak input; **b22** recovers adroitly from a lazy nose. *58.9%. nc ncf sc. 286 bottles.*

⫶⫶⫶ **Scotch Malt Whisky Society Cask 37.54 Aged 27 Years** refill hogshead, dist 24 Apr 85 **(93) n22** at first the muscle on the vanilla signals over-age. Slowly, delicate exotic fruits begin to escape from the cracks; **t24** yep: just about perfect weight on delivery. By the time the second phase of heavy artillery oak arrives, the ground has been perfectly prepared by the light, fruity but always lush malt concentrate on delivery. The mid-ground is unashamed mocha, with a sprig of mint; **f23** any threat of over oaking has receded and the vanilla is now pleasantly topped by a thin layer of orange blossom honey; **b24** stupendous whisky which gives a master class as to why blenders love this beauty to add such subtle flavour pyrotechnics to their blends... *52.4%. nc ncf sc. 215 bottles.*

⫶⫶⫶ **Wemyss 1989 Single Speyside "Evergreen Forest"** hogshead, dist 89, bott 13 **(85.5) n21.5 t22 f20 b21.** As though a light, intensely malty dram has been infused with lemon sherbet. *46%. sc. 326 bottles.*

Wemyss 1989 Single Speyside "Lemon Grove" hogshead, dist 1989, bott 2011 **(94.5) n24** delicate citrus caress the nose from all angles. A very fine dusting of grist ensures the sugars and barley notes meld effortlessly; the lightest throb of smoke offers a degree of backbone; **t24** textbook delivery: clean but by no means neutral as the immediate intensity of the barley is not only apparent, but so too is the fabulous growth in flavour; juicy with a sprinkling of icing sugar melting in the mouth with the grist; the citrus notes dovetail without ever gaining control; **f23** light vanillas remind you of the good age to this; **b23.5** the citrus and sugars have a much bigger say than the distillery usually allows. Sublime. *46%. sc. 371 bottles.*

CRAIGELLACHIE

Speyside, 1891. John Dewar & Sons. Working.

Berry's Own Selection Craigellachie 1991 cask no. 2715, bott 2011 **(83) n21 t22 f20 b20.5.** An oily, eye-watering barley-fest. *55.8%. nc ncf sc. Berry Bros & Rudd.*

Chieftain's Craigellachie Aged 13 Years Oloroso finish, dist Mar 99, bott 2012 **(89) n22** an excellent light smoke backdrop to the honey and citrus lead; **t23** quietly aggressive as the barley displays little subtlety; some jammy fruitiness as well; **f22.5** a tad bitter but good vanilla; **b22.5** seriously satisfying. *43%. nc ncf sc. Ian Macleod Distillers.*

⫶⫶⫶ **Chieftain's Craigellachie Aged 21 Years** hogshead, cask no. 2713, dist Mar 91, bott Apr 12 **(75.5) n19 t19 f18.5 b19.** As hot and aggressive as a tanked up imbiber of the same age falling out of a highland hostelry in the wee hours and looking for a punch up. *50%. nc ncf sc. Ian Macleod Distillers. 292 bottles.*

Duncan Taylor Dimensions Craigellachie 21 Years Old cask no. 5399, dist Aug 90, bott Jan 12 **(89) n22** charming exotic and citrus fruit combo; **t23** ethereal barley though the vanilla is more earthbound; very attractive spice; **f22** lengthened by just so oils. Excellent barley finale. **b22** Craigellachie in very fine fettle. *52%. nc ncf sc. Duncan Taylor & Co.*

⫶⫶⫶ **Gordon and MacPhail Connoisseurs Choice Craigellachie 1997 (91) n23** pancake with lashings of lemon juice; **t23** beware you down drown in your own saliva! As juicy a Speysider as you'll find, with the citrus prominent and the barley pristine; welcome spices and a light touch of hickory; **f22** wanders off towards cocoa and cool mint; **b23** captures this distillery at its most polite yet lively. Really lovely. *46%. ncf.*

Kingsbury "The Selection" Craigellachie 8 Years Old butt, cask no. 900085 & 900086, dist Aug 02, bott Apr 11 **(69.5) n17 t18 f17 b17.5.** Sad to say, but someone has selected a very poor cask. *43%. nc ncf. Japan Import Systems. 1,651 bottles.*

⫶⫶⫶ **Old Malt Cask Craigellachie Aged 13 Years** sherry butt, cask no. 9730, dist 00, bott 13 **(77) n18 t21 f19 b19.** Malty; sweet but off key during the vital movements. *50%. sc. 338 bottles.*

Old Malt Cask Craigellachie Aged 14 Years refill hogshead, cask no. 8185, dist Dec 97, bott Feb 12 **(87) n21.5** light, though busy, malt; **t23** much bigger on delivery: the barley offers a big, slightly oily surge. Spices and vanilla back up pleasantly; **f21** vanilla and cocoa; **b21.5** a very simple malt, but attractive. *50%. nc ncf sc. Douglas Laing & Co. 354 bottles.*

⫶⫶⫶ **Old Malt Cask Craigellachie Aged 15 Years** refill hogshead, cask no. 9344, dist Dec 97, bott Jan 13 **(89) n22** a light mini trace of smoke weaves through the barley and marzipan; **t22.5** exceptional delivery with the oils thickening the salivating barley. The middle ground holds a mocha theme; **f22** the most subtle wisps of smoke reappear amid the vanilla; **b22.5** sometimes this distillery can really sparkle on the palate and wow you. Here is one such juicy, yet gloriously subtle, example. *50%. sc. Douglas Laing & Co. 293 bottles.*

⋅❄⋅ **Old Masters Craigellachie 11 Years Old** cask no. 150, dist 00, bott Oct 12 **(86) n21.5 t22 f21 b21.5**. A competent Speysider with few party tricks. Concentrates almost exclusively on keeping the barley on an even keel. A little citrus zestiness provides the jazz. *57.3%. sc.*

Premier Barrel Craigellachie Aged 12 Years (75.5) n18 t20 f18.5 b19. Not even a tidal wave of barley can entirely overcome the limitations of the cask. *46%. nc ncf sc.*

⋅❄⋅ **Provenance Craigellachie Over 10 Years** sherry refill butt, cask no. 9421, dist 2002, bott 2012 **(74.5) n17.5 t19 f19 b19**. It's 7am. First whisky of my 12 hour tasting day and...bugger! Where's my bed? Despite the attractive smoked mint finale, woefully off key. *46%. nc, ncf, sc.*

Provenance Craigellachie Over 12 Years sherry butt, cask no. 8444, dist 1999, bott 2012 **(84.5) n21 t21.5 f21 b21**. An attractive malt which concentrates on a malty simplicity, but is not beyond adding a degree of sweetened seasoning to get the juices flowing. *46%. nc ncf sc.*

Provenance Craigellachie Over 12 Years sherry butt, cask no. 7607, dist Summer 1999, bott Summer 2011 **(76.3) n18 t19 f20 b19.5**. Worth tasting alongside the provenance cask 7974 just so you can see the difference between decent and very indifferent oak. *46%. nc ncf sc.*

Provenance Craigellachie Over 12 Years sherry butt, cask no. 7974, dist Autumn 1999, bott Winter 2011 **(88.5) n21** dusty, but flecks of fruit fight through; **t23** superb delivery full of understated power and barley at its most vibrant; **f22** attractively long with the spices fading then returning; **b22.5** a lovely dram swimming in personality. *46%. nc ncf sc.*

Scotch Malt Whisky Society Cask 44.50 Aged 18 Years refill barrel, cask no. 5793, dist 1993 **(89) n21.5** sharp and tangy, the barley appears to have been steeped in sea water...; **t23** good grief! the salty tang to the malt almost brings a tear to the eye; the thumping bourbony vanillas are no less saline intense; the middle has a light Walnut Whip feel; **f22** a little sweetened walnut oil creeps in to soften things a little; **b22.5** love to know where this cask has been kept: one of the most coastal Speyside whiskies you'll taste this year... *58.3%. sc.*

Scotch Malt Whisky Society Cask 44.51 Aged 22 Years refill hogshead, cask no. 3876, dist 1989 **(90) n22** a blender's treat: clean, playful barley offering just a little salt to the surviving grist; **t23** a beautiful delivery which draws the best out of both the barley and cask. The sugars are intact and err towards the standard white side; the barley is more complex and fill out to the full as the oils gather; **f22.5** exactly the butterscotch and vanilla style you'd expect. Though the return of the salt is a bit of a surprise; **b22.5** great to find the distillery in excellent form both in production and cask choice. Unostentatiously gorgeous. *53.7%. sc.*

⋅❄⋅ **Scotch Malt Whisky Society Cask 44.57 Aged 22 Years** refill hogshead, dist 13 Aug 90 **(86) n22 t22 f21 b21**. Hardly surprising that a distillery set at the very centre of Speyside should produce a malt which so ably summarises the region's style. Only a less than helpful old bourbon barrel detracts as the spirit is bustling with fresh malty intent and makes for a lively and busy chew. *52.9%. nc ncf sc. 305 bottles.*

The Warehouse Collection Craigellache Aged 10 Years bourbon hogshead, cask no. 212, dist 1999, bott 2009 **(94) n23.5** punchy barley: a little salt adding zest and zip; elsewhere, outstanding crushed walnut and hazel notes are topped by a distant and surprising strawberry jam sweetness; **t24** juicy: the barley is as clean as you can get without even beginning to bore. This is partly because of the complexity of the crisp sugars, as well as the fabulous marriage between the malt and marzipan. Again, though, it is the delicate salt which seems to arouse the complexity into a state of juicy excitement; **f23** long, still a multitude of barley notes but now late spices buzz in; **b23.5** my favourite age and cask type for this distillery. Rarely is Craigellachie these days displayed in better profile. This will be considered the bar all future 10-year-old Craigellachies will have to clear for years to come. *59%. sc. 311 bottles.*

DAILUAINE
Speyside, 1854. Diageo. Working.

Dailuaine 1997 The Manager's Choice db **(87.5) n21.5 t23 f21 b22**. One of the most enjoyable (unpeated!!) Dailuaines I've come across in an age. There is the usual distillery biff to this, but not without a honeyed safety net. Great fun. *58.6%*

Dailuaine Aged 16 Years bott lot no. L4334 db **(79) n19 t21 f20 b19**. Syrupy, almost grotesquely heavy at times; the lighter notes of previous bottlings have been lost under an avalanche of sugary, over-ripe tomatoes. One for those who want a massive dram. *43%*

Archives Dailuaine 1983 28 Years Old First Release hogshead, cask no. 865, dist 23 Feb 83, bott 4 Jan 12 **(85.5) n21 t22 f21 b21.5**. Talk about déjà vu! For a moment I thought I had tasted this before, or at least a more emboldened version of this thin but pleasant offering. Then spotted my Mo Or 1983 notes....!! *47.3%. nc ncf sc. Whiskybase B.V. 265 bottles.*

⋅❄⋅ **Chieftain's Dailuaine Aged 30 Years** hogshead, cask no. 3893, dist Oct 82, bott Jan 13 **(83.5) n21 t21 f21 b20.5**. Even after all this time, remains a malt confined by its own lack of character despite offering an attractive if brief mouth-watering quality. Interesting how some distillates which offer little when young, such as Caperdonich, blossom into grandee malts as the whiskers grey. Not this guy, which perhaps would have served an old blend to more telling effect. *52%. nc ncf sc. Ian Macleod Distillers. 282 bottles.*

⠿ **Master of Malt Dailuaine 15 Years Old** hogshead, cask no. 15562, dist 25 Nov 97, bott 1 Apr 13 **(94.5) n23.5** complex and busy with the vanillas skipping between barley and citrus; **t24** salivating at first, but the lightest of oils ensures fabulous depth to the barley sugar. There is a fabulous spice sub structure and a touch of ulmo honey strengthened with toasted honeycomb; **f23** Maryland cookie, nuts, spice and light chocolate; **b24** Dailuine in the kind of nick and showing a complexity very rarely seen for this distillery. This you must experience..! *55.7%. sc. 282 bottles.*

Mo Ôr Collection Dailuaine 1983 27 Years Old first fill bourbon hogshead, cask no. 869, dist 23 Feb 83, bott 2 Dec 10 **(87.5) n21** thin and vaguely apple-fruity but with the barley still having a say; **t22.5** clean, salivating with a butterscotch lid to the gooseberry pie; **f22** some more plaintiff calls of apple but now the vanilla grips like a vice; **b22** a rough and ready dram. The bite is more young cider brandy than malt. But the overall effect shimmers with pour-me-another-one allure... *46%. nc ncf sc. Release No. 20. The Whisky Talker. 407 bottles.*

⠿ **Provenance Dailuaine Over 10 Years** sherry cask, cask no. 9195, dist Autumn 02, bott Autumn 12 **(88) n22** you can stand the oak up in the oils; some French bread sweetness lightens things, as do the sultanas; **t22** the heavyweight sugars punch hard while the oak offers backbone; some barley sugar refreshes slightly; **f22** long with varying shades of intensity and depth to the vanilla and oil; **b22** though it sticks to its oft repeated style of hefty oils and sugars, enough barley gushes through to make for an enjoyable if obvious malt. Helped along the way by an above average cask. *46%. nc ncf sc. Douglas Laing & Co.*

Provenance Dailuaine Over 11 Years sherry butt, cask no. 8012, dist Spring 2000, bott Winter 2012 **(84) n21 t21 f21 b21.** A pleasant malt in a mildly fruity, juicy nondescript kind of way. *46%. nc ncf sc. Douglas Laing & Co.*

Provenance Dailuaine Over 12 Years sherry butt, cask no. 8434, dist Autumn 1999, bott Spring 2012 **(84.5) n21.5 t20.5 f21.5 b21.** A warming malt where you feel the stills were going at some lick when this was distilled. Attractive mint chocolate on the finish. *46%. nc ncf sc.*

⠿ **Provenance Dailuaine Over 15 Years** refill hogshead, cask no. 9641, dist Summer 97, bott Spring 13 **(83) n20 t21 f21 b21.** Malty, salty and sugary. And thin enough to be on whisky weight watchers..*46%. nc ncf. Douglas Laing & Co.*

Riegger's Selection Dailuaine 1998 bourbon cask, cask no. 3396, dist 31 Mar 98, bott 6 May 12 **(79.5) n20 t19 f20.5 b20.** A distillery known to have its odd off day when distilling. This salty and salivating effort came from one of them. *58.5%. nc ncf sc. 298 bottles.*

Scotch Malt Whisky Society Cask 41.50 Aged 30 Years refill hogshead, cask no. 9135, dist 1980 **(86) n21.5 t21 f22 b21.5.** By no means a shy character and brimming with chocolate nut. Always tangy, a little honeycomb towards the finish, too. *53.5%. sc.*

⠿ **Scotch Malt Whisky Society Cask 41.54 Aged 8 Years** 1st fill barrel, 11 May 04 **(81) n22 t19 f20 b20.** Despite the gooseberry and lime dust, robust to the point of aggressive in its malty single-mindedness. *58.7%. nc ncf sc. 217 bottles.*

⠿ **Scotch Malt Whisky Society Cask 41.56 Aged 24 Years** refill hogshead, 28 Aug 88 **(84) n22.5 t21.5 f20.5 b20.5.** Frantic sugars cool down the fiery-thin spirit. For the odd moment, it seems more like the spirit from an over-excited German column still. Attractive grapefruit and pineapple nose, though. *51.9%. nc ncf sc. 280 bottles.*

Scott's Selection Dailuaine 1983 bott 2011 **(84) n21 t23 f20 b20.** Marked with all the usual ticks and crosses. But a few extra ticks, and even the odd gold star, for the gorgeous exuberance of the honey-sweetened barley on delivery. *57.9%. Speyside Distillers.*

⠿ **That Boutique-y Whisky Company Dailuaine** batch 1 **(83.5) n22.5 t22 f19 b20.** Great that Dailuaine offers a bit of sheen to its normal dose of sugar-barley. Pity about the bitter oak, though. *51.5%. Master Of Malt. 201 bottles.*

⠿ **That Boutique-y Whisky Dailuine 15 Year Old (94.5) n23.5** complex and busy with the vanillas skipping between barley and citrus; **t24** salivating at first, but the lightest of oils ensures fabulous depth and to the barley sugar. There is a fabulous spice sub structure and a touch of ulmo honey strengthened with toasted honeycomb; **f23** Maryland cookie, nuts, spice and light chocolate; **b24** Dailuine in the kind of nick and showing a complexity very rarely seen for this distillery. This you must experience..! *55.7%*

DALLAS DHU
Speyside, 1899–1983. Closed. Now a museum.

Gordon & MacPhail Rare Vintage Dallas Dhu 1979 (94.5) n23 marginally earthy but probably only there for the fruit and nuts to grow in; green banana and toasted yam lead, pecan pie follows behind; **t23.5** how can barley melt in the mouth after 32 years? It defies logic and description. What makes it work so well, is that the base and baritone sugars from the oak never for a moment attempt to drown the tenor from the grist. Often that is the key to a whisky's success and here it is demonstrated perfectly: it means the complexity levels remain high at all times and the depth of oak controlled; f23.5 long, with the vanilla enjoying a nutty depth, moving into a more deliciously praline oiliness. The tannins are firm enough to remind us that 1979 was a long time ago now but not a single hint of oaky degradation. Clear, confident, strident notes from first to last; b24 I can hardly recall the last time a bottling from this distillery popped along – depressing to think I am old enough to remember when they were so relatively common they were being sold on special offer! It was always a class act; it's closure an act of whisky vandalism, whether it be preserved as a museum or not. This, even after all these years, shows the extraordinary quality we are missing day in, day out. 43%

DALMORE
Highands (Northern), 1839. Whyte and Mackay. Working.

The Dalmore 12 Years Old db (90) n22 mixed dates: both dry and juicy; t23 fat, rich delivery with a wonderful dovetailing of juicy barley and thick, rumbling fruit; f22.5 lots of toffee on the finish, but gets away with it thanks to the sheer depth to the barley and the busy sherry sub-plot; b22.5 has changed character of late yet remains underpowered and with a shade too much toffee. But such is the quality of the malt in its own right it can overcome any hurdles placed before it to ensure a real mouth-filling, rumbustious dram. 40%

The Dalmore Dee Dram 12 Years Old db (63.5) n15.5 t17 f14 b16. Words fail me...40%

The Dalmore 15 Years Old db (83.5) n21 t21 f20.5 b21. Another pleasant Dalmore that coasts along the runway but simply fails to get off the ground. The odd off note here and there, but it's the blood orange which shines brightest. 40%

The Dalmore 18 Years Old db (76.5) n19 t21 f18 b18.5. Heaps of caramel and the cask choice might have been better. 43%

The Dalmore 21 Years Old db (87) n22 t23 f20 b22. Bottled elegance. 43%

The Dalmore Forty Years Old db (82) n23 t20 f19 b20. Doubtless my dear friend Richard Paterson will question whether I have the ability to spot a good whisky if it ran me over in a ten ton truck. But I have to say here that we have a disappointing malt: I had left this too late on in writing this year's (2008) Bible as a treat. But it wasn't to be. A soft delivery: but of what? Hard to exactly pin down what's going on here as there is so much toffee and fruit that the oak and barley have been overwhelmed. Pleasant, perhaps, but it's all rather dull and passionless. Like going through the motions with an old lover. Adore the sherry-trifle/toffee mousse nose, though... 40%

The Dalmore Astrum Aged 40 Years db (89) n23.5 t21 f22 b22.5. This guy is all about the nose. The oak is too big for the overall framework and the balance hangs by a thread. Yet somehow the overall effect is impressive. Another summer and you suspect the whole thing would have snapped... 42%

The Dalmore Aurora Aged 45 Years db (90.5) n25 unquestionably an intriguing and engaging nose, full of subtleties and quirky side streets. Initially, all these sub plots and intrigues are to do with oak and very little else. However, the spices once located are a treat and open the door to the delicate boiled fruit which, after making a tentative entrance, begins to inject the required sweetness; give ten minutes in the glass to discover something quite sublime and faultless... t22 rounded on delivery but again it's all about the oak which piles up untidily on the palate, though the odd exotic fruit note can be detected. Salt dovetails with that fruit but it is heading downhill... f21.5 some vaguely malty vanilla but the oak is now dominating though some mocha does come to the rescue; b22 sophisticated for sure. But so huge is the oak on the palate, it cannot hope to match the freakish brilliance of the nose. 45%

The Dalmore 50 Years Old db (88) n21 t19 f25 b23. Takes a while to warm up, but when it does becomes a genuinely classy and memorable dram befitting one of the world's great and undervalued distilleries. 52%

The Dalmore Candela Aged 50 Years db (96) n25 there you go: that's the next half hour to 45 minutes taken up...trying to unravel this one. Fresh fruity frame, but the picture in the middle is far more difficult to understand. Dates – both dried and juicy – mingle with finest quality Lubec marzipan paste (sans chocolate) while a few spices nip in to say 'hullo'; clean, relaxed... and very sprightly for its age; t24 immediate onrush of oaks, offset by a cherry sauce and later plain chocolate fondant to ensure any bitterness is kept in check; elsewhere an improbable layering of barley juice and fruit again makes a mockery of the age; f23.5 for a whisky reaching half a century, curiously reserved with the oaks now really starting to get a degree of bitterness generated; a thin line of chocolate and raisin helps keep that bitterness at acceptable levels; b23.5 just one of those whiskies which you come across only a handful of times in your life. All because a malt makes it to 50 does not mean it will automatically be great. This, however, is a masterpiece, the end of which seemingly has never been written. 50% (bottled at 45%).

The Dalmore Eos Aged 59 Years db (95) n24.5 extraordinary pulsing of rich, dry sherry notes: nutty and polished oak in one of the finer Mayfair antique shops or clubs. The moistest, choicest Lubeck marzipan with a thread of Jaffa jam and, as the whisky settles into its stride, this moves to Jaffa cakes with heavy dark chocolate; very limited spice, but the salt levels grow.; t24 ultra dry delivery despite the juices flowing from the very first moment: the grape is beautifully firm and holds together light oils and burgeoning oak which threaten to inject a weighty toastiness; the mid ground though is a triumph of glorious lightly molassed vanilla notes with strands of barley; spices buzz and fizz and add even further life; f22.5 a light off-key bitterness knocks off a mark or two, but the cocoa and burnt raisin charge to the rescue; b24 for those of you who thought this was a camera, let me put you in the picture. This is one well developed whisky, but by no means over exposed, as it would have every right to be after nearly 60 years. Indeed: it is one of those drams which utterly confounds and amazes. I specially chose this as the 1001st new whisky for the 2012 Bible, and those of us old enough to be young when most of its sister casks were hauled off for blending, there was an advert in the '60s which said: "1,001 cleans a big, big carpet…for less than half a crown." Well this 1001 cleans a big, big palate. But I can't see a bottle of this majestic malt going for as little as that… 44%

The Dalmore 62 Years Old db (95) n23 PM or REV marked demerara potstill rum, surely? Massive coffee presence, clean and enormous, stunning, topdrawer peat just to round things off; t25 this is brilliant: pure silk wrapping fabulous moist fruitcake soaked in finest oloroso sherry and then weighed with peat which somehow has defied nature and survived in cask all these years. I really cannot fault this: I sit here stunned and in awe; f24 perfect spices with flecks of ginger and lemon rind; b24 if I am just half as beautiful, elegant and fascinating as this by the time I reach 62, I'll be a happy man. Somehow I doubt it. A once-in-a-lifetime whisky — something that comes around every 62 years, in fact. Forget Dalmore Cigar Malt — even I might be tempted to start smoking just to get a full bottle of this. 40.5%

The Dalmore 1263 King Alexander III db (86) n22 t22.5 f20 b21.5. Starts brightly with all kinds of barley sugar, fruit and decent age and oak combinations, plus some excellent spice prickle. So far, so good…and obviously thoughtfully and complexly structured. But then vanishes without trace on finish. 40%

The Dalmore 1978 db (89.5) n23.5 t22 f21.5 b22.5. A seriously lovely old dram which is much weightier on the palate than nose. 47.1%. 477 bottles.

The Dalmore 1979 db (84) n21 t21.5 f20 b21.5. Hard to find a more rounded malt. Strangely earthy, though. 42%. 487 bottles.

The Dalmore 1980 db (81.5) n19 t21 f20.5 b21. Wonderful barley intensity on delivery does its best to overcome the so-so nose and finale. 40%

The Dalmore Matusalem 1981 db (91.5) n23 muscular and beautifully primed with soft herbs amid the fruit; marmalade at the bottom of an old jar; t23.5 now, do I love that delivery! Waxy and thick in a uniquely Whyte and Mackay style, there is a clever muscovado-molasses mix which not just ramps up the sugars but the weight and depth, also; f22.5 some tangy notes while the sugars fight a rearguard action with the bittering oak; b22.5 had someone tied me to a rack and kept pulling until I said this could be something other than a W&M production, I would have defied them to the bitter end… 44%. 497 bottles.

The Dalmore 1981 Amoroso Sherry Finesse amoroso sherry wood cask db (85.5) n21 t22 f21.5 b21. A very tight, fruity, dram which gives away its secrets with all the enthusiasm of an agent under torture. Enjoyable to a degree… but bloody hard work. 42%

The Dalmore Mackenzie 1992 American oak/port pipes, bott 2009 db (88.5) n23 t22 f21 b22.5. I suppose you could say that such is the influence of the grape that this is a tad one dimensional. But such is the grim state of wine casks in the industry today, one is forgiven for falling on bended knee and kissing the bottle. Though even this isn't without its sulphury failings… 46%

⠿ **The Dalmore 1995 Vintage Distillery Manager Exclusive** db (87) n22 soft, mildly spiced dates and yam; t22 soft, mildly spiced milk fudge with some lovely malt undertones; f21.5 more milk fudge…sans spice; b21.5 pleasant. But seems stuck in a single gear. 40%. Whisky Shop Exclusive. 1800 bottles.

The Dalmore Vintage 2001 Limited Edition db (84.5) n21 t22 f20.5 b21. Ah… a Dalmore of straw colour displaying such delicate intricacies with the barley…complex, especially with the varying degrees of malt to the oils… What???? I was asleep? I was dreaming…? What do we have here? Oh. Yet another mahogany-coloured Dalmore. Another Dalmore so thick, nutty-toffeed and chewy you can hardly tell where the story starts and ends. Or exactly what the story is that differs from the others… Yes, overall a generally pleasant experience but the feeling of déjà vu and underachievement is depressingly overwhelming. 48%

The Dalmore Rivers Collection Dee Dram Season 2011 db (81.5) n20 t22.5 f19 b20. Where the previous bottling was a complete disaster, this one is friendly and approachable. Still don't expect anything two dimensional on the finish as the caramel attack and a strand of bitterness dries your taste buds to squeaking point. But the delivery is a very pleasant, chewy affair for sure. 40%

The Dalmore Rivers Collection Tweed Dram Season 2011 db (86) n21 t22 f21.5 b21.5. Silky and slinky, a real soup of a malt in which the barley occasionally rises high to deliciously juicy effect. 40%

The Dalmore Rivers Collection Tay Dram Season 2011 db (86.5) n22.5 t23 f20 b21. Despite the house toffee-neutered finale and the odd but obvious cask-related off note, there is still plenty to enjoy here. 40%

The Dalmore Cabernet Sauvignon db (79) n22 t19 f19 b19. Too intense and soupy for its own good. 45%

The Dalmore Castle Leod db (77) n18.5 t21 f18.5 b19. Thumpingly big and soupy. More fruit than you can wave a wasp at. But, sadly, the sting comes with the slightly obvious off note. 46%

The Dalmore Ceti db (91.5) n24 a nose for fruitcake lovers everywhere: ripe cherries and blood orange abound and work most attractively with the slightly suety, muscovado enriched body...; t23.5 the nose demands a silky delivery and that's exactly what you get. Rich fruit notes form the principle flavour profile but the backing salivating barley and spice is spot on; the mid ground becomes a little saltier and more coastal...; f21.5 a vague bitterness to the rapidly thinning finale, almost a pithy element, which is slightly out of sync with the joys of before; b22.5 a Ceti which warbles rather well... 44.7%

The Dalmore Cigar Malt Reserve Limited Edition db (73.5) n19 t19.5 f17 b18. One assumes this off key sugarfest is for the cigar that explodes in your face... 44%

The Dalmore Cromartie dist 1996 db (78.5) n20 t22 f17.5 b19. Always hard to forecast what these type of bottlings may be like. Sadly there is a sulphur-induced bitterness and tightness to this guy which undermines the more attractive marmalade notes. 45%

The Dalmore Gran Reserva sherry wood and American white oak casks db (82.5) n22 t21.5 f19 b20. An improvement on the near nonentity this once was. But still the middle and finish are basic and lacking sophistication or substance outside a broad sweet of oaky chocolate toffee. Delightful mixture of blood orange and nuts on the approach, though. 40%

-:- **The Dalmore Valour** db (85.5) n21 t22 f21 b21.5. Not often you get the words "Valour" and "fudge" in the same sentence. 40%. Whyte and Mackay. Travel Retail Exclusive.

The Dalmore Visitor Centre Exclusive db (95.5) n25 this isn't just about fruit: this is a lesson in a nosing glass in how the marriage and equilibrium between salt, sugars, barley and delicate fruit juices should be arranged. There is not an off note; no party dominates; the complexity is beguiling as the picture shifts and changes in the glass every few seconds. Also, how the weight of the whisky is essential to balance. It is, frankly, the perfect malt whisky nose... t24 so off we go on a journey around about fifteen fruit levels, half that number of sugar intensities and a fabulous salty counter. Close your eyes and be seduced...; f22.5 a minor blemish as a vaguely bitter note from the oak interjects. Luckily, the thick barley sugar is in there to repair the damage; remains salty to the very end; b24 not exactly the easiest distillery to find but a bottle of this is worth the journey alone. I have tasted some sumptuous Dalmores over the last 30-odd years. But this one stands among the very finest. 46%

Master Of Malt Dalmore 14 Year Old dist 1996 (90) n21.5 Digestive biscuit which needs to cut down on the salt content slightly; t24 oh, yes! The lack of caramel means you can see with breathtaking clarity the most fabulous complexity to a delivery: intense, ultra-clean barley with vivid, almost eye-watering salt and sugars opening the way for the zesty praline middle...my God! You want to kiss its very beauty...!! f22 soft vanillas tame the salty fire, alas, but the late cocoa compensates pleasantly; b22.5 always wonderful to meet a exquisitely naked Dalmore, as so often it is wrapped in an opaque gown of caramel. 55.5%. sc.

-:- **Old Malt Cask Dalmore Aged 16 Years** refill hogshead, cask no. 9816, dist Oct 96, bott May (89) n21.5 curious cold sausage meat and oat cakes; t23 back to big malt: a barley and sugar porridge of a dram; light spices weave among the muscovado; f22 excellent length with the rich barley sugar and cocoa-vanilla hand-in-hand; b22.5 deliciously neat and tidy despite the odd nose. Superb! 50%. nc ncf sc. 371 bottles.

Provenance Dalmore Over 10 Years refill hogshead, cask no. 7645, Spring 2001, Summer 2011 (84.5) n21 t21.5 f21 b21. Malty, gristy sweet and very tame. 46%. nc ncf sc.

-:- **Provenance Dalmore Over 11 Years** refill hogshead, cask no. 6879, dist Spring 99, bott Winter 11 (86) n21.5 t22 f21 b21.5. From the sweaty armpit nose, you know this is going to be interesting without hitting the heights. Revels in a rich digestive biscuit graininess but the bitter orange finish dashes hopes of further complexity. 46%. nc ncf sc. Douglas Laing & Co.

-:- **Provenance Dalmore Over 12 Years** refill hogshead, cask no. 9501, dist Summer 2000, bott Spring 2013 (86) n21 t21.5 f22 b21.5. Glutinous, tangy and with the intensity of the malt and barley sugar growing attractively along the road. 46%. nc ncf sc. Douglas Laing & Co.

⁘ **Wemyss 1997 Single Highland "Gooseberry Marmalade"** hogshead, dist 97, bott 13 (**90**) n22 a vague fruitiness polishes the unchecked barley; t22.5 vivid barley at its most uniquely Dalmore intensity: when in good oak like this the malt gets every opportunity to sparkle on the palate, its sheen intensified by the lightest coating of beech honey; f22.5 dries ponderously and, therefore, satisfyingly with the silky sugars battling against the slowly rising spice and oak; b23 a lovely dram for sure. But what on earth is "gooseberry marmalade"? Marmalade, in the English language, is made from citrus, including the peel. The huge Surrey garden in which I spent my formative summers had a great number of gooseberry bushes and I grew up on gooseberry jam made by my mother. And my fridge or larder is seldom out of a commercially made jar of it. Either way, no gooseberries here – jam or "marmalade" - or citrus, either! Apricot and under-ripe greengage...now you're talking...!! 46%. sc. 372 bottles.

DALWHINNIE
Highlands (Central), 1898. Diageo. Working.
Dalwhinnie 15 Years Old db (**95**) n24 sublime stuff: a curious mixture of coke smoke and peat-reek wafts teasingly over the gently honied malt. A hint of melon offers some fruit but the caressing malt stars; t24 that rarest of combinations: at once silky and malt intense, yet at the same time peppery and tin-hat time for the tastebuds, but the silk wins out and a sheen of barley sugar coats everything, soft peat included; f23 some cocoa and coffee notes, yet the pervading slightly honied sweetness means that there is no bitterness that cannot be controlled; b24 a malt it is hard to decide whether to drink or bath in: I suggest you do both. One of the most complete mainland malts of them all. Know anyone who reckons they don't like whisky? Give them a glass of this – that's them cured. Oh, if only the average masterpiece could be this good. 43%

⁘ **Dalwhinnie 25 Years Old Special Release 2012** Rejuvenated American Oak hogshead, dist 1987, bott 2012 db (**92**) n23.5 toasty with lashings of hickory and maple syrup. A little sappy but the busy saltiness lifts the barley; t23.5 a busy delivery of light sugars and spice; red liquorice and acacia honey combine beautifully. The spice rises as the oiliness increases; f22 thins as the impact of the oak lessens. Just the vaguest hint of smoke drifts in; b23 more from the mountains of Kentucky than central Scotland. Anyone with a bourbon bent and a sweet tooth will adore this. As will bee keepers.. 52.1 %. nc ncf. Diageo.

DEANSTON
Highlands (Perthshire), 1966. Burn Stewart Distillers. Working.
Deanston 6 Years Old db (**83**) n20 t21 f22 b20. Great news for those who remember how good Deanston was a decade or two ago: it's on its way back. A delightfully clean dram with its trademark honey character restored. A little beauty slightly undermined by caramel. 40%

Deanston 12 Years Old db (**74**) n18 t19 f18.5 b18.5. It is quite bizarre how you can interchange this with Tobermory in style; or, rather, at least the faults are the same. 46%. ncf.

Deanston Aged 12 Years db (**75**) n18 t21.5 f17.5 b18. The delivery is, for a brief moment, a malty/orangey delight. But the nose is painfully out of sync and finish is full of bitter, undesirable elements. A lot of work still required to get this up to a second grade malt, let alone a top flight one. 46.3%. ncf. Burn Stewart.

Deanston 1967 casks 1051-2, filled Friday 31st Mar 67 db (**90**) n23 t23 f21 b23. The oak is full on but there is so much class around that cannot gain control. A Perthshire beauty. 50.7%

Deanston Virgin Oak db (**90**) n22.5 does exactly what it says on the tin: absolutely brimming with virgin oak. To the cost of all other characteristics. And don't expect a bourbon style for a second: this is sharp-end tannins where the sugars have their own syrupy point of entry; t23 now those sugars dissolve with some major oak attached: many years back, I tasted a paste made from roasted acorns and brown sugar...not entirely dissimilar; f22.5 continues to rumble contentedly in the oakiest possible manner...but now with some fizzy spice; b22 frankly. Don't expect this to taste anything like Scotch... 46.3%

⁘ **Kingsbury Deanston Aged 14 Years** hogshead, cask no. 1989, dist 97 (**88**) n21 two toned thin spirit coupled with a huskier, muskier depth; t22.5 attractive lightly molassed fruit and nut; f22.5 warmed by some marauding stem ginger; b22 a very decent Deanston experience. 55.1%. nc ncf Japan Import System. 281 bottles.

Marks & Spencer Deanston Aged 12 Years db (**84.5**) n20.5 t22 f21 b21. It's been a while since I found so much honeyed malt in a Deanston. Echoes of 20 years ago. 40%. UK.

Marks & Spencer Deanston Aged 17 Years Limited Edition db (**88.5**) n20 t23.5 f22.5 b22.5. Overcomes a taught, off-key nose to open into something full of juice, fruity intrigue. Really enjoyed this one. 46.3%. ncf. 979 bottles.

⁘ **Master of Malt Deanston Aged 19 Years** refill hogshead, dist 16 Dec 92, bott 20 Nov 12 (**86.5**) n21.5 t22 f21.5 b21.5. Technically on the thin side on delivery and finish and possessing a degree of burn. But very hard not to thoroughly enjoy the creamy barley middle and the gamut of sugars surrounding it. A little charmer. *53.4%. sc. 260 Bottles.*

Mo Òr Collection Deanston 1995 15 Years Old first fill bourbon hogshead, cask no. 382, dist 3 Feb 95, bott 28 Jan 11 **(74.5) n18 t20 f18.5 b19**. Fights back from a dreadful nose and at times offers a compensating sweetness to the distinct barley. But not very good whisky is not very good whisky. *46%. nc ncf sc. Release No. 40. The Whisky Talker. 506 bottles.*

Riegger's Selection Deanston 1992 bourbon cask, cask no. 11, dist 16 Dec 92, bott 11 Feb 11 **(94) n23** intricate citrus bolsters the delicate barley tones. The vanillas are clean and supportive; cocoa lurks somewhere in the background; **t24** the salivating barley and sugars engage in the most comfortable harmony; the odd mocha note gives way to a growing display of delicate spices; the overall weight and pace nears perfection...; **f23** drier, but those excellent mildly gristy sugars still hold the upper hand; the mocha returns now for a more dominating role; **b24** easily one of the best Deanstons I have tasted for a very long time. Worth finding! *57.2%. nc ncf sc. Viktor-Riegger GmbH. 178 bottles.*

⠿ **That Boutique-y Whisky Company Deanston** batch 1 **(94) n23** Deanston-by-the-Sea! Where on earth has this salt come from? Sits comfortably with the more usual Perthshire honey....and even a touch of seaweed for the bees to pollinate; **t24** massive honey but what works is the complex oak strata which absorbs the silky barley with aplomb; the middle is a very thick dose of malt...gosh! **f23** a top-notch cask reverberates with tangy salt and a light butterscotch and honey fade; **b24** wow! Not seen Deanston in this kind of nick for about 15 years! I am quite taken aback. Just grab some of that honey...!! *50.8%. 218 bottles.*

The Whisky Agency Deanston 35 Years Old dist 1977 **(78) n21 t20 f18 b19**. A little unlucky. What was clearly good spirit to start off with has gone through the wood. Some decent moments, but doesn't gel. *40.4%. sc.*

DUFFTOWN

Speyside, 1898. Diageo. Working.

Director's Cut Dufftown Aged 30 Years sherry butt, cask no. 8232, dist Mar 1982, bott Mar 2012 **(92) n22.5** near impenetrable nutty sherry which binds and gags the barley like a thief does a bank manager before running off with the loot; **t24** a bulldozer of a slightly dirty malt meets the express train of concentrated sherry head on. The result is almost mesmeric; the taste buds witness some of the biggest flavours of the year crash over them in random fashion. Walnut oil softens the blow...but only by minimal amounts; **f23.5** as the dust settles some spices replace the earlier sugars; **b22** displays all the subtlety of a kick in the nuts. But is strangely and compellingly delicious. *51.7%. nc ncf sc. Douglas Laing & Co. 189 bottles.*

Gordon & MacPhail Connoisseurs Choice Dufftown 1999 **(85.5) n20.5 t22.5 f21 b21.5**. If you are going to find a very drinkable Dufftown, you have to trust Gordon and MacPhail – as usual. Even so, a workmanlike rather than spectacular malt, though the surprise tang of gooseberry amid the barley is more than attractive. *43%*

⠿ **Gordon and MacPhail Connoisseurs Choice Dufftown 2002** **(84.5) n21 t22 f20.5 b21.** Dufftown at its very cleanest. The sugars are full on and spices dip in usefully. Hardly inspirational but will attract barley freaks. *46%. ncf.*

⠿ **Old Malt Cask Dufftown Aged 30 Years** refill hogshead, cask no. 9272, dist Nov 82, bott Nov 12 **(73) n19 t19 f17 b18**. Sweet, thick, hot and unimpressive. The house style, in fact. *50%. sc. Douglas Laing & Co. 174 bottles.*

⠿ **Provenance Dufftown Over 13 Years** refill hogshead, cask no. 9659, dist Autumn 99. Bott Spring 13 **(85) n22 t21.5 f20 b21.5**. Typically syrupy and one dimensional for the distillery with only the spices giving the profound molassed malt an alternative vibe. *46%. nc ncf. Douglas Laing & Co.*

Scott's Selection Dufftown 1988 bott 2011 **(76) n20 t19 f18 b19**. Despite the score, this isn't too bad a mark for this distillery during this era. The trouble was, they were producing a syrupy type of malt, devoid of anything approaching subtlety and displaying a "dirtiness" to the finish in particular (to quote someone who worked there at the time, and who took me through the made back in about 88/89). Even after 23 years in the cask, you can see things have little changed. The sugars, quite simply, are out of control. *58.3%. Speyside Distillers.*

Silver Seal Dufftown Over 28 Years Old dist 1983, bott Dec 2011 **(88.5) n22** light with an attractive mealy composition. Biscuity in a fruit shortcake kind of way; only the odd glimpse of the usual dirtiness; **t23.5** wow! An enormous delivery with the barley in near concentrate form; the mixed sugars are of the molassed and aged maple syrup variety; **f21** dirty and spiced; **b22** always brave to bottle from this distillery. And, for once, it has paid off. Somehow manages to convert its failings into its strengths. *54.2%. sc. Silver Seal Whisky Company.*

Singleton of Dufftown 12 Years Old db **(71) n18 t18 f17 b18**. A roughhouse malt that's finesse-free. For those who like their tastebuds Dufft up a bit... *40%*

EDRADOUR
Highlands (Perthshire), 1837. Signatory Vintage. Working.

Edradour Aged 10 Years db **(79)** n18 t20 f22 b19. A dense, fat malt that tries offer something along the sherry front but succeeds mainly in making a whisky cloyingly sweet and unfathomable. Some complexity to the finish compensates. 43%

Edradour Ballachin #1 The Burgundy Casks db **(63)** n17 t16 f15 b15. A bitter disappointment in every sense. Were the Burgundy casks sulphur treated? I'd say so. Something completely off-key here. A shocker. 46%

Edradour Ballachin #2 Madeira Matured db **(89)** n22 t22 f23 b22. On the nose and entry I didn't quite get the point here: putting a massively peated malt like this in a Madeira cask is a bit like putting Stan Laural into bed with Marylyn Munro. Thankfully doesn't come out a fine mess and the Madeira certainly has a vital say towards the beautifully structured finale. It works! I feel the hand of a former Laphroaig man at work here. 46%

⁘ **Master Of Malt Edradour 27 Years Old Lost Bottlings Series** dist 68, bott 95 **(61)** n13 t18 f15 b16. A shocker. Very similar in character to some Littlemill and Glenora I have encountered over the years where way too much soap was stuffed into the still or washback as a calming exercise. Not saying that happened here, of course...45.8%

FETTERCAIRN
Highland (Eastern), 1824. Whyte and Mackay. Working.

Fettercairn 12 Year Old db **(66)** n14 t19 f16 b17. If the nose doesn't get you, what follows probably will...Grim doesn't quite cover it. 40%

Fettercairn 30 Years Old db **(73)** n19 t18 f18 b18. A bitter disappointment. Literally. 46.3%

Fettercairn 40 Years Old db **(92)** n23 technically, not exactly how you want a 40-y-o to be: a bit like your old silver-haired granny knitting in her rocking chair...and sporting tattoos. But I also have to say there is no shortage of charm, too...and like some old tattooed granny, you know it is full of personality and has a tale to tell... t24 I was expecting dates and walnuts... and I have not been let down. A veritable date and walnut pie you can chew on until your jaw is numb; the sharp raisiny notes, too, plus a metallic sheen which reminds you of its provenance...; f22 those burned raisins get just a little more burned...; b23 yes, everyone knows my views on this distillery. But I'll have to call this spade a wonderfully big, old shovel you can't help loving...just like the memory of me tattooed ol' granny... 40%. 463 bottles.

Fettercairn 1824 db **(69)** n17 t19 f16 b17. By Fettercairn standards, not a bad offering. Relatively free from its inherent sulphury and rubbery qualities, this displays a sweet nutty character not altogther unattractive – though caramel plays a calming role here. Need my arm twisting for a second glass, though. 40%

⁘ **Malts Of Scotland Fettercairn 1990** bourbon hogshead, cask no. 13004, dist May 90, bott Jan 13 **(69)** n16 t18 f17 b18. I am trying to think of something positive to say about this sickly sweet, off-key mess of a pot still malt. I admit defeat. 51.5%. nc ncf sc. 96 bottles.

Old Malt Cask Fettercairn Aged 16 Years refill hogshead, cask no. 7725, dist Nov 95, bott Nov 11 **(71.5)** n18 t18.5 f17 b18. Hot, thin and superficially malty. 50%. nc ncf sc. Douglas Laing & Co. 314 bottles

⁘ **Provenance Fettercairn Over 10 Years** refill hogshead, cask no. 9307, dist Autumn 02, bott Autumn 12 **(73)** n18 t19 f18 b18. Syrupy sweet, rubbery, heavy duty. About as delicate and sophisticated as dropping a brick on your enemy's toe. 46%. nc ncf sc.

GLEN ALBYN
Highlands (Northern) 1846–1983. Diageo. Demolished.

Gordon & MacPhail Rare Vintage Glen Albyn 1976 (96) n22.5 salty and nippy. And the theme thunders into an early Kentuckian drawl, with red liquorice and hickory prominent; t24.5 I am shaking my head in disbelief. Not through disappointment, but wonder! How can something of this antiquity still fill your mouth with so much juice? The barley still offers a degree of grassiness, though this is camouflaged by the softest bourbon characters I have seen in a long time. The honeycomb is in molten form, as is the vanilla which appears to carry with it a fabulous blend of avocado pear and ulmo honey; f24.5 a pathetic degree of oaky bitterness tries to interrupt, but it is swept aside by the residual and very complex sugars. There remains some spicy activity and even some Kentuckian red liquorice and hickory, but that South American honey really does the business b24.5 wow! My eyes really popped out of my head when I spotted this in my sample room. Glen Albyns come round as rarely as Scotsman winning Wimbledon. Well, almost. When I used to buy this (from Gordon and MacPhail in their early Connoisseur's Choice range, as it happens) when the distillery was still alive (just) I always found it an interesting if occasionally aggressive dram. This masterpiece, though, is something else entirely. And the delivery really does take us to places where only the truly great whiskies go... 43%

99

GLENALLACHIE
Speyside, 1968. Chivas Brothers. Working.

Glenallachie 15 Years Old Distillery Edition db **(81)** n20 t21 f19 b19. Real battle between nature and nurture: an exceptional sherry butt has silk gloves and honied marzipan, while a hot-tempered bruiser lurks beneath. 58%

Director's Cut Glenallachie Aged 40 Years sherry butt, cask no. 8217, dist Mar 72, bott Mar 12 **(88)** n23 big sherry; t22.5 big spiced sherry; f22.5 big sweet sherry; b20 Glenallachie 40 years ago made one of Scotland's invisible whiskies. Not because it hardly ever saw the light of day as a single malt – a rare foray in the European market was the best it achieved – but, rather, the spirit was so lacking in personality that blenders told me it was put into blends to cheaply bulk up the malt content rather than give character. So for Glenallachie to shine as a single malt, a good cask is essential. Here we have a clean, uncontaminated sherry butt that is in very fine form. However, any trace of the malt it once contained has entirely vanished. 56.8%. nc ncf sc. Douglas Laing & Co. 146 bottles.

Gordon & MacPhail Connoisseurs Choice Glenallachie 1999 (85) n22 t22 f20 b21. Ingratiatingly clean, monosyllabically malty and in its very finest blending regalia. 43%

Malts Of Scotland Glenallachie 1973 bourbon hogshead, cask no. MoS11018, dist Mar 73, bott Oct 11 **(86.5)** n21 t22.5 f21.5 b21.5. Unusually rich for a Glenallachie and even appears to boast a sultana-fruit sweetness despite its bourbon heritage. The middle ground, when the mocha arrives, is particularly attractive. 44%. nc ncf sc. Malts Of Scotland.

Mo Òr Collection Glenallachie 1973 37 Years Old first fill bourbon hogshead, cask no. DL6746, dist 31 Mar 73, bott 3 Nov 10 **(82)** n22 t21.5 f19 b19.5. Even after nearly four decades, a malt which still has the propensity to cut through the taste buds like a blow torch. Has filled out since its younger days and is especially attractive on the nose and early delivery. But the rest is a battle. 46%. nc ncf sc. Release No. 25. The Whisky Talker. 266 bottles.

Old Malt Cask Glenallachie Aged 16 Years refill hogshead, cask no. 7932, dist May 95, bott Dec 11 **(82.5)** n20 t22 f20 b20.5. Clean, malty, but miserly: with a touch of the new makes about it, more of a 16 month than a 16 year whisky... Even so, there is something crystalline and compellingly attractive about the delivery. 50%. nc ncf sc. Douglas Laing & Co. 295 bottles.

·⫶· **Provenance Glenallachie Over 11 Years** refill hogshead, cask no. 8689, dist Winter 00, bott Autumn 12 **(74)** n19 t19.5 f18 b18.5. Thin, one-dimensional and aggressive: seen more fat on a ship. 46%. nc ncf sc. Douglas Laing & Co.

Scott's Selection Glenallachie 1993 bott 2012 **(82)** n21 t21 f20 b20. Sweet and malty. But as tight as the arse of one of the ducks I used to feed at the distillery... 55.6%.

The Whisky Agency Glenallachie 1973 bott 2011 **(85.5)** n22 t22 f20 b21.5. Heavily perfumed on the nose and laden with barley on delivery. But for all the usual fire midway through and thin finish, you cannot help but enjoy its clean simplicity. 50.4%. nc ncf sc.

GLENBURGIE
Speyside, 1810. Chivas Brothers. Working.

Glenburgie Aged 15 Years bott code L00/129 db **(84)** n22 t23 f19 b20. Doing so well until the spectacularly flat, bitter finish. Orangey citrus and liquorice had abounded. 46%

Chieftain's Glenburgie Aged 12 Years hogsheads, cask Nov 98, bott Sep 11 **(88)** n23.5 exemplary combination of light, playful aromas mixing up rather beautifully with some delicate citrus and even juicier barley. The Middle-Eastern touch of lemon and mint adds a lovely flourish; t22 a much more workaday aspect to the warming, vaguely biting, delivery with the vanillas making the most of a surprisingly thin body; f20 spices blossom as it thins and bites further; b22 one of those malts which is chiefly about the nose. 43%. nc ncf.

·⫶· **Chieftain's Glenburgie 14 Years (86)** n21.5 t22.5 f20.5 b21.5. Solid single malt. And the backbone is pure oak. 59.6%.

Gordon & MacPhail Rare Vintage Glenburgie 1966 (90) n22.5 distinctly floral: a real midsummer's night garden job...complete with creosoted fences; t22 much softer on delivery with cream toffee dominant; there is also a big barley juiciness, too; f23 the Rolo effect clings and expands, complete with milk chocolate which builds its shares. The final moments are quite dry with chalky vanilla seeping in with raw hazelnuts for depth; b22.5 a malt which has reached a point in its life where it is not exactly sure where it is going. You get the feeling the most of the successes are by luck rather than design. But it doesn't really matter: after giving it at least 15 minutes in the glass, simply enjoy! 43%

Kingsbury "The Selection" Glenburgie 17 Years Old hogshead, cask no. 100 & 101, dist Feb 04, bott Apr 11 **(79.5)** n18.5 t21 f20 b20. Sweet and sugary, the brilliance of the original spirit works miracles to make the most of some very ordinary oak. 43%. nc ncf. 852 bottles.

Old Malt Cask Glenburgie Aged 16 Years refill hogshead, cask no. 8005, dist Apr 95, bott Jan 12 **(88.5)** n22 big, very lightly sweetened malt but mainly grassy; t22 salivating, mouth cleansing and bursting with barley; f22 a very polite introduction of drier vanilla and the faintest hint of red liquorice and butterscotch; **b22.5** if I was giving a lecture, I could unveil this malt and reveal exactly why Burgie is such a spot-on blending malt: here the barley is true, clean and persistent....very much in the distillery style. *50%. nc ncf sc. 304 bottles.*

Provenance Glenburgie Over 11 Years refill hogshead, cask no. 7653, dist Autumn 1999, bott Summer 2011 **(92.5) n23** green, under-ripe gooseberry; the very vaguest puff of smoke; **t23** juicy, clean malt attack; slow diffusion of sugars towards the middle; **f23** surprisingly lengthy where just a little phenolic spice tacks on to the vanilla; **b23.5** a quite gorgeous bottling: a whispering, understated gem of no little complexity. *46%. nc ncf sc.*

⫶ **Provenance Glenburgie Over 12 Years** refill hogshead, cask no. 8015, dist Spring 99, bott Winter 12 **(82.5) n20 t21.5 f20.5 b20.5.** Fizzes and frolics on the palate, though it is the simplistic barley doing all the work. *46%. nc ncf sc. Douglas Laing & Co.*

Scotch Malt Whisky Society Cask 71.34 Aged 13 Years refill gorda, cask no. 1580, dist 1998 **(82) n18 t23 f20 b21.** Gorda Bennett!! OK, this whisky does have its charms and the big chocolate fruit and nut explosion is a joy. But the cask is faulty. If you can live with the sub standard nose and finish, give it a go. *56.8%. sc. Scotch Malt Whisky Society.*

Whisky Antique Glenburgie 26 Years Old Special Bottling dist 1983, bott 2009 **(89.5) n22.5** attractive suet, spotted dog pudding; crispened with Demerara sugar; **t23.5** soft, juicy delivery soon backed up with some stinging spices. The fruit arrives early too, making for a gorgeous first half dozen waves; **f21.5** dries a little as the cocoa and mildly burned toast arrives; **b22** a metallic hand in a silky glove... *57.7%. sc. Silver Seal Whisky Company.*

GLENCADAM
Highlands (Eastern), 1825. Angus Dundee. Working.

Glencadam Aged 10 Years db **(95) n24** crystal clarity to the sharp, ultra fresh barley. Clean, uncluttered by excessive oak, the apparent lightness is deceptive; the intensity of the malt carries its own impressive weight and the citrus note compliments rather than thins. Enticing; **t24** immediately zingy and eye-wateringly salivating with a fabulous layering of sweet barley. Equally delicate oak chimes in to ensure a lightly spiced balance and a degree of attitude; **f23** longer than the early barley freshness would have you expecting, with soft oils ensuring an extended, tapering, malty edge to the gentle, clean oak; **b24** sophisticated, sensual, salivating and seemingly serene, this malt is all about juicy barley and balance. Just bristles with character and about as puckeringly elegant as single malt gets...and even thirst-quenching. My God: the guy who put this one together must be a genius, or something... *46%*

Glencadam Aged 12 Years Portwood Finish db **(89.5) n22.5 t22.5 f22 b22.5.** After coming across a few disappointing Port finishes in recent weeks, just wonderful to experience one as you would hope and expect it to be. *46%*

Glencadam Aged 14 Years Oloroso Sherry Cask Finish bott May 10 db **(95) n24** pinch me: I'm dreaming. Oloroso exactly how it should be: classically clean with a dovetailing of dry and sweeter grape notes which are weighty, but not heavy enough to crush the lighter barley and vanillas from adding to the sumptuous and elegant mix; **t23.5** mouth-filling with firstly fat grape then a second flavour round of spices and custardy vanillas; **f24** much drier now with the accent on the barley but still that light spice persists, actually increasing in weight and effect as it goes along; **b23.5** what a total treat. Restores one's faith in Oloroso whilst offering more than a glimpse of the most charming infusion of fruit imaginable. *46%*

Glencadam Aged 15 Years db **(90.5) n22.5** soft kumquats mingle with the even softer barley. A trace of drier mint and chalk dust points towards the shy oak. Harmonious and dovetails beautifully; **t23** sharp, juicy barley - almost fruity - fuses with sharper oak. The mouth-watering house style appears to fatten out as gentle oils emerge and then give way for a spicy middle; **f22** long, with those teasing, playful spices pepping up the continued barley theme. Dries as a 15 year old ought but the usual bitterness is kept in check by the prevailing malt; **b23** the spices keep the taste buds on full alert but the richness and depth of the barley defies the years. Another exhibition of Glencadam's understated elegance. Some more genius malt creation... *46%*

Glencadam Aged 21 Years "The Exceptional" bott May 10 db **(81) n21.5 t22 f17.5 b20.** For a little distillery with a reputation for producing a more delicate malt this is one big whisky. Sadly, the finish is out of kilter, for the delivery is a knife and fork job, offering some extraordinary variations on a fudgy-maple syrup theme which promises much. *46%*

Glencadam Aged 21 Years "The Exceptional" bott 2011 db **(94) n23.5** just so sexy! The sugars have a sparkle in their eye while the malt carries a lemon sharpness which breaks up the heavier aromas. A nose to take a good 10-15 minutes with, as the clarity allows you to see a long way; **t24** the sugars show first. But here there is more complexity: almost a step ladder of intensity. As it climbs, it gets a little heavier in oils, eventually taking on a barley-themed fudge; the whole show is in slow motion, with the odd, short-lived burst of spice, and a very lightweight fruitcake richness; **f23** long, now surprising spice-free and sugar-softened with the accent very much on the vanilla; **b23.5** this distillery is emerging out of the shadows from its bad old Allied days as one of the great Scottish single malt distilleries. So good is some of their whisky, this "exceptional" bottling is almost becoming the norm. *46%. nc ncf.*

⁙ **Glencadam 30 Years Old Single Cask 1982** Limited Edition cask no. 730, dist 10 Jun 82, bott Oct 12 db **(96) n25** try finding the nose of a Glencadam – or any Highland malt - in better shape. Even after three decades, the oak is content to share equal status with the still lemon-fresh barley and pitches in with quiet hints of eucalyptus, kumquat, the mist of distant smoke and exotic fruit. Impossible to find a nose more stable or subtle showing magnificent balance and poise throughout: perfection. **t24** the oak is a little more upfront on delivery, but there is also a wave of delicate peat of surprising, if brief, intensity bursting onto the scene before vanishing under the still juicy barley and richer cocoa tones; **f23** the expected vanillas surface, with the cocoa dust upping in percentages; a few late oils develop to ensure a lubricated, longer finale than first seemed possible; **b24** a rare bottling from a country at war. This was distilled in the very final days of the Falklands War when the conflict was at its most ferocious. Anyone finding a bottle of this can raise a glass to honour the memory to the gallant who are no longer with us. On both sides. *46%. nc ncf sc.*

⁙ **Berry's Own Selection Glencadam 1991** cask no. 4762, bott 2012 **(95.5) n24** it is a warm summer's day outside, and inside, in the cool, I have a glass of fruit salad: freshly diced Somerset apples and Worcestershire pears, fully ripened and dripping with juice; to set them off, a little nutmeg and allspice have given them a dry spiciness...; **t24.5** one of the deliveries of the year! The eye-closingly, low-sighingly impact is an explosion of livewire, juicy fruit. Still with pears, maybe now some cherry and yellow plum. A thick custardy vanilla tops the lot while the spices quiver...; **f23** dark sugars fend off the hickory thrust of the oak; buttery caramels try to soften things. But those warming spices will have their way; **b24** just startlingly beautiful. *53.9%. nc ncf sc.*

Mo Òr Collection Glencadam 1985 25 Years Old first fill bourbon hogshead, cask no. 3997, dist 26 Jun 85, bott 2 Dec 10 **(91) n22** thick with oak; nose blind and you'd be tempted to think bourbon, so intense is the vanilla; **t24** perfect weight and oiliness and then a slow, sexy dissolving of honey and sugar into the ever-building oak; **f22** the rapid drying offers a startling contrast to the delivery; **b23** Glencadam is not overrun with first fill bourbon casks. Always good to see a fine example hit the shelves. *46%. nc ncf sc. Release No. 19. 341 bottles.*

⁙ **Old Malt Cask Glencadam Aged 14 Years** refill butt, cask no. 9633, dist Dec 98, bott Mar 13 **(86.5) n20 t22.5 f22 b22.** The nose is hardly a turn on but there is enough energy in both the cask and barley to make for a mouth-watering interlude. Good body and delicate spice, too. *50%. sc. Hunter Laing & Co Ltd. 256 bottles.*

Old Malt Cask Glencadam Aged 21 Years refill hogshead, cask no. 8167, dist Oct 90, bott Feb 12 **(91) n22** wonderfully clean, powdery malt...though not in a gristy way; **t23.5** full blooded, unadulterated, gorgeously concentrated...malt; **f22.5** a little spice mixed in with the Horlicks; **b23** if you have a soft spot for Maltesers grab two bottles if you can. A real gent of a bottling. *50%. nc ncf sc. Douglas Laing & Co. 304 bottles.*

⁙ **Provenance Glencadam Over 8 Years** refill hogshead, cask no. 9484, dist Spring 2004, bott Winter 2013 **(80) n20 t21 f19 b20.** Decent barley versus under par cask. *46%. nc ncf.*

Provenance Glencadam Over 12 Years refill butt, cask no. 7656, dist Winter 1998, bott Summer 2011 **(87) n22** soft fruits and vanilla; very distant smoke; **t22** a blizzard of delicate spices counter the gentle malt arrival; **f21** a slight harshness to the vanilla; **b22** enticingly delicate despite the limitations of the cask. *46%. nc ncf sc. Douglas Laing & Co.*

⁙ **Provenance Glencadam Over 14 Years** refill butt, cask no. 9634, dist Winter 98, bott Spring 13 **(89.5) n22** basic barley, maybe. But when this clean, so enticing; **t23** supremely tart and mouth-watering: rarely does barley dominate to such effect with under-sweetened rhubarb at the fore; **f22** fabulous spice fade; **b22.5** impossible to fault. *46%. nc ncf sc.*

Scotch Malt Whisky Society Cask 82.19 Aged 13 Years refill puncheon, cask no. 1322, dist 1998 **(76.5) n19.5 t20 f18 b19.** Eye-watering. *55.7%. sc. Scotch Malt Whisky Society.*

Wemyss 1990 Single Highland "Caribbean Fruit" hogshead, dist 1990, bott 2011 **(90.5) n22.5** unusually dry for a Glencadam. But there is spot-on harmonisation between the floral tones and the ever-burrowing oak; **t23** a typical Glencadam in that the mouth-feel to the delivery is about as good as it gets. The barley takes some enticing but eventually displays in full juiciness; **f22** a light sugaring to the vanilla; the pace to the finish is mesmerising; **b23** perhaps the oak has rung the malt a little too dry to over celebrate the fruitiness. But a sophisticated, high quality dram without doubt. *46%. sc. Wemyss Malts. 320 bottles.*

GLENCRAIG
Speyside, 1958. Chivas Brothers. Silent.

⁙ **Cadenhead Glencraig 31 Years Old** bourbon, dist 81, bott 12 **(89) n23** much lighter than any Clencraig I have tasted in the last decade, perhaps due to being filled into a cask which was going to add little to the debate; even after all these years there is a new-makey element to this. A citrus and even very odd grape fruitiness sits comfortably with the barley; **t22** as fresh and salivating as you might expect an eight- or maybe ten-year-old to be. But most noticeable is the sheer weight and thickness of the body which you should always expect from this distillery, but was curiously absent on the nose; **f22** still the oak fashions little personality into the piece. The youth and unchallenged enormity of the malt carries through to the end; **b22** time warp whisky. The last time I tasted Glencraig like this was probably in the late 1980s or very early 1990s. It is a whisky from a dead distillery which appears frozen in time: a ghostly spirit in your glass. *50.8%. sc. 186 bottles.*

Scotch Malt Whisky Society Cask 104.13 Aged 36 Years refill barrel, cask no. 7825, dist 1974 **(96) n24** wonderful aroma: heavyweight stuff with all the characters playing at full throttle but within a seemingly confined space. So the bananas and ripe oranges would explode from the glass, except the thick bourbon is holding them by the lapels. Massive, magnificent... and very different...; **t24** the first oak notes to burn off are over the top and spent. But after about the third wave it settles down with the introduction of telling muscovado sugars and a seemingly roasty maltiness; spices dovetail with an almost cooing gentleness while slowly, but unmistakably, the barley builds up enough intensity to make a salivating contribution; **f23.5** the spices persist while the bourbon characteristics hold sway. The dryness of the sawdusty oak never hints at bitterness while the kumquats and figs ensure a distant softness; **b24.5** don't get many of these guys to the dozen. What a relief this one's a cracker! If you are to buy only one major whisky this year, make it this. *50.6%. sc. 179 bottles.*

GLENDRONACH
Highlands, 1826. The BenRiach Distillery Co. Working.

The GlenDronach Aged 8 Years "Octarine" db **(86.5) n23.5 t23 f19 b21.** Juicy yet bitter: a bipolar malt offering two contrasting characters in one glass. *46%. nc ncf.*

The GlenDronach 12 Years Old db **(92) n22** some pretty juicy grape in there; **t24** silky delivery with the grape teaming with the barley to produce the sharpest delivery and follow through you can imagine: exceptionally good weight with just enough oils to make full use of the delicate sweetness and the build towards spices and cocoa in the middle ground is a wonderful tease; **f22.5** dries and heads into bitter marmalade country; **b23.5** an astonishingly beautiful malt despite the fact that a rogue sherry butt has come in under the radar. But for that, this would have been a mega scorer: potentially an award-winner. Fault or no fault, seriously worth discovering this bottling of this too long undiscovered great distillery *43%*

The GlenDronach Aged 12 Years "Original" db **(86.5) n23 t22 f22 b21.5.** One of the more bizarre moments of the year: thought I'd got this one mixed up with a German malt whisky I had tasted earlier in the day. There is a light drying tobacco feel to this and the exact same corresponding delivery on the palate. That German version is distilled in a different type of still; this is made in probably the most classic stillhouse on mainland Scotland. Good, enjoyable whisky. But I see a long debate with distillery owner Billy Walker on the near horizon, though it was in Allied's hands when this was produced. *43%*

The GlenDronach Aged 12 Years "Revival" db **(83) n20 t22.5 f20.5 b20.** Glendronach at 12 is a whisky which has long intrigued me...for the last three decades, in fact. Always felt Allied had problems dealing with it, though when it was right it was sumptuous. Here it is a distance from being right: odd tobacco notes creeping into the fray, though that rings a bell with this distillery as I'm sure the old "Original" showed a similar trait. A very decent malty middle but elsewhere it flounders somewhat. *43%. nc ncf.*

The GlenDronach Original Aged 12 Years Double Matured db **(88) n23 t21 f22 b22.** Vastly improved from the sulphur-tainted bottling of last year. In fact, their most enjoyable standard distillery bottling I've had for many years. But forget about the whisky: the blurb on the back is among the most interesting you are likely to find anywhere. And I quote: "Founder James Allardice called the original Glendronach, 'The Guid Glendronach'. But there's no need to imitate his marketing methods. The first converts to his malt were the 'ladies of the night' in Edinburgh's Canongate!" Fascinating. And as a professional whisky taster I am left wondering: did they swallow or spit... *40%*

The GlenDronach 14 Years Old Sauternes Finish db **(78.5) n18 t22 f19 b19.5.** That unique Sauternes three dimensional spiced fruit is there sure enough...and some awesome oils. But, with so much out of key bitterness around, not quite I had hoped for. *46%. nc ncf.*

The GlenDronach 14 Years Old Virgin Oak db **(87) n22.5 t22 f21 b21.5.** Charming, pretty, but perhaps lacking in passion... *46%. nc ncf.*

The GlenDronach 15 Years Old db **(77.5) n19 t18.5 f20 b20.** The really frustrating thing is, you can hear those amazingly brilliant sherry butts screaming to be heard in their purest voice. Those alone, and you could, like the 12-y-o, have a score cruising over the 95 mark. I can't wait for the next bottling. *46%*

The GlenDronach 15 Years Old db (83) n20 t22 f20 b21. Chocolate fudge and grape juice to start then tails off towards a slightly bitter, dry finish. 40%

The GlenDronach 15 Years Old Moscatel Finish db (84) n19 t22.5 f21.5 b21. Such is the intensity of the grape, its force of life, it makes a truly remarkable recovery from such a limited start. But it is hard to be yourself when shackled... 46%. nc ncf.

The GlenDronach 15 Years Old Tawny Port Finish db (84.5) n21 t22 f20.5 b21.5. Quite a tight fit for the most part. But when it does relax, especially a few beats after delivery, the clean fruit fairly drips onto the palate. 46%. nc ncf.

The GlenDronach Aged 15 Years "Revival" db (88.5) n22 t23 f21.5 b22. Unambiguously Scottish... A fantastically malty dram. 46%

The GlenDronach 18 Years Old db (96.5) n24 groaning under the weight of sublime, faultless sherry and peppers; t24 puckering enormity as the saltiness thumps home. Black forest Gateaux complete with cherries and blended with sherry trifle. The spices have to be tasted to be believed. The sugars range from Demerara to light molasses; f24 again the sugars are in perfect position to ramp up the sweetness, but the grape, vanilla and spices are the perfect foil; b24.5 the ultimate sherry cask whisky. Faultless and truly astounding! 46%. nc ncf.

The GlenDronach Aged 18 Years "Allardice" db (83.5) n19 t22 f21 b21.5. Huge fruit. But a long-running bitter edge to the toffee and raisin sits awkwardly on the palate. 46%

The GlenDronach 21 Years Old db (91.5) n23.5 thumping sherry of the old fruitcake school; a serious number of toasty notes including hickory of a bourbon style; t23.5 no less lush delivery than the nose portends; the follow up layerings of burnt raisin and cremated fudge are pretty entertaining; f22 like burnt toast, a touch of bitterness at the death; b22.5 a quite unique slant on a 21-year-old malt: some aspects appear very much older, but some elements of the grape occasionally reveal a welcome youth. Memorable stuff. 48%. nc ncf.

The GlenDronach Grandeur Aged 31 Years db (94.5) n23.5 dry, mildly peppery vanilla; crushed golden raisin counter-plot; t24 spice-dusted grapes explode on the palate on entry; the mouth-feel plays a key role as the early lushness carries the fruit only so far before it begins to break up, allowing a fabulous spicy complexity to develop; f23.5 beautiful intertwining between those golden raisins and coffee. The spices are never far away...; b23.5 just one hell of an alpha sherry butt. 45.8%

The GlenDronach Aged 33 Years oloroso db (95) n24 t24 f23 b24. Want to know what sherry should really nose like: invest in a bottle of this. This is a vivid malt boasting spellbinding clarity and charm. A golden nugget of a dram, which would have been better still at 46%. 40%

⋯ **The GlenDronach Cask Strength** batch 2 Oloroso & Pedro Ximenez sherry casks db (94) n23 nosing this without aid of any info on this bottling. But this is a very strange maturation combination, as it appears to have had more than a single life; a tightness suggest some possible PX involvement but the over-ripe greengage and burnt sultana is profound; almost heavy ester, coffee style not uncommon in rums (another PX nod); t24.5 definitely PX (he says, not overly sure at all). Again there is a crispness to the sugars unique to that kind of maturation; but really it is the mix of pure Panama coffee and the milky mocha which knocks you backwards: this really is some mouthful, for the grape contains pips, skin the lot....a bit like a Valpolicella Ripasso on steroids...; f23 the vaguest hint of something furry from a slightly flawed cask. But even so, such is the intensity to the dried grape skins, enclosed in a light cocoa case, that the damage is minimal; b23.5 for those who like their sherried malts to take not a single prisoner. Immense, magnificent and quite unique in flavour profile. 55.2%. nc ncf.

The GlenDronach Single Cask 1971 Aged 41 Years batch 6, cask no. 1247, dist 71, bott 12 db (87) n21 all is so intense that the higher notes are flattened, leaving the duller, over-tired notes too big a say; t22 at first sweet though the spices soon enter like drunken cowboys bursting into the saloon looking for a fight. The salty bite thins out some of the fatter notes; f22 salty and oaky, the grape begins to take a much sturdier direction but leads us only unto a very milky coffee; b22 a lovely whisky, but one which has been worked too hard to be coherent. A malt desperate to find its rhythm but for all the high class fun, it never quite gets there. 47.9%. nc ncf.

⋯ **The GlenDronach Single Cask 1971 Aged 42 Years** batch 8, Pedro Ximenez sherry puncheon, cask no. 1246, dist 71, bott May 13 db (92.5) n22 spiced toffee apple; creosote drying next door; t23.5 the oak doesn't wipe its feet before entering. But the wall of robust fudgy sugar and treacle is up to absorbing any excess. Busy and chewy; f23.5 much more settled and last some distance. A light build up of spice turns this even more into a fruity boiled cough sweet; b23.5 the PX cask leaves so little room for the malt to get a word in. The spices, though, make this when it could so easily have just tipped over the oaky edge. Curiously delicious and different. 44.6%. nc ncf sc.

The GlenDronach Single Cask 1972 Aged 40 Years batch 7, Oloroso sherry butt, cask no. 710, dist 2 Mar 72, bott 2012 db (96) n23 countless strands of aged malt here: so old, the oak could well have woodworm. But the richness of the sherry is almost the stuff of make-believe....though instantly recognisable to those of us who tasted the sherry version of the distillery at 12 years in the 1980s and 90s....; **t24.5** the delivery is of oak crashing in a forest...mighty and all consuming. For a while it is almost eye-watering, if somehow juicy. But, slowly, the more delicate shards of grape appear while the spices blossom and sugars emerge unscathed and celebrating their usual high performance Demerara style; the middle ground is one of both dried and juicy dates and high class Jamaican blue mountain coffee. Wow...this is like a big succulent bourbon matured in a top class sherry butt!! **f24** dries again for a while as the oaks regroup like dazed Triffids. A wonderful briny element appears to soften rather than embolden the oak's impact and allows both the spices and sugars to dampen the work of the vanilla. The fruit remains, even offering black cherry at times; **b24.5** on delivery, there is a puckering of the taste buds which makes you fear that age has done its worst. The recovery is as remarkable as it is magnificent. This is a malt which if you should ever chance upon, you give the guy your coat if you have not money enough; even your under garments if it does the trick! For this is a whisky so complex, so complete, it is almost exhausting... *49%. nc ncf sc.*

The GlenDronach Single Cask 1978 Aged 33 Years batch 6, Oloroso sherry puncheon, cask no. 1068, dist 29 Dec 78, bott 2012 db **(96) n23.5** ever been in a high quality antique shop specialising in 18th century furniture...? **t24.5** from the nose you'd expect an oaky salute. Not a bit of it: the grape juices set you off salivating instead. There are many kinds of old pot still Demerara rum notes to enjoy, especially those with a touch of coffee; and the Demerara sugars there in abundance, too; **f24** a wonderful saltiness begins to make itself felt, at first distantly and then more stridently. But it never offers more than is required...the spices and dark, lengthy sugars see to that; **b24.5** when this distillery gets it right, your taste buds don't stand a chance. Almost brain-explodingly complex... *52.9%. nc ncf sc.*

The GlenDronach Single Cask 1989 Aged 23 Years batch 7, Pedro Ximenez sherry puncheon, cask no. 5475, dist 30 Nov 89, bott 2012 db **(92) n22.5** pithy and dry, the nose is almost the complete opposite of what you might expect; **t23** sensational delivery! The sugars are tight and intense and not free to roam over the big vanilla and spice. The fruit is almost pure grape skin. When a sweetness does evolve there is a touch of the honeycombs about it; **f23** long, with a wonderful interweaving of lightly fruited vanillas and crisp, Demerara crusted barley; **b23.5** a malt which becomes spellbinding as the tale unfolds. *51.6%. nc ncf sc.*

The GlenDronach Single Cask 1989 Aged 23 Years batch 6, Moscatel barrel, cask no. 4885, dist 18 Jan 89, bott 2012 db **(80.5) n19.5 t21 f20 b20.** The muscatel gives a generous injection of fruit. But there is the nagging feeling (and not for the only time with a Glendronach) that, a long time ago, a cask has waited a long while to be filled. *53.9%. nc ncf sc.*

The GlenDronach Single Cask 1990 Aged 22 Years batch 6, Pedro Ximenez sherry puncheon, cask no. 2966, dist 30 May 90, bott 2012 db **(77.5) n20 t20 f18.5 b19.** Tangy...and for all the wrong reasons. Sulphur free, though. *55.1%. nc ncf sc.*

⁘ **The GlenDronach Single Cask 1990 Aged 22 Years** batch 8, Pedro Ximenez sherry puncheon, cask no. 2971, dist 13 Jun 90, bott May 13 db **(86) n21 t22.5 f21 b21.5.** Although a relatively healthy puncheon, there is tightness here where the sugars, for all their intense fruit and fudginess, strangle other development. Enjoyable. But... *50.8%. nc ncf sc.*

The GlenDronach Single Cask 1991 Aged 20 Years batch 7, Pedro Ximenez sherry puncheon, cask no. 3183, dist 15 Nov 91, bott 2012 db **(95) n23** of the mocha and Demerara rum school of Glendronach though this time with extra tight sugars; **t24** thick on delivery and thickens further as the flavours pan out. Almost a coffee cake and Swiss roll marriage with grape jam for filling; **f24** long, thick-bodied until almost the very last moment and a few fudge and mocha-flavoured Lubec marzipan notes sidle in delightfully. The light spices pulse...; **b24** tries to be syrupy and overbearing but fails miserably. Has to settle for being brilliant. *51.3%. nc ncf sc.*

⁘ **The GlenDronach Single Cask 1991 Aged 21 Years** batch 8, Pedro Ximenez sherry puncheon, cask no. 5409, dist 22 Nov 91, bott May 13 db **(81) n20 t21 f20 b20.** A steady stream of treacle. *49.8%. nc ncf sc.*

The GlenDronach Single Cask 1992 Aged 19 Years batch 7, Oloroso sherry butt, dist 92, bott 12 db **(85) n22 t21.5 f20 b21.5.** Distinctly nutty, with walnuts shining on the nose. Very dry and oaky throughout with the grape helped along with some busy spice. *57.8%. nc ncf sc.*

⁘ **The GlenDronach Single Cask 1992 Aged 21 Years** batch 8, oloroso sherry butt, cask no. 145, dist 22 May 92, bott May 13 db **(96) n23.5** excellent balance between the lightweight spice and the grape; citrus darts in and out to ensure subtlety while the heavier oak offer ballast; **t24.5** the delivery of dreams: as near as damn it perfect weight with the grape as juicy as you like and the balancing oils full of malty intent. The sugars are molassed but thin enough for the buttery vanillas to make it to the middle; **f24** much lighter, with a sultana-laced butterscotch sign off; **b24** call me old fashioned, but I really do think there is a vast difference in the quality between whisky matured in good oloroso and PX. The trouble with PX is that it is so intense it often snuffs out the complexity which can make a good whisky great. Here, you can see so many aspects of the malt which has been lost in previous vintages: this is sherried Highland malt of the very highest calibre. 58.1%. nc ncf sc.

The GlenDronach Single Cask 1993 Aged 18 Years Oloroso sherry butt, cask no. 1607, dist 24 Sep 93, bott 2012 db **(78) n18.5 t21 f19.5 b19**. A sulphured butt that despite its grapey riches is off key thanks to sub-standard wood. 56.1%. nc ncf sc. Distillery exclusive.

The GlenDronach Single Cask 1993 Aged 19 Years batch 6, Oloroso sherry butt, cask no. 536, dist 26 Feb 93, bott 2012 db **(95) n23.5** a degree of breakfast business here: some mid roast Java coffee appears to have been sweetened with grape jelly; **t24.5** supremely sweet with the sugars arriving in a rush...just ahead of the pounding spice. The mid ground is an explosion of complexity, and just about perfectly weighted and very lightly oiled. Again coffee at play, but some major bourbon and Demerara rum notes also have a big say; absolutely huge, yet carries itself off with rare grace; **f23** plenty of mocha sweetened with...Demerara, of course...; **b24** another ultra complex gem from this magnificent distillery. 59.4%. nc ncf sc.

⁓ **The Glendronach Single Cask 1993 Aged 20 Years** batch 8, oloroso sherry butt, cask no. 3, dist 15 Jan 93, bott May 13 db **(90.5) n22** pretty heavy and tight. But at its best, a fruitcake on steroids; **t24** melt in the mouth – while your mouth melts into the malt thanks to the spices; sublime range of sugars, topped with manuka honey and dates; **f21.5** a little furry and dull towards the end; **b23** a very slight blemish on the butt, but there are enough stunning moments to make this one to savour. 52.9%. nc ncf sc.

The GlenDronach Single Cask 1994 Aged 18 Years batch 7, Oloroso sherry butt, cask no. 98, dist 28 Jan 94, bott 2012 db **(96) n24** absolutely huge grape: a real Dundee cake dripping with oloroso and Demerara. The spices are profound but sit comfortably with the richness of the fruit; **t24** enormous yet somehow fresh and mouth-watering. For all the fruit and spice the barley is clearly visible and offers a more deft sweetness; the fudgy vanilla heads towards a hickory-style bourbon character; **f23.5** long with a slight sprinkling of salt. Otherwise it rumbles just like the delivery and middle, but now with far more humbleness; **b24.5** a faultless sherry butt. The malt offers an almost perfect accompaniment. As it happens, I had this sample in my hand as the Queen gave her 6pm address on June 5th to round off her 60th anniversary celebrations: I could hardly have had a more fitting dram with which to toast her with...which I gladly did. Congratulations, your Majesty. And thank you. 58.2%. nc ncf sc.

⁓ **The GlenDronach Single Cask 1994 Aged 19 Years** batch 8, oloroso sherry butt, cask no. 101, dist 28 Jan 94, bott May 13 db **(96) n24** a half hour nosing job, this. Apart from the crisp toffee apple and pepper and steamed ginger spice, just look out for the interaction of the bourbon-style liquorice and carrot juice; ulmo honey is on the prowl, also; **t24.5** that is perfect weight and an equally perfect match between the silky fruit and the spice and vanilla led oak; heather honey and molasses thicken the fruitcake; **f23.5** back to ulmo honey and butterscotch, with a confident sultana thread and continuing spice; **b24** proof that great, unspoiled sherry butts were getting into Scotland during this period. And what proof! Magnificent. 58.4%. nc ncf sc.

⁓ **The GlenDronach Single Cask 1996 Aged 17 Years** batch 8, Pedro Ximenez sherry puncheon, cask no. 1490, dist 16 feb 96, bott May 13 db **(76) n19 t20 f18 b19**. Syrupy and too many spent matches. 53.1%. nc ncf sc.

⁓ **The GlenDronach Single Cask 2002 Aged 10 Years** batch 8, Pedro Ximenez sherry puncheon, cask no. 1988, dist 3 Jul 02, bott May 13 db **(94.5) n23.5** probably the cleanest PX puncheon I have yet nosed that's available commercially. Dense, of course. But sufficiently light enough to allow a little coffee and spice to wander in and out; **t23** quite feminine? Sugars and spice and all things nice...; **f24** where the delivery jars sensationally for a moment, this is probably the highlight: the toasted sugars come through in varying degrees of intensity, as does the pulsing spice. Is there even a hint of malt in there...? My imagination, surely...; **b24** a superior PX cask in that it is not so heavy as to blot out some of the more quixotic elements of the whisky and is as clean as a whistle and as spicy as a poppadom. The best PX puncheon I have found on the market in my lifetime. 55.6%. nc ncf sc.

⁓ **The GlenDronach Recherché 1968** oloroso sherry butt, cask no. 5, bott 12 db **(97) n24** unsubtle with in-your-face grape, so thick you can hardly breathe; the sugars are no less loutish and the spices are pure thugs. And you know what? I bloody love it...!!! **t24** the most ridiculously clumsy start to a whisky of all time with the grape notes tripping over each other to get out first. However, they are beaten back into second place by rip-roaring plum treacle and molasses; the degree of oils border on perfect, but then so, too, does the balance between oaky toast and the jammy fruit spread all over it; **f24** you expect spices...and you get spices. Here, though, the fruit is more temperate and even a little ulmo honey kisses and seduces; **b25** once, I admit, I found this kind of cask OTT. And it is a style that was often found with the obsolete Glendronach 12-year-old sherry edition, which compared to other oloroso styles around lacked a little couth. However, with good sherry butts these days being rarer than a Millwall goal at home, I have come to look at this style of malt beyond fondly. In fact this is love. A 44-year-old malt and not one atom of over age: truly incredible. A real once in a lifetime treat for most. And a throwback. *48.6%. 1968 Vintage aged 44 years.*

Cadenhead GlenDronach 21 Years Old bott 2012 **(95.5) n24** promises something special: stewed apple with a little clove seasoning; **t24** I sit here purring. This is exactly what I demand of a 21-year-old from a distillery of this stature and it delivers with frightening ease. Precise and salivating barley, but the busying plot by fragile fruits, quarrelsome spices and multi-toned oils and sugars is mesmerising; **f23.5** settles into something a little more simplistic; malt-nougat and rich barley fade of the highest order; **b24** an effortless essay in magnificence. *51.1%. sc.*

Malts Of Scotland GlenDronach 2002 sherry hogshead, cask no. MoS12004, bott 2012 **(94.5) n23** an enormous, quarrelsome marriage between very fresh oak and dripping, unspoiled sherry. The vanillins actually square up with the grape, neither staring the other down; a highland equivalent of a Mexican Standoff ensues; **t24** the sherry is actually too big and bold for a perfect delivery, crowding out the barley entirely. Slowly the oak gets a toehold and as the spices spread, things become fabulously interesting; **f24** chocolate and jam spread on burnt toast; **b23.5** not even a hint of a fault on this cask. The sherry might be just a little bit of a bully, but you can't but admire the muscle. Not so much a dram as a statement. A bruising whisky experience. And not a single sulphur atom in sight. *54.8%. nc ncf sc.*

GLENDULLAN *(see also below)*
Speyside, 1972. Diageo. Working.

Glendullan Aged 8 Years db **(89) n20 t22 f24 b23.** This is just how I like my Speysiders: young fresh and uplifting. A truly charming malt. *40%*

Singleton of Glendullan 12 Years Old db **(87) n22 t22 f21 b22.** Much more age than is comfortable for a 12-y-o. *40%*

Gordon & MacPhail Connoisseurs Choice Glendullan 1997 (85) n22 t21 f21 b21. Tries hard to impress, and the hayrick nose makes a success of getting the Speyside message across. But a little too syrupy sweet for its own good. *43%. Gordon & MacPhail.*

⠿ **Gordon and MacPhail Connoisseurs Choice Glendullan 1999 (84.5) n21.5 t22 f20 b21.** Nutty, full bodied and unfailingly pleasant, it is a tad too dependent on crystalline sugars for impact. Better oak might have helped here. *46%. ncf.*

Provenance Glendullan Over 12 Years refill hogshead, cask no. 8013, dist 1999, bott 2012 **(82.5) n22 t21 f19 b20.5.** One of those skinny chaps: all barley, no meat. *46%. nc ncf sc.*

Royal British Legion Glendullan 1999 cask no. 16546, bott 2012 **(85.5) n20.5 t23 f21 b21.** The nose leaves you in little doubt what kind of rough ride awaits. But the shimmering intensity of the barley, especially on delivery, is a delicious wonder to behold. *58.8%. nc ncf sc.*

GLENDULLAN *(see also above)*
Speyside, 1898–1985. Closed.

Glendullan 1978 Rare Malt db **(88) n23 t22 f21 b22.** Sherlock Holmes would have loved this one: he would have found it lemon-entry. *56.8%*

GLEN ELGIN
Speyside, 1900. Diageo. Working.

⠿ **Dun Bheagan Glen Elgin Aged 21 Years** sherry butt, cask no. 8294, dist Dec 91, bott 13 **(90.5) n23.5** resplendent in manuka honey and liquorice; the fruit is represented by black cherry: mesmeric; **t23** much fruitier delivery, with the grape having equal billing with banana but the spices play the key role. Good, mildly oily weight with barley and vanilla filling the middle ground; **f21.5** thins out fast, with a mild spiced pulse; **b22.5** clean sherry influence for a typical Glen Elgin picture book malt. *52.5%. nc ncf sc. Ian Macleod Distillers. 558 bottles.*

Glen Elgin Aged 12 Years db **(89) n23 t24 f20 b22.** Absolutely murders Cragganmore as Diageo's top dog bottled Speysider. The marks would be several points further north if one didn't get the feeling that some caramel was weaving a derogatory spell. Brilliant stuff nonetheless. States Pot Still on label – not to be confused with Irish Pot Still. This is 100% malt... and it shows! *43%*

Liquid Sun Glen Elgin 1984 bott 2011 **(85) n21.5 t22 f20.5 b21.** By no means the first cask I have tasted this year where age has got the better of the obvious honey theme. Nor will it be the last. Enjoyable, but obviously not at its zenith. *45.1%. nc ncf sc. The Whisky Agency.*

Malts Of Scotland Glen Elgin 1975 bourbon hogshead, cask no. MoS11024, bott Nov 11 **(91.5) n22.5** pretty tired oak. But beyond that a massive salt and honey mix; some lovely lime jam amid the Jaffa Cake; **t23.5** creaks, cracks and leaks oak in every way thinkable. And yet the acacia honey mixing with toasty honeycomb, Demerara sugar and the oils of Venezuelan cocoa ensure a very special experience; **f22.5** long, and more of the same, but with more spice and less sugars; **b23** despite the biting oak, there is little doubting the once greatness of this cask. A decade ago this would have been a world beater. *46.8%. nc ncf sc.*

⠿ **Milroy's of Soho Glen Elgin Aged 17 Years** hogshead, cask no. 1669, dist 7 Nov 95, bott 15 Apr 13 **(89) n22.5** creamy malt shake and cream soda; **t23.5** thick textured delivery coats the palate with massively intense malt, the sweetness of which flutters in the breeze of tangier tannins and even raisin; **f21** a curious "glassy" texture – usually found in whiskies that have been kept in the bottle for a long time – develops; **b22** a delicious distillery here at its most silky and creamy. *46%.*

⠿ **Old Masters Glen Elgin 16 Years Old** cask no. 1660, dist 95, bott Oct 12 **(92) n23** that gorgeous aroma you sometimes find in antique restoration workshops: a sweet resin mixing with sugared almonds; **t23.5** so sensuously silky. The malt leads in both a rich barley ale style (almost complete with slightly bitter hops) and in a juicier, semi-gristy incarnation; **f22.5** a butterscotch finale beacons from early on and arrives. A hint of lemon curd tart and bittering oak are also present; **b23** a distillery which, in the lab, rarely disappoints. And in bottled form is more likely than not to offer a treat. *56.4%. sc. James MacArthur & Co Ltd.*

The Perfect Dram Glen Elgin 36 Years Old bourbon cask, dist 1975, bott 2011 **(88.5) n22** a close relation to the Malts of Scotland bottling. A little extra salt this time round; **t22.5** eye-watering oak, but just enough sugars and honey to make for a delicious counter; Jaffa cake but now no lime; **f22** salty; **b22** fascinating. It is as though the Malt of Scotland cask has had some of its sugars removed to be replaced by extra salt... *48.2%. sc. The Whisky Agency.*

Scott's Selection Glen Elgin 1995 bott 2011 **(89) n22.5** freshly baled straw sweetened with a honey and lime-marmalade freshness; a hint of smoke; **t23** and again on the delivery, which combines those sweet, fluting fruity notes with a sumptuous texture to match; **f21.5** over enthusiastic bitterness at the death, but only after a vanilla custard fade; **b22** excellent malt which in an even better cask might really have meant business. *57.1%. Speyside Distillers.*

⠿ **The Whisky Agency Glen Elgin 1975** dist 75, bott 12 **(88) n23** saturated with oak but a kiwi fruit and physalis counters results in a stylish experience; **t0** not a particularly happy delivery: the degree of oak shoe-horns out the juicy barley and citrus and has made for an unsettled arrival with little later direction; **f23** now we get there: the tannins settle to allow a rich fudge and spice finale with no little butterscotch; **b22** proof that a whisky, as it develops, goes through an unsettled period not just around its birth. *48.4%*

The Whisky Cask Glen Elgin Aged 25 Years bourbon cask, dist 1984, bott 2009 **(95.5) n23** a finely tuned mix of traditional heavy bourbon notes sweetened with Golden Syrup and lightweight fruit including glazed cherries; **t24** a magnificent delivery with the emphasis on the sugars, but inclusive of complex malt and vanilla; the middle ground is also a riot of light Golden Syrup melting into a toasted fruit loaf; **f23.5** vanilla and butterscotch until it comes out of your ears; **b24** so many strands of Golden Syrup, the dentist might be called in. A superb experience from a superb distillery. *49%. sc. The Whisky Cask.*

GLENESK
Highlands (Eastern), 1897–1985. Diageo. Demolished.
Duncan Taylor Collection Glenesk 1983 cask no. 4930 **(89.5) n22 t23 f22 b22.5.** By far the best Glen Esk I've tasted in years. Perhaps not the most complex, but the liveliness and clarity are a treat. *52.1%*

GLENFARCLAS
Speyside, 1836. J&G Grant. Working.
Glenfarclas 8 Years Old db **(86) n21 t22 f22 b21.** Less intense sherry allows the youth of this malt to stand out. Mildly quirky as a Glenfarclas and enormous entertainment. *40%*

Glenfarclas 10 Years Old db **(80) n19 t20 f22 b19.** Always an enjoyable malt, but for some reason this version never seems to fire on all cylinders. There is a vague honey sheen which works well with the barley, but struggles for balance and the nose is a bit sweaty. Still has distinctly impressive elements with an odd fish. *40%*

Glenfarclas 12 Years Old db **(94) n23.5** a wonderfully fresh mix of grape and mint; **t24** light, youthful, playful, mouthwatering. Less plodding honey, more vibrant Demerara and juiced-up butterscotch; **f23** long, with soft almost ice-cream style vanillas with a grapey topping; **b23.5** a superb re-working of an always trustworthy malt. This dramatic change in shape works a treat and suits the malt perfectly. What a sensational success!! *43%*

Glenfarclas 15 Years Old db **(85.5) n21.5 t23 f20 b21.** One thing is for certain: working with sherry butts these days is a bit like working with ACME dynamite....you are never sure when it is about to blow up in your face. There is only minimal sulphur here, but enough to take the edge off a normally magnificent whisky, at the death. Instead it is now merely, in part, quite lovely. The talent at Glenfarclas is unquestionably among the highest in the industry: I'll be surprised to see the same weaknesses with the next bottling. *46%*

Glenfarclas 17 Years Old db **(93) n23** just so light and playful: custard powder lightens and sweetens, sultana softens, barley moistens, spice threatens...; **t23** the relaxed sherry influence really lets the honey deliver; delightfully roasty and well spiced towards the middle; **f23** when I was a kid there was a candy – pretend tobacco, no less! – made from strands of coconut and sweetened with a Demerara syrup. My, this takes me back...; **b24** an excellent age for this distillery, allowing just enough oak in to stir up the complexity. A stupendous addition to the range. *40%*

⁖ **Glenfarclas 18 Years Old** db (84) **n21 t22 f20 b21.** Tight, nutty and full of crisp muscovado sugar. *43%. Travel Retail Exclusive.*

Glenfarclas 21 Years Old db (83) **n20 t23 f19 b21.** A chorus of sweet, honied malt and mildly spiced, teasing fruit on the fabulous mouth arrival and middle compensates for the few blips. *43%*

Glenfarclas 25 Years Old db (84) **n20 t22 f20 b22.** A curious old bat: by no means free from imperfect sherry but compensating with some staggering age – seemingly way beyond the 25-year statement. Enjoys the deportment of a doddering old classics master from a family of good means and breeding. *43%*

Glenfarclas 30 Years Old db (85) **n20 t22 f21 b22.** Flawed yet juicy. *43%*

Glenfarclas 40 Years Old db (94) **n23** old Demerara rum laced with well aged oloroso. Spicy, deep though checked by vanilla; **t23** toasty fruitcake with just the right degree of burnt raisin; again the spices are central to the plot though now a Jamaican Blue Mountain/ Mysore medium roast mix makes an impressive entrance; **f24** long, with the oak not just ticking every box, but doing so with a flourish. The Melton Hunt cake finale is divine... **b24** couldn't help but laugh: this sample was sent by the guys at Glenfarclas after they spotted that I had last year called their disappointing 40-year-old a "freak". I think we have both proved a point... *46%*

Glenfarclas 40 Years Old Millennium Edition db (92) **n23 t23 f23 b23.** An almost immaculate portrayal of an old-fashioned, high-quality malt with unblemished sherry freshness and depth. The hallmark of quality is the sherry's refusal to dominate the spicy, softly peated malt. The oak offers a bourbony sweetness but ensures a rich depth throughout. Quite outstanding for its age. *54.7%. nc ncf.*

Glenfarclas 50 Years Old db (92) **n24** Unique. Almost a marriage between 20-y-o bourbon and intense, old-fashioned sherry. Earthy, weighty stuff that repays time in the glass and oxidization because only then does the subtlety become apparent and a soft peat-reek reveal itself; **t23** an unexpected sweet – even mouthwatering - arrival, again with a touch of peat to add counter ballast to the intense richness of the sherry. The oak is intense from the middle onwards, but of such high quality that it merely accompanies rather then dominates; **f22** warming black peppers ping around the palate; some lovely cocoa oils coat the mouth for a bitter-sweet, warming and very long finish; **b23** Most whiskies cannot survive such great age. This one really does bloom in the glass and the earthy, peaty aspect makes it all the more memorable. It has taken 50 years to reach this state. Give a glass of this at least an hour's inquisition, as I have. Your patience will be rewarded many times over. *44.4%*

Glenfarclas 105 db (95.5) **n23.5** the youthful grape comes in clean, juicy bunches; the herbs and spices on a rack on the kitchen wall; **t24** any lovers of the old Jennings books will here do a Mr Wilkins explosive snort as the magnificent barley-grape mix is propelled with the force of dynamite into the taste buds; survivors of this experience still able to speak may mention something about cocoa notes forming; **f24** long, luxurious, with a pulsing vanilla-grape mix and a build up of spices; light oils intensify and elongate; **b24** I doubt if any restorative on the planet works quite as well as this one does. Or if any sherry cask whisky is so clean and full of the joys of Jerez. A classic malt which has upped a gear or two and has become exactly what it is: a whisky of pure brilliance... *60%*

Glenfarclas 1953 Aged 58 Years first fill sherry butt, cask no. 1674, dist 1953, bott 2012 db (91) **n24** if you could draw in your mind's eye just how the great old sherry butts of yesteryear nosed at their most complex, you would find facets of that picture here. The grape makes its statement but does not dwell or boast. It allows so many other aroma profiles to the dais: the vanilla is coated in lemon, the dryer hickory accompanied by sweeter blackjacks; a slice of apple, a whiff of bluebell...it is almost an aromatic tapestry of all the things that can make a whisky great; **t23** the delivery is sherry coated and the bold molassed sugars hold out for a while, though the strain shows as the creamy mocha forms. But when the oaks break through, age is writ large; **f21** a creaking finale, though the timber never quite cracks under the strain of nigh on 60 years. Busy spices make a defiant and heroic late charge; **b23** sections of the nose are outstanding. The passing years, though, have crept up with the body. Yet, once you acclimatise, it is a dram you are unlikely to forget. Majestic. Literally. *47.2%. nc ncf sc. 400 bottles.*

Glenfarclas 1961 The Family Casks Release VII sherry hogshead, cask no. 1325 db (87.5) **n23.5** the sherry has taken on a formidable thickness of character, absorbing a degree of creosote from the ancient oak; **t23** the delivery is exactly as the nose promises: big, juicy, salivating grape and then a gravy of oaky tones; dried dates and walnuts abound; **f19** bitters out dramatically; **b22** earlier this year I officially opened an allotment for very young children suffering from cancer (anyone wishing to contribute to this touching cause please contact 0844 879 4247 or visit www.nctlctrust.com). I mention this because one of the most magical aspects of being able to nose, is that it can take you on a journey when you least expect it. I nosed this, and suddenly I was in my dad's wheelbarrow being carried to his old allotment in Surrey. I remember him liberally painting his little shed there in creosote. And the mildly creosoteish nose to this took me back, involuntarily, to that warm Sunday afternoon, probably back in 1961, when, as coincidence will have it, this was made. *47%. sc. 108 bottles.*

Glenfarclas 1961 The Family Casks Release IX sherry hogshead, cask no. 3050 db **(95.5)** **n23.5** a busy junction where many of the darker sugar types meet, though the tannins act like traffic lights to stop them crashing into each other. Surprisingly well ordered and beautifully balanced; the toffee apple is a lovely distraction; **t24** and again on delivery we have those huge tannins and impressive sugars doing the perfect job of cancelling out each others' excesses; almost like a malty porridge with molten muscovado sugar and juicy sultanas; **f24** long and not a hint of bitterness as those dark sugars radiate deeply; the oaks do pop up with a spicy, coconut, treacle edge. Ridiculously yummy for its age.... **b24** where this succeeds and cask 1325 struggles, is that this maintains the sugars and balance throughout: a rare trick for a cask some 50 years of age! *48%. sc. 133 bottles.*

Glenfarclas 1962 The Family Casks Release VIII sherry hogshead, cask no. 2648 db **(85.5) n21.5 t22 f21 b21.** Just strays outside the area of comfort once or twice. The delivery is sublime, but the beauty is fleeting. Plenty still to savour from a clean butt...but just a little too bitter from wear and tear. *49.2%. sc. 135 bottles.*

Glenfarclas 1963 The Family Casks Release VIII sherry hogshead, cask no. 179 db **(89.5) n21.5** of that tomato soup variety of sherry; **t22** a big, eye-watering whack of oak, but the taste buds are kissed better by a juicy grape follow through; **f23.5** at last finds a welcome degree of balance, with the more vigorous elements of the oak now having backed off completely. The mocha is distinctly more high roast Mysore than chocolate; late on some major heavy duty fruitcake; **b22.5** goes round the houses a bit to get to where it wants to go. But we can all celebrate when it finally arrives. *50.4%. sc. 194 bottles.*

Glenfarclas 1964 The Family Casks Release VII sherry hogshead, cask no. 4719 db **(86) n22.5 t23.5 f19 b21.** Time has played some peculiar tricks on this old dram. Both the nose and delivery are draped with a mixture of hugely delicious fresh and ancient grape notes, as well as spice, giving a distinctive two-tone effect. This finish, though, bitters out too violently. *48.5%. sc. 377 bottles.*

Glenfarclas 1965 The Family Casks Release IX sherry butt, cask no. 4502 db **(73.5) n18 t22 f15 b18.5.** A silky assassin. *53.7%. sc. 509 bottles.*

Glenfarclas 1966 The Family Casks Release VIII sherry butt, cask no. 4186 db **(94) n23** it's the bottled aroma of Wembley. Brylcreem. Woodbines. The oak of 100,000 rattles. Of Booby Moore leading the team onto the pitch...of sweat...; **t23.5** a dram that's perfect to experience from a table at home...or off the bar...; **f23.5** as sweet as a devastating shot from Geoff Hurst... mmm... I think it's all over...; **b24** ...it is now..! *51.1%. sc. 461 bottles.*

Glenfarclas 1970 The Family Casks Release VII sherry hogshead, cask no. 6778 db **(90.5) n23** thick grape: the oak punches through, but a cleanly bitten, crunchy toffee apple injects surprising vigour; **t22** the oak arrives in puckering fashion; major league Demerara sugars required to ensure a balance; **f23** settles comfortably with the grapes back on track and a chocolate fudge finale...along with some late warming spice; **b22.5** I think I remember a previous '70 vintage which was among the best I have ever tasted from this distillery. This is big and bold, but the oak now has a much bigger say. *51.7%. sc. 224 bottles.*

Glenfarclas 1971 The Family Casks Release VII sherry butt, cask no. 150 db **(77) n20 t22 f17 b18.** Starts on the palate with a pretty spectacular display of old style sherry and then, as the nose threatens, tightens and bitters dramatically. *51%. sc. 468 bottles.*

Glenfarclas 1972 The Family Casks Release VIII sherry butt, cask no. 3547 db **(95) n23.5** if you have a thing for sticky, over-ripe dates and juicy prunes then this could be your lucky day...! **t24.5** sublime delivery with a texture to die for! Absolute bliss as a fabulous, magnificently even-handed grape shimmies its way around the palate offering some manuka honey here, a little mocha there; the spices are almost too laid back to notice; **f23** as if tired of dispensing various grapey tones, it now concentrates on a semi-bourbony oak depth, even with a touch of liquorice and hickory on display; **b24** class in the glass! *474%. 608 bottles.*

Glenfarclas 1973 The Family Casks Release VIII sherry butt, cask no. 2598 db **(84) n21 t22 f20 b21.** Clean-ish, massively spiced in part but very loose with the grape. Quite bubble gummy on the nose and finish. *56.5%. sc. 456 bottles.*

Glenfarclas 1975 The Family Casks Release IX refill butt, cask no. 1 db **(92.5) n23** green banana...after over 35 years! Deliciously ridiculous! Putty and golden syrup; **t23.5** tart delivery, concentrating on the under-ripe fruits; big barley bite; **f23** long with vanillas worming a way in but the golden syrup staying firm; just a little furry; **b23** mmmmm! *54.7%. sc. 344 bottles.*

Glenfarclas 1978 The Family Casks Release VII refill hogshead, cask no. 590 db **(86.5)** **n22 t22 f21 b21.5.** Never quite hits what I would get when I used to tell a joke to a late old friend of mine, Doris Stokes: a happy medium. Either swimming in supercharged sugars or a little on the sharp and astringent side. *46.3%. sc. 240 bottles.*

Glenfarclas 1981 The Family Casks Release VII plain hogshead, cask no. 57 db **(96)** **n24** orange blossom honey. But that is merely the enticing finger, drawing you in to where red liquorice, glace cherries, treacle sponge cake and delicate shades of hickory await...; **t25** that's it. That is absolute perfection on delivery. I cannot find a fault as the oak is of exquisite quality: seasoned to the very highest standard. Never have I found a whisky which just sits and melts on the tongue quite like this: a meringue made from a mix of ulmo honey, butterscotch, walnut oil, icing sugar and barley grist. With the liberal dosage of citrus and the underlying bourbon-style liquorice depth, not for a moment is it a tad too sweet; **f23.5** just bitters a little as the sweeter elements wear off, but the weight and body remain spot on; **b24** when you find a Glenfarclas in this fettle, it makes you wonder why they don't move away from their sherry bias more often. This is Speyside malt at its zenith. *50.8%. sc. 183 bottles.*

Glenfarclas 1982 The Family Casks Release VIII sherry hogshead, cask no. 4568 db **(94) n23** if you are into sugared stewed gooseberries, this is the malt for you...; **t23.5** the gooseberries have been lost on delivery, but the sugars – full of lively acidity – are in full flow. A wonderful marriage of gristy barley juice and a grape; **f24** the vanillas ensure that a certain decorum controls the naked exuberance of the sugars; **b23.5** possibly one of the sweetest whiskies I have ever seen extracted from the sherry cask....! *54.9%. sc. 233 bottles.*

Glenfarclas 1983 The Family Casks Release IX refill hogshead, cask no. 43 db **(92) n22.5** needs a few minutes in glass to settle. Then a complex citrus dance is performed...; **t24** hi honey! Oh my word: I could chew on this all day. The orange blossom honey sets up camp but allows all kinds of spicy friends along. The buttery vanilla is a welcome guest, not least because it refuses to stay too long; **f22.5** simplifies with those vanillas returning and even appears to offer the vaguest and most tiny of smoky adieus; **b23** just one of those gorgeous drams which stylishly entrances. *51%. sc. 273 bottles.*

Glenfarclas 1984 The Family Casks Release VII plain hogshead, cask no. 6030 db **(94.5)** **n23** surprisingly fresh, even to the extent of a new makey fingerprint, which barely seems possible. But this is helped by the house-style citrus: a fresh zestiness, this time in tandem with a lemon drop sharpness; **t24** I feel that my taste buds are sitting in the most scrotive pool of citrusy malt, slowly having their nerve endings massaged and manicured; any cracks found are filled in with honey and marzipan; **f23.5** the barley juices appear to stretch into the distance, enough to carry the most sublime butterscotch and vanilla; **b24** Glenfarclas does mind-blowing citrus like no other Speyside distillery. *51%. sc. 264 bottles.*

Glenfarclas 1986 The Family Casks Release IX refill sherry butt, cask no. 4336 db **(68) n17 t19 f15 b17.** Oh, Lordy... *58.4%. sc. 574 bottles.*

Glenfarclas 1989 The Family Casks Release IX sherry butt, cask no. 12989 db **(96) n24** probably the most moist Melton Hunt Cake you'll ever find; **t24** a stunning delivery: the oloroso is dripping with greengages and dates, all backed up by lush spiced treacle; **f24** a classy fruity fade concentrating on the burnt raisin especially; **b24** oh, if only all sherry matured malts in Scotland from this era could be as faultless as this... *55.9%. sc. 622 bottles.*

Glenfarclas 1990 The Family Casks Release VIII sherry butt, cask no. 5099 db **(83.5)** **n21.5 t23 f19 b20.** Oh, so many grapey gold medals and a wonderful thread of golden syrup. But the finish is too dry for all the wrong reasons. *56.5%. sc. 615 bottles.*

Glenfarclas 1991 The Family Casks Release IX sherry butt, cask no. 5669 db **(87) n23** toffee apple on speed...; **t22** an enormous delivery of thick caramel and thicker grape; **f21.5** salty and delightfully aggressive; **b20.5** never seems to form a meaningful narrative; just a succession of round or angular shapes pitched together at random. *57.1%. sc. 624 bottles.*

Glenfarclas 1992 The Family Casks Release VIII sherry butt, cask no. 861 db **(81.5) n22 t22.5 f17 b20.** Lands rather beautifully with a late furry nibble; *59.5%. sc. 550 bottles.*

Glenfarclas 1993 The Family Casks Release V cask no. 3942, bott Apr 10 db **(72) n17.5 t19.5 f18 b18.** All over the place. The black sheep of the family... *59.7%. sc. 566 bottles.*

Glenfarclas 1993 The Family Casks Release IX sherry butt, cask no. 74 db **(96) n24** I am not sure if sherry gets any more intense than this without shutting out all other degrees of complexity. But the wonderful drip-feeding of both spice and herbs, ulmo honey and cracked leather really does take this up a few notches; **t24** presumably oloroso: the body is thick and dripping with intense, spiced grape. The vanillas are a perfect foil; **f24** the stunning ulmo honey continues to the very end where it stays arm in arm with the roasted nuts and drying grape skins; **b24** I am on my knees with my head bowed towards this bottle; a cask which would have been very much at home in the 60s and 70s...this offers us something which has now almost entirely been lost to the whisky world. *58.7%. sc. 627 bottles.*

Glenfarclas 1994 The Family Casks Release IX sherry butt, cask no. 2950 db **(93.5) n24** if this was any more sherry-ish it would be...a sherry...; thankfully, given time a whole complex gamut of oaky notes begin to wander in and out; **t23** the clean, unblemished grape on the nose stands the delivery in the highest stead; nutty, lively, full of dates and dried prunes in a molassed setting; **f23.5** my word, how can you say no to that rich chocolate mousse stuffed with walnuts...? **b23** takes me back to the 1970s when you could frolic with unblemished sherry butts to your heart's desire... *57.9%. sc. 629 bottles.*

Glenfarclas 1995 The Family Casks Release IX sherry butt, cask no. 6612 db **(76.5) n18 t21.5 f18 b19.** As bright as a 2012 British summer's day... *52.5%. sc. 650 bottles.*

Glenfarclas 1995 45° The Heritage Malt Collection sherry cask, dist Nov 95, bott Sep 06 db **(94.5) n24 t23.5 f23.5 b23.5.** Exceptional. Absolutely everything you could demand from a sherried malt of this age. Not a single off note and the freshness of comparative youth and complexity of years in the cask are in perfect harmony. *45%. Spain.*

Glenfarclas 1996 The Family Casks Release VII sherry butt, cask no. 1306 db **(80.5) n19 t22.5 f19 b20.** Not exactly perfect. But the sugars hit the heights. *55.6%. sc. 593 bottles.*

⁘ **Glenfarclas 2003** db **(83) n21.5 t23 f18 b20.5.** Some classic oloroso moments here, bounding with rich grape and walnuts. Alas, a little tight and furry. *46%. Whisky Shop Exclusive.*

Glenfarclas 175th Anniversary 2011 db **(94) n23.5** crisp and precise fruit: clean and hedging towards bon bons. The very vaguest hint of smoke adds extra depth; vanilla and spice fly the other way; **t24** fabulous delivery: every aspect dissolves on impact. The fruits are again subtle yet lush, the sweetness initially from gristy icing sugar, though towards the middle more muscovado. Again, the lightest imaginable wisps of smoke and more profound spices; **f23** cream toffee; burnt raisin; **b23.5** hard to imagine an experience more gentle than this where alcohol is concerned. No slam bam stuff here. Every moment is about whispers and brushes of the nerve endings. Sensual whisky. *43%. nc. J&G Grant. 6000 bottles.*

Cadenhead Glenfarclas 21 Years Old dist 1990, bott 2011 **(89.5) n22.5** vanilla, marmalade and a shake of salt; **t22.5** clean, sharp delivery; citrussy with major tang factor; **f22** allows the vanillas a bigger role on the creamy fade; **b22.5** charming. Never stops entertaining. *54.3%. sc. WM Cadenhead Ltd. 222 bottles.*

⁘ **Director's Cut Glenfarclas Aged 46 Years** refill butt, cask no. 9176, dist Jun 66, bott Sep 12 **(90.5) n24** all kinds of kumquat and marmalade lead; thick liquorice and hickory too: exceptionally deep and proud; **t22.5** doesn't take long to get among the spices. The brown sugars are tempered by some pretty shrill oak, but one does a good job of cancelling out the other; **f22** surprisingly short and simplistic with its jam and marmalade mix over buttered, singed toast finale; **b22** if you can take full on oak, you'll marvel at this. *49.7%. 319 bottles.*

⁘ **Malts Of Scotland 1836 - 2001** sherry butt, cask no. MoS 12062, dist Jun 2001, bott Nov 2012 **(81.5) n20 t23 f18.5 b20** Interesting. Laden with fruit. Yet still very tight. *57.8%. nc ncf sc. 96 bottles.*

⁘ **Riegger's Selection Eagle of Spey Glenfarclas 1993 (96.5) n24.5** hard to imagine a Glenfarclas more sexy and alluring than this: carries a gorgeous gooseberry and lemon tart aroma with panache; so delicate: the degree of salt is sublime and uplifting; the sharpness is in equal measure to the shy coconut and thin beech honey sweetness; there are times I actually forget about going on to taste it! One of the great Speyside aromas of the year...; **t24.5** the impact would be extraordinary had not the nose told you of the complexity to come: myriad mini flavour explosions on delivery – perhaps the small grains attack found on six-year-old bourbon from the Tom Moore distillery is the closest relation sensation-wise. Here, there is a bit more honey from the barley, which lets itself be heard by the juiciness which develops at slow-motion pace; **f23** a little tangy as some of the more exhausted tannins get a slight foot-hold. You crave cocoa to compensate. And, inevitably, it is cocoa you get...; **b24.5** you will have to pass a few bottlings to find one from this distillery so fruity yet not from a sherry butt. An absolute masterpiece from this outstanding distillery. *53.6%.*

Scotch Malt Whisky Society Cask 1.160 Aged 11 Years first fill barrel, cask no. 800150, dist 2000 **(88.5) n21.5** dry with a saline lead; **t22** big delivery with no shortage of tannins; the sugars arrive quite late but in good numbers; **f23.5** easily the best part: first milky cocoa and then coffee before the two merge...; **b21.5** A solid malt making the most of the salty tannins dredged from a very fresh cask. Just love the late mocha. *55.6%. sc.*

⁘ **Scotch Malt Whisky Society Cask 1.166 Aged 25 Years** refill hogshead, 3 Dec 86 **(93) n23.5** surprising amounts of fresh barley even after all this time: almost like moist hay; a touch of citrus to the sawdusty oak; **t23** big, punchy intense oak carries attractive light spice and burnt toast qualities; the sugars are even and happy to drive from the back seat; **f23** long, chewy barley once more with a light ulmo honey topping to the butterscotch; **b23.5** sound and steady malt where the sum is much bigger than all the subtle parts. *48.3%. nc ncf sc.*

꠵⠶ **Scotch Malt Whisky Society Cask 1.172 Aged 19 Years** refill hogshead, 23 Sep 93 **(89.5) n22.5** an honest, no nonsense malt fest; **t22.5** huge barley delivery; gristy sugars move towards a grassy freshness; the spices doff a cap to the elegant oak involvement; **f22** bitters very slightly but there is a slight Canadian/Kentucky-style nod towards liquorice and honey towards the very end; **b23** something so stylishly Speyside about this one. *55.7%. nc ncf sc. 230 bottles.*

꠵⠶ **The Whisky Shop Dufftown Glenfarclas The Family Casks 40 Years Old** oloroso sherry cask, cask no. 152, dist 8 Jan 71, bott 14 Feb 11 **(89) n24** almost Demerara pot still rum in its slightly estery intensity; subdued spice...but so much toasted raisin...; **t23** uptight sugars pound the taste buds with some milky mocha hinging around with intent; **f20** bitters out dramatically; **b22** a mottled malt where the toasted raisins turn up here and there but never quite run true. Some serious entertainment and quality early on, though. *51.6%. nc ncf sc. 496 bottles.*

GLENFIDDICH
Speyside, 1887. William Grant & Sons. Working.

Glenfiddich 12 Years Old db **(85.5) n21 t22 f21 b21.5.** A malt now showing a bit of zap and spark. Even displays a flicker of attractive muscovado sugars. Simple, untaxing and safe. *40%*

Glenfiddich 12 Years Old Toasted Oak Reserve db **(92.5) n22.5 t23.5 f22.5 b24.** Another bottling to confound the critics of Glenfiddich. This is as fine an essay in balance, charm and sophistication as you are likely to find in the whole of Speyside this year. Crack open a bottle... but only when you have a good hour to spend. *40%*

Glenfiddich Caoran Reserve Aged 12 Years db **(89) n22.5 t22 f21.5 b23.** Has fizzed up a little in the last year or so with some salivating charm from the barley and a touch of cocoa from the oak. A complex little number. *40%*

Glenfiddich Rich Oak Over 14 Years Old new American & new Spanish oak finish db **(90.5) n23** fascinating: there is a nod towards Japanese oak in the naked wood profile here. Toned down, though, by a huge pithy kumquat presence. That this is virgin oak there can be no doubt, so don't expect an easy ride; **t22** soft oils help for a quiet landing: like lonely oaks falling in a forest...there is a brief sensation of passing barley. Then it returns again to a number of oak-laden notes, especially the spices which move towards a creamy mocha territory; **f23.5** possibly the best phase of the experience. The vivid, surging oak has cooled and some barley oils mingle in a relaxed fashion with the sweetening, very mildly sugared mocha; **b22** from the moment you nose this, there is absolutely no doubting its virgin oak background. It pulls towards bourbon, but never gets there. Apparently European oak is used, too. The result is something curiously hinting at Japanese, but without the crushing intensity. Delicious, thoughtful whisky and one to tick off on your journey of malt whisky discovery. Though a pity we don't see it at 46% and in full voluptuous nudity: you get the feeling that this would have been something really exceptional to conjure with. *40%. William Grant.*

Glenfiddich 15 Years Old db **(94.5) n23** such a deft intermingling of the softer fruits and bourbon notes...with barley in there to remind you of the distillery; **t23** intense and big yet all the time appearing delicate and light; the most apologetic of spices help spotlight the barley sweetness and delicate fruits; **f24.5** just so long and complex; something of the old fashioned fruit salad candy about this but with a small degree of toffee just rounding off the edges; **b24** if an award were to be given for the most consistently beautiful dram in Scotland, this would win more often than not. This under-rated distillery has won more friends with this masterpiece than probably any other brand. *40%*

Glenfiddich Aged 15 Years Cask Strength db **(85.5) n20 t23 f21 b21.5.** Improved upon the surprisingly bland bottlings of old, especially on the fabulously juicy delivery. Still off the pace due to an annoying toffee-ness towards the middle and at the death. *51%*

Glenfiddich Distillery Edition 15 Years Old db **(93.5) n24.5** banana skins, but there is no slip up here as the aroma spectrum moves from ultra fat sultanas on one side to dried coconut on the other. You'll find countless other reference points, including lightly salted celery and even molten candle wax. Quite astonishing and, even with its spice nip, one of the great whisky noses of 2010; **t24** my word!! Just so lively...enormous complexity from the very first mouthful. The mouthfeel is two-toned with heavier fruit not quite outstripping the flightier barley. All kinds of vanilla – both dry and sweet – and a dusty spiciness, too; **f22** tones down rather too dramatically, hedging much more towards the more docile banana-vanilla elements; **b23** had this exceptional whisky been able to maintain the pace through to the finish, this would have been a single malt of the year contender - at least. *51%. ncf.*

Glenfiddich Aged 15 Years Solera Reserve *(see Glenfiddich 15 Years Old)*

Glenfiddich 18 Years Old db **(95) n23.5** the smoke, which for long marked this aroma, appears to have vanished. But the usual suspects of blood orange and various other fruit appear to thrive in the lightly salted complexity; **t24.5** how long are you allowed to actually keep the whisky held on the palate before you damage your teeth? One to really close your eyes and study because here we have one of the most complex deliveries Speyside can conjour: the peat may have gone, but there is coal smoke around as the juicy barley embeds with big fat sultanas, plums, dates and grapes. Despite the distinct lack of oil, the mouthfeel is entirely yielding to present one of the softest and most complete essays on the palate you can imagine, especially when you take the bitter-sweet ratio and spice into balance; **f23** long, despite the miserly 40% offered, with plenty of banana-custard and a touch of pear; **b24** at the moment, the ace in the Glenfiddich pack. If this was bottled at 46%, unchilfiltered etc, I dread to think what the score might be... 40%

Glenfiddich Age Of Discovery Aged 19 Years Bourbon Cask Reserve db (92) n23.5 not just complex, but so delicate one is almost afraid to nose too deeply incase you break the poor thing into a million pieces. The barley skits around like a highly strung actress on the edge of a breakdown; **t24** of such butterfly qualities, it wanders at random around the palate, touching down here and there to offer a barely legible malty weight; the sugars are no less constrained, a thin heather honey style feebly patting away the encroaching oak: the whole thing, like the nose, is wonderfully neurotic; **f22** melts away with limited grace and tact for far too short a finale; **b22.5** for my money Glenfiddich turns from something quite workaday to a malt extraordinaire between the ages of 15 and 18. So, depending on the casks chosen, a year the other side of that golden age shouldn't make too much difference. The jury is still out on whether it was helped by being at 40%, which means the natural oils have been broken down somewhat, allowing the intensity and richness only an outside chance of fully forming. 40%

Glenfiddich Age Of Discovery Aged 19 Years Madeira Cask Finish db (88.5) n22.5 t22.5 f21 b22.5. Oddly enough, almost a breakfast malt: it is uncommonly soft and light yet carries a real jam and marmalade character. 40%

Glenfiddich 21 Years Old db (86) n21 t23 f21 b21. A much more uninhibited bottling with loads of fun as the mouth-watering barley comes rolling in. But still falls short on taking the hair-raisingly rich delivery forward and simply peters out. 40%

Glenfiddich 30 Years Old db (93.5) n23 always expect sherry trifle with this: here is some sherry not to be trifled with... salty, too; **t23.5** the juiciest 30-y-o I can remember from this distillery for a while: both the grape and barley are contributing to the salivation factor...; the mid ground if filled with light cocoa, soft oils and a delicate hickory-demerara bourbon-style sweetness; **f23.5** here usually the malt ends all too briefly. Not this time: chunky grape carries on its chattering with the ever-increasing bourbon-honeycomb notes; a vague furry finale...; **b23.5** a 'Fiddich which has changed its spots. Much more voluptuous than of old and happy to mine a grapey seam while digging at the sweeter bourbon elements for all it is worth. Just one less than magnificent butt away from near perfection and a certain Bible Award... 40%

Glenfiddich 40 Years Old batch 7 db (96) n24 it's the spices which win hands down here. Yes, there is all kinds of juicy, voluptuous fruit...this nose is dripping with it. But the spices are the rudder steering a path through spectacular scenery...; **t24** ...so no surprises it is the eloquent spices which speak first on delivery. Nothing brash. No violence. Just considered and balanced, bringing the most from the oak and allowing a juicy degree of salt to enliven things further; to work properly sugars are required and sublime traces of muscovado sugars appear to bring the fat sultanas to bursting; **f23.5** now we get to the burnt raisin bit of the fruit cake effect. That's just how it should be...; oh, and did I mention the spices...? **b24.5** for the 750th New Whisky for the 2012 Bible, I decided to select a distillery close to my heart...and the age I'll be next birthday... Believe me: this guy didn't let me down. Full frontal fruit and spice. Perfectly toned and all the curves in the right places. Rrrrr!!! 45.8%. 600 bottles.

Glenfiddich Rare Collection 40 Years Old db (86.5) n22.5 t23 f20 b21. A quite different version to the last with the smoke having all but vanished, allowing the finish to show the full weight of its considerable age. The nose and delivery are superb, though. The barley sheen on arrival really deserves better support. 43.5%

Glenfiddich 50 Years Old db (97) n25 we are talking 50 years, and yet we are still talking fresh barley, freshly peeled grape and honey. Not ordinary honey. Not the stuff you find in jars. But the pollen that attracts the bees to the petunia; and not any old petunia: not the white or the red or pink or yellow. But the two-toned purple ones. For on the nose at least this is perfection; this is nectar... **t24** a silky delivery: silky barley with silky, watered down maple syrup. The middle ground, in some previous Glenfiddich 50-year-olds a forest of pine and oak, is this time filled with soft, grassy barley and the vaguest hint of a distant smoke spice; **f24** long, long, long, with the very faintest snatch of something most delicately smoked: a distant puff of peat reek carried off on the persistent Speyside winds, then a winding-down of vanillas, dropping through the gears of sweetness until the very last traces are chalky dry; **b24** for the record, my actual words, after tasting my first significant mouthful, were: "fuck!

This is brilliant." It was an ejaculation of genuine surprise, as any fly on the wall of my Tasting Room at 1:17am on Tuesday 4th August would testify. Because I have tasted many 50-year-old whiskies over the years, quite possibly as many as anyone currently drawing breath. For not only have I tasted those which have made it onto the whisky shelves, but, privately, or as a consultant, an untold number which didn't: the heroic but doomed oak-laden failures. This, however, is a quite different animal. We were on the cusp of going to press when this was released, so we hung back. William Grant blender David Stewart, whom I rank above all other blenders on this planet, has known me long and well enough to realise that the surrounding hype, with this being the most expensive whisky ever bottled at £10,000 a go or a sobering £360 a pour, would bounce off me like a pebble from a boulder. "Honestly, David," he told my chief researcher with a timorous insistence, "please tell Jim I really think this isn't too oaky." He offered almost an apology for bringing into the world this 50-year-old babe. Well, as usual David Stewart, doyen of the blending lab and Ayr United season ticket holders, was absolutely spot on. And, as is his want, he was rather understating his case. For the record, David, next time someone asks you how good this whisky is, just for once do away with the Ayeshire niceness installed by generations of very nice members of the Stewart family and tell them: "Actually, it's bloody brilliant if I say so myself! And I don't give a rat's bollocks what Murray thinks." 46.1%

Glenfiddich Malt Master's Edition double matured in oak and sherry butts db **(84)** n21 t22 f20 b21. I would have preferred to have seen this double matured in bourbon barrels and bourbon barrels... The sherry has done this no great favours. 43%

Glenfiddich Millennium Vintage dist 2000, bott 2012 db **(83.5)** n21.5 t22 f20 b20. Short and not very sweet. Good juicy delivery though, reminiscent of the much missed original old bottling. 40%

Glenfiddich Snow Phoenix bott 2010 db **(95)** n23.5 graceful and delicate, there is obviously some age lurking, lord-like, in the background. But it is the younger malts, reminiscent of the long-lost, original, no-age statement version that steals the show, imprinting the unique grassy, tingly signature into the glass; **t24** a time machine has taken me back 25 years: it is like the original Glenfiddich at its juicy, ultra-salivating youthful finest but now with a honey enriched backbone and some real belief in the oaky spices, where they were once half-hearted a generation ago; **f23** long, with that honeyed sheen remaining impressively attached to the dynamic barley; **b24.5** it is no easy task for blender Brian Kinsman to emerge from the considerable shadow of the now retired David Stewart, the world's finest blender of the last 20 years. But here he has stepped up to the plate to create something which captures the very essence of the distillery. It is almost a deluxe version of the original Glenfiddich: something that is so far advanced of the dull 12-year-old, it is scary. This is sophisticated whisky, have no doubt. And the first clear, impressive statement declaring that Glenfiddich appears to remain in very safe hands. Whatever Brian did from those casks, exposed to the bleak Speyside winter, he should do again. But to a far wider audience. 4.76%. ncf.

GLEN GARIOCH
Highlands (Eastern), 1798. Morrison Bowmore. Working.

Glen Garioch 8 Years Old db **(85.5)** n21 t22 f21 b21.5. A soft, gummy, malt – not something one would often write about a dram of this or any age from Geary! However, this may have something to do with the copious toffee which swamps the light fruits which try to emerge. 40%

Glen Garioch 10 Years Old db **(80)** n19 t22 f19 b20. Chunky and charming, this is a malt that once would have ripped your tonsils out. Much more sedate and even a touch of honey to the rich body. Toffeed at the finish. 40%

Glen Garioch 12 Years Old db **(88.5)** n22 t23 f21.5 b22. A significant improvement on the complexity front. The return of the smoke after a while away was a surprise and treat. 43%

Glen Garioch 12 Years Old db **(88)** n22.5 rich, and full bodied. Fudge with the vaguest hint of fruit. A little earthy; **t22.5** big, bold delivery again with that earthiness working well alongside a big toffee-fudged barley juiciness; **f21.5** thins a little, but still enjoyably earthy; boosted by late spice; **b22** sticks, broadly, to the winning course of the original 43% version, though here there is a fraction more toffee at the expense of the smoke. 48%. ncf.

Glen Garioch 15 Years Old db **(86.5)** n20.5 t22 f22 b22. In the a bottling I sampled last year the peat definitely vanished. Now it's back again, though in tiny, if entertaining, amounts. 43%

Glen Garioch 21 Years Old db **(91)** n21 a few wood shavings interrupt the toasty barley; **t23** really good bitter-sweet balance with honeycomb and butterscotch leading the line; pretty juicy, busy stuff; **f24** dries as it should with some vague spices adding to the vanilla and hickory; **b23** an entirely re-worked, now smokeless, malt that has little in common with its predecessors. Quite lovely, though. 43%

Glen Garioch 1797 Founders Reserve db **(87.5)** n21 t22 f22.5. Excellent mocha accompanies the fruit with aplomb; **b22** impressively fruity and chewy: some serious flavour profiles in there. *48%*

Glen Garioch 1958 db **(90)** n24 t21 f23 b22. The distillery in its old smoky clothes: and quite splendid it looks! *43%. 328 bottles.*

Glen Garioch 1995 db **(86)** n21 t22 f21.5 b21.5. Typically noisy on the palate, even though the malty core is quite thin. Some big natural caramels, though. *55.3%. ncf.*

⋅≔⋅ **Glen Garioch 1997** db **(89)** n22 unusually salty, dry and subtle; **t22.5** just a few semi-gristy sugars make a minor noise while the barley appears in intense bursts but happy to duck behind the oak; some early barley wine oils early on; **f22** a charming fade of caramelised barley; **b22.5** had you tasted this malt as a 15-year-old back in 1997, you would have tasted something far removed from this, with a peaty bite ripping into the palate. To say this malt has evolved is an understatement. *56.5%. Whisky Shop Exclusive. 204 bottles.*

Glen Garioch 1997 db **(89.5)** n22 lively barley bolstered by what appears to be a generous but perfectly acceptable cut on the stills; **t23** huge delivery which makes the most of the 48% abv. This doesn't need water, just time and a strong jaw to chew it. That wide cut on the nose is confirmed on the palate with a feisty oiliness which drags every last nuance from the barley; **f22** long with those oils now intensifying around a cocoa glow; **b22.5** I have to say: I have long been a bit of a voice in the wilderness among whisky professionals as to regards this distillery. This not so subtly muscled malt does my case no harm whatsoever. *56.7%. ncf.*

⋅≔⋅ **Glen Garioch 1999** db **(64)** n16 t17 f15 b16. Massively sulphured. *56.3%. ncf.*

⋅≔⋅ **Glen Garioch Virgin Oak** db **(93)** n22 a salty, unsmoked bacon feel to this with quietly controlled tannins and hickory; **t23.5** a series of complex sugar notes are first to arrive. Then come in second, third and fourth, the complexity levels rising by the second; grated coconut and Brazilian biscuit works well with the maple syrup; **f24** now the complexity peaks with modest spices cranking up the vanilla and countering the light layer of ulmo and manuka honey blend; **b23.5** Glen Garioch as probably never seen before and at its most beautifully complex. *56.7%.*

Archives Glen Garioch 1990 21 Years Old First Release hogshead, cask no. 252, dist 28 Dec 90, bott 5 Jan 12 **(77)** n19 t21 f19 b19. Any sweeter and my teeth will drop out. Never gives the impression of high quality malt. *54%. nc ncf sc. Whiskybase B.V. 267 bottles.*

⋅≔⋅ **Berry's Own Selection 1992** cask no. 3464, bott 2013 **(87)** n23 a light blend of honey and carrot juice shows this will stick to a slightly earthy, complex and balanced style; **t23** good oils to the sugars, in fact a thin syrup engulfs the bright barley and fattening oak; **f19.5** let down by some bitterness from the cask, though spices try to compensate; **b21.5** a distillery with the propensity to make gorgeous whisky without seemingly breaking sweat is at it again...just not helped by a indifferent piece of wood. *46%. nc ncf sc.*

⋅≔⋅ **Liquid Library Glen Garioch 1991** ex-bourbon hogshead, dist 91, bott 12 **(93.5)** n23 an irresistible blend of boiled gooseberries and cordite (non-boiled); **t24** the delicate smoke adds minor ballast to the evocative light fruit and barley mix: just so many mind-blowing layers; **f23** long with a few late oils offering a cocoa bitterness and ever thickening vanilla; **b23.5** an all day any, day show dram showing wonderful sleight of hand. *52.5%. The Whisky Agency.*

Liquid Sun Glen Garioch 21 Years Old dist 1991 **(88)** n21.5 a little bit of distillery nip on the nose; thin barley; **t22.5** fattens up on delivery and surges with a gorgeous and satisfying vanilla and barley oily combo; **f22** warms with an intriguing mix of distillery bite and quite separate spices; the cocoa rounds matters off; **b22** the distillery on its best behaviour for that period. A very even malt. *52.8%. sc. The Whisky Agency.*

⋅≔⋅ **Master of Malt Glen Garioch Aged 21 Years** bourbon cask, dist 16 May 90, bott 8 Feb 12 **(86)** n22 t23 f20 b21. Anyone remember the original 21-y-o produced by the distillery? Not exactly like this one...none of the bite (or even smoke), though that didn't offer the gorgeous fresh malt and gooseberries available here. *48.8%. ncf sc.*

⋅≔⋅ **Old Malt Cask Glen Garioch Aged 21 Years** refill hogshead, cask no. 9809, dist Nov 91, bott May 13 **(85.5)** n21.5 t22 f20.5 b21.5. A sweet, nutty number where the sugars at times seem a little out of control because of the lack of body. Enjoyable, if characteristically thin. *50%. nc ncf sc. 251 bottles.*

Old Malt Cask Glen Garioch Aged 25 Years refill hogshead, cask no. 7866, dist May 86, bott Nov 11 **(88.5)** n22 chunky with an almost Bowmore-style Fisherman's Friend edge to the quagmire malt: curious, seeing they are from the same company....; at times it is like a vaguely peated bourbon; **t22.5** again, Fisherman's Friend...but without any great peat residue, though there is definitely a smokiness. The barley is juicy and brimming with muscovado sugars. Plus more bourbony liquorice and hickory; **f22** long and attractive; **b22** uniquely Geery. And an impressive attempt to unite Scotland with Kentucky. *50%. nc ncf sc. 174 bottles.*

⋅≔⋅ **Provenance Glen Garioch Over 17 Years** refill hogshead, cask no. 9767, dist Spring 95, bott Spring 13 **(87.5)** n21.5 thin. Slightly wallpaper glueish, but gristy, too; **t22** thin start again in the less than impressive delivery but the barley and banana begin to spread; **f22** a surprising number of late sugars make for the easiest of gristy, ultra malty finishes; **b22** Glen Garioch in this mood can win the hearts of anyone. *46%. nc ncf sc.*

⋯ **Wemyss Glen Garioch 1989 Single Highland "Fruit Bonbons"** hogshead **(91.5) n22** loys of zingy barley with a few greengages and under-ripe gooseberries thrown in for good measure; **t23.5** from the nose this had to be salivating...and it is! The barley cuts a juicy dash but there are sufficient oils to help the tannins to gather and intensify, though weak ulmo honey keeps the sugar levels up before the spices arrive; **f23** the barley still retains a vaguely fruity presence, but the pulsing spicy oak lasts longest; **b23** the spirit from the stills at this time had a "fire water" reputation which now, as is so often the case, means we have a malt which is wilful and complex and able to take the two decades of maturation comfortably in its stride. *46%. sc. 325 bottles.*

The Whisky Agency Glen Garioch 20 Years Old bourbon cask, dist 1991, bott 2011 **(85.5) n21.5 t23 f20 b21.** An attractive malt making the most of an intense barley simplicity. Some muscovado sugars balance out the spices. *54.4%. sc.*

GLENGLASSAUGH
Speyside, 1875. The BenRiach Distillery Co. Working.

Glenglassaugh 21 Year Old db **(94) n23.5** elegant and adroit, the lightness of touch between the citrus and barley is nigh on mesmeric: conflicting messages of age in that it appears younger and yet you feel something has to hit this degree of vintage to hit this degree of aloofness. Delicate and charming...; **t24.5** again we have all kinds of messages on delivery: the spices fizz around announcing oaky intentions and then the barley sooths and sweetens even with a degree of youthful juiciness. The tastebuds are never more than caressed, the sugar-sweetened citrus ensuring neither the barley or oak form any kind of advantage; impeccably weighted, a near perfect treat for the palate; **f22.5** white chocolate and vanilla lead the way as the oak begins to offer a degree of comparative austerity; **b23.5** a malt which simply sings on the palate and a fabulous benchmark for the new owners to try to achieve in 2030...!! *46%*

Glenglassaugh 26 Years Old db **(78.5) n19 t21.5 f18.5 b19.5.** Industrial amounts of cream toffee here. Also some odd and off key fruit notes winging in from somewhere. Not quite the gem I had hoped for. *46%*

Glenglassaugh Master Distillers' Selection Aged 28 Years dist 1983 db **(93) n23** seville orange and vanilla. But not quite that simple...don't get me started on the antique leather...; **t24** the body is of the type you might see on a Scandinavian beach in high summer: beautiful tone and delicate curves in all the right places. The barley myriad juices; the oak conjures several layers of vanillas, including a light covering of ulmo honey; **f22.5** just bitters out slightly, though remains busy; **b23.5** knowing Norway as I do, glad to see these lovely people are getting their money's worth! *49.8%. nc ncf sc. Norway exclusive. 400 bottles.*

Glenglassaugh 30 Year Old db **(89) n23 t23 f21 b22.** Sheer poetry. Or not... *43.1%*

Glenglassaugh Rare Casks Aged Over 30 Years db **(86) n22 t21 f21.5 b21.5.** Nearly four decades in an oak cask has resulted in a huge eruption of caramels. Soft oils and citrus abounds but it is the oak which dominates. *43%. nc ncf sc. Actual age 36 years. 280 bottles.*

Glenglassaugh The Chosen Few 1st Edition "Ronnie Routledge" 35 Years Old sherry butt, dist May 76 db **(95) n24** lacking the over enthusiastic oak which might have been expected, it enjoys the freedom with a wonderful display of its trademark orange blossom honey but with extra butterscotch, red liquorice and glace cherries. Very bourbony, but this time with a distinctive barley lilt; **t24** the strength is almost perfect for the degree of intensity proffered by the complex early sugars. The natural caramel forms a medium-depthed layer, but one easily penetrated by myriad further bourbon signatures, the spiced liquorice not being the least of them; **f23.5** long with a near perfect weight to the oil and oaky background. Busy spices and busier sugars, all done with panache; egg custard tart, improbably sprinkled with a little hickory and allspice; **b23.5** I had no idea Ronnie Routledge was 35 years old. Thought he was much younger... *49.6%. 654 bottles.*

Glenglassaugh Aged 37 Years db **(92) n23.5** honeycomb and hickory; burnt (or with the vaguest hint of smoke, is that burning?) date and walnut cake with liberal helpings of Demerara sugar; a hint of spice on the ever thickening vanilla. Not a single off note, or hint of over exertion...; **t23** excellent honey and spice delivery. First-class oils and beeswax ensure the sugars glide around the palate as if on skates; a curious subplot of glazed cherry ups the salivation factor even further; **f22** more vanillas and a little (smoky?) praline for a finale flourish; **b23.5** after all those years, dementia has set in: it thinks it's a bourbon... And not any old bourbon, believe me... *54.8%. nc ncf.*

Glenglassaugh Master Distillers' Selection Aged 37 Years dist 1974 db **(90.5) n23** a complex smattering of oaky tones, almost all of them recognisable in well matured bourbon: the most attractive is the interplay between the orange blossom honey and much drier hickory; **t23** the honey tries to carry on from the nose. But brought to a halt a far more aggressive toasty oak, though a brief early kumquat injection restores balance; **f22** sugar-free mocha; **b22.5** for the US market only, one assumes it was sent to Oakland. And I have just spotted the tasting notes I did for their 37-year-old bottled last year...the characteristics almost identical! Oh well, it is personally reassuring that even with over 1,000 tasting notes completed for the next Bible, my poor old palate is still registering! *56%. nc ncf sc. USA exclusive. 470 bottles.*

⁘ **Glenglassaugh Massandra Collection Aleatico Aged 39 Years** db (96.5) **n24.5** when you have grape in a malt, you really want it to do something and not either ruin it or swamp the barley into silence. Here is that rarest of beasts of a grape which has so much to say, especially in its deep Sumatra and Blue Mountain mix of coffee. The sharpness of the tannin works against the brilliance of the thick barley, yet does so with a soft, always alluring, voice; **t25** this appears to be an old malt (again, I don't have details with the sample) for the layering of the oak is truly exceptional. But where this truly excels is with both the weight, intensity and vivacity of the barley coupling so seamlessly with the much richer grape which, like the nose, is intent on displaying a fabulous coffeed edge, though here much more milky and of a mocha style. We are talking, in short, perfection...; **f23** more vanilla at play, and some courser sugars plus a furry buzz which may be more of a marmalade character than anything more sinister; **b24** if you are looking for something very different, and truly exceptional quality wise, you could do a lot worse. One of the few whiskies this year which has made me sit bolt upright in my seat. A whisky of the very rarest beauty and one of the finest scotch whiskies to land on my tasting desk for a great many years... *50.7%.*

Glenglassaugh 40 Year Old db (96) **n24.5** the kind of oak you'd expect at this age – if you are uncommonly lucky or have access to some of the most glorious-nosing ancient casks in all Scotland - but there is so much else on the fruity front besides: grape, over-ripe yam, fat cherries...And then there is a bourbony element with molassed hickory and sweetened vanilla: wake me, I must be dreaming...on second thoughts, don't; **t24.5** pure silk on delivery. All the flavours arrive in one rich wave of consummate sweetness, a tapestry celebrating the enormity of both the fruit and oak, yet condensed into a few inches rather than feet; plenty of soft medium roast Jamaican Blue Mountain and then at times mocha; on the fruity front there is juicy dates mulched with burned raisin; **f23** the relative Achilles heel as the more bitter, nutty parts of the oak gather; **b24** it is as if this malt has gone through a 40-year marrying process: the interlinking of flavours and styles is truly beyond belief. *44.6%*

Glenglassaugh Aged 43 Years db (91) **n23.5** a nose of rare clarity for its age. Or it is once it has been in the glass for a good 15 minutes. Then the wrinkles vanish and we are left with a vibrant, juicy nose offering a sweetness that runs the full gamut from fruit to biscuit... Not surprisingly there is a death by chocolate feel to this one, too. And even a little smoke; not entire free of the odd gremlin, but not too much damage done; **t24** you really don't spit this kind of whisky, however professional you are. Not sure if the silkworm has been bred yet that can produce something as silky as this guy. A few random spices here, a splash of walnut oil there; **f21** a slight Achilles heel: some weaknesses show as a mild bitterness leaks in. But I am not quibbling; **b22.5** another ridiculously magnificent malt from a distillery which should never have been closed in the first place... *48.7%. nc ncf.*

Glenglassaugh Andrea Cammineci 1972 refill butt db (92.5) **n23.5** spiced bonbons, with some black cherry for good measure; the sweetness is dull, of the liquorice variety as well as toasty raisin; **t24** those looking for a big sherry statement are in for a shock: the delivery is nearer Kentucky with tidal waves of waxy honeycomb and natural caramels; the odd piece of fruitcake can be spotted bobbing around; **f22** enters a no-man's-land for a while where there is a lack of anything much. Then, slowly, a fruitcake toasty dryness emerges, along with walnut oil; **b23** one of those rare hybrids that manages to get the best of both worlds; will appeal to high quality bourbon lovers every bit as those looking for sumptuous sherried drams... *59.1%. nc ncf sc. For German distribution.*

Glenglassaugh 1973 Family Silver db (95) **n23 t24 f24 b24.** From first to last this whisky caresses and teases. It is old but shows no over-ageing. It offers what appears a malt veneer but is complexity itself. Brilliant. And now, sadly, almost impossible to find. Except, possibly, at the Mansefield Hotel, Elgin. *40%*

⁘ **Glenglassaugh The Chosen Few 1978** db (94) **n24** the nose of a malt which has seen probably more summers than it should have done. But it has picked up a creamy, orange blossom honey tan along the way; the multiple vanilla tones are seasoned beautifully with a soft saltiness. Enough to make one swoon...; **t23** despite the early sugars, the delivery is dominated with over-aged oak: punchy tannins which creak around the palate. Thankfully there is enough spotted dog pudding encased in sugar – and coconut cream – to see off the aged excess; **f23.5** settles now with a few spices adding to the sweetened Carnation evaporated milk; **b23.5** hate to say it, and almost impossible to believe: but Mhairi McDonald has not seen off the years quite as well as Ronnie Routledge. Even so, still some looker! *46.5%.*

⁛ **Glenglassaugh Evolution Ex-Tennessee Cask** db (87) **n22** crème brule; **t22.5** an ever increasing intensifying degree of muscovado sugars stirred into the vanilla; **f21** the fondant of a Walnut Whip battling with some random barley and oak notes; **b21.5** a Bambi of a dram, youthfully stumbling around seeking balance with limited success. Interesting: the 10cl sample bottle here tells me only it is ex-Tennessee cask. I'd be willing to bet a wad of this is Dickel over Daniel any day. The giveaway is the fact that the punchier tannins are not in evidence – suggesting older maturation in the US. Nor is the residual oiliness which usually makes its mark. Having said all that, I'm sure someone will now tell me this is a JD cask! *57.2%.*

⁛ **Glenglassaugh Madeira** db (93) **n23.5** spices rarely come sexier: busy, pulsing and of varying tone and heat; mainly appear to be oak led, though the sultana concentrate makes its mark, also; **t23.5** thick grape dulls the expected spice kick; the sugars, at first beaming, are also quickly subdued, though of a lightly molassed style; supremely chewy, though, with just so sugar impact; **f22.5** a gorgeous creamy mocha with a tea spoon of molasses; a slightly muffled, furry finale; **b23.5** a deliciously rich but surprising malt in that the spices fanfared on the nose never quite arrive. Love it, warts and all. *44.8% nc ncf sc. 437 bottles.*

Glenglassaugh The Manager's Legacy No.1 Jim Cryle 1974 refill sherry hogshead db (90.5) **n21.5** citrus and various salty, herbal notes try to prop up a crumbling castle as an incoming tide of oak begins to wash it away...; **t23.5** where did that come from? Early oak, but then a magnificent recovery in the form of sharp old orange peel and a salty, mega malty thrust. Some dried fruit, mainly old dates and plums, build further bridges and as the saline quality intensifies, the juicier it all becomes; **f22.5** long with spices and plenty of cream toffee; **b23** talk about blowing away the cobwebs! The nose trumpets all the hallmarks of a tired old malt in decline. What follows on the palate could not be more opposite. Don't you just love a surprise! *52.9%. nc ncf sc. 200 bottles.*

Glenglassaugh The Manager's Legacy No.2 Dod Cameron 1986 refill sherry butt, dist Dec 86 db (92) **n23.5** the sherry residue must have been as thick as tar when they billed this butt: an enormous welter of pithy and juicy grape married with the aroma one might expect at a Fruitcake Fest. The odd roasty bitter note counters the sweeter Demerara tones. Wow! **t24** a near perfect delivery with that thick grape arriving hand-in-hand with sublime spices; again a burnt toast bitterness battles it out with some macho sugars; **f22** back to a more Dundee cake style, with a few natural caramels thrown in; **b22.5** did anyone mention this was from a sherry butt...? A vague, mildly out of kilter, bitterness knocks the odd mark off here and there, but a dram to kick the shoes off to and savour. *45.3%. nc ncf sc. 500 bottles.*

Glenglassaugh The Manager's Legacy No.3 Bert Forsyth 1968 refill sherry butt, dist Dec 68 db (89) **n22 t23 f22 b22.** A kind of upside down whisky: usually the big oaks arrive at the death. Here they are all upfront... An excellent whisky that, by rights, should never be... *44.9%. nc ncf sc. 300 bottles.*

Glenglassaugh The Manager's Legacy No.4 Walter Grant 1967 refill sherry hogshead, dist May 67 db (86.5) **n19.5 t22 f23 b22.** Despite the oaky wounds to the nose, the palate is far more open and somehow reaches a degree of depth and complexity which makes for an excellent and unexpected experience. *40.4%. nc ncf sc. 200 bottles.*

⁛ **Glenglassaugh Muscat Finish** db (94) **n23** the nose appears to be hit continuously with an oak stave. The blows are softened only by a thick layer of boiled plums and under-ripe dates; **t23. 5** salivating to the point of near incontrollable dribbling...as juicy as any malt you'll taste this year. But, unusually, oak-weighted, too, with that sucked back of pencil unmistakable in its sheer woodiness. Even so, it works..beautifully! And not least because of a fabulous mocha, rum and raisin middle; **f24** at last softens, though the fruits, aided by lemon-topped marzipan, rumble on; the butterscotch fade is truly classic; **b23.5** you'd expect any Muscat finish to be over the top...and it is. Great to see a whisky named after a former Millwall hardman...wasn't it...? *44.1% nc ncf sc. 200 bottles.*

⁛ **Glenglassaugh Red Port** db (85) **n22 t22 f20 b21.** Loads of homemade redcurrant jam on toast here. Excellent texture, good age but an off key finish. *50.2%. nc ncf sc.*

Glenglassaugh Revival new, refill and Oloroso sherry casks db (75) **n19 t20 f17 b19.** Rule number one: if you are going to spend a lot of money to rebuild a distillery and make great whisky, then ensure you put the spirit into excellent oak. Which is why it is best avoiding present day sherry butts at all costs as the chances of running into sulphur is high. There is some stonkingly good malt included in this bottling, and the fabulous chocolate raisin is there to see. But I look forward to seeing a bottling from 100% ex-bourbon. *46%. nc ncf.*

⁛ **Glenglassaugh Sherry** db (87) **n21.5** pure sherry trifle...with an extra dollop of custard; **t22.5** rampant tannins are impressively quelled by a viscous layer of clean, unambiguous sherry which, after untangling, offers greengage and spice; **f21** long, with those oak notes calming down into gentler cocoa tones; no shortage of raisin, too...; **b22** at first the sherry is over dominant, but once it relaxes the complexity and enjoyment levels rise. Technically, a bit of a nightmare. But the impact of the sherry is compelling. *53.3% nc ncf sc. 328 bottles.*

Glenglassaugh The Spirit Drink db (85) n20 t22 f21.5 b21.5. A pretty wide margin taken on the cut here, it seems, so there is plenty to chew over. Richly flavoured and a tad oily, as is to be expected, which helps the barley to assert itself in midstream. The usual new make chocolaty element at work here, too, late on. Just great to see this distillery back in harness after all these years. And a great idea to get the new spirit out to the public, something I have been encouraging distilleries to do since my beard was still blue. Look forward to seeing another version where a narrower cut has been made. 50%. 8,160 bottles.

Glenglassaugh The Spirit Drink Fledgling XB db (91) n22 t23.5 f22.5 b23. The barley arrives unblemished and makes a proud, juicy stand. A surprising degree of early natural caramel. Prefer this over the peat, to be honest, and augers well for the distillery's future. 50%

Glenglassaugh The Spirit Drink Peated db (89.5) n22 t23 f22 b22.5. Enjoyable and doesn't appear close to its 50%abv. But it's not about the bite, for there is a welcome citrus freshness to this, helped along the way by a peatiness which is big but by no means out to be the only important voice. 50%

Glenglassaugh The Spirit Drink That Blushes to Speak Its Name db (85) n22 t21.5 f21 b21. Not whisky, of course. New make matured for a few months in wine barrels. The result is a Rose-looking spirit. Actually takes me back to my early childhood – no, not the tasting of new make spirit. But the redcurrant aroma which does its best to calm the new make ruggedness. Tasty and fascinating, though the wine tries to minimalise the usual sweetness you find in malt spirit. 50%

Mo Òr Collection Glenglassaugh 1983 26 Years Old first fill Oloroso sherry butt, cask no. 171, dist 17 Jun 83, bott 8 Oct 09 (72) n19 t20 f15 b18. Despite the blood orange, this is a dry and nutty affair. But gets drier, and unacceptably so, as the sulphur candle takes hold. 50.4%. nc ncf sc. Release No. 6. The Whisky Talker. 885 bottles.

GLENGOYNE

Highlands (Southwest), 1833. Ian Macleod Distillers. Working.

Glengoyne 10 Years Old db (90) n22 beautifully clean despite coal-gas bite. The barley is almost in concentrate form with a marmalade sweetness adding richness; t23 crisp, firm arrival with massive barley surge, seriously chewy and textbook bitter-sweet balance; but now some oils have tucked in to intensify and lengthen; f22 incredibly long and refined for such a light malt. The oak, which made soft noises in the middle now intensifies, but harmonises with the intense barley; an added touch of coffee signals some extra oak in recent bottlings; b23 proof that to create balance you do not have to have peat at all. The secret is the intensity of barley intermingling with oak. Not a single negative note from first to last and now a touch of oil and coffee has upped the intensity further. 40%

Glengoyne 12 Years Old db (91.5) n22.5 salty, sweet, lightly fruity; t23 one of the softest deliveries on the market: the fruit, gristy sugars and malt combine to melt in the mouth: there is not a single hint of firmness; f23 a graduation of spices and vanilla. Delicate and delightful...; b23 the nose has a curiously intimate feel but the tasting experience is a wonderful surprise. 43%

Glengoyne 12 Years Old Cask Strength db (79) n18 t22 f19 b20. Not quite the happiest Glengoyne I've ever come across with the better notes compromised. 57.2%. nc ncf.

Glengoyne Aged 14 Years Limited Edition oloroso cask db (77) n19 t20 f19 b19. A vague sulphur taint. But rather underpowered anyway. 40%. nc. Marks & Spencer UK.

Glengoyne Single Cask 14 Years Old bourbon hogshead, cask no. 1546, dist 1 May 97 db (91.5) n22 outwardly dull thanks to a big natural caramel injection but there is some honeyed promise; t23 among the rich spiced tannins is a sumptuous honey middle, lightened by a soft citrus edge; f23.5 mocha enters to give a drying Jaffa Cake feel; b23 those lucky Swedes. Not only do they get all those stunning women, but this as well. 57.8%. nc ncf sc. Swedish exclusive.

Glengoyne 15 Years Old db (73.5) n18 t19 f18 b18.5. Some sub-standard, left-out-in-the-rain oak crept in from somewhere. Ouch. 40%. Travel Retail exclusive.

⁙ **Glengoyne 15 Years** sherry casks db (81) n19 t20 f21 b21. Brain-numbingly dull and heavily toffeed in style. Just don't get what is trying to be created here. Some late spices remind me I'm awake, but still the perfect dram to have before bed – simply to send you to sleep. Or maybe I just need to see a Doctor... 43%. nc. Ian Macleod Distillers.

Glengoyne 17 Years Old db (86) n21 t23 f21 b21. Some of the guys at Glengoyne think I'm nuts. They couldn't get their head around the 79 I gave it last time. And they will be shaking my neck not my hand when they see the score here...Vastly improved but there is an off sherry tang which points to a naughty butt or two somewhere. Elsewhere mouth-watering and at times fabulously intense. 43%

⁙ **Glengoyne 18 Years** first-fill sherry casks db (82) n22 t22 f18 b20. Bunches of lush grape on nose and delivery, where there is no shortage of caramel. But things go downhill once the dreaded "s" word kicks in. 43%. nc. Ian Macleod Distillers.

Glengoyne 21 Years Old db (90) n21 closed and tight for the most part as Glengoyne sometimes has a tendency to be nose-wise, with the emphasis very much on coal gas; t22 slow to start with a few barley heads popping up to be seen; then spices arrive with the oak for a slightly bourbony feel. Gentle butterscotch and honey add a mouth-watering edge to the drier oaks; f24 a stupendous honey thread is cross-stitched through the developing oak to deliver near perfect poise and balance at finish; b23 a vastly improved dram where the caramel has vanished and the tastebuds are constantly assailed and questioned. A malt which builds in pace and passion to delivery a final, wonderful coup-de-grace. Moments of being quite cerebral stuff. 43%

Glengoyne 21 Years Old Sherry Edition db (93) n22 t24 f23 b24. The nose at first is not overly promising, but it settles at it warms and what follows on the palate is at times glorious. Few whiskies will match this for its bitter-sweet depth which is pure textbook. Glengoyne as few will have seen it before. 43%

Glengoyne Single Cask 24 Years Old European oak sherry butt, cask no. 354, dist 14 May 87 (96.5) n24 I could almost weep as this is the way a sherry butt should be on the nose: CLEAN and full of rich tannins, pith, spice and complex sugars; t24.5 oh, yes.....YES!!! Brilliant. Exactly how it should be for the age: the barley, oak and grape are all at the very points you would expect them to be. As for the spices: this is swoonable stuff... f24 and again, confirmation that this cask is clean without a single off note. No bitterness, no puckering of the tongue. The juicy grape, bolstered by honey melon and spice, embraces the rich slightly bourbony tannins with relish...; b24 Glengoyne in full pomp. Magnificent. 54.8%. nc ncf sc.

Glengoyne 40 Years Old db (83) n23 t21 f19 b20. Thick fruit intermittently pads around the nose and palate but the oak is pretty colossal. Apparent attempts to reinvigorate it appear to have backfired. 45.9%

⁘ **Glengoyne Cask Strength** db (86) n21.5 t23 f20 b21.5. The grape is nailed to the nose and palate with minimum subtlety. Initial flavour explosion packed with eye-glisteningly intense grape. But a furriness to the finish also plays a part, though not quite so upbeat. 58.7%. nc ncf. Ian Macleod Distillers. batch no. 001.

Glengoyne Port Cask Finish 1996 db (74) n17 t20 f18.5 b18.5. Decent fruit on delivery, but elsewhere proof that in whisky there is no such thing as any port cask in a storm... 46%

Glengoyne Vintage 1996 db (70) n16 t18 f18 b18. Creamy, but off key. 43%. nc ncf. USA.

Glengoyne Vintage 1997 db (68) n16 t18 f17 b17. The "S" word strikes. And with a vengeance. 43%. nc ncf. German release.

Glengoyne 'Glen Guin' 16 Year Old Shiraz Finish db (79) n18.5 t20 f19.5 b20. Some oily depth here. 48%

Glengoyne Burnfoot db (84) n21 t21 f21.5 b21. A clodhopping bruiser of a malt. Good honey, though. 40%. Duty Free Market.

⁘ **A.D. Rattray Glengoyne 2001** sherry butt, cask no. 388, dist 3 Mar 2001, bott Apr 2013 (68) n18 t18 f16 b16. Whenever "sherry butt" and "Glengoyne" are mentioned in the same sentence, I give an involuntary shudder. Here you can see why. 58.4%. sc. Dewar Rattray Cask Collection.

Glengoyne Teapot Dram db (86.5) n23 t22 f20.5 b21. The nose, for its obvious fault, still has a truly classic oloroso-style depth. However, the light sulphur stain is not so easily covered up once tasted. A slightly cracked teapot, I'm afraid. 58.8%. nc ncf. Distillery exclusive.

⁘ **Malts Of Scotland Glengoyne 1997** bourbon hogshead, cask no. MoS 13020, dist Mar 97, bott Apr 13 (86) n21.5 t22.5 f21 b21. Outstanding weight and texture to the body, with the malt offering a gorgeously honeyed sheen. Oak of only fair quality limits further development. 54.6%. nc ncf sc. 96 bottles.

Malts Of Scotland Glengoyne 1998 sherry hogshead, cask no. MoS12003, dist 1 Apr 98, bott Jan 12 (90.5) n23 simplistic oloroso trademark; weighty, distinctly Dundee fruitcake in style, complete with toasted almonds; t23 mouth-filling with excellent black pepper bite to the toasty raisin; limited complexity development, but some late vanilla; f22 more vanilla as it dries; b22.5 a clean, untainted sherry butt offering pure silk. 52.7%. nc ncf sc.

Malts Of Scotland Glengoyne 1998 sherry hogshead, cask no. MoS11006, dist May 98, bott Aug 11 (63) n17 t16 f15 b15. The MOS12003 above thankfully dodged the sulphur bullet. This, alas, did not. 53.7%. nc ncf sc. Malts Of Scotland.

Malts Of Scotland Glengoyne 1998 sherry hogshead, cask no. MoS12024, dist Apr 98, bott Apr 12 (66) n17 t17 f16 b16. Opening a sherry butt Glengoyne is the equivalent of tackling an UXB. This one has exploded in my face... 54.8%. nc ncf sc. Malts Of Scotland.

⁘ **Malts Of Scotland Glengoyne 1998** sherry hogshead, cask no. MoS 12050, dist Apr 98, bott Oct 12 (72.5) n21 t20 f15 b16.5. What could have been an orange fest to remember turns into a sulphury lemon. 54.2%. nc ncf sc. 96 bottles. Exclusive bottling for Aquavitae Die Messe.

Old Malt Cask Glengoyne Aged 14 Years refill hogshead, cask no. 7661, dist Sep 97, bott Sep 11 (83) n21 t21 f20 b21. A dry guy with a spicy clout. 50%. nc ncf sc. 307 bottles.

Provenance Glengoyne Over 11 Years refill hogshead, cask no. 7604, dist Winter 1999, bott Summer 2011 **(89) n22.5** top class barley with controlled dusting of sugar; **t22** fabulous clarity to the malt: crisp, precise and very comfortable as the oak gathers; some delicate citrus fizz; **f22** a hint of medium roast Mysore coffee amid the natural caramel; **b22.5** crystalline and beautifully clean. 46%. nc ncf sc. Douglas Laing & Co.

Provenance Glengoyne Over 12 Years refill hogshead, cask no. 7962, dist Winter 1999, bott Winter 2011 **(81.5) n21 t20 f20 b20.5**. Structurally, the malty weight is very similar to their new 11-year-old. But an inferior cask means far less positive development. 46%. nc ncf sc.

⋯ **Provenance Glengoyne Over 12 Years** refill hogshead, cask no. 8567, dist Winter 99, bott Summer 12 **(84) n21 t21.5 f20.5 b21**. Crispy barley sugar. 46%. nc ncf sc.

⋯ **Provenance Glengoyne Over 13 Years** refill hogshead, cask no. 9517, dist Winter 1999, bott Winter 2013 **(91.5) n22.5** a fabulous mix of delicate and weighty barley; fresh yet with enough oak for depth; **t23** grassy and gristy with the salivating factor entering red on the dial; the lightness of the sugars beggars belief; **f23** sublime, lightly sweetened vanilla with crisp barley lingering to the end; **b23** simple yet ridiculously charming. 46%. nc ncf.

The Whisky Cask Glengoyne Aged 37 Years bourbon cask, dist 1972, bott 2010 **(92.5) n23** we have entered exotic fruit territory here, but there is much more: almost like sniffing at the herb rack; **t23.5** bold sugars see off the bigger tannins. We get back to those dry herbs again, though vanilla pods are in biggest demand; wonderful kumquat and lemon notes; **f23** long with a pretty standard vanilla and butterscotch fade; chalky oak gives a dry send off; **b23** about as busy a malt as you'll find. Full of herb and spicy intent. 51.8%. sc. The Whisky Cask.

GLEN GRANT
Speyside, 1840. Campari. Working.

Glen Grant db **(87) n21.5 t23 f21 b21.5**. This is a collector's malt for the back label alone: truly one of the most bizarre I have ever seen. "James Grant, 'The Major'" it cheerfully chirrups, "was only 25 when he set about achieving his vision of a single malt with a clear colour. The unique flavour and appearance was due to the purifiers and the tall slender stills he designed and the decision to retain its natural colour..." Then underneath is written: "Farven Justeter Med Karamel/Mit Farbstoff"" Doh! Or, as they say in German: "Doh!" Need any more be said about the nonsense, the pure insanity, of adding colouring to whisky. 40%

Glen Grant 5 Years Old db **(89) n22.5 t22 f21.5 b23**. Elegant malt which has noticeably grown in stature and complexity of late. 40%

Glen Grant Aged 10 Years db **(95) n23.5** OK: let's take turns in counting the rungs on the barley ladder here....the usual crisp aroma, but softened by deft, if unspecific fruitiness (maybe the distant aroma of a very old orange and by no means unpleasant!), myriad vanilla and butterscotch notes can do without the toffee one; **t24** magnificent! A malty delivery which simultaneously melts in the mouth, yet offers granite-like barley that crashes into your teeth; the star, perhaps are the sugars which vary from caster, through golden syrup and pans out somewhere in the muscovado range – curiously honey-free, though; **f23** a tad tangy, though the caramel returns to turn out the lights after the butterscotch and marzipan say goodnight..; **b23.5** unquestionably the best official 10-y-o distillery bottling I have tasted from this distillery. Absolutely nails it! Oh, and had they bottled this at 46% abv and without the trimmings...my word! Might well have been a contender for Scotch of the Year. It won't be long before word finally gets around about just how bloody good this distillery is. 40%

Glen Grant Aged 16 Years bott Mar 10 db **(91.5) n23** a lovely under-ripe banana sharpness to this while the malt snuggles up to the crunchy green apple; a playful molecule of smoke wafts around; **t23.5** salivating, fresh, slightly green ...and that's just the first few nano-seconds of the delivery! Next comes a lengthy, relaxed wave of oilier barley, with a coppery, honeyed depth; tangy vanilla fills the middle ground; **f21.5** medium length, more oils and barley but with a degree of bitterness; **b22** again the finish doesn't do justice to the earlier jousting on the nose and palate. The label talks about orchard fruits, and they are absolutely spot on. Apples are order of the day, but not sure about the ripe bit: they appear slightly green to me... and that suits the nature of the crisp malt. A gorgeous whisky I fully expect to see improve over coming batches: it's one that has potential to hit superstar status. 43%

Glen Grant Distillery Edition Aged 19 Years cask no. 17161, dist 12 Feb 92, bott 6 Jan 12 db **(92) n22.5** not the usual brusque nose; much softer than normal with ingratiating chocolate fudge notes tacked to the lemon barley theme; **t23.5** various medium weight tannins try to dampen the onslaught (or rather, not) but a soft molasses and burnt raisin sharpness does nothing to stifle the complexity; **f23** any longer and it'd be like waiting in a Post Office queue. Heads into the delicious direction of the chocolate and coconut side of liquorice allsorts; **b23.5** curiously, it seems I was at the distillery the week (possibly the day) this was distilled! Manager Denis Malcolm was there then, just (thankfully!) as he is today. Wonderful to see there are some consistencies in the changing whisky world... 52.4%. ncf sc. 222 bottles.

⋰ **Glen Grant Distillery Edition Cask Strength Aged 20 Years** cask no. 17165, dist 12 Feb 92, bott 14 Aug 12 db **(95.5) n23.5** oranges and roasted hazelnuts...and distant peat...?; **t24** busy delivery but the improbable smoke on the nose is confirmed on the palate, the peats clinging to the oils on which barley, as usual, abounds. More marmalade which works well with the buttery element. Amazing shape and complexity, all helped by the usual, unique clarity of this glorious distillery; **f23.5** so, so long, with the spices picking up where the smoke leaves off; cream jam doughnuts come to mind late on; **b24.5** I can only assume that this was matured in a cask which once held a high phenol Islay. The underlying peat is as intriguing as it is delicious! Glen Grant as you may never have seen it before...and will definitely want to see again. *55.7%. ncf. sc. 360 bottles.*

Glen Grant Cellar Reserve 1992 bottled 08 db **(94.5) n23** a beguiling array of crisp barley and crystalised sugary notes; if a nose can be crunchy and brittle, then this really is it; **t24** the tastebuds virtually swoon under this glorious bathing of barley and sugar; unbelievably juicy and mouth-watering for its age, the oak is there to ensure backbone and fair play and does nothing to subtract from the most graceful notes, except perhaps to pep up slightly with a teasing spiciness; **f24** more playful spices and a chocolate fudge lending weight to the glassy barley edge; one to close the eyes to and be consumed by; **b23.5** one of the great world distilleries being revealed to the us in its very finest colours. They tend to be natural, with no colourings added, therefore allowing the extraordinary kaleidoscope of subtle sweetnesses to be deployed and enjoyed to their fullest. I defy you not to be blown away by this one, especially when you realise there is not a single big base note to be heard... *46%. nc ncf.*

Glen Grant 170th Anniversary db **(89) n23.5 t23.5 f20 b22.** The odd mildly sulphured cask has slipped through the net here to reduce what was shaping to be something magnificent. Still enjoyable, though. *46%*

⋰ **Glen Grant Five Decades** bott 2013 db **(92) n24** the kind of aroma which leaves you transfixed: the trademark crisp, juicy barley is there in force, but the darker, deeper tones rumble with a spiced orange lead: sublimely complex; **t23.5** the delivery is full of the usual malty zest for life. There is a unique clarity to the barley of Glen Grant and here, on delivery and for a few a few moments after, this goes into overdrive. The mid ground is more muddled with tannin and burnt raisin making their presence felt; **f21.5** tangy marmalade; **b23** a nose and delivery of astonishing complexity. Hardly surprising the fade cannot keep up the pace. *46%*

Glen Grant The Major's Reserve bott Mar 10 db **(85.5) n21.5 t23 f20 b21.** Forget about the so-so nose and finish. This is one of those drams that demands you melt into your chair on delivery, such is the fresh beauty of the malt and stunning honeycomb threads which tie themselves around every taste bud. Pity about the ultra dry, caramel-rich finish, but apparently nearly all the sherry butts have now been used up at the distillery. Thank gawd for that. *40%*

Archives Glen Grant 1975 36 Years Old First Release hogshead, cask no. 5476, dist 18 Apr 75, bott 4 Jan 12 **(94.5) n25** only this distillery and Caperdonich produce fruit as exotic as this...and usually from casks of this vintage; **t23** silky delivery as required by the nose, though these days the oak can nip a bit; **f23.5** tires slightly, hence the light tang. The custardy vanilla and the fruit makes for a superb dessert **b23** I had expected the exotic fruit treatment. But not this Fortnum and Masonesque fruit basket... *46.6%. nc ncf sc. Whiskybase B.V. 81 bottles.*

Berry's Own Selection Glen Grant 1974 cask no. 7643, bott 2012 **(96.5) n25** at 54, am I too old to swoon? That near perfection of thick grape infused with essence of barley malt. The sugars are mere hints: grist here, honeydew melon there. And all emboldened by a smattering of herb and not overly antagonistic spice; **t24** the spices are more upfront now. But before they get a chance to really soar, molten honey fills the palate and dispenses grape in its cleanest form; the middle is a marvellous mix of coconut and raisin chocolate; **f23.5** maybe suffering from not quite knowing where the middle ends and the end begins. But there is no bitterness, no oak trying to have the last say at the cost of all else. Just a slow denouement, perhaps with a sprig of mint attached, of all else that has gone before; **b24** when I come across an unspoiled nugget like this, a malt of timeless magnificence, then the whisky world seems such a wonderful place in which to live. Those responsible for Scotland's whisky future could do worse than invest in a bottle and see what steps have to be taken to continue this glittering tradition. Certainly, the casks which have gone into this bottling represent a high water – or is it grape juice? – mark for Scotch single malt whisky. *478%. nc ncf sc.*

Berry's Own Selection Glen Grant 1974 cask no. 7646, bott 2012 **(79) n20.5 t22 f17.5 b19.** A fascinating and dramatic contrast with Berry's other Glen Grant offering this year. A kind of bottled proof that more is less. Plenty of wonderful spiced orangey-grape notes to get on with and thoroughly enjoy. But the failings are stark. *49.3%. nc ncf sc.*

⋰ **Duncan Taylor Dimensions Glen Grant 17 Years Old** cask no. 85116, dist May 95, bott May 12 **(84.5) n21 t21 f21.5 b21.** The usual chunky barley at play. But rather workmanlike and urbane by Glen Grant standards, concentrating on its fiery element rather than its usual deft complexity. *54.2%. nc ncf sc. Duncan Taylor & Co. 226 bottles.*

Duncan Taylor Dimensions Glen Grant 19 Years Old cask no. 142040, dist 1992, bott 2012 (88.5) n22 an exercise in simplicity: oak and barley...and that's it. Good, though..! t22 just the right yield from the oak to allow the barley full juicy value; f22.5 more complexity as the vanilla and then cocoa arrive in droves; b22 a blenders' delight of a malt possessing just enough tricks and turns to make for an entertainer. 52.7%. nc ncf sc. 242 bottles.

Duncan Taylor Dimensions Glen Grant 21 Years Old cask no. 16973, dist Aug 90, bott Jan 12 (85) n21 t22.5 f21.5 b20. A weirdo whisky. First we start with, if not unattractive, then certainly a fuddled and uncomfortable nose. This is followed with, outside the "Malts of Scotland Whisky Liqueur", one of the sweetest deliveries I've experienced, with your teeth wondering if permanent damage has been done. 55.5%. nc ncf sc.

Duncan Taylor Rare Auld Glen Grant 16 Years Old cask no. 85090, dist 1995 (88) n22.5 solid malt; a wall of the stuff offers at first a sharp crack across the bows before some sugary notes seep out almost shyly; t22.5 intense barley; busy spices arrive just as the vanilla begins to be heard; f21 the malt vanishes quickly leaving the vanilla and spices to fight it out alone; b22 not a malt for the squeamish: the intensity is sometimes challenging. 54.9%. sc.

First Cask Glen Grant 23 Years Old bourbon hogshead, cask no. 10182, dist 12 Jul 85, bott 28 Aug 08 (92.5) n23 barley concentrate with several charming layers of peek-a-boo bourbon; red-liquorice and black cherry; t23.5 lightly oiled barley with just enough attitude from the sugars and spices to crank up the complexity levels; f22.5 reverts back to a genteel maltiness though with enough spice to confirm it still has a pulse; b23.5 a serenely malty yet complex dram which has been around for a while, but there are still stocks left in Holland, apparently! Don't ask me how!! 55.8%. nc ncf sc. Whisky Import Nederland. 187 bottles.

Gordon & MacPhail Distillery Label Glen Grant 1960 (96) n24.5 oh my word! Spices with mufflers attached, oloroso with a few brush strokes of prune juice and molasses. And for all the obvious Spanish influence, we have echoes of Kentucky with liquorice and honey in delicate proportions and pastel shades; t23 the oak makes an early impact, as you might expect. But that is soon buried under layers of melt-in-the-mouth fruit, then a more bitter burnt raisin; f24.5 fabulously long. And the most extraordinary bisection of an ancient, slightly over cooked fruitcake. Which consisted of about 76% raisin; b24 the kind of nose which makes it difficult to get to the next stage. But when you make that next, tentative step, you are so glad you did! Just about perfect oloroso which alone these days makes this a national treasure. 40%

Gordon & MacPhail Distillery Label Glen Grant 1996 (87) n22.5 fragile, with the barley any moment about to give way to the vanilla; t22 a reversal on the nose with the vanillas in early control, but now it's those delicate barley notes which fight back. Just a slight degree of acacia honey, too; f21 and finally the vanilla holds sway...; b21.5 without G&M, it is unlikely Glen Grant would be as well loved as it is today: they carried its torch for decades. However, as lovely as this malt may be, they are doing a slight disservice. This really should be at 46%, as the quality would be increased significantly. 40%. Gordon & MacPhail.

Gordon & MacPhail The Queen's Diamond Jubilee Glen Grant 60 first fill sherry hogshead, cask no. 465, dist 2 Feb 56, bott 2 Feb 12 (92.5) n24.5 stunning smorgasbord of diced aged citrus and other fruit peel sets this off to a delicate and fresh start; the sweetness is supplied by a blend of heather and orange blossom honey; a tantalising trail of distant peat smoke; t23 light, delicate delivery offering early barley and thin, juicy grape. But the oak has a lot to say and makes a resounding vanilla custard statement; f22 thins out as the oaks take sharp command. Enough residual sugars to make for a pleasant if oaky landing; b23 how interesting to see a '52 Glen Grant picked for the Jubilee Celebrations. Back in 1992 I bought my then wife a bottle of Gordon and MacPhail 1952 for her 40th birthday. And I have to say that that bottling, still bristling with vibrancy, is better than this, which for all its charm is feeling the years. How do I know for sure? I still have that bottle. But ssshh! Don't tell my ex....!! 42.3%. sc. Gordon & MacPhail. 85 bottles.

Malts Of Scotland Glen Grant 1972 sherry hogshead, cask no. 8235, dist Nov 72, bott Jun 11 (96) n23 liberal degrees of manuka honey dovetail with the vanilla and fruitcake; t25 textbook! A near perfection of malt and fruit interlinking and then offering up a heady mix of nuts and spices; f23.5 the nuttiness intensifies and adds a degree of salt; the vanillas buzz and glow.; b24.5 Glen Grant boasted some of the finest sherry butts of the 1970s. This is one of them. 48.2%. nc ncf sc. Malts Of Scotland.

Malts Of Scotland Angel's Choice Glen Grant 1972 sherry hogshead, cask no. MoS12006, dist 1972, bott Jan 12 (89) n23 gloriously weighted grape, at times heading off towards a fruitcake complexity, but more happy in being the base of a sherry trifle; t24 thickly knotted oak radiates warm spices; the sugars and grapes are huddled together to form an intense core; f20 the spices continue to pulse while the vanillas, sugars and fruits untangle; furry finale; b22 the surprising slight tang on the nose and finish means that it is not quite in the same class as the Malts of Scotland version. 54.1%. nc ncf sc. Malts Of Scotland.

‹∴› **Master Of Malt Glen Grant 31 Years Old Lost Bottlings Series** dist 64, bott 95 **(97)** n24.5 near perfect. Spices, fruit, mocha and, one fancies, a touch of barley-carrying apple, in all the right places. Not a single atom of sulphur...anywhere...; **t24** you laugh as it delivers: the weight is as it should be, the treacle sugars and burnt raisin understand each other completely; the oils seem to have been weighted to sub-particle exactitude...ohhh, bliss; **f24** lingering, spiced up and suave. The raisin and sultana could not be better matched, with just so toastiness leading to a subtle chocolate fade; **b24.5** by 'eck! Sherry butts like this haven't been seen in Scotland for quite a while, believe me. If you wonder why I'm on the warpath with the modern day rubbish which passes for sherry-matured malt, get a gander at this...and welcome back to the lost world in which I used to belong and the majority of those working in today's industry have never seen, or even have the faintest idea ever existed. *45.8%*

Mo Òr Collection Glen Grant 1972 38 Years Old first fill bourbon hogshead, cask no. 16568, dist 31 May 72, bott 25 Jan 11 **(88)** n23 some pretty hefty layers of tannin, but a light hickory surge softens the attack and appears to underline the sugars; **t22** a big oak and sugar battle heads off into creamy mocha and spices; **f21** dries just a little too violently, though the spices are fine; **b22** a white knuckle ride of a dram. One fears it is going to disintegrate into old age at any moment, but it just manages to keep the wheels on the tracks. *46%. nc ncf sc. Release No. 16. The Whisky Talker. 210 bottles.*

Mo Òr Collection Glen Grant 1985 25 Years Old first fill bourbon hogshead, cask no. 10187, dist 12 Jul 85, bott 2 Dec 10 **(83)** n23 t21.5 f19 b19.5. Great nose, full of pithy crushed grape seeds despite its bourbon cask heritage. But for all its light sugar coating, simply cannot cope with the overwhelming dry oak. *46%. nc ncf sc. Release No. 53. 310 bottles.*

Old Malt Cask Glen Grant Aged 18 Years refill hogshead, cask no. 8006, dist Oct 93, bott Jan 12 **(80)** n19 t21 f19.5 b20.5. Huge, delicious malt. But the cask just isn't up to snuff. *50%. nc ncf sc. Douglas Laing & Co. 311 bottles.*

Old Malt Cask Glen Grant Aged 36 Years brandy finished butt, cask no. 7820, dist Apr 75, bott Nov 11 **(87)** n22 a huge and by no means unattractive pithy grape presence: it is as though the malt has been substituted for crushed grape pips; some lovely spices intervene; **t22** soft and immediately salivating and moderately sweet with the spices galloping in at the double; the dry middle of spice, more grape pip and oaky vanilla is almost inevitable; **f21.5** dry and enclosed; **b21.5** Glen Grant is probably the crispest, the most staccato, of all the malt produced in Scotland. And if I was asked how to enclose a malt and give it the tightest finish possible, my answer might be to finish it in a Cognac or brandy cask. So when I saw the label... *50%. nc ncf sc. Douglas Laing & Co. 268 bottles.*

The Perfect Dram Glen Grant 39 Years Old sherry cask, dist 1972, bott 2011 **(86)** n21 t21.5 f22 b21.5. A dram which will doubtless make some weak at the knees. But, for me, an example of a malt that shows faded greatness but with just not enough sugars present to make a must-have malt. Even so, once you get past the eye-watering oak, there is enough mocha and black pepper to make for a long and entertaining experience. *51.1%. sc.*

Provenance Glen Grant Over 8 Years refill barrel, cask no. 7611, dist Summer 2003, bott Summer 2011 **(88)** n22 a squirt of lemon zest in the crisp barley; **t22.5** beautiful delivery: barley sugar on a yielding, lightly oiled platform of vanilla; **f21.5** light, with spiced custard; **b22** a good example of the distillery showing its lilting maltiness when in that curious age between youth and maturity. *46%. nc ncf sc. Douglas Laing & Co.*

Provenance Glen Grant Over 12 Years refill hogshead, cask no. 7649, dist Autumn 1998, bott Summer 2011 **(83.5)** n21 t22 f20 b20.5. A volley of juicy grains does all it can to overcome the unflattering oak. *46%. nc ncf sc. Douglas Laing & Co.*

Scotch Malt Whisky Society Cask 9.63 Aged 8 Years first fill barrel, cask no. 800547, dist 2002 **(93)** n23.5 absolutely brimming with malty promise. Sweet and sharp, the closest commercial nose to this used to be the old non-age statement Glenfiddich; **t24** few whiskies force you into such rabid salivation. Fresh, clean and the barley simply exploding with lusty juices; **f22.5** the oak finally gets a word in edgeways. It arrives with a spicy butterscotch signature; **b23** this is a distillery very well suited to comparatively young malt. You will not find a more compelling case for a distillery bottling 8-year-old at cask strength than this. *60.9%. sc.*

Scott's Selection Glen Grant 1993 bott 2011 **(94)** n22 the usual tight barley and a very well behaved cask means a technical triumph but the complexity, beyond the simplest green apple tones, is relatively limited. My word, though: what you could do with this in a top class blend...; **t25** there may be relative inactivity on the nose. But it makes amends in scary fashion by going ballistic on the palate. One of the deliveries of the year as the taste buds are flooded under a deluge of the most profoundly clear and juicy barley notes you are ever likely to experience; **f23** cannot match the delivery, and doesn't try. Settles, instead, for a simplistic but very effective vanilla fade...with clean and crisp barley for company to the very end; **b24** a lesson in magnificent Speyside-style malt. The nose is a blender's many Christmases coming at once ...but the delivery is something else altogether. *53.7%. Speyside Distillers.*

The Whisky Agency Glen Grant 1972 bott 2011 **(84) n22 t21 f20 b21.** The softness on the mocha towards the end somewhat glosses over the oaky strain this malt is under from first to last. *52.3%. nc ncf sc. The Whisky Agency.*

The Whisky Agency Glen Grant 1975 bott 2011 **(94) n23.5** diced apple...this could almost be a brandy; just a jot of cinnamon and allspice. Age, and lots of it. Not taking the exotic fruit route, but something much more like home cooking; **t24** silky barley delivery...then there we go again: we are back to the cider brandy. Has that degree of fruity firmness and crisp sugars, coupled with a real small still- styled metallic tang....; **f22.5** the oak kicks in for sure, but does so with more than a degree of good manners, allowing all the fruit, copper and barley to say their piece before leaving; **b24** wonderful whisky: it's as simple as that... *50.7%. nc ncf sc.*

Whisky Doris Glen Grant 38 Years Old refill sherry, cask no. 1650, dist Feb 72, bott Mar 10 **(86.5) n21 t22 f22 b21.5.** Exceptionally oily for a Glen Grant. Even so, pleasingly rough enough to give you a good punch in the kisser where you might have hoped for something a little more delicate and fruity. *53.6%*

GLENGYLE
Campbeltown, 2004. J&A Mitchell & Co. Working.
Kilkerran Single Malt db **(80) n19 t20 f21 b20.** Glyngyle's first offering doesn't rip up any trees. And maybe the odd flaw to its character that you won't see when the distillery is fine-tuned. But this is the first-ever bottling from this brand new Campbeltown distillery and therefore its chances of being a worldbeater as an untried and untested 3-y-o were pretty slim. I will be watching its development with relish. And with heart pounding... *46%. Available exclusively from distillery direct from cask.*

Kilkerran Single Malt bott 22 May 07 db **(84) n20 t21 f22 b21.** Sadly, I was out of the country and couldn't attend the Coming of Age of Kilkerran, when its first casks turned three and became whisky. Very kindly, they sent me a bottle as if I was there and, therefore, these are the notes of the very first bottling handed out to visitors. Interestingly, there is a marked similarity in distillery style to the 46% bottling in that the malt offers a crescendo of quality. This is only three year old whisky, of course, and its fingerprints will alter as it spends longer in the cask. *62%. nc ncf.*

Kilkerran 'Work in Progress' db **(88) n22.5 t22 f21.5 b22** doing very well. *46%*

GLEN KEITH
Speyside, 1957. Chivas Brothers. Working (re-opened 14th June 2013).
Glen Keith 10 Years Old db **(80) n22 t21 f18 b19.** A malty if thin dram that finishes with a whimper after an impressively refreshing, grassy start. *43%*

Berry's Own Selection Glen Keith 1993 cask no. 97100, bott 2012 **(88) n22** ultra grassy and salivating: as refreshing as a malt of this age dare hope to be; **t22.5** ridiculously gristy for a malt of this age; the sugars are so clean, you could clean your teeth with them...; **f21.5** dulls out slightly as the creaking vanilla gets a toe-hold; **b22** if someone asked me to imagine an 18 or 19-y-o Glen Keith in a well-used but very serviceable bourbon cask and distilled to a slightly above average standard, it would be almost exactly like this. *53.8%. nc ncf sc.*

Cadenhead Glen Keith 13 Years Old bott 2011 **(83) n20 t21.5 f21 b20.5.** Pretty one dimensional. But if your preferred dimension happens to be clean, intense, semi-new makey barley then this offers all you need. *54.2%. sc. WM Cadenhead Ltd.*

Cadenhead Glen Keith 18 Years Old bott 2012 **(89) n22.5** the grassiest, most juicy barley you'll ever find; **t22.5** the nose is untroubled by oak, and there is little in evidence on delivery as that juicy barley enjoys supremacy; **f22** the lightest hint of praline shows the cask does offer something quite positive after all; **b22** Glen Keith raising the Speyside colours with singular pride. Quietly adorable. *54.3%. sc. WM Cadenhead Ltd.*

John Milroy Selection Glen Keith 1993 cask no. 97101, bott 2012 **(86.5) n21.5 t22 f21.5 b21.5.** Not entirely dissimilar to the Berry's Own cask 97100, but with more spice and less sparkle. *55.3%. nc ncf sc. Berry Bros & Rudd.*

⁘ Kingsbury Glen Keith Aged 15 Years hogshead, cask no. 72621, dist 97 **(80.5) n20.5 t21 f19 b20.** A good example of a second class blending malt struggling to find another gear beyond some basic barley and icing sugar. *46%. nc ncf. Japan Import System. 378 bottles.*

Liquid Sun Glen Keith 21 Years Old dist 1991 **(82.5) n21 t21 f20 b20.5.** Pleasant. No off notes. But tends to just sit in the glass doing very little other than radiating malt. *51.7%. sc.*

Old Malt Cask Glen Keith Aged 18 Years refill hogshead, cask no. 7671, dist Sep 93, bott Sep 11 **(90.5) n23** the oak plays second lead to the barley, but through its understated gravitas steals the show; the bourbon undercurrent allures; **t23** excellent weight with a touch of honeycomb and delicate bourbon-style liquorice ensuring that the salivating barley dominates only up to a point; **f22** long with the vanillas now in control; a late chocolate coffee bean flourish; **b22.5** an impressive bottling. *50%. nc ncf sc. Douglas Laing & Co. 311 bottles.*

Old Malt Cask Glen Keith Aged 18 Years refill hogshead, cask no. 7963, dist Sep 93, bott Dec 11 (77) n19.5 t20 f18.5 b19. Worth buying both this and cask 7671 above: just astonishing the difference the quality of a cask can make. 50%. nc ncf sc. 320 bottles.

⁘ **Provenance Glen Keith Over 15 Years** refill hogshead, cask no. 9655, dist Winter 97, bott Spring 13 (84) n19 t22 f21.5 b21.5. Glen Keith was once regarded the lightest of all the Chivas Speysiders. With minimal oak interference here, and with the barley at its most sparkling, you can see exactly why. 46%. nc ncf.

Scott's Selection Glen Keith 1996 bott 2011 (90.5) n23 busy, busy, busy! Barley nipping and fluttering about in the most vivid terms with that uniquely toffee apple sharpness as well as white pepper pepping up the celery; t23 not often GK gets into its stride so confidently and so early. The barley is pinging around with a bullet hardness and the salivation levels fly off the scale. As the mocha begins to descend and the sugars transform from grist to Demerara, there are signs that the cask is beginning to play up; f22 vanilla and mocha. The late bitterness, though unwelcome, isn't mean enough to spoil the party; b22.5 magnificent spirit, showing Glen Keith at its very best. Just a shame about the cask, which just fails to last the course. Still, for the most part a fabulous whisky experience. 576%. Speyside Distillers.

Sestante Collection Glen Keith 18 Years Old dist 1991, bott 2009 (77) n21 t19 f18 b19. Hardly recognisable as a Scotch and has all the bizarre and in-your-face characteristics of a malt matured in a barrel made from something other than oak. More likely to find this style in Germany or Austria. Several layers of kumquat save the day. 46%. sc.

Sestante Collection Glen Keith 40 Years Old dist 1970, bott 2011 (87.5) n22 nutty; almost an antique furniture feel to this, complete with some old polish! t22.5 the delivery spells in every way imaginable, o-l-d-a-g-e. Yet enough sugars, tinged by pretty eye-watering zest, help get it through the oaky onslaught; f21 a little spice at the death...but it creaks its way to the finishing line; b22 thought by mistake that this was their 1991 bottling, as I was unaware they had a much older version. Relieved on discovering my mistake, as I wondered what the hell had happened to this to make it age so drastically. 46.1%. sc. Silver Seal Whisky Company.

⁘ **The Whisky Cask Glen Keith Aged 17 Years** bourbon hogshead, dist 95, bott 12 (85.5) n20 t23 f21b21.5. Lightly smoked Love Heart candy fizzes on the palate for a charming, low key malt which overcomes its slightly too underwhelming nose and finish. Anyone who remembers mint chocolate Merlin's Brew lollies from the late 1970s and early '80s will appreciate the mid ground of this malt. 52.9%. nc ncf sc.

GLENKINCHIE
Lowlands, 1837. Diageo. Working.
Glenkinchie 12 Years Old db (85) n19 t22.5 f21.5 b22. The last 'Kinchie 12 I encountered was beyond woeful. This is anything but. Still not firing on all cylinders and can definitely do better. But there is a fabulous vibrancy to this which nearly all the bottlings I have tasted in the last few years have sadly lacked. Impressive. 43%

Glenkinchie Aged 15 Years The Distillers Edition Amontillado finished, dist 1992, bott 2007 db (94) n23.5 t24 f23 b23.5. Now this is absolutely top class wine cask finishing. One of my last whiskies of the night, and one to take home with me. Sophisticated, intelligent and classy. 46%

Glenkinchie 20 Years Old db (85.5) n21 t22 f21.5 b21. When I sampled this, I thought: "hang on, haven't I tasted this one before?" When I checked with my tasting notes for one or two independents who bottled around this age a year or two ago, I found they were nigh identical to what I was going to say here. Well, you can't say its not a consistent dram. The battle of the citrus-barley against the welling oak is a rich and entertaining one. 58.4%

Glenkinchie 1992 The Manager's Choice db (78) n19 t22 f18 b19. Has a lot going for it on delivery with a barley explosion which rocks you back in your chair and has you salivating like a rabies victim. But the rest of it is just too off key. 58.1%. Diageo.

THE GLENLIVET
Speyside, 1824. Chivas Brothers. Working.
The Glenlivet Aged 12 Years db (79.5) n22 t21 f18 b18.5. Wonderful nose and very early development but then flattens out towards the kind of caramel finish you just wouldn't traditionally associate with this malt, and further weakened by a bitter, furry finale. 40%

The Glenlivet Aged 12 Years Old First Fill Matured db (91) n22.5 t22.5 f23 b23. A quite wonderful whisky, far truer to The Glenlivet than the standard 12 and one which every malt whisky lover should try once in their journey through the amber stuff. Forget the tasting notes on the bottle, which bear little relation to what is inside: A gem of a dram. 40%

The Glenlivet Excellence 12 Year Old db (87) n22 clean, gristy barley; slightly chalky and tart; so clean, you fancy you can even detect the very faintest of phenols; t21.5 almost too delicate as the barley tries, but fails, to keep its foothold; some big vanilla; f22 more comfortable and balanced towards the finish as a few sugars and spices step aboard; **b21.5** low key but very clean. The emphasis is on delicate. *40%. Visitor Centre and Asian exclusive.*

The Glenlivet 15 Years of Age db **(80) n19 t21 f20 b20.** Undeniable charm to the countless waves of malt and oak. But don't expect much in the way of complexity or charisma. *40%*

⁘ **Glenlivet Quercus 17 Years Old** db **(93.5) n23.5** Brazilian coconut biscuit and Victoria sponge cake drizzled with lemon...and just love that faintest trail of smoke...; **t23.5** a little more viscous than your average Glenlivet. The barley offers both maltshake and sugar barley candy; again the citrus peps all around it; **f23** more custardy vanilla; the expected spices arrive; **b23.5** someone has cherry-picked a cracker of a cask... *52.1%. Whisky Shop Exclusive.250 bottles.*

⁘ **The Glenlivet Alpha** db **(92) n23.5** a clever use of counter weights here with good aged oak – enter delicate exotic fruit – harmonising with an orange blossom/ulmo honey blend, a sweet sultana fruitiness and marmalade; **t24** just love that delivery! The texture is sublime, boasting a crisp muscovado sugar sheen, with juicy barley being just below the surface: really doesn't get more Speyside than that! The intensity also dazzles, as does the glazed ginger guest appearance, though the exotic fruit makes only a surprisingly brief appearance before a light dusting of spices and Kit Kat milky chocolate-vanilla mix moves in; **f21.5** short and slightly disappointing with a definite furriness to the marmalade; **b23** you get the feeling some people have worked very hard at creating a multi-toned, complex creature celebrating the distillery's position at the centre of Speyside. They have succeeded. Just a cask selection or two away from a potential major Bible award. Maybe for the next bottling.... *50%*

The Glenlivet French Oak Reserve 15 Years of Age Limousin oak casks db **(95) n22.5** oo la la citrus; avec spice; **t23** comme ci comme ca caramels rescued by an uplifting injection of sweet barley; the juicy, salivating qualities are quite startling if not profound; **f22.5** long, with a fabulous butterscotch fade and a slow dissolving of dark sugars; **b23** I have to say that after tasting nearly 800 cask strength whiskies, to come across something at the ancient 40% is a shock to the system. My taste buds say merci... And, what is more, a bottle of this shall remain in my dining room for guests. Having, a lifetime ago, lived with a wonderful French girl for three years I suspect I know how her country folk will regard that... Oh, and forgive a personal message to a literary friend: Bobby-Ann...keep a bottle of this beside the Ancient Age... *40%*

The Glenlivet Nadurra Aged 16 Years batch no. 0911P, bott Sep 11 db **(95) n23.5** one of those teasing noses which revels in its own complexity. The Glenlivet bright barley style is there in abundance, but the layering of the tannins and the sharpness this creates fair makes the heart skip a beat; **t24** puckeringly tart on delivery, those rich tannins are softened by the sugars of the barley; barley sugar candy sucked simultaneously with lemon drops; **f23.5** more vanilla dependent with an almost inevitable butterscotch subplot. A few weightier cough sweets slip in at the end...; **b24** this remains by far and away the finest and most consistent style from this historic distillery. A Speyside must-have for any single malt lover. *53%. ncf.*

The Glenlivet Aged 18 Years bott Feb 10 db **(91) n22** attractive mixture of honeycombed bourbon and fruitcake; **t23.5** oh...just didn't expect that...!! Fabulous, honey-sweet and slightly sharp edge to the barley: excellent weight and mouthfeel with the honeycomb on the nose making slow but decisive incursions; **f23** a very slight technical flaw drops it half a point, but there is no taking away from the improbable length of the dissolving honey and barley...some gentle chewing is required, especially with the late juices and vanilla arriving; **b23** a hugely improved bottling seriously worth discovering in this form. Appears to have thrown off its old shackles and offers up an intensity that leaves you giving a little groan of pleasure. *43%*

The Glenlivet Founder's Reserve 21 Years Old db **(95.5) n23.5** initially tight and, even after 20 minutes in the glass, allows the grape to unfurl in the most niggardly fashion. Thing is: the few notes, in tandem with some gorgeous Columbian cocoa, spices, orange peel and rich dates, reveals that much is to come on the palate... **t24.5** those spices are the first to flee the confines of the thick grape, but so many layers of grape skin and mocha follow that you can sit there for a good five minutes and still not entirely work out what is going on; the spices are not just persistent but simply magnificent; **f23.5** long, with (milky) cocoa and dates (of the juicy rather than dried variety) leading the way; a light sulphur note detracts half a mark, but it is testament to the malt that it barely detracts from the moment; **b24** on this evidence, one of the whiskies of the year for sure. I really don't think my 800th new single malt of the year could have been a more inspired – or lucky - choice. *55.6%. ncf. 1824 bottles.*

The Glenlivet 1973 Cellar Collection bott Oct 09 db **(94.5) n24** luxurious stewed sultanas in a custard tart; yet for a malt heading towards 40, improbable grist, too: clean, complex, thick and simply spellbinding... **t24** just melts into the taste buds with the freshest, cleanest, juiciest charm you could possibly imagine, yet always with a nibbling spice darting around the side of the tongue; **f23** a touch of oaky bitterness, but a mere detail: the late oils are sympathetic and contain a surprising degree of vanilla; **b23.5** for Glenlivet lovers, I point you towards something a little special... *49%. Chivas.*

The Glenlivet Cellar Collection 1980 bott Aug 11 db (**94.5**) **n23** no shortage of chalky oak creating almost a bloom to the fruit. There is citrus, but that fruit has slightly more tropical shades, especially green banana; **t24** one of those deliveries where the mouth-feel actually outpoints the flavours – not that there is anything wrong here. Soft and yielding, even with an early puff of distant smoke, but just enough fibre to ensure a chewy element to those fruits which are now extolling the virtues of grassy barley; **f23.5** it would be easy just to concentrate on the big peppery spices. But then you would be missing the mocha, not to mention the vanilla ice cream with a physalis topping; **b24** some of you in the know will have been expecting exotic fruit from this...and you won't be disappointed! 43.3%. ncf. 500 bottles.

The Glenlivet Master Distiller's Reserve db (86.5) **n22.5 t22 f20.5 b21.5**. I chose this as my 800th whisky to taste for the 2012 Bible against the Founder's Reserve on the strength of the nose over the first 30 seconds. Oh, well. Shows you the pricelessness of time when evaluating a whisky... 40%

⠿ **The Glenlivet Single Cask Inveravon Aged 21 Years** cask no. 10667, bott 25 Oct 11 db (**96.5**) **n24** sophisticated: obviously bourbon cask, but the malt still somehow conjures up a number of fruit notes, including salted cucumber and lime. Delicate, hushed liquorice and hazelnut tones and polite spice. Everything is so understated; **t24** no disappointment on delivery. The weight is sublime: just enough oil to carry the more powerful fruit notes towards the growing cocoa without there being a gap; the spices are equal and busy; **f24** happy to sign off with a simple Neapolitan ice cream vanilla and chocolate finish; **b24.5** this was a single cask for the Taiwanese market I think. Time to get a flight to Taipei...this is Glenlivet at its absolute best. 54.6%

Berry's Own Selection Glenlivet 1973 cask no. 10658, bott 2012 (**94**) **n23.5** despite the fact it pulses antiquity this remains sprightly and nubile, the barley absolutely fizzing on the nose. A few shards of honey offer weight and resonance to the citrus; **t24** demands a mouth-watering delivery after that nose, and that is exactly what you get. The spices flock to the scene so the taste buds are at once drowned, caressed and burnt alive...; **f23** long, with a slow devaluation of the sugars as the vanillas take command; **b23.5** about as salivating a near 40-year-old you are likely to find! 48.6%. nc ncf sc. Berry Bros & Rudd.

Berry's Own Selection Glenlivet 1973 cask no. 10822, bott 2012 (84.5) **n22 t22.5 f19 b21**. The barley and the expected spices do all in their power to enliven, enrich and entertain. But the deeper oak renders it at times a bit of a maudlin dullard. 476%. nc ncf sc.

Berry's Own Selection Glenlivet 1974 cask no. 5247, bott 2012 (83.5) **n20.5 t22 f21 b20**. Sharp, with plenty of malt to go around. But just a little too tangy and off balance for its own good. 46%. nc ncf sc. Berry Bros & Rudd.

Cadenhead Glenlivet 21 Years Old bott 2011 (**95**) **n23.5** what a darling of a nose: the oaks lead the way with a fabulous French toast sweetness, but there is a babbling undercurrent of spice and barley, too.; **t24.5** this is the way a Glenlivet of this age should behave: plenty of barley and all kinds of salivating properties. But the sheer delight is in the puckering sharpness of the spiced apple and semi-bourbony honeycomb. The vanillas enter butterscotch territory and a lemon zesty gristiness still has something to say; even the oak is a little different; **f23** settles into a more subtle denouement where the barley sugars and citrus sit comfortably with a less intense oakiness; **b24** really not the easiest whisky I have ever had to spit out! Absolutely overflowing with flavours. A classic! 55.7%. sc. WM Cadenhead Ltd.

⠿ **Cadenhead Glenlivet 24 Years Old** claret, dist 88, bott 13 (**94.5**) **n23** classic sweaty armpit saltiness; vague fruit of the plummy school; **t24** the juices are in explosive mood thanks to some energetic spice; again the salts are up to all kinds of tricks; the malt is of Malteser-sweet intensity; **f23.5** the spices continue to glow, though the milk chocolate finale settles things; **b24** how good is that! A wine cask with not a single off note: a real collector's item! Another masterpiece for what is a vintage year for Glenlivet lovers. 53.9%. sc. 258 bottles.

Duncan Taylor Octave Glenlivet 21 Years Old cask no. 470899, dist 1970 (86) **n22 t22 f21 b21**. Hate to say it, but for all its wealth of intense barley riches, the oak forces this a little out of tune. If you like to pick a few splinters from between your teeth, then go get, for there is much to enjoy! But for all its compensating blood orange and ribald barley, the oak is just a little too uncouth for where you might prefer it to be. 46.1%. sc. Duncan Taylor & Co.

Gordon & MacPhail Private Collection Glenlivet 1954 (**96**) **n24** Bassett's chocolate liquorice. An outline of earthy smoke plus toffee apple with a surprising degree of Golden Delicious. I really have no idea how a whisky this old can be so devoid of any off notes – well, apart from the fact the oak was so much better in those days; **t23.5** first up come some oak-led spices, but all very civil. A charming soft oil lubricates the taste buds without them really noticing; there is a very brief puckering sharpness from the oak, and a wave of barley-tinged fruitcake fills the middle; **f24.5** such a wonderfully weighted finale it borders on the ridiculous. Understated but evident layers of chocolate sponge, walnut cake (with cream) and a liberal smattering of dates makes for a finish bordering on perfection. Especially if you can pick up on that delicate smoke which re-enters the picture and seems like the glow from a swallowed and well matured Melton Hunt cake... **b24** if there is a heaven, I think I have just entered it. For no company in the world does this kind of veteran whisky better than Gordan and MacPhail and here they have exceeded even themselves. Guessed this would be an outstanding whisky to mark my 700th specifically tasted for the Bible 2012, and 600th new entry. My word: was I right...! *50.6%*

Gordon & MacPhail Rare Vintage Glenlivet 1961 (94.5) **n24** nutty: hazelnut and almonds to the fore, including hints of marzipan. A mix of salted butter and Demerara sugar fills the gaps, long with a a thin spreading of lime jelly; **t23.5** the oak shows a dark, threatening side. But the star quality of the dark, roasty sugars beats back the ravages of time and positively laughs in its face; **f23** the oak, earlier, had threatened to spoil the party. But now it has been tamed and offers a meek contribution to the slow unwinding of the vanillas and surprisingly intact barley, plus the toasted fudge and dried dates. A few pecans and walnuts offer extra oiliness, and all is carried out in slow motion; **b24** a very dear friend and colleague told me today that his mother was diagnosed with Alzheimer's. It was terribly sad news, and something she understood and accepted with fortitude, magnanimity and a courage which came so natural I doubt if she realised she even had it. "They are a different breed" said my friend with unaffected reverence, referring to the generation which survived a World War, so would take whatever low card fate was dealing them with the same innate stoicism. I have a mother who was 91 last week, is mentally sharp as a knife but unable to walk unaided, and a final remaining blood uncle also with Alzheimer's whom I visit whenever in London. So I knew exactly what he meant. And in a far, far less important way, I feel something similar regarding the whiskies of yesteryear and today. I cannot see that many whiskies reaching 50 years with the kind of resilience that this whisky shows me here. The casks of today, both sherry and bourbon, are so much more inferior – weaker - that we can only look upon this vanishing generation of malts, like the one in my glass before me, as we do our own kinfolk. So easily taken for granted. So dreadfully under- appreciated when with us. And to be painfully and immeasurably missed when they are gone. *43%*

Gordon & MacPhail Private Collection Glenlivet 1963 (88) **n23 t21.5 f21.5 b22.** Defies the odds to stay together. A malt that feels its age, but can still get around. *40.6%*

Gordon & MacPhail Rare Vintage Glenlivet 1966 (95) **n24** spices drill into the nostrils and explode; yams sit steaming on a plate; celery is being salted and freshly chopped; plasticine is being kneaded by a child; casks of apple brandy sit 100 yards away in a dank cellar; a cracked old chesterfield is being pushed into an antique showroom; a conker has just split in your hand....; **t23.5** obviously, the oak makes the first play as the body is so thin. But the cask is made of magnificent stuff because it still allows the barley the stage for a while; **f23.5** dries and spices up. The vanillas are brief, quickly replaced by sturdier liquorice and Demerara sugars; **b24** I have never quite understood how whisky from this distillery gets past a dozen years, let alone makes it to such antiquity. Yet when it does, it carries its stardom with the grace of a movie star who understands the value of stage-managed humbleness. *43%*

Gordon & MacPhail Rare Vintage Glenlivet 1967 (83) **n21 t20 f21 b21.** You should get a free white flag with every bottle: this is a whisky which, for all its salty enormity, has surrendered to the oak. *43%. Gordon & MacPhail.*

Gordon & MacPhail Rare Vintage Glenlivet 1977 (86) **n22.5 t22.5 f20 b21.** A delicate dram with improbable degrees of citrus for its age. Sadly, the weak strength helps break up the oils and give the bittering oak a much larger say than it deserves. *43%*

Kingsbury Single Cask Series Glenlivet Aged 17 Years Trois Riviers rum finish (87.5) **n22** almost a Glen Grant brittleness to this with sugar encrusting the bright barley; **t22** pretty sweet delivery with a lovely degree of grassy, salivating sharpness. Again, the sugars are profound; **f21.5** stays on its malty track with the vanillas at last adding weight and a degree of gravitas; **b22** sweet and simplistic, but works rather well. *46%. sc. Japan Import Systems.*

Mo Ór Collection Glenlivet 1977 33 Years Old first fill bourbon hogshead, cask no. 13141, dist 29 Jun 71, bott 2 Dec 10 (87.5) **n20.5** somewhat grizzled with oaky oak. An injection of kumquat keeps the circulation going; **t22** the oak needs no second invitation to shove its wooden foot in the door. Slowly the barley battles back, with a little bit of oil and fudge there; **f23** at last all the pieces fit together and, with a light chocolate and mint flourish, seems to live happily ever after; **b22** you know when a friendly dog jumps slobberingly all over you? Well it's like that, but with the oak... *46%. nc ncf sc. Release No. 28. 274 bottles.*

Old Malt Cask Glenlivet Aged 10 Years sherry butt, cask no. 8191, dist Sep 01, bott Feb 12 (89.5) **n21.5** an excellent clean sherry butt...but where is the malt? The vanilla whipped ice cream isn't it! **t23** soft and satisfying, the grape enters the fray first and, finally, the barley shows its head, injecting a juicy element alongside the more chewy oak; **f22.5** very late spice and fruity mocha; **b22.5** the kind of malt which, even for its lack of major complexity, makes you inwardly purr... *50%. nc ncf sc. Douglas Laing & Co. 387 bottles.*

⠿ **Old Malt Cask Glenlivet Aged 11 Years** sherry butt, cask no. 9210, dist Sep 01, bott Oct 23 **(90)** n23.5 peaches, apricot and marzipan vie for pole position amid the deep, unmistakable grape: about as intense an 11-y-o aroma as you might wish for. Not flawless, but always enticing; **t23.5** succulent delivery with magnificent chewing capabilities; the raisins are positively burnt, though housed in a chocolate shell, the marzipan heaped on with double layering; somewhere some barley seeps through, though this is short lived; **f20** the slight flaw on the nose is re-visited with a little extra introspection now, but the fruit continues to mingle with the gathering vanillas; **b23** as fruity as a nut cake. *50%. sc. 374 bottles.*

⠿ **Old Malt Cask Glenlivet Aged 11 Years** sherry butt, cask no. 9637, dist Spe 01, bott May 13 **(86.5)** n21.5 t22.5 f21 b21.5. An odd one, this. Works on certain delicious fruitcake levels, especially with the extra molasses, but a good example of how the grape and natural caramels from the oak can combine to restrict complexity. *50%. nc ncf sc. 382 bottles.*

Old Malt Cask Glenlivet Aged 16 Years refill butt, cask no. 8214, dist Sep 95, bott Mar 12 **(73.5)** n18.5 t19 f18 b18. The nose tells you what is to come and you won't be disappointed. Or, rather, you will... *50%. nc ncf sc. Douglas Laing & Co. 299 bottles.*

Old Malt Cask Glenlivet Aged 19 Years refill hogshead, cask no. 7609, dist Apr 92, bott Aug 11 **(92)** n23.5 the banana and cherry drop aroma is as delightful as it is invigorating; **t23** mouth-watering with those cherries showing early then giving way to spices and vanilla; the barley is always on the prowl; **f22.5** remains chewy forever; the vanilla really doesn't want to leave the stage; **b23** a right little smasher. *50%. nc ncf sc. Douglas Laing & Co. 283 bottles.*

Old Malt Cask Glenlivet Aged 34 Years refill hogshead, cask no. 7734, dist Jun 77, bott. Sep 11 **(87)** n21.5 a sharp fruity note is dulled by a little distant mustiness; the barley displays a thick core; **t22** the big age is apparent as the oak burrows deep on arrival; tangy and juicy with a refreshing liveliness to the barley; the spices have some major nip and bite; **f21.5** creamy barley and tired oak; **b22** the integrity of the barley has not been breached, but the failing oak ran it close. Still plenty of life left, though. *50%. nc ncf sc. 232 bottles.*

⠿ **Provenance Glenlivet Over 11 Years** sherry butt, cask no. 0000, dist 2001, bott 2013 **(94)** n23.5 a once common aroma of crushed hazelnut and medium baked raisin; a slightly salty, seasoned edge to the barley; **t24** lush in the traditional and present-day meaning of the word: the grape engulfs the palate, even forming a slightly oily layer before a truly to-die-for succession of flavour mechanisms with subtly varying weights and intensity begin to lap against the taste buds. The sugars are restrained, allowing the drier notes of the oloroso and oak to caress with a distinct degree of sophistication; **f23** a delicate furriness confirms the butt did not entirely escape brutal Spanish hands, but the salty, sugar-deprived old farmhouse cake feel continues; **b23.5** what the Scotch whisky industry would give to have all its sherry butts in this wonderful, (nearly) unspoiled form. Thirty years ago, this was pretty close to how 11-year-old sherry matured whisky nosed and tasted. Now it is almost a freak. *46%. nc ncf.*

Riegger's Selection Glenlivet 1973 bourbon cask, cask no. 10474, dist 10 Dec 73, bott 6 Apr 10 **(94)** n24 those who love marmalade on your toast will flock to this one. The barley remains crisp and intact but the citrus, coupled with the light liquorice and hickory, will steal your heart; **t23.5** silky delivery where the barley offers a naked show of its pristine self; the fruits are slower to emerge than on the nose, but do finally make a bow, replaced by creamy mocha; **f23** shy spices confirm the age of the cask yet the barley still offers a juicy freshness; **b23.5** get onto the next flight to Germany. Fast! *47.5%. nc ncf sc. 127 bottles.*

Scotch Malt Whisky Society Cask 2.80 Aged 15 Years first fill sherry butt, cask no. 71354, dist 1996 **(95.5)** n24.5 it is like entering a high class bakers: treacle tart, rhubarb crumble, well-aged fruitcake fortified with sherry and molasses, cinnamon scones...this whisky should be a few thousand calories if the nose is anything to go by; **t23.5** spice on delivery and moving into overdrive in the mid section, but perhaps with not quite the body to match. This is Glenlivet, so it is bound to be juicy one way or another; **f23.5** the weight collects at the finish where those spices dissipate among the black cherry and vanillas; **b24** like the most voluptuous company you prefer to spend an evening with, this has a faultless butt... *60.1%. sc.*

⠿ **Scotch Malt Whisky Society Cask 2.83 Aged 19 Years** refill hogshead, 18 Dec 93 **(94.5)** n23.5 the exotic fruit, diced pear, orange blossom honey, all underscored by a chalky dryness, suggests a malt a whole lot older; **t24** a two-toned delivery. Simultaneously, you are treated to massive juicy barley and spiced tropical fruits; the middle pans out towards superb mocha with a playful, alluring smokiness; **f23** long, and reverts back to the nose; drier with over-ripe banana; **b24** about as spick and span as you could pray for. When this distillery produces good whisky...wow! *55.2%. nc ncf sc. 228 bottles.*

Scott's Selection Glenlivet 1977 bott 2012 **(89)** n21.5 tired...; some chopped roast hazelnut offers something positive; **t22** just enough sugars left in the tank to soften the spicy, oaky blows; a quick, sharp burst of tangy orange before the oak closes in; **f23** vanilla and Horlicks make for a relaxing finale; **b22.5** teetering on the brink of oaky extinction but somehow finds the personality and complexity to make for an enjoyable dram. *43.8%*

Scott's Selection Glenlivet 1978 bott 2012 (94.5) n23 exotic fruit on cue...; t24.5 plenty of action on the palate from the very first moment. A beguiling mix of almost clichéd oak notes for the age and region, again putting its weight behind the rich fruit element. But what works so well is this intermingling with fabulous texture and toffee shortcake butteriness; f23 settles into a much steadier stream of vanilla; b24 the kind of malt which leaves your taste buds in a state of exhaustion. Perennial motion on the palate. 51.1%. Speyside Distillers.

⁂ **Wemyss Glenlivet 1977 Single Speyside "Dark Chocolate Orange"** hogshead, bott 13 (92.5) n23 some serious grey hairs here: a good deal of marmalade and vanilla, no shortage of ulmo honey but weighed down by oak increasing in weight with each sniff; t23.5 a fabulously salivating start with the remnants of the barley making an early salvo. Varying degree of cocoa arrive with both the ever-thickening oils and the tangy spiced citrus; f22.5 thinner now, with the accent back on the vanilla. But that tangy marmalade takes a long time to fade; b23.5 yep. I think Dark Chocolate Orange is a good call for this oldie. 46%. sc. 149 bottles.

The Whisky Cask Glenlivet Aged 33 Years bourbon cask, dist 1977, bott 2010 (94.5) n23.5 a genuine surprise with a distant hint of Arbroath Smokies hanging around the more voluptuous barley notes; the fruity notes are pastel shaded and vulnerable; t24 mouth-watering barley, but every malt atom carries with it two from the oak cask. There is enough muscovado sugar on hand to smooth out any wrinkles, though; f23 dries out in time and allows the spices to develop beautifully; long and remains lush for all the oak's best work; b24 there are some excellent old Glenlivets doing the rounds right now. And this is up there amongst the very best. 56.7%. sc. The Whisky Cask.

GLENLOCHY
Highlands (Western), 1898–1983. Diageo. Closed.

Rarest of the Rare Glenlochy 1980 cask no. 2454 (96) n24 t24.5 f23.5 b24. This does what it says on the tin: this really is the rarest of the rare. I do not often see this stuff either in bottled form or privately through a whisky year. It makes hen's teeth look pretty two-a-penny. But then one must ask the question: why? Any distillery capable of making malt this good should still be working, rather than being turned into a small hotel. (Jim Murray and all at Dram Good Books Ltd would like to assure readers of a nervous disposition that no whisky was spat out during the tasting of this sample.) 54.8%. Duncan Taylor.

⁂ **Gordon & MacPhail Rare Old Glenlochy 1979** (95) n23.5 proudly displays its age with major, but entirely acceptable, oak involvement. A pretty salty affair, lifted by delicate kumquat and wild strawberry (two fruits usually associated with oak) though the natural caramel and nibbling spice also balance beautifully; t24 ridiculously soft delivery, even though the oak insists on at least a dual starring role. The deft and fleeting malt moments are really quite monumental and with the milky chocolate gathering in intensity, the entire piece seems to become like a Malteser liqueur; f23.5 the spices which had a little attitude early on now drift serenely about the melted Malteser. A hint of late butterscotch, but the malt holds firm. Or should that be soft? b24 it has been many years since a bottle from this long lost distillery turned up and that was such a classic, I can remember every nuance of it even now. This shows far greater age, but the way with which the malt takes it in its stride will become the stuff of legend. I held back on tasting this until today, August 2nd 2013, because my lad David this afternoon moved into the first home he has bought, with new wife Rachael and little Abi. It is near Fort William, the remote west coast Highland town in which this whisky was made, and where David will be teaching next year. His first job after moving in, though, will be to continue editing this book, for he worked on the Whisky Bible for a number of editions as researcher and editor over the years. So I can think of no better way of wishing David a happy life in his new home than by toasting him with what turned out to be a stunningly beautiful malt from one of the rarest of all the lost distilleries which, by strange coincidence, was first put up for sale exactly 100 years ago. So, to David, Rachael and little Abigail... your new home! And this time I swallowed.. 46%. ncf.

GLENLOSSIE
Speyside, 1876. Diageo. Working.

⁂ **A.D. Rattray Glenlossie 1992** hogshead, cask no. 3440, dist 18 Nov 92, bott Jun 11 (93) n23 no peat, yet a compelling earthiness to this perhaps helped by freshly diced vegetable mixed with molassed tannin; t23.5 perfect weight on delivery and spices which know just how to get maximum effect with minimum effort. The sugars drive the barley, mainly darkened but lightening as the butterscotch arrives; f23 classic vanilla and spice finish with the oak sturdy and steadfast even after two decades: superb! b23.5 oh, I so love this distillery! And remains so faithful to you, too! 56.6%. sc. Dewar Rattray Cask Collection.

⁂ **Berry's Glenlossie 1992** (87) n23 a light blend of honey and carrot juice shows this will stick to a slightly earthy, complex and balanced style; t23 good oils to the sugars, in fact a thin syrup engulfs the bright barley and fattening oak; **f19.5** let down by some bitterness from the cask, though spices try to compensate; **b21.5** a distillery with the propensity to make gorgeous whisky without seemingly breaking sweat is at it again...just not helped by a indifferent piece of wood. 46%

⁘ **Gordon and MacPhail Connoisseurs Choice Glenlossie 1993 (94) n23.5** the cleanest sherry I have nosed this year; the grape is rampant and full of spiced juice, dates and greengages. And not a single off not...not even a murmur...; **t23.5** silky, oily and fabulous fusion of fruitcake and sherry trifle with heady use of molassed sugars...waiting for the off note...there isn't one; **f23** the oak begins to make a noise of its own beyond the fruit with a gorgeous chocolate pudding contribution...dries, a distant furry mumble but nothing at all to worry about; **b24** the first green shoots of heavy sherry cask involvement but (virtually) no sulphur....? I could almost weep. A whisky to rejoice about...for so many reasons! 46%. ncf.

Liquid Sun Glenlossie 36 Years Old refill sherry cask, dist 1975, bott 2011 **(86) n22.5 t22 f20.5 b21.** The line between greatness and just very good is a pretty fine one in whisky. Just a single summer can represent the border. This, though, has crossed four or five. The charm of the orange and lime aroma and delivery is there for all to see; the excellence of the oils is also a triumph. And the spices, layered with praline, really do delight. But the over-aging takes its toll somewhat on the finish and balance. 48.3%. sc. The Whisky Agency.

The Maltman Glenlossie Aged 19 Years bourbon cask, cask no. 18232, dist Jul 78, bott Jun 97 **(84) n21 t22 f20 b21.** Time warp whisky: this has taken an age to get onto the shelves, having been bottled back in 1997 but just released from bond. Was it worth the wait? Well, don't expect a rip-roaring Lossie: this is pretty tame stuff and, though non-coloured I'm told, there is a bit of old-fashioned toffee here - in this case obviously from the cask. 43%. nc ncf sc. Meadowside Blending Co.

Malts Of Scotland Glenlossie 1975 bourbon hogshead, cask no. MoS11022, bott Nov 11 **(91.5) n22.5** dank stinging nettles, earthy, a hint of pine yet enlivened by acacia honey and suet pudding; **t23.5** much sweeter on the palate. The spices bombard from the first moment, then sugars re-establish themselves with the lazy muscovado weight; **f22.5** dries as those spices continue to attack; the vanilla retains a light citrus edge; just a few waves of mocha completes the experience; **b23** intense and busy, the quality of the whisky is never in doubt. All this fun and aggro and undisguised brilliance without a single peaty particle in sight. There are those out there who will refuse to believe it. 49.8%. nc ncf sc. Malts Of Scotland.

Old Malt Cask Glenlossie Aged 18 Years refill butt, cask no. 7789, dist Sep 93, bott Jan 12 **(91) n22** one fancies one can almost detect a distant hint of smoke...no doubting the spice and less than brilliant oak, though...; **t23** much more clarity on the delivery where the barley rings through as clear as the ring on a crystal tasting glass; **f23** remains mouth-watering and beautifully sweet; **b23** outrageously juicy. 50%. Douglas Laing & Co. 416 bottles.

Scotch Single Malt Circle Glenlossie 1984 cask no. 2534, dist 4 Oct 84, bott 24 Feb 10 **(88.5) n23** it is though the cask has been left to lie in the Dead Sea for a few years; some bourbony tannins; **t22.5** when next in my kitchen I will blend some honey and salt together and see if I can recreate this; tart yet strangely attractive; **f21** a long wind-down of various honey and salt residues...; **b22** forget about the strength. The abruptness of this whisky stems from its extraordinary reliance on all things salty. 60%. sc. Scotch Single Malt Circle.

⁘ **The Whisky Agency Glenlossie 1975** bott 13 **(91.5) n22** massive oak but enough mint around to keep it fresh; **t22** mouth-watering at first as the barley somehow, probably by osmosis, makes it thorough the massive oak; **f24** a fabulous mocha arrival, aided by a squeeze of Chinese gooseberry makes for a brilliant finale; **b23.5** put your ear to the glass and you can hear the timber creaking....comes through though with a fine mocha polish. 46.6%. The Whisky Agency.

GLEN MHOR
Highlands (Northern), 1892–1983. Diageo. Demolished.

Glen Mhor 1976 Rare Malt db **(92.5) n23 t24 f22 b23.5.** You just dream of truly great whisky sitting in your glass from time to time. But you don't expect it, especially from such an old cask. This was the best example from this distillery I've tasted in 30 years...until the Glenkeir version was unleashed! If you ever want to see a scotch that has stretched the use of oak as far it will go without detriment, here it is. What a pity the distillery has gone because the Mhor the merrier... 52.2%

Mo Òr Collection Glen Mhor 1975 34 Years Old first fill bourbon hogshead, cask no. 4036, dist 31 Dec 85, bott 3 Nov 10 **(94) n23.5** not sure what I love most: the happy integration of the barley and oaky vanilla after all these years. Or the playful, now you see it, now you don't, nature of the peat. Add to that the oranges and nutty cocoa and you really have something of rare beauty; **t23.5** so soft and silky: the barley and muscovado sugars form a procession and serene enough to embrace the intense yet never burdensome oak; the spices are little more than an afterthought; **f23** butterscotch sprinkled with a lightly salted oakiness and mildly sugared barley; the mouth-feel remains almost glass-like while the mocha is little more than a very delicious whisper; **b24** it has been a very long time since I have found a Glen Mhor in such fine fettle and so in tune with itself. I suspect there are very few like these remaining... *43.3%. nc ncf sc. Release No. 10. The Whisky Talker. 170 bottles.*

⋰⋱⋰ **Old Malt Cask Glen Mhor Aged 30 Years** refill hogshead, cask no. 9183, dist Aug 82, bott Oct 12 **(89.5) n23** you just know you are in for an oaky battle here: the tannins have teeth cleaned by mint. But the underlying kumquat and Demerara give reason for hope – a lovely aroma, though...; **t23** the oak nibbles from the start, but some Parkin cake offers early respite while the mid ground enters a creamy Victoria sponge fruity sweetness; the sugars apparent on the nose reinforce the good guys; **f21.5** the oak finally finds dominance a piece of cake...; **b22** what a fascinating malt! Yes, it is too old for true greatness, but what a wonderful battle between time and structure. Every glass needs a good 20 minutes (and at body temperature, remember) to realise its full potential. *50%. sc. Douglas Laing & Co. 228 bottles.*

GLENMORANGIE
Highlands (Northern), 1843. Glenmorangie Plc. Working.

Glenmorangie 10 Years Old db **(94) n24** perhaps the most enigmatic aroma of them all: delicate yet assertive, sweet yet dry, young yet oaky: a malty tone poem; **t22** flaky oakiness throughout but there is an impossibly complex toastiness to the barley which seems to suggest the lightest hint of smoke; **f24** amazingly long for such a light dram, drying from the initial sweetness but with flaked almonds amid the oakier, rich cocoa notes; **b24** you might find the occasional "orange variant", where the extra degree of oak, usually from a few too many first-fill casks, has flattened out the more extreme peaks and toughs of complexity (scores about 89). But these are pretty rare – almost a collector's item – and overall this remains one of the great single malts: a whisky of uncompromising aesthetic beauty from the first enigmatic whiff to the last teasing and tantalising gulp. Complexity at its most complex. *40%*

Glenmorangie 15 Years Old db **(90.5) n23** chunky and fruity: something distinctly sugar candy about this one; the barley's no slouch, either; and, just to raise the eyebrows, just the faintest waft of something smoky...; **t23** silky, a tad sultry, and serious interplay between oak and barley; a real, satisfying juiciness to this one; **f22** dries towards the oaky side of things, but just a faint squeeze of liquorice adds extra weight; **b22.5** exudes quality. *43%*

Glenmorangie 15 Years Old Sauternes Wood Finish db **(68) n16 t18 f17 b17** I had hoped – and expected – an improvement on the sulphured version I came across last time. Oh, whisky! Why are you such a cruel mistress...? *46%*

Glenmorangie 18 Years Old db **(91) n22** pleasant if unconvincing spotted dick; **t23** sharp, eye-watering mix of fruit and mainly honeyed barley; nutty and, with the confident vanillas, forming a breakfast cereal completeness; **f23** Cocoa Krispies; **b23** having thrown off some previous gremlins, now a perfect start to the day whisky... *43%*

Glenmorangie 25 Years Old db **(95.5) n24** it's strap yourself in time: this is a massive nose with more layers, twists and turns than you can shake a dart at. Soft, mildly lush Lubec marzipan is sandwiched between fruit bonbons and myriad barley tones. Worth taking half an hour over this one, and no kidding... **t24** the clarity on the nose is matched here. Every single wave of flavour is there in crystal form, starting, naturally, with the barley but this is soon paired with various unidentified fruits. The result is salivation. Towards the middle the oak shows form and does so in various cocoa-tinged ways; every nuance is delicately carved, almost fragile, but the overall picture is one of strength; **f23.5** medium length with the cocoa heading towards medium roast Java **b24** every bit as statesmanlike and elegant as a whisky of this age from such a blinding distillery should be. Ticks every single box for a 25-year-old and is Morangie's most improved malt by the distance of Tain to Wellingborough. There is a hint of genius with each unfolding wave of flavours with this one: a whisky that will go in 99/100 whisky lover's top 50 malts of all time. And that includes the Peatheads. *43%*

Glenmorangie 30 Years Old db **(72) n17 t18 f19 b18**. From the evidence in the glass the jury is out on whether it has been spruced up a little in a poor sherry cask – and spruce is the operative word: lots of pine on this wrinkly. *44.1%*

Glenmorangie Vintage 1975 db **(89) n23 t23 f21 b22**. A charming, fruity and beautifully spiced oldie. *43%*

Glenmorangie 1977 db **(92) n24 t23 f22 b23**. Excellent, but a trifle underpowered...what would this have been like at 46%...??? Shows little of its great age as the oak is always subservient to the sweet barley and citrus. *43%. Exclusively at Harrods.*

Glenmorangie Pride 1981 dist Oct 81, bott 2010, Sauternes barrique db **(77.5) n18 t22 f18 b19.5**. The Pride before a fall...? I know that gifted blender Bill Lumsden feels that a touch of sulphur can sometimes bring good to a dram. He and I share many similar views on whisky. But here we very much part company. For me, sulphur is a fault. Nothing more.

Nothing less. The entire reason for stills to be made from copper is so sulphur compounds are removed. So by adding them back in, as they obviously have here via the barriques, can be nothing other than a negative step. Perhaps I am at fault for having a zero tolerance on sulphur. But when, for me, it spoils the nose, muddies the middle and bitters the finish, how can I do anything other than judge accordingly? The tragedy here is that it is obvious that some astonishing elements are at play. Even through the bitter haze I could detect some gorgeous honey and glazed fruits and stems; so excellent, in fact, that for a few brief moments the faults are silenced. But that is only a respite. Those unable to spot sulphur, through smoking or their DNA, will doubtless find much to enjoy and wonder why I have marked this down. But I cannot join the general back-slapping on this whisky. I have been told that someone has suggested the sulphur on this soon goes away. It doesn't: it never does – that is absolutely ridiculous. And why some whisky critics can't nose sulphur is beyond me. About as useful as a wine writer unable to spot a corked wine; or a music critic unable to hear the cello playing in entirely the wrong key. Sorry. But I have to be the sole dissenting voice on this one. 56.7%

Glenmorangie Artein Private Edition db (**94**) **n24** it's the spices that get you: at first you don't quite notice them. Then you realise there is a background buzz, like peppers slyly added to a gazpacho soup, and there is a slight tomato fruitiness, too; the sweetness is a subtle combination of maple syrup and molten Mars Bars; **t23.5** that sweetness arrives early but in very diluted form and refuses to overtake the barley sugar and chocolate raisin; **f23** the spices on the nose return for the finale which sit deliciously with the malt-nougat fade; **b23.5** if someone has gone out of their way to create probably the softest Scotch single malt of the year, then they have succeeded. 46%. ncf.

⁖ **Glenmorangie Artein Private Edition 15 Years Old** db (**91**) **n23** a beautiful mix of fruit pastilles and coconut lime cake; **t23.5** sensual delivery: soft with a few spices to mix with the developing mocha and raisin; **f21.5** lovely buttery oils to the fade but bitters out slightly; **b23** a truly sensual and complex dram, gorgeously weighted underplaying the fruit and wine aspect to a disarming degree. 46%. ncf.

Glenmorangie Artisan Casks db (**93**) **n23 t23.5 f23 b23.5.** If whisky could be sexed, this would be a woman. Every time I encounter Morangie Artisan, it pops up with a new look, a different perfume. And mood. It appears not to be able to make up its mind. But does it know how to pout, seduce and win your heart...? Oh yes. 46%

Glenmorangie Astar db (**88**) **n21 t23 f22.5 b22.** Decidedly strange malt: for quite a while it is as if someone has extracted the barley and left everything else behind. A star is born? Not yet, perhaps. But perhaps a new breed of single malt. 57.1%

Glenmorangie Burgundy Wood Finish db (**72**) **n17.5 t19.5 f18 b18.** Sulphured whisky de table. 43%

Glenmorangie Burr Oak Reserve db (**92**) **n24 t24 f22 b22.** Fades on the finish as a slightly spent force, but nose and arrival are simply breathtaking. Wouldn't be out of place in Kentucky. 56.3%

Glenmorangie Cellar 13 Ten Years Old db (**88.5**) **n22 t22.5 f22 b22** oh, if only I could lose weight as efficiently as this appears to have done... oh, I have! My love and thanks to Nancy, Nigel and Ann Marie. 43%

⁖ **Glenmorangie Ealanta 1993 Vintage** db (**97.5**) **n24** a near faultless nose, as one might expect from ultra high quality oak and supremely well-made distillate. A kind of elite Stranahan's nose, all black tie and wing collars and without the oils. Here, a mesmerising mix of dried orange peel and lychee flips for the leading role with gristy barley sugar and butterscotch seasoned with drying allspice and a few shavings of hickory: monumental...! **t24** the delivery, tasted blind, is bourbon! The nose whispers it, the palate sings it proudly! A gorgeous intertwining of black and red liquorice leaves no doubt. Most amazing is the weight: just an astonishing degree of oils and sugars with the grist seemingly mixed with an 80% Venezuelan cocoa and molassed and muscovado sugar mix (actually, leaning more towards the muscovado); **f24.5** one of the longest finishes to any Scotch this year and borderline perfection. The sugars are supremely weighted, their trick being not to interfere with the complex permutation of vanilla and barley. I cannot remember a fade so wonderfully orchestrated – like the final dying notes of a Vaughan Williams masterpiece – and so entirely free of distracting side issues of weakness and interference. Assisted perfectly by the lightest but most welcome degree of oil; **b25** when is a bourbon not a bourbon? When it is a Scotch single malt...And here we have potentially the World Whisky of the Year. Free from the embarrassing nonsense which passes for today's sherry butt, and undamaged by less than careful after use care of second-hand bourbon casks, we see what happens when the more telling aspects of oak, the business end which gives bourbon that extra edge, blends with the some of the very finest malt made in Scotland. Something approaching one of the best whiskies of my lifetime is the result... 46%

Glenmorangie Elegance db **(92)** n22 quite herbal and soothing; t24 the thinnest layer of icing sugar coats the silk-soft malt; every bit as gentle as the nose suggests; f22 medium to short with some attractive rolling vanilla; b24 a surprise package that is not entirely dissimilar to the Golden Rum, only a tad sweeter. 43%

Glemorangie Finealta db **(84.5)** n21 t22 f20.5 b21. Plump and thick, one of the creamiest malts around. For what it lacks in fine detail it makes up for in effect, especially the perky oaky spices. 46%

Glenmorangie Lasanta sherry casks db **(68.5)** n16 t19 f16 b17.5. The sherry problem has increased dramatically rather than being solved. 46%

Glenmorangie Madeira Wood Finish db **(78)** n19.5 t20.5 f19 b19. One of the real problems with wine finishes is getting the point of balance right when the fruit, barley and oak are in harmony. Here it is on a par with me singing in the shower, though frankly my aroma would be a notch or two up. 43%

Glenmorangie Margaux Cask Finish db **(88)** n22 t22 f22 b22. Even taking every whisky with an open mind, I admit this was better than my subconscious might have considered. Certainly better than the near undrinkable Ch. Margaux '57 I used to bring out for my birthday each year some 20-odd years ago... 46%

Glenmorangie Nectar D'or Sauternes Finish db **(94)** n23 delicate cinnamon on toast and a drizzle of greengage and sultana; t24 refreshing and dense on the palate as the bitter-sweet battle goes into overdrive; excellent weight and body; f23 remains clean and precise, allowing some custard onto the apple strudel finale; b24 great to see French casks that actually complement a whisky – so rare! This has replaced the Madeira finish. But there are some similar sweet-fruit characteristics. An exercise in outrageously good sweet-dry balancing. 46%

Glenmorangie Quinta Ruban Port Finish db **(92)** n24 typical Morangie complexity, but the grape notes added act almost like a prism to show their varied hues; t23 fruit and spice about as the oak goes in search of glory: barley stands in its way; f22 light, deftly sweetened and juicy to the end; b23 this replacement of the original Port finish shows a genuine understanding of the importance of grape-oak balance. Both are portrayed with clarity and confidence. This is a form of cask finishing that has progressed from experimentation to certainty. 46%

Glenmorangie Sherry Wood Finish db **(84)** n23 t21 f20 b20. Stupendous clean sherry nose, then disappoints with a somewhat bland display on the palate. 43%

Glenmorangie Signet db **(80.5)** n20 t21.5 f19 b20. A great whisky holed below the waterline by oak of unsatisfactory quality. Tragic. 46%

Glenmorangie Sonnalta PX db **(96.5)** n24 now this works: has that heavy-handed feel of a sweet sherry butt (or five) at work here, usually the kiss of death for so many whiskies. But an adroit praline sub-plot really does the trick. So with the malt evident, too, we have a three-pronged attack which somehow meshes in to one. And not even the merest hint of an off-note...goodness gracious: a new experience...!!! t24 Neanderthal grape drags its knuckles along the big vanilla floor before a really subtle light Columbian coffee kick puts us back on course; sharper vanillas from some awkward oak threatens to send us off course again but somehow it finds a settled, common ground; f24.5 now goes into orgasmic overdrive as Demerara sugar is tipped into some gorgeous, cream-lightened mocha. This is obviously to wash down the Melton Hunt cake which is resplendent in its grape and roast nut finery. It is the perfect whisky finish... b24 remains a giant among the tall stills. A mesmeric whisky... 46%

Glenmorangie Traditional db **(90.5)** n22 orange blossom, barley sugar and chalk dust; t23 delicate delivery revelling in gentle complexity: really playful young-ish malt makes for a clean start and middle; f22.5 soft mocha notes play out a quiet finish; b23 an improved dram with much more to say, but does so quietly. 57.1%

Glenmorangie Truffle Oak db **(96)** n24 t24 f25 b23. The Glenmorangie of all Glenmorangies. I really have to work hard and deep into the night to find fault with it. If I am going to be hyper-critical, I'll dock it a mark for being so constantly sweet, though in its defence I have to say that the degree of sweetness alters with astonishing dexterity. Go on, it's Truffle oak: make a pig of yourself...!! 60.5%

Scotch Malt Whisky Society Cask 125.50 Aged 12 Years dechar/toasted hogshead, cask no. 13056, dist 1998 **(92)** n22.5 heavy with bourbony sugars and vanillas; t24 deliciously sweet delivery and much thicker bodied than the norm for this distillery. The slow spice development works in harmony with the budding vanilla; f22.5 soft vanilla ice cream...with a dry wafer...; b23 well, that extracted most of the sugars out of that cask! 50.5%. sc.

Scotch Malt Whisky Society Cask 125.52 Aged 10 Years first fill hogshead, cask no. 2948, dist 2001 **(89)** n22 nutty; some drier wafer, too; t23 what a distillery this is: hardly gets out of second gear, withsheer simplicity and magnificent texture to the barley; f22 vanilla and mocha; b22 for a first fill 'Morangie, a real easy goer. 60%. sc. Scotch Malt Whisky Society.

Scotch Malt Whisky Society Cask 125.53 Aged 14 Years first fill designer hogshead, cask no. 8093, dist 1997 **(84.5)** n22.5 t22 f20 b21. One of those noses which evolves slowly and takes time to unravel. But also one of those malts where the cask just does no favours to the development on the palate. 55.3%. sc. *Scotch Malt Whisky Society.*

Scotch Malt Whisky Society Cask 125.54 Aged 9 Years refill hogshead, cask no. 12209, dist 2001 **(85.5)** n21.5 t22 f21 b21. Fruity. And fat. But, for all its power, a long way from firing on all cylinders. 61.4%. sc. *Scotch Malt Whisky Society.*

Scotch Malt Whisky Society Cask 125.56 Aged 8 Years first fill barrel, cask no. 1703, dist 2003 **(86)** n21.5 t22 f21 b21.5. You roll with the spicy punches with this one. A fascinating look at a Morangie under ten years trying to cope with the richness of a first fill barrel. A slightly unequal battle, as the barley is swamped. 60.8%. sc.

Scotch Malt Whisky Society Cask 125.57 Aged 11 Years first fill barrel, cask no. 1396, dist 2000 **(84)** n21 t22 f20 b21. Not surprised by the late bitterness which throws a wobbly on the overall balance as the nose foretold of this. 55.4%. sc. *Scotch Malt Whisky Society.*

Scotch Malt Whisky Society Cask 125.61 Aged 10 Years refill hogshead, cask no. 12207, dist 2001 **(88)** n22 a big wave of curiously tight sugars, some of which take different paths into mildly fruity territory; t23 the enormity of the sugars on delivery almost pin you back in your chair; a vague fruitiness hovers; f21 a degree of blood orange bitterness; b22 a real mixed bag of a malt very far removed from the classic 10-year-old distillery bottling. 61%. sc.

GLEN MORAY
Speyside, 1897. La Martiniquaise. Working.

Glen Moray Classic 8 Years Old db **(86)** n20 t22 f21 b23. A vast improvement on previous bottlings with the sluggish fatness replaced by a thinner, barley-rich, slightly sweeter and more precise mouthfeel. 40%

Glen Moray 10 Years Old Chardonnay Matured db **(73.5)** n18.5 t19 f18 b18. Tighter than a wine cork. 40%

Glen Moray 12 Years Old db **(90)** n22.5 gentle malt of varying pitch and intensity; t22 a duller start than it should be with the vanilla diving in almost before the barley but the juicy, grassy notes arrive in good time; f23 long, back on track with intense malt and the custardy oak is almost apologetic but enlivened with a dash of lime: mmmmm... pure Glen Moray! b22.5 I have always regarded this as the measuring stick by which all other malty and clean Speysiders should be tried and tested. It is still a fabulous whisky, full of malty intricacies. Something has fallen off the edge, perhaps, but minutely so. Still think a trick or two is being missed by bottling this at 40%: the natural timbre of this malt demands 46% and no less.... 40%

Glen Moray 16 Years Old db **(74)** n19 t19 f18 b19. A serious dip in form. Drab. 40%

Glen Moray 16 Years Old Chenin Blanc Mellowed in Wine Barrels db **(85)** n20 t22 f22 b21. A fruity, oak-shaded dram just brimming with complexity. 40%

Glen Moray 20 Years Old db **(80)** n22 t22 f18 b18. With so much natural cream toffee, it is hard to believe that this has so many years on it. After a quick, refreshing start it pans out, if anything, a little dull. 40%

⠂⠢⠂ **Glen Moray Aged 25 Years Portwood Finish Rare Vintage Limited Edition** bott code. 3153, dist 1986 db **(87.5)** n22.5 very unusual signature: the fruit is tight though spicy, even if it does limit the obvious excesses of the oak; t22 both spice and fruit spring immediately into action but the sugars are subdued due to a wine-must dryness; at least the juices flow, complete with muscovado sugars, for a few magical moments; f21 still a little tight and refuses to open as you might expect. A touch of chocolate raisin for sure, but also a furry bitterness; b22 just get the feeling that the Port pipe has not quite added what was desired. 43%

Glen Moray 30 Years Old db **(92.5)** n23.5 it's probably the deftness of the old-fashioned Speyside smoke in tandem with the structured fruits that makes this so special; t23.5 for a light Speysider, the degree of barley to oak is remarkable: soft, oil-gilde d barley is met by a wonderful, if brief, spice prickle; f22.5 deft layering of vanilla and cocoa; a sprinkle of muscovado sugar repels any darker oak notes; b23 for all its years, this is comfortable malt, untroubled by time. There is no mistaking quality. 43%

⠂⠢⠂ **Glen Moray Peated Spirit Batch #1** cask 141 db **(88.5)** n21 t23.5 f22 b22. A gorgeously jazzed up kindergarten Glen Moray, not so wet behind the ears as it might be thanks to what appears to be a very fresh bourbon cask. Imbalance on nose and finish for sure, but with a mega-delivery of smoked French toast washed down with cocoa and tannin concentrate, who cares whether this is strictly whisky or not? 60.6%. phenol content 18ppm

Glen Moray 1959 Rare Vintage db **(91)** n25 t23 f21 b22. They must have been keeping their eyes on this one for a long time: a stunning malt that just about defies nature. The nose reaches absolute perfection. 50.9%

Glen Moray 1962 Very Rare Vintage Aged 42 Years db **(94)** n23 t24 f23 b24. The first temptation is to think that this has succumbed to age, but a second and a third tasting reveal that there is much more complexity, integrity and balance to this than first meets the tastebuds. The last cask chosen by the legendary Ed Dodson before his retirement from the distillery: a pretty perceptive choice. A corker! 50.9%. sc.

Glen Moray 1984 db **(83)** n20 t22 f20 b21. Mouthwatering and incredibly refreshing malt for its age. 40%

Glen Moray 1989 db **(86)** n23 t22 f20 b21. Doesn't quite live up to the fruit smoothie nose but I'm being a little picky here. 40%

Glen Moray 1992 Single Cask No 1441 sherry butt db **(74)** n17 t21 f18 b18. Oops! Didn't anyone spot the sulphur...? 59.6%

Glen Moray 1995 Port Wood Finish bott Dec 09 db **(95.5)** n23 a surprising liquorice base to the healthy spiced fruit; **t24** vivid grape: clean, intense and, for a while, dominant. The oak surges back with a few tricks of its own, the most impressive being a liquorice-hickory thrust and a soothing custardy topping. Meanwhile, the grape offers spice and a sheen; **f24.5** a wonderful array of spicy chocolate and raisin notes that appear to continue indefinitely. Needs to be tasted to be believed. **b24** possibly the most satisfying wine finish of the year. 56.7%

Glen Moray 1995 Single Sherry Cask sherry butt db **(56)** n15 t14 f13 b14. So stunned was I about the abject quality of this bottling, I even looked on the Glen Moray website to see if they had said anything about it. Apparently, if you add water you find on the nose "the lingering soft sulphury smoke of a struck match." Well, here's the news: you don't need water. Just open the bottle and there's Rotorua in all it's stink bomb finery. And errr...hullo, guys... some further news: that means it's a bloody faulty, useless cask. And has no right to be put anywhere near a bottling hall let alone set loose in a single bottling. This, quite frankly, is absolutely rank whisky, the type of which makes my blood boil. I mean, is this really the best cask that could be found in the entire and considerable estate of Glen Moray..???? Am I, or is it the whisky world going mad...? 59.6%

Glen Moray Classic db **(86.5)** n22 t21.5 f21.5 b21.5. The nose is the star with a wonderful, clean barley-fruit tandem, but what follows cannot quite match its sure-footed wit. ☉

Glen Moray Wine Cask Edition bott Sep 09 db **(83.5)** n20 t23 f20 b20.5. When in full flow this is just bursting with some of the juiciest fruit you are likely to encounter. But a familiar bitter buzz brings down the value. How sad. 59.7%

Berry's Own Selection Glen Moray 1991 cask no. 5654, bott 2012 **(95)** n23 a lovely intertwining of polished oaky floors and muscovado-polished barley; **t24.5** deliveries on the palate rarely come more delicious than this: Glen Moray, when on form, is in the true malty elite of Scotland and here it tops the Premier League. The blend of sugars, some honeyed, spices and cocoa make you groan with pleasure; **f23.5** the vanilla and butterscotch kick in as you suspect they might. But the barley remains steadfast and clean; **b24** I have long regarded Berry's whisky buyer Dougie McIvor one of the genuinely understated gems of the industry and the best whisky writer we never had. Here he demonstrates his understanding of clean, barley-rich malts which has made this year's crop of Berry's Own Selection arguably their best yet. When you taste this you can see why I exploded in rage at the deficiencies of the official "Distillery Manager" bottling a few years back... 57.3%. nc ncf sc. Berry Bros & Rudd.

Duncan Taylor Dimensions Glen Moray 20 Years Old cask no. 9408, dist 1991 **(88.5)** n22.5 finely balanced with the saltiness bringing just enough out of the oak to lighten the weight; **t22.5** the sugars show few inhibitions here; juicy despite some obvious age; **f22** the oak catches up again; **b22** an understated dram. 54.8%. sc. Duncan Taylor & Co.

Duncan Taylor Dimensions Glen Moray 24 Years Old cask no. 2311, dist Sep 86, bott Dec 11 **(90.5)** n23 huge bourbon footprint; that's if you can get footprints on the nose; **t23** brown sugar notes swamp the taste buds. The spices appear to have a muscovado edge. The chocolate liquorice sublime, as is the salivating lime; usually barley is prevalent with Glen Moray: here it is peripheral; **f22** custard tart and icing sugar carries out the farewells; **b22.5** Glen Moray at its most confident and forceful. 51.6%. nc ncf sc. Duncan Taylor & Co.

Duncan Taylor Octave Glen Moray 24 Years Old cask no. 701120, dist 1986 **(93)** n23.5 astonishing esters: a degree of Jamaican pot still rum sweetness to this, especially so far as those spiced honeys are concerned; **t23** rum again! I am in a Jamaican warehouse...actually I'm not: I am in England and hailstones are thumping against my window. Those spices, just like on the nose, infuse with fabulous evenness; **f23** that coppery edge lasts to the very end; **b23.5** I have tasted many Glen Morays in my time: indeed, this was the first distillery I took my son, James, to in 1987 when he was just six months old. But I have never quite experienced one with such a feel of the West Indies. The Octave in question must have been penned by Bob Marley. 50.2%. sc. Duncan Taylor & Co.

Duncan Taylor Rare Auld Glen Moray 24 Years Old cask no. 2306, dist 1986 **(90.5)** n23.5 a lovely cross between butterscotch and bluebells, aided by a delicate earthiness softened by a light spreading of honey; **t23** spot-on weight with the barley displaying a dual role of softness and crispness while a tiny dollop of maple syrup goes a long way; **f21.5** fades just a little too quickly as the vanillas offer a burnt toast finale; **b22.5** a deluxe and hugely enjoyable blueprint for the better Glen Morays distilled during this period. *51.7%. sc.*

Malts Of Scotland Glen Morey 1977 bourbon hogshead, cask no. MoS12021, dist Oct 77, bott Apr 12 **(91.5) n23.5** the highlight of the experience: ripe peaches and some underlying avocado; big, big age on the oak, but so deftly done!; **t23** and this underlined on the lime, fig and black cherry delivery. The latter note is normally associated with sherry, but not here. The mid ground lessens in puckering intensity and is happy to concentrate on the intense malt and butterscotch; **f22.5** more lightly oiled malt. And vanilla; **b22.5** now listen guys. As a Murray, whose name most probably originated from this region a great many centuries ago, may I just ask that you spell Moray correctly on your labels?! Anyway, while your spelling may be crap, your ability to pick a superb cask is not in doubt. *52.1%. nc ncf sc. Malts Of Scotland.*

❖ **Master Of Malt Glen Moray 21 Years Old** cask no. 5661, dist 91, bott 13 **(89) n21.5** some fizzing spice and something oddly earthy for a Moray; **t23** spellbinding spice attack on delivery: like the small grains of a complex bourbon. All other layers represent malt in varying degrees of intensity; **f22** the vanilla must have a say while a squeeze of kumquat doesn't go amiss; **b22.5** a fast talking Glen Moray with an unusually vast amount to say for itself about spice. *60.7%. 260 bottles.*

Mo Ór Collection Glen Moray 1971 39 Years Old first fill bourbon hogshead, cask no. 5, dist 11 Oct 71, bott 21 Jan 11 **(93) n24** varying layers of citrus and a surprising dash of apple. There is also a quite beautiful date and walnut sponge here, too. The barley keeps its integrity despite a tendency to veer off in a Kentucky direction; the oak isn't exactly of a retiring nature; **t23** fingers of sugar-coated liquorice tease the taste buds as thickening oils inject a full barley personality; **f23** even and benefits from the late butterscotch; **b23** so teasingly bourbony, they could re-name it Knob Moray... *46%. nc ncf sc. Release No. 11. 429 bottles.*

Mo Ór Collection Glen Moray 1989 21 Years Old first fill bourbon hogshead, cask no. 7277, dist 24 Oct 89, bott 24 Oct 10 **(82.5) n21 t21 f20.5 b20.** The barley sugar is eclipsed by a dull but persistent bitterness. *46%. nc ncf sc. Release No. 49. The Whisky Talker. 419 bottles.*

Provenance Glen Moray Over 11 Years refill hogshead, cask no. 7603, dist Spring 2000, bott Summer 2011 **(85.5) n22.5 t21 f21 b21.** Clean, youthful and with a few spices up its sleeve. *46%. nc ncf sc. Douglas Laing & Co.*

❖ **Provenance Glen Moray Over 12 Years** refill hogshead, cask no. 8435, dist Autumn 99, bott Spring 12 **(88.5) n22** a squeeze of nectarine amid the barley; **t22** usual malty gush from the off: mid-ground pure barley; **f22.5** fizzes with oak slightly as the fade softens out; **b22** a gentle malt from one of the gentler distilleries, but just enough attitude to make it interesting. *46%. nc ncf sc. Douglas Laing & Co.*

Scotch Malt Whisky Society Cask 35.58 Aged 26 Years refill butt, cask no. 31091, dist 1984 **(93.5) n24** dreamy complexity: the lightness of touch of the lime and tangerine notes takes some believing. All the delicacy of the very lightest of fruit sponge cakes; **t24** so no surprise that the delivery should be equally as deft: the malt merely kisses the taste buds while the even lighter, powdered sugars land like snowflakes; **f22.5** just slightly heavy with the vanilla by comparison and the faintest degree of bitterness; **b23** effortless elegance. *41%. sc.*

Scotch Malt Whisky Society Cask 35.59 Aged 39 Years refill hogshead, cask no. 1571, dist 1971 **(87) n22** kumquats and dry marmalade spread over burnt toast; **t22.5** the delivery is the high point of the experience as the barley simply melts into the palate taking with it myriad sugar notes; for a while the over-aged oak is too stunned to take action... **f21**...though it finally does towards the finish; **b21.5** in reality, over-the-top oak from a cask aged maybe five or six years too many. But some of the jewels on display are quite dazzling. *40.9%. sc.*

Scotch Malt Whisky Society Cask 35.60 Aged 39 Years refill hogshead, cask no. 8942, dist 1971 **(84.5) n22 t21.5 f20.5 b20.5.** Always a shame when you find that the oak has got to the whisky before you... *42.3%. sc. Scotch Malt Whisky Society.*

Scotch Malt Whisky Society Cask 35.65 Aged 10 Years refill Chardonnay hogshead, cask no. 7222, dist 2001 **(84.5) n22 t22 f20.5 b20.** Big oak toastiness with some major buttery elements and a tidal wave of seemingly teeth-rotting sugars. Suspect this was a beauty maybe three or four years back but now almost too much of a good thing. *60.3%. sc.*

❖ **Scotch Malt Whisky Society Cask 35.68 Aged 25 Years** refill hogshead, dist 15 May 87 **(94.5) n23.5** at first the sandpaper bites and threatens; fortunately there is more to the oak with dank, mossy north-facing gardens, bluebells and mint perfectly embracing the Lubek marzipan and sweeter barley sugar; **t24** exceptional delivery. The barley forms a thick layer under which bourbony liquorice and thin molasses sit. Spices strike early and persistently, the mint rising with the developing cocoa; **f23** back to a slightly oily vanilla, but a barley trail can be followed; **b24** the oak shows little sign of compromise; fortunately the barley has more than enough in the tank to match it. A malt of stunning complexity and brinkmanship ensues. *54.2%. nc ncf sc. 92 bottles.*

⠴ **Scotch Malt Whisky Society Cask 35.79 Aged 28 Years** refill butt, dist 22 Dec 83 **(70)** n17 t18 f17 b18. Scarred, sadly, by sulphur. 57.7%. nc ncf sc. 167 bottles.

⠴ **Scotch Malt Whisky Society Cask 35.85 Aged 17 Years** 1st fill barrel, 27 Oct 95 **(88)** n21.5 even the light sprinkling of citrus cannot disguise the intense gristiness; t22.5 a real softie on delivery with the melting, gristy sugars filling the palate with the cleanest barley imaginable; the oak-soaked spices act alone in offering a differing viewpoint; f22 a charming vanilla and barley fade, with the lemon making a surprise reprise; b22 an Elgin gristfest... 56.7%. nc ncf sc. 233 bottles.

⠴ **Scotch Malt Whisky Society Cask 35.89 Aged 17 Years** 1st fill barrel, dist 27 Oct 95 **(91)** n22 simple barley in traditional Glen Moray style; t23.5 the oak interjects early with a fabulous spice and liquorice lift off, penetrating deeply into the thick, slightly oily barley; f22.5 simplistic in the distillery's accepted manner: the barley carries on pounding, accompanied by vanilla and citrus; b23 beautifully made and matured whisky. Technically top notch. 59.7%. nc ncf sc.

Single Cask Collection Glen Moray 21 Years Old bourbon hogshead, dist 1990 **(89)** n22 just a little tart, if you know what I mean, though there is something of a jam tart to this, too! That sharpness steadies as the barley makes a stand; t22 the oak is far too aggressive early on, leaving the malt in the shade; exotic fruit and manuka honey do the trick; f23 reverts to serious oakiness then goes into complexity overdrive; b22 at times, the simplicity of Glen Moray means that it struggles to comfortably wear its age. That's how this one starts, but gradually eases into its antiquity. Look closely, around about the time the jam and Venezuelan cocoa arrives at the back end, and there is great complexity to be enjoyed. 55%. sc.

⠴ **That Boutique-y Whisky Company Glen Moray** batch 1 **(86.5)** n20.5 t23 f21.5 b21.5. Rowntree Toffo with a juicy injection of concentrated malt and glazed cherry. Undone slightly by an indifferent nose. 49.1%. Master Of Malt. 176 bottles.

⠴ **The Whisky Agency Glen Moray 1977** bott 12 **(87.5)** n22.5 the vaguest hint of smoke helps protect the nose from a succession of oaky blows; t22 big, very big oak on delivery with strands of juicy orange mingling with the remaining barley; f21.5 tangy with tired oak; b21.5 a splintery white knuckle ride. 51.8%

The Whisky Agency Glen Moray 35 Years Old dist 1977 **(96)** n23.5 brags about its age with an engaging, exotic fruit-rich display. The chalkier elements suggest that the oak has gone as far as it can, but there are no breaches in excellence; t24 soft delivery with an immediate mouth-watering barley thrust. Those exotic fruits pop up around the palate with a delightful randomness; light oils amplify the delicate sugars; f24 fears of oak dominance are never realised. Instead we have a lovely minty cocoa finish with just the right sprinkling of spice; b24.5 a highly accomplished, absolutely top dollar antique whisky. 51.8%. sc.

GLEN ORD

Highlands (Northern), 1838. Diageo. Working.

Glen Ord Aged 12 Years db **(81)** n20 t23 f18 b20. Just when you thought it safe to go back...for a while Diageo ditched the sherry-style Ord. It has returned. Better than some years ago, when it was an unhappy shadow of its once-great self, but without the sparkle of the vaguely-smoked bottling of a year or two back. Nothing wrong with the rich arrival, but the finish is a mess. I'll open the next bottling with trepidation... 43%

Glen Ord 25 Years Old dist 1978 db **(95)** n24 t24 f23 b24. Some stupendous vatting here: cask selection at its very highest to display Ord in all its far too rarely seen magnificence. 58.3%

Glen Ord 28 Years Old db **(90)** n22 t23 f22 b23. This is mega whisky showing slight traces of sap, especially on the nose, but otherwise a concentrate of many of the qualities I remember from this distillery before it was bottled in a much ruined form. Blisteringly beautiful. 58.3%

Glen Ord 30 Years Old db **(87)** n22 t21 f23 b21. Creaking with oak, but such is the polish to the barley some serious class is on show. 58.8%

Glen Ord 1997 The Manager's Choice db **(93.5)** n24 oh my word...what have we here...? Just the most enticing little fruit pastel number you could ask for, and all played out on the softest malty field imaginable. Genuinely complex and enticing with the nose being teasingly caressed; t23.5 then, just to shock, a real injection of bite and nip on delivery with a tangy blood orange thread which follows from the nose; f23 custard powder oakiness with some late hickory and toffee; b23 when given the chance, Glen Ord offers one of the fruitiest drams on the market. Here it is in its full blood orange element. A beauty! 59.2%

Singleton of Glen Ord 12 Years Old db **(89)** n22.5 t22.5 f22 b22 a fabulous improvement on the last bottling I encountered. Still possesses blood oranges to die for, but greatly enhanced by some sublime spices and a magnificent juiciness. 40%

Singleton of Glen Ord 32 Year Old db **(91)** n23.5 t23 f22 b22.5. Delicious. But if ever a malt has screamed out to be at 46%, this is it. 40%

Cadenhead Ord 15 Years Old bott 2012 **(89.5) n22** pulsing barley; **t23** a riot of flavour on delivery. The salt and barley mix before the sugars arrive is awesome; a super-salivating sample...; **f22** much more sanguine with butterscotch dominant; **b22.5** the spectacular delivery is far from ORDinary... *57.3%. sc. WM Cadenhead Ltd.*

⋰ **Liquid Library Glen Ord 1997** ex-bourbon hogshead, dist 97, bott 11 **(84) n22 t21 f20 b21.** A pretty tired cask even before it was filled back in 1997, the oak involvement here is virtually trace. *50.4%. The Whisky Agency.*

⋰ **Liquid Sun Glen Ord 1997** ex-bourbon hogshead, dist 97, bott 12 **(86) n21 t21.5 f22 b21.5.** Wow! Some of the oldest new make on the market! Like the Liquid Library 50.4% we have what appears to be a third fill cask in play here. The result is a juicy, ultra malty beast. But the oak should be injecting so much extra complexity by now. *49.9%. The Whisky Agency.*

Malts Of Scotland Glen Ord 1999 bourbon hogshead, cask no. MoS110013, dist 9 Mar 99, bott Oct 11 **(88.5) n21.5** typical Ordie fruit and spice; **t23** those of a nervous disposition unable to withstand a malt-spice onslaught should withdraw now. A greengage and boiled apple middle, but the barley and its juices run through with ease; **f22** simplifies back to oak, barley and spice basics; **b22** a long way from perfection, but a dram to keep your senses on alert all night long. *54.4%. nc ncf. Malts Of Scotland.*

Provenance Glen Ord Over 7 Years refill hogshead, cask no. 7644, dist Autumn 2004, bott Autumn 2011 **(82.5) n20 t22 f20 b20.5.** A little celebration of all things citrusy. *46%. nc ncf sc.*

⋰ **Provenance Glen Ord Over 8 Years** refill hogshead, cask no. 9034, dist Autumn 04, bott Autumn 12 **(81.5) n19 t21.5 f20.5 b20.5.** A third fill barrel which makes no attempt to interfere with the development of the malt. For those with a penchant for lightweight mega juicy barley fests. *46%. nc ncf sc.*

Provenance Glen Ord Over 11 Years refill hogshead, cask no. 9008, dist Spring 2000, bott Winter 2012 **(89) n23** a style this distillery does so well: a light fruit salad emboldened by citrus-stained barley with only the most distant rumbles of peat offering weight; **t22.5** mouth-watering, clean and then a fabulous cascade of barley in varying degrees of sweetness; **f21.5** thins slightly but peppery spice compensates; **b22** another cask that is too easy to overlook. Take your time with this and just let it melt in the mouth... *46%. nc ncf sc. Douglas Laing & Co.*

⋰ **Provenance Glen Ord Over 14 Years** refill hogshead, cask no. 9652, dist Spring 99, bott Spring 13 **(87) n22.5 t23 f20 b21.5.** Even the thin, pasty finish cannot fully detract from the vitality of the nose and delivery. Early on its barley, barley everywhere! *46%. nc ncf.*

Scotch Malt Whisky Society Cask 77.26 Aged 23 Years refill hogshead, cask no. 3368, dist 1987 **(92.5) n23** lightly fried yam, with a slightly yolky, salty background. The vanillas are deft and complex; **t23.5** soft oils ensure the barley yields at all the right points. Excellent salt and sugar mix. The middle ground is vanilla concentrate with a touch of nougat; **f23** remains juicy and barley rich to the very end, despite the increased oaky weight; a light sprinkling of honeycomb helps; **b23** a Highland malt refusing to accept its age and still showing an almost imperious vigour. Superb! *55.6%. sc. Scotch Malt Whisky Society.*

Scotch Malt Whisky Society Cask 77.27 Aged 11 Years refill hogshead, cask no. 4, dist 2000 **(86) n21.5 t22 f21.5 b21.** Overflowing with intense barley. Well made and matured. But, though deliciously simplistic, could do with stretching the complexity a little. *55.2%. sc.*

⋰ **Scotch Malt Whisky Society Cask 77.28 Aged 25 Years** 2nd fill hogshead, charred oak, dist 13 Aug 87 **(97) n24** someone has quietly poured some paprika a jar of beech honey and topped it off with oak shavings. The result is enticingly formidable; **t24.5** just ridiculous. No delivery should have quite so many things going on at once. In 20 minutes I have identified four different honey types at work, perhaps the most telling of them all being a light manuka, but blended in with ulmo thinned with clear: probably the most complex set of honey notes I've encountered in the last five or six years. The serious age means the oak injects a dryness which counters any honey-led excess of sweetness; **f24** at last something other than honey holds sway: the oak pitches in late with an almost tarry character, though, in essence, we are feeling the drying strains of spent honey and barley with a half-hearted spiciness seeing in the much broader cocoa; **b24.5** truly amazing. Make a bee-line for this one. No idea of the price, but impossible to get stung way here. For this is, as sure as bee eggs are bee eggs, an award winner of some sort this year! You cannot ask for any more from any single malt, as this is a thing of the very rarest beauty. *54.9%. nc ncf sc. 236 bottles.*

The Warehouse Collection Glen Ord Aged 22 Years refill sherry butt, cask no. 30, dist 19 Jan 90, bott 12 Apr 12 **(84.5) n21.5 t22 f20 b21.** The delivery delights; the finish frustrates. *53.2%. sc. Whisky Warehouse No. 8. 535 bottles.*

GLENROTHES
Speyside, 1878. Edrington. Working.

The Glenrothes 1978 dist Nov 78, bott 2008 db **(90.5) n23** over-ripe gooseberries mixed with dry tobacco; suet pudding and vanilla pods: attractively intriguing; **t23** relaxed, lush barley coats the mouth with a muscovado sugar edge; **f22** mushy sultana and toasty oak; **b22.5** sheer – and delicious – entertainment. *43%*

The Glenrothes 1988 Vintage dist 16 Dec 88, bott 04 Nov 08 db **(93) n22** stunning toasted honeycomb **t24.5** exceptional delivery. Not only is the mouth feel quite perfect, the deft marriage of honey, honeycomb, treacle and maple syrup has to be tasted to be believed...; **f23** dries and spices up as the oaks grab hold; **b23.5** a gorgeous bottling still doing the rounds... and should be hunted down and polished off. *43%*

The Glenrothes 1988 Vintage bott 2010 db **(74) n18.5 t19 f18 b18.5.** For all the obvious high quality sugars present, it still can't overcome the Spanish imposition. *43%*

The Glenrothes 1994 dist Oct 94, bott 2007 db **(77) n19 t20 f19 b19.** The citrus appears as promised on the label, but sadly a few unadvertised sulphured butt-related gremlins are present also. *43%*

The Glenrothes 1995 Vintage dist 26 Oct 95, bott 06 Sep 10 db **(87.5) n20 t22 f23 b22.5.** Like an old grump that takes its time to wake and finally has to be kicked out of bed. Once up, certainly does the biz. *43%*

The Glenrothes 1998 Vintage dist Dec 98, bott Feb 09 db **(66) n16 t20 f14 b16.** Really would have thought they would have got the hang of this sulphur lark by now... *43%*

The Glenrothes 1998 Vintage bott 2010 db **(73.5) n20 t19 f16 b18.5.** Talk about bitter-sweet...!!! *43%*

The Glenrothes Alba Reserve db **(87.5) n22 t22 f21.5 b22.** You know that smartly groomed, polite but rather dull chap you invariable get at dinner parties? *40%*

The Glenrothes John Ramsay bott 2009 db **(89.5) n22.5 t23.5 f21.5 b22.** Elegant and charming. What else did you expect...? *46.7%. 1400 bottles.*

The Glenrothes Robur Reserve db **(81.5) n20.5 t22 f19 b20.** With the youthful barley prominent early on, one of the sweetest distillery bottling from Glenrothes I've come across. Bitter cask fade, though. *40%*

The Glenrothes Select Reserve db **(80) n17.5 t22 f20.5 b21.** Flawed in the usual Glenrothes sherry places, but the brilliance of the sharp barley wins your heart. *40%*

The Glenrothes Three Decades bott 2009 db **(90.5) n23.5 t24 f21.5 b22.5.** Not without a minor blemish here and there, but the overall magnitude of this allows you to forgive quite easily. The distant sulphur apart, a stunner. *43%. Duty Free exclusive.*

Archives Glenrothes 1988 23 Years Old Third Release refill sherry hogshead, cask no. 7318, dist 6 Jun 88, bott 4 Jan 12 **(79) n19 t21 f19 b20.** Tight, dry and short of couth. *53.4%. nc ncf sc. Whiskybase B.V. 80 bottles.*

Cadenhead Glenrothes 15 Years Old (88) n22 it's as though someone has moved the distillery to the seaside...very salty; **t23** no less sharp on delivery with those tangy salty malt notes giving way to mocha – seriously tasty! **f21** a caramel overdose: a boring end to a lovely dram; **b22** from an ex-bourbon cask...thank heavens! *53.8%. sc. WM Cadenhead Ltd.*

⁘ **Director's Cut Glenrothes Aged 18 Years** refill hogshead, cask no. 7958, dist Mar 93, bott Jan 12 **(87) n22.5** a mish-mash of grape and orange...with a blurry something else sherry-related in the background...; **t23** irrepressible spiced grape and a mocha stratum make the most of the moment before the inevitable; **f19.5** dulled by guess what... **b22** a blemish for sure, but an excellent delivery. *54.2%. sc. Douglas Laing & Co. 127 bottles.*

Duncan Taylor Dimensions Glenrothes 20 Years Old cask no. 5154, dist Mar 91, bott Dec 11 **(85.5) n21.5 t22 f21 b21.** For all its liveliness and thrust, there is a slight tangy blight to the cask which relegates this to a lower whisky division. *49.6%. nc ncf sc. Duncan Taylor & Co.*

⁘ **Gordon and MacPhail Collection Glenrothes 8 Years Old (91) n22** sublime if simplistic creamy texture to the buttery barley; **t23.5** salivating with the barley and icing sugar in bon accord; **f22.5** a light lemon zest and spice offers a surprising extra depth; **b23** a malt which combines, with impressive gait, and no little gaiety, that unspoiled Glenrothes really is top class fare, even at this tender age. *43%*

Malts Of Scotland Angel's Choice Glenrothes 1970 bourbon hogshead, cask no. MoS11026, bott Nov 11 **(86.5) n21.5 t22 f21.5 b21.5.** If you don't mind getting a splintered tongue, tuck in! Some wonderful honeycomb moments which soothe and amaze. But the massive oaky imprint is just a little too fierce for greatness. *44.5%. nc ncf sc. Malts Of Scotland.*

⁘ **Malts Of Scotland Glenrothes 1982** bourbon hogshead, cask no. MoS 12065, dist Apr 82, bott Nov 12 **(85) n21 t23.5 f19 b21.5.** An unfriendly bourbon cask picks at and undoes the tangled honey and salt. In a better wood this would have been something a little special. *53.2%. nc ncf sc. 96 bottles.*

Mo Ór Collection Glenrothes 1988 22 Years Old first fill bourbon hogshead, cask no. 7321, dist 1988, bott 2010 **(87) n23.5** Marmalade on pretty well scorched toast; no shortage of lemon and lime, either; **t22** for all the fruit on the nose, the barley is first to break through and makes for a succulent dish; **f19.5** overzealously bitter; **b22** doesn't quite live up to its early expectation. The nose, though, has you setting the table for breakfast... *46%. nc ncf sc. 403 bottles.*

⁖ **Old and Rare Glenrothes Aged 21 Years** sherry hogshead, dist Jun 90, bott Jan 12 **(77)** **n18.5 t22 f17.5 b19**. One of those drams you could weep for. The grape has great richness and integrity. Sadly, the furry, bitter notes reveal its Achilles heel: a problem not uncommon with this distillery. *56.1%. nc ncf sc. Douglas Laing & Co. 94 bottles.*

Old Malt Cask Glenrothes Aged 21 Years refill butt, cask no. 7532, dist Jun 90, bott Sep 11 **(94.5) n22** nougat and raisin; elsewhere there are slightly bizarre hints of marmite and liquorice; **t24** excellent delivery sporting a silky sheen to the barley and then a powering spice-bite to the sherry; some beautiful oils attempt to confuse the two camps but there is enough tension between the juicy barley and ever-thickening fruit to ensure the taste buds are kept working overtime; **f24.5** sheer Melton Hunt Cake roastiness to the fruit. The spices fizz around the palate with abandon. The oils intensify and ensure the molassed sugars carry on for an almost ridiculous amount of time. Drying vanillas soon arrive; **b24** a sulphur-free spicefest. Wonderful! *50%. nc ncf sc. Douglas Laing & Co. 328 bottles.*

⁖ **Provenance Glenrothes Over 8 Years** sherry butt, cask no. 9212, dist Spring 04, bott Autumn 12 **(72) n17 t19 f18 b18**. For a brief second the grape glistens on the palate. But for the remainder...oh, sulphury dear...! *46%. nc ncf sc. Douglas Laing & Co.*

Provenance Glenrothes Over 10 Years refill barrel, cask no. 7917, dist Summer 2001, bott Autumn 2011 **(84) n20 t21.5 f21.5 b21**. A well-made, malty and vaguely spicy individual enjoying scant help from the cask. *46%. nc ncf sc. Douglas Laing & Co.*

Provenance Glenrothes Aged 11 Years (86) n21 t22 f21.5 b21.5. A pithy little number seemingly distilled and matured in an orangery. *46%*

Riegger's Selection Glenrothes 1986 bourbon cask, cask no. 2, dist 15 Dec 86, bott 30 Nov 10 **(86.5) n21.5 t22.5 f21 b21.5**. Slaps on the sweet, thick barley with abandon. Decent spices, too. *53.3%. nc ncf sc. Viktor-Riegger GmbH. 369 bottles.*

⁖ **Scotch Malt Whisky Society Cask 30.74 Aged 11 Years** refill port pipe, dist 27 Mar **(86.5) n21.5 t23 f20.5 b21.5**. Despite the obvious and almost inevitable flaws from the sherry butt, there are some spiced sultana and greengage notes to die for. Close your taste buds to the faults and you have a real spicy treat at work. *60.3%. nc ncf sc. 767 bottles.*

Scott's Selection Glenrothes 1990 bott 2011 **(90.5) n22.5** excellent depth to the chalky, liquorice and leathery bourbon theme; **t23** superb balance to the sugar involvement as the barley and muscovado melt in unison; more bourbon tones as the spice bites deep and the chocolate is smothered liberally around; **f22.5** long and sugary; thins out for a papery finish; **b22.5** the kind of Scotch that would be dearly loved in Kentucky. *58.3%. Speyside Distillers.*

⁖ **The Whisky Shop Dufftown Glenrothes Aged 41 Years** oak octave casks, cask no. 491630, dist 6 Jul 70, bott 21 Sep 11 **(92) n23** lavender and fizzing spice points towards big age; lots of bourbon traits; **t22.5** aggressive oak at first, but slowly relents as, miraculously, juicy malt and even some dark sugars, liquorice and ulmo honey begin to make their presence felt; **f23.5** massive spice and still the crunchy sugars crystallize; **b23** does nothing to hide its age. Luckily the sugars and honey are powerful enough to ensure parity. After 41 years it deserves the extra time in the glass to show itself as the mini star it actually is. *43.5%. nc ncf sc. 69 bottles.*

⁖ **Wemyss 1988 Single Speyside Glenrothes "Ginger Spice"** butt, bott 13 **(88) n22** an imperfect butt with perfectly accentuated dry sherry and freshly ground coffee; **t22.5** the barley and butterscotch link comfortably while the grape assembles juicily with the spice; **f21** Lebkuchen German spiced chocolate cake but with grape instead of jam! Spoiled by a little furriness at the death; **b22.5** only the slight blemish on the cask prevents this score from being a whole lot higher. Excellent, all the same. *46%. sc. Wemyss Malts. 660 bottles.*

GLEN SCOTIA
Campbeltown, 1832. Loch Lomond Distillers. Working

⁖ **Glen Scotia Aged 10 Years** bourbon cask, bott Dec 12 db **(90.5) n22.5** soft salty edge to the brittle, clean barley; **t23.5** one of the cleanest deliveries of the year: the barley is tinged with muscovado sugar and oak plays a back seat role; **f22** such a pleasing mix of spice and sugar; just a pinch of ginger reminds you of the oak; **b22.5** fabulous to see Scotia back in this excellent nick again. *46%. nc ncf.*

Glen Scotia 12 Years Old db **(73.5) n18 t19 f18 b18.5**. Ooops! I once said you could write a book about this called "Murder by Caramel." Now it would be a short story called "Murder by Flavours Unknown." What is happening here? Well, a dozen years ago Glen Scotia was not quite the place to be for consistent whisky, unlike now. Here, the caramel is the only constant as the constituent parts disintegrate. *40%*

⁖ **Glen Scotia Aged 12 Years** bourbon cask, bott Dec 12 db **(89) n22** swaggering oak perks up the barley; **t22** immediate spice explosion, though attractively controlled. The big malty thread is pretty wide; **f23** the spice of a warmer, more rumbling style – balances beautifully against the malt; **b22** simplistic but delicious. *46%. nc ncf.*

⠿ **Glen Scotia Aged 16 Years** bourbon cask, bott Dec 12 db (**87**) n22 warming signs of hot spirit chilled by minty cocoa; t22 glossy sheen to the malt, mainly thanks to a sugary coating; f21 thins slightly; b22 signs of a less than brilliant distillate which has been ironed out to some good effect in the cask. *46%. nc ncf.*

⠿ **Glen Scotia Aged 18 Years** bourbon cask, bott Dec 12 db (**77**) n20 t21 f17 b19. Malty but hot as Hades: a reminder of a less than glorious period in the distillery's history. *46%. nc ncf.*

⠿ **Glen Scotia Aged 21 Years** bourbon cask, bott Dec 12 db (**86.5**) n21.5 t22.5 f21 b21.5. Appears nothing like its age: the very vaguely smoked malt is entirely on top and offers little deviation. A playful spice reminds you oak is involved somewhere. *46%. nc ncf.*

Kingsbury Single Cask Series Glen Scotia Aged 19 Years Trois Riviers rum finish (**86**) n21.5 t22 f21.5 b21.5. Pretty tight in places and in others has a problem to breathe. But the salivating nip and tang to the crisp sugars and insistent barley makes for an interesting dram. *46%. sc. Japan Import Systems.*

Malts Of Scotland Glen Scotia 1991 bourbon hogshead, cask no. MoS12009, dist 22 May 91, bott Jan 12 (**84**) n22 t21 f20 b21. A very high quality cask, injecting molassed tannins, ensures some depth and quality to some very ordinary original spirit. *54.5%. nc ncf sc. Malts Of Scotland.*

Mo Òr Collection Glen Scotia 1992 18 Years Old first fill sherry cask, cask no. 6, dist 25 Mar 92, bott 2 Dec 10 (**61**) n17 t18 f12 b14. Grim degrees of sulphur. *46%. nc ncf sc. Release No. 41. The Whisky Talker. 1076 bottles.*

Scotch Malt Whisky Society Cask 93.47 Aged 9 Years refill barrel, cask no. 152, dist 2002 (**92.5**) n22.5 youthful phenols lightened by some major citrus; t24 melt-in-the-mouth peat which is about as soft as any peaty whisky gets. Milky chocolate also softens the proceedings; f23 a lovely build up of salt and vanilla; the smoke wafts around with a feather-light touch; b23 Scotia confirming it does peat with aplomb. An excellent age to enjoy this, too, as the oak has made little more than a guest appearance. *59.7%. sc.*

Scotch Malt Whisky Society Cask 93.48 Aged 12 Years refill barrel, cask no. 510, dist 1999 (**87.5**) n22 remember Merlin's Brew ice lollies? The one with the outrageously delicious chocolate mint theme? This is like a lightly peated version of that...; t22 after the big, spicy, biting peat comes...Merlin's Brew yet again. There appears to be a theme here...; f21.5 a little on the hot side, but that cocoa and peat finale make amends; b22 an attractive, minty bottling of the new malty Scotia. *62%. sc. Scotch Malt Whisky Society.*

Scotch Malt Whisky Society Cask 93.49 Aged 19 Years refill butt, cask no. 226, dist 1992 (**61**) n15 t16 f14 b16. Dreadful and substandard to an almost legendary degree. *578%. sc.*

Scotch Malt Whisky Society Cask 93.52 Aged 9 Years refill barrel, cask no. 153, dist 2002 (**88.5**) n22 attractive Victoria sponge nose, complete with powdered sugar. The barley is unusual, though...; t23 big, clean, bounding barley showing excellent weight yet not being lost in oils; f21.5 slightly bitters but those persistent malt and sugar notes hang on in; b22 thick and syrupy but the barley does a good job. *58.4%. sc.*

⠿ **Scotch Malt Whisky Society Cask 93.53 Aged 10 Years** refill barrel, dist 30 Apr 02 (**86.5**) n21 t22.5 f20.5 b21.5. Firm almost to the point of being solid. The shimmering saltiness of the juicy barley is underscored, but there are a few scorch marks, especially to the thin finale. *58.7%. nc ncf sc. 233 bottles.*

⠿ **Scotch Malt Whisky Society Cask 93.55 Aged 13 Years** refill barrel, dist 31 Jul 99 (**88**) n22 a sharp acidic bite to the peaty theme; t22 excellent sugars integrate with the modest smoke to strike up some depth; the ground black peppers are well mannered; f22 a little mint to the smoky chocolate; the spices last longer than expected; b22 an attractive, steady-as-she-goes merchant offering mild peat. *61.4%. nc ncf sc. 217 bottles.*

Scott's Selection Glen Scotia 1991 bott 2010 (**81.5**) n19 t20 f21.5 b21. Just looking for a mirror to see if there is any enamel left on my teeth. Violent. *58.7%. Speyside Distillers.*

Scott's Selection Glen Scotia 1991 bott 2012 (**84.5**) n21 t21 f21.5 b21. Resounding oak makes this an eye-watering one...; some trace mocha makes life easier towards the end. *53.8%. Speyside Distillers.*

The Warehouse Collection Glen Scotia Aged 20 Years first fill sherry butt, cask no. 5, dist 25 Mar 92, bott 8 Aug 12 (**86**) n22 t24 f19 b21. Delighted to report sulphur didn't explode in my face. But this has been treated, alas, and the bitterness gathers slowly but surely at the death. Until it gets there, enjoy the chocolate raisin ride! *59.5%. sc. 470 bottles.*

⠿ **Wemyss 1991 Single Campbeltown "Salted Caramels"** barrel, dist 91, bott 13 (**85**) n22 t21 f21 b21. Can't argue with the title this time: a malt swimming in brine and with toffee aplenty. Like the celery on the nose, though. *46%. sc. 279 bottles.*

Wemyss 1991 Single Campbeltown Glen Scotia "Strawberry Ganache" butt, bott 2012 (**83.5**) n20 t22 f20 b21.5. In the US, the film "Whisky Galore" was called "Tight Little Island". This would have starred: it is a tight little whisky...there is plenty of grape and chewability. But there is enough sulphur candle influence to limit the fun. *46%. sc. 833 bottles.*

⁙ **The Whisky Cask Glen Scotia Aged 20 Years** bourbon hogshead, dist 92, bott 12 (**74**) n18 t19 f18.5 b18.5. Not particularly well made spirit though the oak has made a valiant effort to reduce the deficit. Those into sweaty armpits might find this a turn on, though. *50.6%. sc.*

GLEN SPEY

Speyside, 1885. Diageo. Working.

Glen Spey Aged 12 Years db (**90**) n23 the kind of firm, busy malt you expect from this distillery plus some lovely spice; t22 mouthwatering and fresh, a layer of honey makes for an easy three or four minutes; f22 drier vanilla, but the pulsing oak is controlled and stylish; b23 very similar to the first Glen Spey I can remember in this range, the one before the over-toffeed effort of two years ago. Great to see it back to its more natural, stunningly beautiful self. *43%*

Glen Spey Special Release 2010 21 Years Old sherry American oak cask, dist 1988 db (**94.5**) n23 a huge nose by this distillery's standards. There are elements of fruit, but more delicious are the controlled oaky bourbony offerings. Honeydew melon, vanilla and red liquorice abounds...telling you something about the variation of weight; t24 the delivery is silky and positively melts into the taste buds, making a mockery of the strength. The honey is stupendously well proportioned and carries spices which prickle as much as the sugars sparkle; f23.5 long, with a wonderful butterscotch/lemon curd tart ensemble. There is a distant fruitiness, burned raisin more associated with aging oak than grape; b24 Glen Speys of this age tended to find their way into blends where they would beef up the sweeter malt content. Sometimes they were used to impart clean sherry or at least fruit, but otherwise give nothing of themselves. This bottling tends to take both strands and then ties them up in a complex and compelling fashion. Wonderful. *50.4%. nc ncf. Diageo. Fewer than 6000 bottles.*

Old Malt Cask Glen Spey Aged 25 Years refill hogshead, cask no. 8196, dist Nov 86, bott Feb 12 (**94**) n23.5 how evocative! A stroll through bluebell woods; slightly earthy without the smoke and floral without the pungency. Fresh and allows the barley to display a wonderful citrus edge; t24 mouth-watering delivery with the malt growing in intensity by the second... amazing! f23 slackens in pace as the vanillas move in; b23.5 Rarely have I found a Glen Spey so self-assured and intense. Bravo! *50%. nc ncf sc. Douglas Laing & Co. 299 bottles.*

⁙ **Provenance Glen Spey Over 9 Years** refill hogshead, cask no. 8468, dist Summer 00, bott Spring 12 (**77**) n20 t19 f19 b19. Docile even by third fill cask standards. Virtually colourless, the barley is untroubled by oak or the passing years so the new make style remains intact. *46%. nc ncf sc. Douglas Laing & Co.*

GLENTAUCHERS

Speyside, 1898. Chivas Brothers. Working.

⁙ **Chieftain's Glentauchers Aged 20 Years** hogshead, cask no. 6016, dist Sep 92, bott Mar 13 (**95**) n23.5 older 'Tauchers are not unknown to throw up enticing banana notes amid the usual cereal stuff, and this is no exception; slightly salty porridge; distant peat embers... surely not...; t24 I am not particularly fond of cats, I admit. But I cannot help but purr with this near perfect concoction of barley, spice, ulmo honey and marzipan. The delicate oils are not thick enough to interfere with the natural interplay. Just a light vaguely bizarre coastal sea-breeze of salt and peat stir towards the middle; f23.5 all the previous notes scaled down with more accent on grapefruit and cocoa; b24 one of the most consistent distilleries in not just Speyside but Scotland. Yet another treat of a dram: technically flawless. *59.5%. nc ncf sc. Ian Macleod Distillers. 265 bottles.*

Duncan Taylor Dimensions Glentauchers 15 Years Old dist May 96, bott Dec 11 (**92**) n23 classic for the distillery: crisp barley, softened by much more rounded citrus and vanilla notes. Exactly what you should expect at this age; t23.5 the clarity is magnificent. Barley, sugar and vanilla sounds simple enough, but when in this uncluttered, sumptuous form,,,,oh, my word! f22.5 a light degree of oak bitterness is compensated by some late, prickly spices. The barley remains compact and unmolested; b23 I would say this is about as definitive 'Tauchers as you are ever likely to find in bottled form for the age and oak. *46%. nc ncf sc.*

⁙ **Gordon and MacPhail Distillery Label Glentauchers 1994** (**96.5**) n23.5 impossible to imagine a nose more subtle or intrinsic: the barley is so delicate you expect it to shatter if you sniff too hard; t24.5 oh my word! The barley melts on the palate, yet at the same time has enough firmness to crash land into the taste buds...but with the aid of a parachute. Hard to imagine a barley where the flavours are so pronounced, the use of muscovado sugar so well judged. The oak, all buttress and little show, could be knighted for its services to diplomacy; f23.5 relies on the slow burn of egg custard tart and melting muscovado; a little diced coconut is added to the mix, as is citrus; b25 one day someone else who matters in the industry will wake up to just how good this malt is...probably the finest of the G&M Distillery Label fleet. Certainly must find a bottle or two for myself...the perfect early evening accompaniment to life...and a good read... *43%*

　　Old Malt Cask Glentauchers Aged 16 Years refill hogshead, cask no. 8902, dist Jul 96, bott Sep 12 **(88) n22** the smoke is little more than a caress on the vanilla-rich nose; **t21.5** some fizzing bite is soothed by an exhibition of delicate sugars; **f22.5** more complexity and weight as smoke, at last, arrives; **b22** they were skimping on the peat slightly when this one was made. Delightfully layered, though. *50%. sc. Douglas Laing & Co. 229 bottles.*

　　Provenance Glentauchers Over 12 Years refill hogshead, cask no. 8014, dist Winter 2012 **(88.5) n22** lively barley and enlivened further by a stem of ginger; **t22.5** some agreeable diced apple gives the already juicy malt a welcome boost and fits snugly with the lightly honeyed oil; **f22** where did those spices spring from...? **b22** a typical understated 'tauchers offering much more than first meets the eye. Or palate. *46%. nc ncf sc.*

　　Single Cask Collection Glentauchers 17 Years Old bourbon hogshead, cask no. 1155, dist 1 Feb 96, bott 13 Feb 13 **(95.5) n23.5** really beautiful gooseberry and greengage mash; plenty of barley apparent. So clean, with the sweetness restricted to the delicate fruit notes; high tannin, but rounded by those stunning, delicate fruits; **t24** just as salivating as the nose promises, though far more in the way of spice which comes through at its own ambling pace as the tannins begin to bite; the evenness of the brown sugars is truly textbook; **f23.5** a light pulsing of spice works beautifully with the increasing depth of the Venezuelan Criollo cocoa; **b24.5** this distillery is one of the unknown gems of Speyside and rarely does it come better polished than this... *55.2%. nc ncf scl. 167 bottles.*

GLENTURRET

Highlands (Perthshire), 1775. Edrington. Working.

　　Glenturret Aged 8 Years db **(88) n21 t22 f23 b22.** Technically no prizewinner. But the dexterity of the honey is charming, as this distillery has a tendency sometimes to be. *40%*

　　The Glenturret Aged 10 Years db **(76) n19 t18 f20 b19.** Lots of trademark honey but some less than impressive contributions from both cask and the stillman. *40%*

　　The Glenturret Aged 15 Years db **(87) n21 t22 f22 b22.** A beautifully clean, small-still style dram that would have benefitted from being bottled at a fuller strength. A discontinued bottling now: if you see it, it is worth the small investment. *40%*

　　Cadenhead Glenturret 15 Years Old bott 2011 **(83) n20 t22 f20 b21.** The cut from this distillate is pretty wide, so there is plenty of oil and buzz on the palate. Some honey, too, as well as the usual coppery sharpness. *53%. sc. WM Cadenhead Ltd.*

　　Gordon and MacPhail Collection Glenturret 1999 (84.5) n20.5 t22.5 f20.5 b21.5. Lots of small still coppery action, all sharp and angular. Some powdery, gristy sweetness, too, amid the tartness. Yet, curiously, though pleasant, never quite falls together as one might hope or expect. One for those looking for a very different dram. *43%*

　　Liquid Sun Glenturret 1980 bott 12 **(92.5) n23** major sma' still coppery edge to this, with the usual Perthshire heather- depth; some curious earthiness, too; **t23** rounded delivery and follow through. Again, heather-honey leads the way with a lavender and spice back up; **f23.5** soft oils and a return of the coppery edge. Crisp sugars sign off; **b23.5** 'Turret's classic style. *42.4%. The Whisky Agency.*

　　Malts Of Scotland Glenturret 1977 bourbon hogshead, cask no. MoS12007, dist 28 Oct 77, bott Feb 12 **(94) n22.5** the oaks are bit on the heavy side with mint, natural caramels and sap evident. But such is the high quality of malt, and so rich its body, that the citrus-honey still powers through after all this time; **t23.5** wow! Gorgeously silky, with the old trademark acacia honey arriving at the double. There is a coppery thread, but in comfortable balance with the intact, juicy malt; **f24** lengthens with the oils and now the complexity, helped along the way with a delicate touch of Lubec marzipan, goes into overdrive; **b24** finding truly great Glen Turret these days is a bit of an ask. I have just found one. *474%. nc ncf sc.*

　　Malts Of Scotland Glenturret 1980 bourbon hogshead, cask no. MoS12008, dist 14 May 80, bott Feb 12 **(87) n23** so much lemon, I thought some washing up liquid had got onto my hands. It hadn't...; **t22** lemon curd tart...and going easy on the tart.... **f22** ...until now with some late, dry crusty vanilla. Slight spice, too; **b22.5** always great to find a faultlessly made Turret in excellent form. *42.5%. nc ncf sc. Malts Of Scotland.*

　　Master Of Malt Glenturret Aged 34 Years refill sherry hogshead, dist 77, bott 12 **(87) n21** a little soapy and citrusy – and honeyed; **t22.5** makes a big toasted honeycomb statement after the initial lime marmalade on toast delivery; **f21.5** some tangy marmalade hangs around the finish too; **b22** a breakfast malt if ever there was one. *479%. ncf nc. 247 bottles.*

　　Old Malt Cask Glenturret Aged 17 Years sherry butt, cask no. 7972, dist Sep 94, bott Dec 11 **(82) n19 t22 f20 b21.** The odd flaw, as might be expected. But gets away with it and celebrates with some half decent honey. *50%. nc ncf sc. Douglas Laing & Co. 298 bottles.*

⋰⋰ **Old Malt Cask Glenturret Aged 18 Years** sherry cask, cask no. 9037, dist Sep 94, bott Sep 12 **(83.5)** n19 t23 f20.5 b21. One of those heartbreak casks. The delivery lights up in neon the original beauty of the butt, but the nose and finish reveal its Achilles heel. Some, though, may find this a stunningly beautiful oloroso-influenced malt. *50%. sc. Douglas Laing & Co. 288 bottles.*

The Whisky Agency Glenturret 35 Years Old dist 1977 **(84)** n21.5 t21 f21 b20.5. having just tasted this alongside their 1977 Glen Moray, it is fascinating to see how one bottling shows where the oak has been embraced and allowed to be part of the all-round development of nose and flavours, while the other struggles to keep its balance as the wood becomes a little too astringent. I'll let you guess which one this is. *46.7%. sc.*

GLENUGIE
Highlands (Eastern). 1834–1983. Whitbread. Closed.

Deoch an Doras Glenugie 30 Years Old dist 1980, bott 2011 db **(87)** n22 t23.5 f19.5 b22. Now there's something I didn't expect to see again: a distillery bottling of Glenugie. Well, technically, anyway, as Glenugie was part of the Chivas group when it died in the 1980s. As far as I can remember they only brought it out once, either as a seven- or five-year-old. I think that went to Italy, so when I walked around the old site just after it closed, it was a Gordon and MacPhail bottling I drank from and it tasted nothing like this! Just a shame there is a very slight flaw in the sherry butt, but just great to see it in bottle again. *52.13%. nc ncf. Chivas Brothers.*

Scotch Malt Whisky Society Cask 99.13 Aged 31 Years refill hogshead, cask no. 3102, dist 1980 **(92.5)** n22.5 some of the old Glenugie traits: brittle, uncompromising barley with limited yield. New, though, are the softer shades of exotic fruit, some recognisable as fruit salad candy; t23 you could almost use this as a sugar training platform: the common theme is the gristy barley which has defied logic to last years. But it runs through crystallised maple syrup efficiently enough and even hints at molasses; spices begin to articulate; f23 excellent mocha doesn't drown out the spice, but the dark sugars ensure balance; b24 like Littlemill, in its day Glenugie produced a spirit the better blenders treated with caution: a malt you added into blends sparingly. But from unpromising beginnings it has matured in old age into something high class and entertaining. To be savoured. *43.8%. sc. Scotch Malt Whisky Society.*

GLENURY ROYAL
Highlands (Eastern), 1868–1985. Diageo. Demolished.

Glenury Royal 36 Years Old db **(89)** n22 t23.5 f21.5 b22 With so much dark, threatening oak around, the delivery defies belief or logic. Cracking stuff!! *57.9%*

Glenury Royal 36 Years Old db **(89)** n21 t23 f22 b23. An undulating dram, hitting highs and lows. The finish, in particular, is impressive: just when it looks on its last legs, it revives delightfully. The whole package, though far from perfect, is pretty astounding. *50.2%*

Glenury Royal 40 Year Old Limited Edition dist 1970, bott 2011 db **(84)** n20.5 t20 f22 b21.5. Glenury is these days so rare I kept this back as a treat to savour as I neared the end of the book. The finale throws up a number of interesting citrus equations. But the oak, for the most part, is too rampant here and makes for a puckering experience. *59.4%. 1,500 bottles.*

Glenury Royal 50 Years Old dist 1953 db **(91)** n23 marvellous freshness to the sherry butt; this had obviously been a high quality cask in its day and the intensity of the fruit sweetened slightly by the most delicate marzipan and old leather oozes class; a little mint reveals some worry lines; t24 the early arrival is sweet and nimble with the barley, against the odds, still having the major say after all these years. The oak is waiting in the wings and with a burst of soft liquorice and velvety, understated spice beginning to make an impression; the sweetness is very similar to a traditional British child's candy of "tobacco" made from strands of coconut and sugar; f22 masses of oak yet, somehow, refuses to go over the top and that slightly molassed sweetness sits very comfortably with the mildly oily body; b22 I am always touched when sampling a whisky like this from a now departed distillery. *42.8%*

HAZELBURN *(see Springbank)*

HIGHLAND PARK
Highlands (Island–Orkney), 1795. Edrington. Working.

Highland Park 8 Years Old db **(87)** n22 t22 f22 b21. A journey back in time for some of us: this is the orginal distillery bottling of the 70s and 80s, bottles of which are still doing the rounds in obscure Japanese bars and specialist outlets such as the Whisky Exchange. *40%*

Highland Park Aged 12 Years db **(78)** n19 t21 f19 b19. Let's just hope that the choice of casks for this bottling was a freak. To be honest, this was one of my favourite whiskies of all time, one of my desert island drams, and I could weep. *40%*

Highland Park Saint Magnus Aged 12 Years 2nd edition db **(76.5) n18.5 t21 f19 b19.** Tight and bitter 2nd edition. *55%*

Highland Park Aged 15 Years db **(85) n21 t22 f21 b21.** Had to re-taste this several times, surprised as I was by just how relatively flat this was. A hill of honey forms the early delivery, but then... *40%*

Highland Park Earl Magnus Aged 15 Years 1st edition db **(76.5) n20 t21 f17.5 b18.** Tight and bitter. *52.6%. 5976 bottles.*

❖ **Highland Park Loki Aged 15 Years** db **(96) n24** heather honey milling around in a confident, but soft, plume of smoke – but a curious different type of lighter heather! Usual stewed apples at play, but sweetened by the honey rather than sugar; a little stem ginger amid the hickory and vanilla, too; **t24** wonderful HP silkiness, a rasping snort of barley is captured and enwrapped by the heather-ish-honey while those ginger-led spices are pitched at the smouldering smoke; **f23.5** tangy marmalade changes the fruity dimension, but the comforting oils continue to ensure a gentle mouth feel, despite the best efforts of some late herbal interaction. The smoke continues on its cheery but quietly deep way...; **b24.5** the weirdness of the heather apart, a bit of a trip back in time. A higher smoke ratio than the bottlings of more recent years which new converts to the distillery will be unfamiliar with, but reverting to the levels regularly found in the 1970s and 80s, probably right through to about 1993/94. Which is a very good thing because the secret of the peat at HP was that, as puffed out as it could be in the old days, it never interfered with the overall complexity, other than adding to it. Which is exactly the case here. Beyond excellent! *48.7%. Edrington.*

Highland Park 16 Years Old db **(88) n23 t23 f20 b22.** I tasted this the day it first came out at one of the Heathrow whisky shops. I thought it a bit flat and uninspiring. This sample, maybe from another bottling, is more impressive and showing true Highland Park colours, the finish apart. *40%. Exclusively available in Duty Free/Travel Retail.*

Highland Park Thor Aged 16 Years db **(87.5) n22.5** very difficult to pick an easy path through this dense offering: the fruitcake is dank and full of pith, the toffee fudge thick. However, the peat is delicate, allowing full view of a stray cask which will probably cause problems elsewhere; **t23.5** the usual HP silk mouth-feel on delivery. But the spices are far more upfront than normal and the layered cocoa backing is quite sublime; the vague smoke fills up the middle ground; **f19** a disappointing, un-godlike, truly mortal finale. Tangy and off key; **b22.5** now, from what I remember of my Norse gods, Thor was the God of Thunder. Which is a bit spooky seeing as hailstones are crashing down outside as I write this and lightning is striking overhead. Certainly a whisky built on power. Even taking into account the glitch in one or two of the casks, a dram to be savoured on delivery. *52.1%. 23,000 bottles.*

Highland Park Aged 18 Years db **(95.5) n23.5** a thick dollop of honey spread across a layer of salted butter; in the background the ashes of a peat fire are emptied; **t24** eye closing beauty: immediate glossy impact of rich, vaguely metallic honey but upped in the complexity stakes by the subtle intense marbling of peat; the muscular richness, aided by the softness of the oil ensures that maximum intensity is not only reached but maintained; **f24** long continuation of those elements found in the delivery but now radiating soft spices and hints of marzipan; **b24** if familiarity breeds contempt, then it has yet to happen between myself and HP 18. This is a must-have dram. I show it to ladies the world over to win their hearts, minds and tastebuds when it comes to whisky. And the more time I spend with it, the more I become aware and appreciative of its extraordinary consistency. The very latest bottlings have been astonishing, possibly because colouring has now been dropped, and wisely so. Why in any way reduce what is one of the world's great whisky experiences? Such has been the staggering consistency of this dram I have thought of late of promoting the distillery into the world's top three: only Ardbeg and Buffalo Trace have been bottling whisk(e)y of such quality over a wide range of ages in such metronomic fashion. Anyway, enough: a glass of something honeyed and dazzling calls... *43%*

Highland Park Aged 21 Years db **(82.5) n20.5 t22 f19 b21.** Good news and bad news. The good news is that they appear to have done away with the insane notion of reducing this to 40% vol. The bad news: a sulphured sherry butt has found its way into this bottling. *47.5%*

Highland Park Aged 25 Years db **(96) n24** big aged oak amid the smoke and honey: it appears something a lot older has got in here...; uniquely complex and back to its very best; **t24** silky and confident, every usual box is ticked – or even double ticked. Much more honey and smoke than I have seen here for a while and it's not all about quantity. What quality! **f24** long with amazing degrees of oil, almost of the bourbony-corn variety! Helps keep those mind-bending honeys coming! **b24** I am a relieved man: the finest HP 25 for a number of years which displays the distillery's unmistakable fingerprints with a pride bordering on arrogance. One of the most improved bottlings of the year: an emperor of a dram. *48.1%* ⊙

Highland Park Aged 30 Years db **(90) n22** a fascinating balancing act between juicy fruit and very tired, splintered oak; **t22.5** the age waters the eye, so powerful is the oak. But it settles into an oily sweetness displaying both a lazy smokiness and burnt raisin; **f23** some real complexity here with oils filling in the drier vanilla moments; **b22.5** a very dramatic shift from the last bottling I tasted; this has taken a fruitier route. Sheer quality, though. 48.1%

Highland Park 40 Years Old db **(90.5) n20.5** tired and over-oaked but the usual HP traits are there in just enough force to save it from failing with an extra puff of something smoky diving in to be on the safe side; **t22.5** even after 40 years, pure silk. Like a 40-year-old woman who has kept her figure and looks, and now only satin stands in the way between you and so much beauty and experience...and believe me: she's spicy...; **f24** amazing layering of peat caresses you at every level; the oak has receded and now barley and traces of golden syrup balance things; **b23.5** I have to admit to picking splinters from my nose with this one. Some of the casks used here have obviously choked on oak, and I feared the worst. But such is the brilliance of the resilience by being on the money with the honey, you can say only that it has pulled off an amazing feat with the peat. Sheer poetry... 48.3%

Highland Park 50 Years Old dist Jan 60 db **(96.5) n24.5** mint, cloves and a thin coat of creosote usurp the usual deft heather and smoke to loudly announce this whisky's enormous age. Don't bother looking for honey, either. Well, not at first... However, there is a growling sweetness from the start: deep and giving up its part molten Demerara-part treacle character with miserly contempt, as though outraged by being awoken from a 50-year slumber. Of course, as the whisky oxidises there is a shift in pattern. And after about ten minutes a wine effect – and we are talking something much more akin to a First Growth Bordeaux than sherry – begins to make a statement. Then the sugars transmogrify from treacle to molasses to manuka honey; **t24** certain sugars present on the delivery, though at first hard to quite make out which. Some surprising oil ensures suppleness to the oak; there is also a wonderful marriage, or perhaps it is a threesome, between old nutty fruitcake, tangy orange-enriched high quality north European marzipan, and ancient bourbon...; **f24** silky with some wonderful caramels and toasted fudge forming a really chewy finale. As well as ensuring any possible old-age holes are plugged; **b24** old whiskies tend to react to unchartered territory as far as time in the oak is concerned in quite different ways. This grey beard has certainly given us a new slant. Nothing unique about the nose. But when one is usually confronted with those characteristics on the nose, what follows on the palate moves towards a reasonably predictable path. Not here. Truly unique – as it should be after all this time. 44.8%. sc. 275 bottles.

Highland Park 1964 Orcadian Vintage refill hogshead, bott 2009 db **(90.5) n23 t22 f23 b22.5.** At times you think the old oak is going to sink without trace, taking the whisky with it. But such is the pedigree of the HP make, that it not only fights back but regains control. An honour to experience. 42.2%. 290 bottles.

Highland Park 1968 Orcadian Vintage refill casks, bott 2009 db **(88.5) n20 t23.5 f23 b22.** The spicy oak has taken too firm a grip for true greatness. But some of the passages offer wonderful moments of contemplation. 45.6%. 1550 bottles.

Highland Park 1970 Orcadian Vintage db **(94.5) n23.5** much smokier than present day HP..would love to have nosed the new make 40 years ago: it would have been massive; helped along here with a squeeze of blood orange; **t24** splinters on delivery – in both senses - but the silky malt-honey body is able to absorb everything thrown at it; the degrees of sweetness run from honey, through light sugars to subtle Lubec marzipan: sublime; **f23.5** long, again with a distinctive orangey note clinging to the sweet, lightly smoked barley: elegant...; **b23.5** most other malts would have disintegrated under the weight of the oak. This takes it in its stride, and actually uses the extra vanilla to excellent effect. Memorable. 48%

Highland Park 1973 bott 2010 db **(96) n24** what could be better than a standard HP nose, complete with all that delicate smoke and honey? An HP nose with a decent smidgeon of high quality bourbon! Well that's what those extra years in the cask has gone and given you; **t25** mouth-watering barley enters the arena hand-in-hand with pristine acacia honey. Directly behind is two-tone smoke: one firm, lightly peated and spiced, the other a softer, billowing safety net; the middle ground concerns molten manuka honey and muscovado sugar thickened with vanilla and then the lightest hint of mocha. Frankly, perfect...; **f23** lighter, lengthy with toffee and liquorice; **b24** now that, folks, is Highland Park and make no mistake! 50.6%

Highland Park Vintage 1978 db **(95.5) n24** some thumping oak is of such high quality it only adds to the mix, rather than detracts. The smoke level is pretty high considering it's had so long in the cask and this helps fend off any oaky excess. Elsewhere tangy kumquats mix with physalis and greengages. The usual honey has given way to soft molasses; **t24** I hope the flight is a long one if you have bought this Duty Free: you really need a good hour alone with this guy to begin to understand his foibles and complexities. The delivery offers a surprising degree of sharpness and life, in which those citrus notes formulate. Then a gentle mixing of delicate, vaguely weary smoke and an almost bourbony red liquorice and light honeycomb mix...; **f23.5** a very light oiliness has formed and provides all that is required to give an extra polish to those soft oaky tones. An equally understated mocha and molasses creamy sweetness ties up the loose ends; **b24** if you are buying this in Duty Free, a tip: get it for yourself...it's too good for a gift!! This purrs quality from first to last. And is quite unmistakably Highland Park. A noble malt. 47.8%. Available in Global Travel Retail.

Highland Park 1990 bott 2010 db **(90) n23** a sprig of lavender (probably in lieu of standard heather) dovetails jauntily with ubiquitous honey and a puff of smoke; **t23** sublime delivery: an almost perfect degree of oil to help the honey slither into its rightful place at the head of the flavour queue with some toffee vanilla not far behind. Just a hint of soapiness; **f22** long, with a buzzing smokiness...and late toffee pudding; **b22** much more like it...!! 40%

Highland Park 1994 bott 2010 db **(87) n23 t22 f20.5 b21.5.** I am not sure what is happening here. HPs of this vintage should be soaring into the comfortable 90s. But again the finish is dull and the usual complexity of the malt is vanishing behind a murky veil. 40%

Highland Park 1997 "The Sword" db **(79.5) n19 t23 f18 b19.5.** Shows its cutting edge for only a brief while on delivery – when it is quite spectacular. Otherwise, painfully blunted. 43%. Available in Taiwan.

Highland Park 1998 bott 2010 db **(85) n22 t22 f20 b21.** They must have special Orcadian spiders to spin a silk this fine. But, though pleasant, disappointing by HP standards as it never gets to spread its wings. The whisky, that is: not the spider. 40%

Highland Park Earl Haakon db **(92) n22.5** the smoke is unusually fishy – something of the Arbroath Smokie. But there are massive tracts of oak waiting in the wings – fresh, red-blooded and happy to keep the honey company; **t24** even by HP's extraordinary standards, the mouth feel on this guy makes the knees tremble. Aided by spices which shimmy and contort all over the palate, the first five or six waves are as good as any malt I have tasted this year; heads towards a surprisingly lightweight butterscotch middle; **f22.5** caramels are happy to lead the fade; **b23** a fabulous malt offering some of the best individual moments of the year. But appears to run out of steam about two thirds in. 54.9%. 3,300 bottles.

Highland Park Hjärta db **(79.5) n18.5 t22 f19 b20.** In part, really does celebrate the honeycomb character of Highland Park to the full. But obviously a major blemish or two in there as well. 58.1%. 3924 bottles.

Highland Park Leif Eriksson bourbon and American oak db **(86) n22 t22 f21 b21.** The usual distillery traits have gone AWOL while all kinds of caramel notes have usurped them. That said, this has to be one of the softest drams you'll find. 40%. Edrington.

Highland Park New Make Spirit Drink dist Feb 10, bott Mar 10 db **(85.5) n21 t22 f21 b21.5.** Doesn't boast the usual degree of ultra rich texture of new make HP – even when reduced – and though sweet, malty and enjoyable, with its few extra metallic molecules not exactly how I recently tasted new make HP in a blending lab. A curious choice. 50%. Venture Whisky Ltd.

A.D. Rattray Highland Park 1984 cask no. 1753, dist 17 Dec 84, bott Jun 11 **(95) n23** light smoke: tick. Heather: half a tick. Honey: three ticks...; **t24** delicate spice: tick. Light smoke: tick. Juicy barley: two ticks. Honey: three ticks. Perfect weight and body: how many ticks can you find in the box?; **f24** repeat procedure for taste. Except find a tick from somewhere for the vanilla and butterscotch; **b24** this is probably the closest thing to a model HP you will ever come across. For its age, it does everything asked and expected of it in just the right proportions. If you ever see this bottle and don't grab it...give yourself a ticking off...! 58.6%. sc. A.D. Rattray. Dewar Rattray Cask Collection.

⠿ **A.D. Rattray Highland Park 1990** butt, cask no. 577, dist 3 Dec 90, bott Apr 13 **(68.5) n17 t20 f14.5 b17.** Reminiscent of being On the Beach. For, amid the sulphury radiation the salty honey and peat taps out its proud, elegant and ultimately heartbreaking farewell... 58.1%. sc. A.D. Rattray. Dewar Rattray Cask Collection.

Archives Highland Park 2000 11 Years Old Second Release bourbon hogshead, cask no. 800005, dist 2 Jun 00, bott Jan 12 **(85) n22 t21 f21 b21.** Quite smoky. But even the famous HP honey, which is quite abundant here, fails to entirely get to grips with an oak-driven bitterness. 50.9%. nc ncf sc. Whiskybase B.V. 129 bottles.

⠿ **Director's Cut Highland Park Aged 21 Years** refill butt, cask no. 9200, dist Feb 91, bott Oct 12 **(87) n21** the colour may not suggest sherry but a tell-tale matchstick leaves little doubt. The sugars are not entirely unlike old, dried clear honey, breaking down into pollen; **t23** quick blast of muscovado sugars and later a blend of manuka honey and maple syrup. Between and directly after come the drier oak and pith tones; **f21** light mocha with a spice, kumquat and furry fade; **b22** a two-toned malt which errs on the dry side. 53.6%. sc. 285 bottles.

⠿ **Douglas Laing Premier Barrel Highland Park Aged 15 Years** **(91) n22.5** bonfire as well as peat smoke; **t22.5** busy sugars with a smoky bite; **f23** much more complexity with an ulmo and manuka honey blend thickening with the budding peat; **b23** classic HP ticking every required box with a flourish! 46%. nc ncf sc. 483 bottles.

Duthies Highland Park 19 Years Old sherrywood **(69) n17 t19 f16 b17.** Very sweet on delivery. But very sulphured elsewhere. 62.6%. sc. WM Cadenhead Ltd.

⠿ **Gordon and MacPhail Cask Strength Highland Park 2003** (96.5) n23.5 no other distillery on the planet holds a thumbprint quite this recognisable or is able to stroke the heart with such gentle grace: heather-honey and trace peat reek t24.5 the delivery is pretty near perfection: the degree of oils mix with unbelievable aplomb and a light coppery sheen (had they just done some repair work to a still, I wonder?) and then layer upon layer of spice and heather-honey tinged tannin and smoke...; f24 long, with the smoke now radiating with unusual weight and confidence for an HP but still it is that chocolate caramel tart, criss-crossed with honey that just makes you want to curl up and hug this glass to death...; b24.5 oh...my.....gawd....!!!! 57.8%. ncf.

⠿ **Gordon & MacPhail MacPhail's Collection Highland Park 8 Years Old** (74) n18 t20 f17 b19. Completely off the pace for all its groin-fumbling sweetness, with the odd dodgy cask involved here. 43%

Hart Brothers Highland Park Aged 22 Years cask no. 3961, dist 23 Apr 90, bott 30 Apr 12 (92.5) n23 light smoke, honey etc.: the essence of Highland Park in every respect; t23 irresistible combination of juicy barley and then those signature smoke and honey notes; f23 a 22 gun salute of spices; a few light sugars, a little firmer than honey, form to balance superbly; b23.5 excellent quality and unmistakably HP. 46%. sc.

James MacArthur Old Masters Highland Park 13 Years Old cask no. 5790, dist 1998, bott Feb 12 (88) n22 spices prickle the honey; t23 salivating and attractively tart barley as the salt bites deep. The honey is always around to soothe; f21 burned coffee; b22 perhaps not quite matured in the finest oak Scotland has seen, but there is certainly nought wrong with the spirit. 57.5%. nc ncf sc. James MacArthur & Co.

⠿ **Malts Of Scotland Highland Park 1998** sherry hogshead, cask no. MoS 12058, dist Mar 98, bott Nov 12 (92.5) n23.5 spiced coffee – sweetened by a big dollop of Harvey's Bristol Cream; t23.5 for the most part you are drinking high strength sherry, but about two-thirds in, juicy barley does make an impudent entrance; f23 tart marmalade, as opposed to marmalade tart; b22 one of the old-fashioned types of sherry casks which three decades ago would have been regarded as slightly inferior quality for overwhelming and bullying the malt, but is today of a higher class for being generally clean of sulphur. 57.4%. nc ncf sc. 96 bottles.

Mo Ór Collection Highland Park 1986 24 Years Old first fill bourbon hogshead, cask no. 2275, 27 Jun 86, bott 29 Oct 10 (92) n23 slightly more butterscotch than honey this time, though the delicate floral notes star; t24 the smoke is barely noticeable on the nose, but it arrives here on about the fifth or sixth wave to complete an impressive opening; the maple sugars are fragile and very clean; the spices are as gentle as they come; f22 back to butterscotch with the inevitable vanilla whirl; b23 hints and shadows about: as deft as they come. 46%. nc ncf sc. Release No. 8. The Whisky Talker. 300 bottles.

Mo Ór Collection Highland Park 1996 14 Years Old first fill bourbon barrel, cask no. DL6457, dist 13 Sep 96, bott 14 Sep 10 (86.5) n21 t22.5 f21 b22. The limitations of oak only partially block the delicately-smoked complexity. The even-handed sweetness on delivery really is sublime. 46%. nc ncf sc. Release No. 50. The Whisky Talker. 475 bottles.

Old Malt Cask Highland Park Aged 14 Years sherry butt, cask no. 7234, dist Sep 96, bott Jun 11 (90) n22 vanilla and perhaps a very distant degree of smoke; t22.5 almost identical to cask 7865, but with a little extra cocoa; f22.5 peat, honey and cocoa; b23 virtually a re-run on the taste buds of another HP OMC: real peas in a pod! That said, this has a little extra complexity and better use of the sweeter elements. 50%. nc ncf sc. 300 bottles.

Old Malt Cask Highland Park Aged 15 Years sherry hogshead, cask no. 7865, dist Sep 96, bott Nov 11 (88.5) n21.5 the closest to fruit on this is under-ripe tomatoes; a few shards of vanilla; t22.5 lovely spiced honey and even a degree of hickory on hand; lightly oiled; the smoke shows itself subtly through the middle ground; f22 still the peat and honey continues; b22.5 the fruit hangs back allowing the complexity to gather pace. 50%. nc ncf sc. 394 bottles.

⠿ **Provenance Highland Park Over 14 Years** sherry cask, cask no. 9630, dist Summer 98, bott Spring 13 (75) n16 t21 f19 b19. A Lazarus of a dram: from a dreadful nose which is dead in the glass, it rises with eerie aplomb for a heather-honey fanfare which really does treat the palate despite the obvious flaws! 46%. nc ncf. Douglas Laing & Co.

Scotch Malt Whisky Society Cask 4.155 Aged 11 Years first fill barrel, cask no. 800158, dist 1999 (93) n22 relatively light for an HP of this age: someone forgot to add the peat to the kiln, or at least get it to smoke; t23.5 they certainly did forget to add the barley which comes through in the juiciest terms; f24 from somewhere the vaguest hint of spice and smoke arrive...better late than never; b23.5 just a beautifully made malt, even if all the usual HP characteristics take a bit of time to evolve. 58.6%. sc. Scotch Malt Whisky Society.

⠿ **Scotch Malt Whisky Society Cask 4.173 Aged 23 Years** refill hogshead, dist 19 May 89 (94.5) n23.5 a bowl of honey Cheerios for breakfast, though someone has tipped on a little salt: tangy tannins point at the year of distillation with glee; t24 the weave of the honeyed thread is intricate, yet bold. Aided and abetted by the weightier smoke and spice, the honey moves between manuka and beech with a beguiling deftness; the age is underscored by a cocoa-hickory mix; **f23** long, lightly oiled, a hint now of pith but with the spices ensuring a vigorous fade; **b24** in this kind of cask, nonchalantly shows why this is one of the best distilleries in the world... *52%. nc ncf sc. 210 bottles.*

Scott's Selection Highland Park 1989 bott 2012 **(84.5) n22 t20.5 f21.5 b20.5.** Unusual for a HP of this age in that the honey has been outflanked by the oak. *51.4%. Speyside Distillers.*

⋄ **That Boutique-y Whisky Company Highland Park** Batch 1 **(87.5) n23** weighty: fruity with nectarine and honey; lazy smoke; **t22** usual deft delivery with malt entering the fray early to be replaced by tangy fruit; **f21** a tad furry; **b21.5** pleasant, but sometimes doesn't seem to have the will to get the wheels off the ground. *44.7%. 241 bottles.*

The Whisky Agency Highland Park 27 Years Old bourbon cask, dist 1984, bott 2011 **(93) n24** complex with a fascinating smattering of peat and coal dust. Bigger than usual citrus for this distillery, giving the feeling of a room newly cleaned after a visit from the chimney sweep; the spices and soft red liquorice offer just the right weight; **t23.5** distinctive tangerine notes ensure a controlled sweetness to balance against the spices and dusty smoke; the midground is thick with vanilla and barley; **f22** relatively shy and retiring and dependent on the clean barley; **b23.5** soft and satisfying. Pushes all the right buttons. *52.5%. sc.*

The Whisky Agency Highland Park 2000 bott 2012 **(86) n22 t22 f20.5 b21.5.** Some classic honey and light peat moments here ensure a familiar tune on both nose and palate. Thins just a little too enthusiastically. *53.3%. nc ncf sc. The Whisky Agency.*

Whisky Antique Highland Park 22 Years Old Special Bottling dist 1988, bott 2011 **(85) n20 t23 f20.5 b21.5.** The streaks of honeyed greatness here more than compensate for the failings of the over exposed, milky oak. The gorgeous high notes really can shatter the crystal most impressively, though. *53.4%. sc. Silver Seal Whisky Company.*

The Whisky Cask Highland Park Aged 24 Years bourbon cask, dist 1986, bott 2010 **(94.5) n24.5** heather: tick. Peat: tick. Honey: tick: Barley: tick: All in perfect rhythm and order and offering crotch-bulging complexity; **t24** quite superb interplay between the smoke and juicier, fruitier notes, especially the Jaffa Cake and lemon zest; excellent spice in the middle ground; **f22.5** an annoying degree of late cask bitterness. But the light smoke won't be denied, nor the honey and sugars... **b23.5** you're unlikely to find a more Highland Parky Highland Park this year. So much pollen with this honey, I've just had a sneezing fit! *52%. sc.*

IMPERIAL
Speyside, 1897. Chivas Brothers. Silent.

Imperial Aged 15 Years "Special Distillery Bottling" db **(69) n17 t18 f17 b17.** At least one very poor cask, hot spirit and overly sweet. Apart from that it's wonderful. *46%*

Archives Imperial 1995 16 Years Old Third Release bourbon cask, cask no. 50035, dist May 95, bott Apr 12 **(89) n22** sharp, clean, lively barley; just a murmur of bourbon-style liquorice; **t23** salivating, quite brittle in a Glen Grant style maltiness with some citrus sticking to the light oils; **f22** good oak offers just the right degree of clean vanilla; **b22** even, quite simplistic, yet always a delight. *51.7%. nc ncf sc. Whiskybase B.V. 60 bottles.*

Glen Karadag dist 1997, bott 2011, Crimean Madeira cask **(90) n22.5** a mildly tight nose, and not immediately recognisable within the normal Imperial family of characteristics. But I have just noticed this is a Crimean Madeira, so it is not something this distillery sees every day. Most intriguing is the light gooseberry fruitiness tied in with vaguely spiced barley; **t23** much firmer and more confident. The crisp barley surge is superb, the deft almost gristy sweetness a perfect foil for the bubbling spices; **f22** thins as the vanilla takes charge. A thread of pithy fruit, marrying even more spice, reminds you of the Madeira link; **b22.5** after taking three of us two days to open the sample bottle, this needed to be worth waiting for...As it happens, it really was! *46%. Duncan Taylor & Co. Ukraine exclusive. 414 bottles.*

⋄ **Gordon and MacPhail Distillery Label Imperial 1994 (94) n22.5** an unusual example of exact equal input from both barley (some still a little green) and oak: beautifully even and weighted; **t24** resplendent barley on delivery, both at its thickest and with lighter, crispier notes which carry delicate hints of salivating, under-ripe greengage and busy spice; **f23.5** pure American malt shake to the last embers, though with extra, gentle spice; **b24** if anyone can get the best out of this distillery it is G&M. Really is an endearing bottling. *43%*

⋄ **Liquid Sun Imperial 1995** bott 12 **(84) n21.5 t22.5 f19 b21.** Fabulous delivery shows Speyside at its maltiest. The helping required by the oak doesn't really happen. *50.3%*

⋄ **Old Malt Cask Imperial Aged 18 Years** refill hogshead, cask no. 9815, dist May 95, bott May 13 **(86.5) n21.5 t22 f21.5 b21.5.** A firm, compact malt, with a major vanilla theme, very much of the classical Imperial style which refuses to open out too far even with gentle coaxing. But what it does, it does with pleasing aplomb. *50%. nc ncf sc. 346 bottles.*

Old Malt Cask Imperial Aged 35 Years refill butt, cask no. 7431, dist Oct 76, bott Oct 11 **(90) n22** how do you get so many citrus notes on a malt so old...? **t23.5** improbably refreshing for its age with the delivery all about the barley and lime hinted at on the nose; **f22** quite sublime cocoa: almost something of the chocolate liqueur about the finale...; **b22.5** Don't know why. But a bar in Lexington, Virginia, flashed into my mind while tasting this. I must have tasted a malt that evening very close to this in style to cause the flashback. Well, this one certainly doesn't Stonewall... *50%. nc ncf sc. 443 bottles.*

Scotch Single Malt Circle Imperial 1995 cask no. 512690, dist 24 Jan 95, bott 15 Feb 12 **(92)** **n23** a touch of fizzing perry with a sprig of mint; **t24** gorgeous delivery with the barley revelling in its freedom to expand in the juiciest of directions; just about perfect degree of oils and the spice-sugar mix in mid-ground is faultless; **f22** the vanilla and butterscotch which forms is soon lost behind a degree of Allied-style barrel-bitterness; **b23** another imperious stunner from this underestimated distillery. *50%. sc. Scotch Single Malt Circle.*

Sestante Collection Imperial 19 Years Old dist 1991, bott 2011 **(85.5) n22 t21 f21 b21.5.** A very firm malt with limited lateral movement on the palate. But the upfront barley plus cinnamon on the delicate fruit is good enough. *55.3%. sc. Silver Seal Whisky Company.*

The Whisky Agency Imperial 1995 bott 2011 **(78) n21 t20 f18 b19.** Juicy and delicate to start, but the light spirit is no match for the bitterness of the poor quality cask. *46%. nc ncf sc.*

⁖ **The Whisky Shop Dufftown Imperial 16 Years Old** remade refill hogshead. Cask no. 7300, dist 28 Sep 94, bott Aug 11 **(87) n22** light pomegranate thins out further the already sparsely populated barley and oak; **t22.5** the highlight is the extraordinary battering the malt gives the taste buds: relentless and warming on the very coldest days; **f21** thins out again, but you cannot help loving the clarity of the barley even amid the big vanilla; **b21.5** typically stretched and tight for the distillery. *57.4%. nc ncf sc. 267 bottles.*

INCHGOWER
Speyside, 1872. Diageo. Working.

Inchgower 1993 The Manager's Choice db **(84.5) n21 t21.5 f21 b21.** Like your malts subtle, delicate, clean and sophisticated? Don't bother with this one if you do. This has all the feel of a malt that's been spray painted onto the taste buds: thick, chewy and resilient. Can't help but like that mix of hazelnut and Demerara, though. You can stand a spoon in it. *61.9%*

Berry's Own Selection Inchgower 1982 cask no. 6967, bott 2011 **(80) n21.5 t21 f18.5 b19.** An oil-slicked monster reminding us of Inchgower's excesses from its last days at Bell's. Fun, if you want your taste buds to have the crap kicked out of them. *54.5%. nc ncf sc.*

⁖ **Cadenhead Inchgower 22 Years Old** bourbon cask, dist 89, bott 12 **(85) n23 t22 f19 b21.** There is a lovely mix of raspberry jam and bourbon-style clear honey on the nose. The palate, though initially lush and malty, fails to quite match the early magic. *56.5%. sc. WM Cadenhead Ltd. 246 bottles.*

Dun Bheagan Inchgower 29 Years Old hogshead, dist Jun 82 **(91) n22.5** the complex balance between the honey and latent fruitiness is a treat; **t23.5** this distillery usually offers a clunking heavyweight of a start. Here we have a light acacia honey lead, then a full barley-rich juice fest. Spices towards the middle are fabulous; **f22** settles for a more sedate honey-barley finale; **b23** rarely the most gainly of whiskies, this Inchgower overcomes its trademark indelicacies with a dizzying degree of spiced honey. *54.3%. nc ncf sc. Ian Macleod Distillers.*

Duncan Taylor Rare Auld Inchgower 29 Years Old cask no. 6975, dist 1982 **(87.5) n22** as salty as a sailor's armpit; **t21.5** a thudding delivery which biffs the taste buds. Somehow the sugars and barley find common ground amid the mayhem; **f22** settles into a chunky, barley-filled finish; **b22** a macho dram which is reassuringly aggressive. *54.8%. sc. Duncan Taylor & Co.*

Gordon & MacPhail Connoisseurs Choice Inchgower 1997 dist 1997 **(84.5) n21 t21.5 f21 b21.** A plodding malt which does its best to do as little as possible. Yet the cask is good and as enjoyable as a corner shop cheese sandwich. *43%*

⁖ **Old Malt Cask Inchgower Aged 16 Years** sherry butt, cask no. 8827, dist Dec 95, bott Aug 12 **(95) n23.5** something of the Harvey's Bristol Cream to this one, except enough barley and egg custard tart get through to confirm the whisky identity; **t24** a mixture of silk and barb as the spices cut through the oily grape with style. Salivating at first with plump grape, then morphs into barley. The oak tip deep into the middle ground; **f23.5** complex and layered with the vanillas and butterscotch playing a more telling role by the second; **b24** one of the better sherry butt bottlings of recent times: clean as a whistle and complex. *50%. nc ncf sc. 642 bottles.*

⁖ **Old Malt Cask Inchgower Aged 30 Years** refill hogshead, cask no. 8258, dist Jun 82, bott Jun 12 **(84.5) n21.5 t20 f22 b21.** Showing Inchgower at its most exhausted when the distillery was run into the ground to produce Bell's. Hot and thin at first, the almost concentrated intensity of the barley doesn't just save the day but makes for an, ultimately, attractive experience. *50%. nc ncf sc. Douglas Laing & Co. 260 bottles.*

Provenance Inchgower Over 12 Years sherry, cask no. 7654, dist 99, bott 11 **(85) n22 t21 f21 b21.** Ticks all the malty boxes, the nose conjures up a marvellous kumquat and gooseberry combo and the oak is top quality. The spirit, however, is a little stretched. *46%. nc ncf sc.*

Provenance Inchgower Over 12 Years sherry butt, cask no. 7937, dist Spring 1999, bott Winter 2011 **(86)** n21 t22 f21.5 b21.5. Limited in its range across the palate perhaps, but there is no denying its clean, mouth-watering properties. An enjoyable dram. *46%. nc ncf sc.*

⁕ **Wemyss Inchgower 1982 Single Highland "Pears and Almonds"** hogshead, bott 13 **(88.5)** n22.5 a well preserved nose....in that there is some creosote present. Oaky, oily... but entertaining; **t22** big whisky with a kick above its strength on delivery. this is down to the full frontal oak, reinforced with treacle and molasses; **f22** the oak frays a little, but those pounding sugars, backed by a little marzipan, fill in the cracks; **b22** a malt which doesn't just rage against its age...it just rages. A real warts and all character. *46%. sc. 315 bottles.*

⁕ **The Whisky Agency Inchgower 'Sea Life' 1980** refill sherry butt, dist 80, bott 12 **(67)** n17 t18 f15 b17. The only Sea Life I see here is a squid setting off a dozen box of matches... *52%*

INVERLEVEN
Lowland, 1938–1991. Demolished.
Deoch an Doras Inverleven 36 Years Old dist 1973 **(94.5)** n24 just one of those noses where you think twice about tasting: not because it is bad, but quite the opposite...you really don't want the experience to end. Exotic fruit sitting comfortably with bigger oak notes and the juiciest of grassy malt; **t23.5** a slightly ungainly delivery but after the first three or four flavour waves settles into a more rhythmic pulsing of light golden syrup, fresh barley, cocoa and spices; a bourbon sub text is deliciously fascinating; **f23** exemplary dovetailing of the finer details of the malt, with the spices now showing a little more keenly; **b24** as light on the palate as a morning mist. This distillery just wasn't designed to make a malt of this antiquity, yet this is to the manor born. *48.85%. nc ncf. Chivas Brothers. 500 bottles.*

ISLE OF ARRAN
Highlands (Island–Arran), 1995. Isle of Arran Distillers. Working.
The Arran Malt 8 Years Old Pinot Noir Finish db **(79.5)** n19 t21 f19.5 b20. Pleasant enough. But just seems to lack the trademark Arran balance and has a few lopsided moments to boot, especially at the death. *50%. Isle of Arran Distillers.*

The Arran Malt 8 Years Old Pomerol Wine Finish db **(87)** n19 t23.5 f22 b22.5. Full bodied and lush. *50%. Isle of Arran Distillers.*

The Arran Malt Under 10 Years Old db **(89)** n22 t23 f22 b22. This one's kicked its shoes and socks off... *43%*

The Arran Malt 10 Year Old db **(87)** n22.5 t22.5 f20 b22. It has been a while since I last officially tasted this. If they are wiling to accept some friendly advice, I think the blenders should tone down on raising any fruit profile and concentrate on the malt, which is amongst the best in the business. *46%. nc ncf.*

The Arran Malt 12 Years Old db **(85)** n21.5 t22 f20.5 b21 Hmmmm. Surprise one, this. There must be more than one bottling already of this. The first I tasted was perhaps slightly on the oaky side but otherwise intact and salt-honeyed where need be. This one has a bit of a tang: very drinkable, but definitely a less than brilliant cask around. *46%*

The Arran Malt 12 Years Old Cask Strength Batch 1 bott Sep 11 db **(78)** n21 t22 f17 b18. There is no questioning that Arran is now one of Scotland's Premier League quality malts. But the strength of their whisky is in their bourbon casks, not so much their sherry. And to create a batch like this was tempting fate. The sulphur present is by no means huge, but it takes only a single off butt to spoil the party. *54.1%. nc ncf. 12,000 bottles.*

The Arran Malt Aged 14 Years db **(89.5)** n22 t23.5 f21.5 b22.5. A superb whisky, but the evidence that there has been a subtle shift in emphasis, with the oak now taking too keen an interest, is easily attained. *46%. ncf.*

⁕ **The Arran Malt 15 Years Old** sherry hogshead, dist 21 Jul 97, bott 30 Apr 13 db **(90)** n22 banana and custard; oak marauds everywhere...quietly; **t23** gorgeous, silky delivery with a major oaky statement but glazed with barley sugar; **f22** chocolate mint; **b23** a truly lovely whisky which, as is often the case from this distillery, has somewhat become prematurely grey as the oak has made its mark. But enough light fruit and sugar abound to make for a treat. *50.7%. 230 bottles. Whisky Shop Exclusive.*

The Arran Malt 1995 Bourbon Single Cask Distillery Festival Release 2012 cask no. 128 db **(92.5)** n23.5 packs quite an oaky punch for one so relatively young: chunky, chocolaty and brimming with spiced nougat; **t23** doesn't do anything to lessen the pace on delivery: the spices virtually shriek at you as the liquorice takes on an almost fruity edge; **f23** toasty and sharp; the sugars babble and squabble on the big oaky fade which enjoys a wonderful Jaffa Cake finale; **b23** now that really is one profound Isle of Arran... *54.7%. nc ncf sc.*

The Arran Malt 1996 'The Peacock' Icons of Arran bott 2009 db **(96)** n24.5 oh my word: what a shame I have only three or four months to write this book: the degree of complexity will take that time to unravel. Both floral and fruity in almost perfect doses, the white pepper perfectly balances the light saltiness. The big weight is deceptive as the delicate sultana and perry sub plot appears to give more air and space to the overall picture. Outstanding...; **t24.5** what a delicate creature this is: the juicy grape appears to be apparent on a couple of levels, sandwiching the honey and hickory bourbon notes between them; **f23** long, now with that hint of pear on the nose re-surfacing as the finish nestles somewhere between butterscotch tart and buttered toast; **b24** yet again this outstanding distillery delivers the goods: one of the most outstanding malts of the year and certainly one of the most complex. I've not yet spoken to the Arran guys about this, but would happily bet my house that this is a sublime mix of top bourbon cask and faultless sherry. As fabulous as this distillery unquestionably is, they will be hard pressed to keep this standard going... 46%

The Arran Malt 1996 Bourbon Single Cask cask no. 400 db (**93**) **n24** a sawdusty dryness slowly gives way to ultra-delicate maple syrup and coconut notes. But it's all whispers and hints, making it all the sexier; look out for the Mars bars with a sprinkling of salt. When the honey and kumquat starts to weave itself into the picture...wow! **t23** much silkier delivery than the full on and sometimes sparky nose testifies to. Barley resounds first and foremost with the sugars inching their way in alongside the ever darkening oaky tones. There's the familiar chocolate and spice theme towards the middle; **f22.5** much more strait laced and vanilla happy; **b23.5** high quality, complex and rewarding. 46.8%. nc ncf sc. Distillery exclusive.

The Arran Malt 1997 'The Rown Tree' Icons of Arran bott 2010 db (**77.5**) **n18.5 t22 f18 b19.** The key here is balance and harmony. And this, unusually for an Arran, possesses little of either. The bitter finish confirms the unhappiness hinted at on the nose. Someone was barking up the wrong tree when putting this one together and the malt, in this form, even for all the sweet, bright moments on delivery, is ready for the chop. 46% Isle of Arran Distillers

The Arran Malt 1999 "The Eagle" Icons Of Arran bourbon barrels & sherry hogsheads, bott 2012 db (**77**) **n19.5 t20.5 f18 b19.** Don't know about the eagle having landed: this one never took off...the wings have been clipped by sulphur. 46%. nc ncf. 6,000 bottles.

The Arran Malt 1999 Vintage 15th Anniversary Edition finished in amontillado, bott 2010 db (**92.5**) **n24** sherry as you demand it shows on the nose. Clean, confident, a hint of sultana only as this is dry, yet always with enough finesse for the barley to come through loud and clear: an absolute treat...; **t23.5** salivating from the off with a glittering delivery of fresh grape and spice. Waves of vanilla punch through and there is a fabulous malty flourish towards the middle. But those spices continue to pulse...; **f22.5** drier, with vanilla pods and a buttery residue; **b22.5** there is no mistaking excellence. And here it appears to flow freely. 54.6%

The Arran Malt Open Day Single Bourbon Cask Bottling 2011 db (**94**) **n23.5** unbelievable degree of fruit sitting alongside the rich barley and muscovado-enriched bourbon notes; **t24** a match of spice and sugared barley made in heaven; **f23.5** the earlier juiciness evaporates as the vanillas lay claim. But enough spices – and fruit – remain for the finale to be anything but standard; **b23.5** to me, Arran in a high class bourbon cask shows the distillery to its very finest advantage: my case rests... 52%. nc ncf sc. Sold at distillery during 2011 Open Day.

The Arran Malt Ambassador's Choice db (**87.5**) **n22 t22 f21.5 b22.** So heavy with oak I was amazed I could pick the nosing glass up... 46%

The Arran Malt Amarone Cask Finish db (**94.5**) **n23** the buzzing black peppers leave you in no doubt what is to follow. As does the stunning clarity of the grape and crisp, business-like manner of the barley: stirring! **t24** and so it is played out on the palate: the grape is juicy and sweet, the barley is firm and forms the perfect skeleton, the spices pop busily around the palate. No great age evident, but the oak also chimes in with a few choice cocoa notes; **f23** a shard of bitterness, but nothing which subtracts from the gloss; **b23.5** as cask finishes go, this one is just about perfect. 50%. nc ncf.

The Arran Malt Bourgogne Finish db (**74**) **n18 t19 f18 b19.** Arran Malt Vinegar more like... 56.4%

The Arran Malt Chianti Classico Riserva Cask Finish db (**85**) **n19 t23 f21 b22.** Mamma mia: there eeza poco zolfo ina mia malto!! Butta chicco d'uva, ee eez eccellente! 55%

The Arran Malt Devil's Punch Bowl Chapter No. 1 db (**72**) **n17.5 t22.5 f15 b17.** For a few brief moments the delivery shows how Arran can rightly be considered one of the best distilleries in Scotland. But the finish, following on from the faulty nose, suggests they are in danger of blowing their reputation. I don't know what's happened in the last year but there appears to be a new policy of involving sherry butts at every turn. Sadly, they are not weeding out the sulphured ones and the result here is ruinous brimstone for the Devil's Punch Bowl. If you are going to dance with the devil – present era sherry butts – you had better know exactly what you are doing. Otherwise you're be playing with fire 52.3%. nc ncf. 6,600 bottles.

The Arran Malt Fino Sherry Cask Finish db (**82.5**) **n21 t20 f21 b20.5.** Pretty tight with the bitterness not being properly compensated for. 50%

The Arran Malt Fontalloro Wine Cask Finish db (**84.5**) **n20 t22 f21.5 b21.** For a wine cask, the malt really does sing. 55%

The Arran Malt Lepanto PX Brandy Finish db (85) n22 t22 f20 b21. Tight, unusually thin for an Arran, but some lovely sweet fruit amid the confusion. Pretty oaky, too. 59%

The Arran Malt Madeira Wine Cask Finish db (77.5) n19 t21 f18.5 b19. The odd exultant moment but generally flat, flaky and bitter. 50%

The Arran Malt Moscatel Cask Finish db (87) n22 t21.5 f22 b21.5. Arran is pretty full bodied stuff when just left to its own devices. In this kind of finish it heads towards an almost syrupy texture. Luckily, the grape effect works fine. 55%

The Arran Malt 'Original' db (80.5) n19 t22 f19.5 b20. Not the greatest bourbon casks used here. 43%

The Arran Malt Pineau des Charentes Cask Finish db (94) n22.5 wispy barley clouds in a bright, sweet-grapey sky; t24 succulent and spicy. Delivery is first class, allowing full weight to the grassy barley before those fuller, fruitier notes close in. The spices are fabulously subtle and mildly puckering; f23.5 a real chocolate dessert helped by the slow build up of soft oils; b24 I may not be the greatest fan of cask finishes, but when one comes along like this, exhibiting such excellence, I'll be the first to doff my hat. 55%

The Arran Malt Pinot Noir Cask Finish db (73.5) n18 t19 f18 b18.5. A less than efficient cask from the Germans who produced it. Plenty of off key moments on nose and taste, but it does enjoy a too brief, barely redeeming Bird's Angel Delight chocolatey moment. 50%

The Arran Malt Pomerol Cask Finish Bordeux wine casks db (86.5) n20 t23 f22 b21.5. Although the cask is very marginally flawed, the relentlessness of the sweet, juicy grape and barley is a sheer delight. The odd cocoa note does no harm either. 50%

The Arran Malt Port Cask Finish db (85.5) n21 t22.5 f22 b20. One of the real problems with cask finishes is that there is no real or straightforward reference point to knowing exactly when the host flavours and the guest ones are in maximum alignment. For all this one's obvious charms, I get the feeling it was bottled when the balance was pretty low on the graph... 58.3%. nc ncf.

The Arran Malt Premier Cru Bourgogne Cask Finish db (86) n21 t22 f21 b22. An entertaining dram which some would do somersaults for, but marks docked because we have lost the unique Arran character. 56.4%

The Arran Malt Robert Burns 250 Years Anniversary Edition db (91.5) n22.5 mainly floral with just a light touch from the barley; t23.5 unusually light and flighty in body. A dusting of caster sugar softens the vanilla even further: juicy, a touch spicy and quite wonderful; f22.5 a few oils had formed towards the middle and follow through to the end. Again it is barley dominant with a squeeze of something citrussy; b23 curiously, not that far away from the light Lowland style of malt produced in the 60s and 70s in Burns' native Lowlands. Not the usual Arran, but shows that it can change personality now and again and still be a total charmer. 43%

The Arran Malt St. Emilion Cask Finish Grand Cru Classé wine casks db (89) n24 t22 f21.5 b21.5. Not the best balanced whisky you'll ever pour. But such is the sheer force of flavours, you have to doff your beret... 50%

The Arran Malt Sassicaia Wine Cask Finish db (92.5) n22.5 t23.5 f23 b23.5. Unquestionably one of Arran's better wine finishes. 55%

The Arran Malt Sauternes Cask Finish db (86) n21 t23 f21 b21. Plenty of sugars and allure. But natural caramels bring an abrupt halt to the complexity. 50%. nc ncf.

The Arran Malt Sauternes Finish db (84) n21 t22 f20 b21. Strap yourself in for this one: eye-watering sultana and 240 volts of spice. Choked with oak, though. 56%

The Arran Malt "The Sleeping Warrior" bott 2011 db (84.5) n19 t22.5 f21.5 b21.5. Zzzzzzzz. 54.9%. nc ncf. 6000 bottles.

The Arran Malt Tokaji Aszu Wine Cask Finish db (83) n20 t21.5 f21 b20.5. Pleasant enough, but the wine dulls the more interesting edges. 55%

Isle of Arran 'Jons Utvalgte' Aged 7 Years db (87) n22 t21.5 f22 b21.5. The clean intensity of the malt is soup-like. 46%. Norway.

The Peated Arran "Machrie Moor" 1st release db (86.5) n22 t22 f21 b21.5. A bit of a surprise package: I have tasted many peated Arrans over recent years, the majority voluptuous and generous in their giving. Yet this one is strangely aloof. The flavours and nuances have to be sought rather than presented for inspection and there is a hardness throughout which makes for a very solid dram. That said, it has many fine qualities, too. And the mouth-watering unravelling of its slightly cough-sweetish intensity is great entertainment. A fascinating, mixed bag. 46%. nc ncf. 9000 bottles.

Cadenhead Arran 15 Years Old bott Apr 12 (88.5) n21.5 just a little tightness from the cask; t23 the limitation of the oak is shrugged aside by the zingy, eye-watering salty barley. The sugars dissolve beautifully; f21.5 the cask constricts but the salty and spiced custard still has much to offer; b22.5 Arran heading into virtually unknown territory at this age. Perhaps not quite the complete deal but plenty going on here to delight. 56.9%. sc. WM Cadenhead Ltd.

⫶⫶ **Chieftain's Isle of Arran Aged 15 Years** butt, cask no. 935, dist Jun 97, bott Jan 13 **(83.5)** n20 t21.5 f21 b21. Disappointingly dull for an Arran. Shows virtually no coastal flair with both saline and layering conspicuous by their absence. Pleasant and malty enough, but a bit of a one-trick pony. *46%. nc ncf sc. Ian Macleod Distillers. 786 bottles.*

Duncan Taylor Dimensions Isle Of Arran 15 Years Old dist Dec 96, bott Feb 12 **(84.5)** n21 t22 f20 b21.5. Plenty of fizz and citrus to the barley. But probably not quite the best cask Arran has ever been filled into. *46%. nc ncf sc. Duncan Taylor & Co.*

Hart Brothers Isle Of Arran Aged 15 Years sherry wood, cask no. 1312, dist 24 Sep 96, bott 30 Apr 12 **(86)** n21 t23.5 f20 b21.5. As present day sherry butts go, not a bad one. But, then, not a great one either. The finish is dull and a little fuzzy but at least the delivery and follow through gives us a delicious Swiss Roll cream and jam middle to enjoy. *46%. sc.*

⫶⫶ **Malts Of Scotland Isle of Arran 1996** sherry hogshead, cask no. MoS 13002, dist Dec 96, bott Jan 13 **(96)** n24 fantastic array of salted gooseberries and boiled greengages; hint of exotic fruit cocktail; grated Cadbury's milk chocolate; first shoots of high quality bourbon with red liquorice and vague molasses; t24 near perfect weight and mouth feel with the barley radiating from the palate and its sugary juiciness contrasting with the background noise of big aged oak; the mid ground hurtles towards Chinese gooseberries with a growing degree of butterscotch; f23.5 much drier now, but this must have been one high quality cask because the bourbon notes, just like on the nose, take time to form but are unmistakable on arrival with thinned down liquorice and hickory and a thin degree of maple syrup; b24.5 almost premature aging: lots of exotic fruit seeping through: a Speyside style of twice the age...and the result is as mesmerising as it is magnificent. One of the greatest-ever bottlings from this brilliant distillery. *56.3%. nc ncf sc. 96 bottles.*

⫶⫶ **Master of Malt Arran Aged 16 Years** refill sherry hogshead, dist 13 Jun 96, bott 21 Nov 12 **(89)** n21.5 a bit of a salty headlock. Fruit tries to make an entrance, but has limited effect; t22 big, salivating, but also quite puckering as the oak takes hold; f23.5 relaxes into a more complex mode with the salty mocha catching the eye. Well...taste buds...; b22 quite tight and sometimes aggressive. Massively enjoyable, though. *55.4%. sc. 218 bottles.*

Mo Òr Collection Isle Of Arran 1996 14 Years Old first fill bourbon hogshead, cask no. 96/868, dist 5 Aug 96, bott 2 Dec 10 **(87)** n22.5 almost something of a leek and celery broth with plenty of salt added; there is also juicier and floral undertones, too; t22.5 the big juicy barley arrival is no surprise. Nor is the fabulous complexity between the sugars and salts which follow; f20.5 the bitter finish is unusual for a first fill cask; b21.5 an excellent spirit undone slightly by a disappointingly tight cask. *46%. nc ncf sc. Release no 35. 475 bottles.*

⫶⫶ **Old Malt Cask Arran Aged 15 Years** refill hogshead, cask no. 9273, dist Jan 97, bott Nov 12 **(95.5)** n23.5 good grief! A mix of dates and walnuts go into one of the thickest noses I have ever encountered from this distillery: beautiful! t24.5 delivery nears perfection with a massive deployment of spiced fruit on a gloriously thick and silky bed. Even so, the barley peels as distinctly as a church bell, allowing a pleasing degree of salivating. Some soft high roast Papua coffee notes drift through; it is the sultanas, though, which abound and make the most telling contribution; f23.5 longer than it first appears because the sugars, mildly molassed and deft, linger longer than you think. The wonderful clarity allows the gentle spices and vanilla to thrive; b24 if you find a better refill hoggy than this over the next year you will have tasted thousands to get there. A major malt whisky. Just sorry that it is not a distillery bottling... *50%. sc. Douglas Laing & Co. 282 bottles.*

⫶⫶ **Provenance Arran Over 12 Years** refill hogshead, cask no. 9237, dist Spring 00, bott Autumn 12 **(88)** n21.5 a touch of saline to the clear barley; t22 grassy, complex with a distinctive seaweed and salt lilt; f22.5 settles into a far more complex rhythm as the oak adds a broader dimension; b22 a delightful malt without even really trying. *46%. nc ncf sc.*

⫶⫶ **Provenance Arran Over 12 Years** refill hogshead, cask no. 8575, dist Winter 00, bott Summer 12 **(82)** n20 t21 f20.5 b20.5. Malty, if monosyllabic. *46%. nc ncf sc.*

Provenance Arran Over 13 Years refill butt, cask no. 7680, dist Winter 1997, bott Autumn 2011 **(84.5)** n21 t22 f20 b21.5. An attractively made dram but unusual for this distillery by not spreading its wings beyond some charming barley notes. *46%. nc ncf sc. Douglas Laing & Co.*

⫶⫶ **Provenance Arran Over 16 Years** sherry butt, cask no. 9753, dist Summer 96, bott Spring 13 **(88.5)** n22.5 virile oak offers an earthy, floral exterior; t22.5 much sweeter on delivery, though the oak is quick to be counted. Huge natural caramel surge, cream-fudge like though this is balanced by a heather-honey and spice mix later; f21.5 more evidence of splinters but the fudge and honeyed malt shake makes for a soft landing; b22 probably from a first fill bourbon cask, here is one of the first examples of an Arran showing signs of wear and tear having absorbed a little too much oak. That said, what a delight it still is and the honey-barley tandem delights throughout. *46%. nc ncf sc.*

⫶⫶ **Riegger's Selection Arran 1997** bourbon cask, cask no. 1073, dist 21 Jul 97, bott 21 Dec 12 **(94.5)** n23.5 a lovely hint of sandpaper being worked on an old piece of oak: sawdusty but brought to life by a squeeze of lemon and lime and sweetened by a gentle sprinkling of icing sugar; **t24** a magnificent delivery: has to be a first fill bourbon cask for this amount of tannin to be balanced by an orange blossom-ulmo honey mix of such magnitude; red and black liquorice combine to add a lightly sweetened weight; **f23** dries out impressively to give a feeling of controlled age and sophistication; **b24** Arran at absolutely the top of its game – and in a top notch bourbon cask, so it doesn't get any better! *55.5%. nc ncf sc. Viktor-Riegger GmbH. 396 bottles.*

Scotch Malt Whisky Society Cask 121.51 Aged 9 Years refill butt, cask no. 800399, dist 2002 **(90) n22** clean grape: juicy yet just enough vanilla weight for a satisfying depth; **t22** shades of new make on the delivery but this is quickly trampled upon by intense grape and spice; **f23.5** remains mouth-watering, with now far less of a combative feel between barley and fruit. There is even a dusting of cocoa as the spices settle into a more relaxed state; **b22.5** a charming, fresh-faced version brimming with youth and vitality. *61.3%. sc.*

⫶ **Scotch Malt Whisky Society Cask 121.54 Aged 9 Years** refill barrel, dist 15 Jul 02 **(92) n22** tannins start pushing towards a bourbon course but the barley is steadfast, if paradoxically youthful; **t23.5** oh my word! If you find a more malty delivery than this this year, you'll obviously just have fallen into a vat of malt. Maltesers on speed yet still juicy and absolutely full of vim; **f23** now even the chocolate to complete the Malteser effect; **b23.5** Arran as it was intended! Actually, if you had asked my dear recently departed friend, Gordon Mitchell , the start up manager of Arran if he would have accepted this as standard make as the place was being built, he would have shaken your bloody hand off...*58.9%. nc ncf sc. 192 bottles.*

⫶ **Scotch Malt Whisky Society Cask 121.56 Aged 9 Years** refill barrel, dist 15 Jul 02 **(88) n22** unambiguous malt; **t22** more of the same as 121.54, except the body is marginally thinner and the colours are more pastel shaded; **f22** the emphasis is on the vanillas; there is an inevitability to the butterscotch; **b22** an attractive, more simplistic and low key version of 121.54. *58.5%*

⫶ **Scotch Malt Whisky Society Cask 121.58 Aged 10 Years** refill barrel, dist 15 Jul 02 **(86) n21.5 t21 f22 b21.5.** Curious how an off beam cask can completely alter the direction of a malt. It is obvious the spirit is of the same quality as 121.54/56. But the niggardly character of the oak makes for a more aggressive (though still ultra malty) child. *57.8%. nc ncf sc. 131 bottles.*

Scotch Single Malt Circle Arran 1998 cask no. 98/652, dist 11 Jun 98, bott 9 Dec 10 **(89.5) n23.5** more than a single pinch of salt brings out the sharper aspects of the barley. A wonderful marriage of sweet, fresh grist and the creakier resonance of aged oak; the butterscotch topped with diced physalis is a bonus; **t23** invigorating delivery with the taste buds standing to attention, puckering under the onslaught of the salt and spiced honey malt; a lovely sheen thanks to delicate copper notes; **f21** cocoa and vanilla; **b22** the whisky equivalent of a bracing shower under a waterfall to liven you up. *54.9%. sc.*

⫶ **That Boutique-y Whisky Company Arran** batch 1 **(74) n19 t19 f18 b18.** A clumsy, off key whisky at best. *49.1%. Master Of Malt. 211 bottles.*

⫶ **That Boutique-y Whisky Company Arran** batch 2 **(95) n23.5** crushed poppy seeds, diced apple and salted tannin star; **t23.5** massive malt on delivery, pepped up by manuka honey in a hurry and a peppery glow taking it slow; **f24** long, with the persistent barley as well as the vanilla being coated in muscovado sugar; and still those spices sing...; **b24** shimmers like the sun reflecting off the Sound of Bute...from the right cask, one of the truly great distilleries of the world. *494% Master of Malt. 459 bottles.*

The Whisky Agency Arran 1995 bott 2012 **(76) n18 t21 f18 b19.** no matter how good the spirit, if the cask isn't up to the mark. It is a testament to Arran's excellence that some gorgeous honey notes can still be heard through the tart noise. *52.3%. nc ncf sc.*

ISLE OF JURA

Highlands (Island—Jura), 1810. Whyte and Mackay. Working.

Isle of Jura 5 Years Old 1999 db **(83) n19 t23 f21 b20.** Absolutely enormously peated, but has reached that awkward time in its life when it is massively sweet and as well balanced as a two-hour-old foal. *46% The Whisky Exchange*

Isle Of Jura Aged 10 Years db **(79.5) n19 t22 f19 b19.5.** Perhaps a little livelier than before, but still miles short of where you might hope it to be. *40%*

Jura Elixir Aged 12 Years Fruity & Spicy db **(77) n18 t21 f18 b20.** Fruity, spicy and a little sulphury, I'm afraid. Those who can't spot sulphur will love the caramel-fruitcake enormity. *40%*

Isle of Jura Mountain of Gold 15 Years Old Pinot Noir cask finish db **(67.5) n15 t18 f17 b17.5.** Not for the first time a Jura seriously hamstrung by sulphur - for all its honeyed sweetness and promise: there are some amazingly brilliant casks in there tragically wasted. And my tastebuds partially crocked because of it. Depressing. *46%. 1366 bottles.*

Isle of Jura Mountain of Sound 15 Years Old Cabernet Sauvignon finish db **(81) n20 t21.5 f19.5 b20.** Pretty quiet. *43%*

Isle of Jura The Sacred Mountain 15 Years Old Barolo finish db **(89.5) n21.5 t24 f21.5 b22.5** Hoo-bloody-rah! One of the three from this series has actually managed to raise my pulse. Not, it must be said, without the odd fault here and there. But there really is a stunning interaction between grape and barley that sets the nerves twitching: at its height this is about as entertaining a malt as I've come across for some time and should be on everyone's list for a jolly jaunt for the taste buds. Just when I was beginning to lose faith in this distillery... *43%*

Isle Of Jura Aged 16 Years db **(90.5) n21.5** salty, coastal, seaweedy, but with an injection of honey; **t23.5** carries on from the nose perfectly and then ups the stakes. The delivery is malt dependent and rich, the salty tang a true delight; **f23** all kinds of vanillas and honeys carried on a salty wind; **b23** a massive improvement, this time celebrating its salty, earthy heritage to good effect. The odd strange, less than harmonious note. But by far and away the most improved Jura for a long, long while. *40%*

Isle of Jura Aged 21 Years 200th Anniversary db **(74) n19 t19 f18 b18.** Don't know what to say. Actually, I do. But what's the point...? *44%*

Isle of Jura 21 Years Old Cask Strength db **(92) n22 t24 f23 b23.** Every mouthful exudes class and quality. A must-have for Scottish Island collector... or those who know how to appreciate a damn fine malt *58.1%*

Isle of Jura 30 Years Old db **(89) n22.5 t22.5 f22 b22.** A relaxed dram with the caramel dousing the higher notes just as they started to get very interesting. If there is a way of bringing down these presumably natural caramels – it is a 30 years old, so who in their right mind would add colouring? – this would score very highly, indeed. *40%*

Isle of Jura 40 Years Old finished in oloroso wood db **(90) n23** a different species of Jura from anything you are likely to have seen before: swamped in sherry, there is a vague, rather odd smokiness to this. Not to mention salty, sea-side rockpools. As a pairing (sherry and smoke), the odd couple... which works and doesn't work at the same time. Strange... **t22** syrupy sweet delivery with thick waves of fruit and then an apologetic 'ahem' from the smoke, which drifts in nervously. Again, everything is awkward... **f22** remains soft and velvety, though now strands of bitter, salty oak and molasses drift in and out; **b23** throw the Jura textbooks away. This is something very different. Completely out of sync in so many ways, but... *40%*

Isle of Jura 1974 db **(87.5) n23 t22.5 f20.5 b21.5.** Stick your nose in this and enjoy those very first outstanding moments on delivery. *42%*

Isle of Jura 1974 db **(85.5) n22 t23 f18.5 b22.** A case where the unhappy, bitter ending is broadcast on the nose. Talk about warts 'n all...!! *44.5%*

Isle of Jura 1976 db **(94.5) n24.5** a fascinating wisp of smoke acts almost like a thread which stitches together myriad complex, barely discernable facets which make for a nose to be treasured. We are talking pastel shades here, nothing brash or vivid. Vanilla shapes the background but the light herbal notes, marrying with the deft, crushed between the fingers berries makes for the most teasing of experiences. Look out for gooseberries and a butterscotch/honey mix in particular; **t24** works with rare magnificence from the go simply because the barley leads the way with such ease and there is neither OTT oils or oaks to blur the picture; varying types of sugars follow behind and spices are also in close attendance, again with a marvellous hint of smoke lingering; **f22.5** shows an acceptable and understandable degree of oaky bitterness but the spices and barley still ride high; **b23.5** absolutely beautiful whisky which carries its age with unfeigned elegance. *46.1%*

Isle of Jura 1977 first fill bourbon casks finished in Ruby Port pipe db **(94.5) n24** pretty classy: greengages about to explode while soft marzipan and spices form the spine; **t23.5** melt-in-the-mouth delivery with a really impressive meeting of heather-honey, Demerara sugars and sherry trifle, or maybe that should be Port trifle...; **f23** the vaguest hint of spiced praline as the silky essay draws to a close; **b24** now and again something rather special and significant emerges from this distillery. *46%. Whyte and Mackay. 498 bottles.*

Jura Boutique Barrels Vintage 1995 bourbon Jo finish db **(89.5) n24.5 t23.5 f20 b21.5.** There are moments when you wonder if you have a possible malt of the year on your hands. Then the slip shows... Even so, one of the more memorable whiskies of the 2011 Bible. *56.5%*

Jura Boutique Barrels 1996 db **(78) n21 t21.5 f17.5 b18.** A clumsy whisky in which the fruit fits the malt in the same way a size 46 jacket fits a guy with a 40 inch chest. Either too cloyingly sweet or just too viciously bitter. *54%. 493 bottles.*

Jura Boutique Barrels Vintage 1999 heavily peated, bourbon Xu finish db **(84) n21.5 t21 f20.5 b21.** Pretty peat. But not in the same league as the Prophecy, simply because the base spirit is nowhere near as good. *55%*

Jura Elements "Air" db **(76) n19.5 t19 f18.5 b19.** Initially, I thought this was earth: there is something strangely dirty and flat about both nose and delivery. Plenty of fruits here and there but just doesn't get the pulse racing at all. *45%*

Jura Elements "Earth" db (89) n23.5 t22 f21.5 b22. I haven't spoken to blender Richard Paterson about these whiskies yet. No doubt I'll be greeted with a knee on the nuts for declaring two as duds. My guess is that this is the youngest of the quartet by a distance and that is probably why it is the best. The peat profile is very different and challenging. I'd still love to see this in its natural plumage as the caramel really does put the brakes on the complexity and development. Otherwise we could have had an elementary classic. 45%

Jura Elements "Fire" db (86.5) n22.5 t21.5 f21 b21.5. Pleasant fare, the highlight coming with the vaguely Canadian-style nose thanks to a classic toffee-oak mix well known east of the Rockies. Some botanicals also there to be sniffed at while a few busy oaky notes pep up the barley-juiced delivery, too. Sadly, just a shade too toffee dependent. 45%

Jura Elements "Water" db (73.5) n18.5 t19 f18 b18. Oranges by the box-full trying to get out but the mouth is sent into puckering spasm by the same sulphur which spoils the nose. 50%

Jura Prophecy profoundly peated db (90.5) n23.5 something almost akin to birchwood in there with the peat and salt; there is a wonderful natural floral note as well as coastal elements to this one; t23 impressively two-toned: on one side is the sharper, active barley and peat offering an almost puckering youthfulness and zest; on the other, a sweeter, lightly oiled buzz...a treat; f22 thins as the vanillas enter; b22 youthful, well made and I prophesize this will be one of Jura's top scorers of 2011... 46%

Jura Superstition db (73.5) n17 t19 f18 b18.5. I thought this could only improve. I was wrong. One to superstitiously avoid. 43%

⁘ **Jura Turas-Mara** db (82.5) n20.5 t22 f19 b21. Some irresistible Jaffa Cake moments. But the oils are rather too severe and tangy. 42%. Travel Retail Exclusive.

Archives Isle Of Jura 1988 24 Years Old Third Release bourbon cask, cask no. 752, dist May 98, bott May 12 (87) n22.5 interesting balance between sharp, grassy barley and minty old oak; t22 excellent delivery full of juice, then fattens out enormously to a semi-syrupy constitution; f20.5 inelegant oils and oak; b22 a heavy malt resplendent early on in its sugary frock. 51.3%. nc ncf sc. Whiskybase B.V. 60 bottles.

Dun Bheagan Isle Of Jura 11 Years Old St Etienne rum finish, dist May 00 (82) n20 t22 f19 b21. I'm not sure if the rum finish has smoothed out the usual rougher edges form this distillery or dumbed down what appears to be a charming maltiness. A little bit of the chewing gum about this. 46%. nc ncf sc. Ian Macleod Distillers.

⁘ **Gordon & MacPhail Connoisseurs Choice Jura 1997** (84.5) n20 t23 f20.5 b21. Drink plenty before tasting this: few whiskys work on your saliva glands as does the delivery of this guy. Juicy doesn't even begin to half cover it. 46%. ncf.

⁘ **Malts Of Scotland Isle of Jura 1992** bourbon hogshead, cask no. MoS 12064, dist 92, dist 12 (78) n18 t21 f19 b20. A thick, syrupy, overly sweet and, finally, tangy addition to the Jura cannon. Though one which, by and large, fails to hit the target. 50.3%. nc ncf sc. 96 bottles.

Mo Òr Collection Isle Of Jura 1988 22 Years Old first fill bourbon hogshead, cask no. 756, dist 19 Apr 88, bott 15 Dec 10 (87) n20.5 the vague, distant smoke is a surprise package. Not particularly brilliant, but displays an attractive, salty character; t22 the softness of the delivery is yet another surprise; the richness of the malt isn't. A pleasant tang of blood orange; f22.5 soft cocoa, leading into mocha. The vanilla is firm and shuts the gate on further development; b22 a real Jaffa Cake of a dram. 46%. nc ncf sc. Release No. 52. 352 bottles.

Old Malt Cask Isle Of Jura Aged 16 Years refill hogshead, cask no. 7739, dist Apr 95, bott Oct 11 (74.5) n19 t19 f18 b18.5. It may be 16 years old, but it looks nowhere near the age of consent. A gristy, wet behind the ears offering. 50%. nc ncf sc. 207 bottles.

⁘ **Old Malt Cask Jura Aged 21 Years** refill hogshead, cask no. 9806, dist Mar 92, bott May 13 (93) n23.5 wow! Delicate and so complex: steamed pears lead the considerable fruit interest; the merest hint of lychee and ginger underscores the oak; t23.5 fabulous mouth feel with near perfect oil involvement; the tannins have the greater clout, with buttered toast and a shaving of hickory. A brief barley sugar surge, then immediate dry toast and spice; f23 long, and benefitting from a really top quality barrel, with the oak drying to an excellent pitch; b23 oh, if only all Juras were this stunning: as refreshing as the wind blowing in from the sound directly into your face.... 48%. nc ncf sc. 239 bottles.

Provenance Jura Over 9 Years refill hogshead, cask no. 8510, dist Spring 2003, bott Spring 2012 (85.5) n21.5 t22 f21 b21. Chunky, ribald barley with a good dollop of maple syrup. If you are looking for poise or subtlety, move on... 46%. nc ncf sc. Douglas Laing & Co.

⁘ **Scotch Malt Whisky Society Cask 31.24 Aged 24 Years** refill hogshead, dist 27 Sep 88 (85.5) n19 t22 f22.5 b22. Relentlessly coastal with brine hitting the taste buds from every direction. Once past the strangely fishy nose the malt has a big, juicy say before the sea spray takes hold. A little mocha makes a pleasant late flourish. 54%. nc ncf sc. 255 bottles.

⁘ **The Whisky Agency Joint Bottling Bresser & Timmer Isle Of Jura 1988** ex-bourbon hogshead, dist 88, bott 12 (88) n22 light lime pulses like a Jura lighthouse. Sharp barley holds sway; the vanilla is elegant and consistent; t22 the oak offers an unusual bitter burst so early on. But the buttery malt recovers the situation calmly; **f22** a nutty finale works well with the steady barley; **b22** shows the distillery off in a better light than many. *50.8%*

The Whisky Agency Jura 24 Years Old dist 1988 **(85) n21 t22 f21 b21.** A big, thick lump of a malt with major barley juiciness and over oakiness. Never quite sits right, though it does have its fleeting moments of charm. *51.3%. sc.*

KILCHOMAN
Islay, 2005. Kilchoman Distillery Co. Working.

Kilchoman Autumn 09 Release db **(85) n21 t22.5 f20 b21.5.** Still to completely find it's legs: a youthful malt is trying desperately hard to hit the high notes, but falling short. Or perhaps I should say flat as the fruit here is acting like caramel in dumbing down the more complex notes you know are in there somewhere...especially in the final third. Like the Inaugeral Release there is a feinty element to this, not all of it bad, but certainly marks the nose and finish. Also a charming gristiness: you feel as though you are standing there watching the barley being dried. But as yet doesn't quite have the early excellence that Arran, for instance, boasted. But these are early days in the distillery's life. And, for me, anything drinkable at all is a bonus... *46%*

⁘ **Kilchoman 2008** first fill bourbon cask db **(92.5) n23** someone has put some green apples amid the peat; **t23.5** like the nose, sensationally clean and so crystal clear you can even pick out the barley sugar notes quite separately from the phenols; pretty youthful; **f23** dry now the majority of the muscovado sugars are spent with cocoa powder moving in; **b23** as fresh as an autumnal Islay wind on your cheeks... *61%. sc. Whisky Shop Exclusive. 260 bottles.*

Kilchoman Winter 2010 Release fresh and refill bourbon db **(88) n23 t22 f21 b22.** Size doesn't really matter, apparently. Well that is certainly the case here. This may be a big boy, displaying a stonking 50ppm phenols, but it fails to match the overall elegance of the Kilchoman Inaugural 100% Islay...which is a p-challenged 15ppm. The Inaugural showed great purpose throughout. This is a big crash, bang wallop merchant. That said, fully enjoyable stuff! *46%. nc ncf.*

Kilchoman Spring 2011 Release oloroso finish db **(93.5) n23.5** there is no doubting the enormity of the smoke, but that is matched by the deftness of the lightly molassed grape. What a surprisingly well suited marriage; **t24** and there we go again: juicy yet dry at the same time. The delivery offers outstanding early balance and control. Also, very hard to believe this is just three years old: behaves something nearer ten or twelve. Excellent soft oils which act as a reservoir for the melting muscovado sugar; **f22.5** garibaldi biscuit and coffee; the smoke does not act much like a 50ppm giant; **b23.5** have to admit: when I this was a 50ppm phenol malt finished in oloroso, my head was in my hands and my heart was filled with trepidation. This is a story that normally ends in tears... But what a surprise! A faultlessly clean butt helped, but the grape is by no means overplayed and its main function, apart from balance, appears to be to generate a feeling of extra age and tranquillity in the glass. A lovely and genuinely unexpected Islay experience. On this evidence, Kilchoman has well and truly arrived and can hold its head as high as the other Islay distilleries... *46%. nc ncf.*

Kilchoman Inaugural Release db **(87.5) n21 t23 f21.5 b22.** Not by any means perfect but what could have been something of a bumpy ride has been helped along by some very good casks: like an excellent football referee, you don't notice it, but not only is it there, it makes the best of what is on offer. Not a great whisky. But a very promising start. *46%. nc ncf.*

Kilchoman Inaugural 100% Islay 1st fill bourbon db **(91.5) n23.5** a superb nose which takes full advantage of some excellent oak to give weight to the soft gristiness. Young, but no hint of a Bambi here: this has found its feet already...; **t24** fabulous delivery. Soft, genteel peats melt into a light citrus sweetness and then several waves of red-liquorice oak add just the right anchor; **f21.5** pleasant and vanilla-driven though slightly untidy, as one might reasonably expect; **b22.5** in a quite different world to the first two bottlings. Those, falteringly, gave reason for hope. But a slight degree of concern, too. This is unerringly fine: clean and purposeful and making a very clear and eloquent statement. *50%. nc ncf.*

⁘ **Kilchoman 100% Islay The 2nd Edition** db **(93) n23** tannins have kicked in already to create a redcurrant and liquorice dais to the smoke; **t23.5** a pup of a dram, the juices from the barley cascade onto the palate. The sugars are uncomplicated and dripping in phenols before custard cream biscuits take charge; **f23** the custard cream is dunked into milky, muscovado-rich Panama coffee; **b23.5** the first edition of this sent out, I remember, a clear statement as to regards the quality of the spirit being produced at Kilchomen. This doesn't just endorse it, but actually takes us further down the line. Less storms and drama than the previous bottling, but this is far better controlled and weighted with the praline and coffee liqueur mix making for one of the best three-year-olds ever bottled in Scotland. *50%. nc ncf.*

⁘ **Kilchoman Loch Gorm** sherry cask, dist 07, bott 13 db **(92.5) n23.5** anyone who has squelched through the blackest peat bog on a stormy Islay day will recognise parts of this earthy aroma; fruit has tightened the smoky, slightly coal tar creosote aspect; **t23.5** ridiculously soft landing on the palate with those now familiar oils soon aboard and to all parts of the palate; one of the oiliest middles I have tasted in a Scotch; **f22.5** big smoked raisin fudge; **b23** it is never a good idea to be Gorm-less...especially when a whisky is quite this scarily enormous. On this and other evidence, it could be that Kilchomen is not just challenging Caol Ila as the oiliest malt on Islay, but may well have surpassed it. *46%. nc ncf.*

Kilchoman Machir Bay bott 2012 db **(93) n23** fireside peat ash wrapped in sherry; **t23.5** beautifully distilled barley and grist – both youthful and some weighed down with a little vanilla – tapping out some major peaty notes; just a little bitter as it appears the oak has been forced slightly. The sultana fruit maximises the juiciness; **f23** long with a wonderful ulmo honey depth and the now restrained peat taking a support role rather than the lead; **b23.5** it is over 30 years since I first tried to play football on the sands of Machir Bay. I did it because with the winds never ceasing, it was, like a latter day Canute, an attempt at the impossible. A bit like trying to get to the bottom of this malt, in fact. In some respects it works, in others I feel a degree of sherry may just have knocked out some of the more complex characters in an attempt to soften. It is, however, much more successful than my failed attempts at playing "Keepie Uppie" against the perennial winds of Machir Bay... *46%. nc ncf.*

⋙ **Kilchoman Machir Bay** oloroso sherry butt finish, bott 13 db **(90.5) n23** as fat as an Islay goose with the wine helping to turn this chunky; **t22.5** how sweet it is: to be loved by those who want their palate caked Caol Ila style in thick oil with the phenols subdued and trying to get out from under the weight of the juicy sultanas; **f22** the oiliest coffee ever; **b23** I think this was more honeyed last time, but the sultanas ring a bell. Another very different but high quality offering from Kilchomen. *46%. nc ncf.*

Kilchoman Sherry Cask Release bott 2011 db **(83) n21.5 t21.5 f19 b21**. The thumping peat and at times almost syrupy sherry is just too much of a good thing. *46%. nc ncf.*

Kilchoman Vintage 2006 bott 2012 db **(93.5) n24** I close my eyes and allow myself to be consumed by the aroma which takes me away from a freezing, rain-soaked summer in England, to a freezing, rain-soaked summer on Islay, with gulls screeching from a distance, peat on the wind from Port Ellen and midges biting hard with an uncanny accuracy for the most sensitive nerve endings. You are unlikely to find an aroma which so perfectly embodies maritime Islay; **t23.5** the sugars seemingly so tied up with the phenols on the nose appear to have momentarily escaped the smoky masters to make the delivery a sweet one. But the smoke is on its trail and soon has the caster sugar and maple syrup back in custody allowing vanilla to make its presence felt; **f22.5** bitters very slightly; the peat now has the density of an Arbroath smoky while spice rattles in late on; **b23** a sweetly peated triumph. *46%. nc ncf.*

⋙ **Scotch Malt Whisky Society Cask 129.1 Aged 5 Years** 1st fill barrel, dist 28 Jun 06 **(89) n22.5** as earthy as a dank summer garden: the floral notes vie with the peat manure, Palma Violet candy and cough sweet; **t22.5** not quite as bold as the script written by the nose, though perhaps just as well. The oak-inspired muscovado sugars play a bigger part here and after a delivery as silky as sandpaper, the shape oils out sufficiently for a gristy, barley-rich middle; **f21.5** just a little on the short and dry side with the smoke hesitant; **b22.5** a delicious, if different, experience not to be missed. *60.2%. nc ncf sc. 235 bottles.*

⋙ **Scotch Malt Whisky Society Cask 129.2 Aged 4 Years** 1st fill barrel, dist 13 Dec 07 **(92.5) n23** a smashed bottle of TCP... which happens to have conveniently landed in a bowl of grist and freshly squeezed lemon; **t23.5** at first the delivery concentrates on the ashy aspect of the peat, being dry and dusty. The spices fizz like fuse wire for a few seconds but the way in which the oils form to create an entirely different character in mid act is some trick...; **f22.5** continues along its young smoky path but there is a short burst of Demerara sugars to reinvigorate the complexity; **b23.5** probably because of its comparative youth, a malt which somehow bypasses the coastal feel other Kilchomens have conjured in previous bottlings and instead decided to flaunt its peaty charms shamelessly. *61.6%. nc ncf sc. 250 bottles.*

KINCLAITH
Lowlands, 1957–1975. Closed / Dismantled.
Mo Òr Collection Kinclaith 1969 41 Years Old first fill bourbon hogshead, cask no. 301453A, dist 28 May 69, bott 29 Oct 10 **(85.5) n22 t22 f20.5 b21**. Hangs on gamely to the last vestiges of life, though the oak, without being overtly aggressive, is squeezing all the breath of out of it. *46%. nc ncf sc. Release No. 2. The Whisky Talker. 164 bottles.*

KNOCKANDO
Speyside, 1898. Diageo. Working.
Knockando Aged 12 Years dist 94 db **(86) n22 t22 f21 b21**. An unusually light bottling. Here you get full exploration of the attractive, malty skeleton. But Knockando has a tendency towards dryness and the casks here oblige rather too well. A delicate dram all the same. *43%*

Knockando Aged 12 Years dist 1995 db (71.5) n16 t19 f18 b18.5. If there was an award for Worst Nose of the Year, this must be somewhere in the running. *43%*

Knockando Aged 12 Years dist 1996 db (76) n18 t20.5 f18.5 b19. Disappointing. As someone who knows this distillery perhaps as well as anyone working for its current owners, I had hoped for a dry, sophisticated dram to send me into various degrees of ecstasy. Instead, I am left lamenting a few poor casks which have distorted what this distillery stands for. *43%*

Knockando Aged 18 Years sherry casks, dist 1987 db (77) n19 t21 f18 b19. Bland and docile. Someone wake me up. *43%*

Knockando 25 Years Old Special Release 2011 db (77) n20 t22 f16 b19. One or two renegade sherry butts away from what would have been a memorable whisky. *43%. nc ncf.*

Knockando 1990 db (83) n21 t22 f20 b20. The most fruity Knockando I've come across with some attractive salty notes. Dry, but a little extra malty sweetness these days. *40%*

Old Malt Cask Knockando Aged 17 Years refill hogshead, cask no 7762, dist Aug 94, bott Oct 11 (86.5) n22 t23 f20 b21.5. The wonderful depth and complexity to the textbook sharp Knockando style barley is undermined slightly by the bitterness on the finish. *50%. nc ncf sc. Douglas Laing & Co. 175 bottles.*

KNOCKDHU

Speyside, 1894. Inver House Distillers. Working.

AnCnoc 12 Year Old db (94.5) n24 so complex it is frightening: delicate barley; delicate spices; delicate butterscotch-vanilla, delicate citrus... and all the while the lightest discernible sugars melt into the malt; t23 it had to be salivating... and is! Yet there is enough oaky-vanilla roughage to ensure the citrus and barley don't get their own way; f23.5 a slow but telling arrival of spices fit hand in glove with the complex cocoa-barley tones; b24.5 a more complete or confident Speyside-style malt you are unlikely to find. Shimmers with everything that is great about Scotch whisky... always a reliable dram, but this is stupendous. *40%*

AnCnoc 13 Year Old Highland Selection db (85) n21 t23 f20 b21. A big Knockdhu, but something is dulling the complexity. *46%*

AnCnoc 16 Years Old db (91.5) n22 sharp, pithy, salty, busy...; t23.5 those salts crash headlong into the taste buds and then give way to massive spice and barley; soft sugars and vanilla follow at a distance; f23 salted mocha and spice; b23 unquestionably the spiciest AnCnoc of all time. Has this distillery been moved to the coast..? *46%*

⁘ **AnCnoc 22 Year Old** db (87) n22 a classic case of polished oak floor; t21.5 the tingle on delivery is oak concentrate. The sweeter barley recovers and battles to keep it in check, but there are casualties; f22 settles gently towards a cocoa and butterscotch finish. The oaks seem less militant; b21.5 often a malt which blossoms before being a teenager, as does the fruits of Knockdhu; struggles to cope comfortably with the inevitable oakiness of old age. Here is such a case. *Inverhouse Distillers*

AnCnoc 26 Years Old Highland Selection db (89) n23 t22 f23 b21. There is a little flat moment between the middle and finish for which I have chipped off a point or two. That apart, superb. *48.2%*

AnCnoc 30 Years Old db (85) n21 t23 f19 b22. Seat-of-the-pants whisky that is just on the turn. Still has a twinkle in the eye, though. *49%*

AnCnoc 35 Years Old db (86) n21 t21 f22.5 b21.5. Tries to take the exotic fruit route to antiquity but headed off at the pass by a massive dollop of natural caramels. The slow burn on the spice is an unexpected extra treat, though. *43%*

AnCnoc 35 Years Old bourbon and sherry casks db (88) n22.5 any saltier and you'd expect the odd barnacle to be attached...; t22 dry thanks to the oak and for the same reason evolved into a complex malt with the butterscotch providing the sweetness covering a multitude of subtle spice notes; f21.5 barley and vanilla; b22 the usual big barley sheen has dulled with time here. Some attractive cocoa notes do compensate. *44.3%. nc ncf.*

An Cnoc 1993 db (89) n22 t21 f24 b22. Quite an odd one this. I have tasted it a couple of times with different samples and there is a variance. This one takes an oakier path and then invites the barley to do its stuff. Delicious, but underscores the deft touch of the standard 12-year-old. *46%*

AnCnoc 1994 db (88.5) n22.5 t22.5 f21.5 b22. Coasts through effortlessly, showing the odd flash of brilliance here and there. Just get the feeling that it never quite gets out of third gear... *46%. ncf.*

AnCnoc 1995 db (84.5) n21 t22 f20.5 b21. Very plump for a Knockdhu with caramel notes on a par with the citrus and burgeoning bourbon. Some barley juice escapes on delivery but the finish is peculiarly dry for the distillery. *46%*

AnCnoc Peter Arkle first fill sherry casks db (67) n17 t17.5 f16.5 b17. Unattractive and grimly off key. *46%. nc ncf.*

Knockdhu 23 Years Old db **(94) n23 t24 f23 b24.** Pass the smelling salts. This is whisky to knock you out. A malt that confirms Knockdhu as not simply one of the great Speysiders, but unquestionably among the world's elite. *57.4%.*

LADYBURN
Lowlands, 1966–2000. William Grant & Sons. Closed.
Mo Ór Collection Rare Ayrshire 1974 36 Years Old first fill bourbon barrel, cask no. 2608, dist 10 May 74, bott 1 Nov 11 **(89.5) n22** a battering of unpretentious oak. But there is a light sweetened salted butter halo which offers something else; **t23.5** the delivery concentrates on those sugars, the first to arrive being not much more complex than basic icing sugar. But the map changes as a wonderfully complex portfolio of spices make their mark; **f22** virtually croaks on the spot, with, initially, not much more than oak-strewn vanilla. But like Lazarus it rises, with a red liquorice and chalky citrus glint in its once dead eye; **b22.5** I had a feeling it'd be this distillery when I saw the title on the label... it couldn't be much else! Fascinating to think that I was in final countdown for my 'O' levels when this was made. It appears to have dealt with the passing years better than I have. Even so, I had not been prepared for this. For years during the very early 1990s Grant's blender David Stewart sent me samples of this stuff and it was, to put it mildly, not great. Some were the oakiest malt I ever tasted in my life. And, to compound matters further, the distillery's own bottling was truly awful. But this cask has re-written history. *46%. nc ncf sc. Release No. 4. The Whisky Talker. 261 bottles.*

LAGAVULIN
Islay, 1816. Diageo. Working.
Lagavulin 12 Years Old 7th release, bott 2007 db **(92.5) n23 t23 f23 b23.5.** Brooding, enigmatic and just pulsing with quiet sophistication. A dram to drink quietly so all can be heard in the glass... *56.4%*

Lagavulin 12 Years Old 8th release, bott 2008 db **(94.5) n24** heady mixture of coal dust and peat reek, quite dry but not without some fried banana sweetness in the most delicate terms possible; **t24.5** a lightly oiled landing allows the peats to glide around the palate with minimal friction; a light dusting of hickory powder works well with the big, but by no means brooding phenols; the sweetness levels are just about perfect; **f22.5** surprisingly short with a dull toffee flourish to the smoke; **b23.5** sensational malt: simply by doing all the simple things rather brilliantly. *56.4%*

Lagavulin 12 Years Old 10th release, bott 2010 db **(94.5) n23.5** a dusty, gristy combination. As though someone has swept up the remnants of an anthracite pile and mixed it in with powdered peat and grist. And then sprinkled liberally with hickory. Dry with sugars at a premium; **t24** the arrival offers a surprising amount of juice: still enough rich barley still not under the influence of oak. The sugars, so shy on the nose, show all the bashfulness of a teenage wannabe on a TV talent show. Except these sugars do have talent...; all the while the smoke hangs around like reek on a windless winter morn; **f23.5** long with a touch of melted molasses spread over a butterscotch tart; the peat could hardly be more gentile; **b23.5** keeps on track with previous Releases. Though this is the first where the lowering of the ppms from 50 to 35 really do seem noticeable. Quite beautiful, nonetheless. *56.5%*

Lagavulin 12 Years Old Special Release 2011 db **(96.5) n24.5** the kind of perfectly weighted aroma which makes your hairs stand on end and your taste buds salivate. The peat takes neither ashy nor oily form, or maybe it takes both....you decide. And the light mintiness to the lemon....extraordinary! **t24** the oils form with limited density on delivery. Not only do they usher in the controlled peat, but also a milky mocha thread which perfectly absorbs the percussion of most explosive spices; **f23.5** softens out with the deft sugars now in command over the vanilla; the thin, creamy mocha continues; **b24.5** so the peat may not pound as it did when the Whisky Bible began life in 2003: the phenols are noticeably lighter here. But it is not all about size: balance and complexity still reign supreme. *57.5%. nc ncf.*

⁘ Lagavulin 12 Years Old Special Release 2012 Refill American Oak Casks, bott 2012 db **(95) n23** firm peat, firm gristy barley, firm sugar. Yet the subtle oils and underlying vanillas ensure a soft centre; **t24** big and juicy delivery with major barley sparking on delivery. The peat is sublime, appearing on varying waves of intensity and depth: a delivery and follow through which always appears fresh and on the move; **f24** more vanilla and butterscotch; buttery, too – of the salted variety. Like the nose and delivery a fluid finale, with the sugar melting, solidifying and melting again and a mild, smoky manuka honey fade; **b24** truly wonderful. A very clever, sympathetic and professional choice of casks from this superstar distillery. *56.1%. nc ncf. Diageo.*

Lagavulin 16 Years Old db **(95) n24** morning cinders of peat from the fire of the night before: dry, ashy, improbably delicate. Just a hint of Demerara sweetness caught on the edge; **t24** that dryness is perfectly encapsulated on the delivery with the light sugars eclipsed by those countless waves of ash. A tame spiciness generates a degree of hostility on the palate, but the mid-ground sticks to a smoky, coffee-vanilla theme; **f23** light spicy waves in a gentle sea of smoke; **b24** although i have enjoyed this whisky countless times socially, it is the first time for a while I have dragged it into the Tasting Room for professional analysis for the Bible. If anyone has noticed a slight change in Lagavulin, they would be right. The peat remains profound but much more delicate than before, while the oils appear to have receded. A different shape and weight dispersal for sure. But the sky-high quality remains just the same. *43%*

Lagavulin Aged 16 Years The Distillers Edition PX cask, dist 1991, bott 2007 db **(83) n22 t21 f20 b20.** I have oft stated that peat and sherry are uncomfortable bed-fellows. Here, the two, both obviously from fine stock and not without some individual attraction, manage to successfully cancel each other out. One is hard pressed to imagine any Lagavulin this dull. *43%*

Lagavulin 21 Years Old bott 2007 db **(96) n24.5 t24 f23 b24.5.** Big peat and grape rarely work comfortably together and here we a have malt which struggles from the nose to finish to make some kind of sense of itself. There will be some Islayphiles who will doubtless drool at this and while certain aspects of the finish are quite excellent the balance never appears to come into focus. *56.5%*

⫶⫶⫶⫶ **Lagavulin 21 Years Old Special Release 2012** dist 1991, bott 2012 db **(92.5) n23.5** fruity and fresh: toffee raisin meets Rupp cheese; salty and seaside, too...and rather sweet; **t23.5** thick, smoky, juicy fruitcake...and rather sweet; **f23** exceptionally clean fruit and a slow, sweet pulsing smokiness...and rather sweet; **b22.5** the impact of the fruit is truly delicious in its sweet juiciness, but the smoke means complexity is slightly subdued. Fantastic whisky, though...and rather sweet. *52%. nc ncf. Diageo.*

Lagavulin Special Release 2010 12 Years Old refill American oak db **(94) n24.5** unambiguously Lagavulin: the mixture of chalkiness to the gristy peat, all ringed by light oil, is unmistakable. Clean, beautifully shaped and disciplined in its use of spice; **t24** the same can be said here as the nose: it absolutely screams Lagavulin and is bolstered by a clever injection of muscovado sugars which actually boosts rather than relieves the intensity. The oils are so soft, they could come from Leeds...; **f22** just a shade of disappointing bitterness as tired cask cocks a snook at the continuing spices and forming cocoa; **b23.5** Bloody hell! This is some whisky...! *56.5%. nc ncf. Diageo.*

LAPHROAIG
Islay, 1815. Beam Inc. Working.

Laphroaig 10 Years Old db **(90) n24** impossible not to nose this and think of Islay: no other aroma so perfectly encapsulates the island – clean despite the rampaging peat-reek and soft oak, raggy coast-scapes and screeching gulls – all in a glass; **t23** one of the crispiest peaty malts of them all, the barley standing out alone, brittle and unbowed, before the peat comes rushing in like the tide: iodine and soft salty tones; **f20.5** the nagging bitterness of many ex-Allied bourbon casks filled during this period is annoyingly apparent here... **b22.5** has reverted back slightly towards a heavier style in more recent bottling, though I would like to see that old oomph at the very death. Even so, this is, indisputably, a classic whisky. The favourite of Prince Charles apparently: he will make a wise king... *40%*

Laphroaig 10 Years Old Cask Strength batch no. 001 bott Feb 09 db **(91.5) n22.5** like a throbbing 6 litre engine below a still bonnet, you are aware of the peaty power waiting to be unleashed; **t23.5** a stunningly sublime, slightly watered muscovado sugar coating ensures the dry, phenolic explosion conjures myriad variances on a theme; **f23** a quite beautiful milk chocolate quality dovetails to excellent effect with the smoke; **b22.5** a Groundhog Day of a malt with the waves of smoke starting identically but always panning out a little differently each time. Fascinating and fun. *578%*

Laphroaig 10 Years Old Original Cask Strength (with UK Government's Sensible Drinking Limits boxed on back label) db **(92) n22** a duller nose than usual: caramel reducing the normal iodine kick; **t24** recovers supremely for the early delivery with some stunning black peppers exploding all over the palate leaving behind a trail of peat smoke; the controlled sweetness to the barley is sublime; **f23** again there is a caramel edge to the finish, but this does not entirely prevent a fizzing finale; **b23** caramel apart, this is much truer to form than one or two or more recent bottlings, aided by the fresh, gristy sweetness and explosive spices. Wonderful! *55.7%*

Laphroaig Aged 15 Years db **(79) n20 t20 f19 b20.** A hugely disappointing, lacklustre dram that is oily and woefully short on complexity. Not what one comes to expect either from this distillery or age. *43%*

Laphroaig 18 Years Old db **(94) n24** multi-layered smokiness: there are soft, flightier, sweeter notes and a duller, earthier peat ingrained with salt and leather; **t23.5** perhaps it's the big leg-up from the rampant hickory, but the peat here offers a vague Fisherman's Friend cough sweet quality far more usually associated with Bowmore, except here it comes in a milder, Demerara-sweetened form with a few strands of liquorice helping that hickory to a gentler level; **f23** soft oils help keep some late, slightly juicy barley notes on track while the peat dances off with some spices to niggle the roof of the mouth and a few odd areas of the tongue; **b23.5** this is Laphroaig's replacement to the woefully inadequate and gutless 15-year-old. And talk about taking a giant step in the right direction. Absolutely brimming with character and panache, from the first molecules escaping the bottle as you pour to the very final ember dying on the middle of your tongue. *48%*

Laphroaig Aged 25 Years db **(94) n23** the clean - almost prim and proper - fruit appears to have somehow given a lift to the iodine character and accentuated it to maximum effect. The result is something much younger than the label demands and not immediately recognisable as Islay, either. But no less dangerously enticing... **t24** the grapes ensure the peat is met by a salivating palate; particularly impressive is the way the sweet peat slowly finds its footing and spreads beautifully; **f23.5** no shortage of cocoa: a kind of peaty fruit and nut chocolate bar... **b23.5** like the 27-y-o, an Islay which doesn't suffer for sherry involvement. Very different from a standard, bourbon barrel-aged Laphroaig with much of the usually complexity reined in, though its development is first class. This one's all about effect - and it works a treat! *40%*

Laphroaig Aged 25 Years Cask Strength 2011 Edition oloroso and American oak casks db **(96.5) n24** an immense nose with fruit and smoke dished out in equal measure: rarely have I located so much marmalade on a Laphroaig nose. An extraordinary degree of black pepper, too. The smoke, though intense, enjoys a wonderful degree of layering; **t24.5** the peat is, as is so often the case with this distillery, the first to show. But it does so with such a suave sophistication that one is tempted to bow at its majesty. The backdrop to this is a molassed cocoa depth. But it is the light oils bringing in the distinctive vanilla followed by the Jaffa cake orange...; **f24** lengthened by those most delicate oils, the vanilla still has a presence while the smoke forms circular patterns of almost feather-like substance; **b24** quite possibly the finest bottling of Laphroaig I have ever encountered. And over the last 35 years there have been a great many bottles... *48.6%*

Laphroaig Aged 30 Years db **(94) n24 t23 f23 b24.** The best Laphroaig of all time? Nope, because the 40-y-o is perhaps better still... just. However, Laphroaig of this subtlety and charm gives even the very finest Ardbeg a run for its money. A sheer treat that should be bottled at greater strength. *43%*

Laphroaig Aged 40 Years db **(94) n23 t24 f23 b24.** Mind-blowing. A malt that defies all logic and theory to be in this kind of shape at such age. The Jane Fonda of Islay whisky. *43%*

Laphroaig Càirdeas Ileach Edition ex bourbon Maker's Mark casks, bott 2011 db **(90) n23** a beautiful grist theme with spice and floral tones; **t22.5** lounges around the palate as though it owns the place. Just stretches out, brings a few brown sugar notes absent-mindedly into play and dozes off into a toffee-enriched land of nod; **f22** a few bitter oak notes, but the natural caramels and peaty spices tip toe around determined not to cause a scene; **b22.5** the name of the whisky means "friendship". And it is unlikely you will ever find a Laphraoig 101 any friendlier than this... *50.5%*

Laphroaig Càirdeas Origin quarter casks, bott 2012 db **(89) n24** the kind of nose that will send hardcore Islayphiles into near ecstasy: some real iodine clinging to the phenols and a sharp-toothed bite to the oak; something on the nose does worry me for later down the line...; **t22.5** gorgeous mouth-feel with muscovado sugars climbing aboard the smoky train. Barley is evident, as well as a few green apple notes, suggesting something youthful in there; the mid ground starts getting a little rough; **f20.5** irritatingly bitters out: what a shame; **b22** started like a train and hit the buffers for the finish. Still, early on it is quite superb. *51.2%. ncf.*

Laphroaig PX Cask bourbon, quarter and Pedro Ximenez casks db **(96) n23.5** a strangely coal dusty element to this: anthracite, to be precise. The grape effect is a little blunt and monosyllabic. But there is an extra sturdiness to the oak which injects the required complexity and helps identify the figs and physalis against the clearer red liquorice-bourbony background; **t24.5** the delivery is at first muddled, though the texture and shape of the body is never less than superb; the smoke bounces contentedly around the firmer oaks; even a touch of lightly smoked mocha here and there. A harder sugar edge from the PX tries to quieten matters a little too forcefully, but there is enough left in the peaty tank to allow spices to quash any chance of that; **f24** long, perhaps restricted by some uncompromisingly firm sugars, but there is both barley and smoke enough for a satisfying finale which includes some high quality cocoa; **b24** I get the feeling that this is a breathtaking success despite the inclusion of Pedro Ximenez casks. This ultra sweet wine is often paired with smoky malt, often with disastrous consequences. Here it has worked, but only because the PX has been controlled itself by absolutely outstanding oak. And the ability of the smoke to take on several roles and personas simultaneously. A quite beautiful whisky and unquestionably one of the great malts of the year...in spite of itself. *48%. Travel Retail exclusive.*

Laphroaig Quarter Cask db **(96)** n23 burning embers of peat in a crofter's fireplace; sweet intense malt and lovely, refreshing citrus as well; t24 mouthwatering, mouth-filling and mouth-astounding: the perfect weight of the smoke has no problems filling every crevice of the palate; builds towards a sensationally sweet maltiness at the middle; f24 really long, and dries appropriately with smoke and spice. Classic Laphroaig; b25 a great distillery back to its awesome, if a little sweet, self. Layer upon layer of sexed-up peatiness. The previous bottling just needed a little extra complexity on the nose for this to hit mega malt status. Now it has been achieved... 48%

Laphroaig Triple Wood ex-bourbon, quarter and European oak casks db **(86)** n21 t21.5 f21.5 b21. A pleasing and formidable dram. But one where the peat takes perhaps just too much of a back seat. Or, rather, is somewhat neutralised to the point of directional loss. The sugars, driven home by the heavy weight of oak, help give the whisky a gloss almost unrecognisable for this distillery. Even so, an attractive whisky in many ways. 48%. ncf.

⊸ **Dr Jekyll's Laphroaig Aged 7 Years** Pedro Ximenez cask, bott 12 **(78.5)** n21.5 t22 f17 b18. Loads of attitude and has much to say. A giveaway furriness on the tongue reveals an unwanted secret about the cask...and it sticks; the final notes are not at all helpful. 54.5%

A Fine Cigar's Pleasure Laphroaig Aged 10 Years refill hogshead **(88)** n21 minimal oak impact; something of an Arbroath Smoky to this; t22.5 much more lush on delivery with soft oils transporting the big sugars far and wide; the smoke is delicate and even; f22.5 at last a touch of vanilla; the smoke is delicate, almost aloof; b22 enjoyable even to a strict non-smoker like myself... 50%. nc ncf sc. Douglas Laing & Co. 210 bottles.

Archives Laphroaig 1998 13 Years Old Second Release bourbon hogshead, cask no. 700228, dist 14 May 98, bott Dec 11 **(95.5)** n24 the peat is worn much the way a Visa by Robert Piguet is carried by a lady for whom expense and prestige is a right rather than a privilege. Just so delicate and natural....and very high class...; t24 the delivery is every bit as chic and understated. The peat never for a moment tries to upstage the well sugared and beautifully clear barley; f23.5 a light injection of nutty nougat and vanilla adds a slightly drier and weightier feel to what remains a classy act; b24 Laphroaig at its most effortlessly sublime from the first sniff to the final, smoky pulse. 54.2%. nc ncf sc. Whiskybase B.V. 80 bottles.

Chieftain's Laphroaig Aged 14 Years hogsheads, dist May 97, bott Sep 11 **(85)** n21.5 t21 f21.5 b21. Smoky, but never quite relaxes. The dryness overpowers the sweetness just a little too astringently perhaps. 43.3%. nc ncf. Ian Macleod Distillers.

⊸ **Chieftain's Laphroaig Aged 14 Years** hogshead, cask no. 8601,8604, dist Sep 98, bott Feb 13 **(87.5)** n23 dry, compelling peat; a mix of salt and mint ups the complexity; t23 gorgeous delivery; medium weighted, medium smoked but high level complexity as the sweets citrus cuts through the oils; f19.5 bitters out annoyingly, though the spices offer redemption; b22 a very decent dram until the Allied bitter cask curse hits. 44.3%. nc ncf. 1518 bottles.

Director's Cut Laphroaig Aged 15 Years refill hogshead, cask no. 8255, dist Oct 96, bott Mar 12 **(89)** n22 dry phenols bolstered by citrus; t23 superb delivery with a sweet liquorice wave easily coping with the smoke; f22 silky vanilla and mocha; b22 the soft oil smears the sugars and phenols into all the right places... 57.2%. nc ncf sc. Douglas Laing & Co. 193 bottles.

Dun Bheagan Laphroaig 17 Years Old hogshead, dist May 94 **(82)** n20 t21 f20.5 b20.5. A familiar experience of excellent distillate let down by a cask which doesn't match the malt's quality. 49.2%. nc ncf sc. Ian Macleod Distillers.

⊸ **Dun Bheagan Laphroaig Aged 17 Years** hogshead, cask no. 5035,5037, dist May 94, bott 12 **(89)** n22 simplistic dry smoke; a little vanilla; t23 spiced sugars (Worcester source style) out muscle the half-hearted smoke; f22 inevitable big vanilla and cocoa finale; b22 pleasant, sweet but never abandons cruise control. 49.2%. nc ncf. 954 bottles.

First Cask Laphroaig 21 Years Old refill hogshead, cask no. 5936, dist 1990, bott 2012 **(91.5)** n22.5 predominantly dry with a coastal ash to the phenols; t23.5 big, resounding smoke though this time with a few huge waves of fudgy sugars to ram home the weight; f22.5 lightens slowly as the peat turns from smoke to spice; the sugars stay in top gear; b23 with old Allied casks, you actually breathe a sigh of relief when you get to the end and bitterness from a poor barrel doesn't spoil things. Big thumbs up here! 52.6%. nc ncf sc. 280 bottles.

Hart Brothers Laphroaig Aged 22 Years cask no. 3688, dist 26 Apr 90, bott 30 Apr 12 **(88)** n22 about as thick and oily as Laphroaig gets: there is almost a buttery quality to the smoke; t22.5 chewy from the off with that creamy texture coating the peat on thickly; lots of natural cream toffee insuring excellent sweetness; f21.5 relatively lazy and simplistic but the outline of some spice welcome; b22 pleasing and enjoyable without tearing up trees. Other than the ones it had been sitting in for the last 22 years, of course... 46%. sc.

James MacArthur Old Masters Laphroaig 13 Years Old cask no. 700234, dist 1998, bott Feb 12 **(83)** n21 t23 f19 b20. A beauty with a bit of a limp... The delivery of soft, dissolving sugars is mesmeric, especially as the smoke begins to take a grip. However the nose reveals an oaky tightness which predicts bitterness on the finish. 56.2%. nc ncf sc.

Kingsbury Single Cask Series Laphroaig Aged 12 Years Trois Riviers rum finish **(89)** n21.5 seriously needing balance: the smoke and sugars are barely on speaking terms; t23 but now they do! The sugars act as a friendly field while the smoke thickens. Intriguing; f22 now dry and the smoke takes a chewy turn; b22.5 a less than promising nose but the big sugars actually do a job. Genuinely complex. *46%. sc. Japan Import Systems.*

⁙ **Kingsbury Laphroaig Aged 13 Years** hogshead, cask no. 4145, dist 99 **(89.5)** n21.5 ultra dry peat embers; t23 a whiz-bang delivery, punching above its alcohol weight with the smoke unable to soften the landing and consequent tightness; some outstanding sugars form the mid ground; f23 gorgeous smoky mocha with plenty of Demerara stirred in; b22 nippy and, at times, with some serious bite. But acclimatise for a fabulous experience. *46%. nc ncf. Japan Import System. 314 bottles.*

⁙ **Kingsbury Laphroaig Aged 22 Years** hogshead, cask no. 2234, dist 90 **(91)** n21.5 surprisingly low key, almost dull, as butterscotch wafts around almost more than the smoke; t22.5 exceptionally malty. What little oak there is gives way to the deft sugars and natural toffee fudge; f24 light smoke but the complexity heightens as vague spices move in with the chocolate mint; b23 takes time to get going. But it is the lightness of touch which astounds. *53.7%. nc ncf. Japan Import System. 242 bottles.*

Liquid Sun Laphroaig 13 Years Old refill sherry cask, dist 1998, bott 2011 **(58)** n15 t17 f12 b14. For all its thick sugars and smoke, the sulphur dictates grimly. Technically dreadful, but there will be some in Germany who will set up a new religion to worship it... That's my taste buds wrecked for the day...and it's only 9.42am... *56.6%. sc. The Whisky Agency.*

⁙ **Malts Of Scotland Laphroaig 1996** sherry hogshead, cask no. MoS 12041, dist Jun 96, bott Sep 12 **(83.5)** n23 t21.5 f19 b20. The quality of the superb nose and early delivery cannot be maintained. *56.1%. nc ncf sc. 96 bottles.*

⁙ **Malts Of Scotland Laphroaig 1996** bourbon hogshead, cask no. MoS 13028, dist Jul 96, bott Apr 13 **(89.5)** n22.5 touch of menthol amid the smoke; t23 an avalanche of crispy muscovado: astonishingly sweet; f22 the sugars remain to the finish, though there is a curious cocoa and Twiglet finale; b22 a very curious, head-scratching bottling. Amazing delivery. *56.2%. nc ncf sc. 96 bottles.*

Malts Of Scotland Laphroaig 1998 bourbon hogshead, cask no. MoS11002, dist Mar 98, bott Jul 11 **(88.5)** n22 light and citrusy; the smoke offers both sweetness and weight; t22.5 bounding sugars ensure the smoke melts on the tongue; chocolate sponge cake fills the middle; a decent variety of spices; f22 dry, stubbornly spicy and ashy; b22 oak takes a back seat to some simplistic smoke. *56.4%. nc ncf sc. Malts Of Scotland for Aquavitae 2011.*

Malts Of Scotland Clubs Laphroaig 1998 sherry hogshead, cask no. MoS11001, dist Mar 98, bott Aug 11 **(70.5)** n18 t19 f16.5 b17. Pretty raw and off key. *53.4%. nc ncf sc.*

Malts Of Scotland Laphroaig 1998 bourbon hogshead, cask no. 5920, dist May 98, bott May 11 **(94)** n24 classic dry smoke; a mix of both peat and soot; t24 again dry from the off but just enough sugars to first soften the peaty impact, then a few waves of vanilla and walnut oil to add almost perfect weight and depth; f22.5 simplifies considerably and finishes in a surprisingly tame manner, though the salt hanging onto the peaty embers is very attractive; b23.5 the distillery in a nutshell. Well, in a bourbon hogshead... *53.4%. nc ncf sc.*

Malts Of Scotland Laphroaig 1998 bourbon hogshead, cask no. 5921, dist May 98, bott May 11 **(88)** n23.5 an Islayphile's dream: wonderful salt and spices attached to the dry peat... just paints a picture of that beautiful distillery in the glass; a little, well-hidden edge which makes me worry for the finish...; t22 plenty of golden syrup really makes the big peat an easy catch to land: chewy and juicy; f20.5 the smoke carries the full length, but a little bitterness arrives as promised by the nose; b22 overcomes the usual Allied cask problem to deliver a rousing and classic Laphroaig. *52.9%. nc ncf sc. Malts Of Scotland.*

Malts Of Scotland Laphroaig 1998 sherry hogshead, cask no. MoS11007, dist Mar 98, bott Sep 11 **(50)** n13 t14 f10 b13 Absolutely reeking of sulphur. A shocker. So this should double the price in Germany.... *52.5%. nc ncf sc. Malts Of Scotland.*

Malts Of Scotland Laphroaig 1998 bourbon hogshead, cask no. 5922, bott 2011 **(81)** n21.5 t22 f18 b19.5. A more lightly smoked version than the norm for this distillery. A shame, as it allows the bitterness of the poor cask to carry far too much weight. *59.8%. nc ncf sc.*

⁙ **Malts of Scotland Laphroaig 1998** sherry **(69)** n17 t19 f15 b18. All you'll ever need of the four Ss: sugar, sherry, smoke...and sulphur. *56.8%.*

⁙ **Malts Of Scotland Laphroaig 2000** sherry hogshead, cask no. MoS 13010, dist Feb 00, bott Feb 13 **(85.5)** n22 t22 f20 b21.5. One of the oiliest Laphroaigs I have encountered in years: like a dollop of cream sherry in every glass. A tell-tale fuzziness to the finish, but a fulsome, medium-sweet, toffee-ish chew. *57.8%. nc ncf sc. 96 bottles.*

Mo Ôr Collection Laphroaig 1990 20 Years Old first fill bourbon hogshead, cask no. 5941, dist 1990, bott 2010 **(89)** n22.5 dry peat soot lightly sprinkled with Demerara sugar; something of the farmyards about this; t22.5 those sugars on the nose arrive without hesitation: much sweeter and juicier than you could possibly expect; **f22** reverts back to a smoky sootiness again, though those sugars persist; **b22** a real sweetie; literally! 46%. nc ncf sc. Release No. 21.

Old Malt Cask Laphroaig Aged 11 Years refill hogshead, cask no. 8315, dist Feb 01, bott Apr 12 **(89)** **n22.5** trademark Laphroaig dry, salty smoke; **t23** early muscovado sugars make an excellent platform for the vanilla and peat to make a complex middle; **f21.5** bitters out slightly; **b22** does what it says on the tin. 50%. nc ncf sc. Douglas Laing & Co. 289 bottles.

Old Malt Cask Laphroaig Aged 12 Years refill hogshead, cask no. 7806, dist Aug 99, bott Oct 11 **(87.5)** **n22** a touch Fisherman's Friend mixes in with the mint and sugars; **t22.5** deft smoke intertwines with muscovado sugars; **f21** a long fade of vanilla and peat; less dries than shrivels as its bulk is lost unevenly; **b22** warts and all Laphroaig which employs enough old tricks to keep anyone entertained. 50%. nc ncf sc. Douglas Laing & Co. 188 bottles.

⁙ **Old Malt Cask Laphroaig Aged 12 Years** refill hogshead, cask no. 8677, dist Jun 2000, bott Aug 12 **(88)** **n22** the lazy smoke wipes its feet at the door of the gristy, sweet barley; **t22** still surprisingly low key smoke. The peat is there, but is happy to cling to the even sugars without making a great impact; **f22** drier and dustier the smoke now has a more noticeable presence; **b22** lower than the usual 35ppm phenols, this is light, sugar dependent and an easy, clean and non-taxing ride all the way. 50%. nc ncf sc. Douglas Laing & Co. 387 bottles.

⁙ **Old Malt Cask Laphroaig Aged 14 Years** refill hogshead, cask no. 9227, dist Oct 98, bott Dec 12 **(86.5)** **n21.5 t22 f21.5 b21.5.** Not the most complex Laphroaig you'll encounter. But if you are a Peat Freak there are enough phenols here to keep you happy for an hour or two. 50%. nc ncf sc. Douglas Laing & Co. 311 bottles.

⁙ **Old Malt Cask Laphroaig Aged 14 Years** refill hogshead, cask no. 9222, dist Oct 98, bott Oct 12 **(89.5)** **n22** some charming lavender growing from the moss; **t23** not just big, vaguely cough sweetish peat, but a really serious spicy back up from the start; **f22** smoked butterscotch tart; **b22.5** just works on so many levels better than its close relation, cask 9227: great example of how oak makes all the difference. 50%. sc. Douglas Laing & Co. 322 bottles.

Old Malt Cask Laphroaig Aged 15 Years refill hogshead, cask no. 7966, dist Oct 96, bott Dec 11 **(95.5)** **n24** Barratt's chocolate liquorice meets gristy smoke: a real complex number where a subtle dexterity is the key despite the obvious enormity; **t24.5** textbook delivery of soft oils and mixed sugars, including maple syrup. The smoke offers a dual role of offering caressing weight and a punchy spiciness; the middle ground is a fabulous mix of praline, vanilla and honeydew melon.....wow!!; **f23** long with the cocoa playing out with the multi-layered smoke; **b24** pure class. 50%. nc ncf sc. Douglas Laing & Co. 321 bottles.

⁙ **Old Malt Cask Laphroaig Aged 16 Years** refill hogshead, cask no. 9736, dist Oct 96, bott May 13 **(93)** **n23.5** a few violets and salty crushed green olives amid the usual smoke; **t23.5** well behaved peat which shows just enough muscle you hope for from a Laphroaig but no more. German coffee biscuit, and half-hearted hint of spice; outstandingly well-balanced oils; **f23** cinders and molasses; long and chewy all the way with late hickory; **b23** these peaty ashes don't come with a straighter bat than this, or are played with such effortless grace. What a difference a high quality piece of oak can make.... 50%. nc ncf sc. 168 bottles.

Old Malt Cask Laphroaig Aged 18 Years refill hogshead, cask no. 7992, dist Sep 93, bott Dec 11 **(84.5)** **n21.5 t22 f20 b21.** Unusually sweet for a Laphroaig yet struggles against a very tight cask determined to add a bitter edge. 50%. nc ncf sc. 271 bottles.

Premier Barrel Laphroaig Aged 11 Years **(89)** **n22** a real spike to the smoke despite some oils trying to add a sugary weight; **t23.5** zips around the palate with youthful abandon. Little oak present to prevent the barley, smoke and sugars crash into the taste buds like joyriders wrapping themselves into lamp-posts and doing a runner; **f22** relatively short, but full of zesty smoke; **b22** when they say "premier barrel" I think they mean here one that is least likely to alter the course of the spirit. Youthful and delicious! 46%. nc ncf sc. 328 bottles.

Provenance Laphroaig Over 10 Years refill hogshead, cask no. 7566, dist Winter 2001, bott Summer 2011 **(91)** **n23.5** dry, sooty smoke over a vanilla base; **t22.5** the sugars appear under protest; the smoke bathes the taste buds with subtlety; **f22.5** the lack of oils here is reflected by the medium length finish. The dry, dusty smoke never lets up; **b22.5** almost a blueprint for a classic Laphroaig 10-y-o of the very driest variety...!! 46%. nc ncf sc.

Provenance Laphroaig Over 10 Years refill hogshead, cask no. 7841, dist Winter 2001, bott Autumn 2011 **(81.5)** **n20 t22 f19 b20.5.** The miserly cask does little to enhance the crusty peat. Worth buying alongside cask 7566 to show just what oak can do in just ten years to a malt as distinctive as Laphroaig. 46%. nc ncf sc. Douglas Laing & Co.

⁙ **Provenance Laphroaig Over 12 Years** bourbon hogshead, cask no. 475 **(88)** **n22.5** spot on aroma with just the right saltiness to give the peat an extra tweak; **t22** the odd wave of muscovado sugars softens the smoky impact; early vanilla through the middle; **f21.5** a tad bitter but compensated by spices; **b22** a steady-as-she-goes bottling; 46%.

⁙ **Riegger's Selection Laphroaig 2000** bourbon-sherry cask, cask no. 4121, dist 2000, bott 2013 **(90.5)** **n23** like getting a custard pie in the face: except this is dry, ashy peat and even drier sherry...splat! **t23** any drier on the nose and you'd be expecting olives on delivery. But some sugars make it through the spiced peat ash. The grape, in the form of fried raisin, makes it through to the mid ground. A few razor blades are thrown in; **f21.5** drier than a Greek table wine poured out for mutton, perhaps because a little furriness is present; limited muscovado and grape is soon over-run; **b23** it is pretty well known that I'm not the greatest fan of big peat and sherry together. And this is rougher than three day old stubble. But you know what? This works...and is a magnificent journey - a bit like driving a Land Rover over some rocky terrain. *55.2%. ncf sc. Viktor-Riegger GmbH.*

Scotch Malt Whisky Society Cask 29.106 Aged 13 Years refill hogshead, cask no. 700066, dist 1998 **(95.5) n23.5** a sparkling trade off between light yet lively peat and wonderful citrus; **t24** gloriously weighted; the barley and delicate fruits offer a surprising lightness while the peats act as the expected anchor; **f24** long with a dry, ashy finale in perfect harmony to the juicy, sugar-studded barley; a slight, late, bitterness to the oak is the only fly in the ointment; **b24** for what has been a disappointing year for independent bottlings of Laphroaig, this classic bottling has been very badly needed. *57.3%. sc. Scotch Malt Whisky Society.*

Scotch Malt Whisky Society Cask 29.109 Aged 20 Years refill butt, cask no. 10837, dist 1990 **(91.5) n23** No off-notes. Very few other notes than grape....and peat trying to get a word in edgewise; **t23** silky grape on delivery...followed by less silky grape. The peat is found in a chocolate fudge middle; **f22.5** lots more chocolate fudge. With spiced raisins....; **b23** some may regard this as their whisky of the year, so enormous is the sherry input. Yet, for me, balance has been compromised, though there is no denying that this is great fun. *59.2%. sc.*

Scotch Malt Whisky Society Cask 29.110 Aged 10 Years refill hogshead, cask no. 398, dist 2001 **(86.5) n22 t22 f21 b21.5.** A very tight cask where the salt squeezes the living daylights out of all else. Big, eye-watering flavours, uncompromising peat but, eschewing restraint, simply too much of a good thing. *57.2%. sc. Scotch Malt Whisky Society.*

Scotch Malt Whisky Society Cask 29.111 Aged 10 Years refill hogshead, cask no. 400, dist 2001 **(86) n21.5 t22 f21 b21.5.** As soft and soothing a malt as cask 29.110 is a vixen. But the oak is not quite up to scratch, so the bitter lines apparent cannot be outmanoeuvred by the malty talent on show. The softness of delivery is a treat, though. *57.3%. sc.*

⠴⠶ **Scotch Malt Whisky Society Cask 29.125 Aged 17 Years** refill barrel, dist 95 **(89) n21.5** not a positive contribution from the oak, but the spirit is crisp and impressive; **t23** excellent oils help meld Palma Violets with Fisherman's friend and muscovado sugar; **f22** smoked butterscotch tart; **b22.5** no shortage of sugars outflanking the peat. *60.6%. nc ncf sc. 205 bottles.*

⠴⠶ **Scotch Malt Whisky Society Cask 29.128 Aged 21 Years** refill butt, dist 12 Oct 90 **(79) n20 t20 f19 b20.** A big brown sugar bonanza which, with a clean cask, would have been a sherried belter of the very top order. *58.8%. nc ncf sc. 601 bottles.*

⠴⠶ **Scotch Malt Whisky Society Cask 29.136 Aged 17 Years** refill barrel, dist 4 Apr 95 **(86) n22.5 t22 f20.5 b21.** Disappointingly bitter cask influence undermines the sweet charms of the smoke and spice. *59.2%. nc cf sc. 128 bottles.*

Single Cask Collection Laphroaig Aged 13 Years bourbon hogshead, cask no. 1998 **(92.5) n23** a superb combination of sweet gristy barley and citrus-tinted smoke. Even a hint of gooseberry there, too; **t23** salivating and succulent, the barley is oozing with beautifully peated juice; **f23.5** the vanillas arrive to combine with the smoke for a drier finale; **b23** a cracking cask full of lusty intent but showing a great deal of craft, too. *60.8%. sc.*

⠴⠶ **Wemyss 1998 Single Islay Laphroaig "Beach Bonfires"** hogshead, bott 2012 **(92.5) n23** beautiful mix of dry peat and sweeter barley and peach notes; **t23** gorgeously juicy, again, like the nose having a distinctive barley edge to this with the smoke playing second fiddle, if slightly loudly; **f23** the vanilla and late honey is so clear, only a top quality cask can be at work here. The smoke continues to drink lazily and, finally, some spices can be heard; **b23.5** this great distillery has been cursed a little by having technically outstanding spirit maturing in indifferent wood. This beauty, however, is not so constrained. *46%. sc. 357 bottles.*

The Whisky Agency Laphroaig 21 Years Old bourbon cask, dist 1990, bott 2011 **(84.5) n22 t22.5 f19 b21.** A curious malt: enjoyable and sweet early on but little helped by at times appearing weirdly thin with a touch of smoky acetate. *56.8%. sc. The Whisky Agency.*

Whisky Antique Laphroaig 21 Years Old Special Bottling dist 1990, bott 2011 **(91.5) n22** has much to say, yet does so in a confined space where any amount of peat and fruit are crushed together; **t23** the delivery is equally condensed and it is not until the fourth or fifth layer that those gargantuan notes begin to find breathing space; most impressive is the juicy fruit; **f23.5** dries with all kinds of coal and peat dust clogging the palate; **b23** hardly one for the squeamish. Light Speyside lovers beware! *57.7%. sc. Silver Seal Whisky Company.*

⠴⠶ **The Whisky Cask Laphroaig Aged 21 Years** bourbon cask, dist 1990, bott 2011 **(86.5) n21.5 t22 f21.5 b21.5.** One of the more sugar-saturated versions of Laphroaig. It needs to be, with the typical Allied cask bitterness coming through long before the death. But impossible not to love those heavily smoked, chocolatey brown and black Liquorice Allsorts... *52.5%. sc.*

LINKWOOD

Speyside, 1820. Diageo. Working.

Linkwood 12 Years Old db **(94.5)** n23.5 gorgeous malt absolutely bursting at the seems with barley-rich vitality; citrus and anthracite abound; t24 a quite stunning delivery with some of the clearest, cleanest, most crystalline malt on the market. The sugars are angular and decidedly Demerara; f23 a long play out of sharp barley which refuses to be embattled by the oaky vanillas; light spices compliment the persistent sugars; b24 possibly the most improved distillery bottling in recent times. Having gone through a period of dreadful casks, it appears to have come through to the other side very much on top and close to how some of us remember it a quarter of a century ago. Sublime malt: one of the most glittering gems in the Diageo crown. *43%*

Linkwood 26 Year Old port finish dist 1981, bott 2008 db **(85)** n20 t24 f20.5 b20.5. Can't say that either nose or finish do it for me. But the delivery is brilliant: the enormity and luxurious sweetness of the grape leaves you simply purring and rolling your eyes in delight. *56.9%*

Linkwood 26 Year Old rum finish, dist 1981, bott 2008 db **(89.5)** n23.5 t23.5 f21 b21.5. A real touch of the rum toffee raisin candy to this one. *56.5%*

Linkwood 26 Year Old sweet red wine, dist 1981, bott 2008 db **(89)** n22.5 t23 f21 b22. Juicy, spicy: doesn't stint on complexity. *56.5%*

Linkwood 1974 Rare Malt db **(79)** n20 t21 f19 b19. Wobbles about the palate in search of a story and balance. Finds neither but some of the early moments, though warming, offer very decent malt. The best bit follows a couple of seconds after – and lasts as long. *55%*

Boisdale Linkwood 1991 cask no. 10344, bott 2012 **(88)** n22 ginger and clove has been squeezed into a mildly rummy aroma, broadcasting the good age; t21.5 the nose suggests the potential for a spiced up delivery and it doesn't disappoint. The oak really does bite deep, but soon soothing thick barley is on hand; f22.5 a far more comfortable finish with the excesses now dampened down and extra sugars in for balance; b22 a malt aged as far as it can comfortably go. *46%. nc ncf sc. Berry Bros & Rudd.*

⁖ **The Coopers Choice Linkwood 1995 15 Years Old** hogshead, cask no. 9140, dist 95, bott 10 **(88)** n22 barley sugar candy with a custardy fringe; t22 juicy clean salivating barley all the way with some delicate spice pep; f22 silky, but it's the barley still dominating; b22 anyone searching for a typical Speyside clean "grassy" style can end their search here. *46%. nc ncf sc. The Vintage Malt Whisky Co Ltd. 360 bottles.*

⁖ **Duncan Taylor Octave Linkwood 22 Years Old** cask no. 764147, dist 89 **(88)** n22.5 a serious stewed apple kick to this one; t21.5 busy delivery but struggles to find early harmony. Relaxes as the spices and barley entwine; f22 the spice continues, now with an oaky accent; b22 a blender would enjoy this in a 21-year-old creation for the confident barley and controlled spice. *48.9%. sc. Duncan Taylor & Co.*

Duncan Taylor Rare Auld Linkwood 20 Years Old cask no. 8323, dist 1990 **(90)** n24 fabulous and something bordering original! A real mix of lively fruit, chopped aubergine and salted celery; some black peppers and cocoa-vanilla in there, too...; t23.5 beautifully weighted delivery, then a surprising degree of clean, mouth-watering barley; the sugars early on show a textbook degree of poise; f20 fades severely as the vanilla becomes just a little too dominant and tart; b22.5 doesn't quite live up to the promise on the nose and delivery, though remains a hugely enjoyable dram, never short of surprises. *48.3%. sc. Duncan Taylor & Co.*

Gordon & MacPhail Private Collection Linkwood 1991 Cote Rotie finish **(72)** n19 t18 f18 b17. Certainly fruity. But just too many faults from the cask. *45%. Gordon & MacPhail.*

Gordon & MacPhail Rare Vintage Linkwood 1973 (87) n23 caramelised biscuit meets Garibaldi; there are some serious bourbon style kumquat notes amid the big oak kick; t22 enough barley sugars and vague chocolate notes are dredged up to make for a pleasantly chewy experience; f20.5 dries out until your eyes water; b21.5 outrageous, as it is simply over the hill. Or should be. But it gathers enough charisma from somewhere to make for an intriguing battle between the malty remnants and the massive oak. *43%. Gordon & MacPhail.*

Hart Brothers Linkwood Aged 14 Years cask no. 4144, dist 17 Apr 97, bott 15 Apr 12 **(87)** n21.5 thin, with everything pointing to grassy, clean barley; t22 mouth-watering with the barley dominating all aspects of delivery and follow through; f22 a spiced vanilla buzz, but the malt retains control; b21.5 very simple whisky. But attractive all the same. *46%. sc.*

Liquid Sun Linkwood 27 Years Old bourbon cask, dist 1984, bott 2011 **(91.5)** n22.5 gristy, for all its years, and lightly dappled with smoke; t23 beautifully weighted, fabulously juicy and the smoke leads into a complex array of spices; f23 long, thanks to the smoke, but the cocoa confirms the antiquity; b23 this has been a vintage year for decent Linkwood releases and this smoky offering is by no means cowed by its company. *53.2%. sc.*

Malts Of Scotland Linkwood Peated 1987 bourbon hogshead, cask no. MoS11008, dist 1987, bott 2011 **(91)** n22.5 Arbroath Smokies and diced apple; t23 smoky and spiced from the off, but nothing too heavy and the sugars stay until the midway point. Certainly the malt is tangible until the cocoa arrives; **f22.5** dries as the oak takes hold. But the Smokies still have something to say; **b23** an attractive malt unusual for its playful smokiness. *51.4%. nc ncf sc.*

Mo Òr Collection Linkwood 1983 27 Years Old first fill bourbon hogshead, cask no. 5714, dist 17 Nov 83, bott 14 Jan 11 **(92) n22.5** anyone who used to invest in a Wagon Wheel biscuit from their school tuck shop will have memories flooding back from the chocolate and spice combo here: this one is of the jammy variety; **t24** one of the great deliveries of the year: the sweetness accompanying the lightly honeyed barley acts only as the perfect foil for the light peppers and crisp vanilla which descends; the lightest of sheens suggests a sugary glaze to the barley; **f22** pans out with delicate vanillas and almost indelicate butterscotch; **b23.5** clean, bold, purposeful and beautifully weighted, this does slightly more than can be expected of it. *46%. nc ncf sc. Release No. 29. The Whisky Talker. 352 bottles.*

Old Malt Cask Linkwood Aged 21 Years refill butt, cask no. 7102, dist May 90, bott Mar 12 **(64) n16 t18 f14 b16.** Riddled with you-know-what... *50%. nc ncf sc. 450 bottles.*

⊙ **Old Malt Cask Linkwood Aged 21 Years** refill hogshead, cask no. 9218, dist Sep 91, bott Oct 12 **(88.5) n21.5** moist fig roll and barley; **t22** big barley from first mouthful to the thickening middle; usual light spices; **f22.5** some excellent cocoa coats the barley; **b22.5** standard Linkwood without frills, though with the odd spicy thrill. *50%. sc. 252 bottles.*

Provenance Linkwood Over 12 Years bourbon barrel, cask no. 8242, dist Summer 1999, bott Spring 2012 **(88) n21.5** thin barley bolstered with cooked apple; **t22.5** mega-salivating barley with the sugars offering just the right degree of crispness; **f22** light vanilla and the sugars persist; **b22** clean, attractive and simplistic. *46%. nc ncf sc.*

⊙ **Provenance Linkwood Over 15 Years** refill hogshead, cask no. 9661, dist Summer 97, bott Spring 13 **(84) n22 t21 f20 b21.** Built as a blending malt and refuses to stray from the simple barley-intense script. The heat on the finish suggests the stills were at one stage a little too over excited. *46%. nc ncf. Douglas Laing & Co.*

Scotch Malt Whisky Society Cask 39.83 Aged 28 Years refill hogshead, cask no. 5412, dist 1982 **(85.5) n21 t21.5 f21.5 b21.5.** Looking for a docile malt? Back off! Vague fish paste to the aroma but every other nuance clings to something with a barley theme. *53.9%. sc.*

Scotch Malt Whisky Society Cask 39.84 Aged 21 Years refill hogshead, cask no. 8314, dist 1990 **(88.5) n23** unusual to find an exotic fruit touch to a malt which has reached only its early 20s. But it is there, as is a light liquorice bourbon trait and a touch of hickory; **t22** for all the age on the nose, initially a salivating delivery with a malty theme. It is not long before the oak takes command, however; **f21.5** dry and overworked oak; **b22** have you ever seen a grey and balding 21-year-old bloke...? *48%. sc. Scotch Malt Whisky Society.*

⊙ **Scotch Malt Whisky Society Cask 39.88 Aged 22 Years** refill hogshead, dist 29 Oct 90 **(84.5) n22 t22 f19.5 b21.** After the initial delivery, the oak takes too firm a grasp. But for a few brief moments there is a lively fruit and fudge entrance which borders on burnt raisin. *47.8%. nc ncf sc. 231 bottles.*

Scott's Selection Linkwood 1991 bott 2011 **(87.5) n21.5** the creaky oak out performs the malt; **t22** a sharp delivery of petulant oak slowly cut down to size by the juicy barley; well spiced throughout; **f22** from the vanilla and butterscotch school with a late malty flourish; **b22** takes a while to find its feet but is pretty well balanced when it does. *59.3%. Speyside Distillers.*

Single Cask Collection Linkwood 27 Years Old bourbon hogshead, dist 1984 **(92.5) n22.5** a tight nose flaked with oak and linseed. Some red liquorice and cinnamon-apple; **t23.5** big oils on delivery help the maple syrup cover a wider area but are reduced in effect as the spices begin to up the complexity, again cinnamon having an input; **f23** long, with the vanillas showing cleanly and keenly; **b23.5** not just a bourbon hogshead. But gives all the indications of a first-fill because some real Kentucky character leaks into this one, yes-sir-ee! A very decent spirit has spent 27 years in a top cask. *57%. sc. Single Cask Collection.*

The Warehouse Collection Linkwood Aged 11 Years bourbon barrel, dist May 97, bott Jun 08 **(89) n22.5** superb citrus and salt nose; the clean barley links with tingling peppers to provide a complex punch; **t22.5** salivating and crisp, the barley goes steady on the sugars and provide enough muscovado to balance the grapefruit sharpness; **f22** softens towards vanilla and butterscotch with a twinge of spice, too; **b22** apparently still quite a few bottles of this are still around. They shouldn't be for much longer. *46%. sc. Whisky Warehouse No. 8. 271 bottles.*

The Warehouse Collection Linkwood Aged 28 Years bourbon hogshead, cask no. 1620, dist 15 Mar 84, bott 8 Aug 12 **(95) n24.5** Bourbon hoggy it may be, but the prevailing kumquat is the key. Wonderfully coastal, with a sea-breeze saltiness cleansing both the barley and light, dry coconut-oak. Some serious floral note and did I mention the fruit?; **t24** the nose is a hard act to follow, but the fabulous combo of mega-sweetened puckering oak gives it a pretty good shot. The spices in the middle ground are as complex and busy as you'll find with any Speysider this year; **f22.5** dips slightly as the more astringent aspects of the oak are briefly exposed. But still a delicious meal; **b24** rare to start a new tasting day with a treat such as this. Beautiful whisky. *56.7%. sc. Whisky Warehouse No. 8. 171 bottles.*

⚜ **Wemyss 1991 Single Speyside "Apple Pastry"** hogshead, dist 91, bott 13 (83.5) n22 t21.5 f19.5 b20.5. Starts off as boiled pears under a blanket of custard but the aggressive, bitter oak turns this more into a pear-drop...I coughed!! A prickly pear, indeed. 46%. sc. 320 bottles.

⚜ **Wemyss Linkwood 2000 Single Speyside "Summer Orchard"** butt (84.5) n20 t21.5 f22 b21. Less Summer Orchard and maybe more Early Spring: underdeveloped and very green. Little to report beyond the massive barley. 46%. sc. 762 bottles.

Wemyss 2000 Single Speyside "Vanilla Zest" butt, bott 2011 (88.5) n21 sherbet lemon and zest; very clean and a little new makey...) t23 delivers exactly as expected; clean and fresh with a barley juiciness and zesty bite; f22 a slow unveiling of vanilla but remains clean and true; b22.5 the word "zest" had formed in my mind when nosing even before I knew the full name of the brand! Does what it says on the tin... 46%. sc. 792 bottles.

LITTLEMILL
Lowland, 1772. Loch Lomond Distillers. Demolished.

Littlemill Aged 8 Years db (84) n20 t22 f21 b21. Aged 8 Years, claims the neck of the dumpy bottle, which shows a drawing of a distillery that no longer exists, as it has done for the last quarter of a century. Well, double that and you'll be a lot closer to the real age of this deliciously sweet, chewy and increasingly spicy chap. And it is about as far removed from the original 8-y-o fire-water it once was as is imaginable. 40%.

⚜ **Littlemill Aged 21 Years** bourbon cask, bott Dec 12 db (88) n21.5 hard not to miss the nail varnish element to this, but now softened enough to act as a sharpening tool for the barley; t22 simple, salivating barley which warms as expected....; f22 the usual raging fire is now a pleasant glow; b22.5 Littlemill again enjoying an Indian Summer of a dram...after many years of grim rain. 46%. nc ncf. Glen Catrine Bonded Warehouse Ltd.

Littlemill 1964 db (82) n21 t20 f21 b20. A soft-natured, bourbony chap that shows little of the manic tendencies that made this one of Scotland's most-feared malts. Talk about mellowing with age... 40%

⚜ **Littlemill 1990 Vintage Aged 22 Years** bott 2013 db (91) n23 despite a light flame licking at the nose there is enough honey and sugar on the barley to persuade you to dive in head first; t23 peppered barley attacks the taste buds with gusto, leaving behind a trail of tannins and honey; f22.5 butterscotch and watered-down napalm in equal measures; b22.5 a very tasty bit of rough. 50.6%. nc ncf. Glen Contrine Bonded Warehouse Ltd.

Archives Littlemill 1988 23 Years Old Third Release cask no. 08/1077, dist 7 Nov 88, bott May 12 (75.5) n18.5 t20 f18 b19. Much closer in style to a not particularly great slivovitz than a malt. 49.3%. nc ncf sc. Whiskybase B.V. 48 bottles.

Archives Littlemill 1989 22 Years Old Inaugural Release cask no. RTN-11-238, dist May 89, bott Jul 11 (80) n20 t21 f19 b20. Begins ungracefully and moves into a much maltier theme later on before falling away again. 48.3%. nc ncf sc. Whiskybase B.V. 120 bottles.

⚜ **Berry's Own Selection Littlemill 1992** cask no. 10, bott 2013 (86) n21.5 t23 f20 b21.5. Plenty of synthetic raspberry cream a la Swiss role. Bit of a malty belter but the original paint stripper burn is still there. Bless it! 54.9%. nc ncf sc.

⚜ **The Coopers Choice Littlemill 1985 25 Years Old** refill butt, cask no. 105, dist 1985, bott 2011 (75) n19 t19 f18 b19. Big barley and very drinkable. But the clarity of the malt also helps accentuate the whisky's technical problems. 46%. nc ncf sc. The Vintage Malt Whisky Co Ltd. 480 bottles.

⚜ **The Coopers Choice Littlemill 1985 26 Years Old** hogshead, cask no. 99, dist 85, bott 11 (87.5) n22.5 fudge...with salt; t22.5 big barley and tangerine delivery...with fudge; f20.5 bittering oak...and fudge; b22 if you find a fudge with more fudge characteristics than this, I'll buy you a box of the finest fudge I can find. And I won't fudge the issue...53%. nc ncf sc. The Vintage Malt Whisky Co Ltd. 270 bottles.

First Cask Littlemill 20 Years Old bourbon barrel, cask no. 726, dist 7 Mar 90, bott 14 Oct 10 (87) n20.5 sharp, a touch of tobacco, by no means in tune; but saved by a vague nutty-nougat theme not uncommon in Kentucky; t23 salivating barley. Followed by...more barley! Gosh this is one malty beast...; f21.5 the nip and bite of a slightly hot spirit, and some unwelcome oaky tang, too. But the intense malt saves the day; b22 you get a lot of barley to each pour... 56.2%. nc ncf sc. Whisky Import Nederland. 225 bottles.

Hart Brothers Littlemill Aged 20 Years cask no. 19, dist 27 Feb 92, bott Mar 12 (88.5) n23.5 peppery and attractively floral – in a dank forest kind of a way; some bourbon theme, too; t22 thin, sweet barley; watered down barley sugar; f21.5 papery and increasingly warming; b21.5 the palate makes no attempt to hide that slightly gluey side to its personality but a bit of an entertainer, especially on the characterful nose. 46%. sc.

⚜ **Liquid Library Littlemill 1992** ex-bourbon hogshead, bott 12 (84) n21 t22 f20 b21. A few apples in the offing. As well as the standard bug malt kick. But the flames lick just a little too hard on the palate. 51.6%

Malts Of Scotland Littlemill 1989 sherry butt, cask no. 2511, dist 28 Mar 89, bott May 11 **(84) n20 t22 f20.5 b21.5**. Littlemill...in a late 1980s sherry butt! That is like playing Russian Roulette with five loaded chambers.... Yet, this one is a decent cask with no sulphur. Even so, the grape has its work cut out to douse the flames of this napalm malt. Hot doesn't quite do it justice. Though this is a mere vindaloo of a whisky: without the sherry one suspects this would have been a Littlemill Phall! 52.8%. nc ncf sc. Malts Of Scotland.

Old Malt Cask Littlemill Aged 20 Years refill hogshead, cask no. 7099, dist Nov 91, bott Nov 11 **(88) n22** you know those fruit-scented soap bars...; **t22.5** lush and surprisingly sweet on entry. Then a short burst of the flame thrower before all kinds of Maltese notes beckon; **f21.5** those strange, slightly soapy off notes on the nose re-appear; **b22** a distillery that never fails to amaze – one way or another. Overly perfumed. As fiery as a five-foot nothing flamed-haired Scottish midfielder. 50%. nc ncf sc. 121 bottles.

-:⊱- **Old Malt Cask Littlemill Aged 21 Years** refill hogshead, cask no. 9443, dist Nov 91, bott Feb 13 **(84.5) n21 t21 f21.5 b21.** Something of a minor juicy treat. Has much more the feel of east European slivovitz than a single malt. 50%. sc. Douglas Laing & Co. 262 bottles.

-:⊱- **Old Malt Cask Littlemill Aged 21 Years** refill hogshead, dist Nov 91, bott May 13 **(87.5) n22.5** a little bit of glue here, still. But completely forgiven when the attractive strains of carrot cake doused in maple syrup massage the nose buds; **t22.5** two toned with both a chunky barley and vanilla duet and the much thinner layers of the old paint stripper still just about visible. The duet wins...; **f21** now seriously thins out, but enough glycerine and vanilla to still work; **b21.5** despite its obvious charms and sophistication of middle age, the tattoos and scars of a wild childhood are still clearly visible. 50%. nc ncf sc. 315 bottles.

Riegger's Selection Littlemill 1990 first fill sherry butt, cask no. 2, dist 20 Dec 90, bott 24 Nov 10 **(95) n24** a truly faultless sherry butt of the very highest order. Not just from the copious dates and walnut richness but because it allows the barley to make a fabulously malty contribution; **t24** silky beyond words. The spices arrive early but in outstanding shape allowing as much grape and malt as required to fill the middle, complex ground. Softly nutty and chewy, we now head in Melton Hunt Cake direction with a little lardy cake on the side; **f23** much vanilla and barley, but a hint of burnt raisin lurks. The oils work deftly and to excellent effect; **f24** if 25 years ago you had told me I would one day taste a Littlemill as good as this, I would have laughed in your face... 53.6%. nc ncf sc. Viktor-Riegger GmbH. 198 bottles.

-:⊱- **Riegger's Selection Littlemill 1992** bourbon cask, dist 27 Feb 92, bott 2 Nov 12 **(94.5) n23.5** talk about moist fruitcake: all kinds of burnt raisin and molasses at work. Only the remnants of an initially indifferent spirit drops this a point; **t24** what a delivery! Again that little technical blip, pulsing like the distant beat of an extinct star, is evident. But so too is the controlled enormity of a fabulous sherry butt which allows the grape and spice to intermingle with the barley on equal terms; naturally, the molassed sugars play an important part; even a degree of Demerara rum to this; **f23** a mix of sherry trifle and butterscotch; the vanilla has both the tang of the old spirit; **b24** shows you what's possible with a 100% unblemished, clean-as-a-whistle, entirely sulphur-free sherry butt. These guys do this whisky so magnificently well!! Some in the industry – and a few commentators – would do well to find a bottle of this – and learn. 54.5%. nc ncf. Viktor-Riegger GmbH. 629 bottles.

Scotch Malt Whisky Society Cask 97.21 Aged 21 Years first fill barrel, cask no. 732, dist 1990 **(94.5) n23** malt breakfast cereal complete with creamy milk...and a sprinkling of muscovado sugar; a curious – and decidedly attractive – blend of Demerara rum and bourbon whiskey; **t24** you'd expect something Kentuckian maybe but, no, it's intense barley first out of the traps. And then bourbon honeycomb catches up and overtakes; chocolate is not far behind...; **f23.5** long, with a wonderful trailing of diverse sugars, not least coconut syrup; lots of mocha with a dab of vanilla; **b24** what a shame this distillery is so much better dead than when alive...this is Littlemill at its zenith. 54.7%. sc. Scotch Malt Whisky Society.

Scott's Selection Littlemill 1992 bott 2012 **(90) n22** some of the distillery's traditional nip and aggression is still at large, though now works well with so much vanilla to hand; **t22** silky mouth-feel while the barley appears to have the teeth of a crocodile...; **f23** settles down for a friendlier, more sugar-coated finale....topped off with bang on spice; **b23** the recent bottlings of Littlemill have been remarkable for their consistency. And they don't get any more consistent than this...An adorable rogue. 55.6%. Speyside Distillers.

Sestante Collection Littlemill 19 Years Old dist 1990 **(85) n20 t22.5 f21 b21.5**. A fiery little number where the barley pierces the taste buds like an exocet. The resulting explosion, though, is sugar-rich and by no means unpleasant. 57%. sc. Silver Seal Whisky Company.

-:⊱- **Single Cask Collection Littlemill 21 Years Old** bourbon hogshead, cask no. 20, dist 27 Feb 92, bott 28 Feb 13 **(95) n23** a belter of a bourbon influence; a pinch of drying allspice and cloves accentuate the oak without taking it past a point of no return; some stunning marmalade as the whisky warms; **t24** a volley of sugars on delivery, some containing barley, but most dark and seasoned; the spices towards the middle are worth awards on their own;

f23.5 a slow injection of ulmo and manuka honey underlines the butterscotch and spice; the weight and oil involvement is just about perfect; **b24.5** a tamed bruiser which has many similarities to the Scott's 1992 bottling of last year, though this boasts the odd extra gear. World class malt from a failed distillery. *55.6%. nc ncf sc. 318 bottles.*

Single Malts Of Scotland Littlemill 1989 refill sherry cask **(89) n22** just the first nosing of this tells you that life is about to get interesting: some controlled nip and bite with some many things wrong it almost seems right; **t22** fruity and fluting delivery and then promptly rips into your taste buds. Make sure you have a chair with arms attached...; **f22.5** steadies as the sugars and barley finally make an entrance; **b22.5** a bone shaker of a whisky experience; a thuggish bouncer in a £500 whistle and flute. It's rough, tough....and bloody great fun! *55.7%. ncf sc. Speciality Drinks. 183 bottles.*

Silver Seal Littlemill Over 20 Years Old dist 1990 **(84.5) n21.5 t22.5 f19.5 b21.** Time has tamed the bad boy of the Lowlands. No ripping your throat out here. A pleasant, simple malt awaits. Though the bitter finish does knee one in the nuts, somewhat. *46%. sc.*

⁘ **The Whisky Agency Littlemill 1989** bott 12 **(82.5) n21 t21 f20 b20.5.** When distilled, Littlemill was virtually undrinkable: it was more likely to be the fuel to take rockets to Mars than be a decent malt. But years of maturation calmed it and brought out the best of the intense malt. And a number of casks which have surfaced have been top-notch: truly out of this world. However, this one is re-entering earth's orbit...and is hot and burning up... *52.1%*

⁘ **The Whisky Agency Littlemill 'Sea Life' 1990** refill sherry butt, dist 90, bott 12 **(85.5) n22 t22 f20.5 b21.** A little bit of the old trademark wallpaper glue. And the heat cannot be denied. But the barley content will impress anyone who can hone in on the buffering marzipan. *52.2%*

LOCH LOMOND
Highlands (Southwestern), 1966. Loch Lomond Distillers. Working.

Inchmurrin 12 Years Old db **(86.5) n21.5 t22 f21.5 b21.5.** A significantly improved dram which is a bit of a malt soup. Love the Demerara injection. *40%*

⁘ **Inchmurrin Aged 12 Years** bourbon cask, bott Dec 12 db **(88) n22** surprising oak visible; some citrus **t22** Malteser-like maltiness with lovely cocoa thread; **f22** yet more malt, with a vanilla veneer; **b22** a superior dosage of simple, intense malt. *46%. nc ncf.*

⁘ **Inchmurrin Aged 15 Years** bourbon cask, bott Dec12 db **(86) n22 t21.5 f21 b21.5.** Slightly tangy with an edge to the cask which interferes with the usual malty procession. *46%. nc ncf. Glen Catrine Bonded Warehouse Ltd.*

Loch Lomond 18 Years Old db **(78.5) n19 t21 f19 b19.5.** A demanding, oily malt which is a long way from technical excellence but is no slouch on the chocolate nougat front. *43%*

⁘ **Inchmurrin Aged 18 Years** bourbon cask, bott Dec 12 db **(92.5) n22.5** something of the old-fashioned hop-less Barley Wine about this, spiked by warming, vivid white pepper; **t23.5** a fascinating Rowntree Fruit Pastille citrus kick to this. But only after the usual mega-malt delivery; **f23.5** now rambles around the palate with hands in pockets – just so relaxed. Mainly malt at varying levels; natural caramels and two or three different honey tones, orange-blossom the most prevalent. Outstanding late spice, too; **b23** Loch Lomond distillery in its brightest colours. *46%. nc ncf. Glen Catrine Bonded Warehouse Ltd.*

Loch Lomond 21 Years Old db **(89.5) n22.5** a real chunky fella with all kinds of melted fruit and chocolate bar properties; a few oily nuts, too...; **t23** the usual fruitcake feel to this, plus the Demerara sugar topping; **f22** light oils carry vanilla and cocoa; **b22** a little while since I last tasted this, and pretty close to exactly how I remember it. Seems to revel in its own enormity! *43%*

⁘ **Inchmurrin Aged 21 Years** bourbon cask, bott Dec 12 db **(90) n22** big vanilla injection; **t23** profound juice radiating from the barley; the sugars are kept in reserve as the hickory holds court; **f22.5** back to the vanilla again, though now some muscovado turns up to ensure a delicate finale; **b22.5** this has spent 21 years in a very exceptional cask. Not exactly breathtaking complexity, but what it does is completed with aplomb. *46%. nc ncf. Glen Catrine Bonded Warehouse Ltd.*

Loch Lomond Copper Pot Still 1966 db **(92) n23 t23.5 f23 b22.5.** Shows remarkably little wear and tear for its great age. A gentleman of a whisky. *45%*

Loch Lomond Gavin's Single Highland Malt dist 1996, bott 2007 db **(90.5) n23 t23 f22.5 b22.** Ester-fuelled and fabulous. *45%. nc ncf.*

Loch Lomond No Age Statement db **(74.5) n18 t20 f18 b18.5.** Still feinty and out of sync, though the lively sugars try to compensate. *40%*

Loch Lomond Single Highland Peated Malt db **(74) n16.5 t20 f19 b18.5.** Feints and peat simultaneously: not something you happen upon very often. Thankfully. *46%*

Scott's Selection Inchmurrin 1997 bott 2012 **(83.5) n20 t23 f20 b20.5.** All about the delivery. Want to know what malted barley tastes like? Look no further. *55.3%. Speyside Distillers.*

LOCHSIDE

Highlands (Eastern), 1957–1992. Chivas Brothers. Demolished.

The Cooper's Choice Lochside 1967 Aged 44 Years cask no. 807 **(96.5) n24.5** yep. Pretty close to perfection. At first it is the softest of smoke which gets you primed. Then the pastel-shaded fruit begins to take shape, perhaps drawing from the honey blossom honey which is weighted by the butterscotch oak and Nice biscuits; **t24.5** again the smoke makes a very early foray, but it is a ghostly one and does a masterful job of keeping anchored the lighter fruit tones. Astonishingly after all these years the barley is still capable of a big juicy volley. While the oak, though arriving early, is of the most benign type offering a seemingly impossible layering of delicate tannins which emboldens and enriches; **f23.5** just a little thinner here with the oat now showing a slightly more austere trait. However, that priceless and ultra-complex smoke ensures the finale is one of quiet dignity; **b24** it is amazing that I had to travel 6,000 miles to find this in British Columbia. But, this is the kind of whisky you would travel four times that kind of distance to experience. Easily one of the top ten single casks I have tasted in the last five years. *41.5%. 354 bottles.*

First Cask Lochside 46 Years Old 5th Anniversary Bottling refill sherry cask, dist Nov 63, bott Mar 10 **(91) n24** an unashamed fruitcake aroma, absolutely reeking of moist molassed sugar and glazed cherries; the sherry trifle goes easy on the custard but instead we get polished antique furniture and a mild bourbon-style toasted honeycomb; **t23** after all that on the nose, a real softy. The custard missing from the trifle has turned up here and anyone who has tasted melted sugar on their porridge will also recognise a flavour profile here; much less sherry influence than expected, save the inevitable rich oloroso delivery; **f21** fades a little too quickly and a surprising tangy bitterness begins to take hold; **b23** a rare view of Lochside from a sherry butt. And one that will get rarer by the day... *46.6%. nc ncf sc. 71 bottles.*

Malts Of Scotland Lochside 1967 bourbon hogshead, cask no. MoS12016, bott Mar 12 **(96) n24.5** I could keep my beak in the glass forever. A Jamaican medium ester pot still sweetness to this; the oak interweaves majestically. A series of delicate lemon notes remind me of pancakes, thanks probably to the sugars which sweeten it; **t24** not so much melts in the mouth but dissolves and hides in every crevice: the oak tries to make a big play but the mix of three vital ingredients – golden syrup, Greek honey and heather honey – ensures that all we hear from the cask is a buttery, vanilla squeak; **f23.5** a hint of tangy marmalade and blood orange and still that unsalted butter; some late, pernickety spices buzz around the tongue late on; **b24** the Spanish may be the possessors of the World and European Cups through their beautiful football. But why did they have to close a distillery which offered a malt with every bit as much flair and movement? *41.7%. nc ncf sc. Malts Of Scotland.*

LONGMORN

Speyside, 1895. Chivas Brothers. Working.

Longmorn 15 Years Old db **(93) n23** curiously salty and coastal for a Speysider, really beautifully structured oak but the malt offers both African violets and barley sugar; **t24** your mouth aches from the enormity of the complexity, while your tongue wipes grooves into the roof of your mouth. Just about flawless bitter-sweet balance, the intensity of the malt is enormous, yet – even after 15 years – it maintains a cut-grass Speyside character; **f22** long, acceptably sappy and salty with chewy malt and oak. Just refuses to end; **b24** these latest bottlings are the best yet: previous ones had shown just a little too much oak but this has hit a perfect compromise. An all-time Speyside great. *45%*

Longmorn 16 Years Old db **(84.5) n20.5 t22 f21 b21.** This was one of the disappointments of the 2008 edition, thanks to the lacklustre nose and finish. This time we see a cautious nudge in the right direction: the colour has been dropped fractionally and the nose celebrates with a sharper barley kick with a peppery accompaniment. The non-existent (caramel apart) finale of yore now offers a distinct wave of butterscotch and thinned honey...and still some spice. Only the delivery has dropped a tad...but a price worth paying for the overall improvement. Still a way to go before the real Longmorn 16 shines in our glasses for all to see and fall deeply in love with. Come on lads in the Chivas lab: we know you can do it... *48%*

A.D. Rattray Longmorn 1992 cask no. 71783, dist 25 May 92, bott Jun 12 **(86.5) n21.5 t23 f21 b21** Decent enough dram, the best of the 1992 bunch, with good salt and sugar drive on delivery. *58.1%. sc. A.D. Rattray Ltd.*

Archives Longmorn 1992 19 Years Old Third Release bourbon cask, cask no. 86607, dist 1992, bott 2012 **(88.5) n22** busily floral and herbal; **t22.5** not quite so busily malty and sugary; **f22** puts its feet up and enjoys the spice; **b22** a hard-working malt. *48.5%. nc ncf sc. 60 bottles.*

⸳⸙⸳ **Berry's Own Selection Longmorn 1992** cask no. 71775, bott 2013 **(94.5) n23.5** for those who love their fruitcake dripping with toasted almonds; decently spiced and even slightly salted; **t24** sultry delivery with the treacle and manuka honey arm-wrestling the burnt raisins to the death; surprisingly mouth-watering, showing how lively that salt 'n' spice is, and that, amazingly, the barley is able to be heard amid the fruity din; **f23** sticky toffee pudding with thick molasses oozing from every pore. A dusting of cocoa tops it off; few finishes come any chewier...; **b24** at times the oak reminds you that here is a distillery uneasy about the passing years. But the enormity of the principal players overcomes any doubts. *58.6%. nc ncf sc.*

Boisdale Longmorn 1992 cask no. 71762, bott 2012 **(82.5) n21 t21 f20 b20.5.** The perfect dram before going to bed: that's if it doesn't send you to sleep before you even reach the stairs. Bland. *46%. nc ncf sc. Berry Bros & Rudd.*

Cadenhead Longmorn 16 Years Old dist 2011 **(91) n22** lively malt: sharp and pungent... the aroma of a cask being dumped; **t23.5** barley comes neither fresher nor more mouth-watering than this. The oak has added a degree of lemon and vanilla; **f23** fine dust icing sugars stretch the finish and ensure the improbably salivating gristiness sees us through to the end; **b22.5** Longmorn at 16 exactly how it should be, yet is so rarely seen! A personal favourite of its type: sheer uncomplicated but highly effective fun; a malt showing the kind of clarity you find when gazing into the distance after a refreshing rain shower. *53.5%. sc.*

⁘ **The Coopers Choice Longmorn 1992 19 Years Old** hogshead, cask no. 71779, dist 92, bott 12 **(89.5) n23** a little spice punctuates the busy barley; **t22.5** sound delivery: absolutely no cracks to the malty sheen; **f22** a slight oak-induced bitterness. But the barley impact is relentless; **b22** straight-as-a-die, no nonsense Speysider with an extra malty edge. *58.2%. nc ncf sc. The Vintage Malt Whisky Co Ltd.*

⁘ **The Coopers Choice Longmorn 1992 19 Years Old** hogshead, cask no. 48461, dist 92, bott 2011 **(88.5) n22.5** toffee and fruit salad candy mix; **t22** Quality Street cream toffee emboldened by a spice buzz; **f22** multi layers of vanilla; **b22** big and flooded with natural caramel. *46%. nc ncf sc. The Vintage Malt Whisky Co Ltd.*

Duncan Taylor Dimensions Longmorn 19 Years Old cask no. 71738, dist May 92, bott Feb 12 **(85.5) n21.5 t22 f21 b21.** In keeping with this particular batch of '92 Longmorns, pleasant but falls under the spell of the natural caramels. *53.7%. nc ncf sc. Duncan Taylor & Co.*

⁘ **Duncan Taylor Octave Longmorn 15 Years Old** oak cask, cask no. 923352, dist 96 **(96) n23.5** some bourbon elements full of red liquorice and ulmo honey with the tannins showing the right degree of muscovado; **t24** this distillery can offer one of the most complex deliveries in all Speyside. And that's what happens here as the oak churn up the barley-rich procession. Malteser candy mingles with almost eye-watering barley juice; **f24.5** after the pizzazz we now have the sophistication. All the previous qualities, but now drier and in seeming slow motion; the butterscotch is astonishing and the varying shades of controlled oak almost beyond belief; **b24** gosh, I wish Chivas would take note: Longmorn at 15, in an excellent cask with no caramel...my word: you have to go a long way to beat it! One of the single casks of the year. *53.4%. sc. Duncan Taylor & Co.*

First Cask Longmorn 23 Years Old refill sherry hogshead, cask no. 14379, dist 13 Oct 88, bott 9 Jan 12 **(79) n20.5 t20 f19 b19.5.** I'll let you guess....Not ruinously bad, though, and the grape certainly pounds through for a while. *52.6%. nc ncf sc. 259 bottles.*

Gordon & MacPhail Rare Vintage Longmorn 1964 (93.5) n23 half an hour's worth of testing out cracked yet highly polished old chesterfields...; **t23.5** the integrity of the sherry has lasted almost 50 years and here offers the most attractive dark cherry you will find; sweetened by molasses and burnt fudge; **f23.5** when first poured, the finale is pretty oaky aggressive. Leave a while to oxidise and that oak begins to put a protective arm around the surprisingly juicy fruit; the dark sugars and marzipan also join forces and become a little special...; **b23.5** it's waited some 47 years to come out and have a chat with you. So leave it in the glass a good 20 minutes before listening to what it has to say. *43%*

Gordon & MacPhail Rare Vintage Longmorn 1967 (94) n23 I've entered a world of expensive polished Victorian wooden artefacts; **t23.5** a delicate yield of honey allows in far more bourbon liquorice notes and overdone toast; complexity and delicacy are sky high; **f23.5** a layer of Chilean honey is soothingly spread on the toast; **b24** an antique whisky with the aroma of a Dorking antique shop. The notes should be written by Arthur Negus. But he'll tell you it's the residual honey effect that goes for the sweetest song. *43%*

Gordon & MacPhail Rare Vintage Longmorn 1973 (95) n24.5 thinks about heading into fruitcake territory but hangs back: the sherry is just a little too clean, the vanillas a little too sweet...it opts for a trifle, instead...; complex, almost perfectly weighted and a reminder of what a real, untainted sherry butt should smell like; **t24** no spring chicken for sure, but somehow the grape feels as though its juices first flowed only yesterday. The oak, though, does underscore the age with an impressive array of dry toasty notes with hazelnut puree. Remarkably, the barley remains fresh and intact; **f23** dries according to the rules with a vague molasses note to the starchy vanillas; a buttery edge offers a degree of oil; **b23.5** Longmorn has long been a staple of Gordon and MacPhail. Here you can see exactly why. *43%*

Hart Brothers Longmorn Aged 19 Years cask no. 110933, dist 11 Sep 92, bott 30 Apr 12 **(80.5) n21 t22 f18.5 b19.** Sticky toffee and then curiously bitters out. *46%. sc.*

Liquid Library Longmorn 1992 ex-bourbon hogshead, dist 92, bott 12 **(86)** n22 t21.5 f21 b21.5. Despite the house style of bruising, biscuit barley, Longmorn does have a tendency to show puckering oak at the first opportunity. Here is a classic example – could pass for a 30-year-old with no problems. *52.7%*

Malts Of Scotland Longmorn 1975 bourbon hogshead, cask no. 3977, dist Mar 75, bott May 11 **(81.5)** n20 t21 f20.5 b20. For all the spice and almost Mr Whippy-style vanilla, there appears to be a conspiracy to bottle Longmorn older than it should be. It starts with the distillers themselves, and is carried on by the independents. Sure, the citrus and bourbon notes are to be applauded. But it is too old and OTT. Something younger, please! *46.4%. nc ncf sc.*

Malts Of Scotland Longmorn 1992 bourbon hogshead, cask no. MoS12011, idst 22 May 92, bott Jan 12 **(86)** n22 t22 f21 b21. At first very good juicy malt then becomes bogged down in natural caramels. Attractive buzz, though. *52.6%. nc ncf sc. Malts Of Scotland.*

Malts Of Scotland Longmorn 1992 bourbon hogshead, cask no. MoS 13014, dist Mar 92, bott Mar **(95)** n23 dry 'n' spicy; t24.5 much sweeter, though the spices live up to the nose's expectation: beautiful mix of molasses and clear honey for the big sugary thread, though the barley still plays a big, juicy part; the middle dries quickly and covers butterscotch ground; f23.5 more butterscotch, though with a thin muscavado layer; the spices provide the backing to the very end; b24 outwardly a classic honey on toast effort. Further investigation reveals a gem. *54.2%. nc ncf sc. 96 bottles.*

Mo Ôr Collection Longmorn 1988 22 Years Old first fill bourbon hogshead, cask no. 14378, dist 13 Oct 88, bott 21 Jan 11 **(65.5)** n16.5 t18 f15 b16. Probably the most un first fill, bourbon-esque cask I have come across from this distillery. Unimpressive in so many ways I don't quite know where to start... *46%. nc ncf sc. Release No. 44. The Whisky Talker. 411 bottles.*

Old Malt Cask Longmorn Aged 21 Years refill hogshead, cask no. 8256, dist Feb 91, bott Mar 12 **(88.5)** n22 a touch opaque with the sharp barley of jungle-like density; t22.5 like the nose, the barley is so thick it takes time for much else to come into focus. At last some relatively delicate sugars emerge, as do the big oils which reduce chances of further complexity; f22 just a little hot and thins out with pretty standard vanilla; b22 a huge whisky which hides itself well. Quite a trick. *50%. nc ncf sc. 303 bottles.*

Old Masters Longmorn 16 Years Old cask no. 156778, dist 96, bott 13 **(91)** n22 dense barley hogs the limelight; t23.5 malt comes neither thicker or fatter than this: like an American malt shake in concentrate form: you have to keep re-tasting it to believe it! f22.5 some vanilla fights its way to the top, plus some molten brown sugar, the like of which you find on steaming porridge; b23 anyone with a love for malt shakes or Malteser candy will probably take no prisoners to get their hands on this one. Truly idiosyncratic. *56.3%. sc. James MacArthur & Co Ltd.*

Scotch Malt Whisky Society Cask 7.69 Aged 8 Years first fill barrel, cask no. 800279, dist 2003 **(89.5)** n21.5 obviously youthful, and equally obviously of a high standard though in an underdeveloped state; t23.5 age counts for little as the palate is packed with highly charged barley and sugars sporting a caramelised, oaky tint which is not to be found on the nose; quite sharp, almost aggressive in its flavour distribution....but bloody delicious! f23 falls back into the safer zones of muscovado sugar sweetened cocoa and quite rich liquorice. Certainly begins to take a bourbon shape..; b23 the nose may struggle to find its balance, but the delivery spins as many plates as you like. *61.6%. sc. Scotch Malt Whisky Society.*

Scotch Malt Whisky Society Cask 7.70 Aged 19 Years refill hogshead, cask no. 48420, dist **(88.5)** n22 powerful oaky caramels make for a flattish though Kentuckian aroma; t22 explosive delivery with some viperish pepper; after a few waves the natural caramels begin leaving their tide mark; f22.5 plenty of recognisable bourbon characteristics on the long tail; b22 when you get this degree of caramel occurring naturally and the effect it has, you can see why it is suicide to add any to the official bottling. *51.1%. nc.*

Scotch Malt Whisky Society Cask 7.71 Aged 19 Years refill hogshead, cask no. 48423, dist 1992 **(91)** n22.5 less bourbon than 7.70 with the weightier elements broken up by a succession of clean citrus notes; t23 soft and malty delivery, becoming chewier. Excellent medium roast Java offers delicate bitterness which works perfectly with the sweeter malt; f22.5 the barley remains slightly gristy and juicy while the mocha rounds matters off pleasantly; b23 the lack of natural caramels make for a jauntier malt. *53%. sc.*

Scotch Malt Whisky Society Cask 7.75 Aged 27 Years 2nd fill sherry butt, dist 26 Oct 84 **(95.5)** n23.5 dry from both the oloroso and huge oak input. Probably a second fill sherry butt which escaped a sulphury death in Jerez and emptied at three or five years first time around as the oaky fingerprints are massive and unusual; t24.5 bliss! That ultra-rare experience of taking the full value of high quality, untarnished oloroso on board, complete with big spiced sultana, then layer upon layer of cream chocolate wafer, all with a magnificent dusting of grist and Danish marzipan; f23.5 slightly shorter finish than might be expected, but the fade is both elegant and boisterous: the spices warm the ulmo honey and coconut water

mix; **b24** a clean butt, so to speak, and though there are too many rings in the oak, this is a sherry cask not to be trifled with.....If you can get one, buy two...! *51.7%. nc ncf sc. 54 bottles.*

⸙ **Scotch Malt Whisky Society Cask 7.84 Aged 27 Years** refill hogshead, dist 24 Sep 85 **(92) n23** shouldn't be having coffee at this time of the evening, but here it is...no shortage of tannin and hickory, too; **t23** excellent body; the barley and muscavado sugars form a great, almost biscuity, alternative to the oilier theme; **f23** butterscotch and hazelnut conclude an in impressive experience, with the dark sugars rumbling on and on; **b23** Longmorn at its most confident at an age when it can sometimes become oak-soaked and a little jittery. *56.3%. nc ncf sc. 173 bottles.*

⸙ **Scotch Malt Whisky Society Cask 7.86 Aged 27 Years** refill hogshead, dist 24 Sep 85 **(83) n21.5 t20 f21 b20.5.** Disappointing considering the all-round might of the distillery. Hot and at no stage of the proceedings does it ever look remotely in control. *56.7%. nc ncf sc.*

Scott's Selection Longmorn 1992 bott 2012 **(90.5) n22** superb hazelnut spread on toast: creamy yet busy; dank barley offers a very green aspect; **t23.5** beautiful delivery: the nuttiness turns up as expected and there is a degree of bite to the oak, but all very acceptable. Stewed apples then a kind of sweet, barley crumble tart fills the mid ground rather deliciously; **f22** the sugars stay loyal as the barley goes a surprising distance; **b23** simply delicious; one of the better Independent Longmorns, SMWS apart. *58.1%. Speyside Distillers.*

⸙ **Wemyss 1996 Single Speyside Longmorn "Toasted Hazelnuts"** hogshead, bott 13 **(84) n21 t21.5 f20.5 b21**. Elements of chocolate orange and some major oils for a Speysider. But the oak is a little too loud for comfort. *46%. sc. Wemyss Malts. 234 bottles.*

The Whisky Agency Longmorn 1965 bott 2011 **(96) n25** oh, it's one of those!! Longmorn and Glen Grant had gifted upon them 40 to 50 years ago some of the finest sherry butts that those living today can remember. Just one inhalation of this reveals this to be one. Even after all this time the grape is not only intact but radiating equal measures of delicate sugars and spices, especially the white peppers. The oak degredation is zero. Anything less than 25 minutes nosing this is a crime against whisky: to add water – even a teaspoonful deserves - being taken outside and shot...; **t24** the oak is definitely more up to the challenge here and makes sure you know it's around. But, again, so rich is the grape, so confident the sugars attached, that the oak offers little more than a growl before backing off; a wonderful fruitcake, seemingly encased in chocolate pampers the middle ground, luxuriating in a delicate oiliness; **f23** just for a moment the oak catches all else off guard and strikes a slightly bitter note. But it is short lived as wave upon wave of dry dates and liquorice engulf the palate; **b24** this could well be, after all these years, The Fat Lady of Limburg singing for... I looked at the samples that were sent and furrowed my brow. You would never believe that I'd tasted royalty and fame if you saw me now. But my sense of taste is such that I'll distinguish with my tongue the subtleties a spectrograph would miss. And announce my decision, while demanding my reward: a bottle of this. (With thanks and apologies to Brian Eno) *51.8%. nc ncf sc. The Whisky Agency. Joint bottling with Gordon & MacPhail for Limburg Whisky Festival.*

Whisky Antique Longmorn 22 Years Old Special Bottling dist 1988, bott 2011 **(87) n21** salted peanut spread on burnt toast; a twist of lemon; **t22** early on, as barley-biased as you might expect. But there is a real bite in there, also, while the oak shouts rather than whispers its presence; **f22** the sugars begin to make an effort and calm the growing excesses of the oak; **b22** Antique by nature, this one. Seems a great deal older than its 22 years and another summer in the cask will have done some serious damage. *54.4%. sc.*

THE MACALLAN
Speyside, 1824. Edrington. Working.

The Macallan 7 Years Old db **(89) n23 t23 f21 b22**. An outstanding dram that underlines just how good young malts can be. Fun, fabulous and in recent bottlings has upped the clarity of the sherry intensity to profound new heights. *40%*

The Macallan Fine Oak 8 Years Old db **(82.5) n20.5 t22 f20 b20**. A slight flaw has entered the mix here. Even so, the barley fights to create a distinctive sharpness. However, a rogue sherry butt has put paid to any hopes the honey and spice normally found in this brand. *40%*

The Macallan 10 Years Old db **(91) n23** oloroso appears to be the big noise here, but clever, almost meaty, incursions of spice offer an extra dimension; fruity, yet bitter-sweet: dense yet teasingly light in places; **t23** chewy fruit and the old Macallan silk is back: creamy cherries and mildly under-ripe plum ensures a sweet-sour style; **f21.5** traces of vanilla and barley remind us of the oak and barley, but the fruit reverberates for some while, as does some annoying caramel; **b23.5** for a great many of us, it is with the Mac 10 our great Speyside odyssey began. It has to be said that in recent years it has been something of a shadow of its former great self. However, this is the best version I have come across for a while. Not perhaps in the same league as those bottlings in the 1970s which made us re-evaluate the possibilities of single malt. But fine enough to show just how great this whisky can be when the butts have not been tainted and, towards the end, the balance between barley and grape is a relatively equal one. *40%*

The Macallan 10 Years Old Cask Strength db **(85) n20 t22 f22 b21.** Enjoyable and a would give chewing gum a run for its money. But over-egged the sherry here and not a patch on the previous bottling. *58.8%. Duty Free.*

The Macallan Fine Oak 10 Years Old db **(90) n23** finely tuned and balanced: everything on a nudge-nudge basis with neither fruit nor barley willing to come out and lead: really take your time over this to maximise the entertainment; **t22.5** brimming with tiny, delicate oak notes which just brush gently, almost erotically, against the clean barley; **f21.5** drier, chewier and no less laid-back; **b22** much more on the ball than the last bottling of this I came across. Malts really come as understated or clever than this. *40%*

The Macallan Sherry Oak 12 Years Old db **(93) n24** thick, almost concentrated grape with a stunning degree of light spices. Topped with boiled greengage; **t23.5** clean sherry is heralded not just by vanilla-thickened grape but a deft muscovado sweetening and a light seasoning of spice; **f22.5** cocoa, vanilla and fudge. Remains clean and beautifully layered; **b23** I have to say that some Macallan 12 I have tasted on the road has let me down in the last year or so. This is virtually faultless. Virtually a time machine back to another era... *40%*

The Macallan 12 Years Old Sherry Oak Elegancia db **(86) n23 t22 f20 b21.** Promises, but delivers only to an extent. *40%*

The Macallan Fine Oak 12 Years Old db **(95.5) n24** faultless, intense sherry light enough to allow the fabulous apple and cinnamon to blend in with the greengage and grape; **t24** a near perfect entry: firm, rummy sugars are thinned by a barley-grape double act; juicy yet enough vanilla to ensure structure and layering; **f23.5** delicate spice keeps the finish going and refuses to let the muscovado-grape take control; **b24** a whisky whose quality has hit the stratosphere since I last tasted it. I encountered a disappointing one early in the year. This has restored my faith to the point of being a disciple... 40%

Macallan Gran Reserva Aged 12 Years db **(92) n23** massive cream sherry background with well matured fruit cake to the fore: big, clean, luxurious in a wonderfully old-fashioned way. Oh, and a sprinkling of crushed sultana just in case the grapey message didn't get across... **t24** a startlingly unusual combination on delivery: dry yet juicy! The ultra fruity lushness is dappled with soft spices; oak arriving early-ish does little to alter the path of the sweetening fruit; just a hint of hickory reveals the oak's handiwork towards the middle; **f22** dry, as oloroso does, with a vaguely sweeter edge sparked by notes of dried date; the delicate but busy spices battle through to the toffeed end; **b23** well, you don't get many of these to the pound. A real throwback. The oloroso threatens to overwhelm but there is enough intrigue to make for a quite lovely dram which, as all good whiskies should, never quite tells the story the same way twice. Not entirely without blemish, but I'm being picky. A Macallan soaked in oloroso which traditionalists will swoon over. *45.6%*

The Macallan Fine Oak 15 Years Old db **(79.5) n19 t21.5 f19 b20.** As the stock of the Fine oak 12 rises, so its 15-y-o brother, once one of my Favourite drams, falls. Plenty to enjoy, but a few sulphur stains remove the gloss. *43%*

The Macallan Fine Oak 17 Years Old db **(82) n19.5 t22 f19.5 b21.** Where once it couldn't quite make up its mind on just where to sit, it has now gone across to the sherry benches. Sadly, there are a few dissenters. *43%*

The Macallan Sherry Oak 18 Years Old db **(87) n24 t22 f20 b21.** Underpowered. The body doesn't even come close to matching the nose which builds up the expectancy to enormous levels and, by comparison to the Independents, this at 43% appears weak and unrepresentative. Why this isn't at 46% at the very least and unambiguously uncoloured, I have no idea. *43%*

The Macallan 18 Years Old dist 1991 db **(87) n22 t22.5 f21 b21.5** Honestly: I could weep. Some of the sherry notes aren't just textbook...they go back to the Macallan manuals of the early 1970s. But the achievable greatness is thwarted by the odd butt of you know what... *43%*

The Macallan Fine Oak 18 Years Old db **(94.5) n23.5** classic cream sherry aroma: thick, sweet but enlivened by a distinct barley sharpness; **t24** juicy, chewy, clean and intense delivery. Strands of honey and syrup help pave the way for vanillas and spices to get a grip; the complexity levels are startling and the weight just about spot on; **f23** a degree of blood orange bitterness amid the cocoa and raisin; the spices remain lazy, the texture creamy; **b24** is this the new Fine Oak 15 in terms of complexity? That original bottling thrived on the balance between casks types. This is much more accentuated on a cream sherry persona. But this sample is sulphur-free and quite fabulous. *43%*

The Macallan Masters Of Photography Albert Watson 20 Years Old db **(94.5) n24** if there is such a thing as a seismograph for measuring sherry, this would be bouncing from wall to wall. Concentrated noble rot, with a few roasted almonds and spices tossed in; **t24.5** as soft as a 20-year-old sherry... without the whisky. It works beautifully as the required balance between sugars and spice is there in bundles; and as well as sherry trifle, there is blackcurrant on butterscotch, too; **f22.5** just a hint of bitterness but plenty of over-ripe greengage and toasty vanilla to see you off; **b23.5** it's one of those! (Bizarrely, as I wrote that, Milton Jones said exactly the same words on the radio...spooky!) Once I would have marked this down as being simply too sherry drowned. But since clean sherry butts are now at a premium, I am seeing whiskies like this in a very different light: certainly not in the negative... It can still be argued that this is far too sherry driven, with too much else overpowered. And maybe just a little too bitter on the finish. But of its once thought extinct type, staggering. *46.5%. Edrington.*

The Macallan Fine Oak 21 Years Old db **(84) n21 t22 f20 b21.** An improvement on the characterless dullard I last encountered. But the peaks aren't quite high enough to counter the sulphur notes and make this a great malt. *43%*

The Macallan 25 Years Old db **(84.5) n22 t21 f20.5 b21.** Dry with an even drier oloroso residue; blood orange adds to the fruity mix. Something, though, is not entirely right about this and one fears from the bitter tang at the death that a rogue butt has gained entry to what should be the most hallowed of dumping troughs. *43%*

The Macallan Fine Oak 25 Years Old db **(90) n22** coal dusty: the plate of old steam engines; a speckle of raisin and fruitcake; **t23.5** despite the early signs of juicy grape, it takes only a nanosecond or two for a much drier oak-spiced spine to take shape; the weight is never less than ounce perfect, however; **f22** puckering, aged oak leaves little doubt that this is a malt of advanced years, but a few liquorice notes ensure a degree of balance; **b22.5** the first time I tasted this brand a few years back I was knocked off my perch by the peat reek which wafted about with cheerful abandon. Here the smoke is tighter, more shy and of a distinctly more anthracitic quality. Even so, the sweet juiciness of the grape juxtaposes gamely with the obvious age to create a malt of obvious class. *43%*

The Macallan Fine Oak 25 Years Old db **(89) n23 t23 f21 b22.** Very similar to the Fine Oak 18. However, the signature smoke has vanished, as I suppose over time it must. Not entirely clean sherry, but much remains to enjoy. *43%*

The Macallan Fine Oak 30 Years Old db **(81.5) n22 t22 f18 b19.5.** For all its many riches on delivery, especially those moments of great bourbon-honey glory, it has been comprehensively bowled middle stump by the sherry. Gutted. *43%*

The Macallan 40 Years Old dist 10 May 61, bott 09 Sep 05 db **(90) n23** no shortage of oak, as you might expect. But nutty, too (chestnut pure, to be precise). The scope is broadened with a distracted smokiness while oak maximizes the longer it stays in the glass; **t23** soft and yielding, with a lovely dovetailing of vanillins and delicate sherry. The grape appears to gain control with a sweet barley sidekick before the oak recovers; **f22** soft oils formulate with some laite and slightly salted, Digestive-style biscuit. Gentle spices delight; **b22** very well-rounded dram that sees off advancing years with a touch of grace and humour. So often you think the oak will take control, but each time an element intervenes to win back the balance. It is as if the dram is teasing you. Wonderful entertainment. *43%*

The Macallan 50 Years Old dist 29 Mar 52, bott 21 Sep 05 db **(90) n25** we all have pictures in our minds of the perfect grandmother: perhaps grey-haired and knitting in her rocking-chair. Or grandfather: kindly, gentle, quietly wise, pottering about in the shed with some gadget he has just made for you. This, then, is the cliched nose of the perfect 50-year-old malt: time-defying intensity and clarity; attractive demerara (rum and sugar!) sweetened coffee, a tantalizing glimpse at something smoky and sensationally rich grape and old fruit cake. So that the sweetness and dryness don't cancel each other out, but complement each other and between them tell a thousand tales. Basically, there's not much missing here... and absolutely all you could wish to find in such an ancient Speysider...; **t23** dry delivery with the oak making the early running. But slowly the grape and grain fights back to gain more than just a foothold; again telling wisps of smoke appear to lay down a sound base and some oily barley; **f19** now the oak has taken over. There is a burnt-toast and burnt raisin bitterness, lessened in effect marginally by a sweeter vanilla add-on; **b23** loses it at the end, which is entirely excusable. But until then, a fabulous experience full of passion and complexity. I nosed and tasted this for over an hour. It was one very rewarding, almost touching, experience. *46%*

The Macallan Millennium 50 Years Old (1949) db **(90) n23 t22 f22 b23.** Magnificent finesse and charm despite some big oak makes this another Macallan to die for. *40%*

The Macallan Lalique III 57 Years Old db **(95) n24.5** coffee and walnut cake. That's the simple way of looking at this one: but give yourself maybe half an hour and a slightly more detailed picture forms. The fruit conjures dates and walnuts – so walnuts and walnut oil is a pretty common thread here. And truffle oil, amazingly. The oak is toasty liquorice and overcooked fudge. But the delicate smoke I was expecting is conspicuous by its absence... until very late on. Only after a major degree of oxidisation does it add that extra delicate dimension; **t23** a soft landing in the canopy of the oaky trees with those coffee notes noticeable on the nose now really making a stir. Most beautiful, perhaps, is the lightness of touch of the Demerara and muscovado sugar blend, damped in intensity by a sprinkling of vanilla. Some surprising oils form and make for a silky middle ground; **f23.5** some late spices, no more than a smattering, underline the oak without overstating the case while the sugars do their almost invisible job of keeping the dryer notes under control; like on the nose, a little smoke drifts in from seemingly nowhere; **b24** I chose this as my 1,000th new whisky tasted for the 2012 Bible not just because of my long-standing deep love affair with this distillery, but also because I honestly felt it had perhaps the best chance to offer not just a glimpse at the past but also the possibility of a whisky experience that sets the hairs on the back of my neck on end. I really wasn't disappointed. It is almost scary to think that this was from a vintage that would have supplied the whiskies I tasted when getting to first discover their 21-year-old. Then, I remember, I thought the malt almost too comfortable for its age. I expected a bit more of a struggle in the glass. No less than 36 years on, the same thing crosses the mind: how does this whisky find it so easy to fit into such enormous shoes? No experience with this whisky under an hour pays sufficient tribute to what it is all about. Checking my watch, I am writing this just two minutes under two hours after first nosing this malt. The score started at 88.5. With time, warmth, oxidation and understanding that score has risen to 95. It has spent 57 years in the cask; it deserves two hours to be heard. It takes that time, at least, to not just hear what it has to say to interpret it, but to put it into context. And for certain notes, once locked away and forgotten, to be slowly released. The last Lalique was good. But simply not this good. 48.5%

The Macallan 1824 db (**88**) **n24 t23.5 f19 b21.5.** Absolutely magnificent whisky, in part. But there are times my job is depressing...and this is one of them.. 48%

The Macallan 1824 Estate Reserve db (**90.5**) **n22** excellent clean grape with an intriguing dusting of mint; **t23** almost a Jamaican pot still rum sheen and sweetness; beautiful weight and even some barley present; **f22.5** satisfying, gorgeously clean with very good vanilla-grape balance; **b23** don't know about Reserve: definitely good enough for the First Team. 45.7%

The Macallan 1824 Select Oak db (**82**) **n19 t22 f20 b21.** Soft, silky, sometimes sugary... and tangy. Not convinced every oak selected was quite the right one. 40%

The Macallan 1851 Inspiration db (**77**) **n19.5 t19.5 f19 b19.** Flat and uninspirational in 2008. 41%

The Macallan 1937 bott 1969 db (**92**) **n23** an outline of barley can eventually be made in the oaky mist; more defined as a honeyed sweetness cuts in. Fingers of smoke tease. When nosing in the glass hours later the fresh, smoky gristiness is to die for ... and takes you back to the mill room 67 years ago; **t22** pleasantly sweet start as the barley piles in – even a touch of melon in there; this time the oak takes second place and acts as a perfect counter; **f24** excellent weight with soft peat softening the oak; **b23** subtle if not overly complex whisky where there are few characters but each play its part exceptionally well. One to get out with a DVD of Will Hay's sublime Oh Mr Porter which was being made in Britain at the same time as this whisky and Laurel and Hardy were singing about a Lonesome Pine on the other side of the pond; or any Pathe film of Millwall's FA Cup semi-final with Sunderland. 43%

The Macallan Gran Reserva 1981 db (**90**) **n23 t22 f22 b23.** Macallan in a nutshell. Brilliant. But could do with being at 46% for full effect. 40%

The Macallan Gran Reserva 1982 db (**82**) **n21 t22 f20 b19.** Big, clean, sweet sherry influence from first to last but doesn't open up and sing like the '81 vintage. 40%

The Macallan Masters Of Photography Annie Leibovitz 1989 "The Gallery" sherry butt, cask no. 12251 db (**96.5**) **n24.5** just love those pulsing spices and the cloves which gee up the ample grape and apple. Clean, fresh and almost perfectly structured and weighted. Sherry butts of the old school, so very rarely seen these days; **t24** there we go: an almost perfect reflection on the palate of the beautiful aroma. The grape does what all fruit should do in a whisky: lead but not dominate to the cost of all else. Like the nose, there is no sulphur evident: a pristine cask. The barley comes through in tandem with the oak, offering almost a chocolate malt style depth. The spices do as spices should: they simply add resonance and piquancy: they do not scold or burn, or detract from all other complex machinations! **f24** long, chewy and now dried dates inject a sublime fruit and toffee richness; still the barley returns for more; **b24** like that ace photo sitting on a newsroom picture desk, this stands out above all the other Speysiders I have tasted so far this year...Colin Gower, the Richard Paterson of the national newspaper picture desks, grab a bottle, my old friend....!! 56.6%. sc. 285 bottles.

The Macallan Masters Of Photography Annie Leibovitz 1991 "The Bar" sherry oak puncheon, cask no. 7023 db (**87**) **n22** heavy duty, one dimensional though enjoyable clean grape; **t22** sweet, with enough spice to entertain; **f22** chocolate fruit and nut; **b21** enjoyable but astonishingly simple as malt and complexity has been cropped. 50.8%. sc. 285 bottles.

The Macallan Masters Of Photography Annie Leibovitz 1995 "The Library" sherry oak hogshead, cask no. 14007 db (**82.5**) **n21.5 t21 f20 b20.** A clean, unsulphured cask. But the soupy grape is entirely over exposed. Frankly, boring as no meaningful shape or form can be seen. 59.6%. sc. 145 bottles. Exclusive to distillery, Global Travel Retail and private sale.

The Macallan Masters Of Photography Annie Leibovitz 1996 "The Skyline" American oak butt, cask no. 10019 db **(94) n23.5** top grade input from the oak with a colourful array of darker sugars working alongside brooding tannins; **t24** the nose cranks up the expectation, the delivery delivers! Those muscovado sugars saturate the taste buds alongside just the right degree of spice to counter; the tannins pulse and head towards a mocha middle but veer off towards a more banana custard sweetness; **f22.5** not as long as might be hoped, but the quality remains to the end; **b24** quite outstanding oak composition. 55.5%. sc. 285 bottles.

Macallan Cask Strength db **(94) n22 t24 f24 b24.** One of those big sherry babies; it's like surfacing a massive wave of barley-sweetened sherry. Go for the ride. 58.6%. USA.

The Macallan Easter Elchies Seasonal Cask Selection Winter Choice 14 Years Old db **(94) n24 t24 f23 b23.** From a faultless cask and one big enough to have its own Postcode... 54%. Exclusive to visitor centre.

⠶ **The Macallan Amber** sherry oak cask db **(78) n19 t22 f18 b19.** The texture alone shows this should be something truly special. The first few moments of the delivery likewise, with its astonishing Locket's honey filling; honey is the unambiguous theme throughout. But the tangy presence of a few sub-standard sherry butts undermine some great work in the lab. I suspect the next bottling might be a corker. 40%

The Macallan Estate Reserve db **(84) n22 t22 f20 b20.** Doh! So much juice lurking about, but so much bitterness, too. ...grrrrr!!!! 45.7%

The Macallan Fine Oak Master's Edition db **(91) n23** one of the most delicate of all Macallan's house noses, depending on a floral scented theme with a sweetish malty tinge to the dank bracken and bluebells; **t23** so salivating and sensual! The tastebuds are caressed with sugar-coated oaky notes that have a devilish buzz about them; **f22** more malt and now vanilla with a bitter cocoa death... **b23** adorable. 42.8%

The Macallan Fine Oak Whisky Maker's Selection db **(92) n22 t23 f23 b24.** This is a dram of exquisite sophistication. Coy, mildly cocoaed dryness, set against just enough barley and fruit sweetness here and there to see off any hints of austerity. Some great work has gone on in the lab to make this happen: fabulous stuff! 42.8%. Duty Free.

⠶ **The Macallan Gold** sherry oak cask db **(89.5) n22** the accent is on a fabulous blend of clear and ulmo honey; creamed rice; **t23.5** like Macallan Amber, the texture makes great play of the smallness of the copper stills, with a slightly metallic, rich theme; it is the (chocolate) biscuity barley laced with honey and maple syrup which blows you away though...; **f21.5** ulmo honey still, this time spread over farmhouse bread; a late tang; **b22.5** no Macallan I have tasted since my first in 1975 has been sculpted to show the distillery in such delicate form. 40%

The Macallan Oscuro db **(95.5) n24.5** the cleanest, most juicy grape dripping into a puddle of molten muscovado sugar: amazed I have not been attacked by wasps while nosing this; it would be too much on its own, but there is a sprinkling of spice to balance things beautifully; **t24** golden sultanas, ripe fig, exploding greengages and that muscovado sugar and spice again...unreal...; **f23** a little bitter, probably from the oak which until now had hardly got a look in; some toasty vanilla makes a late entry but that juicy, lightly spiced fruit just keeps on going; **b24** oh, if all sherried whiskies could be that kind - and taste bud-blowingly fabulous! 46.5%

⠶ **The Macallan Ruby** sherry oak cask db **(92.5) n23** classic Macallan super-soft cream sherry nose, incorporating rose petals and other Turkish delight traits, as powdered sugar; **t24** sumptuous and just sweet enough to remind one of noble rot grapes before heavier tannins and cream coffee begins to gain the middle ground; **f22** layering of grape and vanilla coffee; the vaguest hint of a treated sherry butt can just be found; **b23.5** those longer in the tooth who remember the Macallan 10 of 30 years ago will nod approvingly at this chap. Perhaps one butt away from a gong! 43%.

⠶ **The Macallan Sienna** sherry cask db **(94.5) n23** another Macallan with honey in its sights: simplistic clear honey this time, though enriched by grated desiccated coconut and vanilla; **t24** soothing texture with the barley bringing forward enough juice to the soft oil to give extra complexity; easy going to the point of falling backwards off its chair, the barley gives way eventually to a gorgeous ulmo honey, vanilla and butterscotch middle; **f23.5** buttery and not unlike uncooked cake mix you scrape from the bowl; **b24** the pre-bottling sample presented to me was much more vibrant than this early on, but lacked the overall easy charm and readily flowing general complexity of the finished article. A huge and pleasing improvement. 43%.

The Macallan The Queen's Diamond Jubilee db sherry cask matured **(94) n23.5** heavy duty grape, but clean as a whistle. Damsons and dates abound; **t23** it's one of those amazingly full, slightly uncouth, types of sherry malts, where the grape is piled on thick and only the fittest barley and oak notes manage to make their way through – and there are few. Tasty, though! **f24.5** now it moves into overdrive. The overbearing grape on delivery has vanished and we are left with a really complex fade, full of massive chocolate which sits atop a plum pudding sweetened by molasses; **b23** a wonderful, high quality sulphur-free zone where Macallan unashamedly nails its sherried credentials to the union flag. 52%. 2012 bottles. UK exclusive.

The Macallan Royal Marriage db **(89)** n23.5 t22.5 f21 b22. Some amazing moments to remember. 46.8%

The Macallan Select Oak db **(83)** n23 t21 f19 b20. Exceptionally dry and tight; and a little furry despite the early fruitiness. 40%

The Macallan Whisky Makers Edition db **(76)** n19 t20 f18 b19. Distorted and embittered by the horrific "S" element... 42.8%

The Macallan Woodlands Limited Edition Estate Bottling db **(86)** n21 t23 f21 b21. Toffee towards the finish brings a premature halt to a wonderfully mollased early delivery. 40%

❖ **Gordon and MacPhail Speymalt Macallan 1991 (89)** n22.5 sumptuous praline and diced kumquat; t23.5 slick delivery with stunning Demerara sugars clinging to the marzipan and malt delivery; a touch of lychee fills the middle ground; f20.5 unravels a little as the tangerine turns a little furry; b22.5 wobbles and bitters out towards the end, but some lovely fruit and nut moments up until then. 43%

❖ **Gordon and MacPhail Speymalt Macallan 2003 (68.5)** n16 t19 f16.5 b17. One to throw back into the river... 43%

Hart Brothers Macallan Aged 14 Years cask no. 84, dist 26 Feb 98, bott 15 Apr 12 **(89.5)** n23 light traces of almonds and nougat work excellently with the subtle spices; t21.5 the complexity on the nose is lost under the intense presence of sweet barley; f22.5 returns to a more symphonic work with trace cocoa elements working well with a return of the nougat and bolstered by delicate honey; b22.5 almost too delicate and understated. You have to listen very carefully and with great patience to hear the full beauty of this malt. 46%. sc.

Heiko Thieme's 1974 Macallan 65th Birthday Bottling cask no. 16807 dist 25 Nov 74 bott Jul 08 **(94)** n23 the clarity of the sherry takes some believing: this malt has obviously been in a good clean home for the last 34 years: not a single off note and the balance between grape, oak, spice and sweetened tomato puree is exceptional...; t23 the arrival is sharp, both in terms of barley and grape. At first it looks shocked to have escaped the cask, or is hunting around for the alcohol to tie it together. But soon it finds harmony, helped along the way by a stunning chocolate and raisin middle which leads to some sweetening molasses; f24 now enters into a class of its own. We all know about the fruitcake cliché: well here it is in glorious roasted raisin brilliance. Melton Hunt cake and trifle combined; the length makes a mockery of the strength. And it looks as though someone forgot to go easy on the burnt cherry. The vanillas are deft, the coffees are medium roast; b24 this is not whisky because it is 38%abv. It is Scottish spirit. However, this is more of a whisky than a great many samples I have tasted this year. Ageism is outlawed. So is sexism. But alcoholism isn't....!! Try and become a friend of Herr Thieme and grab hold of something a little special. 38% 238 bottles.

Malts Of Scotland Macallan 1990 Oloroso sherry hogshead, cask no. 1134, dist 1990, bott 2011 **(95)** n24 dense: like sticking your nose inside a Macallan cask at the distillery in the early '80s. Just a hint of salt, but mainly it's moist fruitcake, ripe and ready to explode greengages, a leaf or two of mint , a touch of lavender and a vague hint of spotted dog pudding; t24 where does one begin? With the almost perfect spices? The ineffective shackles on the sweetness? The measuring of the intensity of the cocoa against the rich fruits? Which kind of fruit cake it reminds you of most...? f23 just a whisky where you run out of superlatives, your brain is over-run with ultra pleasant sensations and the only words which form are '...cor, bugger me...!!' b24 if I could take you back 30 years, you'd find every Macallan 21 tasted something rather similar to this, though not always quite so well appointed in the complexity stakes. Flawless, not a sulphur atom in sight: stunningly made and matured and a malt you spend a very quiet night alone with. For even silk isn't this silky... 49.1%. nc ncf sc. Malts Of Scotland.

Malts Of Scotland Macallan 1990 Fino sherry hogshead, cask no. 1135, dist 24 Jan 90, bott 27 May 11 **(82)** n21 t22 f19 b20. I have spoken and written much about the detrimental effect of sulphur on sherry butts and the resulting spoiling of the whisky it later contains. And have hacked off a number of people in the whisky industry because of it, one or two who, in denial, claim the problem is a figment of my imagination. Nothing I have written, though, has been as eloquent as the unambiguous statement made by these two sister casks. One has been very mildly treated with sulphur. The other, almost certainly, escaped any treatment whatsoever. Try each whisky side by side and I'll let you decide which... 51.5%. nc ncf sc.

Mo Ór Collection Macallan 1991 19 Years Old first fill bourbon hogshead, cask no. 21436, dist 25 Feb 91, bott 24 Nov 10 **(95)** n23.5 a wonderful mix of mocha and Seville orange; a lovely salty tidemark, too; t24 doesn't so much caress the taste buds as pamper them to death; the sugars are a dream, as crunchy as the barley is molten; f23.5 back to the mocha, though pepper has now replaced the salt; b24 a Macallan with no baggage can be a very beautiful thing. 46%. nc ncf sc. Release No. 12. The Whisky Talker. 429 bottles.

Old Malt Cask Macallan Aged 14 Years refill hogshead, cask no. 7738. dist Oct 97, bott Oct 11 **(89.5)** n23 diaphanous citrus; the barley shows remarkable clarity; t23 mouth-watering gristy barley helped along by lush muscovado notes; **f21.5** vanilla and a little oak weariness; **b22** Macallan for the most part at its most sprightly. *50%. nc ncf sc. 365 bottles.*

⠠ **Old Malt Cask Macallan Aged 15 Years** refill hogshead, cask no. 9458, dist Oct 97, bott Feb 13 **(92) n23** thick barley seems as though it is stuck fast to the red liquorice. High quality oak at play...and the pedigree of the initial spirit is pretty impressive, too; **t23.5** classic small still intensity here with the oils tight and copper giving both a lustre and sharpness to the barley. As intense as Speyside malt gets; **f22.5** thins out as the vanilla arrives, though the copper lingers; **b23** Macallan at its most malty and muscular. Really beautiful, if simplistic. *50%. sc. Douglas Laing & Co. 329 bottles.*

⠠ **Old Malt Cask Macallan Aged 16 Years** refill butt, cask no. 8815, dist Mar 96, bott Jul 12 **(84) n22 t21 f20 b21.** A tangy offering from what appears to be a slightly tired cask. *50%. nc ncf sc. Douglas Laing & Co. 189 bottles.*

Old Malt Cask Macallan Aged 18 Years bourbon barrel, cask no. 7700, dist Jun 93, bott Nov 11 **(84.5) n21 t22 f21 b20.5.** Exceptionally sweet and has no pretentions as to balance. *50%. nc ncf sc. Douglas Laing & Co. 192 bottles.*

Old Malt Cask Macallan Aged 18 Years refill butt, cask no. 8210, dist Nov 93, bott Feb 12 **(79) n18 t21 f19.5 b20.5.** For all its obvious failings, has plenty of barley backbone to make for an decent-ish dram. Nose apart, that is. *50%. nc ncf sc. Douglas Laing & Co. 412 bottles.*

⠠ **Old Malt Cask Macallan Aged 18 Years** refill hogshead, cask no. 8678, dist Sep 93, bott Jun 12 **(93) n23** pretty salty, which tends to crank up the oaky side. Plenty of fruitcake, too, complete with nuts..; **t24** now that is one impressive delivery: the grape arrives in bunches but the malt will not be outdone and vies for equal juiciness; **f22.5** perhaps fades in stature as a little bitterness creeps in, but the weight remains exemplary; **b23.5** a treat of a malt. Even the most hard to please Macallan lover will be charmed off his Winchester... *50%. nc ncf sc. Douglas Laing & Co. 349 bottles.*

⠠ **Old Malt Cask Macallan Aged 18 Years** refill hogshead, cask no. 9127, dist Nov 93, bott Sep 12 **(92) n22.5** curiously creamy and a touch spicy; **t23** silky, voluptuously bodied with the malt intensity stoked up to the full; **f23.5** an intriguing hint of late smoke raise the complexity levels – and weight; **b23** blending Macallan in its best single malt suit. *50%. sc. Douglas Laing & Co. 265 bottles.*

⠠ **Old Malt Cask Macallan Aged 18 Years** refill hogshead, cask no. 9202, dist Dec 93, bott Nov 12 **(86.5) n21 t22.5 f21 b22.** Very drinkable with an attractive hyper-malty fizz. But a lazy cask which refuses to stump up on the complexity. *50%. nc ncf sc. 273 bottles.*

⠠ **Old Malt Cask Macallan Aged 20 Years** refill hogshead, cask no. 9449, dist Oct 92, bott Mar 13 **(93) n23** gorgeous cream sherry and intense sultana; **t23.5** slick and thick, the sultana and marzipan dominates; **f23** long and aided by a flawless cask which pulses spice and ginger nut biscuits for quite a while; **b23.5** a crackerjack of a cask. *50%. sc. 131 bottles.*

⠠ **Old Malt Cask Macallan Aged 20 Years** refill hogshead, cask no. 9853, dist Jun 93, bott Jun 13 **(88.5) n22** unusual to find spices leading the team onto the field...; **t22.5** big dose of malt on delivery, just lightly sugared and then the oak really starts to dig in; a late acceleration of spices, all clinging to the gathering oils; **f22** softens towards the end with a Walnut Whip type oily vanilla nuttiness; **b22** a dry, sophisticated Macallan showing a side it rarely reveals. *50%. nc ncf sc. 285 bottles.*

Old Malt Cask Macallan Aged 21 Years refill hogshead, cask no. 7090, dist May 90, bott May 11 **(94.5) n23.5** a stunning amalgam of sultana and sweeter bourbon notes; the fruit also heads towards spiced yam and caramel; **t24** perfect delivery: the barley leaps from the first note and the juiciness just keeps on developing; the middle ground begins hinting of muscovado-sweetened mocha: outrageously refreshing for its age; **f23** long and more and more bourbon tones flex their muscles...with wonderfully good grace; **b24** looking for a magnificent, fault-free Macallan 21? Look no further... *50%. nc ncf sc. 160 bottles.*

⠠ **Provenance Macallan Over 15 Years** refill hogshead, cask no. 9657, dist 97, bott 13 **(85.5) n22 t22 f20 b21.5.** Unusually firm barley for a Macallan with a crisp sugar shell. *46%. nc ncf.*

Scotch Malt Whisky Society Cask 24.114 Aged 21 Years refill butt, cask no. 16520, dist 1989 **(86) n21.5 t22 f21 b21.5.** Thoroughly enjoyable whisky which perhaps just overdoes the sugary caramel to take it into the next level of excellence. *52.3%. sc. 165 bottles.*

Scotch Malt Whisky Society Cask 24.116 Aged 20 Years 1st fill sherry hogshead, cask no. 278057, dist 1990 **(91.5) n22.5** huge spiced sultana; the odd "s" atom, but those peppers and the promise of thick juice is pretty damn sexy; **t23** an early puckering "s" note is blasted into the sidings by a staggering degree of explodingly fat sultana; the grape arrives in layers, as does a rich coffee note; **f23** coffee cake complete with walnuts. A few dates thrown in for good measure; **b23** not quite 100% free of impurity, but still a stonking cask! *55.8%. sc. 202 bottles.*

Scotch Malt Whisky Society Cask 24.117 Aged 20 Years first fill sherry hogshead, cask no. 278046, dist 1990 **(87) n21** grape but very tight with limited growth; **t22.5** surprisingly active with the spices grappling liquorice and barley; **f21.5** a slight off-note buzz, but not enough to spoil the oaky fun; **b22** not quite the perfect cask but clean enough for the grape to make a mouth-watering contribution and the spices to form a delightful backing. *55.4%. sc.*

Scotch Malt Whisky Society Cask 24.118 Aged 20 Years first fill sherry hogshead, cask no. 278047, dist 1990 **(67) n17 t17 f16 b17.** A gruesome tale of dire sulphur. On nosing I held this back to be my last whisky of the day... and with very good reason. *50.7%. sc.*

Scotch Malt Whisky Society Cask 24.119 Aged 26 Years refill hogshead, cask no. 2612, dist 1985 **(94) n23** rich, with the barley, sharp and slightly fruity, interwoven with a light coppery thread; **t23.5** a brain-explodingly complex delivery with all kinds of small flavours popping up here and there, with a light coppery sharpness multiplying the intensity: it's as if a new still or two was being put through its paces; **f23.5** long and now with a fabulous, salivating fruitiness giving the big vanilla and butterscotch a run for its money; **b24** a bottling which captures the small still style of the distillery perfectly. *51.7%. sc. Scotch Malt Whisky Society.*

Scotch Malt Whisky Society Cask 24.120 Aged 20 Years first fill sherry butt, cask no. 278059, dist 1990 **(70) n19 t18 f16 b17.** The sulphury knife cuts deep enough... *56.3%. sc.*

Scott's Selection Macallan 1989 bott 2012 **(88) n21** a few oak shavings amid the barley; **t22** the delivery again shows its full age but the barley digs deep to find the sugars to compliment the peek-a-boo butterscotch; **f23** much happier finish, with soft oils helping the malt form an intense finish; **b22** wobbles around a bit, but the quality and complexity are always there. Just have to be patient and hunt them out a bit... *50.1%. Speyside Distillers.*

Scott's Selection Macallan 1990 bott 2012 **(85.5) n21.5 t21 f21.5 b21.5.** Shows some bright honey touches at times, as well as a distinctive small still richness. Able and pleasant without setting the pulse racing. *46.1%. Speyside Distillers.*

Silver Seal Macallan 22 Years Old dist 1988 **(94.5) n23.5** not quite classic Macallan: certainly has the intense grape and it's untainted, too. But here there is an extra degree of must and spice; **t24.5** for a moment the taste buds reach out and touch Macallan perfection. It lasts but a few seconds, but long enough for you to appreciate the astonishing density and balance to this. Again, the juice and spice are in near perfect accord; **f23** a huge cocoa backlash as the grape dissipates, offering a Cadbury Fruit and Nut finale... **b23.5** if you don't reach some form of ecstasy with this, you might as well stick to vodka. *56.7%. Whisky Antique.*

∴ **That Boutique-y Whisky Company Macallan** batch 3 **(77) n18 t21 f19 b19.** Sweet, malty but dismally underwhelming. *43.4%. Master Of Malt. 245 bottles.*

MACDUFF
Speyside, 1963. John Dewar & Sons. Working.

Glen Deveron Aged 10 Years dist 1995 db **(86) n19 t23 f23 b21.** The enormity of the third and fourth waves on delivery give some idea of the greatness this distillery could achieve perhaps with a little more care with cask selection, upping the strength to 46% and banning caramel. We'd have a malt scoring in the low to mid 90s every time. At the moment we must remain frustrated. *40%*

Glen Deveron Aged 15 Years db **(88.5) n22 t22.5 f22 b22.** For those who like whisky to caress rather than attack their taste buds. *40%*

∴ **A.D. Rattray Macduff 1984** sherry butt, cask no. 3149, dist 18 May 84, bott Apr 13 **(88.5) n23.5** so many things are good here; the integrity of the grape, the liquorice...but....; **t22** the delivery makes you purr as the salivating barley and juicy grape meld together; though mocha, praline and spice form and delicious grouping, there are increasing signs of a weakness; **f21.5** the failures of the cask begin to tell with a furry signature; **b21.5** some aspects of this malt are breathtaking. *51.4%. sc. A.D. Rattray. Dewar Rattray Cask Collection.*

Berry's Own Selection Macduff 2000 cask no. 5774, bott 2011 **(96) n24** pounding and gorgeously clean oloroso-style grape. A really stunning mixture of dried fruit and sweet honey...and a fascinating degree of bourbony liquorice; **t24** just as mouth-filling as the nose promises, though the spices flood in from all directions and pack quite a sting. The remainder is like chewing through ultra moist fruitcake laden with cherries; **f24** so long you could almost doze off counting the flavour waves. The vanilla takes time to get a foothold, but manages in the end. Though the spices remain...; **b24** nuttier and juicier than a fruitcake...and, my word, what a delicious cherry to chew on... Fizzing, fruity, and frankly, fantastic! *60%. nc ncf sc.*

Duncan Taylor Dimensions Macduff 17 Years Old dist Jun 94, bott Nov 11 **(67) n17 t19 f15 b16.** Sweet, but Macduffed up by sulphur. *46%. nc ncf sc. Duncan Taylor & Co.*

Gordon & MacPhail Connoisseurs Choice Macduff 1997 (91.5) n23 a soft nougat and honey interplay; pick any citrus note you like...; **t24** hazelnut and honey: the texture is exceptional; mocha and natural caramel fills things out beautifully; **f21.5** a degree of late barley even offers a juicy richness; a hint of praline and walnut whip; **b23** so delicate, so damned beautiful, you just want this Macduff to carry on... *43%. Gordon & MacPhail.*

Kingsbury "The Selection" Macduff 8 Years Old butt, cask no. 900265 & 900266, dist Aug 02, bott Apr 11 **(71.5) n18.5 t19 f16 b17.** Puts the duff in Macduff... *43%. nc ncf. 1,666 bottles.*

··⑤·· **Kingsbury Macduff Aged 15 Years** hogshead, cask no. 4129, dist 97 **(86.5) n21.5 t22 f21.5 b21.5**. Compact, barley intense and unusually dependent on the malt rather than the usual little honeyed flourishes. *46%. nc ncf. Japan Import System. 354 bottles.*

Mo Òr Collection Macduff 1973 37 Years Old first fill bourbon hogshead, cask no. 20, dist 30 Nov 73, bott 2 Dec 10 **(89.5) n23** drifts towards Kentucky like a moth towards a flame, so telling is the big orange on the liquorice; **t22** big oaky beating of the chest, then a slow diffusion of kumquat notes; **f22** light vanilla, a mounting of spices and citrusy barley sign off; the confident sugars save the day; **b22.5** magnificently complex, but tries to hang onto its youth unconvincingly. *46%. nc ncf sc. Release No. 22. The Whisky Talker. 281 bottles.*

Old Malt Cask Macduff Aged 21 Years refill hogshead, cask no. 8002, dist Dec 90, bott Jan 12 **(90) n22** soft, with varying butterscotch tones; **t23.5** beautifully sharp delivery with some wonderful fragments of honey amid the sublime barley; **f22** long and hangs on to a long honeycomb note; **b22.5** now there's a thing! I absent-mindedly nosed and tasted this without taking note of what whisky exactly I had before me. And images of the old William Lawson 12-year-old blend of maybe two decades ago came flooding into my mind. Imagine my astonishment when I realised just what I had in the glass. For this was the major malt used in that blend... *50%. nc ncf sc. Douglas Laing & Co. 272 bottles.*

Scotch Single Malt Circle Macduff 1980 cask no. 6865, dist 28 Nov 80, bott 1 Sep 11 **(86.5) n21.5 t22.5 f21 b21.5**. The oak has taken a few prisoners. And some quite excellent chocolate orange and honey notes do manage to escape. *52.8%. sc. Scotch Single Malt Circle.*

··⑤·· **Single Cask Collection Macduff Aged 31 Years** sherry hogshead, cask no. 6900, dist 28 Nov 80, bott 7 Mar 12 **(91.5) n23** plenty of green apple as well as grape; **t24** the weight is nigh perfect with the rich, Demerara-mottled sherry rolling in with one breathtaking wave after another; the spices are polite but increasingly assertive; **f21.5** a light blemish, but the grape helps the damage limitation, as does that Demerara concentrate; **b23** when a treated sherry butt comes close to pulling off greatness...; *50%. nc ncf sc. 191 bottles.*

The Whisky Agency Macduff 38 Years Old bourbon cask, dist 1973, bott 2011 **(83) n21.5 t21 f20 b20.5**. Another of a batch of '73s doing the rounds. That was like a moth to the flame with its aging. This one well and truly got its wings singed... *47%. sc.*

MANNOCHMORE

Speyside, 1971. Diageo. Working.

Mannochmore Aged 12 Years db **(84) n22 t21 f20 b21**. As usual the mouth arrival fails to live up to the great nose. Quite a greasy dram with sweet malt and bitter oak. *43%.*

Mannochmore 1998 The Manager's Choice db **(71.5) n18 t18 f17.5 b18**. A very bad cask day... *59.1%.*

Cadenhead Mannochmore 15 Years Old dist 1996, bott Apr 12 **(93.5) n24** one of those all evening noses that takes an hour or so to fully appreciate: in particular, just love the Bakewell tart and the toasted almonds; the very faintest dab of phenol adds both spice and weight; **t23** my palate feels as though it has just slid into a lovely warm bath after a hard day's tasting: luxurious mouth-feel with plenty of barley on the menu and a near perfect salty-sharp/gristy sweet balance; **f23** the late, light tang is not from a poor cask but from further manoeuvrings between the saline and sugary, though some Maryland Cookie dough offers further complexity; **b23.5** a beautifully crafted malt. *56.4%. sc. WM Cadenhead Ltd.*

··⑤·· **Old Malt Cask Mannochmore Aged 13 Years** refill hogshead, cask no. 9230, dist Apr 99, bott Oct 12 **(91.5) n22.5** a dreamy aroma: just the right degree of icing sugar to put a gloss to the sultana, vanilla, barley and tannin; **t23** how crisp and juicy is that?! The barley crackles on the palate and melts into the comfortable vanilla; **f23** just the degree of spice required, as well as the most distant apple and barley; **b23** class at its most simple. Beautiful stuff! *50%. sc. Douglas Laing & Co. 182 bottles.*

Provenance Mannochmore Over 12 Years refill hogshead, cask no. 8189, dist Spring 1999, bott Winter 2012 **(86.5) n22 t22 f21.5 b21**. Refreshing with intense grist and juicy barley. But just a little on the hot but non-spicy side. *46%. nc ncf sc.*

··⑤·· **Provenance Mannochmore Over 14 Years** bourbon barrel, cask no. 9766, dist Spring 99, bott Spring 13 **(89) n22** a dank oakiness is the only variant to the multi-layered barley; **t23** wow! Any blender looking to make the barley content sing in his creation will lap this up: sweet, still vaguely gristy and just the lightest of spicy touches; **f21.5** a slight old oak tang to the finale, but before then its....you've guessed it: malty...; **b22.5** thumbs up for a thumping barley monster. *46%. nc ncf sc.*

Scotch Malt Whisky Society Cask 64.34 Aged 21 Years refill barrel, cask no. 1510, dist 1990 **(96) n24** just how many variations on a honey theme can you spot? I'm at about five, though some are heavily disguised amid the hickory and butterscotch; if that wasn't complex enough, we also have a vivid floral edge with bluebells leading the way; **t24** an almost perfect degree of oil accentuates the sugars but allows the vanillas to do their own thing unimpeded; some crushed nuts, dry dates and spices make for a super-rich middle ground; **f23.5** long and big on the mocha; back to the honeycomb towards the finale; **b24.5** outwardly an understated malt in so many ways, but don't be fooled: this is pure star quality! *56%. sc.*

⁙ **Scotch Malt Whisky Society Cask 64.42 Aged 22 Years** refill barrel, dist 14 Feb 90 **(96) n24** tasting this on a Sunday (yes, I really do taste seven days a week...!), which is rather fitting as this has all the hallmarks of a gorgeous, creamy Victoria sponge, though rather than powdered sugar being sprinkled on top, there appears to be grist; **t25** faultless: the weight is exactly where a mix of beautifully intense, yet gristilly-sweetened barley should be, plus butterscotch oak. The oils are again, like the nose, on the creamy side and the mid ground also hosts diced pistachio and almonds; **f23** a late tinge of ulmo honey does the required as the oak dries to a chalky conclusion; **b24** finding Mannochmores of this vintage is becoming one of my favourite aspects of my work. Another truly memorable, sensational dram. *55.6%. nc ncf sc. 198 bottles.*

The Warehouse Collection Mannochmore Aged 19 Years bourbon hogshead, cask no. 6606, dist 5 May 92, bott 11 Nov 11 **(87) n22.5** clean, teasing barley with a curious vanilla depth; the sugars and salts seem a little compartmentalised...; **t22** ...yet it is they which show first before an outbreak of brittle barley; **f20.5** tangy citrus; late natural caramel; **b22** from the crunchy school of Speysiders.. *49.5%. sc. Whisky Warehouse No. 8. 118 bottles.*

MILLBURN
Highlands (Northern), 1807–1985. Diageo. Demolished.
Millburn 1969 Rare Malt db **(77) n19 t21 f18 b19**. Some lovely bourbon-honey touches but sadly over the hill and declining fast. Nothing like as interesting or entertaining as the massage parlour that was firebombed a few yards from my office twenty minutes ago. Or as smoky... *51.3%*

MILTONDUFF
Speyside, 1824. Chivas Brothers. Working.
Miltonduff Aged 15 Years bott code L00/123 db **(86) n23 t22 f20 b21**. Some casks beyond their years have crept in and unsettled this one. But some real big salty moments to savour, too. *46%*

⁙ **Cadenhead Miltonduff 22 years Old** claret, dist 90, bott 12 **(96) n23** manuka honey points to the age, as does the delicate clove and primrose. Gloriously floral; **t24.5** here we go... we are entering superstar malt land. The delivery carries no shortage of oak. But there is so much honey and treacle to hand, it makes no kind of negative impact at all. The mid ground is a sea of rich barley with a slow mocha growth of Ghana chocolate and Sumatra coffee; **f24** classic ulmo honey fade...with magnificent spices guaranteeing maximum balance and complexity; **b24.5** a great distillery...being truly great... *56.8%. sc. 252 bottles.*

⁙ **Dun Bheagan Miltonduff 24 Years Old** hogshead, dist May 87 **(96) n24** teasing fruity notes of wavering intensity; well matured fruit cake but there are sumptuous greengages and runny honey, too; the spices are perfectly well behaved and the vanillas are graceful **t24** like the nose, the delivery is a fabulous amalgam of all faiths. There are both bourbon honey and liquorice notes harmonising with fruity notes to die for. The spices are almost too perfect in weight; **f23.5** content to move down the old fruitcake washed down with mocha scenario; **b24.5** yet another bottling which makes one wonder why this has never been a malt which has received the backing as a singleton it deserved. Once you've had a glass of this stuff you know it: in many ways the complete dram. *55%. nc ncf sc. Ian Macleod Distillers.*

⁙ **Liquid Sun Miltonduff 1980** ex-bourbon hogshead, dist 80, bott 12 **(85) n22 t21 f21 b21**. Attractive malt in need of a stairlift to hit the heights. The oak creeks from start to finish, but just enough honey and natural caramel filters through to blunt the sharper splinters. *41.9%*

Mo Ór Collection Miltonduff 1980 30 Years Old first fill bourbon hogshead, cask no. 12431, dist 12 Sep 80, bott 24 Nov 10 **(95) n24** a superlative, zesty nose which shows you why blenders prize this as a malt which speaks so much more eloquently than many others: especially with the higher, honeyed notes, perfectly balanced with the earthier tones of salty, lightly peppered bacon: the perfect whisky to return home to and call to your partner: high honey, I'm ham....; **t24** there is no faulting the weight, shape and balance of the delivery; when you get a mouthful of this, the barley seemingly acts like a 19th century native American before fighting the cowboys: it grows in a tent city...; **f23** now it teases you with its roundness, maltiness and chocolate; oh, no that's a malt teaser...; **b24** a whisky which religiously, and quite literally, gets the wrong meaning with any potentially ambiguous tasting note. Oh, no: that's Milton Jones... *46%. nc ncf sc. Release No. 18. 321 bottles.*

Old Malt Cask Miltonduff Aged 21 Years refill hogshead, cask no. 7921, dist May 90, bott Nov 11 **(89.5) n23** superb nose with roasted peanuts on toast and a cup of mocha sitting nearby. The subtlety of the sugars borders perfection; **t22.5** soft barley delivery but there is a firm backbone to this, allowing a crunchy feel to the proceedings. Sharp, almost eye-watering in part with a lightly salted sub-plot; **f22** the creamy mocha on the nose returns; **b22** this distillery doesn't have to work hard to produce excellent whisky. And though this one is relatively simple, it's complex enough... *50%. nc ncf sc. Douglas Laing & Co. 183 bottles.*

⚬⚬⚬ **Premier Barrel Miltonduff Aged 7 Years** (86.5) **n21 t22.5 f21.5 b21.5.** A veritable fruit bomb which explodes on impact. Youthful and not dissimilar to sucking a fruit pastille. The dark ones in particular. *46%. nc ncf sc.*

⚬⚬⚬ **Provenance Miltonduff Over 7 Years** sherry butt, cask no. 9239, dist Autumn 05, bott Autumn 12 (83.5) **n19.5 t21.5 f22 b20.5.** Not a bad butt, in that there are no off notes. But here we have an example where the wine and barley are at an awkward stage of their lives. Plenty to enjoy, though, and no shortage of juicy grape. *46%. nc ncf sc. Douglas Laing & Co.*

⚬⚬⚬ **Scotch Malt Whisky Society Cask 72.25 Aged 29 Years** refill hogshead, dist 15 dec 83 (94) **n23.5** what a bag of tricks: fabulously earthy and with a teasing fruit and veg mix, with crushed watercress and under-ripe greengages and cape gooseberries at the vanguard; **t24** sumptuous, multi-layered and faceted from the very first rumblings on the taste buds. Again, the spices, like on the nose, go into overdrive, yet are never for a moment aggressive – they sit happily with the oily, syrupy mix which keeps the lid on the big oak; **f22.5** much drier with the emphasis now on the cocoa and, much later on, gorgeous and unmistakable Panama high roast coffee; **b24** another of the great undiscovered distilleries of Scotland showing exactly why it should be not just better known but actually revered. This rare bottling from the SMWS for this distillery was more than worth waiting for. *49.9%. nc ncf sc. 174 bottles.*

Scott's Selection Miltonduff 1990 bott 2011 (94.5) **n23.5** displays its usual pastel shaded sugars: everything understated and delicate, though this time with a not quite so usual element of dried dates; **t24.5** almost a nonchalance bordering on arrogance to the way in which the perfectly weighted barley moves across the palate; the sugars are a little fudge-like and thick, the spices are present but shy. But the layering of kumquat and milky mocha borders the sensational; **f23** a thin muscovado-molassed mix sets the tone for the long finish, in which oak gets some kind of dry toe hold but can barely hang on; the complexity and layering remains exceptional; **b23.5** this distillery must, surely, one day be publicly outed by their owners as one of the world's finest, let alone Scotland's... *59.2%. Speyside Distillers.*

Scott's Selection Miltonduff 1990 bott 2012 (86) **n21 t22 f21.5 b21.5.** A lazy, chewy offering with too much toffee dampening down the excellent work of the juicy barley and busy oak. *55.3%. Speyside Distillers.*

Wemyss 1987 Single Speyside Miltonduff "Wild Berry Spice" barrel, bott 2012 (87) **n21.5** the oak threatens darkly but enough malt and liquorice bubbles through...; **t22** certainly spiced, though at first it is calmed by an oily wave of simplistic but attractively sugared barley; a hint of Swiss roll style raspberry jam and cream; **f21.5** the oils and slightly one dimensional spice continue, but complexity is sketchy; **b22** as someone who spends as much spare time as possible rambling in the country, my autumns are spent picking wild berries. And you've got me here, guys...never yet found a wild spiced Swiss Roll...! *46%. sc. 169 bottles.*

The Whisky Agency Miltonduff 1989 bott 2011 (90.5) **n22** leathery and dry without the oak getting any kind of meaningful grip; some freshly baked bread, though lacking the subtle sweetness; **t23** lovely soft oil heralds the dawn of some stunning muscovado sugars; the middle ground offers a subtle mid-roast Java coffee note; **f22.5** a plethora of spices ensure a busy finale; **b23** a malt to take your time with. It will be very well rewarded. *50%. nc ncf sc.*

MORTLACH
Speyside, 1824. Diageo. Working.

Mortlach Aged 16 Years db (87) **n20 t23 f22 b22.** Once it gets past the bold if very mildly sulphured nose, the rest of the journey is superb. Earlier Mortlachs in this range had a slightly unclean feel to them and the nose here doesn't inspire confidence. But from arrival on the palate onwards, it's sure-footed, fruity and even refreshing... and always delicious. *43%*

Mortlach 32 Years Old dist 1971 db (88) **n22 t22 f22 b22.** Big and with attitude... *50.1%*

Berry's Own Selection Mortlach 1998 cask no. 3798, bott 2012 (87) **n19** a little dirty – in the house style; **t24** the taste buds are blanketed by one of the most impenetrable barley experiences known to mankind. It is as though you are sucking on a boiled malt whisky sweet which takes forever to dissolve; **f22** the imperfections on the nose pan out at the very death. But there are some spices to contend with; **b22** a typical knife and fork merchant from Mortlach where the puffy nose wins little for beauty, but is compensated with big personality on delivery. Impossible not to fall in love a little. *56.8%. nc ncf sc. Berry Bros & Rudd.*

Chieftain's Mortlach Aged 18 Years sherry butt, dist May 93, bott Sep 11 (80) **n19 t23 f19 b19.** A shame. The nuttiness and molassed sweetness to the sherry is truly superb. But the darker, drier forces at work drag the overall quality down. *57.2%. nc ncf sc. Ian Macleod.*

⫶⫶ **Chieftain's Mortlach Aged 22 Years** sherry butt, cask no. 5159, dist Aug 90, bott Feb 13 (**92**) n23 virtually Guyanese pot still rum in its almost impenetrable density and big molassed sweetness. But we also have the enormity of a super-rich sherry, spattered, burned raisin-infested Melton Hunt cake complete with over-ripe figs, the most lush dates in syrup imaginable and plums to contend with; not entirely clean, but good enough...; t24 not sure if you are supposed to drink or eat this: just keep chewing until your jaw aches and a wonderful intermingling of melted sugars, French toast and a blend of maple syrup and mollasses; f22 just a little bitter but the toasty oak is now poking through; b23 funny how a type of whisky I used to thoroughly dislike as OTT, I now truly enjoy. Because this shows a form of sherry butt matured once common in Scotland, but now lost under the onslaught of sherry. Here there are only traces of an off note. It is still OTT....but, oh, thank you for that...!!! 50%. nc ncf sc.

⫶⫶ **Chieftain's Mortlach Aged 22 Years** sherry butt, cask no. 5160, dist Aug 90, bott Mar 13 (**95.5**) n23.5 just like the 50% abv version, but cleaner and distinctly nuttier; t24 again, very similar in style to the 50% abv bottling. Here, however, we have a more compact nutty element which fits beautifully with the mocha middle, while the sugars have sharper teeth; f24 again, so similar to the other bottling but cleaner on the finish, with the molasses and raisins taking far longer to drift away; b24 there are going to be some very lucky Americans: they will be tasting an almost extinct Scotch whisky style... 58.1%. For USA nc ncf sc.

Gordon & MacPhail Rare Vintage Mortlach 1971 (**95.5**) n25 as solid and clean a sherry as you are likely to find: mangos, salted lime, grape pith, kumquat peel, thinned molasses, physalis, exploding gooseberry, Crunchie bar,...it's as though someone has taken the lot, crushed them in a mortar and pestle and added ancient oloroso: perfection! t24 black cherries, which don't appear on the nose, most certainly do here. Along with a soft volley of spice and muscovado and molassed sugars; the middle is molten Milky Way topped off with even more honeycomb; f22 it tires somewhat and even the odd degree of bitter oak assembles. But there are still many positives to behold; b24.5 if you don't like a whisky like this, then you should give up. The kind of dram I spend my life searching for... 43%. Gordon & MacPhail.

Gordon & MacPhail Rare Vintage Mortlach 1976 (**84.5**) n22.5 t21.5 f20 b20.5. An underpowered dram which begins with a magnificently dextrous, if sawdusty, nose but falls away slightly as the weakened oils fail to hold honeyed but chalky excesses of the oak. 43%

Hart Brothers Mortlach Aged 14 Years cask no. 12843, dist 1997, bott 2012 (**86**) n22 t22.5 f20 b21.5. Creamily textured and impressively intense especially towards the start. 46%. sc.

⫶⫶ **Malts Of Scotland Mortlach 1994** sherry hogshead, cask no. MoS 12059, dist Aug 94, bott Nov 12 (**76.5**) n18.5 t20 f19 b19. There's a rare beast these days: a sherry butt which doesn't work...and not an atom of sulphur in sight. 55.2%. nc ncf sc. 96 bottles.

Old Malt Cask Mortlach Aged 15 Years refill hogshead, cask no. 7647, dist Aug 96, bott Aug 11 (**81.5**) n18 t22.5 f20 b21. Sweet, buttery and spicy. 50%. nc ncf sc. 350 bottles.

Old Malt Cask Mortlach Aged 21 Years refill puncheon, cask no. 7489, dist Sep 90, bott Sep 11 (**87**) n19 perhaps not the ideal blueprint for a Speyside nose as there is some tired oak in there. But enough sugars to give hope; t23.5 Much juicier and more compact than the nose would lead you to believe. After the initial barley blast, opens out superbly to allow in the spices and begin a breath-taking series of complex waves involving toasty, fudgy notes, myriad spices and even a hint of manuka honey and liquorice; f22.5 the tannins kick in but add just the right degree of dryness; oily and long; b23 from such an unpromising nose, there is much to celebrate afterwards. 50%. nc ncf sc. 271 bottles.

⫶⫶ **Old Malt Cask Mortlach Aged 21 Years** refill hogshead, cask no. 9432, dist Sep 91, bott Feb 13 (**86**) n21 t22 f21.5 b21.5. Typically chunky and glutinous, full of thick brown sugars, liquorice and spice. 50%. sc. Douglas Laing & Co. 259 bottles.

Premier Barrel Mortlach Aged 14 Years (**83.5**) n21 t22.5 f19 b21. An intense malt. A character on the nose suggests this might be heading for a fall further on down the line. But the big malt delivery is a treat. 46%. nc ncf sc. Douglas Laing & Co. 178 bottles.

Premier Barrel Mortlach Aged 14 Years (**92**) n23 a subtle and unexpected pinch of peat to this. Chimes well with the sugary malt; t23.5 soft layers of peat intertwine effortlessly with the barley-vanilla theme. The odd squeeze of something citrusy ensures a clean, salivating experience; f22.5 vanillas offer a drying component but the light sugars persist deliciously while the smoke breaks down to something spicier; b23 elements in the makeup of this remind me of when I first tasted Mortlach over 30 years ago and has been lost for something approaching the last two decades. 46%. nc ncf sc. Douglas Laing & Co.

Provenance Mortlach Over 8 Years Montilla butt, cask no. 7679, dist Spring 2003, bott Autumn 2011 (**88.5**) n22 spotted dog pudding with a layer of molten sugar; t22 thickly coated in malt and fruit, the middle ground fizzes with spice and is not shy in coming forward with the oak; f22.5 more spice, then a superb late dawning of delicate brown sugars; a smattering of cocoa powder tops things off delightfully; b22 a dense malt in which evidence of youth is far from easy to trace. Chunky and chewy from first to last. 46%. nc ncf sc. 163 bottles.

⋄⋄ **Provenance Mortlach Over 10 Years** refill hogshead, cask no. 9520, dist Winter 2002, bott Winter 2013 (79.5) n20 t20.5 f19 b20. No shortage of barley sugar but complexity is at a premium. 46%. nc ncf sc. Douglas Laing & Co.

Scotch Malt Whisky Society Cask 76.85 Aged 15 Years first fill sherry butt, cask no. 4393, dist 1995 (79) n19 t21 f19 b20. No major off notes, other than the inevitable tang on the finish which matches the off-colour nose. Just stupefyingly dull. 55.2%. sc.

Scotch Malt Whisky Society Cask 76.87 Aged 9 Years first fill barrel, cask no. 4532, dist 2002 (85.5) n21 t21.5 f22 b21. Massively malty, gristy and fresh. The spices make do for the complexity interest. 59.5%. sc. Scotch Malt Whisky Society.

⋄⋄ **Scotch Malt Whisky Society Cask 76.100 Aged 19 Years** refill sherry butt, dist 1 Jun 93 (68.5) n16.5 t18 f17 b17.5. I have no notes in front of me today. Just the sample. I assume this is from a sherry butt. Because guess what's spoiling the party... 58.1%. nc ncf sc.

⋄⋄ **Scotch Malt Whisky Society Cask 76.101 Aged 24 Years** refill hogshead, dist 12 Apr 88 (86) n21.5 t22 f21 b21.5. Puckering, eye-wateringly tart fare which enjoys some good moments, especially when the concentrated molasses drive, with deranged viciousness, into the oak concentrate. 55.7%. nc ncf sc.

Silver Seal Mortlach Over 13 Years Old dist 1997 (74) n19 t20 f17 b18. Subtlety, charm, charisma, complexity, class...yes, it has none of those whatsoever. Lumpy, hot and less than brilliantly made whisky: ideal for the persistent visitor who comes to your home to help themselves to your best malt. 46%. sc. Silver Seal Whisky Company.

Silver Seal Mortlach Over 22 Years Old dist 89, bott 11 (83) n21 t20 f21 b21. A wholesome malt despite its propensity to want to pick fights with all your taste buds. Enough peppered sugar character and walnut oil to make for a pleasant-ish, if warming, experience. 58.2%. sc.

The Warehouse Collection Mortlach Aged 11 Years bourbon hogshead, cask no. 9052, dist 29 Jun 00, bott 3 Aug 11 (88) n21.5 a little dirty in the Mortlach style, but a little pineapple to the honey cleanses things somewhat; t23 big, pulsing oily malt with the emphasis on spiced barley. The trick, though, is the kaleidoscopic sugars which twist from an early Demerara style to a later muscovado, taking in the odd golden syrup note at points between. This, though, is beautifully underscored by spice; f21.5 much more simplistic vanilla; b22 hats off to these German bottlers. Mortlach is not an easy distillery from which to locate an entertaining cask. The chaps have achieved it. 59.9%. sc. Whisky Warehouse No. 8. 271 bottles.

⋄⋄ **Wemyss 1998 Single Speyside "Tarte aux Pommes"** hogshead, dist 98, bott 13 (84.5) n21 t22.5 f20 b21. Some appeasing chocolate mint arrives down the line. But by and large about as subtle as being hit around the head with a malt shovel....full of malt. A tart for dirty malt Johnnies more like. 46%. sc. 337 bottles.

⋄⋄ **The Whisky Cask Mortlach Aged 17 Years** hogshead, dist 95, bott 12 (84.5) n22 t21 f21.5 b20. It is as though your taste buds are being crushed under the weight of a runaway tank made entirely of sugar. In some way, more of a liqueur than a malt. 56.4%. nc ncf sc.

MOSSTOWIE
Speyside, 1964–1981. Chivas Brothers. Closed.
Rare Old Mosstowie 1979 (84.5) n21.5 t21 f21 b21. Edging inextricably well beyond its sell by date. But there is a lovely walnut cream cake (topped off with brown sugar and spices) to this which warms the cockles. Bless... 43%. Gordon & MacPhail.

NORTH PORT
Highlands (Eastern), 1820–1983. Diageo. Demolished.
Brechin 1977 db (78) n19 t21 f18 b20. Fire and brimstone was never an unknown quantity with the whisky from this doomed distillery. Some soothing oils are poured on this troubled – and sometimes attractively honeyed – water of life. 54.2%

OBAN
Highlands (Western), 1794. Diageo. Working.
Oban 14 Years Old db (79) n19 t22 f18 b20. Absolutely all over the place. The cask selection sits very uncomfortably with the malt. I look forward to the resumption of normality to this great but ill-served distillery. 43%

Oban Aged 15 Years The Distiller's Edition db finished in Montilla Fino casks, dist 1992, bott 2007 (90) n22.5 t23 f22.5 b22. This isn't all about complexity and layering. It's about style and effect. And it pulls it off brilliantly. 43%

Oban Aged 15 Years The Distiller's Edition db finished in Montilla Fino casks, dist 1993, bott 2008 (91.5) n22 nutty, tight, a little musty; t24 much more assured: the dryness of the grape sports beautifully against the obviously more outgoing and sweeter barley: excellent balance between the two; f22.5 perhaps the Fino wins, as it dries and embraces the oak quite happily; b23 delicate and sophisticated whisky. 43%

PITTYVAICH

Speyside, 1975–1993. Diageo. Demolished.

Pittyvaich Aged 12 Years db (64) n16 t18 f15 b15. It was hard to imagine this whisky getting worse. But somehow it has achieved it. From fire-water to cloying undrinkability. What amazes me is not that this is such bad whisky: we have long known that Pittyvaich can be as grim as it gets. It's the fact they bother bottling it and inflicting it on the public. Vat this with malt from Fettercairn and neighbouring Dufftown and you'll have the perfect dram for masochists. Or those who have entirely lost the will to live. Jesus... 43%. Flora and Fauna.

PORT ELLEN

Islay, 1825–1983. Diageo. Closed.

Port Ellen 1979 db (93) n22 mousy and retiring; a degree of oak fade and fruit on the delicate smoke t23 non-committal delivery but bursts into stride with a series of sublime, peat-liquorice waves and a few rounds of spices; f24 a surprising gathering of oils rounds up the last traces of sweet barley and ensures an improbably long – and refined – finish; b24 takes so long to get out of the traps, you wonder if anything is going to happen. But when it does, my word...it's glorious! 57.5%

Port Ellen 29 Year Old 8th Release, dist 1978, bott 2008 db (90.5) n23 t22.5 f22.5 b22.5. The glory and charisma is still there to cast you under its spell, but some high notes are missed, the timing not quite what it was; yet still we stand and applaud because we recognise it exactly for what it is: beauty and genius still, but fading beauty; receding genius. Something which only those of us of a certain vintage, can remember as being that unique, almost naked, celebration of Islay malt whisky it once so beautifully and so gloriously was. 55.3%

Port Ellen 31 Years Old Special Release refill American & European oak, dist 1978, bott 2010 db (88.5) n22 t23 f22 b21.5 shows some serious cracks now, though that can't be helped; this whisky was never made for this type of age. Still some moments to close the eyes to and simply cherish, however; 54.6%. nc ncf. Diageo. Fewer than 3000 bottles.

Port Ellen 32 Years Old Special Release 2011 db (88.5) n22.5 PE at its drowsiest: not so much the normal ashy notes of old age, but dust. The phenols hang on in there; t22.5 a burst of gristy sugars has been infiltrated by some muscly oak but surprisingly virile lemon; f22 any drier and you could use this for a smoky martini. Actually, anyone found putting anything into a PE, other than more PE, will have to be brought to me for the most severe sentencing. b22 really feeling its age, though there are many superb passages of play. 53.9%. nc ncf.

⠿ **Port Ellen 32 Years Old Special Release 2012** Refill American and European Oak Casks, dist 1979, bott 2012 db (88.5) n23 presumably the use of sherry casks has dampened the fire. The smoke is hard to spot, other than a slightly acrid burned toast bite; t23.5 comes together gorgeously on delivery with a sharp, salty whip to the arrival of both the big malt and feathered grape; pretty mouthwatering and now the smoke really does grab hold...with silk gloves; f20 furry and moist an un-Port Ellenly off key; b22 some mesmerising moments. Not sure what the finish is all about, though. 52.5 %. nc ncf. Diageo.

⠿ **Chieftain's Port Ellen Aged 30 Years** hogshead, cask no. 1518, dist May 82, bott Sep 12 (96.5) n24 exceptional nose: a few strands of citrus and banana delicately sweeten the dry, sooty peat and oak-rich hickory; t25 the delivery amazes: even after 30 years of tasting the rare fruits of this distillery, I was still taken aback by the beautifully fragile nature of the fruit which is first to show. Both tangerine and ordinary oranges show immediately, then a brief cherry note before the honey arrives in both ulmo and heather form. And the peat. At first politely allows the fruit and sugars to lead the way, then slowly takes command first as a base phenol note, then by taking off in smoke form across the palate; f23 thins and tires quite quickly, though the oak is good enough never to detract; b24.5 when you consider first the quality of this malt and then that with each new bottling of Port Ellen the remaining reserves of its whisky shrinks like a puddle in the noonday sun, one is not sure whether to laugh or cry. But like all great whiskies of near perfect balance, it is a bitter-sweet experience. 50.1%. nc ncf sc. Ian Macleod Distillers. 308 bottles.

⠿ **Gordon and MacPhail rare Old Port Ellen 1979** (96) n24 what can you say? Looking at the negative points...a touch of oak-faulted bitterness. But it is a side issue, far, far outweighed by the peat which appears to begin as a single, lonely atom but slowly multiplies hand in hand with the kumquats. Even now, after all these years, the trademark gristy barley can still be detected....truly astonishing...; t23.5 just as on the nose, the smoke begins with little more than a shadow but with a touch of buttercream and muscovado sugar, climbs in weight and depth; immediate spices underline the oak and age; f23 the nose suggested a bitter landing; it was a false call. This is in keeping with all before, concentrating mainly on a soft fondant (Walnut whip-type) with a light degree of cocoa and what little weight there is created by that sophisticated, understated smoke and balanced by that thin thread of ulmo honey; b24.5 a fascinating dram. This is what happens when peat diminishes over the decades. It begins on both nose and palate like a small tattoo, a mark you can see but is indistinguishable. Then, with each sniff and mouthful, that tattoo is added to and is formed into a dragon. But not one breathing fire...just soft, elegant smoke. And a dragon with green, mossy, earthy eyes with flecksof golden honey which draws you in further, deeper....An erotic, beautiful whisky which displays charm and depth in equal measures. And, here's the rub: does so without seemingly knowing. 46%

Malts Of Scotland Port Ellen 1982 sherry hogshead, cask no. MoS12017, dist Feb 82, bott Apr 12 (**96**) **n24** the sultanas are so juicy, the smoke for a moment has a problem competing; a degree of harmony is contrived, though a chunk of hickory tries to intervene; the smokiness is meaty, not dissimilar to certain sausages I have found in Bavaria; even a hint of Rupp cheese; **t24.5** massive delivery, helped along by the surprising strength for its age; with the phenols powering through while they have the chance. Several layers of seriously overcooked Christmas pudding tries to have its cake, so to speak...; the barley flows, the fruit juices flow...spices bombard...; **f23.5** long, with the burnt cherries and raisins coming back with a vengeance; the smoke is now much more ethereal; **b24** stunning whisky. The sherry, even though this time from a faultless butt, dumbs down to a degree and takes the edge off the complexity. But it doesn't matter: this is one very big dram to savour from the very top drawer of Islay malts. 58.6%. nc ncf sc. Malts Of Scotland.

Malts Of Scotland Port Ellen 1983 bourbon hogshead, cask no. MoS11011, dist Feb 83, bott Oct 11 (**91**) **n22** dry and ashy like the other '83 vintages out this year. But this offers a bit more tart aggression; **t23** the sugars gang up fast and true; the smoke helps deflect some of the harder strikes especially from the early spice; **f23** the spices linger, but otherwise calms beautifully, again with the delicate smoke seemingly pulling all the strings; **b23** comes out a snarling fighter, ends a buttercup-sniffing pacifist. 58.9%. nc ncf sc. Malts Of Scotland.

Old Malt Cask Port Ellen Aged 28 Years refill hogshead, cask no. 7244, dist Feb 83, bott Jun 11 (**94.5**) **n23** an ashy dryness is countered by molten liquorice-muscovado; **t24** grist! How does it do that after all this time. I thought that old Port Ellen trademark was a thing of the past; the sugars and smoke in rhapsodic harmony; **f23.5** the gristy effect continues with a degree of lemon now sharpening the smoky barley; **b24** after 28 years not a single blemish. Spectacular! And not least for its understated elegance. 50%. nc ncf sc. Douglas Laing & Co. 292 bottles.

⁘ **Old & Rare Port Ellen Aged 30 Years** refill hogshead, dist 82, bott 12 (**95**) **n24.5** almost perfect: the signature delicate PE gristiness, the peat in butterfly mode, revealing just the odd sprig of mint as a nod towards age; **t23.5** can a whisky be both delicate and intense? This seems to manage it with the muscovado sugars having as much to say as the phenols; **f23** playful smoky butterscotch....little oil, so dry but always elegant; **b24** what can you say? How much longer will we be able to enjoy masterpieces like these? 51.8%. nc ncf sc. 154 bottles.

⁘ **Old & Rare Port Ellen Aged 32 Years** refill butt, dist 79, bott 12 (**93.5**) **n24** lots of tannins but the spice and smoke balance with ease. Lovely sweet-dry interplay; **t23** sweet barley shows first then, like distant smoke signals the phenols send their message; **f23** lots of vanilla and the sugars bite deep as the tannins return; **b23.5** the oak is doing its best to spoil the party but the sheer mastery of the peat foils that plan. Superb. 54.8%. nc ncf sc. 145 bottles.

Whisky Antique Port Ellen 26 Years Old dist 1983, bott 2009 (**89**) **n22** as dry as port Ellen ever get. Not just ashy, but that stringent nose burn that sometimes comes along with embers; a light hint of creosote; **t22.5** sugars at last! A sprinkling of caster sugar melts immediately on the palate; as soon as that has dissolved, a smoky-liquorice substitute dives in; **f22** long, reverting back to that dry ashy persona; a late barley juiciness breaks out only to be replaced by butterscotch; **b22.5** a fascinating dram, at a stage of its life where it cannot sit comfortably for more than a few moments. 53.5%. sc. Silver Seal Whisky Company.

Whisky Antique Port Ellen 28 Years Old dist 1983, bott 2011 (**91**) **n22** obviously a twin cask to their 2009 bottling: very similar but a few extra softening vanillas here; **t23** sugars aplenty but this time not of the superfine variety: much weightier and a little more molassed, heading in a muscovado direction. The smoke eschews the ashy route and joins the oils to form a more voluptuous peatiness, again with caramels at play; **f23** much softer on the finish than its twin with the smoke gliding home, even sporting a degree of citrus, rather than crash-landing; late smoky mocha; **b23** displays the kind of softness of touch that could convert many who think they don't like peaty whisky. 55.5%. sc. Silver Seal Whisky Company.

PULTENEY

Highlands (Northern), 1826. Inver House Distillers. Working.

Old Pulteney Aged 12 Years db (**90.5**) **n22** pungent, busy and full of zesty zap. Enough salt to get your blood pressure up; **t23** beautifully clean barley, again showing little shortage of saltiness, but thriving in its zesty environment; **f22.5** the vanillas and cocoa carry out an excellent drying operation. The sea-breeze saltiness continues to hang on the taste buds...; **b23** a cleaner, zestier more joyous composition than the old 43%, though that has less to do with strength than overall construction. A dramatic whisky which, with further care, could get even closer to the truth of this distillery. 40%

Old Pulteney Aged 12 Years db (85) n22 t23 f19 b21. There are few malts whose finish dies as spectacularly as this. The nose and delivery are spot on with a real buzz and panache. The delivery in particular just bowls you over with its sharp barley integrity: real pulse-racing stuff! Then... toffee...!!! Grrrr!!! If it is caramel causing this, then it can be easily remedied. And in the process we'd have a malt absolutely basking in the low 90s...! 43%

Old Pulteney Aged 15 Years db (91) n21 pretty harsh and thin at first but some defter barley notes can be detected; t24 an attention-grabbing, eye-wateringly sharp delivery with the barley in roasty mood and biting immediately with a salty incision; the barley-sugar effect is mesmerising and the clarity astonishing for its age; f23 long, with those barley sugars working overtime; a slight salty edge there but the oak behaves impeccably; b23 only on about the fourth or fifth mouthful do you start getting the picture here: enormously complex with a genuine coastal edge to this. The complexity is awesome. 54.9%

Old Pulteney Aged 17 Years db (95) n22 tight but does all that is possible to reveal its salty, fruity complexity with pears and lemons to the fore; t25 one of the softest, most beautifully crafted deliveries in the whisky world. Absolutely faultless as it picks the most fabulous course among the honeyed vanilla and barley which is so delicate words simply cannot do justice; f24 near perfect balance between the vanillas and delicate honeys; b24 the nose confirms that some of the casks at work here are not A1. Even so, the whisky performs to the kind of levels some distillers could only dream of. 46%

Old Pulteney Aged 21 Years db (97.5) n25 if you had the formula to perfectly transform salt, citrus, the most delicate smoke imaginable, sharp barley, more gristy barley, light vanilla, toasty vanilla, roasted hazelnut, thinned manuka honey, lavender honey, arbutus blossom and cherry blossom, light hickory, liquorice, and the softest demerara sugar into the aroma of a whisky, you still wouldn't quite be able to recreate this perfection...; t24 the sugars arrive: first gristy and malt-laden, then Demerara. This is followed by a salty, nerve-tingling journey of barley at varying intensity and then a slow but magnificently complete delivery of spice...; f24 those spices continue to buzz, the vanillas dovetail with the malt and the fruit displaying a puckering, lively intensity. Ridiculously long fade for a malt so seemingly light, the salts and spices kiss the taste buds goodnight...; b24.5 by far and away one of the great whiskies of 2012, absolutely exploding from the glass with vitality, charisma and class. One of Scotland's great undiscovered distilleries about to become discovered, I think... and rightly so! 46%

Old Pulteney Aged 30 Years db (93.5) n23 magnificent spectrum of exotic fruits leave no doubts about its age: plenty of mango, especially, while the odd tinned peach appears to have been tossed into the dainty salad; t24 melts-in-the-mouth, aided by the strength. But that means the richer flavours grab only half a hold and soon slip away; the mid-ground has the feel of a chocolate fruit liqueur, except the liqueur might have more attitude; f23 medium length but we are back into exotic fruits territory: an unusual development for a malt. Maybe it is a mixture of the subtle salt and delicate, semi-drowned orange blossom honey which is raising the fruity profile; b23.5 I know there is not too much of this north Scottish nectar, but they would have been brave to have brought this out at 46%...if they were able, that is. 40.1%

Old Pulteney 30 Years Old db (92) n23.5 fabulous mix of Jaffa cake and bourbon, seasoned by a pinch of salt; t23.5 an early, unexpected, wave of light smoke and silkier oak gives immediate depth. But stunning, ultra-juicy citrus and barley ensures this doesn't get all big and brooding; f22 thinner and oakier with a playful oak-spice tingle; plenty of vanilla controls the drier aspects; b23 I had to laugh when I tasted this: indeed, it had me scrambling for a copy of the 2009 Bible to check for sure what I had written. And there it was: after bemoaning the over oaking I conjectured, "As Pulteney has the fascinating tendency to radically shift style over not too long a period, I can't wait for the next instalment." And barely a year on, here it is. Pretty far removed from last year's offering and an absolute peach of a dram that laughs in the face of its 30 years... 45%

Old Pulteney Aged 40 Years db (95) n23.5 gosh! That's pretty aged stuff with the exotic fruit hanging on by a fingernail. Some major bourbon notes now evident – and lip-smacking; t23.5 massive delivery, again with tannins coming from every angle. But a mix of liquorice, dates, burnt raisin and honey cope well while spices tingle; f24 settles for a long essay of happy old bourbon-style led whisky; b24 this malt still flies as close to the sun as possible. But some extra fruit, honey and spice now grasps the tannins by the throat to ensure a whisky of enormous magnitude and complexity 51.3% ⊙ ⊙

Old Pulteney WK209 db (71) n68.5 t18 f16.5 b17. Could well be liked by the Germans. 46%

Old Pulteney WK217 db (88.5) n21 some pretty young notes offer a background "new make" freshness; the salt and delicate, peachy fruits are only half-formed; t22 the delivery reveals unusual youthfulness, amply balanced by a more impressive saline contour which hits you like sea spray in the face: a rare eruption of flavour in a sensual experience; f23 the oaks appear to have ganged together to proffer an oily, praline fade; **b22.5** the WK series is named after the old fishing vessels which used to be based in the town's harbour. I suspect old WK217 rarely had a day at sea in waters as calm as this softy of a malt. *46%*

Cadenhead Pulteney 20 Years Old bott 2009 **(91) n24** what a nose...! Just so delicate and complex. Very lightly salted and coastal, with a nod towards clear rock pools; there is even a touch of distant Pennan peat fires on the wind. The malt is fresh with the sugars crisp and countering the sharper tones. Complex and, frankly, something of a turn on; **t23** wonderful, crystalline clarity to the early barley with almost a fizz to the salt-malt interaction. Just so juicy...! **f21.5** damn! Typically Allied in the finish, in that a slight bitterness develops, though nothing will, ultimately, undoes the overall enjoyment. Also, a really busy, complex and unusually bitty and peppery spice – something not unknown in bourbons - takes off on full damage limitation; **b22.5** I'm glad I have plenty of this left. For the next time I spend an evening with a beautiful woman, I would like to smear this all over her body... *56.9%. sc.*

Gordon & MacPhail Cask Strength Pulteney 1998 **(92) n22** citrusy, with a powerful kumquat element as well as big vanilla and a surprising rumble of natural caramels; **t23** mmmmmm! What a delivery! Barley concentrate eventually giving way to a tangy saltiness missing on the nose; sharp and eye-watering and wonderfully layered; **f23** the barley plays out until the end, but some cocoa and spice make a near inevitable appearance; the salt also sticks around, though seasons with little less gusto than before, keeping the burgeoning sugars honest; good late oils; **b24** the nose may be missing the normal coastal depth to this malt, but it makes up for it elsewhere! Confirmation of what a cracking distillery this is. *56.9%*

ROSEBANK
Lowlands, 1840–1993. Diageo. Closed. (But if there is a God will surely one day re-open)

Rosebank Aged 12 Years db **(95) n24 t24 f23 b24.** Infinately better than the last F&bottling, this is quite legendary stuff, even better than the old 8-y-o version, though probably a point or two down regarding complexity. The kind of whisky that brings a tear to the eye... for many a reason... *43%. Flora and Fauna.*

Rosebank 21 Years Old Special Release db **(94) n24** fabulous interplay between apple and berry fruits, though it's the pear juice which acts as the sweetening agent; a nose to spend a good 20 minutes over; **t23.5** at once fizzing and busy while soft and caressing; natural caramels combine with coconut oil to offer the weightier sheen; **f23** dries but never bitters; healthy vanilla all the way **b23.5** can any Lowland be compared to a fully blossomed Rosebank? This is whisky to both savour and worship for this is nectar in a Rose... *53.8%. nc ncf.*

Rosebank 22 Years Old Rare Malts 2004 db **(85) n22 t23 f19 b21.** One or two Rosebank moments of joyous complexity but, hand on heart, this is simply too old. *61.1%*

Rosebank 25 Years Old db **(96) n24.5 t23.5 f24 b24.** I had to sit back, take a deep breath and get my head around this. It was like Highland Park but with a huge injection of sweetened chocolate on the finale and weight – and even smoke – from a Rosebank I had never quite seen before. And believe me, as this distillery's greatest champion, I've tasted a few hundred, possibly thousands, of casks of this stuff over the last 25 years. Is this the greatest of all time? I am beginning to wonder. Is it the most extraordinary since the single malt revolution took off? Certainly. Do I endorse it? My god, yes! *61.4%*

Chieftain's Rosebank Aged 20 Years butt, dist Oct 90, bott Sep 11 **(88) n22** a little dull with the red liquorice tannins dominating; quite a salty theme to the quiet honey, too; **t22.5** some serious spice prickle injects some major action; a delicate honey thread forms the audience; **f21.5** back to a mildly one-dimensional oaky theme; **b22** a rose with several thorns... *55.7%. nc ncf sc. Ian Macleod Distillers.*

Old Malt Cask Rosebank Aged 21 Years refill hogshead, cask no. 8227, dist Jun 90, bott Mar 12 **(90.5) n23.5** excellent floral depth to the honey and crisp vanillas; the citrus is a delight; **t23** a light, teasing touch where the barley makes the juiciest impact possible with so much oak present; the vanillas are dry but friendly, the honey moves towards a cocoa-nougat middle; **f21.5** the vanillas dry up – like a salt lake in the desert...! **b22.5** molten chocolate-honey candy. *50%. nc ncf sc. Douglas Laing & Co. 136 bottles.*

Old Malt Cask Rosebank Aged 21 Years refill butt, dist Feb 90, bott Aug 11 **(89) n23.5** it's a question of counting the different shades of honey: I can spot three without difficulty. And seemingly on a bed of crushed Digestive biscuit...; **t22** an early spice kick is doused by those varied honeys; takes on a surprising degree of oil; **f21** the honey is usurped by a thin vanilla sign off; **b22.5** unusually oily but those honeys are sublime. *50%. nc ncf sc. 268 bottles.*

Old Malt Cask Rosebank Aged 21 Years refill hogshead, cask no. 8247, dist Jun 90, bott May 12 **(82.5) n21 t21.5 f19 b21.** A seriously bipolar dram. The buttock-clenching tightness on delivery and thereafter is a result of a very tight, uncompromising cask. However, the constant lip-smacking qualities are due to a spirit with more than the ghost of varying shades of honey. *50%. nc ncf sc. Douglas Laing & Co. 116 bottles.*

Scotch Malt Whisky Society Cask 25.59 Aged 20 Years refill barrel, cask no. 2009, dist 1991 (86.5) n21.5 t23 f21 b21. Honey and spice aplenty if you look for it. But this cask is slightly bunged up with natural caramels which give a heavy, restricted feel to the proceedings. A rose which refuses to bloom. 53.8%. sc. Scotch Malt Whisky Society.

Scotch Malt Whisky Society Cask 25.60 Aged 20 Years refill barrel, cask no. 2018, dist 1991 (87.5) n21.5 sluggish and toffee heavy; t23 superb delivery with a sparkling oak-sharpened tang to juicy barley. The odd honey note surfaces but is countered by chunky caramel; f21.5 more creamy toffee; b21.5 similar to 25.59, except here the caramel is marginally less attentive. 51.1%. sc. Scotch Malt Whisky Society.

ROYAL BRACKLA
Speyside, 1812. John Dewar & Sons. Working.

Royal Brackla Aged 10 Years db (73) n18 t20 f17 b18. A distinct lowering of the colours since I last tasted this. What on earth is going on? 40%

Cadenhead Royal Brackla 19 Years Old Demerara rum cask, bott Apr 12 (84.5) n22 t22 f19 b21.5. From the cask type you'd expect a malt as hard as nails. And that's exactly what you get. Enjoys some memorably bold and juicy moments. 55.9%. sc.

Duncan Taylor NC2 Royal Brackla 12 Years Old dist 1999 (86) n21.5 t22 f21 b21.5. Solid and simplistic with much emphasis on the rigid sugars keeping the barley in place. The spice element works quite beautifully. 46%. Duncan Taylor & Co.

Duncan Taylor Dimensions Royal Brackla 14 Years Old dist Sep 97, bott Nov 11 (84) n21.5 t21.5 f20 b21. A distillery which is a bit uptight at the best of times shows little inclination for fun here. 46.1%. nc ncf sc. Duncan Taylor & Co.

Fortnum & Mason Jubilee Royal Brackla Aged 11 Years dist 1999 (89) n21.5 exceptionally light, allowing what little oak influence there is to have a fuller say than you might expect. The barley retains a touch of grist and lemon; t24 shy it may be on the nose, it sweeps onto the taste buds like a 19th century debutant might fill a grand staircase as she enters the ball. Honey and spice and all things thrice as the flavours pound, pound and pound again. Lightly oiled bourbon notes of a red liquorice and mild hickory hue help fill out the petticoats and gown, all covering a thin vanilla body; f21.5 content with idle vanilla and barley chatter; b22 I used to do annual whisky tastings at Fortnum and Mason when this malt was just a twinkle in the distiller's eye. They did not have a house malt this good. They have called it "The Queen's Own Whisky." A charming, elegant, demure princess of a dram. 46%. nc ncf. Fortnum & Mason.

Gordon & MacPhail Connoisseurs Choice Royal Brackla 1995 (88) n22 spotted dog pudding and stewed apple; t22 silky malt and a riot of dark sugars; some evidence of a wide cut by the stillman; f22 the extra oils inject spice and mocha to counter the vanilla; b22 a softer, sweeter and more friendly Brackla than many on the market just now. This one works quite well, though technically not totally sound. 46%. Gordon & MacPhail.

Gordon and MacPhail Connoisseurs Choice Royal Brackla 1997 (84.5) n20.5 t22 f21 b21. An intriguing battle between good, sprightly spirit and so-so oak which offers little and detracts some. 46%. ncf.

Old Malt Cask Royal Brackla Aged 12 Years (77) n20 t20 f18 b19. The tang of an unhelpful cask spoils the party somewhat. 50%. nc ncf sc. Douglas Laing & Co. 250 bottles. In celebration of the Queen's Diamond Jubilee.

ROYAL LOCHNAGAR
Highlands (Eastern), 1826. Diageo. Working.

Royal Lochnagar Aged 12 Years db (84) n21 t22 f20 b21. More care has been taken with this than some other bottlings from this wonderful distillery. But I still can't understand why it never quite manages to get out of third gear...or is the caramel on the finish the giveaway...? 40%

Royal Lochnagar 1994 The Manager's Choice db (89.5) n23 t23.5 f21.5 b21.5. Much more intense and heavyweight than the norm. Also a bit of toffee on the finish brings down the marks slightly. Great stuff, even so. 59.3%

Royal Lochnagar Selected Reserve db (89) n23 t23 f21 b22. Quite brilliant sherry influence. The spices are a treat. 43%

Old Malt Cask Royal Lochnagar Aged 14 Years refill butt, cask no. 7595, dist Apr 97, bott Aug 11 (89.5) n21.5 bizarrely, a vague new make element clings to the barley and citrus; t23.5 a superb delivery with the grist melting on the palate in the sexiest way possible; like a young virgin falling into your arms and craving love...; f23 there is the lightest of vanilla touches here, little more than a threat amid the persistent and almost perfectly sugared barley; b21.5 how can a whisky spend 14 years in a cask, pick up virtually no colour and yet get a very healthy tick of approval from me. Answer: the oak, as well as not imparting too much positive, does nothing negative, either. So there are none of the bitter notes you often find at the tail end of a cask like this to spoil the experience. Just a gorgeously refreshing and bright malt, the like of which you will not find every day... *50%. nc ncf sc. 460 bottles.*

꘎꘎ **Old Malt Cask Royal Lochnagar Aged 15 Years** refill butt, cask no. 9818, dist Jun 97, bott May 13 **(86) n22 t21 f21.5 b21.5.** Pretty even but when the flavours spike, especially with the lemon attached to the heather honey, Queen Victoria – the distillery's greatest advocate – would have been amused. *50%. nc ncf sc. Hunter Laing & Co Ltd. 329 bottles.*

Provenance Royal Lochnagar Over 10 Years refill hogshead, cask no. 7648, dist 01, bott 11 **(89.5) n22** fabulously vibrant. The oak has scarcely made an impact, leaving the barley to celebrate both a malty and juicily fruity edge; **t23** even more mouth-watering than you could hope for. Gristy in part, with the sugars dissolving on the palate. Some lovely lemon adds zip and zest. This has a small still feel and the copper really has a presence; **f22** mocha with a slice of lime; **b22.5** no wonder Prince Albert used to visit this distillery: this bottling looks like a Riesling! But one can certainly be amused on nose and taste. *46%. nc ncf sc.*

Provenance Royal Lochnagar Over 12 Years refill butt, cask no. 8187, dist Summer 1999, bott Winter 2012 **(91) n22** curious mix of honey and stewed, unsalted celery...; some old polished leather, too; **t23** a soufflé-light delivery of watered down acacia honey and an unusual march past of delicate Victoria sponge cake offering varying degrees of vanilla and custard....very different...and delicious! **f23** just more of the same, but with a long fade; **b23** an uncommonly good year for Lochnagar bottlings, and this is the best I have tasted so far. *46%. nc ncf sc. Douglas Laing & Co.*

The Whisky Broker Royal Lochnagar 9 Years Old Queen's Diamond Jubilee hogshead, cask no. 644, dist 8 May 02, bott 26 Jan 12 **(90.9) n22.5** lightly stewed apple with delicate vanilla rather than cinnamon; **t22.5** fresh, salivating, crisp and then a fabulous slow motion explosion of intense barley and spice; lacks the normal coppery sharpness; the sugars are precise and a joy; **f23.5** long clean and uncluttered by anything other than even more concentrated barley and a gorgeous maple syrup and spice wind down; **b22** diamond coloured for the Queen Elizabeth's Diamond Jubilee. But it works for, despite the minimalist oak involvement, it never fails to charm. And for this whisky: we are amused. *55.5%. nc ncf sc. 353 bottles.*

ST. MAGDALENE

Lowlands, 1798–1983. Diageo. Demolished.

Linlithgow 30 Years Old dist 1973 db **(70) n18 t18 f16 b18.** A brave but ultimately futile effort from a malt that is way past its sell-by date. *596%*

꘎꘎ **Mo Ór Collection Linlithgow 1982 28 Years Old** first fill bourbon hogshead, cask no. 2203, dist 5 Oct 82, bott 1 Nov 10 **(88) n21.5** a touch of plasticine, but an agreeable degree of fruit and barley, too; **t23** a gristy, juicy sweetness holds its ground and the spices follow in with impressive timing; **f21.5** fades and bitters slightly with minimal development beyond the oak; **b22** way better than I suspected it might be. The finish is thin, but all else is a treat. *46%. nc ncf sc. Release No. 7 The Whisky Talker. 900 bottles.*

Old Malt Cask St Magdalene Aged 29 Years refill butt, cask no. 7662, dist Oct 82, bott Oct 11 **(92) n22.5** busy and perfectly weighted nose even displaying a surprising – no, astonishing! - element of delicate smoke (and I mean no more than the odd atom or two here) to provide the anchor for the cleanest of vanilla-barley mixes; **t23.5** one of the softest deliveries of the year as the gristy malts melt juicily. This leaves a clear run for the lightest of spice and charming of milk chocolate mousses; **f23** vanilla and butterscotch, as one might imagine, but the spices return to lengthen matters to the max; **b23** unfortunately not a malt that turns up often these days. And this little essay in subtle complexity proved to be a great and very pleasant surprise. A go-grab no brainer! *50%. nc ncf sc. 288 bottles.*

SCAPA

Highlands (Island–Orkney), 1885. Chivas Brothers. Working.

Scapa 12 Years Old db **(88) n23 t22 f21 b22.** Always a joy. *40%*

Scapa 14 Years Old db **(88) n22 t22.5 f21.5 b22.** Enormous variation from bottling to bottling. In Canada I have tasted one that I gave 94 to: but don't have notes or sample here. This one is a bit of dis-service due to the over-the-top caramel added which appears to douse the usual honeyed balance. Usually, this is one of the truly great malts of the Chivas empire and a classic islander. *40%*

Scapa 16 Years Old db **(81) n21 t20.5 f19.5 b20.** For it to be so tamed and toothless is a crime against a truly great whisky which, handled correctly, would be easily among the finest the world has to offer. *40%*

Scapa 'the' Orcadian 16 Years Old db **(87.5) n22 t22 f21.5 b22.** A thin wisp of honey is key to the weight and balance of this malt. *40%. For the Swiss market.*

꘎꘎ **Gordon and MacPhail Distillery Label Scapa 2001 (94.5) n23** the fresh, slightly fruity aromas of a high class bakery on first opening its doors; the barley is so, so young...but equally unblemished; **t24** the delivery is near perfect: a light oil helps spread the juiciest of salty barley notes, young and chock-a-bloc with gristy sugars; a very light, cooling mintiness to the vanilla; **f23.5** more of the same, the oils ensuring a long fade and high quality oak offering weight and keeping things on track; **b24** showing Scapa exactly as it should be. One of the easiest drinking malts currently in the market place, and quite probably the most moreish. Genius. And dangerous... *43%*

Scotch Malt Whisky Society Cask 17.33 Aged 9 Years refill barrel, cask no. 313, dist 2002 **(83.5) n22.5 t22 f19 b20.** Those bitter Allied casks can be heartbreakers. The big honeycomb lead had, until their intervention, been a treat. *57.7%. sc.*

SPEYBURN
Speyside, 1897. Inver House Distillers. Working.

Speyburn 10 Year Old db **(82) n20 t21 f20.5 b20.5.** A tight, sharp dram with slightly more emphasis on the citric. A bit of toffee on the finale. *40%*

Speyside 12 Years Old db **(85) n22 t22 f20.5 b21.5** Copious honey and malt on delivery. Simplistic, effective but a tad bitter on finish. *40%*

Speyburn Aged 25 Years db **(92) n22 t24 f23 b23.** Either they have re-bottled very quickly or I got the diagnosis dreadfully wrong first time round. Previously I wasn't overly impressed; now I'm taken aback by its beauty. Some change. *46%*

Speyburn Bradan Orach db **(76.5) n19 t20 f19.5 b18.** Fresh, young, but struggles to find a balance. *40%*

⁘ **Gordon and MacPhail Connoisseurs Choice Speyburn 1989** **(82.5) n21 t21.5 f20 b20.** A kind of Speyside version of malt gruel. *46%. ncf.*

Provenance Speyburn Over 7 Years sherry butt, cask no. 8498, dist 2004, bott 2012 **(74) n19 t19 f19 b17.** Had to check for a moment if I was tasting Speyside. The malt and oak are not on speaking terms and hard to find a less harmonious youngster. *46%. nc ncf sc.*

⁘ **Provenance Speyburn Over 8 Years** sherry butt, cask no. 9435, dist Autumn 04, bott Winter 13 **(88) n21.5** a touch of boot polish to the raisin; **t22.5** light and thinly malted at first, but gets into its stride as the macadamia nut and spotted dog pudding get into their stride; the malt intensifies dramatically; **f22** impressive oak sign off for a malt so young; **b22** muscles up on the barley. Simple, but effective. *46%. nc, ncf, sc. Douglas Laing & Co.*

THE SPEYSIDE DISTILLERY
Speyside, 1990. Speyside Distillers. Working.

The Speyside 10 Years Old db **(81) n19 t21 f20 b21.** Plenty of sharp oranges around; the malt is towering and the bite is deep. A weighty Speysider with no shortage of mouth prickle. *40%*

The Speyside Aged 12 Years db **(81) n19 t22 f19.5 b20.5.** Unusual to find feints to this degree after twelve years. Some short-lived honey...but it's hard work! *40%*

The Speyside Aged 15 Years db **(75) n19 t20 f18 b18.** A case of quantity of flavours over quality. *40%*

Cú Dhub db **(88) n22 t22.5 f21.5 b22.** Not exactly a thoroughbred and you won't find it winning any prizes at Cruft's. But a malt which has improved beyond recognition in recent years and now even boasts a degree of enjoyable complexity. And you know something else...not a single sulphur note in sight... *40%*

Drumguish db **(87) n18 t22 f19 b19.** Historically, not one of my favourite drams. But I have to say that this has improved by a considerable degree. Still feinty, and the delivery is not promising. But once it settles, there is a very acceptable degree of honey-led complexity before the feints bite back. *40%*

Mo Òr Collection Speyside 1994 16 Years Old first fill bourbon hogshead, cask no. 34, dist 25 Apr 94, bott 2 Dec 10 **(85.5) n19 t23 f22.5 b21.** They have done well to select one of the better casks from this distillery for this period. Straighter than a Roman road, and perhaps a little broader from the oils. But beyond the barley and most simplistic oak there is little to engage the mind or taste buds. But of all the deliveries I have found in bottled form from this distillery, this rates among the best. *46%. nc ncf sc. Release No. 45. 385 bottles.*

Old Malt Cask Speyside Aged 20 Years sherry butt, cask no. 8472, dist May 92, bott May 12 **(81) n21 t21 f19 b20.** A real glassful of dates and walnuts. But the cut is simply too wide to get away with it comfortably. *50%. nc ncf sc. Douglas Laing & Co. 294 bottles.*

⁘ **Provenance Speyside Over 13 Years** refill hogshead, cask no. 9215, dist Winter 99, bott Autumn 12 **(75) n18 t19 f18 b18.** Very big injection of malt and quite brusque sugar; and even a touch of Weetabix on the fade. But, quite patently, poorly distilled spirit. *46%. nc ncf sc.*

⁘ **Riegger's Selection The Speyside 1999** bourbon cask no. 190, bott 2013 **(86) n22 t21.5 f21 b21.5.** A very acceptable rendition of the distillery from this period. A few clumsy notes still can't entirely disrupt the integrity of the intense barley sugar. *45%. sc.*

Scott's Selection Speyside 1993 bott 2011 (89) n21.5 maybe slightly feinty but, with the extra nutty oil it provides, easy to forgive; just dig that juicy date, too; t22 fat, oily and brimming with the most intense sugar-laden barley you'll find this year. Again, at times reverting to a date-like thickness of flesh; so juicy and chewy you want to give the bottle a little kiss...; f23 long, with the expected custardy vanillas arriving. But the Demerara sugars absolutely refuse to be cowered. The last tones are those of the kind of wafer cones you find for ice cream...minus the Mr Whippy...; b22.5 now there you go! We can start to re-write the history books regarding the quality of whisky from this distillery. For this is, though it be made up like an old tart you might find along an unlit canal path, uncommonly fine merchandise worthy of a knee trembler whatever your whisky persuasion, whatever your sex... 61.5%. Speyside Distillers.

⋰⋰⋰ **The Warehouse Collection The Speyside Aged 16 Years** bourbon barrel, cask no. 928, dist 28 Aug 96, bott 30 Apr 13 (92.5) n23 lemon curd spread generously over barley sugar. Lashings of tannins; t23.5 a fizzy start with light muscovado sugars accompany the unusually clean and concentrated barley for The Speyside; the oaks are firm and a little earthy: ersatz coffee and hickory lead; f23 latte coffee sweetened with barley grist; b23 had to look twice at the label here. Rarely does this distillery come across with such easy charm. No great complexity. But everything it does is done with a swagger. 52.7%. nc ncf sc. 171 bottles.

SPRINGBANK
Campbeltown, 1828. J&A Mitchell & Co. Working.

Hazelburn Aged 8 Years bourbon cask, bott 2011 db (94.5) n23 green apple represents the more dashing aspect of the very young barley; t24 fabulously solid barley; intense and complete. The youth shimmers on the palate, the malt mixing contentedly with pleasing early butterscotch; elsewhere there is a real richness seemingly imparted from the stills themselves; f23.5 confirmation of an excellent cask in use here as the lightly spiced vanilla enjoys the odd strand of honey; more light metals breaking into the lengthy barley; b24 a very curious coppery sheen adds extra lustre and does no harm to a very well made spirit filled into top grade oak. For an eight year old malt, something extra special. 46%

Hazelburn Aged 8 Years 3rd Edition (triple distilled) bott 2007 db (89) n22 t22.5 f22 b22.5. Somewhat effete by comparison to last year's big malty number. Here there is a shade more accent on fruit. Very light, indeed. 46%

Longrow Aged 10 Years db (78) n19 t20 f19 b20. This has completely bemused me: bereft not only of the usual to-die-for smoke, its warts are exposed badly, as this is way too young. Sweet and malty, perhaps, and technically better than the marks I'm giving it – but this is Longrow, dammit! I am astonished. 46%

Longrow Aged 10 Years 100 Proof db (86) n20 t23 f22 b21. Still bizarrely smokeless – well, maybe a flicker of smoke as you may find the involuntary twitching of a leg of a dying fly – but the mouthfeel is much better here and although a bit too oily and dense for complexity to get going, a genuinely decent fruit heading towards Hazelburn-esque barley intensity. Love it, because this oozes class. But where's the ruddy peat...?! 57%

Hazelburn Aged 12 Years fresh sherrywood, bott 2012 db (85.5) n22 t21 f21.5 b21. At times nutty. At others, oily. And is that the vaguest hint of phenol I spot bouncing around at one stage...? But overall a malt which does not, at this juncture in its life, seem entirely at ease with either itself or the cask. Some lovely moments of lucidity but for the most part it's an interrupted work in progress. Still, this is the 666th new whisky I have tasted for the 2013 Bible, so it was likely to have a little bit of devil in it... 46%

Longrow 14 Years Old refill bourbon and sherry casks db (89) n24 t23.5 f19 b22.5. Again, a sherry butt proves the Achilles heel. But until then, a charmer. 46%

Longrow Aged 18 Years db (94) n23.5 t23 f24 b23.5. Tries to hide its light under a bushel... but fails. The most subtle and sophisticated Longrow I've come across in 20 years... 46%

Longrow CV bott 2012 db (91) n24 nippy spices infuse with the dry date; the smoke is delicate with an almost dry tobacco edge; the harder peat teams up with the gentle Demerara; t24.5 soft and silky, again the fruit notes intermingle and add a banana and mango juiciness to the oils; the smoke again keeps a low profile, happy to accompany the more telling sugars; f19.5 dries quickly as the furry bitterness from a sherry butt take hold; b23 for a few moments this is heading onto the shortlist of potential Whisky Bible award winners, but a familiar furry rumble – a bit like the distant thunder currently heard from my tasting room – means vital points are lost. Even so, the nose and delivery are something very special, indeed. 46%

Longrow Gaja Barola Wood Expression Aged 7 Years db (91.5) n23.5 t22.5 f23 b22.5. Taking this on is like running around an asylum claiming you're Napoleon. But I have to admit; it's fun! An accidental classic that is unlikely to be repeated...even if they tried..!! 55.8%

Springbank Society Aged 9 Years Rum Wood bott Mar 07 db (93.5) n23 t23.5 f23 b24. A mere pup by Springbank standards. For once its comes through as a real winner in these tender years, doubtless aided by the mercurial charms of the rum and even an unexpected touch of smoke to make for a most complex and entertaining dram. *60.2%*

Springbank Aged 10 Years db **(89.5)** **n22** a surprising hint of peat ash; makes the lemon citrus carry a shade more weight; **t23** that usual Springbank trick at this age of showing oaky depth bouncing off the youthful malt; excellent oil and still a touch of smoke; **f22** thins out with a bitter-ish vanilla tang; **b22.5** although the inherent youthfulness of the 10-y-o has not changed, the depth of body around it has. Keeps the taste buds on full alert. *46%*

Springbank Aged 10 Years (100 Proof) db **(86)** **n21.5 t22 f21 b21.5.** Trying to map a Springbank demands all the skills required of a young 18th century British naval officer attempting to record the exact form and shape of a newly discovered land just after his sextant had fallen into the sea. There is no exact point on which you can fix...and so it is here. A shifting dram that never quite tastes the same twice, but one constant, sadly, is the bitterness towards the finale. Elsewhere, it's one hell of a journey...! *57%*

Springbank 11 Years Old Madeira Wood Expression db **(88)** **n23 t22.5 f21.5 b21.** Madeira perhaps as you've never seen it before: don't go thinking Glenmorangie or Penderyn with this one. As big as the fruit is, the smoke outguns it. *55.8%*

Springbank Aged 15 Years db **(88.5)** **n22.5** full of chunky, malty promise; **t22** big, oily spreads across the palate; dry, a little tart even with limited sweetness; **f22** more oil and huge natural oak caramel; **b22** last time I had one of these, sulphur spoiled the party. Not this time. But the combination of oil and caramel does detract from the complexity a little. *46%*

Springbank Aged 18 Years db **(90.5)** **n23** busy in the wonderful Springbank way; delicate greengage and date; nippy; **t23** yummy, mouthwatering barley and green banana. Fresh with excellent light acacia honey; **f21.5** fabulous oak layering, including chocolate. A little off-key furriness from a sherry butt late on; **b23** just one so-so butt away from bliss... *46%*

Dà Mhile Lost & Found Springbank Organic Aged 20 Years cask no. 237, dist 1992, bott 2012 **(94)** **n23** when first launched as a seven-year-old in 2000 the nose displayed some ungainly feints from where they tried to stretch the unique single run as far they could. Here is proof that time deals with feints in no uncertain manner. And that the casks they filled the historic organic malt in was as good as they get: roast Blue Mountain blended with a medium Java sets the tone and even the mountainous liquorice and Demerara appear dwarfed by the coffee; **t23.5** ever sat down in the morning with the most sublime but heavy roast coffee, the finest natural molassed sugars and beautifully crafted bread baked that morning, freshly toasted and groaning under salted butter....? **f24** absolutely goes into overdrive: the sugars are extraordinary and difficult to translate as there is a criss-crossing of so many styles. Yet late barley juice filters through what appears to be hickory and liquorice. The spices kiss rather than strike. this is wonderful....entirely typical of a Springbank hitting its optimum age between 20 and 25 years. **b23.5** the sun is a circle; the world is a sphere; the greatest fun in existence involves round objects either being kicked or struck by willow. Life, however we look at it, no matter how we try to force to be otherwise, is circular. So how fitting that the very last Scotch whisky to arrive (behind the deadline time!) for this year's 2013 Whisky Bible happens to be the very first whisky I ever wrote about as a professional whisky writer, the first-ever organic malt distilled. It was carried out by award-winning cheese maker John Savage-Onstwedder, who hired Springbank distillery to carry out his dream. And it arrived as I celebrate my 20 years as the world's first full time whisky writer. What goes round, comes round...and here it is again.... re-released 20 years on. *57.3%. sc. J&A Mitchell for Dà Mhile. 87 bottles.*

⁕ **Duthies Springbank 11 Years Old** db **(80)** **n20.5 t21 f19 b20.5.** Malty, fruity and sugary. But never finds the semblance of a rhythm, bitters out and seems about as harmonious and happy as the Australian batting line up. *46%. sc. WM Cadenhead Ltd. 528 bottles.*

Malts Of Scotland Springbank 1998 sherry hogshead, cask no. MoS12014, bott Apr 12 **(85.5)** **n21 t22 f21.5 b20.5.** Well, you can't say this is a shy dram. Indeed, it has much to say, especially on delivery. Then the barley out performs any input by the grape to a massive margin. But, as is so often the case with malts under 15 from this distillery, structure and format appears to have been lost in a sprawling free-for-all. The nose, tight and helped only by a shallow smokiness, is a good indication of what is to follow. *51.5%. nc ncf sc.*

⁕ **Master of Malt Springbank Aged 19 Years** hogshead, cask no. 129, dist 7 May 93, bott 27 Nov 12 **(96)** **n24** beautiful whole-hearted aroma: fills the glass with a thick, digestive biscuit concentrate with extra salt sprinkled in. A hint of kumquat helps lighten the load. Few malts are quite this intense yet intact; **t24.5** the delivery is near perfect: malt concentrate cascades onto the palate with a brown sugar-sweetened mocha hanging on to its coat tails; fabulous black liquorice and hickory middle, sweetened by butterscotch and an ulmo honey trace; **f23.5** long, with a slow degree of building oils which seems only to amplify the barley; spiced French toast drips with late sugars...; **b24** world class whisky. End of... *578%. sc. 221 bottles.*

⁕ **Master of Malt Springbank Aged 19 Years** hogshead, cask no. 482, dist 26 Nov 93, bott 27 Nov 12 **(88.5)** **n22** just a little strained and tight but the saltiness is intriguing;

t23 incredibly sweet delivery; the thick barley is mixed with maple syrup; f21.5 the lesser quality of the oak evident on the nose helps create a sweet but thin finale; b22 thoroughly enjoyable and packed with character. But very much the poor relation of the three Master of Malt bottlings 55.2%. sc. 250 bottles.

⬩ **Master Of Malt Springbank 30 Years Old Lost Bottlings Series** dist 65, bott (95) (77.5) n18 t22 f18.5 b19. A real weirdo for a Springbank. Sign on nose and finish that we are in exhausted oak territory. Big sugars and even a hint of something smoky on palate saves the day...or part of it. 45.6%

Scotch Malt Whisky Society Cask 27.93 Aged 11 Years refill barrel, cask no. 128, dist 2000 (84.5) n21 t22 f20.5 b21. Some of the same tobacco characteristics as 27.95...and I see the casks are related: this is most probably from the same distillate. However, the cask here is nowhere near as accommodating. 51.5%. sc. Scotch Malt Whisky Society.

Scotch Malt Whisky Society Cask 27.94 Aged 11 Years first fill sherry hogshead, cask no. 87, dist 2000 (78) n20.5 t19 f18.5 b19. Not one to be added to this wonderful distillery's annals of greatness.... 54.6%. sc. Scotch Malt Whisky Society.

Scotch Malt Whisky Society Cask 27.95 Aged 11 Years refill hogshead, cask no. 168, dist 2000 (90) n22 a little tobacco perhaps and the most distant phenols. Jumbled, fruity and darkly attractive in an off-beat way...; t23.5 much more clarity on delivery. That tobacco note arrives early before we are treated to a party of busy spices; barley develops healthily and to full juice effect; f22 a touch bitter, but the barley shines under some late salt; b22.5 I have long stated that Springbank doesn't really get out of bed until it's about 18 years old. Here, the combination of lively barley and fruit are irresistible. 50.2%. sc. Scotch Malt Whisky Society.

⬩ **Scotch Malt Whisky Society Cask 27.100 Aged 12 Years** refill barrel, dist 31 Mar 00 (86.5) n22 t22 f21 b21.5. A beautifully constructed spirit plucked from the cask far too ahead of time. The oak makes an impression but it is an unclear one. The youthful nuttiness always charms, though. 52.4%. nc ncf sc. 176 bottles.

⬩ **Scotch Malt Whisky Society Cask 27.102 Aged 12 Years** 1st fill sherry hogshead, dist 31 Mar 00 (85) n21 t22 f21 b21. Another Springbank which lurches uncontrolled around the palate. The toasted fudge is fun and the quality of the cloth is fine. But it is all a little too anarchic and shapeless. 52%. nc ncf sc. 301 bottles.

Scotch Single Malt Circle Springbank 1996 cask no. 77, dist 10 Oct 96, bott 6 Jan 11 (63) n16.5 t16.5 f14 b16. Springbank is a distillery which I feel flies more naturally and elegantly than most other distilleries in the world. This one, though, has crash landed with its wheels up. Accident investigators will hardly know where to start... 53.7%. sc. Scotch Single Malt Circle.

Scotch Single Malt Circle Springbank 1997 cask no. 319, dist 4 Apr 1997, bott 7 Jan 2011 (92.5) n23 you really have to smile when you nose this: it is the aroma of a dank old warehouse in a glass! Incredibly salty, even slightly musty. Plenty of kumquat notes, too; t23 a mildly puckering saline delivery is soon giving way to a fabulous build up of citrus and spice; if you find a middle better weighted than this, let me know...; f23 the oaks take their usual place at the rear but there is also a wonderful, very vaguely metallic, sharpness to the end; b23.5 as ever, a Springbank with much to say and in a unique voice. 55.1%. sc. Scotch Single Malt Circle.

⬩ **That Boutique-y Whisky Company Springbank** batch 1 (93) n23 serious big oak brinkmanship: this spirit has got wood; t23 the delivery is deceptively silky and soft with the malt at almost barley wine intensity. But soon the oak is biting hard and deep adding a far more aggressive and old-bourbon bitterness; f23.5 settles now for a much more contented bourbon-style fade with red liquorice and manuka honey trying to blunt the more jagged oaky edges; b23.5 the taste buds are battered by oak notes which gang up like marauding thugs. Never less than delicious...but not for the squeamish. 54.6%. 252 bottles.

⬩ **That Boutique-y Whisky Company Springbank** batch 2 (91) n22 busy, mildly botanical and unusually phenolic lilt to this; t23 barley rarely arrives thicker on delivery: massive sugar pulse and concentrated grist; f23 long, with some kumquat and marmalade notes settling in for the finale; b23 a very soft Springbank body-wise, but still pulls no punches. 53.1%. 450 bottles.

STRATHISLA
Speyside, 1786. Chivas Brothers. Working.

Strathisla 12 Years Old db (87.5) n22.5 t23.5 f20 b21.5. Still a big, chewy dram which is about as heavy in body as you are likely to find anywhere in Speyside. Very enjoyable, though you know deep down that some fine tuning could take this guy easily into the 90s. 43%

Strathisla Distillery Edition 15 Years Old db (94) n23 flawlessly clean and enriched by that silky intensity of fruity malt unique to this distillery; t23 the malt is lush, sweet and every bit as intense as the nose; a touch of toffeespice does it no harm; f24 just so long and lingering, again with the malt being of extraordinary enormity: these is simply wave upon wave of pure delight; **b24** what a belter! The distillery is beautiful enough to visit: to take away a bottle of this as well would just be too good to be true! *53.7%*

⁙ **Gordon & MacPhail Distillery Label Strathisla 1965 (94.5)** n23.5 punchy old oloroso: nutty and big roast raisin; a few dried dates thrown in; the spices are of the old kitchen larder variety; **t23** a big jolting oakiness is immediately soothed by the united front of molasses and toasted raisin; **f24** some light manuka honey bathed by ulmo honey. Then in comes the several years matured Melton Hunt cake; **b24** needs to be left in the glass for a little while for it to open and reveal its secrets. Gorgeous. *43%*

Gordon & MacPhail Rare Vintage Strathisla 1969 (95.5) n24 fascinating to nose this beside the 1972 vintage. This has embraced the oak to the advantage of the sherry as the grape now has a slightly weightier partner it can show its more deft tones against; less fruitcake here though no shortage of cooked apples and pears seasoned with a little cinnamon; **t23.5** sublime delivery! Again the sherry has excellent body, enjoying a rich texture which makes the most of the light saltiness present, giving all the flavours present a sharper edge. Amazingly, the barley makes a very juicy appearance. Elsewhere, some hints of sherry trifle, as well as a sherry-chocolate mousse, complete with over-ripe banana-custard. But it is the weight of the Demerara sugars against the rich oaky vanillas which offer the most mesmerising battle; **f23.5** sugars remain calm, collected and comfortably in sync with any of the weightier oak notes which offer much more of a spicy, burnt honeycombed bourbon style than anything the fruit can produce; **b24.5** the kind of magical Speyside oldie which, among the independents, only Gordon and MacPhail can conjure. A true classic. *43%*

Gordon & MacPhail Rare Vintage Strathisla 1972 (88) n23 major fruitcake statement (with old Demerara rum added, not whisky!), with the emphasis on the molassed and toasted glazed cherries and overly burned raisin; **t22** much softer body than the nose promises. The sherry shows virtually no backbone. But the initially thin flavours build into something which dominate all else; **f22** some vague hint of chocolate raisin. But they've gone heavy on the raisin; **b21** a real heavyweight sherry butt. But one that bullies rather than coerces. *43%*

⁙ **Gordon and MacPhail Distillery Label Strathisla 1993 (83.5)** n21.5 t22 f19 b21. Honey, oils and fruit combine for a juicy and lively opening but this is a malt which fails to build on its early promise. A bit like a film which starts brightly but within a few minutes you can predict exactly where it is going to go...especially with the fruit influence... *43%*

Hart Brothers Strathisla Aged 14 Years cask no. 78924, dist 19 Jun 97, bott 15 Apr 12 **(89.5)** n22 clean malt with a dash of semi-spiced oak bourbon style; **t22** juicy, grassy barley enjoying a good oily body; **f23** now the spices cascade; chocolate arrives late, presumably to go with the Brazils; **b22.5** benefits hugely from having matured in very good oak. Has "Speyside" tattooed all over it. But this is adorable stuff. *46%. sc.*

Old Malt Cask Strathisla Aged 16 Years (85) n21.5 t21.5 f21 b21. A rolling, undulating experience with the barley and spices filling the contours of the palate. A little off key oak flattens things a little. *50%. nc ncf sc. Douglas Laing & Co.*

⁙ **Old Malt Cask Strathisla Aged 21 Years** refill hogshead, cask no. 9519, dist Jun 91, bott Feb 13 **(86.5)** n21 t22 f22 b21.5. A typically silky Strathisla which, despite some early floral notes, tends to over rely on the big barley for effect. Impossible not to enjoy, though. *50%. sc. Douglas Laing & Co. 155 bottles.*

Provenance Strathisla Over 10 Years refill hogshead, cask no. 6301, dist Winter 99, bott Summer 10 **(72)** n18 t18 f18 b18. Starts off kilter and never corrects itself. *46%. nc ncf sc.*

Provenance Strathisla Over 12 Years refill hogshead, cask no. 7658, dist Summer 1999, bott Summer 2011 **(81.5)** n21 t20.5 f20 b20. A malty Plain Jane. *46%. nc ncf sc. Douglas Laing & Co.*

⁙ **Scotch Malt Whisky Society Cask 58.14 Aged 23 Years** refill barrel, dist 5 Jan 89 **(85.5)** n22.5 t22 f20 b21. A very curious Strathisla which deliciously blasts off all guns blazing down the malt and muscovado sugar road. But after a strangely sugary middle, tails off with surprising rapidity and is positively anorexic by the finish. *57.8%. nc ncf sc. 222 bottles.*

Scott's Selection Strathisla 1989 bott 2011 **(94)** n22 carrot juice with hickory and spice; **t24.5** a classic of its kind; the delivery is shimmering with deep oaky spices yet for all the enormity of the obviously top quality cask the barley has its own agenda and comes through vividly; the mid ground settles towards a walnut oil and lightly molassed sweetness: fabulous!; **f23** long, soft oils spreading every atom of sweetness as far as they will stretch; **b23.5** just shows what this distillery can do when untethered... a sheer delight! *56.5%. Speyside Distillers.*

STRATHMILL

Speyside, 1891. Diageo. Working.

A.D. Rattray Strathmill 1989 puncheon, cask no. 10310, dist 13 Oct 89, bott Jun 12 **(94)** n22.5 sparkling barley: a gorgeous mix of grist and golden syrup; **t24.5** yes...!! Shows exactly why I regard the output from Strathmill as one of the most malty spirits in Scotland: grassy, juicy, clean and almost too salivating. Yet the star turn is the middle where the spices kick in to counter the pulsing acacia honey...fabulous! f23 not a bitter element to this: the oak acts like a gent and offers untainted butterscotch, though it can hardly be seen for the continuing sweet barley chorus; b24 one of the tastiest Puncheons I have seen since Jason scored a hat-trick for Millwall against Crystal Palace a couple of Christmases back....! 58.6%. sc. A.D. Rattray Ltd.

Archives Strathmill 1974 37 Years Old Inaugural Release bourbon hogshead, cask no. 1231, dist Jun 74, bott Jun 11 (85) n22 t21.5 f21 b21.5. The years have not damaged this dram, but the degree of natural caramels and tannins means that meaningful complexity is out of the question. 44.5%. nc ncf sc. Whiskybase B.V. 180 bottles.

⠿ **Duncan Taylor Dimensions Strathmill 21 Years** cask no. 4248, dist Aug 90, bott Jun 12 (90) n22 the most sumptuous sherry trifle....with a distant edge of something undesired; t24 stunning delivery: a fruitcake doused in malt and high ester rum, with the brown sugars and peppery spices running amok; f22 back to a more sombre finish with fruits more circumspect, a lot more suet and the raisins now a touch burnt. But the "S" word rears its head late on, as threatened on the nose; b22 oh, but for the briefest insertion of a sulphur candle 21 years ago – and I mean for a few seconds – we would have had a contender for Malt Whisky of the Year here... 54.4%. nc ncf sc. Duncan Taylor & Co. 280 bottles.

James MacArthur Old Masters Strathmill 21 Years Old cask no. 101112, dist 1990, bott Feb 12 (96.5) n24 fantastically complex: how do you get so many varying sweet notes to work so well together without the nose heavily laden becoming like a candy store? Have fun spotting the differing shades of sweetness, but you should be able to spot the light rum notes, the touch of Irn Bru, the heavy rum notes and the Lubec marzipan complete with cocoa; t24 those rum notes on the nose translate into a light, coppery sheen. Then a plethora of playful spices mingle with the honeycomb....; f23.5 dulls a little as the vanillas take charge. Still enough sugar to go round, though; b24 the old J&B blender Jim Milne always had a special place in his heart for this distillery. Here you can see exactly why. 54.1%. nc ncf sc.

⠿ **Master Of Malt Strathmill 21 Years Old** cask no. 2534, dist 3 Jun 91, bott 7 May 13 (89) n22.5 big oaky throb; attractive acacia honey; t22 slightly tight on delivery thanks to the muscular oak; good barley counter and sugar-rich middle; f22.5 blossoms into a chocolate-orange territory; b22 a malt taken out of its usual comfort zone, age-wise. But gets through the oaky ordeal. 57.7%. sc.

Old Malt Cask Strathmill Aged 35 Years refill hogshead, cask no. 7817, dist Apr 76, bott Feb 12 (93) n23.5 the erstwhile J&B blender and my very dear friend Jim Milne used to take me to this distillery often and he would guide me through the casks at varying ages, explaining just why he adored its malty charisma. Jim would be purring at this one if he was still with us...and he would especially enjoy the most subtle of citrus counter weights; t23 again the malt is of the cleanest and most intense style. It has taken on a little oak, but only enough to offer just the right degree of gravitas; f23.5 maybe a touch of salt now to the tannin, but that lingering malt really does take your breath away...; b23 hang on to your hats: this is one of the most deliciously malty rides in town...! 47.2%. nc ncf sc. 176 bottles.

⠿ **That Boutique-y Whisky Strathmill 21 Years Old** (89) n22.5 big oaky throb; attractive acacia honey; t22 slightly tight on delivery thanks to the muscly oak; good barley counter and sugar-rich middle; f22.5 blossoms into a chocolate-orange territory; b22 a malt taken out if its usual comfort zone, age-wise. But gets through the oaky ordeal. 57%

⠿ **The Warehouse Collection Strathmill Aged 22 Years** bourbon hogshead, cask no. 5349, dist 1990, bott 2013 (91) n22.5 a complex array of dank mushroom, orchids and violets thicken the barley and spice; t23 forceful delivery, borderline roughhouse, with the spiced barley anything but shy; the sugars are crisp, almost vicious in their arrival...the softening by the developing cocoa is a relief and becomes probably the highlight; f22.5 fading chocolate mint; b23 a gorgeous cocoa g-spot for all to enjoy. Rrrrrrr....! 52.8%. nc ncf sc. 219 bottles.

TALISKER

Highlands (Island–Skye), 1832. Diageo. Working.

Talisker Aged 10 Years db (93) n23 Cumberland sausage and kipper side by side; t23 early wisps of smoke that develop into something a little spicier; lively barley that feels a little oak-dried but sweetens out wonderfully; f24 still not at full throttle with the signature ka-boom spice, but never less than enlivening. Some wonderful chocolate adds to the smoke; b23 the deadening caramel that had crept into recent bottlings of the 10-y-o has retreated, and although that extraordinary, that wholly unique finale has still to be re-found in its unblemished, explosive entirety, this is much, much closer to the mark and a quite stupendous malt to be enjoyed at any time. But at night especially. 45.8%

Talisker 12 Years Old Friends of the Classic Malts db (86) n22 t21.5 f21 b21.5. Decent, sweet, lightly smoked...but the explosion which made this distillery unique - the old kerpow! - appears kaput. 45.8%

Talisker Aged 14 Years The Distillers Edition Jerez Amoroso cask, dist 1993, bott 2007 db (**90.5**) n23 t23 f22 b22.5. Certainly on the nose, one of the more old-fashioned peppery Taliskers I've come across for a while. Still I mourn the loss of the nuclear effect it once had, but the sheer quality of this compensates. 45.8%

Talisker Aged 20 Years db (**95**) n24 t24 f23 b24. I have been tasting Talisker for 28 years. This is the best bottling ever. Miss this and your life will be incomplete. 62%

Talisker 25 Years Old db (**88**) n22.5 a sweeter nose than normal despite the raging oaks; the first from this distillery with Fisherman's Friend qualities..; t22 the oak pounds in from all directions, this time giving the sugars less room to manoeuvre than on the nose; f21.5 very distant spiced smoke. But just a little jaded after 25 years of whisky maturation. Mind you, I know how it feels... b22 pretty taken aback by this one: it has taken a fancy to being a bit of a Bowmore, complete with a bountiful supply of Fisherman's Friends. 45.8%

Talisker 25 Year Old bott 2008 db (**92**) n23 lazy smoke drifts over a scene of light citrus and slowly forming ancient oaks; t23.5 soft vanillas arrive first, then a wave of muted peppers stinging only playfully as the sweet barley unfolds just so charmingly; f22.5 the oaks really are revving up, but the sweet barley provides the balance; peat and citrus provide an unlikely fade; b23 busy and creaking but a glass or two of this offers some classy entertainment for the evening. 54.2%

Talisker 25 Years Old db (**88.5**) n23 t22 f21.5 b22. Another Talisker almost choked with natural caramels. Chewy and undoubtedly charming. 54.8%

Talisker 25 Years Old db (**92**) n23.5 t24 f22.5 b22.5. Fabulous stuff, even though the finish in particular is strangely well behaved. 58.1%

Talisker 30 Years Old db (**93.5**) n23 complex and slightly bitty, lemon-lightened phenols, sitting comfortably atop a pile of buttery egg custard tart. A lot sexier than it sounds...! t24 the citrus leads the way here, too. It helps intensify the juiciness of the barley, though a countering liquorice and crunchy Demerara sugar sweetness amplifies the age. The smoke is restrained though not beyond offering a spice throb; f23 just a few shuddering oaky passes, but the smoke, sugar, spice and even a little salted butter ensure the fade is long and satisfying; b23.5 much fresher and more infinitely entertaining than the 25 year old...!!! 45.8%

Talisker 30 Year Old bott 2008 db (**89**) n21 t23.5 f22 b22.5. This malt seriously defies the nose, which gives every indication of a whisky about to peg it. The softness of the experience is memorable. 49%

Talisker 30 Years Old db (**84.5**) n21 t21.5 f21 b21. Toffee-rich and pretty one dimensional. Did I ever expect to say that about a Talisker at 30...? 53.1%

Talisker Special Release 2010 30 Years Old refill American & European oak db (**93**) n23 shards of honeycomb pierce the thin cloud of smoke; some bristling spice suggests daddy may be home; t24 superb delivery: an explosion of rabid spices tear at the taste buds, though some astonishingly refined honey does its best to hold it back; there is a melt-in-the-mouth barley sub plot and the natural caramels one comes to expect from this guy; a late burst of garibaldi biscuit rounds things off efficiently; f23 relatively docile by comparison and perhaps over dependent on the caramel. But at least the spice keeps buzzing...; b23 a Talisker with some snap, grunt and attitude. 573%. nc ncf. Diageo. Fewer than 3000 bottles.

⠿ **Talisker 1977 Special Release 2012** American and European Oak refill casks, bott 2012 db (**86.5**) n22 t21 f22.5 b21 Distilled just two years after I first visited the distillery, I remember being told that they bottled their whisky at 8-years-old as they felt it was the optimum age of the maturing malt. The manager pointed to some very old casks in a warehouse there but said they were for blending, as it tastes better that way rather than as a singleton. Interesting to hear those works echo around my head now. Certainly this is a malt of character, but over the time the majority of the peat has vanished and huge oak has taken its place. The highlight is somewhere near the end, when the sugars have at last come to terms with the tannins and a gorgeous, vaguely smoky mocha theme strikes up. 54.6%. nc ncf.

Talisker 57 Degrees North db (**95**) n24 salty, smoky, coastal, breezy. The distillery's location in a nose... t24.5 peat encased in a muscovado sugar, in the same way a fly might be enveloped in amber, melts to allow the slow blossoming of a quite beautiful and peaty thing...; f23 some welcome whip and bite; the smoke and vanillas hang in there and even the odd hint of mocha puffs around a bit; b23.5 a glowing tribute, I hope, for a glowing whisky... 57%

⠿ **Talisker Dark Storm** charred oak db (**92**) n22 some pretty chunky peat and spice is blown around the glass, certainly big enough to take the muscovado sugars and red liquorice head on...; t23.5 the sugars on the nose appear to multiply on delivery, as does the bourbon-style tannin-led liquorice and hickory. The smoke takes a bit of time to get back into the game, as if hiding behind the sofa until safe to come out again but mildly reasserts itself; f23 even the sugars buckle under the oaky strain. But all is fresh and balanced enough to come good, even with some very late spices; b23.5 much more like it! Unlike the Storm, which appeared to labour under some indifferent American oak, this is just brimming with vitality and purpose. 45.8%.

⫶ **Talisker Port Ruighe** Port cask db **(88)** n22 earthy, boiled tomato and chives; t22 now pretty soupy. The delivery offers that thick, airless delivery which peat and wine uniquely conjour up; the sugars are pretty profound....and very dark; f22 a little saline note enters the fray as well as an inevitable chocolate raisin touch; b22 sails into port without changing course 45.8%. *Diageo.*

⫶ **Talisker Storm** db **(85.5)** n20 t23 f21 b21.5 The nose didn't exactly go down a storm in my tasting room. There are some deft seashore touches, but the odd poor cask –evident on the finish, also - has undone the good. But it does recover on the palate early on with an even, undemanding and attractively sweet display showing malt to a higher degree than I have seen any Talksker before. *45.8%.*

TAMDHU

Speyside, 1897. Ian Macleod Distillers. Working (re-opened 3rd March 2013).

Tamdhu db **(84.5)** n20 t22.5 f21 b21. So-so nose, but there is no disputing the fabulous, stylistic honey on delivery. The silkiest Speyside delivery of them all. *40%*

⫶ **Tamdhu Aged 10 Years** oak sherry cask db **(69.5)** n17 t18.5 f17 b17. A much better malt when they stick exclusively to ex-bourbon casks, as used to be the case. *40%*

Tamdhu Aged 18 Years bott code L0602G L12 20/08 db **(74.5)** n19 t19 f18 b18.5. Bitterly disappointing. Literally. *43%*

Tamdhu 25 Years Old db **(88)** n22 t22 f21 b23. Radiates quality. *43%*

Gordon & MacPhail Cask Strength Tamdhu 2001 (75) n19 t19 f17 b18. Sweet and fruity but slightly off key. *58%. Gordon & MacPhail.*

⫶ **Gordon & MacPhail MacPhail's Collection Tamdhu 8 Years old (84.5)** n21 t22.5 f20 b21. Quintessential Speyside in its simplistic juicy broadside and light vanilla backing. *43%.*

⫶ **Malts Of Scotland Tamdhu 1988** sherry hogshead, cask no. MoS 12029, dist 88, bott 12 **(78.5)** n19 t22.5 f18 b19. One of the myriad heartbreakers we see in Scotland these days. The nose and finish tell a sad story of suicidal sulphur candles, the delivery speaks of a sherry butt that was once made by the hands of Dionysus himself. *52.3%. nc ncf sc. 96 bottles.*

Mo Ór Collection Tamdhu 1987 23 Years Old first fill Oloroso sherry butt, cask 3649, dist 87, bott 10 **(64)** n16 t17 f15 b16. The problem with first fill sherry butts (especially from Tamdhu) in 1987 is that they were likely to be riddled with sulphur. And this is, believe me. *46%. nc ncf sc.*

⫶ **Old Malt Cask Tamdhu Aged 14 Years** refill hogshead, cask no. 9076, dist Mar 98, bott Sep 12 **(90)** n22 spiced strawberry Swiss Roll; t23.5 a few greengages add extra juice to the spiced sultana; vanilla and malt enter at the right points; the weight and light oiliness is exemplary; f22 much maltier at the death with the fruit fading and butterscotch moving in with intent; b22.5 great to see a blending malt step up to the plate and puff out its chest as a singleton. *50%. nc ncf sc. Douglas Laing & Co. 262 bottles.*

Old Malt Cask Tamdhu Aged 21 Years sherry hogshead, cask no. 6956, dist Dec 89, bott Mar 11 **(95)** n24.5 you know when you visit an ancient castle and you spot the two-feet thick walls? Well, this has that kind of substance: something from before our time where you know the people responsible knew what they were doing... almost a lost craft. The grape isn't quite impenetrable... it is pierced by a beam mildly acidic sugar. And molasses...; t24 how many layers of grape? I lost count at six. Each with a varying degree of either fruit, such as juicy, over-ripe greengage or a pulpier, more bitter note... and molasses; f23 long, layered with the drier, chalky oak tones acting as the cement to the grapey brick. The lasting sweetness is supplied by... the molasses b23.5 I don't do price: I have no idea what a bottle of this goes for. But, whatever it may be, rip their arms off... *50%. nc ncf sc. Douglas Laing & Co. 154 bottles.*

Provenance Tamdhu Over 12 Years refill hogshead, cask no. 7657, dist Winter 1998, bott Summer 2011 **(84)** n21.5 t21.5 f20 b21. Hard to imagine more single-mindedly gristy blending fodder if you tried...; *46%. nc ncf sc. Douglas Laing & Co.*

Provenance Tamdhu Over 12 Years refill hogshead, cask no. 8166, dist Spring 1999, bott Winter 2012 **(78.5)** n19 t21.5 f18.5 b19.5. I expect the cask holding this underdeveloped malty whisky to turn up at Garden Centre near you soon... *46%. nc ncf sc. Douglas Laing & Co.*

Riegger's Selection Tamdhu 1988 bourbon cask, cask no. 417, dist 28 Jan 88, bott 8 Mar 12 **(91.5)** n23.5 superb zesty and very moist Lubek marzipan; a fair bit of salt around, too; t23.5 magnificent spice attack quickly followed by rich honeycomb; the middle thickens with soft oils and lilting lime, coconut and maple syrup sweetness; f22 thins out a little too fast towards vanilla; b22.5 reminds me of a heated debate I had with a blender who told me that he thought Tamdhu was a second rate malt and avoided it when possible. I told him I thought he was mistaken: in ex-bourbon it could prove quite bold and had much going for it. He admitted all his limited stock was in sherry, so I certainly understood his point of view. He refused to believe me: wish I had a bottle of this with me at the time! *57.2%. nc ncf sc. 199 bottles.*

Scott's Selection Tamdhu 1984 bott 2011 **(88.5)** n22 buy a box of mini fruit tart pies, sniff the green one and compare... t23 lush malt exclusively concentrates on the barley theme at first before switching its attention to a more salty, eye-watering aspect; spices creep up to excellent effect; **f21.5** bitters out a bit too much; **b22** this distillery has often been accused of making sub-standard malt. Poppycock! Nothing wrong with the distillate here, however, a better cask would have made this something to really remember... *49.6%. Speyside Distillers.*

TAMNAVULIN
Speyside. 1966. Whyte and Mackay. Working.

Tamnavulin 1966 Aged 35 Years cream sherry butt db **(91) n24 t22 f23 b22.** For those who love great old sherry, this is an absolute. Perhaps too much sherry to ever make it a true great, but there is no denying such quality. *52.6%*

Old Malt Cask Tamnavulin Aged 25 Years refill butt, cask no. 8432, dist Dec 86, bott Apr 12 **(82.5) n20 t22 f19.5 b21.** If you taste this blind I doubt if any more than five per cent of you would recognise this as a 25 year old malt: I certainly wouldn't. As youthful and juicily gristy as a malt a third of that age, this is the Cliff Richard of Speyside. Amazing what 25 years in a third filled cask at the bottom of warehouse can do...or not! *50%. nc ncf sc. 302 bottles.*

Riegger's Selection Tamnavulin 1993 bourbon cask, cask no. 1013, dist 24 Mar 93, bott 24 Mar 11 **(86) n21.5 t22 f21.5 b21.** A bit of a sloppy cask means there is an underlying edge. But the salivation factor of the barley rockets through the roof; the spices are a treat. Love the little hint of mint tagging onto the cocoa, too. *56.9%. nc ncf sc. Viktor-Riegger GmbH. 176 bottles.*

The Whisky Agency Tamnavulin 1967 bott 2010 **(86.5) n22 t22 f21 b21.5.** Plenty of surprisingly youthful, almost zesty charm which, initially, defies the years. But the passing summers – and oak – catch up with it in the end. *41%. The Whisky Agency.*

TEANINICH
Highlands (Northern), 1817. Diageo. Working.

Boisdale Teaninich 1973 cask no. 6066, bott 2012 **(85) n22 t21 f21 b21.** The strength of this malt gives some idea of what time has done to this malt. Massively oaky, though there is enough molasses and spice to see it into the next world. *40.1%. nc ncf sc.*

Chieftain's Teaninich Aged 28 Years hogshead, dist Dec 82, bott 2011 **(85) n21 t22 f21.5 b21.5.** A serious oaky infusion boasts enough sugar and salt to make for a complex, if rather over-aged, meal of a dram. Plenty to enjoy for a final nightcap, though. *46.8%. nc ncf.*

⠶ **Director's Cut Teaninich Aged 30 Years** refill butt, cask no. 9323, dist Dec 82, bott Dec 12 **(89) n22** so toasty! Even with lightly salted butter! Look out for a few earthy, fresh cabbage notes, too; **t22.5** the oak makes immediate impact but barley retains enough sugar to balance beautifully; a touch of Jaffa Cake seeps into the middle point; **f22** delicate spices emphasise the oak, though the barley echoes to the end; **b22.5** charming and complex to the point of never tasting the same twice. *47.8%. sc. Douglas Laing & Co. 201 bottles.*

Dun Bheagan Teaninich Aged 28 Years hogshead, dist Dec 82, bott Nov 11 **(94.5) n23.5** fabulous nip to the barley despite its good age and an enticing interplay between the vaguest of phenol notes and a tannin-fuelled saltiness; the sweetness is catered for by a complex intermingling of maple syrup and thin molasses; **t24** those sugars are first at the scene when it comes to delivery though we have excellent barley and vanilla strata as the oak takes a foothold; the spices are only half cocked but the glazed cherry on the sponge cake is adorable; **f23** long, with the molasses taking over from the maple and the vanillas glowing beside the barley; not a single hint of bitterness...superb!; **b24** I have never shared some blenders' dismal view of this distillery. Here is a vivid example as to why. *51.8%. nc ncf sc. Ian Macleod Distillers.*

⠶ **Dun Bheagan Teaninich Aged 30 Years** butt, cask no. 4453, dist May 82, bott 13 **(81.5) n20.5 t21 f20 b20.** Harsh and hot, the butt, though entirely free from sulphur, has done little to add lustre. *47.5%. nc ncf sc. Ian Macleod Distillers. 576 bottles.*

⠶ **Gordon & MacPhail Connoisseurs Choice Teaninich 2004 (84) n21 t22 f20 b21.** Sharp and at times feisty, the barley rolls up its sleeves to give some pretty unsympathetic oak a good bashing. Not for the first time, a sugary sheen helps soften the blows. *46%. ncf.*

John Milroy Selection Teaninich 1982 cask no. 7714, bott 2012 **(87.5) n22** malty ice cream wafer cones; **t21.5** the spice fair pings off the solid barley. Virtually no yield until a little oil arrives carrying sugar; **f22** the oils ensure a chewy vanilla finale; **b21.5** if the water for this whisky ran over granite, then a lot of granite came with it. *45.4%. nc ncf sc. Berry Bros & Rudd.*

⠶ **Malts Of Scotland Teaninich 1973** bourbon hogshead, cask no. MoS 13011, bott 13 **(84.5) n21.5 t22 f20 b21.** Sugared almonds followed by blood orange on the delivery is the highlight. But this is a malt on the way down and was plummeting fast when bottled: the sawdusty oak is just a little too rabid. *41.8%. nc ncf sc. 96 bottles.*

Mo Ór Collection Teaninich 1983 27 Years Old first fill bourbon hogshead, cask no. 7660, dist 29 Nov 83, bott 8 Feb 11 **(92.5) n23** lively barley with a fine salt and honey edge; **t24** sweet, palate-cleansing, ever-sweetening barley. The spices are sublime: almost faultless for its type; **f22** settles down to a contented vanilla-rich and lightly spiced finale; **b23.5** a charming, clean, nubile malt displaying a quite vivid Speyside style: a fine example of how regions mean nothing at all. *46%. nc ncf sc. Release No. 26. The Whisky Talker. 391 bottles.*

⚬ **Scotch Malt Whisky Society Cask 59.43 Aged 29 Years** refill hogshead, dist 8 Nov 83 **(92.5) n23** gorgeous gooseberry and butterscotch tart: mega yummy; **t24** a rare example of a truly faultless delivery. The weight, the sugar levels, the tartness and compelling intensity of the barley meld together to create a seamless beauty; the first 15 seconds offers all you'll ever need from a Highland malt; **f22** altogether more austere with the thin vanillas lording it over the retreating malt; **b23.5** goes to town on the complexity. *56.4%. nc ncf sc. 252 bottles.*

Wemyss 1982 Single Highland "Winter Spice" hogshead, bott 2011 **(87.5) n21.5** spiced suet; diced uncooked green vegetables; **t22.5** heavy duty malt: really thick and would be quite dull were it not for the effervescence of the spices; **f21.5** the inevitable vanilla cannot shake off the peppers; **b22** so weighty and plodding your tongue aches! *44.4%. sc. 201 bottles.*

⚬ **The Whisky Agency Teaninich 1973** bott 12 **(84.5) n22 t21 f20.5 b21.** Excellent kumquat and cocoa. But I just need to find the tweezers for those splinters.... *42%*

⚬ **The Whisky Cask Teaninich Aged 39 Years** bourbon cask, cask no. 6068, dist 1973, bott 2013 **(85) n21 t22.5 f20.5 b21.** Sultry and at times shimmering on the palate, but this has been left in the cask a few years too many as the oak input is just is too overzealous. Even so, a decent layering of heather honey repairs some damage. *40.1%. nc ncf sc.*

TOBERMORY

Highlands (Island–Mull), 1795. Burn Stewart Distillers. Working.

Ledaig 10 Years Old db **(85) n21.5 t22 f20 b21.5.** Some gorgeous and beautifully weighted peat at play here, showcased in full glory on the nose and delivery. Has to paper over some cracks towards the finish, though. *46.3%*

Ledaig Aged 10 Years db **(85.5) n20 t22.5 f21.5 b21.5.** Almost a Bowmore in disguise, such are its distinctive cough sweet qualities. Massive peat: easily one of the highest phenol Ledaigs of all time. But, as usual, a slight hiccup on the technical front. Hard work not to enjoy it, though. *46.3%. nc ncf.*

Ledaig Aged 10 Years db **(63) n14 t17 f15 b17.** What the hell is going on? Butyric and peat in a ghoulish harmony on nose and palate that is not for the squeamish. *43%*

Ledaig Aged 12 Years db **(90) n23** serious farmyard aromas – and as someone who spent three years living on one, believe me...borderline butyric, but somehow gets away with it, or at least turns it to an advantage; **t23.5** the staggering peat on the nose is no less remarkable here: chunky, clunking, entirely lacking poise and posture. And it obviously doesn't give a damn...; **f21.5** strange gin-type juniper amid the smoke; **b22** it has ever been known that there is the finest of lines between genius and madness. A side-by-side comparison of the Ledaig 10 and 12 will probably be one of whisky's best examples of this of all time... *43%*

Tobermory Aged 10 Years db **(67.5) n16 t17 f17.5 b17.** A less than brilliantly made malt totally bereft of character or charm. I have no idea what has happened here. I must investigate. Frankly, I'm gutted. *40%*

Tobermory 10 Years Old db **(73.5) n17.5 t19 f18 b19.** The last time I tasted an official Tobermory 10 for the Bible, I was aghast with what I found. So I prodded this sample I had before me of the new 46.3% version with all the confidence Wile E Coyote might have with a failed stick of Acme dynamite. No explosions in the glass or on my palate to report. And though this is still a long way short, and I'm talking light years here, of the technical excellence of the old days, the uncomplicated sweet maltiness has a very basic charm. The nose and finish, though, are still very hard going. *46.3%*

Tobermory Aged 10 Years db **(85) n20 t22.5 f21 b21.5** Bracing, nutty and malty the oils perhaps overdo it a little but there are enough sugars on hand to steer this one home for an enjoyable experience overall. *46.3%. nc ncf.*

Tobermory Aged 15 Years db **(93) n23.5** dripping with fresh, clean, ultra high quality oloroso there remains enough tangy malt to underscore the island location; **t23.5** a fabulous marriage of juicy grape and thick, uncompromising malt. It is an arm wrestle for supremacy between the two...but it is the delicate spices which win; **f23** salty chocolate raisin; **b23** a tang to the oils on both nose and finish suggests an over widened middle. But such is the quality of the sherry butts and the intensity of the salt-stained malt, all is forgiven. *46.3%. nc ncf.*

Tobermory Aged 15 Years Limited Edition db **(72.5) n17 t18 f19 b18.5.** Another poorly made whisky: the nose and delivery tells you all you need to know. *46.3%*

⚬ **A.D. Rattray Ledaig 2004** butt, cask no. 900161, dist 24 Nov 04, bott 25 Nov 12 **(94) n23.5** there is possibly some barley amid all that smoke... even the influence of the sherry struggles to get a note in edgeways; **t23** the delivery is so thick and intense it takes a little while for things to be distinguished amid the smoke. A real pea-souper, an old fashioned smog of a dram, where the grape does now have an input, though it battles tigerishly to make itself heard. When the spirit is located it is obvious that, technically, it is not Premier league.

But such is the hurly burly of the smoke, it doesn't very much matter; **f24** long with the grape having a chocolate coating. The smoke, though, refuses to stop molesting it; **b23.5** easily one of the most heavily peated Ledaigs I have encountered in the last two decades. Must be well over the 50ppm of the Ardbegs of this world...one for those who prefer the insane Bruichladdichs. *60.5%. sc. A.D. Rattray. DRCC German and Denmark Markets.*

Archives Ledaig 2004 7 Years Old First Release cask no. 900009, dist 04, bott 12 **(94) n23.5** exceptionally clean with a limited coastal feel; a beautiful hickory sweetness to the peat; **t24** outstanding delivery with uncanny balance between the sugars, the peat and oak **f22.5** thins a little, though the smoke doesn't; **b24** a whisky entirely at one with itself. *61.9%. nc ncf sc.*

꘎ **Cadenhead Ledaig 16 Years Old (77.5) n19 t20 f19 b19.5.** Sweet and smoky. But hardly textbook distillate. *46%. WM Cadenhead Ltd. 360 bottles.*

꘎ **Caermory Aged 20 Years** cask 246 **(94) n23.5** lively malt both offers a jaunty juice grain element and a balancing barley sugar counter. The oak is ridiculously well-behaved for its age and ensures just enough vanilla for depth without reducing the crispier, crunchier notes; **t24** I adore this type of malt: the barley is both eye-wateringly fresh, sharp and salivating. Yet there is also enough spice fizz and, eventually, oil creating a secondary personality – almost a parallel whisky universe in the glass; **f23** the very faintest tang from the bourbon cask is the only thing which contradicts the startling clarity of this 20-y-o, and so minor it hardly detracts. Especially when there is enough cocoa and salt around to makes for a lip-smacking finale; **b23.5** Tobermory at its very sprightliest: a malt to get you off to a breezy start to the day, or end it on an up-note. *49.6%*

Gordon & MacPhail Private Collection Ledaig 1993 St Joseph wood finish **(70) n18 t19 f16 b17.** I assume St Joseph is the patron saint of sulphur. *45%*

꘎ **Gordon and MacPhail Connoisseurs Choice Ledaig 1994 (90) n21.5** the odd atom of peat reminds you this is Ledaig, but anyone deaf will be unable to hear; **t23.5** magnificent texture with the butterscotch oak pulling rank over the most distant smoke rumble imaginable; it is the chocolate chip mint lolly middle which really stars, though, helped along by a generous lashing of maple syrup; **f22** a bit of citrus tang on the fade with lemon butter and vanilla dominating; **b23** probably the most miserly peated Ledaig of all time. But don't let that worry you: the chocolate chip mint is a stunner...! *46%. ncf.*

Hart Brothers Tobermory Aged 17 Years cask no. 987, dist 22 Apr 95, bott 30 Apr 12 **(76.5) n20.5 t19 f18 b19.** Ungainly, though some might enjoy the sweet, nutty nose. *46%. sc.*

Kingsbury "The Selection" Ledaig 9 Years Old hogshead, cask no. 900129 & 800130, dist Oct 01, bott Apr 11 **(87.5) n22.5** gristy smoky bacon...with the emphasis on the grist; **t22** more grist; less smoke than on the nose; **f22** vanilla with the vaguest hint of smoke; **b21.5** one of the sweetest peaty malts you'll find. *43%. nc ncf sc. Japan Import Systems. 805 bottles.*

Malts Of Scotland Ledaig 1998 sherry butt, cask no. MoS11010, dist Apr 98, bott Aug 11 **(76) n18 t21 f18 b19.** For a brief moment on the palate I thought this one was going to get away with it: the grape had actually fought its way through to show a juicy clarity and it actually chimed pleasantly with the peat. But that was brief and tantalising. The remainder of the story is one of World War Three on the palate. *61.2%. nc ncf sc. Malts Of Scotland.*

꘎ **Master of Malt Tobermory Aged 17 Years** refill hogshead, dist 26 Apr 95, bott 26 Nov 12 **(84.5) n21 t20.5 f22 b21.** A raucous dram which heaves and pitches on delivery but sails home to safety as the barley and spice take hold. *57%. sc. 274 bottles.*

Mo Ór Collection Tobermory 1995 16 Years Old first fill bourbon hogshead, cask no. 1646, dist 8 Nov 95, bott 2 Dec 10 **(91) n22** a lovely, lilting edge of lemon curd tart on the barley; **t23** richly textured with some early spices which become quite boisterous later on. The barley remains thick and true; **f23** a light touch of cocoa as the spices and growing sugars engage; **b23** one of the better bottlings – official or otherwise – to have made it out of this distillery for quite a while. *46%. nc ncf sc. Release No. 46. The Whisky Talker. 480 bottles.*

Mo Ór Collection Ledaig 1994 16 Years Old first fill bourbon hogshead, cask no. 228066, dist 5 May 94, bott 24 Jan 11 **(93.5) n23** a few miserly phenols add weight to the more flighty salt and barley sugar; **t23.5** salivating from the off with the emphasis on the barley and spices; there is something like a lemon sherbet zing to the middle; **f23.5** thins out though the vaguely smoked chocolate mint is a pretty novel experience; **b23.5** if you are expecting to be blown away with peat like a Ledaig of old, this will disappoint. This almost has all the classic signs of a peated malt where the husk has been removed. That said, well weighted and complex. Very different and never less than delicious. *46%. nc ncf sc. 330 bottles.*

Old Malt Cask Tobermory Aged 15 Years refill hogshead, cask no. 7933, dist 96, bott 11 **(75) n17 t20 f19 b19.** Weighty whisky. But, alas, singularly unattractive. *50%. nc ncf sc. 289 bottles.*

꘎ **Provenance Tobermory Over 6 Years** sherry butt, cask no. 8760, dist Summer 06, bott Summer 12 **(81) n18 t20 f22 b21.** Decidedly odd. The nose is best ignored and doesn't bode well. But on the palate a malt which intrigues, not least with its marzipan, cocoa and cough sweet finale. *46%. nc ncf sc. Douglas Laing & Co.*

⋄ **Provenance Ledaig Over 7 Years** refill hogshead, cask no. 9654, dist Autumn 05, bott Spring 13 **(92) n22.5** youthful – not uncommon for a nose like this on a five-year-old – with the peat sharpened by the crispness of the barley and acrid intensity of the soot; **t24** beautifully salivating: exactly as it should be with the peat acting almost like lead weights to stop the juicier barley from flying off; superb gristy sugars pound the mid ground: magnificently wild! **f22.5** the light oils noticeable throughout cling to the death and help accentuate the little oak present; **b23** feisty, flighty and fun. 46%. nc ncf. Douglas Laing & Co.

⋄ **Single Cask Collection Tobermory 17 Years Old** bourbon hogshead, cask no. 699, dist 6 Jun 95, bott 5 Feb 13 **(80.5) n19 t21.5 f20 b20.** The astonishingly intense barley on delivery is the star of the show here. But don't look for harmony as it is obvious the original spirit was never in tune. 54.9%. nc ncf sc. 251 bottles.

⋄ **That Boutique-y Whisky Company Tobermory** batch 1 **(75.5) n18 t20 f18.5 b19.** Occasionally you come across a magnificent whisky which absolutely makes your day. This isn't one of them. Badly made and good maturation offers only damage limitation. 53.8%. Master Of Malt. 200 bottles.

The Whisky Agency Ledaig 7 Years Old dist 2005 **(73) n18.5 t19 f17.5 b18.** Clumsily made malt. Having tasted it beside the 2004 Archive edition, a lesson in good and bad distillation. 52.1%. sc.

⋄ **The Whisky Agency Ledaig 2005** bott 12 **(86) n21 t22 f21.5 b21.5** No shortage of hazel nuts in toffee to soften the peppery peat. 52.1%.

Wilson & Morgan Barrel Selection Tobermory 1995 refill sherry, bott 2011 **(85) n19 t22.5 f22 b21.5.** Strikingly firm for a Tobermory with a light coating of grape softening some of the harder edges. Love the delicate sweetness. 46%. Wilson & Morgan.

TOMATIN
Speyside, 1897. Takara, Shuzo and Okura & Co. Working.

⋄ **Cù Bòcan Highland Single Malt** virgin oak, bourbon & sherry casks db **(85.5) n21 t21 f22 b21.5.** An old fashioned dram: the type Pitt the Younger, or Pitt the Embryo might remember...and appreciate. Appears to be nearer new make than fully matured Scotch: the big player is the oak which, almost, bourbon-like, shovels cart loads of caramel and muscovado into the mix. Green...and engrossing. 46%

Tomatin 12 Years Old db **(85.5) n21 t21.5 f22 b21.** Reverted back to a delicately sherried style, or at least shows signs of a touch of fruit, as opposed to the single-minded maltfest it had recently been. So, nudge or two closer to the 18-y-o as a style and shows nothing other than good grace and no shortage of barley, either. 40%

Tomatin Aged 15 Years ex bourbon cask, bott 2010 db **(86) n21 t22 f21.5 b21.5.** One of the most malty drams on the market today. Perhaps suffers a little from the 43% strength as some of the lesser oak notes get a slightly disruptive foothold. But the intense, juicy barley trademark remains clear and delicious. 43% Tomatin Distillery

Tomatin 15 Years Old bourbon barrels and Spanish Tempranillo wine casks db **(88.5) n22** the odd rogue note here but it is as if the acacia honey and marmalade are doing all they can to smother them. Red liquorice and barley lend a hand to the good guys; **t23** exceptionally rounded with the malt coming through with that uniquely Tomatin intensity. Jaffa cake orange and cocoa join the ripe figs and muscovado sugars in the middle ground; **f21** dips slightly as the off note detected on the nose resurfaces with a dry austerity. Again the sweeter elements come rushing like white blood cells; **b22.5** not free from the odd problem with the Spanish wine casks but gets away with it as the overall complexity and enjoyment levels are high. 52%

Tomatin Aged 18 Years db **(85) n22 t21 f21 b21.** I have always held a torch for this distillery and it is good to see some of the official older stuff being released. This one has some serious zing to it, leaving your tastebuds to pucker up - especially as the oak hits. 40%

Tomatin 18 Years Old db **(88) n22.5 t22 f21.5 b22.** What a well-mannered malt. As though it grew up in a loving, caring family and behaves itself impeccably from first nose to last whimpering finale; 43%

Tomatin Aged 18 Years sherry finish, bott 2010 db **(92.5) n22.5** busy, thick milkshake maltiness with a touch of fruitcake; **t23.5** cream sherry: creamy + sweet barley + fruity = cream sherry...; **f23** very long with a touch of controlled spicy fizz to the proceedings. But that indomitable barley signature sings to the end; **b23.5** finished in quite superior sherry butts. A malt brimming with character and quality. What a treat! 46%. ncf. Tomatin Distillery.

Tomatin Aged 21 Years created using 6 refill American oak casks and the 7th an ex sherry butt, bott 2009 db **(81) n22 t22.5 f18.5 b19.** A clattering, chattering, cluttering malt never once getting into rhythm to tell a coherent story. The sherry-pitched nose is jumbled but attractive; the delivery is at first rampant and entertaining but the middle and finale fall away, with the odd negative note at the death. A good one to pour your friends while they are blindfolded: this will confuse them. 52% Tomatin Distillery. 2400 bottles.

Tomatin 25 Years Old db (89) n22 t23 f21.5 b22.5. Not a nasty bone in its body: understated but significant. 43%

Tomatin 30 Years Old db (91) n22 if there was a hint of the exotics in the 25-y-o, it's here, five years on, by the barrel load. Evidence of grape, but the malt won't be outdone, either; t23 silky and sultry, there is every suggestion that the oak is thinking of going too far. Yet such is the purity and intensity of the malt, damage has been repaired and/or prevented and even at this age one can only salivate as the soft oils kick in; f23.5 probably my favourite part of the experience because the sheer deliciousness of the chocolaty finale is awesome; b22.5 malts of this age rarely maintain such a level of viscosity. Soft oils can often be damaging to a whisky, because they often refuse to allow character to flourish. Yet here we have a whisky that has come to terms with its age with great grace. And no little class. 49.3%

Tomatin 30 Year Old European & American oak casks db (85.5) n21 t21 f22.5 b21. Unusually for an ancient malt, the whisky becomes more comfortable as it wears its aged shoes. The delivery is just a bit too enthusiastic on the oaky front, but the natural caramels soften the journey rather delightfully. 46%. ncf.

Tomatin 40 Years Old db (89.5) n21.5 t22 f23 b23. Not quite sure how it's done it, but somehow it has made it through all those oaky scares to make for one very impressive 40-y-o!! Often it shows the character of a bourbon on a Zimmer. 42.9%

Tomatin 1997 1st fill bourbon, bott 2009 db (93.5) n23.5 t24 f23 b23. Another outlandishly beautiful malt from this underrated distillery. Had they mixed in a few second fill casks into this, the complexity would have been fearsome and the stuff of legend. 57.1%. 244 bottles.

Tomatin 1999 refill American oak, Tempranillo finish, bott 2009 db (92) n22 t23.5 f23 b23.5. Looking for something different? Give this a whirl around the palate. Fabulous. 57.1%. 302 bottles.

Tomatin Decades European & American oak casks db (91) n23 floral and earthy yet equally fruity and vivid: as if nosing in a greenhouse.. t23 big malt but the strands of toffee become chewier as the oaky theme develops; light, vaguely peaty, spices open out on an increasingly vanilla landscape; f22.5 big age as the oak, in curiously diverse forms, take control. Just love the sugars of the cream toffee; b22.5 an intriguing onion of a malt, of which the layers can, with concentration, be stripped away. The light smoke does its job immaculately. A malt for those with an hour to spare... 46%. ncf. Marriage of 1967, 1976, 1984, 1990 and peated 2005 Tomatins.

⁙ **Tomatin Legacy** bourbon barrels & virgin oak cask db (94.5) n22.5 an even blend of young barley and confidently sugared oak; t24 some of the honey and tannin notes here more easily relate to bourbon than Scotch: there must be exceptionally fresh casks at work! The result is a dram of rare mouth-watering quality, ably assisted by layered cocoa and hickory; the mix of molassed and muscovado sugars is something which makes you want to gasp with pleasure; the spices are almost too much of a good thing...; f23.5 long, with a wonderful fade of clear honey and crystalline barley; b24.5 again, just working here with the sample, I don't have the label to hand. But this screams new oak to me, as the sugars and spice are almost identical to those found in bourbon. Mix that with probably the maltiest distillate in Scotland and the result is something to truly savour. No great age evident, for all the oak input. But as they say: if you are good enough, you are old enough... 43%

Berry's Own Selection Tomatin 1991 cask no. 51, bott 2012 (90.5) n22 strangely breakfast cereal-like in style: some major Malt Shreddies at work here...; t23 Tomatin, like Glen Moray, is among the malty elite. The mind-blowing intensity here underlines the fact....wow!!! f23 not just malty, but some sublime sugars enrich it and fill out the finish... b22.5 plants the Tomatin flag proudly at the summit of Mount Malt... 54.8%. nc ncf sc.

The Clan Denny Tomatin 44 Years Old dist 1967 (67.5) n15 t20.5 f15 b17. A malt which renders me speechless – for all the wrong reasons. Please tell me this was put into a new sherry butt for "freshening" before bottling. Or, rather, please don't... 51.9%. sc. The Whisky Agency joint bottling with Douglas Laing for Limburg Whisky Fair.

⁙ **Director's Cut Tomatin Aged 45 Years** refill butt, cask no. 9315, dist Nov 67, bott Dec 12 (73) n18 t19 f17 b19. Will someone please tell me that this wasn't "freshened" in a present day sherry butt.... 51.6%. sc. Douglas Laing & Co. 175 bottles.

Gordon & MacPhail Connoisseurs Choice Tomatin 1989 (91) n23.5 sweet barley concentrate; lovely citrus and the most delicate liquorice weaves in and out of the malty anthem; t23 here we go again: the nose transferred to the palate, except a little dustier in part in the middle section; f22 bitters very slightly, but almost like a blood orange amid the barley-vanilla theme; b22.5 a just about spot on representation of exactly how I would describe the style demographic for this distillery at that age. 43%. Gordon & MacPhail.

Malts Of Scotland Tomatin 1966 sherry butt, cask no. MoS11021, bott Nov 11 (94) n24 hard to imagine grape could be quite so thick after all this time: spiced up like warm spotted dog; the smell from your lover's bedroom of toast burning in the kitchen: salty, sweaty and just a little acrid...; t23.5 and while previously on the subject of dogs...a bit of an early dog fight between oak and grape, though it is the lovely lemon curd/chocolate hazelnut spread mix which takes the lead; **f23** pulsing spices rise above the deeper oaks while the late burnt grape skids in on the oils; **b23.5** a miraculous dram with the delicate sugars keeping their heads when it could have been so easy to get lost in an oaky forest. 46.1%. nc ncf sc.

Mo Òr Collection Tomatin 1976 34 Years Old first fill sherry butt, cask no. 4, dist 31 Dec 76, bott 7 Feb 11 **(95.5) n24** a touch of blackcurrant to the dates and walnut. Over-ripe greengages are added to the Melton Hunt Cake; **t24** the silkiest of deliveries and each of the first seven or eight flavour waves allows grape, both sweet and of a drier crushed pip variety, to lap upon the taste buds; **f23.5** the fruit meanders a long way down the path towards the finish, but as the spices pick up, so does a minty chocolate theme; the weight remains impressive and even; **b24** an exemplary sherry butt of a type seldom found today. A magnificent malt, indisputably classic old stuff. 46%. nc ncf sc. Release No 14. The Whisky Talker. 954 bottles.

Old Malt Cask Tomatin Aged 21 Years refill hogshead, cask no. 7967, dist May 90, bott Dec 11 **(87) n21.5** a rare example of a 21-y-o malt still showing some new make character: young, fresh, malty clean and lively...; **t22** all kinds of brittle malty sugars crack against the palate as the vanilla takes its time to arrive; even a puff of smoke is detectable; **f22** at last a degree of age as the oak wells and thickens; **b21.5** a 21-year-old whisky going on 21 months. A third fill cask for sure, though of high quality. A few blenders would have killed for this cask...! 50%. nc ncf sc. Douglas Laing & Co. 340 bottles.

The Perfect Dram Tomatin 34 Years Old sherry cask, dist 1976, bott 2011 **(95) n24** mmmmm! Just get those sherry trifle meets Melton Hunt Cake notes: fruity, subtly spiced, yet light, playful and complex: a real rarity for its vintage; it's the sultanas though that will blow you away... **t24** this distillery is one of the maltiest in the world and the barley plays its part in interweaving with the heavier oaky notes. But those spices: Where do they come from? Obviously the oak, and possibly partially from the sherry. But they never, for a moment try to dominate and sugars have an easy time of lightening the middle ground which becomes ridiculously juicy with the fresh barley; **f23** the vanillas and liquorice arrive, but the spices pound their merry beat to the last; **b24** any whisky calling itself "The perfect Dram" is setting itself up for a proverbial punch on the kisser and a spectacular fall from grace. However, knowing the distillery, knowing the year and knowing the type of cask, you really could not ask for much more than this. A dram which should take a year to empty: it is for those special, quiet moments only. It is, quite simply, glorious. 51.9%. sc. The Whisky Agency.

Scott's Selection Tomatin 1993 bott 2012 **(86) n21.5 t22.5 f20.5 b21.5**. Intense barley. But where did all that toffee come from? Delicious, but a bit of a mystery. 56%

⁙ **The Warehouse Collection Tomatin Aged 19 Years** bourbon hogshead, cask no. 7116, dist 17 Jun 93, bott 6 Feb 13 **(94) n23** a few old tangerine peels inject a crusty citrus note to the heather-honey barley; **t24.5** fabulous spiced honey of the very highest order gives way to wave upon wave of clean, juicy barley. That, in turn makes way for a second coming of honey, this time of light ulmo: simple...but so beautifully effective! **f22.5** big vanilla fade, but again no off notes or bitterness from the cask...just a light barley flourish; **b24** Tomatin is one of those few malts which has enough about its barley-intense single mindedness to be able to absorb good oak with alacrity. A good example as to why there is no need to display this malt (ever!) in ex-sherry, as those casks, even those free of sulphur, are invariably inferior to how well it works with ex-bourbon. Indeed, this is always a distillery my pulse rate rises to when confronted with ex-bourbon cask samples on my desk. Again, I have not been let down. For though this is in many ways a simply dram, it is truly stunning. 46.4%. nc ncf sc. Whisky Warehouse No. 8. 228 bottles.

The Warehouse Collection Tomatin Aged 19 Years bourbon hogshead, cask no. 16364, dist 24 Sep 90, bott 19 Feb 10 **(90.5) n23** crush some honeycomb candy in your hand, and you get this. Though I doubt you get the dry banana and barley as well; **t23** either this cask has been sitting by the sea somewhere or every last bit of salt in the cask has been extracted. The result is a heightened flavour profile for the balancing manuka honey; **f22** a touch of praline softens the big oaky fade; **b22.5** another summer and that oak would have crossed the border. A fabulous whisky...in the nick of time 573%. sc. Whisky Warehouse No. 8. 174 bottles.

The Warehouse Collection Tomatin Aged 28 Years refill sherry butt, cask no. 29, dist 12 Jan 82, bott 23 Feb 10 **(85) n23 t21 f20 b21**. A shame. A very clean sherry butt with not a single blemish. But the involvement of the oak has turned this into hard work, especially if you have a problem with searing spices. 55.3%. sc. Whisky Warehouse No. 8. 574 bottles.

The Whisky Agency Tomatin 1966 sherry butt, bott 2011 **(94) n23** at first the aroma seems a touch claustrophobic, but let the air get to this one and the juiciness of the grape is unveiled before your very nose...; **t24** outstanding delivery with a touch of noble rot to the first wave or two, followed by a more traditional degree of fruitcake and then even a degree of oak-puckered barley; the subtle spices do a fabulous job; **f23.5** the big oak at first looks threatening but high quality vanilla sprinkled with sugars ensure a balanced finale; **b23.5** a textbook oldie but with all the twists and turns of a novel... 46.1%. The Whisky Agency.

TOMINTOUL

Speyside, 1965. Angus Dundee. Working.

Tomintoul Aged 10 Years db (83.5) n21 t20 f21.5 b21. Has bucked up recently to offer a juicy, salivating barley thrust. Yet still a little on the thin side, despite some late oak. 40% ⊙ ⊙

Tomintoul Aged 12 Years Oloroso Sherry Cask Finish db (73.5) n18.5 t19 f18 b18. Tomintoul, with good reason, styles itself as "The Gentle Dram" and you'll hear no argument from me about that one. However, the sherry influence here offers a rough ride. 40%

Tomintoul Aged 12 Years Portwood Finish db (87.5) n22 grapes and tangerines vie for dominance; clean with a wonderful threat of spice; t22 soft oils help embolden the juicier malt elements; a hint of plum and peach; f21.5 a light custard note ticks the oak box while the barley outweighs the fruit; b22 as Portwood finishes go, a real lightweight allowing the barley plenty of room to flex its juicier muscles. 46%. nc ncf. ⊙ ⊙

Tomintoul Aged 14 Years db (91) n23.5 t23 f21.5. This guy has shortened its breath somewhat: with the distinct thinness to the barley and oak arriving a little flustered and half-hearted rather than with a confident stride; b23 remains a beautiful whisky full of vitality and displaying the malt in its most naked and vulnerable state. But I get the feeling that perhaps a few too many third fills, or under-performing seconds, has resulted in the intensity and hair-raising harmony of the truly great previous bottlings just being slightly undercooked. That said, still a worthy and delicious dram! 46%. nc ncf. ⊙ ⊙

Tomintoul Aged 16 Years db (94.5) n24.5 a fruity concoction of apples and pears topped with vanilla ice cream; even the vaguest hint of something smoky...one of the noses of the year; t23.5 every bit as gentle as the label promises, as the light oils coat the palate with a fabulously intense and delicately sweetened barley skin. The skeleton is playful oak; f23 a wonderful, multi-layered interplay between malt and oak-vanillas. Long, curiously spice-free, increasingly dry but hugely sophisticated; b23.5 confirms Tomintoul's ability to dice with greatness. 40% ⊙

Tomintoul Aged 21 Years db (94) n24 has all the hallmarks of a malt which contains casks a lot older than the stated age: the fruit is of the exotic variety and the manner in which those fruit and defter floral notes effortlessly intertwine confirms not just the magnificence of quality but also familiarity between oak and malt t24 silky and soft with the balance of the light sugars to barley almost perfect; the vanillas grow, as they should, but the freshness to the barley never diminishes f22.5 a beautiful butterscotch and custard confection b23.5 just how good this whisky would have been at cask strength or even at 46 absolutely terrifies me. 40%. ⊙ ⊙

Tomintoul Aged 27 Years db (87) n22 t22.5 21.5 b21. The last time I saw a colour like this was on antique expert David Dickinson's face. Still, lots of charm and character to go round... and on the whisky, too. 40%

Tomintoul Aged 33 Years db (95.5) n24.5 just about textbook aged high quality malt: exotic fruit at every turn...and displaying extraordinary depth and intensity into the bargain. The level of fruit sweetness against the more lush semi-bourbony brown sugars is an experience to savour. The spices twinkle endearingly; t24.5 the weight on the palate defies belief. Just about perfection in that department while there is almost a sheen to the oaky input. The sugars dissolve readily allowing the spices a controlled lift off. Somehow, after all these years, a salivating element is preserved...virtually faultless; f23 just loses its way a little as a light, tight furriness burrows into the crisp sugars and silky oaks; even so, some stunning moments in the oaky sunset; b24 the point about whiskies of this age is that sometimes you have to deal with what you are given. Some 33 years ago a blender didn't decide to put these to one side for a single malt; this was made to be blended away and have arrived at this point with a pleasing randomness: the casks used here escaped the call of the warehouse foreman. Which means this breathtakingly beautiful 33 Year Old Tomintoul bares virtually no resemblance to the last one I tasted. Which is what makes this job of mine, at times, so bloody fascinating. 43%. ⊙ ⊙

Tomintoul With A Peaty Tang db (94) n23 t24 f23 b24. A bit more than a tang, believe me! Faultlessly clean distillate that revels in its unaccustomed peaty role. The age is confusing and appears mixed, with both young and older traits being evident. 40%

Archives Tomintoul 1969 42 Years Old Third Release bourbon cask, cask no. 4266, dist Jun 69, bott Mar 12 (88.5) n22 oaky seeds are sown: has more in common with Kentucky than Keith; t22 big oak but the barley still has enough life to keep control; f22 quiet and happy to snooze in a vanilla-caramel stupa; b22.5 looks like crashing fatally into the oak, but the integrity of the barley performs miracles. Charming. 42.4%. nc ncf sc. Whiskybase B.V. 60 bottles.

⋅⋅⋅ **Gordon & MacPhail Private Collection Tomintoul 1972** refill sherry hogshead, cask no. 1974 (86.5) n23 t20 f22 b21.5. Such a great nose and, eventually, complex finish. Wonderful. But the senses are elsewhere bombarded and sometimes overwhelmed with just too many oak fundamentalists. 45.1%. ncf.

Liquid Sun Tomintoul Peated 11 Years Old dist 2001 (86) n22 t21.5 f21 b21.5. A straightforward malt: peaty, clean, a touch of citrus but a shade too sweet for great complexity. 47.6%. sc. The Whisky Agency.

Liquid Sun Tomintoul 43 Years Old dist 1969 **(88.5)** n21 aggressive oak; t22 the delivery is none-too promising as splinters of oak are driven into the tongue. But the barley and liquorice notes regroup to find some sugar from somewhere, inevitably molasses; light oils and caramels form to make a softer middle than once seemed possible; f23 mmm! Hard not to love that late citrus which sits with the chocolate very comfortably; b22.5 ever been to a tennis match where the old guy is a set down in a Gland Slam final and being played off the court before switching on the brilliance to storm back to victory....? 476%. The Whisky Agency.

Malts Of Scotland Tomintoul 1967 bourbon hogshead, cask no. MoS11023, bott Nov 11 **(86)** n22.5 t20.5 f22 b21. The oak is just a little too dominant. Even so, this is one very complex old beast with some excellent sugars helping to ensure a degree of balance against the marauding salt. 47.5%. nc ncf sc. Malts Of Scotland.

Malts Of Scotland Tomintoul 1967 rum barrel, cask no. MoS12020, bott Mar 12 **(83.5)** n22 t21 f20 b20.5. I would need Dr Frankenstein, not a rum cask, to inject life back into this guy. Some pleasant sugars, but a little cough syrupy in part. 51.3%. nc ncf sc.

Malts Of Scotland Tomintoul 2001 bourbon hogshead, cask no. MoS12010, dist 25 Jun 01, bott Jan 12 **(84)** n23 t21 f19 b21. The peat is full on - and quite beautiful on the nose - the barley is rock hard and the barrel is not great, hence the bitter finish. 53.9%. nc ncf sc.

⁜ **Master Of Malt Tomintoul 17 Years Old** cask no. 2175, dist 1 May 95, bott 1 Apr 95 **(89)** n22.5 toasty but oiled barley sugar; t22 big malt kick on arrival but the oak is up fast into the action as the vanilla/butterscotch grabs hold; fudge; f22 toasty fudge and spice; b22.5 shares many similar elements as the Boutique-y batch 1...but better tooled up on the oil and barley front. 54.5%. sc.

Mo Òr Collection Tomintoul 1967 43 Years Old first fill bourbon hogshead, cask no. 4691, dist 19 Jun 67, bott 2 Dec 10 **(95)** n23.5 from the marmalade on burnt toast school though with a side dollop of lime jelly; t24 sublime delivery. The oak is right up there, but unlike some others from this distillery it doesn't dominate at any given moment. Instead, it gently persuades the marmalade and sugars to fall into file and then mix gently. The result is a silky, malt-driven treat with very well-mannered spices; f23.5 delicate golden syrup absorbs the vanillas like treacly suspension. No bitterness, no eye-watering oakiness. Just a gorgeous, relaxed fade; b24 improbably good! 46%. nc ncf sc. Release No. 24. The Whisky Talker. 215 bottles.

⁜ **Old Ballantruan The Peated Malt Aged 10 Years** **(86.5)** n21.5 t22 f21.5 b21.5. A busy youngster of a malt whose peaty sweetness nibbles at the taste buds than swamps them. Delicious and well made, with only a surprising lack of complexity development keeping the score down. 50%. ncf. Tomintoul

Old Malt Cask Tomintoul Aged 40 Years refill hogshead, cask no. 8007, dist Mar 71, bott Jan 12 **(94)** n23 as much exotic fruit as could be wished for. A lovely bourbony red liquorice tang represents the oak with aplomb, perhaps with a hint of creosote; the laziest of light phenols hang in the air; t24 ridiculously fragile: the barley is waif-like, the vanillas gentle and planting a row of delicate kisses rather than a big smacker on the chops...; f23.5 long, despite the fragility of the flavours. Against the odds, the sugars seem to gather rather than diminish; b23.5 majestic and magnificent. 45.6%. nc ncf sc. Douglas Laing & Co. 142 bottles.

Old Malt Cask Tomintoul Aged 40 Years refill barrel, cask no. 7731, dist Apr 71, bott Sep 11 **(87.5)** n21 lemon zesty barley...only a sprinkling of saline vanilla hints at the age; t23 mouth-watering and fresh, the barley has the juiciness of a malt a fraction of the 40 given years; f22 tightens rather too quickly as the oak takes command; b21.5 for a whisky of such antiquity, the story is surprisingly one-dimensional and barley bound....though always enjoyable. 46.8%. nc ncf sc. Douglas Laing & Co. 209 bottles.

Scott's Selection Tomintoul 1989 bott 2011 **(84.5)** n21 t22 f20.5 b21. Exceptionally malty. Wonderfully well sugared. But this is a malt whisky over 21–years-old...it has to move on from there... 53.2%. Speyside Distillers.

⁜ **That Boutique-y Whisky Company Tomintoul** batch 1 **(88.5)** n22.5 slightly scorched toast; nutty; t22 vanillas arrive early to show solid oak involvement; fudgy barley, too; f21.5 the spices enliven the natural caramels; b22.5 a lovely distillery showing a somewhat brooding side to its nature. 478%. 172 bottles.

⁜ **The Whisky Agency Tomintoul 1967** bott 12 **(84)** n24 t21 f19 b20. Fantastic spices, all of them oak-derived. But it is all about the nose which is an essay of poise and complexity. There even a brief malt moment in there somewhere. Don't bother drinking. Just sniff..and preferably after it has been in the glass for at least 20 minutes. 44.6%

The Whisky Agency Tomintoul 1968 bott 2011 **(94.5)** n23.5 no doubting the age, but the lack of aggression or bitterness from the oak is unusual. Some slightly overcooked fruit, which almost suggests an old sherry butt, but I suspect this is bourbon thanks to the peaches and apricots; t23.5 more oak evidence on delivery than nose, but the slow meandering among the dates and assorted brown sugars, Demerara especially, ensures the balance is never compromised; f23.5 just like the butterscotch tart I had at school in Surrey, except here some late barley gathers and intensifies to mix with the watered down ulmo honey; **b24** you dangerously exotic little thing, you! Defies the years to entice and finally seduce. Let it sit in the glass for 15 minutes before tackling. *43.2%. nc ncf sc. The Whisky Agency.*

The Whisky Agency Tomintoul 1969 bott 2011 **(88) n21** no-one at home: dull; **t22.5** the oak shows a few early knots but soft, sweetened mocha soothes the way; a light citrus tang offers much needed complexity; **f22** soft, bereft of great depth, but content in its sugary vanilla fade; **b22.5** makes up for the nothing nose with an electrifying display of delicate sugars and juicy citrus. Although it doesn't ramp up quite the complexity you might hope for a malt this age , its gentle nature is very attractive. *53.1%. nc ncf sc. The Whisky Agency.*

The Whisky Agency Tomintoul 1972 bott 2011 **(95) n24** a degree of exotic fruit, except much more sophisticated than that; a drizzle of peat blends beautifully with the mocha. All is understated and with the soft caresses almost as erotic as exotic; **t24** the barley is remarkably agile and salivating, though soon thin strands of manuka honey and honeycomb are attaching themselves to a cocoa backbone; the subtlety of sweetness astonishes while the texture makes you purr; **f23** yet more cocoa, getting milkier by the minute: a wonderful finale of Brazilian biscuit; **b24** I have had the good fortune over a great many years to meet quite a few veteran actresses who somehow retained a beauty that the passing of time could not tarnish. This immaculate whisky reminds me of them. *45.7%. nc ncf sc. The Whisky Agency.*

The Whisky Agency Tomintoul Peated 2001 bott 2011 **(85) n21.5 t22.5 f20 b21.** A lightly peated, slightly creamy dram which is done few favours by a tired cask which adds little to the table except a late bitterness. The delicate gristy smokiness is a delight, however. *49.7%. nc ncf sc. The Whisky Agency.*

⫶⫶⫶ **The Whisky Cask Tomintoul Aged 43 Years** bourbon hogshead, dist 69, bott 12 **(86) n20.5 t21.5 f22.5 b21.5.** Tired, limping whisky. But enough muscular sugars − helped by an unusual degree of oil for its age − allows the more subtle oak notes to come through as well. *42.7%. sc.*

TORMORE

Speyside, 1960. Chivas Brothers. Working.

Tormore 12 Years Old db **(75) n19 t19 f19 b18.** For those who like whisky in their caramel. *40%*

Tormore Aged 15 Years "Special Distillery Bottling" db **(71) n17 t18 f19 b17.** Even a supposed pick of choice casks can't save this from its fiery fate. *46%*

⫶⫶⫶ **Gordon & MacPhail Connoisseurs Choice Tormore 1997 (86) n21.5 t22 f21 b21.5.** Easy going malt with a big lemon curd kick early on but soon reverts to simple, clean barley throughout. *46%. ncf.*

⫶⫶⫶ **Malts Of Scotland Tormore 1988** sherry butt, cask no. MoS 12043, dist Sept 1999, bott Sept 2012 **(92.5) n23** black peppers rubbed into thin creosote and raisin-soaked tannin; **t23.5** great body; some real oloroso-cream sherry style oiliness at play, and it gets creamier by the moment; a short burst of juicy barley then the cocoa in the fore- and middle-ground becomes also Cadbury-like; **f23** more creamy chocolate, though some spices offer an edge. The fruit is now more date-like; **b23** Tormore does not offer the greatest spirit known to Scotland. But when in a top grade, almost (though not quite) faultless sherry butt like this, there is just sufficient juiciness to make the most of the grape. *55.4%. nc ncf sc. 96 bottles.*

⫶⫶⫶ **Master of Malt Tormore Aged 28 Years** ex-bourbon cask, dist 24 Feb 84, bott 21 Nov 12 **(83.5) n21 t20 f21.5 b21.** The intense malt and concentrated sugars save it. But it is as hot as Hades...and that has nothing to do with the strength. *60.2%. sc. 182 bottles.*

Mo Ór Collection Tormore 1996 14 Years Old first fill bourbon hogshead, cask no. DL6868, dist 30 Nov 96, bott 9 Feb 11 **(84) n21.5 t21 f21.5 b20.** Malty, pleasant and clean. But puckeringly sharp and limited in overall complexity, except for a surprise twist of a vaguely bourbony sweetness on the finish. *46%. nc ncf sc. Release No. 47. 500 bottles.*

Provenance Tormore Over 11 Years refill hogshead, cask no. 6861, dist Autumn 1999, bott Winter 2011 **(78) n18 t20 f21 b19.** Cumbersome and unexpectedly oily, though the grist on the finale entertains. *46%. nc ncf sc. Douglas Laing & Co.*

⫶⫶⫶ **Old Malt Cask Tormore Aged 17 Years** refill hogshead, cask no. 9036, dist Jun 95, bott Sep 12 **(77.5) n19 t20 f19 b19.5.** You can count on this distillery to rarely satisfy you, and this off beam (if very malty) offering is no disappointment...if you see what I mean... *50%. sc. Douglas Laing & Co. 340 bottles.*

Scotch Malt Whisky Society Cask 105.16 Aged 28 Years first fill sherry hogshead, cask no. 900008, dist 1983 **(78.5) n18.5 t21 f19 b19.** Surprised to find a slight sulphury note in a cask from this vintage, but it was there on the nose to the extent that I decided to make this the last one I'd taste before lunch. Disappointing, though those unable to detect sulphur should be able to enjoy with abandon. *54.5%. sc. Scotch Malt Whisky Society.*

Scotch Malt Whisky Society Cask 105.17 Aged 28 Years first fill sherry hogshead, cask no. 900003, dist 1983 **(83)** n20 t22 f20 b21. Rich, voluptuous grape dominates. But a vague, bitterish off note rains on the party. *55.3%. sc. Scotch Malt Whisky Society.*

⋙ That Boutique-y Whisky Company Tormore batch 1 **(88)** n22 spotted dog pudding... but spotless; **t22** a playful barley hint on the nose becomes more substantial on delivery; clean; **f22** simplistic vanilla with a twist of lemon; late cocoa at the death; **b22** easy going Tormore with enough zest to the barley to make for an interesting and pleasant experience. *50%. Master Of Malt. 226 bottles.*

⋙ Wemyss 1988 Single Speyside Tormore "White Chocolate Torte" barrel, bott 2012 **(91)** n22.5 diffused cracked black pepper and pink grapefruit; **t23** mega intense barley, in some ways intensified by the usual thinness of the spirit. But this has lived in a top quality cask for a good while and the oak balances beautifully, helped along by just-so oil involvement; **f22.5** surprising degree of salt gives a tang to the evolving cocoa; **b23.5** not my favourite distillery, but here the elements work together like a charm. An absolute little beauty cluttered with surprising nooks and crannies. *46%. sc. 251 bottles.*

TULLIBARDINE
Highlands (Perthshire), 1949. Tullibardine Ltd. Working.

Tullibardine 1988 John Black Edition 4 bott 2008 db **(91.5)** n23.5 gosh!! How about this for ultra ripe figs and greengages? Wonderfully spiced, honeyed - in an intriguingly understated style - and clean for good measure. One of those you leave the empty glass to give any room's aroma a touch of class to for a few days... **t23** the grape cascades onto the taste buds in a thick, dizzying regiment of fruitiness, by no means all grape, either. The spices hinted at on the nose are here ramrod hard and unyielding; **f22.5** the intensity on delivery fades quite dramatically to leave an almost new-makey cocoa residue. Surprising... and delicious...; **b22.5** An altogether superior and much more complex animal to J B's disappointing No 3 Selection. *46%*

Tullibardine 1992 Rum Finish bott 2009 db **(89.5)** n22 t23 f22.5 b22. Cracking stuff! *46%*

Tullibardine 1993 bott 2009 db **(91.5)** n22 t23.5 f23 b23. Intrinsically sweet barley. But spellbindingly charming all the way. *40%*

Tullibardine 1993 Moscatel Finish bott 2007 db **(92.5)** n23.5 t23.5 f23 b22.5. This really is how wine casks should integrate. A minor stunner. *46%*

Tullibardine 1993 Oloroso Sherry Finish bott 2008 db **(89)** n23 t23 f21 b22. Almost a trip down Memory Lane: once a pretty standard sherry butt, but now a treat. *46%*

Tullibardine 1993 Pedro Ximénez Sherry Finish bott 2009 db **(87)** n21 t23 f20.5 b22.5. Sticky and enjoyable. *46%*

Tullibardine 1993 Port Finish bott 2008 db **(83.5)** n21.5 t21 f20 b21. A bumbling, weighty kind of dram with indistinct shape and purpose, even to the extent of displaying a more bourbony gait than a fruity one. Enjoyable, decently spiced but limited in scope. *46%*

Tullibardine 1993 Sauternes Finish bott 2008 db **(84.5)** n22 t22 f20 b20.5. Sleepy and soft with the expected major grape input. Yet rather flattens out too early and to too great a degree. Pleasant, but a little disappointing, too. *46%*

⋙ **Tullibardine Aged 20 Years** db **(92.5)** n22.5 busy and can't decide which weight to adopt; ethereal hazelnut and citrus rise above the languid tannins; **t24** no doubting the richness of body and the exceptional weight: first it is scorched yet juicy barley by the cartload, then thudding oak with just enough ulmo honey to oil the wheels. And then rampaging spice; **f22.5** settles for more prosaic butterscotch but the spices continue to bristle; **b23.5** while there are whiskies like this in the world, there is a point to this book... *43%*

⋙ **Tullibardine Aged 25 Years** db **(86.5)** n22 t22 f21 b21.5. There can be too much of a good thing. And although the intricacies of the honey makes you sigh inwardly with pleasure, the overall rigidity and fundamentalism of the oak goes a little too far. *43%*

⋙ **Tullibardine 225** sauternes cask finish db **(85)** n20 t22.5 f21 b21.5. Hits the heights early on in the delivery when the honey and Lubeck marzipan are at full throttle. *43%*

⋙ **Tullibardine 228** Burgundy cask finish db **(82)** n21 t22 f18 b21. No shortage of bitter chocolate. Flawed but a wow for those looking for mega dry malt. *43%*

⋙ **Tullibardine 500** sherry cask finish db **(79.5)** n19 t21 f19 b20.5. The usual problems from Jerez, but the grape ensures maximum chewability. *43%*

Tullibardine Aged Oak bott 2009 db **(86)** n21.5 t21 f22 b21.5. Aged oak maybe. But early on this is all about the malt which is faultless. Major oaky buzz later. *40%*

Tullibardine Aged Oak Edition bott 2010 db **(88)** n21 t22 f22.5 b22.5. Beautifully made malt which is full of life. *40%. nc.*

Tullibardine Banyuls Finish bott 2011 db **(68)** n16 t18 f17 b17. I saw the sulphur coming on this. A steaming mug of intense black coffee and a cool glass of taste bud restorative coconut water wait in the wings. *46%. nc ncf.*

Tullibardine Banyuls Finish bott 2012 db **(71)** n17 t19 f17 b18. A minor tragedy: take away the sulphur and you have what would have been a serious juicefest. Not for the first time with a banyuls cask, I could cry! 46%. nc ncf.

Tullibardine John Black db **(84.5)** n20 t21.5 f22 b21. Young, clean and bursting with all kinds of delicious maltiness. An almost perfect first dram of the day. 40%. nc.

Tullibardine John Black Edition No. 6 bourbon barrel, cask no. 10002, dist 1993, bott Dec 2011 db **(94.5)** n24 t23 f23.5 b24. There are very few whiskies which, professionally, I find impossible to spit out. Here is one. 55.1%. nc ncf sc.

Tullibardine Premier Cru Classé Finish Chateau Lafite casks, dist 92, bott 10 **(89.5)** n21.5 t22.5 f23 b22.5. A quite fascinating whisky which will keep you entertained for hours. It's like having War Games in a glass. Curiously, I tasted this from the cask when it was a few months younger. At full strength and with the malt having more telling depth and confidence there was more harmonisation. 46%. nc ncf.

Tullibardine Pure Pot new make db **(90.5)** n24 t23 f21.5 b22. Pure delight! Not whisky, of course, but a great example of how new make malt should be. 69%

Tullibardine PX Finish dist 1993, bott 2008 db **(85)** n23 t22 f20 b20. A big, at times bone-hard, whisky which, like many which have spent time in Pedro Ximénez casks, have found it difficult to acquire the kind of balance hoped. The nose offers great promise with a real old-fashioned fruitcake flourish but after the melt-in-the-mouth delivery gets past the barley lead, the degree of bitterness outweighs the growing soft fig notes. For equilibrium, needed less – or more – time in cask: we'll never know. 46%

Tullibardine Sauternes Finish bott 2012 db **(90.5)** n22 quite tight with fruit and barley bound together; a mild spearmint sweetness lightens things; t23 the balance between the juicier grape, diced apple and the keynote light sugars is excellent, as is the soft oils and ever buzzing spices; f22.5 butterscotch tart with a light chocolate topping; b23 the spices attached to the richness of the body makes for a very satisfying and quite intriguing malt. 46%. nc ncf.

⁖ **Tullibardine Sovereign** bourbon barrel db **(89.5)** n22.5 a kind of 'what's what' of bourbon aromas: an entire regiment of delicate oaky tones from the standard butterscotch through to polished oak floors. But all tinged with a green-ish barley note. Always light and a little chalky; t23 the nose is transferred almost in identical form to the delivery: more light sugars at play here and a little nutty, too; f21.5 a slight tang to the fading milky Sugar Puffs; b22.5 beautifully salivating despite the intricate oak notes. 43%

Tullibardine Vintage Edition Aged 20 Years dist 1988, bott 2008 db **(86)** n22 t22 f21 b21. The malt sparkles on the nose and delivery. Fades as caramels kick in. 46%

⁖ **Cadenhead Tullibardine 19 Years Old Chateau Lafitte** dist 93, bott 13 **(89)** n23 big statement here: one of the most peppered aromas of the year. The fruit is dripping from the glass; t22.5 Superb delivery. The malt steps up to the plate to ensure the wine doesn't have it all its own way. Toffee nougat middle before big spices begin to bite; f21.5 not entirely flawless but still enough pepper to keep the dry finish going; b22 sometimes these wine finishes can anything other than to pop your cork for. This, though, has enough depth to handle the majority of the massive grape. 48.3%. Wm Cadenhead Ltd. 210 bottles.

Mo Òr Collection Tullibardine 1965 44 Years Old Oloroso sherry butt, cask no. 959, dist 23 May 65, bott 26 Nov 09 **(95.5)** n23 big fruitcake with burnt raisins, yet the whole seems to have been cooked beautifully; t23.5 a silk delivery with some pins left in it: the thick grape seems to glide over the palate but the spices ensure it is not plain sailing; there is lush Demerara sugars to ensure stability; other fruits abound in this juicy set up, not least black cherry and dates; f24 the kind of fade that stretches far into the distance. At last more gentle vanillas emerge while those gorgeous, now molassed sugars thinly coat both the oak and the persistent fruit. You would feel hard done by if cocoa didn't form somewhere, and it dutifully does with a light praline touch late in the day; b25 a riveting malt which just gets better and better. After the procession of underwhelming Scotch singletons I have been tasting today, it is so good to at last find one of undisputed quality. 48.8%. nc ncf sc. Release No. 3. 197 bottles.

Scott's Selection Tullibardine 1989 bott 2012 **(86.5)** n22 t22 f21 b21.5. An attractive all rounder with a comfortable oak supporting act warming up the big barley lead. Lovely spices, too. 55.7%. Speyside Distillers.

Wemyss 1989 Single Highland "Rum & Raisin" hogshead, bott 2011 **(87)** n22 t22 f21 b22. A malt which lives dangerously: on the edge so far as the oak involvement is concerned, but enough complexity and fun for a few extra ticks. 46%. sc. Wemyss Malts. 299 bottles.

UNSPECIFIED SINGLE MALTS (Campbeltown)

Cadenhead's Campbeltown Malt (92) n22 t24 f23 b23. On their home turf you'd expect them to get it right... and, my word, so they do!! 59.5%

Cadenhead's Classic Campbeltown (92) n23 t24 f22 b23. What a dram! Must be what they gave Lazarus... 50%

UNSPECIFIED SINGLE MALTS (Highland)

Ailein Mor (84) n21 t22 f20 b21. An ultra soft malt with plenty of chew to it and a honey-caramel sweetness. 40%. Robert Graham.

⁂ **Elements of Islay BR4** (93) n22.5 a saline drip of cucumber and barley; t24 wow! The sharpness of the barley hits puckering levels helped by massive salt seasoning. Massive and as sizzling as an Islay sunrise; f23 long with a salted custard tart finale; a few strands of cooking apple; b23.5 non-peated Islay at is most deliciously coastal. 54.7%

⁂ **Elements of Islay BW1** (89) n22 good salty edge to the peat soot; a minor citrus sub note; t22 early oils and tangy gristy sweetness. The smoke hangs above and below the juicy, sugary norm; f22 a lovely light orange touch to the clean barley. Late oak complexity; b23 pretty regulation oily peat, but with helpful oak. 52.9%. Speciality Drinks Ltd.

⁂ **Elements of Islay CL4** (92.5) n23.5 good grief...!! A rock pool of salt water on a very hot day with all kinds of seaweed breaking down on the surrounding boulders; the smoke opens up properly after about 15 minutes in the glass and offers a cocoa edge to the sublime phenols; t23.5 intense delivery. The salt and sugars are in primary form: no honey around, just a massive Demerara/molasses mix. The smoke doesn't come through as on the nose, but leaves no doubt it's around; f22.5 a Demerara-cocoa blend...and still the malty salt shimmers; b23 astonishing. If you are looking for a soft, easy going peat job with polite smoke, go somewhere else. This is bold as brass. Massive and magnificent. 58.7%. Speciality Drinks Ltd.

⁂ **Fortnum and Mason Highland Aged 10 Years** (88.5) n23 generous dollop of heather honey spread on freshly cut farmhouse bread; t22 beautifully silky with an immediate spice impact which surprisingly lessens rather than expands. Burnt fudge may be to blame, though toasted honeycomb does make an appearance; f21.5 more chewy toffee; b22 a very soft ride around the Highlands. Dangerously easy drinking in Mayfair. 43%

⁂ **Glen Marnoch Aged 18 Years Limited Edition Release Cask Reserve** (88.5) n23 wonderful gooseberry jam and seasoned sultana; the custard tart vanilla underlines the age; t22.5 pure silk on delivery, though made interesting by a double burst of staccato spice and salivating fruit; f21 quietens with toffee; b22 quite beautiful. Distilled hot cross bun. 40%. Aldi.

⁂ **Glen Turner Aged 12 Years Exclusive Reserve** bott code. L206557A (87) n22 good nose. Though flattened by a touch of caramel, there is still room for a light, spicy and engagingly fruity roll call; t22 jaunty barley trips juicily off the tongue; the mid-ground is melted icing sugar; f21 toffee; b22 charming and showing delicate complexity in all the right places. 40%

Glen Turner Aged 21 Years Limited Edition (94.5) n24 t23 f23.5 b24.5. Oddly enough I grew up with a name like this involved in my everyday life. Len Turner was my late father's best friend. And as a small boy both he and his wife, Maude, unofficial uncle and aunt, showed me untold kindness. They have both been gone over 30 years now...but it would have been lovely to present them with a bottle of this very beautiful whisky, just to say: "thanks". 53.1%. ncf. La Martiniquaise. 500 bottles.

The Grangestone Whisky Collection Highland Single Malt 21 Years Old (89) n23.5 t22.5 f21 b22. What a softie! Not sure whether to drink this or pat and pet it...Think it's one to drink – some aspects are superb. 40%. Quality Spirits International.

Highland Queen Majesty Classic (84.5) n21.5 t21 f21 b21. The horse on the label somehow perfectly represents the plodding nature of this whisky. A single malt bottling of the old-fashioned school in that it is well made and matured with no off notes at all. But shy coming forward, too, and never quite makes it from a walk to a trot. 40%

Highland Queen Majesty Aged 8 Years (84) n22 t21 f20 b21. Another soft, silky and safe malt, though complexity is lost under a big toffee theme. Well made and decently matured though. 40%. Highland Queen Scotch Whisky Company.

Highland Queen Majesty Aged 12 Years (86.5) n22 t22 f21 b21.5. The most gentle and easy going malt, though the toffee notes have much to do with that. Even so, some charming characteristics bubble underneath. The nose benefits from its apple and pear fruitiness and the usual silky texture is punctured by some lively spices. 40%

Highland Queen Majesty Aged 16 Years (90.5) n24 t22.5 f22 b22. Your majesty! I am impressed! Benefits from the toning down of the caramel character and doubtless would benefit further from being at the 46%abv its age warrants. 40%

Highland Queen Majesty Distiller's Selection Limited Edition 1989 ex-bourbon hogsheads, bott 2009 (87) n22.5 t22 f21 b21.5. Again, good casks helping out a well-made malt. But, for all the main sugar and spice theme, complexity remains at a premium. 40%. Highland Queen Scotch Whisky Company.

Master Of Malt Highland Single Malt (86.5) n23 t21.5 f21 b21. Enjoys a distinctly sma' still constitution with copper being as much part of the makeup as the chalky malt. 40%

⁂ **Maxwell 33 Year Old Highland Single Malt** (95) n24.5 rarely does exotic fruit come quite so exotic! The oak is pulling out every trick in the book to underscore its great age with an aroma as softly enveloping as it has any right to be. Those who remember fruit salad candy will also be seduced by this one. As well rounded as any malt you'll find this year and probably as labyrinthine, too. And, just to prove it, a few peat notes escape from their fruity clutches to add weight and depth, the intensity increasing as the temperature and oxidisation increases. Has to be nosed to be believed...here is a chance to have a sniff at something nearing perfection; **t24** all the fruits registered on the nose are present and correct, but it is the spices which momentarily take the breath away. A fabulous mouth feel alternating between crisp and mouth-watering – aided and abetted by some staccato Demerara sugar notes - and always no less than feather-pillow soft. The mid ground starts allowing the oak to show some intense vanilla and that lazy smoke to gain a foothold, a more solid one with each mouthful; **f22.5** dry and sophisticated, the fruit is now spent and a slight tang reminds us of the great age here. A light, delicate fade with the peat withdrawing surprisingly early on; **b24** Last year Lidl unearthed a couple of stunning whiskies to be sold at an improbably economic price to the consumer. They have done it again for Christmas 2012 with a malt destined to be another collectors' item. At times towards the end the age is apparent. But no less so is a malt which has on the nose and delivery a marriage between oak and barley matured in heaven. A very softly smoked, delightfully fruity gem. *40%. sc. Lidl. 5280 bottles.*

Sainsbury's Single Highland Malt 12 Years Old Unchillfiltered (84.5) **n20 t22 f21 b21.5.** Love it! Admittedly, not technically the best spirit ever distilled (as the nose confirms rather too proudly), but that extra width of cut ensures a malt you can contentedly chew on for an age. *46%. nc ncf. Ian Macleod for Sainsbury's UK.*

Wemyss Aged 14 Years Single Highland "A Day at the Coast" hogshead, bott Aug 11 (90.5) **n23 t23 f22 b22.5.** The day at the coast certainly wasn't Margate. Worthy of a "wish you were here" postcard! *46%. sc. 354 bottles. USA exclusive.*

❖ **Wemyss Aged 16 Years Highland "Beachcomber"** hogshead, bott 11 (90) **n23** apples both diced and boiled, then mixed; a slight "milky" sign of an overused cask, but nothing too serious; might lead to some bitterness at the death, however...; **t23.5** irresistible delivery: fresh and younger than its years given a big clear honey polish and then an intense, oily barley concentrate middle; **f21.5** long, thanks to that soft oil, with the old, solidified honey and fresher barley bowling along to the, literally, bitter end (surprise, surprise); **b22** the honey elements are to die for. Not sure where the beach comes in, though; such fanciful and, frankly, pretentious names does the brand no favours whatsoever and imbues a degree of amateurism which does the brand and whisky a disservice... *46%. sc. 257 bottles. USA exclusive.*

Wemyss Aged 29 Years Single Highland "The Dunes" hogshead, bott Aug 11 (75.5) **n19 t19.5 f18 b19.** Lost in a burning vanilla desert... *46%. sc. 202 bottles. USA exclusive.*

❖ **Wemyss Glen Garioch 1989 Single Highland "Fruit Bonbons"** hogshead (91.5) **n22** lots of zingy barley with a few greengages and under-ripe gooseberries thrown in for good measure; **t23.5** from the nose this had to be salivating...and it is! The barley cuts a juicy dash but there are sufficient oils to help the tannins gather and intensify, though weak ulmo honey keeps the sugar levels up before the spices arrive; **f23** the barley still retains a vaguely fruity presence, but the pulsing spicy oak lasts longest; **b23** the spirit from the stills at this time had a "fire water" reputation which now, as is so often the case, means we have a malt which is wilful and complex and able to take the two decades of maturation comfortably in its stride. *46%. sc. 325 bottles.*

Wemyss 1990 Single Highland "Tropical Spice" refill butt, bott Sep 09 (95) **n24.5 t24 f23 b23.5.** A peach of a barrel. Highly unusual in character and never seemingly the same any two times you taste it. *59.4%. Wemyss Malts Ltd. 767 bottles.*

UNSPECIFIED SINGLE MALTS (Island)

Master Of Malt Island Single Malt (91.5) **n22.5 t23 f22.5 b23.5.** Don't know about Lord of the Isles. More like Lord of the Flies...Fruit flies, that is...! They would be hard pressed to find even an over-ripe mango any juicier than this gorgeous malt... *40%*

UNSPECIFIED SINGLE MALTS (Islay)

Adelphi Breath Of The Isles 15 Years Old cask no. 1792, dist 95, bott 10 (94.5) **n24** excellent honey-smoke combo; floral pollen-like notes; spices take a little time to arrive but when they do, they no more than complete the picture; **t24** sublime honeycomb: actually breaks down honey constituents thanks to a manuka-acacia mix; a liquorice layer; **f22.5** threatens to bitter up, but instead light spices and more honeycomb edge it closer to a bourbon-style finale; **b24** take a breath of this every day and you'd live for ever... *58%. sc. 245 bottles.*

Adelphi's Liddesdale Aged 18 Years Batch 1 sherry butt, bott 2010 (94) **n23.5 t24 f23 b23.5.** An exceptional Islay where complexity and balance are the key. *46%. 2962 bottles.*

Auld Reekie Islay Malt (95) **n24 t24 f23 b24.** My last whisky of the day and a dram I shall be tasting all the way to when I clean my teeth. On second thoughts... I'll do them in the morning. Only kidding. But this is a must have dram for Islayphiles: true genius. *46%*

Elements Of Islay Br2 (87.5) n22 t22 f21.5 b22. A malt with an identity crisis. Off key in part, absolutely on the ball elsewhere. *49.3%. ncf. Speciality Drinks.*

⁙ **Elements of Islay BR4 (93)** n22.5 a saline drip of cucumber and barley; **t24** wow! The sharpness of the barley hits puckering levels helped by massive salt seasoning. Massive and as sizzling as a Islay sunrise; **f23** long with a salted custard tart finale; a few strands of cooking apple; **b23.5** non-peated Islay at is most deliciously coastal. *54.7%.*

⁙ **Elements of Islay BW1 (89)** n22 good salty edge to the peat soot; a minor citrus sub note; **t22** early oils and tangy gristy sweetness. The smoke hangs above and below the juicy, sugary norm; **f22** a lovely light orange touch to the clean barley. Late oak complexity; **b23** pretty regulation oily peat, but with helpful oak. *52.9%. Speciality Drinks Ltd.*

⁙ **Elements of Islay CL4 (92.5)** n23.5 good grief...!! A rock pool of salt water on a very hot day with all kinds of seaweed breaking down on the surrounding boulders; the smoke opens up properly after about 15 minutes in the glass and offers a cocoa edge to the sublime phenols; **t23.5** intense delivery. The salt and sugars are in primary form: no honey around, just a massive Demerara/molasses mix. The smoke doesn't come through as on the nose, but leaves no doubt its around; **f22.5** a Demarara-cocoa blend...and still the malty salt shimmers;; **b23** astonishing. If you are looking for a soft, easy going peat job with polite smoke, go somewhere else. This is bold as brass. Massive and magnificent. *58.7%. Speciality Drinks Ltd.*

Elements of Islay Pe1 (95.5) n24 t24.5 f23.5 b23.5. This is a fabulous, nigh faultless, example of the purest element of Islay: its whisky... *58.7%. Speciality Drinks Ltd.*

⁙ **Finlaggan Old Reserve Cask Strength (94)** n23 a bold, macho nose with a peatiness which could chip diamonds; **t23.5** weirdly enough the sugars on parade on delivery are almost identical to those found in better rye whiskies: crisp, juicy yet brooding. Then the smoke goes into eye-watering overdrive; **f23.5** just so long...hope you have a good ten minutes to spare. Begins to move towards a drier, more sooty style, but those maple syrup and beech honey notes have their say, first; **b24** I can imagine even people who proclaim not to like peaty whisky slowly falling in love with this...it is so enormous, that it would be a case of kill or cure. *58%. The Vintage Malt Whisky Co Ltd.*

First Cask Isle Of Islay 21 Years Old first fill sherry butt, cask no. 12, dist 24 Dec 90, bott 9 Jan 12 **(77)** n19 t21 f18 b19. Back in 1990, only one distillery on Islay was filling non-peated spirit into sherry butts as often as not sulphur treated. This one has been, but not so badly affected as others and the grape is still quite profound. *54%. nc ncf sc. 360 bottles.*

⁙ **Fortnum and Mason Islay Aged 10 Years (90.5)** n23 soft oily, smoke. A hint of butter toffee and seaweed make unusual bedfellows these days, but were once often found side by side; **t23** silky toffee honey softens down even further the oily delivery...if that was possible. The brown sugars with the caramel and butter make almost for a smoky version of your mum's old cake mixing jar; **f22** medium length, stunted by the toffee, but an ashy finale balances out the earlier sugars rather well; **b22.5** it is nearly 20 years since I began giving whisky tastings at Fortnum and Mason. And I remember when I unleashed the first big Islay malt the majority of the veritable patrons of Mayfair had ever tasted. It was not unlike this, though less oily. The shock in the room could be felt all the way to my hat suppliers, Bates, about 250 yards away. And not all were convinced. Amazing how the same clientele, or at least their heirs, demand that a malt like this should be available to them. Times have changed drastically over two decades... *43%*

⁙ **Milroy's of Soho Peated Single Malt** hogshead, cask no. 8099, dist 4 Dec 08, bott 13 Apr 13 **(84)** n22 t21 f21 b20. Semi new-makey on nose and delivery, this enormous whisky positively flops around the palate with little discernible balance. Some thick sugar battles out the bitter oak and ash influence. Very different. *40%. 497 bottles.*

⁙ **Mystery Lochside (95)** n24.5 oozes age. Yet the delicate presence of gooseberries sweetened with light manuka honey ensures the oak never takes on more than a bourbon-tannin weight. A playful wafting of orange blossom beneath the nose completes an aroma which less than ten minutes deliberation would be an affront to great whisky. Watch out for the odd, irregular, lavender note as well as a gathering of distant smoke as the temperature and oxygen begin to kick in; **t24** evidence of the odd peat particle from yesteryear still clings to the ever-intensifying oak. The barley somehow still sits centre stage and radiates some stunning juiciness. The sugars are varied, deft, quick, melt-in-the mouth but never outmuscled by the hints of citrus working in tandem with the barley; **f22.5** light, perhaps a little thin and on the gluey side before the vaguest hint of dry cocoa powder plays its part. The steady late bite is a positive rather than a hindrance, a reminder that this oldie is still alive and possessing attitude; **b24** the kind of malt that deserves all the time you can afford it. It will repay you handsomely, especially on the nose and delivery and will never come at you at the same speed or angle. Subtle and sublime.

⁙ **Port Askaig Harbour Aged 12 Years (84.5)** n21.5 t22 f20 b21. Perfect if you are looking for a peaty fix. But the quality of the bittering oak doesn't do the malt many favours. *45.8%*

⁘ **Port Askaig Harbour Aged 19 Years** (94) n23.5 one of those wonderful aromas full of peaty promise and intent, yet still light enough to allow the salty citrus full scope; t23.5 and there, right on cue, is the lemon-rich delivery, but now divest of salt and full of delicate sugars. The saltiness arrives later, holding hands with the medium but sparkling spices and the growing barley; f23 much oakier and drier at the death and the spices now become busier and a little hotter; b24 one of those gorgeous offerings which basks in its simplicity, but takes what it does to the max. 50.4%. Speciality Drinks Ltd.

⁘ **Port Askaig Harbour Aged 30 Years** (89) n22 doesn't try to hide its age: the oak is every bit as prominent as the smoke and is now hinting at entering the realms of eucalyptus and creosote; t23 the sugars form a formidable guard of honour for the forthcoming onslaught of oak. They are of the lightly molassed variety, backed by smoked treacle and some remnants of butterscotch: all in all a decent line up; f22 the oak throbs, but enough sugar and smoke does the trick; b22 a barrel of brinkmanship: the oak influence is immense, but the quality of the spirit and profound sugars make relatively light work of it. 51.1%.

Sainsbury's Single Islay Malt 12 Years Old Unchillfiltered (94) n24 t23.5 f23 b23.5. I still remember the days when some British supermarkets would use only unpeated Islay whisky for their own label bottlings as they were too terrified that a big peat attack would scare their customers off. Let's just say that the evidence of this is that times have changed... A beast of a bottling! 46%. nc ncf. Ian Macleod for Sainsbury's UK.

Smokehead Extra Black Aged 18 Years (94) n23 t24 f23.5 b23.5. Doubtless some will prefer the in-your-face standard version. This is for those seeking a bit of grey-templed sophistication. 46%

⁘ **Wemyss Aged 14 Years Islay "Smoke on the Rocks"** hogshead, bott Aug 11 (87) n22 busy phenols which break down to smaller parts, exposing a light lime fruitiness; t22.5 slight cream soda kick to the delivery: fat textured with liquorice and latte; f20 milky mocha with a bitter oak finale; b22.5 Laphroaig-style smoke dispersal...and even complete with late cask bitterness. 46%. sc. 338 bottles. USA exclusive.

Wemyss Aged 15 Years Single Islay "A Matter of Smoke" hogshead, bott Aug 11 (84) n22 t21 f20 b21. Dishes out the peat in spades. Very little yield either from cask or spirit, though. 46%. sc. 337 bottles. USA exclusive.

⁘ **Wemyss Aged 30 Years Islay "Heathery Smoke"** hogshead, bott Aug 11 (95.5) n24 elegant, where the smoke has reached a stage in its life when it is simply part of the surroundings, rather than dominating; a lovely mix of coffee cake, soft lychee and lime plus gently spiced manuka honey makes for an unforgettable opening; t24 salivating delivery where the barley is upfront; the mouth feel is silky, almost glassy while the sugars are crystalline and tinged with the softest smoke imaginable; some ancient oak hits the middle, but soothed by the gentle complexity of the mocha and praline; f23.5 a light tangerine tang to the lightly oiled vanilla...a distant choir of spices serenade us out; b24 one of those magical malts which never noses or tastes the same twice and always offers a different perspective and new facets each time it is sampled. A true gem. 46%. sc. 272 bottles. USA exclusive.

⁘ **Wemyss 1997 Single Islay "Seaspray"** hogshead, bott 11 (74) n18 t21 f17 b18. The furry bitterness on the finish tells you all you need to know: a reject cask has got through. 46%. sc. 373 bottles. France exclusive.

Wemyss 1981 Single Islay "Whispering Smoke" hogshead, bott 2011 (94) n23 a beautiful meeting of butterscotch, salt, lemon peel and surprisingly crisp barley; t24 fabulous texture: a real golden syrup and burned fudge sweetness to the barley with busy spices popping around the palate; f23 earthy, chewy and wards off any oaky excess without breaking sweat; b24 just one of those really magnificent malts which cannot be ignored. 46%. Wemyss Malts. 228 bottles.

The Whisky Broker Islay Malt first fill sherry butt, cask no. 3, dist 17 Dec 90, bott 29 Mar 12 (80) n19 t22 f19 b20. Voluptuous grape and busy spice. Just a little too tight in part, though, for obvious reasons. 54.5%. nc ncf sc. 739 bottles.

The Whisky Broker Islay Malt first fill sherry butt, cask no. 54, dist 24 Dec 90, bott 9 Jan 11 (85.5) n23 t22 f19.5 b21. A two-toned sherry. Magnificent sultana and cinnamon-rich juicy grape to drool over. But a bitter taint takes away some of the gloss. 54.8%. nc ncf sc.

UNSPECIFIED SINGLE MALTS (Lowland)

Master Of Malt Lowland Single Malt (86) n22 t21.5 f21 b21.5. If one was to paint in one's mind's eye a delicate, grassy, inoffensive Lowlander, this would just about be it. 40%

⁘ **Master of Malt Lowland Single Malt 2nd Edition** (87) n23 some trace lime, lightening further the big acacia honey lead; t22.5 the honey makes the early running and displays early like a peacock, though dulled slightly by growing vanilla; f20.5 dries but some major chalky oak shows big cask involvement; b21 for a malt seemingly light in body, it appears to put on weight like a pie shop regular. 40%. ncf.

⋯ **McClelland's Lowland** (87.5) n22 tangy, imperfect, citrusy...enticing; **t22.5** fabulously juicy, with a mix of citrus and pears. The malt is rich and even offers some ginger as well as muscovado sugars; **f21** a dull finish, showing the limitations on the nose; **b22** a lovely, relaxed Lowlander which doesn't claim greatness but offers modest distinction. 40%

UNSPECIFIED SINGLE MALTS (Speyside)

A.D. Rattray Whisky Experience Malt 1 dist 2003 (87.5) n22 t22.5 f21 b22 Well made and richly textured malt. 40%. sc.

Ben Bracken Aged 12 Years (86.5) n22 t22.5 f20.5 b21.5. A classically easy going Speyside with no bumps or surprises. Accentuates its delicate nature attractively and makes the most of its juicy barley core. 40%. Lidl.

Celtique Connexion Saussignac Double Matured 1997 bott 2010 (95) n24 the vaguest degree of smoke drops anchor on the fruit. Freshly cleaned mature plums and tangy fruit cubes from the boiled sweet jar; Clean, lively, intense; **t24** thrilling delivery full of fresh, spicy grape, salivating barley and meaningful caramel; **f23** long with the caramels continuing the cream toffee theme, but with extra spices arriving late... and that irrepressible grape...; **b24** dreamy. Faultless. Just bloody fantastic! Displays more life, vitality and reasons to live than the entire main stand at Selhurst Park... 46%. nc ncf sc. Celtic Whisky Compagnie. 381 bottles.

Glenbridge 40 Years Old European oak sherry casks (95.5) n24 t24 f23.5 b24. Appears to be related in style to the 24-year-old and shows many similar characteristics. This, however, has dried in the extra 15 years and although the spices still rumble, there is slightly less on the sugary front to ensure an exact balance. That said, another malt showing no signs of ill health; obviously beautifully made and whoever put this into wood knew something about buying in good quality casks. 40%. Aldi. 3,000 bottles.

Glenbrynth Twenty One Limited Release first release, bott 2011 (84) n21 t21 f21 b21. I can understand why it is called 21. Not sure how to say how disappointed I am with this malt. Has the odd lively moment and a few juicy ones, too. But they are too few and far between: this is a whisky which gets into second gear but no further. Just too many blind alleys and, literally, bitter endings. 43%. OTI Africa.

Glen Marnoch 24 Years Old dist 1987 (94) n23.5 t23.5 f23 b24. A magnificent malt showing an age greater than its given years but with no off notes or signs of weariness. A malt which keeps the taste buds working hard and long. 40%. Aldi. 3,000 bottles.

Lidl Speyside Single Malt Aged 18 Years (84) n21.5 t21.5 f20 b20.5. At first silky sweet but then a dull fellow riddled with caramel character at the cost of most else. 40%.

Malts Of Scotland "1836" 1995 sherry hogshead, cask no. 37, dist Dec 95, bott May 11 (68) n17 t19 f15 b17. Sweet. But badly sulphur stained. 50.5%. nc ncf sc. Malts Of Scotland.

Malts Of Scotland Angel's Choice "1836" 1970 sherry hogshead, cask no. MoS11025, bott Nov 11 (94) n23 t23.5 f24 b23.5. An ace dram. 53.5%. nc ncf sc. Malts Of Scotland.

Malts Of Scotland Whisky Liqueur 20 Years Old (75) n21 t18 f18 b18. What the hell was THAT.....!!!! At first I thought they meant Liqueur Whisky, having been told this is a single malt. But, no: having tasted it, the word order is right. If this is pure single malt whisky, then it is the sweetest I have ever encountered. As though matured in a cask still dripping with maple syrup when filled. I can see a few women going wild over this. 40%. Malts Of Scotland.

Master Of Malt Speyside Single Malt (82.5) n20.5 t21.5 f20 b20.5. Sweet, lightly oiled but troubled by a bitter finish and wilfully refuses to crank up the complexity. 40%

⋯ **Master of Malt Speyside 30 Years Old 5th Edition** (89) n22.5 a massive flood of oak, plus a odegree of over-ripened raspberry; given time settles down to radiate manuka honey and coconut water; **t21.5** oooff!!! Like being bludgeoned by an oak stave; **f23** now moves into a gorgeous, massively sensuous mocha dripping with with muscovado sugar; **b22** a whisky moving in and out of acceptable oak like a how patient might drift in and out of consciousness. 43%.

⋯ **Master Of Malt Speyside 40 Years Old 2nd Edition** (95) n23.5 find me a Dundee fruit cake that smells more Dundee fruit cake than this, and you'll have done well; **t24** there we go. A malt 40 years old and still the juices cascade. Yes, the oak nips and ticks here and there, but the oils plus the freshness of the raisin and the vibrancy of the spice makes for something a little special; **f23.5** you expect this to bow out with a cocoa signature...and it does. But it's a long way down the track and the finish seems endless; **b24** magnificent. has no problem mastering the years. 43%.

⋯ **Master Of Malt Speyside 50 Years Old 3rd Edition** (96.5) n24 an aroma which could so easily head fatally into over-oakiness. But steps back just in time as a few layers of marmalade arrive like the 7th cavalry to lighten the load and unlock the door other more delicate tones, including Sharron fruit and butterscotch; but like all the great old whiskies, leave for about half an hour and take another look...it will have then developed a genteel life of its own...; **t23.5** a sizzing oakiness grips onto the silkymuscovado sugars for support; the middle is dry and one fears the worst...; **f24.5** and then, with spices fizzing and a weak layer of ulmo honey soothing and cajoling, the finish decides to take on the nuances of an elder statesman, with complexity levels not just amazingly high, but the elegance rendering you almost speechless; **b24.5** like many an old 'un, it seems to forget where it's going for a while. But when it reaches its destination, it just charms you to death. *43%.*

Muirhead's Silver Seal Aged 8 Years (75.5) **n18.5 t20 f18 b19.** Just too lacking in character and complexity to get away with the harshness of the feints. *40%*

Muirhead's Silver Seal Aged 12 Years (87) **n22 t22 f21.5 b21.5.** Doesn't try to be flash. Just does Speysidey things very well indeed! *40%. Highland Queen Scotch Whisky Company.*

Muirhead's Silver Seal Chassagne Montrachet Burgundy Wood Finish (89) **n23 t22.5 f21.5 b22.** Oh, guys! Had you only gone at 46%, then you would have had a real winner. As it is, charming, delicate and delicious... *40%. 5,000 bottles.*

Muirhead's Silver Seal Limited Edition 1987 (86.5) **n21.5 t22.5 f21 b21.5.** A delicate and characterful malt which pays a price for not finding a cask which could just give a fuller finish more in keeping with what had gone on before. Certainly the use of the bourbony honey and hickory notes are compelling on the nose and delivery. All the same, an attractive any-time-of-the-day malt. *40%. Highland Queen Scotch Whisky Company. 3,500 bottles.*

Muirhead's Silver Seal Special Edition 1993 (89.5) **n23 t23 f21.5 b22.** Just so delicate and sexy. *40%. Highland Queen Scotch Whisky Company.*

Old Malt Cask Speyside's Finest Aged 43 Years sherry butt, dist Jun 66, bott Oct 09 (96.5) **n24 t24.5 f24 b24.** As near as damn it faultless... *48.2%. For The Whisky Show 2009.*

Old Malt Cask Probably Speyside's Finest Distillery Aged 18 Years refill hogshead, cask no. 6376, dist Nov 96, bott Jul 10 (73) **n18 t20 f17 b18.** Maybe arguably the finest distillery. But no disputing it is a long way from being their finest cask...the "s" word has reared its ugly head again. *50%. nc ncf sc. Douglas Laing & Co. 313 bottles.*

Sainsbury's Single Speyside Malt 12 Years Old Unchillfiltered (91.5) **n22.5 t23.5 f22.5 b23.** Absolutely gorgeous! *46%. nc ncf. Ian Macleod for Sainsbury's UK.*

Sansibar Single Speyside Malt 8 Years Old sherrywood, dist 2003 (78) **n20 t22 f17 b19.** For a few moments on delivery the honey and almost sultana-sweet fruitiness hold together beautifully. The nose also shows some outstanding fruit and nut quality, though usually well hidden. I once interviewed the legendary American comedian and actor Bob Hope. But with the bitter taint hovering around, this is one road to Zanzibar he might not have enjoyed... *52.9%. sc. The Whisky Agency.*

Shieldaig Aged 10 Years (85.5) **n21.5 t22 f21 b21.** If this was a dog, it'd be one of those silly ones that'd lie on its back all day awaiting a tickle. Friendly, sweet, bursting with barley. But complexity has gone walkies.... *40%. Booker.*

Spey River Eight Years Matured bourbon oak (89) **n23 t23 f21 b22.** Simplistic, but what it does, it does with genuine panache. *40%. Quality Spirits International.*

Tesco Speyside 18 Year Old (84) **n21 t22 f20 b21.** Pleasant, but enough unwelcome tangy notes to ensure this will not be talked about in a decade's time. Chewy, thick-bodied, decent honey and spice here and there though the finish dies a little feebly. *40%. Tesco.*

⁖ **That Boutique-y Whisky Company Secret Distillery Number One** batch 1 (92.5) **n23** moist fruit cake with no shortage of roasted almonds: hard to know whether to drink or eat what is to come next...; **t24** a procession of classic oloroso notes: almost glutinous grape, just allowing a mere shadow of barley; the sugars are strictly second-layer and supportive; **f22.5** the ending has been allocated the oak influence which has been patient in waiting to foist its vanilla-rich flag; **b23** a pretty satisfying experience for those with an oloroso bent. *55.4%. 486 bottles.*

Wemyss Aged 20 Years Single Speyside "Winter Larder" butt, bott 11 (63.5) **n16 t16.5 f15 b16.** Only for those who seasonally stock up on sulphur. *46%. sc. 654 bottles. USA exclusive.*

⁖ **Wemyss Linkwood 2000 Single Speyside "Summer Orchard"** butt (84.5) **n20 t21.5 f22 b21.** Less Summer Orchard and maybe more Early Spring: underdeveloped and very green. Little to report beyond the massive barley. *46%. sc. 762 bottles.*

The Whisky Agency Housemalt Single Speyside 8 Years Old refill sherrywood, dist 2003 (91.5) **n23 t23.5 f22 b23.** Forget the age: enjoy the charisma. *52.9%. sc.*

The Whisky Agency Speyside Single Malt 1969 bott 2010 (92.5) **n22** at first, appears weighed down with wood. But boiled molassed sweetness is evident, as well as overcooked gooseberry tart; **t24** fabulous delivery: grip tightly to your chair as the spices rip around your palate. But the balancing sugars do a near perfect job and we are back with hint of a fruit pie again...; **f23.5** calms down with a creamy mocha...with an extra sugar; **b23.5** one of the spiciest drams of the year. Delicious! *54.3%. The Whisky Agency.*

⁖ **The Whisky Agency Speyside House Malt 1995** refill sherry wood, bott 12 (88) **n22.5** tight, but loose enough to display massive barley and gooseberry; **t23.5** gorgeous weight, oils and initial balance, too, but peaks as the chocolate and raisin middle evolves; **f20** sharpens before becoming a little furry; **b22** sublime fruit early on. *50.8%*

UNSPECIFIED SINGLE MALTS (General)

Chieftain's The Cigar Malt Aged 15 Years hogshead, dist Apr 95, bott 2011 (**94**) **n24** a spicy affair: delicate with fascinating tangy tangerine oak complexity; **t22.5** a muddled delivery, but within a beat or two it has set its course. And that is to the heart of a cocoa bean. Massive waves of milky chocolate; **f23.5** fantastically long finish with deft oak spices piling on those sugars and cocoa; **b24** must be one of those chocolate cigars I used to eat when I was a kid. Seemingly distilled from 100% malted cocoa and matured in a cask coopered by the gods. A gun to the head would never induce me to smoke a cigar or even cigarette (I did once have one put to my head by a weirdo to force me to smoke dope, and I turned that down, too – but that's another story). But just try and stop me drinking this stuff... *46%. nc ncf. USA release.*

Clan Sinclair Aged 16 Years (**94.5**) **n23.5 t24 f23 b24**. I have subsequently learned this is a Speysider, though not mentioned on the bottle. Must surely be Benriach at its most charming...and peaty! *43%. Scotia Blending Co. India exclusive.*

The Whisky Agency Housemalt 16 Years Old sherry cask, dist 1995, bott 2011 (**61**) **n15 t17 f14 b15**. Ex-sherry maybe. But, alas, there is nothing ex about the sulphur. *46%. sc.*

Scottish Vatted Malts
(also Pure Malts/Blended Malt Scotch)

100 Pipers Aged 8 Years Blended Malt (**74**) **n19 t20 f17 b18**. A better nose, perhaps, and some spice on arrival. But when you consider the Speysiders at their disposal, all those mouth-wateringly grassy possibilities, it is such a shame to find something as bland as this. *40%*

Ballantine's Pure Malt Aged 12 Years bott code. LKAC1538 (**88.5**) **n22.5** spicy mixture of honey, light smoke and added orange; **t23** stupendous mouth-feel with the fruit re-inserted alongside the honey; **f21** pretty thin with almost a grainy feel alongside the bittering oak; **b22** no sign of the peat being reintroduced to major effect, although the orange is a welcome addition. Remains a charmer. *40%. Chivas.*

⬥ **Bally Delicious 23 Year Old** refill hogshead, cask no. 288, dist 10 Mar 89, bott 26 Nov 12 (**86**) **n22 t21 f22 b21**. A vatted malt in that this comes from one distillery (probably Balvenie) and has a minute amount of its sister malt (Glenfiddich) entered into the cask – thus making it impossible for the single cask Balvenie to enter into the market place as this is made for other blending companies. And, somewhat typically for the distillery, the oak plays too grand a part in affairs when it gets to this kind of advanced age. That said, there are some majestic honey and marmalade moments amid the barley. But the oak is simply far too loud for a malt so delicate. *54%. sc. Master of Malt. 288 bottles.*

Barrogill (**90**) **n22.5 t23 f22.5 b22**. Prince Charles, who allows the name to be used for this whisky, is said to enjoy this dram. Hardly surprising, as its pretty hard not to: this is wonderful fun. Curiously, I have just read the back label and noticed they use the word "robust". I have employed "lusty". Either way, I think you might get the message. *40%*

Barrogill North Highland Blended Malt Mey Selections bott code PO12630 (**79**) **n18 t21 f20 b20**. Recovers attractively – helped by a mighty dose of concentrated maltiness - from the disappointing nose. *40%. Inver House Distillers for North Highland.*

Bell's Signature Blend Limited Edition bott 2009, bott no. 42515 (**83.5**) **n19 t22 f21 b21.5**. The front label makes large that this vatted malt has Blair Athol and Inchgower at the heart of it as they are "two fine malts selected for their exceptionally rich character". Kind of like saying you have invited the Kray twins to your knees up as they might liven it up a bit. Well those two distilleries were both part of the original Bell's empire, so fair dos. But to call them both fine malts is perhaps stretching the imagination somewhat. A robust vatting to say the least. And, to be honest, once you get past the nose, good back-slapping fun. *40%. 90,000 bottles.*

Berrys' Best Islay Vatted Malt Aged 8 Years (**82**) **n20 t21 f20 b21**. Smoky, raw, sweet, clean and massive fun! *43%. Berry Bros & Rudd.*

Berry's Own Selection Blue Hanger 5th Release bott 2010 (**81**) **n20 t21 f20 b20**. Not a lot – but enough – sulphur has crept in to take the edge of this one. *45.6%. nc ncf.*

Berry's Own Selection Islay Reserve 2nd Edition (**86.5**) **n22 t22 f21 b21.5**. Maybe an Islay reserve but has enough smoky weight and hickory/chocolate charisma to be pushing for the first team squad. *46%. nc ncf. Berry Bros & Rudd.*

Berry's Own Selection Speyside Reserve 2nd Edition (**79.5**) **n21 t21.5 f18 b19**. Some excellent early sharpness and honey depth but falters. *46%. nc ncf. Berry Bros & Rudd.*

Big Peat (**96**) **n25** magnificent array of salt and bitty peat; heavy yet light enough for the most delicate of citrus. Hard to find a nose which screams "Islay" at you with such a lack of ambiguity: it is, frankly, perfect. **t24** the delivery is constructed around a fabulous bourbon

Demerara sugar and liquorice framework; the peat enters as soon as this is in place and in varying layers of oiliness and depth. The mid ground sees the re-emergence of the more complex Ardbeg and Port Ellen factions, a bourbon style, small grains busyness; **f23.5** long, softly oiled still and then a slow dissolving liquorice and spice; vanillas pop up very late, still accompanied by soft Demerara; **b23.5** I suppose if you put Ardbeg and Port Ellen together there is a chance you might get something rather special. Not guaranteed, but achieved here with the kind of panache that leaves you spellbound. The complexity and balance are virtually off the charts, though had the Caol Ila been reduced slightly, and with it the oils, this might well have been World Whisky of the Year. *46%. ncf Douglas Laing & Co.*

Big Peat Batch 20 Xmas 2011 (96) **n24 t23.5 f24.5 b24**. I haven't got a television these days as my life is simply too busy. And with entertainment like this in the glass to keep you occupied, who needs one...? I doubt if any Christmas Special on the box came remotely close to matching this...! *578%. nc ncf.*

Big Peat Batch 26 (83.5) **n21.5 t21.5 f20 b21**. Not quite as big a peat as some, suffering from over-active oils and a bitter rear-guard. Still has the odd powerful puff. *46%. nc ncf.*

Big Peat Batch 27 (88) **n22 t22 f22 b22**. Well weighted sugars and just the right degree of smoked vanilla bate. Just spotted that this, the 888th new whisky for the Bible 2013 scored...88. It had to be ...!! *46%. nc ncf. Douglas Laing & Co.*

Big Peat Batch 28 (84.5) **n22 t22 f20 b20.5**. Pleasant. But appears to possess a bit too much Caol Ila style oiliness to set the peaty pulse racing. *46%. nc ncf. Douglas Laing & Co.*

Big Peat Batch 29 (89.5) **n22.5 t23 f22 b22**. A peaty massage. *46%. nc ncf.*

Big Peat Batch 30 (92) **n23 t22 f23.5 b23.5**. That's much more like it! This is far more how I expect this dram to be. *46%. nc ncf. Douglas Laing & Co.*

⁖ **Big Peat Batch 31** (90.5) **n23** love it: superb mix of allotment bonfire and peat reek. Some young spirit offering great energy; **t22** gristy sweet delivery pounded by spicy attitude; a blast of hickory and cocoa; **f22.5** the smoke rumbles along, but there is no letting up in intensity of peat or spice; **b23** good to see it has maintained its cheery high standard. Youthful, boisterous and challenging throughout. *46%. nc ncf. Douglas Laing & Co.*

The Big Smoke 40 (83) **n22 t21 f20 b20**. Pure grist. *40%*

The Big Smoke 60 (92) **n23 t23.5 f22.5 b23**. Much more delicate and in touch with its more feminine self than was once the case. A real beauty. *60%. Duncan Taylor & Co.*

Black Face 8 Years Old (78.5) **n18.5 t22 f19 b19**. A huge malt explosion in the kisser on delivery, but otherwise not that pretty to behold. *46%. The Vintage Malt Whisky Co Ltd.*

Burns Nectar (89.5) **n22 t22 f23 b22.5**. A delight of a dram and with all that honey around, "Nectar" is about right. *40%*

Carme 10 Years Old (79) **n21.5 t20 f18.5 b19**. On paper Ardmore and Clynelish should work well together. But vatting is not done on paper and here you have two malts cancelling each other out and some less than great wood sticking its oar in. *43%*

Cask Islay Vatting No. 1 (89) **n23 t22 f22 b22**. Those looking for a soft, smoky, inoffensive little Islay to keep them company had better look elsewhere... *46%. ncf A.D. Rattray Ltd.*

Castle Rock Aged 12 Years Blended Malt (87) **n22.5 t23 f19.5 b22**. Stupendously refreshing: the finish apart, I just love this style of malt. *40%*

Cearban (79.5) **n18 t21.5 f20 b19**. The label shows a shark. It should be a whale: this is massive. Sweet with the malts not quite on the same wavelength. *40%. Robert Graham Ltd.*

Celtique Connexion Sauternes 16 Years Old dist 1995, bott 2012 (95) **n24 t24 f23 b24**. Not many whiskies make me cough, and hardly any at all at just 46%abv. But this, though only because the intensity caught me by surprise. And what a pleasant one! This horse chestnut-coloured malt is one you are unlikely to forget in a hurry. As sweetly balanced and beautiful to enjoy as Josh Wright's stunning volley for Millwall at Burnley in February 2012.... *46%. nc ncf.*

Clan Campbell 8 Years Old Pure Malt (82) **n20 t22 f20 b20**. Enjoyable, extremely safe whisky that tries to offend nobody. The star quality is all on the complex delivery, then it's toffee. *40%. Chivas Brothers.*

Clan Denny (Bowmore, Bunnahabhain, Caol Ila and Laphroaig) (94) **n24 t23 f23 b24**. A very different take on Islay with heavy peats somehow having a floating quality. Unique. *40%*

Clan Denny Islay (86.5) **n21.5 t23 f21 b21**. A curiously bipolar malt with the sweetness and bitterness at times going to extremes. Some niggardly oak has taken the edge of what might have been a sublime malt as the peat and spices at times positively glistens with honey. *46.5%. nc ncf sc. Douglas Laing & Co.*

Clan Denny Speyside (87) **n22 t22 f21 b22**. A Tamdhu-esque oiliness pervades here and slightly detracts from the complexity. That said, the early freshness is rather lovely. *46%*

Compass Box Canto Cask 10 bott Jul 07 (86.5) **n20.5 t21 f23.5 b21.5**. One the Canto collection which slipped through my net a few years back, but is still around, I understand. Typical of the race, this one has perhaps an extra dollop of honey which helps keep the over vigorous oaks under some degree of control. Sublime finish. *54.2%. nc ncf. 200-250 bottles.*

Compass Box Eleuthera Marriage married for nine months in an American oak Hogshead **(86) n22 t22 f20 b22.** I'm not sure if it's the name that gets me on edge here, but as big and robust as it is I still can't help feeling that the oak has bitten too deep. Any chance of a Compass Box Divorce...? 49.2%. *Compass Box for La Maison du Whisky.*

Compass Box Flaming Heart second batch, bottling no. FH16MMVII **(95.5) n23.5 t24.5 f23 b24.5.** The Canto range was, I admit, a huge over-oaked disappointment. This, though, fully underlines Compass Box's ability to come up with something approaching genius. This is a whisky that will be remembered by anyone who drinks it for the rest of their lives as just about the perfect study of full-bodied balance and sophistication. And that is not cheap hyperbole. 48.9%. nc ncf. 4,302 bottles.

⋅∺⋅ **Compass Box Flaming Heart 4th Edition** bott Aug 12 **(95) n23.5** here we go again: that familiar FH earthy smokiness, as usual backed up handsomely with a citrus charge down the wicket; **t24.5** fabulous delivery: not just that lilting smokiness, but an eye-watering ramping of blazing barley, juicy, fresh, sugar laden and trailing smoke all the way; **f23** gorgeous mocha – and smoke of course; **b24** vatted malt at its very best. A genuine celebration of great Scotch malt whisky. 48.9%. *Compass Box Whisky Co. 9,147 bottles.*

Compass Box Flaming Heart 10th Anniversary bott Sep 10 **(92) n24 t23 f22 b23.** This one, as Flaming Heart so often is, is about counterweight and mouth feel. Everything appears just where it should be... 48.9%. nc ncf. 4186 bottles.

Compass Box Lady Luck American white oak hogshead, bott Sep 09 **(91) n22 t24 f23 b22.** Just a shade too sweet for mega greatness like The Spice Tree, but quite an endearing box of tricks. 46%. *Compass Box Whisky Co.*

Compass Box Oak Cross bott May 10 **(92.5) n23 t24 f22.5 b23.** The oak often threatens to be just too big a cross to bear. But such is the degree of complexity, and cleverness of weight, the overall brilliance is never dimmed. Overall, a bit of a tart of a whisky... 43%. nc ncf.

Compass Box The Peat Monster bott May 10 **(82) n21.5 t21.5 f19 b20.** It is as though Victor Frankenstein's creation has met Bambi. Monsters don't come much stranger or more sanitised than this... 46%. nc ncf.

⋅∺⋅ **Compass Box The Peat Monster** first fill and refill American Oak Casks, bott 18 Aug 12 **(94) n23.5** the last one I had of these was a pretty sweet affair, I remember: this is soot dry; just embers of a peat fire, complete with acrid sharpness; **t23.5** lights oils on parade, then a procession of sugars, mainly maple syrup, which induces a distinct juiciness. The smoke is lesser than on the nose, but certainly builds and begins to offer a spicy pep, too; **f23** simply more of the same, though a degree of butterscotch and burnt fudge begins to up the chewiness, even this late on; **b24** wonderful to see peat working on so many levels. The sugars are perhaps more judicially used this time around. 46%. nc ncf.

Compass Box The Peat Monster Reserve (92) n23 t23.5 f22.5 b23. At times a bit of a Sweet Monster...beautiful stuff! 48.9%

Compass Box The Spice Tree first-fill and refill American oak. Secondary maturation: heavily toasted new French oak **(95.5) n24.5 t24.5 f23 b23.5.** Having initially been chopped down by the SWA, who were indignant that extra staves had been inserted into the casks, The Spice Tree is not only back but in full bloom. Indeed, the blossom on this, created by the use of fresh oak barrel heads, is more intoxicating than its predecessor – mainly because there is a more even and less dramatic personality to this. Not just a great malt, but a serious contender for Jim Murray Whisky Bible 2011 World Whisky of the Year. 46%

Compass Box The Spice Tree Inaugural Batch (93) n23 t23 f23 b24. The map for flavour distribution had to be drawn for the first time here: an entirely different whisky in shape and flavour emphasis. And it is a map that takes a long time to draw... 46%. 4150 bottles.

Co-operative Group (CWS) Blended Malt Aged 8 Years (86.5) n22 t22 f21 b21.5. Much, much better! Still a little on the sticky and sweet side, but there is some real body and pace to the changes on the palate. Quite rich, complex and charming. 40%

Cutty Sark Blended Malt (92.5) n22 a salty, sweaty armpit doesn't fill you with confidence at first, but then light smoke descends as well as some prime grassy barley; **t24** magnificent! The mouth feel is close to perfection, as there is a dazzling sheen to this one thanks to a just-so squirt of something a little oily; the vaguest of smoke wrestles with the more clear-cut barley; **f23** thinner, but maintains the malty sheen, though dried now by vanilla; the building of the spices is quite wonderful; **b23.5** sheer quality: as if two styles have been placed in the bottle and told to fight it out between them. What a treat! 40%.

Douglas Laing's Double Barrel Ardbeg & Glenrothes (91) n23 t23 f22 b23. A feather-light whisky offering subtlety throughout; 46%

⋅∺⋅ **Douglas Laing's Double Barrel Ardbeg & Glenrothes 8th Release** (85.5) n22.5 t22 f20 b21. Nothing like as perky as the bottling I tasted last year: the Glenrothes appears to blunt the more intricate machinations of the Ardbeg after a beautifully choreographed nose and very early delivery. 46%

Douglas Laing's Double Barrel Ardbeg & Glenrothes Aged 10 Years product no. MSW2685 **(92) n22 t24 f23 b23.** Not what I was expecting. But a lovely experience nonetheless. *46%*

Douglas Laing's Double Barrel Ardbeg & Glenrothes Aged 10 Years product no. DBS0003 **(88.5) n23 t22 f21.5 b22.** An uncompromising but fun way to bring up New Whisky no. 750 for Bible 2011... *46%. Douglas Laing.*

Douglas Laing's Double Barrel Braeval & Caol Ila Aged 10 Years (78) n18 t21 f20 b19. The Mike and Bernie Winters of double barrelled whisky. *46%. Douglas Laing & Co Ltd.*

∹ **Douglas Laing's Double Barrel Caol Ila & Braeval 4th Release (92.5) n23** the smoke appears to hug every contour of the nose with its slick, oily presence but extra barley is crumbled into the mix. Rather lovely; **t23.5** absolutely superb delivery: one that demands mouthful after mouthful just to repeat the experience. The smoke is gorgeously diffused into the sparkling barley with the oils really making sure there is a lingering, yet soft, intensity; **f22.5** tamed easily, the smoke settles for a lighter presence while the vanilla takes control; **b23.5** after a few failures with this combination, a hit. A real egg and bacon of a vatted malt with the two personalities this time complimenting each other beautifully. *46%*

Douglas Laing's Double Barrel Caol Ila & Braeval Aged 10 Years (84.5) n23 t21 t22 f20.5 b21. It is probably impossible to find a malt which is more friendly and inoffensive. Or two malts which have done such a first class job of cancelling each other's personalities out. *46%*

Douglas Laing's Double Barrel Caol Ila & Tamdhu (89) n22 t23 f22 b22. Put two oily malts together and you get...an oily whisky... *46%*

∹ **Douglas Laing's Double Barrel Glenallachie & Bowmore 1st Release (89) n22** young, grassy barley; toasty smoke; **t22.5** a slight Glenallachie trademark burn on delivery, but settles as the barley sugars arrive; **f22** the smoke drifts in for a satisfying finale; **b22.5** the delicate smoke of the Bowmore has tamed the wilder elements of the Glenallachie. A good mix. *46%*

Douglas Laing's Double Barrel Glenrothes & Ardbeg Aged 10 Years 4th Release (89.5) n21.5 t23 f22.5 b22.5. Despite the average nose the charmingly effete palate is another matter entirely. *46%. Douglas Laing.*

Douglas Laing's Double Barrel Highland Park & Bowmore (95) n23 t24.5 f24 b23.5. The vital spark of fury to this one keeps the palate ignited. A standing ovation for such a magnificent performance on the palate. *46%. Douglas Laing & Co Ltd.*

Douglas Laing's Double Barrel Ledaig & Bowmore (87) n22.5 t22 f21.5 b21. About as sweet a marriage as you are likely to find. For some, it may be too sweet! *46%*

Douglas Laing's Double Barrel Macallan & Laphroaig 5th Release (93) n23.5 t24 f22.5 b23. As if born to be together. *46%*

Douglas Laing's Double Barrel Macallan & Laphroaig Aged 9 Years (83.5) n21 t22 f20 b20.5. Curiously muted. Sweet with the natural caramels outweighing the smoke. *46%*

Douglas Laing's Double Barrel Mortlach & Laphroaig 2nd Release **(83.5) n20 t22 f20.5 b21.** Compared to the Ardbeg/Glenrothes match, about as subtle and delicate as a smoky custard pie in the face. Hot and snarling fare. *46%*

∹ **Douglas Laing's Double Barrel Mortlach & Laphroaig 3rd Release (82.5) n22.5 t21 f19 b20.** Its sweet nose and soft touch in the opening seconds promises so much, but fails to deliver – especially on the finish. *46%*

∹ **Douglas Laing's Double Barrel Mortlach & Laphroaig 4th Release (85.5) n21.5 t21.5 f21 b21.5.** All kinds of sugars heading off every which way. Juicy and punchy, interests and entertains without harmonising. *46%*

Douglas Laing's Double Barrel Talisker & Craigellachie (73) n19 t19 f17 b18. Should be divorced on the grounds of adultery with a poor cask. *46%*

∹ **Douglas Laing's Double Barrel Talisker & Craigellachie 2nd Release (94.5) n23** strangely fizzy smoke with a big impact despite being lightened by citrus; **t24** fabulous marriage of juicy barley and peaty spice: rarely is the palate cleaned so beautifully while under such smoky bombardment; **f23.5** long, with that fabulous citrus and smoke interplay going the full term; **b24** these two malts go together like bacon and eggs. And very smoky bacon at that... *46%*

Duncan Taylor Regional Malt Collection Islay 10 Years Old (81) n21 t22 f19 b19. Soft citrus cleanses the palate, while gentle peats muddies it up again. *40%*

The Famous Grouse 10 Years Old Malt (77) n19 t20 f19 b19. The nose and finish headed south in the last Winter and landed in the sulphur marshes of Jerez. *40%. Edrington Group.*

The Famous Grouse 15 Years Old Malt (86) n21 t22 f21.5 b21.5. Salty and smoky with a real sharp twang. *43%. Edrington Group.*

The Famous Grouse 15 Years Old Malt (86) n19 t24 f22 b21. There had been a hint of the "s" word on the nose, but it got away with it. Now it has crossed that fine – and fatal – line where the petulance of the sulphur has thrown all else slightly out of kilter. All, that is, apart from the delivery which is a pure symphony of fruit and spice deserving of a far better introduction and final movement. Some moving, beautiful moments. Flawed genius or what...? *40%*

The Famous Grouse 18 Years Old Malt (82) n19 t21.5 f21 b20.5. Some highly attractive honey outweighs the odd uncomfortable moment. 43%. Edrington Group.

The Famous Grouse Malt 21 Years Old (91) n22 candy jar spices, green apple and crisp barley. t24 spot on oak offers a platform for the myriad rich malty notes and now, in the latest bottlings, enlivened further with an injection of exploding spice... wow! f22 flattens slightly but muscovado sugar keeps it light and sprightly; b23 a very dangerous dram: the sort where the third or fourth would slip down without noticing. Wonderful scotch! 43%. Edrington Group.

The Famous Grouse 30 Years Old Malt (94) n23.5 brain-implodingly busy and complex: labyrinthine depth within a kind of Highland Park frame with extra emphasis on grape and salt; t24 yesssss!!!! Just so magnificent with the theme being all about honeycomb...but on so many different levels of intensity and toastiness; so juicy, too...; f23 now the spices dive in as the barley resurfaces again; long, layered with spot on bitter-sweet balance; b23.5 whisky of this sky-high quality is exactly what vatted malt should be all about. Outrageously good. 43%

Glenalmond 2001 Vintage (82.5) n22 t21.5 f19 b20. Glenkumquat, more like: the most citrusy malt I have tasted in a very long time. 40%. The Vintage Malt Whisky Co Ltd.

Glenalmond "Everyday" (89.5) n21.5 t23.5 f22 b22.5. They are not joking; this really is an everyday whisky. Glorious malt which is so dangerously easy to drink. 40%

Glen Brynth Aged 12 Years Blended Malt (87) n22.5 t23 f19.5 b22. Deja vu...! Thought I was going mad: identical to the Castle Rock I tasted this morning, right down to the (very) bitter end ..!!! 40%. Quality Spirits International.

Glenbrynth Blended Malt 12 Years (87.5) n22.5 t22.5 f21 b21.5. Heavyweight malt which gets off to a rip-roaring start on the delivery but falls away somewhat from the mid ground onwards. 43%. OTI Africa.

Glenbrynth Ruby 40 Year Old Limited Edition (94) n23.5 t24 f23 b23.5. Has all the hallmarks of a completely OTT, far too old sherry butt being brought back to life with the aid of a livelier barrel. A magnificent experience, full of fun and evidence of some top quality vatting at work, too. 43%. OTI Africa.

Glendower 8 Years Old (84) n21.5 t21 f20.5 b21 Nutty and spicy. 43%

The Glenfohry Aged 8 Years Special Reserve (73) n19 t19 f17 b18. Some of the malt used here appears to have come from a still where the safe has not so much been broken into, but just broken! Oily and feinty, to say the least. Normally I would glower at anyone who even thought of putting a coke into their malt. Here, I think it might be for the best.. 40%

-⋅⊱- **Glen Turner Heritage Double Wood** Bourbon & Madeira casks, bott code. L311657A (85.5) n21.5 t22 f21 b21. A very curious amalgamation of flavours. The oak appears to be in shock with the way the fruit is coming on to it and offers a bitter backlash. No faulting the crisp delivery with busy sugar and spice for a few moments brightening the palate. 40%

Glen Turner Pure Malt Aged 8 Years L525956A (84) n20 t22 f22 b20. A lush and lively vatting annoyingly over dependent on thick toffee but simply brimming with fabulously mouth-watering barley and over-ripe blood oranges. To those who bottle this, I say: let me into your lab. I can help you bring out something sublime!! 40%

Glen Orchy (80.5) n19.5 t21.5 f19.5 b20. Not exactly the most subtle of vatted malts though when the juicy barley briefly pours through on delivery, enjoyable. 40%. Lidl.

-⋅⊱- **Glen Orchy 5 Year Old Blended Malt Scotch Whisky** (88.5) n22 screams malt at you, juicy and grassy all the way; t22.5 clean, fresh barley again on delivery. Superb, mouth-watering gristy sugars; f22 late spices offer the first and only degree of complexity; b22 excellent malt plus very decent casks equals light-bodied fun. 40%. Lidl.

Glen Orrin (68) n16.5 t17.5 f17 b17. In its favour, it doesn't appear to be troubled by caramel. Which means the nose and palate are exposed to the full force of this quite dreadful whisky. 40%. Aldi.

Glen Orrin Six Year Old (88) n22 t23 f21 b22. A vatting that has improved in the short time it has been around, now displaying some lovely orangey notes on the nose and a genuinely lushness to the body and spice on the finish. You can almost forgive the caramel, this being such a well balanced, full-bodied ride. A quality show for the price. 40%

Hedges and Butler Special Pure Malt (83) n20 t21 f22 b21. Just so laid back: nosed and tasted blind I'd swear this was a blend (you know, a real blend with grains and stuff) because of the biting lightness and youth. Just love the citrus theme and, err...graininess...!! 40%

Imperial Tribute (83) n19.5 t21.5 f21 b21. I am sure – and sincerely hope – the next bottling will be cleaned up and the true Imperial Tribute can be nosed and tasted. Because this is what should be a very fine malt... but just isn't. 46%. Spencer Collings.

Islay Trilogy 1969 (Bruichladdich 1966, Bunnahabhain 1968, Bowmore 1969) Bourbon/Sherry (91) n23 t23 f22 b23. Decided to mark the 700th tasting for the 2007 edition with this highly unusual vatting. And no bad choice. The smoke is as elusive as the Paps of Jura on a dark November morning, but the silky fruits and salty tang tells a story as good as anything you'll hear by a peat fire. Take your time...the whiskies have. 40.3%. Murray McDavid.

J & B Exception Aged 12 Years (80) n20 t23 f18 b19. Very pleasant in so many ways. A charming sweetness develops quickly, with excellent soft honeycomb. But the nose and finish are just so...so...dull...!! For the last 30 years J&B has meant, to me, (and probably within that old company) exceptionally clean, fresh Speysiders offering a crisp, mouth-watering treat. I feel this is off target. *40%. Diageo/Justerini & Brooks.*

J & B Nox (89) n23 t23 f21 b22. A teasing, pleasing little number that is unmistakably from the J&B stable. *40%. Diageo.*

John Black 8 Years Old Honey (88) n21 t22.5 f22.5 b22. A charming vatting. *40%*

John Black 10 Years Old Peaty (91) n23 salty and peaty; t23 soft and peaty; f22 delicate and peaty; b23 classy and er...peaty. *40%. Tullibardine Distillery.*

John McDougall's Selection Islay Malt 1993 cask no. 103 (94.5) n23.5 t24.5 f22.5 b24. Complex, superbly weighted and balanced malt which just keeps you wondering what will happen next. *54.7%. House of Macduff.*

Johnnie Walker Green Label 15 Years Old (95) n24 kind of reminds me of a true, traditional Cornish Pasty: it is as though the segments have been compartmentalised, with the oak acting as the edible pastry keeping them apart. Sniff and there is a degree of fruit; nose again and there is the Speyside/Clynelish style of intense, slightly sweet maltiness. Sniff a third time and, at last you can detect just a hint of smoke. Wonderful... t23.5 no compartmentalisation here as the delivery brings all those varying characters together for one magnificently complex maltfest. Weightier than previous Green Label events with the smoke having a bigger say. But the oak really bobs and weaves as the palate is first under a tidal wave of juicy malt and then the fruit and smoke – and no little spice – take hold...; f23.5 soft smoke and grumbling spice latch on to the fruit-stained oak; plenty of cocoa just to top things off; b24 god, I love this stuff...this is exactly how a vatted malt should be and one of the best samples I've come across since its launch. *43%. Diageo.*

Jon, Mark and Robbo's The Rich Spicy One (89) n22 t23 f22 b22. So much better without the dodgy casks: a real late night dram of distinction though the spices perhaps a little on the subtle side... *40%. Edrington.*

Jon, Mark and Robbo's The Smoky Peaty One (92) n23 t22 f23 b24. Genuinely high-class whisky where the peat is full-on yet allows impressive complexity and malt development. A malt for those who appreciate the better, more elegant things in life. *40%. Edrington.*

The Last Vatted Malt bott Nov 11 (96.5) n24 the work of both oak and the peat kiln appear to be well matched here. Though perhaps it is the orange blossom and pear fruitiness that really makes the heart skip a beat; t25 a sublime delivery. The Compass Box marque of oakiness is stamped prominently, but couched this time by a stunning mix of cream cocoa, lightly sweetened by Demerara. Improbably, half way in there is a steady stream of juicy barley...about the same time you notice how well balanced the smoke is: like a great football referee, you don't actually notice him being there, but makes all else run beautifully; f23.5 doesn't try to develop. Just allows the elements that make up this complex whisky the space to run their own course...; b24 being an American, Compass Box founder and blender, John Glaser, knows a thing or two about pouring two fingers of whisky. So I join John in raising two fingers to the SWA and toast them in the spirit they deserve to thank them for their single-minded and successful quest to outlaw this ancient whisky term. *53.7%. nc ncf. 1,323 bottles.*

Mackinlay's Rare Old Highland Malt (89) n22 t22 f22 b23. Possibly the most delicate malt whisky I can remember coming from the labs of Whyte and Mackay. Thought it still, on the palate, must rank as heavy medium. This is designed as an approximation of the whisky found at Shackleton's camp in the Antarctic. And as a life-long Mackinlay drinker myself, it is great to find a whisky baring its name that, on the nose only, briefly reminds me of the defter touches which won my heart over 30 years ago. That was with a blend: this is a vatted malt. And a delicious one. In case you wondered: I did resist the temptation to use ice. *473%*

Matisse 12 Year Old Blended Malt (93) n23.5 t23 f22.5 b23. Succulent, clean-as-a-whistle mixture of malts with zero bitterness and not even a whisper of an off note: easily the best form I have ever seen this brand in. Superb. *40%. Matisse Spirits Co Ltd.*

Matisse Aged 12 Years (79) n17 t21 f20 b21. Not sure if some finishing or re-casking has been going on here to liven it up. Has some genuine buzz on the palate, but intriguing weirdness, too. Don't bother nosing this one. *40%. The Matisse Spirits Co Ltd.*

Milroy's of Soho Finest Blended Malt (76) n18 t19 f20 b19. Full flavoured, nutty, malty but hardly textbook. *40%. Milroy's of Soho.*

Mo'land (82) n21 t22 f19 b20. Extra malty but lumbering and on the bitter side. *40%.*

Monkey Shoulder batch 27 (79.5) n21 t21.5 f18 b19. Been a while since I lasted tasted this one. Though its claims to be Batch 27, I assume all bottlings are Batch 27 seeing as they are from 27 casks. This one, whichever it is, has a distinctive fault found especially at the finale, which is disappointing. Even before hitting that point a big toffeed personality makes for a pleasant if limited experience. *40%. William Grant & Sons.*

"No Age Declared" The Unique Pure Malt Very Limited Edition 16-49 Years (85) n22.5 t19.5 f22 b21. Very drinkable. But this is odd stuff: as the ages are as they are, and as it tastes as it does, I can surmise only that the casks were added together as a matter of necessity rather than any great blending thought or planning. Certainly the malt never finds a rhythm but maybe it's the eclectic style on the finish that finally wins through. 45%. Samaroli.

Norse Cask Selection Vatted Islay 1992 Aged 16 Years hogshead cask no. QWVIM3, dist 92, bott 09 (95) n24 t24 f23 b24. The recipe of 60/35/5 Ardbeg/Laphroaig/Bowmore new make matured in one cask is a surprise: the oiliness here suggests a squirt of Caol Ila somewhere. This hybrid is certainly different, showing that the DNA of Ardbeg is unrecognisable when mixed, like The Fly, with others. Drinkable...? Oh, yes...!! Because this, without a single negative note to its name, is easily one of the whiskies of the year and a collector's and/or Islayphile's absolute must have. 56.7%

Norse Cask Selection Vatted Islay 1991 Aged 12 Years (89) n24 t23 f21 b21. Fabulous, but not much going in the way of complexity. But if you're a peat freak, I don't think you either notice...or much care...!! 59.5%. Quality World, Denmark.

Old St Andrews Fireside (88.5) n22 delicate, bright, the faintest hint of distant smoke; t22.5 sharp, clean and full of malty freshness; f21.5 custard creams dunked in spiced milk; b22.5 beautifully driven... 40%. Old St Andrews Ltd.

Old St Andrews Nightcap (89) n21.5 t24 f21 b22.5. Some delightful weight and mass but perhaps a bit too much toffee takes its toll. 40%. Old St Andrews Ltd.

Old St Andrews Twilight (94.5) n24 t23.5 f23 b24. Less Twilight as Sunrise as this is full of invigorating freshness which fills the heart with hope and joy: Lip-smacking Scotch malt whisky as it should be. Anyone who thinks the vatted malt served up for golf lovers in these novelty bottles is a load of old balls are a fair way off target... 40%. Old St Andrews Ltd.

Poit Dhubh 8 Bliadhna (90) n22.5 t23.5 f21.5 b22.5. Though the smoke which marked this vatting has vanished, it has more than compensated with a complex beefing up of the core barley tones. Cracking whisky. 43%. ncf. Pràban na Linne.

Poit Dhubh 12 Bliadhna (77) n20 t20 f18 b19. Toffee-apples. Without the apples. 43%. ncf. Pràban na Linne.

Poit Dhubh 21 Bliadhna (86) n22 t22.5 f21 b20.5. Over generous toffee has robbed us of what would have been a very classy malt. 43%. ncf. Pràban na Linne.

The Pot Still Scotch Vatted Malt Over 8 Years Old (90) n22 t24 f22 b22. Such sophistication: the Charlotte Rampling of Scotch. 43.5%. ncf. Celtic Whisky Compagnie, France.

Prime Blue Pure Malt (83) n21 t21 f21 b20. Steady, with a real chewy toffee middle. Friendly stuff. 40%

Prime Blue 12 Years Old Pure Malt (78) n20 t20 f19 b19. A touch of fruit but tart. 40%

Prime Blue 17 Years Old Pure Malt (88) n23 clever weight and a touch of something fruity and exotic, too; t21 thick malt concentrate; f22 takes a deliciously latte-style route and would be even better but for the toffee; excellent spicing; b22 lovely, lively vatting: something to get your teeth into! 40%

Prime Blue 21 Years Old Pure Malt (77) n21 t20 f18 b18. After the teasing, bourbony nose the remainder disappoints with a caramel-rich flatness. The reprise of a style of whisky I thought had vanished about four of five years ago 40%

Rattray's Selection Blended Malt 19 Years Old Batch 1 Benrinnes sherry hogsheads (89.5) n22 t23.5 f21.5 b22.5. Absolutely love it! Offers just the right degree of mouth-watering complexity. not a malt for those looking for the sit-on-the-fence wishy-washy type. 55.8%. Auchentoshan, Bowmore, Balblair & BenRiach. A.D. Rattray Ltd.

Sainsbury's Malt Whisky Finished in Sherry Casks (70) n18 t19 f16 b17. Never the greatest of the Sainsbury range, it's somehow managed to get worse. Actually, not too difficult when it comes to finishing in sherry, and the odd sulphur butt or three has done its worst here. 40%. UK.

Scottish Collie (86.5) n22 t23 f20.5 b21. A really young pup of a vatting. Full of life and fun but muzzled by toffee at the death. 40%. Quality Spirits International.

Scottish Collie 5 Years Old (90.5) n22 t22.5 t23 f22 b23. Fabulous mixing here showing just what malt whisky can do at this brilliant and under-rated age. Lively and complex with the malts wonderfully herded and penned. Without colouring and at 50% abv I bet this would have given a right wolf-whistle. Perfect for one man and his grog. 40%.

Scottish Collie 8 Years Old (85.5) n22 t21.5 f21 b21. A good boy. But just wants to sleep rather than play. 40%. Quality Spirits International.

Scottish Collie 12 Years Old (82) n20 t22 f20 b20. For a malt that's aged 84 in Collie years, it understandably smells a bit funny and refuses to do many tricks. If you want some fun you'll need a younger version. 40%. Quality Spirits International.

Scottish Leader Imperial Blended Malt (77) n20 t20 f18 b19. Now don't be confused here: this isn't Imperial malt from Speyside. And although it says Blended, it is 100% malt. What is clear, though, is that this is pretty average stuff. 40%. Burn Stewart.

Scottish Leader Aged 14 Years (80) n21 t21 f19 b19. A cleaner, less peaty version than the no-age statement vatting, but still fails to entirely ignite the tastebuds 40%. *Burn Stewart*.

Scott's Selection Burnside 1994 bott 12 (93) n23.5 a whisky for Dundee cake lovers the world over, especially those with a soft spot for toasted almonds; certainly doesn't go easy on the glazed sherries and molasses; perhaps a little unwelcome dryness is in the air, too; t24 the famous integrity of the Balvenie malt shows to sublime effect here: so much fruit and yet the barley has such a big say, too. Toasty, for sure, and eye-wateringly fruity. But a light salty tang brings out the sharper aspects of the honeycomb; f22.5 tightens a little until the Glenfiddich makes its mark...only joking!! Maybe some evidence of not quite the perfect cask, but its mild failings are easily forgiven; b23.5 I may well be wrong. But I think this is the first time I have seen a Burnside, which is a cask of Balvenie spoiled as a single malt by having a spoonful of same age Glenfiddich added to it, in a commercial bottling rather than as a sample in my blending lab! Believe me: it was well worth waiting for...! 56.7%.

Sheep Dip (84) n19 t22 f22 b21. Young and sprightly like a new-born lamb, this enjoys a fresh, mouthwatering grassy style wth a touch of spice. Maligned by some, but to me a clever, accomplished vatting of alluring complexity. 40%

Sheep Dip 'Old Hebridean' 1990 dist in or before 1990 (94) n23 every aspect has the buoyancy of an anchor, the subtlety of Hebridean Winter winds. Thick peat offering both smoke and a kippery saltiness is embraced by honey; t24 big, weighty delivery with an immediate spice and honey delivery; a butterscotch barley theme appears and vanishes like a small fishing craft in mountainous waves; f23.5 that honey keeps the pace and length, while a beautiful bourbon red liquorice beefs up the vanilla; b23.5 you honey!! Now, that's what I call a whisky...!! 40%. *The Spencerfield Spirit Co.*

The Six Isles Pomerol Finish Limited Edition French oak Pomerol wine cask no. 90631-90638, dist 03, bott 10 (85.5) n19 t23 f21.5 b22. What makes the standard Six Isles work as a vatted malt is its freshness and complexity. With these attributes, plus the distinctive distilleries used, we consistently have one the world's great and truly entertaining whiskies. With this version we have just a decent malt. The wine finish has levelled the mountains and valleys and restricted the finish dramatically, while the nose doesn't work at all. Perfectly drinkable and the delivery is extremely enjoyable. But as a Six Isles, delighted it's a Limited Edition. 46%.

◊ **The Six Isles St Etienne Rum Cask Finish** American oak & Caribbean rum casks, cask no. 92011/920110, bott 12 (96.5) n24 smoke nibbles and tickles, making it absolutely impossible not to enjoy; jam tart, passion fruit and sharon fruit adds the sex appeal; t24 you could almost swoon! What a fabulous delivery: turns like a Root delivery into the rough. What makes this work is the manner in which the sugars develop, like plants growing when filmed on time lapse. Almost incredible; because although it is smoky, the depth of the gristy barley, melted into muscovado sugar is astounding; a secondary crispness to the sugar represents the rum casks; f24 mocha with a light sultana fruit thread; the smoke continues to bamboozle; b24.5 Six Isles rarely lets you down; these rum casks are distilled sugar icing on the cake. Most probably the best use of rum casks I have ever encountered in the Scotch whisky industry. Bloody well done, chaps! 46%. nc ncf. *Ian Macleod Distillers. 3161 bottles.*

S'Mokey (88) n22.5 t22 f21.5 b22. Delicate, sweet and more lightly smoked than the nose advertises. 40%.

◊ **Smokey Joe Islay Malt** (87) n21.5 a tangy mix of Fisherman's Friend and smoked Demerara; t22 silky mouth feel with varied brown sugars peddling insanely; the Fisherman's Friend character persists, but underpinned by some steady smoke; f21.5 tangy, smoky marmalade; b22 a soft, soporific version of a smoky Islay. No thumping of waves here: the tide is out. 46%. ncf. *Angus Dundee Distillers.*

Tambowie (84.5) n21.5 t21.5 f20.5 b21. A decent improvement on the nondescript bottling of yore. I have re-included this to both celebrate its newly acquired lightly fruited attractiveness...and to celebrate the 125th anniversary of the long departed Tambowie Distillery whose whisky, I am sure, tasted nothing like this. 40%. *The Vintage Malt Whisky Co Ltd.*

Treasurer 1874 Reserve Cask (90.5) n23 t23 f22.5 b22. Some judicious adding has been carried out here in the Robert Graham shop. Amazing for a living cask that I detect no major sulphur faultlines. Excellent! 51%. *Live casks available in all Robert Graham shops.*

◊ **Triple Wood Blended Malt Scotch Whisky** (77) n17.5 t22 f18.5 b19. At least one wood too many. Tangy...for all the wrong reasons. 42%. *Lidl.*

Vintner's Choice Speyside 10 Years Old (84) n21.5 t22 f20 b20.5. Pleasant. But considering the quality of the Speysiders Grants have to play with, the dullness is a bit hard to fathom. 40%. *Quality Spirits International.*

Waitrose Pure Highland Malt (86.5) n22 t22 f20.5 b22. Blood orange by the cartload: amazingly tangy and fresh; bitters out at the finish. This is one highly improved malt and great to see a supermarket bottling showing some serious attitude...as well as taste!! Fun, refreshing and enjoyable. 40%

Wemyss Malts "The Hive" Aged 8 Years bott Nov 11 (85.5) n21 t23 f20 b21.5. You may get stung on the nose but the delivery is pure nectar. Sadly, the bitter finish lives up to the nose's prediction. 40%. Wemyss Malts.

Wemyss Malts "The Hive" Aged 12 Years (93) n23 t24 f22.5 b23.5. Mixing different malt whiskies is an art form – one that is prone to going horribly wrong. Here, though, whoever is responsible really is the bees-knees... 40%

Wemyss Malts "Peat Chimney" 5 Years Old (82.5) n20.5 t21 f20 b21. Rougher than the tongue of a smoking cat. 40%. Wemyss Malts Ltd.

Wemyss Malts "Peat Chimney" 8 Years Old (85) n21.5 t21.5 f21 b21. Delightful chocolate amid the attractively course peat. 40%. Wemyss Malts Ltd.

Wemyss Malts "Peat Chimney" Aged 12 Years bott Oct 10 (90.5) n22.5 good vanilla depth to the clunking phenols: the peat is positively lashed to the aroma; t23 beautifully made malt with an outstanding understanding between the light but silky oils, phenols and sympathetic sugars; f22.5 the vanillas return but retain their smoky chaperone; b22.5 gorgeous: does what it says on the tin... 40%. Wemyss Malts.

Wemyss "Smooth Gentleman" 5 Years Old (80) n20 t21 f19 b20. A bit of a schoolkid with an affectation. 40%. Wemyss Malts Ltd.

Wemyss Malts "Smooth Gentleman" 8 Years Old (89) n21 sweet but a little bland; t23.5 much better arrival with a gorgeous barley-toffee impact assisted, naturally, by a spoonful of acacia honey; f22 returns to a more middle-of-the-road character, but still deliciously soft and rich...and a little juicy; b22.5 more of a Kentuckian George Clooney than a Bristolian Cary Grant. 40%. Wemyss Malts Ltd.

Wemyss Malts "Smooth Gentleman" Aged 12 Years 1st fill bourbon cask, bott Oct 10 (88.5) n23 t22 f21.5 b22. A very attractive and competent, vaguely spicy gentleman who has a bit of a penchant for butterscotch and chocolate. 40%. Wemyss Malts.

Wemyss Malts "Spice King" 5 Years Old (76) n18.5 t20 f18.5 b19. A little on the mucky, tangy side. 40%. Wemyss Malts Ltd.

Wemyss Malts "Spice King" 8 Years Old (87) n22 plenty of butterscotch and fudge; t22 chewy toffee with a malty, honeyed strata; f21.5 more toffee. Just when you start wondering where the spice is, it appears very late on through the tradementen's entrance, though does the best it can not to disturb those at home; b21.5 hard to believe this lush malt is in any way related to the 5-y-o...!! 40%. Wemyss Malts Ltd.

Wemyss Malts "Spice King" Aged 12 Years bott Oct 10 (85) n22.5 t21 f21 b21. Thoroughly enjoyable sugar edge to the decent smoke. A bit thin on the complexity front, though. 40%. Wemyss Malts.

Wemyss Vintage Malt The Peat Chimney Hand Crafted Blended Malt Whisky (80) n19 t22 f20 b19. The balance is askew here, especially on the bone-dry wallpapery finish. Does have some excellent coffee/coffee moments, though. 43%. Wemyss Vintage Malts Ltd.

Wemyss Vintage Malt The Smooth Gentleman Hand Crafted Blended Malt Whisky (83) n19 t22 f21 b21. Not sure about the nose: curiously fishy (very gently smoked). But the malts tuck into the tastebuds with aplomb showing some sticky barley sugar along the way. 43%

Wemyss Vintage Malt The Spice King Hand Crafted Blended Malt Whisky (84) n22 t22 f20 b20. Funnily enough, I've not a great fan of the word "smooth" when it comes to whisky. But the introduction of oily Caol Ila-style peat here makes it a more of a smooth gentleman than the "Smooth Gentleman." Excellent spices very late on. 43%. Wemyss Vintage Malts.

Wholly Smoke Aged 10 Years (86.5) n22.5 t22.5 f20 b21.5. A big, peaty, sweat, rumbustuous number with absolutely no nod towards sophistication or balance and the finish virtually disintegrates. The smoke is slapped on and the whole appears seemingly younger than its 10 years. Massive fun, all the same. 40%. Macdonald & Muir Ltd for Oddbins.

Whyte & Mackay Blended Malt Scotch Whisky (78) n19 t22 f18 b19. You know when the engine to your car is sort of misfiring and feels a bit sluggish and rough...? 40%. Waitrose.

Wild Scotsman Scotch Malt Whisky (Black Label) batch no. CBV001 (91) n23.5 t23.5 f21 b23. The type of dram you drink from a dirty glass. Formidable and entertaining. 47%

Wild Scotsman Aged 15 Years Vatted Malt (95) n23 t24 f24 b24. If anyone wants an object lesson as to why you don't screw your whisky with caramel, here it is. Jeff Topping can feel a justifiable sense of pride in his new whisky: for its age, it is an unreconstituted masterpiece... 46% (92 proof). nc ncf. USA.

Mystery Malts

Chieftain's Limited Edition Aged 40 Years hogshead (78) n22 t22 f16 b18. Oak-ravaged and predictably bitter on the death (those of you who enjoy Continental bitters might go for this..!). But the lead up does offer a short, though sublime and intense honey kick. The finish, though... 48.5%. Ian Macleod.

Cu Dhub (see Speyside Distillery)

Scottish Grain

It's a bit weird, really. Many whisky lovers stay clear of blended Scotch, preferring instead single malts. The reason, I am often told, is that the grain included in a blend makes it rough and ready. Yet I wish I had a twenty pound note for each time I have been told in recent years how much someone enjoys a single grain. The ones that the connoisseurs die for are the older versions, usually special independent bottlings displaying great age and more often than not brandishing a lavish Canadian or bourbon style.

Like single malts, grain distilleries produce whisky bearing their own style and signature. And, also, some display characteristics and a richness that can surprise and delight. Most of the grains available in (usually specialist) whisky outlets are pretty elderly. Being made from maize and wheat helps give them either that Canadian or, depending on the freshness of the cask, an unmistakable bourbony style. So older grains display far greater body than is commonly anticipated.

Light whiskies, including some Speysiders, tend to adopt this north American stance when the spirit has absorbed so much oak that the balance has been tipped. So overtly Kentuckian can they be, I once playfully introduced an old single grain Scotch whisky into a bourbon tasting I was conducting and nobody spotted that it was the cuckoo in the nest ... until I revealed all at the end of the evening. And even had to display the bottle to satisfy the disbelievers.

Younger grains may give a hint of oncoming bourbon-ness. But, rather, they tend to celebrate either a softness in taste or, in the case of North British, a certain rigidity. Where many malts have a tendency to pulverise the taste-buds and announce their intent and character at the top of their voice, younger grains are content to stroke and whisper.

Scotch whisky companies have so far had a relaxed attitude to marketing their grains. William Grant had made some inroads with Black Barrel, though with nothing like the enthusiasm they unleash upon us with their blends and malts. And Diageo are apparently content to see their Cameron Brig sell no further than its traditional hunting grounds, just north of Edinburgh, where the locals tend to prefer single grain to any other whisky. And the latest news from that most enormous of distilleries...it is getting bigger. Not only are Diageo planning to up their malt content by building a new Speyside distillery, but Cameronbridge, never a retiring place since the days of the Haigs in the 1820s is set for even grander expansion. Having, with Port Dundas until recently, absorbed the closure of a number of grain distilleries over the last 30 years something had to be done to give it a fighting chance of taking on the expansion into China, Russia and now, most probably, India. It is strange that not more is being done. Cooley in Ireland have in the past forged a healthy following with their introduction of grain whiskies at various ages. They have shown that the interest is there and some fresh thinking and boldness in a marketing department can create niche and often profitable markets. Edrington entered the market with a vatted grain called Snow Grouse, designed to be consumed chilled and obviously a tilt at the vodka market. The first bottling I received, though, was disappointingly poor and I hope future vattings will be more carefully attended to. All round, then, the news for Scottish grain lovers has not been good of late with the demolition of mighty Dumbarton and, controversially, closure of Port Dundas itself. With the expansion of Cameronbridge and a 50% stake in North British, Diageo obviously believe they have all the grain capacity they require.

The tastings notes here for grains cover only a few pages, disappointingly, due to their scarcity. However, it is a whisky style growing in stature, helped along the way not just by Cooley but also by more Independent bottlers bringing out a succession of high quality ancient casksThere has even been an organic grain on the market, distilled at the unfashionable Loch Lomond Distillery. Why, though, it has to be asked does it take the relatively little guys to lead the way? Perhaps the answer is in the growing markets in the east: the big distillers are very likely holding on to their stocks to facilitate their expansion there.

At last the message is getting through that the reaction to oak of this relatively lightweight spirit - and please don't for one moment regard it as neutral, for it is most certainly anything but - can throw up some fascinating and sometimes delicious possibilities. Blenders have known that for a long time. Now public interest is growing. And people are willing to admit that they can enjoy an ancient Cambus, Caledonian or Dumbarton in very much the way they might celebrate a single malt. Even if it does go against the grain...

Single Grain Scotch
CALEDONIAN

Clan Denny Caledonian 45 Years Old bourbon barrel, cask no. HH6294, dist 1965 **(89)** n22 t23.5 f21.5 b22. For all its obvious tiredness, there is plenty of rich character. 46.1%. nc ncf sc.

Clan Denny Caledonian 45 Years Old refill hogshead, cask no. HH6228, dist 1965 **(96)** n23.5 fascinating – and quite stunning – mix of light Canadian and deeper bourbon characteristics; almost a buttery quality to the corn; t25 that is about as good as you might ever expect the delivery of an ancient grain to be: perfect weight, perfect balance between light sugars, oily corn and other oak; perfect timing to its slow unveiling of its many complexities...in fact, simply perfect...; f23.5 simplifies, as a grain really has to but those delicate sugars ensure the oak remains honest; **b24** Super Caley...my prayers have been answered... 476%. nc ncf sc.

Clan Denny Caledonian Aged 45 Years bourbon barrel, cask no. HH7501, dist 1965 **(94)** n23.5 a curious though not unpleasant mix of bourbon whiskey warehouse and my dad's old-train imbued clothes in the early '60s after he got in from work...; t24 a Kentuckian character from the moment it touches the lips; the sugars are delicate and diverse, the liquorice building in boldness. By the midway point the sugars have moved into fully-fledged honeys; light and brain-explodingly complex; f23 a wee bitter note from tired oak. But that is outflanked by those oils carrying a gorgeous fruit and nut character and vanilla to die for; **b23.5** anyone who managed to get their hands on the very oldest maturing stocks of Barton bourbon from twenty years ago (and there were very few of us who managed it) would recognise it immediately. The similarities are uncanny. 473%. nc ncf sc. Douglas Laing & Co.

⁘ **Scotch Malt Whisky Society Cask G3.3 Aged 26 Years** refill barrel, dist 29 Apr 86 **(87)** n21.5 vanilla yoghurt; salty for a grain; t22 very simple sugars sweeten the light corn flour; f21.5 dry oaky yet slightly nutty with beeswax; **b22** no frills: a straight up and downer other than the unusual coastal twang. 56%. sc. 174 bottles.

Scott's Selection Caledonian 1965 bott 2011 **(89.5)** n24 t22.5 f20.5 b22.5. How about that? The nose belongs to Kentucky, the flavours carry a Maple Leaf flag. Aaah, pure Scotch! 45%

CAMBUS

⁘ **Clan Denny Cambus Vintage Aged 25 Years** refill hogshead, cask no. HH9320 **(96.5)** n24 you would not expect to get estery notes from a grain, but they certainly waft through here, not entirely dissimilar to a lighter Guyanese pot still. But the corn not only holds sway, but brings in the oak like a link-up striker brings in the wingers. Always sweet, always vanilla rich, always Canadian in its style, the weight and complexity both arouses and stuns in equal measure; t24.5 silky delivery, then so many layers of sugar the brain almost wilts trying to cope with the complexity; there is honey there, too. But of the clearest kind and offers no protection for the spices which makes a beautifully mannered entry; f23.5 medium length with citrus now forming a fresher element to the vanilla and corn..; **b24.5** nosed blind, this would be mistaken for absolutely top notch Canadian, and in particular the finer output from the now entirely lost LaSalle Distillery. But that rarely engaged its sugars in such a breathtakingly, almost outrageously, attractive way. One of the grain bottlings that will be remember among those in the know until the last one amongst us follow the Path of LaSalle...and, no less tragically, Cambus. 53.1%. ncf sc. Douglas Laing & Co. DEN0093.

Clan Denny Cambus Aged 36 Years bourbon barrel, cask no. HH7252, dist 1975 **(89.5)** n22 t23.5 f22 b22. Flawless grain limited only by its simplicity. 52.1%. nc ncf sc.

Clan Denny Cambus 45 Years Old refill bourbon barrel, cask no. HH5638, dist 1965 **(88.5)** n22 t23 f21.5 b22. A grain which has learned to deal with the impact of age in its very own, sweet way... 45.9%. nc ncf sc. Douglas Laing & Co.

Clan Denny Cambus 47 Years Old bourbon barrel, cask no. HH7029, dist 1963 **(97)** n24.5 a mesmeric blending of classic liquorice-bourbony tones, the vivid vanilla of a great Canadian and the sharp, lively precision of a massive scotch... t25 if you spent a dozen years of your life trying to create a whisky with absolutely perfect weight on delivery, you'd still fail to match the natural genius of this. The oils have just enough body to coat the palate with a delicate fretwork of the finest light liquorice and honeycomb lustre, but whose fragility is exposed by the orange-citrus sharpness which etches its own, impressive course; the sugars mingle with the spices with 47 years of understanding...; f23 after almost 50 years in the barrel, there is no surprise that a degree of bitter tightness comes into play. But the compactness of the vanilla keeps damage to a minimum; **b24.5** if this wasn't a Scotch single grain, it might just qualify as Bourbon of the Year. Proof that where a whisky is made, matured, or from makes absolutely no difference: it is the quality which counts. And there will be very few whiskies I taste this year that will outgun this one in the quality stakes... 49.7%. nc ncf sc. Douglas Laing & Co.

Clan Denny Cambus Aged 48 Years bourbon barrel, cask no. HH 7863, dist 1963 **(93)** n24 an old Buffalo Trace from the bottom third of the warehouse? Well it has complexity enough. The clever mixing of the red and black liquorice, that distant, dull rumble of molasses, the teasing spice, the exceptional balance between sweet and dry....; absolutely nothing short of fabulous....; **t23** the tiredness is evident early on, but there is sufficient dark sugars and thumping vanilla to place a delicious sticky plaster over the wounds; a highly unusual oil-led sharpness breathes all the life that is required back into this; **f22.5** dry with the oak gathering pace but thwarted from a full attack by those persistent oils and charming sugars; some diced hazelnut works wonders; **b23.5** no wonder they closed down the Cambus distillery; they must've plain gone and shipped it to Kentucky... 49.5%. nc ncf sc. Douglas Laing & Co.

Scotch Malt Whisky Society Cask G8.1 Aged 21 Years refill hogshead, cask no. 41759, dist 1989 **(85.5) n22.5 t22 f20 b21.** Decent enough, but a relatively underwhelming way to kick off the Society's account with this legendary grain distillery. A less than endearing piece of oak keeps any chance of the distillery's usual ability to tantalise with clever use of weight and complexity. A few kumquat and delicate clove notes do shake up the caramels on the nose, though. 61.2%. sc. 272 bottles.

⋅∵⋅ **Scotch Malt Whisky Society Cask G8.2 Aged 23 Years** refill hogshead, dist 12 Jun 89 **(94.5) n24** one of the most floral notes of the year: summer evening gardens with violets in particular; earthy but scented sweetness; **t23** big texture with many a mocha note. The usual rummy, estery pot still note hangs around, emboldened by the molassed sugars on the loose; the spices create a pleasing rhythm; **f23.5** softens down as vanilla-thickened ulmo honey moves in; **b24** not as complex as some Cambus you'll find but just ridiculously pleasing and steady, while the attitude and bite is a turn on.. Wow! 62.4%. sc. 252 bottles.

CAMERONBRIDGE

Clan Denny Cameronbridge Aged 21 Years refill butt, cask no. HH7541, dist 1990 **(85.5) n21.5 t22 f20.5 b21.5.** Creamy textured and sweet. Possibly filled into an old – and tired - Islay cask as there is the odd strand of smoke. 58.2%. nc ncf sc. Douglas Laing & Co.

⋅∵⋅ **Clan Denny Cameronbridge Aged 38 Years** refill barrel, cask no. HH9488 **(94) n23.5** the corn oils are so thick, it's amazing they can escape from the glass; **t24** denser than the forest the oak came from. Immediate spices show the depth of the aging but the subtle muscovado sugars enrich the corn to stay in control; just so thick and chewy; **f22.5** tangs out slightly as a few excesses of the oak come home to roost. But again the oils, aided now with fudge and butterscotch, fill in the gaps; **b24** some kind of Canadian and corn whiskey orgy. And a bit of a turn on it is, too...52.4%. sc. Douglas Laing & Co.

Clan Denny Cameronbridge 45 Years Old bourbon, cask no. HH6805, dist 1965 **(78) n21 t20 f18 b19.** Even grains can feel the cold hand of Father Time on their shoulder... 40.5%. nc ncf sc.

Rare Auld Grain Cameronbridge 32 Years Old cask no. 3597, dist 1979 **(92) n23 t23.5 f22.5 b23.** Anything but the norm. 48.8%. sc. Duncan Taylor & Co.

Scott's Selection Cameron Bridge 1973 bott 2010 **(77) n19 t21 f18 b19.** Good grain + poor cask = 77. 41.4%. Speyside Distillers.

Scott's Selection Cameron Bridge 1973 bott 2010 **(85) n23.5 t21 f20 b20.5.** Worth getting just for the nose alone, which is top rate Canadian with the corn leaping from the glass. A disappointing bitterness from the oak creeps in to spoil the party somewhat. 44.9%

CARSEBRIDGE

Clan Denny Carsebridge 29 Years Old 1st fill hogshead, cask no. HH6609, dist 1981 **(82) n22 t22 f18 b20.** The intensity of the corn is profound. So too, alas, is the bitter retribution of the tired cask. 53.1%. nc ncf sc. Douglas Laing & Co.

Clan Denny Carsebridge Aged 30 Years refill hogshead, cask no. HH7780, dist 1981 **(91.5) n21.5** light for its age with the odd vegetable note; **t23.5** the astonishing strength for its age does no harm as the mouth-watering grain is driven purposefully into the taste buds; the spices begin midway and show little sign of abating; **f23** good length, though the extended vanillas cannot outrun the spice; **b23.5** is there such a thing as a juicy 30-year-old grain? On this evidence, indubitably. 59.1%. nc ncf sc. Douglas Laing & Co.

Clan Denny Carsebridge Aged 45 Years bourbon barrel, cask no. HH7500, dist 1965 **(95) n24** absolutely no doubting the corn used in this whisky: a gently honeyed cross between a Canadian and bourbon, alternating in intensity between the two styles; **t24** the delivery comes down firmly in the bourbon camp; or perhaps I should say softly but decidedly: the oils are sumptuous yet feather-light, the sugars no more than sprinkled; **f23** and now we have the Canadian, with the banana vanillas dominating though the spices warm; **b24** as we have so often seen in Kentucky and Canada, old grains maturing in high quality casks rank among the best whiskies in the world: here is a stunning example. 44.7%. nc ncf sc.

⋅∵⋅ **Clan Denny Carsebridge Aged 47 Years** refill barrel, cask no. HH9489 **(91) n23.5** fabulous nutty lead, fresh hazelnuts in particular, also a Play Doh sweetness as well as a corny gristyness you rarely see outside Kentucky; **t23.5** good, sweet corn oils spread evenly. Only vanilla offers a complexity; **f22** the cask is hanging on by a thread, but the sugars fill in the cracks deliciously; **b22** a simple grain, despite the antiquity, doing the easy things attractively. 45.3%. sc. Douglas Laing & Co.

DUMBARTON

⫶ **Cadenhead Dumbarton 24 Years Old** bourbon, dist 87, bott 12 **(93)** **n24** that has to be one of the most alluring grain noses bottled for a while. As fruity as you could ever get from an ex-bourbon cask with the accent all bendy banana; **t22.5** light and delicate delivery, ridiculously juicy for a grain nearly a quarter of a century old; **f23** now the complexity begins to start cranking up with a lovely Milky Way cocoa softness building behind the corn and honey outer wall; **b23.5** for those of you who adore the older Ballantine's, you can certainly see the square root of some of the complex flavour profiles. Dumbarton grain was, to me, the best of the industrial-sized grain plants by a distance. Try this for proof. 49.5%. sc. 210 bottles.

Clan Denny Dumbarton 45 Years Old refill hogshead, cask no. HH7001, dist 1965 **(89.5)** **n23 t23 f21.5 b22.** A lovely grain bottled in the nick of time and happy to display the remnants of its zesty vigour. 49.5%. nc ncf sc. Douglas Laing & Co.

Clan Denny Dumbarton Aged 46 Years refill hogshead, cask no. HH7542, dist 1964 **(86.5)** **n22 t23 f20 b21.5.** The tiredness on the finish, confirming the big oaks on the nose, still cannot entirely overcome the beauty of the honey and golden syrup delivery: some of the early moments in the mouth are akin to the soaring strings of a John Barry score. The finish is pure Bay City Rollers. 474%. nc ncf sc. Douglas Laing & Co.

⫶ **Clan Denny Dumbarton Aged 48 Years** refill hogshead, cask no. HH9345 **(96.5)** **n25** frightening. How is something so simple and imperfect as a human brain supposed to unravel something so spellbindingly complex as this? All at the same level, there is an earthy vegetable weight, not in a "gone off" style, but in a gentle, slightly salted leek, as well as a delicate fruit cocktail with the emphasis on honeydew melon and tangerine; the sugars are spectacular. They range from thin maple syrup, running through to a light manuka honey with seemingly half a dozen variations between. One of the great noses of 2013/14; **t24** of all the honeys, ulmo now comes out tops on delivery. But we also have some surprising oils at work, carrying a buttery corn meal infused with light salt and vanilla; **f23.5** long, again with the corn at the lead. Enormous butterscotch and vanilla interplay, inevitable cocoa...but those sugars...just so ridiculously deft; **b24** truly great whisky. Forget this being a grain: excellence is excellence. Full stop. 50.1%. sc.

Scott's Selection Dumbarton 1986 bott 11 **(94)** **n24.5** complex? Doesn't even touch upon what is going on here. Most ungrain like in the manner by which a complex prickle teases the nose. A bit like the small grains working wonders in a bourbon. Not overly sweet, but the cooked molassed sugars do add depth as well as balance; butterscotch in a mildly overcooked tart; **t24** initially a silkier delivery than the nose suggests will happen. But those corn oils are relatively brief and a combination of sugars, of varying degree of intensity, begin to box with the fizzing spices; **f22** some bitterness as one comes to expect from old Allied casks, but the clarity of the grain and now honeyed sugars negates the worst and has a little to spare; **b23.5** when this distillery was closed I was almost beside myself with disappointment...and rage. Following the closure of Cambus, this left Dumbarton as the brightest star in the collapsing grain whisky galaxy. This bottle will give you some insight into just why I treasured it so greatly; certainly more so than the bead counters at Allied who saw its potential as prime real estate over its ability to keep making arguably the best blended Scotch whiskies in the world. My main point of surprise now is why so few bottlings from this giant of a distillery ever see the shelves. 51.5%.

GARNHEATH

Clan Denny Garnheath 43 Years Old refill hogshead, cask no. HH6642, dist 1967 **(94)** **n24.5** a charming mix of very old Georgian corn whiskey and no less young Demerara column still rum; it would be hard to fine tune the spices to better effect; **t23.5** rare for a grain, the barley is detectable briefly but distinctly early on. It is then lost under a silo of corn but the juiciness never dissipates; **t22.5** fabulously controlled, bristling spice keeps a hint of oaky burnout to a minimum; **b23.5** what a treat: not just a whisky as rare as budgie teeth, but one in tip-top nick for its age. A rare delight. 44.4%. nc ncf sc. Douglas Laing & Co.

⫶ **The Coopers Choice Golden Grains Garnheath 1967 45 Years Old (94.5) n23.5** the nose is found more often in Kentucky: rich corn absorbing ulmo and manuka honey and a little coconut with the red liquorice; **t24** so soft on delivery you would not think it possible: just the most amazing mixture of ulmo honey (sans manuka) with icing sugar. The corn clings to the oils beautifully; **f23.5** a fabulous example of difference between quality of oak then and now: not a hint of bitterness just a sensuously slow fade on the sugars, plus some Danish marzipan; **b24** I remember the last time I tasted Garneath it was Atlanta corn whiskey coming back at me from the glass. Now we have top grade bourbon... 42%. nc ncf sc.

GIRVAN

 Girvan Single Grain 22 Years Old cask no. 110633, dist 89, bott Oct 11 **(88)** n21.5 corn oil and light vanilla; t22.5 fat delivery at first with a quick peppery burst before the sugars arrive in force; f22 simple oak-strewn vanillas; b22 safe and conservative. *63%. sc.*

Berry's Own Selection Girvan Aged 46 Years cask no. 37532, bott 2011 **(94.5)** n24 takes me back to a kitchen in Surrey in the early '60s with my mother boiling the cooking apples from the tree from the back garden, sharp and slightly under-sugared; elsewhere a gallery of spices hang in the air; I may have just broken into a Crunchie bar; t23.5 silky and magnificent, this is a grain which envelopes the taste buds, caressing them with such delicate oils and oaks, the latter apparent thanks to both a vanilla dryness and a tangier pepper attack; f23 vanilla ice cream with a dab of honeycomb; the oils keep their shape and weight ensuring the sugars see off any oak attack; b24 if you have not yet crossed the divide and got into grain whisky, here really is your chance. What a stunner! *46%. nc ncf sc.*

Berry's Own Selection Girvan 1989 cask no. 37530/1, bott 2010 **(82.5)** n21 t22 f19.5 b20. Thick, sweet but a little on the tardy side... *45.1%. nc ncf sc. Berry Bros & Rudd.*

 Clan Denny Girvan Aged 21 Years refill barrel, cask no. HH9451 **(92)** n23 the oak has stirred up a hornets' nest of busy tannins which prick the delicate moist coconut and Demerara sweetness; t23.5 lush delivery with the sugars probing then soothing; vanilla arrives with just a hint of spice alongside; f22.5 a slight bitterness to the barrel but the oily Venezuelan cocoa holds court; b23 complex, busy and compelling. *59.6%. sc.*

Clan Denny Girvan 45 Years Old refill hogshead, cask no. HH6276, dist 1965 **(90)** n23 t23.5 f21.5 b22.5. Laid on with a golden trowel. *47.3%. nc ncf sc.*

Clan Denny Girvan 45 Years Old refill hogshead, cask no. HH6923, dist 1965 **(88.5)** n23 t23 f20.5 b22. Simplistic, certainly. But as you get older, you learn to appreciate the more simple things in life... *45.3%. nc ncf sc. Douglas Laing & Co.*

Clan Denny Girvan Aged 46 Years refill hogshead, cask no. HH7669, dist 1965 **(94.5)** n23 the tannins sticking to the vanilla lessen the sugars on the acacia honey; liquorice underlines the great age; a small squeeze of lime offers an improbable freshness; t24 a fabulous delivery which for the first few moments holds a Canadian line of soft corn oil and vanilla. But soon that liquorice on the nose heads the vanguard of the bourbon characteristics, including melt-in-the-mouth manuka honey, which soon take command. The spices fizz but refuse to fully explode; f23.5 breathtakingly elegant fade with caresses of honeyed vanilla all the way; b24 sublime. *49.7%. nc ncf sc. Douglas Laing & Co.*

Riegger's Selection Girvan 1964 bourbon cask, cask no. 86, dist 2 Sep 64, bott 7 Feb 11 **(87)** n22.5 some evidence of crumbling oak and tiredness but there is enough dry allspice and coriander to inject life and complexity back into the light corn; t22.5 lightly oiled texture; soft corn oil and delicate muscovado sugars. The vanillas turn from heavy to stark; f20 just a little bitterness from the fading cask; b22 lovers of corn whisky will enjoy many aspects of this oldie. *48.7%. nc ncf sc. Viktor-Riegger GmbH. 189 bottles.*

 Scotch Malt Whisky Society Cask G7.5 Aged 28 Years refill hogshead, dist 84 **(91)** n23.5 hard to imagine grain going into better oak: the orange-blossom honey is just about faultless; some perky spice, too; t23.5 from the nose you can tell the texture will be both rich and delicate – and it is. So juicy, with maple syrup hanging off the tannins; f22 minor bitterness – unusual: didn't see that coming. But enough honey in reserve. Just; b22 keep bottling gems like this and they'll have to form the Grain Whisky Society. *58.9%. sc. 275 bottles.*

Scott's Selection Girvan 1964 bott 2011 **(92.5)** n23.5 t24 f22 b23. Girvan, like Invergordon, is grain which takes full advantage of its sumptuous persona. Here, though, it adds some controlled sharpness. But it's the lordly sugars which really win the day. Superb. *48.8%*

 The Whisky Agency Girvan Aged 48 Years ex-sherry butt, dist 64, bott 12 **(87.5)** n23 astonishing mix of old-style bourbon and salty, rich grape. Just a little milky tiredness from the oak, but this was once a top class butt; t22.5 full bodied richness of sugared almond and sugar-glazed grape; the oak is a bit confused though the butterscotch is excellent; f20 tired, bitter oak; b22 outwardly like a Macallan from the early 1980s. Except with a bourbon rather than malt background...the oak is just leaking a little bitterness, though. *49.5%. ncf. 487 bottles.*

INVERGORDON

Berry's Own Selection Invergordon 1971 cask no. 2, bott 2011 **(91.5)** n24 more of a high quality column still rum than a whisky...; Demerara in both rum type and sugars evident with the vanillas showing a delicious citrus tinge; some real butterscotch in there, too; t23 back to being grain whisky now: toffee, toasted fudge and spices; some soft oils glue the busy flavours to the roof of the mouth; f22 the peppers keep peppering, but the toffee-vanillas dominate; b22.5 a beautiful experience. *46.7%. nc ncf sc. Berry Bros & Rudd.*

Clan Denny Invergordon 44 Years Old refill barrel, cask no. HH4995, dist 1966 **(95.5)** n23.5 corn dough and carrot juice; a light smattering of spice ensures some real complexity here;

t24 as soft and sweet as you might imagine an Invergordan to be. But also offers a surprising degree of countering sharpness with a salivating quality of a grain more than half its age **f23.5** a wonderful build up of tingling, busy spice offers an excellent exit; **b24.5** almost quicksand-ish in its softness. But an amazing degree of complexity, too. A true gem of a whisky. *46.8%. nc ncf sc. Douglas Laing & Co.*

Clan Denny Invergordon 45 Years Old bourbon barrel, cask no. HH7254, dist 1966 **(88)** **n22 t22 f22 b22.** Played with an absolutely straight bat: over 45 years every kink appears to have been ironed out. *47.1%. nc ncf sc. Douglas Laing & Co.*

Clan Denny Invergordon Aged 45 Years bourbon barrel, cask no. HH7864, dist 1966 **(88.5)** **n22.5** a touch of exotic fruit; **t22** soft and delicately oiled; a huge wave of Canadian-style vanilla tinged with citrus; **f22** more echoes of Canada; the vanilla is curiously sweetening as well as drying; **b22** an unspectacular, well-made and matured grain offering quiet gracefulness. *47.5%. nc ncf sc. Douglas Laing & Co.*

⁙ **Clan Denny Invergordon Vintage Aged 46 Years** barrel, cask no. HH9077 **(91.5) n24** the coconut mixed in with the red liquorice and soft hickory offers the base to the acacia honey which sings so sweetly; **t23** lilting sugars ensure the oak doesn't show even a slight degree of wear or tear. Just soft vanilla and natural caramel all the way; **f22** a short finish as there are so few oils around, other than a slight corn bread and egg custard mix; **b22.5** about a quiet a dram you could wish to bring into your house. Open late at night...it will disturb nobody. *44.2%. sc. Douglas Laing & Co.*

Duncan Taylor Octave Invergordon 38 Years Old cask no. 520883, dist 1972 **(86.5) n24 t21 f20 b21.**5. Some serious Demerara sugars knit tightly into the intense vanilla. A few bitter notes amid the booming spice. The nose, however, excels and conjures myriad bourbon images. *47.8%. sc. Duncan Taylor & Co.*

First Cask Invergordon 37 Years Old American oak, cask no. 63641, dist 1 Jul 72, bott 3 Jul 09 **(85) n23.5 t21 f20 b20.**5. A dram which conjures up clearer pictures of ice cracking on the Great Lakes than it does water coursing through the Scottish glens. The corn works beautifully on the nose in particular but the oak bitters from delivery onwards. *44%. nc ncf sc. 135 bottles.*

⁙ **Malts Of Scotland Invergordon 1973** bourbon hogshead, cask no. MoS 12063, dist 73, bott 12 **(90) n22** butterscotch tart: the pastry is thick; **t22** melts in the mouth. No complexity. Just satisfying lightly sugared effect; **f23** the oak grows layer by layer and the spice arrives; **b23** a grain which makes you groan with pleasure. How soft is that! *42%. 96 bottles.*

Rare Auld Grain Invergordon 38 Years Old cask no. 96251, dist 1972 **(88.5) n22.5 t22.5 f21.5 b22.** Ramrod straight and beyond the nose eschews any grand design of complexity. *44%. sc. Duncan Taylor & Co.*

Scotch Malt Whisky Society Cask G5.2 Aged 17 Years virgin toasted oak hogshead, cask no. 53285, dist 1993 **(90.5) n23 t23 f21.5 b23.** Oils apart, barely representative of the distillery at this age but bourbon lovers will be thrilled. *65.3%. sc. 248 bottles.*

Scotch Malt Whisky Society Cask G5.3 Aged 18 Years virgin toasted oak, cask no. 53289, dist 1993 **(95.5) n23.5** a fabulous cross between bread pudding and a well-aged Canadian whisky; **t24.5** the delivery may be soft in texture. But there is no holding back on the flavour front as myriad oak notes pour onto the palate with sugars offering varying degrees of intensity and comfort, though all of them sitting very comfortably with the buzzing spice; the main flavour profile constantly hovers between top notch bourbon and ultra fine Canadian; **f23.5** much more simplistic vanilla. But the weight remains almost perfect; **b24** there aren't many grain whiskies so gorgeously influenced by oak to the dozen. Invergordon as you have probably never seen before...and are unlikely to see again... *65.6%. sc.*

Scotch Malt Whisky Society Cask G5.4 Aged 18 Years virgin toasted oak, cask no. 53288, dist 1993 **(92) n23** you often get Canadian style grains. This is much nearer a Kentuckian with the breakfast marmalade fruitiness jousting with the big oaky liquorice. The sugars are molassed. As heavyweight a nose on a grain as you'll ever find; **t23** the delivery is a kaleidoscope of delicate and indelicate sugars, mostly of the crisp and crunchy variety but offering variations of hues from icing sugar down to Demerara; spices nip and kiss while the vanillas boil up some custard; **f22.5** long with the accent firmly on those darker sugars and bourbony hickory; **b23.5** I must admit I gave the whisky a bit of a quizzical look after both clapping my eyes on its rich colour and breathing in that intense marmalade nose. Only on reading the small print did it all make sense. *65.6%. Scotch Malt Whisky Society.*

Scotch Malt Whisky Society Cask G5.5 Aged 18 Years virgin toasted oak hogshead, cask no. 53286, dist 1993 **(94.5) n24** obviously Invergordon has been moved to Kentucky... the diced orange peel and blood orange suggests a bourbon, as does the hickory and spice. How about that manuka, too! Above all, it's like being inside a Victorian or Edwardian cupboard; **t24** there is no distillery in Kentucky which ensures such an oily delivery (mind you, I know one in Tennessee), so Invergordon it must be! But there is no let up to the North American theme, now with various cocoa notes dominating, Jamaican Blue Mountain coffee taking a stroll through the mid-range and burnt raisin – without the fruit element, if you know what I mean, heading us towards the finale...; **f23** which is a slow switching out of the lights...; **b23.5** a whisky I've had to taste to hit deadline without being supplied with cask details. From the way this is behaving it must be some kind of super first fill or even virgin oak: it is much nearer bourbon than Scotch! *65.3%. sc.*

⁖ **Scotch Malt Whisky Society Cask G5.7 Aged 19 Years** refill hogshead, dist 20 May 93 **(92) n24** neo-bourbon, except just too much timber; the thick citrus and leather saves the day while the green tea leaves are just about a master stroke; reminds me of when I first entered Indian spice stores in the late '70s...; you have to leave it for half an hour in the glass to get the honey properly; **t23** big blood orange and beech honey; butterscotch and ulmo honey middle...then splinters...; **f22** a fascinating mix of sugar and sawdust...; **b23** for those who like a little whisky in their oak....Outrageous. But somehow works! *64.6%. sc. 234 bottles.*

Scott's Selection Invergordon 1964 bott 2011 **(92) n24 t24 f21 b23.** Another which keeps faithfully to the distillery's yielding, melt-in-the-mouth style. But here we have a deep Kentucky drawl and a nose from heaven... *43.8%. Speyside Distillers.*

Scott's Selection Invergordon 1964 bott 2012 **(94) n22.5** just a little flat with the vanillas having dragged out a few elements from the oak I would preferred not have seen. Even so, there is no denying the virtues of the unusual sugar peanut candy and corn oil also on view; **t24** oooh! Didn't see that coming. After the flat delivery I knew was on its way, several thick waves of lightly salted, melt-in-the-mouth and highly intense barley sugar (in a corn-fuelled grain!!) notes flood through. Next the corn oils themselves burst their banks, an episode those of you who enjoy Corn Whisky will recognise and appreciate; the mid-ground is a matter of coping with the toasty liquorice; **f23.5** silky to the last with the corn and vanilla contentedly holding hands; **b24** when I first nosed this, my instinct was that it would have been better off propping up an ancient old blend. Having now fully tasted it, I am not so sure... *42.3%.*

⁖ **Single Cask Collection Ivergordon Aged 24 Years** bourbon barrel, cask no. 18589, dist 22 Feb 88, bott 22 Aug 12 **(89.5) n21.5** typical unobtrusive, soft Canadian style from this distillery. Few peaks or troughs but displays an enigmatic sweetness; **t23.5** nothing enigmatic about the muscovado sugars and ulmo honey which bombard the delivery; gorgeous, Canadian-styled, softly oiled middle; **f22** bitters slightly as the oak tires; a light mocha fade fits well; **b22.5** softly, softly all the way. *55.5%. nc ncf sc. 188 bottles.*

⁖ **That Boutique-y Whisky Company Invergordon Batch 1 (93) n23** soup-like with sweet oaky thickness; hints of my old Winchester in my Bristol office; **t23.5** this would be way over the top were not the sugars and spices so profound; love the wonderful burnt fudge and crème brûlée; **f23** a strange sherry trifle finale though the fruit appears to be from toasty burnt raisin sugars; **b23.5** an ancient old bourbon in all but name. *41.6%. 252 bottles.*

The Whisky Agency Invergordon 1965 bott 2010 **(90) n23.5 t23 f21 b22.5.** A glorious old timer, showing some quality Canadian-style manoeuvres. *44.7%. The Whisky Agency.*

LOCH LOMOND

Rhosdhu 2008 Cask No. 2483 re-char bourbon, dist 17/03/08, bott 27/07/11 **(86.5) n22 t22 f21 b21.5.** Delicately clean barley with a touch of lemon and, though engagingly soft, is not beyond showing some sugary teeth. *45%. nc ncf sc.*

Rhosdhu 2008 Cask No. 2484 bourbon barrel, dist 17/03/08, bott 27/07/11 **(84) n21.5 t21.5 f20.5 b21.** The barley battles with some aggressive oak, even at this tender age. The spice count is pretty high. *45%. nc ncf sc.*

LOCHSIDE

⁖ **The Coopers Choice Lochside 1964 47 Years Old** sherry, bott 12 **(95.5) n24.5** The softest of fruitcakes, one with juicy rather than roasted raisin and the dough a bit like a Huffkins Lardy Cake; the spices are impeccable; **t24** silk, wrapped in silk, wrapped in silk... wrapped in silk. The corn oil has ensured the framework of the whisky has bones of jelly, the fruit rounding off any possible interference from the oak; the sugars are sublime: mainly muscovado, but a little maple syrup, too, and a few strains of citrus; **f23.5** again, has all the firmness of quicksand but those sugars a wonderful job; **b23.5** there are still some around who remember 1964 as a very special year in Montrose. First, their distillery, Lochside, was working. Secondly, they were receiving top quality sherry butts, long before the days they were ruined by reckless, unforgivable – and unforgiving - sulphur treatment. And, thirdly, for a while their football team enjoyed rare success on the park. In fact, in 1964 the guys at the distillery would have seen their blue-hooped heroes thrash neighbours Forfar 5-0 (having already murdered them 8-2 earlier in the season), would have made the short journey to next door Brechin for victory there as well as seen their lads annihilate Raith 8-3 and Stenhousemuir 7-1 back on home soil. The only thing they were denied was victory over the upstarts down the coast at Arbroath. But you can't have everything. Obviously happy workers make happy whisky. Amazing how those goals – and sound sherry butts - of 1964 can come back and heighten our enjoyment now. *41.5%. ncf sc. Cask Strength.*

NORTH BRITISH

Berry's Own Selection North British 2000 cask no. 4312, bott 2011 **(87.7) n22** gorgeously structured: firm, if understated, sweetness; dank stinging nettles; gooseberry tart; **t22.5** crisp skeleton on which a fatter outer layer of spiced golden syrup hangs; **f21** bitters thanks to some indifferent oak; **b22** neutral whisky....? I don't think so. *46%. nc ncf sc.*

Director's Cut North British Aged 50 Years refill butt, cask no. 8228, dist 1962 **(82.5) n21 f19 b20.5**. How truly bizarre that the whisky waits 50 years to be tasted. And on the day I get round to it, the distillery is closed in the national gaze during a Legionaire's disease outbreak: certainly not what the distiller who made this would have expected two generations ago. I don't think he would have expected this whisky either. Now I may be completely wrong. But I suspect this has been finished in a pretty fresh sherry butt to spruce the dear old thing up before bottling. Sadly, the sherry cask has a light sulphur taint, so the bitterness creeps in. Leave these whiskies well alone, is my motto... *571%. nc ncf sc. 222 bottles.*

⚬⚬ **Malts Of Scotland North British 1962** bourbon hogshead, cask no. MoS 13017, dist May 62, bott Mar 13 **(95.5) n23.5** Guyana's finest...no, wait a minute we are in Scotland. Massive crisp sugar wrapped in a crisper kumquat shell; a slight ester softness among the looser sugar; **t24** superb! Again the sugars get off to a cracking start, carrying now with the lightest oak veneer, mainly vanilla but soft liquorice, too; **f24** long, the elegance continues, as does that distinctive rummy feel; a light hint of mocha but the Demerara sugars are in control; **b24** a faultless whisky for rum lovers. Tasted blind, no difference. Fabulous grain, breathtaking, continuous and still Demerara in style. Who cares? Hang on: come to think of it, both come from Coffey stills...interesting... *41.5%. 48 bottles.*

⚬⚬ **Master of Malt North British 18 Years Old** bourbon, cask no. 309896, dist 23 Dec 94, bott 1 Apr 13 **(77) n17.5 t22 f18 b19.5**. From around this time a number of blenders were bemoaning the sulphurous qualities of North British. Even taking into account the oily, sugary charge on the palate, you can see why. This, I have just discovered, is the 777th new whisky for the 2014 Bible. And it scores 77...how weird is that! But this 777, a very lopsided grain, never takes off. *52.3%. 240 bottles.*

Master Of Malt North British 20 Year Old cask no. 3228, dist 1991 **(85.5) n22 t22 f20.5 b21.** Some decent, slightly syrupy sugars but bitter at death. *54.1%. sc. Master Of Malt.*

⚬⚬ **Scotch Malt Whisky Society Cask G1.10 Aged 21 Years** refill hogshead, dist 14 dec 90 **(85) n22 t22 f20 b21.** Absolutely standard and non-spectacular without enough grain character to see off the massive caramels dragged from the oak. Pleasant and easy going, though the finish is on the bitter side. *61.1%. sc. 137 bottles.*

Scott's Selection North British 1989 bott 2011 **(86) n21.5 t22.5 f20.5 b21.5.** Threatens to break out and expand on its vanilla-led theme but remains pretty tight throughout. Some puckering saltiness early on. *54%. Speyside Distillers.*

⚬⚬ **That Boutique-y Whisky Company North British Batch 1** (73.5) **n18 t19 f18 b18.5.** Really didn't know they were making gin at North British. What the bloody hell is this...? 51.1%. 117 bottles.

The Whisky Agency North British 1962 (93) n24 t23.5 f22.5 b23. Full of traits and characteristics as rare as this type of whisky. But, above all, absolutely refuses to admit its age. This grain is an inspiration to us all... *479%. The Whisky Agency.*

NORTH OF SCOTLAND

⚬⚬ **Clan Denny North Of Scotland Vintage Aged 38 Years** barrel, cask no. HH9078 **(94.5) n23** big tannin with liquorice and, nondescript honey mixed with maple syrup doing battle with some engagingly brutal spices; **t24** close your eyes and you could be in Frankfort allowing some pretty old Ancient Age pass through your teeth. again, like on the nose, the sugars are profound, earthy, toasty yet never too precious to allow in the far duskier, toastier elelments of the oak; **f23.5** lightens with surprising rapidity into a more chalky and a little tangy marmalade on the fade; **b24** fascinating how some grains, like the Cambus, head in a Canadian style of direction, while this is pure Kentucky. And superb Kentucky at that... *52%. sc. DEN0030*

Late Lamented North of Scotland 37 Years Old **(94.5) n23.5** sweet and nutty, there is a crisp sheen to the more sugary Canadian vanilla notes. Just a slight drizzle of something spicy makes for a beautifully balanced aroma; **t23.5** a sumptuous mouth feel cannot disguise the busy interplay between the weighty vanillas and slicker sugars, which run the range from refined to muscovado; ridiculously clean, a rare clarity on the palate for a whisky of such great age; **f23.5** textbook complexity of an old-fashioned Canadian. Beautiful corn dots the I and crosses the T, finding the spots still not filled by the sugary vanillas. An almost lazy, apologetic spiciness ramps up the complexity and the expected semi-gluey finale has a surprising mouthwatering quality; **b24** an astonishing whisky completely devoid of the bitterness often found in a whisky of such antiquity, or over the top oakiness. One of the great Scottish Single Grains of recent years and a bottling that Canadian whisky devotees of a near lost style of half a century ago will relish. Monumentally magnificent and, of its type, almost flawless. 44.2%

Scott's Selection North Of Scotland 1971 bott 2012 (87) **n21** a bizarre lightly smoked edge to this. There is relatively little there, but so surprising to find it at all that it is hard to concentrate on much else... **t22** hard as granite. The grains appear to have locked together to allow little to pass or escape. A few sugars do dodge the guards; **f22** maybe a little bitterness to the cask. But vanillas and soft nougat dominate. Until a lightly smoked spiciness makes an entry; **b22** what a weirdo. If grain is filled into an old Islay cask, over 40 years the phenols will vanish. What they are still doing here, though in minor quantities, is open to debate...! 45.1%

Scott's Selection North Of Scotland 1973 bott 2012 (92) **n23.5** black cherries; dripping in molasses and a minty oakiness; muscovado-sweetened Madagascan cocoa of the top order; **t23** huge shape and presence on delivery: thick oils thickened further by oaky vanilla concentrate but enough dark sugars to ensure balance; the mid-ground allows the grain and spice to form comfortably; **f22.5** the oak tires a little but now a few strands of Jaffa cake make for a pleasant finale; **b23** you just know you've had one hell of a big whisky... 48.5%

PORT DUNDAS

Port Dundas 20 Years Old Special Release 2011 db (90) **n21.5** a little nip, but mostly alcohol related. Otherwise a bit of a damp squib, though there is no doubting the overall quality; **t22** pure silk with a few sugars giving a slightly rummy gesture of intense sweetness; the vanillas start forming thickly towards the middle; **f23.5** a sublime finish: varying spices get to grips with the big fruit and tannin and now we have something approaching a blend between pot still Guyana rum and an old bourbon. In its own way, quite brilliant...; **b23** can a whisky be a little too silky. This one tries, especially on the non-committal nose and over friendly delivery. But once the spices rise, things get very interesting... 574%. nc ncf sc.

∴ **Clan Denny Port Dundas Aged 21 Years** refill hogshead, cask no. HH9452 (93) **n23** honeycomb on speed: sharp, toasty, crispy sweet; lime on vanilla ice cream; **t23.5** although the oak has dug in and makes an early impact, the spreading of what appears to be soft corn oils helps the ever-intensifying sugars to see off the underlying toastiness; **f23** the sugars are now crystalline and persistent; **b23.5** astonishingly invigorating. Leaps from the glass with intent and purpose. Wonderful! 55.7%. sc. Douglas Laing & Co.

∴ **Clan Denny Port Dundas Vintage Aged 24 Years** hogshead, cask no. HH9079 (94.5) **n23** don't get many noses like that to the dozen: pure fruitcake thanks to the Demerara and a sweetness that indirectly fits alongside burnt raisins. Yet not fruity, if you see what I mean...; **t24** gorgeous structure; light oils allowing the Demerara and butterscotch to gel beautifully; the sweetnes is enormous, yet the toastiness of the tannins keeps everything in shape; **f23.5** toasty with a more structured dryness which balances sublimely with the deliverythe spices take their time to get there, but arrive at long last;; **b24** a typical Coffey still heavyweight which never thinks of stinting on the dark sugars. 52.2%. sc. Douglas Laing & Co. DEN0091

Clan Denny Port Dundas Aged 34 Years refill hogshead, cask no. HH7543, dist 1978 (92) **n22** simplistic vanilla and toffee; **t23** lazy start then slowly shifts into gear. By the midway point the spices have arrived to keep the growing sugars company; **f23.5** full on complexity and brimming with mocha; shows ever-increasing Canadian tendencies; **b23.5** one of those deliciously rare beasts that just gets better and better as it goes along. 54.2%. nc ncf sc.

Clan Denny Port Dundas Aged 34 Years refill hogshead, cask no. HH7543, dist 1978 (94.5) **n23.5** corny Canadian in hyper show off mode: the sugars are bristling and the vanilla almost pulses; **t24** even more silky than the nose suggests with the corn oil ensuring the friendliest of greetings. Excellent "Milky Way" chocolate nougat middle; **f23.5** moves unexpectedly towards a pot still rum character before the corn returns again; **b23.5** not many single malts can match this for sheer deliciousness. 58.6%. nc ncf sc. Douglas Laing & Co.

Director's Cut Port Dundas Aged 30 Years refill hogshead, cask no. 8416, dist 1982 (87) **n21** untidy and tight, the oak constrains just a little too forcefully **t23.5** relaxes on the palate... and how! The slow opening up of the corn oils and accompanying sugars is superb and though complexity is at a premium, the gradual strengthening of the citrus notes is superb; **f20** retracts slightly as the tightness on the nose is repeated at the death; **b22.5** no shortage of action...but, oh! for a better cask!! 58.7%. nc ncf sc. Douglas Laing & Co. 207 bottles.

Duncan Taylor Octave Port Dundas 38 Years Old cask no. 600952, dist 1973 (86) **n23** **t21.5 f20.5 b21.5.** One very strange grain whisky. An equal tugging between fruit and bourbon which ensures a fascinating nose. But it never quite gels after the initial rich, biscuit delivery, though always enjoyable and even occasionally juicy, tails off a little. 55.6%. sc.

Scotch Malt Whisky Society Cask G6.2 Aged 18 Years refill barrel, cask no. 20061, dist 1993 **(82) n22 t21 f19 b20.** For all the early sweetness, never quite succeeds in shrugging off an ultimately debilitating bitterness. *55.2%. sc. Scotch Malt Whisky Society.*

Scott's Selection Port Dundas 1965 bott 2011 **(91) n24 t23 f21.5 b22.5.** If you ever see a witch's chest in Holland...this is even flatter than that... No peaks or troughs. Just one flavour rolling, seemingly without a second glance, hesitation or join into the next... Not sure whether to adore this incredibly delicate whisky or try to thrash some life into it. Certainly, as I come up to tasting my 1,000th whisky of the year (this is no. 972) I can safely say there has been no other one quite like it. Which must be a good thing. So, upon reflection, one to get to know and love. For it is a thing of rare beauty. Flat chest or not... *43.3%. Speyside Distillers.*

STRATHCLYDE

Clan Denny Strathclyde 33 Years Old refill butt, cask no. HH6144, dist 1977, bott 2010 **(94.5) n23.5** pithy grape and pepper; **t23.5** fresh fruit and then an avalanche of pepper and bread pudding spices, complete with a topping of crunchy brown sugars; succulent mouth feel with a superb touch to the delicate oil; **f24** so un-33-year old! No tired oak and the spices still lightly buzz. But more fruity notes now draining away **b23.5** I am not told it has been, but imagine an old grain finished in a lively, fresh and very clean wine cask... A stunner! *57.2%. nc ncf sc.*

⁘ **Clan Denny Strathclyde Aged 38 Years** refill barrel, cask no. HH9486 **(88) n23.5** clever interplay between nougat and marzipan. The distant aroma of cordite springs a surprise; **t22** beautifully weighted and powerfully spicy, suggesting early wheat. The sugars are distinctly in the muscovado mould, with a little liquorice thrown in; **f20.5** the usual Allied poor bourbon barrel bitterness ruins the fun; **b22** appears to be wheated grain as opposed to corn. Very early if so. *55.5%. sc. Douglas Laing & Co.*

⁘ **Scotch Malt Whisky Society Cask G10.1 Aged 23 Years** refill hogshead, dist 31 Aug 89 **(94) n24** dates and greengages abound, as do walnuts; leathery Winchester chairs and leather-bound Millwall: Lions of the South...; **t23** soft, radiating malt hits the ground running, then an immediate second wave of concentrated fudge and raisin; **f23.5** this is so un-Strathclyde like, even to the end. I was expecting a mild sulphury bite from the stills at least, but the closest we come is a busy, vaguely discordant croakiness to the otherwise harmonious molassed sugars and vanilla; **b23.5** oh, if only the majority of malts could offer such clarity from the cask! *59.6%. sc. 280 bottles. Scotch Malt Whisky Society.*

UNSPECIFIED SINGLE GRAIN

⁘ **Lady of the Glen Twenty Four Year Old (89.5) n21.5** a stark, basic nose which screams: "I am grain!" Absolutely no pretentions or complexity whatsoever; **t23** mouth-filling, soft, with spiced maple syrup; that pleasant, synthetic cream filling in a Swiss roll; **f22.5** long, oily with a vapour trail of varying sugars, mainly muscovado; the spices are a gorgeous accompaniment; **b22.5** squelchy-sift Invergordon at its sugary best. *56%. Hannah Whisky Merchants.*

The Last Vatted Grain bott Nov 11 **(88.5) n23** some biting fizz to the vanilla; a procession of delicate and indelicate sugars; someone has added some banana and lemon for freshness; **t22** takes a bit of time to find a rhythm on delivery with the softer grains clashing a little with the firmer ones. Settles picturesquely with the sugars dominant and the spices playing along behind; **f21.5** a little bit of tired oak bitterness but the fussing spices, battling with the now muscovado-weighted sugars is a delight; **b22** not just sad that the term "vatted" is now pointlessly outlawed on the bottle. But also that half of the four grain distilleries used in this vatting are equally consigned to history. *46%. nc ncf. Compass Box.*

Scottish Spirits Single Grain 3 Years Old (Canned) **(82.5) n21 t21.5 f20 b20.** An absolutely standard, decent quality grain whisky with an attractive sweetness and latent youthful zesty fizz. Ill-served, however, by what I presume is caramel to give it a clichéd scotch look which dulls the finish in particular. In its natural form, this would have scored a lot higher. *40% (80 Proof).*

Vatted Grain

⁘ **Compass Box Hedonism** first fill American oak cask, bott 20 Feb 13 **(84) n22 t22 f19 b20.** Just too fat, too sweet and too bitter at the finale to work to great effect. Some decent oak on both nose and delivery, though. *43%. nc ncf. Compass Box Whisky Company.*

Compass Box Hedonism Maximus (93.5) n25 t22.5 f23 b23. Bourbon Maximus... *46%*

⁘ **Compass Box The Entertainer Limited Edition** Aug 12 **(88.5) n21.5** intriguing mix of butterscotch and smoke; **t22.5** rich bodied, early sugars parade themselves and a small layer of fruit pastilles; some mid ground cocoa begins to grow; **f22** slightly tangy but the vanilla is inevitable; **b22** a pleasant blend, though the tanginess is perhaps a little too sharp. *46%. Compass Box Whisky Company. 1000 bottles. Commissioned by Selfridges.*

Scottish Blends

For the first time in my career, I got a bit of an ear-bashing from a dissatisfied customer at one of my blind whisky tastings. And, of all things, it was because I had not included a blended Scotch in the line-up. My-oh-my! How times change.

Actually the guy was good natured about it, especially when I told him it was because the samples had been lost in transit, but his sense of loss was real. Apparently, he had attended one of my tastings a few years before, arriving as a self-confessed malt snob. He left converted to the blended whisky cause... to the extent it was now his favourite whisky style. As much as it is annoying when things go slightly wrong at an event, I still felt a thrill that more hardcore whisky lovers find experimenting in blends every bit as enjoyable as finding new malts. This implies blended scotch is as good as single malt. And, for my money, that is entirely the case; and if the blender is really doing his or her job, it should often be better. However, that job is getting a little harder each year. Once it was the standard joke that a sulphured sherry butt that had once been marked for a single malt brand would be dumped into a large blend where it would work on BP Chief executive Tony Hayward's "drop in the ocean" principle. However, there is now a lot more than just the odd off sherry butt finding their way in and blenders have to take guard that their blends are not being negatively affected. Certainly, during the course of writing the Whisky Bible I discovered this was becoming a much more common occurrence from the 2010 edition onwards. Indeed, one or two brands which a few years back I would have expected to pick up awards on a regular basis have been hit badly: disappointing and a great loss to whisky lovers.

However, Ballantine's 17 – a blend that has been on a higher plane than most other world whiskies for a very long time – again stood out as the best blended scotch I'd tasted all year. Over time it has, by necessity, had to vaguely change style but quality has been a constant.

Over 90 out of every 100 bottles of Scotch consumed is a blend, and therefore rather common. That has brought about some cold-shouldering from certain elitist whisky lovers who convince themselves that a blend must be inferior. Well, not in my books. In fact, perhaps the opposite is true. Until you get to grips with blends you may well be entitled to regard yourself knowledgeable in single malts, but not in Scotch as a whole. Blends should be the best that Scotland can offer, because with a blend you have the ability to create any degree of complexity. And surely balance and complexity are the cornerstones of any great whisky, irrespective of type.

Of course there are some pretty awful blends created simply as a commodity with little thought going into their structure – just young whiskies, sometimes consisting of stock that is of dubious quality and then coloured up to give some impression of age. Yes, you are more likely to find that among blends than malts and for this reason the poorest blends can be pretty nasty. And, yes, they contain grain. Too often, though, grain is regarded as a kind of whisky leper – not to be touched under any circumstances. Some writers dismiss grain as "neutral" and "cheap", thus putting into the minds of the uninitiated the perception of inferiority.

But there really is nothing inferior about blends. In fact, whilst researching The Bible, I have to say that my heart misses more than one beat usually when I received a sample of a blend I have never found before. Why? Well, with single malts each distillery produces a style that can be found within known parameters. With a blend, anything is possible. There are myriad styles of malts to choose from and they will react slightly differently with certain grains.

For that reason, perhaps, I have marked blends a little more strictly and tighter than I have single malts. Because blends, by definition, should offer more.

The most exciting blends, like White Horse 12 (why, oh, why is that, like Old Parr 18, restricted mainly to Japan?) Grant's and the perennially glorious Ballantine's show bite, character and attitude. Silk and charm are to be appreciated. But after a long, hard day is anything better than a blend that is young and confident enough to nip and nibble at your throat on its way down and then throw up an array of flavours and shapes to get your taste-buds round? Certainly, I have always found blends ultimately more satisfying than malts. Especially when the balance, like this year's Scotch Blend of the Year, Ballantine's 17, simply caresses your soul. And they do more: they paint pictures on the palate, flavour-scapes of extraordinary subtlety and texture. No two bottles are ever exactly the same, but they are usually close enough and further illustrate the fascination of a beautifully orchestrated variation on a theme.

With Blended Scotch the range and possibilities are limitless. All it takes is for the drinker not just to use his or her nose and taste-buds. But also an open mind.

Scottish Blends

"10 Years and a Bit" Blended Scotch (84) n21.5 t22 f20 b20.5. Matured in oloroso and finished in a Cognac quartercask. Explains why this blend lurches drunkenly all over the palate. Enough honeycomb, though, for a pleasant few minutes 42%. *Qualityworld, Denmark.*

100 Pipers (74) n18.5 t18 f19 b18.5. An improved blend, even with a touch of spice to the finish. I get the feeling the grains are a bit less aggressive than they for so long were. I'd let you know for sure, if only I could get through the caramel. 40%. *Chivas.*

Aberdour Piper (88.5) n22 t23 f21.5 b22. Always great to find a blend that appears to have upped the stakes in the quality department. Clean, refreshing with juicy young Speysiders at times simply showing off. 40%. *Hayman Distillers.*

Adelphi Private Stock Loyal Old Mature (88) n21 t23 f22 b22. A very attractive number, especially for those with a slightly sweet tooth. 40%

Antiquary 12 Years Old (92) n23.5 t23.5 f23 b22 A staggering about turn for a blend which, for a very long time, has flown the Speyside flag. 40%. *Tomatin Distillery.*

Antiquary 21 Years Old (93) n23.5 t23.5 f23 b23 A huge blend, scoring a magnificent 93 points. But I have tasted better, and another sample, direct from the blending lab, came with even greater complexity and less apparent caramel. A top-notch blend of rare distinction. 43%

Antiquary 30 Years Old (86) n22 t23 f20 b21. Decidedly odd fare but the eccentric nose and early delivery are sublime, with silky complexity tumbling over the palate. 46%

Antiquary Finest (79.5) n20 t21 f19 b19.5. Pleasantly sweet and plump with the accent on the quick early malt delivery. 40%. *Tomatin Distillery.*

Arden House Scotch Whisky (86) n19.5 t22 f22.5 b22. Another great bit of fun from the Co-op. Very closely related to their Finest Blend, though this has, for some reason or other, a trace of a slightly fatter, mildly more earthy style. If only they would ditch the caramel and let those sweet malts and grains breathe! 40%. *Co-Operative Group.*

Asda Blended Scotch Whisky (76.5) n19 t21 f17.5 b19. A scattergun approach with sweet, syrupy notes hitting the palate early and hard. Beware the rather bitter finish, though. 40%

Asda Extra Special 12 Years Old (78) n19 t21 f19 b19. Pleasantish but dragged down by the dreaded S word. 40%. *Glenmorangie for Asda.*

The Bailie Nicol Jarvie (B.N.J) (95) n24 the sharpest barley has been taken to a barley-sharpening shop and painstakingly sharpened; this is pretty sharp stuff...the citrus gangs together with the fresh grass to form a dew which is pretty well...er... sharp...; t24 mouth-watering, eye-closingly, mouth-puckeringly sharp delivery with the barley pinging off the tautest grain you can imagine; f23 softens with a touch of vanilla and toffee; the late run from the citrus is a masterpiece of whisky closing; b24 I know my criticism of BNJ, historically one of my favourite blends, over the last year or two has been taken to heart by Glenmorangie. Delighted to report that they have responded: the blend has been fixed and is back to its blisteringly brilliant, ultra-mouth-watering self. Someone's sharpened their ideas up. 40%

Ballantine's Aged 12 Years (84.5) n22.5 t22 f19 b21. Attractive but odd fellow, this, with a touch of juniper to the nose and furry bitter marmalade on the finish. But some excellent barley-cocoa moments, too. 43%. *Chivas.* ☉

Ballantine's 12 Years Old (87) n21 t22 f21 b23. The kind of old-fashioned, mildly moody blend Colonel Farquharson-Smythe (retired) might have recognised when relaxing at the 19th hole back in the early '50s. Too good for a squirt of soda, mind. 40%. *Chivas Bros.*

Ballantine's 17 Years Old (97.5) n24.5 deft grain and honey plus teasing salty peat; ultra high quality with bourbon and pear drops offering the thrust; a near unbelievable integration with gooseberry juice offering a touch of sharpness muted by watered golden syrup; t24 immediately mouthwatering with maltier tones clambering over the graceful cocoa-enriched grain; the degrees of sweetness are varied but near perfection; just hints of smoke here and there; f24 lashings of vanilla and cocoa on the fade; drier with a faint spicey, vaguely smoky buzz; has become longer with more recent bottlings with the most subtle oiliness imaginable; b25 now only slightly less weighty than of old. After a change of style it has comfortably reverted back to its sophisticated, mildly erotic old self. One of the most beautiful, complex and stunningly structured whiskies ever created. Truly the epitome of great Scotch. 43%. ☉

⠿ **Ballantine's Aged 17 Years Limited Edition Miltonduff Signature Distillery** (91.5) n22.5 gooseberry tart sans sugar; dry and pretty heavy handed with the fruit; t24 much more like it: the first eight or nine waves are the stuff of greatness. The mouth feel nudges perfection and there is a real coppery weight here, too. The malt content appears to be pretty high as barley sugar abounds and links early with the liquorice and hickory; f21.5 reverts to a fruitier cannon, a little muffled and fuzzy; b23.5 the usual alto libretto of the Ballantine's 17 has been replaced here by a much weightier composition, even though the usual subtle smoke is missing. Using sherry butts is to enter a minefield in this day and age, one I'm afraid, there is no clear path through. The ones here are of mixed quality, but the overall effect is pleasing. 43%

Ballantine's Aged 21 Years (93) n24 t24 f22 b23 One of the reasons I think I have loved the Ballantine's range over the years is because it is a blenders' blend. In other words, you get the feeling that they have made as much, and probably more, as possible from the stocks available and made complexity and balance the keystones to the whisky. That is still the case, except you find now that somehow, although part of a larger concern, it appears that the spectrum of flavours is less wide, though what has been achieved with those available remains absolutely top drawer. This is truly great whisky, but it has changed in style as blends, especially of this age, cannot help but doing. 43% ☉

Ballantine's Aged 30 Years (94) n23.5 satisfying interplay between spiced grape and vanilla-clad smoke; t24 quite sublime: the delivery simply melts in the mouth. Mainly grain on show early, again with all the attendant vanilla, then a juicier network of sharper barley and fruit. The weight is outstanding; f23.5 long, with a real grain-malt tug of war. Spices persist and the vanilla ups a gear; b23.5 quite a different animal to that which I tasted last year...and the year before. Having come across it in three different markets, I each time noted a richer, more balanced product: less a bunch of old casks being brought together but more a sculpted piece from preferred materials. That said, I still get the feeling that this is a work in progress: a Kenny Jackett-style building of a team bit by bit, so that each compartment is improved when it is possible, but not to the detriment of another and, vitally, balance is maintained. 43% ☉

Ballantine's Christmas Reserve (72) n18 t19 f17 b18. Not quite what I asked from Santa. A rare sulphury slip up in the Christmas day snow from the Ballantine's stable. 40%

Ballantine's Finest (96) n24 a playful balance and counter-balance between grains, lighter malts and a gentle smokiness. The upped peat of recent years has given an extra weight and charm that had been missing; t24 sublime delivery: the mouthfeel couldn't be better had your prayers been answered; velvety and brittle grains combine to get the most out of the juicy malts: a lot of chewing to get through here; f23.5 soft, gentle, yet retains its weight and shape with a re-emergence of smoke and a gristy sweetness to counter the gentle vanillas and cocoa from the oak b24.5 as a standard blend this is coming through as a major work of art. Each time I taste this the weight has gone up a notch or two more and the sweetness has increased to balance out with the drier grain elements. Take a mouthful of this and experience the work of a blender very much at the top of his game. 40%. Chivas Bros. ☉

Ballantine's Limited brown bottle, bott code D03518 (94.5) n23.5 a gentle patchwork quilt of fruit and surprisingly nippy spices. The odd stewed greengage chimes in, as well as toffee apple. And there is something of the early opened bakers too, with that sweet smell of warm cakes and pies...; t24 obscenely beautiful delivery, perhaps bordering on the delivery of the year. When you taste as many whiskies as I, you sometimes forget that it is, under exceptional circumstances, possible to create a mouth-feel so soft; icing sugars and diluted golden syrup offer moisture to the burnt raisin; f23 a very slight bitter fade but there are now oaky vanillas to contend with, though they no more than breeze around the palate; b24 when it comes to Ballantine's I am beginning to run out of superlatives. The last time I tasted Limited, I remember being disappointed by the un-Ballantine's-like bitter finish. Well, from nose to finale, there is a barely perceptible trace of a rogue cask costing half a point from each stage: indeed, it may have cost it World Whisky of the Year. But so magnificent are all those keeping it company there has been no such falling at the last hurdle here. This bottle, rather than finding its way back into my warehouse library, will be living at my home for offering an ethereal quality unmatched by any other whisky in the world. 43%. Chivas.

Ballantine's Limited 75cl royal blue bottle (89) n22 t24 f21 b22. Hadn't tasted this for a little while but maintains its early style and quite glorious delivery. 43%

Ballantine's Master's (82) n21 t22 f19 b20. Excellent lively grain and chewy malt, but the always suspect, grain-drizzled finish has become even more nondescript in recent bottlings. 40%

Ballantine's Rare Limited (89.5) n23.5 t22.5 f21.5 b22 A heavier, more mouth watering blend than the "Bluebottle" version. 43%. ncf. Chivas.

Barley Barony (83) n21.5 t21 f20 b20.5. A faintly furry finish follows from a firm, fruity front. 40%. Quality Spirits International.

Bell's Original (91) n23 t22.5 f22.5 b23 Your whisky sleuth came across the new version for the first time in the bar of a London theatre back in December 2009 during the interval of "The 39 Steps". To say I was impressed and pleasantly surprised is putting it mildly. And with the whisky, too, which is a massive improvement on the relatively stagnant 8-year-old especially with the subtle extra smoky weight. If the blender asks me: "Did I get it right, Sir?" then the answer has to be a resounding "yes". 40%

Bells 8 Years Old (85) n21.5 t22.5 f20 b21. Some mixed messages here: on one hand it is telling me that it has been faithful to some of the old Bells distilleries – hence a slight dirty note, especially on the finish. On the other, there are some sublime specks of complexity and weight. Quite literally the rough and the smooth. 40%. Diageo.

Benmore (74) n19 t19 f18 b18. Underwhelming to the point of being nondescript. 40%

Berrys' Blue Hanger 30 Years Old 3rd Release bott 2007 **(90.5)** n23 t22.5 f22.5 b22.5 Much improved version on the last, closer to the original in every respect. Excellent. 45.6%. Berry Bros & Rudd.

Big "T" 5 Years Old (75) n19 t20 f18 b18. Still doesn't have the finesse of old and clatters about the tastebuds charmlessly. 40%. Tomatin Distillery.

Black & White (91) n22 t23 f22.5 b23.5 This one hasn't gone to the dogs: quite the opposite. I always go a bit misty-eyed when I taste something this traditional: the crisp grains work to maximum effect in reflecting the malts. A classic of its type. 40%. Diageo.

Black Bottle (74.5) n18 t20.5 f17 b18. Barely a shadow of its once masterful, great self. 40%. Burn Stewart.

Black Bottle 10 Years Old (89) n22 t23 f22 b23 A stupendous blend of weight and poise, but possessing little of the all-round steaming, rampaging sexuality of the younger version... but like the younger version showing a degree less peat: here perhaps even two. Not, I hope, the start of a new trend under the new owners. 40%

Black Dog 12 Years Old (92) n21 t23 f24 b24. Offering genuine sophistication and élan. This minor classic will probably require two or three glass-fulls before you take the bait... 42.8%

Black Dog Century (89) n21 t23 f23 b22. I adore this style of no-nonsense, full bodied bruising blend which amid the muscle offers exemplary dexterity and finesse. What entertainment in every glass!! 42.8%. McDowell & Co Ltd. Blended in Scotland/Bottled in India.

The Black Douglas bott code 340/06/183 **(84)** n19 t20 f23 b22. Don't expect raptures of mind-bending complexity. But on the other hand, enough chewability and spice buzz here to make for a genuinely decent whisky, especially on the excellent finish. Not dissimilar to a bunch of blends you might have found in the 1950s. 40%. Foster's Group, Australia.

The Black Douglas Aged 8 Years bott code 348/06/187 **(79)** n20 t21 f19 b19. Slightly lacking for an 8-y-o: probably duller than its non-age-statement brother because of an extra dollop of caramel. 40%. Foster's Group, Australia.

The Black Douglas Aged 12 Years "The Black Reserve" bott code 347/06/188 **(87)** n21 t21 f23 b22. The toffee does its best to wreck the show – but there are simply too many good things going on to succeed. The slight smoke to the nose delights and the honeycomb middle really does star. 40%. Foster's Group, Australia.

Black Grouse (94) n23 outwardly a hefty nose, but patience is rewarded with a glorious Demerara edge to the malt and oak: superb, understated stature; t24 again the smoke appears to be at the fore, but it's not. Rather, a silky sweet delivery also covers excellent cocoa and spice f23 so gentle, with waves of smoke and oak lapping on an oaky shore. Brilliant... b24 a superb return to a peaty blend for Edrington for the first time since they sold Black Bottle. Not entirely different from that brand, either, from the Highland Distillers days with the smokiness being superbly couched by sweet malts. A real treasure. 40%

The Black Grouse Alpha Edition (72.5) n17 t19.5 f17 b18. Dreadfully sulphured. 40%

Black Knight (85.5) n21 t22 f21 b21.5. More of a White Knight as it peacefully goes about its business. Not many taste buds slain, but just love the juicy charge. 43%. Quality Spirits Int.

Black Ram Aged 12 Years (85) n21 t23 f21 b20. An upfront blend that gives its all in the chewy delivery. Some major oak in there but it's all ultra soft toffee and molasses towards the finish. 40%. Vinprom Peshtera, Bulgaria.

Blend No. 888 (86.5) n20 t21.5 f23 b22. A good old-fashioned, rip-roaring, nippy blend with a fudge-honey style many of a certain age will fondly remember from the 60s and 70s. Love it! 40%. The House of MacDuff.

:·: **Boxes Blend (90)** n22.5 soft smoke, shaved sandalwood and black liquorice; t23.5 mega sweet delivery couched in a silky amalgamation of manuka honey and dryer black strap molasses; the vanillas form towards the middle; f21 a rougher finale as it dries. Remarkable for its entire lack of spice, which seemed promised on the nose; b23 a box which gets plenty of ticks. 40.9%. ncf. Master of Malt.

Broadford (78.5) n19 t19.5 f20 b20. Boringly inoffensive. Toffee anyone? 40%. Burn Stewart.

Buchanan's De Luxe 12 Years Old (82) n18 t21 f22 b21. The nose shows more than just a single fault and the character simply refuses to get out of second gear. Certainly pleasant, and some of the chocolate notes towards the end are gorgeous. But just not the normal brilliant show-stopper! 40%. Diageo.

Buchanan's Red Seal (90) n22 t23 f22 b23 Exceptional, no-frills blend whose apparent simplicity paradoxically celebrates its complexity. 40%. Diageo.

Budgen's Scotch Whisky Finely Blended (85) n21 t22 f21 b21. A sweet, chunky blend offering no shortage of dates, walnuts, spice and toffee. A decent one to mull over. 40%

Callander 12 Years Old (86) n21 t22 f21.5 b21.5. No shortage of malt sparkle and even a touch of tangy salt. Very attractive and enjoyable without ripping up trees. 46.3%. Burn Stewart.

Campbeltown Loch Aged 15 Years (88) n22.5 t22.5 f21 b22 Well weighted with the age in no hurry to arrive. 40%. Springbank Distillers.

Castle Rock (81) n20 t20.5 f20 b20.5. Clean and juicy entertainment. *40%*

Catto's Aged 25 Years (87.5) n23 t22.5 f20.5 b21.5. A hugely enjoyable yet immensely frustrating dram. The higher fruit and spice notes are a delight, but it all appears to be played out in a padded cell of cream caramel. One assumes the natural oak caramels have gone into overdrive. Had they not, we would have had a supreme blend scoring well into the 90s. *40%*

Catto's Deluxe 12 Years Old (79.5) n20 t21.5 f18 b20. Refreshing and spicy in part, but still a note in there which doesn't quite work. *40%. Inverhouse Distillers.*

Catto's Rare Old Scottish (92) n23.5 t23.5 f22 b23 Currently one of my regular blends to drink at home. Astonishingly old-fashioned with a perfect accent on clean Speyside and crisp grain. In the last year or so it has taken on a sublime sparkle on the nose and palate. An absolutely masterful whisky which both refreshes and relaxes. *40%. James Catto & Co.*

Chequers Deluxe (78.5) n19.5 t20 f19 b20. Charm, elegance, sophistication...not a single sign of any of them. Still if you want a bit of rough and tumble, just the job. *40%. Diageo.*

Chivas Regal Aged 12 Years (83.5) n20.5 t22.5 f20 b20.5. Chewy fruit toffee. Silky grain mouth-feel with a toasty, oaky presence. *40%. Chivas.*

Chivas Regal Aged 18 Years (73.5) n17.5 t20 f17.5 b18.5. The nose is dulled by a whiff of sulphur and confirmation that all is not well comes with the disagreeably dry, bitter finish. Early on in the delivery some apples and spices show promise but it is an unequal battle against the caramel and off notes. *40%*

Chivas Regal 25 Years Old (95) n23 exotic fruit of the first order: some pretty serious age here, seemingly older than the 25 years; t23.5 mesmerisingly two-toned, with a beautiful delivery of velvety grains contrasting stunningly with the much firmer, cleaner malts. Softly chewable, with a gentle spice fizz as the vanilla begins to mount; unbelievably juicy and mouth-watering despite its advanced age; f24 long, wonderfully textured and deft; some cocoa underlines the oak involvement, but there is not once a single hint of over-aging; b24.5 unadulterated class where the grain-malt balance is exemplary and the deft intertwining of well-mannered oak and elegant barley leaves you demanding another glass. Brilliant! *40%*

Clan Campbell (86.5) n21.5 t22.5 f21 b21.5. I'll wager that if I could taste this whisky before the colouring is added it would be scoring into the 90s. Not a single off note; a sublime early array of Speysidey freshness but dulls at the end. *40%. Chivas.*

Clan Gold 3 Year Old (95) n23.5 shimmering elegance; delicate enough to allow both grain and malt a clear voice with a light mintiness and seasoned celery well at home with those gently honeyed vanilla-oaked notes; t24 an eye closing, mouth-puckering delivery as those fabulous, sharp Speyside-style barley notes get to work. Beyond the obvious malt come several layers of spices of varying intensity and a much drier oak signature; f23.5 seemingly dry at first but some late crystalised demerara and waves of pristine barley ensure a sublime balance; b24 a blend-drinkers blend which will also slay the hearts of Speyside single malt lovers. For me, this is love at first sip... *40%*

Clan Gold Blended 15 Years Old (91) n21.5 t23 f23.5 b23 An unusual blend for the 21st century, which steadfastly refuses to blast you away with over the top flavour and/or aroma profiles and instead depends on subtlety and poise despite the obvious richness of flavour. The grains make an impact but only by creating the frame in which the more complex notes can be admired. *40%*

Clan Gold Blended 18 Years Old (94.5) n23 a light background coating of dusty oak but the freshness of the barley startles and pleases. Its trademark is the crushed green apple of a whisky almost half its age though the softening custardy sweetness is an unmistakable sign of antiquity; t24 bristles on the palate: all kinds of peppery spices lead the malty surge. Gloriously mouthwatering: the lushness of the grains make the hairs stand on end as the mouth feel is the stuff of dreams. Apples lead the fruity fray but that intense barley is never far away; a delightful formation of muscovado sugars, then more apples...; f23.5 chewy, clean and truly rejoicing in the complex dovetailing of the malt and chalk. The oak remains refined throughout, the grains polishing the last of the fading malts. The smattering of light muscovado sugar continues until near the end. Then the slightly drier oaks reintroduce the now intense spices apparent on delivery; b24 almost the ultimate preprandial whisky with its at once robust yet delicate working over of the taste buds by the carefully muzzled juiciness of the malt. This is the real deal: a truly classy act which at first appears to wallow in a sea of simplicity but then bursts out into something very much more complex and alluring. About as clean and charming an 18-year-old blend as you are likely to find. *40%*

Clan MacGregor (92) n22 t24 f23 b23 Just gets better and better. Now a true classic and getting up there with Grant's. *43%*

Clan Murray Rare Old (84) n18 t23 f21 b22. The wonderful malt delivery on the palate is totally incongruous with the weak, nondescript nose. Glorious, mouth-watering complexity on the arrival, though. Maybe it needs a Murray to bring to perfection... *40%. Benriach Distillery.*

Clansman (80.5) n20.5 t21 f19 b20. Sweet, grainy and soft. *40%. Loch Lomond.*

Clansman (78.5) n20 t21.5 f18 b19. Plenty of weight, oil and honey-ginger. Some bitterness, too. 43%. *Loch Lomond Distillers.*

The Claymore (85) n19 t22 f22 b22. These days you are run through by spices. The blend is pure Paterson in style with guts etc, which is not something you always like to associate with a Claymore; some delightful muscovado sugar at the death. Get the nose sorted and a very decent and complex whisky is there to be had. 40%. *Whyte & Mackay Distillers Ltd.*

Compass Box Asyla 1st fill American oak ex-bourbon, bott May 10 (93) n24 t24 f22.5 b23.5 If you can hear a purring noise, it is me tasting this... 40%. nc ncf.

Compass Box Asyla Marriage married for nine months in an American oak barrel (88) n22 t23 f21 b22 A lovely blend, but can't help feeling that this was one marriage that lasted too long. 43.6%. *Compass Box Whisky for La Maison du Whisky in commemoration of their 50th Anniversary.*

⠿ **Compass Box Delilah's Limited Release** American oak, bott Jul 13 (89.5) n23 pulped sharron fruit plus a salty toasty tannin nip; t22 teasing, tickling delivery: a brief wave of malt passes through but the grains score highest and loudest. Those are silk soft and allow the brighter sugars to outpoint the more docile vanilla; f22 those sugars now engage spice cordially, allowing the citrus to sing freely at the death; b22.5 a clean and satisfying blend which ramps up the sugars when need be. I'll be surprised if you get to the point where you couldn't take any more... 40%. 6400 bottles.

⠿ **Compass Box The Entertainer Limited Edition** Aug 12 (88.5) n21.5 intriguing mix of butterscotch and smoke; t22.5 rich bodied, early sugars parade themselves and a small layer of fruit pastilles; some mid ground cocoa begins to grow; f22 slightly tangy but the vanilla is inevitable; b22 a pleasant blend, though the tanginess is perhaps a little too sharp. 46%. *Compass Box Whisky Company. 1000 bottles. Commissioned by Selfridges.*

Compass Box Great King St. Artist's Blend (93) n24 now there's a way to start the day: stunningly enticing with every nuance of the delicate young barley laid bare. A light coating of bourbon oakiness is enhanced by the scrumptious cinnamon apple pie; t23 even as a hardened pro, I find it is difficult to spit this one. The delivery is firm, juicy and compelling; few blends these days are half so salivating! The grains try not to hide and weigh in with some lovely cocoa and bourbon stratum, allowing the barley to spread the grassy freshness gospel; good weight throughout; f22.5 just a slight fault here: a little milkiness from a tired bourbon cask, a distant echo on delivery now makes itself heard, but has the good grace to remain in the background as the spices and late Demerara and liquorice notes hold court; b23.5 the nose of this uncoloured and non-chill filtered whisky is not dissimilar to some better known blends before they have colouring added to do its worst. A beautiful young thing this blend: nubile, naked and dangerously come hither. Compass Box's founder John Glaser has done some memorable work in recent years, though one has always had the feeling that he has still been learning his trade, sometimes forcing the issue a little too enthusiastically. Here, there is absolutely no doubting that he has come of age as a blender. 43%. nc ncf.

⠿ **Compass Box Great King St. New York Blend** bott Aug 12 (89.5) n22.5 lovely minty smoke hiding behind the tangy orange skirts; t23.5 excellent weight thanks to light oils and broad sugars; pleasing juices mingle with the silky grain; f21.5 good length with the spices travelling with the smoke; a little late bitterness; b22 another thoughtful blend with Compass Box making good use of Caol Ila-style oiliness. 46%. nc ncf. 1,840 bottles. USA exclusive.

Consulate (89) n22 t22 f22.5 b22.5. One assumes this beautifully balanced dram was designed to accompany Passport in the drinks cabinet. I suggest if buying them, use Visa. 40%

Co-operative Finest Blend (92.5) n23.5 t23 f22.5 b23.5 A fabulous and fascinating blend which has divested itself of its peaty backbone and instead packed the core with honey. Not the same heavyweight blend of old, but still one which is to be taken seriously – and straight – by those looking for a classic whisky of the old school. 40%

Co-operative Premium Scotch 5 Years Old (91.5) n22 t24 f22.5 b23 From the nose I thought this blend had nosedived emphatically from when I last tasted it. However the delivery remains the stuff of legend. And though it has shifted emphasis and style to marked degree, there is no disputing its overall clout and entertainment value remains very high. 40%

Craigellachie Hotel Quaich Bar Range (81) n20 t21 f20 b20. A delightful malt delivery early on, but doesn't push on with complexity as perhaps it might. 40%

Crawford's (83.5) n19 t21 f22 b21.5. A lovely spice display helps overcome the caramel. 40%.

Cutty Black (83) n20 t23 f19 b21. Both nose and finish are dwarfed and flung into the realms of ordinariness by the magnificently substantial delivery. Whilst there is a taint to the nose, its richness augers well for what is to follow; and you won't be disappointed. At times it behaves like a Highland Park with a toffeed spine, such is the richness and depth of the honey and dates and complexity of the grain-vanilla background. But those warning notes on the nose are there for good reason and the finish tells you why. Would not be surprised to see this score into the 90s on a different bottling day. 40%. *Edrington.*

Cutty Sark (78) n19 t21 f19 b19. Crisp and juicy. But a nipping furriness, too. 40%

Cutty Sark Aged 12 Years (92) n22 t24 f23 b23 At last! Cutty 12 at full sail...and blended whisky rarely looks any more beautiful! 40%. Edrington.

Cutty Sark Aged 15 Years (82) n19 t22 f20 b21. Attempts to take the honey route. But seriously dulled by toffee and the odd sulphured cask. 40%. Edrington.

Cutty Sark Aged 18 Years (88) n22 t22 f22 b22 Lost the subtle fruitiness which worked so well. Easy-going and attractive. 43%

Cutty Sark Aged 25 Years (91) n21 t23.5 f22.5 b23 Magnificent, though not quite flawless, this whisky is as elegant and effortlessly powerful as the ship after which the brand was named... 45.7% Berry Bros & Rudd.

⋄⋄⋄ **Cutty Sark Storm (81.5)** n18 t23.5 f19.5 b20.5. When the wind is set fair, which is mainly on delivery and for the first six or seven flavour waves which follow, we really do have an astonishingly beautiful blend, seemingly high in malt content and really putting the accent on ulmo honey and marzipan: a breath-taking combination. This is assisted by a gorgeous weight to the silky body and a light raspberry jam moment to the late arriving Ecuadorian cocoa. All magnificent. However, the blend, as Cutty sadly tends to, sails into sulphurous seas. 40%. Edrington.

Demijohn's Finest Blended Scotch Whisky (88) n21 t22 f23 b22 A fun, characterful blend that appears to have above the norm malt. Enjoy. 40%. Adelphi.

Dew of Ben Nevis Blue Label (82) n19 t22 f20 b21. The odd off-key note is handsomely outnumbered by deliciously complex mocha and demerara tones. Ditch the caramel and you'd have a sizzler! 40%. Ben Nevis Distillery. Replacement for Dew of Ben Nevis Millennium Blend.

Dew of Ben Nevis Special Reserve (85) n19 t21 f23 b22. A much juicier blend than of old, still sporting some bruising and rough patches. But that kind of makes this all the more attractive, with the caramel mixing with some fuller malts to provide a date and nuts effect which makes for a grand finale. 40%. Ben Nevis Distillery.

Dew of Ben Nevis Supreme Selection (77) n18 t20 f20 b19. Some lovely raspberry jam swiss roll moments here. But the grain could be friendlier, especially on the nose. 40%

Dewar House Experimental Batch No. A39 Age 17 Years sherry finish, cask no. 001, bott 17 Jul 12 (96) n24 faultless grape, but not overly heavy or too sweet. Instead a busy procession of spices, some of them quite peppery and nippy, binds rather beautifully with a delicate vanilla, date and walnut base; t24 you feel you have been flung to the bed and your hands tied while wave upon wave of sensual flavours wash over you, one moment juicy and soft, the next attacking with as much controlled aggression as you can withstand...and all the times the plums and dates and walnuts continue on their ultra-rich fruitcake way; f23.5 you'd expect – demand – a long finish after all that. And you get it thanks to a sublime mix of all those delicate fruits. Alas, a minor build up of sulphur has accumulated, knocking off half a point or so. But if you keep on drinking this stuff, you don't get to the point of noticing...; b24.5 like old Tommy Dewar himself, a unique and classy, classy act. To be honest, when I saw "finished in sherry" on the label I had got to the point this year where I was terrified of opening the bottle. But this shows how it should be done: I'd like to shake the blender by the hand! This was exactly the whisky the scotch industry needed at this precise moment, well that vague residue on the finish apart...(one that probably robbed it of World Whisky of the Year). Even so, unforgettable and truly magnificent. And as experiments go, it knocks the relatively unimportant goings on at Cern into a cocked hat... 58.9%. sc. 30 bottles.

Dewar's Special Reserve 12 Years Old (84) n20 t23 f19 b22. Some s... you know what... has crept onboard here and duffed up the nose and finish. A shame because elements of the delivery and background balance shows some serious blending went on here. 40%

Dewar's 18 Years Old (93) n23 t24 f22.5 b23.5 Here is a classic case of where great blends are not all about the malt. The grain plays in many ways the most significant role here, as it is the perfect backdrop to see the complexity of the malt at its clearest. Simply magnificent blending with the use of flawless whisky. 43%. John Dewar & Sons.

Dewar's 18 Year Old Founders Reserve (86.5) n22.5 t22 f20.5 b21.5. A big, blustering dram which doesn't stint on the fruit. A lovely, thin seam of golden syrup runs through the piece, but the dull, aching finale is somewhat out of character. 40%. John Dewar & Sons.

Dewar's Signature (93) n24 t23.5 f22 b23.5. A slight departure in style, with the fruit becoming just a little sharper and juicier. Top range blending and if the odd butt could be weeded out, this'd be an award winner for sure. 43%

Dewar's White Label (78.5) n19 t21.5 f19 b19. When on song, one of my preferred daily blends. But not when like this, with its accentuated bitter-sweet polarisation. 40%

⋄⋄⋄ **Dhoon Glen** (85.5) n21 t22 f21 b21.5 Full of big flavours, broad grainy strokes and copious amounts of dark sugar including toffee. 40%. Lombard Brands Ltd.

Dimple 12 Years Old (86.5) n22 t22 f21.5 b21. Lots of sultana while the spice adds aggression. 40%. Diageo.

Dimple 15 Years Old (87.5) n20 t21 f24 b22.5. Only on the late middle and finish does this particular flower unfurl and to magnificently complex effect. The texture of the grains in particular delight while the strands of barley entwine. A type of treat for the more technically minded of the serious blend drinkers among you. *40%. Diageo.*

Drummer (81) n20 t21 f20 b20. Big toffee. Rolos...? *40%. Inver House Distillers.*

Drummer Aged 5 Years (83) n19 t22.5 f20.5 b21. The nose may beat a retreat but it certainly gets on a roll when those fabulous sharp notes hit the palate. However, it deserves some stick as the boring fudge finishes in a cymbal of too much toffee. *40%. Inver House.*

Duncan Taylor Auld Blended Aged 35 Years dist pre 70 (93) n23 t24 f22 b24 An infinitely better dram than previous bottlings, due mainly to the fact that the dangers of old oak appear to have been compensated for. *46%. 131 bottles.*

Duncan Taylor Collection Black Bull 12 Year Old (88.5) n22.5 t22.5 f21.5 b22 Black Bulls enjoy a reputation for being dangerous. So does this: once you pour yourself a glass, it is difficult not to have another...and another... *50%. Duncan Taylor & Co Ltd.*

Duncan Taylor Collection Black Bull Deluxe Blend Aged 30 Years (93) n24 t24 f22 b23. This pedigree Black Bull doesn't pull its horns in... *50%. Duncan Taylor.*

Duncan Taylor Collection Rarest of the Rare Deluxe Blend 33 Years Old (94) n24 a fusion of rich bourbon and old Canadian characteristics beefed up further with diced exotic fruit and a dash of ancient Demerara rum; t24 the bourbon hits the track running, closely followed by some silky barley couched in velvet grain; invariably some spices pitch in to ramp up the complexity even further; f22 no great length, but no off notes, either. Instead the oak adds an unsweetened custardy grace; b23 outstanding and astounding blended whisky. An absolute must for blend lovers...especially those with a bourbony bent. *43.4%*

Duncan Taylor Collection Black Bull 40 Year Old batch 1 (86.5) n23 t21 f21.5 b21. Almost certainly whisky which had dipped below 40%abv in the cask has been included in this blend. That would account for the occasional spasm of ultra intense natural caramels, a kind of tell-tale fingerprint indicating this is likely to have been done. The nose is exotic fruit; the delivery is a battle to keep the oak at bay. One which is happily won. *40.2%*

Duncan Taylor Collection Black Bull 40 Years Old batch 2 (94) n23 a barrel-load of exotic fruitiness that is not unexpected from a whisky of this antiquity; light but with banana and custard the main theme; t24 ridiculously fresh delivery for its massive age with a brilliant eye-watering quality to the barley. Slightly coppery, too; f23 virtually no ill effect from the cask, as one might expect from something this delicate. Instead, we are treated to a touch of freshly squeezed orange alongside the lightly creamed mocha; b24 just sit back and marvel at something so old...yet so young at heart. *41.9%. Duncan Taylor & Co. 957 bottles.*

Duncan Taylor Collection Black Bull Special Reserve batch 1 (86) n21 t22.5 f21 b21.5. Juicy in just the right areas. Some charming spice and vanilla, too. *46.6%*

⁙ **Duncan Taylor Black Bull Special Reserve Batch 2** (87.5) n23 thick set and muscular – Bullish, in fact – with a husky Valpolicella grapiness amid the blackcurrant and butterscotch; t23.5 the sugars delay their entry by a few seconds, allowing a curious, dullish toffee delivery; the molten muscavdo sugars embrace the growing spice, though chewy toffee fills the late mid ground; f19 a lingering, furry blur to the toffeed finish; b22 has seriously upped the fruit and spice from the original version to make for a compelling blend. *50%*

⁙ **Duncan Taylor Smokin'** (85) n21 t22 f21 b21. On one hand phenolic, on the other surprisingly lightweight. Attractively sweet and friendly, though. *40%. Duncan Taylor.*

The Famous Grouse (89) n22 t23 f21.5 b22.5 It almost seems that Grouse is, by degrees, moving from its traditional position of a light blend to something much closer to Grant's as a middle-weighted dram. Again the colouring has been raised a fraction and now the body and depth have been adjusted to follow suit. Have to say that this is one very complex whisky these days: I had spotted slight changes when drinking it socially, but this was the first time I had a chance to sit down and professionally analyse what was happening in the glass. A fascinating and tasty bird, indeed. *40%. Edrington Group.*

⁙ **The Famous Grouse Aged 16 Years Special 2013 Edition** (84) n22 t22 f19 b21. A completely different type of Grouse which on one hand offers a pretty comprehensive guide to all the sugar shelves, yet somehow manages, for all its apparent esters, to bitter out violently at the finish. Intriguing, to put it mildly. *40%. Edrington Group.*

The Famous Grouse Gold Reserve (90) n23.5 t23 f21.5 b22 Great to know the value of the Gold Reserve is going up...as should the strength of this blend. The old-fashioned 40% just ain't enough carats. *40%. Edrington Group.*

The Famous Jubilee (83.5) n21.5 t22.5 f18.5 b21. A heavyweight, stodgy, toffee-laden kind of blend a long way from the Grouse tradition. With its ham-fisted date and walnut middle I would have sworn this was the work of another blender entirely. There are redeeming rich honey tones that are a joy. But the dull, pulsing sulphur on the finish has almost an air of inevitability. I promise you this: go back 60 years, and there would have been no blend created with this signature...not only did the style not exist, but it would have been impossible to accomplish. *40%. Edrington.*

The Formidable Jock of Bennachie (82) n19 t22 f21 b20. "Scotland's best kept secret" claims the label. Hardly. But the silky delivery on the palate is worth investigating. Impressive roastiness to the malt and oak, but the caramel needs thinning. *40%. Bennachie Scotch Whisky.*

Fort Glen The Blender's Reserve Aged 12 Years (88.5) n21.5 t23 f21.5 b22.5 An entirely enjoyable blend which is clean and boasting decent complexity and weight. *40%*

Fort Glen The Distiller's Reserve (78) n18 t22 f19 b19. Juicy, salivating delivery as it storms the ramparts. Draws down the portcullis elsewhere. *40%. The Fort Glen Whisky Company.*

Fraser MacDonald (85) n21 t21.5 f21 b21.5. Some fudge towards the middle and end but the journey there is an enjoyable one. *40%. Loch Lomond Distillers.*

Gairloch (79) n19 t20 f20 b20. For those who like their butterscotch at 40% abv. *40%*

Glen Brynth (70.5) n18 t19 f16 b17.5. Bitter and awkward. *43%*

⁙ **Glenbrynth 8 Year Old (88)** n21.5 light but with a Digestive biscuit bent; t22 much better weight on delivery with the sweet barley far from shy; f22.5 serious complexity as we now move towards chocolate digestive biscuit; b22 an impressive blend which improves second by second on the palate. *40%. OTI Africa.*

Glenbrynth Pearl 30 Year Old Limited Edition (90.5) n22.5 t23.5 f21.5 b23 Attractive, beautifully weighted, no off notes...though perhaps quietened by toffee. Still a treat of a blend. *43%. OTI Africa.*

Glen Gray (84.5) n20 t22.5 f21 b21. A knife and fork blend you can stand your spoon in. Plain going for most of the way, but the area between delivery and middle enjoys several waves of rich chocolate honeycomb...and some of the cocoa resurfaces at the finale. *43%*

Glen Lyon (85) n19 t22.5 f22 b21.5. Works a lot better than the nose suggests: seriously chewy with a rabid spice attack and lots of juices. For those who have just retired as dynamite testers. Unpretentious fun. *43%. Diageo.*

⁙ **Glen Orrin Aged 5 Years (77)** n19 t21 f18 b19. Glen Orrible more like. A step up from the no age statement version, thanks mainly to a very delicate underlying smokiness. But the core malt is still of that ilk that will drive people to bourbon. *40%. Aldi.*

⁙ **Glen Orin 30 Years old Blend (95)** n24 the grains have made a first-class job of drawing out the most lively vanillas and when fully warmed in the hand the delightfully sharp marmalade is at its zenith. The malt is no less graceful and dovetails majestically and at times almost covertly, injecting a delicate maple syrup sweetness to soften the richer elements of the grassy barley; t24 crisp, firm grain ensures a cracking delivery and a very old-fashioned style. Despite its early ramrod rigidity, it softens slowly – almost tantalizingly - with first mouth-watering barley then a volley of the vanillas promised on the nose. The sugars are delicate, still offering a degree of maple but more inclined now towards a thin layer of acacia honey; f23 the same grainy crispness which makes the delivery so strident ensures a less dramatic, more peaceful finale. Here, the influence of the oak is underlined with a drier, chalkier feel to the persistent vanillas. A light barley frame ensures that drier oak, patiently sculpted over three decades, is seen to its fullest advantage; b24 a clean, charming blend from the old school and of a style too rarely seen today, alas. The accent, as it should be, is on the grain, and its very brittleness accentuates just how delicate this whisky is. A perfect pre-prandial dram to be taken straight and at body temperature, without water or ice, so its astonishing complexity can be fully explored. Or very late at night when you might find time for all its mysteries to unravel. Top notch Scotch where subtlety is the watchword. Delicacy and understatement is the key; yet with enough life and juiciness to entertain even the most fatigued taste buds. Truly outstanding. *40%. Aldi*

Golden Piper (86.5) n22 t21 f22 b21.5. A firm, clean blend with a steady flush through of diverse sugars. The grain does all the steering and therefore complexity is limited. But the overall freshness is a delight. *43%. Whisky Shack.*

Grand Sail (87) n21 t22 f22 b22 A sweet, attractive blend with enough bite to really matter. *40%*

Grand Sail Aged 10 Years (79) n20 t(22.) f18 b19. Pleasant and at times fascinating but with a tang that perhaps the next vatting will benefit from losing. *40%. China market.*

Grand Sail Rare Reserve Aged 18 Years (94) n23 slightly waxy and bourbony; t24 fabulous silky grain delivery which offers no little early cocoa; as it moulds into the palate, the mix of corn and spice forms a beautifully textured layering to the roof of the mouth; brown sugars slowly form; f23 long, as the earlier oils suggest, and the chocolate lightly sweetened by brown sugars go into overdrive; a desired degree of late bite, too; b24 a truly beautiful whisky which cuts effortlessly and elegantly through the taste buds. *40% Angus Dundee. China market.*

Glenross Blended (83) n20 t22 f20 b21. Decent, easy-drinking whisky with a much sharper delivery than the nose suggests. *40%. Speyside Distillers.*

Glen Simon (77) n20 t19 f19 b19. Simple. Lots of caramel. *40%. Quality Spirits International.*

The Gordon Highlanders (86) **n**21 **t**22 **f**21 **b**22. Lush and juicy, there is a distinctive Speysidey feel to this one with the grains doing their best to accentuate the developing spice. Plenty of feel good factor here. *40%. William Grant & Sons.*

Grand Macnish (79) **n**19 **t**21 **f**19 **b**20. Welcome back to an old friend...but the years have caught up with it. Still on the feral side, but has exchanged its robust good looks for an unwashed and unkempt appearance on the palate. Will do a great job to bring some life back to you, though. *43%. MacDuff International Ltd.*

Grand Macnish 12 Years Old (86) **n**21 **t**22 **f**21.5 **b**21.5. A grander Grand Macnish than of old with the wonderful feather pillow delivery maintained and a greater harmonisation of the malt, especially those which contain a honey-copper sheen. *40%. MacDuff.*

Grant's Aged 12 Years bott 30/09/10 (89.5) **n**23 **t**23 **f**21.5 **b**22 Can't argue too much with the tasting notes on the label (although I contend that "full, rich and rounded" has more to do with its body than taste, but that is by the by). Beautiful whisky, as can be reasonably expected from a Grant's blend. If only the sharpness could last the distance. *40%.*

Grant's Cask Edition No.1 Ale Cask Finish Edinburgh ale casks (88.5) **n**22 **t**23 **f**21.5 **b**22. always loved this concept: a whisky and chaser in one bottle. This was has plenty of cheer in the complex opening, but gets maudlin towards the end. *40%. William Grant & Sons.*

Great MacCauley (81) **n**20 **t**20.5 **f**20 **b**20.5. Reminds me of another whisky I tasted earlier: Castle Rock, I think. Identical profile with toffee and spice adding to the juicy and youthful fun. *40%. Quality Spirits International.*

Green Plaid 12 Years Old (89) **n**22 **t**23 **f**22 **b**22 Beautifully constructed; juicy. *40%.*

Guneagal Aged 12 Years (85.5) **n**21 **t**22.5 **f**20.5 **b**21.5. The salty, sweaty armpit nose gives way to an even saltier delivery, helped along by sweet glycerine and a boiled candy fruity sweetness. The finish is a little roughhouse by comparison. *40%. William Grant & Sons.*

Haddington House (85.5) **n**21 **t**21.5 **f**22 **b**21. Mouth-watering and delicate. *40%*

Haig Gold Label (88) **n**21 **t**23 **f**22 **b**22 What had before been pretty standard stuff has upped the complexity by an impressive distance. *40%. Diageo.*

Hankey Bannister (84.5) **n**20.5 **t**22 **f**21 **b**21. Lots of early life and even a malt kick early on. Toffee later. *40%. Inverhouse Distillers.*

Hankey Bannister 12 Years Old (86.5) **n**22 **t**21.5 **f**21 **b**22. A much improved blend with a nose and early delivery which makes full play of the blending company's Speyside malts. Plenty of toffee on the finish. *40%. Inverhouse Distillers.*

⁙ **Hanky Bannister Regency 12 Year Old** (84.5) **n**22.5 **t**22 **f**19 **b**21 Plenty of honey and some fine, silky structuring. Just a tad too bitter and furry on the finish, though. *40%.*

Hankey Bannister 21 Years Old (95) **n**23.5 a fruity ensemble, clean, vibrant and loath to show its age **t**24 as juicy as the nose suggests, except for the odd rumble of distant smoke; a firm, barley-sugar hardness as the grains keep control; **f**23.5 the arrival of the oak adds further weight and for the first time begins to behave like a 21-y-o; long, now with decent spice and with some crusty dryness at the very death; **b**24 with top dressing like this and some obviously complex secondary malts, too, how can it fail? *43%.* ☉ ☉

Hankey Bannister 25 Years Old (91) **n**22.5 **t**24 **f**21.5 **b**23 Follows on in style and quality to 21-year-old. Gorgeous. *40%*

Hankey Bannister 40 Years Old (89.5) **n**23.5 **t**24 **f**19.5 **b**22.5 Not sure where the finish came from. But the fruit symphony leading up to it is a thing of beauty. *43.3%.*

Hankey Bannister 40 Years Old (89) **n**22 **t**23 **f**22 **b**22. This blend has been put together to mark the 250th anniversary of the forging of the business relations between Messrs. Hankey and Bannister. And although the oak creaks like a ship of its day, there is enough verve and viscosity to ensure a rather delicious toast to the gentlemen. Love it! *44%. Inverhouse.*

⁙ **Hanky Bannister 40 Year Old** (94) **n**23.5 brilliantly playful; spiced carrot cake, a touch of Parkin cake and several layers of torched honeycomb; **t**23.5 the sugars are first to arrive, though tight and slightly molassed; a busy malt surge and weight provided by beech honey and hickory. Butterscotch evens the middle; **f**23 more bourbon-style liquorice and honey; **b**24 pure quality. The attention to detail is sublime. *44.3%. Inverhouse Distillers.*

⁙ **Hanky Bannister Heritage** (84.5) **n**21 **t**22 **f**20.5 **b**21. So softly spoken sometimes you struggle to hear it. Makes a juicy, malty chuntering mid-way through, though. *46%.*

Hedges & Butler Royal (92) **n**22.5 **t**23.5 **f**23 **b**23 Massively improved to become a juicy and charming blend of the very highest order. *40%*

High Commissioner (88.5) **n**22.5 **t**22.5 **f**20.5 **b**22.5 Now I admit I had a hand in cleaning this brand up a couple of years back, giving it a good polish and much needed balance complexity. But I don't remember leaving it in quite this good a shape. Just a bitter semi-off note on the finish, otherwise this guy would have been in the 90s. What a great fun, three-course dram this is... *40%. Loch Lomond Distillers.*

Highland Baron (85.5) **n**21 **t**22 **f**21 **b**21.5. A very clean, sweet and competent young blend showing admirable weight and depth. *40%. Loch Lomond Distillers.*

Highland Bird (77) n19 t19 f19 b20. I've has a few of these over the years, I admit. But I can't remember one quite as rough and ready as this... 40%. *Quality Spirits International.*

Highland Black 8 Years Old Special Reserve (85.5) n22 t22.5 f20 b21. A lovely blend which has significantly improved since my last encounter with it. A touch too much grain on the finish for greatness, perhaps. But the nose and delivery both prosper from a honey-roast almond sweetness. 40%. *Aldi.*

Highland Dream 12 Years Old bott Jan 05 **(94.5)** n23.5 t24 f23 b24. Now that is what I call a blend! How comes it has taken me two years to find it? A wet dream, if ever there was one... 43%. *J & G Grant. 9000 bottles.*

Highland Dream 18 Years Old bott May 07 **(88.5)** n22.5 t22.5 f21.5 b22. Perhaps doesn't get the marks on balance that a whisky of this quality might expect. This is due to the slight over egging of the sherry which, while offering a beautiful delivery, masks the complexities one might expect. Lovely whisky, and make no mistake. But, technically, doesn't match the 12-year-old for balance and brilliance. 43%. *J & G Grant. 3000 bottles.*

Highland Earl (77) n19 t20 f19 b19. Might have marked it higher had it called itself a grain: the malt is silent. 40%. *Aldi.*

Highland Gathering Blended Scotch Whisky (78) n19 t20 f19 b20. Attractive, juicy stuff, though caramel wins in the end. 40%. *Lombards Brands.*

Highland Glendon (87.5) n21.5 t22.5 f21.5 b22 An honest, simple but effectively attractive blend. 43%. *Quality Spirits International.*

Highland Harvest Organic Scotch Whisky (76) n18 t21 f19 b18. A very interesting blend. Great try, but a little bit of a lost opportunity here as I don't think the balance is quite right. But at least I now know what organic caramel tastes like... 40%

Highland Mist (88.5) n20.5 t23 f22.5 b22.5 Fabulously fun whisky bursting from the bottle with character and mischief. Had to admit, broke all my own rules and just had to have a glass of this after doing the notes... 40%. *Loch Lomond Distillers.*

Highland Piper (79) n20 t20 f19 b20. Good quaffing blend – if sweet - of sticky toffee and dates. Some gin on the nose – and finish. 40%

Highland Pride (86) n21 t22 f21.5 b21.5. A beefy, weighty thick dram with plenty to chew on. The developing sweetness is a joy. 40%. *Whyte & Mackay Distillers Ltd.*

⋰ **Highland Queen Blended Scotch Whisky (86.5)** n22 t21 f21.5 b22. Lots of grains at play here. But what grains?! Clean and crisp with a superb bite which balances the softening mouth feel attractively. Old fashioned and delicious. 40%

⋰ **Highland Queen Aged 8 Years Blended Scotch Whisky (90)** n22.5 full and rounded with a disarming squeeze of apple juice; t23.5 silky delivery followed by an onslaught of superb spices; a touch of Demerara sweetens the drier oaks; f21.5 the caramel kicks in slightly, as does the grain, but age is apparent; b22.5 lots of entertainment value from a high quality whisky. The blender has done a great job in the lab. 43%

⋰ **Highland Queen Aged 12 Years Blended Scotch Whisky (87)** n22 fruit candy and rhubarb tart; t22 silky a la the 8-year-old, and then the same configuration of spice..but without the same impact; f21 back to the silky stuff with some decent late vanilla; b22 a polite, slightly more sophisticated version of the 8-year-old...but without the passion and drama! 40%

Highland Reserve (82) n20 t21 f20 b21. You'll probably find this just off the Highland Way and incorporating Highland Bird and Monarch of the Glen. Floral and muddy. 40%

Highland Reserve Aged 12 Years (87) n21 t22 f22 b22 Anyone who has tasted Monarch of the Glen 12 will appreciate this. Maybe a bit more fizz here, though, despite the big caramel. 43%. *Quality Spirits International.*

Highland Warrior (77.8) n19 t19 f19.5 b20. Just like his Scottish Chief, he's on the attack armed with some Dufftown, methinks... 40%. *Quality Spirits International.*

Highland Way (84) n19 t20.5 f22.5 b22. This lovely little number takes the High Road with some beautiful light scenery along the way. The finish takes a charming Speyside path. 40%

Inverarity Limited Edition cask no. 698, dist 1997, bott 2009 **(84.5)** n20.5 t22 f21 b21. A heady, heavy-duty blend where honeycomb rules on the palate and thick dates offer a more intense sweetness. But don't go looking for subtlety or guile: those whose palates have been educated at the Whyte and Mackay school of delicate sophistication will have a ball. 40%

Islay Mist 8 Years Old (84) n20 t22 f21 b21. Turned into one heavy duty dram since last tasting a couple of years back. This appears to absorb everything it touches leaving one chewy, smoky hombre. Just a little tangy at the end. 40%. *MacDuff International Ltd.*

Islay Mist 12 Years Old (90) n22 t23 f22 b23 Adore it: classic bad cop - good cop stuff with an apparent high malt content. 40%

Islay Mist 17 Years Old (92.5) n22.5 t23.5 f23 b23.5 Always a cracking blend, this has improved of late into a genuine must have. 40%. *MacDuff International Ltd.*

Islay Mist Delux (85) n21.5 t22 f21.5 b20. Remains a highly unusual blend with the youthful peat now more brilliant than before, though the sugar levels appear to have risen markedly. 40%

Isle of Skye 8 Years Old (94) n23 Isle of Skye? Or Orkney? Honey and smoke play tag; the grain is firm and clean; t24 just so beautiful. Honeycomb and light fudge form a rich partnership, the smoke is little more than ballast and a shy spice; the grains play a fabulous role in allowing the maltier notes to ping around and increase the salivating qualities; f23.5 the spice is now pretty warming but the honeycomb and vanilla dominate the finale; b23.5 where once peat ruled and with its grain ally formed a smoky iron fist, now honey and subtlety reigns. A change of character and pace which may disappoint gung-ho peat freaks but will intrigue and delight those looking for a more sophisticated dram. 40%. Ian Macleod.

Isle of Skye 21 years Old (91) n21 t23.5 f23 b23.5 What an absolute charmer! The malt content appears pretty high, but the overall balance is wonderful. 40%. Ian Macleod.

Isle of Skye 50 Years Old (82.5) n21.5 t21 f20 b20. Drier incarnation than the 50% version. But still the age has yet to be balanced out, towards the end in particular. Early on some distinguished moments involving something vaguely smoked and a sweetened spice. 41.6%

The Jacobite (78.5) n18 t18.5 f22 b20. Neither the nose or delivery are of the cleanest style. But comes into its own towards the finish when the thick soup of a whisky thins to allow an attractive degree of complexity. Not for those with catholic tastes. 40%. Booker.

⸰⸰⸰ **Jackson McCloud Premium Blended Scotch Whisky (81)** n20 t21 f20 b20. Absolutely standard fare, full of grainy bite and caramel. 40%. Galleon Liqueurs.

⸰⸰⸰ **Jackson McCloud Rare Batch Blended Scotch Whisky (85.5)** n20 t22.5 f22 b21. Pleasant, but with little or no effort to overcome the dominating grain. As it happens, it turns out to be pretty decent silky grain with some attractive fruit notes. 40%. Galleon Liqueurs.

James Alexander (85.5) n21 t21.5 f21.5 b21.5. Some lovely spices link the grassier Speysiders to the earthier elements. 40%. Quality Spirits International.

James King (76.5) n20 t18 f20 b18.5. Young whiskies of a certain rank take their time to find their feet. The finish, though, does generate some pleasant complexity. 43%

James King Aged 5 Years (85) n21 t21.5 f21 b21.5. Very attractive, old fashioned and well weighted with a pleasing degree of fat and chewy sweetness and chocolate fudge. Refreshingly good quality distillate and oak have been used in this: I'd drink it any day. 40%

James King 8 Years Old (78.5) n18.5 t21.5 f19 b19.5. Charming spices grip at the delivery and fine malt-grain interplay through the middle, even showing a touch of vanilla. But such a delicate blend can't fully survive the caramel. 43%. Quality Spirits International.

James King 12 Years Old (81) n19 t23 f19 b20. Caramel dulls the nose and finish. But for some time a quite beautiful blend soars about the taste buds offering exemplary complexity and weight. 40%. Quality Spirits International.

James King 15 Years Old (89) n22 t23 f21.5 b22.5. Now offers extra spice and zip. 43%

James King 21 Years Old (87.5) n20.5 t23.5 f22 b22. Attractive blend, but one that could do with the strength upped to 46% and the caramel reduced if not entirely got rid of. One of those potentially excellent yet underperforming guys I'd love to be let loose on! 43%

James Martin 20 Years Old (93) n21 t21.5 t23.5 f24.5 b24. I had always regarded this as something of an untamed beast. No longer: still something of a beast, but a beautiful one that is among the most complex found on today's market. 43%. Glenmorangie.

James Martin 30 Years Old (86) n21.5 t22 f21 b21.5. Enjoyable for all its exotic fruitiness. But with just too many creaking joints to take it to the same level as the sublime 20-y-o. Even so, a blend worth treating with a touch of respect and allowing time for it to tell some pretty ancient tales... 43%. Glenmorangie.

J&B Jet (79.5) n19 t20 f20.5 b20. Never quite gets off the ground due to carrying too heavy a load. Unrecognisable to its pomp in the old J&B days: this one is far too weighty and never properly finds either balance or thrust. 40%. Diageo.

J&B Reserve Aged 15 Years (78) n23 t19 f18 b18. What a crying shame. The sophisticated and demure nose is just so wonderfully seductive but what follows is an open-eyed, passionless embrace. Coarsely grain-dominant and unbalanced, this is frustrating beyond words and not worthy to be mentioned in the same breath as the old, original J&B 15 which, by vivid contrast, was a malty, salivating fruit-fest and minor classic. 40%. Diageo.

J&B Rare (88.5) n21.5 t22.5 f22 b22.5 I have been drinking a lot of J&B from a previous time of late, due to the death of their former blender Jim Milne. I think he would have been pretty taken aback by the youthful zip offered here: whether it is down to a decrease in age or the use of slightly more tired casks – or both – is hard to say. 40%. Diageo.

Jim McEwan's Blended Whisky (86.5) n20 t22 f22.5 b22. Juicy and eye-watering with clever late spices. 46%. Bruichladdich.

John Barr (85.5) n20 t22 f21.5 b22. I assume from the big juicy dates to be found that Fettercairn is at work. Outwardly a big bruiser; given time to state its case and it's a bit of a gentle giant. 40%. Whyte & Mackay Distillers Ltd.

Johnnie Walker Black Label 12 Years Old (95.5) n23.5 pretty sharp grain: hard and buffeting the nose; a buffer of yielding smoke, apple pie and delicate spice cushions the encounter; **t24.5** if there is a silkier delivery on the market today, I have not seen it: this is sublime stuff with the grains singing the sweetest hymns as they go down, taking with them a near perfection of weighty smoke lightened by brilliantly balanced barley which leans towards both soft apple and crème broulee; **f23.5** those reassuringly rigid grains re-emerge and with them the most juicy Speysidey malts imaginable; the lovely sheen to the finish underlines the good age of the whiskies used; **b24** here it is: one of the world's most masterful whiskies back in all its complex glory. A bottle like this is like being visited by an old lover. It just warms the heart and excites. 40%. Diageo.

Johnnie Walker Blue Label (88) n21 t24 f21 b22 What a frustrating blend! Just so close to brilliance but the nose and finish are slightly out of kilter. Worth the experience of the mouth arrival alone. 43%. Diageo.

Johnnie Walker Blue Label The Casks Edition (97) n24.5 now that is a nose: absolutely brimming with intent and character, this obviously has no designs to just sit there and look pretty. A blend where the malts have a far bigger say than the grains, especially the honeydew melon and red berries. The phenols are surprisingly laconic, but that gives more scope for the duskier notes from the oak to come through, especially the more bourbon-style liquorice and hickory. There is also something there which would be appreciated by lovers of high ester Jamaican pot still rum; **t24.5** the great blends have, traditionally, offered a little nip and bite...and the delivery here shows as many teeth as it does soothing fingers of honey. Wonderful walnut oil and marzipan offer the nuts to go with the delicate fruit and chocolate; the mid range carries on with this high ester, slightly oily sweetness which coats the mouth with kumquats and liquorice; the spices are shallow but offer excellent variance to the vanilla; **f23.5** long, languid, delicately oiled and bowing out with a stunning display of spiced heather honey, mocha, dates, walnuts and the lightest of smoky fades...; **b24.5** this is a triumph of scotch whisky blending. With not as much as a hint of a single off note to be traced from the tip of the nose to tail, this shameless exhibition of complexity and brilliance is the star turn in the Diageo portfolio right now. Indeed, it is the type of blend that every person who genuinely adores whisky must experience for the good of their soul....if only once in their life. 55.8%.

Johnnie Walker Double Black (94.5) n23 sweet, distinctly malty and salty (salted celery, to be precise); there is an earthiness to this unlike any other JW. Weighty, but light and aloof enough for hints of honey and orange to blossom; **t23.5** superb mouth-feel on delivery: silky and suave with the malt immediately apparent through the spiced smoke and buttery barley; a string of vanilla notes punctuate the mid ground; the melting of the brown sugars is a dream; **f24** long and confidently spiced. But the trick is in the light oils carried on the smoke (presumably Caol Ila displaying its party piece) and the ambiguity of age: some younger notes play havoc with the more mature tannins. Complex and keeps the palate on full alert from delivery to the very last spice buzz; **b24** double tops! Rolling along the taste buds like distant thunder, this is a welcome and impressive addition to the Johnnie Walker stable. Perhaps not as complete and rounded as the original Johnnie Walker Black...but, then, what is? 40%.

⁘ **Johnnie Walker Explorers' Club Collection The Gold Route (89) n23.5** understated – which is always good – fruit, though the grains are used rather well here to magnify the effects of the more estery malts and flag up the apricot, spice and very delicate smoke; **t24** the sweet softness of the grains are again first to show, then a dazzling display of lighter brown sugars, muscovado in particular. There is a Clynelish-style injection of mildly exotic fruit, especially guava, followed by a more simplistic vanilla thread; **f19.5** the somewhat off-key finale does not fit with what has gone on before, again revealing a furry bitterness; a buttery, oily body tries to remedy the situation; **b22** much of this blend is truly the stuff of golden dreams. Like its Explorer's Club stable mate, some attention has to be paid to the disappointing finish. Worth sending out an expedition, though, just for the beautiful nose and delivery... 40%. Diageo.

⁘ **Johnnie Walker Explorers' Club Collection The Spice Road (84.5) n22 t23.5 f18 b21.** Sublime delivery of exceptionally intense juiciness: in fact, probably the juiciest blend released this year. But the bitter, fuzzy finish reveals certain casks haven't helped. 40%.

Johnnie Walker Gold Label Reserve (91.5) n23 just a little extra weight by comparison to its 18-y-o predecessor. Delicate heather honey, though the higher notes are clipped by caramel. Both are out-performed by the nutty Danish marzipan; a little bitter marmalade also makes a bow; **t24** the star moments of this blend are reserved for the delivery. The texture is the stuff of dreams and the slow opening of the delicate honey tones are sublime, especially as both a juicy Speyside style barley and an encircling vanilla from the grains offer the perfect accompaniments; the spices are reserved, but present; **f22** much duller as the toffee on the nose returns and a light furry bitterness rumbles; **b23** moments of true star quality here, but the finish could do with a polish. 40%. Diageo.

Johnnie Walker King George V db (88) n23 t22 f21 b22 One assumes that King George V is no relation to George IV. This has genuine style and breeding, if a tad too much caramel. 43%

Johnnie Walker Platinum Label Aged 18 Years (88) n22 the delicate smoke appears to have as much tobacco as peat; earthy, a sprig of mint and a little nip to the spice; t23 busy, playfully spiced and gorgeously weighted delivery with excellent orange blossom honey hanging on the oils; the caramels give something else to chew on; f21 just a bit tight and furry on the finale from the wine cask influence; b22 this blend might sound like some kind of Airmiles card. Which wouldn't be too inappropriate, though this is more Business than First... 40%. *Diageo.*

Johnnie Walker Red Label (87.5) n22 t22 f21.5 b22 The ongoing move through the scales quality-wise appears to suggest we have a work still in progress here. This sample has skimped on the smoke, though not quality. Yet a few months back when I was in the BA Business Lounge at Heathrow's new Terminal Five, I nearly keeled from almost being overcome by peat in the earthiest JW Red I had tasted in decades. I found another bottle and I'm still not sure which represents the real Striding Man. 40%. *Diageo.*

❖ **Johnnie Walker X.R Aged 21 Years** (94) n23.5 silky marmalade and vanilla sent me to North America. Wonderful thread of peat reveals the Scottish credentials. Some very serious complexity going on; t24 one of the most sublime examples of spiced ulmo honey on delivery, revelling in its gorgeous waxy texture offered by some top quality grain; huge vanilla thread through the middle; f23 chocolate fruit and nut, backed by a massive vanilla backbone and echoes of that astonishing ulmo honey; a little furry and bitter apricot; b23.5 how weird! I nosed this blind before seeing what the brand was. My first thought was: "mmm, same structure of Crown Royal XR. Canadian??? No, there's smoke!" Then looked at what was before me and spotted it was its sister whisky from the Johnnie Walker stable. A coincidence? I don't think so... 40%. *Diageo.*

Kenmore Special Reserve Aged 5 Years bott code L07285 (75) n18 t20 f19 b18. Recovers to a degree from the poor nose. A must-have for those who prefer their Scotch big-flavoured and gawky. 40%

King Robert II (77) n19 t19 f20 b19. A bustier, more bruising batch than the last 40 per cent version. Handles the OTT caramel much better. Agreeably weighty slugging whisky. 43%.

Kings Blended 3 Years Old (83) n21 t21.5 f20 b20.5. A young, chunky blend that you can chew forever. 40%. *Speyside Distillers.*

King's Crest Scotch Whisky 25 Years Old (83) n22 t22 f19 b20. A silky middle weight. The toffee-flat finish needs some attention because the softly estered nose and delivery is a honey-rich treat and deserves better. 40%. *Speyside Distillers.*

Label 5 Aged 18 Years (84.5) n20.5 t22 f21 b21. A big mouthful and mouth-feel. Has changed course since I last had this one. Almost a feel of rum to this with its estery sheen. Sweet, simple, easy dramming. 40%. *La Martiniquaise, France.*

Label 5 Classic Black (75) n18 t20 f18 b19. The off-key nose needs some serious re-working. Drop the caramel, though, and you would have a lot more character. Needs some buffing. 40%. *The First Blending for La Martiniquaise, France.*

❖ **Label 5 Classic Black** bott code L3060 (84.5) n20.5 t22 f21 b21. A better whisky than when last tasted with more even use of the date and walnut theme. Caramel still substantial, but complexity levels are higher. 40%. *La Martiniquaise, France.*

❖ **Label 5 Classic Black** bott code L3084 (83.5) n20 t21.5 f21 b21. Like L3060. Except the nose is even harsher and here the grain have a much more jarring effect. 40%. *La Martiniquaise, France.*

❖ **Label 5 Classic Black** bott code L3144 (85) n20.5 t22 f21 b21.5. Stays in the same areas as the two previous bottlings, but slightly better use of spices. Still needs a nose job, though... 40%. *Glen Turner.*

❖ **Label 5 Reserve No. 55** sherry cask finish, bott code B-3695 (89) n22 soft smoke offers surprising weight; sweet, diced apple; t23 oh, yes! That's what you want to see from a blend: makes a smoky statement yet enough complexity elsewhere, especially from the gooseberry and greengages to add lines of texture; f21.5 a very slight fuzziness amid the toffee, but the sugars are true; b22.5 the last one of these I had a couple of years back was a sulphur-damaged disaster. This is anything but. A real bold treat. 43 %. *La Martiniquaise, France.*

❖ **Label 5 Reserve No. 55** sherry cask finish, bott code F-4482 (87) n20.5 some anthracite dust; dry; t22.5 busy with the sugars spiky and battling with the early spice; the fruit is little more than a whisper; f22 remains dusty with the oak vying with the late Demerara sugars; b22 lacking the suave sweetness of the B-3695 bottling, but excellent spice. 43%.

Label 5 Reserve No. 55 Single Cask sherry cask finish, bott code no. E-1067 (75) n19 t20 f18 b18. The cordite on the nose suggests fireworks. But somehow we end up with a damp squib. 40%. *La Martiniquaise, France.*

❖ **Label 5 Aged 12 Years** bott code L307157A (82) n21 t20 f21 b20. Heavy duty date and walnut. Loads of caramel, too. For those looking for a weighty and chewy, rather complex dram. 40%. *Glen Turner.*

Lang's Supreme Aged 5 Years (93.5) n23.5 t23.5 f23 b23.5. Every time I taste this the shape and structure has altered slightly. Here there is a fraction more smoke, installing a deeper confidence all round. This is blended whisky as it should be: Supreme in its ability to create shape and harmony. 40%. Ian Macleod Distillers Ltd.

The Last Drop (96.5) n24 t25 f23.5 b24. How do you mark a whisky like this? It is scotch. Yet every molecule of flavour and aroma is pure bourbon. I think I'll have to mark for quality, principally, which simply flies off the graph. I'll dock it a point for not being Scotch-like but I feel a pang of guilt for doing so. This, by the way, is a blend that was discovered by accident. It had been put away many years ago for marrying – and then forgotten about in a warehouse. The chances of finding another whisky quite of this ilk are remote, though I'm sure the hunters are now out. It is a one off and anyone who misses this one will kick themselves forever. Astonishing. A freak whisky at its very peak. 52%. The Last Drop Distillers Ltd.

The Last Drop 50 Years Old (96.5) n25 where once there was bourbon only, now we have a cross fertilisation of aromas. Certainly, once you allow it to breathe, the grape engulfs most else. It is as if the whisky has undergone a fruity polish and shine. On first pouring, the oak has the ability to cause splinters; allow to settle for a while and we are talking a much softer, less senile Drop; and slowly the spices unravel...; **t24.5** perhaps what is so astounding about this, is the way that the balance does not, even for a second, waiver under the occasional oaky onslaught: as it bites, from somewhere a grapey honeycomb flies in to the rescue offering just-so compensatory sugars which perfectly match the most delicate spices imaginable...; **f22.5** now we edge towards a drier finale than before. The original was remarkable for not having a degree of bitterness, though it had every right to be there. Now, alas, there is. The bitterness is slightly furry and dusty, but to make amends we are treated to one very old Melton Hunt cake, indeed; **b24.5** I tend to stick to the old adage: if it isn't broke, don't fix it. However, I do admire what has been done here. Because it was a gamble for the right reasons, which has paid handsomely in many ways, yet has just fallen short in others. Here, they took a magnificent whisky which for no other reason than pure serendipity, like Adam Adament, had awoken in another age but instead of, like our Victorian hero, being lost in a strange new world, found itself in one ready to appreciate and embrace its manifold beauty. This whisky was thrown back for a few extra summers in oak to take it to 50 years. A bold move. And it remains a quite astonishing, for life-remembering dram of labyrinthine complexity. 52%. 198 bottles.

Lauder's (74) n18 t21 f17 b18. Well, it's consistent: you can say that for it! As usual, fabulous delivery, but as for the rest...oh dear. 40%. MacDuff International Ltd.

Lauder's Aged 12 Years (93.5) n23 t24 f23 b23.5 This is every bit as magnificent as the standard Lauder's isn't. 43%

Loch Lomond Blended Scotch (89) n22 t22.5 f22 b22.5 A fabulously improved blend: clean and precise and though malt is seemingly at a premium, a fine interplay. 40%.

Lochranza (83.5) n21 t21.5 f21 b20. Pleasant, clean, but, thanks to the caramel, goes easy on the complexity. 40%. Isle of Arran.

Lochside 1964 Rare Old Single Blend (94.5) n24 sensual citrus: thick cut marmalade thinned by delicate lime. Hints of bourbony liquorice fits the style perfectly; **t23.5** mainly a corn lead: sweet, yielding yet salivating. Momentarily shows signs of wilting under the oak, but responds immediately by slamming the door shut and upping the fruit and vanillas; **f23** remains improbably delicate with the corn and vanilla dovetailing with aplomb; **b24** a unique and entirely fitting tribute to a distillery which should never have been lost. 42.1%. nc ncf. Speciality Drinks Ltd.

Logan (78.5) n19 t19 f20 b19.5. Entirely drinkable but a bit heavy-handed with the grains and caramel. 40%. Diageo.

Lombard's Gold Label (85) n21 t22 f21 b21. Big and chewy, not as complex as of old but those who like chunky toffee will be in for a treat. 40%. Lombard Brands Ltd. ⊙ ⊙

⋯⋅ **Lord Elcho Aged 15 Years** (84) n21 t21 f21 b21. A straight wicket with no turn at all. A degree of coppery sharpness and caramel, but low key. 40%. Wemyss Malts.

Lord Hynett (85) n21.5 t23 f22 b22 Just perfect after a shitty day. 40%.

⋯⋅ **Lord Hynett** (87) n22 excellent grain cuts through the toffee; **t22** sharp, earthy but a pleasing sugary bite of the old school; **f21.5** clean, Jammie Dodger biscuit; **b21.5** an honest, beautifully made blend with a welcome degree of attitude. 43%. Loch Lomond Distillers.

Lord Scot (77.5) n18.5 t20 f19.5 b19.5. A touch cloying but the mocha fudge ensures a friendly enough ride. 40%. Loch Lomond Distillers.

Lord Scot (86.5) n20 t22 f22.5 b22. A gorgeously lush honey and liquorice middle. 43%

⋯⋅ **The Lost Distilleries Batch 2** (94) n22.5 get the trowels out and dig that ginger; **t24** a stunner. What a beautifully rounded delivery with near perfect maple syrup mingling with vibrant yet polite spice; **f23.5** back to ginger again, a dash of salt and liquorice which caresses; **b24** whoever lost it better find it again: this is how you dream every whisky should be. 53.2%.

Mackessack Premium Aged 8 Years (87.5) n21.5 t23 f21.5 b21.5. Claims a high Speyside content and the early character confirms it. Shoots itself in the foot, rather, by overdoing the caramel and flattening the finish. *40%. Mackessack Giovenetti. Italian Market.*

Mac Na Mara (83) n20 t22.5 f20 b20.5. Absolutely brimming with salty, fruity character. But just a little more toffee and furriness than it needs. Enjoyable, though. *40%*

Mac Na Mara Rum Finish (93) n22 t24 f23 b24 High quality blending, and the usage of the rum appears to have retained the old Mac Na Mara style. *40%. Praban na Linne.*

MacQueens (89) n21.5 t22.5 f22.5 b22.5. I am long enough in the tooth now to remember blends like this found in quiet country hotels in the furthest-flung reaches of the Highlands beyond a generation ago. A wonderfully old-fashioned, traditional one might say, blend of a type that is getting harder and harder to find. *40%. Quality Spirits International.*

Master of Malt 8 Years Old (88) n22.5 t22.5 f21 b22. Understated and refined. *40%*

⁘ **Master Of Malt 8 Year Old Blended Whisky** (83.5) n21 t22 f20.5 b20. Never quite makes up its mind what it wants to do, or where it wants to go. A few intriguing vaguely Irish Pot Still-style moments on delivery, though. *40%*

Master Of Malt St Isidore (84) n21 t22 f20 b21. Sweet, lightly smoked but really struggles to put together a coherent story. Something, somewhere, is not quite right. *41.4%*

Master Of Malt World Whisky Day Blend (86) n21.5 t22 f21 b21.5. Limited complexity and depth but it gets the Orange Aero bit right.... 40.18%. Master Of Malt.

Matisse 12 Years Old (90.5) n23 t23 f22 b22.5 Moved up yet another notch as this brand continues its development. Much more clean-malt oriented with a Speyside-style to the fore. Majestic and charming. *40%. Matisse Spirits Co Ltd.*

Matisse 21 Years Old (86) n23 t22 f20 b21. Begins breathtakingly on the nose, with a full array of exotic fruit showing the older bourbon casks up to max effect. Nothing wrong with the early delivery, which offers a touch of honeycomb on the grain. But the caramel effect on the finish stops everything in its tracks. Soft and alluring, all the same. *40%*

Matisse Old (85.5) n20 t23 f21 b21.5. Appears to improve each time I come across it. The nose is a bit on the grimy side and the finish disappears under a sea of caramel. But the delivery works deliciously, with a chewy weight which highlights the sweeter malts. *40%*

Matisse Royal (81) n19 t22 f20 b20. Pleasant, if a little clumsy. Extra caramel appears to have scuppered the spice. *40%. Matisse Spirits Co Ltd.*

McArthurs (89.5) n22 t22.5 f22 b23 One of the most improved blends on the market. The clever use of the peat is exceptional. *40%. Inverhouse Distillers.*

Michael Jackson Special Memorial Blend bott 2009 (89) n24 t22.5 f20.5 b22. Whenever Michael and I had a dram together, his would either be massively sherried or equally well endowed with smoke. This is neither, so an odd tribute. Even so, there is more than enough here for him to savour. *43%. Berry Bros & Rudd. 1000 bottles.*

Mitchell's Glengyle Blend (86.5) n21.5 t22 f21.5 b21.5. A taste of history here, as this is the first blend ever to contain malt from the new Campbeltown distillery, Glengyle. Something of a departure in style from the usual Mitchell blends, which tended to put the accent on a crisper grain. Interestingly, here they have chosen one at least that is soft and voluptuous enough to absorb the sharper malt notes. *40%. Springbank Distillers.*

Monarch Of The Glen Connoisseurs Choice (80) n20 t21 f19 b20. Has changed shape a little. Positively wallows in its fat and sweet personality. *40%. Quality Spirits International.*

Monarch Of The Glen Connoisseurs Choice Aged 8 Years (76.5) n19 t20.5 f18 b19. Leaves no doubt that there are some malts in there... *40%. Quality Spirits International.*

Monarch Of The Glen Connoisseurs Choice Aged 12 Years (88) n21.5 t22.5 f22 b22 Charming, fruity and a blend to put your feet up with. *40%. Quality Spirits International.*

Monarch Of The Glen Connoisseurs Choice Aged 15 Years (83) n21 t22 f19 b21. Starts off on the very same footing as the 12-y-o, especially with the sumptuous delivery. But fails to build on that due to toffee and bitters at the death. *40%. Quality Spirits International.*

Montrose (74.5) n18 t20 f18 b18.5. A battling performance but bitter defeat in the end. *40%. Burn Stewart.*

Morrisons The Best 8 Years Old (87) n21 t23 f22 b21. Some of the traces of its excellence are still there, it remains highly drinkable, but that greatness has been lost in a tide of caramel. When, oh when, are people going to understand that you can't just tip this stuff into whisky to up the colour without causing a detrimental effect on the product? Is anybody listening? Does anyone care??? Someone has gone to great lengths to create a sublime blend – to see it wasted. Natural colour and this'd be an experience to die for. *40% Wm Morrison Supermarket.*

Morrisons Fine Blended Whisky (77) n18.5 t21 f18.5 b19. Sweet, chewy but a few rough edges. *40%. Wm Morrison Supermarket.*

Muirhead's (83) n19 t22 f23 b21. A beautifully compartmentalised dram that integrates superbly, if that makes sense. *40%. MacDonald & Muir.*

Muirhead's Blue Seal (83) n21 t21 f20.5 b20.5. Goes to town quite heavily on the grain. If this is the new version of the old McDonald and Muir brand, then this is a lot oilier, with a silkier mouthfeel. *40%. Highland Queen Scotch Whisky Company.*

The Naked Grouse (76.5) n19 t21 f17.5 b19. Sweet. But reveals too many sulphur tattoos. *40%. Edrington.*

Northern Scot (68) n16 t18 f17 b17. Heading South bigtime. *40%. Bruce and Co. for Tesco.*

Old Crofter Special Old Scotch Whisky (83) n18 t22 f21 b22. A very decent blend, much better than the nose suggests thanks to some outstanding, velvety grain and wonderfully controlled sweetness. *40%. Smith & Henderson for London & Scottish International.*

Old Masters "Freemason Whisky" (92) n24 t23 f22 b23. A high quality blend that doesn't stint on the malt. The nose, in particular, is sublime. *40%. Supplied online. Lombard Brands*

Old McDonald (83.5) n20 t22 f20.5 b21. Attractively tart and bracing where it needs to be with lovely grain bite. Lots of toffee, though. *43.%. The Last Drop Distillers. For India.*

Old Mull (84.5) n22 t21 f20.5 b21. With dates and walnuts clambering all over the nose, very much in the house style. But this one is a shade oilier than most – and certainly on how it used to be – and has dropped a degree or two of complexity. That said, enjoyable stuff with the spices performing well, as does the lingering sweetness. *40%*

Old Parr 12 Years Old (91.5) n21.5 t23.5 f23 b23.5 Perhaps on about the fourth of fifth mouthful, the penny drops that this is not just exceptionally good whisky: it is blending Parr excellence... *40%. Diageo.*

Old Parr Aged 15 Years (84) n19 t22 f21 b22. Absolutely massive sherry input here. Some of it is of the highest order. The nose, reveals, however, that some isn't... *43%*

Old Parr Classic 18 Years Old (84.5) n21 t21.5 f21 b21. A real jumbled, mixed bag with fruit and barley falling over each other and the grains offering little sympathy. Enough to enjoy, but with Old Parr, one expects a little more... *46%. Diageo.*

Old Parr Superior 18 Years Old batch no. L5171 (97) n25 a nose with just about a touch of everything: especially clever smoke which gives weight but allows apples and bourbon to filter through at will. Perfect weight and harmony while the complexity goes off the scales; t25 voluptuous body, at times silky but the grains offer enough jagged edges for a degree of bite and bourbon; mouthwatering and spicey with the peats remaining on a slow burner. Toasty and so, so chewy; f23 the vanilla is gentle and a counter to the firmness of the combined oak and grain. A flinty, almost reedy finish with spices and cocoa very much in evidence; b24 year in, year out, this blend just gets better and better. This bottling struck me as a possible Whisky of the Year, but perhaps only an outsider. Familiarity, though, bred anything but contempt and over the passing months I have tried to get to the bottom of this truly great whisky. Blended whisky has long needed a champion. This grand old man looks just the chap. This is a worthy, if unexpected (even to me), Jim Murray' Whisky Bible 2007 World Whisky of the Year. *43%.*

Old Smuggler (85.5) n21 t22 f21 b21.5. A much sharper act than its Allied days with a new honeyed-maple syrup thread which is rather delightful. Could still do with toning down the caramel, though, to brighten the picture further. *40%. Campari, France.*

Old St Andrews Clubhouse (82) n18 t22 f21 b21. Not quite the clean, bright young thing it was many years back. But great to see back in my nosing glass after such a long while and though the nose hits the rough, the delivery is as sweetly struck as you might hope for. *40%*

Old Stag (75.5) n18.5 t20 f18.5 b18.5. Wants shooting. *40%. Loch Lomond Distillers.*

The Original Lochlan Aged 8 Years (80.5) n19 t21 f20 b20.5. Doused in caramel. So much so it's like a toffee and nut bar. One to chew on until your fillings fall out, though the spices compensate on the finish to a degree. Pleasant and sweet, but don't expect great refinement. *40%. Tesco.*

The Original Mackinlay (83) n19 t21 f22 b21. A hard nose to overcome and the toffee remains in force for those addicted to fudge. But now a degree of bite and ballast appears to have been added, giving more of a story to the experience. *40%. Whyte & Mackay Distillers Ltd.*

Passport (83) n22 t19 f21 b21. It looks as though Chivas have decided to take the blend away from its original sophisticated, Business Class J&B/Cutty Sark, style for good now, as they have continued this decently quaffable but steerage quality blend with its big caramel kick and chewy, rather than lithe, body. *40%. Chivas.*

Passport v (91) n23 23.5 f22 b22.5. Easily one of the better versions I have come across for a long time and impressively true to its original style. *40%. Bottled in Brazil.*

Passport v (91) n22.5 t22 f23.5 b23.5. A lovely version closer to original style with markedly less caramel impact and grittier grain. An old-fashioned treat. *40%. Ecuador.*

Parkers (78) n17 t22 f20 b19. The nose has regressed, disappearing into ever more caramel, yet the mouth-watering lushness on the palate remains and the finish now holds greater complexity and interest. *40%. Angus Dundee.*

Prince Charlie Special Reserve (73) n17 t20 f18 b18. Thankfully not as cloyingly sweet as of old, but remains pretty basic. *40%. Somerfield, UK.*

Prince Charlie Special Reserve 8 Years Old (81) n18 t20 f22 b21. A lumbering bruiser of a dram; keeps its trademark shapelessness but the spices and lush malt ensure an enjoyable experience. *40%. Somerfield, UK.*

Queen Margot (86) n21 t22 f21.5 b21.5. A lovely blend which makes no effort to skimp on a spicy depth. Plenty of cocoa from the grain late on but no shortage of good whiskies put to work. *40%. Wallace and Young for Lidl.*

Queen Margot v (83.5) n20.5 t22 f20 b21. Same brand, but a different name on the back label. And certainly a different feel to the whisky with the grains having harsher words than before. *40%. Clydesdale Scotch Whisky Co for Lidl.*

Queen Margot Aged 8 Years (89) n22 green banana sits well with the vanilla and gentle citrus; t22.5 the best blends offer a degree of nip and bite and this doesn't disappoint. A touch of juiciness early on and then the lightest coating of oil soothes - even as the grains gain the upper hand; f22 a light cocoa element is attractively applied; b22.5 a satisfying blend with a delicious clarity to the light malts and high class grains. Just the right touch of sweetness, too. *40%. Wallace and Young for Lidl.*

Queen Margot Aged 8 Years (84) n20.5 t21 f21.5 b21. Here's the variant. Darker in colour I notice and a bit of a dullard and simpleton by comparison, though not without an acceptable degree of charm. Much weightier. *40%. Clydesdale Scotch Whisky Co for Lidl.*

Real Mackenzie (80) n17 t21 f21 b21. As ever, try and ignore the dreadful nose and get cracking with the unsubtle, big bruising delivery. A thug in a glass. *40%. Diageo.*

Real Mackenzie Extra Smooth (81) n18 t22 f20 b21. Once, the only time the terms "Real Mackenzie" and "Extra Smooth" were ever uttered in the same sentence was if someone was talking about the barman. Now it is a genuine descriptor. Which is odd, because when Diageo sent me a sample of their blend last year it was a snarling beast ripping at the leash. This, by contrast, is a whimpering sop. "Killer? Where are you...???" *40%. Diageo.*

Red Seal 12 Years Old (82) n19 t22 f20 b21. Charming, mouthwatering. But toffee numbs it down towards the finish. *40%. Charles Wells UK.*

Reliance PL (76) n18 t20 f19 b19. Some of the old spiciness evident. But has flattened out noticeably. *43%. Diageo.*

Robert Burns (85) n20 t22.5 f21 b21.5. Skeletal and juicy: very little fat and gets to the mouthwatering point pretty quickly. Genuine fun. *40%. Isle of Arran.*

Robertson's of Pitlochry Rare Old Blended (83) n21 t20 f21 b21. Handsome grain bite with a late malty flourish. Classic light blend available only from Pitlochry's landmark whisky shop. *40%*

The Royal & Ancient (80.5) n20 t21.5 f19 b20. Has thinned out dramatically in the last year or so. Now clean, untaxing, briefly mouth-watering and radiating young grain throughout. *40%*

Royal Castle (84.5) n20 t22 f21 b21.5. From Quality Street, or Quality Spirits? Sweet and very well toffeed! *43%. Quality Spirits International.*

Royal Castle 12 Years Old (84.5) n22 t22 f20 b20.5. Busy nose and delivery with much to chew over. Entirely enjoyable, and seems better each time you taste it. Even so, the finish crumbles a bit. *40%. Quality Spirits International.*

Royal Clan Aged 18 Years (85) n21.5 t21 f21.5 b21. For those giving up gum, here's something to really chew on. Huge degree of cream toffee and toasted fudge which makes for a satin-soft blend, but also one which ensures any big moves towards complexity are nipped in the bud. Very enjoyable, all the same. *40%. Quality Spirits International.*

Royal Household (90.5) n21.5 t23 f23 b23 We are amused. *43%. Diageo.*

Royal Park (85) n21.5 t22.5 f20 b21. Pretty generic with an attractive silky sheen, Demerara sugars and decent late spice swim around in an ocean of caramel. *40%*

Royal Salute 21 Years Old (92.5) n23 t23.5 f23 b23.5 If you are looking for the velvety character of yore, forget it. This one comes with some real character and is much the better for it. The grain, in particular, excels. *40%. Chivas.*

Royal Salute 62 Gun Salute (95.5) n24.5 prunes and apples plus a little cinnamon. And grapes, of course. All this in a bed of seemingly natural caramels. It is a smoke-free environment where every oak note is rounded and friendly, where you fancy you can still find the odd mark of barley and yet although being a blend, the grain is refusing to take it down a bourbon path, despite the peek-a-boo honeycomb; t24 the oak is relatively full on, but early on adds a toasty quality to the marmalade and plum jam. The mid ground casts off any sherry-like clothes and heads for a more honey-rich, vaguely bourbon style without ever reaching Kentucky; f23 the fade is on the gentle side with sugars dissolving against a slightly bittering background as some of the oak rebels, as you might expect at least one or two of these old timers to do. At the very death comes the one and only sign of smoke...that is some parting shot; b24 how do you get a bunch of varying whiskies in style, but each obviously growing a grey beard and probably cantankerous to boot, to settle in and harmonise with the others? A kind of Old People's Home for whisky, if you like. Well, here's how...*43%. Chivas.*

⚬⚬⚬ **Royal Salute The Diamond Tribute** (91) n23.5 docile cherry, linseed oil and plums – sounds like a cricket match...; t23 silky delivery, like a liquidised Melton Hunt fruitcake; f21.5 some very late spice...and a small degree of furriness; b23 ironic that a diamond is probably the hardest natural creation, yet this whisky is one of man's softest... 40%. Chivas.

Royal Salute The Hundred Cask Selection Limited Release No. 7 (92) n22 t23.5 f23 b23.5 As blends go, its entire countenance talks about great age and elegance. And does so with a clipped accent. 40%. Chivas.

Royal Silk Reserve (93) n22 t24 f24 b23 I named this the best newcomer of 2001 and it hasn't let me down. A session blend for any time of the day, this just proves that you don't need piles of peat to create a blend of genuine stature. A must have. 40%

Sainsbury's Basics Blended Scotch Whisky (78.5) n19 t20.5 f19.5 b19.5. "A little less refined, great for mixing," says the label. Frankly, there are a lot of malts out there far less enjoyable than this. Don't be scared to have straight: it's more than decent enough. 40%

Sainsbury's Scotch Whisky (84.5) n20 t22 f21 b21.5. A surprisingly full bodied, chewy blend allowing a pleasing degree of sweetness to develop. No shortage of toffee at the finish – a marked improvement on recent years. 40%. UK.

Sainsbury's Finest Old Matured Aged 8 Years (86) n21.5 t21 f22 b21.5. A sweet blend enjoying a melt-in-the-mouth delivery, a silky body and toffee-vanilla character. The spices arriving towards the end are exceptionally pleasing and welcome. 40%. UK.

Sandy Mac (76) n18 t20 f19 b19. Basic, decent blend that's chunky and raw. 40%. Diageo.

Scots Earl (76.5) n18 t20 f19 b19.5. It's name is Earl. And it must have upset someone in a previous life. Always thrived on its engaging disharmony. But just a tad too syrupy now. 40%. Loch Lomond Distillers.

Scottish Chief (77) n19 t19 f19 b20. This is one big-bodied chief, and not given to taking prisoners. 40%. Quality Spirits International.

Scottish Collie (77) n19 t19 f19 b20. Caramel still, but a Collie with a bit more bite. 40%

Scottish Collie 12 Years Old (85) n22 t22 f20 b21. On the cusp of a really classy blend here but the bitterness on the finish loses serious Brownie points. 40%. Quality Spirits Int, UK.

Scottish Collie 18 Years Old (92) n24 t23 f22 b23. This, honey-led beaut would be a winner even at Crufts: an absolute master class of how an old, yet light and unpeated blend should be. No discord whatsoever between the major elements and not a single hint of over-aging. Superb. 40%. Quality Spirits International, UK.

Scottish Glory dist 2002, bott 2005 (85) n21 t21 f22 b21. An improved blend now bursting with vitality. The ability of the grain to lift the barley is very pleasing. 40%. Duncan Taylor.

Scottish Leader Original (83.5) n17.5 t22.5 f22.5 b22.5. About as subtle as a poke in the eye with a spirit thief. The nose, it must be said, is not great. But I have to admit I thoroughly enjoy the almost indulgent coarseness from the moment it invades the palate. A real chewathon of a spicy blend with a wicked, in-yer-face attitude. Among all the rough-'n-tumble and slap-'n-tickle, the overall depth, weight, balance and molassed charm ain't half bad. 40%. Burn Stewart.

Scottish Leader Aged 12 Years (91) n22.5 t23 f22 b22.5 Absolutely unrecognisable from the Leader 12 I last tasted. This has taken a plumy, fruity route with the weight of a cannonball but the texture of mallow. Big and quite beautiful. 40%. Burn Stewart.

Scottish Leader 30 Years Old (87) n23.5 t21.5 f20.5 b21.5 A little too docile ever to be a great whisky, but the nose is something rather special. A bit of attention on the finish and this could be a real corker. 40%. Burn Stewart.

Scottish Leader Select (91.5) n23 t23.5 f22.5 b22.5 Don't make the mistake of thinking this is just the 40% with three extra percentage points of alcohol. This appears to be an entirely different bottling with an entirely different personality. A delight. 43%. Burn Stewart. For the South African Market.

Scottish Leader Select (74) n18.5 t19 f18 b18.5. I assume the leader is Major Disharmony. 40%. Burn Stewart.

Scottish Leader Supreme (72.5) n17 t19 f18 b18.5. Jings! It's like an old-fashioned Gorbals punch-up in the glass – and palate. 40%. Burn Stewart.

Scottish Piper (80) n20 t20 f20 b20. A light, mildly- raw, sweet blend with lovely late vanilla intonation. 40%

Scottish Prince (83.5) n21 t22 f20 b20.5. Muscular, but agreeably juicy. 40%

Scottish Reel (78.5) n19 t19 f20 b19.5. Non fussy with an attractive bite, as all such blends should boast. 40%. London & Scottish International.

Scottish Rill (85) n20 t20.5 f22.5 b22. Refreshing yet earthy. 40%. Quality Spirits Int.

Sheep Dip Amoroso Oloroso 1999 Oloroso sherry casks, bott Mar 12 (92) n23.5 big toffee apple fanfare and then a slow development of juicy dates and prunes...topped with treacle. A thick aroma, but not too intense for subtlety; t24 after a nose like that how could it be anything other than lush? Those big sugars are kept in check by an excellent sub-woofer oak; the midground enjoys an outbreak of creamy chocolate, with a little fruit and nut mixed in; **f21** as this matured in Spain, just a touch puzzled by the bitter-ish, furry finale; **b23.5** more like Sherry Dip than Sheep Dip. Actually, chocolate dip wouldn't be too far off the mark, either. To create this, malt which had spent three years maturing in bourbon cask was then shipped to Jerez where it spent a further nine years in presumably fresh sherry. It was worth the trouble... *41.8%. Spencerfield Spirits.*

Something Special (85) n21.5 t22 f20.5 b21. Mollycoddled by toffee, any murderous tendencies seem to have been fudged away, leaving just the odd moment of attractive complexity. You suspect there is a hit man in there somewhere trying to get out. *40%. Chivas.*

Something Special Premium Aged 15 Years (89) n22 t23 f21 b23 Fabulous malt thread and some curious raisiny/sultana fruitiness, too. A blend-lover's blend. *40%.*

Spar Finest Reserve (90.5) n21.5 t22.5 f23.5 b23 One of Britain's best value for money blends with an honest charm which revels in the clean high quality grain and earthier malts which work so well together. *40%*

Stewart's Old Blended (93) n22.5 t24 f23 b23.5 Really lovely whisky for those who like to close their eyes, contemplate and have a damned good chew. *40%*

Storm (94) n23 a clarion call of clean grain amid decimated coconut; t23.5 superb delivery: the structure is a joy with a lush mouth-feel but the complexity by no means stilted. The odd salty note appears to maximise the oaky depth and that light oiliness ensures the barley-sweetness lasts; superb light spicing begins to intensify towards the middle; f24 fabulous finale with that spice hanging on in there and acting as the perfect foil for the deft honeycomb and sugars; so clean you feel your teeth are being polished while drinking this; b23.5 a little gem of a blend that really will take you by storm. *43%. Whisky Shack.*

Swords (78) n20 t21 f18 b19. Beefed up somewhat with some early smoke thrusting through and rapier grains to follow. *40%. Morrison Bowmore.*

Talisman 5 Years Old (85.5) n22 t22 f20.5 b21. Unquestionably an earthier, weightier version of what was once a Speyside romp. Soft peats also add extra sweetness. *40%*

Teacher's 50 - 12 Years Old batch 2-16, bott Sep 11 (85.5) n20.5 t22.5 f21.5 b21. Once, before entering the Indian bottling hall, this must have been a strutting peacock of a Scotch blend. But after being doused in a far too liberal amount of caramels it has been reduced to a house sparrow: outwardly common and dull but at least with an engaging personality. The usual Teacher's smoke shows itself only at the death, alas. And all else is a silky honeyed sweetness pleading for an extra degree of complexity. The very complexity, indeed, which was almost certainly there before being coloured to death. If they could sort out the caramel levels in the bottling hall, this would be a blend that would put on a spectacular display.... *42.8%*

Teacher's Aged 25 Years batch 1 (96.5) n24 at first this Teacher's lectures malt to you; not any old malt, but delicately smoked and as light with citrus as it is heavy with phenol. Then slowly the grains emerge, offering weighted consistency to the sweeter, maple syrup elements, until there is a satisfying fusion between the two....; t24.5 not sure one can quite nose silk, though that's what it appeared to be. But you can certainly spot it on the palate, and that's exactly what we have on delivery: every atom, be it smoky or marmalade orangey, simply melts in the mouth though unusually for a 25-y-o, it does not leave an oaky residue; f23.5 long, spicy, a little tangy; b24.5 only 1300 bottles means they will be hard pushed to create this exact style again. Worth a go, chaps: considering this is India bound, it is the karma sutra of blended scotch. *46%. Beam Inc. 1300 bottles. India & Far East Travel Retail exclusive.*

Teacher's Highland Cream (90) n23 t23 f22 b22 Not yet back to its best but a massive improvement on the 2005 bottlings. Harder grains to accentuate the malt will bring it closer to the classic of old. *40%*

Teacher's Highland Cream v (90) n23 t22.5 f22 b22.5 A very curious, seriously high grade, variant. Although the Ardmore distillery is on the label, it is the only place it can really be seen. Certainly - the least smoky Teacher's I've come across in 35 years of drinking the stuff: the smoke is there, but adds only ballast rather than taking any form of lead. But the grain is soft and knits with the malts with ease to make for a sweeter, much more lush version than the rest of the world may recognize. *40%*

Teacher's Origin (88.5) n22 t23.5 f21 b22 A fascinating blend which probably ranks as the softest on the market today. That is aided and abetted by the exceptionally high malt content, 65%, which makes this something of an inverted blend, as that, for most established brands, is the average grain content. What appears to be a high level of caramel also makes for a rounding of the edges, as well as evidence of sherry butts. The bad news is that that has resulted in a duller finish than perhaps might have been intended, which is even more pronounced given the impressive speech made on delivery. Lovely whisky, yes. But something, I feel, of a work in progress. Bringing the caramel down by the percentage points of the malt would be a very positive start... *42.8%. ncf. Beam Global.*

Té Bheag (86) n22 t21 f21.5 b21.5. Classic style of rich caramels and bite. *40%. ncf. Pràban na Linne.*

261

Tesco Finest Reserve Aged 12 Years (74) n18.5 t19 f18 b18.5. The most astonishing thing about this, apart from the fact it is a 12 year-old, is that it won a Gold "Best in Class" in a 2010 international whisky competition: it surely could not have been from the same batch as the one before me. Frankly, you have to go a long way to find a whisky as bland as this and for a 12-y-o it is monumentally disappointing. 40%.

Tesco Special Reserve Minimum 3 Years Old (78) n18.5 t21.5 f19 b19. Decent early spice on delivery but otherwise anonymous. 40%. Tesco.

Tesco Value Scotch Whisky (83) n19 t21 f22 b21. Young and genuinely refreshing whisky. Without the caramel this really would be a little darling. 40%

Traquair (78) n19 t21 f19 b19. Young, but offering a substantial mouthful including attractive smoke. 46%. Burn Stewart.

The Tweeddale Blend Aged 10 Years (89.5) n22 t23.5 f21.5 b22.5 The first bottling of this blend since World War 2, it has been well worth waiting for. 46%. ncf. 50% malt. Stonedean.

The Tweeddale Blend Aged 12 Years bott Jun 11 **(94.5)** n23.5 a sumptuous mixture of diced apples with berry fruit. The sugars and honeys are of the lightest variety but complex and perfectly in harmony with the friendly vanillas: a triumph! t24 boasts that beguiling and entirely disarming mixture of passive aggression, where your taste buds think they are being lulled into an easy, silky ride before being stormed by troops fully armed with spicy vanilla. Always clean, so you get a clear view of the deepening honey in the middle ground; f23 light oils carry the spices and chewy vanilla the full course. And it is a very long one...; b24 bravo! A blend which sets out to maximise the (in this case) high quality whiskies used. An engrossing and massively enjoyable celebration of blended scotch. A minor classic, in fact. And not entirely dissimilar, curiously, to a blend I occasionally concoct for my own enjoyment... 46%. ncf. Stonedean.

⬩⬩⬩⬩⬩ **The Tweeddale Blend Aged 12 Years** bott code 28 Feb 13 **(95)** n23.5 t24 f23 b24.5 For the tasting notes see the 2011 bottling above. Very, very similar, except more crisp grain on the nose and a slightly more clever use of citrus throughout. How heart-warming to see a blend not just keep faithfully to its style, but appears to somehow up the quality a fraction. A treat of a whisky experience. 46%. nc ncf. Stonedean. 3rd release.

Ushers Green Stripe (85) n19 t22.5 f21.5 b22. Upped a notch or two in all-round quality. The juicy theme and clever weight is highly impressive and enjoyable. 43%. Diageo.

VAT 69 (84.5) n20 t22 f21 b21.5. Has thickened up in style: weightier, more macho, much more to say and a long way off that old lightweight. A little cleaning up wouldn't go amiss. 40%

White Horse (90.5) n22 t23 f22.5 b23 A malt which has subtley changed shape. Not just the smoke which gives it weight, but you get the feeling that some of Diageo's less delicate malts have been sent in to pack a punch. As long as they are kept in line, as is the case here – just – we can all enjoy a very big blend. 40%. Diageo.

White Horse Aged 12 Years (86) n21 t23 f21 b21. enjoyable, complex if not always entirely harmonious. For instance, the apples and grapes on the nose appear on a limb from the grain and caramel and nothing like the thoroughbred of old. Lighter, more flaccid and caramel dominated. 40%. Diageo.

Whyte & Mackay 'The Thirteen' 13 Year Old (92) n22.5 t23.5 f23 b23. Try this and your luck'll be in...easily the pick of the W&M blended range. 40%. Whyte & Mackay Distillers Ltd.

Whyte & Mackay Luxury 19 Year Old (84.5) n21 t22 f20 b21.5. A pleasant house style chewathon. Nutty, biting but with a tang. 40%. Whyte & Mackay Distillers Ltd.

Whyte & Mackay Supreme 22 Year Old (87) n21 t23 f20.5 b22.5. Ignore the nose and finish and just enjoy the early ride. 43%

Whyte & Mackay Oldest 30 Year Old (87.5) n23 t23 f20 b21.5. What exasperating whisky this is. So many good things about it, but... 45%

Whyte & Mackay Original Aged Blended 40 Years Old (93) n23 t24 f22 b24. I admit, when I nosed and tasted this at room temp, not a lot happened. Pretty, but closed. But once warmed in the hand up to full body temperature, it was obvious that Richard Paterson had created a quite wonderful monster of a blend offering so many avenues to explore that the mind almost explodes. Well done RP for creating something that further proves, and in such magnitude, just how warmth can make an apparently ordinary whisky something bordering genius. 45%

Whyte & Mackay Special (84.5) n20 t23 f20 b21.5. If you are looking for a big-flavoured dram and with something approaching a vicious left uppercut, this might be a useful bottle to have on hand. The nose, I'm afraid, has not improved over the years but there appears to be compensation with the enormity and complexity of the delivery, a veritable orgy of big, oily, juicy, murky flavours and tones if ever there was one. You cannot but like it, in the same way as you may occasionally like rough sex. But if you are looking for a delicate dram to gently kiss you and caress your fevered brow, then leave well alone. 40%

William Grant's 12 Years Old Bourbon Cask (90.5) n23 lively and floral. The drier notes suggest chalky oak but the sweet spiciness balances beautifully; t22.5 flinty textured with both malts and grains pinging around the teeth with abandon; f22 remains light yet with a clever, crisp sweetness keeping the weightier oaks in check; **b23** very clever blending where balance is the key. *40%*

William Grant's 15 Years Old (85) n21 t23 f20 b21. Grain and, later, caramel dominates but the initial delivery reveals the odd moment of sheer genius and complexity on max revs. *43%*

William Grant's 25 Years Old (95.5) n23.5 some serious oak, but chaperoned by top quality oloroso, itself thinned by firm and graceful grain; **t24** sheer quality: complexity as the shovel-load as juicy fruits interact with darting, crisp barley; again the grain shows elegance both sharpening increasingly mouth-watering malt and softening the oak; **f24** medium length, but not a single sign of fatigue: the sweet barley runs and runs and some jammy fruits charm. Just to cap it all, some wonderful spices dazzle and a touch of low roast Java enriches; **b24** absolutely top-rank blending that appears to maximize every last degree of complexity. Most astonishing, though, is its sprightly countenance: even Scottish footballing genius Ally MacLeod struggled to send out Ayr Utd. sides with this kind of brio. And that's saying something! A gem. *40%*

William Grant's 100 US Proof Superior Strength (92) n23 sublime chocolate lime nose, decent oak; **t24** big mouth arrival, lush and fruity with the excellent extra grain bite you might expect at this strength, just an extra degree of spice takes it into even higher orbit than before; **f22** back to chocolate again with a soft fruit fade; **b23** a fruitier drop now than it was in previous years but no less supremely constructed. *50% (100 US proof)*

William Grant's Ale Cask Reserve (89) n21 t23 f22 b23. A real fun blend that is just jam-packed with jagged malty notes. The hops were around more on earlier bottlings, but watch out for them. Nothing pint-sized about this: this is a big blend and very true in flavour/shape to the original with just a delicious shading of grain to really up the complexity. *40%*

William Grant's Family Reserve (94) n25 this, to me, is the perfect nose to any blend: harmonious and faultless. There is absolutely everything here in just-so proportions: a bit of snap and bite from the grain, teasing sweet malts, the faintest hint of peat for medium weight, strands of oak for dryness, fruit for lustre. Even Ardbeg doesn't pluck my strings like this glass of genius can; **t23** exceptionally firm grain helps balance the rich, multi-layered malty tones. The sub-plot of burnt raisins and peek-a-boo peat add further to the intrigue and complexity (if it doesn't bubble and nip around the mouth you have a rare sub-standard bottling); **f22** a hint of caramel can be detected amid returning grains and soft cocoa tones: just so clean and complex; **b24** there are those puzzled by my obvious love affair with blended whisky - both Scotch and Japanese - at a time when malts are all the rage. But take a glass of this and carefully nurture and savour it for the best part of half an hour and you may begin to see why I believe this to be the finest art form of whisky. For my money, this brand - brilliantly kept in tip-top shape by probably the world's most naturally gifted blender - is the closest thing to the blends of old and, considering it is pretty ubiquitous, it defies the odds for quality. It is a dram with which you can start the day and end it: one to keep you going at low points in between, or to celebrate the victories. It is the daily dram that has everything. *40%*

William Grant's Sherry Cask Reserve (82) n20 t22 f20 b20. Raspberry jam and cream from time to time. Attractive, but somewhat plodding dram that's content in second gear. *40%*

William Lawson's Finest (85) n18.5 t22.5 f22 b22. Not only has the label become more colourful, but so, too, has the whisky. However that has not interfered with the joyous old-fashioned grainy bite. A complex and busy blend from the old charm school. *40%*

William Lawson's Scottish Gold Aged 12 Years (89) n22 t23 f22 b22. For years Lawson's 12 was the best example of the combined wizardry of clean grain, unpeated barley and good bourbon cask that you could find anywhere in the world: a last-request dram before the firing squad. Today it is still excellent, but just another sherried blend. What's that saying about if it's not being broke...? *40%*

Windsor 12 Years Old (81) n20 t21 f20 b20. Thick, walloped-on blend that you can stand a spoon in. Hard at times to get past the caramel. *40%. Diageo.*

Windsor Aged 17 Years Super Premium (89) n23 t22 f22 b22. Still on the safe side for all its charm and quality. An extra dose of complexity would lift this onto another level. *40%*

Windsor 21 Years Old (90) n20 fruity and weighty but something a bit lactic and lethargic from some old bourbon casks has crept in; **t23** excellent oils surround the silk to help amplify the intensity of the fruit and drifting smoke; **f24** some spiciness that shows towards the middle really takes off now as drying vanilla counters the sweet grains; **b23** recovers fabulously from the broken nose and envelopes the palate with a silky-sweet style unique to the Windsor scotch brand. Excellent. *40%. Diageo.*

Ye Monks (86) n20 t23 f21.5 b21.5. Just hope they are praying for less caramel to maximize the complexity. Still, a decent spicy chew and outstanding bite which is great fun and worth finding when in South America. *40%. Diageo.*

Yokozuna Blended 3 Years Old (79.5) n18.5 t20.5 f20 b20.5. It appears the Mongols are gaining a passion for thick, sweet, toffeed, oily, slightly feinty whisky. For a nation breastfed on airag, this'll be a doddle... *40%. Speyside Distillers. Mongolian market.*

Irish Whiskey

Of all the whiskies in the world, it is Irish which probably causes most confusion amongst both established whisk(e)y lovers and the novices.

Ask anyone to define what is unique to Irish Whiskey – apart from it being made in Ireland – and the answers, if my audiences around the world at my tastings are anything to go by, are in this order: i) It is triple distilled; ii) It is never, ever made from peat; iii) They exclusively use sherry casks; iv) It comes from the oldest distillery in the world; v) It is made from a mixture of malted and unmalted barley.

Only one of those answers is true: the fifth. And it is usually the final answer extracted from the audience when the last hand raised sticks to his guns after the previous four responses have been shot down.

There was no shortage of Blarney when the Irish were trying to market their whiskey back in the 1950s and early 60s. Hence the triple distilled/non-peated myth was born. The Irish had had a thin time of it since the 1920s and seen their industry decimated. So the marketing guys got to work.

As much of Ireland is covered in peat, it is hardly surprising that in the 19th century smoky whiskey from inland distilleries was not uncommon. Like Scotland. Some distilleries used two stills, others three. Like Scotland. Sherry butts were ubiquitous in Ireland before World War 2. Just as they were in Scotland. And there are distilleries in Scotland older than Bushmills, which dates from 1784. However, the practice of using malted and unmalted barley, begun so less tax had to be paid on malted grain, had died out in the Lowlands of Scotland, leaving it for Ireland to carry on alone.

It is hard to believe, then, that when I was researching my Irish Whiskey Almanac way back in 1993, Redbreast had just been discontinued as a brand leaving Green Spot, an ancient gem of a bottling from Mitchell and Son, Dublin's legendary high class wine and spirit merchants, as the sole surviving Pure Irish Pot Still Whiskey. At first Redbreast's owners refused to send me a bottle as they regarded it a pointless exercise, seeing as the brand had gone. After I wrote about it, first in my Almanac and then in newspapers and magazines elsewhere, they had no option other than to reverse their decision: interest had been whetted and people were asking for it once more.

When it was relaunched, the Pot Still came from Midleton. The Redbreast they were discontinuing was Pure Pot Still from the long defunct original Jameson Distillery in Dublin. Jameson may once have been locked in commercial battle with their neighbouring Power's distillery, but they united in the late 19th century when they brought out a book called: "The Truth About Irish Whiskey" in which they together, along with other Dublin distillers, fought against blended and other types of what they considered adulterated whiskey to tell the world that the only true Irish whiskey was Pure Pot Still.

The last direct descendent of the true Irish distilling DNA from that era is Barry Crockett. He and I first met 20 years ago when he took me around the very Midleton Distillery in whose grounds he had been born long before the present plant of 1975 had been as much as a glint in an accountant's eye. Barry, myself, Irish Distillers blender Barry Walsh and Green Spot owners Mitchell and Son were then the only people in the entire industry who knew just how great true Irish pot still whiskey was and the deadly threat it was under with Redbreast having been discontinued.

The two Barrys had their hands tied: one had to blend in a certain way and for set markets, the other to produce to order. But I was more than aware of the sorrow in both men that they could not produce more pot still (there was simply not enough capacity), or make extra available to be tasted in its own unmolested glory. So when I met up with Barry Crockett in Stockholm a year or two back and we posed for photos with the new Pot Still range, there was a quiet sense of achievement between us. He had been granted his wish and produced more of the world's most esoteric whiskey style, and my long campaign to see it back on the shelves (begun with a flaming row with the directors of Irish Distillers) had born fruit.

In March 2013 Barry retired, ending nearly 50 years in Irish whisky production, more than 30 of them as distillery manager at Midleton. A nation's loss is a Nation's gain – his deputy Brian Nation takes over after a decade's mentoring. But Barry, who will be now found burrowing into the distillery's archives, will be able to look back proudly at a lifetime's work quite magnificently done.

Pure Pot Still
MIDLETON (old distillery)

Midleton 25 Years Old Pot Still db (92) n24 t24 f21 b23. A really enormous whiskey that is in the truest classic Irish style. The un-malted barley really does make the tastebuds hum and the oak has added fabulous depth. Interesting when tasted against an American rye – the closeness of the character is there to be experienced, but also the differences. A subtle mature whiskey of unquestionable quality. Superb. 43%

Midleton 30 Years Old Pot Still db (85) n19 t22 f22 b22. A typically brittle, crunchy Irish pot still where the un-malted grains have a telling say. The oak has travelled as far as it can without having an adverse effect. A chewy whiskey which revels in its bitter-sweet balance. An impressively tasty and fascinating insight into yesteryear. 45%

Midleton 1973 Pure Pot Still db (95) n24 t24 f23 b24. The enormous character of true Irish pot still whiskey (a mixture of malted and unmalted barley) appears to absorb age better than most other grain spirits. This one is in its element. But drink at full strength and at body temp (it is pretty closed when cool) for the most startling – and memorable effects. I have no idea how much this costs. But if you can find one and afford it... then buy it!! 56%

MIDLETON (new distillery)

⁙ **Midleton Single Pot Still Single Cask 1991** cask no. 48750, dist Nov 91, bott Oct 12 db (96.5) n23.5 usual mix of beech honey, manuka honey and an indistinguishable fruit-like sweetness, somewhere between pear and strawberry; a fascinating blend of bourbon and rye styles; t24 just one of those deliveries you pray for: magnificent mouth feel and weight, just about perfect in fact. Then that unique iron rod of sweet barley couched in velvet. The salivation levels are off the scale, while the hard-nosed unmalted barley offers up their standard crisp honey tones. The enormous age is supported by a crypto-bourbon attack of liquorice and hickory; f23.5 softens, elongates and really kicks in with more bourbon/ rye-style molasses, though this only adds weight to the strawberry and chocolate mousse towards the very death; b24.5 like the majority of Pot Still whiskeys, takes a little time to settle in the glass: always give it time to breath and come alive. When it finally does...just....wow!! 54.1%. ncf. Irish Distillers. Warehouse No. M09, exclusive to The Whisky Exchange.

Midleton Single Pot Still Single Cask 1994 cask no. 74060, dist 15 Nov 94 db (93) n23 delicate and clean yet far more happy to trot out the caramels from the oak than the biting grain from the pot still; a few spices carry the unmistakable Irish on the wind, though...; **t23** firms up slightly on delivery, but this is still a softie as IPS goes. Again, the caramel dictates and it takes a little while for the harder grains to force their way through. They arrive in a cocoa-nougat cloak when they do..; **f23.5** some balmy sugar and a slight hint of honey makes this about as silky an IPS as you'll ever come across despite the late oak arrival; **b23.5** probably a mod pos as opposed to a heavy one. A charming bottling, though if only they had been braver and gone for full cask strength... *46%. ncf. Irish Distillers. Exclusive to the Celtic Whiskey Shop.*

Midleton Barry Crockett Legacy db (**94**) **n23.5** spices nip and thrust; delicate fruits form a series of gentle layers; a light bourbon liquorice adds depth...; **t24.5** the delivery provides the sweetness missing from the nose but only after an early surge of oak and soft oils. The middle ground is a battlefield between spices and peachy fruit, with just a touch of honey moving in when it thinks no one is watching...; **f22.5** relatively short and duller than you might expect. The caramels cap the higher points and though spices rumble there is little for it to echo against; **b23.5** another fabulous Pot Still, very unusual for its clever use of the varied ages of the oak to form strata of intensity. One very sophisticated whiskey. *46%. ncf.*

⁘ **Paddy Centenary Edition** db (**93**) **n22** strangely busy with distinct dry tobacco leaf and even a German-esque nougat element to this; **t23.5** from the fascinating to the point of weird nose, we are now thrown back into a land we recognise: mouth-filling with a tart fruitiness countering an outbreak of balmy brown – mainly muscovado – sugars. The usual hardness to a Pot Still is at first AWOL, but slowly builds as the barley asserts itself; **f24** this is the business end where we now have a complexity alert with walnut oils dripping into grittier sugars and barley grain. The oak also display itself with a light, tangy overlay and egg custard tart – complete with a light sprinkling of cinnamon; inevitably, almost, there is a very late hint of milky cocoa, **b23.5** this 7-year-old Pure Pot Still whiskey really is a throwback. All Paddy's original whiskey from this era would have been from the old Midleton distillery which sits, in aspic, beside the one opened in 1975. Even with the likelihood of oats being in the mash in those days, still can't believe the original would have been quite as sweet on the palate – and soul – as this. *43%*

Powers John's Lane Release Aged 12 Years db (**96.5**) **n24** unmistakable. Unique. Utopian. Irish pure pot still at its most embracing and magnificent. That bizarre bipolar character of rock hard grain so at home in the company of silky, molten honey. Some light, non-specific fruit – a bit like boiled sweets in a candy shop. But a vague menthol note, too...; **t25** as Irish whiskey goes: perfection! The delivery can come only from Irish Pot still – I have encountered it nowhere else. And it is a replay of the nose: soft, dissolve-on-the-palate honey and elsewhere strands of something much firmer – hardening more and more as it moves to the middle ground; **f23.5** wonderful fade: a distant medium roast Java, the Lubec marzipan which you just knew would be coming; a little caramel; some orangey notes... **b24** this is a style of Irish Pot Still I have rarely seen outside the blending lab. I had many times thought of trying to find some of this and bottling it myself. No need now. I think I have just tasted Irish Whiskey of the Year, and certainly one of the top five world whiskies of the year. *46%*

⁘ **Powers John's Lane Release Aged 12 Years** bott 13 Nov 12 db (**91**) **n24** a breath-taking display of major bourbon cask credentials with huge tannins sparking off liquorice and hickory storms, as well as polished leather and manuka honey. The firmness which, for a second, you might think is rye, is actually the pot still un-malted barley in action; **t23.5** initially soft, then breaks up fast on delivery so spices pounce. Honey dominates, as does treacle and walnut; the fruit has a degree of dried dates and figs; **f21** dries and bitters out a tad with furry marmalade and cocoa; **b22.5** researchers some time ago discovered the American accent is derived from an Irish one (and the Canadian from Scots). As pure Irish pot still is the foundation stone of all Irish whiskey, there is no little irony that so many aspects of this bottling is more recognisable as Kentuckian than it is from Cork. Only a slightly off beam cask undermines the finish a tad. Otherwise, superb. *46%. Irish Distillers.*

⁘ **Powers Signature Release** bott code. L3065 db (**91**) **n23.5** such an old-fashioned nose. Juicy fruit abounds, especially passion fruit and pear, and there is no shortage of herbs, either, with allspice at the vanguard; **t22.5** a big, bold sugary statement on delivery, a mix between molasses and muscovado; busy spices flit around as figs and dates begin to point to the sherry influence; **f22** a slight Achilles heel of fuzzy marmalade, reveals a less than perfect sherry butt. But the cocoa and ulmo honey does all it can to compensate; **b23** when I first tasted pure pot still over three decades ago, virtually all that I came across was maturing in oloroso butts. Often, the quality of the casks was better than the spirit from the dilapidated distilleries which produced it. Here again the sherry butts are of the highest quality. Maybe one is below par and this is evidenced, very vaguely, on the finish. But, overall, superb! *46%*

Redbreast 12 Years Old db (**96**) **n23.5** lively and firm, this one offering a gentle fruity swetness not too dissimilar to a rye, ironic as there is light bourbony kick off the oak, too; **t24.5** wonderfully clipped and correct in delivery: firm at first - very firm!!! - but slowly the barley melts and light muscovado sugars dovetail with a flinty fruitiness and pillow-soft vanilla; incorrigibly mouthwatering and the build up of spices is just showing off; **f24** remains spicy but clean, allowing a clear view of those varying barley tones drifting away; **b24** Yess...!!! Back to its classically classy, brilliant best. No sulphur casks this time (unlike last year). Just juicy pot still all the way. An old loved one has returned... more gorgeous than ever. *40%. Irish Distillers.*

⋅⊗⋅ **Redbreast Aged 12 Years** bott 7 Jan 13 (code: L3007) db **(89) n22** almost grainy in its lightness; sweet, slightly minty; **t23.5** Redbreast at its most genteel: such a clean delivery and follow through with a distinct and unusual maltiness; **f21.5** vanishes surprisingly quickly leaving a light sugar and vanilla coating; **b22** this one took me aback. One of the softest Irish pot stills I have encountered, in or outside a lab. Delicious, but displaying very little of the trademark steel which sets this whiskey apart. *40%. Irish Distillers.*

Redbreast Aged 12 Years Cask Strength batch B1/11 db **(96) n24.5** just about the ultimate in Irish whiskey noses. Absolutely rock hard: you feel you could cut diamonds with an aroma like this. It is curiously fruity in that unique Irish Pot Still way, and not just from the obvious sherry involvement, yet shows clearly it's a relation to another whiskey style: American rye. A little hint of mint and lavender goes a long way and offers the only softness in this glorious bitter-sweet aroma; **t24.5** my, oh my, oh my, oh my...one of those deliveries which takes your breath away and it is a few moments before you can compose yourself to think. Or, in my case, to compose myself to compose. The first thing is the sweetness which is never apparent on the nose: here we have the crunchiest Demerara sugar meeting even crunchier muscovado; then a litany of varied fruit and quasi-rye juicy bits...mmmmmm; **f23** majestically long and moves in fabulously mysterious chocolatey ways - chocolate and raisin to be more precise - generating even more salivating moments right until the big chocolate sponge/sherry trifle finale. Late spices, even the faintest possible bitterness of a rogue treated sherry butt, though for once it does no serious damage, other than costing it a possible place in the world's top three. The vanillas come into action for the first time here, too...; **b24** this is Irish pot still on steroids. And sporting an Irish brogue as thick as my great great grandfather John Murray's. To think, had I not included Redbreast in Jim Murray's Irish Whiskey Almanac back in 1994, after it had already been unceremoniously scrapped and discontinued, while championing the then entirely unknown Irish Pot Still cause this brand would no longer have been with us. If I get run over by a bus tomorrow, at least I have that as a tick when St Peter is totting up the plusses and minuses... And with the cask strength, he might even give me two... *57.7%. ncf. Irish Distillers.*

⋅⊗⋅ **Redbreast Aged 12 Years Cask Strength Edition** batch B1/12 bott 4 Apr 12 (code: L2095) db **(97) n24.5 t24 f24 b24.5**. For the sake of space, it is best I refer you to the tasting notes for Batch B1/11. Except here there is less fruit and absolutely no off notes. It is, as Irish whiskey is concerned, nigh-on perfection. *58.6%. ncf. Irish Distillers.*

Redbreast 15 Years Old db **(94) n23 t24 f23 b24**. For years I have been pleading for Irish Distillers to launch a pot still at 46%, natural colour and unchillfiltered. Well, I've got two out of three wishes. And what we have here is a truly great Irish whiskey and my pulse races in the certain knowledge it can get better still... *46%. ncf. France.*

⋅⊗⋅ **Redbreast Aged 15 Years** bott 12 Nov 12 (code: L2317) db **(96) n23.5** soft fruits from peaches to strawberry with boiled yam and molasses as back up. Rich, intense, vaguely spiced yet so, so gentle...; **t25** how does this happen...? Take all of the following ingredients but in their most delicate individual form: treacle, banana (or is it yam again?), liquorice, molasses, manuka honey, ulmo honey, maltshake, raisin, dates, vanilla....and stir until your arm drops off; **f23.5** just a thinner, less oily version of the delivery and middle; the vaguest hint of furriness; **b24** just so far better than the original 15-year-old it is hard to know where to start. You get the feeling there is wider stock to choose from and the casks are peaking, showing no sign of regressive traits. The delivery, though, is something you are unlikely ever to forget. *46%. ncf. Irish Distillers.*

Green Spot (94.5) n23.5 mouthwatering and fresh on one level, honey and menthol on another; **t24** crisp, mouthwatering with a fabulous honey burst, alarmingly sensuous; **f23.5** the caramel has receded, leaving the finer, sharper pot still character to battle it out with the honey. The spices are now much clearer too; **b23.5** this honeyed state has remained a few years, and its shar ness has now been regained. Complex throughout. Unquestionably one of the world's greatest branded whiskies. *40%. Irish Distillers for Mitchell & Son, Dublin.*

Green Spot 10 Year Old Single Pot Still dist 1993 **(92) n23 t22 f24 b23**. Launched to celebrate the 200th anniversary of this wonderful Dublin landmark, this is bottled from three mixed bourbon casks of Irish Pot Still. The extra age has detracted slightly from the usual vitality of the standard Green Spot (an 8-y-o) but its quality still must be experienced. *40%*

Green Spot 12 Year Old Single Pot Still dist 1991 **(93) n24 t24 f22 b23**. A single cask restricted to exactly 200 bottles to mark the 200th anniversary of the grand old man of Kildare Street, this is the first Middleton pot still I have seen at this strength outside of a lab. A one-off in every sense. *58%*

❖ **Irish Whiskey Society Single Cask Aged 17 Years** cask no. 1038, dist 13 Jan 1995, bott 12 Jul 2012 **(91.5) n22** toasty. As in toasted mallows and heather-honey on toast. Lots of toffee, too; **t23.5** livelier delivery than the relatively inert nose; firm spice and a rod of honey form the spine; marmalade and chocolate fill the middle; **f23** long with a touch of Cadbury chocolate mini-rolls but set off with a degree of maple syrup; **b23** even in the lab, I have encountered very few pure pot still whiskies of this age. The degree the sugars take over is a bit of a surprise. Delicious, to be sure. 55.2%. sc. *Irish Distillers.*

Yellow Spot Aged 12 Years bourbon, sherry and Malaga casks db **(88.5) n23.5** my nose is sifting through the layers of fruit to get a glimpse of the IPS.... Much has sunk without trace, like a head in an eiderdown pillow. As an archaeologist tenderly scrapping away at a find might, the apricot and orange blossom has to be moved to one side before a degree of brittle grains shows; the spices soon follow...; **t22.5** big initial flavour profile. Enjoyable, fun, lush. But, like the nose, muddled and without a defined structure. Definitely a crispness at work in there late on, but takes its time to arrive; **f20** a little unplanned as bitterness joins in with the apricot, though the complex part of the finale is over quite quickly; **b22.5** if anything, just a shade too many wine casks used which somewhat drowns out the unique IP character. Reminds me of when Barry Walsh was working on the triple maturation theme of the Bushmills 16, probably about 15 years ago. Not until the very last days did all the components click. Just before then, it went through a phase like this (though obviously with malt, not IPS). Knowing current blender Billy Leighton as I do, I can see this whiskey improving in future batches as lessons are learned. not that there isn't already much to enjoy... 46%. *Irish Distillers.*

OLD COMBER

Old Comber 30 Years Old Pure Pot Still (88) n23 t24 f20 b21. A classic example of a whiskey spending a few Summers too many in wood: increasing age doesn't equal excellence. That said, always very drinkable and early on positively sparkles with a stunning mouthfeel. Out of respect for the old I have made the markings for taste cover the first seven or eight seconds... 40%

Single Malt
COOLEY

Connemara bott code L9042 db **(88) n23 t22.5 f20.5 b22.** One of the softest smoked whiskies in the world which though quite lovely gives the impression it can't make its mind up about what it wants to be. 40%

Connemara Aged 8 Years db **(85) n22.5 t21.5 f20 b21.** Another Connemara lacking teeth. The peat charms, especially on the nose, but the complexity needs working on. 46%

Connemara Aged 12 Years bott code L9024 db **(85.5) n23 t21.5 f20 b21.** The nose, with its beautiful orange, fruity lilt, puts the shy smoke in the shade. 40%

Connemara Bog Oak bott 26 July 2011, batch V11/07 db **(93) n24** the ancient Bog Oak dug up and fitted to the end of the barrels has definitely made an impact, for there has never been a Connemara nose like this before. It is sweeter for a start, and the iodine character seems more pronounced....a little more concentrated. Just a very different – and hugely enjoyable – twist on a well-known tale...; **t24** again...Connemara, but not quite as we have ever known it. A decidedly molten Mars Bar feel to this, with cocoa and caramel mixing in with the ever-sweetening phenols; **f22.5** silky, but a little tang here, slightly musty...perhaps it needs some new heads...; **b22.5** I guessed with the hand of Cooley blender Noel "Nosher" Sweeney (the man who can put away a roast dinner more quickly than most of us can successfully open a bar of Nutri Grain) behind this it would be anything other than bog standard...And Noel: well done on successfully getting your ancient ends away... 57.5%

Connemara Cask Strength bott code L9041 db **(90) n21.5 t23 f22 b22.5.** A juicy negative of the standard bottling: does its talking on the palate rather than nose. Maybe an absence of caramel notes might have something to do with that. 57.9%

Connemara Distillers Edition db **(86) n22 t22.5 f20 b21.5.** When I give whisk(e)y tastings around the world, I love to include Connemara. Firstly, people don't expect peated Irish. Secondly, their smoked whisky stock is eclectic and you never quite know what is going to come out of the bottle. This is a particularly tight, sharp style. No prisoners survived... 43%

Connemara Single Cask 18 Years Old Amontillado Sherry Finish Solera Amontillado sherry cask, cask no. 155, dist 31 Aug 92, bott 12 May 92 db **(70) n18 t19 f16 b17.** Blast! I hoped to finally get through an entire day without sulphur for once. Failed! 46%. sc.

Connemara Turf Mór Limited Edition Small Batch Collection bott code L10215 db **(94) n23.5 t23.5 f23.5 b23.5.** At Burnley FC, the wine served in their boardroom is The Claret's Claret, naturally. I will not be surprised to find this the whiskey on offer... The tasting notes to this just about perfectly match the ones above. 58.2%

Cooley Poitín Origin Edition dist 26 July 2011, rotation 232/11 db **(92.5)** n23.5 t23 f23 b23. Full bloodied and rumbustious, this is high quality new make Irish that absolutely thumps the salivation button on palate. And, apparently, a mix of malted and unmalted barley in the traditional Irish Pot Still style....though this neither noses nor tastes anything like the new spirit from Midleton. The label waffles on about 1,000 years of Irish tradition. But the use of unmalted barley came into use only when distillers found a way of avoiding tax on the malted stuff. Were there taxes on alcohol in Ireland 1,000 years ago...? 65%

Inish Turk Beg Maiden Voyage db **(91.5)** n22 punchier and saltier than the normal Cooley malt, this is quite a heavyweight with some Demerara sugars adding to thickening oak; t23.5 a lot of chewing required, even for the delivery which, though soft, is also a weighty beast; again a saltiness persists bringing out the full flavour of the barley; f22.5 some shades of fudge and natural caramels; b22.5 brooding and quite delicious. 44%

Locke's Aged 8 Years bott code L9005 db **(88)** n22.5 t22 f22 b21.5. A beautiful malt at probably this distillery's optimum age. 40%

Locke's Aged 8 Years Crock (92) n23 t24 f22 b23. Much, much better cask selection than of old: some real honey casks here. A crock of gold...! 40%

Locke's Aged 9 Years Grand Crew cask no. 700, dist Feb 00, bott Sep 09 db **(91.5)** n23 t23.5 f22.5 b22.5. This took me back a few years. Having the three new Locke's lined up was like the days when I went through the Cooley warehouses looking for casks to put into Knappogue. This wasn't far off the style I was searching for. The right age, too. 58.9%. Cooley for The Irish Whisky Society. 233 bottles.

Locke's Aged 10 Years Premier Crew cask no. 713, dist Feb 00, bott Jul 10 db **(88)** n22 t23 f21 b22. The cask does its best to try and spoil the barley fun. Here's a tip: stick to younger malts. Cooley is brilliant and relatively undiscovered at between seven and nine years. And there is less time for cask to bite back... 46%. Cooley for The Irish Whisky Society. 292 bottles.

Tullamore Dew Single Malt 10 Years Old db **(91.5)** n23 t23 f22.5 b23. The best whiskey I have ever encountered with a Tullamore label. Furtively complex and daringly delicate. If only they could find a way to minimise the toffee... 40%. William Grant & Sons.

The Tyrconnell bott code L9074 db **(86)** n21 t22 f22 b21. Sweet, soft, chunky and with a finely spice finale. 40%

The Tyrconnell Aged 10 Years Madeira Finish bott code L8136 db **(91)** n23 t23 f22 b23. Not quite the award-winning effort of a few years back, as those lilting high notes which so complimented the baser fruit tones haven't turned up here. But remains in the top echelon and still much here to delight the palate. 46%

The Tyrconnell Aged 10 Years Port Finish bott code L8167 db **(81.5)** n21.5 t21 f19 b20. Toffee all the way. 46%

The Tyrconnell Aged 10 Years Sherry Finish bott code L8168 db **(84)** n22 t21 f21 b20. Like the Port Cask in this present series we have a thick malt that is friendly, toffeed and generally flat. This one, though, does have the odd peak of grapey richness, but you have to travel through a few plateaux to reach them. 46%

Tyrconnell Aged 11 Years sherry cask finish, cask no. V09-10 #336 db **(95)** n23.5 my word! This bodes very well! Black pepper notes ginger up the intense marmalade and honey. Clean and brimming with undisguised intent; t24 magnificent. The palate is left salivating and, if you are not careful, you are left dribbling as a glorious delivery of rich grape and sweetened orange paste offers the juicy introduction while a slow rumbling of ever-increasing spice shakes you to the core; f23.5 long with a slow build up of oils and further fruit. Very late on a succession of bourbon-style honeycomb and molassed notes begin to make their mark; b24 a thrilling virtuoso performance. Those who bought a bottle of this when they had the chance are unlikely to have regretted it. 58.5%. Bottled for Whisky Live 2011.

The Tyrconnell Aged 14 Years cask no. 3179, rotation K92/25 db **(93)** n23 t23 f23 b24. By rotation, K92 means it was distilled in 1992. Which just proves this distillery really has come of age, because, make no mistake, this is a belter... 46%

The Tyrconnell Single Cask 11 Year Old db **(95.5)** n23.5 sings the house style with a voice of rare clarity. The thin orange blossom honey is divine; t25 of the great Irish whiskey malt deliveries for this and many years: perfection. The weight of the barley and oak cannot be bettered while the clarity of the malt and pink grapefruit is faultless; f23 long, but concentrates purely on winding down the charming complexity of all that has gone before. And not an atom of bitterness from the oak...; b24 well, if there weren't enough reasons to go to Dublin, you now have this... 46%. sc. Exclusive to the Celtic Whiskey Shop.

The Tyrconnell Single Cask 11 Year Old Anima Negra Mallorcan Wine Cask Finish db **(86)** n21.5 t22 f21 b21.5. Loads going on here and those who like a boiled fruit candy feel to their malt will appreciate this one. 46%. sc. Exclusive to the Celtic Whiskey Shop.

The Tyrconnell Aged 15 Years Single Cask cask no. 1854/92 db **(92.5)** n24 t23 f22.5 b23. Infinitely more comfortable in its aging skin a similar malt I tasted in Canada last year. 46%

The Tyrconnell Aged 17 Years Single Cask cask no. 5306/92 db **(87) n22 t22 f21.5 b21.5.** Attractive barley all the way but barely deviates. *46%*

The Tyrconnell Aged 18 Years Single Cask cask no. 592/93 db **(94.5) n24** wow! What a nose! A half hour aroma, with the myriad variances in the shades of honey and marmalade taking an age to unravel; **t23.5** melt-in-the-mouth delivery, but there is a superb sharpness which really allows the barley to stand out after all these years and those kumquat notes to positively fizz; the complexity quotient increases as the vanilla joins to the spices in beating out an oaky tattoo; **f23** lemon curd tart and marmalade mix now works alongside the spice; **b24** "beautiful in its simplicity" trills the label. Guys: are you kidding? Don't undersell yourselves. This is a very complex dram, indeed! And a fitting swan song to this wonderful distillery's final days of independence... *46%. sc.*

The Tyrconnell Single Cask cask no. 9571/1992 db **(85.5) n23 t21 f20.5 b21.** The wonderful citrus notes on the nose are swamped by the oak further down the line. There is no doubting the age of this Cooley! *46%*

Clonmel Peated Aged 8 Years (86) n22 t23 f20 b21. Take the toffee away and you would have one hell of an Irish. Claims to be "Pure Pot Still". It isn't (in Irish terms): it's malt. *40%*

Craoi na Mona Irish Malt Whiskey (68) n16 t18 f17 b17. I'm afraid my Gaelic is slipping these days: I assume Craoi na Mona means "Feinty, badly made smoky malt"... (that's the end of my tasting for the day...) *40%*

Glen Dimplex (88) n23 t22 f21 b22. Overall, clean and classically Cooley. *40%*

Knappogue Castle 1990 (91) n22 t23 f22 b24. For a light whiskey this shows enormous complexity and depth. Genuine balance from nose to finish; refreshing and dangerously more-ish. Entirely from bourbon cask and personally selected and vatted by a certain Jim Murray. *40%. nc. Great Spirits.*

Knappogue Castle 1991 (90) n22 t23 f22 b23. Offers rare complexity for such a youthful malt especially in the subtle battles that rage on the palate between sweet and dry, malt and oak and so on. The spiciness is a great foil for the malt. Each cask picked and vatted by the author. *40%. nc. Great Spirits.*

Knappogue Castle 1992 (94) n23 t23 f24 b24. A different Knappogue altogether from the delicate, ultra-refined type. This expression positively revels in its handsome ruggedness and muscular body: a surprisingly bruising yet complex malt that always remains balanced and fresh – the alter-ego of the '90 and '91 vintages. I mean, as the guy who put this whiskey together, what do you expect? But it's not bad if I say so myself and was voted the USA's No. 1 Spirit. Virtually all vanished, but worth getting a bottle if you can find it (I don't receive a penny – I was paid as a consultant!). *40%. nc. Great Spirits.*

Knappogue Castle 1993 *(see Bushmills)*

Knappogue Castle 1994 *(see Bushmills)*

Liquid Sun Cooley 1999 bott 2012 **(87) n22** cream toffee raisin...without the raisin...; **t22** peated cream toffee....without the peat.... **f21.5** complex cream toffee...with the complexity... **b21.5** awash with natural caramels and enjoyable in a horrible way...without the horrible. *53.2%. nc ncf sc. The Whisky Agency.*

Magilligan Cooley Pure Pot Still Single Malt (91) n22 t22 f24 b23. A touch of honey for good measure ...or maybe not..!! *43%. Ian MacLeod Distillers.*

Magilligan Irish Whiskey Peated Malt 8 Years Old (89) n21 t23 f22 b23. Such a different animal from the docile creature that formally passed as Magilligan peated. Quite lovely...and very classy. *43%. Ian Macleod Distillers.*

Merry's Single Malt (83) n20 t22 f20 b21. Ultra-clean barley rich nose is found on the early palate. The finish is flat, though. *40%*

Michael Collins Irish Whiskey Single Malt db **(68) n17 t18 f17 b16.** Bloody hell, I thought. Didn't anyone get my message from last year? Apparently not – and it's our fault as the tasting notes above were accidentally edited out before they went in. Sorry. But the caramel in the latest bottling has been upped to take the whisky from deep gold to bronze. Making this among the most over-coloured single malt I have tasted in years. Please guys. For the love of whiskey. Please let us taste exactly what a great malt this could be. *40% (80 proof)*

⋰ **Milroy's of Soho Single Malt Cooley Aged 11 Years** first fill bourbon, cask no. 3442, dist 22 Oct 01, bott 5 Nov 12 **(91) n23.5** strangely, reminds me of cough syrup from when I was a kid, yet I have to say, it is sweet and rather lovely – some strawberries at play; **t23** a real juicy statement, malt all over the place. Again, there is that strawberry-flavoured medicine: odd; **f22.5** long, long fade. Massive barley sugar finale; **b23** seriously enjoyable. Just what the doctor ordered...! *46%*

Sainsbury's Single Malt Irish Whiskey bott code L10083/16 **(87.5) n22 t22 f21.5 b22.** Classic Cooley showing its big, malty depth. *40%*

Sainsbury's Dún Léire Aged 8 Years Single Malt (95.5) n24 the score for this crept upwards as I investigated the aroma like the thermometer in my back garden on a bright

Summer's day. The first thing to throw itself at you is Seville blood orange, backed up by a clever layering of barley at varying intensity and sweetness; the delicate oak acts as no more than a buffer in between; **t24** just about the perfect mouth feel: silky and melting on the palate. Again, it was an orangey citrus first to show, then again followed by some stunning malt. Everything dissolves: you don't have to do anything but close your eyes and enjoy, indeed: marvel...but it is hard work to stop yourself chewing; **f23.5** dries slightly, but the bitterness threatened on the label fails to materialise...thankfully. The fruit and barley ride off into the sunset in tandem; **b24** when I read "notes of bitter orange" on the label I feared the worst and expected a sulphurous whiskey. Well maybe there is a molecule or two hanging around, but so minor is it, it is impossible to tell exactly where it comes from. This is one of the great whiskeys from Cooley, ever. And as a supermarket Irish... unsurpassed. One of the surprise packages of world whisky for 2010. Magnificent. 40%. *Cooley for Sainsbury's Supermarket.*

Shannahan's (92) n23 t22 f24 b23. Cooley natural and unplugged: quite adorable. 40%

Slieve Foy Single Malt Aged 8 Years bott code L9108 **(88) n23 t22.5 f21 b21.5.** Never deviates from its delicate touch. 40%. *Cooley for Marks & Spencer.*

Vom Fass Cooley Irish Single Malt 8 Years Old (88) n22 t22.5 f21.5 b22. A very decent, if undemonstrative, example of the distillery at an age which well suits. 40%

The Wild Geese Single Malt (85.5) n21.5 t21 f22 b21. "A Rare Blend of Pure Aged Irish Malt Whiskies" says the front label. Yet it is a single malt. Confusing. And very unhelpful to a whisky public already being totally bamboozled by the bizarre and misguided antics of the Scotch Whisky Association. It is not a blend. It is a mixing of Cooley malt whiskey, as I understand it. The back label's "Smoother Because We Distil it Longer" is also a bit of a blarney. It's made in a pot still and whilst it is true that if you distil faster (by higher temperatures) you could well end up with "hot" whiskey, I am not aware of this being distilled at a significantly slower rate than at either Bushmills or Midleton. Or do they mean the cut of the run from the spirit still is longer, which would impart more oils – not all of them great? Just ignore the Wild Goose chase the labels send you on and enjoy the malt, with all its failings, for what it is (and this is pretty enjoyable in an agreeably rough and ready manner, though not exactly the stiff of Irish whiskey purists): which in this case for all its malt, toffee and delicate smoke, also appears to have more than a slight touch of feints - so maybe they were right all along...!!! 43%. *Cooley for Avalon.*

OLD KILBEGGAN

Kilbeggan Distillery Reserve Malt matured in quarter casks, batch no. 1, bott Jun 10 db **(89) n22.5 t22.5 b22.** An endearingly soft malt to see Kilbeggan distillery back into the whiskey world. Shame it has been reduced to 40%, as this one demanded to be at least 46% - indeed, preferably naked - and allowing those delicate, elegant but marginalised characters a chance to bloom. But welcome back...and I look forward to many an evening with me tasting you as you blossom, as I am sure you will. It has been nearly 20 years since I first discovered the beauty of Kilbeggan Distillery and I have countless times since dreamed of that moment. 40%. 1500 bottles. Available only in the distillery gift shop.

The Spirit of Kilbeggan 1 Month (90.5) n22 t23 f23 b22.5. Wow!! They are really getting to grips with the apparatus. Full bodied and lush small still feel to this but radiating complexity, depth, barley and cocoa in equal measures. The development of the oils really does give this excellent length. Impressed! 65.5%

The Spirit of Kilbeggan 1 Year (85) n20.5 t21 f22 b21.5. A veritable Bambi of a spirit: a typical one year old malt which, as hard as it tries, just can't locate its centre of gravity. Even so, the richness is impressive and some highly sugared chocolate mousse near the end is a treat. 62.7%

The Spirit of Kilbeggan 2 Years (84) n20 t21 f22 b21. A tad raw and a little thin. There is some decent balance between oak and malt, but the overall feeling is that the still has not yet been quite mastered. 60.3%

OLD BUSHMILLS

Bushmills Aged 10 Years matured in two woods db **(92.5) n23** has maintained that big sultana and honey signature; **t23** rich delivery, delicately oiled and beautifully rounded. Slightly more two-toned than previously, with the old-fashioned barley-bourbon oak notes coming through in its traditional flaky manner; **f23** very accomplished finish with a wonderful even-ness between barley and fruit. Much more recognisable as a traditional Bushmills than when they first changed the oak recipe; **b23.5** absolutely superb whiskey showing great balance and the usual Antrim 19th century pace with its favour development. The odd bottle of this I have come across over the last couple of years has been spoiled by the sherry involvement. But, this, as is usually the case, is absolutely spot on. 40%

Bushmills Select Casks Aged 12 Years married with Caribbean rum cask db **(95)** n23 unusual moist rum and raisin cake effect: effective and just enough spice to deliver extra complexity. Just the very slightest hint of bourbon, too; **t24** adorable malt richness; biscuity and stupendously seasoned yet always remains fresh and mouthwatering. The sweetness is very cleverly controlled; **f24** there are just so many layers to this: the oak is a growing force, but restricts itself to a vanilla topping; **b24** one of the most complex Bushmills in living memory, and probably since it was established in 1784. 40%

Bushmills Aged 16 Years db **(71)** n18 t21 f15 b17. In my days as a consultant Irish whiskey blender, going through the Bushmills warehouses I found only one or two sulphur-treated butts. Alas, there are many more than that at play here. 40%

Bushmills Aged 21 Years db **(95.5)** n24.5 this remains something of a Chinese puzzle on the nose: just how do all those different notes , sometimes soft and rounded, sometimes hard and angular, many of them fruity, manage to intertwine...yet never clash? And why can you never detach one without another clinging on to it. If Sherlock Holmes tried to solve it, this would be a three pipe conundrum...except the use of tobacco would ruin the experience. Just marvel at the greengage and physalis, the flaked vanilla and liquorice, the ulmo honey and hickory...so much else besides; **t24** as melt-in-the-mouth as a whiskey can be: amazingly juicy barley offers the cutting edge and lead while a plethora of delicate sugars dissolve on impact; the fruit is served as a perpetual mixed salad; **f23.5** this is where I am really impressed. Despite all the complexity of the nose and delivery, at the finish the Bushmills trademark flaky vanilla and delicate barley comes through...a signature unique to one distillery in the world; **b24** an Irish journey as beautiful as the dramatic landscape which borders the distillery. Magnificent. 40% ☉

Clontarf Single Malt (90.5) n23 barley concentrate with a squeeze of orange and distant juniper; **t23** beautifully fresh barley, almost barley sugar, with light sinews of oak; **f22** long, intense barley but with the vanilla standing tallest at the death as welcome spices finally gather; **b22.5** beautiful in its simplicity, this has eschewed complexity for delicious minimalism; 40%. Clontarf Irish Whiskey Co.

The Irishman Single Malt bottle no. E2496 **(83)** n20 t21 f21 b21. Highly pleasant malt but the coffee and toffee on the finish underline a caramel-style whiskey which may, potentially, offer so much more. 40%. Hot Irishman Ltd.

⁘ **The Irishman Single Malt 12 Years Old** 1st fill bourbon barrels, casks no. 70691&70692, bott Nov 2012 **(88)** n22 soft with huge toffee; a gentle, orangey breeze; **t22.5** fabulous delivery with the malt kicking off, though the amount of juiciness is muted by a tsunami of caramels; the early heather honey polish also wears off quite fast; **f21.5** short finish, caramels apart, as most of what has been said has been said early on...; **b22** very pleasant but, ultimately, docile thanks to the caramels at work. Putting my Irish blender's hat on for a moment, I think the whiskey would had offered a lot more had it been carefully selected first and second fill bourbon casks at play, rather than two very similar B1s. 43%. ncf. Hot Irishman Ltd.

Knappogue Castle Aged 12 Years bourbon cask matured **(90)** n23.5 the oak has got in amongst the barley. It means this is a double edged aroma: on one hand bright and malt sharp, on the other there is a duller, more caramel-rich, almost biscuity base. Hugely attractive, though, and the toffee apple sideline is a treat; **t23** this translates perfectly on delivery. Hard and crisp interior (the closest you'll find to an Irish pot still style!) which really ups the salivation factor. Then outside a softer, duller toffee effect; **f21** a touch of crème brulee, but just too much toffee; **b22.5** the massive toffee influence deflects from the huge character elsewhere which springs a few surprises. 40%. Castle Brands Group.

Knappogue Castle Aged 16 Years sherry finished, dist 1994, bott 2010 **(84)** n23 t23 f18 b20. The nose: love it! Beautifully spiced, windfall apples piled into a barrow...just wonderful! The delivery: soft, chewy, deftly spiced again, even a sexy touch of Turkish Delight, with the malt having so much to say still....then, the finish. The finish..Oh dear, oh dear.. Let's just say, the perfect malt to have before bedtime, because if this doesn't send you to sleep, nothing will. As flat and lifeless as the nose and delivery are rich with invention. And, to make matters worse, a sulphury sub plot bites with bitterness. What a shame. Someone took their eye off the ball, and a potential award has gone begging... 40%. ncf.

Knappogue Castle 1990 (see Cooley)
Knappogue Castle 1991 (see Cooley)
Knappogue Castle 1992 (see Cooley)
Knappogue Castle 1993 (91) n22 b22 f23 b24. A malt of exceptional character and charisma. Almost squeaky clean but proudly contains enormous depth and intensity. The chocolate finish is an absolute delight. Quite different and darker than any previous Knappogue but not dwarfed in stature to any of the previous three vintages. Created by yours truly. 40%. nc. Great Spirits.

Knappogue Castle 1994 lot no. L6 **(89)** n23 t24 f20 b22. A wonderful whiskey in the Knappogue tradition, although this one was not done by its creator. That said, it does have an Achilles heel: the finish. This is the most important bit to get right, especially as this is the oldest Knappogue yet. But not enough attention has been paid to getting rid of the oak-induced bitterness. 40%. *Castle Brands.*

Knappogue Castle 1995 bott 2007 **(88)** n23 t22 f21 b22. A charming malt showing Old Bushmills in very unusual colours. Lacking the charisma, clarity and complexity of the first Knappogues simply because they were designed to extol the virtues of young (8-year-old) malt. Naturally, extra oak has crept in here, forcing out – as it must – the sharpness and vitality of the barley. A decent effort, but perhaps more should have been done to keep out the aggressive bitterness. 40%

Single Grain
COOLEY

Greenore 6 Year Old bott code L9015 db **(89)** n23.5 t22.5 f21 b22. Very enjoyable whiskey. But two points: cut the caramel and really see the baby sing. And secondly, as a "Small Batch" bottling, how about putting a batch number on the label...? 40%. *Cooley.*

Greenore 8 Year Old bott code L8190 db **(86.5)** n20 t22 f23 b21.5. The vague hint of butyric on the nose is more than amply compensated by the gradual build up to something rather larger on the palate than you might have expected (and don't be surprised if the two events are linked). The corn oil is almost a meal in itself and the degree of accompanying sugar and corn flour is a treat. 40%. *Cooley.*

Greenore 10 Years Old dist 1997, bott 2007 db **(87.5)** n22 f21.5 b22. Well made grain and always enjoyable but perhaps not brought to its fullest potential due to some less than inspired oak. 40%

Greenore 15 Years Old bott code L8044 **(90)** n23 t22.5 f22 b22.5. The advent of the Kilbeggan 15 reminded us that there must be some grain of that age around, and here to prove it is a superb bottling of the stuff which, weirdly, is a lot better than the blend. Beautiful. 43%

Greenore 18 Years Old db **(91)** n22.5 t22.5 f23 b23. This continuous still at Cooley should be marked by the State as an Irish national treasure. One of the most complex grains you'll ever find, even when heading into uncharted territory like this one. 46%. ncf. 4000 bottles.

Blends

Bushmills 12 Years Old Distillery Reserve db **(86)** n22.5 t22.5 f20 b21. This version has gone straight for the ultra lush feel. For those who want to take home some 40% abv fruit fudge from the distillery. 40%

Bushmills 1608 anniversary edition **(94)** n23.5 the grain barely gets a look in as the malt and oak dominates from the first whiff. Toasted oak and bread form a dense background, sweetened by muscovado sugar melting on porridge; t23.5 now that's different: how many blends do you know kick off with an immediate impact of sweetness that offers about four or five different levels of intensity, and each accompanied by a toasted oakiness? Very, very different, charming, fascinating...and delicious; f23 long, mocha with the emphasis on the coffee and then, at the very end some firm grains at last get a toe-hold; b24 this whiskey is talking an entirely different language to any Irish blend I have come across before, or any blend come to that. Indeed, nosed blind you'd not even regard it a blend: the malt calls to you like a Siren. But perhaps it is the crystal malt they have used here which is sending out such unique signals, helping the whiskey to form a thick cloak of roasty, toasty, burnt toffeed, bitter-sweetness which takes your breath away. What a fabulous whiskey! And whether it be a malt or blend, who cares? Genius whiskey is genius whiskey. 40%

Bushmills 1608 400th Anniversary **(83)** n21 t21.5 f20 b20.5. Thin-bodied, hard as nails and sports a peculiarly Canadian feel. 46%. *Diageo.*

Bushmills Black Bush **(91)** n23 a firmer aroma with less evident malt and the spices have also taken a back seat. But the gentle, toffee apple and night garden scent reveal that the malt-grain interaction is still wonderfully alluring; t23 busy delivery, much softer than the nose indicates with the malt first to show. The oak is no slouch either, offering excellent spices; some burnt, raisiny notes help confirm this is Black Bush on song; f21.5 still over the top caramel interfering but not before some honeycomb makes a small stand; b23.5 this famous old blend may be under new management and even blender. But still the high quality, top-notch complexity rolls around the glass and your palate. As beautiful as ever. 40%

Bushmills Original **(80)** n19 t21 f20 b20. Remains one of the hardest whiskeys on the circuit with the Midleton grain at its most unflinching. There is a sweeter, faintly maltier edge to this now while the toffee and biscuits qualities remain. 40%

Cassidy's Distiller's Reserve bott code L8067 **(84.5)** n21.5 t22 f20 b21. Some salivating malt on flavour-exploding delivery, but all else tame and gentle. 40%. *Cooley.*

Clancey's bott code L8025 **(87) n22 t21 f22 b22**. Remains an excellent blend for all the toffee. The spice balance excels. *40%. Cooley for Wm Morrison.*

Clontarf Classic Blend (81) n20 t22 f19.5 b19.5. A hard as nails blend softened only by the heavy use of caramel which, though chewy, tends to obliterate any complexity from elsewhere. Ouch! *40%. Castle Brands Group.*

Delaney's (85.5) n20 t21.5 f22 b22. Young, clean, citrusy, refreshing and proud. Thoroughly enjoyable and dangerously moreish. *40%. Cooley for Co-operative UK.*

Delaney's Special Reserve (84) n21.5 t20.5 f22 b21. An attractive blend with a big late spicy blast. The toffee dominates for long periods. *40%. Cooley for Co-operative Group.*

Feckin Irish Whiskey (81) n20 t21 f20 b20. Tastes just about exactly the feckin same as the Feckin Strangford Gold... *40%. The Feckin Drinks Co.*

Golden Irish bott code L7064 **(93) n23 t23 f23.5 b23.5**. By far one of the most enjoyable Irish blends around. Simple, but what it does, it does deliciously well. *40%. Cooley.*

The Irishman Rare Cask Strength bott 2010 **(81.5) n20 t22.5 f19 b20**. Fabulous crescendo of weighty malt on delivery. But just too much bitterness and toffee hits this one. *53%. Hot Irishman Ltd. 2850 bottles.*

The Irishman Rare Cask Strength bott 2011 **(94.5) n23** flecks of honey intermingle perfectly with the lightest blush of greengage. A touch of bourbon liquorice is sweetened by a hint of molasses; a piquancy is added by a sprinkle of salt; seemingly light, yet weighty...; **t24** excellent body with the soft barley circling around the more rigid middle. This profound gentle-firm balance is the main feature, as those salty sugars also dazzle. Egg custard tart middle makes for a friendlier environment; light honey is threaded throughout; **f23.5** more vanilla and custard, but now some excellent light spices, too; **b24** the back labels of Hot Irishman whiskeys are always entertaining, not least for their unique use of the English language. A free Jim Murray's Whisky Bible 2012 for the first person to e-mail in and tell us what the cock-up is on this label. Back to the whiskey: this blend of malt whisky and Pure Irish Pot still, is a mildly more lilting, more lightly coloured, version of Writer's Tears. And, just like the first bottling, a must-have stunner. *53%. Hot Irishman. 2400 bottles.*

The Irishman Superior Irish Whiskey bott code L6299L059 **(93) n23 t23 f23 b24**. What a quite wonderful blend: not of the norm for those that have recently come onto the market and there is much more of the Irish Distillers about this than most. Forget about the smoke promised in the tasting notes on the label...it gives you everything else but. And that is one hell of a lot!! *40%. Hot Irishman Ltd.*

Jameson (95) n24.5 Swoon...bizarrely shows even more Pot Still character than the Redbreast I tasted yesterday. Flinty to the point of cracking. The sherry is there but on reduced terms, allowing the firm grain to amplify the unmalted barley: truly brilliant; **t24** mouth-watering delivery and then wave upon wave of diamond-hard barley and grain; the odd eclectic layer of something sweetish and honeyed, but this is eye-watering stuff; **f22.5** an annoying touch of caramel creeps in, costing points, but even beyond that you still cannot other than be charmed by the layering of cocoa, barley and light grape; **b24** I thought I had detected in bottlings I had found around the world a very slight reduction in the Pot Still character that defines this truly classic whiskey. So I sat down with a fresh bottle in more controlled conditions...and was blown away as usual. The sharpness of the PS is vivid and unique; the supporting grain of the required crispness. Fear not: this very special whiskey remains in stunning, truly wondrous form. *40%* ⊙

Jameson 12 Years Old Special Reserve (88) n22 t23 f21 b22. Much more sherry than of late and the pot still makes inroads, too. Just needs to lose some of the caramel effect; *40%.*

Jameson 18 Years Old Limited Reserve eighth batch bott code JJ18-8 **(91) n23 t22.5 f22.5 b22.5**. The astonishing degree of bourbon on the nose thankfully doesn't make it to the palate where Ireland rather than Kentucky rules. *40%*

⌁ **Jameson 18 Years Old Limited Reserve** bott 13.07.12 **(89.5) n22** digestive biscuit meets Toffee Crisp; **t23.5** a sultry delivery with stupendous thick malt and a bourbon-style honeycomb and caramel back up; juicy in part with half-hearted spice for support; **f22** some tingle remains but vanilla and toffee rule; **b22** this guy has changed shape since the last time I tasted it. Toffee has a far bigger say these days. *40%. Irish Distillers.*

Jameson Black Barrel (91.5) n23 enticing, with the oaky grain pulsing out a firm spiciness while a subtle almost gristy sweetness balances matters. Curious mint and juniper notes offer a curveball; **t23** the grain again dominates, but the sugars are out in force: on one hand barley-rich, elsewhere much more of a toffee nature. Again, just straying towards something juniper.; **f22.5** softens for the first time as the oily toffee and coffee massage; **b23** here's the problem faced by any Jameson blender: the column still grain from Midleton is the hardest on the palate made anywhere in the world. So how do you get it to mould into what you want? Usually you can't, so you have to make the whiskeys around it reflect and deflect for maximum effect. And that's what's going on here: a brittle whisky where the pot still element is magnified very cleverly indeed. Lovely stuff: New Yorkers are a lucky bunch! *40%. NY exclusive.*

Jameson Gold Reserve (88) n22 t23 f20 b22. Enjoyable, but so very different: an absolute re-working with all the lighter, more definitively sweeter elements shaved mercilessly while the thicker oak is on a roll. Some distance from the masterpiece it once was. 40%

Jameson Rarest 2007 Vintage Reserve (96) n24.5 the crispest, cleanest, most beautifully defined of all the Jameson family: orange peel, hickory, spotted dog pudding, lavender – they're all there mushed around and in near-perfect proportions; t24 ditto the arrival with the mouth puckering under the onslaught of very old Pot Still: the bitter-sweet sharpness one would expect from this is there in spades; oak present and correct and edged in thin muscovado layer; f23.5 vanilla by the barrel-load, pithy fruit and softly spiced barley b24 is this the whiskey where we see a blender truly come of age. Tall green hats off to Billy Leighton who has, as all the better blenders did in the past, worked his way from quality-testing barrels on the dumping room floor to the lab. With this stupendous offering we have a blender in clover for he has earned his Golden Shamrocks. If the blending alone wasn't stellar enough, then making this a 46%, non chill-filtered offering really does put the tin hat on it (so Billy: you really have been listening to me over the years...!!!) This is truly great whiskey, among the pantheon of the world's finest. 46%

Jameson Signature Reserve (93) n23.5 t23.5 f22.5 b23.5. Be assured that Signature, with its clever structuring of delicate and inter-weaving flavours, says far more about the blender, Billy Leighton, than it does John Jameson. 40%. Irish Distillers.

Kellan American oak cask (84) n21 t22 f20 b21. Safe whisky which is clean, sweet and showing many toffeed attributes. Decent spices, too. 40% (80 Proof). Cooley.

Kilbeggan bott code L7091 (86) n21 t22 f21.5 b21.5. A much more confident blend by comparison with that faltering one of the last few years. Here, the malts make a significant drive towards increasing the overall complexity and gentle citrus style. 40%. Cooley.

Kilbeggan 15 Years Old bott code L7048 (85.5) n21.5 t22 f21 b21. My word! 15 years, eh? How time flies! And on the subject of flying, surely I have winged my way back to Canada and am tasting a native blend. No, this is Irish albeit in sweet, deliciously rounded form. However, one cannot help feeling that the dark arts have been performed, as in an injection of caramel, which, as well as giving that Canadian feel has also probably shaved off some of the more complex notes to middle and finish. Even so, a sweet, silky experience. 40%. Cooley.

Kilbeggan 18 Year Old db (89) n23 t21.5 f22.5 b22. Although the impressive bottle lavishly claims "From the World's Oldest Distillery" I think one can take this as so much Blarney. It certainly had my researcher going, who lined this up for me under the Old Kilbeggan distillery, a forgivable mistake and one I think he will not be alone in making. This, so it appears on the palate, is a blend. From the quite excellent Cooley distillery, and it could be that whiskey used in this matured at Kilbeggan... which is another thing entirely. As for the whiskey: apart from some heavy handedness on the toffee, it really is quite a beautiful and delicate thing. 40%

Kilgeary bott code L8063 (79) n20 t20 f19 b20. There has always, and still proudly is, something strange about this blend. Cold tea on the nose and a bitter bite to the finish, sandwiches a brief flirtation with something sweet. 40%. Cooley.

Locke's bott code L8056 (85.5) n21 t22 f21.5 b21. Now, there you go!! Since I last really got round to analysing this one it has grown from a half-hearted kind of a waif to something altogether more gutsy and muscular. Sweeter, too, as the malts and grains combine harmoniously. A clean and pleasant experience with some decent malt fingerprints. 40%

Michael Collins A Blend (77) n19 t20 f19 b19. Michael Collins was known as the "big fellow". This pleasant, impressively spiced dram, might have enjoyed the same epithet had it not surrendered to and then been strangled by caramel on the finish. 40% (80 proof). Cooley.

Midleton Distillery Reserve (85) n22 t22 f20 b21. A whiskey which, for all its muscovado sweetness offers some memorable barley moments. 40%. Irish Distillers Midleton Distillery only. Changes character slightly with each new vatting. This one is some departure.

Midleton Very Rare 1984 (70) n19 t18 f17 b16. Disappointing with little backbone or balance. 40%. Irish Distillers.

Midleton Very Rare 1985 (77) n20 t20 f18 b19. Medium-bodied and oily, this is a big improvement on the initial vintage. 40%. Irish Distillers.

Midleton Very Rare 1986 (79) n21 t20 f18 b20. A very malty Midleton richer in character than previous vintages. 40%. Irish Distillers.

Midleton Very Rare 1987 (77) n20 t19 f19 b19. Quite oaky at first until a late surge of excellent pot still. 40%. Irish Distillers.

Midleton Very Rare 1988 (86) n23 t21 f21 b21. A landmark MVR as it is the first vintage to celebrate the Irish pot-still style. 40%. Irish Distillers.

Midleton Very Rare 1989 (87) n22 t22 f22 b21. A real mouthful but has lost balance to achieve the effect. 40%. Irish Distillers.

Midleton Very Rare 1990 (93) n23 t23 f24 b23. Astounding whiskey: one of the vintages every true Irish whiskey lover should hunt for. 40%. Irish Distillers.

Midleton Very Rare 1991 (76) n19 t20 f19 b18. After the Lord Mayor's Show, relatively dull and uninspiring. 40%. Irish Distillers.

Midleton Very Rare 1992 (84) n20 t20 f23 b21. Superb finish with outstanding use of feisty grain. 40%. Irish Distillers.

Midleton Very Rare 1993 (88) n21 t22 f23 b22. big, brash and beautiful – the perfect way to celebrate the 10th-ever bottling of MVR. 40%. Irish Distillers.

Midleton Very Rare 1994 (87) n22 t22 f21 b22. Another different style of MVR, one of amazing lushness. 40%. Irish Distillers.

Midleton Very Rare 1995 (90) n23 t24 b21 b22. They don't come much bigger than this. Prepare a knife and fork to battle through this one. Fabulous. 40%. Irish Distillers.

Midleton Very Rare 1996 (82) n21 t22 f19 b20. The grains lead a soft course, hardened by subtle pot still. Just missing a beat on the finish, though. 40%. Irish Distillers.

Midleton Very Rare 1997 (83) n22 t21 f19 b21. The piercing pot still fruitiness of the nose is met by a countering grain of rare softness on the palate. Just dies on the finish when you want it to make a little speech. Very drinkable. 40%. Irish Distillers.

Midleton Very Rare 1999 (89) n21 t23 f22 b23. One of the maltiest Midletons of all time: a superb blend. 40%. Irish Distillers.

Midleton Very Rare 2000 (85) n22 t21 f21 b21. An extraordinary departure even by Midleton's eclectic standards. The pot still is like a distant church spire in an hypnotic Fen landscape. 40%. Irish Distillers.

Midleton Very Rare 2001 (79) n21 t20 f18 b20. Extremely light but the finish is slightly on the bitter side. 40%. Irish Distillers.

Midleton Very Rare 2002 (79) n20 t22 f18 b19. The nose is rather subdued and the finish is likewise toffee-quiet and shy. There are some fabulous middle moments, some of flashing genius, when the pot still and grain combine for a spicy kick, but the finish really is lacklustre and disappointing. 40%. Irish Distillers.

Midleton Very Rare 2003 (84) n22 t22 f19 b21. Beautifully fruity on both nose and palate (even some orange blossom on aroma). But the delicious spicy richness that is in mid launch on the tastebuds is cut short by caramel on the middle and finish. A crying shame, but the best Midleton for a year or two. 40%. Irish Distillers.

Midleton Very Rare 2004 (82) n21 t21 f19 b21. Yet again caramel is the dominant feature, though some quite wonderful citrus and spice escape the toffeed blitz. 40%.

Midleton Very Rare 2005 (92) n23 t24 f22 b23. OK, you can take this one only as a rough translation. The sample I have worked from here is from the Irish Distillers blending lab, reduced to 40% in mine but without caramel added. And, as Midleton Very Rares always are at this stage, it's an absolute treat. Never has such a great blend suffered so in the hands of colouring and here the chirpiness of the pot still and élan of the honey (very Jameson Gold Label in part) show just what could be on offer given half the chance. Has wonderful natural colour and surely it is a matter of time before we see this great whiskey in its natural state. 40%

Midleton Very Rare 2006 (92) n22 t24 f23 b23. As raw as a Dublin rough-house and for once not overly swamped with caramel. An uncut diamond. 40%

Midleton Very Rare 2007 (83) n20 t22 f20 b21. Annoyingly buffeted from nose to finish by powering caramel. Some sweeter wisps do escape but the aroma suggests Canadian and insufficient Pot Still gets through to make this a Midleton of distinction. 40%. Irish Distillers

Midleton Very Rare 2008 (88.5) n22 t23 f21.5 b22. A dense bottling which offers considerably more than the 2007 Vintage. Attractive, very drinkable and without the caramel it might really have hit the heights. 40%. Irish Distillers.

Midleton Very Rare 2009 (95) n24 oh, wow! the best post bottling nose I have ever found on a Midleton, though a few pre-bottlings have exceeded it in grace. Just. This is the fruitiest I can remember, for sure, with a wonderful sherry trifle feel, only with the extra firmness of Irish pot still. A little avocado pear creaminess also goes a long way; t24 it is that creaminess which shows first on delivery, alongside a plethora of crisp, dark sugary notes which appear to shadow the pot still character; the star is the contra deal between the soft oils and the rock hard pot still...stunning f23 remains clean with far more complexity than a Midleton usually retains; the spices are busy and appear to pulse and vary in intensity; b24 I've been waiting a few years for one like this to come along. One of the most complex, cleanest and least caramel-spoiled bottlings for a good few years and one which makes the pot still character its centre piece. A genuine celebration of all things Midleton and Barry Crockett's excellence as a distiller in particular. 40%. Irish Distillers.

Midleton Very Rare 2010 (84) n21 t22 f20 b21. A case of after the Lord Mayor's Show. Chewy and some decent sugars. But hard to make out detail through the fog of caramel. 40%

Midleton Very Rare 2011 (81.5) n22.5 t20 f19 b20 Another disappointing version where the colour of its personality has been compromised for the sake of the colour in the bottle. A dullard of a whiskey, especially after the promising nose. 40%. Irish Distillers.

⁘ **Midleton Very Rare Irish Whisky 2012** db (89.5) n22 the usual lashing of toffee, but some really lovely mint and apple in the oaky frame, too; t23 sumptuous delivery with a spiky, juicy sub strata which really gets the honey and copper fully into play. Wow! The middle ground ambles back towards the safety of caramel; f22 some juicy moments reprised while some Demerara sugars dig deep into the caramel; b22.5 that's much more like it! After a couple of dud vintages, here we have a bottling worthy of its great name and heritage. 40%. Irish Distillers.

Millars Special Reserve bott code L8069 (86) n21 t22 f21.5 b21.5. Now that's some improvement on the last bottling of this I found, with spices back with abandon and grains ensuring a fine mouthfeel. Even the chocolate fudge at the death is a treat. 40%. Cooley.

Morrisons Irish Whiskey bott code L10028 (78) n19 t20 f19 b20. Sweet, pleasant and inoffensive. 40%. Wm Morrison Supermarket.

Paddy (74) n18.5 t20 f17.5 b18. Cleaned its act up a little. Even a touch of attractive citrus on the nose and delivery. But where does that cloying sweetness come from? As bland as an Irish peat bog but, sadly, nothing like so potentially tasty. 40%. Irish Distillers.

Powers (91) n23 t24 f22 b22. Is it any coincidence that in this bottling the influence of the caramel has been significantly reduced and the whiskey is getting back to its old, brilliant self? I think not. Classic stuff. 40%. Irish Distillers.

Powers Gold Label (87) n22 t22 f21 b22. The solid pot still, the very DNA of what made Powers, well, Powers is vanishing in front of our very noses. Yes, still some pot still around, but nothing like so pronounced in the way that made this, for decades, a truly one-off Irish and one of the world greats. Still delightful and with many charms but the rock hard pot still effect is sadly missed. What is going on here? 40%. Irish Distillers.

⁘ **Powers Gold Label** db (93) n23 fascinating mix between big Irish pot still hardness, incorporating manuka honey, and a big toffee and walnut weight; dusty caramels put a lid on things; t24 eye-rollingly superb: magical weight, not quite heavy, a bit more than medium with the sublime mix of dates and honey. The crispness through the middle really shows up the impressive pot still present; f22.5 treacle and toffee; b23.5 now, that's much more like it! The last Gold Label I had was pleasant, but just so not like a Power's in style. This is right back on track. Nothing to do with the extra alcohol. It's to do with the extra pot still, which here acts as backbone and muscle. Cut the caramel down, and it'd be a real world superstar whiskey. 43.2%

Redbreast Blend (88) n23 t23 f20 b22. Really impressed with this one-off bottling for Dillons the Irish wine merchants. Must try and get another bottle before they all vanish. 40%. Irish Distillers for Dillone IR (not to be confused with Redbreast 12 Years Old Pure Pot Still)

Sainsbury's Blended Irish Whiskey (86.5) n22 t22 f21 b21.5. A beautifully relaxed blend showing pretty clearly – literally, thanks to an admirable lack of colouring - just how good the Cooley grain whiskey is even at no great age. Clean with a deceptively busy and intense flavour profile. Far too good for the cola the back label says this should go with... 40%. UK.

St Patrick bott code L030907 (77) n19 t20 f19 b19. Good grief! No prisoners here as we have either a bitter oakiness or mildly cloying sweetness, rarely working in tandem. A few gremlins for the Kremlin. 40%. Cooley for Russia.

Strangford Gold (81) n20 t21 f20 b20. A simplistic, exceptionally easy drinking blend with high quality grain offering silk to the countering spice but caramel flattens any malt involvement. 40%. The Feckin Drinks Co.

⁘ **The Teeling Whiskey Company Poitin** (85) n21 t22 f21 b21. Intense and makes the eyes water to the required levels. Much cleaner, if not as sweet, though a lot safer than the illegal stuff I've tasted over there for the last 20-odd years! 61.5%

Tesco Special Reserve Irish Whiskey bott code L8061 (89.5) n21.5 t23.5 f22 b22.5. A cracker of a blend which allows the malts full scope to do their juicy bit. Possibly more malt than usual for a Cooley blend, but as they say: every little bit helps. 40%. Cooley.

Tullamore Dew (85) n22 t21.5 f20.5 b21. The days of the throat being savaged by this one appear to be over. Much more pot still character from nose to finish and the rough edges remain, attractively, just that. 40%. Campbell & Cochrane Group.

Tullamore Dew 10 Years Old (81.5) n21 t21.5 f19 b20. A bright start from this new kid on the Tullamore block. Soft fruit and harder pot still make some kind of complexity, but peters out at the death. 40%. Campbell & Cochrane Group.

Tullamore Dew 12 Years Old (84.5) n21.5 t21.5 f20 b21.5. Silky thanks to some excellent Midleton grain: there are mouthwatering qualities here that make the most of the soft spices and gentle fruit. An improved whiskey, if still somewhat meek and shy. 40%. Campbell & Cochrane Group.

Tullamore Dew Black 43 (85) n19 t22 f22.5 b21.5. "Black". Now there's an original name for a new whiskey. Don't think it'll catch on, personally: after all, who has ever heard of a whisky being called "This or That" Black...?? But the whiskey might. Once you get past the usual Tullamore granite-like nose, here even more unyielding than usual, some rather engaging and complex (and especially spicy) things happen, though the caramel does its best to neuter them. 43%. William Grant & Sons.

Tullamore Dew Heritage (78) n20 t21 f18 b19. Tedious going with the caramel finish a real turn off. 40.0%. Campbell & Cochrane Group.

Waitrose Irish Whiskey (86.5) n21.5 t22 f21.5 b21.5. Cooley's grain whiskey, about as good a grain made anywhere in the world, is in fine voice here. Pity some toffee stifles it slightly. 40%

Walker & Scott Irish Whiskey "Copper Pot Distilled" (83) n20 t22 f20 b21. A collectors' item. This charming, if slightly fudgy-finished blend was made by Cooley as the house Irish for one of Britain's finest breweries. Sadly, someone put "Copper Pot Distilled" on the label, which, as it's a blend, can hardly be the case. And even if it wasn't a blend, would still be confusing in terms of Irish whiskey, there not being any traditional Irish Pot Still, that mixture of malted and unmalted barley. So Sam's, being one of the most traditional brewers in Britain, with the next bottling changed the label by dropping all mention of pot still. Top marks, chaps! The next bottling can be seen below. 40%. Sam Smith's.

Walker & Scott Irish Whiskey (85) n21 t22 f21 b21. Oddly, sharper grain has helped give his some extra leap through the toffee. A very decent blend. 40%

The Wild Geese Classic Blend (80.5) n20 t21 f19.5 b19. Easy going, pretty neutral and conservative. If you are looking for zip, zest and charisma you've picked the wrong goose (see below). 40%. Cooley for Avalon.

The Wild Geese Limited Edition Fourth Centennial (93) n23 t23.5 f23 b23.5. A limited edition of unlimited beauty. One of the lightest, subtle, intriguing and quite simply disarming Irish whiskeys on the market. As a bird and whiskey lover, this is one goose that I shall be looking out for. 43%. Cooley for Avalon.

The Wild Geese Rare Irish (89.5) n22 t23 f22 b22.5. Just love this. The Cooley grain is working sublimely and dovetails with the malt in the same effortless way wild geese fly in perfect formation. A treat. 43%. Cooley for Avalon.

Writers Tears (93) n23.5 a glossy Pot Still character: rather than the usual fruity firmness, the recognisable Pot Still traits are shrouded in soft honey tones which dovetail with lightening kumquat-citrus tones. Quite a curious, but always deliciously appealing animal...; t24 works beautifully well: the arrival is an alternating delivery of hard and soft waves, the former showing a more bitter, almost myopic determination to hammer home its traditional pot still standpoint; the sweeter, more yielding notes dissolve with little or no resistance, leaving an acacia honeyed trail; towards the middle a juicier malt element mingles with soft vanilla but the Pot Still character never goes away; f22 relatively short with perhaps the Pot Still, with an old-fashioned cough sweet fruitiness, lingering longest, though its does retain its honeyed accompaniment for the most part; b23.5 now that really was different. The first mix of pure Pot Still and single malt I have knowingly come across in a commercial bottling, but only because I wasn't aware of the make up of last year's Irishman Blend. The malt, like the Pot Still, is, I understand from proprietor Bernard Walsh, from Midleton, but the two styles mixed shows a remarkably similar character to when I carried out an identical experiment with pure pot still and Bushmills the best part of a decade ago. A success and hopefully not a one off. Which is more than I can say for the label, a whiskey collectors – sorry, collector's – item in its own right. There is a wonderfully Irish irony that a whiskey dedicated to Ireland's extraordinary literary heritage should be represented by a label, even a brand name, so punctually inept; it's almost brilliant. The reason for the Writers (sic) Tears, if from the spirits of James Joyce, Samuel Beckett, George Bernard Shaw, Oscar Wilde and perhaps even Maurice Walsh, whose grandson became a legendary blender at Irish Distillers, will be open to debate: we will never know whether they laughed or cried. As far as the actual whiskey is concerned, though, I am sure they, to a man, would have no hesitation but to pen the most luminous and positive critiques possible. 40%. Writers Tears Whiskey Co.

Writer's Tears Cask Strength bott 2011 (90.5) n23 a thick nose with honey and butterscotch, but dulled by caramels; t22 a mouth-watering delivery is mildly out of context with the degree of acceleration of toffee and vanilla f22.5 livens up towards the finish as some world-class spices begin to fizz. More accent on the hard-guy/soft-guy approach the two Pure Irish Pot still and malt whiskey styles evoke; b23 sometimes seems a rabble of whiskey, with the flavours and shapes never quite deciding where it wants to go. But the randomness of the style is also a strength as you are entertained from first to last, though the caramels do keep the lid on some of the more honeyed moments. And memo to brand proprietor Bernard Walsh: only one mistake on your back label this time... 53%. 1200 bottles.

American Whiskey

That green – and slightly blue – baized undulating block of limestone known as Kentucky is not much known for high magnitude earthquakes.

It may get the odd tremor to test the loosest tiles, but they are very few and far between. However, the State's whiskey industry was rocked by a couple of massive jolts just seven weeks apart when two of the all-time giants of bourbon were lost to us.

Between them Elmer T Lee and Lincoln Henderson had clocked up over 100 years' experience in the making and blending of bourbon; and in Linc's case the shockwaves were felt as far as Tennessee where he had worked for decades on Jack Daniels.

Though Elmer was 93 and Lincoln 75 both treated their retirements almost as if they had never happened and continued working to the very end. Elmer kept his hand in by once a week visiting the blending lab at Buffalo Trace which, as the George T Stagg distillery on the banks of the Kentucky River in his home town of Frankfort, he had joined in 1949. There, for the last few years, he would sample the possibles and probables of what had become his signature brand, Elmer T Lee single barrel. Tasting samples was nothing new to Elmer, even though he was a technical guy with an engineering degree who had worked his way from the maintenance department to the stillroom by becoming distillery manager in 1969. He made his last visit a fortnight before his death. But his legacy to the distillery – indeed the industry and whisky lovers everywhere – was bringing out the first regular single barrel brand by a whisky company, as opposed to an independent bottler. In 1985 he officially retired from the distillery, by then known as Ancient Age. But a year earlier he had pioneered the Blanton's brand, a labour-intensive, hand-bottled single barrel bourbon which proved to be the pathfinder for much-needed high quality Kentucky whiskey when the industry was at its nadir.

After his retirement Elmer could often be spotted under his trademark flat cap doing this and that around the distillery, especially in the warehouses and lab. He was as much a part of the historic building's structure as any of the salmon pink bricks which form the eclectic contours of an entire nation's distilling heritage. Indeed, there was something touchingly fitting yet other worldly that just two days after his death on July 16th 2013 Buffalo Trace were at liberty to announce that the distillery had the honour of having been designated a National Historical Landmark, the highest and rarest award for any structure or place in the USA. For we who had spent a long time in the whiskey industry already knew that this funny, warm, articulate, whisky-passionate, highly professional and deeply knowledgeable old gent had been a living National Historical Landmark for a great many years.

Where Elmer was the consummate traditionalist to the last, Lincoln Henderson, by contrast, ended his long and distinguished career blending avant-garde whiskeys for the new family concern, Angel's Envy. Linc and I spent quite a lot of time together in the 1990s where he took me through his work in Kentucky for Brown-Forman's bourbon brands and in Tennessee with Jack Daniels, where I found him to be a blender by instinct, the best type of them all. But we spent many months together as an old pile of limestone bricks on McCracken Pike near Frankfort was miraculously transformed back into the historic Labrot and Graham distillery, later to be renamed Woodford Reserve. And with distillery manager Dave Scheurich we would raid the warehouses at random times during day and night, epecially night, to test how the first, embryonic spirit was maturing.

Being in Linc Henderson's company was, for me, the highlight of over two decades in the world whisky industry. A smile and Linc were always in close proximity, his gentle voice never lost its Oklahoma warmness and his charm, wit, one-liners and innate kindness meant you always looked forward to being around him. Linc was even an honorary grand-dad to my son James while I lived in Kentucky for a while; and he treated him like his own.

After his retirement in 2004 Linc was always a little perplexed and disappointed that the bourbon industry did not make use of his vast knowledge and insight. Instead it was the Japanese, through Suntory, who deployed him to spread the word of their whiskies around the globe, a strange situation which was not lost on him. Especially after, back in 1994, I gave him his first-ever taste of a peated whisky... which he instantly loathed. After one judging session at the International Wine and Spirit Competition some years later I took Linc on a drive around my native Surrey and mischievously asked him how he liked Suntory's more heavily peated malts. With trademark Henderson timing he replied without skipping a beat: "What peat?" The crinkled,disguised smile below his manicured moustache said it all.

The pity was that just weeks before his passing I wrote the piece in Bible Thumping criticising the type of whisky he was creating for the Angel's Envy. I had planned to see Linc in November to debate with him his thinking. What was certain, no matter how far apart we may have been in the argument it would have been one carried out amid a flurry of laughs and smiles.

I make no apology for admitting that I loved that man as he was unquestionably the kindest, most gentle and decent person I have met in the last three decades. And the Angel's Envy now is that there will be none of them up there able to hold a candle to him.

Farewell, then Elmer and Linc. Two very special, dearly loved friends who painstakingly went out of their way to teach me so much. And who between them raised the bar in American whiskey to an extent that has never been fully recorded or appreciated. But in time, that most vital ingredient in all things whiskey, surely will.

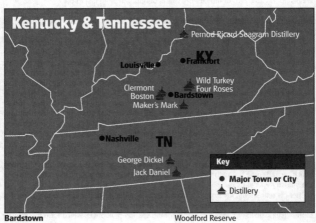

Bardstown	Woodford Reserve
Heaven Hill	**Louisville**
Tom Moore	Early Times
Frankfort	Bernheim
Buffalo Trace	Stitzel Weller

Bourbon Distilleries

Bourbon confuses people. Often they don't even realise it is a whiskey, a situation not helped by leading British pub chains, such as Wetherspoon, whose bar menus list "whiskey" and "bourbon" in separate sections. And if I see the liqueur Southern Comfort listed as a bourbon one more time I may not be responsible for my actions.

Bourbon is a whiskey. It is made from grain and matured in oak, so really it can't be much else. To be legally called bourbon it must have been made with a minimum of 51% corn and matured in virgin oak casks for at least two years. Oh, and no colouring can be added other than that which comes naturally from the barrel.

Where it does differ, from, say Scotch, is that the straight whiskey from the distillery may be called by something other than that distillery name. Indeed, the distillery may change its name which has happened to two this year already and two others in the last three or four. So, to make things easy and reference as quick as possible, I shall list the Kentucky-based distilleries first and then their products in alphabetical order along with their owners and operational status.

BUFFALO TRACE Leestown, Frankfort. Sazerac. Operating.

BROWN-FORMAN Shively, Louisville. Brown-Forman. Operating.

FOUR ROSES Lawrenceburg. Kirin. Operating

HEAVEN HILL BERNHEIM DISTILLERY Louisville. Heaven Hill. Operating.

JIM BEAM Boston and Clermont. Fortune Brands. Operating.

MAKER'S MARK Loretto. Fortune Brands. Operating.

TOM MOORE Bardstown. Sazerac. Operating.

WILD TURKEY Lawrenceburg. Campari Group. Operating.

WOODFORD RESERVE Near Millville. Brown-Forman. Operating.

Bourbon

Ancient Age (74.5) n18 t18.5 f19 b19. Basic: no frills and certainly no thrills until some late oils and spices kick in. 40%

Ancient Age 90 Proof (86.5) n21 t23 f21.5 b22. If this is supposed to be the same whiskey as standard AA, but with just extra strength, you wouldn't know it. Here the oils have reduced considerably and in their place a quite beautiful tapestry of lively spice and rich, sweetened tannins arrive from the first moment...and last most of the course. More than just a passing nod to this distillery's glory. 45%

Ancient Ancient Age 10 Star (94.5) n23 t24 f23.5 b24. A bourbon which has slipped effortlessly through the gears over the last decade. It is now cruising and offers so many nuggets of pure joy this is now a must have for the serious bourbon devotee. Now a truly great bourbon which positively revels in its newfound complexity: a new 10 Star is born... 45%

Ancient Age Bonded (92) n23 t24 f23 b23. Unmistakably Buffalo Trace... with balls. 50%

Ancient Ancient Age 10 Years Old (96) n23.5 t24 f24 b24.5. This whiskey is like shifting sands: same score as last time out, but the shape is quite different again. Somehow underlines the genius of the distillery that a world class whiskey can reach the same point of greatness, but by taking two different routes...However, in this case the bourbon actually finds something a little extra to move it on to a point very few whiskeys very rarely reach... 43%

Baker's Aged 7 Years bott no. L1074CLA (89.5) n23 t22.5 f22 b22. Infinitely more intense and complex than a few years back: further proof that Beam whiskey is very much improving. Superb whiskey but, if anything, too old for its age... 53.5%

Basil Hayden's 8 Years Old (78) n20 t20 f19 b19. A thin bourbon which never quite finds anchor. Certainly one of the most citrusy bourbons around, but, overall, more Basil Fawlty as this is a bit of a strange, mildly neurotic character. 40%

Benchmark (86) n21 t22 f21.5 b21.5. Unquestionably a better whiskey than once it was with now an entirely well constructed vanilla-sugar depth adding ballast where once there was none. Lovely unexpected spices, too. A real surprise after not having tasted for a couple of years...as, frankly, it hadn't been worth it. Now it is... 40%

Benchmark No. 8 (79) n20 t21 f19 b19. Thinner in body and character than the standard Benchmark. Papery sweetness, but little of the balancing spice of its stablemate. 40%

Benjamin Prichard's Double Barrelled Bourbon 9 Years Old (94.5) n24.5 double chocolate, it appears... as usual a stunning nose from Prichard. Crisp rye and crisper apple teams with equally firm Demerara and liquorice but that chocolate plus corn and vanilla offers the countering softness required; a mega bourbon nose...; t24.5 like the nose, absolutely breathtaking intensity which spells bourbon with every atom; spellbinding balance between the maple syrup sweetness and the drier vanillas; the corn really does have a major input in flavour f22 oils and dries out a fraction and some cocoa returns, but remains chewy; b23.5 if only they could bottle that nose...oh, they have...!!! Just wonderful whiskey. 40%

⁖ **Big Bottom Straight Bourbon 91** (95) n23 tight, in that small grain dominates over the corn, while making the most of its oils, and the oak is chunky, salty and chocolaty; t24 again, a big salty tang to this, but this then serves to bring out the enormity of the grains, in which the corn has fought back pole position; the middle is full of honey, liquorice and burgeoning spices; f24 and now the small grains are back behind the wheel for a tantalisingly complex finale; b24 stupendous bourbon. 45.5% (91 proof) ncf

⁖ **Big Bottom Straight Bourbon 111** (85.5) n21.5 t20.5 f22.5 b21. An aggressive bourbon and that has nothing to do with the strength. The delivery is tart and lopsided. The sharpness recedes towards the middle and, finally, the lights shine as the praline and mocha enter the fray on the spicy finish. 55.5% (111 proof) ncf

Blanton's (92) n21.5 t24 f23 b23.5. If it were not for the sluggish nose this would be a Whisky Bible Liquid Gold award winner for sure. On the palate it shows just why little can touch Buffalo Trace for quality at the moment... 40%

Blanton's Gold Original Single Barrel (96.5) n24 a thumping barrage of old honey forgotten in a jar with lavender and leather; t24.5 rarely does a flavour profile follow the nose so faithfully. Here it also confirms the weight and texture; this is pure chewability. One of the most honeyed middles on the circuit with liquorice, usually ballast, here actually thinning things down a little; the spices hit an early crescendo and then buzz contentedly; f24 long and remains absolutely unblemished and on a steady course. The honey remains intact; soft vanillas joins the liquorice while the spices just carry on...and on... b24 it is improbable that a whiskey this enormous and with so many star turns can glide so effortlessly over the palate. One of the best Blanton's in years, this is true Gold standard... 46.5% (93 Proof)

Blanton's 80 Proof (89) n22 t23 f22 b22. Simplistic, soft and full of water-down honey. I doubt you'd say no to a second one... 40%

Blanton's Takara (91.5) n24.5 t23 f22 b22. Not quite how many people might envisage a bourbon: certainly not butch enough to keep the wild west gunslingers happy. No this is a bourbon which searches for your feminine side. And being so light, leaves itself open for any off-key bitter notes which might just happen along the way. *49% (98 proof)*

Blanton's Uncut/Unfiltered (96.5) n25 t24 f23.5 b24. Uncut. Unfiltered. Unbelievable. *65.9%*

Booker's 7 Years 0 Months batch C03-1-16 **(92.5)** n22.5 honey on toast; t23.5 a rumbling, rambling thickly coated feast of spiced liquorice, handsomely topped with vanilla and a late infusion of molasses; f23 superb oils ensure a long, classy and silky textured finale. Some burned toast is crumbled into the mix for the finish which shows age well above its years; b23.5 the alcohol may be big but it hardly makes an impact against the enormity of the huge ok statement. Big, seriously fascinating whiskey. *63.7% (1274 Proof)*

Booker's 7 Years 4 Months batch no. C03-1-17 **(95.5)** n24 t25 f22.5 b24. The best Booker's I have tasted for a very long while, probably ever. Absolutely world class whiskey. *64%*

Booker's 7 Years 4 Months batch C04-A-28 **(92.5)** n23 the usual butch bourbon biffing: meaty, high octane liquorice; manuka honey; t24 a delivery which sends you flying back against your seat: about as roasty as they come with hickory doused in chilli-spiced Demerara sugar; f22 perhaps a little too raw with the sugars vanishing quickly; b23.5 you can always guarantee Booker's to entertain and wow you. No exception here. *64.55% (129.1 proof)*

Bowman Brother's Virginia Straight Bourbon (90) n21 t23 f23 b23. Quietly confident and complex: a bit of a gem waiting to be discovered. *45% (90 proof)*

Buffalo Trace (92.5) n23 t23 f23.5 b23. Easily one of the lightest BTs I have tasted in a very long while. The rye has not just taken a back seat, but has fallen off the bus. *45%*

Buffalo Trace Master Distiller Emeritus Elmer T Lee Collector's Edition bott. 06/09/11 **(96)** n24.5 t24 f23.5 b24. Simply spellbinding. One of the best BT bottlings I have ever enjoyed for bourbon rarely comes more understatedly complete and complex than this. This is the bottle with a nickel coin glued to it. And each complex character within this whiskey gets more than its five cents worth... *45%*

Buffalo Trace Single Oak Project Barrel #132 (r1yKA1 *see key below*) db **(95)** n24 t23.5 f23.5 b24. This sample struck me for possessing, among the first batch of bottlings, the classic Buffalo Trace personality. Afterwards they revealed that it was of a profile which perhaps most closely matches their standard 8-year-old BT. Therefore it is this one I shall use as the tasting template. *45% (90 Proof)*

Key to Buffalo Trace Single Oak Project Codes

Mash bill type: r = rye; w = wheat
Tree grain: 1 = course; 2 = average; 3 = tight
Tree cut: x = top half; y = bottom half
Warehouse type: K = rick; L = concrete

Entry strength: A = 125; B = 105
Seasoning: 1 = 6 Months; 2 = 12 Months
Char: All #4 except * = #3

Buffalo Trace Single Oak Project Barrel #1 (r3xKA1*) db **(90.5)** n22 t23 f23 b22.5. Soft corn oil aroma, buttery, big sugars building, silky texture, long. *45% (90 Proof)*

Buffalo Trace Single Oak Project Barrel #3 (r2xKA1) db **(90.5)** n22.5 t23 f22.5 b22.5. Nutty, dry aroma; apple fruitiness and brown sugars. *45% (90 Proof)*

Buffalo Trace Single Oak Project Barrel #4 (r2yKA1) db **(92)** n23 t23 f23 b23. Exceptionally crisp; sharp rye, honeycomb, big liquorice. *45% (90 Proof)*

⊰⊱ **Buffalo Trace Single Oak Project Barrel #5** (r2xLA1*) db **(89)** n23 t22.5 f21.5 b22. Dullish after a rye-intense and busy nose. Early muscovado followed by vanilla and spice. *45%*

⊰⊱ **Buffalo Trace Single Oak Project Barrel #6** (r3yLA1*) db **(90)** n22.5 t22 f23 b22.5. Toast with salted butter and maple syrup. Prickly, mildly aggressive spice throughout. *45%*

Buffalo Trace Single Oak Project Barrel #8 (r3yLA1) db **(92.5)** n23 t23 f23.5 b23. Crisp rye aroma. Fruity, firm, salivating. Spiced toffee and muscovado; toasty. *45% (90 Proof)*

⊰⊱ **Buffalo Trace Single Oak Project Barrel #9** (r3xKA2*) db **(90)** n22 t22.5 f23 b22.5. Marmalade on singed toast. Soft oils: slow release of natural caramels and mocha. *45%*

Buffalo Trace Single Oak Project Barrel #10 (r3yKA2*) db **(93)** n23.5 t23.5 f22.5 b23.5. Rich, delicate rye. Complex, busy body; rye oils, tannins; slow sugar build. Bitters. *45%*

Buffalo Trace Single Oak Project Barrel #14 (r3yLA2*) db **(95)** n24 t24 f23 b24. Chocolate rye nose and body; silky texture; brown sugar and vanilla; rye-rich sweet finish. *45%*

Buffalo Trace Single Oak Project Barrel #17 (r3xKB1)db **(88.5)** n21.5 t22.5 f22.5 b22. Liquorice nose; oily body sweetens; big vanilla, caramel; dull spice. *45% (90 Proof)*

⊰⊱ **Buffalo Trace Single Oak Project Barrel #18** (r3yKB1*) db **(92.5)** n23 t23 f23.5 b23. Full bodied from nose to finish. Cocoa mingles with rye and rich corn oil. Deep, intense, even. *45%*

Buffalo Trace Single Oak Project Barrel #24 (r3xLB1) db **(90)** n22 t23 f22 b22.5. Big liquorice nose and delivery; toffee raisin; big corn oil; even ulmo honey. *45%*

⊰⊱ **Buffalo Trace Single Oak Project Barrel #25** (r3xKB2*) db **(90.5)** n22.5 t23 f22.5 b22.5. Much more accent on the rye and a slow revealing of rich caramels and Demerara. *45%*

⫶⫶ **Buffalo Trace Single Oak Project Barrel #26** (r3yKB2*) db (89.5) n22 t23.5 f22 b22. A sugary volley follows a shy nose. Quietens quickly; small grains add complexity. *45%*

⫶⫶ **Buffalo Trace Single Oak Project Barrel #27** (r3xKB2) db (95.5) n23 t24 f24.5 b24. Bold timber on nose and delivery; hickory and liquorice evident; a big spiced honey finale. *45%*

⫶⫶ **Buffalo Trace Single Oak Project Barrel #28** (r3yKB2) db (94.5) n23 t24 f23.5 b24. Sublime balance between sugars and grains on body. Controlled spice; layered cocoa. *45%*

Buffalo Trace Single Oak Project Barrel #29 (r3xLB2*) db (91) n23 t22.5 f23 b22.5. Crisp rye nose; more precise grain. Excellent spices. *45% (90 Proof)*

⫶⫶ **Buffalo Trace Single Oak Project Barrel #30** (r3yLB2*) db (95.5) n23.5 t24 f24 b24. One of the most delicate yet: crisp rye and sugars, minty forthright oak. Clean yet deep. *45%*

Buffalo Trace Single Oak Project Barrel #31 (r3xLB2) db (87.5) n22 t22 f21.5 b22. Dull, rumbling and herbal; oily caramel and sugars. Soft. *45% (90 Proof)*

⫶⫶ **Buffalo Trace Single Oak Project Barrel #32** (r3yLB2) db (90.5) n23.5 t23 f21.5 b22.5. Soft corn oils dominate. Buttery, molten muscovado. Late hickory. Bitterish finish. *45%*

Buffalo Trace Single Oak Project Barrel #33 (w3xKA1*) db (94.5) n24 t23.5 f23 b24. Huge, busy baking spiced cake; muscovado sugar delivery; remains sweet, silky and spicy; *45%*

Buffalo Trace Single Oak Project Barrel #35 (w3yKA1) db (89.5) n22 t22 f23 b22.5. Soft mint, yeasty; soft toffee delivery, builds in spice. *45% (90 Proof)*

Buffalo Trace Single Oak Project Barrel #36 (w3yKA1) db (91.5) n23 t23 f22.5 b23. Vague rum and toffee; bold, salivating, slow spice. *45% (90 Proof)*

⫶⫶ **Buffalo Trace Single Oak Project Barrel #37** (w3xLA1*) db (90) n21 t23 f22 b22. Typical big spice beast. Complex, doughy middle with accent on butterscotch and citrus. *45% (90 Proof)*

⫶⫶ **Buffalo Trace Single Oak Project Barrel #38** (w3yLA1*) db (87.5) n22 t22.5 f20.5 b21.5. Fizzy, busy nose matched by massive spice attack on delivery. Bitter, thin finish. *45%*

Buffalo Trace Single Oak Project Barrel #40 (w3xLA1) db (93) n23 t23 f23.5 b23.5. Soft, spiced cake, big citrus; silky, oily, bananas and golden syrup; late spice, balancing bitters. *45%*

⫶⫶ **Buffalo Trace Single Oak Project Barrel #41** (w3xKA2*) db (92.5) n22 t23 f23.5 b24. Less spice than expected. Docile start, builds in intensity. Buttery, big sugars. Balanced. *45%*

Buffalo Trace Single Oak Project Barrel #42 (w3yKA2*) db (85.5) n22 t21.5 f21 b21. Tight nose opens slowly; sultana pudding with maple syrup. Sweet, late bitterness. *45%*

Buffalo Trace Single Oak Project Barrel #46 (w3yLA2*) db (88) n21.5 t22 f22.5 b22 Doughy aroma. Big corn oils and sugars. Late spice growth. Big vanilla. Quietly complex. *45%*

Buffalo Trace Single Oak Project Barrel #49 (w3xKB1) db (93) n24 t23 f23 b23. Chocolate spice, apples, oaky aroma; treacle pudding, soft oils; banana and custard; bitters. *45%*

⫶⫶ **Buffalo Trace Single Oak Project Barrel #50** (w3yKB1*) db (88) n21.5 t23 f23.5 b22. Flat nose. Muscovado delivery. Slow spices. Late liquorice. Even. Limited depth. *45% (90 Proof)*

Buffalo Trace Single Oak Project Barrel #56 (w3yLB1) db (91) n24 t22.5 f22 b22.5. Chocolate vanilla and tannins; soft, slow build up of spice, oily; bitters. *45% (90 Proof)*

⫶⫶ **Buffalo Trace Single Oak Project Barrel #57** (w3xKB2*) db (94) n23 t23.5 f23.5 b24. Immediate spice kick on nose and delivery. Caramels and marmalade. Busy, balanced. *45%*

⫶⫶ **Buffalo Trace Single Oak Project Barrel #58** (w3yKB2*) db (90.5) n22.5 t23 f22.5 b22.5. Liquorice and Fisherman's Friend nose; molassed middle and big spice finish. *45%*

⫶⫶ **Buffalo Trace Single Oak Project Barrel #59** (w3xKB2) db (92) n22 t23.5 f23 b23.5. Lighter Fisherman's Friend; roasted fudge; busy small grains attack. Mega complex. *45%*

⫶⫶ **Buffalo Trace Single Oak Project Barrel #60** (w3yKB2) db (87.5) n22.5 t22.5 f21 b21.5. Aggression to spice nose; tame delivery and body. Soft corn oil and muscovado. *46%*

Buffalo Trace Single Oak Project Barrel #61 (w3xLB2*) db (94.5) n24 t23 f23.5 b24. Classic spiced wheat; Demerara sugars and spices abound. Big. *45% (90 Proof)*

Buffalo Trace Single Oak Project Barrel #62 (w3yLB2*) db (88) n22 t22.5 f21.5 b22. Caramel is leading theme; soft, big wheated spice. Oily. *45% (90 Proof)*

⫶⫶ **Buffalo Trace Single Oak Project Barrel #63** (w3xLB2) db (95.5) n24 t23 f24 b24.5. Subtle dates, spice, cocoa; gentle, oily, perfect spice build. Ultra complex. *45% (90 Proof)*

⫶⫶ **Buffalo Trace Single Oak Project Barrel #64** (w3yLB2) db (91) n22.5 t23.5 f22.5 b23. Citrus nose. Big oak and spice delivery; treacle tart and liquorice. Softens into caramel. *45%*

Buffalo Trace Single Oak Project Barrel #65 (r2xKA1) db (91) n23.5 t22 f23 b22.5. Small grain nose; crunchy muscovado, corn oil; liquorice, vanilla; late spice. Complex. *45%*

Buffalo Trace Single Oak Project Barrel #67 (r2xKA1) db (89.5) n22 t23 f22 b22.5. Blandish nose; tart, tight, sharp, some toffee raisin. *45% (90 Proof)*

Buffalo Trace Single Oak Project Barrel #68 (r2yKA1) db (92) n22.5 t23 f23.5 b23. Rye depth; deeper, warmer spices, liquorice and light molasses. *45% (90 Proof)*

⫶⫶ **Buffalo Trace Single Oak Project Barrel #69** (r2xLA1*) db (94.5) n23 t24 f23.5 b24. Crisp, sharp rye on nose and delivery. Jagged muscovado and spice. Goes down a treat... *45%*

⫶⫶ **Buffalo Trace Single Oak Project Barrel #70** (r2yLA1*) db (91.5) n22.5 t23 f23 b23. Yielding caramel and vanilla. Rye and hot spice breaks up the sleepy theme. *45% (90 Proof)*

Buffalo Trace Single Oak Project Barrel #72 (r2yLA1) db **(89)** n22.5 t23 f21.5 b22. Floral nose; juicy, tangy, citrus. Liquorice, sugary vanilla. Bitter marmalade finish. 45%

◌⋮⋗ **Buffalo Trace Single Oak Project Barrel #73** (r2xKA2*) db **(87.5)** n21.5 t22 f22 b22. Tight, unyielding nose. Initially crisp rye then thick vanilla and baked apple blanket. 45%

Buffalo Trace Single Oak Project Barrel #74 (r2yKA2*) db **(88)** n22 t22 f22 b22. Corny nose; more corn oil early on; syrup, huge rye sure on finish; bitters slightly. 45% (90 Proof)

Buffalo Trace Single Oak Project Barrel #78 (r2yLA2*) db **(89)** n22.5 t22 f22.5 b22. Small grain busy nose; light spice to oils; light rye, late sugars; chewy caramels. 45% (90 Proof)

Buffalo Trace Single Oak Project Barrel #81 (r2yKB1*) db **(94)** n23 t23 f24 b24. Candy shop fruitiness; delicate oils and flavour development; big yet subdued brown sugars. 45%

◌⋮⋗ **Buffalo Trace Single Oak Project Barrel #82** (r2yKB1*) db **(91.5)** n22.5 t23.5 f22.5 b23. Liquoice, manuka honey; lurid rye bite and lychee fruitiness; mocha and Demerara. 45%

Buffalo Trace Single Oak Project Barrel #88 (r2yLB1) db **(89)** n23.5 t22 f21.5 b22. Hickory, rye nose; liquorice delivery big caramel surge; bitters on finish. 45% (90 Proof)

◌⋮⋗ **Buffalo Trace Single Oak Project Barrel #89** (r2xKB2*) db **(89.5)** n22 t22.5 f22 b22.5. Rye radiates on nose and delivery. Big spice surge to the middle. Late mocha, liquorice. 45%

◌⋮⋗ **Buffalo Trace Single Oak Project Barrel #90** (r2yKB2*) db **(94)** n23.5 t24 f23 b23.5. Big tannin, cocoa and caramel throughout. Major peppery spice. Complex. 45% (90 Proof)

◌⋮⋗ **Buffalo Trace Single Oak Project Barrel #91** (r2xKB2) db **(86.5)** n21.5 t22 f21.5 b21.5. Half-cooked: dull caramel throughout. Short spice peak. Sweet, oily, lacking complexity. 45%

◌⋮⋗ **Buffalo Trace Single Oak Project Barrel #92** (r2yKB2) db **(91)** n22 t23 f23 b23. Silky texture. Big corn oil but intense tannin thinned by beech honey. Hickory and maple syrup. 45%

Buffalo Trace Single Oak Project Barrel #93 (r2xLB2*) db **(89)** n22.5 t22 f22 b22.5. Soft rye and sugars; juicy grain, tangy citrus, muscovado. 45% (90 Proof)

◌⋮⋗ **Buffalo Trace Single Oak Project Barrel #94** (r2yLB2*) db **(92.5)** n22.5 t24 f23 b23. Rich, hefty. Slightly salty, crisp rye. Light caramel, hint of Guyanese rum. Delicate spice. 45%

Buffalo Trace Single Oak Project Barrel #95 (r2xLB2) db **(94)** n23 t23.5 f23.5 b24. Citrus, banana; soft vanilla, profound rye sharpness, spices. Big. 45% (90 Proof)

◌⋮⋗ **Buffalo Trace Single Oak Project Barrel #96** (r2yLB2) db **(89)** n22 t23.5 f21.5 b22. Bright, grainy delivery in contrast to oily nose and finish. Heavy, dry molasses at the death. 45%

Buffalo Trace Single Oak Project Barrel #97 (w2xKA1*) db **(87)** n22.5 t22 f21.5 b21.5. Toffee apple nose; heavy corn oil, light muscovado sugar, bitters out; 45% (90 Proof)

Buffalo Trace Single Oak Project Barrel #99 (w2xKA1) db **(86.5)** n22 t22 f21 b21.5. Malty, vanilla; thin maple syrup, caramel. Dull. 45% (90 Proof)

Buffalo Trace Single Oak Project Barrel #100 (w2yKA1) db **(94)** n23 t23.5 f23.5 b24. Busy, green, fresh; big juicy, vanilla, muscovado, spices. 45% (90 Proof)

◌⋮⋗ **Buffalo Trace Single Oak Project Barrel #101** (w2xLA1) db **(96)** n23.5 t24 f23.5 b25. Unerring chocolate and mint aided by even muscovado, vanilla and spice. Hugely complex. 45%

◌⋮⋗ **Buffalo Trace Single Oak Project Barrel #102** (w2yLA1*) db **(88.5)** n22 t22 f22.5 b22. Insane tannin on nose; overcooked caramel. Massive sugar-spice mix. 45% (90 Proof)

Buffalo Trace Single Oak Project Barrel #104 (w2xLA1) db **(91)** n23 t23 f22.5 b22.5. Apple, cinnamon; light spice; corn oil; vanilla and ulmo honey; spices, bitters out. 45%

◌⋮⋗ **Buffalo Trace Single Oak Project Barrel #105** (w2xKA2*) db **(89)** n22.5 t22 f22.5 b22. Spiced, lively nose; hot cross buns; oils and sugars build slowly; spices intensify at end. 45%

Buffalo Trace Single Oak Project Barrel #106 (w2yKA2*) db **(92.5)** n24 t23 f23 b23.5. Mega complex nose: busy sugars and spices; silky texture; nougat, caramel. 45%

Buffalo Trace Single Oak Project Barrel #110 (w2yLA2*) db **(90)** n22 t22.5 f22.5 b23. Intense caramel; liquorice and toffee middle; citrus and salt; caramel finish. 45% (90 Proof)

Buffalo Trace Single Oak Project Barrel #113 (w2xKB1*) db **(88)** n22.5 t22 f22 b21.5. Big vanilla nose; minor spice, oily, buttery vanilla. Simple. 45% (90 Proof)

◌⋮⋗ **Buffalo Trace Single Oak Project Barrel #114** (w2yKB1*) db **(90)** n22 t23 f22 b23. Elements of citrus. Oily corn. Controlled spice. Earthy and sweet. 45% (90 Proof)

Buffalo Trace Single Oak Project Barrel #120 (w2xLB1) db **(89.5)** n23 t22 f22.5 b22. Controlled oak throughout. Intermittent dry vanilla. Delicate sugars. 45% (90 Proof)

◌⋮⋗ **Buffalo Trace Single Oak Project Barrel #121** (w2xKB2*) db **(89)** n22.5 t23 f21.5 b22. Citrusy corn oil apparent and dominates. Sugars rampant, spices shy. Rather flat finale. 45%

◌⋮⋗ **Buffalo Trace Single Oak Project Barrel #122** (w2yKB2*) db **(93)** n22 t23.5 f23.5 b24. Serious wheat-spice with cocoa back up. Demerara sugars evenly spread. Complex. 45%

◌⋮⋗ **Buffalo Trace Single Oak Project Barrel #123** (w2xKB2) db **(85.5)** n21 t22 f21 b21.5. One of the dullest yet: limited sparkle despite light spice. Big caramel. 45% (90 Proof)

◌⋮⋗ **Buffalo Trace Single Oak Project Barrel #124** (w2yKB2) db **(90.5)** n22.5 t23 f22.5 b22.5. The startling, extra sugars over #123 impact hugely. Juicy; oak (liquorice) support. 45%

Buffalo Trace Single Oak Project Barrel #125 (w2xLB2*) db **(93)** n24 t23 f22.5 b22.5. Heavy oak, spices; firm, juicy. Softer caramel fade. 45% (90 Proof)

⠿ **Buffalo Trace Single Oak Project Barrel #126** (w2yLB2*) db (**90**) n22 t23 f22.5 b22.5.
Floral nose (primroses); elaborate delivery of spice and creamed mocha plus molasses. *45%*

Buffalo Trace Single Oak Project Barrel #127 (w2xLB2) db (85.5) n21.5 t22 f21 b21.
Off balance, citrus; juicy at first, bitters later. *45% (90 Proof)*

⠿ **Buffalo Trace Single Oak Project Barrel #128** (w2yLB2) db (89) n21.5 t22 f22.5 b22.5.
Conservative nose, OTT spice on delivery. Molassed dates and walnut. *45% (90 Proof)*

Buffalo Trace Single Oak Project Barrel #129 (r1xKA1*) db (88) n22.5 t22 f22 b22. Firm
grainy, tannin nose; nougat, nutty, corn oil; clean but dim vanilla fade. *45% (90 Proof)*

Buffalo Trace Single Oak Project Barrel #131 (r1xKA1) db (92.5) n23 t23 f23.5 b23.
Relaxed vanilla, light tannin; corn oily, icing sugars, marzipan. *45% (90 Proof)*

Buffalo Trace Single Oak Project Barrel #132 *See above.*

⠿ **Buffalo Trace Single Oak Project Barrel #133** (r1xLA1*) db (89) n22.5 t23 f21 b22.5.
Small grain busyness does the business: rye leads the dark sugar procession. Bitters out. *45%*

⠿ **Buffalo Trace Single Oak Project barrel #134** (r1yLA1*) db (91.5) n22 t23.5 f23 b23.
Velvet delivery: big spice cushioned by muscovado and butterscotch. Mixed honey finale. *45%*

Buffalo Trace Single Oak Project Barrel #136 (r1yLA1) db (92) n23.5 t22.5 f23 b23.
Liquorice on nose and delivery. Spicy. Richer oils. Demerara. Spice. *45% (90 Proof)*

⠿ **Buffalo Trace Single Oak Project Barrel #137** (r1xKA2*) db (90.5) n22 t23.5 f22 b23.
Fruity opening with a hardening rye presence and emphasis on muscovado. Late cocoa. *45%*

Buffalo Trace Single Oak Project Barrel #138 (r1yKA2*) db (87) n22.5 t21.5 f21.5 b21.5.
Marzipan, citrus nose; dull delivery, slow build of muscovado and vanilla. Soft. *45%*

Buffalo Trace Single Oak Project Barrel #142 (r1yLA2*) db (89.5) n22.5 t22.5 f22 b22.5.
Light tannin nose; oils, liquorice, spice bite. More corn oil. Sugars, spicy vanilla. *45%*

Buffalo Trace Single Oak Project Barrel #145 (r1xKB1*) db (91) n22.5 t22 f23.5 b23.
Nougat, cocoa; busy small grains; oily corn; spiced chocolate. *45% (90 Proof)*

⠿ **Buffalo Trace Single Oak Project Barrel #146** (r1yKB1*) db (93) n23 t24 f22 b24.
Rye dominates with clarity and aplomb. Crystal clean nose and delivery: Dundee cake. *45%*

Buffalo Trace Single Oak Project Barrel #152 (r1yLB1) db (81.5) n21 t20.5 f20 b20.5.
Vaguely butyric; harsh, hot fat corn, light rye; bitters out. *45% (90 Proof)*

⠿ **Buffalo Trace Single Oak Project Barrel #153** (r1xKB2*) db (94) n23.5 t23.5 f23 b24.
Complex nose, delivery. Big spice with crisp, juicy rye. Praline, delicate oils. Big but elegant. *45%*

⠿ **Buffalo Trace Single Oak Project Barrel #154** (r1yKB2*) db (92) n23.5 t23 f23 b23.5.
Rye dominates. Hard on palate; yet burnt raisin, lychee and muscovado soften. *45% (90 Proof)*

⠿ **Buffalo Trace Single Oak Project Barrel #155** (r1xKB2) db (93) n23 t24 f22.5 b23.5.
Fierce spice. Dynamic rye shapes all directions. Hickory and manuka honey combine. *45%*

⠿ **Buffalo Trace Single Oak Project Barrel #156** (r1yKB2) db (85.5) n22 t21 f21.5 b21.
Doesn't work. Spices too hot. Caramels and oils negate development. *45% (90 Proof)*

Buffalo Trace Single Oak Project Barrel #157 (r1xLB2*) db (84.5) n21 t21.5 f20.5 b21.
Vague butyric; sharp, juicy corn with slow rye build. Bitter. *45% (90 Proof)*

⠿ **Buffalo Trace Single Oak Project Barrel #158** (r1yLB2) db (88) n22 t22 f22 b22.
Another brawny, corn-oily, oaky effort. Excellent cocoa, citrus and spice development. *45%*

Buffalo Trace Single Oak Project Barrel #159 (r1xLB2) db (88) n20.5 t22.5 f22 b22.5.
Vague butyric; firm sugars then watery, confident spices, soft honey. Complex. *45% (90 Proof)*

⠿ **Buffalo Trace Single Oak Project Barrel #160** (r1yLB2) db (92.5) n23.5 t23 f22 b23. A
salty style with fruity, crisp rye right behind. Steady and firm. *45% (90 Proof)*

Buffalo Trace Single Oak Project Barrel #161 (w1xKA1*) db (87) n21 t22 f22 b22. Cream
caramel candy; juicy corn, oily; more caramel, Light spice. *45% (90 Proof)*

⠿ **Buffalo Trace Single Oak Project Barrel #163** (w1xKA1) db (90) n23 t22.5 f22 b22.5.
Citrus, bubble gum; spiced muscovado sugars at first, bitters. *45% (90 Proof)*

Buffalo Trace Single Oak Project Barrel #164 (w1yKA1) db (94.5) n23.5 t23 f24 b24. Citrus
and vanilla; massive spice, building. Demerara. Warm and complex. *45% (90 Proof)*

⠿ **Buffalo Trace Single oak Project Barrel #165** (w1xLA1*) db (91.5) n22.5 t23 f23 b23.
Lively, spice dominated. Ulmo honey offers superb back up. *45% (90 Proof)*

⠿ **Buffalo Trace Single Oak Project Barrel #166** (w1yLA1*) db (91) n22 t23 f23 b23.
Heady, leathery. Sublime spice middle; molasses and liquorice enrich the tail. *45% (90 Proof)*

Buffalo Trace Single Oak Project Barrel #167 (w1yLB1) db (94) n23.5 t23.5 f23 b24.
Demerara, rummy; intense liquorice, hickory; dark sugars and big spice. *45% (90 Proof)*

⠿ **Buffalo Trace Single Oak Project Barrel #169** (w1xKA2*) db (94) n23.5 t23.5 f23 b24.
Spice, lavender and leather on delivery; nibbly, spicy nose. Good honey and corn oil follow
through. *45% (90 proof)*

Buffalo Trace Single Oak Project Barrel #170 (w1yKA2*) db (92.5) n22.5 t23 f23.5 b23.5.
Sweet, spiced nose; firm, spicy delivery; Demerara and ulmo honey. *45% (90 Proof)*

Buffalo Trace Single Oak Project Barrel #174 (w1yLA2*) db (89) n22 t22.5 f22.5 b22.
Delicate oak; juicy corn, liquorice, light spices, buttery corn. Bitter marmalade. *45% (90 Proof)*

Buffalo Trace Single Oak Project Barrel #177 (w1xKB1*) db (87) n21.5 t22 f22 b21.5. Vaguely spiced corn oil; soft, nutty, marzipan sweetness, citrus. Late mocha. 45% (90 Proof)

⠿ **Buffalo Trace Single Oak Project Barrel #178** (w1yKB1*) db (88.5) n22.5 t23 f21.5 b21.5. Complex marzipan and Demerara nose and delivery; runs out of things to say. 45%

Buffalo Trace Single Oak Project Barrel #184 (w1yLA1) db (93) n23.5 t23 f23 b23.5. Tannins, walnut oil; nutty, corn oils. Light spice, firm Demerara. Late fruity spice. Complex. 45%

Buffalo Trace Single Oak Project Barrel #185 (w1xKB2*) db (92.5) n23 t23.5 f23 b23. Dry, riveting nose; liquorice dominates the palate. Cocoa, hickory enlivened by sugars. 45%

⠿ **Buffalo Trace Single Oak Project Barrel #186** (w1yKB2*) db (90) n23 t22.5 f22 b22.5. Rampant spice from delivery onwards. Burnt fudge and toasted raisin. 45% (90 Proof)

⠿ **Buffalo Trace Single Oak Project Barrel #187** (w1xKB2) db (88) n22 t22 f22 b22. Exceptionally even and caramel rich. Unbalanced tannin and lack of spice. 45% (90 Proof)

⠿ **Buffalo Trace Single Oak Project Barrel #188** (w1yKB2) db (90) n21.5 t23/5 f22.5 b22.5. Lazy nose. Bright delivery; citrusy corn oil and muscovado. Late mocha and liquorice. 45%

Buffalo Trace Single Oak Project Barrel #189 (w1xLB2*) db (88.5) n24 t22 f21 b21.5. Complex citrus, delicate yet big; tart, sweet, fresh, strangely off balance. 45% (90 Proof)

⠿ **Buffalo Trace Single Oak Project Barrel #190** (w1yLB2*) db (94) n23.5 t24 f23 b23.5. Ulmo/manuka honey mix on nose and delivery; silky corn oil; spiced mocha. Complex. 45%

Buffalo Trace Single Oak Project Barrel #191 (w1xLB2) db (94.5) n23 t23.5 f24 b24. Big, spicy, classic; firm wheaty spiciness, juicy, thick caramels. Complex. 45% (90 Proof)

⠿ **Buffalo Trace Single Oak Project Barrel #192** (w1yLB2) db (94.5) n23 t24 f23.5 b24. Demerara rum nose; heavy, dry liquorice body; late spice; molassed butterscotch finish. 45%

⠿ **Buffalo Trace Experiment #7 Heavy Char Barrel** charred white oak, dist 21 Jan 97, bott Oct 12 db (77) n20 t21.5 f17 b18.5. The very nature of experiments means that, sometimes, they go wrong. Perhaps a bit harsh for this one which, to be more precise, has not gone right. The nose has an almost bizarre sherry feel to it, the fruitiness really striking home on the attractive delivery. From then on, it's downhill, leaving an unattractive tang at the death. 45%

⠿ **Buffalo Trace Experiment Hot Box Toasted Barrel** charred white oak, dist 2 Jun 96, bott 22 Oct 12 db (95.5) n24 very unusual: almost a seaside saltiness to this and the fruit from the rye grains emphasised; sensual and almost too delicate for words; t24 it is probably on about the third mouthful that you begin to realise this is very different: where the small grains can sometime be quite angular when not lost against an oak of this age, and where the tannins are usually just begging to get a little over boisterous, you recognise that all the sharp edges and undulations expected have been worn down like a pebble. This is as soft and rounded as any 16-y-o bourbon you will taste in your lifetime, with not even the hint of a splinter; the sugars and the spices are entirely in sync, the maple syrup just melting around the palate; f23 moves into cocoa and mocha territory. Still the dark sugars fashion the shape, but not the overall outcome...especially when a citric tang is reprised; b24.5 I remember having this experimental barrel-making process explained to me what seems a lifetime ago – so long, I'd actually forgotten all about it. But nearly 17 years on, here it is, whiskey from a barrel where the staves were steamed into shape after undergoing some major roasting. The end product is definitely a different kind of BT, where the accent is on softness and pastel-shaded cocoa: a gentle, slightly erotic massage of a bourbon. 45% (90 Proof)

⠿ **Buffalo Trace Experimental Collection Wheat 90** charred white oak, dist 24 Oct 01, bott 15 Jun 13 db (84.5) n21.5 t22.5 f20.5 b20. A curious exhibition of wheated BT, where the sugars appear to have been separated at birth from the dryer elements of the oak. Pleasant, but not up to the usual BT greatness and really not bothered about balance. 45% (90 Proof)

⠿ **Buffalo Trace Experimental Collection Wheat 105** charred white oak, dist 24 Oct 01, bott 14 Jun 13 db (93.5) n24 toasted honey-glazed almonds, lavender and ginger....wow! t22.5 just gorgeous oils to the delivery; muscovado sugars going ape; f23.5 all kinds of caramel and vanilla balancing out with the growing spice; the sugars stay the pace; b23.5 just look at the difference between this and the 90: amazing....!!!! 45% (90 proof)

⠿ **Buffalo Trace Experimental Collection Wheat 115** charred white oak, dist 24 Oct 01, bott 17 Jun 13 db (90) n22 softer vanilla on a very light frame; a drizzle of citrus, a little milky sap from the oak; t24 the initial soft vanilla is soon swamped by a more familiar old guard personality for an 11-year-old bourbon: tannin-leather and liquorice, all weighted gorgeously with deep molasses; f21.5 feels just a little jaded towards the finish, as though someone had over-mined the oak; b22.5 this is like the 105 in reverse: the nose not working so well, but the delivery showing some impressive muscle. 45% (90 proof)

⠿ **Buffalo Trace Experimental Collection Wheat 125** charred white oak, dist 24 Oct 01, bott 17 Jun 13 db (94) n23 so attractively crisp and clean: maple syrup and treacle crystallised; almost a green tea earthiness to the busy herbs at play; t23.5 immediate wheated bourbon style spice on delivery: a kind of abstract fizz about the lightly oiled muscovado and molassed sugar mix; pretty deep, dark with the sugars present but holding back; f23.5 light spices still, just the liquorice and hickory towards the finish emphasises the age; **b24** sensationally satisfying. Bourbon with knobs on...!! *45% (90 proof)*

Bulleit Bourbon (89) n23 t23 f21 b22. A very easy going bourbon which makes the most of any rye in the recipe. *Dangerously drinkable. 45%*

⁙ **Calhoun Bros Straight Bourbon** (84.5) n20.5 t22 f21 b21. Very different! A much wider cut than the norm on straight bourbon whisky results in an oily fellow which you can chew until your jaws ache. Massively toasty, vanilla gorged and intense. *43% (86 proof)*

Charter 101 (95.5) n23.5 standard Charter 101 evening flowers? Check. Usual spices? Check. Obvious lack of honey on the nose? We have a negative, Frankfort. This is just brimming with all the pollen collected from those evening flowers... **t24.5** the lush mouth feel betrays the strength of this bourbon. Again, this has much to do with the honey which absolutely oozes into every crevice of the mouth it can find. Honey was always around on Charter 101, but never like this. Emboldened, it seems, by beautiful blending of lively liquorice and voluptuous vanilla...all with a softly spoken spiciness. But once that settles − even allowing in a chewy fudge sweetness − those honey notes begin to blow you away...simply adorable stuff; **f23.5** long? How long have you got? A sublime layering of Demerara and muscovado sugars embraced by custardy oak...with a cocoa edge throughout. But once that melts you are back to the soft honeyed centre...; **b24** now here is a whiskey which has changed tack dramatically. In many ways it's like the Charter 101 of a year or two back. But this bottling suggests they have turned a warehouse into a giant beehive. Because few whiskeys offer this degree of honey. You can imagine that after all these years, rarely does a whiskey genuinely surprise me: this one has. No wonder there is such a buzz in the bourbon industry right now... *50.5%*

⁙ **Clarke's Old Kentucky Straight Sour Mash Whisky Bourbon** (88.5) n22.5 classic hickory-marmalade-Demerara nose: can't ask for more; **t22** silk-soft and slow spice pulse as the acacia honey radiates; **f22** liquorice and mallows; **b22** honest and hugely impressive bourbon. The rich colour − and remember straight bourbon cannot be falsely coloured − tells its own tale. *40%. Aldi.*

Colonel E H Taylor Barrel Proof (91) n23.5 t23 f22 b22.5. A big boy which turns out to be a bit of a softy in the end... *67.25% (134.5 Proof). nc ncf.*

Colonel E. H. Taylor Old Fashioned Sour Mash (94) n24 t23.5 f23 b23.5. When they say "old fashioned" they really aren't joking. This is a style which takes me back to my first bourbon tasting days of the mid 1970s. And, at the moment, it is hard to name another bourbon offering this unique, technically brilliant style. Outstanding! *50% (100 Proof)*

Colonel E H Taylor Single Barrel (93) n23.5 t23 f23 b23.5. An exceptionally bright barrel that's a bit of a tease. *50% (100 Proof)*

⁙ **Colonel E.H. Taylor Small Batch** (94.5) n23 pretty effortlessly classic: a friendly layering of crisp sugars and teasing spice as well as a thin hint of mint and eucalyptus; the natural vanillas are out in force, too; **t24** pretty perfect weight: the oils have just enough clout to ensure the sugars remain in check and on the Demerara side of things; the small grains do stir, also, and herald the arrival of the toastier elements; **f23.5** long, again with the sweetness in harmony with the butterscotch tart and late peppery bite; **b24** from first nose, to last, the exemplary high quality of this bourbon is not for a second in dispute. *50% (100 Proof)*

Colonel E H Taylor Warehouse C Tornado Surviving (90) n22.5 t23 f22 b22.5. This must be the eye of the storm: a peaceful bourbon that goes about its business with an endearing gentleness. *50% (100 Proof)*

Colonel Lee (70) n17.5 t18.5 f17 b17. The Colonel and I have known each other for a great many years, though it has been a while since I last spent time in his company. A few minutes of his very limited conversation is all I need to remember why... *40%*

Corner Creek Reserve (86) n22 t22 f21 b21. Honeyed with some striking small grain action. *46%. Corner Creek Distilling Company.*

Cougar Bourbon Aged 5 Years (95) n25 t24 f23 b23. If Karl Kennedy of Neighbours really is the whisky buff he reckons he is, I want to see a bottle of this in his home next to Dahl. By the way: where is Dahl these days...? (And by the way, Karl, the guy who married you and Susan in London is a fan of mine. So you had better listen up...!) *37% (74 proof). Foster's Group, Australia.*

Daniel Stewart 8 Years Old (92.5) n22 t23 f23.5 b24. Stellar sophistication. Real complexity here, and, as 8-year-olds go, probably among the most complex of them all. A deep notch up on the previous bottling I encountered. *45%*

Eagle Rare Aged 10 Years Single Barrel (89) n21.5 t23 f22 b22.5. A surprising trip, this, with some dramatic changes en route. *45%*

Eagle Rare Kentucky Straight Bourbon 17 Years Old bott Fall 2010 (92.5) n24 t23.5 f22 b23. The corn hardly makes itself heard and oils at a premium. But for those who love bourbon in their rye...wow!! Oddly enough, while tasting this I am watching, from my sample room, a pair of black vultures circling a bluff at Frankfort, Ky, a short glide from the distillery where this whiskey was made. They are not exactly eagles, I grant you. But, with its eagle-esque deportment and chunkiness, close enough for the moment not to be lost...The Turkey Vultures, meanwhile, are probably waiting until I start on the samples from Lawrenceburg... 45%

Eagle Rare Kentucky Straight Bourbon Whiskey 17 Years Old dist Spring 1993, bott Fall 2011 **(94) n23.5 t24 f23 b23.5.** A marked improvement on previous bottlings, this goes out of its way to show some macho Kentuckian muscle. *45% (90 Proof)*

:::- **Eagle Rare Kentucky Straight Bourbon Whiskey 17 Years Old** bott Spring 2012 **(92) n23** a nuttier fellow than usual, hazelnuts and walnut oil in particular, but it's the dark, liquorice-edged sugars which strike the right cords; **t24** a very controlled delivery, soft, yet ticking all the right sugary boxes without losing its depth; **f22** chewy, toffeed and a touch bitter; **b23** Eagle Rare is the big BT brand which appears to have the widest range. Hit and miss you might say...but always seeming to hit some part of the bull's-eye. *45% (90 proof)*

Elijah Craig 12 Years Old (79) n20 t21.5 f18.5 b19. Once upon a time this whiskey was as resolute, dependable, unshakable and constant as the cliffs which guide the mighty Kentucky River. And every bit as impressive and memorable. Those were in the days when the bourbon was made at Bardstown, with its massive copper input from unerringly fine stills. Then came the fire. And the distillery was lost. 13 years after the event the whiskey had to change: there was no way it could not. This bottling is a considerable distance in style from the original. Superficially, plenty of rye and Demerara. But it is hot and untidy. So unlike Elijah Craig 12. 47%

:::- **Elijah Craig Barrel Proof Bourbon 12 Years of Aging** db **(95.5) n23.5** heavy duty and fudgy, the fruits are all about plums fit to burst and the sweetness from molasses and reduced manuka honey; **t24** Batman would love the ker-pow factor to this. Everything so intense and the balancing sugars and the enormity of the liquorice make this one to remember. Spices punctuate at every point...just astonishing...; **f24** slightly overcooked toast with treacle spread and washed down with a sublime Javan coffee; **b24** not sure when I saw a darker bourbon at 12 years commercially available. Remember that in straight bourbon colour represents interaction between spirit and barrel. So expect big oak presence and you will not be disappointed! A bourbon for bourbon lovers with very hairy chests – male or female.. *671% (134.2 proof) ncf.*

Elijah Craig 18 Years Old Single Barrel barrel no. 3328, dist 8/9/91 **(94.5) n25 t23.5 f22.5 b23.5.** Masterful. Don't even bother opening the bottle unless you have an hour to spend. 45%

Elmer T Lee Single Barrel (91) n22 t23.5 f(22.5) b23. A sturdy, dense bourbon with above average sweetness. So effortless, it is hard to immediately realise that greatness has entered your glass. 45%

European Bourbon Rye Association Kentucky Straight Bourbon Whiskey 16 Years hogshead, cask no. 1.1, dist 1994 **(95.5) n24.5** a Kentucky bourbon offering sublime Danish marzipan coated with Venezuelan cocoa and Demerara sugar. If that isn't enough, there is a touch of New Zealand manuka honey and Chilean ulmo honey. Does a nose really get more international than this...? **t24.5** the delivery is nothing as scary as it seems: keep your mouth open while tasting and the alcohol burns off quickly leaving a stunning residue of fabulously concentrated toasted honeycomb and ulmo honey notes. Next a slow deployment of slightly sweetened marmalade tones. Incredible! **f23** finishes like most 16 years olds...quickly! That is once you get past the enormous middle; **b23.5** mind-blowing whisky; the sort of stuff you can trust good ol' Mr Bourbon in Germany to unearth. A stunner..The whiskey ...not Mr Bourbon... *82.7% (1654 Proof). sc. EBRA. 77 bottles.*

European Bourbon Rye Association Kentucky Straight Bourbon Whiskey 18 Years hogshead, cask no. 1.2 **(85.5) n21.5 t22 f21 b21.** Just 78.1%abv...pathetic! But whatever the strength, the main difference between this and the 16-y-o is that the younger, more powerful whiskey is still in beautiful nick. This, sadly, is showing too many signs of old age and has allowed the giant oak input to destabilise the experience. That said, there is enough natural caramel and tannin here, all blasted into orbit at ultra high strength, to offer something very rarely experienced. *78.1% (156.2 Proof). sc. EBRA. 84 bottles.*

Evan Williams (76.5) n18 t20 f19 b19.5. Unrelentingly sweet and simplistic. *43.3%*

Evan Williams 12 Years (90) n21.5 t23.5 f22.5 b22.5. Perhaps not the force it recently was, but enough grunt here to emphasise the important bits. Namely the enormity of the rye and the sharp spices. Much more at home than, say, the 12-year-old Elijah Craig, for so long its match for quality. *50.5%*

Evan Williams 23 Years Old (94) n22 t23.5 f24.5 b24. Struts his stuff, refusing to allow age to slow him or dim the shine from his glowing grains. Now oak has taken its toll. This seems older than its 23 years... Or so I first thought. Then a light shone in my soul and it occurred to me: hang on...I have wines going back to the last century. For the older ones, do I not allow them to breathe? So I let the whiskey breathe. And, behold, it rose from the dead. This Methuselah of a whiskey had come alive once more...and how!! 53.5% ☉

Evan Williams 1783 (81) n19 t20.5 f21 b20.5. Much improved and now an exceptionally spicy offering. 43%

Evan Williams Single Barrel Vintage 2001 dist Jul 01, bott Oct 10, barrel no. 001 (85) n21.5 t21 f21 b21.5. One thing is for absolute certain: this was not distilled at the long lost Heaven Hill distillery in Bardstown. Those were whiskeys which leapt at you from the glass and pulled your face into its enormity. This, by contrast, is most un-Single Barrel-esque. It is a huge outpouring of cream toffee. Enlivened by some layering of delicate citrus. But all rather sweet and monosyllabic...and soft. 43.3% (86.6 Proof)

Evan Williams Single Barrel Vintage 2002 barrel no 1. barrelled 7 Jun 02 bott 1 Nov 11 (92.5) n23.5 t23.5 f22.5 b23. An altogether different animal to the Evan Williams single barrel which came from the original Heaven Hill distillery: that was incapable of making a bourbon as feminine as this... 43.3% (86.6 Proof)

⁙ **Evan Williams Single Barrel Vintage 2003** barrel no 1. barrelled 11 Feb 03, bott 28 Nov 12 (84.5) n22 t22 f20 b20.5. How curious. When this brand was first launched, the whiskey came from the original Heaven Hill distillery and the big copper content showed through its luxurious complexity. Here we have a great deal of honey and a brash sugary lead on delivery. But the lack of copper is evident further down the line. 43.3% (86.6 Proof)

Fighting Cock Aged 6 Years (82.5) n21 t21.5 f20 b20. I have just gone straight from Virgin Bourbon to Fighting Cock...such are the vagaries of my life. But while the virgin seduced or, rather, raped me, this old Cock leaves me underwhelmed. With its rich colour I had expected untold layering and depth. Instead, it is all rather corn-led and slightly OTT bitter oak. 51.5%

Four Roses (Yellow Label) (89) n23 subtlety is the key here: small grains bristling and jostling for position against the softer honeyed vanilla; t23 steady on, there! The delivery is much weightier and altogether thicker than a couple of years back and that honey note (yes, I do mean honey!) is contrasting vitally against the crisper rye; f21 the fog of vanilla descends; b22 seriously impressed: this whiskey was always pleasant but afraid to say boo to a goose. Now a honey injection has actually helped ramp up the rye content and the complexity has benefitted. The nose and delivery are exceptional. 40%

Four Roses (Black Label) (88) n20 t23 f23 b22. A whiskey which starts faltering on the nose recovers with a sublime delivery of all things bourbon. 40%

⁙ **Four Roses Limited Edition 2012 Small Batch Barrel Strength** (96) n24 if someone asked me to show exactly how a rye-included mashbill bourbon should nose, I could do no better than to pour this: it is truly classic with a fascinating, almost bottomless depth to the dark sugars which works in breath-taking tandem with one of the most subtle and disarming citrus and strawberry sub plots you will find; t24.5 crisp, salivating and bulging with the rye present: clean, yet so amazingly complex; f23.5 Phase II: ditch the crispness and replace it with a soft toffee finale; b24 the improvement of Four Roses has been one of the highlights of recent world whisky events. I was curious to see if this 2012 edition could carry on where the sublime 2011 left off. It has. 57.5% (115 Proof). 4000 Bottles approx.

Four Roses Single Barrel warehouse US cask no. 10-2A (96.5) n25 t24.5 f23 b24. If you have ever wondered if Four Roses has the wherewithal to play amongst the super-elite of the whiskey world, then track down this particular bottling and all will be revealed...For me, the finest Four Roses I have ever come across. 50%

Four Roses Single Barrel barrel 11-3T (94) n23.5 t23 f23.5 b24. In so many ways the quintessential delicate bourbon. But one of the most attractive for chocoholics, too.... 50%

⁙ **Four Roses Single Barrel** barrel no 8-1 Q (91) n22.5 not sure bourbons come any more citrusy on the nose; t23.5 ultra salivating delivery: the palate greets lush, melt-in-the-mouth sugars with essence of lime; the midground hints at ulmo honey but grasps molasses; f22 manuka honey meets some major charring toastiness and hickory; b23 this bourbon reminds you of how Four Roses was a decade ago when it embraced a lighter style. Except it now has a chunkier depth. 50% (100 proof)

⁙ **Four Roses Single Barrel** barrelled 11 Apr 01 35% rye mashbill barrel 4-1F (95) n23.5 bristling rye and barley nibbles, nips and bites in all the right places; t24.5 textbook – no, make that advanced textbook – delivery with the ryes really punching out the crisp, sugary lead while the sub plot of chocolate malt shake and crème brûlée fill in the spaces with pure joy; f23 much more even, even slightly tangy with kumquats; very light spice and liquorice; b24 brims with small grain complexity. A classy act. 61% Binny's, Chicago.

⁙ **Four Roses Single Barrel 9 Years 4 Months** bott July 13 20% rye mashbill barrel 85-3Q (94) n23.5 the tasting says cherries, and cherry juice definitely leads the way. Crushed pine nuts and dried leaves continue the garden and forest theme; t24 a startling delivery which is both crisp and soothing. The crisper notes continue on the fruit theme and up the salivation rate; the heavier tones are distinctly molassed and toasty; f23 tones down towards custard topped with ulmo honey; b23.5 a wonderful bourbon, alternating between full-on and reserved. 58.8% Four Roses Gift Shop.

⁙ **Four Roses Single Barrel 11 Years** bott July 13 20% rye mashbill barrel 47-4Q (95) n23 cream wafer biscuits; fig roll cookies; t24 oh, wow! Same mashbill as the 9-y-o, but very different delivery and personality: fabulously brittle, spiced and salivating delivery with oak interweaving from the very off; creamy textured, toffee-rich and chewy; **f23.5** now we enter cream toffee, a few toasted raisins and high cocoa content chocolate – with Demerara sugars at every corner; **b24.5** a three course bourbon. *61.1% Four Roses Gift Shop.*

Four Roses Single Barrel 11 Years bott July 13 35% rye mashbill barrel 29-3I **(86.5) n21.5 t21 f23 b21.** A serious pea souper of a bourbon. Perhaps a little bit too much of everything. The oak is all pervading, though the mocha and spice firestorms it sets off are lovely. I know some will die for a bourbon like this. But just feel it needs to breathe from time to time. The finish, though, where it gets a chance to stretch, is truly superb. *58.6 %*

Four Roses Single Barrel 12 Years 5 Months bott July 13 35% rye mashbill barrel 22-2F **(96.5) n24** a ridiculous nose for its age. So delicate with citrus, kiwi fruit and steamed yam so soft it could crumble; rhubarb tart offers bite while crisp sugars back off; **t24** just sit back and enjoy the glow...and after glow. The ryes are bursting out from every direction, offering an unspecified fruit, muscovado sugars and spice; the oak does the liquorice thing well; **f24** a gentle fade, but pointing at all the highlights before, with a little extra Bassett's chocolate liquorice for good measure; **b24.5** pretty hard to imagine a single barrel of bourbon outflanking this for all round sex appeal. Majestic and marvellous. *54.6%*

Four Roses 16 Years Old Single Barrel Barrel Strength barrel 78-3B, bott Nov 11 **(96.5) n24.5 t23.5 f24 b24.5.** In all honesty, 17 years ago – based on previous experience – if someone had asked if Four Roses had it in it to produce a top-drawer 16-year-old bourbon, I would have said: "probably not". Their whisky, then, was a little on the sparse side and struggled to add body to the oak. This, though, is not of a type that was around back in those days. The mix of fruit and chocolate is sublime. But above all, it's the silky texture and balance that have you scratching your head in amazement. *55.5%*

Four Roses 16 Years Old Single Barrel Barrel Strength barrel 78-5A, bott Dec 12 **(87) n22 t22 f21.5 b21.5.** Enjoyable, but just so tight by comparison to 78-3B and not on the same planet complexity-wise. *61.7%*

Four Roses Single Barrel Limited Edition 2012 Aged 12 Years Barrel Strength barrel 81-2B **(89.5) n23 t23 f21.5 b22.** Lovely whiskey which takes something of the lazy way out as soon as the caramels grab hold. *52.5%*

Four Roses Small Batch (86) n20.5 t22.5 f21 b21.5. It is odd that while the standard Yellow Label has massively increased its personality, this one has, if anything, moved towards a much more neutral stance thanks to the vanillas dominating the nose and finish. The delivery is by no means so restricted, though. Good spice, too. *45% (90 proof)*

Four Roses Limited Edition Small Batch 2011 Barrel Strength oldest 13-y-o, youngest 11-y-o **(95.5) n23.5 t24 f24 b24.** The bottles of Four Roses I have been working through this year have been one of the most extraordinary treats it has been my privilege to enjoy for a very long time. This, on top of the 16-year-old is simply blowing me away... *55.1%*

George T Stagg dist Winter 1993, bott Fall 2011 **(96.5) n24 t25 f24 b24.5.** Before the bottling of each George T Stagg, the stirring process can shake the dice somewhat, and the scores can be different. Here we see Stagg with fewer oils than normal. This has shifted its stance very slightly. But you have only to ask an astronomer what happens if a planet changes its orbit by only fractions of a degree... *71.3% (142.6 Proof)*

George T. Stagg (97.5) n24 t25 f24 b24.5. Astonishing how so much oak can form and yet have such limited negative impact and so few unpleasant side effects. These tasting notes took nearly four hours to compile. Yet they are still in a simplified form to fit into this book... George T Stagg is once again... staggering. *71.5% (143 Proof). ncf.*

George T. Stagg Limited Edition (96.5) n24 it is as if someone has come up with the quintessential bourbon aroma...and then multiplied it by itself. This is huge, yet the small grains are busy enough to ensure the complexity levels go spinning off the chart. Even a few apples at play. Interestingly low in oils for a Stagg; **t24.5** if you want to know what a big game bourbon should taste like, just take a small mouthful of this. The rye ensures a degree of sharpness present; there are eye-wateringly bright sugars and some serious toasted honeycomb; the tannins nibble; at last the oils form though the spices allow them only so far; **f24** beautifully toasty, all kinds of mocha and hickory and even the outlines of a rather overcooked blackberry tart; **b24** as spectacular as a sunset from the hilltop village of Coldharbour in my beloved Surrey *71.4% (142.8 proof). ncf.*

Hancock's Reserve Single Barrel (92) n25 t23 f21.5 b22.5. A slightly quieter example of this consistently fine brand. The nose, though, is the stuff of wet whiskey dreams... *44.45%*

Heaven Hill Old Style Bourbon (81) n20 t20 f21 b20. a sweeter, more citrusy number than before. Still a lightweight, but offers much more entertainment and style. *40%*

Heaven Hill 6 Years Old (83) n20 t20 f22 b21. An infinitely more satisfying bourbon than its Old Style stable mate at this age. The battle between crisp rye and compact caramel is intriguing and pretty tasty to boot. *40%*

Heaven Hill Old Style Bourbon 6 Years Old Bottled in Bond (81.5) n18 t21.5 f21 b21. What a strange beast. Sluggish on the nose and vanilla-bound on the finish it tends to hurtle around the palate without thought. The delivery, though, is sharp and enjoyably mouth-watering. 50%

Heaven Hill Mild and Mellow (90) n22 t23 f22.5 b22.5. You never know what you are going to get with this one: for that it is consistent. This version is full of colour and vitality and is a real (very pleasant) surprise package. A corker. 43%

Heaven Hill Ultra Deluxe Aged 36 Months (80) n20 t21 f19 b20. I remember a surprising liquorice backbone to this last time out. Not now. Lighter all round with corn dominating but the delicate spices are a treat. 40%

Henry McKenna Aged 10 Years Single Barrel barrel no. 642, dist 11/08/11 (86) n21 t22.5 f21.5 b21. Much more interesting than the last bottle of this I sampled. Here, as before, the sugars are king. But there is a charming kumquat note on both nose and delivery which burrow into the ever thickening liquorice. Superficially, appears to have much in common with the Virgin 7. But tasted side by side... Even so, good stuff. 50%

Hogs 3 (86.5) n21.5 t22 f21 b22. Have to say this is above average 3-year-old fare, with generous lashings of honey and red liquorice at regular intervals. A note about the label: the commendable sweetness of the whisky comes from the sugars that have melted into the alcohol from the oak and nothing, as claimed, from the water. But that nonsense apart, top-range for age, high-class daily bourbon. 40% (80 Proof). Quality Spirits International.

Jefferson's Reserve batch no. 84 (91) n23 t23.5 f22 b23. Once a 15-year-old, no age statement here. But this has seen off a few Summers, and sweetened with each passing one. 45.1%. 2400 bottles.

Jim Beam (86) n21 t21 f22 b21. After a few years kicking its heals, JB White Label has returned to something closer to how I remember it a couple of decades back. Not just a welcome degree of extra weight, but much more honey intensifying and lengthening: someone has been climbing higher up in the warehouse to find this four-year-old... Impressed. 40%

Jim Beam Black Aged to Perfection (89.5) n22 t23 f22.5 b22.5. Jim Beam Black. But, teasingly, with no age statement! Does it live in the shadow of the sublime 8-years-old? Well, perhaps not quite. Lacks the lushness and the peaks and troughs of complexity. But, though a lot more even in temperament, it never fails to delight, even if the standard rye kick is conspicuous by its absence. As a bourbon, excellent. As a Jim Beam Black, a little disappointing. 43% (86 proof)

Jim Beam Black Double Age Aged 8 Years (93) n23 t24 f22.5 b23.5. Rather than the big, noisy, thrill-seeking JB Black, here it is in quiet, reflective, sophisticated mode. Quite a shift. But no less enjoyable. 43% (86 proof)

Jim Beam Choice Aged 5 Years (89) n22 t22 f23 b22. A hugely improved whiskey which is no longer betwixt and between but now strikingly makes its own bold statements. Makes noises on both nose and palate way above its five years. A bourbon to grab whilst in this expansive and impressive mood. 40%

Jim Beam Devil's Cut 90 Proof (89) n22.5 t24 f20.5 b22. Beautifully thrusting with the palate both ran ragged and soothed by a devilish degree of silky complexity and intensity. The finish, though, needs a little attention. 45%

John B. Stetson Straight Bourbon Whiskey (92) n23.5 quite irresistible volley of small grains ensures complexity, despite the light character; the spices are exemplary; t23.5 superb delivery of marmalade and complex spice; lightweight but the sugars shield the corn, though little oil apparent; it's the small grains churning away which really star, though; f22 much more simplistic, almost lazy caramels; b23 absolutely love it! Quality: I take my hat off to you...42%

John E. Fitzgerald Larceny (94) n23 a gorgeous marriage of floral tones, mint especially, and toffee – leading to a sweet mint humbug persona – plus a choir of thin liquorice and Demerara; t23.5 silk-textured with a fabulously understated array of sugar and spice... the spice especially. Cream toffee middle; f23.5 the corn oils spread invitingly around the palate and refuse to budge. The fade sees them clinging fast and the spices really working overtime as the chocolate notes accumulate; b24 if this doesn't win a few converts to wheated bourbon, nothing will. A high quality, stunningly adorable whiskey, pulsing with elegance and personality. Every drinks cabinet should have this wonderful new addition to the bourbon lexicon. 46%

John J Bowman Virginia Straight Bourbon Single Barrel (94) n23 Dense and intense; John J means business...plenty of liquorice to accentuate the oak. Dry and toasty; t24 the delivery is an essay in deportment: big weight, but so evenly balanced that the burnt honey and spice have no problems in showing to the full...chewy and multi-layered; f23 long with the drying processes giving the honey all the time it needs to make its exit; b24 one of the biggest yet most easily relaxed and beautifully balanced bourbons on the market. 50%

Johnny Drum (Black Label) (89.5) n22 similar to the Green Label, but easier on the flowers; t23 again, takes a similar course to the Green Label, except here there is a bigger liquorice thread hammering home the bourbon tag; f21.5 again, like the Green Label, dries and thins; b23 how often does that happen? The same whiskey, different strength, virtually same quality (though this has a little more depth) but gets there by a slightly different route. 43%

Johnny Drum (Black Label) 12 Years Old (78) n20 t22 f18 b18 Attractive early, crusty sugars. But bitters out and loses balance later on. 43%

⁘ **Johnny Drum (Green Label)** (89) n22.5 sultry, perfumed, heavy flower shop aromas; t23 excellent oils make a gentle landing for the fabulous Demerara sugar and honey arrangement. Heather, orange blossom and a light sliver of ulmo honeys....even becoming mildly herbal as the small grains get going in mid-stream; f21 dries out remarkably; b22.5 much more honey these days. Worth making a bee-line for. 40%

Johnny Drum (Green Label) (87.5) n21.5 t22 f22 b22. Has changed direction since I last tasted this one. Now true as a die. And even outperforms the Johnny Drum Black! 43%

Johnny Drum Private Stock (90.5) n22.5 t22.5 f23 b22.5. One of those bourbons where a single glass is never quite enough. Great stuff! 50.5% (101 proof)

J.T.S Brown (83.5) n21.5 t21.5 f19.5 b21. Mr Brown has been on a diet. The thin finish doesn't live up to the early muscovado promise. 40%

J.T.S Brown Bottled in Bond (86.5) n22 t22.5 f21 b21.5. Much busier and fuller than the 40% version, though I tend to think that here the ryes have made a greater impact from a different distillation. Still could do with more oils on the finish though late spices compensate somewhat. 50%

Kentucky Gentleman (86) n19 t22.5 f22 b22.5. Once you get past the disjointed nose, you are in for a very pleasant surprise. The highlight is the delivery on palate and follow-through: a silky-textured (hazelnut) nutty experience with a delightful honeycomb wake. There is a lovely small grain busyness, too. A minor gem of a gentleman. 40%

Kentucky Supreme Number 8 Brand (76) n18 t19 f20 b19. Simplistic and undemanding with massive emphasis on a barley sugar-style tartness and sweetness. 40%

Kentucky Tavern (84) n20 t22 f21 b21. Another juicy little number which appears almost to have a young malt feel to it. Clean, with just the right amount of rye sparkle to offer buzz and complexity. 40%

Kentucky Vintage batch 08-72 (94.5) n23.5 delicate to the point of brittle. Playful spice prickles as the small grains dance and tease; beautiful citrus notes are just showing off; t24.5 the whole thing just melts in the mouth. No grating oak nor rabid spices. No bitter char. Just an intricate and delicate mix of grain and vanilla interweaving...and then melting along with some accompanying butterscotch and muscovado sugar. Quite stunning; f23 both the bitterness and spices grow. But all is balanced and genteel; b23.5 staggered! I really didn't quite expect that. Previous bottlings I have enjoyed of this have had hair attached to the muscle. This is a very different Vintage, one that reaches for the feminine side of a macho whiskey. If you want to spend an hour just getting to know how sensitive your taste buds can be, hunt down this batch... 45%

Knob Creek Aged 9 Years (94.5) n23.5 almost arrogantly consistent: you know pretty well what you are going to get...and there it is. In this classic whiskey's case a whole bunch of honeycomb and vanilla, always more delicate than it first appears...; t24 salivating delivery with rye and barley absolutely hammering on the palate. The corn oil is there not for flavour but effect – it is a fabulous mixture of dates and Demerara rum having the biggest say; f23.5 wonderfully long with the oak toastiness now really beginning to bite...; b23.5 no whiskey in the world has a more macho name, and this is not for the faint-hearted. Big, high in character and expansive, it drives home its point with gusto, celebrating its explosive finish. 50%

Knob Creek Aged 9 Years Single Barrel Reserve bottling batch no. L1017CLH (89) n22.5 t22.5 f22 b22. The point often overlooked by people, even in the industry, is that a single cask is often a part of the sum. So this bottling just shows a single fragment into what will make up the usual Knob Creek small batch bourbon. This particular barrel – and sadly they don't name which one it is for further comparison (a bit of a marketing mistake that, as there are thousands out there dying to compare different styles) is all about depth and weight. Complexity, therefore, does not play a significant role, especially with the rye taking a back seat. Even so, an impressive ride. 60%

Maker's Mark (Red Seal) (91) n22.5 t23.5 f22 b23. The big honey injection has done no harm whatsoever. This sample came from a litre bottle and the whiskey was darker than normal. What you seem to have is the usual steady Maker's with a helping hand of extra weight. In fact this reminds me of the old Maker's Gold wax. 45%

Maker's 46 (95) n23.5 crushed toasted hazelnuts dappled with honeycomb and delicate hickory; beautifully even and well mannered; t24.5 quite superb: an initially thick, intense delivery which fans out in directions; excellent weight as those honeycomb notes go into overdrive; a dotting of wheaty and oaky spices but it's the way the softest of silky and highly complex flavours crash feather-like into the taste buds which cranks up the points;

f23 surprisingly light and simplistic with the accent firmly on vanilla; **b24** some people have a problem with oak staves. I don't: whisky, after all, is about the interaction of a grain spirit and oak. This guy is all about the nose and, especially, the delivery. With so much controlled honey on show, it cannot be anything other than a show-stopper. Frankly, magnificent. I think I've met my Maker's... *47% (94 proof)*

Most Wanted Kansas Bourbon Mash Whiskey (83) n18 t20 f23.5 b21.5. A sweaty armpit nose is the unlikely overture for an attractively flavoursome and delicately sweet bourbon. Highly unusual and rather gristy in style, the superb finish offers hugely attractive chocolate. One that really grows on me. *40% (80 proof)*

Noah's Mill batch 10-170 **(93) n23.5 t23.5 f23 b23.** This monster of a bourbon just rumbles along on the palate like one of the four thunderstorms I have encountered in Kentucky today... *5715%*

⁖ **Noah's Mill** batch 13-81 **(93.5) n23** gorgeous glazed almonds; a little citrus and cold coffee; **t23.5** oddly enough, doesn't taste like the nose: much more macho, with the full blooded hickory and Demerara; enormous weight and depth and assorted honey notes begin to form; **f22.5** gentle finale, reverting back to the style of the aroma. Excellent vanilla on sugars and weightier liquorice; **b23.5** a full bodied classic bourbon which undulates over the palate. *5715% (114.3 proof)*

Old 1889 Royal Aged 12 Years (78) n19 t20 f19 b20. A curiously ineffectual and ultimately frustrating bourbon which still needs to feel loved for its small grain complexity but succeeds only in demanding a slap for being so lily-livered. In the end it falls between the delicate and full-blown fruity stools. *43% (86 proof)*

Old Bardstown Black Label (85.5) n21.5 t22.5 f21.5 b21.5. Lush and overtly simplistic there is enough old honey and busy small grains to keep you very pleasantly entertained. *43%*

Old Bardstown Black Label (88) n21.5 t23 f21.5 b22. Forget about the 2% difference in strength. On this showing, a whiskey with a different mindset and a more muscular body and liberal use of spice. I'm a sucker for this style of bourbon: love it! *45%*

Old Bardstown Estate Bottled (86.5) n22.5 t22.5 f21 b20.5. Just a tad too sweet for greatness, though there is plenty to enjoy along the way. Can't help feeling the complexity levels are lost en route. *50.5%*

Old Bardstown Gold Label (83) n20.5 t21.5 f20 b21. Sweet, citrusy, juicy, uncomplicated, session whiskey. *40% (80 proof)*

Old Charter 8 Years Old (78) n19 t22 f18 b19. Sweetened up of late and even has a bit of pulse early on. But the finish is dull. *40% (80 proof)*

Old Charter 10 Years Old (84) n20.5 t23 f19.5 b21. From a dazed Brontosaurus, as I described it previously, to one that's been prodded awake. Still cumbersome, but now attacks those citrus and liquorice leaves with a spicy relish. Dozes off again at the end, though, for all the chocolate. *43% (86 proof)*

Old Crow Reserve Aged 4 Years (86) n21.5 t22.5 f21 b21. Huge colour for a 4-year-old. Loads of mocha and fruit on the nose and plenty of toffee on the finish. But the star attraction is the big, oily, fat delivery full of liquorice and brown-sugared coffee. *43% (86 proof)*

Old Fitzgerald (83.5) n19 t21 f22 b21.5. A greatly improved bourbon that is beginning to feel more at home in its sweet, vaguely spicy surroundings. *43%*

Old Fitzgerald's 1849 (85.5) n21 t22 f21 b21.5. That's much more like it! After a time in the doldrums, this bourbon has fought back in style. Still one of the sweetest on the market. But the intensity of the spice and the manner in which it dovetails with the Demerara sugars is most enjoyable. Fitz beautifully... *45% (90 proof)*

Old Fitzgerald Very Special 12 Years Old (93) n24 t23.5 f22.5 b23. There is always something that makes the heart sing when you come across a whiskey which appears so relaxed in its excellence. At the moment my heart is in the shower merrily lathering itself... *45%*

Old Forester Birthday Bourbon dist Spring 93, bott 2005 **(94) n24 t23 f23 b24** One of the most rye-studded stars in the bourbon firmament and wholly in keeping with the fabulous quality for which this brand has now become a byword. *40%*

Old Grand-Dad (90.5) n22 t23 f23 b23.5. This one's all about the small grains. A busy, lively bourbon, this offers little to remind me of the original Old Grand-Dad whiskey made out at Frankfort. That said, this is a whisk(e)y-lover's whiskey: in other words the excellence of the structure and complexity outweighs any historical misgivings. Enormously improved and now very much at home with its own busy style. *43%*

Old Grand-Dad Bonded 100 Proof (94.5) n22.5 light rye spices and citrus fruit pop around the glass. One of those weighty yet delicate bourbons, but here the small grain appear at full throttle; **t24** impossible not to be blown away. Exactly like the nose, you are expecting from first impact thundering, almost bullying oak. Instead your taste buds are mesmerised by a fabulous infusion of busy rye: a thousand tiny, crisp explosions in every quarter of the mouth followed by a layering of coconut strands dipped in lightly charred, molten sugars...; **f23.5**

very toasty with the oak now unflinchingly taking the rye on; **b24.5** obviously Old Grand-dad knows a thing or two about classy whiskey: this is a magnificent version, even by its own high standards. It was always a winner and one you could bet your shirt on for showing how the small grains can impact upon complexity. But this appears to go a stage further. The base line is a touch deeper, so there is more ground to cover on the palate. It has been a whiskey-lover's whiskey for a little while and after a few barren years, has been inching itself back to its great Frankfort days. The fact that Beam's quality has risen over the last decade has played no insignificant part in that. *50% (100 proof)*

Old Heaven Hill Bottled in Bond (79) **n**18.5 **t**20.5 **f**20 **b**20. Doesn't have much to choose from flavour-wise. But what it has, it has in spades...especially the maple syrup and vanilla. *50%*

Old Heaven Hill Very Rare Old Aged 8 Years (88) **n**23 **t**22 **f**21 **b**22. Now that is very different! In fact, I can't say I have ever come across a flavour profile quite like it. Maybe it's all from one distillery. I may be wrong, but I get the feeling that the complexity indicates the influence of more than DSP type. *43%*

Old Heaven Hill Very Rare Old Aged 10 Years Bottled In Bond (77.5) **n**19 **t**20 **f**19 **b**19.5. Good Heavens...!! What happened here? I remember this as the mad dog of the whiskey world, thrashing around my palate like something demented. Now it appears the men in the white coats have injected a sedative. Plenty of goody-two-shoes corn and vanilla...but where's the chemistry? *50% (100 proof)*

Old Kentucky Aged 4 Years (84) **n**22 **t**22.5 **f**19 **b**20.5. Hugely enjoyable, busy bourbon where the small grains run amuck for a while. Perhaps over-sweetens towards the middle and runs out of steam towards the end. But as 4-year-olds go, quite a little treat. *40% (80 proof)*

Old Pogue Master's Select batch 6816 (87.5) **n**23 lashings of cream toffee with a lemon and vanilla freshness; **t**22 cranks up the crème brulee even further with big corn oils for accompaniment; **f**21 thin vanilla; **b**21.5 pleasant and simplistic, showing good oils and early sweetness. *45.5%*

Old Rip Van Winkle 10 Years Old (93) **n**24 **t**23 **f**23 **b**23. A much sharper cookie than it once was. And possibly a Maryland Cookie, too, what with the nuts and chocolate evident. As graceful as it is entertaining. *45% (90 Proof). Buffalo Trace.*

Old Taylor Aged 6 Years (89) **n**23 **t**23 **f**21 **b**22. The curiously thin finish is in telling contrast to the superbly honeyed middle that simple dances with small-grain charm. So much lighter than the original Old Taylor *(see below)* of McCracken Pike. But certainly has enough weight and fruit punch to make this better than the cheap brand it is perceived to be. *40% (80 proof)*

Old Virginia Aged 6 Years (79) **n**20 **t**21 **f**18.5 **b**19.5. Old Virginia because of the drying tobacco leaf on the aroma? Sweet, but a lot flatter than the state... *40%. La Martiniquaise.*

Old Virginia Aged 8 Years L434401A (85) **n**22 **t**21 **f**21 **b**21. Vanilla-rich and never quite lives up to the bold nose. *40%. La Martiniquaise, France.*

Old Weller Antique 107 (96) **n**24.5 only pour this one if you have a good half hour to spare: the nose absolutely mesmerises as it changes shape and depth continuously. The honeys are soft and graceful, never dominating but rounding edges. The spices are well mannered yet condiment. The fruit takes the direction of apple and mango. Together they create a near faultless harmony; **t**24 the wheat is vibrant, pressing bold spices into a honeyed core. The layering accentuated by the liquorice and hickory which balance the sweeter elements with rare panache; **f**23.5 long with varying textures of oak. Never dries too much while refusing to allow the bountiful sugars the upper hand. All the time the spices throb... **b**24 this almost blew me off my chair. Always thought this was pleasant, if a little underwhelming, in the past. However, this bottling has had a few thousands volts past through it as it now comes alive on the palate with a glorious blending of freshness and debonair aging. One of the surprise packages of 2012. *53.5% (107 proof)*

Pappy Van Winkle's Family Reserve 15 Years Old (96) **n**24.5 the usual blood oranges by the cartload...the lilting mix of plum juice and white bread kneaded until it has become a sweet, sugary ball. All that plus a shy spiciness and some broad oak. But what makes it all work is the lightness of the mix...so big...yet so delicate...; **t**23.5 lush but with those threatening oaks on the nose exploding on impact. For a moment just a little OTT, but then several huge waves of cocoa-lined vanilla and marmalade puts the world to rights again...; **f**24 long and back to unbridled elegance. Cocoas flit around, as do those wheated softly, softly spices and layers of thinned manuka honey... stunning...; **b**24 at a book signing in Canada earlier this year a Bible enthusiast asked me which well-aged, wheated bourbon he should look for. I told him Pappy 15. He looked at me quizzically and said: "Well, that's what I thought, but in the Bible you have it down as rye-recipe." I told him he was wrong... until I checked there and then. And discovered he was right. Of course, Pappy has always been wheated and the lushness on the palate and spices radiating from it has always confirmed this. I'll put it down to not spitting enough. Or perhaps the speed at which I type whilst tasting. Sometimes you mean one thing – then another word comes out. Like when a member of my staff asks for a pay rise. I mean no. But somehow say yes. So apologies to any other I fooled out there. For not only is this a wheated bourbon. With its improbable degree of deftness for something so big, it has edged up a notch or two into a truly world great whiskey...whatever the recipe. *53.5% (107 proof)*

Pappy Van Winkle's Family Reserve 20 Years Old (85) n19.5 t22 f22 b21.5. Definitely a marked improvement upon recent years with the sugars and spices finding far better synchronisation and harmony than in many previous bottling. And the lushness to the mouth feel has distinctly improved. But the oak remains too powering, thereby upsetting the balance. I know I am a loan voice among commentators here, but... *45.2% (90.4 proof)*

Pappy Van Winkle's Family Reserve 23 Years Old (78) n18 t24 f17 b19. If I remember correctly, the last time I tasted this guy, the nose was a turn on while the body left me pretty cold. Bit of an about face here. Now the aroma shows signs of some of the soapier elements of the oak being exposed (much like a Scotch malt which has lived too long in a third-filled cask), and that in turn has, as is usually the case, a negative knock-on effect with the finish. But the delivery, vibrant with spice and trade mark blood orange, is nothing short of stunning. *47.8% (95.6 proof)*

⚬⚬ **Parker's Heritage Collection Sixth Edition Master Distillery's Blend Of Mashbills Aged Since 2001** db **(94.5)** n24 my word! The small grains have a field day: the rye really ups the crisp fruit levels while the wheat shovels on the spice; elsewhere its big, sweetened liquorice to confirm the dozen years in barrel; t23.5 the sugars arrive as though blasted from a cannon: hard as rock and crystalline they positively burrow into the taste buds and if explosives are required the wheat provides it with some wicked spices; that all said, the mid-ground is a depositary for the more elegant, teasing by-products; f23 settles contentedly along a vanilla route. Some burnt toasty notes, as expected; the sugars more even now, almost quiet with a lovely fried yam fade...and spice, of course! b24 shows plenty of muscle, but subtlety and sophistication in equal measures, too. *63.5% (127 proof). ncf.*

Parker's Heritage Collection Wheated Mash Bill Bourbon Aged 10 Years (97) n24 t24 f24.5 b24.5. Hard to find the words that can do justice. I know Parker will be immensely proud of this. And with every good reason: I am working exceptionally hard to find a fault with this either from a technical distillation viewpoint or a maturation one. Or just for its sheer whiskeyness...A potential World Whisky of the Year. *62.1% (124.2 Proof). ncf.*

Peach Street Bourbon (86) n19 t22 f23 b22. The nose, though the weak link, is not without its charms; the delivery offers excellent spice and a real fruit cake quality, complete with juicy dates. The finish, as the oak finds a home, really is a joy. Impressive stuff from a small batch distiller and a two-year-old bourbon. *48%. Peach Street Distillers, Colorado.*

Pure Kentucky Batch 10-96 (77) n20 t20 f19 b18. Surprisingly fruity but lacks cohesion and direction from first to last. *53.5% (107 proof)*

Ridgemont Reserve 1792 Aged 8 Years (94.5) n23.5 throbbing, pulsing oak is kept comfortably in check with a soft honey and mint restraint. Fabulous depth and even a hint of salt to season the effect; t24 Barton's unique rye and Demerara combo is in full swing here and contrasts fascinatingly with the deeper, vaguely bitterish oak notes; f23.5 back to a vanilla and rye thread here, oscillating with the house brown sugars; the pulsing of the spice is sublime; b23.5 now here is a whiskey which appears to have come to terms with its own strengths and, as with all bourbons and malts, limitations. Rarely did whiskey from Barton reach this level of maturity, so harnessing its charms always involves a bit of a learning curve. Each time I taste this it appears a little better than the last...and this sample is no exception to the rule. Excellent. *46.85% (93.7 Proof)*

Rock Hill Farms Single Barrel (85.5) n22 t22 f20 b21.5. An interesting, but perhaps little known point, is that I never read tasting notes of a brand from previous years until after I have tasted the present whiskey. I can usually remember anyway. But this struck me as being a bit odd, even before I referred back, as it seemed to have an extra summer or two to ramp up the intensity, especially of the sugared-marmalade delivery. But the finish still struck me as typically corn led and stubbornly docile. Pleasant, though, if pretty true to type. *50%*

Rowan's Creek batch 10-109 **(67)** n17.5 t19 f15 b16 Pity: the odd barrel in here should not have got through. Definite soapy quality on the nose is countered by a big maple syrup kick on delivery. But the finish confirms all is not well. Talk about up the creek... *50.05% (100.1 proof)*

⚬⚬ **Rowan's Creek** Batch 13-88 **(82)** n20 t21.5 f20.5 b20. A modest bourbon short on complexity and weight but big on spice and delicate sugars. *50.05% (100.1 proof)*

⚬⚬ **Russell's Reserve Single Barrel (94)** n23.5 you are not only talking bourbon, but you are sniffing it, too! Classic heavyweight hickory and tannin; t24 superb liquorice delivery, with a Fisherman's Friend cough sweet follow up. Molassed, though with some of the sweetness strained from it by the toastier elements of the oak; the weight could hardly be better, or the spices and honey meeting in the mid ground; f23 dries as the hickory evolves. Long with superb corn oil; b23.5 old-fashioned, thick as treacle bourbon. Delicious... *55%. ncf. Wild Turkey.*

Russell's Reserve Small Batch 10 Year Old (92.5) n24.5 t23 f22 b23. Had the quality and complexity on the palate followed on from the nose I may well have had the world's No 1 whisky for 2012 in my glass. Just slum it with something quite wonderful, instead. Still waiting for an official explanation as to why this is a miserly 90 proof, when Jimmy Russell's preferred strength is 101, by the way... 45%. Wild Turkey.

Sainsbury's Kentucky Bourbon 3 Year Old (76.5) n19 t19.5 f19 b19. About the most caramel-flattened bourbon I have tasted in a very long time. 40%. Sainsbury's UK.

Speakeasy Select dist 28 Jan 93 (87) n22 t22.5 f21.5 b21. pleasant, but one or four Summers too long for this barrel. 58.1%. Steelbach Hotel, Louisville, Kentucky.

⬦ **Spring 44 Straight Bourbon** batch 2 (84.5) n21 t22.5 f20.5 b20.5. A straight Kentucky bourbon blended from two distinctly different rye recipe styles. The result is something very different, indeed – and sadly doesn't always work. In short, chocolate orange meets Yorkshire Tea. Odd. 45% (90 proof)

⬦ **Spring 44 Single Barrel Bourbon** batch 2, barrel no 8 (93) n22 sharp, grainy with a thick vanilla surge; t23.5 impressive rye on delivery with softer, ulmo honey massaging where the spices have strafed; massively salivating; f23.5 where the ulmo honey ends and the butterscotch/vanilla begins in hard to say, but the spices continue throbbing and some pear and corn oil stretch the finish deliciously; b24 pure entertainment. Ticks many of the boxes the Spring 44 bourbon misses. And, to be brutally honest, barrels properly blended should always outperform a single one. 50% (100 proof)

⬦ **Stagg Jn** (91.5) n22.5 massive spice, all of it oak inspired. Rarely do you see so much tannin on the nose unchecked by covering sugar. A little clove confirms the forest-like influence; t24 ahh! Just enough molasses holds ground on delivery to absorb those thumping tannins. The spice immediately flies off the scale: arguably the spiciest bourbon on delivery today. Some hickory and ersatz coffee grinds into the mid-ground, a slight nuttiness, too. The sugars just skim the surface; f22.5 dry and drying. The spices still pound and bite and the tannins grip and refuse to release. The sugars present are badly outnumbered; b22.5 a whiskey of staggering brinkmanship. Who will blink first? The massive oak or the taste buds. To be honest, this is the kind of bourbon that sorts out the men from the boys, the women from the girls. Doesn't have quite enough covering sweetness of varying type and intensity to match the complexity found in the original Stagg. One that needs a very long time to get to the bottom of. 67.2% (134.4 proof) Buffalo Trace.

Temperance Trader distilled in Indiana, batch 005, released Mar 12 (89) n22 happy to stick to a corny theme; liquorice is making an entrance; t23 amazingly heavy on the corn oil, the delicate, diluted golden syrup goes a long way; f22 the oils and sugars remain but the corn-laden vanillas dominate; b22 a soft, easy goer which concentrates on charm over complexity. 41.83%. Bull Run, Portland.

Ten High (68) n17.5 t16.5 f17 b17. Always one of the lighter bourbons, now sporting a curious sweetness which does little to engage. Still a good mixer, though. 40%

Tom Moore (85.5) n20 t22 f21.5 b22. An improved and engaging whiskey happy to display its increased fruit and complexity. The babbling on the palate of the small grain is a treat. 40%

Tom Moore 100 Proof (88.5) n21 t23 f22 b22.5. Another bourbon showing the inimitable Barton 1792 Distillery house style. The majority entertain but fall short in one department or another. Here, thanks to a little less water added in the bottling hall, we can really see how this whiskey can really tick. 50% (100 Proof)

Van Winkle Special Reserve 12 Years Old lot B (77.5) n18.5 t22 f18 b19. A very curious bottling: the nose and finish are both lacking in substance. But the delivery offers brief, spicy, slightly jammy riches. 45.2% (90.4 proof)

Van Winkle 23 Years Old (89.5) n23 t23 f21.5 b22. More of a Van Wrinkle: this is showing a lot of age. But enough of a pulse for one last enthralling show. 57% (114 proof). Buffalo Trace.

Very Old Barton (85.5) n21 t22 f21 b21.5. A fair slab of vanilla to go with the busy-ish spice. Attractive, but nothing like as complex as the 6-y-o label. 40% (80 Proof)

Very Old Barton 90 Proof (94) n23 a bit of mint in the tea this time. And perhaps an extra spoonful of sugar; t24 the rye and small grain have gone into overdrive. One of the busier Kentucky whiskeys with no shortage of layering...and spice; f23.5 tons of vanilla to bring the curtain down on the budding hickory and liquorice; b23.5 one of the most dangerously drinkable whiskeys in the world... 45% (90 proof)

Very Old Barton 100 Proof (86) n22 t22 f21 b21. Enjoyable and well made for sure. But by VOB standards pretty dense and one dimensional with the light liquorice-vanilla note having too big a say. Lacking the usual small grain and rye intensity, this cannot be explained by the extra strength alone. 50% (100 proof)

Very Old Barton 6 Years Old (92) n23 t23 f23 b23. One of those seemingly gifted bourbons that, swan-like, appears to glide at the surface but on closer inspection has loads going on underneath. 43%

Virgin Bourbon 7 Years Old (96.5) n24 so Wild Turkey-esque in style it is almost untrue: just loads of honey spilling out of the glass, backed up by big rye and leathery oak; t24.5 hold on to the arm of your seats...the mouth feel is massive with chocolate honeycomb surrounded by juicy dates and figs; liquorice has been piled high with really thick molasses...quite incredible; f24 the corn oils carry the sugars to the very end. But like distant thunder beyond the limestone hills, comes the spices and that liquorice, now with a touch of hickory, rumbling to the last...; b24 this takes me back nearly 40 years to when I first began my love affair with bourbon and was still a bit of a whisky virgin. This was the very style that blew me away: big, uncompromising, rugged...yet with a heart of honeyed gold. It is the type of huge, bold, honest bourbon that makes you get on your hands and knees and kiss Kentucky soil. 50.5% (101 proof)

Virgin Bourbon 15 Years Old (92.5) n23.5 t23 f23.5 b23. The kind of bourbon you want to be left in a room with. 50.5% (101 proof)

Virginia Gentleman (90.5) n22 t23 f23 b23.5. A Gentleman in every sense: and a pretty sophisticated one at that. 40% (80 Proof)

Walker's DeLuxe 3 Years Old (86) n22 t22 f21 b21. Excellent by 3-y-o standards. 40%

Weller Special Reserve 7 Years Old (83) n20 t21 f21 b21. Pleasant stuff which sings a fruity tune and is ably backed by subtle spice. Perhaps a little too sweet, though. 45%

Weller 12 Years Old (93) n24 t23.5 f22.5 b23. Sheer quality. And an enormous leap in complexity and grace from the 7-y-o. 45%

Western Gold (85.5) n21 t22 f21 b21.5. A young, citrusy, light bourbon which concentrates on the delicate honey side of things. Perfect for those who find full-bodied bourbon not to their style....yet! 40%. Lidl.

Wild Turkey (77) n19 t19 f20 b19. As sweet and simple as bourbon gets. Shows few of the qualities that make it such astonishing whiskey when older. 40% (80 proof)

Wild Turkey 101 (91) n22 t23.5 f22.5 b23. By far the best 101 I have tasted in a decade: you simply can't do anything but go weak at the knees with that spice attack. 55.5% (101 proof)

Wild Turkey American Spirit Aged 15 Years (92) n24 t22.5 f22.5 b23. A delightful Wild Turkey that appears under par for a 100 proofer but offers much when you search those nooks and crannies of your palate. 50.0% (100 proof)

Wild Turkey Kentucky Spirit Single Barrel barrel no. 96, bott. 5/13/09, warehouse rick 16 (86.5) n21.5 t22.5 f21 b21.5. More dense from nose to finish than the type of forest the real Wild Turkey prefers to inhabit. Lots of delicious butterscotch and mocha on show, but surprisingly little development. 50% (100 proof)

Wild Turkey Rare Breed bott code L0049FH (94) n22.5 the oak and fruit is of that firm, almost smoky, variety that will be readily recognised and appreciated by devotees of Oregon Pino Noit. However, this is a very different bird to the one I last spotted: the butterscotch and honey are absent leaving berry fruits to dominate. Attractive but very odd; t24.5 much more like it! The puckering oaks are immediately set upon by pots of acacia honey and slightly overcooked butterscotch tart. Reminiscent of the Rare Breed of the early 2000s with the oak pulling up trees, so to speak. The rye notes kick in at about midpoint and dig in satisfyingly deeply; f23 very long with the burned elements offering the required gravitas. Also overcooked prunes are lightened by under-ripe dates...; b24 it is hard to credit that this is the same brand I have been tasting at regular intervals for quite a long while. Certainly nothing like this style has been around for a decade and it is massively far removed from two years ago. The nose threatens a whiskey limited in direction. But the delivery is as profound as it is entertaining. Even on this bottling's singular though fabulous style, not perhaps quite overall the gargantuan whiskey of recent years. But, seeing as it's only the nose which pegs it back a point or two, still one that would leave a big hole in your whiskey experience if you don't get around to trying. 54.1%

Wild Turkey Tradition Aged 14 Years db (89) n23 t21.5 f22.5 b22. Something of a departure in style for a Wild Turkey (which is why it is a little odd it is called "Tradition"): this one makes a point of being an old bird. 50.5% (101 proof)

Willett Family Estate Bottled Single Barrel Bourbon 6 Years Old white oak barrel, cask no. 672 (88) n22.5 some beautiful flaked coconut in golden syrup; teasing, nibbling spices; t21.5 an early delivery of muscovado sugars and then a surge of natural caramels soften; f22 custard tart all the way...; b22 never quite matches the nose for all round balance but impossible not to love. 60.5% (121 Proof). sc. Special bottling for "Mr Bourbon" (Heinz Taubenheim). 196 bottles.

Willett Family Estate Bottled Single Barrel Bourbon 7 Years Old barrel no 3667 (88.5) n23 a dazzling vanilla and caramel duet; good spice prickle; t22.5 resounding Demerara sugars show early with busy spices in tip-top form; still it is the vanilla which dominates; f21 thins out for a finale of austerity; b22 an Early Times style barrel where spice dominates over complexity. 61.05%. 168 bottles.

Willett Family Estate Bottled Single Barrel Bourbon 14 Years Old white oak barrel, cask no. 1067 (96) n24 drier, more liquorice; t23.5 intense delivery with a superb balance between the drier hickory-liquorice combo and the much more open, wider-reaching sugar. Some serious maple syrup in with the molasses here..; **f24.5** that is brilliant: exactly what bourbon should be about! No off notes, no bitterness.; Just a complex but fading massaging of the taste buds, with neither those drier tones nor the sweeter ones – and all with the same characteristics as earlier) dominating...classic stuff..; **b24** if I hadn't have a book to write I could taste this all day... 57.6%. sc. Special bottling for "Mr Bourbon" (Heinz Taubenheim). 72 bottles.

Willett Pot Still Reserve barrel no. 2421 **(95.5) n24.5 t23 f24 b24.** Another fabulous whiskey from Willett. You can so often trust them to deliver and here they have given us a bourbon showing serious oak injection, yet a sweetness which counters perfectly. 47%. 273 bottles.

William Larue Weller dist Fall 1998, bott Fall 2011 **(97.5) n24 t24 f25 b24.5.** Wow! This is becoming a must experience whiskey for hardcore bourbon lovers. Well, whisk(e)y lovers period, really! A bourbon which absolutely takes you to the wire with a "will it or won't it" type brinkmanship taking the flavours as far as they will go in an oaky direction without veering off the road and crashing down the cliff side. Majestic. Or, as it's American, perhaps I should say: Presidential.. 66.75% (133.5 Proof)

William Larue Weller (97) n24 t24 f25 b24. Among the best wheated mash bill bourbon I have ever encountered. Why some whiskeys work better than others is the stuff of long debate. The reason for this particular bottling is relatively simple: you have an almost breathless intensity, yet somehow the constituent parts of the complexity can be individually identified and savoured. That is quite rare in any whiskey with this degree of weight. 67.4% (134.8 proof). ncf.

⋰⋰ **William Larue Weller (97.5) n24** weightier than last time out, though only fractionally, and here much more dependent on a coffee framework backed by wonderfully crystallised dark sugars. Plenty of hickory and little cough sweet thicken the soup; **t24.5** it is probably impossible to get more types of dark sugars into the delivery of whiskey. This is so mesmerizing, you find yourself chuckling as the taste buds are asked to identify the myriad sugar and honey styles which pass through. I have counted eight with some form of certainty...though I'm sure I've missed a few, too; **f24** to make this whiskey work, you now need the finale to be moderately dry...to the point of sophistication. And that is exactly what you get. You can almost taste the char, though it is, like on the nose, the hickory which shapes the finish, comfortably cradling the spices which are dying to burst out; **b25** for any whiskey with a proof of 123.4, the only way is up...! Last year's Whisky Bible World Whisky of the Year Runner-up is going for the full title big time, no holds barred. Again, this is absolutely supreme class. 61.7% (123.4 proof). ncf.

Winn Dixie Bourbon (84.5) n19 t22 f21.5 b22. An entirely agreeable and more-ish bourbon which makes the most of its delicious kumquat and spice backbone. 40%

Woodford Reserve Distiller's Select batch 59 **(85) n22 t21.5 f20.5 b21.** Nutty on nose and delivery with plenty to chew on. The sweetness is limited, perhaps by the degree of feints which ensure an oily, slightly bitter finale. 43.2%

⋰⋰ **Woodford Reserve Distiller's Select** batch 95 **(91) n23** excellent, truly classic aroma of crisp muscovado sugar bathed in red liquorice; soft butterscotch and even a hint of French toast cranks up the complexity; **t23** a deftly sweet delivery, at times seeming powerful on the molasses, but the sublime layering of the tannins ensures a countering dryness which fits beautifully with the spices; **f22** emphasis on the tannin and spice, though a little short; **b23** few bourbons so beautifully pits sweet against dry to such excellent effect. 43.2%

Woodford Reserve Master's Collection Four Grain (95) n24 t24 f23 b24. Sod's law would have it that the moment we removed this from the 2006 Bible, having appeared in the previous two editions without it ever making the shelves, it should at last be belatedly released. But a whiskey worth waiting for, or what? The tasting notes are not a million miles from the original. But this is better bourbon, one that appears to have received a significant polish in the intervening years. Nothing short of magnificent. 46.2%

Zachariah Harris (89) n22 t23 f22 b22. Very good quality, not overly taxing fayre where the spices harmonise comfortably with the generous honey on show. Lovely, every day drinking. 40%

Tennessee Whiskey
BENJAMIN PRICHARD

Benjamin Prichard's Tennessee Whiskey (83) n21.5 t21 f20 b20.5. Majestic fruity rye notes trill from the glass. Curiously yeasty as well; bounding with all kinds of freshly crushed brown sugar crystals. Pleasant enough, but doesn't gel like Prichard's bourbon. 40% ⊙

GEORGE DICKEL

George Dickel Superior No 12 Brand Whisky (90.5) n22.5 t23 f22.5 b22.5. A different story told by George from the last one I heard. But certainly no less fascinating. 45%

JACK DANIEL

Gentleman Jack Rare Tennessee Whiskey (77) n19 t20 f18 b19. A Tennessee that appears to have achieved the impossible: it has got even lighter in character in recent years. A whiskey which wilfully refuses to say anything particularly interesting or go anywhere, this is one for those prefer their hard liquor soft. *40% (80 proof). Brown-Forman.*

⁙ **Jack Daniel's 120th Anniversary of the White Rabbit Saloon** (91) lighter ulmo honey to this, which just lowers the temperature and intensity of the liquorice. Complex stuff...; **t23.5** magnificent delivery: early corn oil carries the deft molasses; both black and red liquorice slowly builds but the middle is pure vanilla; **f22** a mix of dry molassed notes and a little muscovado. Excellent late balance; **b23** on its best-behaved form. After the delivery, the oils are down a little, so not the usual bombastic offering from JD. Nonetheless, this is pure class and the clever use of sugars simply make you drool... *43%. Brown-Forman.*

Jack Daniel's (Green Label) (84) n20 t21 f22 b21. A light but lively little gem of a whiskey. Starts as a shrinking violet, finishes as a roaring lion with nimble spices ripping into the developing liquorice. A superb session whiskey. *40% (80 proof)*

Jack Daniel's Old No.7 Brand (Black Label) (92) n23 t23 f22.5 b23.5. Actually taken aback by this guy. The heavier oils have been stripped and the points here are for complexity...that should shock a few old Hell's Angels I know. *40%*

Jack Daniel's Single Barrel barrel no.7-3915, bott 28 Sep 07 (87) n21.5 t22 f22 b21.5. Pleasant, yet perhaps not the most inspiring single cask I have come across from JD. This one refuses to offer up the usual oily weight. *45% (90 proof). Brown-Forman.*

⁙ **Jack Daniel's Single Barrel 12-5660** bott 15 Oct 12 db (92.5) n23.5 such clarity to the crystallised Demerara sugar, even though some molasses seems to have got into the act; slight cloves and hickory fumble the mocha's blouse buttons; **t23.5** silk delivery, very much putting the onus on the crisp sugars to forge a bright path, along which the very light oils (certainly lighter than of old) travel, as well as a gentle fruit rye kick which acts as the rudder; **f22.5** much gentler than of yore with some spices amid the vanillas; **b23** I'll tell you something about JD. A number of "whisky specialist" I know rubbish this whiskey. With a passion. In fact, they can barely bring themselves to call it whiskey at all. But their single barrel range really does show what magnificent stock they have maturing in their warehouses. As this random bottling testifies... Magnificent stuff. And sod the so-called experts, I say...just enjoy it! *45%*

Jack Daniel's Single Barrel Select cask no. 11-3758, bott 2 Aug 11 (86) n21.5 t22 f21.5 b21. Pleasant, sweet but heavy on the natural caramels. Impedes complexity, a delight if you're into the sweeter side of Jack. *45% (90 proof)*

Jack Daniel's Single Barrel Select cask no. 11-5065, bott 6 Oct 11 (89.5) n22 t23 f22 b22.5. One of those laid back Jacks which does all the good things effortlessly. *45% (90 proof)*

Jack Daniel's Single Barrel Select cask no. 12-0451, bott 31 Jan 12 (93.5) n23.5 t23.5 f23 b23.5. Absolutely bang on the money. Gets the liquorice bite and sugars in superb combination to create a signature like no other distillery in the world. *45% (90 proof)*

Corn Whiskey

Dixie Dew (95) n22.5 corn whiskey...???? Really...??? The corn oils form a bit of a sweet blob, but elsewhere it is all about graduated degrees of cocoa and hickory...and all rather lovely. **t24** good grief!! Have not tasted a profile such as this: healthy corn oils but then a welter of Columbian Santander Cacao and rye-rich spices interject. Absolutely unique and astonishing...; **f24** the corn plays out its long farewell but the spices don't listen and take up the main ground; a few juicy sultanas fly in...from goodness knows where; **b24.5** I have kept in my previous tasting notes for this whiskey as they serve a valuable purpose. The three matured corn whiskeys I have before me are made by the same distillers. But, this time round, they could not be more different. From Mellow Corn to Dixie we have three whiskeys with very differing hues. This, quite frankly, is the darkest corn whiskey I have ever seen and one of world class stature with characteristics I have never found before in any whiskey. Any true connoisseur of whisk(e)y will make deals with Lucifer to experience this freak whiskey. There is no age statement...but this one has gray hairs attached to the cob... *50%*

Georgia Moon Corn Whiskey "Less Than 30 Days Old" (83.5) n21.5 t22 f20 b20. If anyone has seen corn whiskey made – either in Georgia or Kentucky – then the unique aroma will be instantly recognisable from the fermenters and still house. Enjoyable stuff which does exactly what it says on the jar. *50%*

J. W. Corn (92.5) n23 t23.5 f23 b23. In another life this could be bourbon. The corn holds the power, for sure. But the complexity and levels are so far advanced that this – again! – qualifies as very high grade whiskey. Wonderful that the normal high standard is being maintained for what is considered by many, quite wrongly, as an inferior spirit. *50%*

Mellow Corn (83) n19 t21 f22 b21. Dull and oily on the nose, though the palate compensates with a scintillating array of sweet and spicy notes. *50%*

Single Malt Rye
ANCHOR DISTILLERY

Old Potrero Single Malt Straight Rye Whiskey Essay 10-SRW-ARM-E (94) n24 t23 f24 b23 The whiskey from this distillery never fails to amaze. With the distillery now under new management it will be fascinating to see what lands in my tasting lab. Even at 75% quality we will still be blessed with astonishing whiskeys. *45% (90 proof)*

Straight Rye

Abraham Bowman Limited Edition dist 4/3/98, bott. 12/15/09 **(85)** n21 t22 f21 b21. For those who like rye with their vanilla. *63.2%*

⁂ **Benjamin Prichard's Tennessee Rye Whiskey (86)** n20 t21.5 f23 b21.5. Bit of a scruffy nose, but polishes up pleasantly. The rye itself is not of the sharp variety and at times is hard to identify. But the ulmo honey and lush butterscotch offer the gloss at the finish. *43%*

Bulleit 95 Rye (96) n25 only the rye from the Lawrenceburg Indiana distillery can conjure a perfect rye aroma such as this...and that is exactly where it is from. Cinnamon and crunchy muscovado sugar crystal on green apple...so soft...so rigid...so unique...; t24.5 exactly as the nose is fashioned, so is the delivery. At once liltingly soft yet absolutely granite hard...the rye offers both fruity and spicy branches...both lead to a salivating trunk; f22.5 echoes of firm grain and fruit but pretty quick by comparison to what has gone on before...23.5 this is a style of rye, indeed whiskey, which is unique. Buffalo Trace makes an ultra high-quality rye which lasts the course longer. But nothing compares in nose and delivery to this...in fact few whiskies in the world get even close... 45%. Straight *95% rye mash whiskey.*

⁂ **Colonel E.H. Taylor Straight Rye (97)** n24 how can a breezy whiskey, seemingly so light and full of sparkle, also have such an intensely dark side? The rye grains appear to have a spotlight on them following their every elegant movement; the spices, at first docile, build and build. Yet all the time, the grain appears to revel in its cut-glass sugary clarity. A little mystifying, too, as the vague clove and eucalyptus lurking in the background reveals an oak presence found nowhere else in the tasting experience; t24.5 almost all you want from a rye: so clean, so intent in purpose, that the grain seems to transform into Demerara granules with the most polite oils and (for the oak) ulmo honey notes spreading all far and wide and with sensational eight; f24 all is left to the muscovado sugar and quietly persistent ulmo honey to ensure no bitterness or any other wayward notes can infringe upon the charmingly sweet and still lively finish; b24.5 reminds me of the younger ryes when Sazerac Handy first hit the shelves, with the emphasis on the clarity of the grain and the fallout of oak and spice. Really, a bottle which should never be left on a liquor store shelf. *50%*

Cougar Rye (95) n25 t24 f23 b23. The Lawrenceburg, Indiana Distillery makes the finest rye I have ever tasted - and that is saying something. Here is a magnificent example of their astonishing capabilities. Good luck hunting the Cougar. *37%. Foster's Group, Australia.*

Devil's Bit Seven-Year-Old Single Barrel (93.5) n22.5 t24 f23 b24. A must-find rye from one of the most impressive small distilleries in the world. *47.7%. Edgefield Distillery.*

Fleischmann's Straight Rye (87.5) n22 t22.5 f21.5 b21.5. One of the most spiceless ryes I have come across. But a lovely mouth-watering touch. *40%*

High West 12 Years Old Rye (92.5) n22 t24 f23 b23.5. A very clever rye which will hit a chord of appreciation for those who savour this whiskey style. *46%*

High West Double Rye a blend of straight rye whiskeys, batch 12G/9 **(76.5)** n18 t21 f18.5 b19. A rye designed for cowboys. I'll get a dirty glass... *46%*

High West Rendezvous Rye a blend of straight rye whiskeys, batch 12DO-1 **(82)** n22 t22 f19 b19. You would think that just adding one good whiskey to another would bring straightforward results. But blending a very old rye with a young one is one of the most difficult tricks in the book....as this whiskey demonstrates. Better than previous batches....but a long way to go before the trick is mastered, let alone perfected. *46%*

High West Rocky Mountain 16 Years Old Rye (86.5) n20 t22.5 f22 b22. Here and there, the nose being a good example, the rye and vanilla cancel each other out. But there is enough viperfish spice and juicy fruit to keep you salivating for a good while. *46%*

High West Rocky Mountain 21 Year Old Rye (95) n23 how sexy is that dance between the milky cocoa and the piercing rye...? t25 just about everything you could wish for: the rye (as is the case in the very best ones) offers a dual role: it both firms up and fruit enriches, and here refuses to overly play either hand. The sugars are pure melt in the mouth; honeydew melon and liquorice dry out towards a toasty butterscotch-hickory middle; f23 relaxes to let the vanillas (aided by a little cocoa) take charge; b24 bizarrely, tastes a whole lot younger than the 16-years-old. Lighter in both colour and character, here you get to see the full personality of an absolutely outstanding rye whiskey. *46%*

Jim Beam Rye (89) n22.5 t23 f21.5 b22. It seemed that when Beam changed the colour of the label from bright, road-marking, yellow to a wash-out, over milked custard hue, the vividness had also mysteriously – and tragically - vanished from the rye. Still more caramel than the glory days of old, but unquestionably a very welcome, if limited, move back to its sharper old self. Great stuff once more...now let's see what they can do about the label... 40%

Old Overholt Four Years Old (85) n22 t21 f21 b21. Still little sign of this returning to its old rip-roaring best. Duller and less challenging with a frustrating dustiness to the proceedings. 40%

Pappy Van Winkle's Family Reserve Rye 13 Years Old (94) n24 outwardly, the aroma basks in a crisp rye flourish; scratch below the surface and there are darker, more sinister oaky forces at work; t23.5 crisp, almost crackling rye offers both the fruity-clean and burned fruitcake options; f23 dulls out a bit as the liquorice/toffee oak takes hold but remains alluringly spicy and sensual; b23.5 uncompromising rye that successfully tells two stories simultaneously. A great improvement on the Winkle rye of old. 4/78%

Pikesville (77.5) n17.5 t21.5 f19 b19. The freshness is absent here and instead we have a grumpy dustiness which limits development. Know when you have left your car lights on all night and you can't start engine next day? Yep...it's that flat... 40%

(ri)¹ (94) n23 now that's more like it from Beam: the rye is a solid mass, radiating all kinds of fruity notes. But there are intriguing spices, too, ranging from light cloves to varying peppers; t24 spot on delivery: as stark as a Kentucky cliff face and just as porous, too: the rye is crisp for sure and the citrus-induced salivating levels sublime. There is a slow build up of mildly milky chocolate, occasionally bordering on praline; f23.5 the cocoa continues all the way, now with vanilla edging its way in but those light citrus notes balancing against the increasing spice presence...just so complex... b23.5 (ri)ght up my alley. A fabulous meeting of crispy rye and much softer cocoa: an irresistible and ultra high quality addition to Kentucky's rye whiskey cannon. 46%

Rittenhouse (78.5) n18.5 t21.5 f19 b20. Juice and spice but lacking sharpness. 40%

Rittenhouse 100 Proof Rye db (83) n22 fruit and veg! t22.5 chewy delivery with a degree of cocoa. Then crisps out at the rye, with its usual Demerara sugar foot soldiers panning out; more earthiness later on; f18.5 and now there is a definite buzz and light bitterness; b20 the nose is so, so fruity. But there is also a curious steaming asparagus vegetable edge. At first this is by no means unpleasant and adds a certain salty earthiness to the crisp rye. However, the finish displays a definite buzz and vegetable edge which I can't believe is unassociated. Partly enjoyable but perhaps the cask is, for some reason, getting a little stale. 50%. sc.

Rittenhouse 100 Proof Bottled in Bond (86.5) n20 t23 f21.5 b22. The nose labours for a Rittenhouse 100. But the salivating delivery and sweetly fashioned and richly-spiced rye makes a delightful impact on the palate. 50%

Rittenhouse Very Rare Single Barrel 21 Years Old (91) n25 t23 f21 b22. I may be wrong, but I would wager quite a large amount that no-one living has tasted more rye from around the world than I. So trust me when I tell you this is different, a genuine one-off in style. By rights such telling oak involvement should have killed the whisky stone dead: this is like someone being struck by lightning and then walking off slightly singed and with a limp, but otherwise OK. The closest style of whisky to rye is Irish pot still, a unique type where unmalted barley is used. And the closest whiskey I have tasted to this has been 35 to 50-year-old pot still Irish. What they have in common is a massive fruit base, so big that it can absorb and adapt to the oak input over many years. This has not escaped unscathed. But it has to be said that the nose alone makes this worthy of discovery, as does the glory of the rye as it first melts into the tastebuds. The term flawed genius could have been coined for this whisky alone. Yet, for all its excellence, I can so easily imagine someone, somewhere, claiming to be an expert on whiskey, bleating about the price tag of $150 a bottle. If they do, ignore them. Because, frankly, rye has been sold far too cheaply for far too long and that very cheapness has sculpted a false perception in people's minds about the quality and standing of the spirit. Well, 21 years in Kentucky equates to about 40 years in Scotland. And you try and find a 40-year-old Scotch for £75. If anything, they are giving this stuff away. The quality of the whiskey does vary from barrel to barrel and therefore bottle to bottle. So below I have given a summary of each individual bottling (averaging (91.1). The two with the highest scores show the least oak interference...yet are quite different in style. That's great whiskey for you. 50% (100 proof). ncf. Heaven Hill.

Barrel no. 1 (91) n25 t23 f21 b22. As above. 50%
Barrel no. 2 (89) n24 t23 f20 b22. Dryer, oakier. 50%
Barrel no. 3 (91) n24 t23 f22 b22. Fruity, soft. 50%
Barrel no. 4 (90) n25 t22 f21 b22. Enormous. 50%
Barrel no. 5 (93) n25 t23 f22 b23. Early rye surge. 50%
Barrel no. 6 (87) n23 t22 f20 b22. Juicy, vanilla. 50%
Barrel no. 7 (90) n23 t23 f22 b22. Even, soft, honeyed. 50%
Barrel no. 8 (95) n25 t24 f23 b23. The works: massive rye. 50%
Barrel no. 9 (91) n24 t23 f22 b22. Sharp rye, salivating. 50%

Barrel no. 10 (93) n25 t24 f22 b22. Complex, sweet. *50%*
Barrel no. 11 (93) n24 t24 f22 b23. Rich, juicy, spicy. *50%*
Barrel no. 12 (91) n25 t23 f21 b22. Near identical to no.1. *50%*
Barrel no. 13 (91) n24 t24 f21 b22. Citrus and toasty. *50%*
Barrel no. 14 (94) n25 t24 f22 b23. Big rye and marzipan. *50%*
Barrel no. 15 (88) n23 t22 f21 b22. Major oak influence. *50%*
Barrel no. 16 (90) n24 t23 f21 b22. Spicy and toffeed. *50%*
Barrel no. 17 (90) n23 t23 f22 b22. Flinty, firm, late rye kick. *50%*
Barrel no. 18 (91) n24 t24 f21 b22. Big rye delivery. *50%*
Barrel no. 19 (87) n23 t24 f21 b21. Major coffee input. *50%*
Barrel no. 20 (91) n23 t24 f22 b22. Spicy sugar candy. *50%*
Barrel no. 21 (94) n23 t24 f24 b23. Subtle, fruity. *50%*
Barrel no. 22 (89) n23 t22 f22 b22. Mollased. *50%*
Barrel no. 23 (94) n24 t24 f24 b22. Soft fruit, massive rye. *50%*
Barrel no. 24 (88) n23 t22 f21 b22. Intense oak and caramel. *50%*
Barrel no. 25 (93) n25 t22 f23 b23. Heavy rye and spice. *50%*
Barrel no. 26 (92) n23 t23 f23 b23. Subtle, delicate rye. *50%*
Barrel no. 27 (94) n23 t23 f23 b23. Delicate rye throughout. *50%*
Barrel no. 28 (96) n25 t24 f23 b24. Salivating, roasty, major. *50%*
Barrel no. 29 (88) n23 t22 f21 b22. Hot, fruity. *50%*
Barrel no. 30 (91) n24 t23 f22 b22. Warming cough sweets. *50%*
Barrel no. 31 (90) n25 t22 f21 b22. Aggressive rye. *50%*

Rittenhouse Rye Single Barrel Aged 25 Years bott Nov 09 (93.5) n24.5 t24 f22 b23. This is principally on the nose: a thing of rare beauty even in the highest peaks of the whiskey world. The story on the palate is much more about damage limitation with the oak going a bit nuts. But remember this: in Scottish years due to the heat in Kentucky, this would be a malt well in excess of 50 years. But even with the signs of fatigue, so crisp is that rye, so beautifully defined are its intrinsic qualities that the quality is still there to be clearly seen. Just don't judge on the first, second or even third mouthful. Your taste buds need time to relax and adjust. Only then will they accommodate and allow you to fully appreciate and enjoy the creaky old ride. At this age, though, always worth remembering that the best nose doesn't always equal the best tasting experience... *50% (100proof). Heaven Hill.*

Barrel no. 1 (93.5) n24.5 t24 f22 b23. As above. *50%*
Barrel no. 2 (88) n22 t24 f20 b22. Intense. Crisp, juicy; a tad soapy, bitter. *50%*
Barrel no. 3 (89.5) n23 t23.5 f21.5 b21.5. Fabulously crisp. Fruity. Mollassed. *50%*
Barrel no. 4 (85) n21.5 t21.5 f21 b21. Subdued fruit. Massive oak. *50%*
Barrel no. 5 (90.5) n25 t22.5 f21.5 b21.5. Complex. Mega oaked but spiced, fruity. *50%*
Barrel no. 6 (91.5) n24.5 t22 f23 b22. Tangy. Honeyed and hot. Spiced marmalade. *50%*
Barrel no. 7 (83.5) n20 t22 f20.5 b21. Treacle toffee amid the burnt apple. *50%*
Barrel no. 8 (90) n23.5 t23.5 f21 b22. Flinty, teeth-cracking rye. Crème brulee. *50%*
Barrel no. 9 (91) n23.5 t23.5 f22 b22. Massive ryefest. Mocha coated. *50%*
Barrel no. 10 (86.5) n22 t23 f20 b21.5. Early zip and juice. Tires towards caramel. *50%*
Barrel no. 11 (89) n24 t22 f21 b22. Honeycomb. Hickory. Caramel. Oil. *50%*
Barrel no. 12 (84.5) n22.5 t21 f20 b21. Delicate. Vanilla and caramel. Light. *50%*
Barrel no. 13 (89.5) n22.5 t23 f22 b22. Succulent. Yet rye remains firm. *50%*
Barrel no. 14 (88) n22 t23 f21 b22. Very similar to 13 but with extra caramel. *50%*
Barrel no. 15 (86) n21 t23 f20.5 b21.5. Lazy grain. Warming but flat. Caramel. *50%*
Barrel no. 16 (92) n23 t23 f23 b23. Sculpted rye: sugared fruit; a twist of juniper. *50%*
Barrel no. 17 (86.5) n22.5 t21.5 f21 b21.5. Fizzy, fruity spice calmed by caramel. *50%*
Barrel no. 18 (91) n23.5 t23.5 f21.5 b22.5. Pristine rye. Spice. Juicy molasses. Crisp. *50%*
Barrel no. 19 (96) n24 t23.5 f24.5 b23.5. Concentrated honeycomb and chocolate. *50%*
Barrel no. 20 (89.5) n23 t22 f22.5 b22. Cream toffee. Fruit and spice. *50%*
Barrel no. 21 (85) n21 t20 f23 b21. Severe oak delivery. Recovers with mocha toffee. *50%*
Barrel no. 22 (81) n20 t20 f21 b20. Mild sap. Fruity. Oily. *50%*
Barrel no. 23 (94) n23.5 t24 f23.5 b23. Rich. Fruity. Juicy. Clean. Corn oil. Cocoa. *50%*
Barrel no. 24 (88.5) n22.5 t22 f21 b22. Huge vanilla. Slow spice. *50%*
Barrel no. 25 (88) n22.5 t21.5 f22 b22. Custard and sugared fruit. Sharpens. *50%*
Barrel no. 26 (90.5) n22 t23 f22.5 b21.5. Classic crisp rye. Big, manageable oak. *50%*
Barrel no. 27 (88) n23 t22 f21.5 b21.5. Huge, honeyed oak. Oily. Dries at end. *50%*
Barrel no. 28 (91) n22 t23.5 f22.5 b22.5. Exemplary honeycomb-rye delivery. Spices. *50%*
Barrel no. 29 (94) n23.5 t24 f23 b23.5. Juicy rye; crisp sugar-vanilla-hickory fade. *50%*
Barrel no. 30 (94.5) n23 t24 f24 b23.5. Thick rye. Cocoa. Spices. *50%*
Barrel no. 31 (79) n21 t20 f19 b19. Lethargic. Bitter. *50%*
Barrel no. 32 (88) n21.5 t22.5 f22 b22. Relaxed honeycomb. Hint of mint. *50%*

Barrel no. 33 (88.5) n22.5 t22 f22 b22. Powering oak-rye battle. *50%*

Barrel no. 34 (84) n23 t21 f20 b20. Thick oak throughout. Corn oil. *50%*

Barrel no. 35 (93.5) n22.5 t23.5 f24 b23.5. Big rye. Demerara-hickory. Complex. *50%*

Barrel no. 36 (77) n21 t19 f18 b19. Bitter oak. *50%*

Russell's Reserve Rye 6 Year Old Small Batch bott. code L0194FH) (93.5) n24 t23.5 f22.5 b23.5. Has lost none of its wit and sharpness: in fact has improved a notch or two in recent times. Wonderful! *45% (90 proof)*

Sazerac Kentucky Straight Rye Whiskey 18 Years Old bott Fall 2010 (95) n23.5 t24 f23.5 b24. Some ego-driven, know-nothing commentators who for some mysterious reason claim an expertise with whiskey wonder how people can give different scores each year for a rye which has been living in a stainless steel vat. Of course, it would not occur to them that each time the vat is stirred before bottling the mix reveals subtle differences, depending on where the molecules fall. Line up Sazerac 18, one after the other from the last few years, and tell me which one is identical to the other. They are all quite different, and this one appears to have more than its fair share of sawdust and tannin. *45% (90 Proof)*

Sazerac Kentucky Straight Rye Whiskey 18 Years Old dist Spring 1985, bott Fall 2011 (96.5) n24.5 t24 f24 b24. If you are looking to climb the Everest of rye whiskeys, then good luck in scaling the lofty, jagged peaks. *45% (90 Proof)*

⁖ **Sazerac Kentucky Straight Rye Whiskey 18 Years Old** bott 2012 (95.5) n24 yet again a fascinating, subtle difference to previous years. This time a vague nougat toffee underpins the much brighter fruity and crispy rye; a little more earthy, also; t23 probably a first: wild cherries are plucked ripe and bulbous from the delivery, the intense fruity sharpness – with a just so touch of sweetness - masking the semi-aggressive roasty oak which accompanies it, though about half a beat behind. The mid-ground, despite a launching of tingling spices, remains juicy and mouth-watering, even though the grumbling oak tries to negate the freshness; f24 the vanillas which show first midway through now make a much more confident grip. Like a kind of cherry trifle, the finale sweetens and delights; b24.5 unquestionably showing a different side to its personality this time out, allowing the rye to show its fruity personality to the full. *45%*

Thomas H. Handy Sazerac Straight Rye Whiskey (97) n24 t25 f24 b24. It has taken me over three hours to taste this. Were all whiskies and whiskeys like this, the Bible, quite simply, would never see the light of day. Beyond enormous. A whiskey which located taste buds I had no idea I actually possess... Just like his near namesake, Thomas Hardy, Thomas Handy has come up with a rambling, immortal classic. *64.5% (129 proof). ncf.*

Thomas H Handy Sazerac Straight Rye Whiskey dist Spring 2005, bott Fall 2011 (97.5) n24 t24.5 f24.5 b24.5. A real slow burner. Takes a bit of time on the nose to leave the launch pad. But once off the ground it just doesn't stop travelling. Superb! *64.5% (128.6 Proof)*

⁖ **Thomas H. Handy Sazerac Straight Rye Whiskey** (97.5) n24 heavy on the spice and honey and quite light on the flinty rye which can often be found here. Entangled, enticing, beguiling....; t24.5 hold on to your hats, the chair...nail yourself to the ground...this is going to be some ride. The rye appears to have been to the gym and grown a few extra muscles: this is big and the spice will demolish the lily-livered beyond comprehension. The rye grains are always at the centre, even when a little liquorice forms towards the midpoint; f24.5 long and now back to the grain once more with the varying sugar strains head in all directions; a slightly dry finish as, at last, the oak gets a word in but the countering sweetness is ulmo honey at its deftest; b24.5 this was World Whisky of the Year last year and anyone buying this on the strength of that will not be disappointed. Huge whiskey with not even the glimmer of a hint of an off note. Magnificent: an honour to taste and rye smiles all round... *66.2%. ncf.*

Van Winkle Reserve Rye Aged 13 Years Old (94.5) n23.5 beautiful amalgamation of floral and fruit; t24.5 juicy, crisp brown sugar laced with hickory and then a storming middle of spice, tannin and toffee-liquorice; so like an ultra first class Jamaican pot still rum...; f23 with so little corn evident the twilight is shortish, but the sunset is nothing but pure dazzling rye; b23.5 magnificent. *45% (90 proof)*

Wild Turkey (80.5) n18 t22.5 f20 b20. Shackled by a dusty, cocoa-vanilla lethargy, breaks out into its sparkling old self only on delivery. Just not in the same league as the current Russell's Reserve... *50.5%*

⁖ **Whistlepig Aged 10 Years** db (88) n21 a little untidy and, though clean, a little short of rye character; t22 much better with the grain making the firm impact demanded and the right kind of firm brown sugars hit the target; f23 very pleasant blend of vanilla and intensifying grain; b22 having tasted this after the Sazerac beasts, this could have disappeared without trace. But had enough sharpness and rye freshness to make for a very pleasant and worthwhile experience. *50% (100 proof)*

Willet Family Estate Bottled Rye Barrel Proof Single Barrel 3 Years Old (91.5) n23.5 t24 f21.5 b22.5. What it loses in complexity, it makes up for in bay-faced freshness and charm. Ryes rarely come more juicy or puckering than this...a must locate rye! *57.7% (115.4 proof)*

⠿ **Willett Family Estate Bottled Single Barrel Rye 4 Years Old Barrel no 45** (94) n23.5 pretty much how you'd like a 4-y-o rye to show: crisp, uncluttered, the rye pounding out crystalline dark sugars and hints of spice; t24 spot on. Again, almost too clean with all the desired sharp cutting edges yet with truly magnificent mouth-watering qualities. Just as you begin salivating, the spices kick in. Some real boiled sweet quality here while the oak softens the grain only a fraction; f23 relatively short, though the oils are fuller and spices consistent; even some cocoa filters through; b23.5 truly satisfying rye which has in style more than a passing resemblance to the old Jim Beam yellow label rye of about 15 years ago. 55%

Straight Wheat Whiskey
Bernheim Original (91.5) n22 t23 f23 b23.5. By far the driest of the Bernheims I have encountered showing greater age and perhaps substance. Unique and spellbinding. 45%

American Microdistilleries

ALASKA DISTILLERY Wasilla, Alaska
⠿ **Alaska Outlaw Whiskey** (78.5) n20 t20 f19 b19.5. A surprisingly clean whiskey with a thin body and even thinner finale. So clean, in fact, that if you put it in a dirty glass, it'll probably end up sparkling. 40%

ALLTECH Lexington, Kentucky.
⠿ **Pearse Lyons Reserve** (85) n22 t21 f21 b21. A fruity, grainy, pleasant whisky with the higher notes citrus dominant. Never quite finds a place to land or quite tells its story. Attractive but incomplete. 40% (80 proof)
⠿ **Town Branch Kentucky Straight Bourbon** (88.5) n22.5 red liquorice, under-ripe greengages, nutmeg and polished oak floors...mmmm! t21.5 a soft landing with lashing of vanilla and muscovado; f23 thickens out as the treacle and liquorice re-emerge; some kumquats, too; b22 a delicious Kentucky bourbon of considerable depth and charm. I think they have found their niche: bourbon. In Kentucky. Go for it, guys! 40% (80 proof)

AMERICAN CRAFT WHISKY DISTILLERY Redwood Valley, California.
Low Gap Clear Malted Bavarian Wheat Whiskey batch 2010/3B, dist 30/07/10, aged 357 minutes in oak (90.5) n23 t23 f22 b22.5. In 20 years of doing this professionally, I'm pretty sure I have never come across something that has spent so little time in the oak. Very impressed and pray they have set some of this distillate aside for proper maturation. 42.7%
⠿ **Low Gap Whiskey** Distilled from Malted Rye Aged 204 Minutes dist 20 Sep 2012 (87.5) n22 t22 f21.5 b22. Very attractive and working on a surprising number of levels despite the lack of body. Excellent sugars throughout while the rye generates shape and backbone. 42.6%
⠿ **Low Gap Bavarian Hard Wheat** Aged 2 Years dist 31 Dec 10, bott 23 Jan 13 (76.5) n18 t21 f18.5 b19. There appears to be butyric on the nose and the finish bitters uncompromisingly. Despite the odd juicy, spicy high spot, not this distillery's finest moment. 43.1%

ARIZONA DISTILLING Tempe, Arizona
⠿ **Desert Derum Wheat Whiskey** 10 gallon cask barrelled 2013 (89) n22 toasted...toast! A few old barrels comes to mind, too; t22.5 the delivery lulls you somewhat , as the sugars and oils are playful. Then....whuuumph!!! Along comes the spice, rammed home with the full weight of the oak; f22 still a little oaky bitter, the spices sizzle, the sugars sooth...; b22.5 a desert storm of a whiskey. The small barrel punches some pretty towering tannins into the mix, but credit to the distiller for producing a spirit with enough balls to take it. 46%. ncf.

BAINBRIDGE ORGANIC DISTILLERS Bainbridge Island, Washington
⠿ **Battle Point Organic Washington Wheat Whiskey** (88.5) n21 surprisingly placid with a light spice nibble; t23 brilliant delivery, full of quick-tempered spicy attitude. The oils are sublime and the sugars mostly of a muscovado bent; f22 some vanilla and butterscotch show light oaky intent while the sugars remove the spices completely; b23 soft and satisfying. The spices demanded from wheat whiskey, though short-lived, hit all the right spots. Very well made and impressive. 43%

BALCONES DISTILLERY Waco, Texas.
⠿ **Balcones Baby Blue Corn Whisky** batch no. BB 12.9, bott 10 Oct 12 db (79.5) n20 t21 f19 b19.5. A small move in the right direction. The oils are still too cumbersome but the sugars at least outbox the nougat. 46%
Balcones Brimstone Texas Scrub Oak Smoked Corn Whisky batch no. BRM11-2, bott. 1/11/11 (94) n23 t23.5 f24 b23.5. Smoked bacon lovers, or devotees of Rupp smoked Alpine cheese, will be in their element. 53%

Balcones Brimstone Texas Scrub Oak Smoked Corn Whisky batch BRM 1200, bott 10 July 12 **(95.5)** n24 t24 f23.5 b24. When a distillery goes out of its way to offer something different, and then does so on a silver platter, one can only stand back and applaud. Take a bow distiller Chip Tate and the team: you are doing the whisky world a great service. *61.5%*

⫶ **Balcones Brimstone Texas Scrub Oak Smoked Corn Whisky** batch no. BRM 12.9, bott 12 db **(95.5)** n23.5 once had a smoky bacon aroma. Now the stakes have risen and we have a real Arbroath Smokie feel to this that anyone from the north east of Scotland will recognise and swoon at, though there is some serious sugars at play, too; t24 just adore that delivery: no prisoners taken, no compromise. It is all about the toasty oak with, it seems every last piece of burnt sugar extracted. The corn oil remains the perfect conduit through which the sweetness travels; f23.5 the usual hints of chocolate and fruit. But the smoke lasts the course now with a degree of elegance; b24.5 probably one of the most satisfying of all the world's whiskies. *53%*

Balcones Texas Single Malt Whisky Special Release finished in yard aged American/ French oak, batch SM12-3, bott 24 Apr 12 **(91)** n22 t23.5 f22.5 b23. A delicious malt that needs a lot of time and chewing. *52.9%. ncf*

⫶ **Balcones True Blue 100 Corn Whisky** batch no. TB100 12.4, bott 25 Oct 12 db **(86)** n21.5 t22 f21 b21.5. Strangely, a more conservative bottling than others. Maybe the strength, maybe just the batch. Certainly a little extra nougat instead of honeycomb and I feel, also, the fermentation had a bit to play in this. *50%*

Balcones True Blue Cask Strength Corn Whisky batch no. TB10-5, bott. 11/05/10 **(93.5)** n22 t23.5 f24.5 b23.5. Made from 100% Blue Corn, you could call this cornagraphic. It is certainly naked and gives you a rough, full-bodied ride...but also seduces you and caresses more tenderly than you could ever believe. A fabulous experience that will have you gasping for more...Believe me: a Texas star is born... *63%*

Balcones True Blue Cask Strength Corn Whisky batch TB/6/3 1 date: 10 July 12 **(95.5)** n24 t24.5 f23 b24. When they get it right, Balcones are unquestionably the masters of big whisky in the USA outside Kentucky and Tennessee. And certainly ahead of the game in the use of feints to positively steer the experience. What a character whisky...! *68.6%*

BALLAST POINT San Diego, California
⫶ **Devil's Share Single Malt Aged Four Years** (batch 001) **(84)** n20 t22.5 f20.5 b21. Enough feints on the nose and finish to take the gloss off an attractive first bottling from Ballast Point. Beyond the nougat, plenty of honey around to enjoy. But every distiller should remember that to move from a decent to a very good whiskey, the devil is in the detail... *46%*

BENJAMIN PRICHARD'S DISTILLERY Kelso, Tennessee.
Benjamin Prichard's Double Barrelled Bourbon 9 Years Old *(see bourbon section)*
Benjamin Prichard's Lincoln County Lightning Tennessee Corn Whiskey (89) n24 t22.5 f21 b22. Another white whiskey. This one is very well made and though surprisingly lacking oils and weight has more than enough charm and riches. *45%*
Benjamin Prichard's Tennessee Whiskey *(see Tennessee whiskey)*

BERKSHIRE MOUNTAIN DISTILLERS Great Barrington, Massachusetts.
Berkshire Bourbon Whiskey (91.5) n23 t23.5 f23 b23. A bourbon bursting with character: I am hooked! Another micro-gem. *43%*

BRECKENRIDGE DISTILLERY Breckenridge, Colorado.
Breckenridge Colorado Bourbon Whiskey Aged 2 Years (86) n22.5 t22 f20.5 b21. Full of character, big-hearted, chewy, slightly rugged bourbon where honey and cocoa thrives and spices make a telling impact. How apposite that probably the one and only town in Colorado named after a Kentuckian should end up making bourbon. Being close to 10,000 feet above sea level you'd think ice would come naturally with this one. But it does pretty well without it, believe me... *43%*

CATOCTIN CREEK DISTILLERY Loudoun County, Virginia.
Catoctin Creek Cask Proof Roundstone Rye Organic Single Barrel Whisky batch B12E1 **(88.5)** n21 enormous, but about as clumsy a rye as you'll find. Probably an age thing, but the grains and the premature liquorice on the oak notes aren't the greatest bedfellows...; t23 hold tight: this is one delivery taking no prisoners. A real mishmash of assorted, mildly aggressive tones, but again with that hickory-liquorice element coming out on top; f22 returns to a spicier, more grain dominant feel. The vanillas have the odd moment of glory; b22.5 a truly huge rye that, from a technical standpoint, fails its exams. But through a combination sheer delicious belligerence and chutzpah has your taste buds swooning. Great fun! *58%. Distilled from 100% rye. 134 bottles.*

CEDAR RIDGE DISTILLERY Swisher, Iowa.

Cedar Ridge Iowa Bourbon Whiskey barrel no. 124 **(87.5)** n21.5 sweetened broad leaf greens; earthy; **t23** hits its stride on delivery with the ryes making the most telling impact. A little fruity with soft vanilla and sugars; **f21** heavy oils from the distillate coats the busy grains, ramping up the spices a little; **b22** intriguing and entertaining, a complex bourbon which really maximizes the input of the small grains. *40%*

CHARBAY DISTILLERY Napa Valley, California.

Charbay Hop Flavoured Whiskey release II, barrels 3-7 **(91)** n22 t22 f23 b24. Being distilled from beer which includes hops, it can — and will - be argued that this is not beer at all. However, what cannot be disputed is that this is a rich, full-on spirit that has set out to make a statement and has delivered it. Loudspeaker and all. *55%*

CLEAR CREEK DISTILLERY Portland, Oregon.

McCarthy's Oregon Single Malt batch W11-01, bott 11 **(95)** n23 t23.5 f24.5 b24 Simply adorable whiskey. Not only consistent - has stayed exactly on course though I hadn't tasted it for a couple of years - but refuses to stint on its complexity. Remains an American institution. *42.5%*

McCarthy's Oregon Single Malt Single Barrel Cask Strength cask no. 158, bott 1 Nov 10 **(94.5)** n23.5 t24 f23 b24. Probably the most Islay-style of all the McCarthy offerings. Rather than the trademark smoky bacon, here we get an unmistakable sea-salty edge to this both on nose and delivery. But, above all, it is the evenness of the smoke, its patient building of phenols which impresses most. Attach that to the sublime softness of the mouth feel and you have a single malt cask of almost outrageous elegance. *49%. sc.*

McCarthy's Oregon Single Malt Aged 3 Years batch W10-01, bott 8 Nov 10 **(95)** n23.5 t24 f23.5 b24. I am not sure any micro whisky distillery in the US can do charm and elegance quite like Clear Creek does with its McCarthy's. Here is another bottling which puffs out far bigger smoke than you at first realize, rather in the way Ardbeg does. And in this non-smoky bacon style, Ardbeg is its closest relation in style. A masterful single malt which keeps you smokily spellbound. *42.5%*

McCarthy's Oregon Single Malt Aged 3 Years batch W12-01, bott 7 May 2012 **(95)** n24 t23 f24 b24. I doubt if you could find, outside of the tropics, such a relatively young whisky with so vibrant and complex a personality. *42.5%*

⁖ **McCarthy's Oregon Single Malt Aged 3 Years** batch W13-01 bott Feb 13 **(93.5)** n23.5 no one does smoky bacon quite like Clear Creek...; **t23** the smoke arrives upfront and vanishes for a second before regrouping. The intervening moments are filled with thick fudge and vanilla; **f23.5** the spice and sugars which had been around since the first moments now get a chance to shine in the smoke...if you see what I mean...; **b23.5** McCarthy's in its usual irresistible form. *42.5%*

⁖ **McCarthy's Oregon Single Malt Aged 3 Years** batch W13-02 **(90.5)** n22 a very modest degree of smoke this time round, with the sugars also curiously absent; **t22.5** silky delivery with the accent firmly on the fudge; toasty dry middle; **f23** the smoke and spice take time to gather, but when they arrive, they do so with some zip and intent; **b23** one of the lighter bottlings I have come across over the years. The spices, though, don't take a day off. *42.5%*

COLORADO GOLD DISTILLERY Cedaredge, Colorado.

Colorado Gold Straight Bourbon Over Two Years Old Single Barrel bott 8 Oct 11 **(86.5)** n21 t23 f21 b21.5. A bit of a whippersnapper of a bourbon. The nose and finish may lack depth. But it is a whiskey bursting with personality and the delivery is an understated treat. A light mocha thread weaves in and out of the muscovado. Fun. *40%*

COPPER FOX DISTILLERY Sperryville, Virginia.

⁖ **Copper Fox "Rye Whisky" Aged 14 Months** bott 11 Jul 13 **(91)** n22.5 crisp, meaningful rye with bells on. Minty spice and earthy, too; **t23** those rye notes really do gang together. Sublime firmness; all you could wish for. The mint is back for the middle, pleasantly cradled in chocolate; **f22.5** soft oils, and a few muscovado notes trill with the rye; **b23** when is rye whisky not a rye whisky? When it is matured in ex-bourbon barrels, rather than virgin oak for a start. Like this whisky is. So the quote marks are mine, not the label's. That said, purely from a tasting perspective: beautiful! Probably as good a rye type yet to come out of Sperryville. Just need to work on the label... *45%*

Wasmund's Distiller's Art Series Single Malt Spirit dist 03/03/11, less than 30 days old **(92)** n23.5 t23 f22.5 b23. The light smoke of 60% applewood and 40% cherrywood really makes itself count, especially in the quite sexy nose. A beautifully characterful and superbly weighted spirit. *62%*

⋯ **Wasmund's Single Malt Whisky 13 Months Old** batch 94 **(94.5)** n23 the cherry wood both offers tannin and sweetness in equal measure, while the apple grapples with the spice; t23.5 sublime oils and sugars on delivery making the weight spot on and enough sweetness around to absorb the big tannin session which crashes like a tree in a forest; the middle now really concentrates on the ulmo honey, complete with light waxy train; f24 almost perfect. The smoke has gathered softly, the honey glows, the wood elements join the heavier phenols to create the base...gorgeous! b24 distiller Rick Wasmund gets flavours into and out of his whisky like a magician conjures a dove from a hat. Here he has exceeded himself by removing the taughtness which comes with over aging or overdoing the apple and cherry wood smoke. Here he has called it right. Superb. 48% (96 Proof) ncf

Wasmund's Single Malt Whisky 14 Months Old Batch No. 52 (91.5) n22 t23 f23 b23. Makes a huge lightly honeyed statement: superb! 48%. ncf.

CORNELIUS PASS ROADHOUSE DISTILLERY Hillsboro, Oregon.
McMenamins C.P.R. White Owl Distillery (93) n23.5 t23 f23 b23.5. Top dollar White Dog. Huge amount of copper helps expose all the honey available, especially on the nose. Superbly distilled and surging with barley and spice. 49.3%

CORSAIR ARTISAN DISTILLERY Nashville, Tennessee.
Corsair Rye Moon (85) n20 t22.5 f21 b21.5. A sweet, well-weighted white dog with surprisingly little bite. The odd intense, crystalline rye moment is a joy. 46% (92 proof)

Corsair Aged Rye (73.5) n18 t18 f19 b18.5. Hot and anarchic, not as well made as the Rye Moon. But has enough playful character to keep you guessing what's coming next. 46%

Corsair Triple Smoke (92.5) n24 t23 f22 b23.5. The odd technical flaw, to pick nits. But, overall, a lovely whiskey with a curiously polite smoke style which refuses to dominate. Teasingly delicate and subtle...and different. 40%

DARK CORNER DISTILLERY Greenville, South Carolina
Dark Corner Moonshine Corn Whiskey (77.5) n18.5 t22 f18 b19. Full blooded sweet corn on delivery. But could do with some extra copper elsewhere. 50%

Lewis Redmond Bourbon Aged 10 Months batch 1, dist Oct 11, bott Jul 12 **(76.5)** n19 t21 f18 b18.5. Big, almost creamy sugar surge early on. But struggles again without sufficient copper to ensure richness and balance. 43%

DARK HORSE DISTILLERY Lenexa, Kansas
⋯ **Dark Horse Reserve Bourbon Less Than Four Years Old** Batch 2 **(93)** n23 huge vanilla and toffee apple; ticks every bourbony box with a lovely toasted honey buzz; t23.5 exceptional. The tannins arrive in tandem with the molasses. The liquorice is clean and deep, the manuka honey keeps a watchful eye. A slow spice arrival; f23 back to colossal vanilla with a spiced cream toffee finale; b23.5 Even though they appear to have used oak chips to bolster the overall richness of this bourbon, there is no taking away that this is the closest any whiskey produced by a microdistiller comes to the true Kentucky style. But even there, there are few which display so much vanilla. 44.5% (89 proof)

⋯ **Dark Horse Reunion Rye Less Than Four Years Old** Batch 2 **(89)** n22 rye on heat and a hint of clove; t23 the rye grain is so sharp you can cut your tongue on it: it is first to hit the taste buds and the last to leave. There is a little more extra oil than desired, bringing toasted honeycomb; f22 big oils again, though remains juicy and spicy; b22 another enormous, and truly memorable, offering from Dark Horse which is unambiguous in its style. Here, though, the cut was perhaps a little over generous (costing a point or two) with the very sharpest notes sacrificed. That said: just so big and delicious! 44.5% (89 proof)

⋯ **Long Shot White Whiskey** distilled from bourbon mash **(88.5)** n22 t22.5 f22 b22. Seriously good, honest white dog: well made and gives the corn a free hand to shine. Love it. 40% (80 proof)

DISTILLERY 291 Colorado Springs, Colorado.
⋯ **291 Fresh Colorado Whiskey** Batch 13 **(87.5)** n21.5 t22 f22 b22. As near as damn it identical to the notes above! Talk about consistency! 45% (90 proof)

⋯ **291 Colorado Rye Whiskey White Dog** Aged Less than a week, batch 10 **(86.5)** n21 t21 f23 b21.5. A much tamer version of the last one I got my hands on. The rye gets bullied by other factors more easily, too. The finish, though, is superb. 50.8% (101.7 proof)

291 Colorado Whiskey Aspen Stave Finished rye malt mash, barrel no. 2 **(94)** n23 t24 f23.5 b23.5. A superb, enigmatic rye which ticks every box: they are obviously fast learners! 50.8%

⋯ **American Whiskey** Aged 3 months **(73)** n18 t19 f18 b18. Busy. Spices aplenty. But nothing sits right. 43% (86 proof)

∵ **Bad Guy Bourbon** aged 379 days barrel # 1 **(95.5)** n23.5 huge cloves (from oak, usually!) abound; massive wall of rye and muscovado sugar... just so bloody enticing; **t24.5** what the f***!!! Flip, that's the word I was looking for... How can you get such an avalanche of advanced flavours from something so juvenile? Again, cloves and cinnamon to the fore followed by a gallery of crisp sugars. The ulmo honey moving in just takes the Mickey. Pure, clean, intense, fruity, sugary and...stunning! **f24** the spices are in overdrive, the sugars act only as a counterpoint. Still the cinnamon and cloves rumble. How the heck have they done that? **b24** arguably the most astonishing whisky of its age worldwide of the year. That a whiskey just a year old can be this good is obscene. But just proves: the bad guys always win... 56.1%

∵ **Black Mountain Colorado Bourbon** aged 9 months barrel #1 **(87)** n22 big rye and cloves; **t21.5** so young, it should be illegal! Mouth-watering, fresh and youthful with firm corn and firmer rye; **f22** now oils up dramatically with cinnamon and cloves at finale; **b21.5** oily and in your face, despite the big colour, it has been unable to entirely shrug of the white dog bark. That said, the sheer abandon of the cough sweet sugars combined with surging spice – with cinnamon and cloves prevalent - makes for gripping sipping. 46% (92 proof)

∵ **Colorado Bourbon** (Aspen stave finished) **(85)** n20.5 t21.5 f22 b21. A very young, sweet dude but thin bodied and, though attractive, somewhat over reliant on the manuka honey. 52.5% (105 proof)

∵ **Colorado Whiskey** from rye malt mash **(86.5)** n19 t22 f23 b22.5. The nose may be worryingly thin and young. But the magnificence and intensity of the stark rye on delivery and follow-through makes for astonishing drinking. For all of its obvious limitations, its mixture of intensity and youth somehow catapult you back to a time when Colorado was first being colonised. This is probably the closest thing to true, unadulterated, frontier whiskey I've ever tasted. Now, where've I put those dirty glasses....? 56.8% (113.6 proof)

∵ **Colorado Whiskey** from rye malt mash **(84)** n20 t22 f21 b21. This soaring eagle of a whiskey is just too bald, too often. 57.5% (115 proof)

DELAWARE PHOENIX DISTILLERY Walton, New York.

Rye Dog Batch 11-1 (78.5) n19 t21.5 f18 b19. Sweet, distinctive rye tang but a little short on copper sheen. 50% (100 proof)

DOWNSLOPE DISTILLING Centennial, Colorado.

∵ **Double Diamond** aged 3 Years American/French oak batch RV-003 dist 1 June 2010 **(91.5)** n22.5 all kinds of fruit and fruitcake covers the nose, but burnt raisin mostly; the oak is profound...; **t22** and on the delivery, also, though it settles quickly into a more creamy mocha-style; the fruit forms a healthy sub stratum; **f23** the spices grab hold and give the fudge and raisin attitude; finishes with chocolate milkshake; **b24** the degree of oak is a challenge. But in the end you finish shaking your head in wonderment as to how so many vastly different and unlikely aspects of a whiskey somehow fit together. Good going, guys! 50.5% (101 proof)

∵ **Double Diamond** aged 3 Years French oak batch SR-005A dist 10 May 2010 **(87)** n21.5 any more oak and I'll be having splinters extracted from my nose for the next six months...a little fruit soothes; **t21.5** puckering oak – no surprise. Didn't see that juicy malt and grape coming, though; **f22.5** at last settles into a rhythm as the spices dig into the figs and sultanas; **b21.5** in your face oak. Yet somehow salivating. You don't find that very often! A drunkard of dram, staggering without a script...but what fun! 52% (104 proof)

Double Diamond Whiskey Limited Edition French oak, batch MW-001, dist 8 Jan 10, bott 1 Apr 12 **(90)** n22 t23.5 f22 b22.5. For a young whisky this packs a fabulous degree of complexity and depth. Can't wait until it's a grown up... 43%. 225 bottles.

DRY FLY DISTILLING Spokane, Washington

∵ **Dry Fly Bourbon 101 (88)** n21.5 busy tannin: very heavy oak bias with the corn an afterthought; **t23** superb delivery using its power to good effect. Here the small grains twinkle and the oak goes through some sugary gears before going into a cocoa-based autopilot; **f21.5** like the nose, thins to surprisingly basic elements; **b22** a well made bourbon which, with a bit of extra complexity, would stand above some of its Kentucky colleagues. 50.5%

∵ **Dry Fly Cask Strength Straight Wheat Whiskey (94.5)** n23 busy aroma, similar to the Washington wheat bottling with toasted Hovis, except here a couple of slices have been forgotten for a minute or so in the toaster; **t24** beautifully intense sugar and spice on delivery. The same rich sugar cane, except with a little molten muscovado in the mix as well; a cake mix with gentle oils and a squeeze of citrus forms the middle; **f23.5** back to lightly salted butter on brown toast...with a drizzle of sugars; **b24** quite beautiful whiskey. One every whisky lover should experience to further their understanding of this multi-faceted spirit. 60%

❊ **Dry Fly Port Finish Wheat Whiskey** (89) n22 plum and strawberry jam on toast; t23 silky delivery allowing soft sugars to form before the spices punch their way through; f22 chocolate liqueur finale; b22 if you mixed whiskey and jam you might end up with this little charmer. 50% (100 proof)

❊ **Dry Fly Straight Triticale Rye Wheat Hybrid** (86) n22 t22 f21 b21. Pleasant and easy going. But very surprising degree of natural caramels fill in the gaps and shaves off the higher notes expected from the rye. 44% (88 proof)

❊ **Dry Fly Washington Wheat Whiskey** (89) n22 beautifully toasty: warm Hovis with a caramel and maple spread; t22 succulent with a slow release of the expected spices. Juicy sugar cane begins to gather weight as the drier oaky elements begin to form; f22.5 superb bittersweet fade just as the first light oils gather. Some rich Dundee fruit cake makes a late stand; b22.5 hugely impressive, well weighted and balanced and a much better use of wheat than bread, for instance... 40%

EASTSIDE DISTILLING Portland, Oregon

Burnside Bourbon 4 Year Barrel-Aged bott 2012 (92) n24 beautiful! So complex with the small grains performing somersaults to ensure balance remains the key; t23.5 delicate muscovado sugars and ulmo honey get this one off to a flyer. Just fades in the middle as the oils come through, though not before a liquorice and honeycomb surge delights; f22 happy to settle for a vanilla-led finale; b22.5 "Put some sideburns on your face!" screams the back label. Well, a whiskey far too gracious to put hairs on your chest though it would be a close shave to choose this or a Kentucky 4-y-o as one of the best young bourbon noses of the year...Just bristles with charm. 48%

EDGEFIELD DISTILLERY Troutdale, Oregon.

Edgefield Hogshead Whisky 100% malted barley, batch 12-B (94) n23.5 chocolate and Lubec marzipan; honeycomb nougat; a little kumquat accumulates with air; t24 superb texture with an almost perfect degree of oil. The barley has as much scope as it needs to shine; there is a juicy element as well as a weightier oakiness, inevitably heading towards a heather-honey sweetness; f23 an elegant fade with more nougat honey and mocha; still heavy on the oils; b23.5 been a little while since I lasted tasted Edgefield. At that time they were seriously getting their act together. Now they deserve star billing in any bar. This is sheer quality and even though the cut is very fractionally wide, the two years in new oak has ensured something bordering magnificence. 46%

FINGER LAKES DISTILLING Burdett, New York.

Glen Thunder Corn Whiskey (92.5) n23.5 t23 f23 b23. Beautifully distilled, copper rich, Formula 1 quality, absolutely classic corn white dog. 45% (90 proof)

❊ **White Pike Whiskey Aged 18 Minutes** (91) n22.5 t23.5 f22 b23. Top notch white dog more full of flavour than any pike you are ever likely to catch. Maybe 19 minutes in cask might have just taken the edge of the complexity. So well done, boys. Beautifully made distillate, even if slightly copper challenged, where the grains really do stand and be counted and the sugars are slick and sing to you. Created from organic spelt, corn and malted wheat ostensibly as a mixing spirit: that would be a waste. 40%

FLORIDA FARM DISTILLERS Umatilla, Florida

❊ **Palm Ridge Reserve Handmade Micro Batch Florida Whiskey** orange and oak wood Less the 1 Year Old batch 29 (94.5) n23 big rye signature to the nose: fruity, light and easy on the corn oils. Some hints of marzipan, trimmed apple and very old marmalade; aggressive tannin; t24 I doubt if I will experience a more gentle landing on the palate for any US whiskey this year. Just enough oil to absorb the impact of the small grains and, again, the ryes run riot ensuring a juicy, spicy theme throughout. A little Parma Violet candy represents an earthiness which balances the complex, non-specific fruit doing the rounds; f23.5 no great age to this guy (and I wrote that before I spotted the admitted maturation!), but the way the ulmo, manuka and orange-blossom honeys combine, depth is maintained; b24 I can see why everyone heads to Florida in the winter: obviously to try and grab one of the meager 6,000 bottles of this on offer each year. This is beautifully crafted, truly adorable whiskey where fruit appears to constantly have its hand on the tiller. And rather than blast in like a Hurricane from the sea, it breezes gently around the glass and palate with an easy elegance. I have relatives in Florida: about time I gave them another visit... 45% (90 proof)

GARRISON BROTHERS Hye, Texas.

❊ **Garrison Brothers Texas Straight Bourbon 2010 Aged Two Years** Spring 2013 (91) n23 what an improvement over two years! Virtually feint free and bursting with bourbon-ness in every direction. Particularly big on the manuka honey and cough sweet departments, some spice also makes an introductory ahem; **t23** similar to how I remember it a couple of years back with a big, oily statement and massive Demerara sugars. A little marmalade and marzipan also take a bow; **f22** the "virtually" bit of the feint free turns up, but so intense is the hickory and cocoa, it remains seriously enjoyable; **b23** a fascinating bourbon, made from local organic corn, which for a two-year-old is simply brimming with personality. The intensity and balance of the sugars and more bitter toastiness is a constant delight. Still room for improvement, but just love this magnificent stuff. Mind you, still waiting for the Hye Rye... *47%*

⊹ **Cowboy Bourbon Texas Straight Bourbon Whiskey Aged Three Years** (96) **n23.5** could be a blueprint for a solid bourbon aroma: beautifully waxy and nutty with a gathering of ever more intensifying tannins, the spice always well proportioned; **t24** massive. Not exactly Stagg like, as this has some very helpful sweetness to lessen the impact. And there is obviously less age involved. But, again, the weight and pace of the heavier notes, the citrus-studded hickory, even hints of burnt fruit cake (presumably from the rye) are all set to ensure maximum flavour fulfillment; treacle tinged with ulmo honey; **f24** now lightens to allow the liquorice and Sumatra coffee to mix and relax; the treacle lessens to Demerara and manuka honey; the waves just keep on lapping for a ridiculously long finish; **b24.5** I always know when I have a truly great whiskey on my hands: it takes every ounce of my professionalism to spit it out! This has, and make no mistake, raised the bar for bourbon made by the micro distillers: it is truly world class, three year old or not. In fact the name is a misnomer: there are no cowboys at work here. This is darned tootin' fine whiskey. Yesiree! *68%. 600 bottles.*

GOLDEN NORTHWEST DISTILLERY Bow, Washington.
⊹ **Golden Artisan Spirits Single Barrel Cask Strength** (88) **n20.5** a little gruff, but redeemed by some coconut and maple syrup; **t22.5** and it's the maple syrup which is first out of the trenches backed by decimated coconut drenched in manuka honey; **f23** the highpoint by a distance as the honey is joined by deep liquorice...and welcome spice; **b22** much more like it! Not exactly textbook but excellent body and some lovely honey touches. *62.3%*

⊹ **Golden Reserve Samish Bay Single Malt** (85.5) **n20 t23 f21 b21.5**. From the nougat, molasses and chocolate school of distilling. Some honeycomb around, too. Actually, quite like its roughhouse antics on the palate. *40% (80 proof)*

⊹ **Samish Bay Peated Single Malt** (79) **n19 t20 f20 b20**. The lightest smoke imaginable is somewhat overshadowed by the nougat and honey feints. Pleasant if a bit rough and unready. *43% (86 proof)*

GRAND TRAVERSE DISTILLERY Traverse City, Michigan
⊹ **Bourbon Whiskey** (88.5) **n21** a bit of youth makes for a slightly green, peppery aroma with limited harmony....; **t22** which cannot be said of the delivery. Young, for sure, but small-grain punchy and with chocolate honeycomb. The spices sprint off from the start while muscovado sugars form; **f23** we are now in deepest bourbon territory; thick liquorice, huge surges of vanilla, hints of molasses; **b22.5** an absolute charmer which just gets better as it goes along. *46% (92 proof)*

⊹ **Ole George Straight Rye Whiskey** (80) **n19 t21 f20 b20**. Hard to mark this one. As a rye, it marks relatively low. As a gin, it would be higher. Not sure why, but there seems to be all kinds of botanical aromas and flavours involved here. Pleasant as a spirit – and I love the mouth feel. But the flavour make up is skewed. *46.5% (93 proof)*

GREAT LAKES DISTILLERY Milwaukee, Wisconsin.
KinnicKinnic A Blend of American Whiskies (87) **n21.5 t22.5 f21 b22**. The bitterness is replaced by an extra dollop of nougat and honey. *43% (86 proof)* ⊙ ⊙

HIGH WEST DISTILLERY Park City, Utah.
High West Silver Oat (86) **n20 t22 f22 b22**. A white whiskey which at times struggles to find all the copper it needs. But so delicious is that sweet oat – a style that has enjoyed similar success in Austria – that some of the technical aberrations are forgiven. Soft and friendly. *40%*

HOUSE SPIRITS DISTILLERY Portland, Oregon
⊹ **Westward Oregon Straight Malt Whiskey 2 Years Old** batch 1 (92.5) **n23** a coating of vanilla to the intense barley and maple syrup; **t23.5** superb degree of oils ensure the barley clings thickly to the plate. Ulmo honey and light hickory intermingle as the spices begin a gentle journey; **f23** the spices now fizz a little and a delicate, non-specific fruit tang attaches to the dry barley; the vanillas are confident and creamy; just a tad too much lasting bitterness; **b23.5** two years old, perhaps. But absolute star quality with the barley pulsing at every turn: just so satisfyingly mouth-filling and palate teasing. Another great whiskey from Portland. *45%*

KINGS COUNTY DISTILLERY Brooklyn, New York.
Kings County Moonshine Corn Whisky (92) n23 t23 f23 b23. Absolutely spot on corn whiskey: sweet, clean, berry-fruity, very well made; does exactly what it says on the tin. 40%

KOVAL DISTILLERY Chicago, Illinois.
Lion's Pride Dark Millett Whiskey (86) n19 t23 f22 b22. Borat, my late and deeply missed budgie, was occasionally known to stick his beak in a glass of whisky when I was looking... and always tried to come back for more. Well, we'd be fighting over this one. Again the nose is hardly enticing. But this time on the palate we have shards of honeycomb among tangy spices. Much more oil, too, which helps the finish distribute the sugars to the very death. Get the nose cleaned up, and this would be a whiskey worth squawking about. 40%. 100% millett.

Lion's Pride Rye (88) n21 t23 f22 b22. A really enjoyable, well distilled whiskey. But you'd never guess it was a rye.. 40% (80 Proof)

MISSISSIPPI RIVER DISTILLERY Le Claire, Indiana
❖ **Cody Road Bourbon 2013** Batch 1 (91.5) n23.5 toasted brown wheat bread with a perfectly understated sublime manuka- and ulmo honey sweetness. Wow! t23 the delivery offers both spice and molten muscovado sugars in equal measure; the midground thickens and becomes almost doughy; f22 a little bitterness counters the continuing sugars; b23 you really don't need to be told this is a wheat recipe bourbon! A fabulously made whiskey of rare character. 45% (90 proof)

❖ **Cody Road Rye 2013** Batch 4 (86.5) n23 t22.5 f20 b21. The clean, fruity unambiguous rye on the nose is stunning. There is nothing too shoddy about the crisp, juicy grain on delivery, either. Just bitters out a little too enthusiastically from the midpoint onwards. 40%

MOYLAN'S DISTILLING COMPANY Petaluma, California.
Moylan's 2004 Cherry Wood Smoked Single Malt Cask Strength (94) n24 easily one of the most subtle of all America's micro distillery whiskeys and is unusual in not trying to make an early statements of intent. The smoke does no more than furnish a thin, earthy gloss to the delicate array of lightly fruited vanillas: absolutely beguiling; t23.5 more of the same: a distinctive sharp kumquat note injects life into the vanilla; f23 long yet without a hint of oil with light spices and cocoa playing happily together; again there is a faint, fruity glass to the finale; b23.5 a top drawer, quite beautifully distilled and matured, malt which goes much easier on the smoke than you'd expect but is bubbling with personality...and quality. Bravo! 49.5%

NEW HOLLAND BREWING COMPANY Holland, Michigan.
❖ **Beer Barrel Bourbon** (86.5) n21.5 t22 f21.5 b21.5. A distinctly different bourbon, not least because it has been finished for three months in beer barrels. This really only becomes evident on the latest moments of the finish, when a slightly hoppy roast barley character emerges. The base Indiana-originating bourbon is decent enough, though you get the feeling the higher notes and rough edges have been blunted by the beer. 40% (80 proof)

❖ **Bill's Michigan Wheat** (85.5) n22 t21 f21.5 b21. A wheat whisky named in honour of an old friend of mine, Bill Owens, a shining beacon in the world of micro distilling. Kind of a fitting tribute, too, as the somewhat oily and bitter marmalade characteristics are always more likely to be found on a small still than from the big Kentucky boys. 45% (90 proof)

❖ **Brewer's Whiskey Malt Whiskey Aged Six Months** batch 3 (87) n21.5 a curious mix of mocha and distant hop; t22.5 beautiful delivery; the body is exceptional, as is the early, teasing spice. The sugars start out alone but are eventually caught up by pleasing praline and more spice; f21 a hint towards kumquats towards the end...as well as hard, semi-bitter hop!! b22 in the previous Bible, we had batch 1 of their Double Down Barley: this is, effectively batch 3. A better working this time, though the late finish is still challenging. 45% (90 proof)

Zeppelin Bend Straight Malt Whiskey (87.5) n21 a very simplistic marriage of malt and sugar; t22 so sweet and juicy: grist on steroids with a real spicy charge; f22 light citrus mixes into the malt meal; becomes quite edgy and bitter towards the last moments; b22.5 a massively improved whiskey, though untaxing. Shows off the malt like no other in the US. 45% (90 proof) ⊙ ⊙

PEACH STREET DISTILLERS Pallisade, Colorado.
Colorado Straight Bourbon Aged More Than 2 Years batch 21 (89.5) n22 t23 f22 b22.5. A gentle, beautifully made bourbon where the characters evolve in super slow-mo. The flavours are a decibel lower than the norm: seemingly a club under par throughout. 46%

❖ **Colorado Straight Bourbon Aged More Than Two Years** batch 40 (92.5) n22.5 sharp hickory and caramel, flinty fruit and almost Indian-style spiced nuts; t23.5 has that soothing mouth-feel on delivery of the oozy inside of a throat lozenge, except the flavours differ dramatically. For the odd moment you feel that malt is present, but soon we go into familiar manuka honey territory, as well as liquorice; the spices pick up pace with aplomb; **f23** a quality finale, with the spices gently raging, the rye notes riling and other familiar bourbon tones tantalising...; **b23.5** the last bottle I tasted was around the batch 20 mark and was an impressive intro to this distillery. Remarkably, this batch enjoys an almost identical thumb print. But now there is much more sharpness and definition. Superb! 46% (92 proof)

RANGER CREEK DISTILLING, San Antonio, Texas

⸭ **Ranger Creek .36 Texas Bourbon** batch 13 **(93) n23** mega honey and liquorice: superbly weighted; **t23.5** again huge liquorice, perhaps pepped by the odd aniseed ball, before manuka honey and treacle weigh in; there are chewy vanillas to break up the intensity as well as chocolate toffee; **f23** scorched honeycomb and marzipan with just the right amount of sugars to make for a comfortable finale; **b23.5** I would so love to get back to Texas and have this wash down a plate-filling, half cooked ribeye. It's pretty obvious they have used small barrels to create a gentle giant like this – even before you find confirmation on the bottle. This comes under their Small Caliber series of whiskeys. Don't you believe it: this is a howitzer of a bourbon. 48% (96 proof)

⸭ **Ranger Creek Rimfire Mesquite Smoked Texas Single Malt** batch 1 **(85) n21.5 t22 f20.5 b21.** As I have never tasted anything smoked with mesquite before – especially whiskey – I will have to guess that it is the tree of the semi-desert which is imparting a strange, mildly bitter tang on the finish. Whether it is also responsible for the enormous degree of creamed toffee, I am also not sure. Enjoyable, fascinating even...but something the ol' taste buds need a bit of acclimatising to. 43% (86 proof)

RANSON SPIRITS Sheridan, Oregon.

Whipper Snapper Oregon Spirit Whisky (86.5) n21.5 t22 f21.5 b21.5. A curiously thin offering for all the obvious corn apparent. Some walnut oil and light Demerara do offer some meat on the vanilla. 42%

ROCK TOWN DISTILLERY Little Rock, Arkansas.

⸭ **Arkansas Hickory Smoked Whiskey** batch 8 **(87.5) n21.5** a very different kind of sweet smoke, spreading sugar on the bacon; **t21** thin delivery and sharp. Takes about the fourth flavour wave for the oils to gather and the smoke to fall back into place; **f23** delicious smoked chocolate; **b22** a bit of a screwball whiskey on delivery but the finale is to die for. 45%

⸭ **Arkansas Young Bourbon Whiskey** batch 12 **(89) n22.5** now that has a very serious bourbon thumbprint; **t22** fizzing, nipping tannin and then a line of soft brown sugars and maple syrup to kiss the taste buds better; **f22** corn oily and late liquorice; **b22.5** gentle, sweet and all-round adorable. 46% (92 proof)

ROGUE SPIRITS Newport, Oregon

⸭ **Dead Guy Whiskey Aged One Month (73) n21 t22 f14 b16.** Salt and honey, especially on delivery, make for a lovely opening gambit. The finish, alas, takes you via the graveyard. 50%

⸭ **Shatoe Rogue Oregon Single Malt Aged 3 Months (76.5) n18.5 t19 f20 b19.** Needs a bit more copper to brighten the experience. The growing sugars help. 40% (80 proof)

ROUGHSTOCK DISTILLERY Bozeman, Montana.

Roughstock Black Label (92.5) n22.5 t23.5 f23 b23.5. A very beautiful malt whiskey very well made which underlines the happy marriage between barley and virgin oak. A stunner! 64%

ST GEORGE SPIRITS Alameda, California.

St George Single Malt Lot 10 (90) n22 t23 f22.5 b22.5. Welcome back, my old friend! One of the grand-daddies of the micro distilling world and sticking to its guns for one of the fruitiest of all the malts out there. Even if not technically perfect, this is a three course meal of a malt. And so fruity, this one will appeal to rye lovers, too. In fact, it'll slay you... 40%

SAINT JAMES SPIRITS Irwindale, California.

Peregrine Rock (83.5) n21 t20.5 f21.5 b20.5. Fruity and friendly, the wine and smoke combo work well-ish enough but the thumping oak injection highlights that maybe there isn't quite enough body to take in the aging. Perhaps less time in the barrel will reduce the bitter orange finale. 40%

SANTA FE SPIRITS Santa Fe, New Mexico.

Silver Coyote Pure Malt Whiskey (72.5) n16 t21 f17.5 b18. This is made from malted barley, has never seen the inside of an oak barrel yet is called whiskey. Most probably there is some law I am unaware of regarding definitions of whiskey...especially in New Mexico. Even so, not a bad first attempt and on delivery gives a pretty good account of itself as the oils kick in. But somewhere along the line, to significantly up the quality, they have to, among other things (like sorting out the cut), get the spirit to enjoy a lot more contact with copper. A noble effort and I am sure they will improve as they get to know their distillery. Good luck, guys! *40% (80 Proof)*

STEIN DISTILLERY Joseph, Oregon.

Straight Rye Whiskey Aged 2 Years cask no. 7 (88) n23 no doubting the grains at work here: big fruity rye at that lovely stage between sharp and sweet; t22 silky, oily, mildly feinty delivery but the excellence of the rye powers through; f21 the oils offer a spicy buzz; softening caramels; b22 a whiskey which offers up the grains to the full spotlight. A little more care with the cut and we have something special on our hands. *40%*

STONE BARN BRANDYWORKS DISTILLERY Portland, Oregon.

Hard Eight Unoaked Rye Whiskey (86.5) n22.5 t21.5 f21 b21.5. The excellent fruity-rye nose does not quite show the width of the cut which creates a buzzing oiliness. Good brown sugar balance. *40%*

STRANAHAN DISTILLERY Denver, Colorado.

Stranahan's Colorado Whiskey Small Batch dist Dec 05, cask no. 225 (94.5) n24 t23.5 f23 b24. Absolutely magnificent; a malt which never stays still in the glass. By the way, boys: the message on the label to me brought a lump to my throat. Thank you. *47% (94 Proof). sc.*

Stranahan's Colorado Whiskey Batch No. 59 dist Jul 08 (92) n21.5 t24 f23 b23.5. Very complex. Very classy. The interplay of the sugars and spice is utterly world class and the bourbon notes which sing at regular intervals do so with a very clear voice. *47%*

Stranahan's Colorado Whiskey Batch No. 60 dist Jul 08 (94.5) n23 t24.5 f23 b24. Two whiskeys obviously distilled on the same day (see Batch 59)...and a fascinating variance... This is Stranahan at its most communicative. And brilliant! *47% (94 Proof)*

Stranahan's Colorado Whiskey Batch No. 61 dist Aug 08 (90.5) n22 t22.5 f23 b23. Back to its mega fudge state. Lovely whisky. *47% (94 Proof)*

Stranahan's Colorado Whiskey Batch No. 62 dist Sep 08 (92) n23 t23.5 f22.5 b23. They appear to have hit a rich seem of consistency. My word: I love this distillery...! *47% (94 Proof)*

Stranahan's Colorado Whiskey Batch #65 dist 1 Dec 08 (87.5) n23 t21.5 f21.5 b21.5. The superb honeys on the nose fail to fully manifest themselves on the palate. Big and caramel rich, but not without being spicy. *47%*

Stranahan's Colorado Whiskey Batch #66 dist 15 Jan 08 (87.5) n21 t22.5 f22 b22. Earthy and offering more vegetables on nose before heading off to gather the honey. *47%*

Stranahan's Colorado Whiskey Batch #67 dist 30 Dec 08 (96) n24 t24.5 f23.5 b24. You can tell Colorado is in the mountains: this rocks! *47%*

Stranahan's Colorado Whiskey Batch #68 dist 15 Feb 09 (91) n22 t23 f23 b23. Mines every last caramel atom from the oak. Soft, sexy, understated and complex. *47%*

Stranahan's Colorado Whiskey Batch #69 dist 31 Mar 09 (79) n18 t22 f19 b20. Recovers beautifully from an awful nose, thanks to a sugary injection. Relapses, though. *47%*

Stranahan's Colorado Whiskey Batch #70 dist 19 Apr 09 (84) n19.5 t22 f21 b21.5. Oily: a wide cut dishes out the nougat, slaps on the honeys and spices up. *47%*

Stranahan's Colorado Whiskey Batch #71 dist 20 Mar 09 (81.5) n19 t22 f19.5 b21. Returns to its recent vegetable theme. Honey injection at times harsh and bitter. *47%*

Stranahan's Colorado Whiskey Batch #72 dist 20 Mar 09 (92) n22.5 t23.5 f23 b23. Honey-nut bar nose and delivery; complex sugars; silky, spiced mocha finish. Superb! *47%*

Stranahan's Colorado Whiskey Batch #73 dist 7 July 09 (85) n19 t23 f21 b22. Lush and loud on delivery: a real depth to the acacia honey and liquorice. Still a tad too earthy on nose and finish. *47%*

Stranahan's Colorado Whiskey Batch #74 dist 2 Sept 09 (90.5) n22.5 t23 f22 b23. Full bodied, mouthwatering and chewy. Celebrates the sugar and spice element to the max. *47%*

Stranahan's Colorado Whiskey Batch #75 dist 11 Oct 09 (94.5) n23 t24 f23.5 b24. A striking whiskey which stops you in your tracks. Glorious! *47%*

Stranahan's Colorado Whiskey Batch #76 dist 2 Nov 09 (83) n20 t22 f20 b21. Too much generosity on the cut has upped the buzz on the experience a little too profoundly. *47%*

Stranahan's Colorado Whiskey Batch #77 dist 11 Nov 09 (87) n21 t22 f22 b22. Another Stranahan's that works overtime to maximize the sugars from the oak. Releases the caramels, too. *47%*

Stranahan's Colorado Whiskey Batch #78 dist 17 Dec 09 (91.5) n22 t24 f22.5 b23. Relaxed, softly spoken, classy and brimming with sugary intent. Muscovado sugars meet liquorice and manuka honey head on. *47%*

Stranahan's Colorado Whiskey Batch #79 dist 7 Jan 10 (87.5) n21.5 t23 f21 b22. Earthy and oily, wide cut spice. The sugars are thick, the vanilla deep. Feinty finale. 47%

Stranahan's Colorado Whiskey Batch #80 dist 13 Jan 10 (88.5) n22.5 t22 f22 b22. Caramel city, Colorado. 47%

Stranahan's Colorado Whiskey Batch #81 dist 14 Feb 10 (82) n19 t21 f21 b21. Huge whisky with the usual Demerara avalanche down the Rockies. But the feints are just too aggressive. 47%

Stranahan's Colorado Whiskey Batch #82 dist 7 Mar 10 (88) n21 t22.5 f22 b22.5. Clean, simplistic, sugary and another which concentrates on the oaky caramel. 47%

Stranahan's Colorado Whiskey Batch #83 dist 20 Mar 10 (95) n23.5 t23.5 f24 b24. A rare example of where the malt element of the whisky overcomes the bourbon aspect. Magnificent complexity: just shows what a marginally thinner cut can do... 47%

Stranahan's Colorado Whiskey Batch #84 dist 4 Apr 10 (84.5) n21 t22 f20 b21.5. Lots of liquorice but also on the bitter side. 47%

Stranahan's Colorado Whiskey Batch #85 dist 4 Apr 10 (84.5) n21.5 t22 f20 b21. Similar to #84, even to the bitter off-key finish. Suggests the problem is not a rogue barrel. 47%

Stranahan's Colorado Whiskey Batch #86 dist 10 May 10 (92.5) n22.5 t24 f23 b23. Clean, malty with brown sugars which decorate the big vanilla spine. Elegant, intense, complex. 47%

Stranahan's Colorado Whiskey Batch #87 dist 16 May 10 (85.5) n19 t22 f22.5 b22. All kinds of Maryland Cookie chocolate, sugars and spices to see off a slight roughness around the gills. 47%

Stranahan's Colorado Whiskey Batch #88 dist 7 June 10 (76) n19 t20 f18 b19. Earthy, cooked spicy vegetables but generally struggling to find its balance. 47%

Stranahan's Colorado Whiskey Batch #89 dis 13 June 10 (88) n22 t22 f22 b22. Another slightly earthy offering; this time ulmo honey and molasses spring to the rescue. 47%

Stranahan's Colorado Whiskey Batch #90 dist 19 Apr 09 (96) n23.5 t24 f24 b24.5. One of those liquid golden nuggets they find now and then in them thar Rocky Mountain hills. 47%

⁘ **Stranahan's Colorado Whiskey Batch #91** (85.5) n21 t21 f22 b21.5 Curious with a much lighter body. Picks up in flavour intensity as the sugars merge with the spicy mocha. 47%

⁘ **Stranahan's Colorado Whiskey Batch #92** (88.5) n22 t22 f22.5 b22 All about the sugars and the acacia honey and liquorice middle. Good oils from a brave cut. Chewy. 47%

⁘ **Stranahan's Colorado Whiskey Batch #93** (83) n20 t21 f21.5 b20.5 Similar to #91 except the thicker build carries a vague feint. Some nougat and chocolate towards the end. 47%

⁘ **Stranahan's Colorado Whiskey Batch #94** (94) n23.5 spot degrees of muscovado sugars amid the thick malt; the oak offers a little kumquat to lighten things; t23 soft oil, glide over the plate while spices sparkle. the sugars stand guard; f23.5 fabulous complexity as the malt goes into Malteser overdrive, the milk chocolate silky; b24 there you go: 94 points for #94. If Stranahan's could hit this style complex, clean as a benchmark and stick to it, they'd be world beaters! 47% (94 Proof)

⁘ **Stranahan's Colorado Whiskey Batch #96** (87.5) n22.5 t22 f21.5 b21.5 Back to something a little more austere, despite the efforts of the sugary oils. Enjoyable, though. 47%

⁘ **Stranahan's Colorado Whiskey Batch #97** (88.5) n21 t22.5 f22 b23 Recovers wonderfully from a feinty nose to offer a glittering assortment of heavy brown sugars to chew on and teasing spice. 47% (94 Proof)

⁘ **Stranahan's Colorado Whiskey Batch #99** (84) n20 t22 f21 b21 They appear to have got the slight OTT feints on nose and finish and irresistible big sugared middle off pat. 47%

⁘ **Stranahan's Colorado Whiskey Batch #100** (93) n23.5 nutty: walnut oil and top quality north European marzipan; t23 textbook oils show both malt and vanilla in a rich light. Biscuity...; f23 the finish takes a surprise turn towards tangy marmalade b23.5 a three course meal of a malt. And leaves you wanting seconds... 47% (94 Proof)

⁘ **Stranahan's Colorado Whiskey Batch #101** (87.5) n22 t22 f21.5 b22 More playing dare with the cut. Here it pays off as the oils go into molasses overdrive. A dessert whiskey. 47%

⁘ **Stranahan's Colorado Whiskey Batch #102** (92) n22.5 butterscotch, toffee, ulmo honey and spice; t23 juicy barley which spices up beautifully; f23 long, back to the ulmo honey again; the vanillas are creamy and complex; b23.5 superb whisky of almost perfect weight and pace. 47% (94 Proof)

⁘ **Stranahan's Colorado Whiskey Batch #103** (88) n21 t22.5 f22 b22.5 Another vanilla, butterscotch and honey-ladened gem once the light feints are overcome. 47% (94 Proof)

⁘ **Stranahan's Colorado Whiskey Batch #104** (84.5) n21 t21.5 f21 b21 Just a little tight with the crisp sugars outflanked by the slightly bitter, blood-orange feints. 47% (94 Proof)

⁘ **Stranahan's Colorado Whiskey Batch #105** (90) n22 t22 f23 b23 Interesting to see them continue along this orangey-citrus route. Malts show integrity. Spiced. Complex. 47%

⁘ **Stranahan's Colorado Whiskey Batch #106** (86) n21.5 t22 f21 b21.5 Back to the big oils and cumbersome sugars and nougat. Marmalade on the finale, though. 47% (94 Proof)

Stranahan's **Colorado Whiskey Batch #109** (92) n22 t23.5 f23 b23.5 Beautifully flighted malt with a rich seam of molassed sugars and raisins. Vanilla topping and spice. 47%

Stranahan's **Colorado Whiskey Batch #110** (91.5) n22 t23 f23 b23.5 Lovely interplay between crispy grain and even crispier sugars. Two-toned . Juicy and gorgeously spiced. 47%

Stranahan's **Snowflake Cab Franc** dist Sep 05 (95.5) n24 t24.5 f23 b24. Not only is this a celebration of great whiskey, but a profound statement of what the small distilleries of the USA are capable of. 47%. sc.

Stranahan's **Snowflake Conumdrum Peak** dist 1 Oct 09 (86.5) n22 t22 f21 b21.5. Well made, enjoyable whiskey though perhaps a little too simplistic for greatness. Relies too heavily on the natural caramels. 47%. sc. 330 bottles.

Stranahan's **Snowflake Desire** dist 3 Jan 07 (94.5) n24 t24 f23 b23.5. These guys do know how to pick a good barrel... And, frankly, make an exceptional whiskey... 47%. sc.

Stranahan's **Snowflake Maroon Bells** dist 21 Feb 10 (85.5) n21.5 t21 f22 b21. Hell's bells, more like! Ribald in its fruitiness, it never quite hits the required balance with the intense caramel. A shock to the system for Stranahan lovers. 47%. sc. 552 bottles.

Stranahan's **Snowflake Mount Shavano** (85.5) n22 t21 f21.5 b21 The malt vanishes under a cartload of plums. Flat. 47% (94 Proof)

Stranahan's **Snowflake Mount Silverheels** (89) n22.5 t22 f22.5 b22 Another fruity job showing a pithy dryness in tandem with liquorice and treacle. A real mouthful of a malt. 47%

Stranahan's **Snowflake Paladise/Grand Mesa** dist Apr 05 (94) n23 t24 f23 b24. Seriously impressive. I know this distillery makes something a little special, but this is such a sure footed move away from the norm I am stunned. This is my first-ever Stranahan Snowflake... so named because it simply dissolves on touch...? 47%. (94 Proof). sc.

Stranahan's **Snowflake Solitude** dist Mar 08 (93) n23 t23 f23.5 b23.5 I chose this as my 1,111th new whisky of the 2012 Bible, because there is a lot of ones in that. And when you spend three months on your own, virtually cut off from all others, one is number you get used to. So sampling a whisky called "Solitude" strikes home...whatever it tastes like. 47%. sc.

Stranahan's **Snowflake Tempranillo** (91) n21.5 t22 f24 b23.5 A bold malt with a liquorice and greengage delivery backed by a big treacle middle. Molasses wherever you look! 47%. (94 Proof)

SQUARE ONE BREWERY & DISTILLERY St. Louis, Missouri

J J Neukomm Missouri Malt Whisky Single Barrel (88.5) n21 sharp, smoky, intriguing – but a bit of a mess; t23 juicy sugars with seemingly cherry at the heart make for soft footfall on delivery, but the intensity of the malt really surprises; f22 rabidly spicy and threatens to bitter out. But cherry drops to the rescue; b22.5 it was like being transferred back to Sperryville, Virginia, where Copper Fox whiskey is made. The cherry wood smoked malt has a highly distinctive voice, and here it is again. Except this really does appear to have dark cherry notes at work on the palate. Annoyingly, although single barrel, there is no distinguishing reference number. 45% (90 proof)

TRIPLE EIGHT DISTILLERY Nantucket, Massachusetts.

The Notch Aged 8 Years dist 2000, bott Aug 08 db (93) n24 t23.5 f22.5 b23. Very few distilleries make their international bow with a single malt this sublime and superbly constructed. $888 dollars a bottle it may be, but for a taste of America's very first island malt... well, is there really a price? A head turner of a whisky, and every time it's towards the glass. Do we have a world classic distillery in the making...? 44.4% (88.8 proof)

The Notch Aged 8 Years db (95.5) n24.5 t24.5 f23 b23.5. Only six bottles of this were produced for a special dinner at the distillery. It is possible one escaped. I admit I had a hand in putting this one together, selecting samples from about half a dozen casks on the warehouse and blending them to certain percentages. Perhaps the closest it might be compared to is a Cardhu, though with a touch extra fruit. For the doubters, proof that this distillery is quite capable of whisky of the very highest calibre. 40% (80 proof)

WILLIE HOWELL SPIRITS

WH32137 (73.5) n15 t21 f18.5 b19. As big and intense as you'd expect from any spirit with a cut as wide as this. Very sweet corn oil ensures an uplifting body. 42.5%

WOODINVILLE WHISKEY CO. Woodinville, Washington

Mash Bill No 9 Bourbon Batch 2 (90) n22 no shrinking violet here. And on the subject of violets: pretty floral, though the spice rack has much to say too. Genuinely oak-laden and busy; t23.5 if the nose has a lot to say, this positively grinds out the speeches and proclamations. Massive whiskey choc-a-bloc with varied citrus notes of different weights and density. The spices are outwardly delicate but cluster into something serious and meaningful, though the corn has a slightly miserly quality; **f22** thins a shade too fast, though the natural caramels and residual sugars do their best to keep the party going; **b22.5** a bourbon quite impossible not to love. Excellent fare from a new distillery to watch! 46%

WOODSTONE CREEK DISTILLERY Cincinnati, Ohio.

Woodstone Creek 10 Year Old Peated Malt (92) 24 23 22 23. Just read the previous tasting notes. There is nothing I can either add nor subtract. Quite, quite wonderful... 46.25%

Woodstone Microspirit 5 Grain Straight Bourbon Single Barrel No. 3 (95) **n24** mega complex nose with just the right degree of liquorice and manuka honey to get you in a bourbon mood. The small grains are in dizzying perpetual motion; **t24** small still copper sharpness meets a rye-recipe style small grain juiciness with a wheat-recipe style spice. The oak also digs deep and does nothing to lessen the complexity, chipping in with a molten chocolate filling; **f23** softens as the oils filter through but we are back now to a liquorice/hickory feel, sweetened with orange blossom honey; **b24** you can tell Cincinnati borders Kentucky: of all the micro distillery bourbons I have ever tasted, this comes closest to the original big distiller style. Had I tasted blind, for the odd moment or two I might have called this as well aged stock from the Tom Moore distillery in Bardstown. Astonishing. And delightful! 47%

YAHARA BAY DISTILLERY Madison, Wisconsin.

Sample No 1 (87) **n22.5 t22 f20.5 b22.** A disarmingly elegant whiskey. 40%

American/Kentucky Whisky Blends

Ancient Age Preferred (73) **n16.5 t19 f19.5 b18.** A marginal improvement thanks mainly to a re-worked ripe corn-sweet delivery and the cocoa-rich finish. But still preferred, one assumes, by those who probably don't care how good this distillery's whisky can be... 40%

Beam's Eight Star (69.5) **n17 t18 f17 b17.5.** If you don't expect too much it won't let you down. 40%

Bellows (67) **n17 t17.5 f16 b16.5** Just too thin. 40%

Calvert's Extra (79) **n19 t20 f20 b20.** Sweet and mega-toffeed. Just creaking with caramel but extra marks for the late spice. 40%

Carstair's White Seal (72) **n16.5 t18.5 f19.5 b17.5** Possibly the cleanest blend about even offering a cocoa tang on the finale. Pleasant. 40%

Hobble Creek (64) **n16 t17 f15 b16.** Sweet, soft, easy drinking. Total shortage of complexity. 40%

Kentucky Dale (64) **n16 t17 f15 b16.** Thin and spineless, though soft and decently sweet on delivery. The grain spirit completely dominates. 40%

Kessler (84.5) **n20 t21 f22 b21.5.** "Smooth As Silk" claims the label. And the boast is supported by what is in the bottle: a real toffee-mocha charmer with a chewy, spicy depth. 40%

PM Deluxe (75) **n18 t18 f19 b18.** Pleasant moments as the toffee melts in the mouth. 40%

Sunny Brook (79.5) **n20 t21 f19 b19.5.** An entirely agreeable blend with toffee and lightly oiled nuts. Plus a sunny disposition... 40%

Whiskey Distilled From Bourbon Mash

❖ **Angels Envy Bourbon Finished in Port Barrels** (84) **n20 t22 f21 b21.** Almost like a chocolate raisin candy and fruitcake. Silky textured and juicy. 43.3% (86.6 proof)

❖ **Angels Envy Cask Strength Bourbon Finished in Port Barrels Cask Strength** (86.5) **n21.5 t24 f20 b21.** The problem with cask finishing most things, and bourbon in particular it seems, is that something is lost in the complexity - especially the small grain interaction, as well as balance between the spirit and oak - which is not quite compensated for with the lushness of extra fruit. Much better than the standard bottling, though, and the juiciness and cushioned enormity on delivery and spice at the midpoint is certainly worth discovering. 60.5%

❖ **Big Bottom Straight Bourbon Finished in Port Casks 91** (86.5) **n21.5 t24 f20 b21.** Subtract over enthusiastic toastiness and withering dryness and for a while we have a genuinely stunning mouth feel backed by spectacular spiced apricot and ulmo honey. The odd few moments of genius here. 45.5% (91 proof) ncf

❖ **Big Bottom Straight bourbon Finished in Zinfandel Casks 91** (85) **n21 t22 f21b21.** A flat nose and delivery comes alive about eight or nine flavour waves in when the fruit comes to a compromise with the grains. The burnt raisin finish is just a little too bitter. 45.5% ncf.

Whiskey Distilled From Rye Mash

❖ **Angels Envy Rye Finished in Caribbean Rum Casks** (78) **n18.5** truly a unique nose in my 24 years of professional tasting and 38 years of sampling the world's whisk(e)ys. Kind of perfumed burnt orange and toasted vanilla mallow filling in the rye peaks...; **t20.5** what the hell...?? Yes, the rye bites through the clutter, and does it well. But there is still a bizarre background noise that just about defies description. Oily, sugary...odd; **f20** a soft, lightly pulsing oil; **b19** frankly, I was hardly expecting to have any teeth left after this sample. The hardest, most crisp of all whiskeys is rye. And if you want to give any whisk(e)y an extra degree of exoskeleton, then just finish it in a rum cask. And here we have the two together : yikes! Some twenty years ago I gave then Jack Daniel's blender Lincoln Henderson his first-ever taste of peated whisky: a Laphroaig. He hated it! I think he's waited a long time to return the compliment by showing me a style I did not know could exist. Beyond fascinating. Weird, even - hence the full tasting notes. One for the ladies with this liqueur-style smoothie. *50%.*

Other American Whiskey

‑⁖‑ **Buffalo Trace Experimental Collection 19 Year Old Giant French Oak Barrel** 135 gallon French oak barrel, dist 27 Jan 93, bott 28 Jun 12 db **(84.5) n21.5 t22 f20 b21.** Conservative and tight on the nose and finish in particular. But for the sugary rush on delivery, not something you would have hoped to have uncovered after 19 years... *45% (90 Proof). sc.*

‑⁖‑ **Buffalo Trace Experimental Collection 23 Year Old Giant French Oak Barrel** 135 gallon French oak barrel, dist 16 May 89, bott 27 Jun 12 db **(91) n23** big, winey number with a touch of the noble rot about it; **t23** ballsy delivery with the oak and fruit right up there, tight and compact, rounded and determined to hang about together. A touch of salt...; **f22.5** more salty fruit: figs, dates and, finally, rye crispness; **b22.5** different. And, unlike the 19-y-o, this works... *45% (90 Proof). sc.*

Buffalo Trace Experimental Collection 1989 Barrels Rediscovered white oak with seasoned staves, dist Nov 89, bott Dec 10 **(91.5) n24 t23 f22.5 b22.5.** A whispering bourbon of exceptional subtlety which makes minimum fuss of its antiquity. *45% (90 Proof)*

Buffalo Trace Experimental Collection 1991 Barrels Rediscovered white oak with seasoned staves, dist Oct 91, bott Dec 10 **(93.5) n24 t23.5 f23 b23.** Pretty classic stuff. *45%*

Buffalo Trace Experimental Collection Made With Oats white oak, dist 29 April 2002 **(85.5) n20 t22 f21.5 b22.** Oats had been used by the Irish in whiskey making for over 100 years. So it is hard to believe that some early American settler or other didn't use this particular recipe somewhere along the line...This, curiously, has a very similar texture on the palate to Sam Smith's celebrated Oat Stout from Yorkshire, England...though this is much more on the sweet side. The nose is a curious affair being both a little smoky but also vaguely butyric and thick with linseed oil. If it's an acquired nose, I haven't quite got there yet. The oats really come into play with the texture, which is a delight. Just lacks the development hoped for. *45% (90 Proof)*

‑⁖‑ **Buffalo Trace Experimental Collection Other Oak Barrel** 135 gallon French oak barrel, dist 27 Jan 93, bott 28 Jun 12 db **(84.5) n21.5 t22 f20 b21.** Conservative and tight on the nose and finish in particular. But for the sugary rush on delivery, not something you would have hoped to have uncovered after 19 years... *45% (90 Proof). sc.*

Buffalo Trace White Dog Mash #1 (93) n23 t23 f24 b23. Exceptionally high quality spirit, fabulously weighted, neither too sweet nor dry and with the distinctive cocoa character of the very best grain distillate. Beats the crap out of vodka. "White Dog" is the name for spirit which has run off the still but not yet been bottled: "New Make" in Scotland. It is not, therefore, whiskey as it has not been in any form of contact with oak. But what the hell... It must be at least 15 years ago that I told the old plant manager, Joe Darmond, that he should bottle this stuff as it would sell fast. BT brought it out initially for their distillery shop...and now it is in demand worldwide?! If you are reading this, what did I tell you? and about rye come to that! *62.5%*

High West Son of Bourye a blend of bourbon and rye **(95) n23** the rye notes are as crunchy as a muscovado sugar driveway; **t24.5** the kind of salivation factor that brings you to your knees in a state of grainy euphoria. The radiating brown sugars are as clean as they are exemplary; **f23.5** only now does the bourbon get a word in edgeways, though can offer only a half-hearted honey, caramel and liquorice mix; the spices are sublime; **b24** this son, presumably called Ryebon, is a stunningly stylish chap which comprehensively eclipses its lacklustre parent... *46%*

High West Campfire rye, bourbon & Scotch malt, batch no. 3 **(93) n23.5** busy and beautifully balanced; **t22.5** salivating rye strikes first and hard. An armada of honey and caramel types sail softly into view; **f23.5** at last a hint of smoke begins to unravel and sits beautifully, almost Highland Park style, with the oaked honey; the rye ensures a rigidity is maintained as spices form; **b23.5** an enchanting, hugely complex dram...the sort of thing I conjure up in my tasting room every day, in fact, by mixing differing whisky styles from around the world. Here the rye dominates by some margin, creating the backbone on which the sweeter bourbon tones hang. The peated malt ensures a wonderful background rumble. Well blended...and great fun! *46%*

Canadian Whisky

It is becoming hard to believe that Canadian was once a giant among the world whisky nations. Dotted all over its enormous land large distilleries pumped out thousands upon thousands of gallons of spirit that after years in barrel became a clean, gentle whisky.

It was cool to be seen drinking Canadian in cocktail bars on both sides of the pond. Now, sadly, Canadian whisky barely raises a beat on the pulse of the average whisky lover. It would not be beyond argument to now call Canadian the forgotten whisky empire with column inches devoted to their column stills measured now in millimetres. It is an entirely sad, almost heartbreaking, state of affairs though hopefully not an irreversible one. The finest Canadian, for me, is still whisky to be cherished and admired. But outside North America it can be painfully hard to find.

Especially seeing how whiskies containing the permitted 9.09% of non-Canadian whisky (or whisky at all) had been barred from the European market. So just to ensure Jim Murray's Whisky Bible remained on the ball I spend as much time in Canada as possible keeping abreast of any changes I can find in the limited range of new bottlings to emerge each year. There appears now to be a distinct divergence of styles between traditionalist whisky like Alberta Premium, which realy is made from rye, and a more creamy textured, fruit-enhanced corn or wheat distilled product once confined to the USA but now found in Canada itself. The trouble is, apart from the Bible, there is little way of knowing which is which.

BRITISH COLUMBIA

ALBERTA

MANITOBA

▲ Alberta
● Calgary

●Vancouver

▲ Okanagan

▲ Palliser

Gimli ▲

Key

● **Major Town or City**
▲ Distillery
† Dead Distillery

However, there is no doubt that we are seeing a change in the perception of Canadian by drinkers who had previously confined themselves to top quality Scotch malt. Following the award of Jim Murray's Whisky Bible Canadian Whisky of the Year 2006 to Alberta Premium, I had the chance to spend time in television and radio studios around the country talking about the exceptionally high quality of top Canadian whiskies. It led to a string of emails from readers telling me they had since tasted Alberta and been somewhat shocked to find a world classic whisky lurking so unobtrusively - and cheaply - on their shelves. For many, this had led to further exploring of Canadian, and uncovering of further gems. For the Jim Murray's Whisky Bible 2013 and 2014 the winning Canadian whisky asked many questions of just what is happening at Alberta. In July 2012 a knock out blind tasting of 16 award-winning whiskies from around the world I conducted had the people of Sun Peaks in British Columbia's Rocky Mountains speechless when they discovered they had voted Alberta Premium the finest whisky of the evening. No surprise, then, that it is rye from Alberta that not only won top Canadian billing in the Bible, but got through to the last six taste off for World Whisky of the Year. Yet, Masterson's 10-year-old is a label owned by an independent bottler: Alberta's official own new offering, Dark Horse, was anything but a thoroughbred by comparison.

Perhaps one of the things that makes Canadian whisky compelling is its ever-changing face. Many brands do have a tendency to move around in style slightly more than you might expect. However, there is an interesting development from Kentucky which contradicts that in an unorthodox manner. Buffalo Trace have decided to bottle some casks of Canadian in their inventory as a single barrel product. They sent me and others some samples back in their developmental stage and asked us for our input. Now, contrary to what anyone tells you, or claim they know, a Canadian single cask whisky called Bush Pilot was around some 15 years ago, the product of Canadian Club's Okanagan distillery. And each bottling was natural and fascinatingly different. The same can't quite be said for the new Caribou Crossing, a pleasant enough whisky which sports a thumping degree of unionizing caramel while the Canadian whisky lover, or potential convert, is little helped by every bottle looking identical with no cask details. Buffalo Trace have done little wrong in the last decade; indeed, in that time have become the most consistently excellent and exciting distillers in the world taking both bourbon and rye to new heights in my lifetime, and in Drew Mayville (a Canadian, incidentally) they have a blender at the top of his game. But the usual BT sure-footedness appears to have found a hole in the ice - for you can't help thinking that this perfect chance to win over hearts and minds to Canadian has not been fully grasped. Both Drew and I learned our Canadian from the very same school of past Canadian blending masters – and I use the term carefully – so we tend to have very similar views on matters Canadian/Canadien. When last in Frankfort I was unable to discuss this with him as we had the small matter of the Single Oak Project to dissect. Next time though I will be locking friendly Caribou horns with him.

QUEBEC

ONTARIO

Glenora

NOVA SCOTIA

●Quebec

Valleyfield ●Montreal

Canada Mist ●Toronto

Kittling Ridge

Walkerville

Canadian Single Malts
GLENORA

Glen Breton db **(81)** n19 t21 f20 b21. Ultra sweet malt, in almost concentrated form with a tantalising whiff of smoke hanging around; mildly spiced and slightly oily, soapy finale. *43%*

Glen Breton Ice Aged 10 Years db **(85.5)** n21.5 t21 f22 b21. Tasting both a full strength bottled Canadian, and one that had been matured in Icewine barrels, I was nearly blown through the back of my seat and into the wall. One of the biggest shocks to hit you on the Canadian whisky scene today, there is no denying that this whisky offers sufficient panache and lucidity to genuinely impress. Hardly an exercise in perfect balance, it certainly celebrates the art of surprise and, late on, charm. The cocoa-dusted butterscotch really is a rare treat and, thanks to the fruity world it finds itself in, a truly unique and enjoyable experience. *57.2%*

Glen Breton Rare db **(80)** n18 t21 f20 b21. Caramel nose a bit soapy but the buttery, sweet malt, with its vanilla fizz, makes for a pleasant experience. *43%*

Glen Breton Rare Aged 10 Years bott 2010 db **(89.5)** n22 a slight feintiness is soon blown away by a little warming in the hand. This allows the malt to positively sing in the glass, though the choir contains a fruit toffee bass; t23 ye Gods! Didn't expect the malt to come through so beautifully clear and embellished by a light creamy texture. Even something of the Cardhus about this. So much to chew; the spices rattle up a good pace as the oaks begin to arrive; f22 dries and thins with the accent on toffee vanilla; **b22.5** an impressive whisky: one of the best bottlings of this age for some while and showing the malt at full throttle. *43%*

Glen Breton Rare Aged 14 Years db **(92)** n23.5 probably the most Scottish style of any nose I have encountered from a Glenora bottling. Even a delicate degree of spice on hand to maximise the clean barley intensity; the oak used is top notch, showing a delicate trace of bourbon and a gorgeous lime jelly to the butterscotch... wow! t22.5 melt-in-the-mouth barley reverberates around the palate; f23 long, a charming light oiliness helping the sweeter elements of the barley to fuse with the warming oak; soft liquorice and Greek honey flourish; **b23** what is there not to enjoy? Some exceptionally good casks involved here. *43%*

Glen Breton Battle Of The Glen Aged 15 Years Special Edition db **(94)** n23.5 t23.5 f23 b24. I really did know they were capable of bottling something this good: there isn't a single barrel of this vintage I have not tasted in their warehouse at one time or another during its maturation cycle. This watermark bottling from then is an essentially sweet whisky, tasting all the sweeter as it marks the little distillery's victory over the Goliath that is the Scotch Whisky Association in their rightful battle to retain the right to use the name of their brand. Just sometimes there is evidence there just may be a god... *43% 4200 bottles.*

Glen Breton Ice Aged 17 Years aged in Icewine barrels bott 2010 db **(90.5)** n22.5 a fascinating mix of inelegance and sharp, fruity focus. More thumbs up than down...; t24 I am stunned: on delivery alone this is world class whisky without a shadow of doubt: natural elegance such as this comes along only too rarely in whisky. The degree of oil to the malt borders perfection, the intensity and sharpness of the clean apple and pear fruit are exceptional; soft muscovado sugars melt naturally into the buttery mix; f21.5 such a complicated creature, it is no surprise when the balance collapses under the weight of the bitterness; **b22.5** a different animal to the 10-y-o Icewine version, though having much more to do with the spirit than the casks. Yet never before has this distillery sent me such a box of wonderful delights such as these before. It is as though their victory over the Scotch industry has lifted a cloud of self-doubt. Glenora appears to have come of age. *54.6%*

Glen Breton Rare Cabot Links Reserve Aged 19 Years db **(86.5)** n21 t22.5 f21 b22. You know when astronomers build a super-powerful new telescope that gives them a clearer view of when the universe began. This bottling is a bit like that... taking us back to the days of the Glen Breton Big Bang. Lots of dramatic barley to view. But, naturally, all the more basic and primitive elements are there on show, also... *46%*

Canadian Blended Whisky

Alberta Premium (95.5) n24 throbbing, pulsing rye on a variety of levels: full and juicy, dull and dusty, firm and flinty. Unique and unmistakable; t25 my first whisky of the day – and it needs to be. The tastebuds are given such a working over that they need to be fully tuned and fit to take this on. Again it is all about the rye: the first three flavours to pound the mouth are all rye-related. The very first are juicy with a minute sweetness. The second, hanging onto the coattails of the first are Rockies hard and brittle, clattering into the tastebuds with zero yield. Next comes a quick follow through of explosive peppers, but again leaving in their wake a semi-sweet juicy, fruitiness, almost certainly from the malted rye. No other whisky unleashes this combination of grainy punches around the palate. The words beautiful and complex don't even begin to do this whisky justice; f22.5 dulls down, probably because of the needless caramel added, but there is slightly more depth than before thanks most probably to the malted rye. The spices continue to fizz as the Demerara-tipped vanillas make their mark; **b24** it has just gone 8am and the Vancouver Island sky is one of clear blue. My windows are open to allow in some chilly, early Spring air and, though only the first week of March, an American robin sits in the arbutus tree, resplendent in its now two-toned leaves, calling for a mate, as it has done since 5.15 this morning, his song blending with the lively trill of the house finches and the doleful, maritime anthem of the gull. It seems the natural environment of Alberta Premium, back here to its rye-studded best after a couple I tasted socially in Canada last year appeared comparatively dull and restrained. I am tasting this from Bottle Lott No L93300197 and it is classic, generating all I expect and now demand. A national treasure. *40%*

Alberta Premium bott lott L1317 **(96) n24 t25 f23 b24.** Tasting this three years on from the sample above, there is absolutely nothing to add or subtract (except the finish is fractionally more engrossing): the consistency and brilliance defies belief. *40%*

Alberta Premium bott lott L2150 **(94) n23.5 t24 f23 b23.5.** Fractionally duller than the 2011 bottling sampled above with less emphasis on the crystalline rye and more on cane sugar. Still a treat! *40%*

Alberta Premium 25 Years Old (95) n24 t23 f23 b25. Faultless. Absolutely nothing dominates. Yet every aspect has its moment of conquest and glory. It is neither bitter nor sweet, yet both. It is neither soft nor hard on the palate yet both elements are there. Because of the 100% rye used, this is an entirely new style of whisky to hit the market. No Canadian I know has ever had this uncompromising brilliance, this trueness to style and form. And, frightening to think, it could be improved further by bottling at least 46% and un-chillfiltered. For any whisky lover who ever thought Canadian was incapable of hitting the heights among the world's greats. *40%. Alberta Distillers.*

Alberta Premium 30 Years (88.5) n23 t23.5 f20 b22. It doesn't take much to tip the balance of a whisky this delicate on the nose and delivery. Five extra years in the cask has nudged the oak just a little too far. However, savour the nose and delivery which are to die for. *40%*

Alberta Premium Dark Horse (84) n18 t22 f22 b22. The blurb on the back says it is crafted for the "next generation of whisky connoisseur". Fine. But personally, I'd always shape a whisky for the true connoisseurs of today... I have not spoken to the blending team at Alberta to discuss this and, as the book has to be finished within a week or two, I won't get a chance. But this is the most extraordinary development in Canadian I have seen for a while. The nose is not great: it really does seem as though fruit cordial has been given the lead role. But the taste really does challenge, and I have to say there are many aspects I enjoy. It is as though some peated malt has been added to the mix as the finish does have distinctive smokiness. And the balance has been expertly worked to ensure the sugars don't dominate while the spices are persistent. But if it falls down anywhere, the over reliance on the fruit apart, it is the fact that Alberta makes the best spirit in Canada by a very great distance....yet someone has forgotten to ensure that fact is made clear in the taste and the nose especially. *45%*

Alberta Springs Aged 10 Years (83) n21 t21 f20 b20. Really appears to have had a bit of a flavourectomy. Sweet but all traces of complexity have vanished. 40%.

Barton's Canadian 36 Months Old (78) n19 t20 f19 b20. Sweet, toffeed, easy-going. *40%*

Bowman's Canadian Whisky (90.5) n22 t22 f23.5 b23. A delicious, honest Canadian for chocoholics. *40%*

Black Velvet (78) n18 t20 f20 b20. A distinctly off-key nose is compensated for by a rich corn and vanilla kick on the palate. But that famous spice flourish is a distant memory. Another big caramel number. *40%*

Campbell & Cooper Aged a Minimum of 36 Months (84.5) n21.5 t22 f20 b21. Huge flavour profile. An orchard of oranges on the nose and profound vanilla on delivery. *40%*

Canadian Club 100 Proof (89) n21 t23 f22 b23. If you are expecting this to be a high-octane version of the standard CC Premium, you'll be in for a shock. This is a much fruitier dram with an oilier body to absorb the extra strength. An entertaining blend. *50%.*

Canadian Club Premium (92) n23 a comfortable marriage of fruit and drier, almost chalky vanilla; **t22.5** delicate, impressively rounded with just enough firm fruitiness to suggest a semi rye character as well as what now appears to be a ubiquitous sherry-cum-grape note and then a fabulous warming as the spices make an elegant entry; **f23** long, superbly spiced **b23.5** a greatly improved whisky which now finds the fruit fitting into the mix with far more panache than of old. Once a niggardly whisky, often seemingly hell-bent on refusing to enter into any form of complexity: but not now! Great spices in particular. I'm impressed. *40%*

Canadian Club Aged 6 Years (88.5) n21.5 t22 f22.5 b22.5. Not at all bad for a Canadian some purists turn their nose up at as it's designed for the American market. Just brimming with mouth-watering enormity and style. Dangerously moreish. *40%*

Canadian Club Reserve Aged 10 Years (86) n20 t22 f21.5 b22. Odd cove, this. The nose is less than welcoming and offers a hotchpotch of somewhat discordant notes giving a jumbled message and less than well defined statement of intent. Decent delivery, though, shifting through the gears with some impressive and sultry fruit tying in well with a rare grain onslaught found in Canadian these days. The finish, though, just can't steer away from the rocks of bitterness, alas. Again, as so often appears to be the case with CC, the spices star. 40%

Canadian Club Classic Aged 12 Years (91.5) n22 t24 f21.5 b23.5. A confident whisky which makes the most of a honeycomb theme. 40%

Canadian Club Small Batch Classic 12 Aged 12 Years batch C12-020 (75.5) n21 t22 f15 b17. A syrupy whisky which talks a great game on the back label, but fails to deliver in reality. Big fruit, perhaps a little too heavily accented as other avenues of complexity are limited. The bitter, tangy finish is not great at all. 40%

Canadian Club Aged 20 Years (92.5) n24 t21 f23.5 b23. In previous years, CC20 has ranked among the worst whiskies I have tasted, not just in Canada, but the world. Their current bottling, though, is not even a distant relation. Sure, it has a big sherry investment. But the sheer elan and clever use of spice make this truly magnificent. Possibly the most pleasant surprise in my latest trawl through all Canada's whiskies. 40%

Canadian Club Sherry Cask batch no. SC-018 (76) n18 t20 f20 b18. Twice as strong as you can normally buy Sherry yet somehow has only half the body. As I say, I really don't know what to make of this. Nor do I get the point. 41.3%

Canadian Five Star Rye Whisky (83) n21 t22 f20 b20. An entirely tame, well behaved Canadian which celebrates the inherent sweetness of the species. That said, the immediate impact on the palate is pretty delicious with a quick, flash explosion of something spicy. But it is the deft, satin-soft mouthfeel which may impress most. 40%

Canadian Hunter (85.5) n20.5 t21 f22 b22. Remains truly Canadian in style. The toffee has diminished, allowing far more coffee and cocoa to ensure a delightful middle and finish. 40%

Canadian Mist (78) n19 t20.5 f18.5 b20. Much livelier than previous incarnations despite the inherent, lightly fruited softness. 40%

Canadian Pure Gold (82) n21.5 t20.5 f20 b20. Full-bodied and still a notably lush whisky. The pure gold may have more to do with the caramel than the years in cask but the meat of this whisky still gives you plenty to chew over. I especially enjoy the gradual building of spices. 40%

Canadian Spirit (78) n20 t20 f19 b19. A real toffee-fest with a touch of hard grain around the edges. 40%. Carrington Distillers (Alberta Distillers).

Caribou Crossing Single Barrel (84) n20 t22.5 f20 b21.5. While the nose offers an unholy battle between some apple-fruity rye notes and dry, dusty caramel, there is a real pulsating delivery with the sharper spices helped along the way by the silkiness of the body. Though the caramel offers a toffee-fudge backdrop, a countering dry date sweetness does more than enough to keep it at bay. However, the finish dulls out as the caramel gains the upper hand, though the twitching spices do ensure a light, throbbing beat. An enjoyable Canadian, undoubtedly, I am somewhat perplexed by it. There is no reference to the barrel number so you won't know if you are buying from different casks. Also, if it is single barrel what is the point of the caramel? If it is to make all the casks taste the same, or similar, then why not just blend them together. A badly missed opportunity. 40%. Sazerac.

Centennial 10 Year Limited Edition (88.5) n21.5 t23 f22 b22. Retains its usual honey-flavoured breakfast cereal style, but the complexity has increased. Busy and charming. 40%

Century Reserve 8 Years Old Premium (82) n20 t21 f20 b21. Clean vanilla caramel. 40%

Century Reserve Custom Blend 15 Years Plus (88.5) n21.5 t22 f23 b22. After two days of being ambushed in every direction, or completely steamrollered by Canadian caramel, my tastebuds are in total shock. Caramel kept to an absolute minimum so that it hardly registers at all. Charming and refined drinking. 40%

Century Reserve 21 Years Old (91.5) n23.5 t23 f23 b22. Quite beautiful, but a spirit that is as likely to appeal to rum lovers as whisky ones. 40%

Century Reserve Custom Blend lot no. 1525 (87) n21.5 t22 f21.5 b22. An enjoyable whisky which doesn't quite reach its full potential. 40%

Corby's Canadian 36 Months Old (85) n20 t21 f22 b22. Attractive with fine bitter-sweet balance and I love the late spice kick-back. 40%. Barton. Interesting label: as a keen ornithologist, I had no idea there were parrots in Canada. Must be related to the Norwegian Blue.

Crown Royal (86) n22 t23.5 f19.5 b21. The Crown has spoken and it has been decreed that this once ultra grainy old whisky is taking its massive move to a silky fruitiness as far as it can go. It was certainly looking that way last time out; on this re-taste (and a few I have unofficially tasted) there is now no room for doubt. If you like grape, especially the sweeter variety, you'll love this. The highpoint is the sublime delivery and starburst of spice. The low point? The buzzy, unhappy finale. The Grain Is Dead. Long Live The Grape! 40%

Crown Royal Black (85) n22 t23 f18.5 b21.5. Not for the squeamish: a Canadian which goes for it with bold strokes from the off which makes it a whisky worth discovering. The finish needs a rethink, though. 45%

Crown Royal Cask No 16 Finished in Cognac Casks (85.5) n21.5 t21 f22 b21. Clean cut and very grapey. The nose is unique in the whisky world: it is one of Cognac. Otherwise struggles to really find its shape and rhythm. A perfect Canadian for those who prefer theirs with an air of grace and refinement but very limited depth. In fact, those who prefer a Cognac. 40%

Crown Royal Limited Edition (87) n22 t22.5 f20.5 b22. A much happier and productive blend than before with an attractive degree of complexity but the more bitter elements of the finish have been accentuated. 40%

Crown Royal Special Reserve (96) n24 a clean and attractively spiced affair with cinnamon and the faintest pinch of allspice leading the way: rye at work, one presumes; the fruit is clean and precise with weightier grape overshadowing a green apple freshness; t24 a spicier element to the usual rye and fruit delivery, much more in keeping with the nose, but that fabulous, contrary mouth-feel of harder grain and softer fruit continues to do the business. The spices build slowly but with an impressive evenness and determination: one of the most outstanding Canadians on the palate of them all; f24 the finish has been tidied up and with stunning effect: no more sawdust and eye-watering dryness. Both grain and soft fruit ensure a magnificently mouth-watering end to an amazing journey; b24 complex, well weighted and simply radiant: it is like looking at a perfectly shaped, gossamer clad Deb at a ball. The ryes work astonishingly well here (they appear to be of the malted, ultra-fruity variety) and perhaps to best effect after Alberta Premium, though now it is a hard call between the two. 40%

Crown Royal XR Extra Rare lot no. L7064 N4 (93.5) n24 t23 f23 b23.5. Just about identical to the previous bottle above. The only difference is on the finish where the rye, fortified with spice, decides to hang back and battle it out to the death; the toffee and vanilla make a controlled retreat. Either the same bottling with a slightly different stance after a few years in the bottle, or a different one of extraordinary high consistency. 40%

Danfield's Limited Edition Aged 21 Years (95) n24 t24 f23.5 b23.5. A quite brilliant first-time whisky. The back label claims this to be small batch, but there is no batch number on the bottle, alas. Or even a visible bottling code. But this is a five star performer and one of this year's whiskies of the world. 40%

Danfield's Private Reserve (84.5) n20 t21.5 f22 b21. A curious, non-committal whisky which improves on the palate as it goes along. An overdose of caramel (yawn!!) has done it no favours, but there is character enough for it to pulse out some pretty tasty spice. Seamless and silky, for all the toffee there underlying corn-rich clarity is a bit of a turn on. 40%

8 Seconds Small Batch (86) n20 t22 f22.5 b21.5. Fruity, juicy, luxurious. And perhaps one of the few whiskies on the market anywhere in the world today which could slake a thirst. 40%

Forty Creek Barrel Select (86.5) n21.5 t22 f21 b21.5. Thank goodness that the sulphur taint I had found on this in recent years has now vanished. A lush, enjoyable easy-goer, this juices up attractively at the start and ends with an almost sophisticated dry pithiness. 40%

Forty Creek Confederation Oak Reserve lot 1867-B (94.5) n23.5 much more confidence to the fruit than in the previous bottling: clean and sculpted to fit rather beautifully with the delicate dry coconut and moist golden syrup, muscovado sugar and thinned heather honey; some walnut oil tops off a very attractive experience; t24 one of Forty Creek's all time great deliveries: you cannot even begin to fault the sublime balance between the corn oil, the sugars and peppers. All this framed by salivating ultra-ripe fruits and a countering vanilla oakiness. Fabulous texture and depth; f23.5 spiced fruit chocolate pulses like the afterglow of a particularly enjoyable experience...; b23.5 those who tasted the first batch of this will be intrigued by this follow up. The shape and intensity profile has been re-carved and all now fits together like a jigsaw. 40%

Forty Creek Copper Pot Reserve (91.5) n23 clean juicy fruit cascades into a spicy hollow; exceptional sweet-dry balance; t23.5 a big whisky couched in velvet: the delivery bristles and pulses with spiced greengages held on a fabulously firm backbone of what seems like rye (that last statement made me look at the back label...rye is in there!!) with a soothing massage of soft corn oils for the mid-ground; f22 dry and perhaps a hint of tobacco smoke; the oak shows itself in a sawdusty way, but with a light hint of cocoa and raisin; b23 one of the beauties of John hall's whiskies at Forty Creek is that they follow no set pattern in the whisky would: they offer flavour profiles really quite different from anything else. That is why they are worth that bit of extra time for your palate to acclimatise. Here you are exceptionally well rewarded... 43%

Forty Creek Double Barrel Reserve lot 247 (86) n21.5 t22.5 f20.5 b21.5. The usual juicy ride and plenty to savour early on. But there is something slightly off balance about the finish here. 40%

Forty Creek Port Wood Reserve lot 61 (95.5) n24.5 oh my word! Very highest quality Turkish Delight with some pretty top score chocolate; the fruit hangs off the frame full of juice and muscovado sugars. It demands spices...and gets them – with the right pizzazz! t24 the delivery is pure silk in texture and the most stunning fruit and spice on delivery. Hard to know whether to suck as it melts in the mouth, or chew as the background depth is outrageously nutty, with more cocoa to thicken. It is the astonishing spice that really mesmerises, as it is of almost perfect intensity; **f23** dries into an attractive crushed grape pip dryness, again with the spices lingering; **b24** John P Hall has got his ducks in a row. Magnificent! *45%*

Forty Creek Three Grain (76) **n19 t20 f18 b19**. Not quite as well assembled as some Three grains I have come across over the last few years. There is a lopsidedness to this one: we know the fruit dominates (and I still haven't a clue why, when surely this of all whiskies, just has to be about the grains!) but the bitterness interferes throughout. If there have been sherry casks used here, I would really have a close look at them. *40%*

Fremont Mischief Whiskey batch MPJ-0803, bott 11 (77) **n19 t20 f19 b19**. Though this was from the Mischief distillery in Seattle, USA, the whiskey was produced in Canada. Overly sweet, overly toffeed and bereft of complexity. Like Alberta Springs on a very bad day. *40%*

Gibson's Finest Aged 12 Years (77) **n18 t20 f19 b20**. Unlike the Sterling, going backwards rather than forwards. This is way too syrupy, fruity and toffee impacted. Despite the very good spice, almost closer to a liqueur than a true whisky style. *40%*

Gibson's Finest Rare Aged 18 Years (95.5) **n24** close your eyes and sniff and you would swear you have a bourbon-rye mix: simultaneously crisp and soft, the sharpness of the rye and apple-style fruitiness is sublime and as enticing as it gets; **t24.5** and a perfect transfer onto the palate: spectacularly juicy with all kinds of clean rye and corn notes bobbling around in a gorgeous gentle Demerara sugar backdrop; **f23.5** impressive vanilla and long strands of grain and bitter liquorice; **b23.5** so far ahead of both Sterling and the 12, it is hard to believe they are from the same stable. But make no mistake; this is pure thoroughbred: truly world class. *40%*

Gibson's Finest 100th Grey Cup Special Edition (87) **n21** the touch of Kentucky on the nose isn't of bourbon but drying tobacco leaf; no shortage of dusty toffee, either; **f23** a string of intense sugar notes — yes, including maple! — makes for a rattling start, with spices pouring in at the first opportunity. The middle is a bit of a No Man's Land...; **f21** dry and bitters as the caramel bites deeper; **b22** when the label tells you there is a hint of maple, they aren't joking... *40%*

Gibson's Finest Canadian Whisky Bourbon Cask Rare Reserve (89) **n23 t21 f23 b22**. A much better version than the first bottling, the depth this time being massively greater. *40%*

Gibson's Finest Sterling (86.5) **n22 t22.5 f20.5 b21.5**. A massively improved Canadian that had me doing the equivalent of a tasting double take: had to look twice at this to check I had the right stuff! Much firmer now in all the right places with the corn making sweeping statements, the golden syrup melting into all the required crevices and spices exploding at the appropriate moments. Just need to sort the heavy toffee and bitter finish out and this would be up in the Canadian Premier League. *40%*

Gibson's New Oak (88) **n22 t21 f23 b22**. Distinctly different from any other Canadian doing the rounds: the oak influence makes a wonderful and clever impact. *40%*

Highwood Pure Canadian (84) **n20 t21 f22 b21**. A decent, ultra-clean Canadian with markedly more character than before. Certainly the caramel has been seriously reduced in effect and the wheat ensures a rather attractive spice buzz while the cane juice sweetness harmonises well. Perhaps most delightful is the wonderful and distinct lack of fruit. *40%*

Hiram Walker Special Old (93) **n22.5 t24 f23 b23.5**. Even with the extra degree of all-round harmony, this remains the most solid, uncompromising Canadian of them all. And I love it! Not least because this is the way Special old has been for a very long time with obviously no intentions of joining the fruity bandwagon. Honest, first class Canadian. *40%*

James Foxe (77.5) **n20 t19.5 f19 b19**. James could do with putting some weight on... *40%*

Lord Calvert (72.5) **n19 t18.5 f17 b18**. Truly eccentric aristocracy, this. Comes from the most noble of homes, Alberta Distillery, and the pedigree of the rye is evident in patches on both nose and delivery. Then marries something very fruity well beneath its class. *40%*

❖ **Lot No 40 Malted Rye Whisky** (93) **n24** the intensity of the malted rye element powers through, offering several variations of sharp honey concentrate, from manuka down to acacia. The tannins are pretty staggering for a Canadian and much more of the Kentucky/ Indiana style. Simplistic yet so devastatingly beautiful... **t23.5** there we go...like a rocket of rye, firing off in three stages with the softer intensity of the oilier malted rye being propelled by the far more rigid unmalted into orbit; about half way through they meld and then the cocoa-vanilla oak stage bursts through, as well as a playful spiciness which dries towards a serious dark chocolate middle; **f22.5** being a miserable git, I'd say the oak tries too hard for world dominance here, allowing the bitterness to slightly overpower and over dry the crisper, toastier brown sugars. But on the other hand, those cocoa notes are pretty gorgeous and just enough oil allows it to level out across the palate; **b23** an old friend — almost a long lost son — has returned and has brightened up my glass with colossal Canadianness. This is of a style unique to this country, though here the high levels of oak have perhaps dimmed the flame of the rye slightly. Welcome home, my son...!!! *40%*

Masterson's 10 Year Old Straight Rye Whisky batch 003 **(96.5)** n24 fizzing with fruity finesse, there is little doubting the grain involved here; almost a bubble gum sweetness to the fruit and through the melting softness lurks a note as firm and sharp as a sabre; t24 just about as mouth-watering as it is spellbinding, the taste buds are immediately immersed in a stellar degree of crisp, sparkling rye notes; vanilla pods pop as it soaks in the juicy, clean rye; f24 if you want to see an almost perfect degree of spice at work in a whisky, you really can't do better than savour the finish of this gorgeous bottling. Helped along by deft oil, the crystalline sugars and light vanillas just carry on their hypnotic dance; b24.5 a magnificent whisky without any shadow of doubt. Rye is my favourite whisky type and this displays the style to a degree of excellence which is truly memorable in terms of a commercial bottling. Someone has done an outstanding job in selecting these casks. Interesting, however, that they don't actually state on the bottle that this is Canadian and confuse things a little further by spelling it "whiskey". My understanding is that this is unmalted rye from the outstanding Alberta Distillery in Calgary. What is certain is that this is a true classic of its style. And not so much Masterson's but Masterful. 45% ⊙

McGuinness Silk Tassel **(79.5)** n20 t21 f19.5 b19. Silk or satin? The corn oils offer a delightful sheen but still the caramel is over enthusiastic. 40%

McLoughlin and Steele Blended in the Okanagan Valley **(87.5)** n22 clean vanilla tinged with grapefruit; t22 more citrus on the juicy delivery. Corn oil fills the mid ground; f21.5 big, drying vanilla; spice; b22 as straight as a die: a Canadian Rye... without any discernible rye. 40%. McLoughlin and Steele.

Wm Morrison Imported Canadian Rye **(87.5)** n22 t22 f21.5 b22. Still a lovely Canadian, though the toffee needs toning down. Not sure what "Full Strength" is doing on the label when bottled at 40%, though... 40%.

Mountain Rock **(87)** n22 t20.5 f22.5 b22. Still a soft Canadian cocking a melt-in-the-mouth snook at its name. But this time the fruit is just over anxious to be heard and a degree of its old stability has been eroded. 40%. Kittling Ridge.

Okanagan Spirits Canadian Rye **(88.5)** n23 one of the most delicate and teasing of Canadian noses: a beautiful and quite natural marriage between the grains and vanillas with just the right squeeze of lemon; t22.5 seriously juicy. Just as light on the nose with a lovely coating of lemon drops. The vanilla really does show at its very cleanest; f21 vanilla now left alone for a quick finale; b22 a crisp, quite beautiful whisky with a youthful strain. Sort the thin finish out and we'd have something to really remember! Not, by the way, a whisky distilled at their new distillery. 40%

Pendleton Let'er Buck **(91.5)** n22.5 t23 f22.5 b23.5. A significantly improved whisky from the ultra-sweet, nigh on syrupy concoction of before. Here the surprisingly complex and sensual grains take star billing, despite the caramel: it almost makes a parody of being Canadian, so unmistakable is the style. For those who affectionately remember Canadian Club from 20-30 years ago, this might bring a moistening of the eye. 40% (80 proof). Hood River Distillers.

⋄⋄⋄ **Pike Creek 10 Years Old** finished in port barrels **(80)** n21.5 t22.5 f17 b19. The delivery is the highlight of the show by far as the fruit takes off backed by delicate spices and spongy softness. The nose needs some persuading to get going but when fully warmed, gives a preview of the delivery. The furry finish is a big disappointment, though. 40%

Potter's Crown **(83)** n19 t21.5 f21.5 b21. Silky and about the friendliest and most inoffensive whisky on this planet. The dusty aroma and thick, chewy toffee backbone says it all but still impossible not to enjoy! 40%

Potter's Special Old a blend of 5 to 11 year old rye whisky **(91)** n23.5 t23 f22 b22.5. More Canadian than a hockey punch-up – and, for all the spice, somewhat more gentle, too. 40%

Potter's Special Old Rye **(85.5)** n21 t23.5 f20 b21. Not quite the force majeure of a year or two back, the grains are now thinner and starker despite the beautifully striking delivery on the palate. The soft honey tones are an attractive compensation but the austerity on nose and finish takes a little getting used to when remembering previous incarnations. 40%

⋄⋄⋄ **Proof Whisky** charred oak barrels **(87.5)** n22 massive lemon and almost gin-like botanicals at work; t22 again citrus from every direction and a big spice compliment; the mid-ground is a series of satisfying sugars, mainly of the Demerara type; f21.5 thin, clean with a vague cocoa fade; b22 the Proof is in the tasting, and this is a Canadian which should attract those who enjoy Bombay-style gin, too. 42%. Proof Brands Inc.

Rich and Rare **(79)** n20 t20 f20 b19. Simplistic and soft. One for toffee lovers. 40%

Rich and Rare Reserve **(86.5)** n19.5 t21 f23.5 b22.5. Actually does what it says on the tin, certainly as to regard the "Rich" bit. But takes off when the finish spices up and even offers some ginger cake on the finale. Lovely stuff. 40%

Royal Canadian **(87.5)** n22 t22.5 f21 b22. Now there's a whisky which is on the up. 40%

Royal Canadian Small Batch **(88)** n22 t22.5 f21.5 b22. A big Canadian with a pleasing silk and steel pulse. 40%. Sazerac.

Royal Reserve (84.5) n19 t22.5 f21.5 b21.5. No question that the delivery is much richer, fresher and entertaining than before with the spices, dovetailing with subtle fruit, ensuring a complexity previously lacking - especially at the death. Frustratingly, the caramel seems to be biting deeper on the nose, which has taken a backward step. A much more enjoyable and satisfying experience, though. *40%*

Royal Reserve Gold (94.5) n24 this was already one of the better Canadian noses. And with this latest bottling the grain complexity has moved up a gear. Bereft of the tacky toffee which dulls so many Canadian whiskies, we have here a joyous mixture of rye and citrus notes beautifully embedded in decent, vanilla-clad oak and the most tantalising of light honey tones; t23.5 a glorious composition of juicy, salivating rye in tandem with a honey-biscuit note gets this off to a stupendous start. It gets better still as the spices lift off and that honey begins to stick to the roof of the mouth; f23 magically light: a dusting of oak gives a nod towards a respectable, aged dryness but then this acts only as a foil to the delicate lime and Fruit Pastille juiciness and late, radiating rye; b24 retains its position as a classy, classy Canadian that is an essay on balance. Don't confuse this with the much duller standard bottling: this has been moulded in recent years into one of the finest – and among its country's consumers - generally most underrated Canadians on the market. *40%*

Sam Barton Aged 5 Years (83.5) n19 t21.5 f22 b21. Exceptionally sweet session whisky with a lovely maple syrup glow and some complexity on the finish. Friendly, hospitable and impossible not to like. *40%. La Martinquaise, France.*

Schenley Golden Wedding (92) n22 t24 f22 b23. Like a rare, solid marriage, this has improved over time. Always consistent and pleasant, there now appears to be a touch of extra age and maturity which has sent the complexity levels up dramatically. Quite sublime. *40%*

Schenley OFC (90) n22 t22.5 f23 b22.5. Notice anything missing from this whisky? Well the 8-year-old age statement has fallen off the label. But this is still a truly superb whisky which would benefit perhaps from toning down the degree of sweetness, but gets away with it in spectacular fashion thanks to those seductive oils. Not as complex as the magnificent old days, but a whisky that would have you demanding a refill nine time out of ten. *40%*

Seagram's Canadian 83 (86.5) n21 t22 f21.5 b22. A vastly improved blend which has drastically cut the caramel to reveal a melt-in-the-mouth, slightly crisp grain. There are some citrusy edges but the buttery vanilla and pleasing bite all go to make for a chic little number. *40%*

Seagram's VO (91) n22 dried banana skin, a touch of waffle and a complex layering of drier, oaky notes; t23.5 mouth-filling, lush corn oil and a slow, sensual build up of brown sugar and spice; f22.5 back to its oaky promise on the nose as it dries with a mixture of niggly spice and vanilla; b23 with a heavy heart I have to announce the king of rye-enriched Canadian, VO, is dead. Long live the corn-dominant VO. Over the years I have seen the old traditional character ebb away: now I have let go and have no option other than to embrace this whisky for what it has become: infinitely better than a couple of years back; not in the same league as a decade ago. But just taking it on face value, credit where credit is due. This is an enjoyably playful affair, full of vanilla-led good intention, corn and complexity. There is even assertive spice when needed and the most delicately fruity edge...though not rye-style. Thoughtfully blended and with no little skill, I am impressed. And look forward to seeing how this develops in future years. A treat which needs time to discover. *40%*

Snake River Stampede 8 Years Old dist 12 Dec 99, bott. 18 Jul 08 (87.5) n22.5 t22.5 f21 b21.5. A bit concerned when I read in the blurb that they finish this Canadian whisky in sherry butts. But no need; as clean as a perfectly lassoed colt. As silky as a cowboy's kerchief. *40%*

Still Waters Special 1+11 Blend batch 1204, bott 2012 (92) n23.5 superb weaving of deep vanilla, heather honey, corn and cocoa oils and muscovado sugars...I must be in Canada..! t23 the most gorgeous texture and complex sugars. Yet, somehow not overly sweet as the drying, chalky vanillas and sharp citrus breaks up the monopoly; f22.5 the vanilla and caramel on its own with the sugars spent leaves a bitter but manageable finale; b23 if the boys at Still Waters distillery end up with a whisky as enjoyable as this when theirs has matured, Canadian whisky will have flourished. *40%. 1200 bottles.*

Tangle Ridge Aged 10 Years (69) n18.5 t19.5 f15 b16. Decidedly less in your face than of old, unless you are thinking custard pies. For all the cleaned up aroma and early injection of spiced sultana, the uncompromisingly grim finish remains its usual messy self. An unpleasant reminder as to why I only taste this when it's Bible time... *40%*

Tesco Canadian Whisky (75) n18 t18 f20 b19. Sweet, clean, uninspiring. *40%*

Western Gold Canadian Whisky (91) n23 a lovely intertwining of delicate, slightly citrusy vanilla and light corn oils. With toffee, of course...; t23 clean, sweet, delicate with outstanding oils from the grain. The thin honey is a treat; f22.5 long and back to citrus vanilla again; b22.5 clean and absolutely classic Canadian: you can't ask for much more, really. *40%*

White Owl (77.5) n19 t19.5 f20 b19. White whisky: in others words, a whisky the same colour as water. To both nose and taste somewhat reminds me of the long gone Manx whisky which was casks of fully matured scotch re-distilled and bottled. Sweet and pleasant. But I doubt if connoisseurs will give two hoots... *40%*

Windsor (85.5) n21 t22 f21 b21.5. A whisky you could usually bet your week's wages on for consistency and depth. Here, though, the usual rye fruity, crispness has been dumbed down and though there are enough spices to make this a pleasant affair, the impact of the caramel is a tad too significant. The usual custard sweetness has also changed shape and dry vanilla at the death is the compromise. *40%*

Windsor (86) n20 t21 f23 b22. Pleasant but with the majority of edges found on the Canadian edition blunted. Some outstanding, almost attritional, spice towards the middle and finale, though. Soft and desirable throughout: a kind of feminine version of the native bottling. *40%. For US market.*

Winn Dixie Canadian Whisky (80) n19 t20 f21 b20. Soft, sweet, toffeed and boasting a little spice...but with minimum fuss. *40%*

Wiser's Very Old 18 Years Old (90.5) n24 t23 f21.5 b22. Much better than the last bottling I encountered, which in itself was no slouch. Here, though, the blender has written bolder what he is trying to achieve. *40%*

Wiser's De Luxe (86) n20 t22.5 f21.5 b22. Still nothing like the classic, ultra-charming and almost fragile-delicate Wiser's of old. But this present bottling has got its head partly out of the sand by injecting a decently oaked spiciness to the proceedings and one might even fancy detecting shards of fruity- rye brightness beaming through the toffeed clutter. Definitely an impressive turn for the better and the kind of Canadian with a dangerous propensity to grow on you. If they had the nerve to cut the caramel, this could be a cracker... *40%*

Wiser's Legacy (95) n24 even by Canadian standards, a little different: coriander and juniper give a slight gin-style edge to this, though waiting in the wings is a subtle, spicy wine quality. The teasing sweetness, not entirely without a bourbon style new-oakiness and hint of rye-fruitiness, has all the intensity of Mona Lisa's smile...; **t24.5** there is a crystalline quality to the nose, and it transfers immediately to the palate. One is reminded of absolutely unblemished First Growth Bordeaux in the way the grape–fruitiness announces itself before progressing into greatness. After that, it takes, thankfully, a very different course except perhaps in the way the spices unfold: first no more than a shadow, then blossoming out into something profound, deep and always in sync with all else that is going on. Cocoa notes arrive early and stay while the grains offer a salivating edge...nothing short of glorious...; **f22.5** serious but high quality and contained oak: dry and toasty but always a light dusting of slightly sweetened vanilla; **b22.5** when my researcher got this bottle for me to taste, she was told by the Wiser's guy that I would love it, as it had been specially designed along the lines of what I considered essential attributes to Canadian whisky. Whether Mr Wiser was serious or not, such a statement both honoured and rankled slightly and made me entirely determined to find every fault with it I could and knock such impertinence down a peg or two. Instead, I was seduced like a 16-year-old virgin schoolboy in the hands of a 30-year-old vixen. An entirely disarming Canadian which is almost a whisky equivalent to the finest of the great French wines in its rich, unfolding style. Complex beyond belief, spiced almost to supernatural perfection, this is one of the great newcomers to world whisky in the last year. It will take a glass of true magnificence to outdo this for Canadian Whisky of the Year. *45%*

Wiser's Red Letter (95) n24 t24 f23.5 b23.5. The recent trend with Canadian whisky has been to do away with finesse and cram each bottle with fruit. This returns us to a very old fashioned and traditional Canadian style. And had the rye been upped slightly and the caramel eschewed entirely it might have been a potential world whisky of the year...Even in this form, however, it is certainly good enough to be Canadian Whisky of the Year 2010. *45%*

Wiser's Reserve (75) n19 t20 f18 b18. The nose offers curious tobacco while the palate is uneven, with the bitterness out of tandem with the runaway early sweetness. In the confusion the fruit never quite knows which way to turn. A once mighty whisky has fallen. And I now understand it might be the end of the line with the excellent Wiser's Small Batch coming in to replace it. So if you are a reserve fan, buy them up now. *43%*

Wiser's Small Batch (90.5) n21.5 much bigger in the fruit department than of yore with the grains struggling to be heard; soft to the point of borderline flat; **t24** that's more like it!! Back online with the huge, salivating, juicy, mouth-enveloping delivery. The spices spark and ark around the palate and for a while the fruits are lost. Layers of grain dominate and the balance between the brown sugar sweetness and the pounding peppers is sublime; **f22** much harder and crisp with the fruit having now fallen by the wayside. Even the spices burn out leaving firm vanilla; **b23** a real oddity with the nose and taste on different planets. The fruity onslaught promised by the drab nose never materialises – thankfully! – and instead we are treated to a rich, grainy explosion. It's the spices, though, that take the plaudits. *43.4%*

Wiser's Special Blend (78) n19 t20 f19 b19. A plodding, pleasant whisky with no great desire to offer much beyond caramel. *40%*

Japanese Whisky

At Edinburgh Castle in 2010 a fanfare of pipes heralded the launch of the first 70-year-old whisky certainly within living memory. A Speyside scotch single malt, it deservedly brought great acclaim and an enormous degree of publicity. Elsewhere, sneaking in through the back door, came a Japanese single malt bottled by the Whisky Exchange in London as part of their 10th anniversary celebrations. It was 42 years old and from the Karuizawa distillery.

Now Japan tends to get hot... very hot. Certainly a lot hotter than anywhere in Scotland. And though the Winters can sometimes be equally if not more cold than Speyside, I would be quite confident in saying that 42 Japanese Summers is worth at least 70 Scottish in terms of whisky maturation. Ironically, I sat next to WE's owner, Sukhinder Singh, at the Edinburgh event but didn't have time to chat about the Karuizawa. Perhaps the Mortlach edges it in terms of finesse and overall star quality, but for sheer fun the freaky Karuizawa 1967 wins hands down and, for me, and despite its obvious oaky input, was the Japanese Whisky of the Year. I am not the only one praying that this has opened the door for other grandiose Japanese malts to follow.

Yet still there is a great frustration that the myriad types of Japanese whisky is unlikely to be seen outside the mother country, so slow has the expansion of their whisky empire been.

I have met a number of whisky shop owners around the world who will stock only a handful of Japanese simply because they cannot get assurances that what they are being sent does not contain Scotch. Certainly, these mind-blowing single malts which had lorded it with the world's elite were 100% from the land of the rising sun. But until exchanging whiskies within Japanese companies becomes a natural part of their culture it is hard to see how the confidence generated by the excellence of the single malt and grains available as singletons can be extended to the blends.

Part of the problem has been the Japanese custom of refusing to trade with their rivals. Therefore a Japanese whisky, if not made completely from home-distilled spirit, will instead contain a percentage of Scotch rather than whisky from fellow Japanese distillers.

This, ultimately, is doing the industry no favours at all. The practice is partly down to the traditional work ethics of company loyalty and an inherent, and these days false, belief that Scotch whisky is automatically better than Japanese. Back in the late 1990s I planted the first seeds in trying to get rival distillers to discuss with each other the possibility of exchanging whiskies to ensure that their distilleries worked more economically.

In the meantime word is getting round that Japanese whisky is worth finding. It is now not uncommon for me to discuss with whisky lovers at a fair or book signing the merits and differences of Yoichi and Hakushu, two distilleries which are now being correctly recognised for their world-class brilliance. And, increasingly, Yamazaki which has moved away from a comfort zone it operated in for many years and is now offering malts of great magnitude: indeed, it was recently the producer of one of the two

Yamazaki
●Osaka

●Fukuoka

Yoichi

●Sapporo

Sendai ▲

Shirakawa ▲

▲ Karuizawa

Hakushu ▲   ▲ Hanyu

▲ Mars Shinshu   ●Tokyo

Gotemba ▲

Key
● **Major Town or City**
▲ Distillery

Japanese whiskies which was considered as a possible Whisky Bible World Whisky of the Year. And I still get a small thrill when I hear Yoichi's name mentioned around the world: I'm proud to have first brought it to the world's attention way back in 1997 – though these days the distillery, like all others in Japan, has to be a little more careful with their use of sherry.

Mind you, the same didn't have to be said about the Karuizawa 1967. That may have been matured in a sherry butt, but it was filled in the good old days when they were sent from Jerez to Japan still full of the fortified wine, so arrived fresh. Further evidence that there is just no beating the old traditions...

The success of India's Amrut has opened people's minds to the possibility of great whisky being made in lands far from the Scottish glens. Yet still the main problem for whisky lovers is the availability and price of Japanese whisky outside its own borders. The latter is hardly surprising, seeing as the cost of making a litre of spirit in Japan is higher than any other country in the world. But as for availability... even we at the Whisky Bible have problems tracking down many of the great whiskies the country has to offer. It is as though no-one has yet been told there is a huge international market full of people just wanting to discover if the whiskies are as good as I and others have been saying for the last two decades.

Single Malts
CHICHIBU

Golden Horse Chichibu Aged 12 Years bott July 08 db **(95.5)** n24 a majestic nose: crushed nuts on a big malt plane; diced Slovakian milk chocolate and a bourbon injection of mild honeycomb, hickory and toasty Demerara. Sounds like bourbon, but there is a certain something that is purely Japanese. Meanwhile, a slab of drying dates guarantees immortality, despite a inter-planetary distant, nagging bitterness. Sublime... **t24.5** a fruity delivery intensified by spice and a build up of oils that borders on the obscene. I am salivating and having my mouth coated with intense barley all at the same moment: a near unique experience; the letters at the command of my keyboard can't quite describe the depth of the honey or the subtle layering of sugars; **f23** the malt and vanillas become inseparable while the spices ramp up an extra couple of gears. The delicate sugars and drier oaks absolutely match each other stride for stride. Some very late bitterness, but it hardly matters (actually, it probably does), especially when the honeycomb is making a late comeback. How long can a finish be...? **b24** immaculate, faultless (OK, nearly faultless), whisky. And, rarely for Japanese, bottled at exactly the right age. Had this not been bottled in 2008, a contender for World Whisky of the Year. Guys! You have to get this to me sooner!!! For the record, it kind of took me back to the mid 1970s when I was first studying whisky, for here I felt I was learning about this distillery for the very first time...Oh, and for the best effects: don't bother warming in the glass – just pour...and score... *56%*

⁘ **Ichiro's Malt Chichibu Floor Malted 2009** **(85.5)** n22 t22.5 f20 b21. Big, pre-pubescent malt and barley statement, though barely in unison. The bitterness on the finish is unchecked. *50.5%*.

⁘ **Ichiro's Chichibu Peated 2009** **(91.5)** n23 shows way more oaky thrust than the non-peated version. Overcooked kippers, actually, a little burnt. Little sign of its tender age...; **t23.5** massive cascades of muscovado sugars begin to grow into something more assertively smoky; the next stop is a glorious mix of honeydew melon and sugar glazed smoked bacon... wow! **f22** the sheer lack of years suggests this should run out of puff and it does towards the vanilla clad finish; **b23** you can stand your chopsticks up in this one...works so beautifully in so many department. *50.5%*

⁘ **Number One Asama 1999/2000** **(71)** n17 t19 f16 b19. Sulphured. *46%*

FUJI GOTEMBA 1973. Kirin Distillers.

The Fuji Gotemba 15 Years Old db **(92)** n21 t23 f24 b24. Quality malt of great poise. *43%. Kirin.*

HAKUSHU 1973. Suntory.

Hakushu Heavily Peated Aged 9 Years bott 2009 db **(92.5)** n22.5 t23.5 f23 b23.5. Nothing like as heavily peated as some Hakushus it has been my pleasure to sample over the years. But certainly superbly orchestrated and balanced. *48%*

Hakushu Single Malt Whisky Aged 12 Years db **(91.5)** n22.5 t23.5 f22.5 b23. Just about identical to the 43.3% bottling in every respect. Please see those tasting notes for this little beauty. *43.5%*

Hakushu Single Malt Aged 12 Years db **(91)** n22 t23 f23 b23. An even more lightly-peated version of the 40%, with the distillery's fabulous depth on full show. *43.3%*

Hakushu Single Malt Whisky Aged 12 Years bott 2011 db **(95.5)** n24 light but offering enough to really get the nose twitching: complex oaky tones offering subdued vanilla as a platform for the brighter barley, some of which is offering little more than a soupcon **t23.5** salivating, crisp malt turns towards a sugary, gristy very mildly smoky form; spices engage the vanilla in the middle ground; **f23.5** subtle, teasing spices infiltrate the soft lemon jelly and vanilla sponge cake; **b24.5** a prime example of what makes this such a magnificent distillery. One of the most complex and clever 12 year old malts to be found anywhere in the world this year: a great whisky that could be easily overlooked. *43%*

The Hakushu Single Malt Whisky Aged 15 Years Cask Strength db **(95)** n24 pure, unmistakable Hakushu: intense, powering, yet clean and refined. Loads of citrus to lighten matters but the local oak ensures enormity; **t23** big, initially oak-threatened but the barley comes flooding back with light oils helping to soften the early scratchiness; first mouthful is dry, the second shows a much truer picture; **f24** now goes into complexity overdrive as all those fruity-barley-oaky- elements continue to jostle for supremacy, only for late spices and gorgeous milky mocha to come in and steal the thunder; **b24** last time round I lamented the disappointing nose. This time perhaps only a degree of over eagerness from the oak has robbed this as a serious Whisky of the Year contender. No matter how you look at it, though, brilliant!! *56%*

The Hakushu Single Malt Whisky Aged 25 Years db **(93)** n23 t24 f23 b23. A malt which is impossible not to be blown away by. *43%*

Hakushu Single Malt Whisky Aged 25 Years bott 2011 db **(91)** n23.5 t23.5 f21 b23. Just one slightly off butt away from total magnificence. 43%

Hakushu 1984 db **(95)** n22 t25 f24 b24. A masterpiece of quite sublime complexity and balance. The sort of experience that gives a meaning to life, the universe and everything... 61%

Hakushu 1988 db **(92)** n21 t24 f23 b24. Like all great whiskies this is one that gangs up on you in a way you are not expecting: the limited complexity on the nose is more than compensated for elsewhere. Superb. If this were an Islay malt the world would be drooling over it. 61%

Scotch Malt Whisky Society Cask 120.05 Aged 17 Years 1st fill barrel, dist Dec 91 **(94)** n23 subtly peated in a way Hakushu possibly does best of all; t24 it's all there: the most deft smoke; firm, eye-watering barley; explodingly over-ripe cherries; an Arbroath Smokie saltiness; oil laced with honey...; f23.5 remains bullet hard and mercurially smoky to the last departing atom; b23.5 amazingly, this is a less than perfect cask deployed. But so absurdly good was the spirit filled into it, you barely notice...or care. 59%. 104 bottles.

Suntory Pure Malt Hakushu Aged 20 Years db **(94)** n23 fresh, mildly grapey fruit combined with subtle waves of peat; t24 the peat is now less subtle: wave upon wave of it bringing with it flotsam of drifting oak and then a very sharp malt tang; f23 long, sweet spice but the oak forms a chunky alliance with the firm peat. The bitter-sweet compexity almost defies belief; b24 a hard-to-find malt, but find it you must. Yet another huge nail in the coffin of those who purport Japanese whisky to be automatically inferior to Scotch. 56%

HANYU

Hanyu Final Vintage 2000 cask no. 6309, bott 2010 **(94.5)** n23.5 t24 f23.5 b23.5. A fabulous exhibition in just how a sherry whisky should be: blemish free and exploding from the glass with personality. A fabulous malt made for this kind of strength. 59.7%. sc. Venture Whisky Co.

Hanyu Single Malt 2000 hogshead refilled into Japanese oak, bott 2011 db **(91.5)** n21.5 t24; f23.5 b23.5. About as sweet a whisky can go and still be in total control. An after dinner malt if ever there was one... 60.9%. For 'Whisky Live Tokyo 2011'.

Ichiro's Card "Four of Spades" Japanese oak "Mizunara" puncheon finish, dist 2000, bott 2010 **(95)** n24 t24.5 f23.5 b23.5. I have often heard the Japanese accused of trying to mimic scotch whisky. On this evidence, it's the Kentuckians who should be looking over their shoulder... 58.6%. Venture Whisky Ltd.

Ichiro's Card "King of Hearts" PX finish, dist 1986, bott 2009 **(95.5)** n23.5 t24 f24 b24. This King of Hearts had some smoky tarts...delicious and complex almost beyond measure! 55.4%

Ichiro's Card "Ten of Hearts" Hanyu 2000 Madeira hogshead finish, bott 2011 **(91)** n22.5 t23 f22.5 b23. Thank you, Madeira... 61%

Ichiro's Card "Three of Hearts" Hanyu 2000 Port pipe finish, bott 2010 **(90)** n23 t23.5 f21 b22.5. Delicious, but an astonishing degree of toffee is created in the process. 61.2%. Venture Whisky Ltd.

Ichiro's Malt Aged 20 Years **(95.5)** n24 a magnificent portrait of complexity. The malt stands proud and clean, offering a mildly crusty light sugariness; the oaks are a model of good manners: vanilla and honey, but in the most modest amounts; here and there the odd molecule of smoke; t24 a delivery to pray and die for: such spices, such juiciness after so many years: remarkable. The middle ground is taken up by a quite glorious concentrated Malteser candy...but with better milky cocoa than found in the bag; f23.5 long and brimming with so many layers of barley the head spins. The Malteser story continues; b24 no this finish; no that finish. Just the distillery allowed to speak in its very own voice. And nothing more eloquent has been heard from it this year. Please, all those owning casks of Hanyu: for heaven's sake take note... 57.5%. Venture Whisky Ltd.

Ichiro's Malt Aged 23 Years **(92.5)** n23 t23.5 f23 b23. A fabulous malt you take your time over. 58%

One Single Cask Hanyu 1990 cask no. 9305, bott 2009 **(90.5)** n23 t23 f22.5 b22. Huge whisky but borderline OTT oak. The infused sugars do the trick. 53.4%. Number One Drinks Co.

One Single Cask Hanyu 1991 Japanese oak, cask no. 370, bott 2009 **(91.5)** n22 t23.5 f23 b23. Unmistakable style: I found myself muttering " ah, local oak!" to myself (tasting close on 800 malts in a couple of months does that to you...) before I spotted the label. Quite beautiful. 57.3%. Number One Drinks Co.

KARUIZAWA 1955. Mercian.

⁙ **Karuizawa 1964** sherry cask, cask no. 3603, dist 1 Sep 64, bott 24 Dec 12 **(95.5)** n24.5 much more than just massive, well-aged fruit cake. The spices are from another planet: probably the planet Pepper and Paprika; all kinds of advanced fruit notes, including kumquat and kiwifruit. A stick of salted celery on hand too; t24 the spices stimulate a cascade of saliva...so old yet so mouth-watering! Huge fruit follow through and now we get to a Melton Hunt cake matured for maybe two years with some 25-year-old Macallan (bottled in the mid '80s) tipped in to moisturise; **f23** the toasty, scorched raisin bitterness underscores the vintage but just enough Demerara sugar and marzipan (from the fruitcake?) survive to see no damage is done; **b24** a number one example of premier class, unsullied sherry butt from the Number One company. And Japanese Whisky of the Year without doubt. *57.7%. nc ncf sc. Number One Drinks Company. 143 bottles. Poland.*

Karuizawa 1967 Vintage sherry cask, bott 2009 db **(96) n24 t24.5 f23.5 b24.** Another engaging, engrossing and frankly, brilliant malt from this distillery, equalling the oldest I have ever encountered from Karuizawa. If you find it, sell your body, sell your partner's body... anything...just experience it! *58.4%*

Karuizawa 1982 sherry, bott 2009 db **(90) n23 t24 f22 b22.** Forget the sherry. Forget the distant, nagging "S" word. Just home in on that astonishing middle: like a million Maltesers dissolving in your mouth all at once...there is nothing else like it in the whisky world. And no other distillery is capable. Alas. *56.1%. Speciality Drinks Ltd bottled for TWE's 10th Anniversary.*

Karuizawa 1983 Noh Bottling cask no. 7576, bott 2012 **(90.5) n23** good grief....!!! I think I have nosed something remotely like this only at Ardbeg with the sherry butts closest to the ocean. But even those pale by comparison. So salty, I am not sure I like it...(sniff, sniff...).. actually, I think I do...; **t23** taste this only when sitting in chairs with an arm rest. You need something to drip on to as the salt and fruit seer through you...; luckily, there is just enough molasses to ensure balance, but it takes a while for the shell-shocked taste buds to re-align and spot it; **f22** dry, toasty, burnt fruitcake..where salt appears to have partially replaced the sugar on top...; **b22.5** truly astonishing: an absolute one off. Unquestionably the most sea-salty whisky – malt or otherwise – I have ever tasted in my life. By several thousand fathoms... *57.2%. sc. Number One Drinks Company.*

Karuizawa Pure Malt Aged 17 Years db **(90) n20 t24 f23 b23.** Brilliant whisky beautifully made and majestically matured. Neither sweetness nor dryness dominates, always the mark of a quality dram. *40%*

Noh Whisky Karuizawa 1976 cask no. 6719, bott 09 **(91) n22 t24 f22.5 b22.5.** Sticks religiously to the malty house style despite the grape trying to enter from every angle. A beautiful whisky, reminding me what a special year 1976 was for Japan. Happy 35th in April. *63%.*

⋰⋱ **The Spirit Of Asama** sherry cask **(71.5) n17 t19 f17 b18.5.** Sulphur hit. *48%.*

⋰⋱ **The Spirit Of Asama** sherry cask **(75) n18 t20 f18 b19.** Lots of sultanas. Sweet. Pleasant in part. But it isn't just Scotland suffering from poor sherry butts. *55%.*

KIRIN

Kirin 18 Years Old db **(86.5) n22 t22 f21.5 b21.** Unquestionably over-aged. Even so, still puts up a decent show with juicy citrus trying to add a lighter touch to the uncompromising, ultra dense oak. As entertaining as it is challenging. *43%. Suntory.*

KOMAGATAKE

Komagatake 1992 Single Cask American white oak cask, cask no. 1144, dist 1992, bott 2009 db **(93.5) n24.5 t23 f22.5 b23.5.** You know when you've had a glass of this: beautiful and no shrinking violet. *46%. Mars.*

MIYAGIKYO *(see Sendai)*

SENDAI 1969. Nikka.

Miyagikyo 15 Years Old batch 02I10D db **(91.5) n23 t23.5 f22 b23.** A much lighter, more refined and elegant creature than before. Despite a minor sherry butt blemish, fabulous. *45%*

⋰⋱ **Scotch Malt Whisky Society Cask 124.03** Aged 13 Years refill butt, dist 20 Jul 99 **(88) n22.5** one of those noses you just know is going to be better than what will follow next on the palate: a real bourbony marmalade on toast number but with the hint of a spitfire to come; **t22** yep! Buckle yourself in for the ride, guys. That explosion on the palate has little to do with strength: this is all about the speed of the run through the stills. And this orangey-malty inferno was fast; **f21** thin, gluey; **b21.5** seriously feisty. I'm off to chew a jalapeno to cool down... *61.9%. nc ncf sc. 509 bottles.*

SHIRAKAWA

Shirakawa 32 Years Old Single Malt (94) n23 ripe mango meets a riper, rye-encrusted bourbon. We are talking a major aroma here; **t24** the most intense malt you'll ever find explodes and drools all over your tastebuds. To make the flavour bigger still, the oak adds a punchy bourbon quality. Beautiful oils coat the roof of the mouth to amplify the performance; **f23** long, sweet and malty. Some fruitiness does arrive but it is the oak-malt combination that just knocks you out; **b24** just how big can an unpeated malt whisky get? The kind of malt that leaves you in awe, even when you thought you had seen and tasted them all. *55%. Takara.*

WHITE OAK DISTILLERY

White Oak Akashi Single Malt Whisky Aged 8 Years bott 2007 db **(74.5)** n18.5 t19.5 f17.5 b19. Always fascinating to find a malt from one of the smaller distilleries in a country. And I look forward to tracking this one down and visiting, something I have yet to do. There is certainly something distinctly small still about his one, with butyric and feintiness causing damage to nose and finish. For all the early malty presence on delivery, some of the off notes are a little on the uncomfortable side. *40%*

YAMAZAKI 1923. Suntory.

Yamazaki 1984 bott 2009 db **(94)** n24 t24 f22.5 b23.5. If you like your whisky boringly neutral, lifeless and with nothing to say other than that it has been ruined by sulphur, then this will horrify you. Though there is a little blemish at the very death, there is still no taking away from this being a sublime 25-year-old. When this distillery is on form it makes for compelling whisky and here we have a bottling showing Yamazaki at its brightest. *48%*

The Yamazaki Single Malt Whisky Aged 12 Years bott 2011 db **(90)** n23 t22 f22.5 b22.5. A complex and satisfying malt. *43%*

The Yamazaki Single Malt Whisky Aged 15 Years Cask Strength db **(94)** n23 just a hint that its gone OTT oak-wise, but there is a wisp of smoke to this, too. All in all, wonderful brinkmanship that pays off; **t24** stunning: a massive injection of bourbon-style liquorice and honeycomb plays perfectly against the softer malts. The most controlled of malty explosions... **f23** long, lascivious, the tastebuds are debauched by ingots of honeycomb, molasses and dark sugary notes balanced by the drier oaks; **b24** an extraordinary bottling that far exceeds any previous version I have encountered. Stunning. *56%*

Suntory Pure Malt Yamazaki 25 Years Old db **(91)** n23 t23 f22 b23. Being matured in Japan, the 25 years doesn't have quite the same value as Scotland. So perhaps in some ways this can lay claim to be one of the most enormously aged, oak-laden whiskies that has somehow kept its grace and star quality. *43%*

YOICHI 1934. Nikka.

Yoichi Key Malt Aged 12 Years "Peaty & Salty" db **(95)** n23 t25 f23 b24. Of all the peated whiskies of the world, only Ardbeg can stand shoulder to shoulder with Yoichi when it comes to sheer complexity. Here is an astonishing example of why I rate Yoichi in the best five whiskies in the world. Forget the odd sulphur-tarnished bottling. Get Yoichi in its natural state with perfect balance between oak and malt and it delivers something approaching perfection. And this is just such a bottling. *55%. Nikka.*

Yoichi Single Malt 12 Years Old batch 14F36A db **(91)** n22 t23 f23 b23. Best when left in the glass for 10-15 minutes: only then does the true story emerge. *45%*

Yoichi 15 Years Old batch 06I08B db **(91.5)** n22 t23 t23.5 f23 b23. For an early moment or two possibly one of the most salivating whiskies you'll get your kisser around this year. Wonderfully entertaining yet you still suspect that this is another Yoichi reduced in effect somewhat by either caramel and/or sherry. When it hits its stride, though, becomes a really busy whisky that gets tastebuds in a right lather. But I'm being picky as I know that this is one of the world's top five distilleries and am aware as anyone on this planet of its extraordinary capabilities. Great fun; great whisky – could be better still, but so much better than its siblings... *45%*

Yoichi 20 Years Old db **(95)** n23 t23 f25 b24. I don't know how much they charge for this stuff but either alone or with mates get some for one hell of an experience. What makes it all the more remarkable is that there is a slight sulphury note on the nose: once you taste the stuff that becomes of little consequence. *52%. Nikka.*

Nikka Whisky Yoichi 1986 20 Years Old db **(94)** n23 age, the salty sea air of Hokkaido and sweet oak have accounted for the more excessive possibilities of the peat: weighty but restrained; **t24** no holding back here, though, as the delivery is one first of juicy fruit and then silky waves of peat; chunky heavy-duty stuff which, for some reason, appears to float about the palate; the spices shoot on sight; **f23** a sweeter, more sober finale with liquorice and molasses joining forces with the salty oakiness to keep the lid on the smoke; **b24** now this is unambiguous Yoichi :exactly how I have come to know and adore this distillery. *55.0%*

⁖⁖ **Scotch Malt Whisky Society Cask 116.17 Aged 25 Years** 1st fill sherry butt **(96)** n24.5 I have very rarely encountered a nose like it: every last atom is oak enriched. Unlikely you'll find so many orange notes in one glass, all of them intensifying to the point of creating their own black holes; elsewhere green tea from a Sahara campfire permeates proceedings; **t24.5** wonderful maple-syrup infused oils cushion the palate for the oaky onslaught. Spices threaten but vanish as quickly as they arrive while an unusual Turkish Delight with sugar almonds middle pulse complex layers of depth; f23 the drying over-exuberance of the oak begins to take its toll. But still plenty of vanilla to make for a picturesque final journey; b24 not as mouth-puckering as I expected from the nose. The sugars ensure this incredible celebration of all things oak works memorably well. 59.2%. nc ncf sc. 485 bottles.

⁘ **Scotch Malt Whisky Society 116.18 Aged 18 Years** refill butt, dist 2 Feb 94 (89) n23 sweet chestnut and major creamy, salty tannin; t23 a coastal saltiness pervades as cream soda and insane butterscotch dig in; f21 just a little off key bite; b22 not one of the truly great Yoichis in its traditional style but a salty, beast of a malt. 64.4%. nc ncf sc. 410 bottles.

Unspecified Malts

"Hokuto" Suntory Pure Malt Aged 12 Years (93) n22 t24 f23 b24. Another example of Suntory at its most feminine: just so seductive and beautiful. Although a malt, think Lawson's 12-y-o of a decade ago and you have the picture. 40%

Nikka Whisky From the Barrel batch 12F32C db (91) n22 t24 f22 b23. Truly great whisky that mostly overcomes the present Japanese curse of big caramel finishes. 51.4%

Nikka Whisky Single Coffey Malt 12 Years (97) n23.5 forget all about the malt: it's the big bourbony, hickory and honey sweet oak which wins hands down; t25 hold on to your hats: it's flavour explosion time...on first tasting it's simply too much to comprehend. Only on third or fourth mouthful do you really get an idea. First, the delivery is pretty close to perfection: the soft oils seem to draw every last nuance from the barley; then when it has done that, it manages to mix it with myriad delicate sweet notes radiating from the oak. This includes some of those allied to bourbon, especially chocolate honeycomb and very deep molassed notes usually associated with Demerara Coffey still rum; a unique combination absolutely perfectly displayed; f24 long...just so long. One mouthful, especially at 55%, last for about six or seven minutes. So impressive here is the delicacy of the fade: after a delivery so large, the finesse is extraordinary. The flavours in effect mirror the earlier delivery. Except now some vanilla does come in to dry things a little; b24.5 the Scotch Whisky Association would say that this is not single malt whisky because it is made in a Coffey still. When they can get their members to make whisky this stunning on a regular basis via their own pots and casks, then perhaps they should pipe up as their argument might then have a single atom of weight. 55%

Vatted Malts

All Malt (86) n22 t21 f21 b22. The best example by a mile of an almost unique style of vatted whisky: both malt and "grain" are distilled from entirely malted barley, identical to Kasauli malt whisky in India. Stupendous grace and balance. 40%. Nikka.

All Malt "Pure & Rich" (89) n22 t24 f21 b22. Not unlike some bottlings of Highland Park with its emphasis on honey. If they could tone down the caramel it'd really be up there. 40%. Nikka.

All Malt Pure & Rich batch 14F24A (77) n19 t20 f19 b19. My former long term Japanese girlfriend, Makie (hope you enjoyed your 30th birthday in April, by the way), used to have a favourite saying, namely: "I am shocked!" Well, I am shocked by this whisky because it is much blander than the previous bottling (04E16D), with all that ultra-delicate and complex honeycomb lost and lovely gristiness removed. For me, one of the biggest surprises – and disappointments - of the 2007 Bible. But proof that, when using something so potentially dangerous as caramel, it is too easy to accidentally cross that fine line between brilliance and blandness. Because, had they gone the other way, we might have had a challenger for World Whisky of the Year. 40%. Nikka.

Hokuto Pure Malt Aged 12 Years (86) n20 t22 f22 b22. An oaky threat never materialises: excellent mixing. 40%. Suntory.

Ichiro's Malt Double Distilleries bott 2010 (86.5) n22.5 t22 f21 b21. Some imperious barley-rich honey reigns supreme until a bitter wood note bites hard. 46%. Venture Whisky Ltd.

Ichiro's Malt Mizunara Wood Reserve (76) n19 t21 f18 b19. I have my Reservations about the Wood, too... 46%. Venture Whisky Ltd.

Malt Club "Pure & Clear" (83) n21 t22 f20 b20. Another improved vatting, much heavier and older than before with bigger spice. 40%. Nikka.

Mars Maltage Pure Malt 8 Years Old (84) n20 t21 f21 b22. A very level, intense, clean malt with no peaks or troughs, just a steady variance in the degree of sweetness and oak input. Impossible not to have a second glass of. 43%. Mars.

Nikka Malt 100 The Anniversary Aged 12 Years (73) n18 t19 f18 b18. The depressing and deadly fingerprint of sulphur is all over this. Shame, as the spices excel. 40%

Nikka Pure Malt Aged 21 Years batch 08I18D db (89) n23 t22.5 f21.5 b22. By far the best of the set. 43%

Nikka Pure Malt Aged 17 Years batch 08I30B db **(83) n21 t21 f20 b21**. A very similar shape to the 12-years-old, but older - obviously. Certainly the sherry butts have a big say and don't always do great favours to the high quality spirit. *43%*

Nikka Pure Malt Aged 12 Years batch 10I24C db **(84) n21.5 t21 f20 b21.5**. The nose may be molassed, sticky treacle pudding, but it spices up on the palate. The dull buzz on the finish also tells a tale. *40%*

Pure Malt Black batch 02C58A **(95) n24** an exquisitely crafted nose: studied peat in luxuriant yet deft proportions nestling amid some honeyed malt and oak. The balance between sweet and dry is faultless. There is neither a single off-note nor a ripple of disharmony. The kind of nose you can sink your head into and simply disappear; **t23** for all the evident peat, this is medium-weighted, the subtlety encased in a gentle cloak of oil; **f23** long, silky, fabulously weighted peat running a sweet course through some surging malt and liquorice tones with a bit of salt in there for zip; **b25** well, if anyone can show me a better-balanced whisky than this you know where to get hold of me. You open a bottle of this at your peril: best to do so in the company of friends. Either way, it will be empty before the night is over. *43%. Nikka.*

Pure Malt Black batch 06F54B **(92) n24 t24 f21 b23**. Not the finish of old, but everything else is present and correct for a cracker! *43%. Nikka.*

Pure Malt Red batch 02C30B **(86) n21 t21 f22 b22**. A light malt that appears heavier than it actually is with an almost imperceptible oiliness. *43%. Nikka.*

Pure Malt Red batch 06F54C **(84) n21 t22 f20 b21**. Oak is the pathfinder here, but the oily vanilla-clad barley is light and mouth-watering. *43%. Nikka.*

Pure Malt White batch 02C30C **(92) n23 t24 f22 b23**. A big peaty number displaying the most subtle of hands. *43%. Nikka.*

Pure Malt White batch 06J26 **(91) n22 t23 f22 b24**. A sweet malt, but one with such deft use of peat and oak that one never really notices. Real class. *43%*

Pure Malt White batch 10F46C **(90) n23 t23 f22 b22**. There is a peculiarly Japanese feel to this delicately peated delight. *43%*

Southern Alps Pure Malt (93) n24 t23 f22 b24. This is a bottle I have only to look at to start salivating. Sadly, though, I drink sparingly from it as it is a hard whisky to find, even in Japan. Fresh, clean and totally stunning, the term "pure malt" could not be more apposite. Fabulous whisky: a very personal favourite. *40%. Suntory.*

Super Nikka Vatted Pure Malt (76) n20 t19 f19 b18. Decent and chewy but something doesn't quite click with this one. *55.5%. Nikka.*

Taketsuru Pure Malt 12 Years Old (80) n19 t22 f19 b20. For its age, heavier than a sumo wrestler. But perhaps a little more agile over the tastebuds. Lovely silkiness impresses, but lots of toffee. *40%. Nikka.*

Taketsuru Pure Malt 17 Years Old (89) n21 t22 f23 b23 Not a whisky for the squeamish. This is big stuff – about as big as it gets without peat or rye. No bar shelf or whisky club should be without one. *43%. Nikka.*

Taketsuru Pure Malt 21 Years Old (88) n22 t21 f22 b23. A much more civilised and gracious offering than the 17 year old: there is certainly nothing linear about the character development from Taketsuru 12 to 21 inclusive. Serious whisky for the serious whisky drinker. *43%. Nikka.*

Zen (84) n19 t22 f22 b21. Sweet, gristy malt; light and clean. *40%. Suntory.*

Japanese Single Grain

Kawasaki Single Grain sherry butt, dist 1982, bott 2011 db **(95.5) n23.5** clean thick grape offering several layers of depth and intensity. Salty and sharp, too. My god, this is very much alive and kicking...; **t24** classic! Faultless grape arm in arm with rich, fruity fudge. Some spices arrive on impact and slowly spread out with the marauding sugars; **f24** chocolate fudge and garibaldi biscuit...carried far on usual oils for a grain...amazing! **b24** my usual reaction to seeing the words "sherry" and "whisky" when in the context of Japanese whisky, is to feel the heart sinking like the sun. Sulphur is a problem that is no stranger to their whiskies. This, however, is a near perfect sherry butt, clean and invigorating. Grain or malt, it makes no difference: excellent spirit plus excellent cask equals (as often as not) magnificence. *65.5%*.

Blends

Ajiwai Kakubin (see Kakubin Ajiwai)

Black Nikka Aged 8 Years (82) n20 t21 f21 b20. Beautifully bourbony, especially on the nose. Lush, silky and great fun. Love it! 40%. Nikka.

The Blend of Nikka (90) n21 t23 f22 b24. An adorable blend that makes you sit up and take notice of every enormous mouthful. Classy, complex, charismatic and brilliantly balanced. *45%*

Evermore (90) n22 t23 f22 b23. Top-grade, well-aged blended whisky with fabulous depth and complexity that never loses its sweet edge despite the oak. 40%. Kirin.

Ginko (78.5) n20.5 t20 f19 b19. Soft – probably too soft as it could do with some shape and attitude to shrug off the caramel. 46%. Number One Drinks Company.

Golden Horse Busyuu Deluxe (93) n22 t24 f23 b24. Whoever blended this has a genuine feel for whisky: a classic in its own right and one of astonishing complexity and textbook balance. 43%. Toa Shuzo. To celebrate the year 2000.

Hibiki (82) n20 t19 f23 b20. The grains here are fresh, forceful and merciless, the malts bouncing off them meekly. Lovely cocoa finale. A blend that brings a tear to the eye. Hard stuff – perfect after a hard day! Love it! 43%. Suntory.

Hibiki Aged 12 Years bott 2011 (89) n22.5 t22 f22 b22.5. A sensual whisky full of lightly sugared riches. 43%. Suntory.

Hibiki 17 Years bott 2011 (84.5) n22 t21 f20.5 b21. Big oaks and a clever degree of sweetness. But takes the lazy big toffee option. 43%. Suntory.

Hibiki 50.5 Non Chillfiltered 17 Years Old (84) n22 t22 f20 b20. Pleasant enough in its own right. But against what this particular expression so recently was, hugely disappointing. Last year I lamented the extra use of caramel. This year it has gone through the roof, taking with it all the fineness of complexity that made this blend exceptional. Time for the blending lab to start talking to the bottling hall and sort this out. I want one of the great whiskies back...!! 50.5%. Suntory.

Hibiki Aged 21 Years bott 2011 (96) n24 cherry fruitcake...with more black cherries than cake. Spiced sherry notes embrace the oak with a voluptuous richness; t24.5 virtually perfect texture: seemingly silk-like but then a massive outbreak of busy oaky vanilla and juicy barley; the creamy mouth feel supports a mix of maple syrup and muscovado sugars; the middle moves towards a walnut oiliness; f23.5 long, spicy with a gentle date and walnut fade; b24 a celebration of blended whisky, irrespective of which country it is from. Of its style, it's hard to raise the bar much higher than this. Stunning. 43%. Suntory.

Hibiki Aged 30 Years (88) n21 t22 f22 b23. Still remains a very different animal from most other whiskies you might find: the smoke may have vanished somewhat but the sweet oakiness continues to draw its own unique map. 43%

Hokuto (86) n22 t24 f19 b21. A bemusing blend. At its peak, this is quite superb, cleverly blended whisky. The finish, though, suggests a big caramel input. If the caramel is natural, it should be tempered. If it is added for colouring purposes, then I don't see the point of having the whisky non-chillfiltered in the first place. 50.5%. ncf. Suntory.

Ichiro's Blend Aged 33 Years (84) n20 t22 f21 b21. Silky and sweet. But the creamy fudge effect appears to wipe out anything important the oak may have to say. Pleasing spices towards the end, though. 48%. Venture Whisky Ltd.

Ichiro's Malt & Grain bott 2011 (85) n21 t22 f21 b21. A clean though curious blend with the grain dominating and forming a jammy-sweet but thin structure. Pleasant throughout. 46%. Venture Whisky Co.

Imperial (81) n20 t22 f19 b20. Flinty, hard grain softened by malt and vanilla but toffee dulled. 43%. Suntory.

Kakubin (92) n23 lemon zest and refreshing grain: wonderful; t23 light, mouthwatering, ultra-juicy with soft barley sub-strata; true melt-in-the-mouth stuff; f22 long, with charming vanilla but touched by toffee; b24 absolutely brilliant blend of stunningly refreshing and complex character. One of the most improved brands in the world. 40%. Suntory.

Kakubin Ajiwai (82) n20 t21 f20 b21. Usual Kakubin hard grain and mouthwatering malt, with this time a hint of warming stem ginger. 40%. Suntory.

Kakubin Kuro 43° (89) n22 t23 f22 b22. Big, chewy whisky with ample evidence of old age but such is the intrusion of caramel it's hard to be entirely sure. 43%. Suntory.

Kakubin New (90) n21 t24 f21 b24 seriously divine blending: a refreshing dram of the top order. 40%. Suntory.

Kirin Whisky Tarujuku 50° (93) n22.5 t24 f23 b23.5. A blend not afraid to make a statement and does so boldly. A sheer joy. 50%. Kirin Distillery Co Ltd.

Master's Blend Aged 10 Years (87) n21 t23 f22 b21. Chewy, big and satisfying. 40%.

New Kakubin Suntory (see Kakubin New)

Nikka Master Blend Blended Whisky 12 Years Old 70th Anniversary (94) n24 nothing shy or retiring here: big oak, big sherry. A little nervousness with the smoke, maybe; t23 lush, silky grain arrives and then carries intensely sweet malt and weightier grape; f24 dries as the oak takes centre stage. But the peripheral fruit malt, gentle smoke and grain combine to offer something not dissimilar to fruit and nut chocolate; b23 an awesome blend swimming in top quality sherry. Perhaps a fraction too much sweetness on the arrival, but I am nit-picking. A blend for those who like their whiskies to have something to say. And this one just won't shut up. 58%. Nikka.

The Nikka Whisky Aged 34 Years bott 1999 (93) n23 t23 f24 b23. A Japanese whisky of antiquity that has not only survived many passing years, but has actually achieved something of stature and sophistication. Over time I have come to appreciate this whisky immensely. It is among the world's greatest blends, no question. 43%. Nikka.

Nikka Whisky Tsuru Aged 17 Years (94) n23 the usual fruity suspects one associates with a Tsuru blend, especially the apple and oranges. But the grains are now making a bourbony impact, too; t24 advanced level textbook delivery here because the marriage between fruit, grain and oak is about as well integrated as you might wish for; simperingly soft yet enough rigidity for the malts to really count and the palate to fully appreciate all the complexities offered; f23 brushed with cocoa, a touch of sultana and some gripping spices, too; only the caramel detracts; b24 unmistakingly Tsuru in character, very much in line, profile-wise, with the original bottling and if the caramel was cut this could challenge as a world whisky of the year. 43%

Robert Brown (91) n22.5 t23 f22.5 b23. Just love these clean but full-flavoured blends: a real touch of quality here. 43%. Kirin Brewery Company Ltd.

Royal 12 Years Old (91) n23 t23 f22 b23. A splendidly blended whisky with complexity being the main theme. Beautiful stuff that appears recently to have, with the exception of the nose, traded smoke for grape. 43%

Royal Aged 15 Years (95) n25 soft ribbons of smoke tie themselves to a kumquat and sherry flag; supremely well weighted and balanced with the grains and malts united by invisible strands; t24 few whiskies achieve such a beautifully soft and rounded delivery: there is no dominance on arrival as the tastebuds are confronted by a silky marriage of all that is found on the nose, aided and abetted by luxurious grain; f22 a degree of toffee slightly hinders the fade but the lightness of touch is spellbinding; b24 unquestionably one of the great blends of the world that can be improved only by a reduction of toffee input. Sensual blending that every true whisky lover must experience: a kind of Japanese Old Parr 18. 43%

Shirokaku (79) n19 t21 f20 b19. Some over-zealous toffee puts a cap on complexity. Good spices, though. 40%. Suntory.

Special Reserve 10 Years Old (94) n23 t24 f23 b24. A beguiling whisky of near faultless complexity. Blending at its peak. 43%. Suntory.

Special Reserve Aged 12 Years (89) n21 t24 f21 b23. A tactile, voluptuous malt that wraps itself like a sated lover around the tastebuds, though the complexity is compromised very slightly by bigger caramel than the 10-y-o. 40%. Suntory.

Suntory Old (87) n21 t24 f20 b22. A delicate and comfortable blend that just appears to have over-simplified itself on the finale. Delicious, but can be much better than this. 40%

Suntory Old Mild and Smooth (84) n19 t22 f21 b22. Chirpy and lively around the palate, the grains soften the crisp malts wonderfully. 40%

Suntory Old Rich and Mellow (91) n22 t23 f23 b23. A pretty malt-rich blend with the grains offering a fat base. Impressive blending. 43%

Super Nikka (93) n23 t23 f23 b24. A very, very fine blend which makes no apology whatsoever for the peaty complexity of Yoichi malt. Now, with less caramel, it's pretty classy stuff. However, Nikka being Nikka you might find the occasional bottling that is entirely devoid of peat, more honeyed and lighter in style (21-22-23-23 Total 89 – no less a quality turn, obviously). Either way, an absolutely brilliant day-to-day, anytime, any place dram. One of the true 24-carat, super nova commonplace blends not just in Japan, but in the world. 43%. Nikka.

Super Nikka Rare Old batch 02I18D (90.5) n22 t23 f22.5 b23. Beautiful whisky which just sings a lilting malty refrain. Strange, though, to find it peatless. 43%. Nikka.

Torys (76) n18 t19 f20 b19. Lots of toffee in the middle and at the end of this one. The grain used is top class and chewy. 37%. Suntory.

Torys Whisky Square (80) n19 t20 f21 b20. At first glance very similar to Torys, but very close scrutiny reveals slightly more "new loaf" nose and a better, spicier and less toffeed finale. 37%. Suntory.

Tsuru (93) n23 t24 f22 b24. Gentle and beautifully structured, genuinely mouthwatering, more-ish and effortlessly noble. If they had the confidence to cut the caramel, this would be even higher up the charts as one of the great blends of the world. And with Japanese whisky becoming far more globally accepted and sought after, now would be a very good time to start. As it is, in my house we pass the ceramic Tsuru bottle as one does the ship's decanter. And it empties very quickly. 43%. Nikka.

The Whisky (88) n22 t22 f21 b23. A rich, confident and well-balanced dram. 43%. Suntory.

White (80) n19 t21 f20 b20. Boring nose but explodes on the palate for a fresh, mouthwatering classic blend bite. 40%. Suntory.

Za (79) n19 t21 f19 b20. Some lively boisterous grain offers a suet-pudding chewiness. A little bitter on the finish. 40%. Suntory.

European Whisky

The debate about what it means to be European is one that seemingly never ends. By contrast, the discussion on how to define the character of a European whisky is only just beginning.

And as more and more distilleries open throughout mainland Europe, Scandinavia and the British Isles the styles are becoming wider and wider.

Small distillers in mainland Europe, especially those in the Alpine area, share common ground with their US counterparts in often coming into whisky late. Their first love, interest and spirit had been with fruit brandies. It seemed that if something grew in a tree or had a stone when you bit into it, you could be pretty confident that someone in Austria or California was making a clear, eye-watering spirit from it somewhere.

Indeed, when I was writing Jim Murray's Complete Book of Whisky during 1996 and 1997 I travelled to the few mainland Europe distilleries I could find. Even though this was before the days of the internet when research had to be carried out by phone and word of mouth, I visited most – which was few – and missed one or two... which was fewer still.

Today, due mainly to the four solid months it now takes to write the Bible, I can scarcely find the time to go and visit these outposts which stretch from southern Germany to Finland and as far abreast as France to the Czech Republic. It is now not that there is just one or two. But dozens. And I need my good friend Julia Nourney to whizz around capturing samples for me just to try and keep up to date.

It is a fact that there is no one style that we can call European, in the way we might be able to identify a Kentucky bourbon or a Scotch single malt. That is simply because of the diversity of stills – and skills – being deployed to make the spirit. And a no less wide range of grains, or blends of grains, and smoking agents, from peat to wood types, to create the mash.

The distillers who have made major financial investments in equipment and staff appear to be the ones who are enjoying the most consistent results. In the Premier League we have the now firmly established Mackmyra in Sweden and Penderyn in Wales, both of whom use female blenders or distillers, curiously. Newly promoted to the highest tier comes St George's in England and just joining them quality-wise, though not quantity, alas, is their British counterpart Hicks and Healey. In fact, St. George's this year established themselves quality-wise in the world's whisky elite. All but the odd one or two of their bottlings have been staggeringly good and their Chapter 6 suite of bottlings is probably the best ever not to pick up a major gong in the Whisky Bible's history. Never before have I been confronted with one bottling after another meriting a score of 90 plus: so unusual was the phenomenon that I had to taste them all over again a week later to ensure my radar was working correctly. It was. Remarkable, of course, is the youth of the whisky itself. But also the way in which a man fresh to making whisky has so seemlessly copied from an old master. The first distiller to set the distillery on the right path was Iain Henderson of Laphroaig fame. He was also, incidentally, the distillery manager who made the malt at Old Pulteney which over 21 years later was to be awarded World Whisky of the Year in the 2012 Whisky Bible. His successor, David Fitt, a former brewer at Greene King, has now proved himself to be unquestionably one of the best distillers in the world. The fact his spirit has matured into something so technically excellent in so short a time is truly remarkable. Iain Henderson obviously did a very good teaching job. Norfolk gets plenty of snow and frost. So the fact a whisky so young has moved to a place where it is snugly comfortable with the oak speaks volumes. St George's is not just a distillery to watch. It is also in many respects an inspiration to would-be major distillers. ·

Another distillery which maintains exceptionally high standards is the Belgian Owl. This is smaller concern than some, but the output of their single malt is consistent, beautifully made, and brimming with personality. It may be true that you can count internationally famous Belgians on one hand, but the whisky-loving world would immediately recognise two fingers of its owl... Some of the most remarkable whisky came from Liechtenstein, the country which was once unable to furnish me – anywhere within its borders – with a decent hotel room but now offers a three-year-old malt which, but for the wideness of its cut, nearly walked off with an award. The Telser distillery has a long history and its move into whisky has been an impressive one. Perhaps that big, malty, slightly oily and lush style is something of an Alpine trait: another distillery to watch is Interlaken with their Classic, Swiss Highland Single Malt. Which, with a brand name like that, is as likely to stir up the good folk at the Scotch Whisky Association as anything else.

AUSTRIA

ACHENSEE'R EDELBRENNEREI FRANZ KOSTENZER Maurach. Working.

⁘ **Whisky Alpin Grain Whisky Hafer** db (86.5) n20.5 t23 f21 b22. A glutinous dram, full of thick wheat oils but a surprising lack of spice, though the little which forms works well within the hot cross bun sweetness. 40%

⁘ **Whisky Alpin Rye & Malt** db (88) n22 an early oily pungency burns off with time to allow a sharp rye note to blossom; t22 chunky, rich and buttery, not dissimilar to fruit shortcake biscuits; f22 here the raisins are a bit over toasted; b22 needs to settle in the glass a little while for the malt to be at its best. But worth the wait. 40%

⁘ **Whisky Alpin Single Rye Malt** db (81) n19 t21 f20 b21. Creamy and spicy. Good Demerara sugar thread, but the rye itself struggles to convince. 45%

DESTILLERIE GEORG HIEBL Haag. Working.

George Hiebl Mais Whisky 2004 db (93) n23 t23.5 f23 b23.5. More bourbon in character than some American bourbons I know...!! Beautifully matured, brilliantly matured and European whisky of the very highest order, Ye..haahhhh!! 43%

DESTILLERIE KAUSL Mühldorf, Wachau. Working.

Wachauer Whisky "G" Single Barrel Gerste (Barley) bott code L6WG db (90.5) n22 t23 f22.5 b23. Absolutely charming and well made malt. 40%

DESTILLERIE ROGNER Rappottenstein. Working.

Rogner Waldviertel Whisky 3/3 db (86.5) n20 t22 f22.5 b22. Plane sailing once you get past the tight nose. A beautiful display of crisp sugars and come-back-for more grainy juiciness. Lovable stuff, for all its gliches. 41.7%. ncf.

Rogner Waldviertel Rye Whisky No. 13 db (80) n18.5 t20 f21 b20.5. If memory serves, the last time I had this guy I was met by an oily tobacco note. It is a unique feature and this reminds me of it. 42.5%. ncf.

DESTILLERIE WEUTZ St. Nikolai im Sausal. Working.

Franziska bott code. L070206/02 db The 5% elderflower means this is 100% not whisky. But a fascinating and eye-opening way to create a spirit very much in the young Kentucky rye style, especially in the nose. They certainly can do delicious... For the record, the scoring for enjoyment alone: (93) n23.5 t23 f23.5 b23. 48%. Malt refined with 5% elderflower.

White Smoke sherry finished, bott code. L062411/01 db (90) n22.5 t22.5 f22 b23. At times, seems more like sherry finished in whisky. Not a single off note from the cask (though the same can't quite be said for the actual spirit itself) – a completely sulphur free experience. Wonderful and borderline sophisticated. 40%

REISETBAUER Axberg, Thening. Working.

Reisetbauer Single Malt 7 Years Old Chardonnay and sweet wine cask, bott code LWH 099 db (85.5) n19 t21 f23.5 b22. A less than impressive nose is followed by a rocky delivery. But the panning out is truly spectacular as harmony is achieved with a rich honey and nougat mix, helped along the way with pecan nuts and figs. The finish is like a top rank trifle and fruitcake mix. A whisky of two halves. 43%

WHISKY-DESTILLERIE J. HAIDER Roggenreith. Working.

Single Malt J.H. bott code L SM/06 (91.5) n22 t23 f23.5 b23. It must be over a dozen years now since I first went to their distillery. But this is their best batch of whiskies yet... 41%

⁘ **Single Malt Selection J.H.** bott code L7/02 db (94) n23 a brilliant nose combining the more refined bourbon blue prints, allowing the honey to shine thorough with unobtrusive elegance; t23 the house nougat style flickers momentarily, as do caramels from the cask. The remainder is sophisticated honey; f24 a juicy spiciness merges with developing liquorice; b24 one of their cleanest, most understated bottlings to date. A gem. 46%

⁘ **Special Single Malt Selection J.H.** bott code L15/02 db (93) n22.5 a unique mix of nougat and bourbon, with accent on the honeycomb. Pretty salty, too; t23 and those salts are first over the line, giving a tangy blast to the barley. The palate, though, is excited by a procession of spiced manuka honey which keeps the sweetness levels down to tasteful amounts; full bodied, vigorous yet controlled and classy; f23.5 long, with a return to those light hickory, bourbon tones which underscore the good oak used; the spices persist engagingly; b24 it is obvious that the JH whiskies are coming of age: they are consistently now of a very high standard – and just full of honeyed riches. 46%

Original Rye Whisky J.H. L19/05 db (91.5) n23.5 t23 f22 b23. Their Original Rye was last year close to bringing home to Austria the Bible's European Whisky of the Year. This is another outstanding bottling. Perhaps not as sharp and mouth-watering as last time, but the marriage between the rye and toffee-honeycomb is a blissful one. Superb yet again! 41%

Original Rye Whisky J.H. bott code L R/06 **(92.5) n23** t23.5 f23 **b23.** This distillery can produce a Kentuckian style rye better than any other distillery outside the US. here is another gorgeous example. 41%

⊰⊱ **Pure Rye Malt J.H.** bott code LPR 07 db **(95.5) n24** stunning clean rye fruitiness, seemingly wrapping itself in bright citrus, too; **t24** crisp and delicate with a gorgeous outpouring of muscovado sugar topped with unmistakable, almost Kentucky-style rye – just so mouth-watering! **f23.5** the spices come out to play – and they play hard; beautiful creaminess to the sugars; **b24** clean, unerring and screams "rye" at you. Magnificent. 41%

⊰⊱ **Special Rye Malt Selection Nougat J.H.** bott code L SPR 07 SL db **(84.5) n20** t22 f21 **b21.5.** Big and cumbersome, the nougat effect dulls the rye to a telling degree. No shortage of spices, though. 46%

DESTILLERIE WEIDENAUER Kottes. Working.

Waldviertler Dinkel (2008 Silber Medaille label on neck) db **(90) n19.5** t23 f23.5 **b24.** The nose apart, the odd feint note here and there can't seriously detract from this majestically attractive whisky and towards the end even helps! Classy, classy whisky...!!! 42%

Waldviertler Hafer-Malz (2007 Gold Medaille label on neck) db **(91) n22** t22.5 f23 **b23.5.** One of those whiskies that just gets better the longer it stays on the palate. Also, a master class in achieving near perfection in the degree of sweetness generated. 42%

BELGIUM
THE BELGIAN OWL

The Belgian Owl Single Malt Age 4 Years 1st fill bourbon cask, bott code. 270910 db **(94.5) n24** gorgeous marriage between delicate oak and even more delicate barley. Dissolved Lubeck marzipan melts into a lime jam. Youthful, yet almost impossible to see how a four-year-old malt could possibly be more attractive; **t23.5** silky, vaguely juicy maltiness and then any number of complex oaky tones. Again, a light fruitiness threads its way into the picture; **f23** much drier, though both the caramels and oaks remain light; a hint of Belgian chocolate...? **b24** a Belgian treat. 46%. nc ncf.

⊰⊱ **The Belgian Owl Single Malt 48 Months** 1st fill bourbon cask, bott code. L 260312 db **(86) n21.5** t22 f21.5 **b21.** A much thinner bottling than of recent years with the sugars in the ascendancy and the barley devoid of muscle. Attractive and easy, though. 46%. nc ncf.

The Belgian Owl Single Malt 48 Months 1st fill bourbon cask no. 4275933 db **(90.5) n22.5** t23 f22 **b23.** This is quite probably the most powerful bottled whisky I have encountered anywhere in the world in my entire career. Perhaps what is most remarkable is the beautifully delicate nature of the nose and flavour profile, despite the scary alcohol levels. A unique and, if you have the nerve, wonderful experience. 76.5%. nc ncf sc.

The Belgian Owl Single Malt Age 55 Months 1st fill bourbon cask no. 4275890 db **(92.2) n22** t23.5 f23.5 **b23.5.** Fantastic whisky with more twists and turns than a corkscrew. At times like the Hubble telescope looking back to the Belgian Big Bang – the beginning of the dedicated whisky universe in the country. The picking up of extra copper shows it is getting closer to those very first moments at Belgian Owl... 74.3%. nc ncf sc.

The Belgian Owl Single Malt Age 53 Months 1st fill bourbon cask no. 4275986 db **(90.5) n23** t23 f22 **b22.5.** Enormous whisky, unsurprisingly, as deeply satisfying. 74.1%. nc ncf sc.

⊰⊱ **The Belgian Owl Single Malt 60 Months** 1st fill bourbon cask no. 4276140 db **(94) n23.5** a near George T Stagg intensity to the Demerara sugar and apple bourbon aspect of this; some lighter vanillas align with the delicate barley, too; **t23** explosive, as one might expect for a whisky nearly twice the strength of a standard Scotch. The apples on the nose transfer here unscathed while the barley begins with a juicy outline but steadily builds in thickness; **f24** with the alcohol gone, the malt now skips into overdrive as the liquorice and creamy mocha give weight to the malt shake richness and Tunnock's wafer finale; **b23.5** carries out the dual purpose of giving you the big barley fix of the day...and dissolves any plaque that may have formed around your gums. Breathtaking...in every sense... 76.1%. nc ncf sc.

⊰⊱ **The Belgian Owl Single Malt 64 Months** 1st fill bourbon cask no. 4275982 db **(90.5) n23** lovely hazelnut and kiwi fruit lead; **t23.5** silky barley, making the most of a wider than normal cut for this distillery; the barley gangs up slowly but surely, aided by Demerara; **f22** remains soft and barley rich to the end; **b22.5** demure and elegant. 50%. nc ncf sc.

DESTILLERIE RADERMACHER

Lambertus Single Grain Aged 10 Years db **(44) n12** t12 f10 **b10.** This is whisky...? Really???!!!!????? Well, that's what it says on the label, and this is a distillery I haven't got round to seeing in action (nor am I now very likely to be invited...). Let's check the label again... Ten years old...blah, blah. Single grain... blah, blah. But, frankly, this tastes like a liqueur rather than a whisky: the fruit flavours do not seem even remotely naturally evolved: synthetic is being kind. But apparently, this is whisky: I have re-checked the label. No mention of additives, so it must be. I am stunned. *40%*

FILLIERS DISTILLERY
Goldly's Belgian Double Still Whisky Aged 10 Years db **(88)** n21.5 t23 f21.5 b22. Having actually discovered this whisky before the distillers – I'll explain one day...!! – I know this could be a lot better. The caramel does great damage to the finish in particular, which should dazzle with its complexity. Even so, a lovely, high-class whisky which should be comfortably in the 90s but falls short. *40%*

CZECH REPUBLIC
Single Malt
RUDOLF JELÍNEK DISTILLERY
Gold Cock Single Malt Aged 12 Years "Green Feathers" bott 27/05/09 db **(89.5)** n22 t23.5 f22 b22. From my first ever malt-related trip to the Czech Republic nearly 20 years ago, it was always a pleasure to get hold of my Gold Cock. I was always told it went down a treat. And this is no exception. Not a particularly big whisky. But since when has size counted? *43%*

STOCK PLZEN - BOZKOV S.R.O.
Hammer Head 1989 db **(88.5)** n22 t22.5 f22 b22. Don't bother looking for complexity: this is one of Europe's maltiest drams...if not the maltiest... *40.7%*

Blends
Gold Cock Aged 3 Years "Red Feathers" bott 22/06/09 **(86)** n22 t21 f21.5 b21.5. Sensual and soft, this is melt-in-the-mouth whisky with a big nod towards the sweet caramels. *40%*.
Granette Premium **(82)** n21 t22 f19 b20. Lighter than the spark of any girl that you will meet in the Czech Republic. Big toffee thrust. *40%*
Printer's Aged 6 Years **(86.5)** n21.5 t22.5 f21 b21.5. Blended whisky is something often done rather well in the Czech Republic and this brand has managed to maintain its clean, malty integrity and style. Dangerously quaffable. *40%*

DENMARK
STAUNING DISTILLERY Skjern. Working.
Stauning 1st Edition Peated dist 2009, bott 2012 **(94)** n22.5 t24 f24 b23.5. I didn't know whether to taste this, the first whisky from Stauning on the first birthday of my first grand-daughter, Islay-Mae, or make this the 999th new whisky I have tasted for 2013 Whisky Bible in recognition that I played a (very!) small part in its foundation....though only by offering encouragement. As fate dictates, both fell on the same day. Ah, this dram before me really is the stuff of history...and though not technically spot on, is the equivalent to half an hour in the gym for the taste buds. A malt of genuine character. Absolutely adore it! *62.8%*

⸭ **Stauning 2nd Edition Traditional** dist 2009, bott 2013 db **(85)** n20 t21 f22.5 b21.5. Always interesting to see how a malt develops with time. Compared to a year ago, this has lost a little balance, with the barley just a little too ferocious on the nose and the sugars, though ultimately enjoyable, almost to a liquor-ish degree, are too far removed from the hay-like malt. *55%*

⸭ **Stauning 2nd Edition Peated** dist 2009, bott 2013 db **(94.5)** n23 big peat...or is it? Seems big, yet you can easily pick up the individual smoky bacon (how fitting, from Denmark) layers. A little spice, but gristy, too; t23.5 that gristiness is found on the sweet delivery. Subtle oils have a part to play, but less than in the first version if memory serves me correctly; f24.5 at last settles into a delightful narrative of lightly smoked mocha and a succession of brown sugars of which muscovado is key. A treat of a finale; b24 if there are awards given for sheer cleverness within peaty malt, then this would win hands down. No matter how many times you taste it, you can never quite decide whether the smoke is simply a charming accompaniment, or actually has its hands on the tiller of the direction of the whisky. Now that is what I call complexity...and a very classy act! *55%*

Stauning Rye Third Solution dist 2009/2010, bott 2012 **(92)** n23 t23.5 f23 b22.5. No doubting the grain used here: the rye bursts from the glass with massive, sharp fruity intent. Unlike some I have seen made elsewhere, this is very much in the Kentuckian mould and if the cut had been a little more precise, may well even have passed off as such. Not yet whisky, some of the spirit being a little less than the required three years, this bottling sends a very clear message: clean the distillate very slightly and bottle at full age and they will have one of Europe's great whiskies on their hands. This is beautiful stuff which even in this form delights from a multitude of angles. Also, this could well be their trademark whisky as it has the potential to out polish the peated and unpeated barley styles. Are we seeing the formative process of a potential world classic? It wouldn't surprise me. *50.5%*

⁘ **Stauning Young Rye** dist 10 & 11, bott Oct 12 db **(92.5) n23 t23 f23.5 b23.** An interesting change in gear from the last bottling, with this being far more in brown sugar-beech honey mode *49.3%*

⁘ **Stauning Young Rye** dist 2010, bott Aug 12 *db* **(94.5) n23.5 t24 f23.5 b23.5.** As this is too young be a whisky, no room for tasting notes. But there deserves to be. This is absolutely brimming with all the in-your-face chocolate-fruitiness you expect from a top rye. Not difficult to see an award-winner of the near future here. The intensity of the kumquat/liquorice/spice as the rye gets into full stride has been one of my treats of the year. Magnificent. *50.8%*

ENGLAND
HEALEY'S CORNISH CYDER FARM Penhallow. Working.

Hicks & Healey Cornish Single Malt 2004 Cask #29 (94.5) n24.5 quite possibly an aroma I could spend all day getting to know. The interweaving between the soft apples and the softer honeys alone is enough to keep you entertained for a good hour at least. What makes this so special is the shading and texture; this is not a simple canvas on which one side is painted an apple in still life, the other honey. Every hue imaginable appears to be in there; the apples, for instance, appear from crisp green form to sluggish, sweeter brown and bruised. And just to intrigue you further is the slow showing of the spices. Not quite cinnamon, which might have been just too much of a cliché (though in the mix there appears to be a kind of relation), but a dribble of clove oil and linseed. These seem tied in with a burgeoning bourbon characteristic as the red liquorice grows beside the waxed leather. Faultless and almost beautiful beyond words...; **t24** after that astonishing nose it just had to be mouth-watering...and, my word, it is! The spices make an immediate impact, first feisty and then backing off. The delicate fruits refuse to take control and the lightly oiled barley has a bigger role here than on the nose. Again the honey (mainly of the clear, runny English type) waxes and wanes, like on the nose, from one moment being rich and bold, to watery and delicate the next; after a hint of cocoa a few cream caramel notes begin to fill the middle ground; **f22.5** just a hint of oaky bitterness arrives, but the natural caramels are now in the ascendency and offer the desired countering sweetness; late vanilla signs the whisky off; **b23.5** fascinatingly, picking up much more apple here than I did at the distillery, mainly because of the ambient aromas around me there: a great example why all tasting notes I carry out are in controlled environments. Back in January I headed down to the distillery and after going through their casks suggested this one was, like their very finest apples, exactly ripe for picking. The most noticeable thing was that there, in the still house, I picked up only a fraction of the apple I get here in the controlled environment of my tasting room. The distillery makes, above all else, cider brandy, so the aroma is all pervasive. However, my instincts were probably correct, for the apple (doubtless absorbed from the environment of maturing with apple brandy casks, something like the fruit apparent on the whisky of St George's distillery, California) to be found here only contributes positively rather than detracts, especially on the nose...which I have upgraded from excellent then to near faultless now. As new distilleries go, this rates among the best debut bottlings of the last decade. That is not least because most distillers try and launch on three years to get money back as soon as possible. Here they have more than doubled that time and are reaping the benefit...with interest. A dram, then, to keep your nocturnal cinema going on classic mode: "Last night I dreamt I went to Penhallow again." Hang on: twelve syllables... I feel a book coming on... and a film... *61.3%. sc.*

Hicks & Healey Cornish Whiskey 2004 Cask #32 dist 13 Feb 04, bott Feb 12 db **(96) n24** oh...oh... scrumped apple with rainwater, a sprinkling of cinnamon and barley sugar. The vanilla is no more than cold custard on apple crumble...an aroma unique to Hicks and Healey; **t24.5** a mouth feel to die for: almost a perfect degree of soft oil spreads the sugar-crusted apple to all parts of the palate; a slow honey build thickens further and keeps check on the spices; in mid term the barley at last escapes its apple-rich shadow for a clean, juicy rant: superb! **f23.5** strangely short, leaving a busy taste echo and dry, chalky vanilla; **b24** I picked this one up absent-mindedly, nosed...and was carried to Cornwall. I knew what it was without even opening my eyes. Unmistakable. And just so stunningly beautiful... *60.2%. ncf.*

ST. GEORGE'S Rowdham. Working.

The English Whisky Co. Chapter 6 English Single Malt (unpeated) cask no. 163, 165, 171 & 173, dist May 07, bott Jun 10 db **(91) n22 t23 f23.5 b22.5.** Further confirmation that this distillery is on course for true excellence. Here, by comparison to earlier bottlings, the distillate shows some evidence that the stills have been run just a little faster and the cut thinned a little, meaning a laser-sharp crispness to the barley. So reminds me of Glen Grant at this age. *46%*

The English Whisky Co. Chapter 6 English Single Malt ASB casks, cask no. 573, 574, 613 & 614, dist May 08, bott Sep 11 db (92) n23 t23.5 f22 b23.5. Hugely enjoyable, very well made, excellently matured single malt. As simple as that! 46%. nc ncf.

The English Whisky Co. Chapter 6 English Single Malt ASB casks, cask no. 478, 479, 480 & 481, dist Aug 08, bott Oct 11 db (92.5) n24 t23 f22.5 b23. But for one cask betraying the rest with that loose bitterness on the finish and this would have been Liquid Gold.... 46%. nc ncf.

⊙ **The English Whisky Co. Chapter 6 English Single Malt Not Peated** ASB casks, cask no. 001, 002, 003, 004, dist May 09, bott Jan 13 db (95) n23.5 if you find cleaner malt and kinder casks this year let me know: classic for its style; t24 you know from the nose that this is going to be a juice fest and you are not left disappointed. The barley is almost pristine: it is unlikely you can get malt to taste maltier. The spices are a superb add on; f23.5 does not try to be flash. Perhaps you want a little extra complexity. But you happily settle for the top dog, truly flawless, cocoa and spice on offer; b24 shows what maturing in truly great casks can do. Any more stylishly English and you'd think it was distilled in Jermyn Street... 46%. nc ncf.

⊙ **The English Whisky Co. Chapter 6 English Single Malt Not Peated** ASB casks, cask no. 005, 006, 007, 008, dist May 09, bott Feb 13 db (96) n24 there is a rare sparkle to the barley here which many a distillery in Scotland can only dream of: barley sugar, but the accent is on the barley which is of a grassy, Speyside style yet of a diamond-bright three dimensional quality which truly astonishes. My, oh, my....! t24 the sparkle on the nose is somehow amplified on the palate: crystalline sugars adhering to intense yet somehow delicate barley; if you possess a salivation metre, unplug it...it is likely to explode...; f24 settles here to a gristier, deeper delivery, bringing on board the oak through a lightly minty chocolate character. A touch of Crème brûlée to the vanilla; b24 you taste the Chapter 6 casks 1-4 and think it doesn't get any better...and then...this!!! Truly flawless distillate matured in high quality casks. Not just free of a single off note...free of a hint of a rumour of an off note. Truly sublime whisky showing that youth, when well brought up, can only delight. One of the finest examples of unpeated single malt whisky to have hit the market worldwide in the last three or four years... 46%. nc ncf.

⊙ **The English Whisky Co. Chapter 6 English Single Malt Not Peated** ASB casks, cask no. 0193, 0194, dist Apr 10, bott Apr 13 db (95) n23.5 a tad oilier than the norm, but no bad thing as the extra weight seems to favour the tannins slightly to give another view of this malt; t25 a near perfect delivery of barley concentrate and thick, milky cocoa in perfect harmony; sublime sugar and spice combo, too...actually...what the hell: it is perfect! f23 long, again with the oils stretching every element as far they will go. Butterscotch, almond oil and cocoa are the last to be outstared...; b23.5 I'm not sure if anything since Supertramp brought out Crime of the Century and Crisis What Crisis? back in the mid 1970s has two, or in this case three, back to back releases been so seamless or faultless. Let me say it and, as an Englishman, say it proudly: this whisky borders genius. 46%. nc ncf.

⊙ **The English Whisky Co. Chapter 7 Cask Strength** rum casks, cask no. 0457, 0458, dist May 09, bott Apr 13 db (94.5) n23 t24.5 f23.5 b24. If you want proof that adding water to whisky does not necessary improve it, try this cask strength version against the friendly fellow at 46%, above. Here a fruitier element comes into play while some heavier oak notes, via cocoa, batters away with greater success at the inherent sugars offered by the rum. The spices also play their part with far more conviction while the barley has more freedom to shine. Another bottling which is showing that St George's has moved into the very highest echelons of world whisky. 59.9%

The English Whisky Co. Chapter 7 Rum Finish ASB & rum cask nos. 024/025, dist Mar 07, bott Oct 10 db (94) n23.5 t24 f23 b23.5. Absolutely exceptional. A near faultless whisky where the youth of the malt and the sweet finesse of the rum casks were born for each other. The kind of light and juicy whisky I, frankly, adore. 46%. nc ncf.

⊙ **The English Whisky Co. Chapter 7 Rum Finish** ASB & rum casks, cask no. 0457, 0458, dist May 09, bott Apr 13 db (91.5) n22 typically restricted as most rum casks prove to be. Crisp sugar does lead the way with a light butterscotch second gear; t23.5 fabulous impact on delivery. The malt is bright to the point of sparkling, the spices a peppery variety and leading into a mocha-rich middle; f23 this is where so many rum cask finishes go wrong: at the death. Very often little is left to be said. This, though, still shows a keen barley sugar depth and overcomes the earlier spice; b23 you have to be confident when maturing in rum: this has a propensity to tighten a malt until little but the sugars are heard. This though is 92% proof that St George can slay that particular dragon. 46%. nc ncf.

The English Whisky Co. Chapter 7 Rum Cask Limited Edition bott 2011 db (94) n23.5 t23.5 f23 b24. Tight, disciplined, crisp...I have never had the experience, but this (I have been told) seems just what it is like when bound and whipped by a mistress. Britain's judiciary should be on their way to Norfolk en masse... Absolutely delicious!! 46%. nc ncf sc.

The English Whisky Co. Chapter 9 English Single Malt (peated) cask no. 102, 115, 124 & 144, dist May 07, bott May 10 db **(93.5) n23 t23.5 f24 b23**. Frankly, it would be churlish to ask any more of a malt whisky of this age. Three years old only, yet going through the gears of complexity like an old 'un. The secret, though, is in the quality of the distillation and the very decent casks used. So exceptional is this, you would almost think that this was created by the guy who made Laphroaig for many a year... 46%

The English Whisky Co. Chapter 9 Peated/Smokey ASB casks, cask no. 0501 & 0489, dist 08, bott 12 db **(95) n23.5 t24 f23.5 b24**. World class whisky with the weight and finesse making all the right noises. For its age, it writes itself in the annals of English whisky folklore. Beyond superb, this wins my Percy Award for things of stunning beauty coming from Norfolk! 46%. nc ncf.

⚜ **The English Whisky Co. Chapter 9 Peated/Smokey** ASB casks, cask no. 62, 65, 449, 451, dist Jun 12, bott Apr 09 **(88) n22** lightweight smoke, but big enough to dominate over the shy coconut biscuit (see what I did there!) and vanilla; **t23** the sugars gather to momentarily dominate until the smoke begins to form a fog. A liquorice and Demerara middle really entertains; **f21** bitters out slightly and dries as the fog clears; **b22** as sweet as a peaty nut! Just the odd sub-standard cask lets the side down a little. 46%. nc ncf.

⚜ **The English Whisky Co. Chapter 9 Peated** ASB casks, cask no. 064, 065, 066, 103, dist Oct 09, bott Feb 13 db **(92.5) n23.5** like entering a room in which a peat fire had burned until the early hours...; a little citrus lightens the load; **t23** surprisingly juicy: some serious grists at play here as the sugars are at full capacity. The smoke rumbles rather than dominates, drying the palate by the second; **f23** a dusty, powdery finish. Egg custard tart baked alongside some Arbroath smokies...; **b23** a growling, grumbling, curmudgeonly dram which wants to keep to a separate path from the sugars. 46%. nc ncf.

The English Whisky Co. Chapter 10 Sherry Finish Oloroso sherry hogshead, cask no. 488/489, dist Oct 07, bott Oct 10 db **(91) n23.5 t23 f22 b22.5**. A spotlessly clean oloroso cask ensures a beautiful malt, though not quite hitting the very highest forms of excellence as the host whisky has not yet formed sufficient muscle to carry the grape without the odd sideways stagger. That said, not a whisky you'd ever say "no" to the offer of a top-up... 46%. nc ncf.

The English Whisky Co. Chapter 11 "Heavily Peated" ASB cask no. 645/647/648, dist 08, bott 11 db **(92) n23 t23.5 f22.5 b23**. As the 59.7% version below. Only for wimps. 46%. nc ncf.

The English Whisky Co. Chapter 11 Heavily Peated ASB casks, cask no. 639, 640, 641 & 642, dist Mar 08, bott Nov 11 db **(91.5) n22.5 t23 f23 b23**. One of the sweetest English whiskies for the last century... 46%. nc ncf.

⚜ **The English Whisky Co. Chapter 11 Heavily Peated** ASB casks, cask no. 0062, 0065, dist Apr 09, bott Jul 12 db **(81) n19 t22 f21 b19**. A rare blemish. This malt is very much less than the sum of its parts as not enough attention was made in balancing out the peats and the sugars. Brief harmony as the sugars and oils hit the palate, but on the nose and for long periods in the mouth this is a free for all: young malts are temperamental. And here the balance has not been found. 46%. nc ncf.

⚜ **The English Whisky Co. Chapter 11 Heavily Peated** ASB casks, cask no. 0104, 0107, dist Nov 09, bott Feb 13 db **(93) n22** wow! smoked ulmo honey...that's a first! **t24** the silkiest, friendliest delivery imaginable and then the most sensational melting of the ulmo honey promised on the nose. Wonderful, smoky grist turns that into a sandwich, escorting the sweetness from above and below; **f23.5** light vanillas, more clever layering of smoke and now some late liquorice to dry matters; **b23.5** superbly made and makes the most of some honey casks. If anything, perhaps too much honey...! 46%. nc ncf.

The English Whisky Co. Chapter 11 "Heavily Peated" Cask Strength ASB cask no. 645/647/648, dist 08, bott 11 db **(94) n23.5 t24 f23 b23.5**. What can you say? A whisky only three years old yet carrying itself with the wisdom of an elder statesman. The pace of the peat is absolutely textbook; the marriage between the smoke and sugars the stuff of dreams. Proof that great – or even intermediate - age is not always the deciding factor. Sometimes, when a distiller has got all his sums right, a whisky can be plucked from the cask at a positively infantile age and still it can have the capacity to knock you off your chair. As this, indeed, does. And if you require proof that adding water to whisky doesn't do a whisky many favours, just try the 46% version... 59.7%. nc ncf.

The English Whisky Co. Chapter 11 Heavily Peated Cask Strength ASB casks, cask no. 639, 640, 641 & 642, dist Mar 08, bott Nov 11 db **(93) n23 t23.5 f23 b23.5**. Feels very at home at this strength. impossible not to enjoy! 59.7%. nc ncf.

⚜ **The English Whisky Co. Chapter 14 English Single Malt (unpeated)** cask no. 582-585, dist 08, bott 13 db **(95) n23.5** the first strands of a bourbon-style red liquorice are beginning to form: already a surprising degree of balance between darker oak notes and more trilling barley; naturally, citrus gets in on the act somehow; **t23.5** picture perfect use of barley sweetness against a tarter, semi-fruity freshness; sugars exemplary, helping to ensure the softest of landings despite the intensity of the malt; **f24** every form of vanilla and custard you can imagine, all interlaced with soft citrus. Just so clean with an understated but unmissable depth; **b24** this is great whisky in its simplest form – even the complexity, though evident, is untaxing. If you are not an age snob, this, for its gentle elegance, will blow you away. *58.8%. nc ncf.*

⚜️ **The English Whisky Co. Chapter 14 English Single Malt (unpeated)** cask no. 582-585, dist May 08, bott Jul 13 db **(93) n23 t23 f23.5 b23.5**. Now there's a rarity. Nosed and tasted this and thought: "that's weird! Just about identical to the last one. Gorgeous, but just doesn't quite hit the high notes when singing, or have quite so much bass." Then discovered it was the same whisky, but reduced to 46%. Says it all, really. *46%. nc ncf.*

⚜️ **The English Whisky Co. Chapter 15 English Single Malt (peated)** cask no. 615-618, dist 08, bott 13 db **(94.5) n23.5** of the two-toned peat variety, with spice and smoke on equal terms; some pear, maple syrup and liquorice form the back up; maybe a slight lactose note, to subtract half a point; **t24** hard to imagine a better delivery. Or a malt of nearly 60% alcohol, handing so softly on the plate, cushioned not just by a fog of peat reek but molten muscado and ulmo honey. Absolutely sensational; **f23** long, with the sugars happy to lead the smoke wherever possible. The finale definitely confirms that touch of oaky lactose from one of the bourbon casks; **b24** if you could take that single flaw out of the equation, you'd have just about perfect whisky for a five-year-old. As it is, you'll just have to make do with bloody magnificent.... And make no mistake: this is no poor man's Islay. It stands up with the world's elite. *58.4%. nc ncf.*

⚜️ **The English Whisky Co. Chapter 15 English Single Malt (peated)** cask no. 615-618, dist Apr 08, bott Jul 13 db **(92.5) n23.5 t23.5 f22.5 b23**. A drier, more inert version of the cask strength bottling. Here the peat is a little more dusty, though the gristy sugars do show up better. Simply enjoyable, high class peaty whisky however you look at it. *46%. nc ncf.*

⚜️ **The English Whisky Co. Classic (unpeated)** db **(88.5) n22** pretty new makey, but this is clean and deliciously malt heavy; **t22** every bit as salivating as would be expected; the crisp barley is virtually three dimensional; **f22.5** long, thanks to the soft oils and a multitude of melt-in-the-mouth grist and light brown sugars; **b22** sweet, young and innocent. 43%. nc ncf.

The English Whisky Co. Limited Edition "Ibisco Decanter" bourbon cask, dist Nov 06, bott Dec 09 db **(91.5) n22 t24 f23 b22.5**. Quite adorable. Beautifully made whisky from stills small enough to add almost invisible but vital weight. One of the true fun whiskies of the year which further raises the expectations of what this distillery is capable of. *46%*

⚜️ **The English Whisky Co. Peated** db **(93) n23** could almost be a juvenile Laphroaig, this. Gristy with the smokiness both dry and spicy; **t23.5** much sweeter on delivery than on any point on the nose: gently smoked and gristy with the sugars on a muscovado theme, with even a touch of heather honey; the finale, though, is an unusual sensation of chewing peated barley straight from the maltings; **f23** remains soft with a wonderful degree of cocoa and orange-tinged toffee; **b23.5** a young whisky which proves, again, that it is the quality of the distillate – especially when peated – which can count over the years. 43%. nc ncf.

Founders Private Cellar cask no. 0005 db **(94.5) n23.5 t24 f23 b24**. This is the first whisky from this distillery to be bottled at the grand old age of five! And this old timer bears the most eloquent testimony possible to the skills of veteran distiller Iain Henderson: it is a stunner! I drink this to your health, old friend. 60.8%. nc ncf sc.

⚜️ **Founders Private Cellar** cask no. 0116, dist 12 Sep 07, bott 8 Apr 13 db **(94.5) n24** young, but get this up to body temperature and you will see malt at its most three dimensional: apple-rich, astonishing and not short of a wow factor or three; **t23.5** groan-in-pleasure degree of juicy barley and dissolving muscovado sugar - as intense and pure in taste as anything you will find worldwide this year: mega-lip-smacking; **f23** dries in dramatic fashion with a few cocoa notes joining the boiled, unsweetened cooking apple; **b24** yet another bottling from this remarkable distillery which almost defies belief. So clean and proffers the innocence of youth with unsullied beauty. 60.8%. nc ncf sc.

⚜️ **Founders Private Cellar Port Cask**, cask no. 0859, dist 20 Jun 07, bott 10 Apr 13 db **(88.5) n22** takes a while to settle: there are so many crushed grape pips in there it looks as though Percy, my parrot (who was hatched only a mile or two from this distillery, by odd coincidence) has been let loose on it. Very tight and intense, even circumspect; **t23** rough, biting, rudderless first stroke or two then blossoms into something ultra special: the intensity of the fruit is pepped further by an astonishing spice attack which takes the edge off the leading sugars; **f21.5** chocolate fruit and nut; **b22** technically, this is not A1 spirit at work. However the influence of the Port pipe is so impressive, much, if not all, is forgiven... 59.3%. nc ncf sc.

⚜️ **St George's to Commemorate the Royal Coronation** db **(87) n21** slightly dull despite the fruit and quiet smoke on display; **t23.5** youth is the essence here with a glittering display of soft sugar notes tripping over the tongue. Because of the tender years, these tend to be molten white rather than dark sugars but the gristiness which also comes into play delights; some spice tingle and nectarine complete the impressive middle; **f20.5** a slight fault of a sherry butt comes into play giving a degree of furriness to the late cocoa and raisin; **b22** it has just gone 8.30pm on Monday July 22nd 2013 and BBC Radio 4 has just announced that Kate the Duchess of Cambridge, has given birth to a baby boy, and both mother and child are doing well. Of course, that baby boy will be a future King of England; one, as a man in his mid-fifties, I hope never to see on the throne as his father should still be fully ensconced when it my time to grab my percentage of the angel's share. However, such joyous news meant that I made a rapid change to the whiskies I was due to taste. And I thought it only fitting that I should taste from the distillery closest to Cambridge and in which county the royal family have long had a family home, Sandringham. I not only taste this whisky but raise a glass of it to Prince Charles, with whom I have had the pleasure of meeting on several occasions, and welcome him to the joyous world of grandfatherhood. And of course the little, as yet un-named, baby in London, his eyes still unopened, and all around him a confused, cotton wool-minded, mystery. I wish you, Your little Highness, a long, happy and healthy life. Oh, and here's a little exclusive: just spoke to David Fitt who created this whisky. Originally it was meant to be bottled to celebrate the announcement of the expected royal baby. But they decided to switch it to the Coronation in order not to jinx the birth. So, how Fitting.... 46%. 1850 bottles.

⁘ **Stephen Notman Whisky Live Taipei 2013 The English Whisky Co** db (95.5) n24 the hint of youth is just that: a top quality first fill bourbon cask has sent some serious marzipan and lavender into the darkest recessess of the two-toned, occasionally intense peat; t24 mouth-filling and simply pulsing, a perfect peaty storyline. Few malts arrive at a sublimely sweet and dry pitch so early, especially when the malt element is still so juicy; f23.5 dries marginally more as the smoke becomes powdery and the coca-dusted, and lasting the distance as the light oils cling. Enough Demerera sugar to ensure balance, though; b24 a ridiculously stunning cask which I selected from St George's to celebrate Stephen Notman's impressive five year stewardship of Whisky Live in Taipei... making this a very English Whisky affair. Bewildering and beguiling for a four-year-old, where the peat is confident yet elegent, the body crisp yet lush and the complexity and balance beyond comprehension for its age. It was a pleasure to help promote not just the best of Bristish, but truly world-class whisky to an appreciative Taiwanese audience. And just shows what magic happens when near perfect spirit meets a near perfect cask. 50.6%

⁘ **Whisky Live Taipei 2013 Founders Release** B1/416 7/4/09 (93) n23.5 as soft and graceful as any peaty malt you'll find: gentle grist with a sprig of mint; t23 a light oiliness melds the playful peat to the palate for maximum effect; the sugars are of the melt-in-the-mouth, gristy sort, backed by richer muscovado; f23.5 the introduction of vanilla only adds weight and consistency to the understated smokiness; b23 beautifully made; excellent sweetness and beautifully smoky. A quietly satisfying malt. 50.6%

FINLAND
PANIMORAVINTOLA BEER HUNTER'S Pori. Working.
Old Buck cask no. 4, dist Mar 04, bott Apr 10 db (95) n24 t23 f24 b24. Just read the tasting notes to the second release because, a dose of what almost seems like corn oil and ancient Demerara rum combined apart, oh - and an extra dose of oak, there is barely any difference. I will never, ever forget how I got this sample: I was giving a tasting in Helsinki a few months back to a horseshoe-shaped audience and a chap who had been sitting to my right and joining in with all the fun introduced himself afterwards as I signed a book for him as non other than Mika Heikkinen, the owner and distiller of this glorious whisky. I had not been told he was going to be there. His actual, touchingly humble words were: "You might be disappointed: you may think it rubbish and give it a low score. It just means I have to do better next time." No, I am not disappointed: I am astonished. No, it isn't rubbish: it is, frankly, one of the great whiskies of the year. And if you can do better next time, then you are almost certainly in line for the Bible's World Whisky of the Year award. 70.6%

TEERENPELI
⁘ **Teerenpeli Single Malt Aged 8 Years** oak cask db (86) n21.5 t22 f21 b21.5. Has moved on a notch or two from the five-year-old. A soft, simplistic experience, dependent on fudgy cream toffee and hazelnut. 43%

⁘ **Teerenpeli Kaski Single Malt** sherry cask db (90.5) n23 busy, spicy, salted celery rounded off by busy, spicy salted greengage; t23.5 while the big grape delivery melts-in-the-mouth, you melt in the chair! The prime sugars turn this into a powerful cherry boiled sweet; f21.5 loses some focus as the oils from the cut begin to impact slightly; b22.5 a pristine sherry butt ensures massive fruit. Impressed. 43%

FRANCE
Single Malt
DISTILLERIE BERTRAND
Uberach db (77) n21 t19 f18 b19. Big, bitter, booming. Gives impression something's happening between smoke and grape... whatever it is, there are no prisoners taken. 42.2%

DISTILLERIE DES MENHIRS

Eddu Gold db (93) n22 t23 f24 b24. Rarely do whiskies turn up in the glass so rich in character to the point of idiosyncrasy. Some purists will recoil from the more assertive elements. I simply rejoice. This is so proud to be different. And exceptionally good, to boot!! 43%

DISTILLERIE GLANN AR MOR

⸫ **Glann Ar Mor Taol Esa 3ed Gwech 12** first fill bourbon barrel db (76) n18 t20 f18 b18. Sweet, oily, feinty. 46%. nc ncf. 674 bottles.

⸫ **Glann Ar Mor Taol Esa 4ed Gwech 12** first fill bourbon barrel db (80.5) n19 t21 f20.5 b20. A very generous cut, but I can live with this. The malt is intense and is well backed by brooding, spiced tannins. 46%. Nc ncf. Celtic Whisky Ccompagnie. 949 bottles.

⸫ **Glann Ar Mor Taol Esa 2l Gwech 13** first fill barrel db (73) n17 t19.5 f18 b18.5. I had hoped the feints might have taken a backward step: they haven't. 46%. nc ncf. 955 bottles.

Kornog Single Malt Whisky Breton Sant Ivy 2011 db (94) n23 t24 f23.5 b23.5. The nose, at least, says it was distilled on Islay. To a Frenchman, is that an honour or an insult...? For I have to say, this is the closest to a Scotch whisky I have ever tasted outside those cold, windswept lands...To be honest, this is better than your average Caol Ila, as the oak is of finer quality. Frankly, this is a never to be forgotten whisky. 57.8%. nc ncf sc. 249 bottles.

⸫ **Kornog Single Malt Tourbé Whisky Breton Sant Erwin 2013** first fill bourbon barrel db (87.5) n22.5 hickory and deft smoke; t22 accent on the brown sugars; f21.5 dries, bitters slightly; b21.5 kind of lurches around the palate a bit. 50%. nc ncf sc. 309 bottles.

Kornog Single Malt Tourbé (Peated) Whisky Breton Sant Ivy 2012 first fill bourbon barrel db (92) n22.5 t23 f23 b23.5. With the usual time constraints of writing this book and the number of awful, sulphured whiskies which blight my path, I had kept this back as something to look forward to: last year their 2011 bottling was a masterpiece: out-Islaying Islay. This, though, has its own French fingerprint upon it. Sweeter, more diffuse. But, Mon Dieu! A corker nonetheless! 59.9%. nc ncf sc. 260 bottles.

⸫ **Kornog Single Malt Whisky Breton Sant Ivy 2013** first fill bourbon barrel db (94.5) n23.5 sumptuous Caol Ila and Laphroaig mix of oil and soot; t24 mouth-filling with a surprising date and walnut fruitiness to proceedings...and no little molasses; f23 perhaps a distant echo of a wide cut, for the oils have a lumpiness to them. But the smoke continues to waft in the most tantalisingly of traditional, Celtic ways; b24 an Ivy Leaguer in every respect. Remembered this from last time out....in some ways this is even better: as precise as a Michel Platini shot in off the post... 58.6%. nc ncf sc. Celtic Whisky Compagnie. 271 bottles.

⸫ **Kornog Single Malt Tourbé Whisky Breton Taouarc'h An Hañv 2012** first fill ex bourbon cask db (93) n23 dry peat soot sweetened vaguely by powdery, crushed muscovado; a curious beetroot sweetness, too; t23.5 liquorice and cocoa confront the raging spice and kumquat-tinged peat; f23 settles into a smoked vanilla; b23.5 pulsing, phenolic and phenomenal. 58.7%. Celtic Whisky Company. 263 bottles.

Kornog Single Malt Tourbé (Peated) Whisky Breton Taourc'h Trived 12BC first fill bourbon barrel db (95) n24 t23.5 f23.5 b24. No off notes. No bitterness. Complexity on fill volume. I really do have to get to their distillery this year... now, where's that British Airways timetable...? 46%. nc ncf sc. 334 bottles.

Kornog Taouarc'h Kentan db (94.5) n24 t24 f23 b23.5. Not sure there has been this number of perfectly rhapsodic notes coming out of France since Saint Sans was in his pomp... 571%

⸫ **Kornog Taourc'h Kentan 13 BC** first fill barrel db (90) n22 salty smoke; vanilla sweetness; t22.5 healthy oils have a distinctly coastal feel; the smoke is little more than a caress; f22 milky chocolate towards the finale; b23.5 as soft as sun cream being spread over you while basking on a French beach. 46%. nc ncf. 907 bottles.

⸫ **Kornog Taourc'h Pevared 12 BC** first fill barrel db (92) n23.5 perhaps the most Islay nose I ever encountered from mainland Europe: a touch of Ardbeg-ish citrus and the drier, sootier tones of Laphroaig; t23 a touch gristy and just love that squeeze of lemon on the melting sugars; the smoke is playful yet very present; f22.5 even a slight Laphroaig-esque bitterness to the smoky flourish; b23 the language of peat is pretty universal. Laphroaig lovers in particular will rather like this one... 46%. nc ncf. 1007 bottles.

DISTILLERIE GUILLON

Guillon No. 1 Single Malt de la montagne de Reims db (87) n22 t21 f22 b22. Right. I'm impressed. Not exactly faultless, but enough life here really to keep the tastebuds on full alert; By and large well made and truly enjoyable. Well done, Les Chaps! 46%

DISTILLERIE MEYER

Meyer's Whisky Alsacien Blend Superieur db (88.5) n22.5 t22.5 f21.5 b22. Impressively clean, barley-thick and confident: a delight. 40%

DISTILLERIE WARENGHEM

Armorik db **(91) n23 t22 f23 b23.** I admit it; I blanched, when I first nosed this, so vivid was the memory of the last bottling. This, though ,was the most pleasant of surprises. Fabulous stuff: one of the most improved malts in the world. 40%

Armorik Classic db **(88) n22.5** the oak is confident enough to go head to head with the big barley: complex, lively stuff; **t22** attractive gristy sweetness. Subtle oils spread the Barley intensity; **f21.5** dries towards a powdery vanilla; **b22** quietly sophisticated malt. 46%. ncf.

⁙ **Armorik Double Maturation** finished in oloroso casks db **(75) n18.5 t20 f18 b18.5.** Dull and decidedly out of sorts. 46%. ncf.

⁙ **Armorik Millésime Matured for 10 Years** cask no. 3261 db **(92) n22.5** very unusual: a little lemon sherbet dust lightens the marmalade and tannin mix...; **t23** beautiful weight with an immediate spice impact on delivery. The barley is on a pedestal and offers a juicy edge; a little kumquat also ups the sharpness; a number of dark sugars ramp up the sweetness levels; **f23** a dull thudding of spice as vanilla and caramel bites back for a surprisingly dry finish; **b23** never quite know what you are going to get from these messieurs. Didn't expect this bottle of delights, I must say. The sweetness is a bit OTT at one point, but just copes. 56.1%. sc.

Armorik Sherry Finish db **(92) n22.5 t23.5 f23 b23.5.** The first sherry finish today which has not had a sulphur problem...and I'm in my eighth working hour...! Bravo guys! If their Classic was a note on sophistication, then this was an essay. 40%

Breizh Whisky Blended 50% malt/50% grain db **(85.5) n22 t21 f21 b21.5.** A safe, pleasant whisky which happily remains within its sweet, clean and slightly citrusy parameters. 42%

DOMAINE MAVELLA

⁙ **P&M Corsican Single Malt Aged 7 Years** dist 05, bott 12 **(95) n23.5** hefty tannin with a sweet edge: a wonderful saltiness suggests pretty new oak, and European by birth. I adore the (neat!) mandarin and Chinese gooseberry mix; **t24** an attractive, silky delivery at first appears in neutral, bar a faint nod towards cocoa. Soon, though, it slips through the gears and the early beech honey is reinforced with a molasses and liquorice blend, then further Demerara sugars; **f23.5** calms down and eases off the pedal with light tannin-stained maple syrup and a thin date fruitiness accompanying us to the softest of finishes; **b24** not been to this distillery yet and I don't speak much meaningful French. So not sure about the oak, though if I was a gambling guy (which I'm not) then it has the resonance of French oak, and it is this which appears to give the whisky its bold character. A distillery I must get to soon: it is rare to find a malt with this level of complexity and charm. Delightful: an absolute, near faultless joy of a malt. 42%

KAERILIS

⁙ **Kaerilis Le Grand Dérangement 15 Ans** db **(78) n18 t22 f19 b19.** A breakdown of the oils doesn't help reveal the weaknesses from the distillate. A must for fans de nougat. 43%. nc ncf sc.

⁙ **Kaerilis l'Aube du Grand Dérangement 15 Ans** db **(83.5) n20 t22.5 f20 b21.** Miss fires when the revs are up, but purrs for moment on two on delivery as the sugar and barley kicks in to delicious effect. An enigmatic fruitiness enriches. 57%. nc ncf sc.

WAMBRECHIES DISTILLERY

Wambrechies Single Malt Aged 8 Years db **(83) n20 t21 f21 b21.** There's that aroma again, just like the 3-y-o. Except how it kind of takes me back 30 years to when I hitchhiked across the Sahara. Some of the food I ate with the local families in Morocco and Algeria was among the best I have ever tasted. And here is an aroma I recognize from that time, though I can't say specifically what it is (tomatoes, maybe?). Attractive and unique to whisky, that's for sure. I rather like this malt. There is nothing quite comparable to it. One I need to investigate a whole lot more. 40%

Blends

P&M Blend Supérieur (82) n21 t21 f20 b20. Bitter and botanical, though no shortage of complexity. 40%. Mavela Distillerie.

P&M Whisky (89) n22 t23 f22 b22. No mistaking this is from a fruit distillery. Still quite North American, though. 40%

Vatted Malts
KAERILIS

⁙ **Kaerilis Ster Vraz No 9 4 Year Old** db **(80) n22 t21 f18 b19.** Plenty of salt and no little citrus. But undone by an oaky bitterness. 45%. nc ncf.

⋙ **Kaerilis Ster Vraz No 9 4 Year Old** db **(87)** n21.5 no wonder why they have seashell on the bottle: gristy malt reduced by sea water, surely...! The most coastal aroma I have ever encountered! **t23.5** fabulous sharpness to the vivid barley that puts salivation levels to almost record-breaking levels; **f20** tangy and hangs on grimly to the vanilla; **b22** what the hell was that...??? Something different, for sure. At its best, quite stunning. At its worst – at the death – hmmm, not great. Get your bucket and spade out for this one. *61.8%. nc ncf.*

GERMANY
AV BRENNEREI ANDREAS VALLENDAR Wincheringen. Working.
Threeland Whisky dist 2007, bott code L-Wtr200701 db **(83)** n19.5 t22.5 f20 b21. Whilst pleasant enough in its own right, my eyes opened up at this one, as I remember last year's bottling as being one of the best from anywhere in Europe. That, I recall, was so wonderfully fresh and clean. This one, sadly, is bigger and oilier with evidence that the distiller has included some heads and tails which were excluded last time out. Still malty and mouth watering. But a useful lesson in learning the vital difference between good and great whisky. *46%*

BIRKENHOF-BRENNEREI Nistertal. Working.
Fading Hill The Fourth bourbon casks, cask no. 22 & 23, dist Jul 08, bott 14 Mar 12 **(90.5)** n22.5 anyone of a certain age will remember this aroma of green Rowntree Fruit Pastels: this is almost identical...; **t22** mouth-watering barley almost with an effervescent quality before the slightly oily vanilla kicks in, then chocolate, then walnut....it's Walnut Whip... good grief..!! **f23** returns to a more fruity depth, with the vanillas and light spice a pleasant accompaniment; **b23** less Fading Hill: more F***ing Hell...!! Can't remember when I was taken down such a scary part of my past before: some of the aromas and flavours are like a time machine...! beautiful stuff. *45.7%. nc ncf.*

BOSCH EDELBRAND Unterlenningen. Working.
Bosch Edelbrand Schwäbischer Whisky lot 9105 db **(83.5)** n19 t22.5 f21 b21. Could really do with making the cut a little more selective: has the promise to become a pretty high quality whisky. This shows some outstanding depth and honey for some time after the first, impressive delivery. *40%*

BRANNTWEINBRENNEREI WEINBAU ADOLX KELLER Ramsthal.
A.K Whisky bott code L10209 db **(89.5)** n22 t23 f22 b22.5. Hardly faultless from a technical point of view. But if you can't enjoy something as raunchy and ribald as this, you might as well stop drinking whisky. *40%*

BRENNEREI ANTON BISCHOX Wartmannsroth. Working.
Bischof's Rhöner Whisky bott code L-24 db **(75.5)** n17.5 t20 f18 b19. That unique blend of feints and intense, biscuity grains. Just checked: I see I gave it the same score as last year. Not only unmistakable, but consistently so! *40%*

BRENNEREI DANNENMANN Owen. Working.
Danne's Schwäbischer Whisky dist 2002 db **(89)** n22 t23 f22 b22. An exhausting whisky to try and understand. You crack the code only when you fathom that there are two entirely different songs being played at the same time. *54.6%*

Schwäbischer Whisky vom Bellerhof db **(88)** n21 t22 f23 b22. Easy drinking clean and deliciously sweet malt with that indelible touch of class. *43%*

BRENNEREI ERICH SIGEL Dettingen. Working.
Original Dettinger Schwäbischer Whisky db **(88)** n21.5 t22.5 f22 b22. Softly sophisticated. *40%*

BRENNEREI FABER Ferschweiler. Working.
Whisky aus der Eifel Aged 6 Years American oak, dist 2003 db **(91)** n23 t23 f22.5 b22.5. A riveting whisky of uncommonly high quality. *46%*

BRENNEREI FRANK RODER Aalen - Wasseralfingen. Working.
Frank's Suebisch Whisky dist 2005 db **(86)** n21 t22.5 f21 b21.5. Impossible not to be charmed by the disarming citrus note. Every aspect of this whisky is low key and delicate. *40%*

⋙ **Frank's Suebisch Cask Strength 2008** db **(91)** n22 distilled from Lubeck's finest...? **t23** stunning weight; the oils and sugars hold on perfectly, a clean gristiness melts perfectly onto the tongue; **f23** after the marzipan comes the dark chocolate...! **b23** Frank has really got the hang of how to make the most of his still...a little stunner! And his cleanest yet. *57%*

⫶⫶⊱ **Frank's Suebisch Single Grain 2007** db (86.5) n21.5 t22 f21.5 b21.5. Consistent, gristy, mouth-watering fare. Does not try to be spectacular. More dissolving sugars this time. 40%

BRENNEREI HACK Pinzberg. Working.
Walburgis Franken db (78) n17 t20 f21 b20. While the nose puts the 'aahhhh!' in nougat, the sweet walnut-cake nuttiness on delivery and beyond makes some amends. 40%

BRENNEREI HENRICH Kriftel, Hessia. Working.
⫶⫶⊱ **Gilors Fino Sherry Cask** sherry cask, bott code L13032, dist Apr 10, bott May 13 db (89.5) n21 soft sultana and, pointing out an oily cut, nougat; t22.5 bumpy delivery with little accord, then finds its rhythm in mid ground as the grape finds a chocolaty home; f23 lovely finish which is soft and cherubic, the fruit having full scope to drift in and out of the vanilla and cocoa; b23 bravo! A sherry butt with not a hint of sulphur! 44%. sc. 866 bottles.

⫶⫶⊱ **Gilors Port Cask** sherry, bott code L13033, dist 10, bott 13 db (86) n20 t22 f22.5 b21.5. Thoroughly enjoyable and full of depth and no little fruit and spice. But the wide cut, apparent in the sherry version, is not tamed in quite the same effortless way. 44%. sc. 893 bottles.

BRENNEREI HÖHLER Aarbergen, Kettenbach. Working.
Whesskey Hessischer aus Stammwürze 4 Years Old db (90) n21 t22.5 f24 b22.5. There are so many things right with this whisky, but you also get the feeling – even when it as amazing as this - that something is wrong. Either way, bottling like this enliven any evening and give tired taste buds a new lease of life and a will to live... 57%

BRENNEREI HÖNING Winnweiler, Donnersbergkreis. Working.
Taranis Single Cask Limited Edition Aged 3 Years Limousin-Eiche barrel, cask no. 1, dist Sep 08 (84) n21 t21.5 f20 b21.5. Anyone for sweetened lemon tea? Pretty refreshing dram – though unusual! 46%. sc. 679 bottles.

BRENNEREI HÜBNER Stadelhofen, Steinfeld. Working.
Hubner Los Nr 3 db (80.5) n20 t22.5 f18 b20. Overwhelmed by fruit as far as complexity is concerned, but there is a distinctive smoky, salivating theme to this nonetheless. The balance has been trashed and if it were a novel, you'd have to read it three times...and still make no sense of it. A David Lynch film of a whisky...and I love it, though I have no idea why. 40%

BRENNEREI LOBMÜLLER Talheim. Working.
Schwäbischer Whisky Single Grain cask no. 7 db (86.5) n20 t22.5 f22 b22. A friendly, big-hearted, soul full of toffee-chocolate chewiness. Highly enjoyable. 41%

BRENNEREI MARTIN MEIER Neuravensburg. Working.
Mein 9. Fass db (84) n19 t21.5 f22 b21.5. The light spices and dissolving sugars melt beautifully into the malt. Nose apart, this is a ja, nicht ein 9... 42%

BRENNEREI MARTIN ZIEGLER Baltmannsweiler. Working.
Esslinger Single Malt Aged 8 Years db (85) n20.5 t22 f21 b21.5. Malty, nutty, a decent degree of sweetness and toffee marzipan. A well-made malt which you appreciate more as you acclimatise to its compact style. 42%

BRENNEREI RABEL Owen. Working.
Schwäbischer Whisky db (76.5) n17 t21.5 f18 b20. Here's something different. While the nose, or at least the getting it right, is a work in progress, the delivery and body are much more on the ball thanks mainly to a rich treacle and prune element which sees off the thicker distillate. The finish, though, confirms the fault lines. 40%

BRENNEREI VOLKER THEURER Tübingen-Unterjesingen. Working.
Sankt Johann Single Barrel Aged 8 Years bott code BL-2010 db (85) n19.5 t22 f21.5 b22. Fabulous fun. Once it gets over the drying tobacco nose the inevitable nougat is delivered. But it comes with a milk-creamy mocha which develops in intensity and with just the right doses of treacle to keep the sweetness at desired levels. Good background spices too. A very likeable character, this Saint Johann. 46.5%

BRENNEREI ZAISER Köngen. Working.
Zaiser Schwäbischer Whisky db (83) n23 t21.5 f19 b19.5. Surprisingly dry and constricted in development considering the beautiful soft sugars on the nose which also boast excellent clarity. 40%

BRENNEREI ZIEGLER Freudenberg, North Württemberg. Working.

⁙ **Aureum 1865 Single Malt 5 Years Old** db (86) n20.5 t22.5 f21.5 b21.5. Mocha with plenty of grist and muscovado stirred in. 43%

⁙ **Aureum 1865 Vontage Single Malt 2008** db (90.5) n20 off key, though the barley screams from a distance; t24 chair-gripping stuff! An uncomfortable oily start, but then wave upon wave of coconut and honey turn into something a lot more spicy and heady: the barley rips into the taste buds with near full frontal nudity...; f23 still one enormous barley orgy, though a little bit of chalky butterscotch and cocoa tries to offer a towel of modesty; b23.5 after a less than great start on the nose it truly blows you away with a massive impact. 53.9%. ncf.

DESTILLERIE DREXLER Working.

Drexler Arrach No. 1 Bayerwald Single Cask cask no. 262, dist May 07, bott May 10 db (88.5) n21 t23 f22 b22.5. Very good bitter-sweet marriage, but better still is the luxuriant mouth-feel. A well constructed malt. 46%. 210 bottles.

DESTILLERIE HERMANN MÜHLHÄUSER Working.

⁙ **Mühlhäuser Oberwalder Single Grain** bott code L0612 db (86.5) n22 t22 f21 b21.5. An enjoyable whisky, showing sturdy and at times sophisticated oak and good early sugar structure. The grain is a bit on the shy side, though: may have had a better chance to shine at 46%. 40%

⁙ **Mühlhäuser Schwäbischer Whisky aus Korn** bott code L1012 db (85) n21 t21 f21.5 b21.5. Clean, crisp, sweet, honeyed: am I the only one who thinks this tastes like distilled Golden Grahams...? 40%

Mühlhäuser Schwäbischer Whisky aus Korn db (90.5) n23 t23 f22 b22.5. Another stunning bottling from this excellent distiller. You have to admire the subtlety of the complexity of this whisky. 41%

Mühlhäuser Schwäbischer Whisky aus Korn db (90) n22.5 t23 f22 b22.5. So different! If you are into this, it'll be pastoral perfection. 40%

EDELBRAENDE-SENFT

⁙ **SENFT** American white oak, bott code L-SW36, dist Jun 09, bott Aug 12 db (76.5) n18 t20.5 f19 b19. From the chewy nougat school of malt. Lots of toffee, too. But limited in scope. 42%. nc ncf. 7000 bottles.

EDELBRENNEREI PETER HOHMANN Nordheim, Rhön. Working.

Rhöner Grain Whisky Aged 6 Years db (89) n21 t22.5 f23 b22.5. Impressively made and matured with a quite lovely marriage between the sugars and spices. 40%

EDELOBST-BRENNEREI ZIEGLER Freudenberg. Working.

AVREVM db (83) n21.5 t21 f20 b20.5. A most peculiar, though not unattractive, marriage of marmalade and hops. 43%. 1000 bottles.

FEINBRENNEREI SEVERIN SIMON Alzenau-Michelbach. Working.

Simon's 10 Years Old Bavarian Pure Pot Still db (86.5) n21.5 t21.5 f22.5 b21. Not a whiskey to rush. Takes several hours to get to know this chap. When they say Pure Pott Still, I am sure they mean a mixture of malted and unmalted barley. Because that is the only style that offers a whiskey as rock hard as this with virtually no give on the palate. If there is any yield, it comes in a vaguely fruity form but this is a whiskey which sets up an impenetrable barrier and defies you to pass. Fascinating and very different. 40%

FINCH HIGHLAND WHISKY DISTILLERY Nellingen, Alb-Donau. Working.

Finch White Label barrique barrels db (91) n23 t22.5 f22 b23 When I read my first books on archaeology and Iron Age man some 45 years ago, I wondered why they grew spelt and tried to imagine what it tasted like. Now I understand. I look forward to someone unearthing the first Iron Age pot still... A Finch which sings most beautifully. 40%. Spelt and wheat.

Finch Destillers Edition barrique matured/bourbon finish, bott Apr 12 db (94.5) n24 t23.5 f23 b24 These guys know exactly what they are doing... 40%

⁙ **Finch Schwäbischer Highland Whisky** dist 06, bott 13 db (88) n23 a cherry fruitcake; lots of black pepper; t21.5 eye-wateringly dry and pulsing with pith; f21 remains dry, develops along a spiced vanilla line; b22.5 not quite a perfect sherry butt, but one that adds an interesting spice side show. 41%. 449 bottles.

⁙ **Finch Schwäbischer Highland Whisky Destillers Edition** dist 07, bott Feb 13 db (87.5) n22.5 promising with the juicy crispness of the malt dovetailing with light pineapple and muscovado; t22.5 juicy delivery. The sugars gather, and then recede quickly as a chalkier, dry sponge cake style middle takes hold; **f21** some oils from the distillate merge with the vanilla; **b21.5** chirpy, but not entirely on song... *41%. Special Edition "Finest Spirits 2013".*

GUTSBRENNEREI AGLISHARDT Nellingen. Working.

HFG Dinkelwhisky Single Cask No 2 db **(87.5) n21.5 t22 f22 b22.** good, honest whisky with plenty of charm from the grain. *41.5%*

HAMMERSCHMIEDE Zorge. Working.

The Alrik Smoked Hercynian Single Malt 4 Years Old PX casks, dist 2008, bott 2012 db **(95) n24 t23.5 f23.5 b24** Beautiful weight, just-so sweetness, different...and simply adorable. *52.3%. nc ncf. Smoked with alder and beech.*

··⊱· **The Glen Els Dark Sherry Aged 5 Years** woodsmoked, cask no. 77, dist 17 jan 08, bott 15 Feb 13 db **(82) n22 t22 f18 b20.** At its best when the smog (or should that be frog?) of the syrup of dates and prunes and smoke begins to thin slightly. But a faulty cask doesn't help. *47.1%. nc ncf sc. 244 bottles.*

··⊱· **The Glen Els Dulce Negro Malaga Aged 5 Years Cask Strength** cask no. 42, dist 26 Sep 07, bott 26 Oct 12 db **(87.5) n22** a soup of an aroma with syrup of figs, syrup of dates... well. just syrup, really...; **t23** a classic case of a malt so wrapped in fruit that the barley has completely vanished. The caramel and chocolate notes, though, are quite irresistible: almost a chocolate liqueur; **f22** here one hopes for a degree of barley. Nope. But at least some oak comes out to play with more cocoa and now vanilla. But the syrupy fruit lingers...; **b20.5** the single malt whiskies of Glen Els are not exactly shrinking violets: indeed, it is hard to think of any malt distillery in the world bottling such hairy-chested, challenging drams. As is the nature of the beast, some work, others don't. This, once the taste buds have time to overcome the shock and adjust, works. Just... *45.8%. nc ncf sc. 258 bottles.*

The Glen Els Elements Air db **(90.5) n22.5 t22 f23 b23.** A beautifully refined malt. But I just hope that Glen Els is the name of the actual living, breathing distiller, not the brand... otherwise I see the good ol' Scotch Whisky Association finding another reason not to tackle their own problems and instead try to drown at birth a foreign distiller straying into the dangerous field of Scottish nomenclature... *45.9%. 600 bottles.*

··⊱· **The Glen Els Ember** woodsmoked, bott code. L1541 db **(93) n23** denser than the Black Forest...on fire...; **t23.5** fabulous chocolate sultana arrival with a warming, spicy follow through. Some cherry fondant and walnut oil appears to be in the offing; **f23** huge surge of vanilla which begins in the middle ground really does spread far and wide. The spices are beautifully consistent, as are the Demerara sugars which have paced themselves superbly; **b23..5** bold, rich and proudly idiosyncratic. Really can't fault it! *45.9%. nc ncf.*

··⊱· **The Glen Els Four Seasons 2013** claret, bott code. L1546 db **(89.5) n22** salty, with fudge and raisin; **t23** light spices lift the low hanging fruit; **f22.5** caramel wafer; **b22.5** vintage toffee... *45.9%. nc ncf sc. 250 bottles.*

··⊱· **The Glen Els Four Seasons 2013 Dark Sherry** bott code. L1530 db **(77) n19 t20 f19 b19.** I know, I know...some will ram raid any store carrying this. But for me: simply doesn't work as the profound sugars, the smoke and grape just never gel and find a happy balance. *45.9%. nc ncf sc. 250 bottles.*

··⊱· **The Glen Els The Journey** European oak casks, bott code L1532 db **(94) n24** massive: syrupy dates with some intriguing armpit saltiness..; **t24** date and walnut cake...without the walnuts. Maple syrup, treacle and ulmo honey chatter amongst themselves until the spices arrive; **f22.5** long, not entirely relaxed but the sherry trifle and butterscotch tart mix is helped by a faint cocoa fade...and dried dates; **b23.5** so date rich, probably the first whisky that'd appeal to a Tuareg... Ironically, as I taste this my parrot, Percy, is in the next room listening to Rachmaninoff's Piano Concerto #2 – which was used, I think, in Brief Encounter. I assume The Journey, then, is by train...to the Tuaregs... *43%. nc ncf sc.*

··⊱· **The Glen Els Moscatel Aged 5 Years** cask no. 79, dist 17 Jan 08, bott 18 Jan 13 db **(86.5) n21.5 t22.5 f21 b21.5.** Oddly enough, this comes from a cask which is in supreme nick and displaying not the vaguest hint of sulphur: a rarity. However, the smoke and the Moscatel are not the happiest of bed fellows: very tight, especially with the eye-watering sugars, with niggardly development. The more harmonious passages, aided by sultana and praline, are a treat, though. *46.1%. nc ncf sc. 257 bottles.*

··⊱· **The Glen Els Pedro Ximenez Woodsmoked Aged 5 Years Cask Strength** cask no. 65, dist 6 Nov 07, bott 17 Apr 13 db **(77) n19 t21 f18 b19.** Not technically the greatest butt of all time. But the enormity of the PX, the chocolate and the smoke...just too much. Of everything. *46.6%. nc ncf sc. 252 bottles.*

··⊱· **The Glen Els Rich Claret Aged 5 Years** woodsmoked, cask no. 78, dist 17 jan 08, bott 18 Jan 13 db **(92) n23.5** heavy wine fortification to the barley...a kind of port in reverse. Some chunky cocoa notes amid the raisin and Rup cheese; **t24** pure silk of delivery...the kind that makes you groan out loud. My word! A kind of heavily fruited barley wine which remains thick on the palate with some buzzing spices making a subtle but most definite entry; **f21.5** long, with the sugars crisp, jagged and showing both fruit and barley at irregular angles; late cocoa mixes with mid roast Jamaican coffee. But all the time the sultana and raisin drip-drips onto the scene; a late buzzing reveals a late minor flaw to the barrel; **b23** as though distilled by Dali, there are wonderful eccentricities to the overall piece. The secret, though, is the superb barrel choice: breathtakingly high quality despite having been treated, gently, somewhere en route. A Grand Cru of European whisky... *45.9%. nc ncf sc. 261 bottles.*

⸫ **The Glen Els Unique Distillery Edition** First Fill Sherry Casks, bott code. L1547 db **(89)** **n22** reminds me of the days a quarter of a century ago, when I used to nose the sherry butts as they were unloaded from the lorry on arrival at a distillery...; maybe a bit tighter here or there, though; **t23** mouth-filling delivery with exceptional weight. Rich at first, but a slow build up of vanillas lowers the grapey intensity; when the sugars are working though, as though trying to counter the pulsing spices, we have fruitcake ahoy! **f21.5** dulls slightly and loses its sugars fast; **b22.5** truly awash with sherry. But the pounding spices and rich cherry fruitcake makes up for the slight furriness towards the end. *45.9%. nc ncf sc.*

The Glen Els Unique Single Dulce Negra Malaga cask no. 93, dist 08, bott 12 db **(92) n22.5** **t23.5 f22.5 b23.5.** Glen Els may have got a few of their other wine casks slightly around their necks. But this has worked astonishingly well. In over 15,000 whiskies tasted in the last decade, I cannot find another whisky as a reference point. Truly unique. *44.4%. nc ncf sc. 384 bottles.*

HELMUT SPERBER Rentweinsdorf. Working.

Sperbers Destillerie Malt Whisky dist 2002 db **(77.5)** **n17.5 t20 f21 b19.** Very similar to the 46% except the sugars are much more eccentric. *59%*

KINZIGBRENNEREI MARTIN BROSAMER Biberach. Working.

Kinzigbrennerei Martin Brosamer Single Malt oak cask, dist Apr 05, bott Sep 08 db **(84)** **n20.5 t21 f21.5 b21.** For all the obvious nougat, the barley is given a clear stage from which to make its sweet speech. *42%. 120 bottles.*

KLEINBRENNEREI FITZKE Herbolzheim-Broggingen. Working.

⸫ **Derrina Dinkel Schwarzwälder Single Grain** bott code. L11108 db **(85) n22 t22 f20** **b21.** Many European distillers working with spelt have come unstuck over the years. This is a better bottling than most, as they have coped better with the grain during fermentation. There a genuinely complex layering to the understated sugars which allows the soft chewiness of the grain to come through with ease. However, unusually for this distillery, less than wonderful oak has a deleterious effect on the finale. *43%*

⸫ **Derrina Einkorn Schwarzwälder Single Grain** bott code. L11209 db **(96) n23.5** a study of citrus: zesty lemon and lime merges beautifully with the icing sugar; a blend of heather honey and muscovado sugars give extra depth to the sweetness; **t24.5** beautifully clean: the grain immediately salivates, while a massive spice kick heralds the arrival of a spectacular chocolate mousse middle; just so much honey, ranging from the clearest possible to Greek with even a touch of soft manuka stirred in; **f24** long, with the oak offering a vanilla and butterscotch prop. But just enough oils escape the strict cut to ensure a magnificently long finale; the lasting cocoa notes are distinctly Venezuelan and even a little medium roast Mysore coffee...sweetened with honey, of course...; **b24** not every day one gets to taste Einkorn whisky. On this evidence, and when so carefully distilled, a great pity. For this is one of the great whiskies of the world. *43%*

⸫ **Derrina Gerste Schwarzwälder Single Grain** bott code. L5508 db **(80.5) n19 t21 f20** **b20.5.** No little irony that a distillery which specialises so brilliantly in obscure grains gets it slightly wrong when it comes to barley. The juniper on the nose gets this off to a gin-style start...and finish. The intervening cocoa is the high spot. *43%*

⸫ **Derrina Grünkern Schwarzwälder Single Grain** bott code. L11009 db **(94.5) n23** so many variations of salt, hard to know where to begin. The grain offers a just-so countering sweetness' there's a slight vegetable note, too, but not in a rotting negative way – perhaps "earthy" is a better description; **t24** ridiculous! the nose shows little sweetness, yet the delivery is a fabulous catwalk of semi-naked sugars on display before a subtle saltiness creeps into play, giving a sea-breeze tang; the muscovado sugars attached to the gristy juice is wonderful; **f23.5** long with the familiar chocolate nougat attached to the distillery, but much more refined here – literally! The bitter-sweet balance is majestic, but the piquancy upped by the delicate salt; **b24** this may be Green Spelt from the Black Forest. But this tastes as though it has been matured by a Blue Lagoon by Golden Sands. The most coastal whisky I have ever encountered from a land-locked European mainland distillery. Ein stunner! *43%*

⸫ **Derrina Hafer Schwarzwälder Single Grain** bott code. L6205 db **(91) n22.5** busy aroma, a blend of porridge and marzipan; **t24** stunning texture, allowing both the soft sugars and playful spice to mingle and balance; good oak arrival to the mid ground, the oats really do spread luxuriously; f22 bitter chocolate; b22.5 no faulting a beautifully made, complex malt. Any fan of oak whisky, like myself, will not be disappointed. 43%

⁙ **Derrina Hirse Schwarzwälder Single Grain** bott code. L6507 db (87.5) n21 pungent, impossible to describe other than...millet! What more can you say...??? OK, I'll give it a go: old Kiwi boot wax, with a touch of clear honey; t22.5 a strange, intense, boiled sweet fused with humbug-type spiciness; waxy; f22 long with manuka honey and butterscotch, and a bitterish, spiced tang; b22 by strange coincidence, my Meyer's parrot, Perseus, is tucking into some millet while I sample its distilled form. This is enjoyable (and very different!) but I think Percy is enjoying his experience more than me... 43%

⁙ **Derrina Reis Schwarzwälder Single Grain** bott code. L10309 db (84) n21 t21.5 f20.5 b21. Purists argue that distilled rice isn't whisky. Well it's a grain, so surely, in my book, that counts. Whether it makes good distillate is another matter and the lack of body, complexity and anywhere for it to go is clear for all to see. Some pleasant sugary, chocolate moments, though. 43%

⁙ **Derrina Triticale Schwarzwälder Single Grain** bott code. L 10409 db (95) n23 rock hard aroma, almost unmalted rye in style but with a salted vanilla underbid; almost bourbon in style (from the Tom Moore distillery); t23.5 fabulous small grain arrival: as busy and chattering on the palate as you could possibly believe, all held together with a sublime Venezuelan cocoa and lime cement; f24 long with just the most delicate rye-style sharpness, the crisp hardness now joined with some crisper muscovado sugars; b24.5 a very different, but wonderful experience, conjured by a very rare and unusual grain. On this evidence, would love to see it in greater use for this, make no mistake, is a world classic... 43%

⁙ **Derrina Dinkelmalz Schwarzwälder Single Malt** bott code. L5509 db (93.5) n22 crackers with black peppers; a light molassed sub plot; oily thanks to a little extra generosity at the still; t23.5 near perfect weight with oils to die for. The arrival of the muscovado sugars and lightly oiled spelt is a dead heat; the lifting of the spices and the slow growth of a coconut biscuit and Fererro Rocher chocolate duet astounds; the relatively wide cut works well with the oils ensuring both weight and depth; f24.5 one of the most complex finishes produced on mainland Europe this year with the highest quality Lubeck marzipan dabbed with a light coating of ulmo honey; the oak is unobtrusive and is happy to display rich butterscotch; b23.5 a wonderful essay in flavour development. A genuine treat of a malt. 43%

⁙ **Derrina Emmermalz Schwarzwälder Single Malt** bott code. L6809 db (90) n22 nutty nougat, but adore the lime and glazed cherry; t23 early praline on delivery, helped along by an oiliness on which the citrus notes cling unfailingly; walnut and cream cake fills the mid-ground; f22.5 big oils but the spelt really is there for the chewing, its slight grassiness gleaming amid the moist date and walnut cake; for once the light powdering of cocoa represents the spirit rather than the cask; b22.5 another form of spelt and this one is comfortable and relaxed on the palate, allowing a really pleasing complexity. 43%

⁙ **Derrina Gerstenmalz Schwarzwälder Single Malt** bott code. L5409 db (89) n20 plenty of chocolate nougat suggests a wide cut; t22 big malty delivery with the barley offering a juicy middle; f24 absolutely enters overdrive as the oils from that wide cut add brazil nut oil into the even gathering cocoa; molasses and heather honey absorb the custardy vanilla. Fabulously long and complex; b23 splutters around on the nose and delivery but when it finds the map it finds the most satisfyingly complex of all routes. 43%

⁙ **Derrina Hafermalz Schwarzwälder Single Malt** bott code. L6709 db (87.5) n21.5 for a malted oak whisky the degree of light fruit is surprising; t22 much bigger here: the delivery is sumptuous and soon full of spice. The oats become apparent mid-range; warming and thick; f22 much more oaky here with vanilla dominating; b22 lush and far from shy. 43%

⁙ **Derrina Roggenmalz Schwarzwälder Single Malt** bott code. L5609 db (85.5) n21 t21 f22 b21.5. The oils are heavy and ponderous, swamping many of the more intrinsically fruity tones to be expected from the grain. Enjoyable, but could have been so much better. 43%

⁙ **Derrina Torf-Rauchmalz Schwarzwälder Single Malt** bott code. L11309 db (85.5) n19 t22 f22.5 b22. Not quite the greatest nose, with the peat offering a stale tobacco aroma. But pedals hard to make up for lost ground with a sweet, gristy smokiness which charms as it relaxes. Lots of maple syrup fills in the cracks. 43%

⁙ **Derrina Weizenmalz Schwarzwälder Single Malt** bott code. L5709 db (88) n22 a tight aroma, almost like a cold fruit loaf with a little marmalade spread on top; t21.5 a wider cut than normal means some bigger oils than you might expect. A little nougat and molasses and then a big spice expansion; f22.5 spiced honey and nougat, all wrapped in cocoa; b22 you expect spice from wheat whisky – and here you get it, believe me! 43%

Schwarzwälder Whisky Weizenmalz bott code. L5706 db (94) n23 t23 f24 b24. Superbly made whisky with thumping character despite its fresh and delicate nature. One of Europe's finest, for sure. 43%

KORNBRENNEREI WAGNER Dauborn. Working.
Golden Ground Grain Whisky Original Dauborner dist 2005 db (88) n21 t23 f22 b22. A little extra feints has worked well for the rich and complex body. 46%

KOTTMANN´S EDELDESTILLAT-BRENNEREI Bad Ditzenbach. Working.
Schwäbischer Whisky lot no. 120705 (78.5) n19 t20 f19 b19.5. Heavy, oily and with much nougat to chew on. 40%

MÄRKISCHEN SPEZIALITÄTEN BRENNEREI Hagen. Working.
⁂ **Bonum Bono New Make Fassgelagert** db (89) n22 t23 f22 b22. Malteser candy in distilled form. Unbelievably malty, helped along by thin milk chocolate and some compelling beech honey. 55%

NORBERT WINKELMANN Hallerndorf. Working.
Fränkischer Rye Whisky db (93.5) n24 t24 f22.5 b23. For the record, the nose is so good to this that I kept it with me one evening after a badly sulphured cask from another distillery had ruined my tasting for the day. The fruity beauty of this was not just balm, but a reminder of just how wonderful whisky should touch you. 42%

OBSTBRENNEREI MÜCK Birkenau. Working.
Old Liebersbach Smoking Malt Whisky bott code. L1105 db (83.5) n21 t21.5 f21 b20. Good heavens! Don't find many whiskies like this one around the world. Almost a Sugar Fest in part, especially in the earlier stages, then bitters out with an almost shocking suddenness. Fascinating and dramatic, though perhaps not for the purist. 43%

PRIVATBRENNEREI SONNENSCHEIN Witten-Heven. Demolished.
Sonnenschein 15 db (79.5) n19.5 t21 f19 b20. So, it's back!! In its youth, this was a tough whisky to entertain. Many years on and some of the old faults remain, but it has picked up a touch of elegance along the way. 41%

BRENNEREI REINER MÖSSLEIN Zeilitzheim. Working.
Fränkischer Whisky db (91) n23 t23 f22.5 b22.5. Rich, earthy, pungent, full of character and quite adorable. Perhaps an acquired taste for single malt stick-in-the muds, though... 40%

SEVERIN SIMON Alzenau-Michelbach, Aschaffenburg. Working.
Simon's Bavarian Pure Pot Still Whiskey bott code L0011 db (84) n20 t22.5 f20 b21.5. Have been looking forward to locking horns with this one again; the last time we met my teeth almost shattered against its rigidity. A different animal this time, with the pine and lemon nose reminding me I have washing up to do. The first minute after delivery is the high point, where for a short while everything comes together for a sweet and tart chewy treat. But the finish carries on with the pine... 40%

SLYRS Schliersee-Neuhaus. Working.
⁂ **Slyrs Bavarian Single Malt Sherry Edition No. 1** finished in Oloroso, lot no. L00354, bott 2013 (86) n20 t22 f22 b22. Anyone out there who loves cream toffee and spice? This malt has your name on it. 46%

⁂ **Slyrs Bavarian Single Malt Sherry Edition No. 1** finished in Pedro Ximénez, lot no. L02491, bott 2013 (88.5) n21 an unhappy, mixed bag with the slightly wayward cut at odds with the entangled grape; t23 that's much more like it: the massively thick fruit fills in some obvious holes in the distillate and positively zips around the palate thanks to some high quality spice; the liquorice and clean honey middle is a treat; f22 the slight imbalance found on the nose returns, but now some barley comes to the rescue; b22.5 can't say PX is usually my favourite cask for whisky maturation. But I doff my feathered hat to these clever Bavarians: it has done the trick here! 46%

SPREEWALD-BRENNEREI Schlepzig. Working.
Sloupisti 4 Years (Cask Strength) db (94) n23 t24 f23 b24. A mind-blowing fruitfest. Just love the clarity to the flavours. This is such great fun...!! 64.8%

STAATSBRAUEREI ROTHAUS AG Grafenhausen-Rothaus. Working.
Black Forest Single Malt Whisky bourbon cask, dist Dec 07, bott Mar 11 db (79.5) n19 t20.5 f20 b20. This is one of the distilleries in Germany I haven't yet visited. So puzzled by what was in my glass, I called my dear friend Julia Nourney who sent me the sample. "Julia. Do they distill from beer, including the hops?" "You asked me exactly the same question last

year", she replied. I had forgotten, until she reminded me. Apparently they don't. But it kind of tells a story in itself. 43%

STAUNING

⚬ **Brigantia 3 Years Old** bott code L-12/12 db **(79) n19 t21 f19 b20**. Huge malt statement, as is the distillery style. But it appears someone decided to try and extract as much spirit as possible, because the cut seems to be a little too wide for comfort here: the oils are unforgiving. 43%

⚬ **Stauning Peated Single Malt** oloroso cask finish, dist 10, bott 13 **(93) n22.5** a hefty, heady, slightly frightening nose: a peat cake studded with burnt raisin; **t23** an initially tight delivery as smoke and sherry try to outmuscle each other. Opens slowly with the grape at the tiller but soon sails into a foggy bank; some outstanding ulmo honey and molassed sugar notes combine for balance; **f23.5** at last relaxes, perhaps aided by those sublime sugars. The smoke now moves into more cocoa-infested waters...; **b24** can't say I'm the world's greatest fan of peat and sherry. But the finish on this one really is the stuff of smoky dreams. So impressive. 49.4%

⚬ **Stauning Peated Single Malt** Pedro Ximenez cask finish, dist 2010, bott 13 **(85) n21 t22 f21 b21**. Can't say I'm a fan of PX and big peat being thrown together and this does little to alter my view. Simply too much: the tightness of the sugars appears to strangle the life out of any further development. Decent delivery and early shockwaves. But your taste buds feel like they are in a sugary straightjacket. 47.1%

⚬ **Stauning Young Rye** dist 10/11, bott Jun 13 **(77) n19 t20 f19 b19**. Time to be a little careful, guys. The nougat on the nose means that perhaps a few corners have been cut...and the oils clinging to the finish confirms this. Maybe, after making some earlier excellent make, an eye went off the ball: it is too easy to think that the making of great whisky has been mastered and it is easy. It never is! For rye to achieve its greatest clarity and crispness, the cut has to be precise and never too early. The intensity of the rye goes some way to saving the day. 51.2%

STEINHAUSER DESTILLERIE Kressbronn, Baden-Württemberg. Working.

Brigantia 3 Years Old bott code L-11/11 db **(83.5) n21 t22.5 f19 b20.5**. The beautiful maltiness of delivery does well until a violent bitterness erupts on the finish. Love the fact that this has turned up in a classic old Cardhu-style bottle from the 1980s, complete with same colour spirit. A bit like an Austin Montego being kitted out like a 1930s Mercedes... although this offers a far better journey than any Montego I travelled in... 43%

⚬ **Brigantia 3 Years Old** bott code L-12/12 db **(79) n19 t21 f19 b20** Huge malt statement, as is the distillery style. But it appears someone decided to try and extract as much spirit as possible, because the cut seems to be a little too wide for comfort here: the oils are unforgiving. 43%

STEINWÄLDER BRENNEREI SCHRAML Erbendorf. Working.

Stonewood 1818 dist 1999 db **(91) n22.5 t23 f22.5 b23**. Consistant throughout with a superb and endearing degree of sweetness. High quality stuff. 45%

UNIVERSITÄT HOHENHEIM Working.

Hohenheim Universität Single Malt (82) n21 t20 f20 b21. The aroma is atractively nutty, marzipan even, and clean; the taste offers gentle oak, adding some weight to an otherwise light, refreshing maltiness. Pleasant if unspectacular. 40%. Made at the university as an experiment. Later sold!

WEINGUT MÖßLEIN Kolitzheim. Working.

Weingut Mößlein Fränkischer Whisky 5 Years Old bott code L01/11 db **(91.5) n22.5** chocolate cherry and strawberry liqueur; **t23** creamy strawberry liqueur filling....with a dash of coffee; **f23** ...with yet more chocolate. But never a moment of over-sweetness. **b23** a joyous whisky but something very odd about it.... 40%

WHISKY DESTILLERIE LIEBL Bad Kötzting. Working.

Coillmór Kastanie Single Cask chestnut cask, cask no. 19, dist 24 Feb 06, bott code. LB0311 db **(91.5) n22 t23 f23.5 b23**. This is a distillery capable of making whisky at both ends of the quality scale. This beautifully intense malt is the best yet produced by the distillery and most definitely Bundeslige...! Hang on! Just noticed it is from a chestnut cask (hence the chestnuts????) Bugger! It ain't whisky, folks! 50.2%. 60 bottles.

WHISKY-DESTILLERIE ROBERT FLEISCHMANN Eggolsheim. Working.

Austrasier Single Cask Grain cask no. 1, dist Jun 98, bott May 11 db **(91) n22 t22.5 f23.5 b23**. I really don't know whether the Germans are able to knight someone for their services to whisky. But if they can't they should change the law. Another wonderful piece of high quality whisky fun. *40%. sc.*

Austrasier Single Cask Grain cask no. 1, dist Jun 98, bott Apr 12 db **(95.5) n23.5 t24 f24 b24.5.** Big, thick, pulsing... this is one macho whisky that is sweet enough for the ladies to like. This distillery's finest hour... or two... *40%. nc ncf sc.*

⁙ **Blaue Maus 20 Years Old** cask no. 1, db **(89) n23** salty, dry, deft. Tannins are tamed by thick molasses; **t22** soft yet enjoying an immediate spice explosion; **f22** the tannins return, as does a dry caramel edge; **b22** doesn't enjoy the same bourbon-rich vibrancy of the 20-y-o Spinnaker, which is a sweeter herr altogether. *40%. sc.*

⁙ **Blaue Maus 20 Years Old** db **(87) n22** pungent fruitcake bathed in oils and molasses; quite a few slices of apricot adorn the cake; **t22.5** a wide cut was taken here, so the oils on the nose immediately take effect; bitter walnut and raisin kept honest by the molasses; **f21** the oily onslaught recedes sufficiently for a big date and walnut chew; **b21.5** the first whisky of the longest day of the year – and it might take me all the hours the sun is up to work my way through this one...Good grief...technically flawed, yet compelling and strangely enjoyable!!! *45.5%*

⁙ **Blaue Maus 25 Years Old** cask no. 1, dist Apr 88 db **(94) n23.5** distilled dates...dipped in syrup of dates...and hanging from a date tree. **t24.5** beautiful amalgamation of golden syrup and treacle, all poured over a date and walnut cake; **f22.5** dries towards liquorice and burnt raisin...very burnt...!! **b23.5** try not to adore this: Mission impossible. *40%. sc.*

⁙ **Blaue Maus Single Cask Malt** cask no. 2, dist Jun 02 db **(88) n21** nougat and errr... nougat..; **t23** nougat of course, but now some superb and distinctive acacia honey plus a light squeeze of lime; **f21.5** some oils play catch up and bring some cocoa in its train; now switches to ulmo honey at the death; **b22.5** the mouse is at its nibbly-est. *40%. sc.*

Blaue Mause Single Cask Malt 2 Fassfüllung cask no. 1, dist May 98, bott May 11 db **(92.5) n22.5 t24 f23 b23.** Methinks Blau Mause has sailed recently to Jamaica. *40%. sc.*

⁙ **Blaue Maus Single Cask Malt 2 Fassfüllung** cask no. 1, dist Mar 04 db **(89.5) n21.5** the nougat is softer here, a bit like a Milky Way; **t23.5** wonderful honey notes dominate from the off, mainly manuka in style; the vanilla traipses along with a light fruitiness adding to the barley; **f22** dries with a few hints of bitterness; **b22.5** all round, just lovely whisky of its style. *40%. sc.*

Blaue Maus Single Cask Malt Fassstärke cask no. 2, dist Jun 92, bott Apr 12 db **(91) n22 t23 f23 b23.** Suffers a bit of early identity crisis. Whatever it thinks it is, it ends up as a very big experience. *49.3%. nc ncf sc.*

Elbe 1 Single Cask Malt cask no. 1, dist Jun 97, bott Jun 12 db **(91) n22 t23.5 f23 b23.** One of the most restrained, simplistic yet effective malts I have seen from this distillery for a while. *40%. nc ncf sc.*

⁙ **Elbe 1 Single Malt Cask** cask no. 1, dist Jul 00 db **(88) n20** banana and nougat...and biscuit; **t23** superb delivery of spiced honeycomb; **f22.5** excellent length. The spices wear off but the fudge and vanilla add elegance; **b22.5** deep, complex and satisfying. Distilled Ledkuchen biscuit, in fact. *40%. sc.*

⁙ **Grüner Hund Single Cask Malt** cask no. 2, dist Jun 01 db **(79) n20 t19 f20 b20.** All kinds of German style biscuit spices. But the oil runs too deep. *40%. sc.*

⁙ **Krottentaler Single Cask Malt** cask no. 2, dist May 02 db **(88.5) n22.5** a lovely spearmint lilt to the eucalyptus and muscovado; **t22** chewy from the off with an ever-increasing fudginess to the theme; the spices tingle to good effect; **f22** more gentle spice and a slow vanilla burn; **b22** another big oily Germanic beast, but works the toffee to full advantage. *40%. sc.*

Old Fahr Single Cask Malt cask no. 2, dist Jun 00, bott May 11 db **(94.5) n23.5 t23.5 f24 b23.5.** An object lesson in excellent whisky making. Robert, you have excelled...! *40%. sc.*

Old Fahr Single Cask Malt cask no. 5, dist Jun 00, bott Jun 12 db **(89) n22.5 t22.5 f22 b22.** Beginning to become one of my favourites from this distillery. Very consistent. *40%. nc ncf sc.*

⁙ **Old Fahr III** dist Jul 02 db **(89) n22.5** moist ginger cake and nougat; **t22** steady, though sturdy, oils grip the palate with intent; the drier oaky tones have a good deal to say and battle the honeycomb manfully; **f22** much drier now with Madeira cake vanilla; a late hint of hazelnut oil soothes; **b22.5** a complex battle of a dram. *40%*

⁙ **Schwarzer Pirat Single Cask Malt** cask no. 2, dist Jun 99 db **(81.5) n20 t21 f20 b20.5.** Loads of molassed sugar at work and pretty nutty, too. *40%. sc.*

⁙ **Seute Deern Single Cask Malt** cask no. 1, dist May 00 db **(86.5) n22 t22 f21.5 b21.5.** Incredibly soft. And one of the most single-mindedly toffeed whiskies on the market. Especially after the early sugars burn off. *40%. sc.*

Seute Deem Single Cask Malt cask no. 2, dist 00, bott 12 db **(94) n23.5 t23 f23.5 b24.** Gets its act together with some of the distiller's softer themes effortlessly uniting. Leave this in the glass for about 15-20 minutes in a warm room for the most beautiful results. *40%. nc ncf sc.*

⠿ **Spinnaker 20 Years Old** cask no. 1, dist Jul 92 db **(95) n23** sweet chestnut and myriad high quality bourbon tones, especially the toasted honeycomb and hickory mix; **t24** massive bourbon character, except few arrive on the palate wrapped in such high quality silk. Where the standard Spinnaker is a confusion of sweetness, this is much more delicate and layered. In fact, the controlled honey and embedded earthier tannin notes seem to have no end...; **f24** long, drier with the accent of spiced vanilla; **b24** the softest and most elegant of German malts. One to remember. *40%*

⠿ **Spinnaker 25 Years Old** cask no. 1, dist May 88 db **(94.5) n23.5** diced orange peel lightens the deep bourbon theme, though there is a distinctive pot still rum element, too; the spices again have a Ledkuchen biscuit edge – odd, as it is made in the same region! **t24** almost perfect weight. The oils impact with style and ensure a big honeycomb middle; dusty tannins are invigorated by liquorice and hickory; **f23** long, with the spices really now having the most telling say; **b24** tasted on the day Sabine Lisicki made it through to the Wimbledon final (indeed, just been interrupted by a phone call from someone who has just left the centre court), and although this may not be as graceful, powerful or beautiful, it may make you smile like tennis' most charming competitor of all time. *40%. sc.*

Spinnaker Single Cask Malt cask no. 2, dist Jul 99, bott May 11 db **(93) n22 t23.5 f24 b23.5**. Aha! Spinnaker's back! Seams a couple of years since I last had a new bottling of this German whisky mainstay. A much cleaner version than I remember: none of the normal nougat and better distillation. Quite superb! *40%. sc.*

Spinnaker Single Cask Malt cask no. 2, dist Jul 96, bott Jun 12 db **(91) n22 t23.5 f22.5 b23**. Seriously yummy whisky. *40%. nc ncf sc.*

⠿ **Spinnaker Single Cask Malt** cask no. 2, dist Jun 01 db **(86) n22 t21.5 f21 b21.5**. A big honey and spice job, though sometimes the sweetness becomes a tad too enthusiastic and borders a little too close to the liqueur line. Delicious, though! *40%. sc.*

ITALY
PUNI

⠿ **The Italian Single Malt White** marsala casks db **(87.5) n22 t22 f21.5 b22**. Not whisky. Yet. But a very promising early marriage between spice and fruit with perhaps the rye making the only noticeable impact of the three grains used - though the spice may be a wheat by-product. Can't wait to see the distillery in action... their maturation process in particular. *40%*

⠿ **The Italian Single Malt Red** 3-36 months Italian Marsala Cask db **(86) n21.5 t21.5 f21.5 b21.5**. A decent new make from the vanguard of Italian whisky. The grains of local barley, wheat and rye could do with making more of an impact but good scope for the oak to make an early entry. Might be much more interesting at full strength. *40%*

⠿ **Puni Alba Masala** pinot noir & muscat d'alexandrie db **(84) n20 t22 f21 b21**. The nose has the new make somewhat accentuated but the delivery is far more harmonious with a soothing combination of soft oils, sugars and grape. *43%*

⠿ **Puni Pure Italian Triple Malt** pot stills db **(86.5) n20.5 t22.5 f22 b22**. Forget the neo-grappa nose, the spontaneity of the barley on delivery and the richness of the maltshake follow through is a joy! *43%*

LATVIA
LATVIJAS BALZAMS Riga. Working.

L B Lavijas Belzams db **(83) n20 t22 f20 b21**. Soft and yielding on the palate, this is said to be made from Latvian rye, though of all the world's rye whiskies this really does have to be the softest and least fruity. I'll be astonished if there isn't a fair degree of thinning grain in there, too. *40%*

LIECHTENSTEIN
TELSER Triesen. Working.

Telsington IV 3 Years Old dist 2008 db **(94) n23.5 t23 f23.5 b24**. It seemed only right that the 999th new whisky for the 2012 Whisky Bible, a very big number I think you agree, should come from the world's smallest whisky distilling nation. And also because they have the ability to make above average spirit and this, technically, is their best yet. For good measure they have matured it in a first rate cask. The result is a distinguished malt of rare sophistication worthy of the trust I placed in it. *42%. sc.*

⠿ **Telsington V 4 Years Old** Pinot Noir Cask db **(88.5) n22** buttery nougat and fruit; **t22.5** the fruit prods around looking for an opening to expand and expound: it fails...; **f22** buttery again, almost scone like with a light spread of Nutella; **b22** an exceptionally friendly malt. The pinot is a bit tight, but the fruit has just enough shine and clarity to make for a satisfying experience. *43.5%. sc.*

LUXEMBOURG

DISTILLERIE DIEDENACKER Niederdonven. Working.

Diedenacker Number One 2006 Aged 5 Years Luxembourg white wine French oak barrique, cask no. 2, dist Jan 06, bott Apr 11 db **(90.5) n22.5 t23.5 f22 b22.5.** Congratulations to this new distillery – and what a way for Luxembourg to become a whisky nation. A whisky bursting with character and complexity. *42%. nc ncf sc. 450 bottles.*

⁖ **Diedenacker Number One Rye Malt 2008** Aged 5 Years db **(86) n22 t22 f21 b21.** Not quite hitting the heights of their first bottling, but the nut and nougat is balanced well by crystallised treacle. *42%. 450 bottles.*

THE NETHERLANDS

ZUIDAM Baarle Nassau. Working.

⁖ **Millstone 1999 Aged 14 Years** sherry cask, cask no. 1355, dist 26 Feb 99, bott 15 Mar 13 **(73) n18.5 t19 f17 b18.5.** Those with a penchant for German spiced biscuits will love this. Personally, I have a problem with those types of spices which can also be tasted in some Indian whiskies. *46%. sc. Distillery Region Netherlands. Milroy's Of Soho.*

Zuidam Dutch Rye Aged 5 Years cask no. 446-683, bott no. 81, dist Jan 05, bott Aug 10 **(92.5) n23.5 t23 f22.5 b23.5.** This bottle stays in my dining room. There is a new classic European to be found. *40%*

⁖ **Zuidam 2007 Dutch Rye** virgin American oak barrel, cask no. 449, dist 07, bott 13 **(91.5) n24** truly classic rye signature: at once uniquely crisp and fruity with strands of cinnamon and liquorice: an aroma any Kentucky distiller would be proud of; **t23** firmer than I last remember it, with a cracking muscovado sugar and spice backbone; **f22** those spices continue to roll with a touch of late oak bitterness; **b22.5** another impressive bottling from a distillery which proves it certainly knows how to make rye. *46%. sc. Distillery Region Netherlands.*

SPAIN

DYC Aged 8 Years (90) n22 t23 f22.5 b22.5. I really am a sucker for clean, cleverly constructed blends like this. Just so enjoyable! *40%*

SWEDEN

MACKMYRA Gästrikland. Working.

Mackmyra Brukswhisky db **(95.5) n24 t24 f23.5 b24.** One of the most complex and most beautifully structured whiskies of the year. A Mackmyra masterpiece, cementing the distillery among the world's true greats. *41.4%*

Mackmyra Den Första Utgåvan (The First Edition) Swedish oak db **(93.5) n23.5 t23.5 f23 b23.5.** Only Mackmyra combines voluptuousness and severity in such knee-weakening proportions. Like being whipped by a busty blond dominatrix with a thick Scandinavian accent. Or so a judge friend of mine tells me... *46.1%*

⁖ **Mackmyra Moment "Glod" (Glow)** bott code MM-011 db **(96.5) n24.5** do you use an electron microspope to dive in to get close and understand...or a telescope because it appears to form its own galaxy of aromas... Marmalade leads, just, with a sub plot of earthiness bordering, but not quite reaching smoke. Salty. Tangy; a vague butyric fault line hiding behind the noise, maybe...? With so much happening...where's that electron microscope when you need it...? **t24.5** your eyes close with delight: no less than four types of honey at play – ulmo, acacia, orange blossom and manuka, all on low volume but playing a role. The oak growls and grumbles, but finally adds no more than ballast; **f23** long, with the pollen in the honey seemingly breaking up to form a complex structure; butterscotch, vanilla and cocoa powder; and a lingering earthiness prodded by delicate spice; **b24.5** technically, from a fermentation, distillation and maturation perspective: outstanding. From a blending viewpoint: masterful. Truly idiosyncratic: uniquely Mackmyra! *51.2%. 1088 bottles.*

Mackmyra Moment "Jord" bott code MM-004 db **(93) n23 t24 f23 b23.** Anyone with a fondness for bourbon might just have to get a case of this... hard to believe better casks have been used in maturation anywhere in the world this year. *55.1%*

⁖ **Mackmyra Moment "Källa"** bott code MM-010 db **(89) n22** dense, juicy dates; youthful barley; **t23** thicker than an oil slick. Massive molten sugars, mainly muscovado, vie with liquorice for control. The sugars win; some real youth to this malt, despite the muscularity of it all; **f22** strains of oaky depth as it dries; **b22** a bit pie-in-the-face with the avalanche of syrupy sugar. The vaguest fruitiness, but really a whisky for those looking for deliciously unsubtle sugar. *53.4%. 1065 bottles.*

⁖ **Mackmyra Moment "Mareld" (Sea Fire)** bott code MM-013 db **(95) n23.5** the saltiest of all Scandinavia's whiskies by a few fathoms; there is a wonderful citrus sub layer which at first seems at odds, but soon marries: almost like lemon on a fish...but without the fish, just the sea-salt... if that makes sense; elsewhere an earthier note ensures gravity; **t24** such a massive delivery: at first barley in its most concentrated form, followed by a wonderful minty chocolate middle; **f23.5** long, with the oak now having its say. It did that earlier with cocoa, but in a sharing way. Here it dominates... but carefully. The tannins still offer a light salty sappiness, but a mix of liquorice and manuka honey, too; **b24** mesmerising. They say not all the wonders have been yet discovered from the sea. Here is one that apparently just has....A malt for people with time on their hands. Anything less than an hour will do you and the whisky a disservice... *52.2%. 1600 bottles.*

⬩⬩⬩ **Mackmyra Moment "Morgondagg" (Morning Dew)** bott code MM-012 db **(93) n24** if you can imagine clear water running off a sun-shrivelled grape, you might get the idea: busy spices doing all possible to turn this into a heavy duty, moist fruitcake, though the sugars are attractively restrained; yeasty; **t23** a plummy blitz on the palate settles into a far more juicy barley-rich theme by the middle; heavily spiced cocoa and burnt raisin occupy the majority of the mid ground; **f22.5** pounding spices; thins towards vanilla; **b23.5** another masterful Mackmyra experience. Above all, you get the feeling of a heavyweight pulling its punches... *51.1%. 1600 bottles.*

Mackmyra Moment "Rimfrost" db **(95.5) n24 t24 f23.5 b24.** I thought that they had got the name "Rimfrost" from sitting on a Stockholm park bench in the middle of a Swedish winter. Apparently not. *53.2%. 1,492 bottles.*

Mackmyra Moment "Skog" db **(95.5) n24 t24.5 f23 b24.** With a name like "Skog" I wasn't sure if I was supposed to taste this stuff or simply wield the hefty bottle above my head and brain somebody in good Viking tradition. Fortunately I settled for the former...and made the correct choice. Although the latter always remains an open option to anyone who tries to steel this bottle from me. It is by far one of the most beautiful whiskies I have tasted this year... *52.4%. 3,000 bottles.*

Mackmyra Moment "Solsken" db **(92.5) n22.5 t23.5 f23 b23.5.** A treat of a malt. Scandinavian sophistication at its height. *52.6%. 3,000 bottles.*

Mackmyra Moment "Urberg" bott code MM-002 db **(95) n24 t23.5 f23.5 b24.5.** Beautifully distilled, superbly matured, clever flavour profile, first-rate packaging: the complete deal. Certainly one of the most intense, complex, compelling and simply enjoyable whiskies I have tasted this year. Truly a magic Moment... *55.6%*

⬩⬩⬩ **Mackmyra Reserve Cask** ex-sherry cask, cask no. 08-0689, dist 22 Dec 08, bott 28 Aug 12 **(89) n23** salty, heavy duty peat...any more coastal and you'd be tasting this in a fishing boat...with kippers sizzling...! **t22** sweet grists followed by a wave of soft sultana; the smoke arrives flanked by cocoa; surprisingly dry, as though the cut is wider than first appeared on the nose; **f22** a demure finale. Looks as though it is about to explode with spice...but can't be bothered...; **b22.5** the first ever Mackmyra which, on tasting blind, I mistook for an Islay. A very easy mistake to make. *51.7%. Carpets Crawlers Choice.*

⬩⬩⬩ **Mackmyra Special 09: "Vildhallon" (Wild Raspberries)** bott Autumn 12, bott code MS.009 db **(89.5) n22.5** big, chunky, meaty yet with a secondary character of light fruit dusted with cocoa. Busy and integrated with an ever deepening apple and pear complexity as the nose becomes accustomed to the thinner but by no means less significant notes, **t22** when one normally says "manuka honey" that is a close approximation. Here it is exact....; **f22.5** long, with the players in this mystery now showing themselves more clearly, especially the vanillas. That meatiness confirms itself as being from a slightly wider cut, as the chewability rises; barley appears late on; **b22.5** how interesting. First words to enter my head on nosing this was "meaty, cocoa" and on since checking the Special 08, I see I noted identical attributes. Absolutely no coincidence, that: the hallmark of a blender knowing exactly what she is setting out to achieve. *46.1%*

⬩⬩⬩ **Mackmyra Special 10: "Kaffegök"** bott Spring 13, bott code MS.010 db **(81.5) n19 t23.5 f19 b20.** Mackmyra do this from time to time: throw in a bottling which, I think, misses the target. The problem is the use of a cask or two of spirit which is not distilled with quite the same accuracy as normal. The plus side is that you are unlikely to find any malt this year which kicks off offering such a gorgeous and uninterrupted stream of acacia honey. But those extra oils are ultimately a little too burdensome for greatness. *46.1%*

⬩⬩⬩ **Mackmyra Svensk Rök** bott code MR-001 db **(93) n23** fnd strands of crisp muscovado sugar; **t23.5** the malt is pure silk. But yet again the smoke and sugars are busy, stringy and appear to have a life of their own; **f23** not just the smoke and sugar theme continued but mint and cocoa too....; **b23.5** a very different Mackmyra in both style and sensory texture. Subtlety is the key and time is the lock. Definitely need a good half hour to unpick this one. *46.1%*

SPIRIT OF HVEN

⬩⬩⬩ **Hven Dubhe Seven Stars Single Malt No 1** db **(84) n21 t21.5 f20.5 b21.** Very light malt displaying rich fudgy caramels. As simple as it gets, with a slight bitterness at the death. *45%*

SWITZERLAND

BRAUREREI LOCHER Appenzell. Working.

⁘ **Säntis Malt Swiss Highlander** cask no. 1144, bott 26 Apr 13 db (96.5) n23.5 the big oaky signals being sent are more than tinged with layers of clear honey and liquorice; surprising saltiness leads to a bigger honey theme, this time toasted honeycomb; t23.5 massively chewable on delivery...and for about two minutes thereafter. Like Date and Walnut cake on steroids and one with lashings of manuka and ulmo honey thinned slightly by a lime cream; early spices pop and fizz, then quieten; f25 one of the best finishes in Europe which hits the heights, a bit like the summit of Monte Rosa. Date and walnut cake, as before, but no longer on steroids, instead slowly unravelling bit by ultra complex bit.... with a buttery heather-honey sweetness adding another sublime dimension. As finishes go...perfection! b24.5 when this distillery gets it right, their malt really is something to behold. An absolute joy and one of the great whiskies of 2013/14. 57.5%. sc. 570 bottles.

⁘ **Säntis Malt Swiss Highlander Edition Alpstein 5 Aged 6 Years** Merlot finish, 15 Apr 13 db (87) n22.5 angular and irregular marriage between bourbon honeycomb and raisin; t22.5 deft, with a massive outpouring of intense muscovado sugar and maple syrup; a hint of juniper; f20 bitters out at the death; b22 a real softie. 48%. 700 bottles.

⁘ **Säntis Malt Swiss Highlander Edition Alpstein 9 Aged 6 Years** Merlot finish db (88.5) n22 huge natural caramel; t22.5 silky strike, a juicy spice and barley surge then fudge and raisin; f21.5 more fudge and raisin, though now burnt at the edges; b22.5 note; I tasted this at the pre-bottling 48.5%. I don't see it changing much from this toffee fest, though. 48%. 455 bottles.

Säntis Malt Swiss Highlander Edition Dreifaltigkeit db (96.5) n24 t24.5 f24 b24. Such is the controlled enormity, the sheer magnitude of what we have here, one cannot help taste the whisky with a blend of pleasure and total awe. 52%

Säntis Malt Swiss Highlander Edition Sigel oak beer casks db (91.5) n23.5 t23 f22 b23. High quality whisky which balances with aplomb. 40%

BRENNEREI HOLLEN Lauwil. Working.

Hollen Single Malt Aged Over 6 Years matured in white wine casks db (90.5) n23 t23.5 f21.5 b22.5. Many facets to its personality, the nose especially, shows more rum characteristics than malt. A won't-say-no glassful if ever there was one, though, and made and matured to the highest order. Indeed, as I taste and write this, my BlackBerry informs me that Roger Federer is on his way to another Wimbledon title: the similarities in the quiet dignity, elegance and class of both Swiss sportsman and whisky is not such a corny comparison. 42%

BRENNEREI SCHWAB Oberwil. Working.

Bucheggberger Single Malt cask no. 23, bott no. 10 db (74) n17 t21 f17 b19. Decent malty lead, but the intensely bitter finish makes hard work of it. 42%

BRENNEREI URS LÜTHY Muhen. Working.

Dinkel Whisky pinot noir cask db (92.5) n23 t24 f22 b23.5. A big, striking malt which is not afraid to at times make compellingly beautiful statements. 61.5%

BURGDORFER GASTHAUSBRAUEREI Burgdorf. Working.

Reiner Burgdorfer 5 Years Old cask no. 4 db (82.5) n18 t22 f21 b21.5. Recovers from the mildly feinty nose to register some wonderfully lush cocoa notes throughout the coppery, small still development on the palate. 43%

DESTILLERIE EGNACH Egnach. Silent.

Thursky db (93) n24 t23.5 f22.5 b23. Such a beautifully even whisky! I am such a sucker for that clean fruity-spice style. Brilliant! 40%

DESTILLERIE HAGEN-RÜHLI Hüttwilen. Working.

Hagen's Best Whisky No. 2 lot no. 00403/04-03-08.08 db (87) n19 t23.5 f22 b22.5. Much more Swiss, small still style than previous bottling and although the nose isn't quite the most enticing, the delivery and follow through are a delight. Lovely whisky. 42%

BRENNEREI-ZENTRUM BAUERNHO Zug. Working.

Swissky db (91) n23 t23 f22 b23. While retaining a distinct character, this is the cleanest, most refreshing malt yet to come from mainland Europe. Hats off to Edi Bieri for this work of art. Moving stuff. 42%

Swissky Exklusiv Abfüllung L3365 db (94) n23 t23 f24 b24. A supremely distilled whisky with the most subtle oak involvement yet. Year after year this distillery bottles truly great single malt, a benchmark for Europe's growing band of small whisky distillers. 40%

ETTER SOEHNE AG Zug. Working.

⁘ **Johnett Swiss Single Malt 2008** dist May 08, bott Aug 12 db (84.5) n21.5 t22.5 f20 b20.5 Peaks on delivery with a series of gorgeous rich sugar, semi-gristy notes. Just not enough body, though, to sustain the complexity. 42%

HUMBEL SPEZIALITÄTENBRENNEREI Stetten. Working.

Farmer's Club Finest Blended db (85.5) n22 t22 f20.5 b21. Clean, well made, astonishingly Scotch-like in its style. In fact, possibly the cleanest whisky made on mainland Europe. Lashings of butterscotch and soft honey; even a coppery sheen while the oak makes delightful conversation. But there appears to be lots of caramel which dulls things down somewhat. 40%

KOBELT Marbach, St. Gallen. Working.

Glen Rhine Whiskey db (88) n21 quite a variance between the sweeter and more bitter aromas...hmmm; t22.5 all the delicate sugars can't arrive quick enough. Light dusting of powdered sugar quickly absorbs the gathering juicy citrus; vanillas spread into the mid ground; f21.5 the late bitterness arrives on cue... b22 try and pick your way through this one... can't think of another whisky in the world with that kind of fingerprint. 40%. Corn & barley.

LANGATUN DISTILLERY Langenthal, Kanton Bern. Working.

Langatun Old Bear Châteauneuf-du-Pape cask, dist Apr 08, bott Jan 12, bott code L1201 db (96) n24 three types of honey detectable: ulmo, orange blossom and heather. Which tends to suggest a fair degree of complexity, especially when you add in a few phenols for good measure; t24 the texture, the weight, the sugar to oak ratio...it just can't be true. Spices enter the fray, but in tempo to the extraordinary beat of the emerging grape; f23.5 relatively short and just a little bitter, though an echo of ulmo honey does stay to the last; b24.5 whisky for the gods... 64%

RUGENBRAU AG Matten bei Interlaken. Working.

Interlaken Swiss Highland Single Malt "Classic" oloroso sherry butt db (95) n23.5 moist raisins on a toasted teacake; t24 the palate is engulfed by a soft and friendly blanket of light grape. But what really impresses is the structure of the lightly honeyed vanilla, enriched by the walnut oil and Bassett's chocolate liquorice on which the grape is embedded; f23 plateaus out with those soft oils but the lightest dusting of spice allows the drying of the oak a natural progression; b24 hugely impressive. I have long said that the finest whiskies made on mainland Europe are to be found in Switzerland. Game, set and match... 46%

Top Of Europe Swiss Highland Single Malt "Ice Label" bott 2011 (93.5) n23 t24 f23 b23.5. I get a lot of stick for heaping praise on European whisky. OK, there is the odd technical flaw in the distillation – though in some ways it works to its advantage. But how many casks do you find like this in Scotland? For sheer quality of its output, this distillery must rate as high as an Alpine peak... 58.9%. sc.

SPEZIALITÄTENBRENNEREI ZÜRCHER Port. Working.

Zürcher Single Lakeland 3 Years Old dist Jul 06, bott Jul 09 db (88.5) n21.5 t23 f21.5 b22.5. This distillery never fails to entertain. Not as technically perfect as usual, but none of the blemishes are seriously damaging and even add a touch of extra character. 42%

WHISKY CASTLE Elfingen. Working.

Whisky Castle Vintage cask no. 485, dist Sep 06 db (90.5) n22 t23 f23 b22.5. Imagine a whisky angel gently kissing your palate...this is all about very good spirit (with a slightly wide cut) spending time in what appears to be either a high quality virgin cask, or something very close to one. Brimming with character and charisma. 43%

Vatted Malts
LANGATUN DISTILLERY

⁘ **Langatun Old Eagle Cask Proof Pure Rye Whisky** French oak charred, bott code L0113, dist 08, bott 13 db (92) n21.5 as chunky as the mountain on the label, the obvious orange-blossom honey just clipping the wings of the heavier notes from the generous cut. The rye tries to fly like the depicted eagle, but stays in the oaky branches; t24 much more like it! The delivery nearly knocks you off your seat: one of the biggest of any whisky this year. Anyone who remembers Birds Instant Whip chocolate from the 1960s will be transported back in time here, so powering is the cocoa middle. Before then, though, we have to scale some rugged rye peaks...and from there you get some view of the blistering sugars below; f23 long, with that wide cut now ensuring a dusty edge to the Demerara sugar and flinty rye; b23.5 to be honest, not quite a perfect distillation here and doesn't hit the unbelievable heights of the bottling last year. But this is infused with so much character that when it gets it right, as on the palate it pretty often does, you are lavishly and sometimes outrageously entertained. 51.7%. nc sc. 200 bottles.

⁘ **The Swiss Malt (95.5)** n23 Lubeck marzipan interlaced with lime fondant and liquorice; a sprig of mint juts out like a feather from a Swiss hat; t24 it's not that it just melts in your mouth, it's the fact it does so with so many layers of spice, blowing you away in the process. The barley sits on a cushion of its own oils and molten muscovado sugars....; f24... which leads into a glorious ulmo honey fade...wow!! b24.5 Sumptuous and the stuff for late night naval gazing. When Orson Welles, as Harry Lime in the immortal Third Man, made a disparaging summary of all Switzerland's achievements over the centuries as the invention of the cuckoo clock, it was obvious he had never tasted this. A whisky the Swiss distilling nation can be rightly proud of. 50.2%. From 20 Swiss Distillers. 175 miniatures.

WALES
PENDERYN Penderyn. Working.

Penderyn bott code 092909 **(93.5)** n23 t23.5 f24 b23. Just couldn't have been more Welsh than any potential offSpring of Catherine Zeta Jones by Tom Jones, conceived while "How Green Is My Valley" was on the DVD player and a Shirley Bassey CD playing in the background. And that after downing three pints of Brains bitter after seeing Swansea City play Cardiff City at the Liberty Stadium, before going home to a plate of cawl while watching Wales beating England at rugby live on BBC Cymru. Yes, it is that unmistakably Penderyn; it is that perfectly, wonderfully and uniquely Welsh. 46%. ncf. Imported by Sazerac Company.

Penderyn bott code 1131008 (750ml) db **(93.5)** n22.5 t23.5 f23.5 b24. The light cocoa infusion just tops this off perfectly. A truly classic Penderyn; more charm than Tom Jones, hitting just as many pure notes...and just being a fraction of his age 46%. US Market.

⁘ **Penderyn Bourbon Matured Single Cask** cask no. 227B, dist 06 db **(89.5)** n22 heady and heavy, a slightly wider cut here than is the norm for a Penderyn. The oak injects a degree of stability with some kumquat and vanilla; t23 as chewy and mouth-filling as you'll ever see from this distillery, the barley could take the weight of a male voice choir from the valleys.... and show them something about harmony, too; f22 those extra citrus-fused oils are still evident and add a degree of spice to the gathering cocoa; b22.5 definitely a much bigger Penderyn than you might be used to, and that is only partly because of the cask. 62%. ncf sc.

⁘ **Penderyn Grand Slam Edition 2012** bott 3 Dec 12 db **(91)** n22.5 one of the drier versions, this time depending on a chalkiness to the oak as well as a dry wine grapiness; balancing sweetness offered by the most subtle orange blossom honey imaginable; t23 great weight on the delivery with just-so oils spreading the gristy barley evenly. Likewise the muscovado and grape are beautifully matched in overall impact; f22.5 long, exceptionally clean with a tapering and attractive dryness; b23 like the Welsh XV of 2012: tries...and succeeds. 46%

⁘ **Penderyn Icon of Wales Red Flag** Madeira Finish bott Nov 12 db **(94)** n22.5 light, teasing fruit, sultana-centred but some pears and greengages around the edges; t24 oh, yummy! Old fashioned fudge and raisins rain down on the palate to form a creamy textured, lightly sugared delivery and middle – amazing! f23.5 retains the creamy texture, a few half-hearted spices nibble, a touch of burnt raisin and the vanillas intensify but with not a hint of bitterness. Superb! b24 I thought this was dedicated to Cardiff City, the "red birds" for their promotion to the Premiership. But apparently not... though this year I was in the boardroom there watching Millwall and celebrating Neil Kinnock's 70th birthday. So maybe the whisky should represent both these landmarks, after all... 41%. ncf.

Penderyn Madeira released 7 Jul 10 db **(92)** n21.5 t23.5 f23.5 b24. This bottling is a testament to how far this whisky has moved over the years. There appears to be much more Madeira influence than was once the case, indicating that the malt is being allowed a little longer to mature. This is lush, beguilingly complex whisky of the very top order. 46%. ncf.

Penderyn Madeira released 4 Aug 10 db **(89)** n21 t22.5 f23 b22.5. Understated, clever and sophisticated. 46%. ncf.

Penderyn Madeira released 9 Sep 10 db **(91)** n21.5 t23.5 f23 b23. Practically a re-run of the July bottling, with the odd tweak here and there. My curiosity spiked, I contacted the Welsh Whisky Company who confirmed they were now, as I was very much suspecting, using a tank to store the vatted casks before bottling... and thus creating a minor solera system. This explains the continuity of style with the slight variation from month to month, rather than the sometimes violent lurches in style from one bottling to the next that had hitherto been the hallmark of Penderyn. Higher quality, for sure...if slightly less excitement and nosing into the unknown for me...! I shall miss its Russian roulette idiosyncrasy... 46%. ncf.

Penderyn Madeira released 4 Oct 10 db **(92.5)** n22 t23.5 f23 b23.5. Very much in the same mould as the September release, above, but here the fruit has a warmer, softer, say while the milk chocolate is ramped up a notch or two. A very classy act. 46%. ncf.

Penderyn Madeira bott code 8 Dec 10 db **(90)** n22 t23 f22.5 b22.5. I believe this saw the light of day only in miniature form. But there is no challenging the size of the whisky: Penderyn in its silkiest mode and allowing the fruit massive scope for flexing its grapy muscle...which it does with style. Big but simply charming. 46%. ncf.

Penderyn Madeira released 1 Feb 11 db **(94.5)** n23.5 t23.5 f23.5 b24. One of the great standard Peneryn bottlings. 46%. ncf.

Penderyn Madeira bott code. Mar 11 db **(92)** n22.5 t23 f23.5 b23. Almost like a chocolate mousse poured over a fruit pudding. And a spicy one at that. Not quite hitting the overall heights of the previous monster bottling. But sensational nonetheless. 46%

Penderyn Madeira bott 11 db **(95)** n23.5 t23.5 f24 b24. Concentrates on the fruity side of matters; the nose is a wonderful marriage (did I just put the words" marriage" and "wonderful" in the same sentence?....(shudder)) of rather over-ripe mango and fit-to-burst greengage while the delivery makes maximum gain from the sublime grape and peach lucidity. The finish is aided by the softest oils imaginable which inject the barley this is crying out for. Then a cocoa and raisin fade. It is a whisky that makes you sigh...and for all the right reasons. 46%. ncf.

Penderyn Madeira bott Jul 11 db **(91.5)** n23 t23 f22.5 b23. Perhaps if I was asked to pour a Penderyn to display its expected personality in full swing, with little grapey twists here, lightly sugared oaky turns there, this would sum the distillery up almost too well... And not least because of some extra viscosity allowing those sugars to expand as far as they are ever likely to go. 46%. ncf.

Penderyn Madeira bott Sep 11 db **(91)** n23 t23 f22 b23. You really have to take your hats off to these guys: the consistency is now absolutely top draw and here they appear to have that delicate balance between drier crushed grape pithiness of the Madeira completely in harmony with the sweeter elements of both oak and barley. Here, though, the spices season, entertain and bring alive, something like pepper on a piece of Welsh Rarebit. 46%. ncf.

Penderyn Madeira bott Oct 11 db **(94)** n23 t23.5 f24 b23.5. Penderyn with its tie off and top button undone. Relaxed from the moment it hits the palate – or I should say caresses – with a wonderfully soft barley-led fruitiness and then a mercurial display of complex spices and then vanilla-topped mocha. In this form unquestionably one of the easiest-drinking whiskies in the world. the remainder of this bottle won't be going back into my warehouse: this will be sitting in my dining room amid some accomplished others! 46%. ncf.

Penderyn Madeira bott Nov 11 db **(93)** n22.5 t24 f23 b23.5. Never quite settles like the October bottling, but through choice and design rather than fault. Edgy, dry and at times pretty nutty, with gorgeous walnut oil and chocolate fudge ramping up the complexity on the vanilla and burnt raisin. A malt which fidgets from one part of the palate to the next. But the quality is stunning. We have entered, without doubt, a purple period for Welsh Whisky. It is a bit like the national rugby team of the early 70s and Swansea City of the present: just a joy to behold. 46%. ncf.

Penderyn Madeira bott Feb 12 db **(92)** n21.5 t23 f24 b23.5. It is as though the gratingly dry character of the previous bottling had been noted and something has been done to make amends. The texture is much softer yet the grape both sturdier and sultana intense. The spices here are as big as any I can remember from this distillery and though they take no prisoners they successfully riddle the malt with complexity. Quite brilliant! 46%. ncf.

Penderyn Madeira bott Mar 12 db **(91.5)** n22.5 t22.5 f23.5 b23. The even-ness here suggests more casks than normal as we have a white noise on the nose of many of the Penderyn fixtures, though some cancelling others out. There is enough left over, though, to mesmerise. The delivery is also astonishingly well composed with barley and madeira striking an unusual balance of practically going halves in dominance. With the clear, grassy barley actually making this one of the most juicy Penderyns of all time, it is a malt which takes a little time to learn to fly, but when it does, it swoops and rises with elegant abandon. 46%. ncf.

⠴ **Penderyn Madeira** bott 2 Jun 12 db **(76)** n18 t21 f18 b19. Juicy in part. And some cocoa notes. But way, way off the pace by Penderyn's normal spot on standards. 46%

⠴ **Penderyn Madeira** bott 3 July 12 db **(94.5)** n23.5 wonderful marriage of juicy grape, crushed raisin and stewed plums plus Swiss-style chocolate and nougat; t24.5 wow! Penderyn had been trying to get a consistency from bottling to bottling. But this boyo heads into new ground with the depth of its fruit intensity, and its near perfect marriage with spice. Like on the nose, cocoa plays a big part. Never chewed a standard Penderyn quite so long or hard; f23 great length despite virtually no oils apparent. Superb light cherry fruitcake and molassed sugar; b23.5 probably the best delivery of any standard Penderyn since the product was launched. Absolutely marvellous whisky just bursting with depth and character. 46%. ncf.

⠴ **Penderyn Madeira** bott 7 Aug 12 db **(87.5)** n22.5 carrot juice thins the lightly spiced grape; t22 a juicier, fizzier version than we've seen for a while; the mid ground thickens slightly and a big barley surge adds weight; f21.5 vanilla and a little bitterness; b21.5 big barley lift, attractive, but not quite up to the ever-improving standards. 46%. ncf.

❖ **Penderyn Madeira** bott 10 Oct 12 db **(88)** n23 beautiful orange and lime amid the clear barley; some serious tannins, too; t23 a much richer delivery than the nose offers; again the barley is absolutely at maximum volume not only at the vanguard but even outlasting the impressive spice attack; the toasty raisin kicks in to reinforce the fruit theme; f20 back to basic barley and a light sherry trifle. Tangy blood orange kicks in late; b22 what's Welsh for "a juicy beast..."? 46%. ncf.

❖ **Penderyn Madeira** bott 2 Jan 13 db **(91)** n22.5 soft vanilla and kumquat; t23.5 stunningly silky with the toffee from the oak acting as a go-between the milky butterscotch and the firm black cherry; the spices lurk beneath the oil, working well with the crème brûlée; f22 excellent weight to the vanilla which enriches the growing oil and late "new make" notes; b23 a rumbustious version which peaks several times before the final fade. 46%. ncf.

❖ **Penderyn Madeira** bott 4 Feb 13 db **(95)** n23 superb mocha and hickory. The light fruity fringe of sultana is a treat; t24 spot on barley on two levels; crisp and full of juicy grist. This melts into the orange blossom honey and growing spice; the oils are nearly perfect; f23.5 rich tannins lengthen and spice the finish. After a degree of mocha, a light covering of glazed sugars complete the mixed fruit and Madeira cake finale; b24.5 just gorgeous! And simply faultless. 46%. ncf.

Penderyn 41 db **(91.5)** n22 t23 f24 b22.5. Don't think for one moment it's the reduction of strength that makes this work so well. Rather, it is the outstanding integration of the outlandishly good Madeira casks with the vanilla. At usual strength this would have scored perhaps another couple of points. Oh, the lucky French for whom this was designed... 41%

Penderyn 41 Madeira bott Jun 11 db **(90.5)** n22 t23 f22.5 b23 Penderyn at its most demure but also in this case showing it has a few claws, too. Works better at this strength than the Port Wood, probably because there is far more going on between the counter weight of grape and oak . The delivery, though, is the star as early cocoa notes pop up, welded to crunchy muscovado sugars and even a hint of stem ginger. 41%. ncf.

Penderyn Bourbon Matured Single Cask dist 2000 **(96)** n24 t24.5 f23.5 b24. Penderyn as rarely seen, even by me. This is as old a Welsh whisky that has been bottled in living memory. And it is one that will live in the memory of this current generation. For I have encountered very few whiskies which revels in a controlled sweetness on so many levels. This is so good, it is frightening. 61.2%

Penderyn Peated bott Oct 11 db **(90.5)** n22 t23 f22.5 b23. So few whiskies are quite so well-mannered as this... 46%. ncf.

Penderyn Peated bott Nov 11 db **(93.5)** n23.5 t23 f23 b24. The nose has rarely been the ace in the deck for Penderyn, but here it strengthens the hand considerably. This is the first Penderyn with some genuine peaty grunt. 46%. ncf.

❖ **Penderyn Peated** bott 2 Nov 12 db **(95)** n23.5 just the lightest pockets of smoke drift over the citrus lead: in some ways one of the most beautifully textured noses this year and certainly among the most sensuous; t24 just so juicy, with the barley bursting out all over the palate, no more than shadowed by teasing fingers of smoke; again citrus leads the sub plot, helped along by a delicate shading of orange blossom honey; f23.5 the fact that there is no big surge of either tannins or bitterness confirms the high integrity of the oak; the smoke drifts to the final fade, helped along by the most gentle of spices; b24 one of the most delicate whiskies you will experience this year. The fact it is smoked makes it even more remarkable. 46%. ncf.

❖ **Penderyn Peated** bott 3 Feb 13 db **(88)** n22 more blatant smoke than the November 2012 bottling and amid the ashy peat, a light bitterness suggests slightly more aggressive oak, too; t22.5 delicious mixture of citrus and ash; f21.5 quite a surprising degree of smoke on the cool finish which moves towards cocoa before it bitters out slightly; b22 almost a Laphroaig-style malt, complete with oaky bitterness at the death, too. 46%. ncf.

❖ **Penderyn Portwood** bott 1 Nov 12 db **(96)** n23 beautifully dry and pithy, a chalkiness to the grape leaves one wondering the direction this malt will go on the palate...; t24.5 perhaps the silkiest of all the whiskies yet produced at Penderyn. The velvet and ermine delivery salivates from the word go. Normally it is barley which achieves that. Here, it is unmistakably the lushness of the fruit which triggers the juices. The startling complexity is highlighted by the deft interplay between the blackberries and the drier, ultra-high quality marzipan which offers the least sugars required. The balance has to be experienced to be believed...; f23.5 long, one might say dry, but there is just enough sugary glow to the marzipan and milky mocha to tick all the required boxes. As all along, the fruit is understated but there, almost like a plum tart which is mainly pastry; b25 oh, the colour...the colour...!!! The most Port wood Rose I have ever seen...what would this have been like at 46 or cask strength? I wonder. Probably nearer Port...Curiously the blurb on the label describes the colour as "golden". Must have been looking at a ring. For "ruby", like the Port, might have been closer. As for the whisky itself, more importantly, what can one say? Another bottling which is truly world class for sure.

Certainly one of the greatest variations of this distillery, the subtlest and best balanced without doubt, and one that now sits in my dining table amongst the world's elite drams. *41%. ncf.*

Penderyn Portwood Swansea City Special cask no. PT68 db **(96.5) n23.5 t24.5 f24 b24.5.** On Saturday 30th April 1966 I was taken by my father to see my very first football game: Millwall versus Swansea Town, as they were then known. On 30th April 2011 I celebrated 45 years of agony and ecstasy (though mainly agony!) with my beloved Millwall with a dinner at The Den as we hosted.... would you believe it? Yep, Swansea! The Swans won that day on their march to deserved promotion to the Premier League and it was my honour to be at Wembley to see them overcome Reading in the Play Off Final to book their place among the elite. I have met their Chairman Huw Jenkins on occasion but not yet had the chance to wish him well in his new rarified environment. I toast you and your grand old club, Huw, with this quite stunning, absolutely world class malt, as Welsh now as laverbread, and look forward to the day when the Lions are back among the Swans...Oh, and in the newly acquired knowledge from a discovery I made while tracing back some of my family history over Christmas 2011 that, as fate would have it, my paternal grandmother's family hail in the 19th century from Neath, on the outskirts of Swansea...; that there is not a jot of Scots in me as Murray's previously believed, but a whole load of Welsh! Perhaps goes to explain why I have so long been such a fan of Penderyn! Or, just maybe, this fabulous whisky does... *594%. ncf sc.*

Penderyn Sherrywood released 1 Jan 11 db **(94) n23 t23.5 f23.5 b24.** Drier than the lips of a Welsh Male Voice Choir singing in the Sahara. But a whole lot more harmonious. *46%. ncf.*

Penderyn Sherrywood bott Feb 12 db **(94) n22 t24 f24 b24.** Fascinating how this sherry works in an entirely different way to the one bottled in October, offering different structure and focus points. But certainly no less quality. I am delighted for Penderyn when I taste this. But I wish some key people from the scotch whisky industry, as well as one or two commentators, would grab hold of this to learn just how a clean, entirely non-sulphured, sherry butt should actually be...if they have the ability to tell the difference (which in some cases I doubt), they will be in for a major shock. Mind you: there are none so blind than those who wish not to see... *46%. ncf.*

⋙ **Penderyn Sherrywood** bott 20 oct 12 db **(89.5) n21.5** just a little disharmony between the spirit and some very high quality grape (but with not a single hint of sulphur, hurrah!); **t23** ahhh, that's more like it! A sweet, toffeed, cream sherried coating of the cleanest variety really does bring some lovely muscovado sugar and nougat into play; **f22.5** about as soft a landing as you'll find this year: you can hardly feel the bump! Some late barley and butterscotch bids an enjoyable farewell; **b22.5** a faultless sherry butt ensures some marvellous moments, but the scope is a little limited. So enjoyable, though. *46%. ncf.*

⋙ **Penderyn Sherrywood** bott 1 feb 13 db **(93) n23.5** the soft sprig of mint suggests the oak itself and not just the intense sherry is a major player here; **t24** good grief! Springing back in time here: so rare you get an opening gambit like that on delivery, though once common in Speyside a couple of decades back. The sherry, thick and fabulously dry, threatens to swamp, then gives way gracefully to a series of molasses and liquorice notes: really a clever replay of the theme on the nose; **f22** dries again, a touch of burnt raisin though the custardy vanilla balances; **b23.5** a malt which really must be tasted at body temperature for the very best results. *46%. ncf.*

Penderyn Sherrywood Limited Edition cask no. 546 db **(95) n24 t24 f23 b24.** This is one of the world great whiskies. Penderyn's consultant, Jim Swan, is responsible for the use and selection of this cask. As was the case with the other single cask selections. It meant an entire four hour tasting afternoon was been spent simply analysing three astonishing casks. If all the world's whiskies were this good I'd never be able to get even close to completing the Bible. The three single casks included here confirm that Penderyn has entered the stratosphere of magnificent whisky. Ignore this distillery entirely at your peril. *50%. ncf sc.*

Scotch Malt Whisky Society Cask 128.1 Aged 6 Years 1st fill port barrique, cask no. PT3, dist 2003 **(93.5) n21.5 t24.5 f23.5 b24.** For those single malt fundamentalists who think the SMWS have welshed on their ideals, here is confirming proof: Welsh whisky. But tell me. The drunken nose apart, which has probably robbed it of an award, just which part of this whisky is not fabulous...? *55.6%. sc. 233 bottles.*

Scotch Malt Whisky Society Cask 128.3 Aged 5 Years first fill barrel, cask no. 600, dist 06 **(96) n24 t24 f24 b24.** If this doesn't get Penderyn to bring out a succession of full strength cask whiskies, I don't know what will. This is, without question, world class... *61.3%. sc.*

Scotch Malt Whisky Society Cask 128.4 Aged 7 Years first fill port barrique, cask no. 32, dist 2004 **(92) n22 t22.5 f24 b23.5.** Hardly a malt for the faint-hearted, but one many in the Scotch whisky industry, along with 128.3, can take a long hard look at. I'll give you a clue, boys: it is the quality of the casks. That area where the Scotch whisky industry has let us down so badly... *594%. sc.*

World Whiskies

I have long said that whisky can be made just about anywhere in the world; that it is not writ large in stone that it is the inalienable right for just Scotland, Ireland, Kentucky and Canada to have it all to themselves. And so, it seems, it is increasingly being proved. Perhaps only sandy deserts and fields of ironstone can prevent its make physically and Islam culturally, though even that has not been a barrier to malt whisky being distilled in both Pakistan and Turkey. While not even the world's highest mountains or jungle can prevent the spread of barley and copper pot.

Outside of North America and Europe, whisky's traditional nesting sites, you can head in any direction and find it being made. South America may be well known for its rum, but in the south of Brazil, an area populated by Italian and German settlers many generations back, malt whisky is thriving. In even more lush and tropical climes it can now also be found, with Taiwan and Thailand leading the way.

Japan has long represented Asia with distinction and whisky-making there is in such an advanced state and at a high standard Jim Murray's Whisky Bible has given it its own section. But while neighbouring South Korea has ended its malt distilling venture, further east, and at a very unlikely altitude, Nepal has forged a small industry to team up, geographically, with fellow malt distillers India and Pakistan. The one malt whisky from this region making inroads in world markets is India's Amrut single malt. Actually, inroads is hardly doing them justice. Full-bloodied trailblazing, more like. So good now is their whisky they were, with their fantastically complex brand, Fusion deservedly awarded Jim Murray's Whisky Bible 2010 Third Finest Whisky in the World. That represented a watershed not just for the distillery, but Indian whisky as a whole and in a broader sense the entire world whisky movement: it proved beyond doubt that excellent distilling and maturation wherever you are on this planet will be recognised and rewarded.

Africa is also represented on the whisky stage. There has long been a tradition of blending Scotch malt with South African grain but now there is single malt there, as well. Two malt distilleries, to be precise, with a second being opened at the Drayman's Brewery in Pretoria. I was supposed to have visited it a little while back, but the distiller, obviously not wanting to see me, went to the trouble of falling off his horse and breaking his thigh the actual day before. Wimp.

One relatively new whisky-making region is due immediate further study: Australia. From a distance of 12,000 miles, the waters around Australia's distilleries appear to be muddied. Quality appears to range from the very good to extremely poor. And during the back end of 2004 I managed to discover this first hand when I visited three Tasmanian distilleries and Bakery Hill in Melbourne which perhaps leads the way regarding quality malt whisky made south of the Equator. Certainly green shoots are beginning to sprout at the Tasmania Distillery which has now moved its operation away from its Hobart harbour site to an out of town one close to the airport. The first bottlings of that had been so bad that it will take some time and convincing for those who have already tasted it to go back to it again. However, having been to the warehouse – and having tasted samples from every single cask they have on site – I reported in previous Bibles that it was only a matter of time before those first offerings would be little more than distant – though horrific – memories. Well, as predicted, it is now safe to put your head above the parapet. The last cask strength bottling I tasted was a bloody beaut.

For Jim Murray's Whisky Bible 2014 I was again flooded with a disarming array of excellent malt whiskies with all the usual suspects chipping in with deliveries far better their cricketing countrymen. Limeburners, Old Hobart, Heartwood and Bakery Hill came out with staggeringly beautiful bottlings; Nant threw down the gauntlet with one of the most massive yet gorgeous malts yet from the Southern Hemisphere. It was Timboon who stole the show, though, with a like-for-like bottling of last year's winner, the Sullivans Cove French Oak Port Cask. Together they represent some of the highlights of world whisky. That is a quite staggering achievement and one which means that I now have no option but to start thumbing through an Atlas and flight timetable to get back over there pronto. The remaining casks of Wilson's malt from New Zealand are disappearing fast and when in New Zealand I discovered the stills from there were not just making rum in Fiji but whisky as well. We are all aware of the delights of island whisky, but a Pacific Island malt? Which leaves Antarctica as the only continent not making whisky, though what some of those scientists get up to for months on end no one knows.

ARGENTINA
Blends

Breeders Choice (84) n21 t22 f21 b20. A sweet blend using Scottish malt and, at the helm, an unusually lush Argentinian grain. 40%

AUSTRALIA
BAKERY HILL DISTILLERY 1999. Operating.

⁙ **Bakery Hill Classic Malt** cask no. 5710 db (87.5) n22 nougat wrapped in maple syrup; t22.5 big barley, bigger acacia honey; f21 dries as the cocoa gathers around the nougat; b22 not far off how I remember David's previous Classic malt, except now sporting a higher honey level. 46%

⁙ **Bakery Hill Classic Malt** cask no. 8212 db (94) n23 diced pear and apple salad lightening the barley; t22.5 early nougat, but this burns off as the gristy/muscovado sugars arrive in mouth-watering form; f24.5 now goes into complexity overdrive: sublime marzipan edged by apricot jam...wow! b24 just so elegant and playful! Will win any heart. 46%

⁙ **Bakery Hill Classic Malt Cask Strength** cask no. 5710 db (96) n23.5 t23 f25 b24.5. As the 46% version, only here just about every aspect here is more vivid, the flavours brighter – polished by the most sublime oils which offer also a degree of spice absent at the lower strength. Just pour, and nose and taste at body temperature and...you'll never see Australian whisky quite the same way again...Magnificent! 60%

⁙ **Bakery Hill Classic Malt Cask Strength** cask no. 9112 db (90.5) n23 almost minty, so powering are the oaks, but light ulmo honey retrieves what could get out of hand; t22.5 the gentle oils absorb the impact of the spirit while the cream toffee soothes further; f22 again the oak tries to strike up with big liquorice but a fudge and honey balance again; b23 ooh, that mix of tannin and honey...makes you come over all unnecessary...! 60%

⁙ **Bakery Hill Double Wood** cask no. 5591 db (82.5) n20.5 t22.5 f19 b20.5. Not quite exact cut makes for an ungainly malt full of sultanas. 46%

Bakery Hill Double Wood bourbon & French oak cask no. 5855 db (86.5) n22.5 t22.5 f20.5 b21. Substantial whisky with a delightful chocolate fruit and nut core. 46%

⁙ **Bakery Hill Double Wood** cask no. 8256 db (88.5) n21.5 spotted dog pudding; t23 juicy and exceptionally malty. A slight tartness to the fruit makes it interesting; f21.5 butterscotch and caramel; b22.5 placid. 46%

⁙ **Bakery Hill Double Wood** cask no. 9078 db (94.5) n24 gorgeous, marmalade with the vaguest hint of something smoky. Soft, with playful barley and a light sliver of ulmo honey; t24 a delivery you could raise the Australian flag for. Date syrup with the standard honey and a touch of prune juice; f22.5 burnt raisin; b24 this light fruit cake number is one of the better Double woods from Bakery Hill yet. And on the subject of Double Wood, Haddin has just been castled by my old nets partner Graham Swann for 1 (112 for 6), the double wood, presumably the two stumps hit by the ball...) actually, this whisky is so good, TWO wickets have fallen while tasting it...David: how about calling it "Bakery Hill Double Wicket"...? Actually, as I write this a third wicket has just gone.. 114 for 8...any Aussie will get through a bottle of this just to get over the shock!) 46%

⁙ **Bakery Hill Peated Malt** cask no. 6512 db (94.5) n24 easy does it on the smoke; steady, steady, little more...not too much...yep! That's it! t23.5 luscious, gristy melt-in-the-mouth with now trademark ulmo honey...and just the odd shaving of liquorice; f23 a complete unwinding with smoke in the covers; b24 like the cask strength version, only at medium pace. 46%

⁙ **Bakery Hill Peated Malt** cask no. 7011 db (86) n22 t22.5 f20.5 b21. After the usual honey-rich machinations, bitters out quite tellingly (just as Smith loses his wicket to Anderson to make it five down for just 109..how bitter can an Aussie get?). 46%

⁙ **Bakery Hill Peated Malt** cask no. 9212 db (85.5) n21.5 t22 f21 b21. The same as the cask strength version...only not quite so loud... 46%

⁙ **Bakery Hill Peated Malt Cask Strength** cask no. 6512 db (92.5) n24 busy with sublime intermingling between the rotted Root and what any good Cook would be proud of if the plan was to mix up a complex amalgamation of sharp dark sugars, ulmo honey and warming spice; a little hickory-type tannin helps soften; the phenols also has that peat fire ashes sharpness, too: how fitting... t23.5 excellent sugars on delivery and a slow blossoming of smoke. Natural caramels display the vanilla also; f23 soft, just a delicate reminder of peat and lots of cream toffee; b24 began tasting this first Australian whisky of the year at exactly 11am on Wednesday 10th July. Henry Blofeld, Blowers, is at one end of a BBC microphone, I, Sniffers, exactly 46 miles away as one of his pigeons fly. It is the moment Pattinson bowled a wide for the first ball of the 2013 Ashes series. There is smoke in the air at Trent Bridge, with the Red Arrows having flown past displaying red white and blue. The first Ashes Test I ever saw was also at Trent Bridge, Nottingham, where these present day combatants have set up camp. Roughly about the same time I got the exclusive story about a guy who crashed his bi-plane into the River Trent having flown, illegally, under the bridge next to the historic ground with a girl walking the wing at the time...oh, the days of my comparative youth. A bit like this beaut of a malt. A touch of youth, but wily enough to entertain with aplomb. As I sign off from this first Australian of this edition, England, having decided to bat, have progressed to 16 for no wicket. Oh, and that 1981 test at Trent Bridge? England lost, their only defeat in a 3-1 series victory. Bowling for Australia was Dennis Lilley; batting for England Ian Botham. You get the feeling they both would enjoyed a macho malt like this... *60%*

⁘ **Bakery Hill Peated Malt Cask Strength** cask no. 9212 db **(86.5) n22 t22.5 f21 b21.** A real softie for its strength. Let down a little by the bittering oak. But the light honey lift to the smoke is delightful. *60%*

BOOIE RANGE DISTILLERY
Booie Range Single Malt db **(72) n14 t20 f19 b19.** Mounts the hurdle of the wildly off-key nose impressively with a distinct, mouth watering barley richness to the palate that really does blossom even on the finish. *40%*

HEARTWOOD DISTILLERS
⁘ **Convict Unchained 11 Years Old** port cask, cask no. HH0613, dist 01, bott 12 db **(88.5) n23.5** high quality wine melts, with a few spicy waves for fun, into the high quality distillate... or is it the other way round...? **t23** lively, rich delivery, juicy barely, peaches, greengages with a fruitcake and cocoa shape; **f20** just a little bitter and off key; **b22** had this cask been technically on the mark, this would have been a world beater. *58%. sc. Batch 1. 220 bottles.*

⁘ **Release The Beast** sherry cask, bott 7 Aug 12 db **(95.5) n24** more pot still Demerera rum evident that grape: the sugars are intense yet allow mocha and vanilla notes to filter through: much more a Caribbean or Fijian rum style than whisky (even though there appears to be deft flicker of something smoky) ....but when it's this good, who cares? **t24.5** massive delivery, yet controlled and unfailingly polite. There is a background growl of smoke, but the way the huge Melton Hunt fruit cake, moistened by Guyana's finest old pot still rum and embroidered with the juiciest dates on the planet, it plays a very peripheral role; **f23** the mocha is laced with sultana. Some late vanilla....and a little furriness; **b24** as beasts go, for all its power, is a tame and gentle one. Just too gorgeous. *65.4%. sc.*

⁘ **Vat Out of Hell** sherry/bourbon, cask no. LD446 & HH0040, dist Mar 03 & Nov 99, bott May 13 db **(89) n22** very tight sultana clinging thick tannin; **t24** like licking the inside of an oloroso butt. Massive chocolate and fruit cake mix, all spruced up with molasses...wow! **f21** a flaw to the butt brings down the sweetness; **b22** rather than tasting this today, I had planned to be at The Oval to see the Tasmanian former Aussie skipper Ricky Pontin, representing my beloved Surrey, bring the curtain down to his first class career. But with the deadline looming I eschewed, with heavy heart, my natural instincts to catch the train to St Pancras and travel on to Kennington in order to carry on tasting and get this book out on time. So, as a compromise, I spent his batting hours tasting Tas whisky. Ponting finished the day and his career of gritty plundering with an extraordinary 169 not out, having batted the entire day. To mark the end of his magnificent career on the very same day that a young lad on debut called Ashton Agar created Test history by making 98 as a number eleven (oh, for the fearlessness of youth...!) the next bottling should be in their honour: Bat Out of Hell... *67.4%. nc ncf. cask strength. 320 bottles.*

⁘ **Velvet Hammer 13 Years Old** bourbon cask no. HH0072, dist Nov 99, bott Mar 13 db **(95) n23.5** every last bit of natural caramel has been extracted but enlivened by a salty hickory charge...; **t24.5** a rare example of a salivating malt with the juices stimulated by both grain and oak. A light gooseberry fruitiness adds a light jam sharpness to the mix. Muscovado sugar and beech honey mingles contently...; **f23.5** the high quality oak hang around as long as possible; some late spices, too; **b24** absolutely superb! Bill Lark, my old mate...you have excelled yourself! *68.8%. sc. Cask strength, 172 bottles.*

HELLYERS ROAD
⁘ **Hellyers Road Original Aged 10 Years** ex-American cask db **(80) n18.5 t22.5 f19 b20.** A degree of citrus and a light Demerara helps overcome some of the feintier, oilier aspects of the distillate. *46.2%. ncf. Hellyers Road Distillery.*

⁘ **Hellyers Road Peated** ex-American white oak casks db **(87) n22** distinctly dry and powdery; sooty peat. Chopped hazelnut and the merest whiff of orange-blossom; **t22.5** a gristy sugar allows the smoke to escape slowly; very powdery vanilla; **f20.5** a little tangy from apparent lack of copper; **b22** clunky and dry...a very unusual whisky experience. *46.2%. ncf.*

⁘ **Hellyers Road Pinot Noir Finish** ex-American cask db **(87.5) n22** the spices compliment the crisp grape; **t22.5** a volley of muscovado sugars and warming spice herald in the green Rowntree Fruit Pastilles...; **f21** tightens as the vanilla moves in...; **b22** lovely fruit... Hell, yes! *46.2%. ncf. Hellyers Road Distillery.*

⁕ **Hellyers Road Original Roaring Forty** ex-American cask db **(84.5) n21.5 t22 f20 b21.** Dry and a little creaky, as is the wont of the house style. But enough cream caramel and muscovado sugars around to soften the experience. 40%. ncf. Hellyers Road Distillery.

LARK DISTILLERY

The Lark Distillery Single Malt Whisky Cask Strength cask no. LD140, bott Feb 10 db **(80) n19.5 t18.5 f22 b20.** From tip to tail there is a note on this I can't quite put my finger on, or say I much approve of. But there is also a real coppery small still feel to this, bolstered by a late-developing honeycomb and Demerara sheen. 58%

The Lark Distillery Single Malt Whisky Distillers Selection cask no. LD109, bott Apr 10 db **(86.5) n21.5 t21 f22.5 b21.5.** A chunky affair with some attractive nougat and orange; the star turn is the Rolo candy finale. 46%

LIMEBURNERS

Limeburners Single Malt Whisky Barrel M23 bott no. 78 db **(90.5) n22.5 t23.5 f22 b22.5.** First time I've tasted anything from this Western Australian mob. Gday fellas! I have to admit, thought it might have been from France at first, as the aroma on nosing blind reminded me of brandy. And not without good reason, it transpires. This no age statement malt spent an unspecified amount of time in American brandy cask before being finished in bourbon casks. Does it work? Yes it does. But now that's torn it lads. You are supposed to start off with a bloody horrible whisky and get better. Now you have gone and made a rod for your own back. Good on you! 61%

⁕ **Limeburners Single Malt Whisky Peated Barrel M58** ex-bourbon American oak cask db **(89) n22.5** low flying smoke grumbles around the glass; some muscovado sugars, vanilla and grist are also heard; **t23.5** superb delivery! Curiously fruit intense with the rich sugars taking the smoke on in combat: those gristy sugars win; **f21** smoked tangy marmalade; **b22** taken aback when I nosed this: saw the Limeburners tag, but hadn't spotted the style. The smoke gave me a jolt: not seen this from these guys before. Peatburners, more like...and an attractive smoky style the like of which I have never encountered before. 48%. ncf. 133 bottles.

Limeburners Single Malt Whisky M64 Muscat Finish db **(92) n23.5 t23 f22.5 b23.** Macho malt keeps in touch with its feminine side. Tasty and beautifully made. 61%. ncf.

⁕ **Limeburners Single Malt Whisky Barrel M79** ex-bourbon American oak cask and finished in an old Australian sherry cask db **(93.5) n23** what appears a vigorous fruitiness enjoys a soft side, too: moist but well aged fruitcake with an oaky drizzle; **t24** stunning delivery: the grape is profound yet enough manuka honey hangs in there to seemingly thin, yet thicken the mouth feel! **f23** bitters slightly, as the generous cut pinches through. A late toffee and barley rally; **b23.5** a rare exhibition of a happy marriage between bourbon cask and sherry. 61%. ncf. Great Southern Distilling Company. 113 bottles.

⁕ **Limeburners Single Malt Whisky Barrel M91** ex-bourbon American oak barrique and finished in an old Australian sherry cask db **(80) n19 t21 f20 b20.** The stale tobacco on the nose and rumbling, off key finish says something about the feints involved. The delicious clarity of the fruit is a tick for the "sherry" cask. 43%. ncf. 355 bottles.

THE NANT DISTILLERY

The Nant Single Malt First Release bott 2010 db **(91.5) n24 t23 f22 b22.5.** Beyond excellent for a first go. The flavours and style could not be more clearly nailed to the mast. I'll be watching this distillery closely. 43%

The Nant 3 Year Old American oak/Port db **(91.5) n22.5 t22 f23 b24.** Beautifully well made whisky. Has the sophistication of a dry martini, but without the olive...yet maintaining the salt. Last year I set out to keep my eyes on these chaps. Not a bad move. 43%

The Nant 3 Years Old Cask Strength American oak bourbon db **(95.5) n23 t24 f24 b24.5** I have really got to get back to Oz to visit these guys. Something majestic is happening here. Whatever it is they are doing, I have to discover first hand...World class. 61.6%

⁕ **The Nant Distillery 5 Years Old** French oak/Port db **(92.5) n23.5** blackberries filched from a late autumn hedgerow and seasoned with white pepper. An almost rummy sub plot with esters and tannins on the loose; **t23.5** very tight delivery for a nanosecond, then soon relaxes to allow sugar-encrusted prunes to dominate. Exceptionally juicy but then the middle dries quite fast, making the spices more noticeable along with vanilla and non-sweetened almond milk; **f22** the foot comes off the complexity levels, but the spices stay on pretty high revs; **b23.5** not sure if this is talking French, Portuguese, Oz or a strange dialect incorporating all three. Lovely to listen to, whichever, and makes itself fully understood. 43%

⁕ **The Nant Distillery 5 Year Old Cask Strength** American oak/sherry **(86.5) n21.5 t23 f20.5 b21.5.** A bit of a lollipop of a malt: suck at it and you get plenty of fruity sugar. However, unlike most Nants I have tasted previously, there is a bit of an imbalance between the intense sugar, spices and fuzzy oils from the cut. No faulting the juiciness of the fruit or liveliness of the spice, though. 63%

⠿ **The Nant Distillery 5 Year Old Cask Strength** French oak/Port (94) n23.5 much less open fruit than you might expect. Instead, the ball is carried by a very healthy barley vanguard on a dais of hefty tannins. A delicate coating of ulmo honey and spice helps move this almost towards a bourbon style nose...; the fruit is there, of course, but curled up into one sultana-rich ball; t24 oh, oh, oh...!!! The highlight....and some! For a good ten seconds we have a delivery equal to almost any other whisky in the world this year with a near perfect unison of juicy fruit, muscovado sugars and spice. All singing at the top of their voice and in total harmony; once the oak begins to take hold, the more bitter cocoa is quickly noticed; f23 dries into a pithy, vanilla-rich, chalky-textured finale; the cocoa is determined to linger; b23.5 if you are looking for a simple, straight up and down dram, you have opened the wrong bottle. This is one very complex offering... 63%

OLD HOBART DISTILLERY

Overeem Port Cask Matured heavily charred quarter cask finish, cask no. OHD-010, dist 15 Aug 07, bott 15 May 12 db (89) n23 t23 f21 b22. A supreme toastiness works so well with the big fruit. 43%. sc.

⠿ **Overeem Port Cask Matured** heavily charred ex-Port, French oak quarter cask, cask no. OHD-026, dist 08, bott 13 db (90) n22 as thick a non-peated nose as you'll find: glutinous fruit doused in molasses; t23.5 you expect enormity on the palate, and that's what you get. The fruit sugars are so intense that the actual fruitiness becomes almost invisible; somehow some barley notes somehow pop through; big, lush clear honey middle; f22 dries and becomes big on burnt toast and molasses; b22.5 heavily alcoholic sticky treacle pudding... 43%. sc.

Overeem Port Cask Matured Cask Strength heavily charred quarter cask finish, cask no. OHD-008, dist 15 Aug 07, bott 15 May 12 db (95) n24 t24.5 f23 b23.5 Just get it if you see it: a no brainer! 60%. sc.

⠿ **Overeem Port Cask Matured Cask Strength** heavily charred ex-Port, French oak quarter cask, cask no. OHD-029, dist Apr 08, bott Jan 13 db (91) n21.5 salty – in a touch of the sweaty armpit variety – with a curious, near unscalable, wall of tannin and reduced plum; t24 wow! I think they have discovered something denser than osmium – presumably Ausmium. The thickness of the grape is such that it takes maybe three or four pulses of flavour before it begins to break up and allow us to see that it is concentrated fruit and no little hickory-led oak which is causing the blockage. As it breaks down, sublime molasses give the feeling of the richest jam you'll ever find; f22.5 reconfigures with a big vanilla and chocolate presence; b23 you don't get many whiskies like this turning up in a lifetime. A completely unique finger print for any malt, believe me. Hope I can find a full working day in the next year or so to give this the analysis it deserves. 60%. sc.

Overeem Sherry Cask Matured medium charred quarter cask finish, cask no. ODG-005, dist 5 Jun 07, bott 1 Jun 12 db (85.5) n21.5 t22 f21 b21. No frills. No thrills, either. 43%. sc.

⠿ **Overeem Sherry Cask Matured** heavily charred ex-sherry, French oak quarter cask, cask no. OHD-030 db (88.5) n21.5 toffee raisin fudge; t23 toffee raisin fudge, with a few more raisins and dark sugars; f22 bitters slightly in a caramel, cocoa kind of way..; late spice; b22 clean, massively enjoyable...but just needing a top up of complexity for greatness. 43%. sc.

Overeem Sherry Cask Matured Cask Strength medium charred quarter cask finish, cask no. OHD-003, dist 6 Jun 07, bott 2 Mar 12 db (91.5) n23 you salty little fruit bomb, you!! t23 massive viscosity to this voluptuous siren ensuring the intense, spiced grape quite literally sticks around; the oak behaves like a cask three times its age; f22 the sugars have by now been lost and terse dryness begins to make itself known; b23.5 must have stolen all the complexity and charisma from cask ODG-005. A treat! 60%. sc.

⠿ **Overeem Sherry Cask Matured Cask Strength** heavily charred ex-sherry, French oak quarter cask, cask no. OHD-032 db (95) n23 great to see barley visible on a sherry cask; plenty of oak, too, setting off a spicy sub plot; t24.5 initially dense, you cannot be other than entirely blown away by the complexity of the layering...and just how many layers there are! – of the fruit. Adorned by muscovado sugars and an ulmo and beech honey mix, the spices (literally!) pepper the entire event, providing a 3-D feel to the proceedings; f23.5 long, with a liquorice and hickory strand. Still thick grape can be found, while the sugars are more oblique as the spices buzz; b24 the key is the spice: from the first nose to the final pulse on the palate it intrigues and enriches. Brilliant! 60%. sc.

SMALL CONCERN DISTILLERY

Cradle Mountain Pure Tasmanian Malt db (87) n21 t22 f21 b23. A knock-out malt from a sadly now lost distillery in Tasmania. Faultlessly clean stuff with lots of new oak character but sufficient body to guarantee complexity. 43%

SOUTHERN COAST DISTILLERS

Southern Coast Single Malt Batch 001 db (92.5) n23 t24 f22 b23.5. "A hint of bushfire in the barley" claims the back label. Well, that one's got me stumped; I pride myself in nosing anything and everything, but that particular aroma has passed me by. Perhaps they mean the heather aroma...? Mind you, I did get pretty close to some scary forest fires near Marseilles nearly 30 years ago, but probably not the same thing... Anyway, back to this fabulous first effort. Wow! Could ask for more in a study of crisp brown sugars and sweet cocoa...; 46%

Southern Coast Single Malt Batch 002 db (96) n24 t23.5 f24.5 b24. Is this the best Australian whisky ever to shamelessly masquerade as Demerara pot still rum? I should think so. Will it ever be beaten? I doubt it. In fact, just how many Demerara rums have I ever tasted of this refinement. One or two, at most. And I have probably tasted more than anyone in the whisky trade living. One of the most astonishing whiskies it has been my honour to taste. Frankly, I am on my knees... 46%

Southern Coast Single Malt Batch 003 db (79.5) n18 t19 f23 b19.5. Third time unlucky. Lots of oils and berserk honey. But too feinty, though this went to some finishing school, believe me...! 46%. ncf.

Southern Coast Single Malt Batch 004 db (82.5) n20 t22 f20.5 b20. An earthy, slightly musty dram with a pleasing essence of honey but struggles to find structure or balance. 46%

Southern Coast Single Malt Batch 005 db (83.5) n21.5 t22 f20 b20. Starts off like a Jack Hobbs or Brian Lara or Alec Stewart taking the Aussie quick bowling apart. There is even an unusual, but mightily attractive, sweetened Vegemite hint to this (not as strange as it sounds, actually). But the middle stump is removed by the hefty finish: the cricketing equivalent of an ungainly, head-up hoick to cow corner.... 46%

Southern Coast Single Malt Batch 006 db (95) n24 t24 f23.5 b24. When I saw these Southern Coast Whiskies before me, my eyes lit up. Here was my journey to Demerara. Much cheaper and less problem-riddled than any trip I normally make to Guyana..and with less chance of coming away with my normal stomach complaint. Batches 4 and 5 let me down. But Batch 6... even the sun has come out for the first time in three days as I nose this... Georgetown, here I come... 46%

TASMAN DISTILLERY

Great Outback Rare Old Australian Single Malt db (92) n24 t24 f21 b23. What can you say? An Australian whisky distillery makes a malt to grace the world's stage. But you can't find it outside of Australia. This will have to be rectified. 40%

TASMANIA DISTILLERY

Old Hobart db (69) n16 t19 f17 b17. The nose still has some way to go before it can be accepted as a mainstream malt, though there is something more than a little coastal about it this time. However, the arrival on the palate is another matter and I must say I kind of enjoyed its big, oily and increasingly sweet maltiness and crushed sunflower seed nuttiness towards the end. Green (and yellow) shoots are growing. The whisky is unquestionably getting better. 60%

Sullivans Cove db (61) n13 t15 f17 b16. Some malt but typically grim, oily and dirty; awesomely weird. 40%. Australia.

⠿ **Sullivans Cove American Oak Single Cask** cask no. HH0152, dist 28 Jan 00, bott 25 Sep 12 db (86) n21.5 t23 f20.5 b21. A slightly wider cut than required makes for slightly more aggressive oils than required. But you can't help loving the trademark orange-blossom honey, especially when it ends up as tangy marmalade...! 47.5%. nc ncf sc.

⠿ **Sullivans Cove American Oak Single Cask** cask no. HH0211, dist 10 Mar 00, bott 10 Jan 13 db (82) n20 t23 f19 b20. Not quite up to their normal standards on the distilling side. But such is the intensity of the grist and fruity sugars, the delivery simply takes the breath away. Overly sweet to a degree, but that repairs some damage. 47.5%. nc ncf sc.

⠿ **Sullivans Cove American Oak Single Cask** cask no. HH0257, dist 14 Apr 00, bott 25 Sep 12 db (91.5) n23 gorgeous interweaving of shimmering barley and apple; t23.5 perfectly juicy: barley sugar on delivery and for the next four or five flavour waves. And lifted above the norm by spot on spice. Again, light fruits drift in and out with a relaxed, almost arrogant; indifference; f22 bitters down slightly as the custard tart and butterscotch kicks in; b23 about as relaxed and natural (and slightly imperfect) as a 19-year-old making his test debut for Australia at number eleven after the last five wickets have fallen for nine runs... 47.5%

⠿ **Sullivans Cove American Oak Single Cask** cask no. HH0258, dist 14 Apr 00, bott 17 Aug 12 db (90.5) n23 massive barley kick. Thin but useful butterscotch stratum and a few green diced apples freshens it up further; t23 gloriously gristy with an irresistible smattering of Demerara and marzipan; f22 ulmo honey and vanilla; dries on the light oils; b22.5 I know

I shouldn't say it. But the most Scotch single malt in style of all the Aussie drams: try and distinguish blind between this and very decent Speysider. 47.5%. nc ncf sc.

Sullivans Cove Bourbon Matured Cask Strength Single Cask barrel no: HH0602, barrel date 21 Feb 01, bott 10 Sep 09 **(81) n18 t24 f20 b19.** An outrageous maltfest, for all its obvious faults. "Distilled with Conviction" the label proudly states, a reference to Tasmania's penal past. But it looks as though the stillman has made his escape as the nose suggests the eye wasn't being kept on the ball as feints abound. Ironically, the resulting extra oils mean the youthful but hugely intense malt simply blows you away. Technically, a nightmare. But you know what? I just love it...!!! (To ramp it up about five or six points, pour into a glass and place in hot water to burn off the higher alcohols. What remains after about five minutes, depending on the temperature of the water, is a much cleaner, more honeyed version). 60%

Sullivans Cove Rare Tasmanian Single Cask American oak bourbon cask, cask no. HH0128, dist 25 Jan 00, bott 21 Sep 11 db **(86) n21 t22.5 f21 b21.5.** A slightly wider cut that normally means a subtle degree of extra oil is floating around, enough to dull the sharper edges of the more complex notes from an obviously top quality cask. As usual from the distillery, though, the sugars make you groan with delight. 47.5%. sc. 246 bottles.

Sullivans Cove Rare Tasmanian Single Cask American oak bourbon cask, cask no. HH0326, dist 30 May 00, bott 12 Jan 12 db **(90.5) n22 t23 f22.5 b23.** Easy going, sweet enough and with sufficient weight to be an anytime kind of a malt. Put it this way: I'd say yes to it anytime, for one...! 47.5%. sc. 256 bottles.

Sullivans Cove Rare Tasmanian Single Cask American oak bourbon cask, cask no. HH0329, dist 2 Jun 00, bott 17 Feb 12 db **(91.5) n23.5 t23 f22.5 b22.5.** Complex, in a limited kind of way. But beautifully made and the barley is a delight. 47.5%. 168 bottles.

Sullivans Cove Rare Tasmanian Single Cask American oak bourbon cask, cask no. HH0330, dist 2 Jun 00, bott 17 Feb 12 db **(92) n23 t23.5 f22.5 b23.** Makes muted attempts to head into Kentucky territory. Complex. 47.5%. 238 bottles.

Sullivans Cove Rare Tasmanian Single Cask French oak port cask, cask no. HH0425, dist 2000, bott 2012 **(86) n20.5 t23 f21 b21.5.** Huge wine involvement with the chocolatey grape running amuck with a gorgeously soft and rounded assault on the palate. Perhaps, though, could just do with another trick. Still, I'm happy to enjoy the unusual charms offered! 47.5%. sc. 487 bottles.

Sullivans Cove Rare Tasmanian Single Cask French oak port cask, cask no. HH0429, dist 11 Aug 00, bott 21 Sep 11 **(84) n21 t21 f21 b21.** Pleasant. But straight lines just a little too much thanks to the natural caramels. 47.5%. sc. 453 bottles.

Sullivans Cove Rare Tasmanian Single Cask French oak port cask, cask no. HH0430, dist 15 Aug 00, bott 17 Feb 12 **(77.5) n19 t20 f19 b19.5.** Just never quite gets its act together or feels right. 47.5%. sc. 546 bottles.

Sullivans Cove Rare Tasmanian Single Cask French oak port cask, cask no. HH0509, dist 6 Oct 00, bott 17 Feb 12 **(96.5) n24 t24 f24 b24.5.** Although this comes from a wine cask, the dominant forces at work here have much more in common with bourbon style whisky than malt. It is also, unquestionably, one of the world whiskies of the year... 47.5%. sc. 494 bottles.

TIMBOON RAILWAY SHED DISTILLERY

⁘ **Timboon New Make** bott 16 Jun 13 db **(89) 22 t23 f21.5 b22.5.** Plenty of fruit on this clean make. Hard to find sweet barley in more concentrated form, either. 71.4%. sc.

⁘ **Timboon Single Malt Whisky** Port cask, dist 12 Jul 2009, bott 16 Jan 2013 db **(96.5) n24.5** rarely nose a vintage Port this fruity! So intense: like a sweet shop specialising in fudge, boiled fruit and spiced chocolate; **t24** here's the trick: big mouthful (at body temperature, of course), chew for about twice the time you normally keep whisky in your mouth, making sure it never settles in the same spot for more than a second or two, then either spit, or swallow...very, very slowly. And just let that fruit and manuka honey talk to you...; **f24** the afterglow... here the more delicate grape and even a smidgeon of barley lingers and lingers. Red liquorice, followed by black liquorice and hickory. The spice carries on cheerfully, as does the toasty fudge; **b24** way, way better bottling than their last Port cask offering. Huge doesn't even begin to tell the story....with plenty of character. And no fear of giving the taste buds a biff and a kiss almost at the same moment. Easily one of the whiskies of 2013. 68%. sc.

Timboon Single Malt Whisky dist Aug 08, bott May 11 db **(93) n24.5 t23 f22 b23.5.** Imagine Tim Boon, the cricketer, going out to face the current England pace attack with one of those foot-long bats used exclusively for players to sign. That, basically, is what we have here with a malt underpowered for the type of job it is capable of doing. Yes, its technique is extraordinary. Certainly, it has moved to the pitch of the barley and is in line with what's coming with rare textbook elegance. But the strength is too feeble to translate into the highest score that it deserves. That said, quality is quality. And this is strictly First Class. 40%

⸙ **Timboon Single Malt Whisky** bourbon barrel, dist 12 May 09, bott 17 Jun 13 db **(91)** n23 apricots and Chinese gooseberries vie with under-ripe pears for top dog on the fruit front...where are the fruit flies...? t23.5 light delivery at first, then a series of superb waves of maple syrup-mottled grist; there are strains of delicate fruit throughout; f22 long, helped by the faintest of oil and more comprehensive Dominican cocoa; b22.5 a thinner offering than last time round. But the nuttiness, perhaps underlined by the slightest lack of copper, is a treat. Not sure if they mature the whisky in the same environment as fruit spirits, because the otherwise inexplicable fruitiness is quite telling... 70.4%. sc.

YALUMBA WINERY
Smith's Angaston Whisky Vintage 1997 Aged 7 Years db **(88)** n20 t22 f23 b23. Easily one of the most delicate whiskies of the year and one that puts Samuel Smith on the map. Perfect for the hipflask for a night at the ballet. 40%

Smith's Angaston Whisky Vintage 1998 Aged 8 Years db **(86)** n20 t22 f22 b22. Perhaps conscious that their first offering, a genuine touch of culture that it was, wasn't quite Australian enough; this one's showing bit of aggression. And I mean a bit, as this is no tackle from Lucas Neil. Because after the delivery it's back to the girlie stuff with some admittedly delicious Swiss Roll filling fruitiness. Lovely malt from a distillery I'm going to have to keep my eyes on. 40%

Vatted Malts
Tasmanian Double Malt Whisky Unpeated (87.5) n22 t22 f21.5 b22. Not a chance of getting bored with this guy. A sweet tooth would be useful. 43%. The Nant Distillery.

BRAZIL
HEUBLEIN DISTILLERY
Durfee Hall Malt Whisky db **(81)** n18 t22 f20 b21. Superbly made whisky; the intensity of the malt is beautifully layered without ever becoming too sweet. Very light bodied and immaculately clean. Good whisky by any standards. 43%

UNION DISTILLERY
Barrilete db **(72)** n18 t19 f18 b17. Nothing particularly wrong with it technically; it just lacks vitality. Thin but extremely malt intense. 39.1%

Blends
Cockland Gold Blended Whisky (73) n18 t18 f19 b18. Silky caramel. Traces of malt there, but never quite gets it up. 38%. Fante.

Drury's Special Reserve (86.5) n21.5 t22 f21 b22. Deceptively attractive, melt-in-the-mouth whisky; at times clean, regulation stuff, but further investigation reveals a honeycomb edge which hits its peak in the middle ground when the spices mix in beautifully. One to seek out and savour when in Brazil. 40%. Campari, Brasil.

Gold Cup Special Reserve (84.5) n21 t22.5 f20 b21. Ultra soft, easily drinkable and, at times, highly impressive blend which is hampered by a dustiness bestowed upon it by the nagging caramels on both nose and finish. Some lovely early honey does help lift it, though, and there is also attractive Swiss roll jam towards the finish. Yet never quite gets out of third gear despite the most delicate hint of smoke. 39%. Campari, Brasil.

Gran Par (77) n19.5 t22 f17.5 b18. The delivery is eleven seconds of vaguely malty glory. The remainder is thin and caramelled with no age to live up to the name. And with Par in the title and bagpipes and kilt in the motif, how long before the SWA buys a case of it...? 39%

Green Valley Special Reserve batch 07/01 **(70)** n16 t19 f17 b18. A softly oiled, gently bitter-sweet blend with a half meaty, half boiled sweet nose. An unusual whisky experience. 38.1%.

Malte Barrilete Blended Whisky batch 001/03 **(76)** n18 t20 f19 b19. This brand has picked up a distinctive apple-fruitiness in recent years and some extra oak, too. 39.1%.

Natu Nobilis (81.5) n22.5 t20 f19 b20. The nose boasts a genuinely clean, Speyside-style malt involvement. But to taste is much more non-committal with the soft grain dominating and the grassy notes restricted the occasional foray over the tastebuds. Pleasant, but don't expect a flavor fest. 39%. Pernod Ricard, Brasil.

Natu Nobilis Celebrity (86) n22.5 t22 f20.5 b21. A classy blend with a decent weight and body, yet never running to fat. Some spice prickle ensures the flavor profile never settles in a neutral zone and the charming, citrus-domiated malt on the nose is immediately found on the juicy delivery. A cut above the standard Natu Nobilis and if the finish could be filled out with extra length and complexity, we'd have an exceptionally impressive blend on our hands. Another blend to seek out whenever in Brazil. 39%. Pernod Ricard, Brasil.

O Monge batch 02/02 **(69)** n17 t18 f17 b17. Poor nose but it recovers with a malty mouth arrival but the thinness of the grain does few favours. 38.5%. Union Distillery.

Old Eight Special Reserve (85.5) n20 t21 f22.5 b22. Traditionally reviled by many in Brazil, I can assure you that the big bite followed by calming soft grains is exactly what you need after a day's birding in the jungle. *39%. Campari, Brasil.*

Pitt's (84) n21 t20 f22 b21. The pits certainly aint!! A beautifully malted blend where the barley tries to dominate the exceptionally flinty grain whenever possible. Due to be launched later in 2004, this will be the best Brazil has to offer – though some fine tuning can probably improve the nose and middle even further and up the complexity significantly. I hope, when I visit the distillery early in 2005, I will be able to persuade them to offer a single malt: on this evidence it should, like Pitt's, be an enjoyable experience and perfect company for any World Cup finals. *40%. Busnello Distillery.*

Wall Street (84) n23 t22 f19 b20. Fabulous nose with a sexy citrus-light smoke double bill. And the arrival on the palate excels, too, with a rich texture and confident delivery of malt, again with the smoke dominating. But falls away rather too rapidly as the grains throw the balance out of kilter and ensures too much bitter oak late on. *38%. Pernod Ricard, Brasil.*

INDIA
AMRUT DISTILLERY

⁘ **Amrut Bourbon** cask no. 3436, dist 2 Jun 09, bott 2 Aug 13 (84.5) n21 t23 f19.5 b21. A classic case of a cask where the good has been extracted and we are now getting down to some milky undesirables. The astonishing sugar array on delivery is worth the experience alone, though. *41%*

⁘ **Amrut Bourbon**, cask no. 3441, dist 2 Jun 09, bott 1 Aug 13 (94) n23.5 interesting half Canadian/half bourbon aroma: big on ulmo honey and thinned liquorice; t24 absolutely teeming with flavours, most of them delicate sugars dissolved into a salivating mix of barley concentrate and butterscotch; the build up of spice is just so elegant! f23 a little tangy but re-settles as the vanillas find a more comfortable path; b23.5 simple impossible not to love: just so much that's good to keep you entertained. *46%*

Amrut Cask Strength oak barrels, bott 01, bott Jul 09 db (89.5) n23 t22.5 f22 b22. Another big malty tale from India. But there is a big surge of natural, oily caramels to this one which keeps the complexity levels marginally down. *61.8%*

Amrut Cask Strength batch 5, bott 10 db (84) n21 t22 f20 b21. Just a little extra aging here has brought a telling degree of caramel into play, swamping much else. Pleasant, but a reminder of just how fragile the line between greatness and just plain, old-fashioned good. *61.8%. nc ncf.*

Amrut Double Cask ex-bourbon cask no. 2874/2273, bott no. 44, bott Feb 10 db (96) n23 t24.5 f24 b24.5. Frankly, a malt I thought I'd never see: how can a whisky survive seven years under the unremitting Bangalore sun? I am proud of the very small part I played in seeing this wonderful whisky see the world: I tasted both casks, containing the oldest whisky Amrut had ever produced, in a cellar at the distillery earlier in the year and passed both not only fit but exceptional. But I made the observation that they would certainly be better still if mixed together as the personalities of both casks very much complimented the other. On the day the younger of the two casks turned seven years old, this they did and bottled it. And just to show how wonderful this whisky is, from now what must surely be from one of the top two or three malt whisky distilleries in the world, simply leave an empty glass of it by your bedside table and smell it first thing in the morning. *46%. 306 bottles.*

Amrut Fusion batch no. 01, bott Mar 09 db (97) n24 t24 f24 b25. One of the most complex and intriguing new whiskies of 2010 that needs about two days and half a bottle to get even close to fathoming. Not exactly a textbook whisky, with a few edges grinding together like tectonic plates. And there is even odd note, like the fruit and a kind of furry, oaky buzz, which I have never seen before. But that is the point of whiskies like this: to be different, to offer a unique slant. But, ultimately, to entertain and delight. And here it ticks all boxes accordingly. To the extent that this has to be one of the great whiskies found anywhere in the world this year. And the fact it is Indian? Irrelevant: from distillation to maturation this is genius whisky, from whichever continent... *50%*

Amrut Fusion batch 10, bott Mar 11 db (94.5) n24 t24 f22.5 b23.5. Superb whisky, though to be plotted on a different map to the now legendary Whisky Bible award-winning Batch 1. This is a much more delicate affair: more hints and shadows rather than statements and substance. Still, though, a fabulous malt whisky in Amrut's best style. *50%. nc.*

⁘ **Amrut Greedy Angels** dist 3 Oct 04, bott 15 Nov 12 db (96) n25 how odd: matured inland, yet distinctly coastal in its light saltiness. This sits wonderfully well with the most delicate of blood orange notes...which after a while sweetens towards a Jaffa cake middle. The spices hint and tease while the vanilla fades in and out, taking turns with thin ulmo honey: perfection; t24 soft delivery with the accent at first jointly shared between the barley and vanilla, then the oak takes control moving towards a lightly spiced cocoa. Elsewhere a thin layer of ulmo honey secures the required sweetness; f23 some tangy orange returns, a distant echo of spice hangs off the persistent barley oil; **b24** so here we have it: an 8-year-old Indian whisky. Matured in a cellar, luckily, but still has the hallmarks often seen on certain Speysiders in their late 30s...a series of Caperdonichs from about five or six years ago spring to mind. Except their noses were never this good: in fact, few noses have ever been better – it is certainly unsurpassed this year...wonderful. A true whisky great of the last decade. *50%*

Amrut Herald cask no. 2857 db **(92) n23 t24 f22 b23.** Here is the news: Amrut have come up with another fabulous whisky. Actually, the news these days is when they don't... *60.8%. sc.*

⁙ **Amrut Herald** cask no. 3030 db **(93) n23** the tannins are absolutely at their nuttiest with intense red liquorice where I think marzipan once was...; **t24** massive! The delivery is an onrush of hugely spiced thick malt grist of near perfect weight; the oak pounds and pounds on the multi-shock waves which follow, but the dark sugars keeps everything intact; **f22.5** still spicy, but bitters very slightly, too; **b23.5** here's the news: this has outscooped the last Herald I tasted! *58.4%. 219 bottles.*

Amrut Intermediate Sherry Matured bott no. 01, bott Jun 10 db **(96.5) n24.5 t24 f23.5 b24.5.** How do you get three freshly emptied oloroso butts from Jerez to Bangalore without the casks spoiling, and not use sulphur? Answer: empty two cases of Amrut cask strength whisky into each of the butts before shipping them. Not a single off note. No bitterness whatsoever. And the fruit is left to impart its extraordinary riches on a malt matured also in American oak. Amrut is spoiling us again... *57.1%*

Amrut Peated batch no. 1, bott Sep 08 db **(94) n23 t24 f23.5 b23.5.** Absolutely everything you could ask for a peated malt at this strength. The length and complexity are matched only by a train journey through this astonishing country. *46%*

Amrut Peated Cask Strength bott 08 db **(92) n22 t22.5 f24.5 b23.** A touch of youth to this guy but the finish, entirely uncluttered by unnatural caramel or deprived by filtration, confirms a degree of greatness. By the way: if you want to experience something really stunning, trying mixing the 07 and 08 peated. When you get the proportions right...well, watch out Islay! *62.78%*

⁙ **Amrut Peated Port Pipe**, cask no. 2713, dist 2 Jun 09, bott 2 Aug 13 **(88.5) n22** about as thick as any nose gets: the smoke and the grape clot up the nose...it is almost impossible to breath! **t22** a smoky, grapey sugary soup...; **f22.5** my tongue actually aches from chewing this. At the death some complexity as the components stop talking at once and you can hear what they are individually saying; **b22** so big, it's exhausting... *41%*

Amrut Portonova db **(93) n22 t24 f24 b23.** This is a whisky so big, so blinding that when I first tasted it I was so dazzled I could barely see a thing. It was like coming out of the pitch black into a fierce light. My first instincts, while recoiling, was that there was too much oak at work. Only on acclimatisation did I work out what was going on here...and fall helplessly in love. There is still way too much oak, however you look at it and the nose, which neither improves nor worsens over time confirms that. Indeed, the entire thing is outrageous: I have never come across such a flavour profile before anywhere in the world. But my word: what a statement this makes... Unique. *62.1%*

⁙ **Amrut PX Sherry**, cask no. 2701, dist 2 Jun 09, bott 2 Aug 13 **(80) n20 t21 f18.5 b20.5.** Big, cloying, fruity but the sugar makes this a little tart. Not the finest finish, either. Just not really my cup of Darjeeling. *43%*

⁙ **Amrut PX Sherry**, cask no. 2702, dist 2 Jun 09, bott 2 Aug 13 **(71) n18 t19 f16 b18.** A poor, sulphury butt gives the fruit no chance to come alive. Dance with the devil...and you get burned... *42%*

Amrut Single Malt batch 27, bott Mar 11 db **(92.5) n23 t24 f22.5 b23.5.** An assured, elegant malt which now strides greatness with nonchalance. *46%. nc ncf.*

⁙ **Amrut Single Malt** batch 41 Apr 12 db **(94.5) n23.5** so complex; a gorgeous mix of salt and citrus, mainly kumquat. The spices sit lazily on the mounting vanillas; **t24** explosive malt notes offer both a juicy freshness and a more sanguine oak base; a few layers of coppery sheen enrich; light honey on toast plus a few oils fill in the middle to satisfaction; the odd strand of toasty sugars remind you, along with red liquorice, that a sublime bourbon effect is at play, too; **f23** slightly overcooked butterscotch tart; the fade is the soft inside of a walnut whip...complete with walnut...; **b24** just another Amrut bottling. Just another reminder of how good whisky should be. *46%*

Amrut Two Continents Limited Edition bott Feb 09 db **(95) n23.5 t24 f23.5 b24.** Here we have a malt distilled in India and matured first on the sub-continent and then Scotland. Let's just say that it is a malt which has travelled exceptionally well...and arrived at greatness. This is exactly how I like my whisky to be. *46%. 786 bottles.*

Amrut Two Continents 2nd Edition bott Jun 11 db **(95) n23.5 t24 f23.5 b24.** I didn't expect their 2nd edition of this to get anywhere near the first in quality: it has. Not because of any loss in faith in the distillery – quite the contrary, in fact – but because, if I have learned anything in 20 years reviewing whisky, distillers find it near enough impossible to recreate the sublime. This is a vaguely fruitier effort and all the more fascinating for that. *50%. nc ncf. 892 bottles.*

Amrut 100 Peated Single Malt ex-bourbon/virgin oak barrels db **(92)** n23 t23 f23.5 b22.5. Ironically, though one of the older whiskies to come from this distillery, the nose shows a little bit of youth. A quite different style from Amrut's other peated offerings and it was obviously intended. Further proof that this distillery has grown not only in stature but confidence. And with very good reason. 57.1%. nc ncf.

The Ultimate Amrut 2005 Cask Strength bourbon barrel no. 1641, bott no. 174, dist Dec 05, bott Apr 10 db **(94.5)** n23.5 t24 f23.5 b23.5. It makes no difference whether made and matured in Islay or India, great malt whisky is just that. And this is near faultless. And, what's more, it appears to have a character and personality all its own. 62.8%

Blackadder Amrut Rum Cask Finish cask BA5/2009, bott Jul 09 **(91.5)** n23 t24.5 f21.5 b22.5. For every action there is an equal and opposite reaction; so sweet to start, so dry on the finish. 62.% nc ncf. 245 bottles.

⁘ **Bold (94)** n24 soft smoke wraps itself around the bolder tannins until that is almost completely enveloped. A lovely dry-sweet interplay helps disguise the subtle intensity of the peat; t23.5 mouth-watering and yielding on delivery with a commanding peat presence, far bolder than on the shyer nose; a much more crisp firmness, in which the sugars appear to arrive, ensures there is something for the tongue to work with and against. Chewy, yet so soft... and hard; complex; f23 a touch bitter, almost like fresh cocoa, then a little milky and some teasing spices shyly emerge. Long, aided with chocolatey oils; b23.5 as peaty whiskies go, this is an elegant number which will do the reputation of this distillery little harm. Quite lovely... 46%

⁘ **Brilliance** (test run) **(92)** n23 spotted dog pudding – without the sultanas. Sweet, doughy, lots of vanilla. The barley is bright and a little gristy but with a delicate earthy sub strata. A lovely custard tart flourish works a treat; t23 the delivery has an enormous wave of intensity for a malt so outwardly light. A coppery spine is soon carrying the barley in varied forms, again with a light gristiness and then a mouth-watering eruption of intense malt. Both the oak and the most delicate of smoke ensures depth and balancing weight; f22 long, thanks to that ever-developing earthiness and the copper notes appear to sparkle alongside the rich, biscuit, barley fade. More vanilla and custard towards the end of the very long finish; b24 a complex malt which most of the time lives up to its name, as the fresh malt occasionally dazzles. But it has an intriguing darker side, too, which, though not overpowering, adds an attractive counter measure and ensures both the copper and oak are kept as much in their place as possible considering new stills are at work and the heat the casks have matured in. Complex and very enjoyable...even if I say so myself... 46%

Milroy's of Soho Amrut 2003 cask no. 08/08/30-1, dist Jul 03, bott Jan 09 **(84)** n21 t22 f20 b21. Juicy in part and very malty. But this whisky struggles at this kind of age with the oak, especially through the flattening natural caramels, dumbing the beauty down. 46%. 210 bottles.

⁘ **Select Cask Peated (96)** n24 a sexy, sultry, sympathetic exhibition of smoke on varying levels...though all of them soft. A tantalising chocolate mint hangs of the embers, which glow both sweet and dry. Peated whisky from outside Islay rarely comes as complex and beautiful as this, or as deliciously gristy; t24 a massive delivery. Massive yet tender and subtle. How does that happen? Again, cocoa quickly fills the middle but there is more than enough molasses to counter. The weight and depth are spot on, as are the spices which get off to a delicate start but soon get into the swing of things; f24 long, fabulously oiled and just-so amounts of gristy sugars clinging to the smoke. As charming and impressionistic as an Indian kitchen fire wafting its smoke over a remote village in the nearby valleys; b24 a peated malt whisky which will make a few people sit up and take even further notice of Indian whisky. World class... 46%

JOHN DISTILLERIES

A new single malt distillery in Cuncolim, Goa, which will have three single casks bottled while this book is being printed. Indeed, these cask strength malts are likely to be the first bottles sampled for the 2014 edition! I managed to get hold of samples direct from the cask a few days prior to bottling. Each barrel is from the first batch ever produced and turned three years old on 1st August 2012. The scoring I give is therefore of the pre-bottled whisky. **Cask 161** scores a provisional **(94)** n22.5 t24.5 f23 b24, offering sweet malty intensity on its big delivery. **Cask 163** is better still, scoring **(94.5)** n24 t24 f23 b23.5, full of complex vanilla and bourbon notes. Best of all, though, is a real stunner: the massively honeyed **Cask 164** which scores **(96)** n24 t24 f24 b24. A typical Indian beast of a malt having matured way beyond its years. But, coming from coconut-strewn Goa, one with a hint of paradise...

⁘ **Paul John Brilliance** db **(94.5)** n23.5 a complex amalgam of nougat, spotted dog pudding (sans sultanas!) and orange blossom honey with the vanilla spinning tangled webs just beneath. Honey is captured as the bourbon element expands...; a delicate gristiness ushers in a freshness to the custard tart; t24 the mouth feel exudes star quality with the barley generating all kinds of juicy riches and the light Demerara sugars forming an elegant accompaniment. A coppery spine is soon carrying the barley in varied forms while a gorgeous cocoa sub strata heralds in the spices which buzz the taste buds at will; **f23.5** beautifully relaxed: a light tingle from the spices pulses contentedly, the vanillas gather in deeper intensity yet the barley and copper stretches to the end; **b23.5** yet another astonishing malt from India. 46%

⁂ **Paul John Edited** db **(96.5) n24.5** chocolate mint evolves from the delicate peats which sit beautifully with the lesser oaky theme; a comfortable, yet always complex, nose with the smoke soft and relaxed and refusing to bully the juicier barley; **t24.5** grassy barley shows first, but then slowly gives way as those most gentle peat notes dissolve onto the palate and begin to build momentum and intensity. Again there is a chocolate mint/mocha theme, as well as a sublime molassed note which injects all the sweetness required; **f23.5** long, helped by to-die-for oils, some hints of spice and now some tannins, plus the vanilla. But all is beautifully weighted, patient and poised; Oh, and did I mention the chocolate mint...? **b24** a new Indian classic: a sublime malt from the subcontinent. To be more precise: a world classic! Think of Ardmore at its most alluring: one of Scotland's finest and most complex single malts, yet somehow possessing a saltiness and depth more befitting Islay. Then stir in a small degree of ulmo honey and bourbon-style hickory and liquorice. Plus subtle chocolate mint. And there you have it...the smoke drifting around stirring up spicy tales of the east. A world class whisky to be talked about with reverence without doubt... 52.9%

⁂ **Paul John Single Malt Cask No 161** Non Peated **(94) n22.5** as delicate as it comes: layered vanilla and marmalade. The honey boasts gentle acacia and manuka while a bourbon liquorice adds extra weight; excellent oils and depth throughout; **t24.5** mouth-filling and malty, the oils work into every crevice, taking with them first butterscotch and then those varying styles of honey; the middle ground owes much to a bourbon style; **f23** drier with the vanilla holding fort then a bigger, more lush staging of natural caramels; late mocha adds to slightly salty complexity late on; **b24** a malt which has much to say but does so with a quiet intensity. This really is a class act... 57%

⁂ **Paul John Single Malt Cask No 163** Non Peated **(94.5) n24** the house style of vanilla and marmalade is enhanced with salt and spice; a complex dryness offers an excellent counter point to honey: some serious sophistication at play. And no shortage of barley, too; **t24** you might be forgiven for expecting the complexity to drop from the nose. But not a bit of it! Wonderful sweet-dry interplay thanks to the oils amplifying the liquorice and Demerara sugars; **f23** the relative youth of the malt, just three years, can be felt here as the barley returns for a slightly salivating finish; still those light, toasty bourbon notes offer depth; **b23.5** a sublime whisky which, just as it appears to be heading off into deepest Kentucky land, veers back on course with a malty explosiveness. Magnificent complexity...57%

⁂ **Paul John Single Malt Single Cask No 164** Non Peated **(96) n24** you hardly notice the weight at first but as the oils build, and with it the sharpness of the kumquats and marmalade, you begin to realise just how much is going on. You'd expect honey from this distillery, and here you get it in abundance, yet almost teasingly understated. A gorgeous, almost exotic, mix of malt and bourbon style...; **t24** a near faultless delivery and follow through. It is unlikely you will find a better weighted malt this year, or one that reveals its honeyed beauty in the same teasing manner a lover might reveal her secrets. Rich hardly does this justice: the weight and roundness of the oils are, frankly, magical; **f24** some major spices slowly unravel, as do the usual liquorice and manuka honey of its innate bourbony style; **b24** it is hardly believable that this is a three year old single malt: the unstinting high humidity of Goa and even higher temperature, perhaps helped along by three months of monsoons, appears to have given this whisky a degree of complexity which, even in Kentucky, it might have taken a dozen years to compile. This is single malt, but one with a hint of paradise...57%

⁂ **Paul John Peated Single Malt** db **(89) n23** light peat wafting from the sweet grist handles the oak-induced date and walnut cake with aplomb; **t22** the smoke is not slow coming forward and acts as a cushion to the multi layers of crisp sugars, muscovado- and Demerera-type which follow in its train. An excellent spice radiates from the developing hickory and Dominican-style cocoa; **f21.5** a bitter marmalade edge; **b22.5** one of those delicately peaty guys which gangs up on you slowly. The smoke-infused layering of sugars is the star turn, though. 55.5%

⁂ **Paul John Single Malt-Classic (Un Peated)** db **(95) n23.5** an essay in complexity: softly sizzling lightly salted bacon mingles easily with tannins. The barley, offering the vaguest hint of grist, is almost in pastel, so delicate is it, with the deftest touch of citrus and moist syrup cake; **t24** much more salivating on delivery than might be expected: the barley shows early and with pride. A bourbony manuka, honey-liquorice mix makes for an attractive spine with toasted honeycomb arriving in the mid ground; **f23.5** an elegant finish again with the barley chirping surprisingly brightly on the oak branches. The tannins remain checked and under control with juicy Demerara tones ensuring the softest and friendliest of finishes; **b24** further evidence that Indian whisky is on the rise. Just so charming...and irresistible. *55.2%*

PONDA DISTILLERY

Stillman's Dram Single Malt Whisky Limited Edition bourbon cask no. 11186-90 **(94)** **n23** beautifully soft peats fuse with lime-led citrus notes. At once delicate and enormous; **t23** softly smoked malts dissolve into honeyed pools on the palate. Sexier and more relaxing than a Goan foot massage; **f24** the way the delicate oak washes gently against the palate, the manner in which the soft peats build to a crescendo - and yet still refuse to overpower – the entrancing waves of muscovado-sweetened coffee, all make for a sublime finale; **b24** well, I thought I had tasted it all with the Amrut cask strength. And then this arrived at my lab...!! I predicted many years back that India would dish out some top grade malt before too long. But I'd be stretching the truth if I said I thought it would ever be this good... *42.8%. McDowell & Co Ltd, India.*

Blends

Antiquity Blue Ultra Premium Whisky batch 175, bott 16 Sep 11 **(77) n19.5 t20 f18.5 b19**. Busy and nutty, a blend which sets its stall out by depending on a creamy, lush texture. Juicy malt-tinged delivery before spices develop. Bitters out towards the end. *42.8%.*

McDowell's Single Malt batch 33, bott June 11 **(82) n20.5 t21.5 f20 b20**. The malt is hugely intense and offers a degree of gristy juiciness and on the nose something approaching a faint puff of peat. The show is let down by what appears to be very old casks which refuse to offer the support and complexity the decent malt deserves. *42.8%*

McDowell's Single Malt batch 33, bott May 11 **(78) n19 t21 f19 b19**. A sharp, salivating malt which works hard to shrug off the tart intrusiveness of some baser cask notes. Silky in part, smoky in others, this malt struggles to find its balance. Curiously, this claims the same batch, 033, as the June bottling. Yet they are like chalk and cheese. This is much darker, too. *42.8%*

McDowell's No 1 Diet Mate batch 103, bott 24 Jun 11 **(76.5) n18 t19.5 f19 b20**. A genuinely odd whisky. The nose is scented like a tart's boudoir while the finish is simply tart. The delivery, though, does offer a nimble malt effect while the spices rumble with attractive intent. As a fan of McDowell, I can't say this is quite their finest moment. *42.8%. Blended with Scotch and select Indian malts.*

Old Oak Aged 12 Years Premium Malt Whisky batch 76, bott Oct 11 **(72) n19.5 t18 f17.5 b17**. It claims "unique taste". Indeed, it has: a malt whisky totally devoid of any discernable malt flavour. Soft and big on caramel. As a whisky of sorts, OK. As an "Aged 12 Years Premium malt whisky" a bit pathetic. *42.8%. Adinco Distilleries.*

Peter Scot Malt Whisky (84) n20 t21 f22 b21. Enjoyable balance between sweetness and oak and entertainingly enlivened by what appears to be some young, juicy malt. *42.8%.*

⁘ **Rendezvous (95.5) n24** chocolate mint evolves from the delicate peats which sit beautifully with the lesser oaky theme; a comfortable nose with the smoke soft and relaxed and refusing to bully the juicier barley; **t24** grassy barley shows first, but then slowly gives way as those most gentle peat notes dissolve onto the palate and begins to build momentum and intensity. Again there is a chocolate mint/mocha theme, as well as a sublime molassed note which injects all the sweetness required; **f23.5** long, some hints of spice and now some tannins. But all is beautifully weighted, patient and poised; Oh, and did I mention the chocolate mint...? **b24.5** a new Indian classic. A sublime malt from the subcontinent. *46%*

Royal Challenge batch 276, bott 31 Jan 11 **(82) n21.5 t20 f20 b20.5**. The Challenge appears to have been to spread the malts as thinly as possible across the grains yet still make an impact: a kind of malty comb over. The malts used are pretty delicious, though, and makes for a satisfying and attractive blend. *42.8%. A blend of rare Scotch, select grain and mature Indian malts. Mandovi Distilleries for United Spirits Ltd.*

Royal Stag Barrel Select batch 212, bott 17 Feb 12 **(75.5) n20.5 t19 f17 b18**. Thin and sweet. But should be shot to put it out of its misery. *42.8% Mix of Scotch malt and India grain spirit.*

Seagram's Blender's Pride batch 672 bott 12/12/11 **(85) n21.5 t21 f21 b21.5**. A thoughtful composition of soft sugars and caramels. Excellent texture and, rare for an Indian admix, the finish actually ups in complexity and weight. Good spices and attractive playful smoke on the nose especially. *42.8%. Mix of Scotch malt and India grain spirit.*

⁘ **Seagram's Blenders Pride Reserve Collection (77) n19 t20 f19 b19**. Way too reliant on the grain and th malt submerged under the caramel. Soft, clean and painfully non-committal. *42.8%. Mix of Scotch malt and India grain spirit.*

Signature batch 285, bott 05 Jan 12 **(81.5) n22.5 t22 f17.5 b19.5**. Excellent, rich nose and delivery helped along with a healthy display of peat reek. But more attention has to be paid to the brutally thin finish. *42.8% Mandovi Distilleries for United Spirits Ltd.*

NEW ZEALAND
THE NEW ZEALAND WHISKY COMPANY

⦂⦂⦂ **The New Zealand Whisky Collection Milford Single Malt Aged 15 Years** (86.5) n21 t23 f20.5 b22. Exceptionally malty, succulent and enjoys a decent malt-oak balance despite the lack of further complexity. *43%. Gordon and Macphail.*

⦂⦂⦂ **The New Zealand Whisky Collection South Island Single Malt Aged 21 Years** (95) n24 you would be forgiven for thinking this was a 30 or even 35-year-old Speysider: almost a grassy maltiness melding into the light, exotic fruit and freshly chopped celery. Clean, delicate and elegant beyond words...; t23.5 beautiful weight with the barley forming the lightly sweetened top layer and then some drier liquorice and creamed rice below; the sugars offer a fabulous buoyancy to the enormous oak input; f23.5 for a while, it looks as though the oak will take control. But the custardy sweetness retains its integrity to the last. Even at the death, the taste buds can pick off the barley notes with ease: extraordinary! b24 if someone asked me how I would like my 21-year-old non-peated malt to come to me, it would probably be something like this: a top of the range 40-year-old!! Proof that the country in which a whisky is made is totally irrelevant... Great whisky is great whisky. End of.... *40%.*

⦂⦂⦂ **The New Zealand Whisky Collection 1988 Single Malt** (84) n21.5 t21 f21 b20. The hotness of the malt has nothing to do with the spice...much more the double quick speed at which this was distilled. Enough crusty barley and tannin to make for an attractive experience, though. *56.4%. sc. Gordon and Macphail.*

⦂⦂⦂ **The New Zealand Whisky Collection 1989 Single Malt** (86.5) n21.5 t22 f21.5 b21.5. Another competent and richly malted New Zealander which lacks some of the backbone of G&M's other bottlings. The central theme of juiciness is a delight, though. *52.8%.*

⦂⦂⦂ **The New Zealand Whisky Collection 1990 Single Malt** (91) n22 heady stuff: a crunching thickness to the oakiness but subtle traces of fruit inject levity; no doubting we are talking some serious age here... t24 salivating barley launched from a spicy dais; dry cocoa infiltrates the middle ground; the crispness of the muscovado sugar is something to behold; f22.5 long, dry, every bit as oak dominated as the nose, yet no threat of tiredness; b22.5 a curious single malt which reminds me of some of the better rare Irish whiskies uncovered in the late 1980s. The oak treads that fine line between dominance and ruinous intrusiveness with a rare assuredness. *61.7%. Gordon and Macphail.*

⦂⦂⦂ **The New Zealand Whisky Collection 1993 Single Malt** (92.5) n24 timid traces of smoke hang on the intriguing cherry and orange blossom mix. Strands of butterscotch of varying intensity as well as marmalade on (slightly overdone) toast. Light, complex yet with a pleasing sub weight; t23 the delivery courses with rich, biscuit barley followed by a delicate smokiness. The sugars are brown but riddled with spices, black pepper in particular; f22.5 a bourbony liquorice element arrives but the barley and oak thins quickly; b23 I probably saw and tasted this cask when just a few months old. Always great to meet an old friend after many years apart...and even better to find them in tip-top shape. *51.9%.*

⦂⦂⦂ **The New Zealand Whisky Collection Doublewood 10 Years Old** (78.5) n21 t20.5 f18 b19 *40%. Gordon and Macphail.*

⦂⦂⦂ **The New Zealand Whisky Collection Doublewood 10 Years Old** (78.5) n21 t20.5 f18 b19 Any thinner and it would vanish. *40%. Gordon and Macphail*

⦂⦂⦂ **The New Zealand Whisky Collection South Island Single Malt Aged 18 Years** (89) n22 just wonderful interplay between soft, custardy oak and lively, though lightly weighted barley; the thin maple syrup fits a treat; t22.5 and it's the sugars to show first with the gristy barley and delicate spice not far behind; f22 some surprising light oils emerge and take the spicy butterscotch route; b22.5 minimal complexity. Maximum charm. *40%.*

THE SOUTHERN DISTILLING CO LTD

The Coaster Single Malt Whiskey batch no. 2356 (85) n20 t22 f21 b22. Distinctly small batch and sma' still with the accent very much on honey. Nosed blind I might have mistaken as Blue Mouse whisky from Germany: certainly European in style. Recovers well from the wobble on the nose and rewards further investigation. *40%*

The MacKenzie Blended Malt Whiskey (85) n20 t22 f21 b22. A vaguely spicier, chalkier, mildly less honeyed version of Coaster. Quite banana-laden nose. *40%*

THOMSON WILLOWBANK

⦂⦂⦂ **Thomson Single Malt 10 Years Old** ex-bourbon barrel (71) n18.5 t19 f16.5 b17. The sugars are working hard. But have nothing to work with. *40%. Thomson Whisky.*

⦂⦂⦂ **Thomson Single Malt 18 Years Old** (77) n19.5 t20 f18.5 b19. Pleasant, sweet but absolutely no body whatsoever. *46%. sc. Thomson Whisky.*

⦂⦂⦂ **Thomson Single Malt 21 Years Old** (84) n21 t22.5 f20.5 b20. Bit of a bimbo whisky: looks pretty and outwardly attractive but has picked up very little in its 21 years... *46%. sc.*

⁘ **Thomson Whisky Two Tone** European Oak & American White Oak (86) n22 t22 f21 b21. This one had promise. Started full of intent on both nose and delivery, boasting attractive citrus notes. But after a quick rush of clear honey, thins out like the most basic of blends. 40%.

WILSON DISTILLERY
Cadenhead's World Whiskies Lammerlaw Aged 10 Years bourbon, bott 07 (91.5) n22 t23.5 f23 b23. Stunning bottlings like this can only leave one mourning the loss of this distillery. 48.9%

Blends
Kiwi Whisky (37) n2 t12 f11 b12. Strewth! I mean, what can you say? Perhaps the first whisky containing single malt offering virtually no nose at all and the flavour appears to be grain neutral spirit plus lashings of caramel and (so I am told) some Lammerlaw single malt. The word bland has been redefined. As has whisky. 40%.

Wilson's Superior Blend (89) n22 t23 f21 b23. Apparently has a mixed reception in its native New Zealand but I fail to see why: this is unambiguously outstanding blended whisky. On the nose you expect a mouthwatering mouthful and it delivers with aplomb. Despite this being a lower priced blend it is, intriguingly, a marriage of 60% original bottled 10-y-o Lammerlaw and 40% old Wilson's blend, explaining the high malt apparent. Dangerous and delicious and would be better still at a fuller strength...and with less caramel. 37.5%.

SOUTH AFRICA
JAMES SEDGWICK DISTILLERY
Three Ships 10 Years Old db (83) n21 t21 f20 b21. Seems to have changed character, with more emphasis on sherry and natural toffee. The oak offers a thrusting undercurrent. 43%

Three Ships Aged 10 Years Single Malt Limited Edition db (91) n22.5 t22.5 f23 b23.5. If you are looking for a soft, sophisticated malt whose delicate fingers can sooth your troubled brow, then don't bother with this one. On the other hand, if you are looking for a bit of rough, some entertaining slap and tickle: a slam-bam shag of a whisky - a useful port in a storm - then your boat may just have sailed in... Beware: an evening with this and you'll be secretly coming back for more... 43%

Bain's Cape Mountain Single Grain Whisky db (85.5) n21 t22 f21 b21.5. A lively, attractively structured whisky with more attitude than you might expect. Some lovely nip and bite despite the toffee and surprising degree of soft oils. 43%

Blends
Drayman's Solera (86) n19 t22 f23 b22. For a change, the label gets it spot on with its description of chocolate orange: it is there in abundance. If they can get this nose sorted they would be on for an all round impressive dram. As it is, luxuriate in the excellent mouthfeel and gentle interplay between malt and oak. Oh and those chocolate oranges... 43%.

Harrier (78) n20 t20 f19 b19. Not sure what has happened to this one. Has bittered to a significant degree while the smoke has vanished. A strange, almost synthetic, feel to this now. 43%. South African/Scotch Whisky.

Knights (83) n20.5 t21 f20 b20.5. While the Harrier has crashed, the Knights is now full of promise. Also shows the odd bitter touch but a better all-round richer body not only absorbs the impacts but radiates some malty charm. 43%. South African/Scotch Whisky.

Knights Aged 3 Years (87) n22 t22 f22 b22. This now appears to be 100% South African whisky if I understand the label correctly: "Distilled Matured and Bottled in South Africa." A vast improvement on when it was Scotch malt and South African grain. Bursting with attitude and vitality. When next in South Africa, this will be my daily dram for sure. Love it. 43%. James Sedgwick Distillery.

Three Ships Bourbon Cask Finish (90) n22 t23 f22.5 b22.5. A soft, even whisky which enjoys its finest moments on delivery. Clean with a pressing, toasty oakiness to the sweeter malt elements. Always a delight. 43%

Three Ships Premium Select Aged 5 Years (93) n23 t23.5 f23 b23.5. What a fabulous whisky. The blender has shown a rare degree of craft to make so little smoke do so much. Bravo! 43%. James Sedgwick Distillery.

Three Ships Select (81) n19 t21 f20 b21. Busy and sweet. But I get the feeling that whatever South African malt may be found in Knights does a better job than its Scotch counterpart here. 43%. James Sedgwick Distillery.

TAIWAN
KAVALAN DISTILLERY
Kavalan db (91) n23 t23 f22 b23. A high quality, confident malt which underlines this distillery's enormous potential. 40%

Kavalan Concertmaster Single Malt Port cask finish db **(87) n22 t23 f20.5 b21.5.** A malt which will split its audience. In Germany, for instance, the light sulphur note will win all kinds of standing ovations; to the purist there will be a preference that it was not there. Because this piece has many moments of beauty as the malt and grape mingle and interlink: together they are company, anything else is a crowd. Even so I envisage many an encore for this... 40%

Kavalan King Car Conductor db **(89.5) n22.5 t23 f22 b22.** Not quite sure where the salt comes from; this distillery is far enough inland not to be affected. But it is there and does no harm whatsoever. Not quite technically perfect, as at least some of the characteristics are so contra they occasionally jar. But still fabulous whisky and a journey entirely worth embarking on. 46%

⁘ **Kavalan Podium Single Malt** bott 27th Nov 12 db **(96.5) n24** complex and gorgeously weighted, the nose is like an evening in which Richard Strauss and Ralph Vaughan Williams are on the same bill: subtle notes and ranges being practised and perfected...in an air bursting with expectation; **t24** the cherry and malt concentrate mix opening bars are not quite what are expected, but there is never less than harmony. The degree of oiliness, which is able to ramp up the maple syrup and treacle sweetness is also a surprise package; **f24** the start may have exploded like a Strauss in full melodramatic mode, but the finish is Williams at his most pastoral. The toasty and elegant sugars and baser tannins have here formed a cord, one that fades to the death, but not before a few false endings. The use of the molasses brings in the inevitable vanilla so that you barely notice until a light ulmo honey entry is the last note standing.. **b24.5** bravo! Encore!!! 46%. nc ncf.

⁘ **Kavalan Single Malt ex-Bourbon Oak** bott 12th Dec 12 db **(93) n23** presumably first-fill bourbon because there is more than an echo of Kentucky at play here: traces of red liquorice hickory and (heather) honey. And some rousing butterscotch, too; **t23** massive oak and barley interface from the very first moment: who, if anyone, will win? Certainly the early, oily rounds are taken by the malt, but by degree the oak gains ground: a few moments of molasses moves towards softer ulmo honey, which spreads the sweetness evenly while allowing the spices full range; throughout a lovely apricot thread ensures a fruity representation; **f23** tangy and dries as those oak lines really take a grip, thinks about heading towards cocoa but shies away late marmalade; **b24** big oak with a quite dynamic sweetness, always beautifully controlled with the accent invariably on complexity. 46%. nc ncf.

⁘ **Kavalan Single Malt Whisky Sherry Oak** bott 13th Dec 12 **(95) n24** thick, uncompromising, mega-graped, and nutty while gently spiced. A lovely strand of molassed mocha and strawberry, too; **t24** soft, silky delivery – with certain but unmistakable shades of a big, coffee-laden , Guyana rum - with some bigger spice now; the grape uncompromisingly dominates until the middle. Even so, the ability for the juicier and more treacle-led sugars to sing clearly is outstanding; **f23** dries as oloroso tends to, and dies to a more intense oak; that heavy roast coffee lasts the distance with ease; **b24** the type of sherry-heavy malt not uncommonly found on Speyside over 20 years ago before the quality if the butts nosedived dramatically. I feel the judicious hand of Jim Swan at work here who has somehow managed to make this Taiwanese malt more top quality Scottish in character than anything of its age you can find in the Highlands. What a rare treat: not too rare in future one hopes! 46%. nc ncf.

Kavalan Solist Barique db cask no. W080218037 **(90.5) n23 t24 f21 b22.5.** This distillery is, in all the world, my favourite to visit. The drama of the geology in which it is set appears matched only by what one discovers from time to time in their warehouses. It has the potential for true world greatness, though this bottling, for all its magnificence, only nudges rather than grasps at the prospect. 59.2%. nc ncf sc. 237 bottles.

Kavalan Solist Fino Sherry Cask db cask no. S060814045, bott no. 079/500 **(95) n24.5 t24.5 f22.5 b23.5.** When Dr Jim Swan, the distillery's consultant, told me he thought he'd found a cask which could well be a world-beater, I had mixed feelings. On one hand he'd been right when he'd said the same thing when he found a port pipe for Penderyn which has now entered Welsh whisky folklore. But, on the other, there are many times during the year when those I have long known in the game, including some good friends, have called me after reading my review and asked why I had marked their Great Hope down. Jim, though, has got this one spot on. The natural colour is astonishingly un-fino-esque and the overall experience is one that you come across only too rarely in life – especially with sherry butts. The marriage between the sweeter malt and drier grape notes is a thing of not just beauty, but awe. This is a bottling which will place the King Car Yuan-Shan distillery on the world map of truly great distilleries. Because having an exceptional cask is one thing. You also have to have a spirit excellent enough to maximize the potential of that cask and not be overwhelmed by it. That is exactly what you have here. A great new whisky dynasty has been born... 58.5%. ncf nc.

Kavalan Solist Fino Sherry Cask db cask no. S060814021 **(97) n24.5 t24 f24 b24.5.** It might be argued that the one and only thing that makes this exceptional is the quality of the cask, rather than the actual malt it contains. Well, let me set the record straight in this one. Earlier this week I made a very rare escape from my tasting room and visited the Royal Albert Hall for the 34th Prom of the 2011 season. The highlight of the evening was Camille Saint-Saens Symphony No 3 – "Organ". Now some critics, when they can find time to extract themselves from their own rear ends, dismiss this as a commoners' piece; something to amuse the plebeian. What they appear to not have is neither the wit nor humanity to understand that Saint-Saens sewed into this work a degree of such subtle shade and emotion, especially in the less dramatic second movement, that it can, when treated correctly, affect those capable of normal warmth and feeling. With so many nerve endings tingling and nowhere to go Saint-Saens seemingly recognised that he required something profound – in this case the organ – to create a backbone. And someone able to use it to maximum effect. And there we had it the other day: the Royal Albert Hall's awe-inspiring organ, and Thomas Trotter to make it come alive: The Solist. And this is what we have here: a perfect fino sherry selected by the maestro Dr Jim Swan. But able to display its full magnificence only because the host spirit is so beautifully composed. Good whisky is, without question, a work of art; great whisky is a tone poem. And here, I beg to insist, is proof. *58.4%. nc ncf sc. 513 bottles.*

Ka Va Lan Solist Vinho Barrique cask W080218011 bott 08 Nov 11 (93) n23 t24 f22.5 **b23.5** this distillery in a very short time has already planted its flag firmly at the peak of the world's best whiskies. *60%*

Other Brands Available In Taiwan

Eagle Leader Storage Whisky (81.5) **n**20 **t**21 **f**21 **b**20.5. Attractively smoky with a surprisingly long finish for a whisky which initially appears to lack body. By no means straightforward, but never less than pleasant. *40%*

Golden Hill Single Malt (75) **n**18 **t**20 **f**19 **b**18. An unwieldy heavyweight. *40%*

Good Deer (in Chinese Characters) *see McAdams Rye Whisky*

McAdams Rye Whisky bott Nov 09 (85.5) **n**21 **t**22 **f**21.5 **b**21.5. Thoroughly delicious stuff absolutely brimming with juicy, crisp grain notes. The body is lightly oiled and shapely while the finish is sweet and attractive. The odd green apple note, too. *40%. Note: Says it's made in Taiwan, but possesses a maple leaf on the label.*

Sea Pirates (77) **n**18 **t**21 **f**19 **b**19. More Johnny Depp than Errol Flynn. Attractive smoke, though. *40%*

URUGUAY

Dunbar Anejo 5 Anos (85.5) **n**20 **t**22.5 **f**21.5 **b**21.5. A clean, mouth-wateringly attractive mix where the grain nips playfully and the Speyside malts are on best salivating behaviour. Decently blended and boasting a fine spice prickle, too. *40%*

Seagram's Blenders Pride (83) **n**20.5 **t**22 **f**20b20.5. The busy, relatively rich delivery contrasts with the theme of the silky grains and caramel. Easy drinking. *40%*

MISCELLANEOUS

House of Westend Blended Whisky (67) **n**17 **t**18 **f**16 **b**16. No more than OK if you are being generous; some tobacco-dirty notes around. Doesn't mention country of origin anywhere on the label. *40%. Bernkasteler Burghof, Germany.*

Jaburn & Co Pure Grain & Malt Spirit (53) **n**14 **t**13 **f**13 **b**13. Tastes like neutral grain and caramel to me. Some shop keepers, I hear, are selling it as whisky though this is not claimed on the label. Trust me: it isn't. *37.5%. Jaburn & Co, Denmark.*

Prince of Wales Welsh Whisky (69) **n**17 **t**18 **f**17 **b**17. Syrupy aroma is compounded by an almost liqueurish body. Thin in true Scotch substance, probably because it claims to be Welsh but is really Scotch with herbs diffused in a process that took place in Wales. Interestingly, my "liqueur" tasting notes were written before I knew exactly what it was I was tasting, thus proving the point and confirming that, with these additives, this really isn't whisky at all. *40%*

Shepherd's Export Finest Blend (46) **n**5 **t**16 **f**12 **b**13. A dreadful, illdefined grain-spirit nose is softened on the palate by an early mega-sweet kick. The finish is thin and eventually bitter. Feeble stuff. *37.2%. "A superb blend of Imported Scotch Malt whiskies and Distilled N.Z. grain spirit", claims the label which originally gives the strength as 40%, but has been over-written. Also, the grain, I was told, was from the USA. Southern Grain Spirit, NZ.*

⠿ **The Teeling Whisky Co. Hybrid Malt Whiskey No. 1 Edition** (90) **n**23 such playful peat: rarely gets softer without playing a significant part; the juicier barley is one about equal terms as the oak; some youthful apple; **t**22.5 excellent mouth feel and delivery: like on the nose, the smoke presents itself shyly at first then allows the juicier, mouth-watering barley to get stuck in; **f**22 long with minty mocha and smoke; **b**22.5 adorable vibrancy and use of smoke. *44.1%. nc ncf.*

Slàinte

It seems as though you can't have a Bible without a whole lot of begetting. And without all those listed below – stadia swarming full of all the world's whisky people – this Jim Murray's Whisky Bible 2014 would never have been begot at all. A huge amount of blood, sweat and tears go into the production of each edition, more than anyone not directly involved could even begin to comprehend. So, as usual, I must thank my amazing team: James Murray, Dean Ayotte, Billy Jeffrey and David Rankin. Also special thanks to the indefatigable Julia Nourney for once again dredging the distilleries of Europe on my behalf. For the North American sections, my heartfelt appreciation goes to the staff and management of the Union Club of British Columbia in Victoria, something of my second home these days, and my dearest friends and supporters of long-standing, Mick and Tammy Secor of the Highland Stillhouse in Oregon City. A special mention also to two heartwarmingly wonderful people: Gerrit and Andi Boyle: thank you. This tenth anniversary edition of the Whisky Bible could also not have been completed without the unstinting support and friendship of Heiko Thieme and Lawrence Graham, heroes both. Because the list of thank yous had exceeded two pages, we are starting again with those who have helped in providing help and samples for the 2013 Bible onwards. For all those who have assisted in the previous decade, we remain indebted.

Mitch Abate; Ally Alpine; Duncan Baldwin; Clare Banner; Kirsteen Beeston; Annie Bellis; Menno Bijmolt; Rich Blair; Hans Bol; Etienne Bouillon; Birgit Bournemeier; Phil Brandon; Stephen Bremner; Stephanie Bridge; James Brown; Sara Browne; Michael Brzozowski; Alexander Buchholz; Ryan Burchett; Amy Burgess;; Kimla Carsten; Bert Cason; Jim Caudill; Yuseff Cherney; Julia Christian; Nick Clark; Dr Martin Collis; Jason Craig; David Croll; Stephen Davies; Alasdair Day; Dick & Marti; Rob Dietrich; Angela D'Orazio; Jean Donnay; Camille Duhr-Merges; Mariette Duhr-Merges; Gemma Duncan; Ray Edwards; Carsten Ehrlich; Ben Ellefsen; James Espey; Jennifer Eveleigh; Thomas Ewers; Joanna Fearnside; David Fitt; Kent Fleischman; Martyn Flynn; Danny Gandert; Patrick Garcia; Carole Gibson; John Glaser; John Glass; Emily Glynn; Rebecca Groom; Jasmin Haider; Georgina Hall; Scott E Harris; Alistair Hart; Andrew Hart; Donald Hart; Stuart Harvey; Ailsa Hayes; Ross Hendry; Roland Hinterreiter; Bernhard Höning; Emma Hurley; Kai Ivalo; Amelia James; Michael John; Celine Johns; Karen Kushner; Sebastian Lauinger; Christelle Le Lay; Lars Lindberger; Steven Ljubicic; Alistair Longwell; C. Mark McDavid; John Maclellan; Dennis Malcolm; Leanne Matthews; Stephen R McCarthy; Angela Mcilrath; Douglas McIvor; Maggie Miller; Euan Mitchell; Paul Mitchell; Henk Mol; Nick Morgan; Maggie Morri; Fabien Mueller; Michael Myers; Andrew Nelstrop; Alex Nicol; Jane Nicol; Rachel Showalter Inman; Soren Norgaard; Tom O'Connor; Casey Overeem; Ted Pappas; Richard Parker; Sanjay Paul; Amy Preske; Rachel Quinn; Guy Rehorst; Carrie Revell; Kay Riddoch; Massimo Righi; Patrick Roberts; James Robertson; David Roussier; Ronnie Routledge; Jim Rutledge; Caroline Rylance; Paloma Salmeron Planells; Phil Prichard; John Savage-Onstwedder; Ian Schmidt; Rubyna Sheik; Caley Shoemaker; Jamie Siefken; Sam Simmons; Alastair Sinclair; Sukhinder Singh; Barbara Smith; Gigha Smith; Phil Smith; Cat Spencer; Vicky Stevens; Karen Stewart; Katy Stollery; Henning Svoldgaard; Tom Swift; Chip Tate; Marko Tayburn; Celine Tetu; Sarah Thacker; Hamish Torrie; Richard Urquhart; Stuart Urquhart; CJ Van Dijk; Aurelien Villefranche; Anna Wilson; Nick White; Arthur Winning; Stephen Worrall; Kate Wright; Frank Wu; Tom Wyss; Junko Yaguchi; Ruslan Zamoskovny. And, of course, in warm memory of Mike Smith.